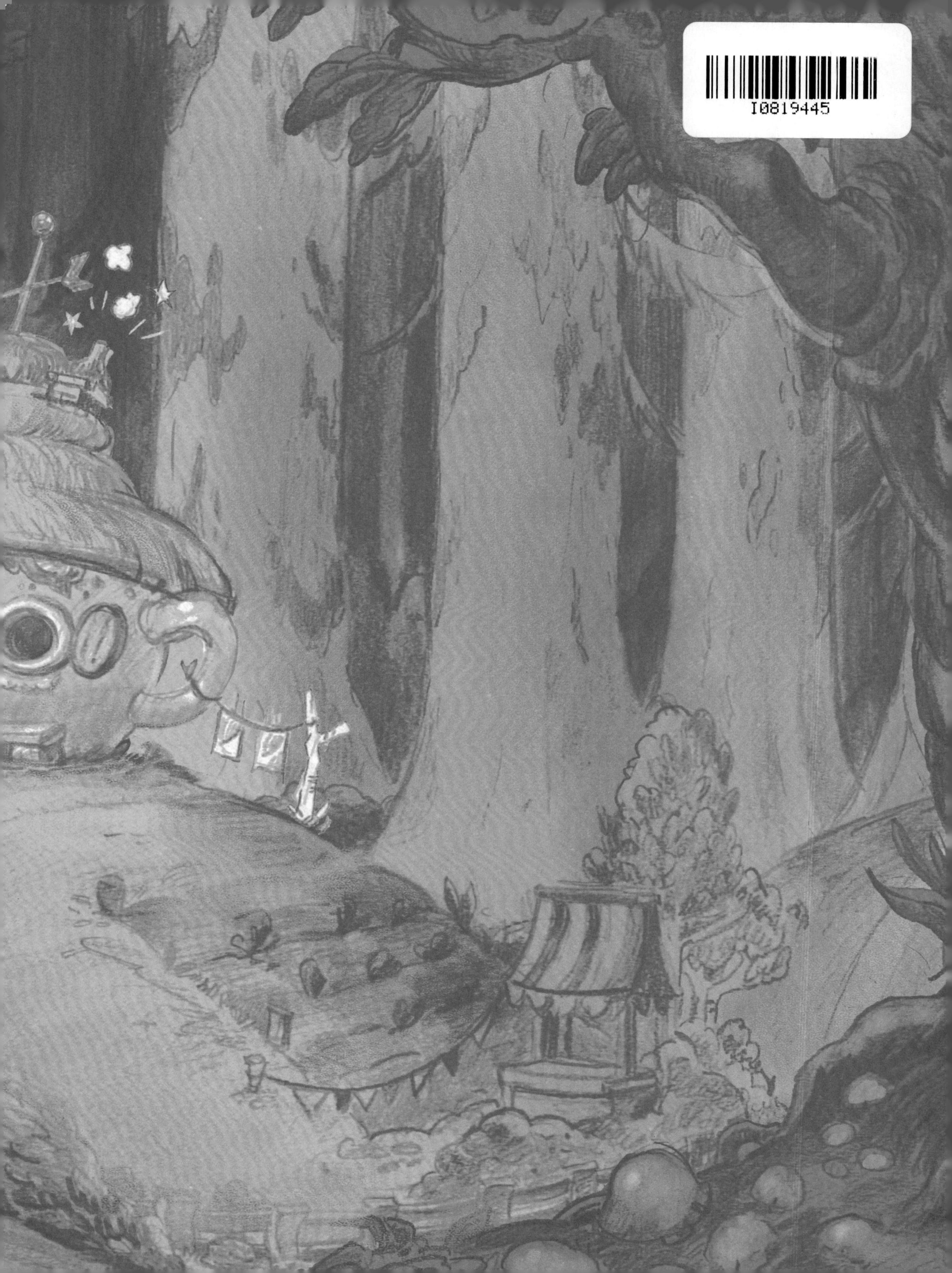

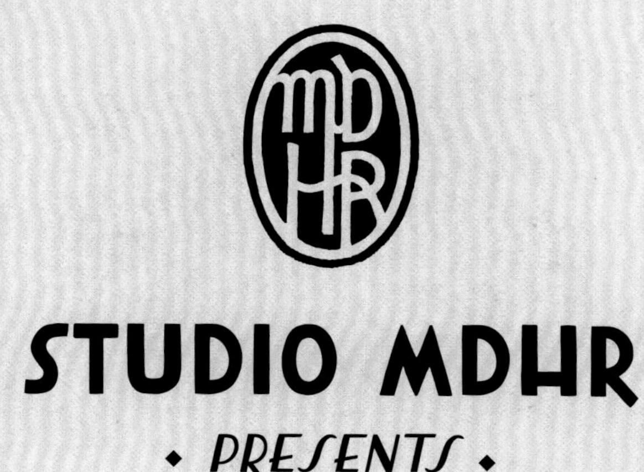
STUDIO MDHR
PRESENTS

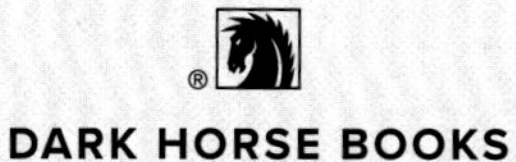
DARK HORSE BOOKS

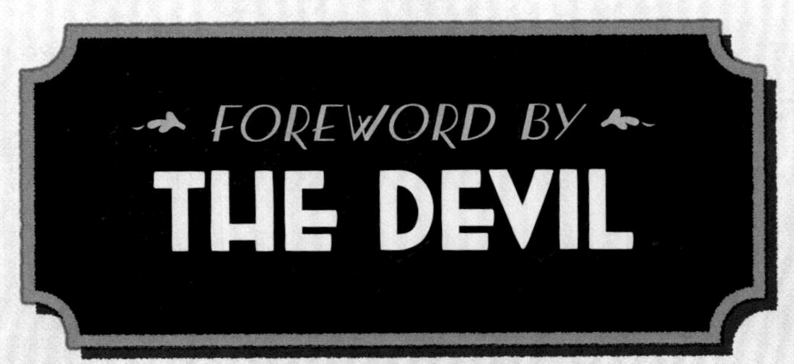

It was late 2018 when my ears began to burn . . .

Talk of the adaptation had been building, with rumors trickling down to the underworld. But after millennia in show business, one learns to be cautious about getting one's hopes up. Still, one had to wonder . . . Would they do a series? Could they do a series? Would it be possible to execute modern animation that stays true to the aesthetics of a bygone era, paying homage to the meticulously hand-drawn source material—and on a television budget? And, most crucially, what is my allotment of costume changes and musical numbers per episode?

As you well know, the series did indeed come to fruition, and I am both honored and humbled to compose the foreword—while also settling a few scores. First and foremost, the individual who purports to have "developed" the series, Dave Wasson. Yet nowhere is there a title card for my development of pure evil. How such a fundamental contribution fails to merit an executive producer credit I will never understand.

I maintain similar disdain for the entire creative team. While I am cognizant of the necessity of conflict in storytelling, I reject the assertion that an all-powerful, eternally immortal, showstoppingly spectacular being such as myself should be subjected to the indignity of interacting with despicable dinnerware for the purposes of entertainment.

I take particular umbrage with one Andrea Fernandez and her team of artists for putting such extensive effort and resources into the non-Devil aspects of the series. While they are painstakingly rendered and simply breathtaking to behold, it must be said that these elements lack a certain . . . this guy. Especially those elements involving a horrible cup and a hideous cottage. Which brings me to the deeper meaning of the series, and this book . . .

You see, underneath the glitz, the glamour, and the showstopping musical numbers, what "The Devil Show!" is truly about is . . . me! Not just "a" Devil, but THE Devil. I suppose you could say I not only bring the Devil to "The Devil Show!" but I also bring the Show! Furthermore, I

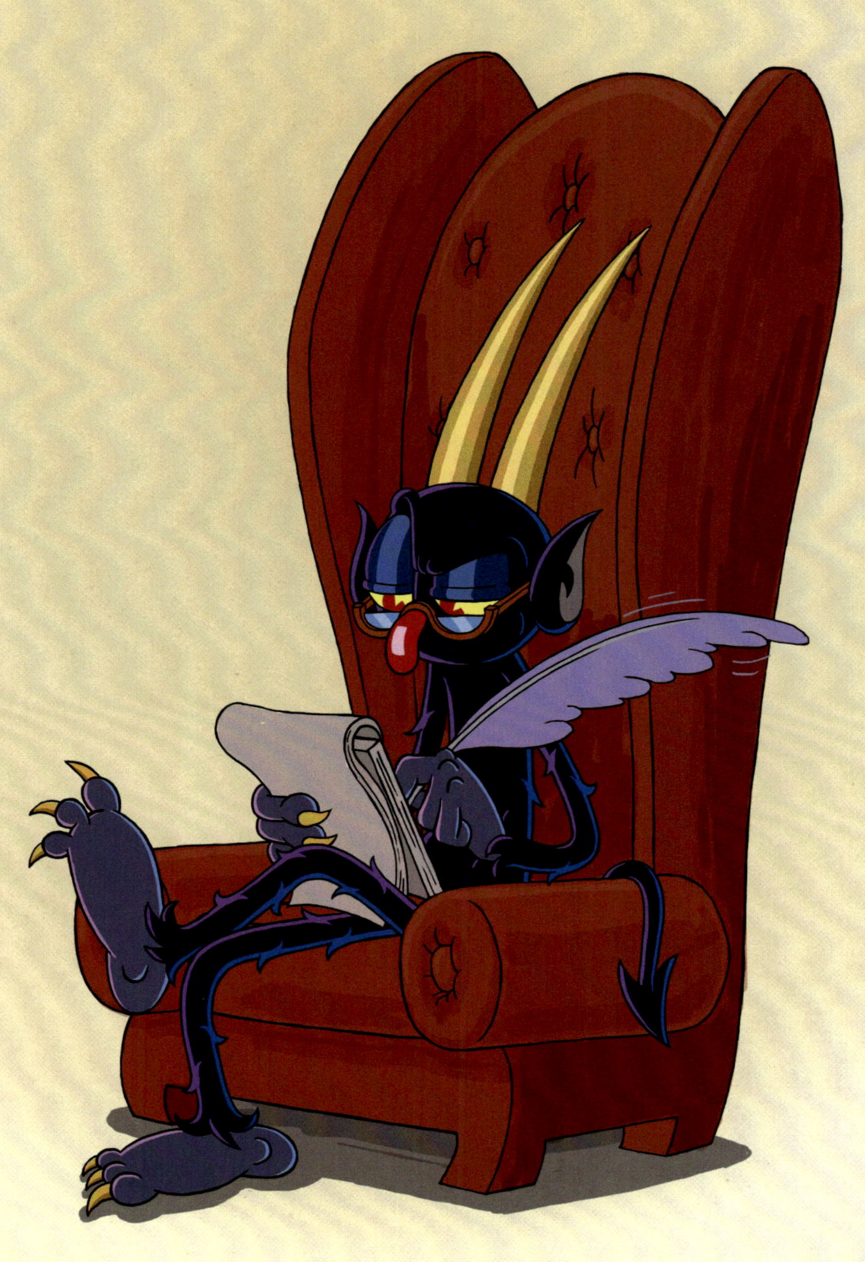

THE ART OF THE CUPHEAD SHOW!

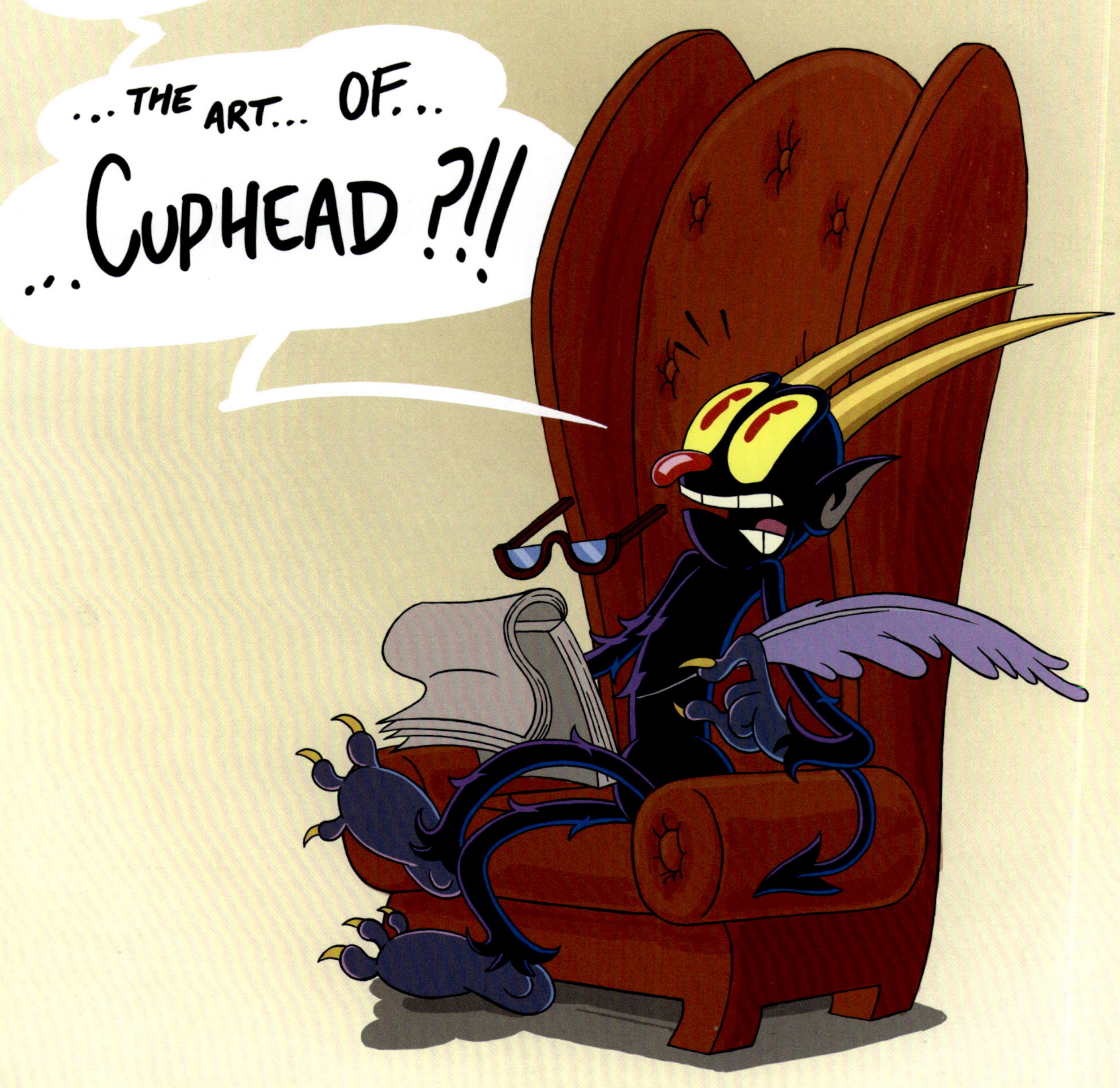

WRITTEN BY DEEKI DEKE

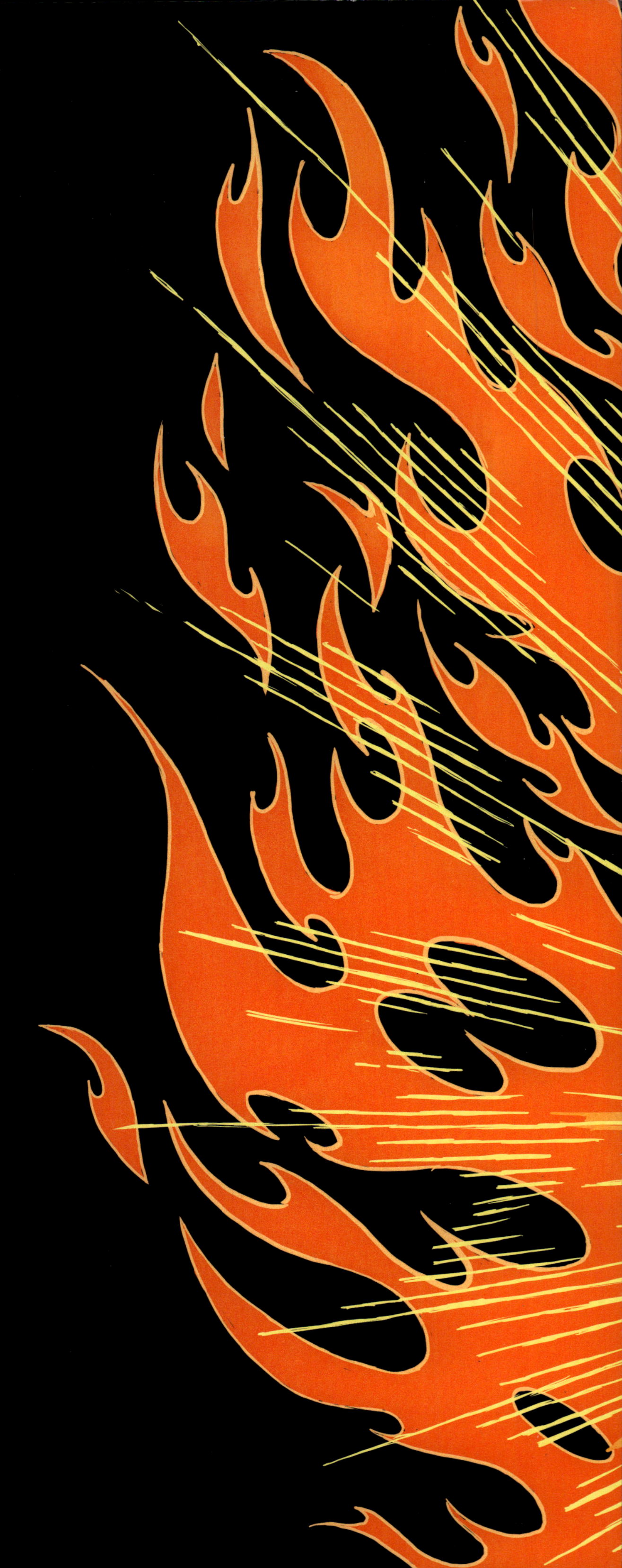

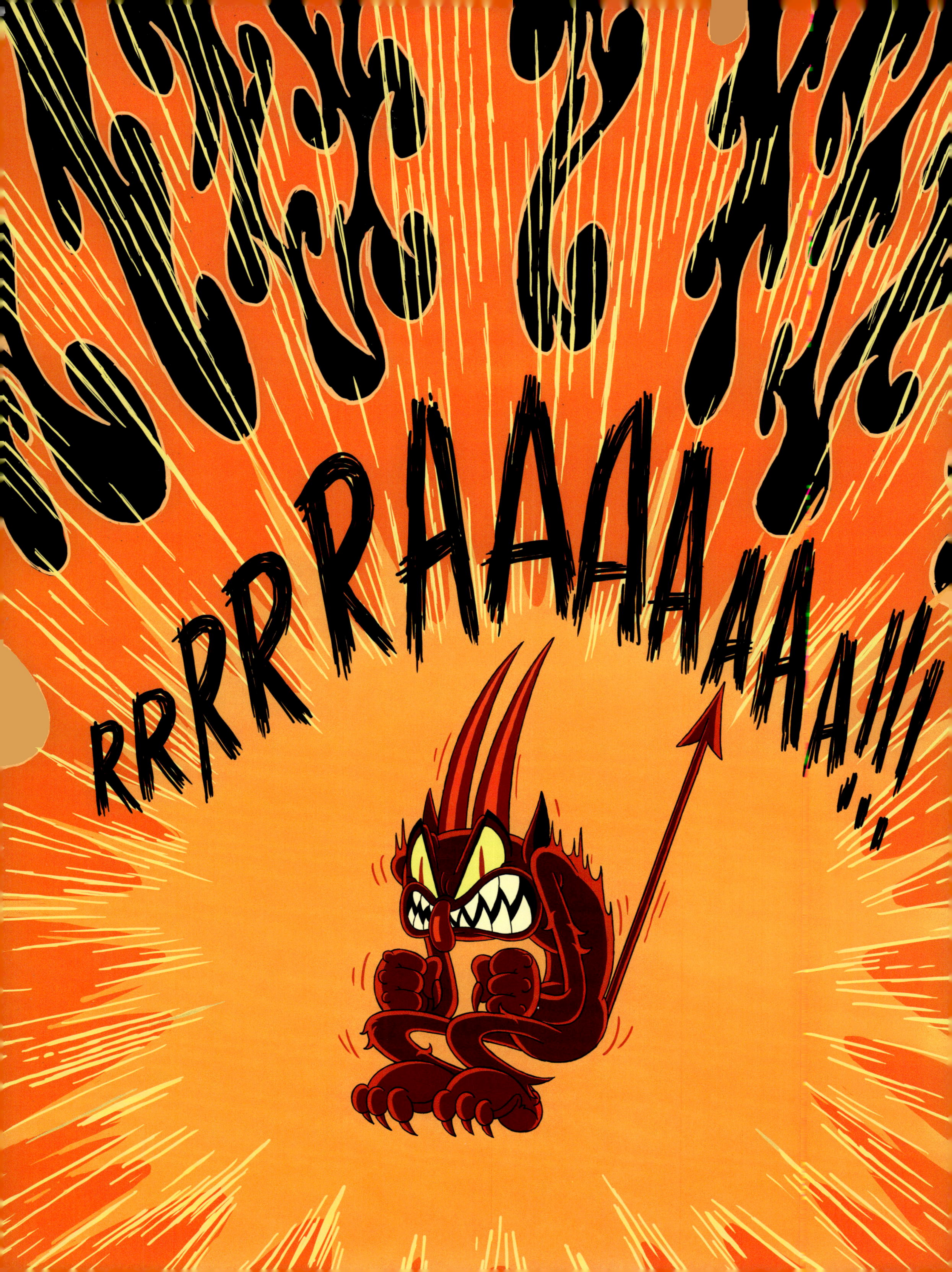
RRRRRAAAAAAA!!!

THE CUPHEAD SHOW! WAS MADE THROUGH THE TALENTS OF:

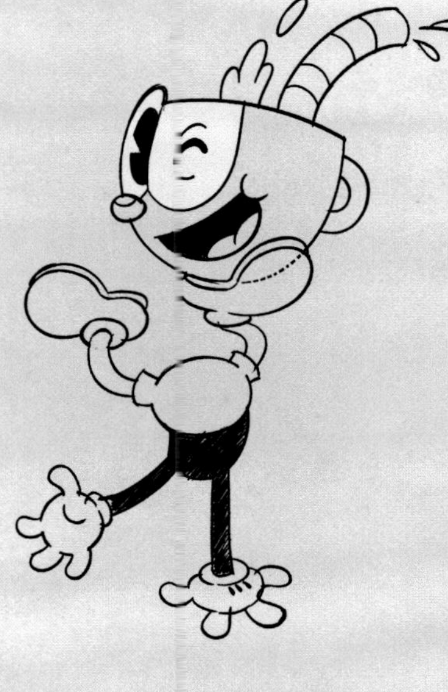

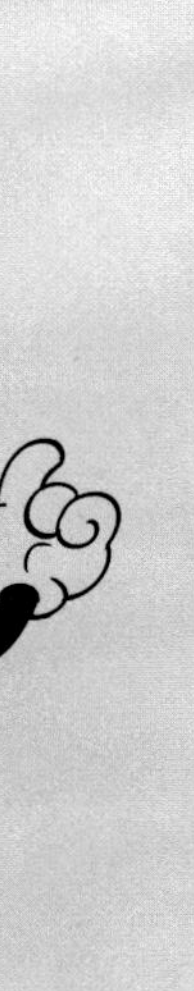

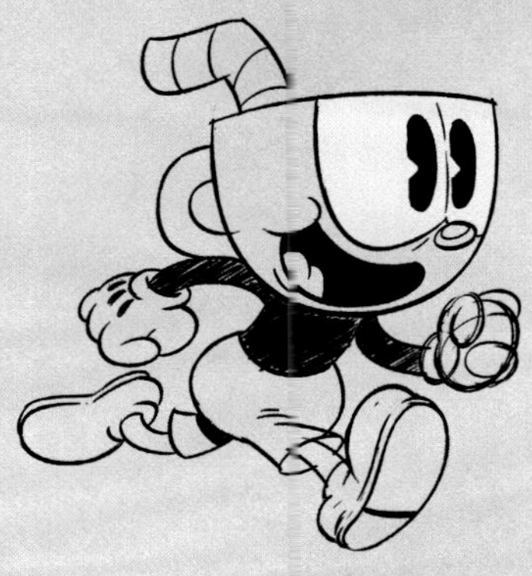

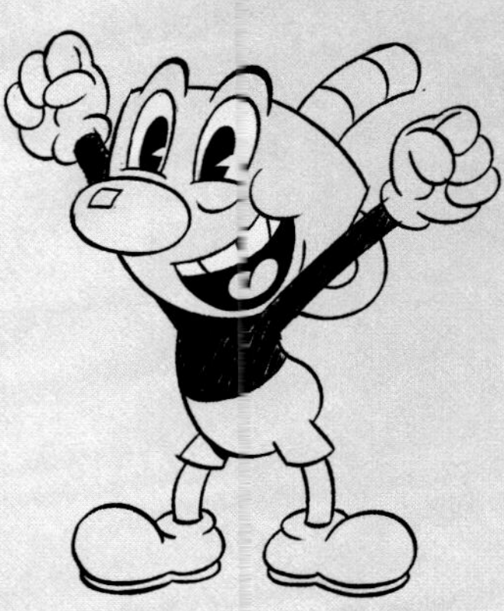

Series Developer
Showrunner
Executive Producer........................ Dave Wasson
Cuphead Creators
Executive Producers............... Chad Moldenhauer
Jared Moldenhauer
Cuphead Executive Producer ....Maja Moldenhauer
Cuphead Producer .... Eli Cymet
President, King Features
Executive Producer ....CJ Kettler
Co-executive Producer................ Cosmo Segurson
Supervising Directors................... Clayton Morrow
Adam Paloian
Retakes Director........... Mitchel Preston Kennedy
Line Producers ....Carolyn Roach
Jackie Watson
Lily Sechrist
Art Director........................ Andrea Fernandez
Story Editor................................Deeki Deke
Script Coordinator...... Margaret "Mugsy" Hoffman
Production Manager........................Libby Smith
Production Coordinators.........................Brian Hill
Justin Connolly
Thalia Nalapraya
Kristen Woods
Production Assistants.................Nadia Garbosky
Allison Pineda
David "Baby Dave" Fonseca
Storyboard Supervisors.................. Jeremy Polgar
Michael Ruocco
Storyboard Artists ....Benjamin Arcand
Ian Vasquez
Dan Becker
Kennedy Tarrell
Karl Hadrika
Zoë Moss
Megan Boyd
Fernando Puig
Jared Morgan
Nick Lauer
Austin Faber

Storyboard Revisionists ....Allen Zhang
Sam Kessler
Animatic Editors........................... Lauren Crist
David Woody
Lauren Hecht
Nicole Rola
Lead Character Designers ....Shakeh Haghnazarian
Martin Wittig
Character Designers.......................Tapan Gandhi
Adam Fay
Mike Fontanelli
Bradley Lewis
Prop Designer ....Adam Dix
Background Designers.............Benjamin Anderson
Laisay Bond
Lauren Duda
Jessica Hong
Pat Marconett
Background Painters....................... Ivan Aguirre
Mallory Carlson
Michelle Thies
Gregory Miller
Leah Chun
Sebastian Guerra-Martinez
Jeff Palm
Color Stylists .... Christopher Hacker
Chelsea Jauregui
Picture Editor ....Amy Blaisdell
Assistant Editor .... Kristen Garris
Assistant Animatic Editor ....Lauren Fan
Post Production Supervisor...........Meghan Caporali
Post Production Assistant...................Joanna Ting
Composer.................................... Ego Plum
Main Title Vocalist............Gizzelle Andrea Becerra
Technical Directors.................. Brianne VanTuyle
Ryan Langelier
Animators...............................Marco Rivera
Sydney Yang

THE ART OF THE CUPHEAD SHOW!

i hate that cup...

WRITTEN BY DEEKI DEKE

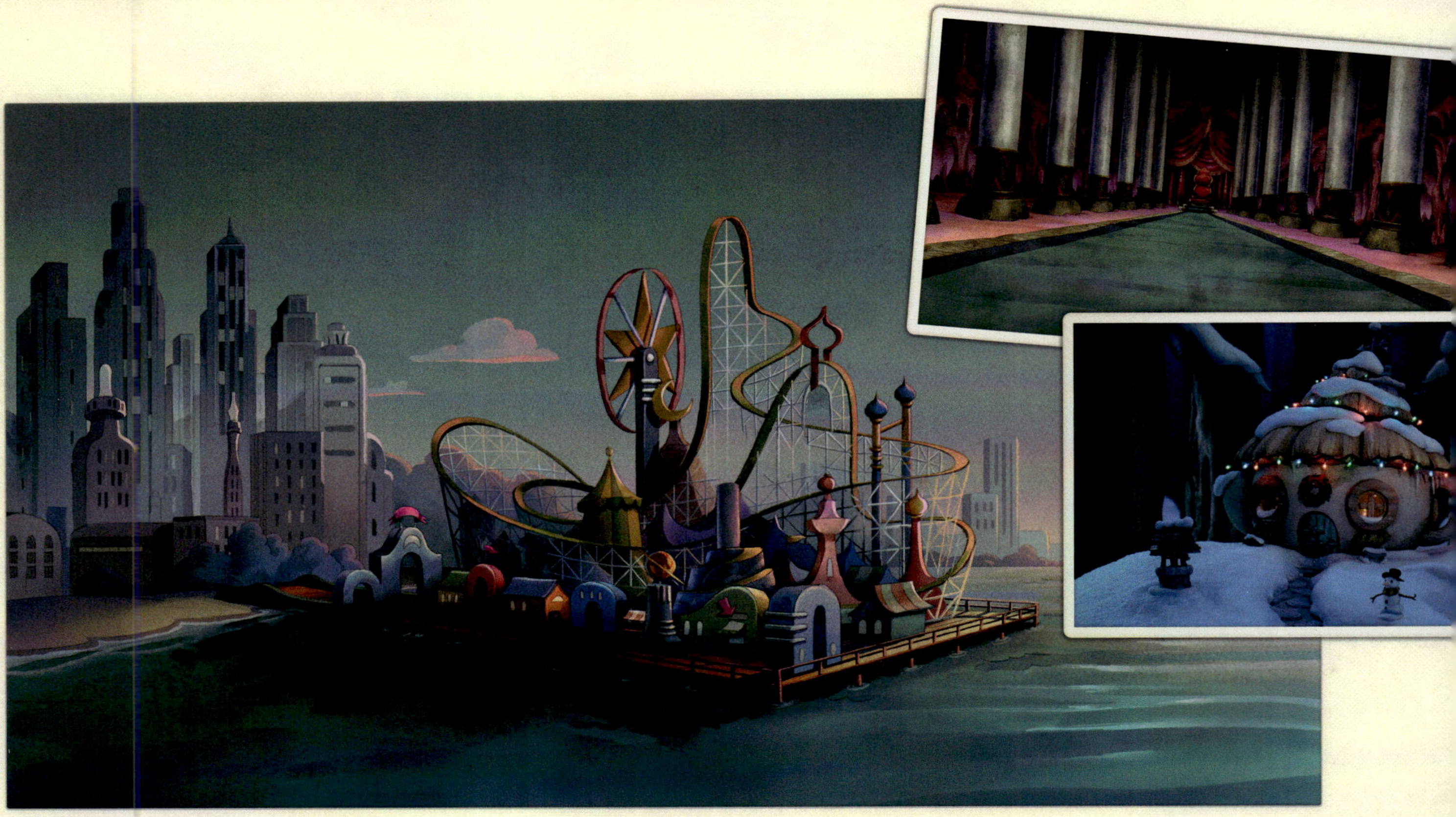

President & Publisher .... Mike Richardson
Editor .... Ian Tucker
Assistant Editor............... Anastacia Ferry
Concept Designer .... Anita Magaña
Designers....................... Anita Magaña
Cindy Cacerez-Sprague
Ethan Kimberling
Lin Huang
Sarah Terry
Digital Art Technician............. Betsy Howitt
Book Cover Artwork .... Dave Wasson
Andrea Fernandez
Michelle Thies
Devil's Foreword Artwork......... Dave Wasson

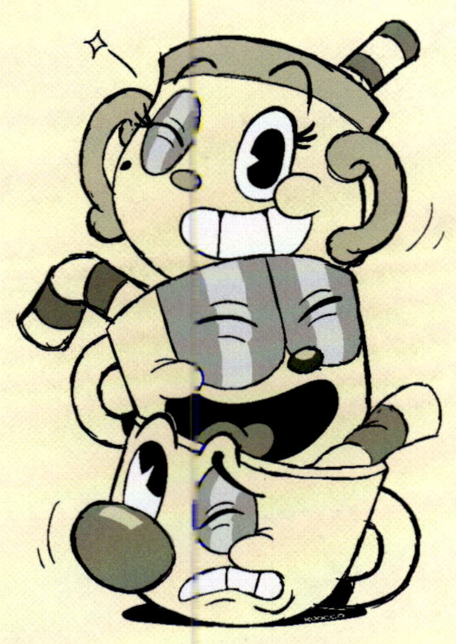

STACK OF CUPS BY MICHAEL RUOCCO.

THE ART OF THE CUPHEAD SHOW!

Published by Dark Horse Books. A division of Dark Horse Comics LLC.
10956 SE Main Street, Milwaukie, OR 97222

DarkHorse.com Facebook.com/DarkHorseComics
X Twitter.com/DarkHorseComics

First edition: September 2024
Ebook ISBN 978-1-50673-300-5
Hardcover ISBN 978-1-50673-299-2

10 9 8 7 6 5 4 3 2 1
Printed in China

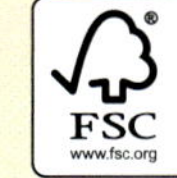

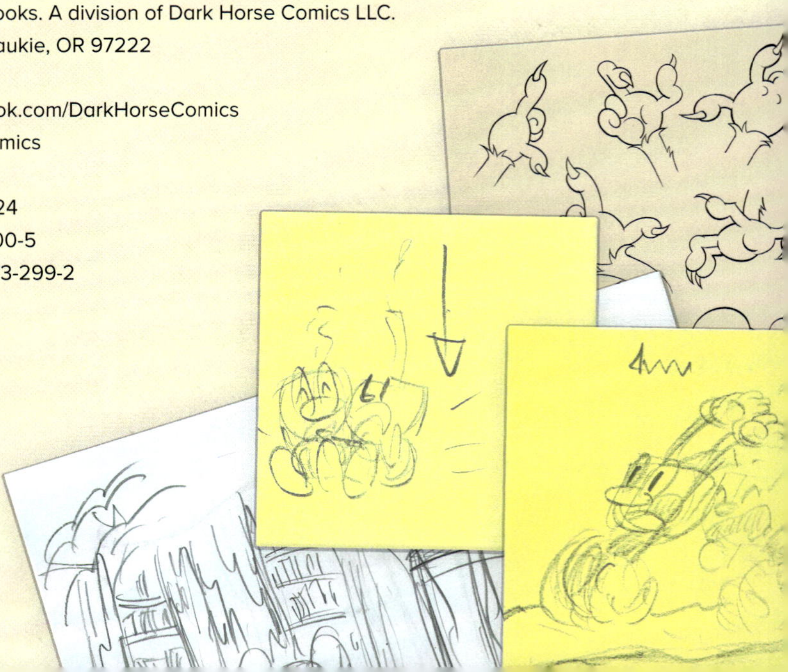

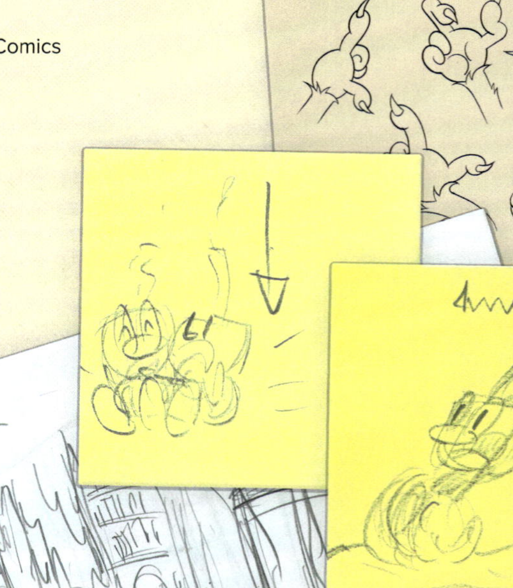

TABLE OF CONTENTS

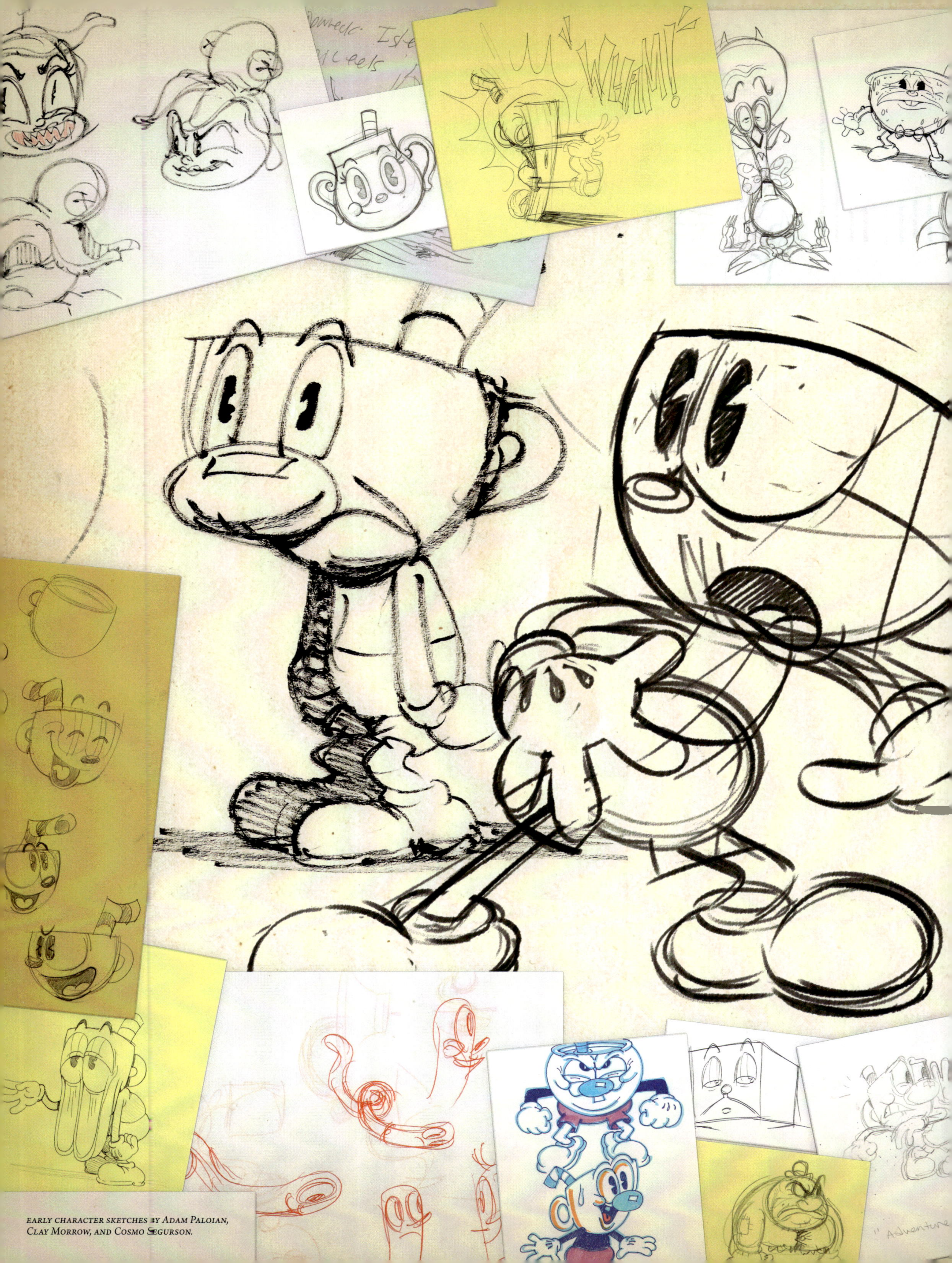

EARLY CHARACTER SKETCHES BY ADAM PALOIAN, CLAY MORROW, AND COSMO SEGURSON.

CHAPTER 1
EARLY DEVELOPMENT

ENTER

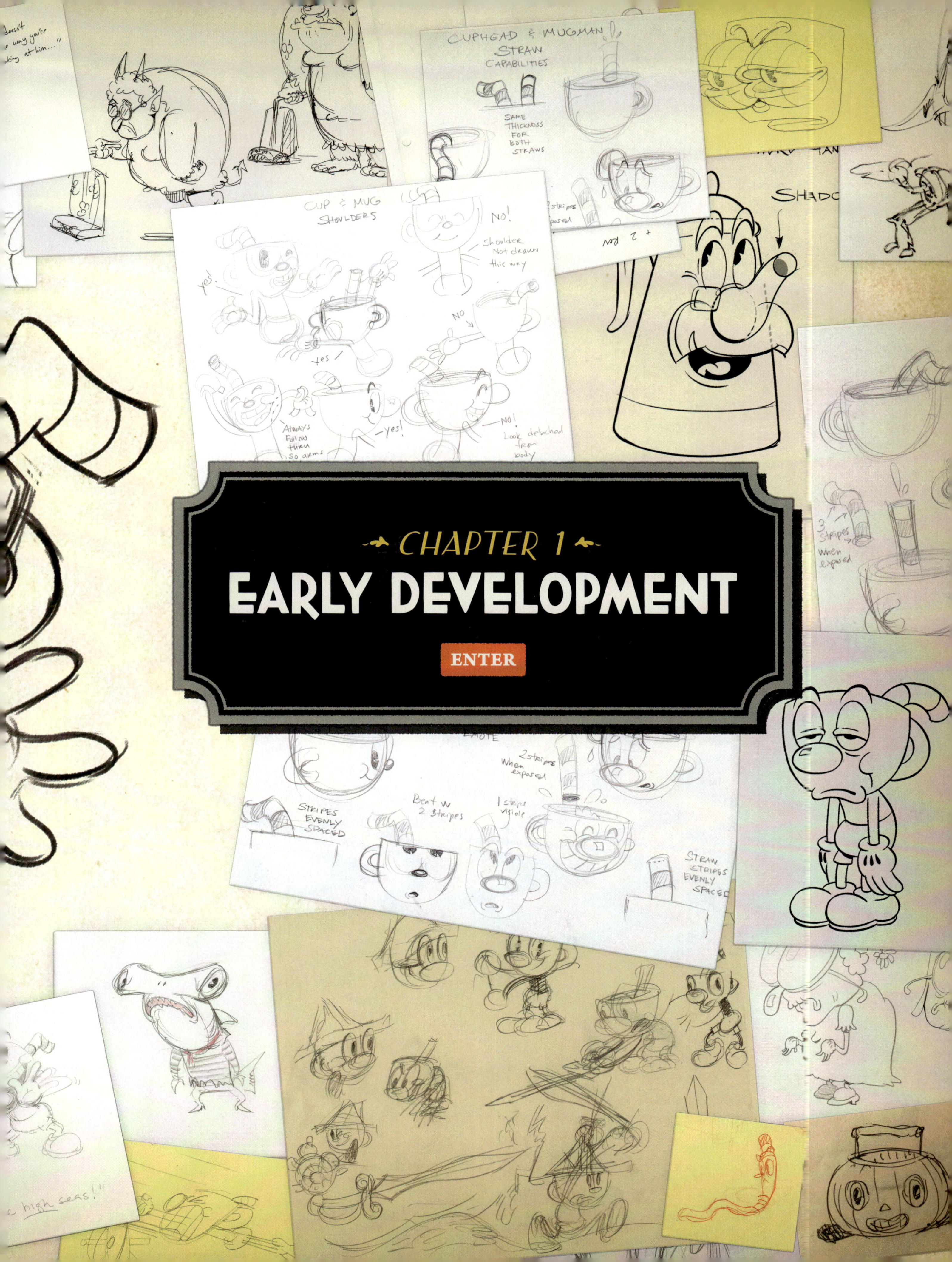

→ **DAVE WASSON, *THE CUPHEAD SHOW!* SERIES DEVELOPER / SHOWRUNNER / EXECUTIVE PRODUCER:** When I first saw the game, I had an emotional, visceral reaction to it. The animation is so well done, the characters are so well drawn, and they all have perfect 1930s timing. They captured the spirit of that era so completely. I was really blown away!

ANDREA FERNANDEZ, *THE CUPHEAD SHOW!* ART DIRECTOR / PRODUCTION DESIGNER: I'd watch the play-throughs while I'd work and listen to old jazz records to give me a jolt of inspiration. Even though I was working on something totally different, I found it so inspiring.

ADAM PALOIAN, *THE CUPHEAD SHOW!* SUPERVISING DIRECTOR: The art was traditionally drawn and painted, and it followed all the steps to be authentic. Just looking at it, you could tell it was a true labor of love.

CLAY MORROW, *THE CUPHEAD SHOW!* SUPERVISING DIRECTOR: For once, it was something my brain could understand, as opposed to some new futuristic app. It was back to paper and pencil.

CJ KETTLER, *THE CUPHEAD SHOW!* EXECUTIVE PRODUCER / PRESIDENT, KING FEATURES: The combination of this extraordinarily successful video game, unbelievably relatable sibling characters, and the style of animation in the game . . . I said, "Clear the decks, we're going to LA." There was no question this property was going to make great television.

ELI CYMET, *CUPHEAD* PRODUCER, STUDIO MDHR: All of the things people love about *Cuphead* the game are things we really wanted them to love about *Cuphead* the show.

CHAD MOLDENHAUER, *CUPHEAD* CREATOR AND *THE CUPHEAD SHOW!* EXECUTIVE PRODUCER, STUDIO MDHR: When making the game, we always wanted people to care about the world we had created and to feel like it brought them joy. The same had to be imbued into a prospective show.

JARED MOLDENHAUER, *CUPHEAD* CREATOR AND *THE CUPHEAD SHOW!* EXECUTIVE PRODUCER, STUDIO MDHR: The artifices for creating a game are not necessary for telling a story. If you get too focused on the actions of gaming, like they're always running and jumping and they have finger guns, then you end up forcing every episode to feel redundant, because you're chasing a similar action.

CHAD: I think our biggest priority heading into such an unfamiliar process was authenticity. More than anything, we didn't want *The Cuphead Show!* to be treated like some video games that we had seen turned into series in the past, where it almost felt as if a production company said, "This video game IP is cool, so let's make a show!" and then asked, "What do you know about the IP?" only to have a room of executives say, "Nothing! But it doesn't matter, we've hired some company, so let's go!"

ANDREA: Before coming on to *The Cuphead Show!* I was on *UniKitty!* for three years. Aesthetically, that show is all sparkles and Legos, and it's amazing in its own way, and I loved working on it. But I was wanting to do something a little more sophisticated, something really nostalgic.

ELI: There is an almost ubiquitous nostalgia with *Cuphead*—you feel nostalgic for an era you never even experienced. That is what I think draws fans to *Cuphead*: it evokes within them this sense of nostalgia and joy and surprise and delight. It evokes a bygone era of artistry.

MAJA MOLDENHAUER, DIRECTOR AND EXECUTIVE PRODUCER FOR *CUPHEAD*, STUDIO MDHR: I think that's a big part of what captured people's attention with *Cuphead*—it felt in a way like it had never been done before, despite ultimately being an homage to something that had been done a long time ago. On a long-enough timeline, what is old becomes new again, and I think it made people stop in their tracks and take notice.

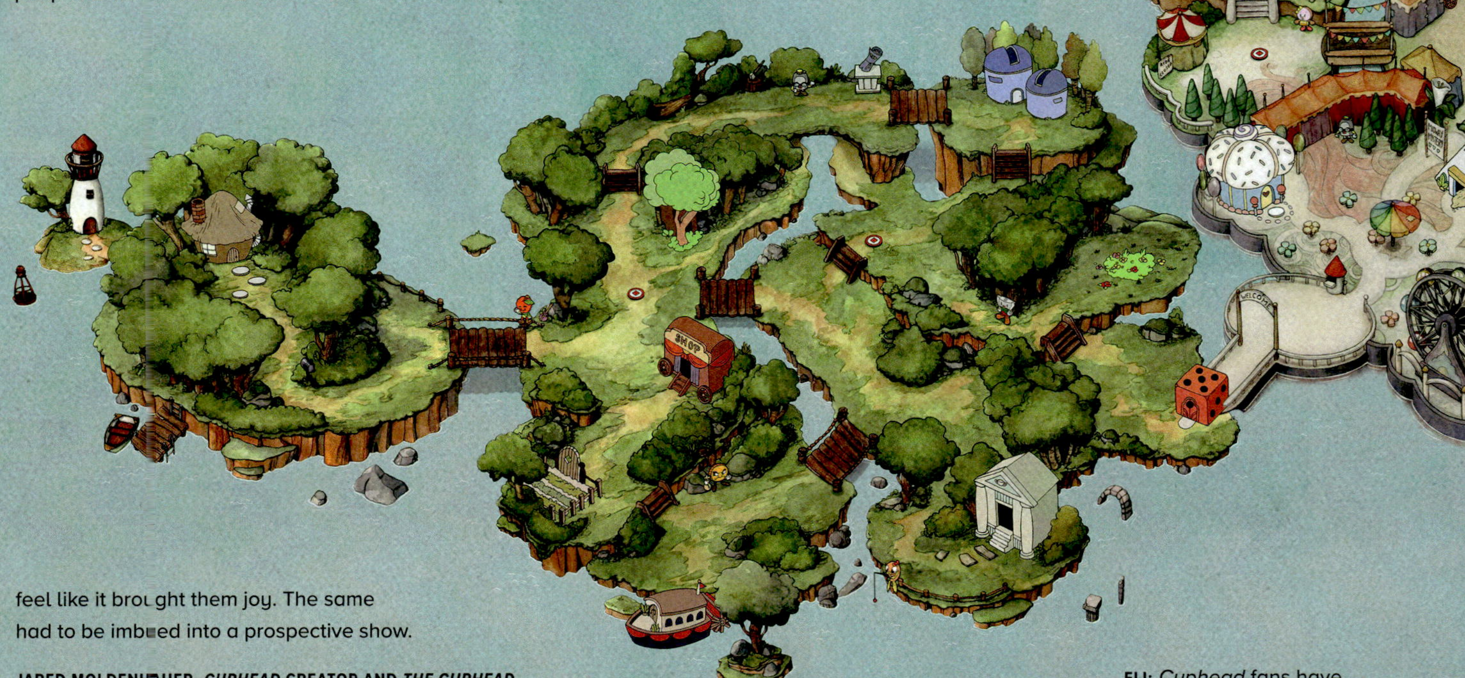

ELI: *Cuphead* fans have an extreme nose for anything that doesn't feel authentically part of that world. It is the double-edged sword of having built *Cuphead* not just as an homage to the 1930s but as if it had been made in the '30s. Now, anything we make is held to this standard.

DAVE: There was a full-blown talent search to find a showrunner. The competition was really stiff. I had to pitch to Netflix, then CJ at King Features, then to Chad and Jared.

CHAD: We liked how structured and down to earth Dave was. It felt like he could take on the biggest film or the smallest series and steer them with his eye on quality above all else.

COSMO SEGURSON, *THE CUPHEAD SHOW!* CO-EXECUTIVE PRODUCER: I told them about my collection of 16 mm shorts that I'd been collecting over the last twenty years, focusing on the *Popeye* cartoons made by Max and Dave Fleischer at Fleischer Studios from 1933 to 1942.

CJ: I remember being sold on Cosmo when he told me he projects old *Popeye* cartoons on the side of his apartment building. He had a deep love and appreciation for 1930s cartoons that he shared with the team. That helped make the series so authentic.

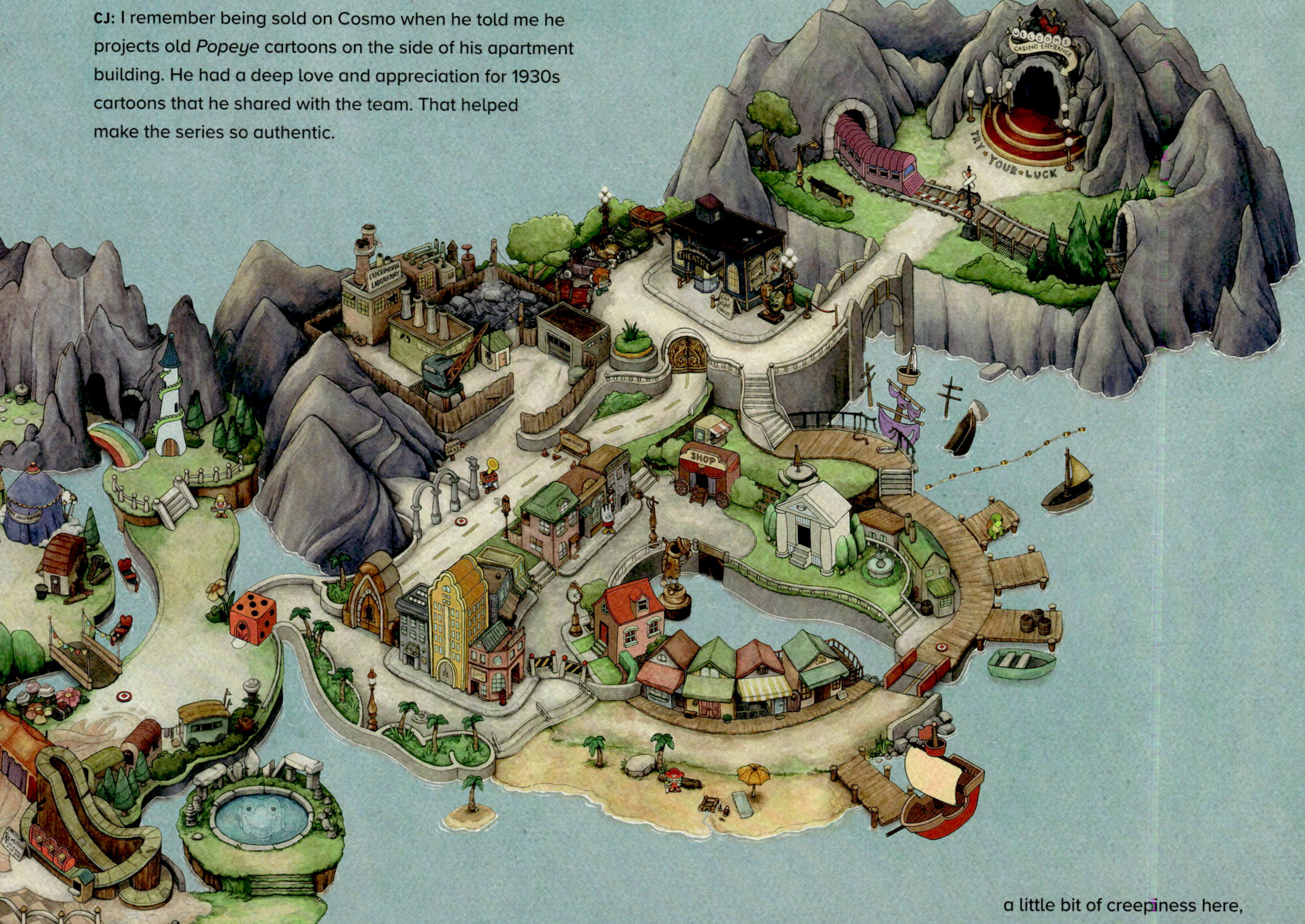

CHAD: Cosmo hosted Fleischer screenings, and some of the shorts that he worked on were quite twisted and off kilter.

CJ: The alchemy of the team is the most important piece of the puzzle. If you don't have a team that gels and genuinely collaborates, that's when you really do have some friction.

JARED: Deeki sort of walked between both worlds, having worked on everything from animated shows to scripts for renowned B horror movie production company Troma.

DEEKI DEKE, *THE CUPHEAD SHOW!* HEAD WRITER: I worked with Dave and Clay on season 1 of the *Mickey Mouse* shorts. Usually, that's the thing on my résumé that people bring up. When Chad and Jared brought up the weird Troma movies I wrote, I knew I had to be a part of this team.

JARED: We saw him from very early in production as someone who could make sure the episodes of *The Cuphead Show!* had elements of all the things we loved growing up—a little bit of creepiness here, an homage to Stephen King there, the change of a camera angle to really make Elder Kettle feel manic in a certain scene. All those things, we think, helped make a fresher cartoon with a sensibility that had been lost to time, in a way. How else do you stand out when there's ten thousand things released every year for kids?

ANDREA: The order was tall. When I interviewed with Dave and Cosmo, they asked me, "Can you do this?" and part of me thought, "I don't know . . ." And I *didn't* know—but I just said yes.

DAVE: She said, "Absolutely, no problem!"

Background painting of the Inkwell Isles from The Cuphead: Don't Deal with the Devil *video game.*

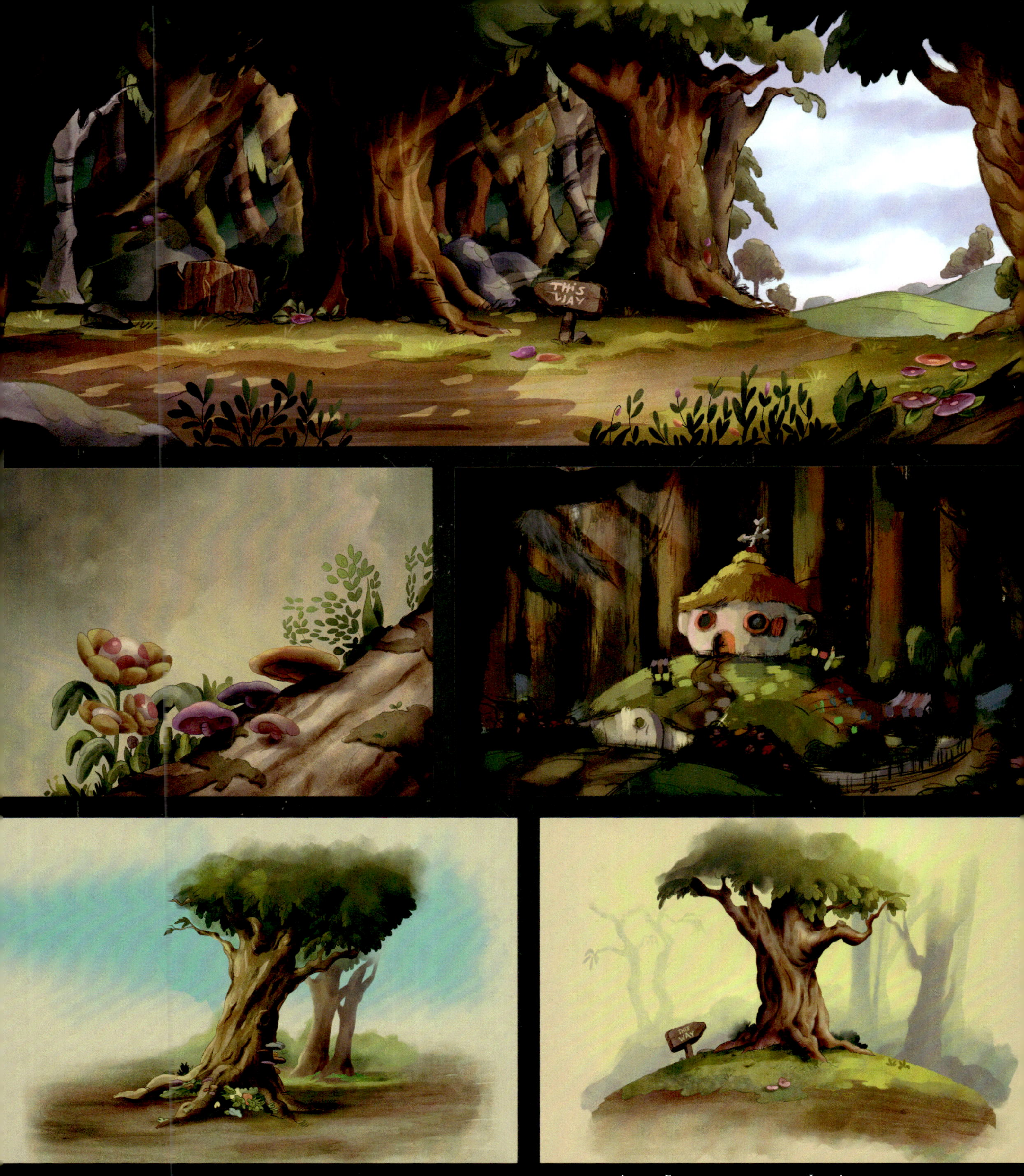

Some of the earliest color keys painted while developing the look of the show. Sketches by Andrea Fernandez; paintings by Ivan Aguirre.

INSPIRATION AND INFLUENCES

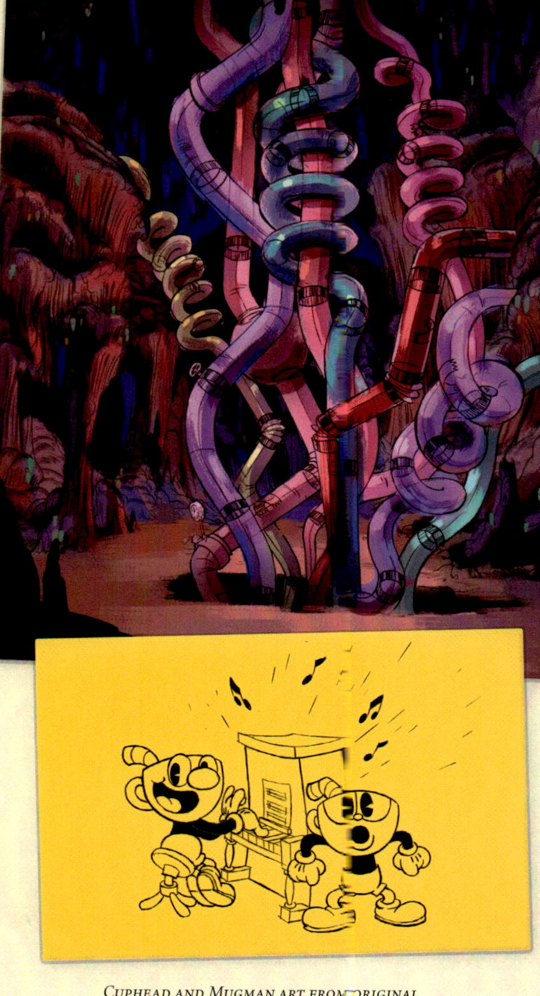

ANDREA: I always get asked what it's like translating a game into a cartoon, but I think people forget that the game was inspired by cartoons in the first place. The idea was always to go back to the source, to read about what MDHR was inspired by, and we'd be inspired by that—rather than only taking inspiration from the game.

SHAKEH HAGHNAZARIAN, *THE CUPHEAD SHOW!* LEAD CHARACTER DESIGNER: The '30s was a time when animation was super experimental and theatrical. Characters were mostly simple shapes without much bone structure and sometimes noodly limbs (hence the term *rubber hose*). There was a rhythm to how they moved and even how they spoke.

ANDREA: Figuring out our unique style based on a decade of animation took a lot of R&D. You have to be practical and pragmatic in terms of the limitations and mathematical in terms of where the energy and the focus will be. It's not just about style but about how you're going to pull off the execution of that style.

SHAKEH: When you watch old cartoons, they have a disclaimer that it doesn't represent current standards. You can't turn a blind eye or try to change what's been done in the past. Back then, it was mostly men working together creating these cartoons. Like when Betty Boop passes by a candle, you'd see her naked silhouette. Sneaky stuff like that.

ANDREA: When people think of 1930s animation, they typically think of a pretty narrow aesthetic, but there's actually a ton of different aesthetics. I started looking at everything from, like, 1928 to 1942. I was mostly inspired by the color *Popeyes*, the color *Donald Ducks*, and the color *Silly Symphonies*.

DAVE: I wanted to be true to the things that were really appealing to me about the game. We looked at the stuff that influenced them and tried to be true to that, like Gustaf Tenggren, the illustrator who was really influential on the backgrounds of *Snow White* [1937] and *Pinocchio* [1940]. That stuff is incredibly well rendered, like you can reach in and touch it. It's really juicy.

ELI: You see the way a lot of modern animated television shows are developed, from a budgetary standpoint, from a narrative standpoint, from a production standpoint, and there obviously were concerns: Are we going to be able to nail the look of the '30s? Can we capture that pre–Hays Code eccentricity? Can it also appeal to a modern, young audience? Can we build a "kitchen sink" show that does it all? There were concerns about how feasible that was.

ANDREA: Today, you can do whatever you want making cartoons because they're mostly done digitally. You can add any texture, you can add any color—but this show's style is really about restricting yourself to what they had back then.

DAVE: That was the golden age of animation. It was artists at the height of their craft. We didn't even know if we could pull it off, but we knew we had to try.

Top: Early color key; background design by Jessica Hong; painting by Ivan Aguirre.

Cuphead and Mugman art from original series bible by Dave Wasson, 2018.

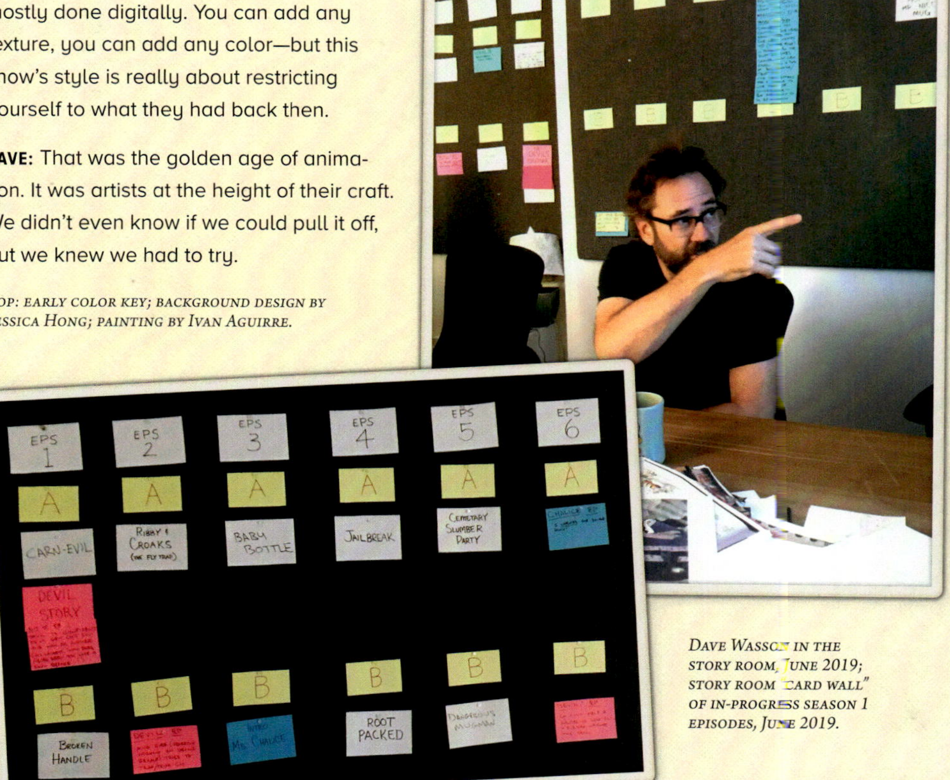

Dave Wasson in the story room, June 2019; story room "card wall" of in-progress season 1 episodes, June 2019.

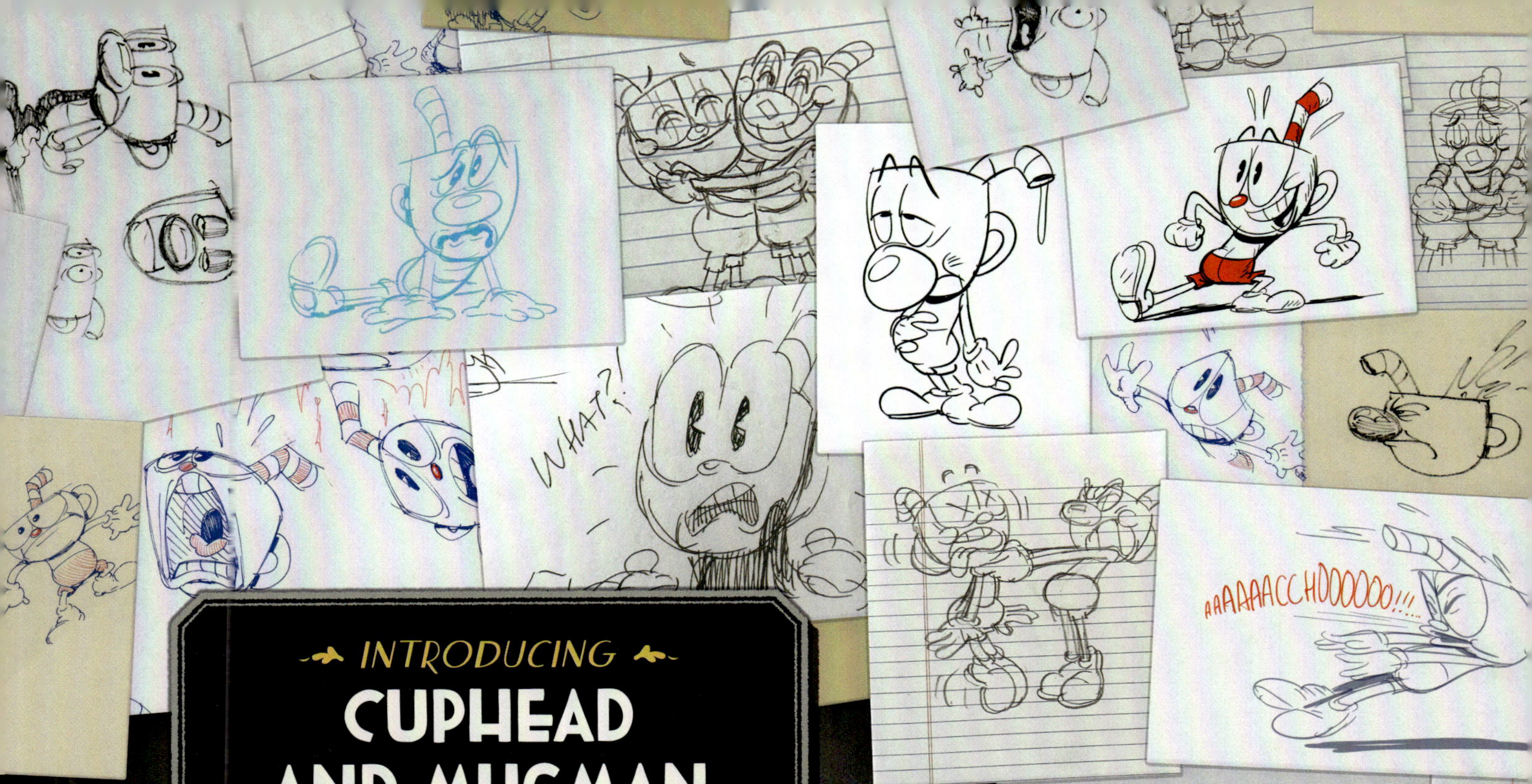

Early Cuphead and Mugman sketches by Adam Paloian and Clay Morrow.

INTRODUCING CUPHEAD AND MUGMAN

(voiced by Tru Valentino and Frank Todaro)

DAVE: We inherited this incredible visual world that was just loaded with great designs, fun action, and beautiful backgrounds, and it was our job to make sense of it and organize the madness into some kind of world you could follow and tell stories with. Even though we were influenced by the cartoons of the 1930s, we wanted to tell stories that were really character driven. It's a character-driven buddy comedy at its core.

JARED: Our characters clearly weren't fully explored in the game. We very purposefully didn't add too much backstory. The characters shine more because they have a little bit of open-endedness, and who they are comes equally from what we tell players and what they invent themselves. We wanted to make sure the show felt like the game in spirit and had room to grow in exciting new narrative directions, but we also don't want to overcook these characters. I didn't ever want to hear the backstory to how Cuphead and Mugman came to live with Elder Kettle, because the ambiguity is what makes it accessible to everyone's imagination.

DAVE: We're not sure what age they actually are—we intentionally left it vague, but they definitely have a childlike mentality. Their wants are pretty simple. They love excitement and adventure and ice cream and candy. They want stuff that any kid would want.

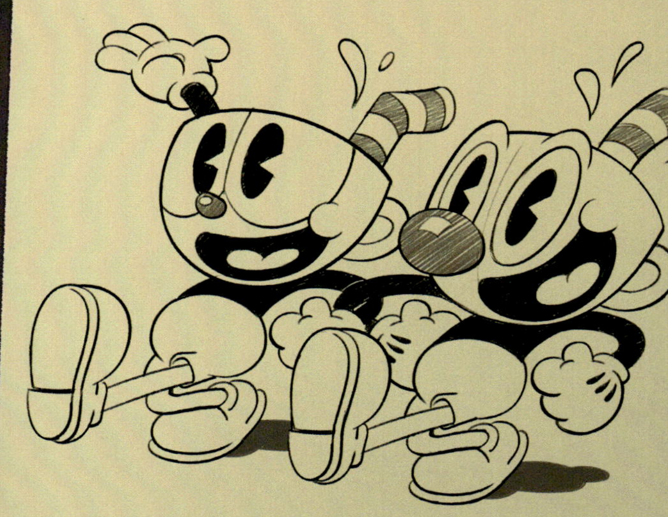

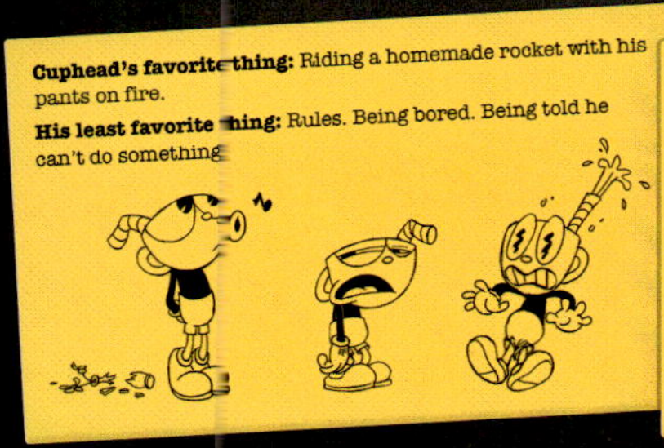

Cuphead's favorite thing: Riding a homemade rocket with his pants on fire.

His least favorite thing: Rules. Being bored. Being told he can't do something.

Mug Man's favorite thing: Getting back home safely after another crazy adventure.

His least favorite thing: Riding a homemade rocket with his pants on fire.

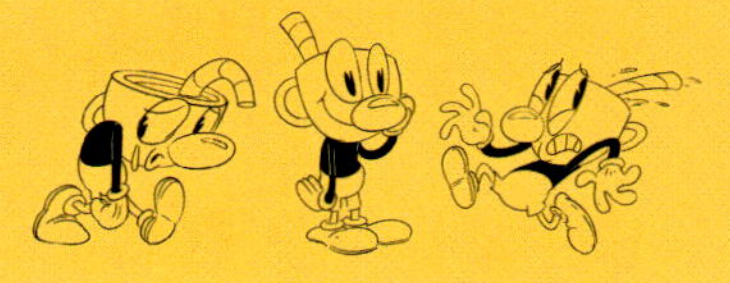

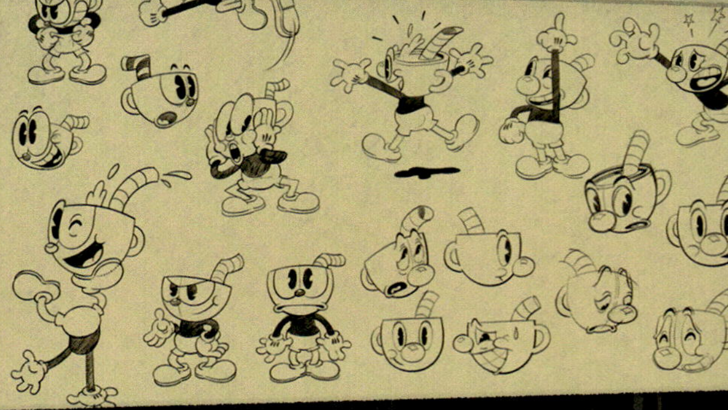

Cuphead and Mugman art from original series bible by Dave Wasson, 2018.

Early design by Shakeh Hachnazarian.

→ **ANDREA:** From a design perspective, the idea was always that Cuphead and Mugman were like kids in this world. The design language was cartoony and the proportions were cartoony, but they always had to feel like they're the size of kids.

DAVE: We took the character designs the Moldenhauers had for the game and pushed them further—into characters we could get more facial expressions and acting from.

ANDREA: Whenever I'm thinking of the style of an episode, I take my cues from Cuphead and Mugman—whatever they're doing, I will fit around them. They're the stars of the show.

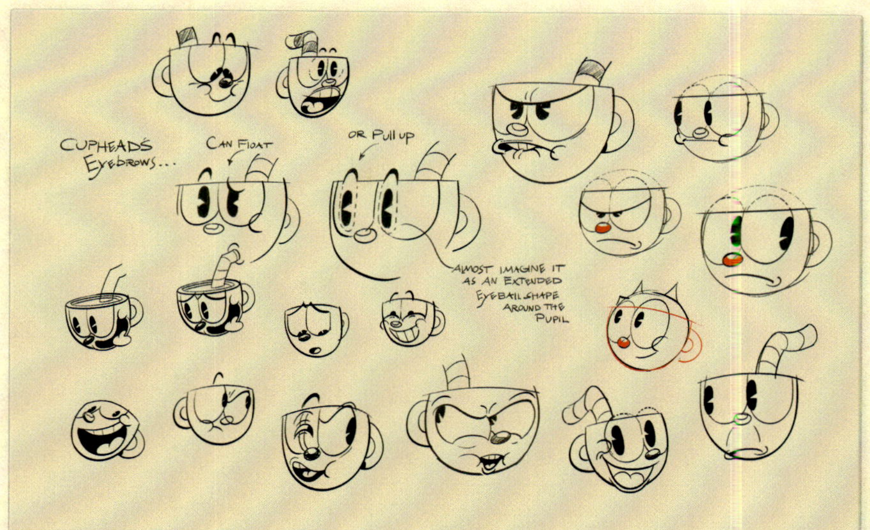

Early sketches and explorations by Shakeh Haghnazarian.

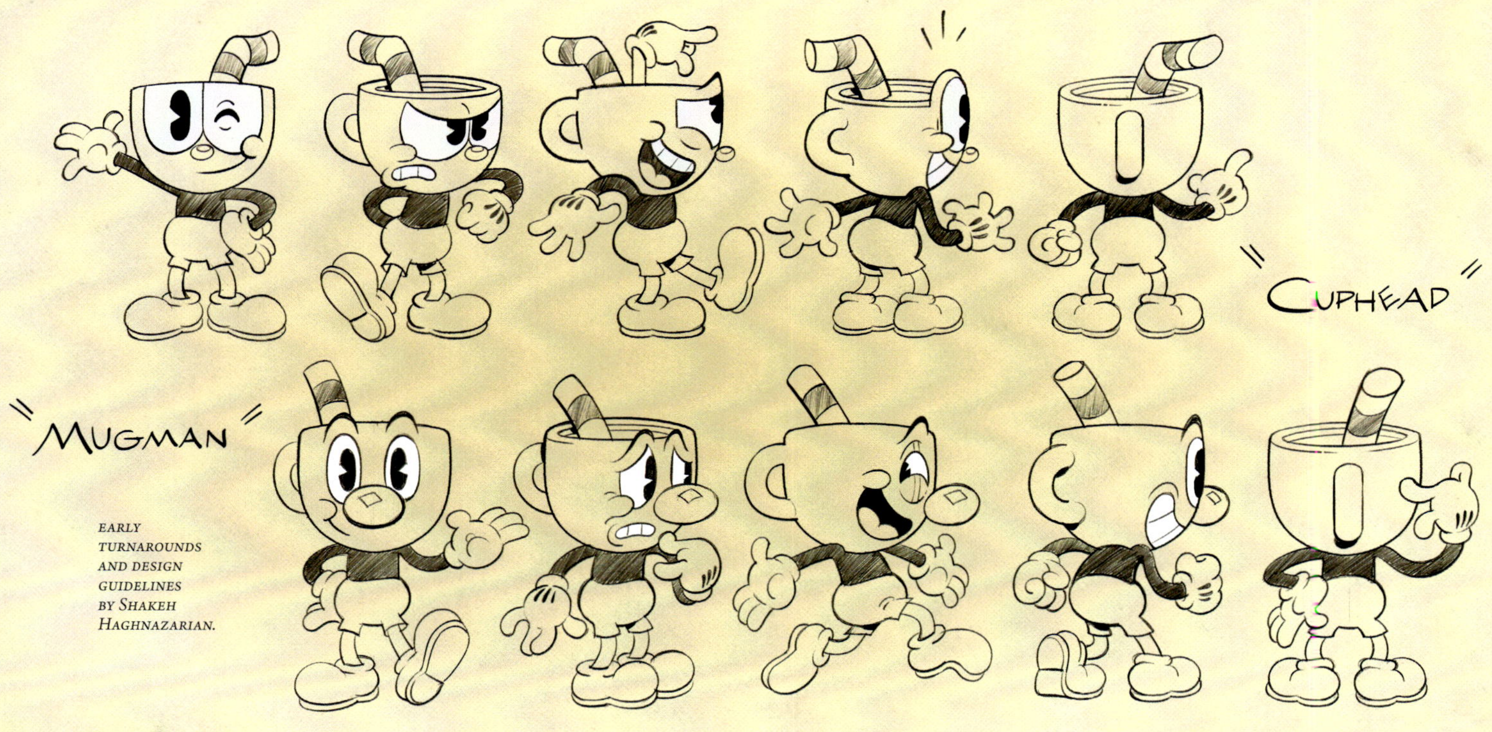

Early turnarounds and design guidelines by Shakeh Haghnazarian.

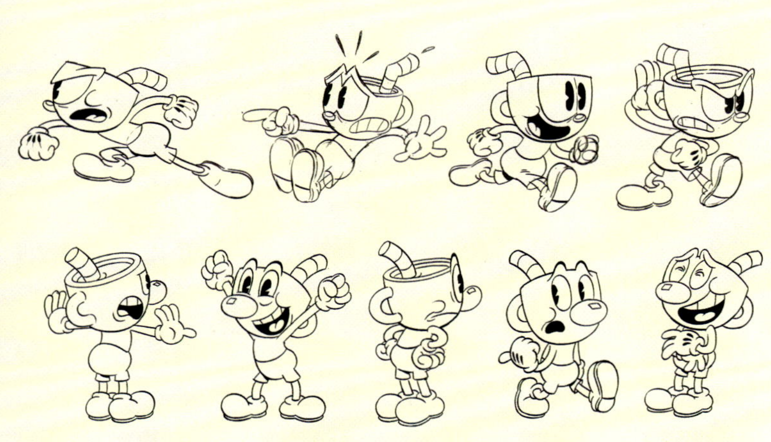

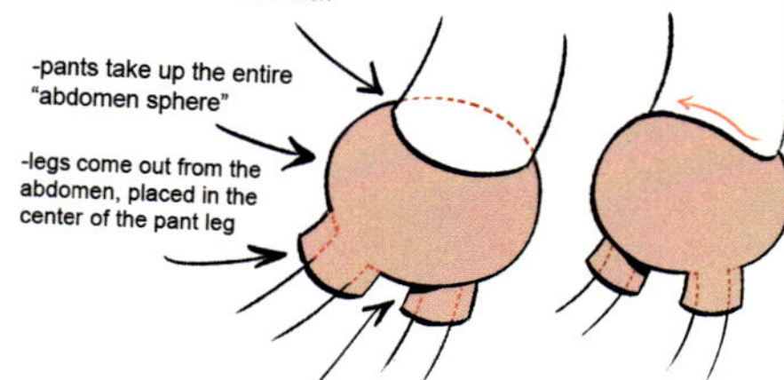

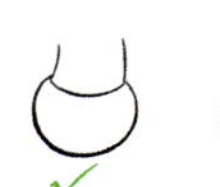

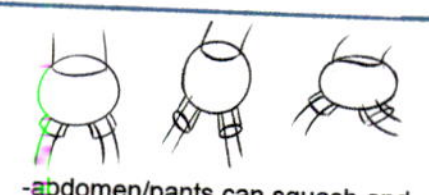

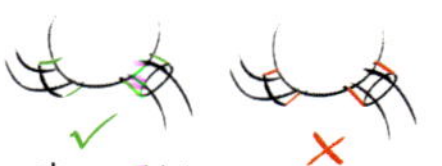

Early special poses by Tapan Gandhi; dos and don'ts by Adam Paloian.

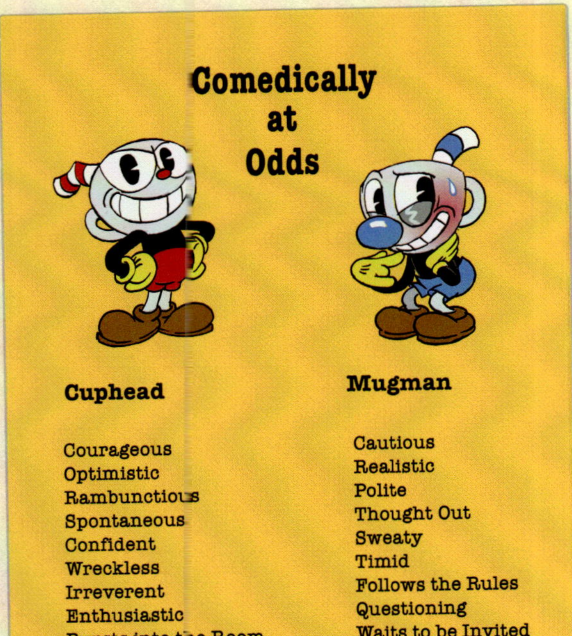

Excerpt from original series bible by Dave Wasson, 2018.

COSMO: The game didn't offer a whole lot in terms of the relationship. We know they live with their Elder Kettle, and that's about it. We really tried to figure out a comedy engine—how would Cuphead react to this? How would Mugman react to that?

DAVE: In the game, Cuphead was the bolder, more risk-taking brother, and Mugman was the slightly meeker and more sensible brother that could be talked into anything. Those were our jumping-off points.

COSMO: Cuphead has really specific goals: adventure and fun. But Mugman is so sweet that he wants to help Cuphead all the time but also can fall into the trap of wanting to have fun as much as Cuphead does. Where Mugman would be more interested in the safe route and a nice meal, Cuphead would run through the joint, grab what he wants, and keep moving.

JARED: Cuphead and Mugman are the perfect contrast as characters—their dynamic as older brother and younger brother offers up a lot of great story opportunities, where you can show them growing and learning things without making it feel ham fisted. That sort of brash, adventurous personality and more cautious personality you see in the show mirrors who we were when we were kids.

DAVE: With brothers, they can fight and they can betray each other in the moment, but at the end of the day, they're best friends.

CLAY: I like that we often keep Mugman as selfish as Cuphead. They're both still in development. They haven't matured to the point where they can be thoughtful all the time.

DEEKI: They can disagree or fight or drop pianos on one another, but the heart of the show is that the two of them always have one another's backs.

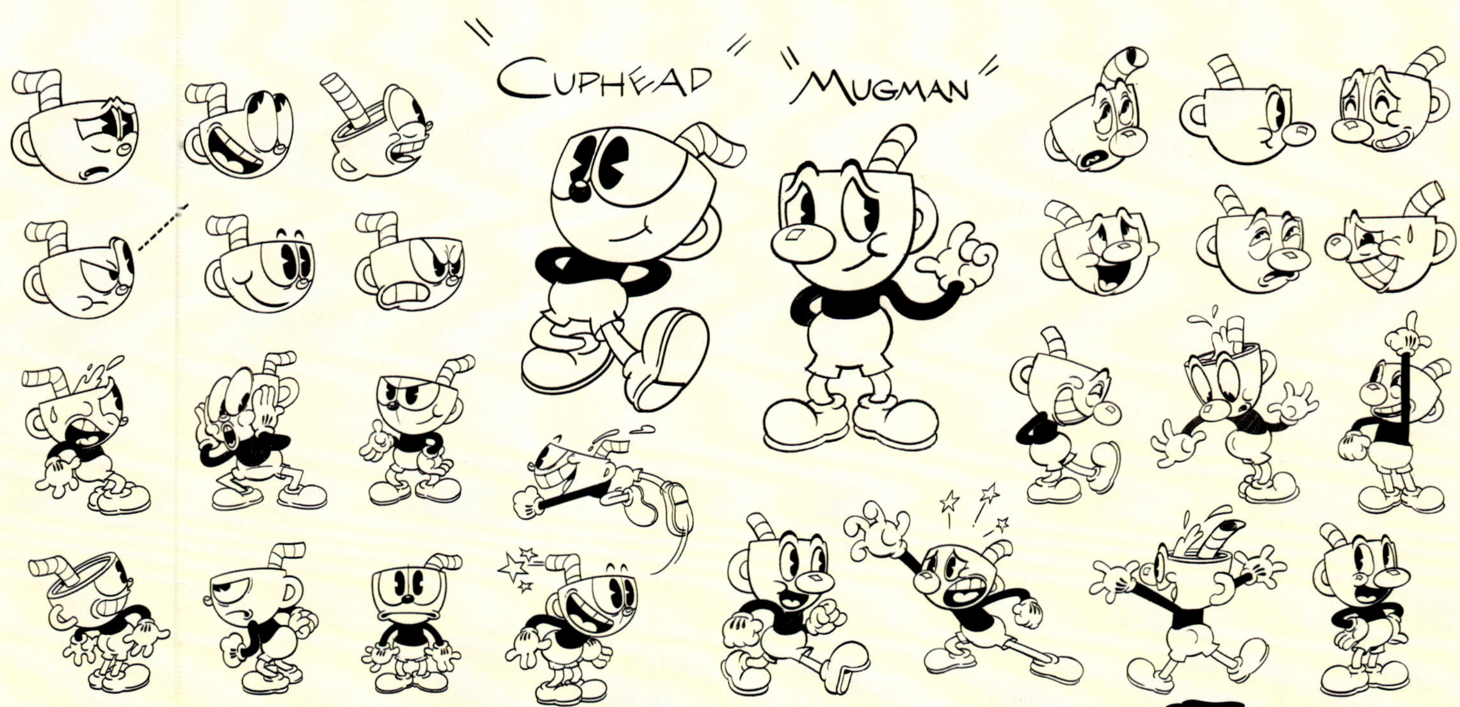

SHAKEH: It's tricky, because they're porcelain, but they still look like they have skin. When their eyebrows would bunch up or when they smiled, their cheeks would pop out. Everything had to feel like it had mass and weight—but then they have [what looks like] milk, so there's a lot of components, like, how does the straw work? I try to make that work to my advantage, because the straw can turn into a telescope, or it could grow into something else, like a weapon. You can just do so much with it. It was open, there was nothing holding me back, so I just went for it.

Original series poses and expression sheets by Shakeh Haghnazarian.

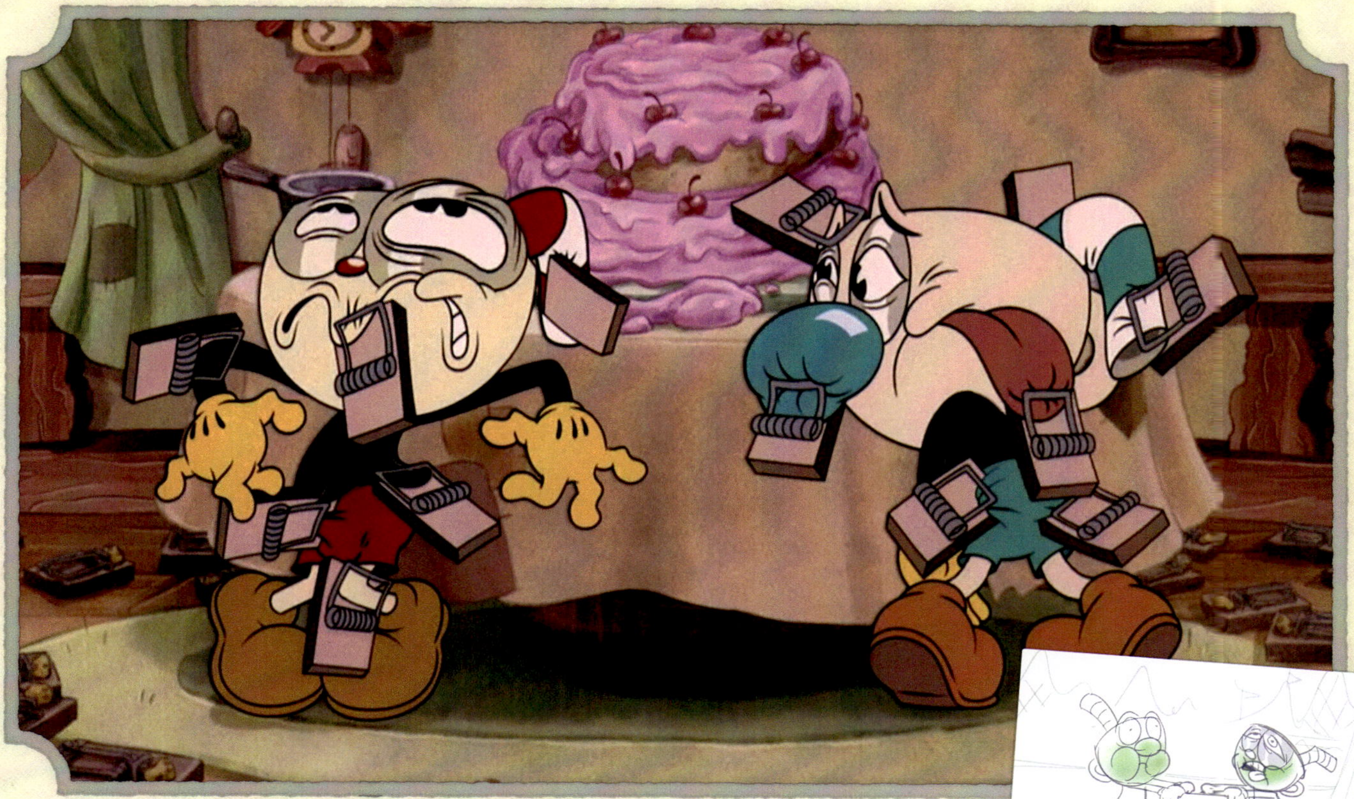

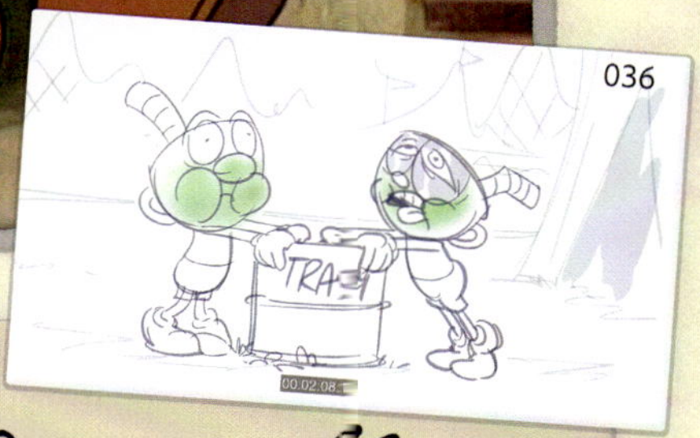

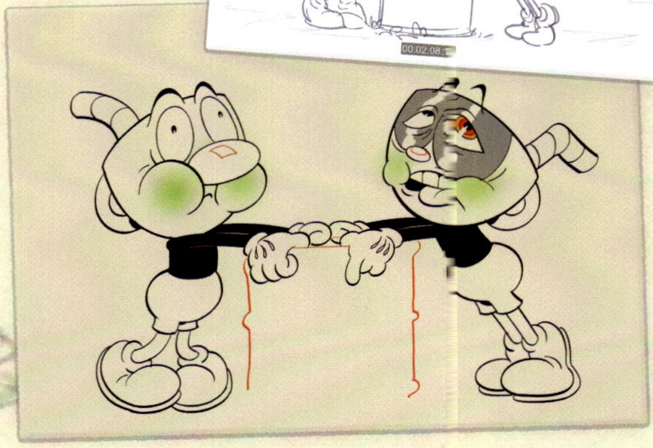

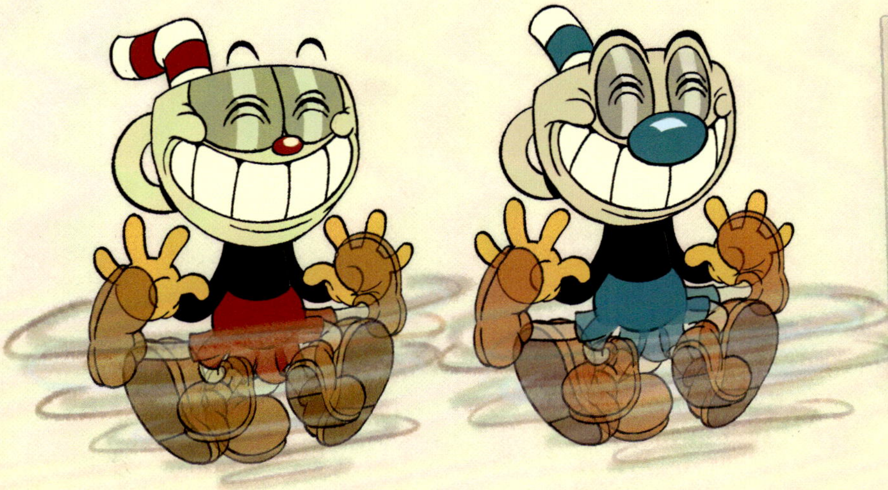

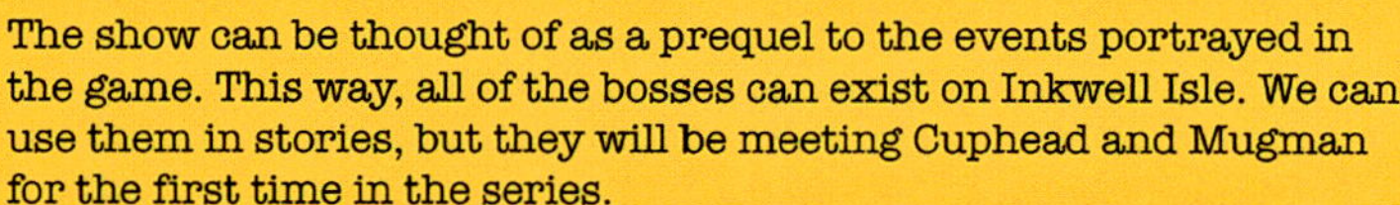
The show can be thought of as a prequel to the events portrayed in the game. This way, all of the bosses can exist on Inkwell Isle. We can use them in stories, but they will be meeting Cuphead and Mugman for the first time in the series.

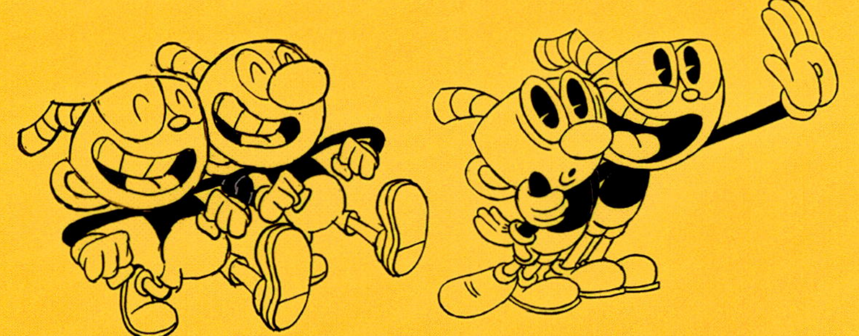

→ **SHAKEH:** All the characters in the game were pretty much working off a side-scrolling pan. So here was a chance to place them in a more dimensional environment, giving them personalities and quirks and breathing life into them.

DAVE: The visual style just lends believability to the world, so you don't question whether this guy with a cup for a head could really be running around doing this stuff. They seem real.

SHAKEH: I kept drawing the characters to get more familiar with them. I tried to sketch them, push them as much as I could, and see how they looked.

Special pose designs by Mike Fontanelli, Bradley Lewis, and Shakeh Haghnazarian; storyboard panel by Adam Paloian; excerpt from original series bible by Dave Wasson, 2018.

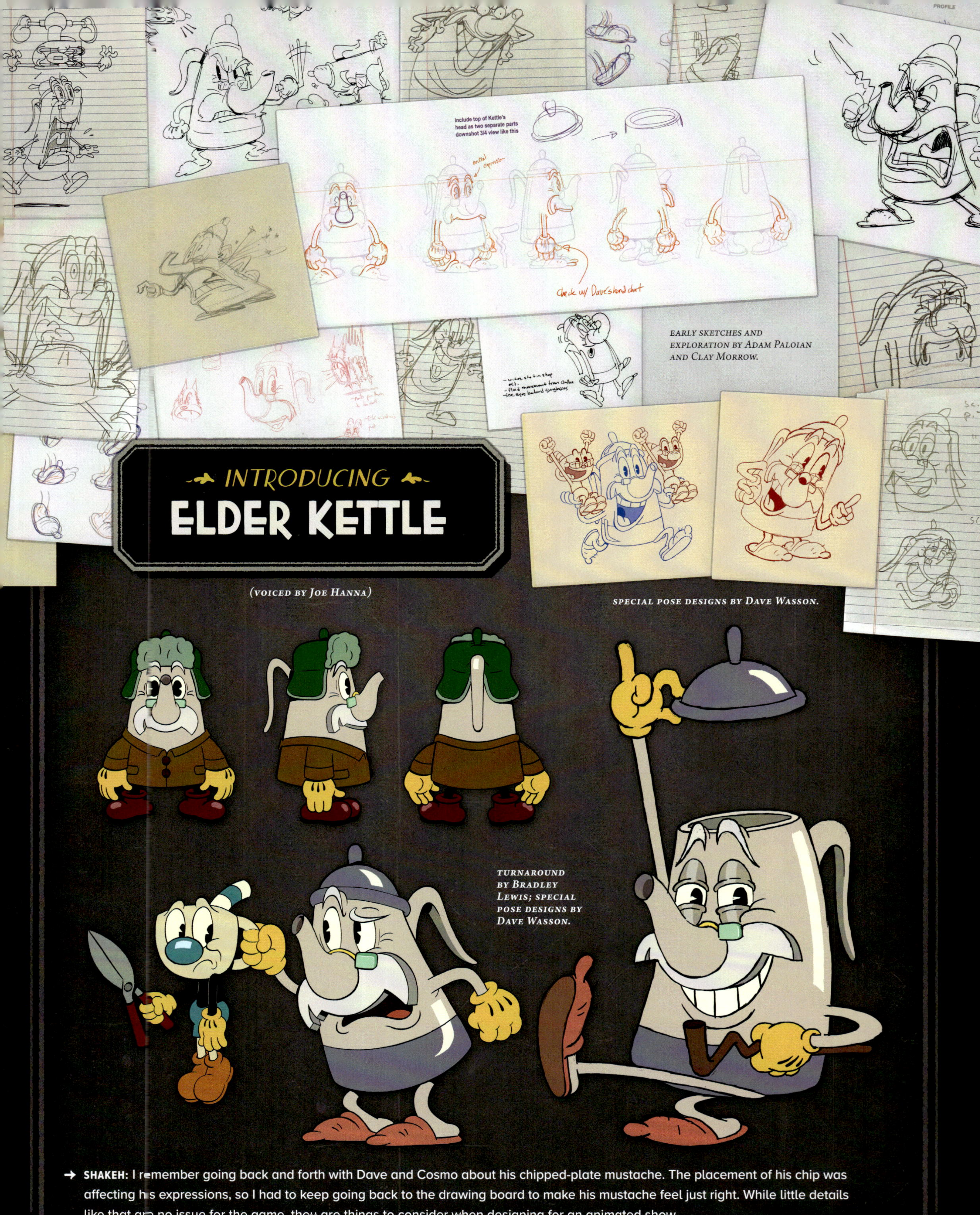

EARLY SKETCHES AND EXPLORATION BY ADAM PALOIAN AND CLAY MORROW.

INTRODUCING
ELDER KETTLE

(VOICED BY JOE HANNA)

SPECIAL POSE DESIGNS BY DAVE WASSON.

TURNAROUND BY BRADLEY LEWIS; SPECIAL POSE DESIGNS BY DAVE WASSON.

→ **SHAKEH:** I remember going back and forth with Dave and Cosmo about his chipped-plate mustache. The placement of his chip was affecting his expressions, so I had to keep going back to the drawing board to make his mustache feel just right. While little details like that are no issue for the game, they are things to consider when designing for an animated show.

→ TAPAN GANDHI, *THE CUPHEAD SHOW!* CHARACTER DESIGNER: I was impressed with the game designs, as we all were, but seeing how Shakeh warmed the characters up and made them more expressive—she made them very accessible for a modern audience. In 1930s cartoons sometimes characters can look kinda walleyed or spacy. She brought them into focus while still retaining the 1930s flair. I was blown away.

SHAKEH: Sometimes it's an out-of-body experience. I'll do something where I get so into the character and afterward, I think, "Oh, I drew that—wow, it looks good!" It's like acting—you're given lines, and you have to deliver those lines. If you're a bad actor, then you're gonna come off blank. So you try to put as much life into the characters as possible. It's about giving them life through your poses and what you choose to bring into them.

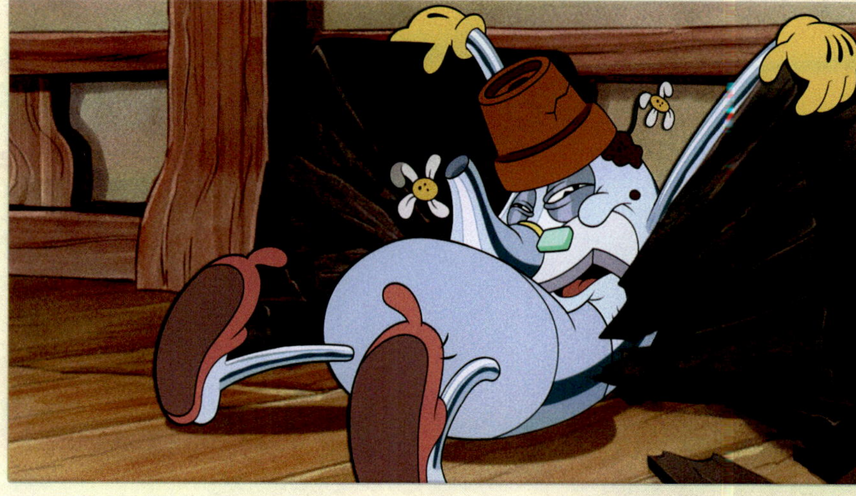

Original Kettle turnaround by Tapan Gandhi; expression sheets by Shakeh Haghnazarian; special pose designs by Martin Wittig.

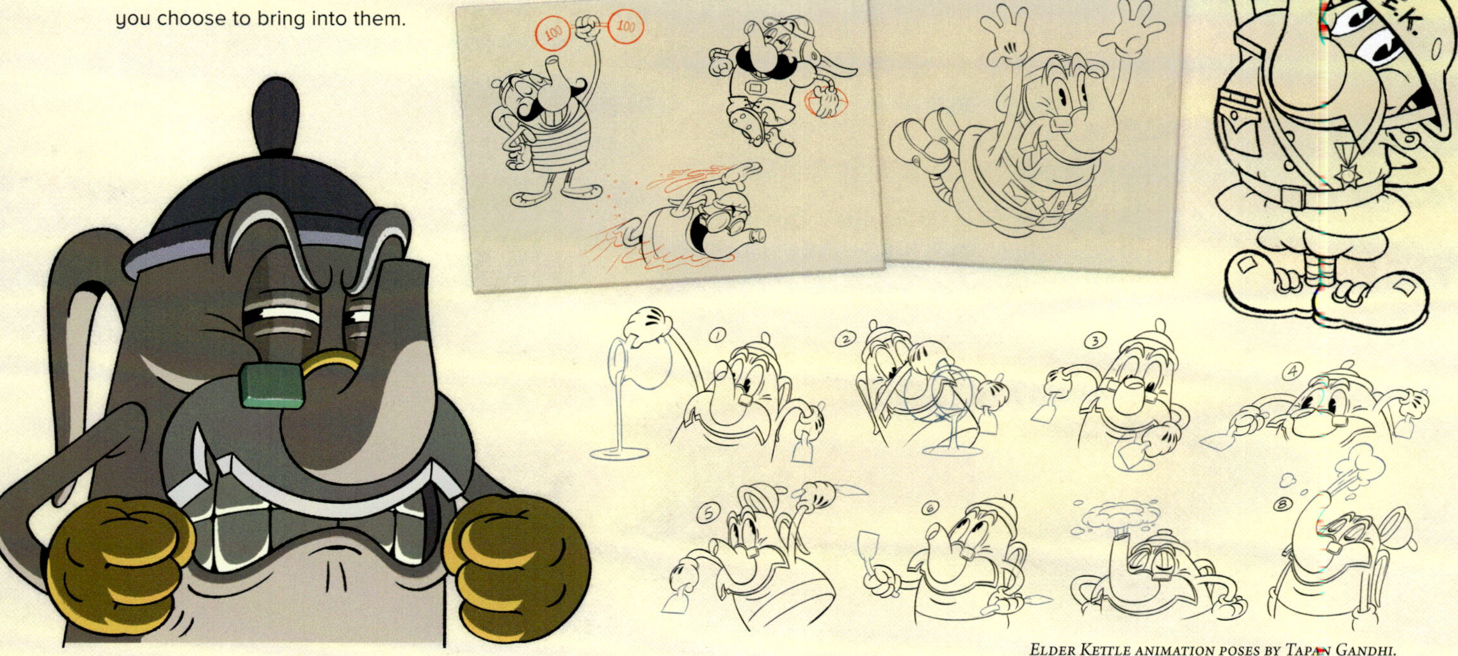

Elder Kettle animation poses by Tapan Gandhi.

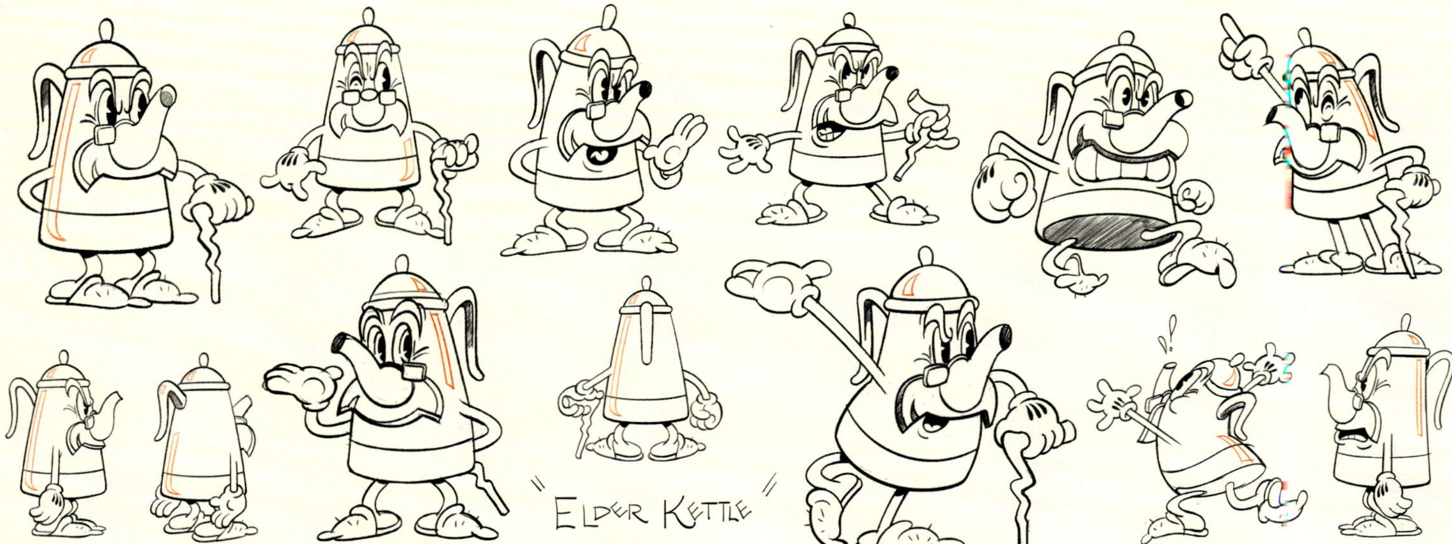

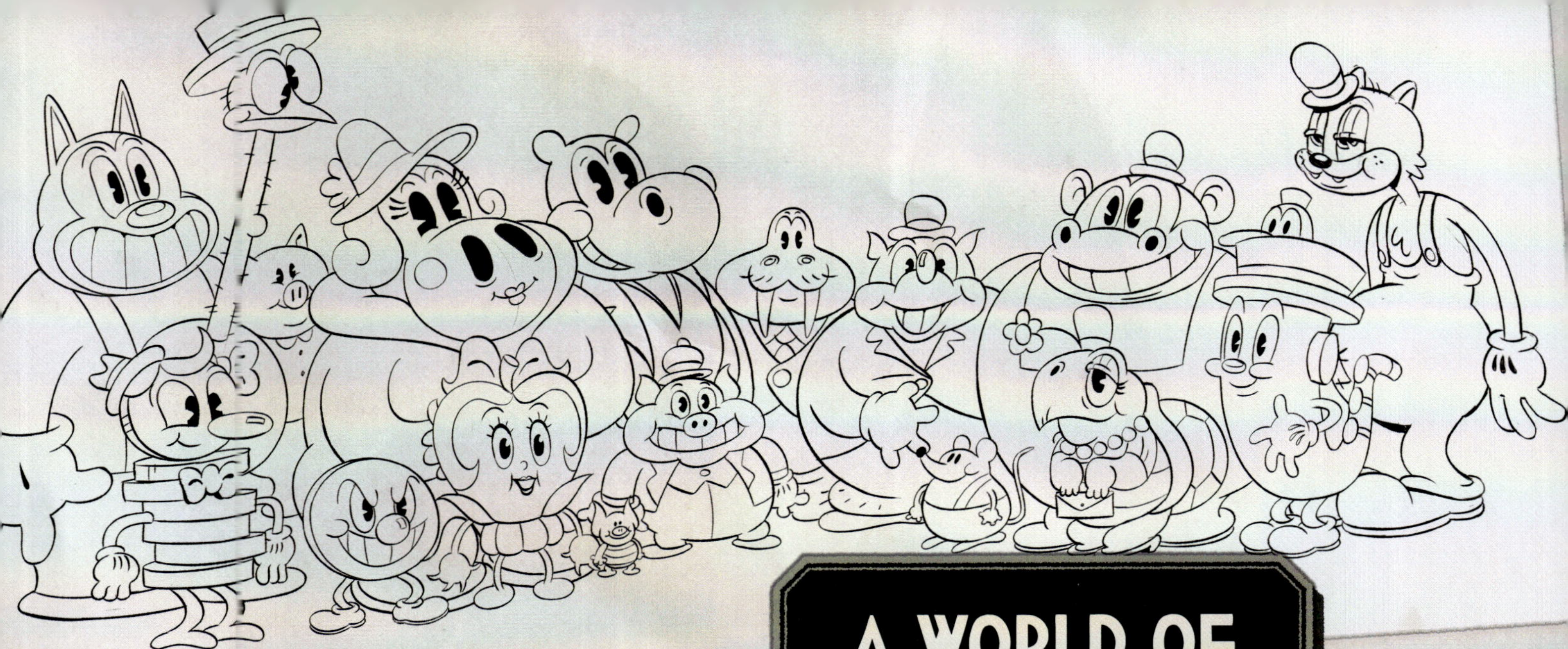

A WORLD OF CHARACTERS

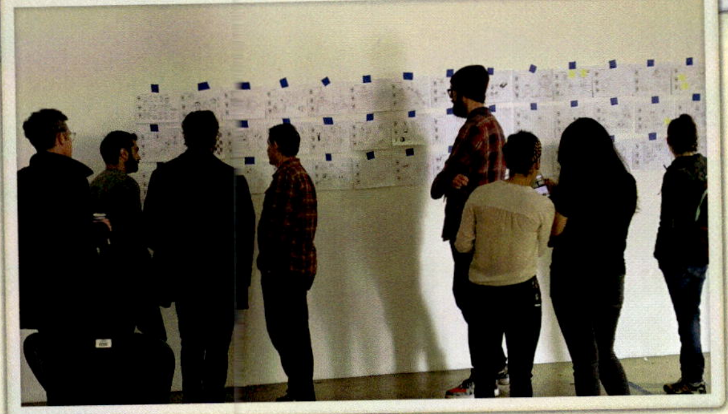

EARLY CREATIVE MEETING AT THE "WALL OF CHARACTERS," 2019.

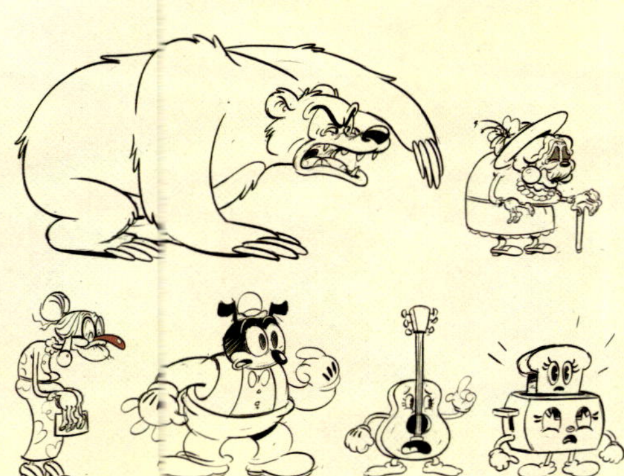

→ **DEEKI:** The world of the Inkwell Isles is incredibly expansive. We couldn't include everything from the game and had to make some difficult choices.

ANDREA: One of the first meetings I went to, we were just cutting characters.

DAVE: The production team pinned up an entire wall of characters from the game. We had to start somewhere.

ANDREA: There were so many characters on the wall, and we were all saying, "Cut, cut, cut, oooh very cool, cut, cut . . ." It was actually a really fun meeting!

DAVE: Andrea had some pretty strong opinions and she wasn't shy about sharing them. She was pretty hilarious, actually.

ANDREA: It was my "production brain" asking, what can we actually achieve onscreen on a TV budget? If this were a feature, we'd have a big budget. But this is episodic TV, so I get two weeks to figure out how each episode will look, and each episode has to fit the scope of what we're doing overall.

DEEKI: On that note, do you have any comment regarding the rather conspicuous absence of the game's first boss, Goopy Le Grande?

ANDREA: Absolutely no comment.

CLAY: We do not speak about Goopy.

→ **TAPAN:** Right in the beginning, I was tasked with making a list of incidentals to populate the show. I had never had so much creative freedom to just draw whatever characters popped into my head.

SHAKEH: We had to stay true to what the existing characters were, but at the same time, we had the freedom to go off and create something new that would fit into that world.

TAPAN: You have to remember they're characters first, and whatever species or object they are is secondary.

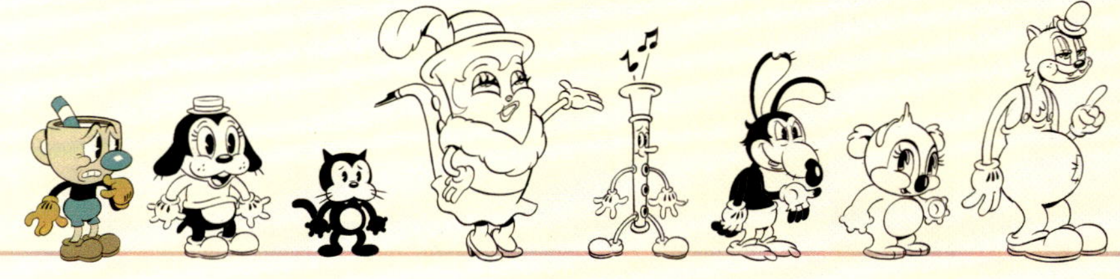

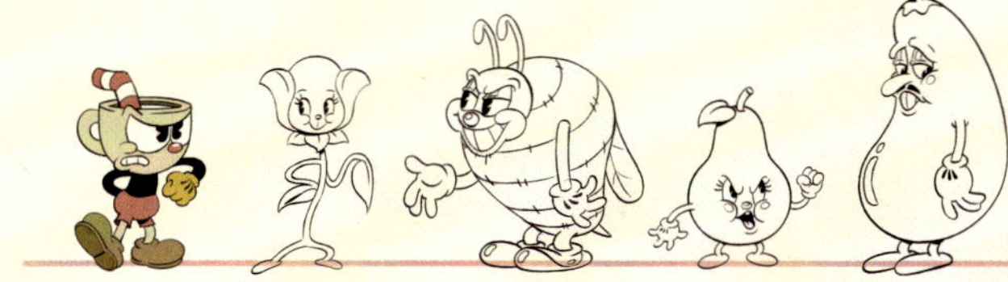

INCIDENTAL INKWELLIAN DESIGNS BY TAPAN GANDHI.

→ **JARED:** One of the key hooks for the game itself was the creativity—the sense that at any moment anything could happen. It's an inherent trait that most people have, and that children in particular have a massive amount of, and the '30s style allowed us to approach different creative ideas in animation. Taken on its own, seeing a blimp turn into a moon that lets out UFOs is sort of nonsense—but in that moment of experiencing it, I think it brings back some of that childhood joy. And I feel like there is a similar vein of seeking out the unexpected and off kilter that runs through *The Cuphead Show!*

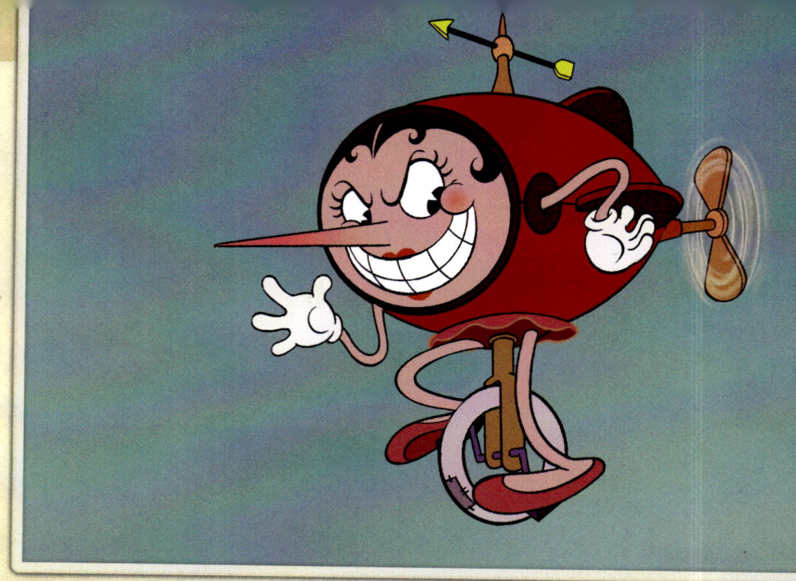

Hilda Berg's cameo in "Charmed and Dangerous"; special pose design by Mike Fontanelli.

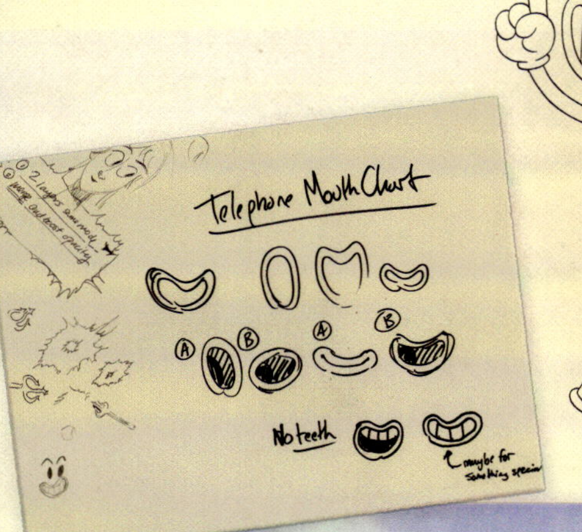

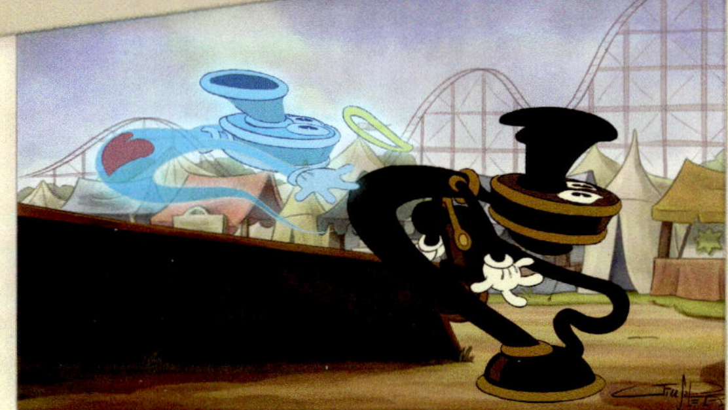

Telephone mouth chart sketch by Adam Paloian; Telephone turnaround by Tapan Gandhi; Telephone special pose designs by Adam Fay and Adam Paloian.

→ **DAVE:** I originally thought that we would have lots of background characters and that we'd keep adding to them throughout the series. Then some production realities set in, and we had to limit the background characters, but this turned out to be a good thing: it forced us to adapt even the incidental characters into personalities.

ADAM P: We reused most of those characters throughout the whole show. They were not supposed to be recurring characters, but Deeki wrote them into other stories and as we got to know them, characters like Telephone became a running gag.

DEEKI: Telephone is born to lose. Whenever he showed up, we felt compelled to punish him.

ANDREA: Especially after Dave was cast as Telephone's voice.

ADAM P: It's nice to see the incidental characters come back, because it starts to feel like you're living in this world and you know all these people.

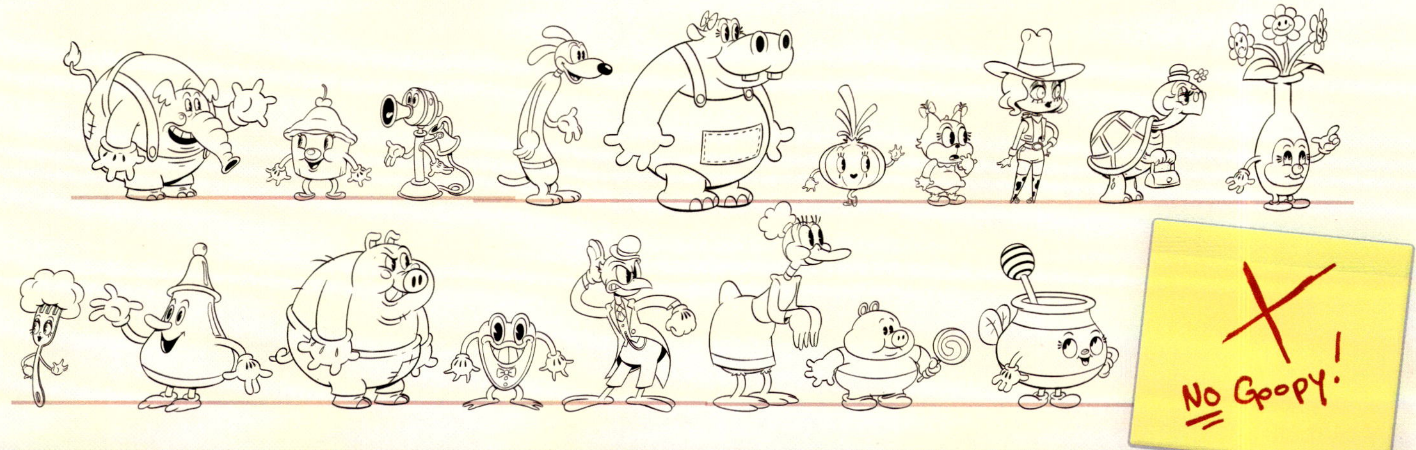

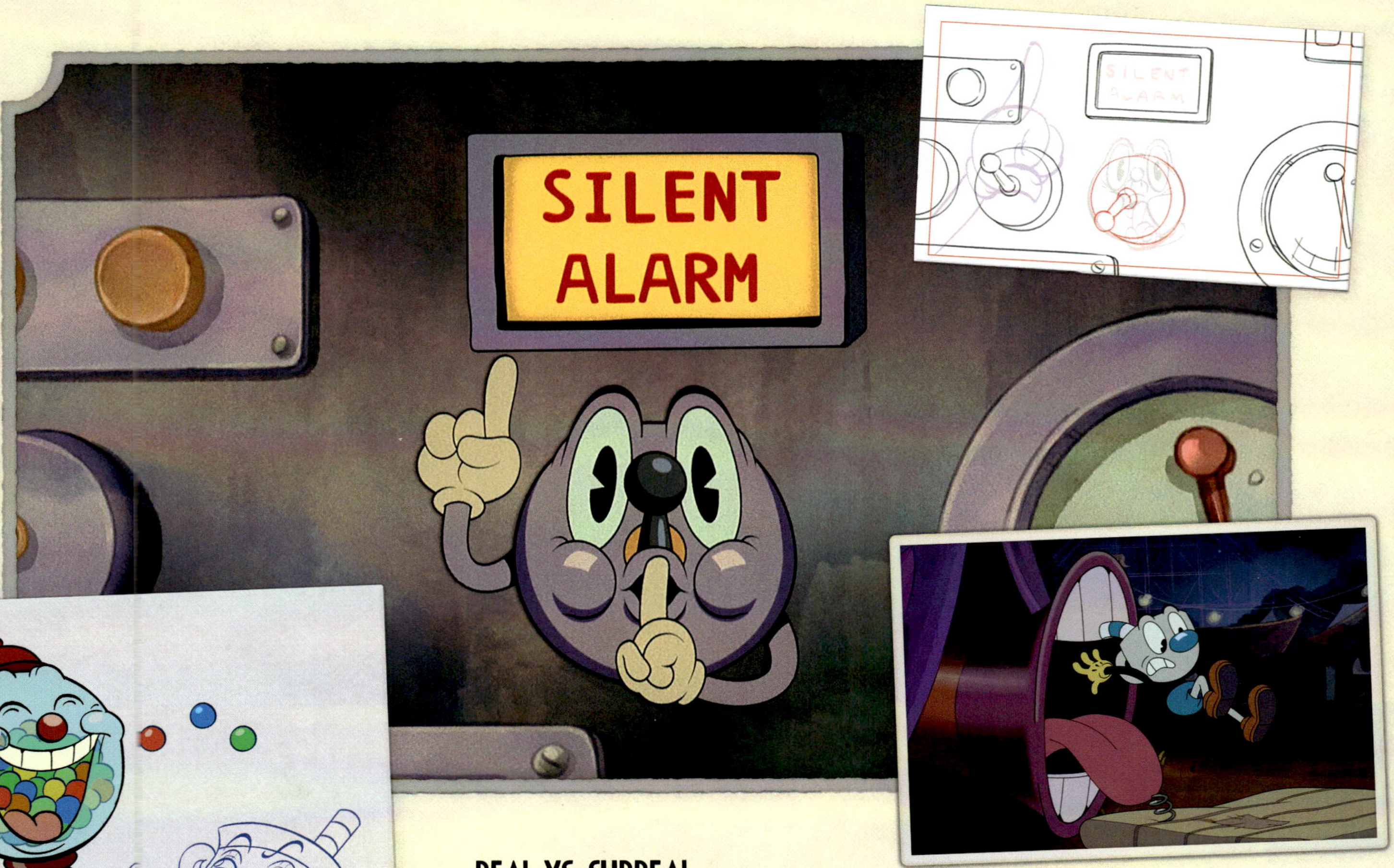

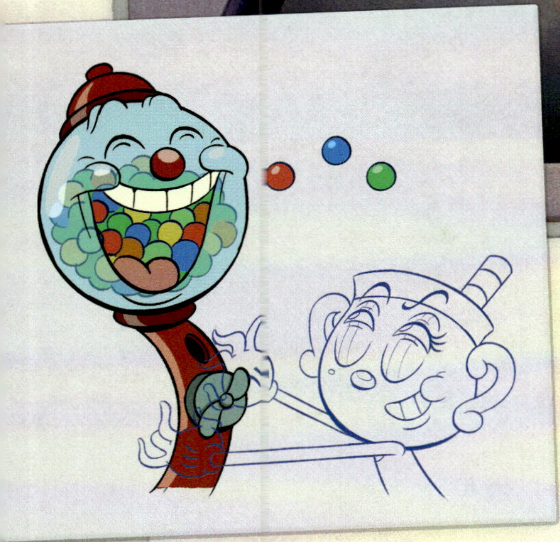

REAL VS. SURREAL

→ **SHAKEH:** The best part was that any inanimate object could potentially be a character.

TAPAN: It's a 1930s world where anything can have eyes pop out and start talking. That concerned me, because then we're mixing character design, prop design, layout, background—everything becomes one thing, and it can get messy quickly.

DAVE: Early on we talked a lot about surreal anthropomorphic gags, where somebody reaches for a doorknob, and a face morphs onto it—we initially thought there would be more of that. But since we were telling character-driven stories, it was harder to find places for that sort of thing, because they tended to interrupt the story flow.

ANDREA: I don't want the world to be more distracting than Cuphead and Mugman. If I take attention from them with the design of the world, it would take people out of the show.

ADAM P: If it's wall-to-wall surreal, it's harder to get the audience to care about the stakes.

CLAY: I think we all appreciated the abstract mind melt of some of the 1930s animation. But it is so difficult for that *and* grounded storytelling to share the same space. If you want to go surreal, you really have to carve out room to get to that point and then back again.

ANDREA: We do get surreal on the show, but there's a specific formula to get surreal. Keeping the world not as wall-to-wall goofy lets it be funnier when we do push it there. If you think a car can come alive at any moment, it's not as funny or unexpected as when it happens intermittently. But because we don't do that all the time, it becomes a more unique moment. I don't want people to be thinking, "Is that chair behind them going to come alive?" I want them to be focused on Cuphead and Mugman. Let Cuphead and Mugman be the stars of the show.

DAVE: My idea of the series evolved as we continued to talk and write stories, but ultimately the thing that was always the most interesting to me was the relationship between Cuphead and Mugman—it just felt the best. The way it naturally evolved, character comedy won out over a more surreal cartoon.

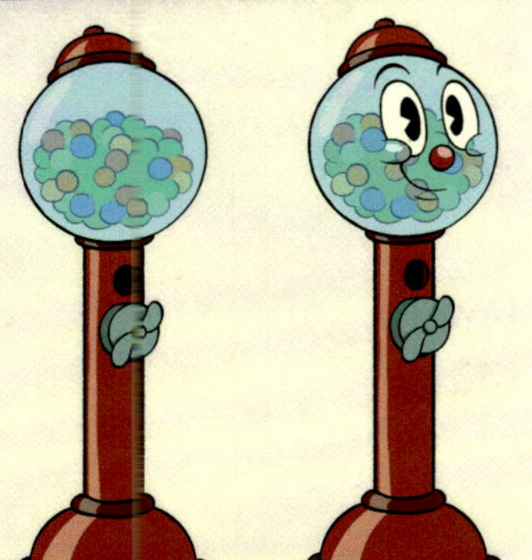

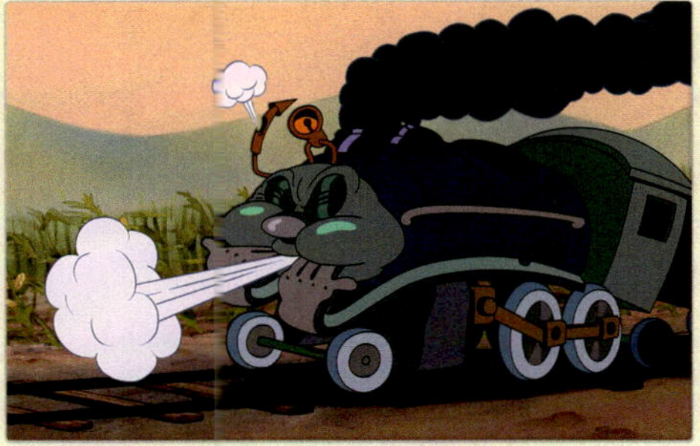

CHARACTER DESIGNS AND SPECIAL POSES BY TAPAN GANDHI AND MIKE FONTANELLI.

Previs tree sketches by Andrea Fernandez; background designs by Andrea Fernandez and Lauren Duda; paintings by Michelle Thies.

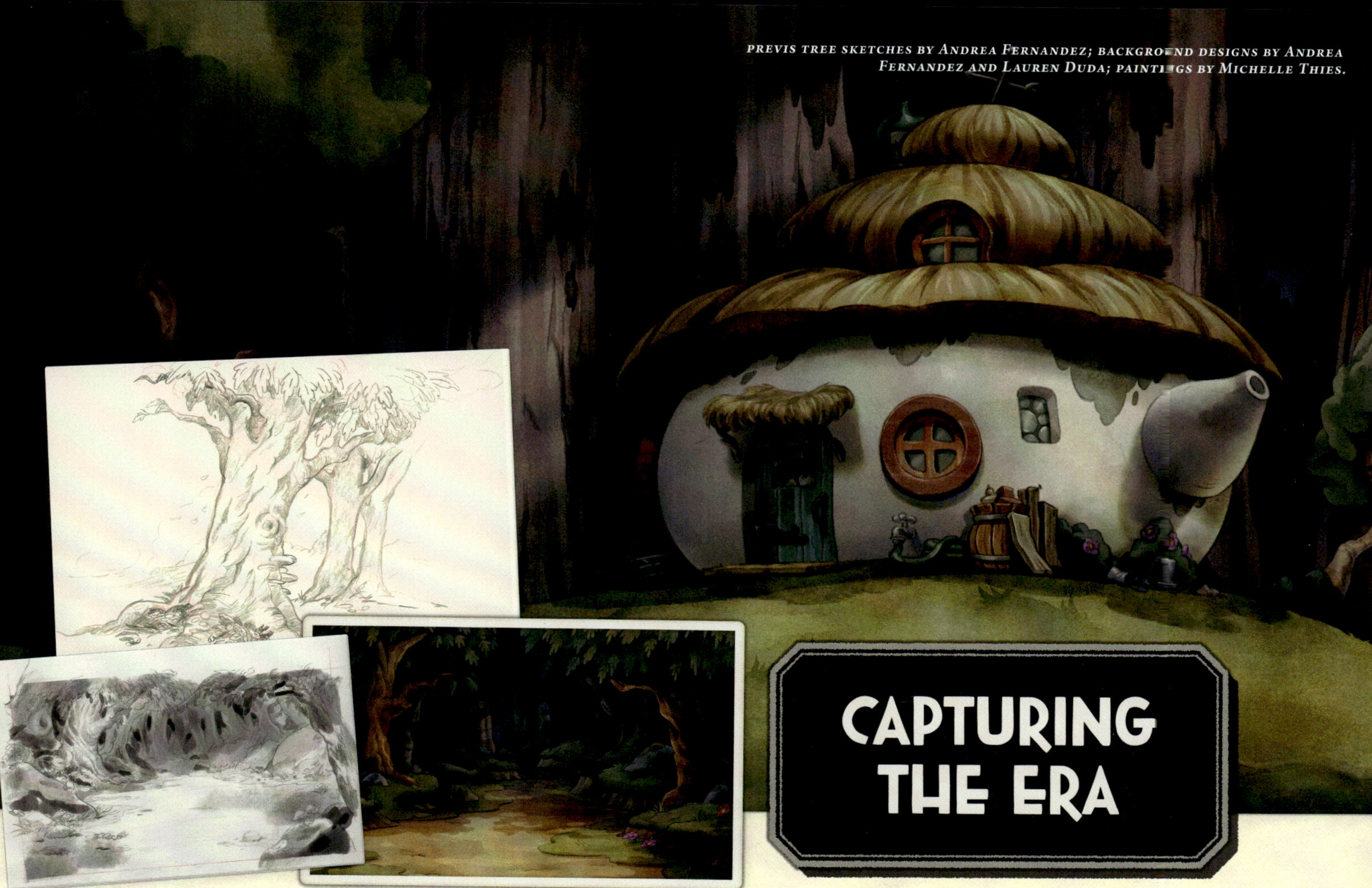

CAPTURING THE ERA

→ **ANDREA:** When they were doing these styles in the 1930s, they weren't stylizing. They were essentially life drawing. They were taking from life, so we had to get into that mindset. A huge part of keeping this world lush was also keeping it realistic. What I would always tell the team was "Know where animation was going." Yes, it's cartoony—but it's not so cartoony that it's excessively stylized. It's kind of like rudimentary realism. It's not stylized, it's not streamlined, but it is a simplified realism, a fun realism with movement and character to it. We really leaned on that thought for the entire design for the show.

CAROLYN ROACH, *THE CUPHEAD SHOW!* LINE PRODUCER: After a show gets the green light, you have to find about fifty insanely talented people really fast. Not only do they have to be insanely talented; they also have to get along with each other. That's a really difficult process in the best of circumstances.

DAVE: I always say it's like you're getting into a submarine, and you're going to be in there with these people for the next two and a half years. You definitely don't want any jerks onboard.

CJ: When you start off on a series and you say, "This is an opportunity to bring back the golden age of animation," you can *say* that to an art director, but you don't know if you're going to find someone who can *do* that. Andrea figured out how to do that.

DAVE: The game is very eclectic—it's a bunch of mismatched ideas thrown together, and I liked that you could go to one location, and it wouldn't look like anything else. Andrea came up with design language and shape language that helped pull it together.

ANDREA: In the first month of development, I have a lot to say and a lot to draw and a lot to give to a project visually, until I start getting other people in the mix. And then my job quickly shifts from being the star player to the coach. I make the plays, I analyze the game, I do the research, and I empower these artists with the best environment for them to create by removing obstacles. That doesn't sound very glamorous, but it really means that I make sure they have everything they need—the time, the information, the confidence to execute their best work. I worry about the rest: the notes, talking to executives, talking to producers.

CJ: Andrea brought great female energy to the team, especially for a show about two brothers—and Ms. Chalice. She had a very clear vision and was very astute in using the source material for inspiration.

ANDREA: I absorb a lot of the feedback—I filter it and create a game plan. I make sure I give clear direction in every aspect of the pipeline, give clear notes, and I put my bumpers up at the beginning and make sure people don't go outside those lanes. That allows everyone to create with confidence and deliver their best work.

DAVE: One of the things that make Andrea such an incredible art director is how she was practical in understanding the process and the limitations. She approached it mathematically: how many paintings can we get done in a week?

ANDREA: This show ran in two teams that ran concurrently. Each person brought a different flavor, so we could really rely on a certain aesthetic coming from each team while still having an umbrella aesthetic over the entire show.

BACKGROUND DESIGN AND COLOR THEORY

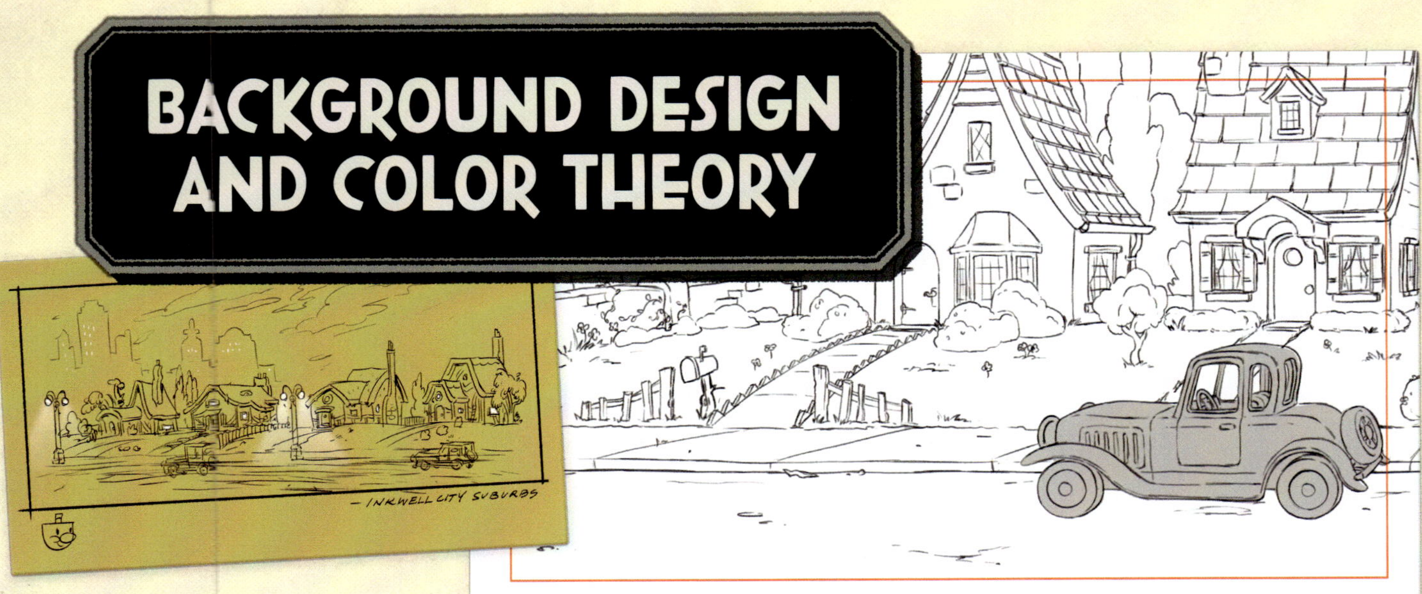

BACKGROUND DESIGN

→ **ANDREA:** I don't like artists who can't make creative decisions on their own or don't push the boundaries of their work. I try to get people who are great at what they do, feel good about what they do, and bring their very best to each piece.

PAT MARCONETT, *THE CUPHEAD SHOW!* BACKGROUND DESIGNER: We had to hold back from zooming in too far when we were cleaning stuff up, because with digital tools you can keep magnifying a small section over and over again.

LAUREN DUDA, *THE CUPHEAD SHOW!* BACKGROUND DESIGNER: I like doing my roughs without a perspective grid to get more character into it, and then I'll slap a grid on there to make sure nothing's way off.

ANDREA: Lauren has a real vibe for things that are shabby. Whether it's a barn, a carnival, a woodsy interior, or Brineybeard's boat, she totally nails those locations. I don't know if it's her East Coast woodsy vibe, but it comes out in the show.

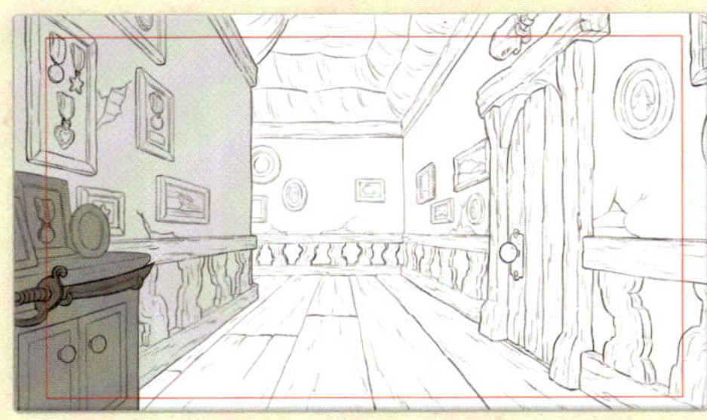

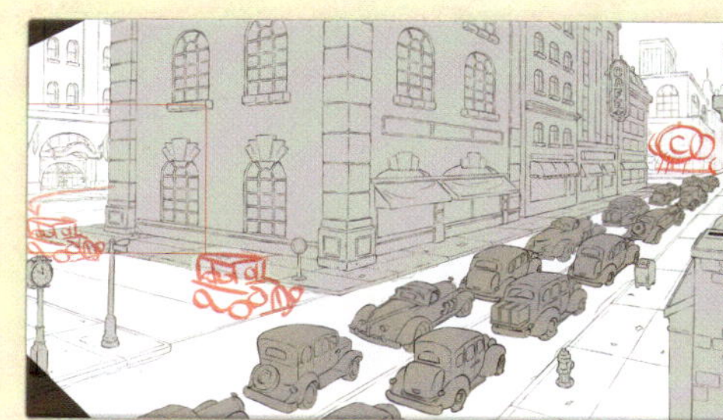

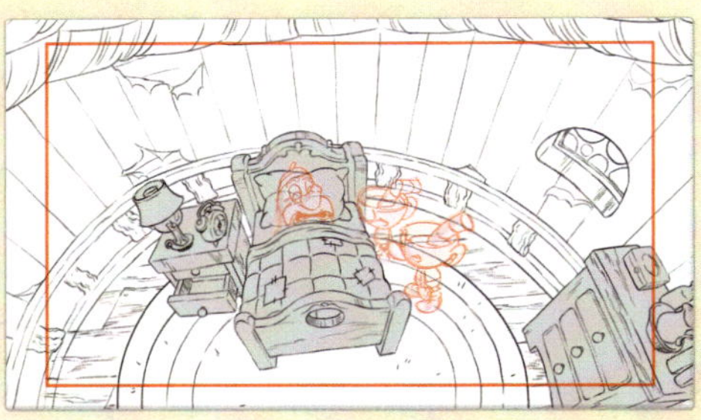

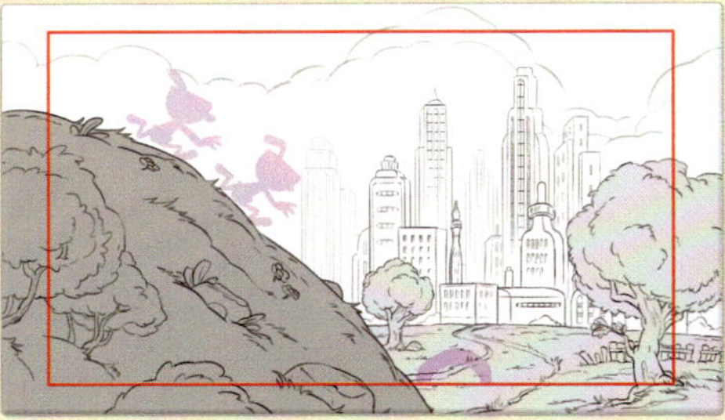

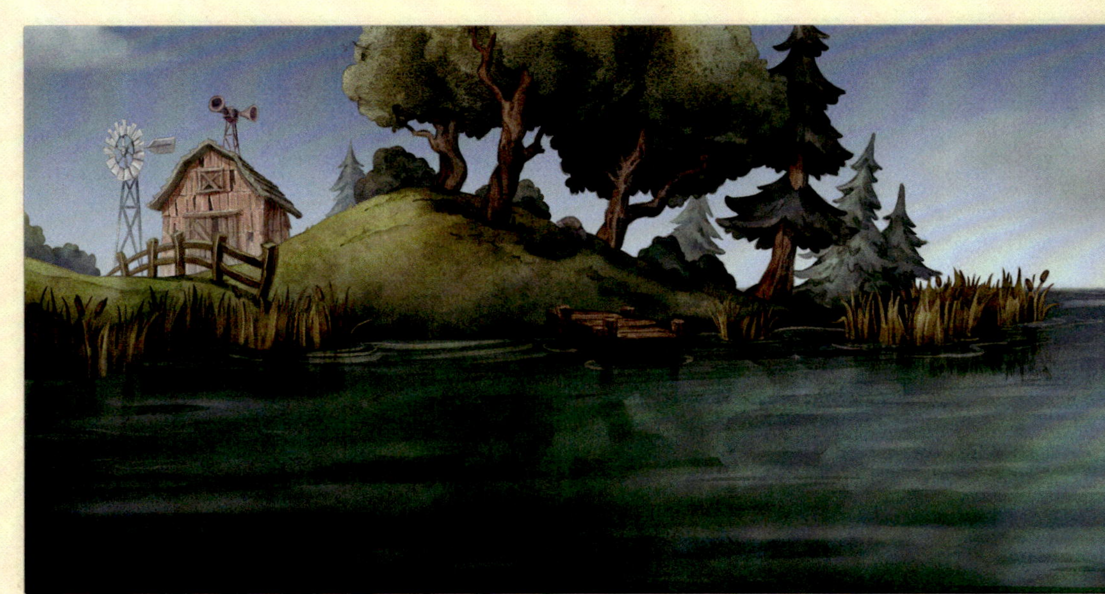

Previs by Cosmo Segurson; background designs by Jessica Fong and Laisay Bond; paintings by Gregory Miller and Mallory Carlson.

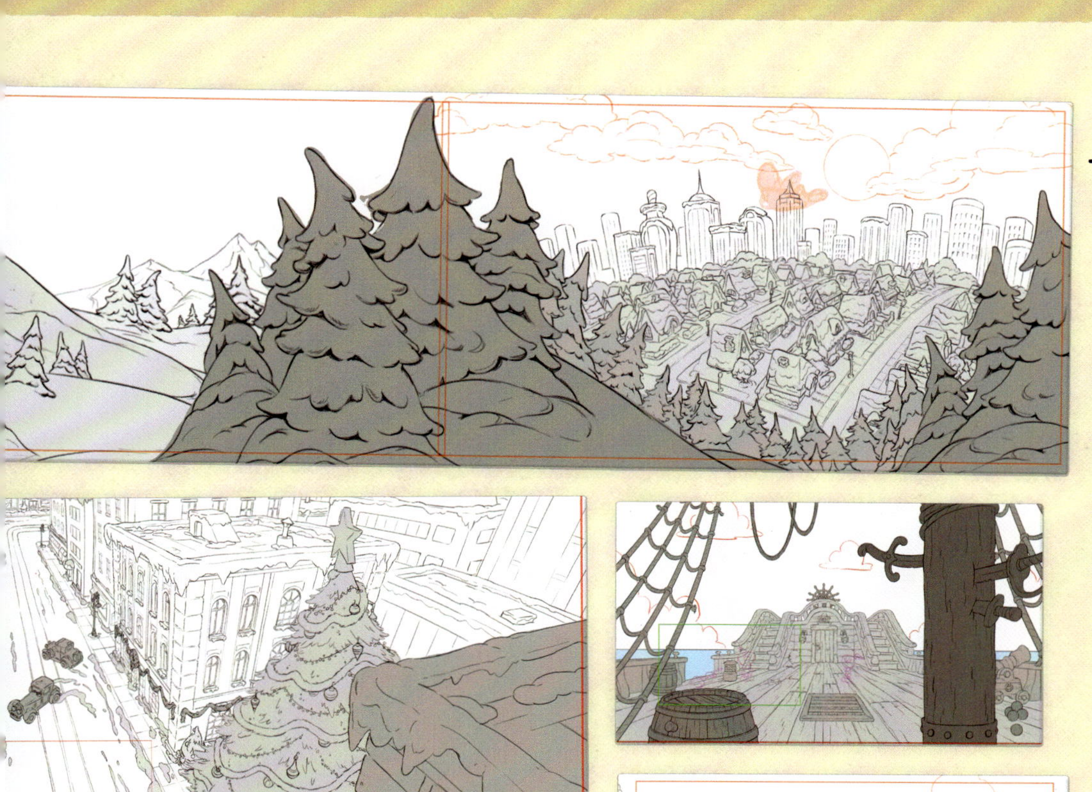

→ **ANDREA:** We had to figure out how to make this world look rich using digital tools but make it *feel* traditional. Most importantly, I wanted to make sure my artists weren't pushed to exhaustion, that we could be successful and make good on our promise of figuring it out, so I took all that into consideration, not just with the style but with the entire process of how to put it all together.

LAUREN: My favorite part of the show was being involved really early with Andrea and ironing out the style of the backgrounds. That exploration period was difficult but rewarding at the same time.

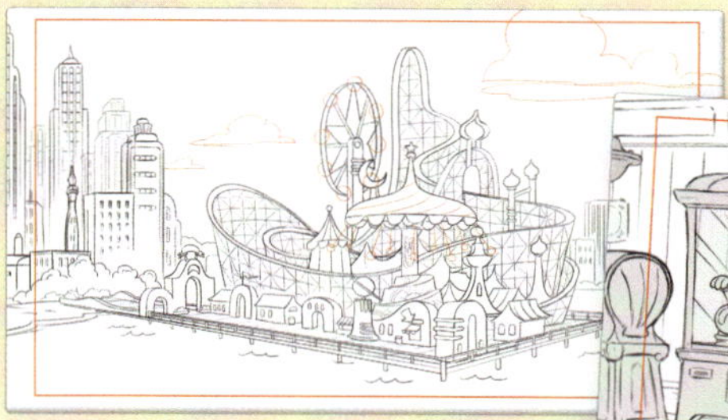

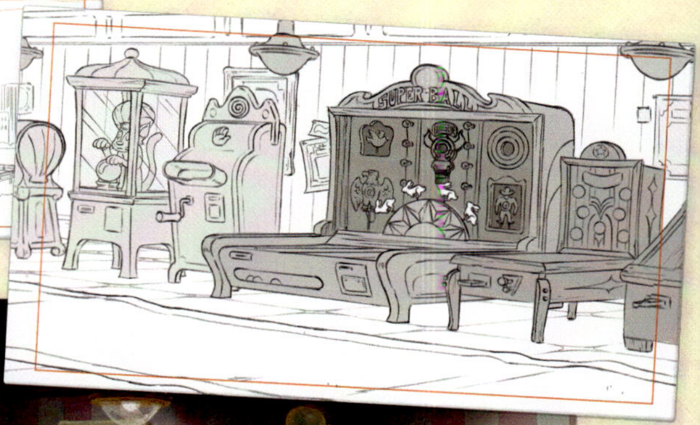

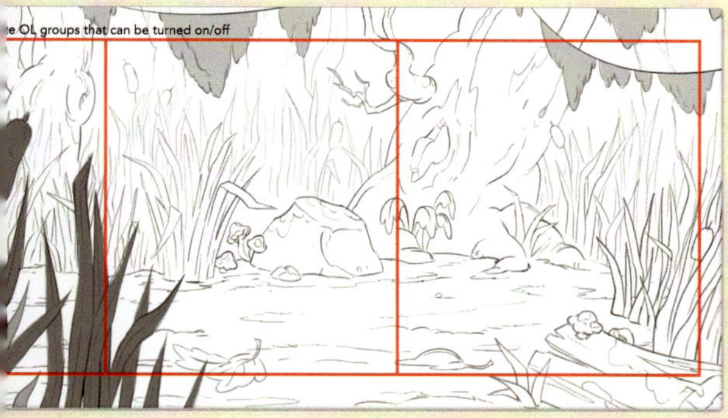

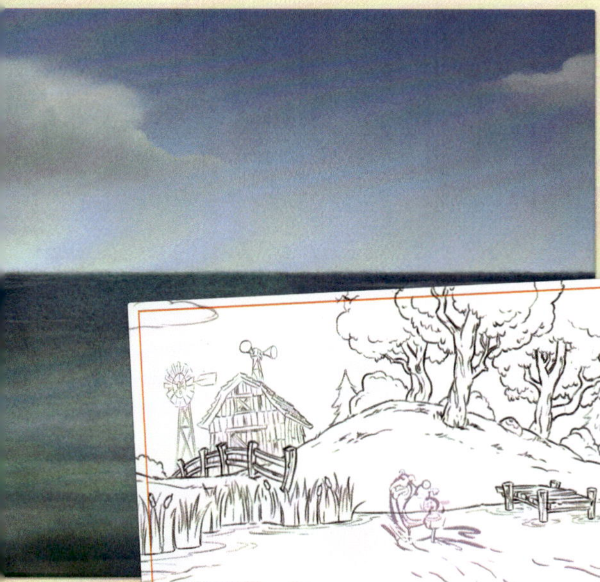

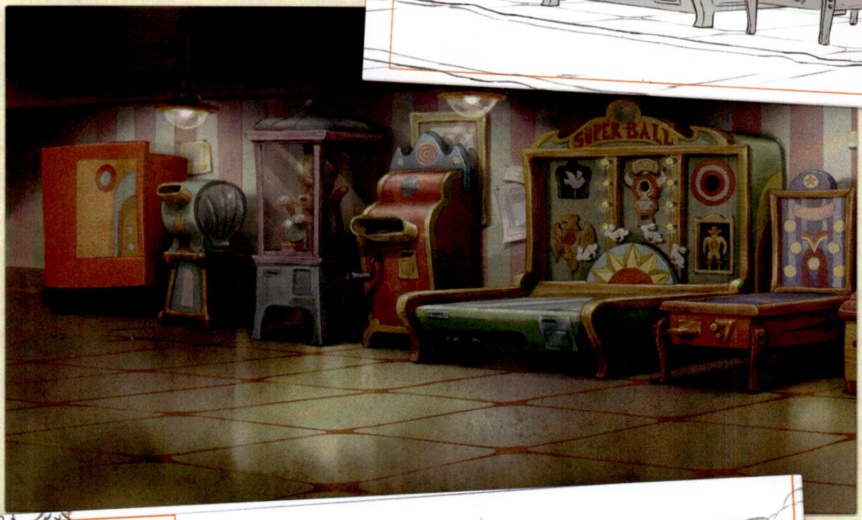

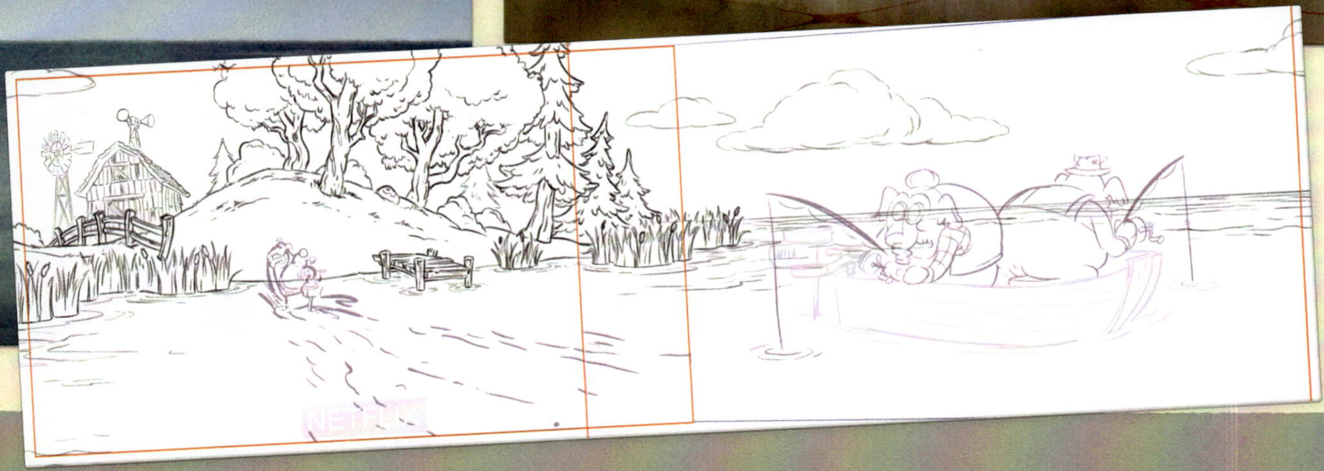

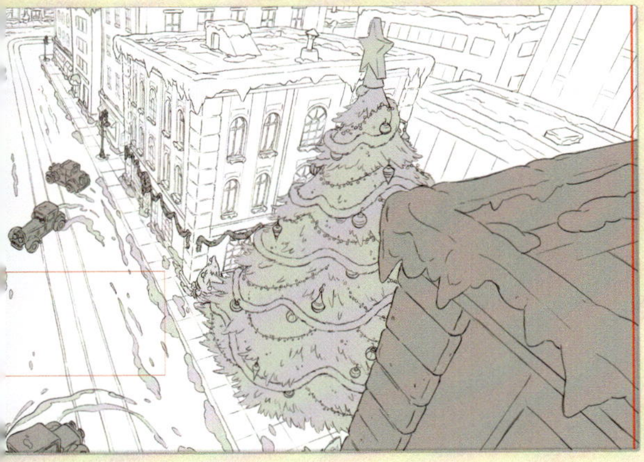

BACKGROUND DESIGNS BY LAUREN DUDA, JESSICA HONG, AND LAISAY BOND.

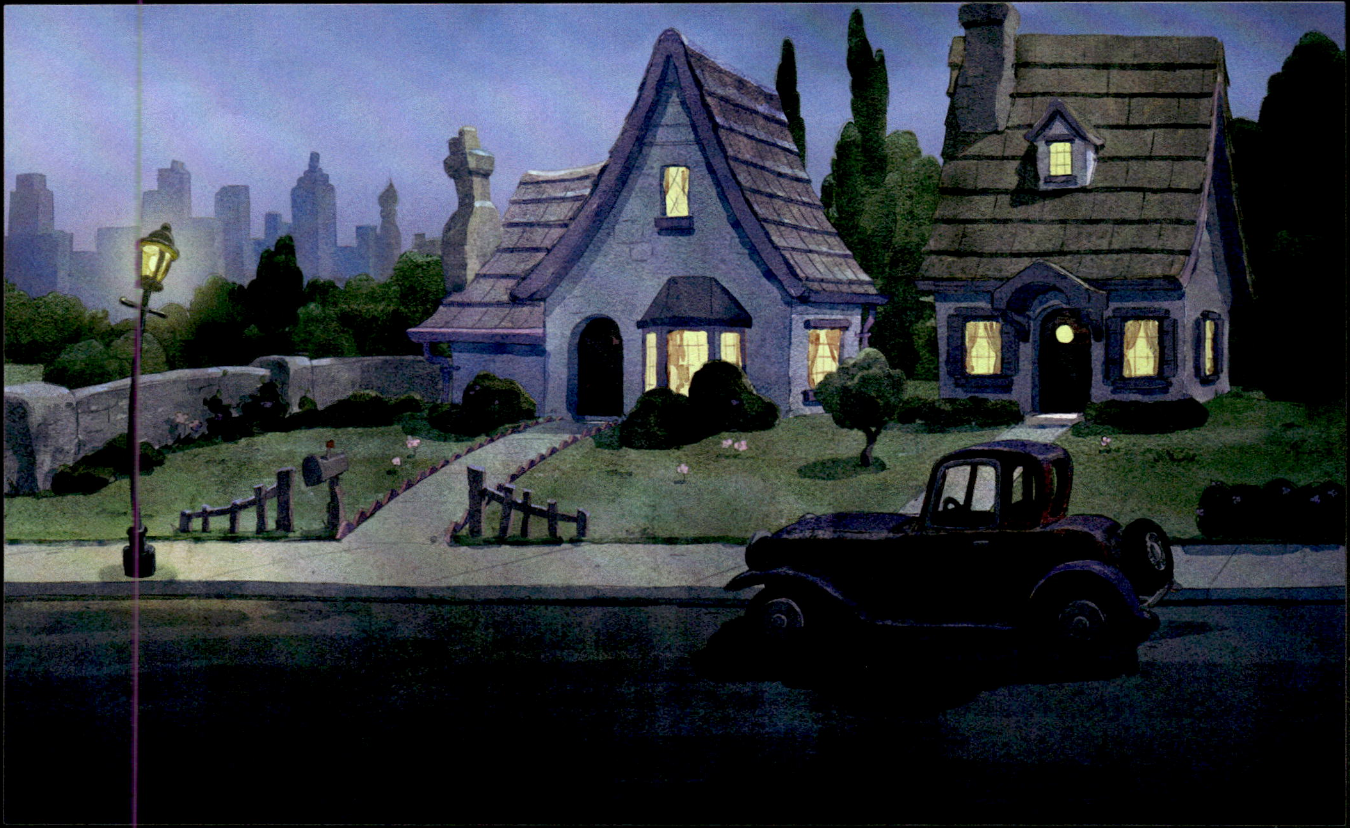

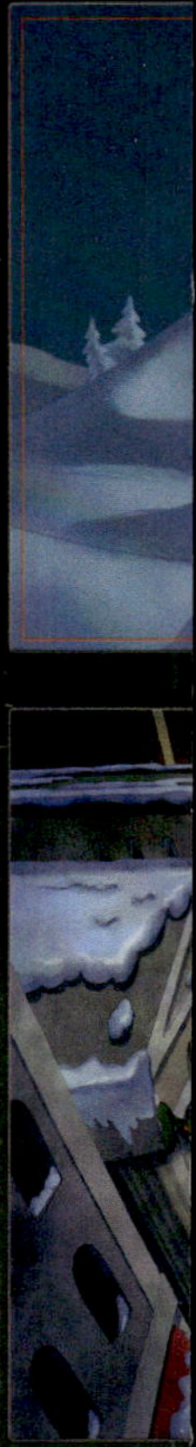

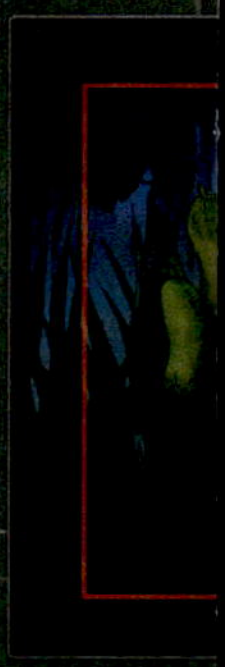

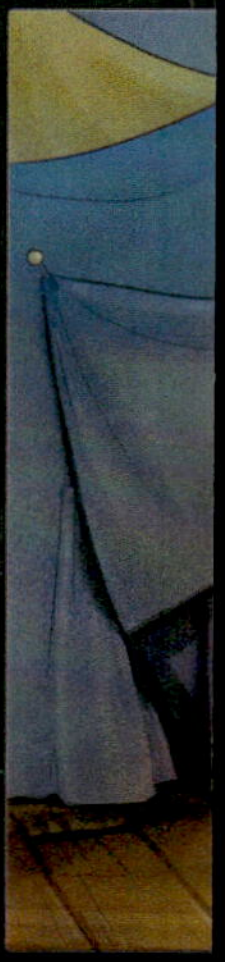

COLOR THEORY

ANDREA: The biggest difference between the show and the game is not necessarily in palette but more in the rendering and the lushness of the painting, which is dialed up on the show. When you look at the game, it's charming, because it's watercolor on paper. But we couldn't replicate that kind of charm from natural materials, not in a modern production pipeline. The painters had to step it up a notch, so the production value felt high quality.

DAVE: We felt like it really had to be a 1930s watercolor background look—but it also seemed like, How in the world are we going to pull that off? Everybody who can do that has been dead for a *very* long time.

ANDREA: When you're working with real materials—like an ink background or graphite background or a fully painted watercolor—there's a certain charm to it that's difficult to replicate when you're working digitally. What was charming and effective in pencil and paper now feels bare for the wrong reasons, like it's just low production quality. There are sometimes over one hundred backgrounds per episode, and thousands of backgrounds for the run of the show. It would have been impossible to do that many traditional paintings. Modern production is not set up to deal with that.

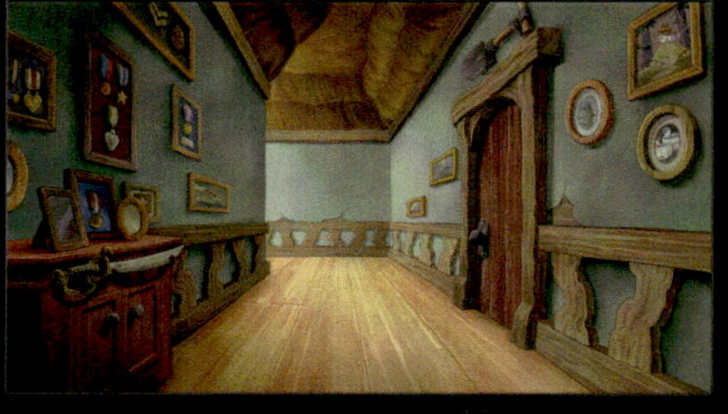

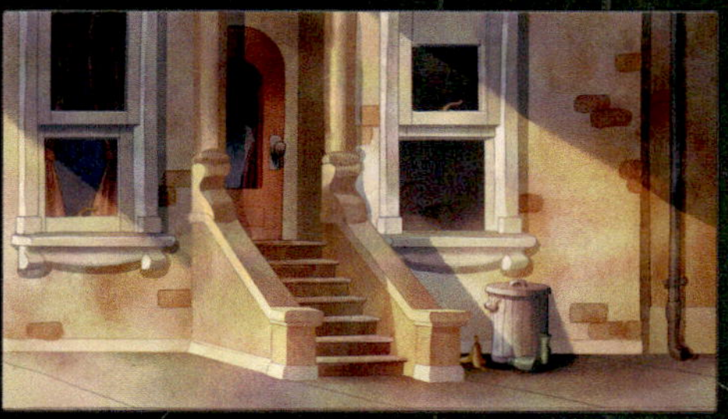

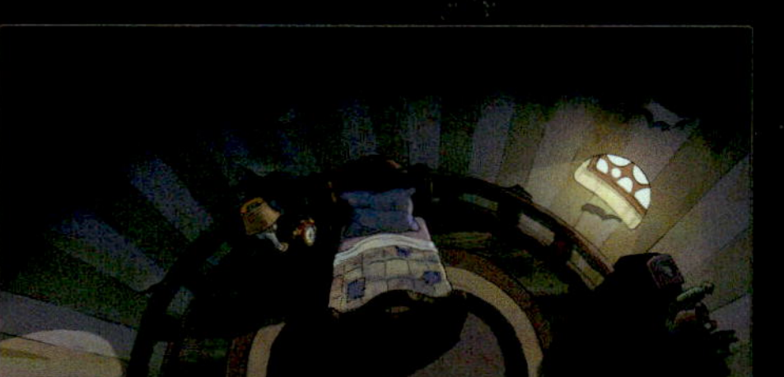

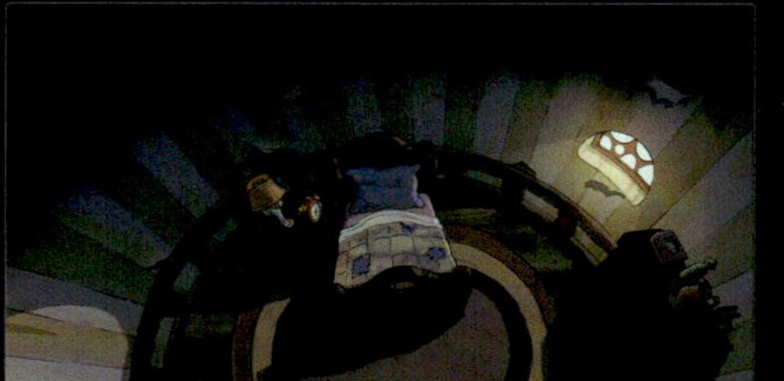

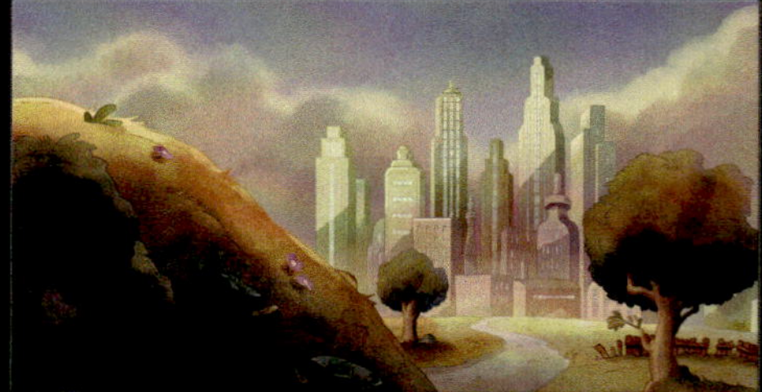

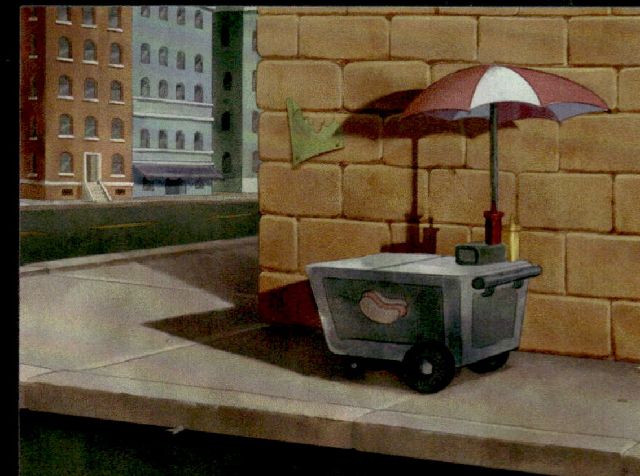

Background designs by Jessica Hong and Laisay Bond; paintings by Gregory Miller and Mallory Carlson.

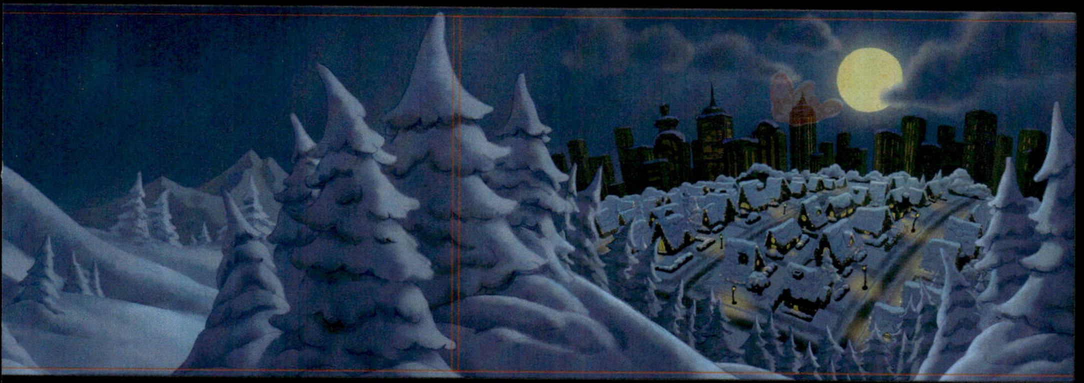

→ **ANDREA:** There were not a ton of surreal cartoons in color. When we get crazy on *Cuphead*, colorwise I had to lean more toward mid to late 1940s. There was no 1930s reference for really "out there" color. That's when I started looking at the early Disney features, like *Snow White* and *Pinocchio*, because I had to edge in on a higher production value in order to give the show the feeling that it's an event.

IVAN AGUIRRE, *THE CUPHEAD SHOW!* BACKGROUND PAINTER: We're trying to really make it look traditional and as organic as possible. It's very time consuming, but it's fun to be on a show that really challenges your skills.

ANDREA: Ivan has always been the best painter I know, so I needed him onboard. For those initial paintings with Ivan, we spent a good three weeks just debating and deciding—just being able to sit together and look at stuff makes a huge difference in the early stages. Once the whole team came on, all that groundwork helped them get the look we were going for and enabled them to start painting like one another much quicker.

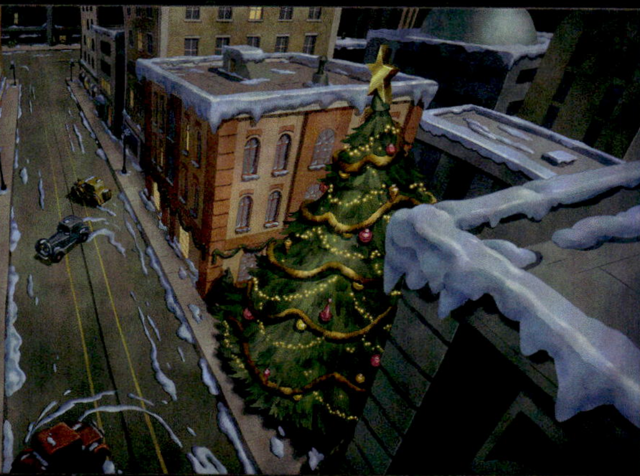

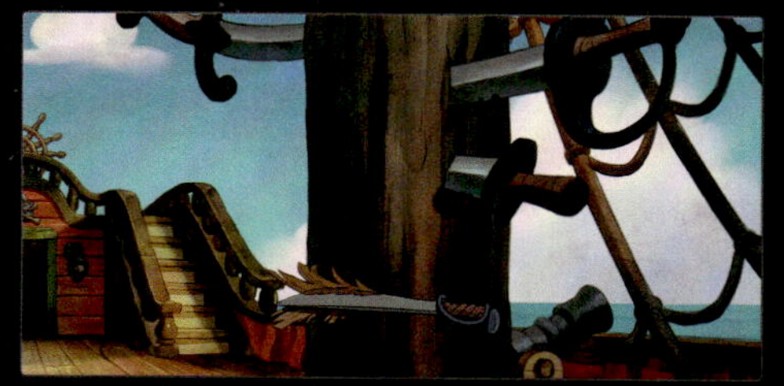

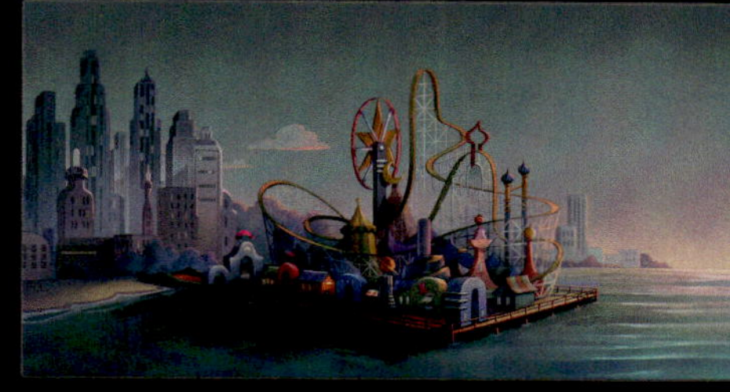

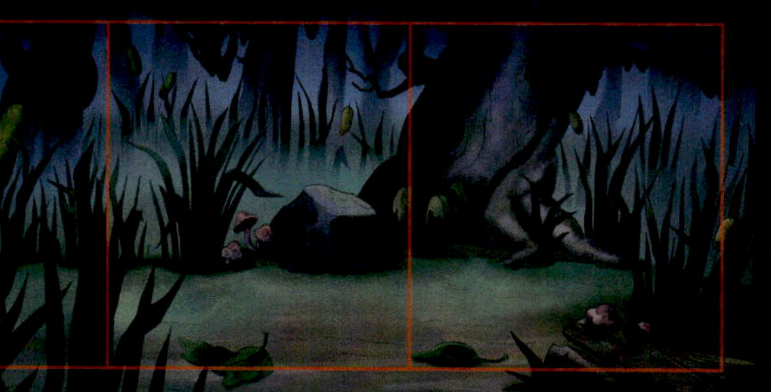

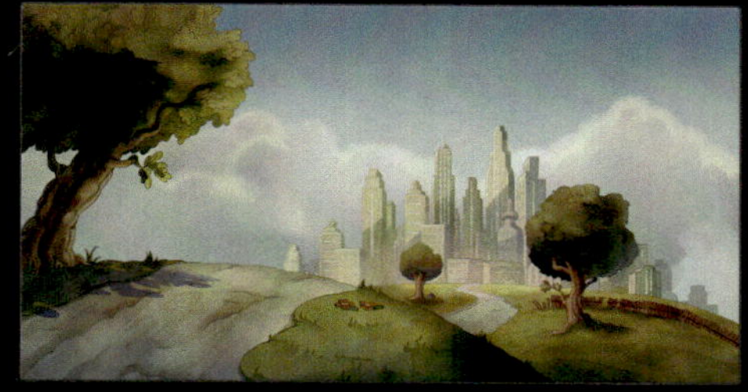

BACKGROUND DESIGNS BY JESSICA HONG, LAISAY BOND, AND LAUREN DUDA; PAINTINGS BY GREGORY MILLER AND MALLORY CARLSON.

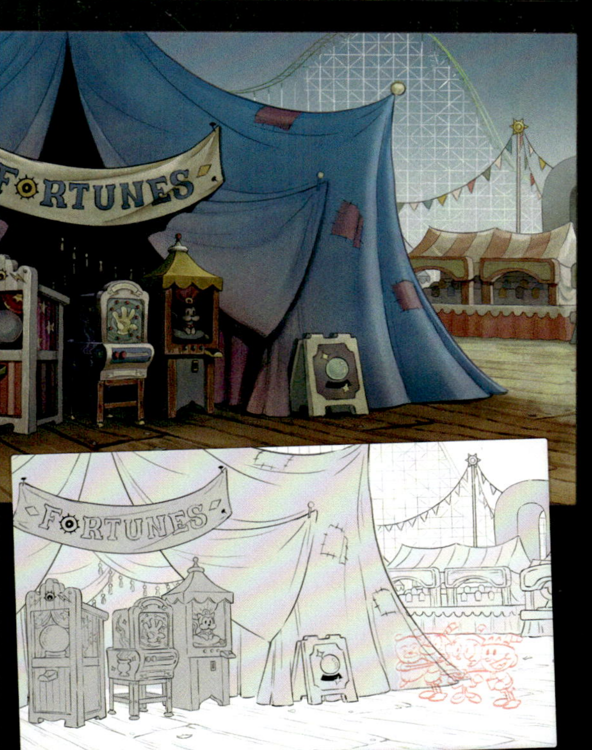

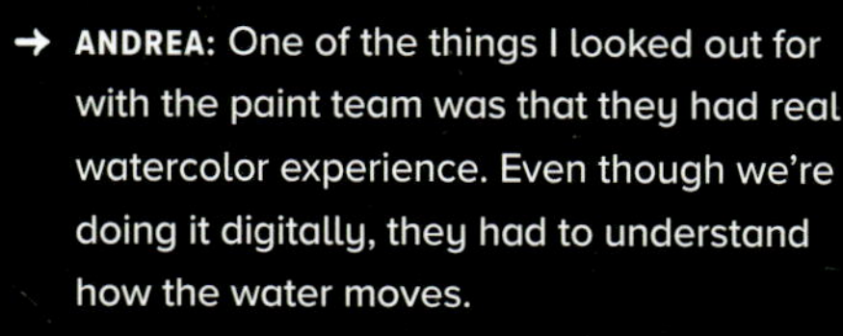

→ **ANDREA:** One of the things I looked out for with the paint team was that they had real watercolor experience. Even though we're doing it digitally, they had to understand how the water moves.

MICHELLE THIES, *THE CUPHEAD SHOW!* BACKGROUND PAINTER: The style is very intuitive for me—what drew me to animation were these elaborate watercolor-wash backgrounds in traditional media.

CHRIS HACKER, *THE CUPHEAD SHOW!* COLOR DESIGNER: In color design for the characters, a lot of our color choices are dictated by the background we're keying to. So we play off what the painting looks like, and that will often dictate the lighting or any kind of palette changes. It's up to us to finish the puzzle.

MALLORY CARLSON, *THE CUPHEAD SHOW!* BACKGROUND PAINTER: The moments that were really satisfying were when I'd finish a certain painting and think, "Wow, it *does* look like watercolor . . ."

GREG MILLER, *THE CUPHEAD SHOW!* BACKGROUND PAINTER: The naturalistic palette is a little unusual for modern TV animation, which usually tends to overdo it. It's nice to work with a more limited palette. The backgrounds aren't ever going too far. Pushing the color too far in backgrounds and environments doesn't help most animation. The characters tend to get lost.

ANDREA: Our whole background team is amazing. I'm enamored with everything they brought to the show.

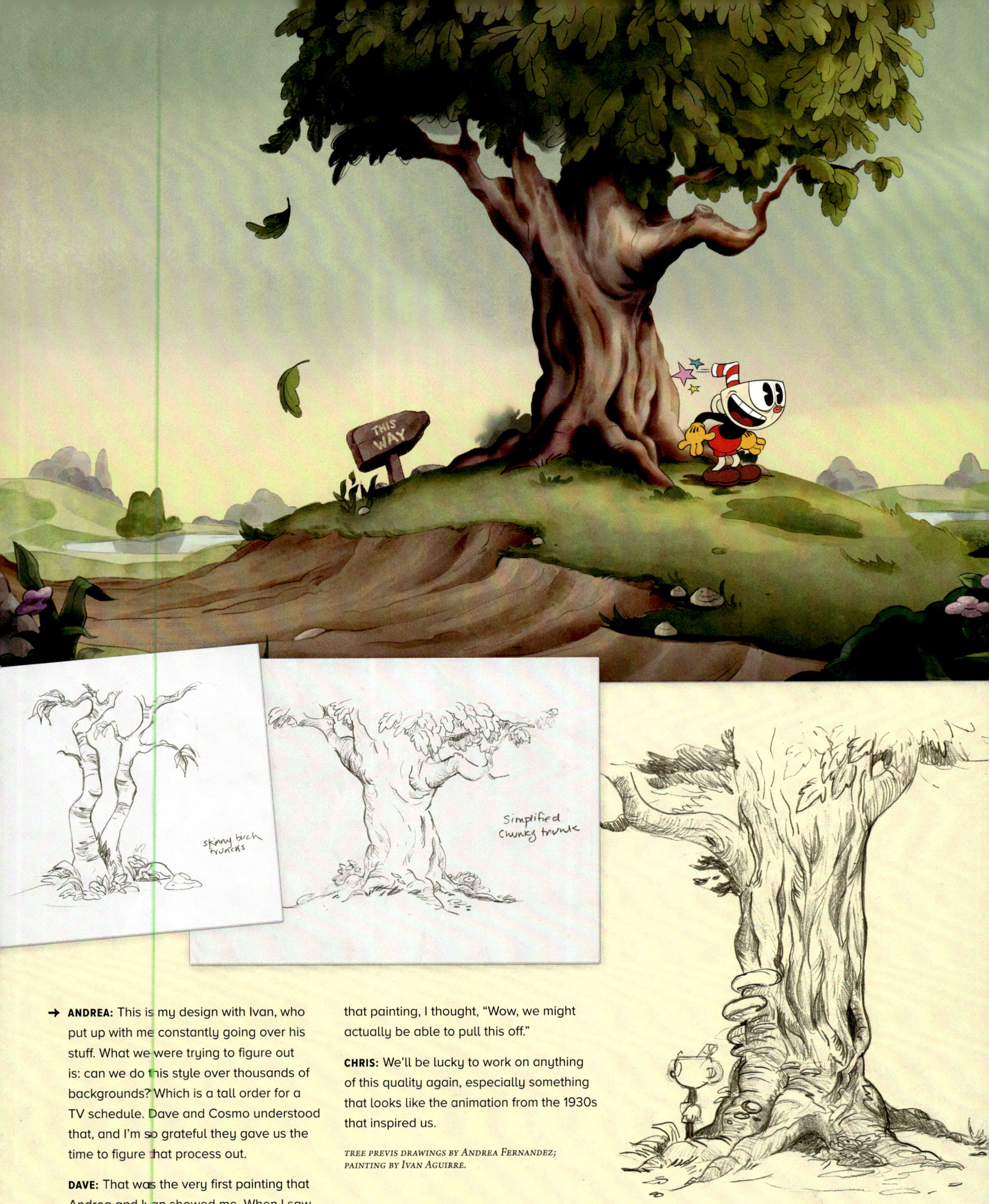

ANDREA: This is my design with Ivan, who put up with me constantly going over his stuff. What we were trying to figure out is: can we do this style over thousands of backgrounds? Which is a tall order for a TV schedule. Dave and Cosmo understood that, and I'm so grateful they gave us the time to figure that process out.

DAVE: That was the very first painting that Andrea and Ivan showed me. When I saw that painting, I thought, "Wow, we might actually be able to pull this off."

CHRIS: We'll be lucky to work on anything of this quality again, especially something that looks like the animation from the 1930s that inspired us.

TREE PREVIS DRAWINGS BY ANDREA FERNANDEZ; PAINTING BY IVAN AGUIRRE.

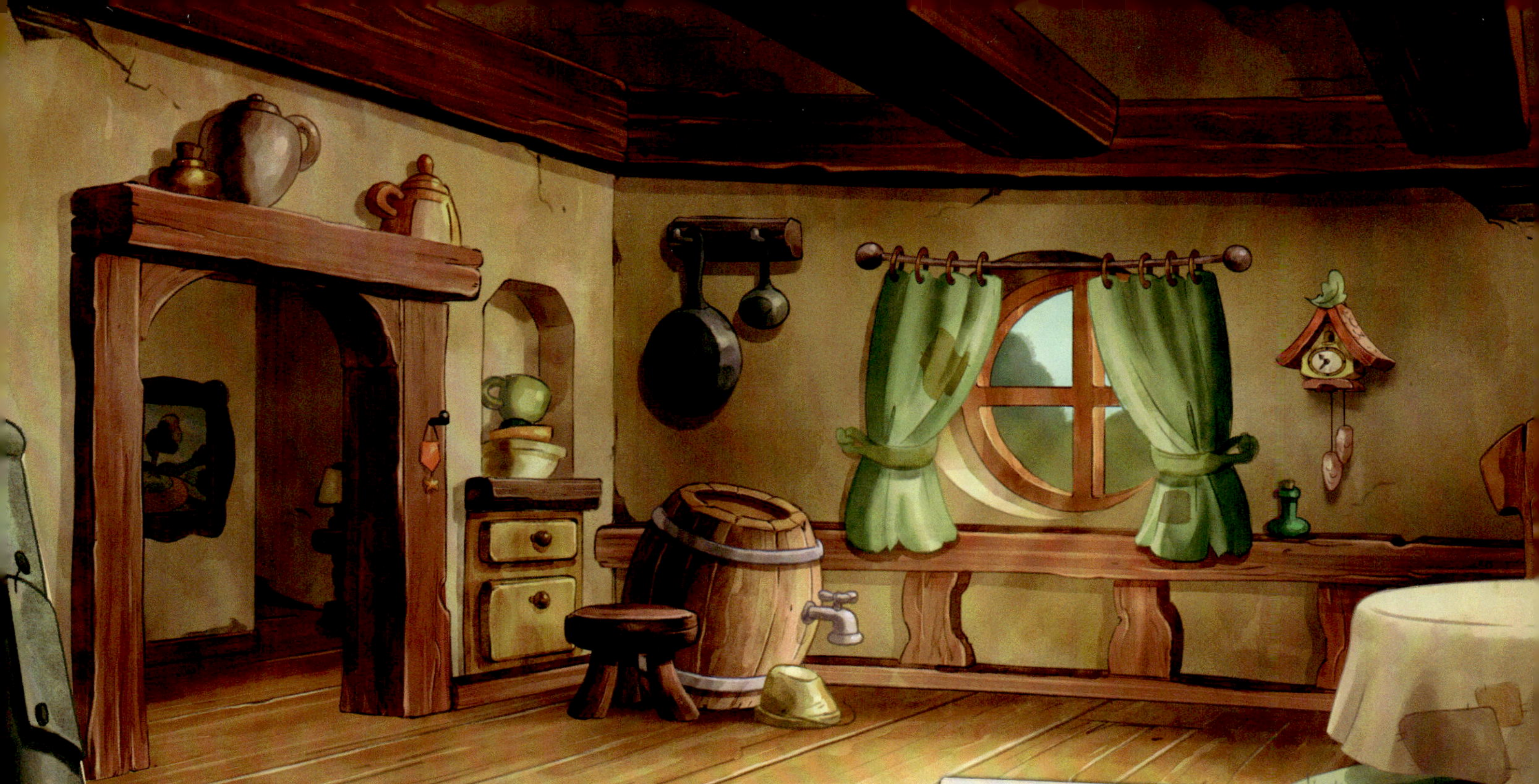

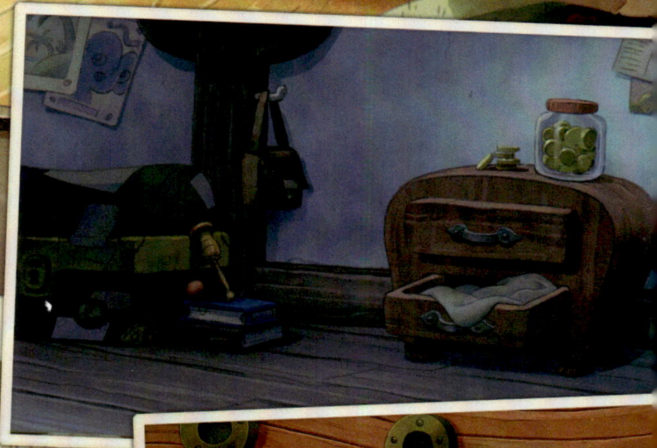

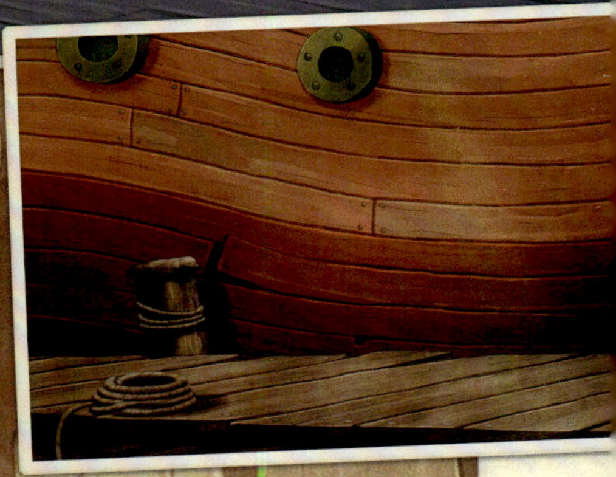

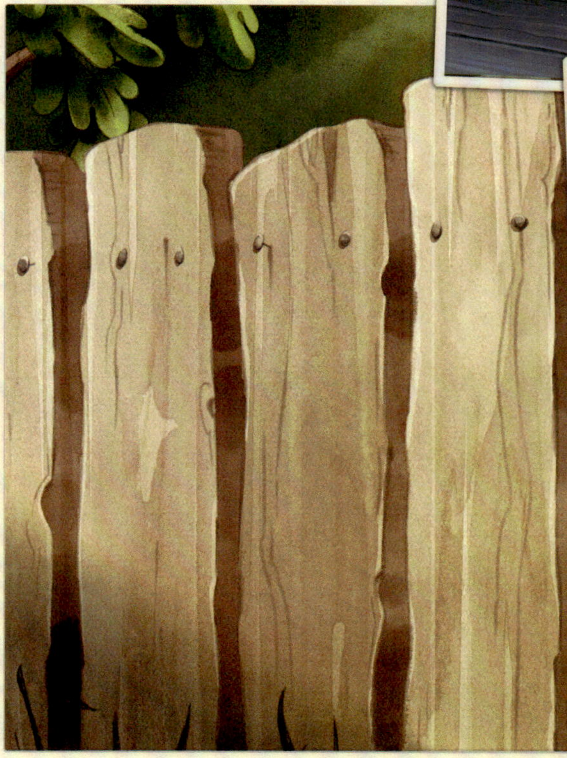

→ **IVAN:** I got to create a lot of custom brushes and wood textures. I make those with real watercolor washes and splatters. There were about two hundred brushes I tested for a week to narrow them down.

ANDREA: When it comes to the "feel" of the color in the show, we usually strive for a balance between three top-line things: naturalistic, nostalgic, and nondistracting. At times it got too splotchy or too graphic. I kept telling Ivan, "Less! Build up the watercolor as if it's coming from a hand, layer by layer. Do not add extra digital flourish. You have to do it like you're painting on paper, building up layer by layer of translucent color—and then leave it! Don't add a bunch of stuff."

BACKGROUND DESIGNS BY LAISAY BOND; PAINTINGS BY IVAN AGUIRRE.

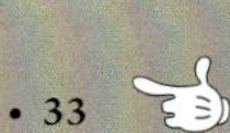

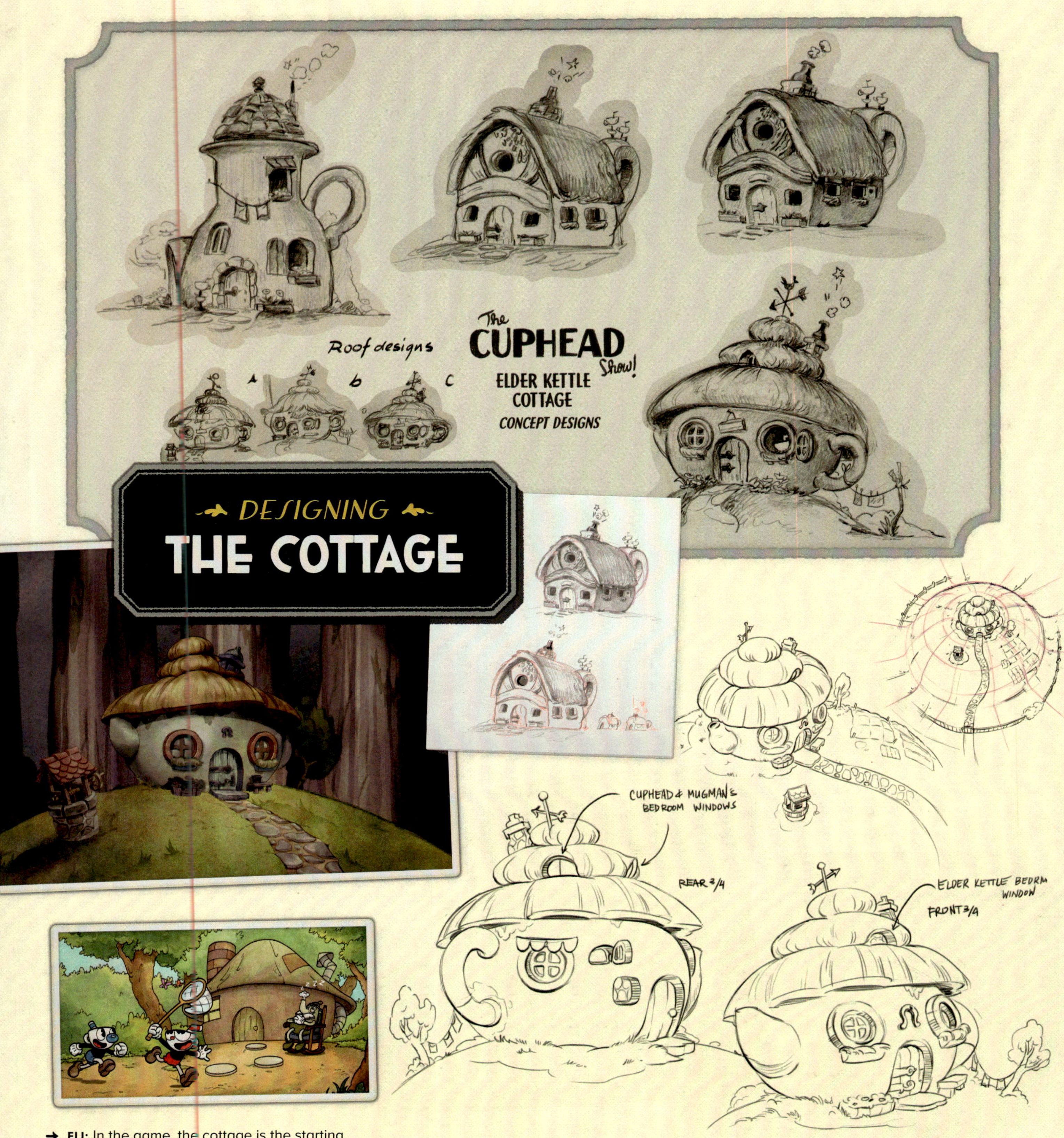

DESIGNING THE COTTAGE

→ **ELI:** In the game, the cottage is the starting point of what is going to be a grand adventure; in the show, often it's the site of a grand adventure unto itself.

ELDER KETTLE'S COTTAGE CONCEPT DESIGNS BY ANDREA FERNANDEZ. LOWER LEFT: ORIGINAL COTTAGE FROM THE GAME.

→ **ANDREA:** The cottage holds a lot of what I think I bring to the show—the cuteness, the nostalgic Disney feel, a Beatrix Potter vibe. It tells you this is home, this is safety, this is the charming part of each episode. I wanted it to feel like you're going through the woods, you discovered this delightful, quirky little place, and now it's yours. Then, traveling to different places, I can bring in new aesthetics as long as they don't clash with the cottage.

Background design by Andrea Fernandez; final painting by Michelle Thies.

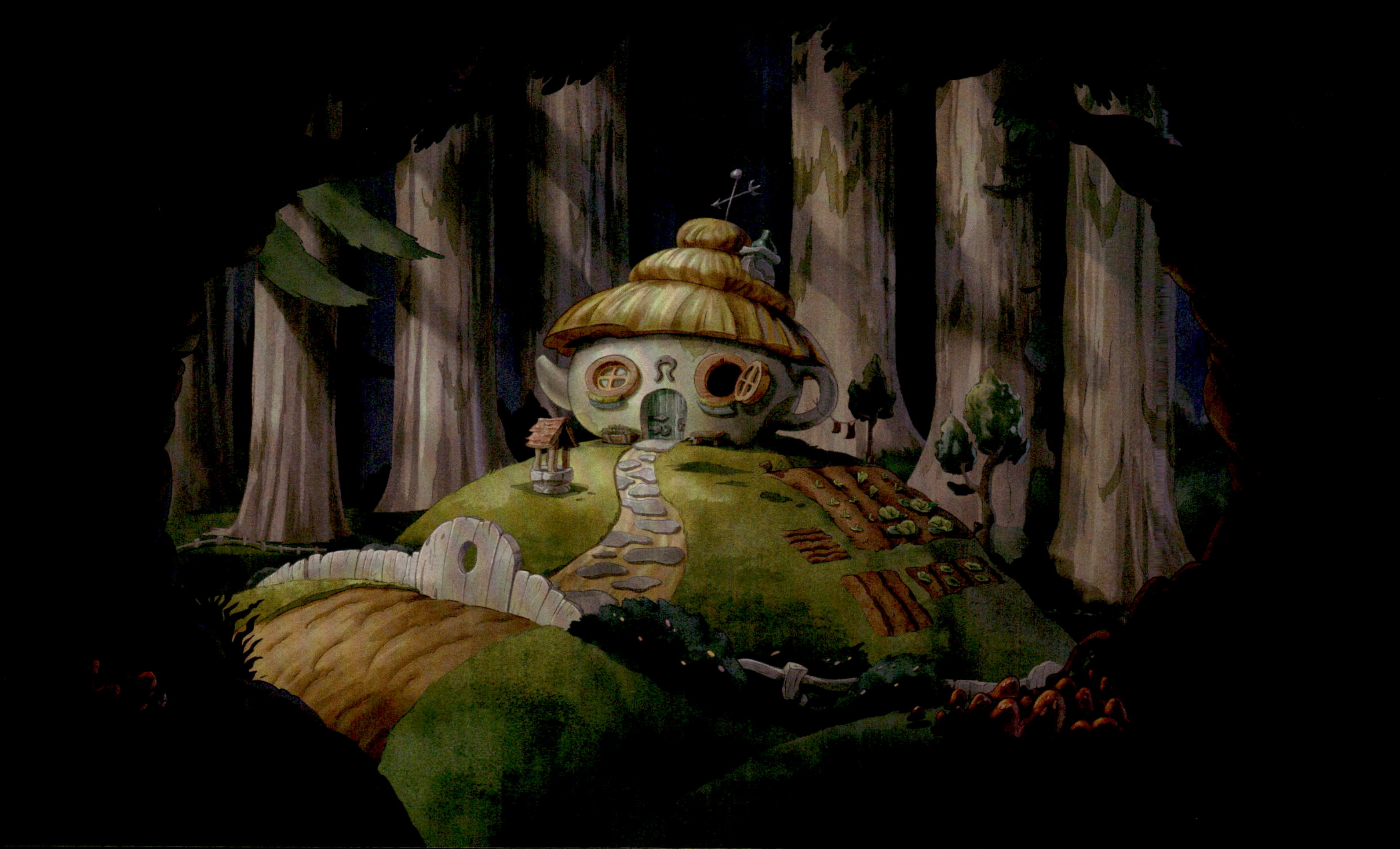

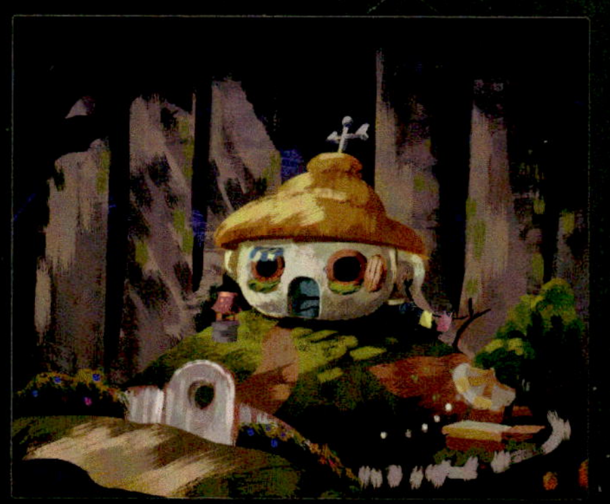

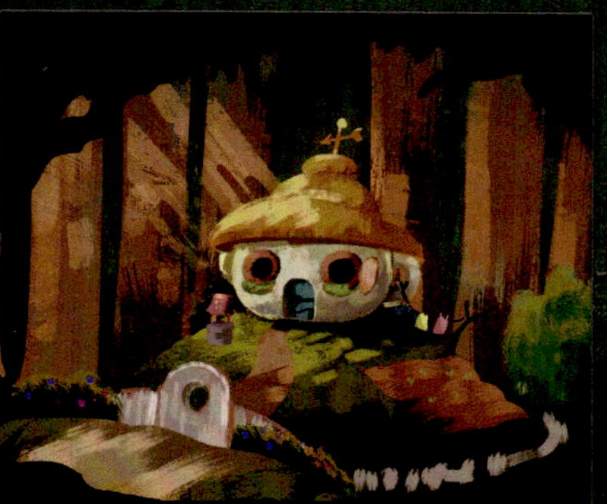

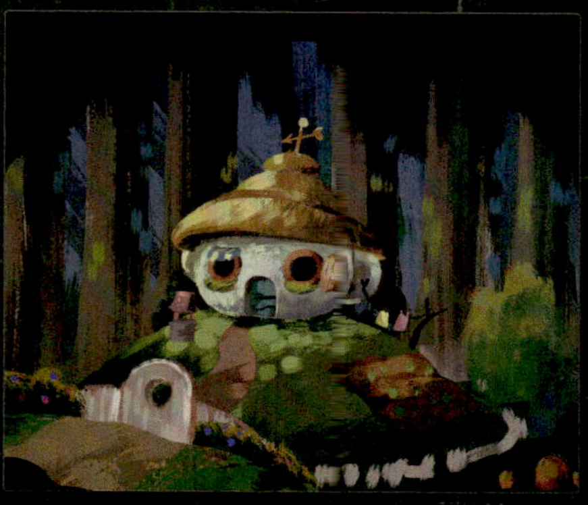

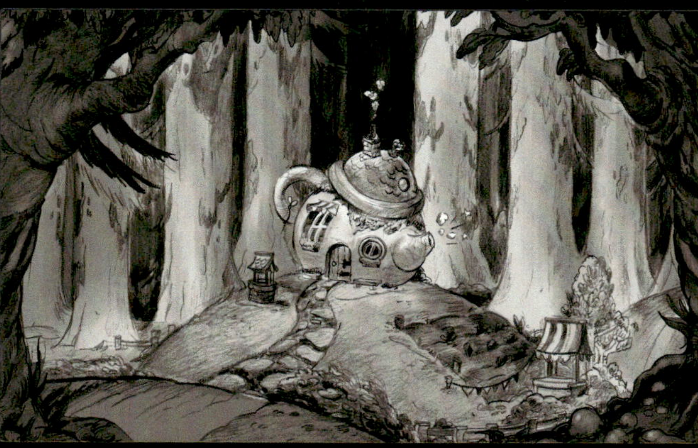

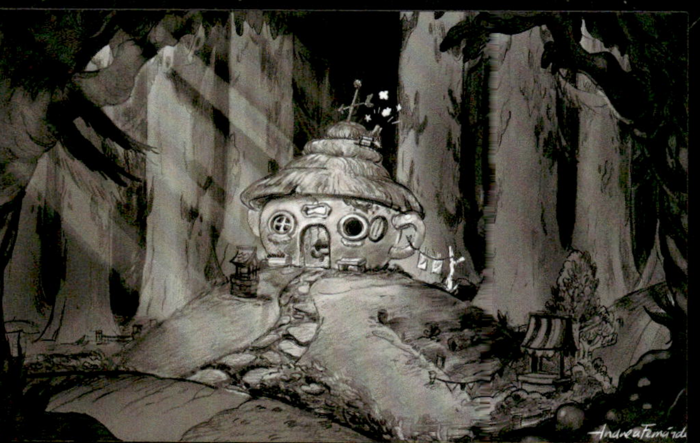

Previs color studies and drawings by Andrea Fernandez.

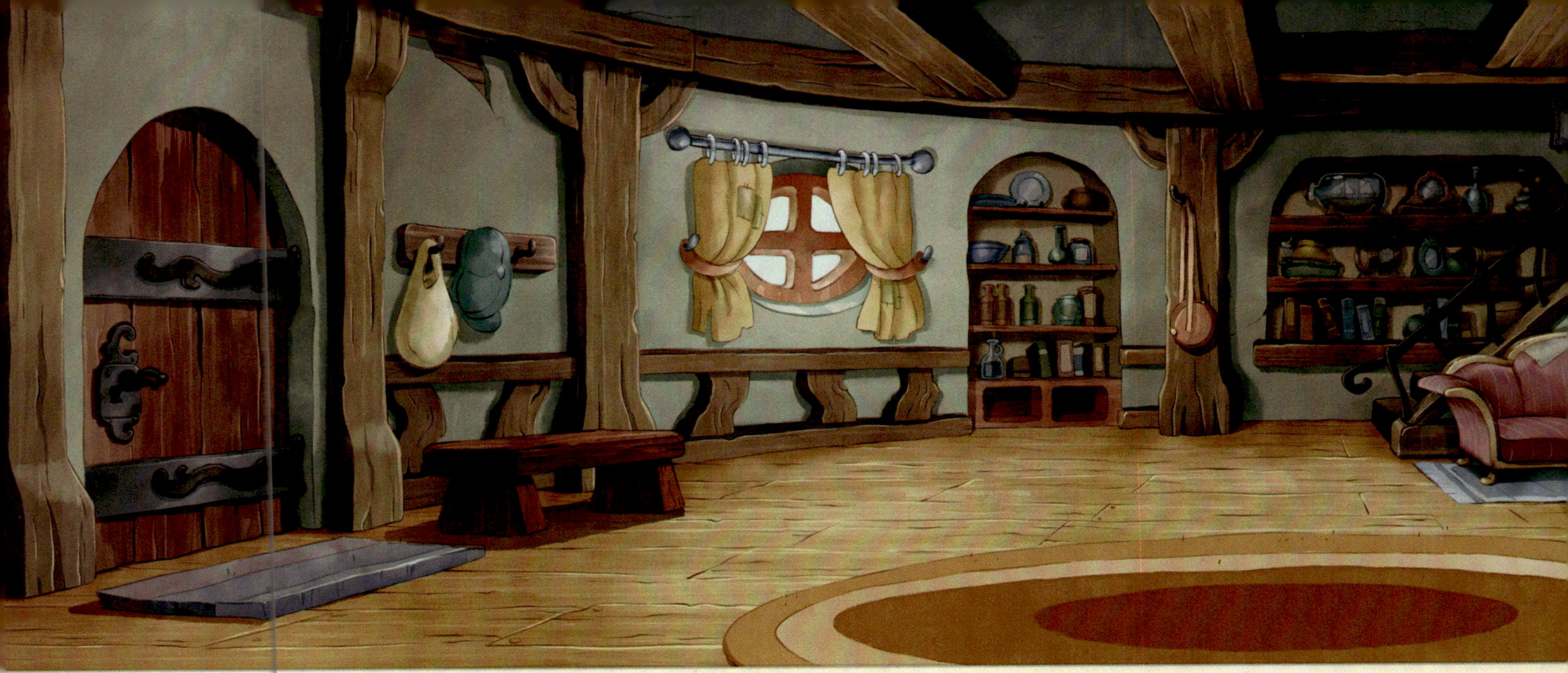

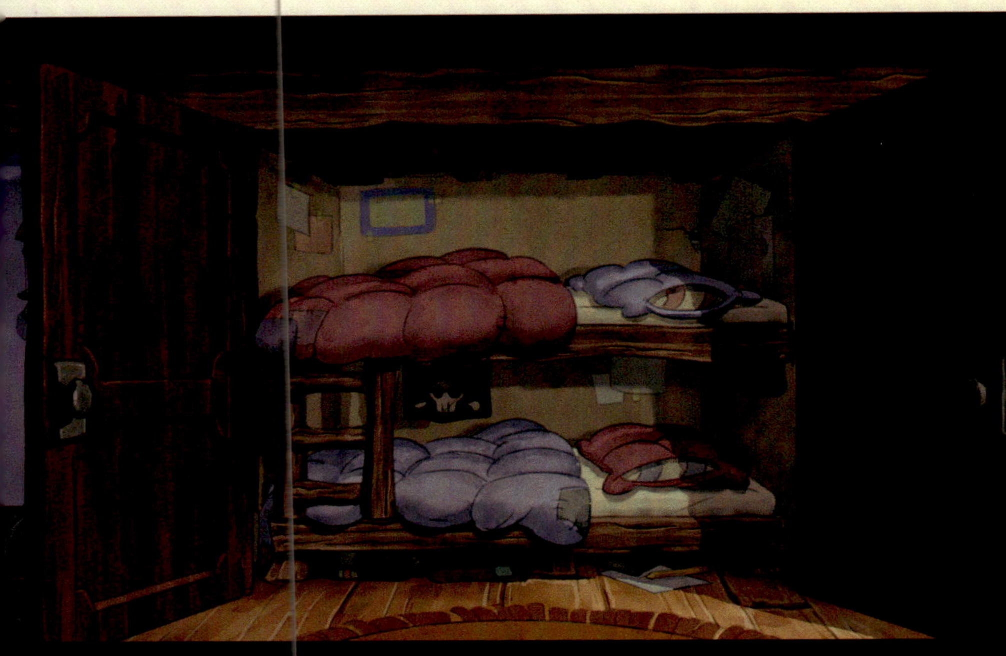

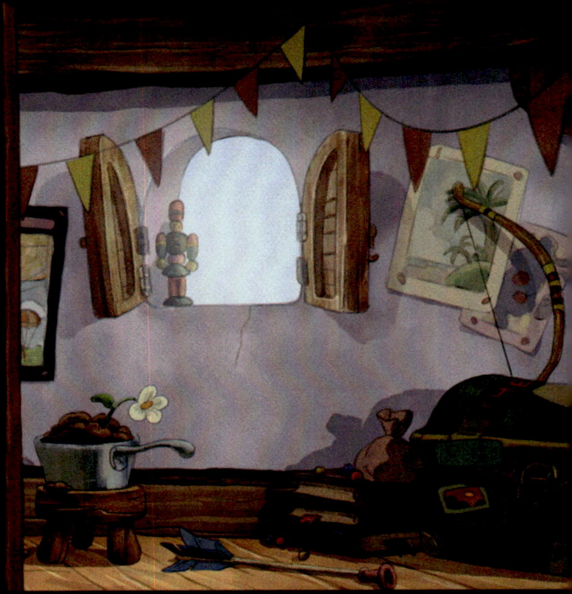

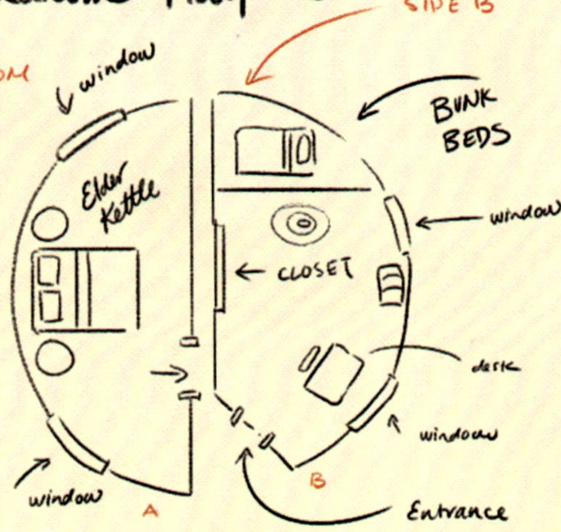

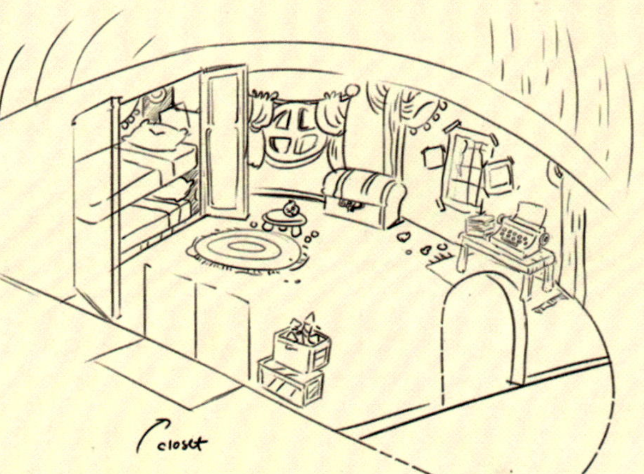

PREVIS DESIGNS BY ANDREA FERNANDEZ; BACKGROUND DESIGNS BY JESSICA HONG; PAINTINGS BY MICHELLE THIES AND GREGORY MILLER.

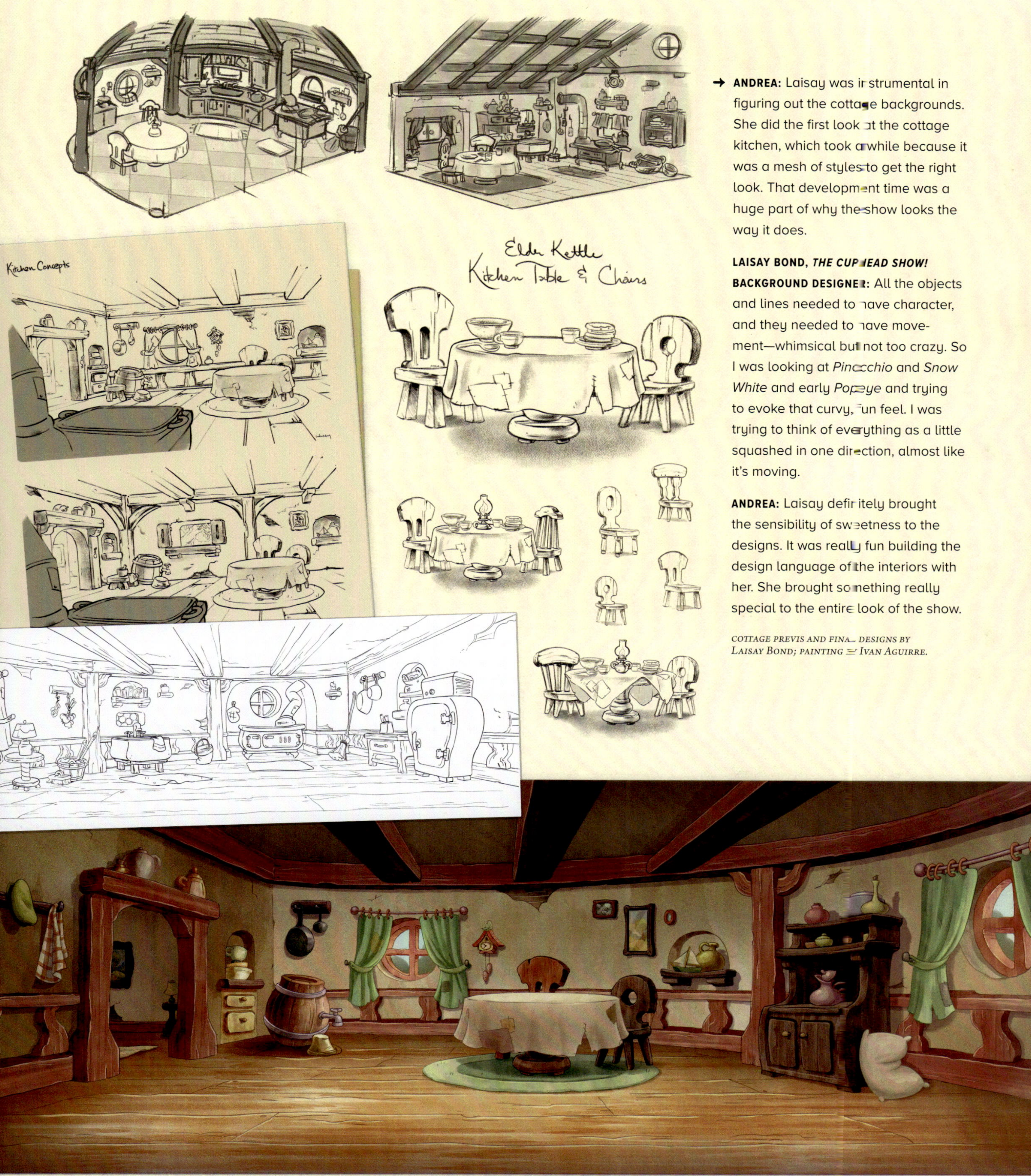

→ **ANDREA:** Laisay was instrumental in figuring out the cottage backgrounds. She did the first look at the cottage kitchen, which took a while because it was a mesh of styles to get the right look. That development time was a huge part of why the show looks the way it does.

LAISAY BOND, *THE CUPHEAD SHOW!* BACKGROUND DESIGNER: All the objects and lines needed to have character, and they needed to have movement—whimsical but not too crazy. So I was looking at *Pinocchio* and *Snow White* and early *Popeye* and trying to evoke that curvy, fun feel. I was trying to think of everything as a little squashed in one direction, almost like it's moving.

ANDREA: Laisay definitely brought the sensibility of sweetness to the designs. It was really fun building the design language of the interiors with her. She brought something really special to the entire look of the show.

Cottage previs and final designs by Laisay Bond; painting by Ivan Aguirre.

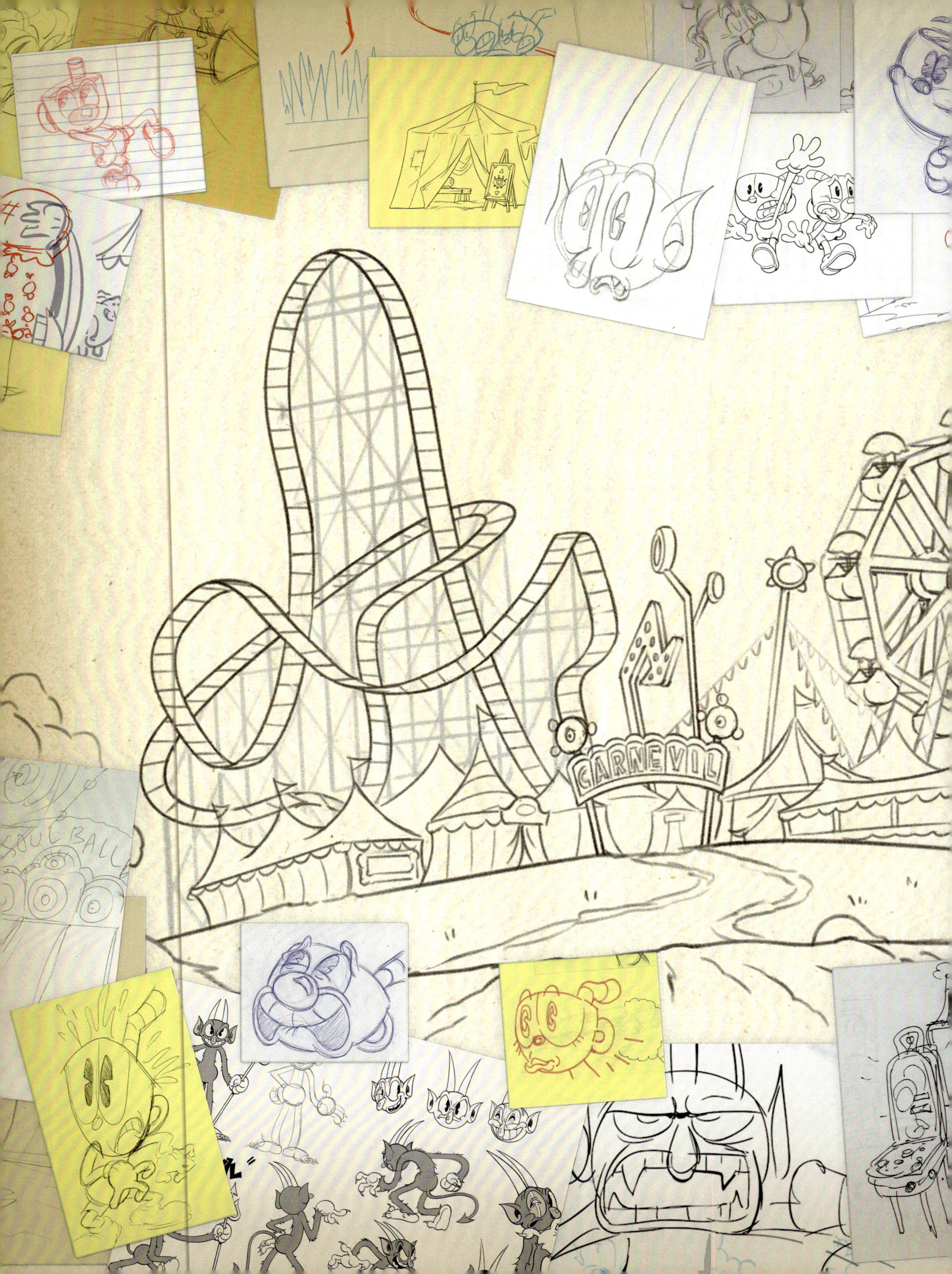
CARNEVIL
SOUL BALL

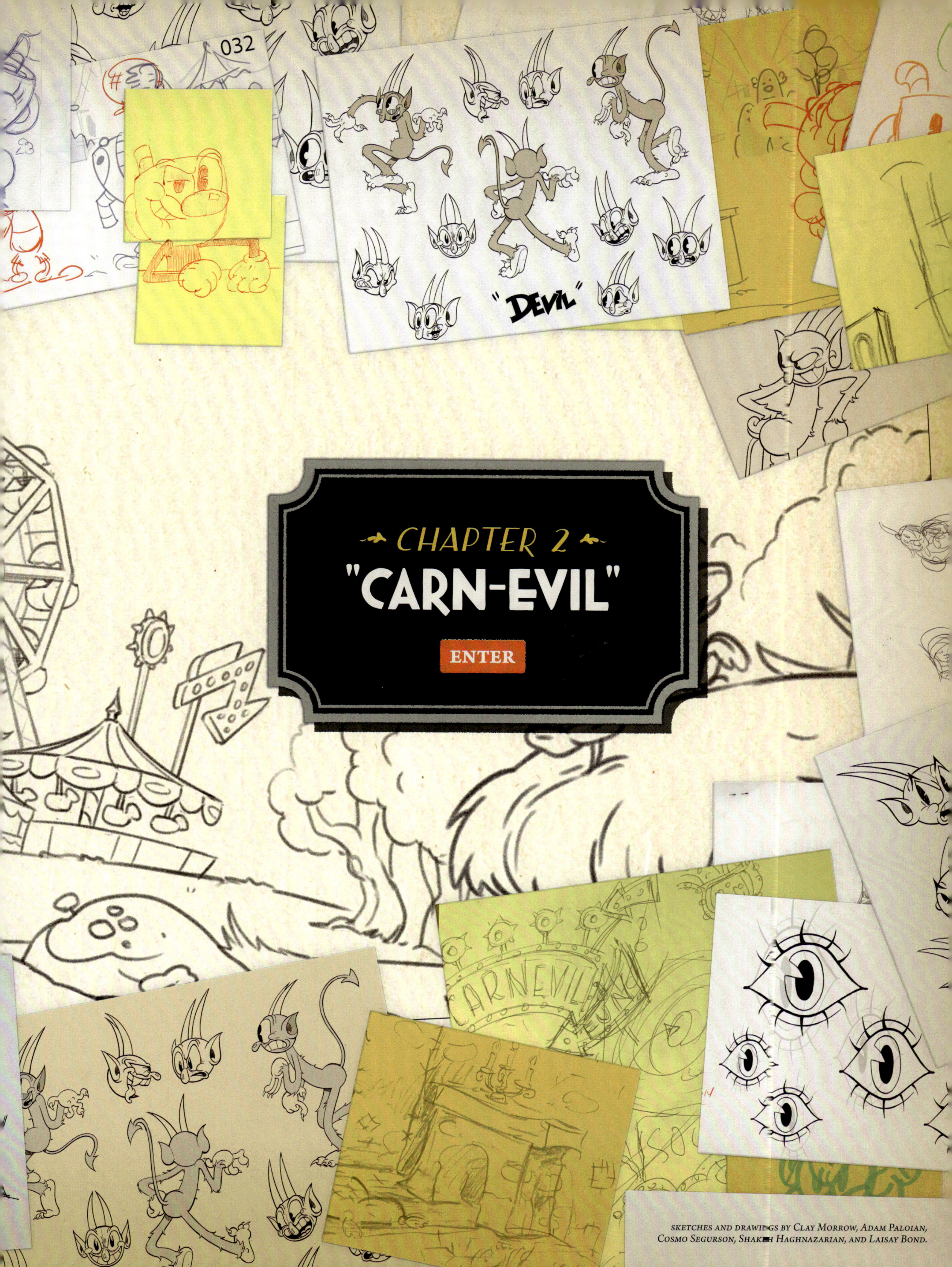

CHAPTER 2
"CARN-EVIL"

ENTER

Sketches and drawings by Clay Morrow, Adam Paloian, Cosmo Segurson, Shakeh Haghnazarian, and Laisay Bond.

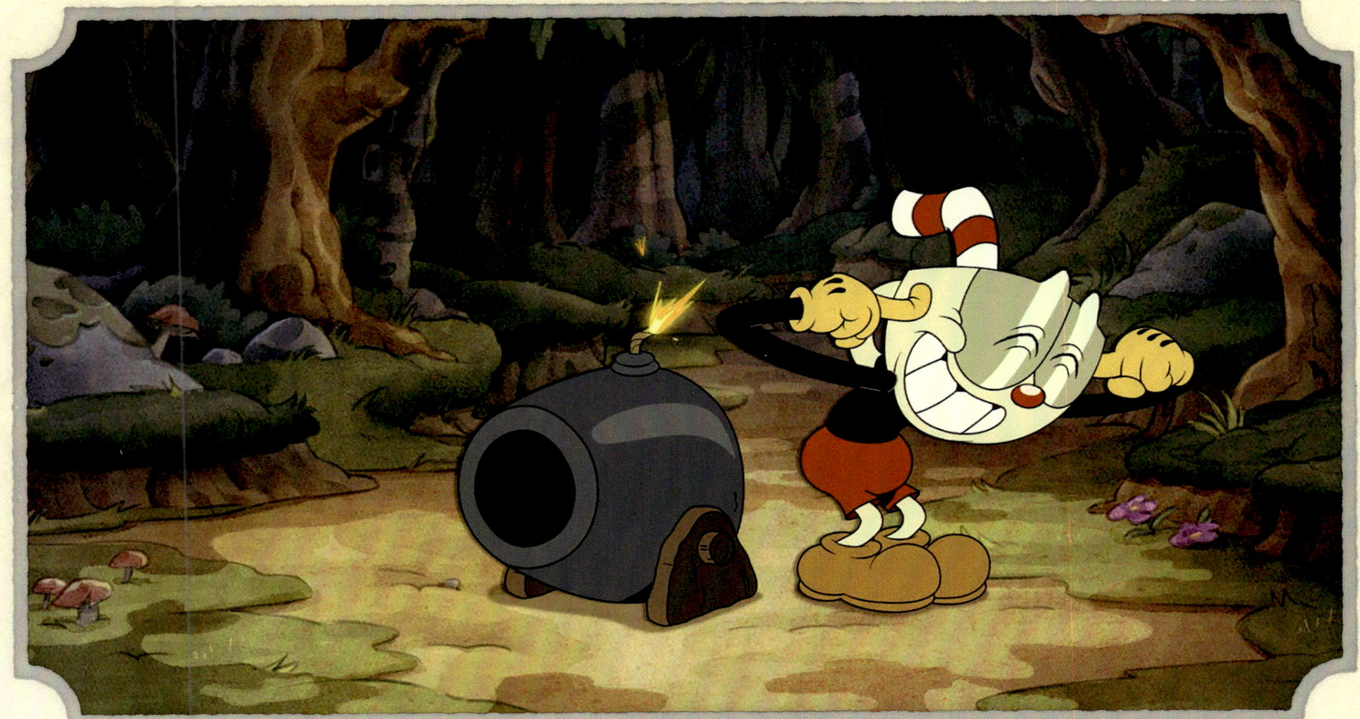

→ **DAVE:** The catalyst for the whole show is the cups' desire for something more than just living in the woods in a cottage with their Elder Kettle. I grew up in Arkansas in the middle of nowhere. I also had a brother, and we were always hiking through the woods, or we'd find a construction site and explore that and make clubs out of two-by-fours and pretend to be warriors . . . Immediately this all made sense to me, growing up in the middle of nowhere and longing for a more exciting life.

COSMO: For the first episode, we wanted to show the dynamic between Cuphead and Mugman, where Cuphead isn't thinking about the consequences, and Mugman is trepidatious—but also establish the relationship with Elder Kettle, introduce the Devil, and get the boys lost in a surreal, grotesque Fleischer-style world.

Layout by Andrea Fernandez; painting by Michelle Thies; special pose design by Shakeh Haghnazarian.

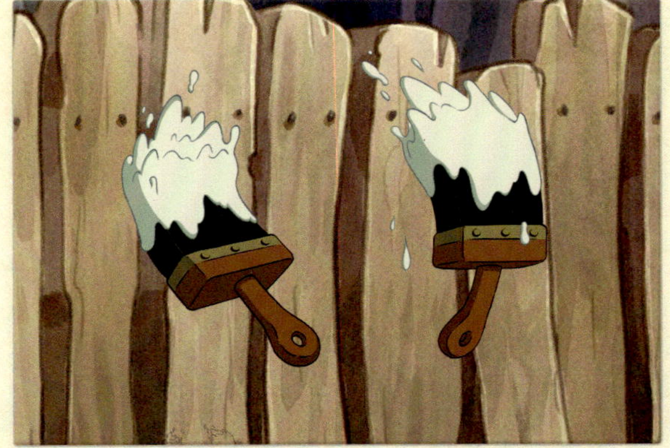

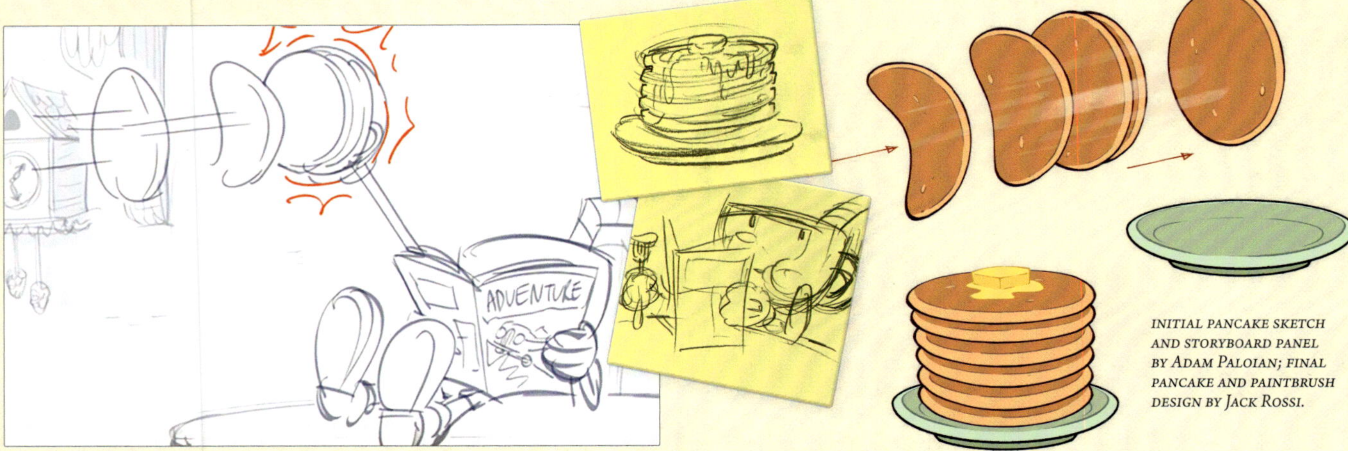

Initial pancake sketch and storyboard panel by Adam Paloian; final pancake and paintbrush design by Jack Rossi.

→ **ADAM P:** The pancake sequence evolved a few times. We wanted to make sure we established our main characters in one shot, since it's the first time the audience would be seeing them. I hid Cuphead's face behind the comic so his introduction was a reveal. It's also part of his personality that he catches the pancakes without even trying. In contrast, Mugman is clearly paying more attention and yet still fails.

Character and props color design by Chris Hacker.

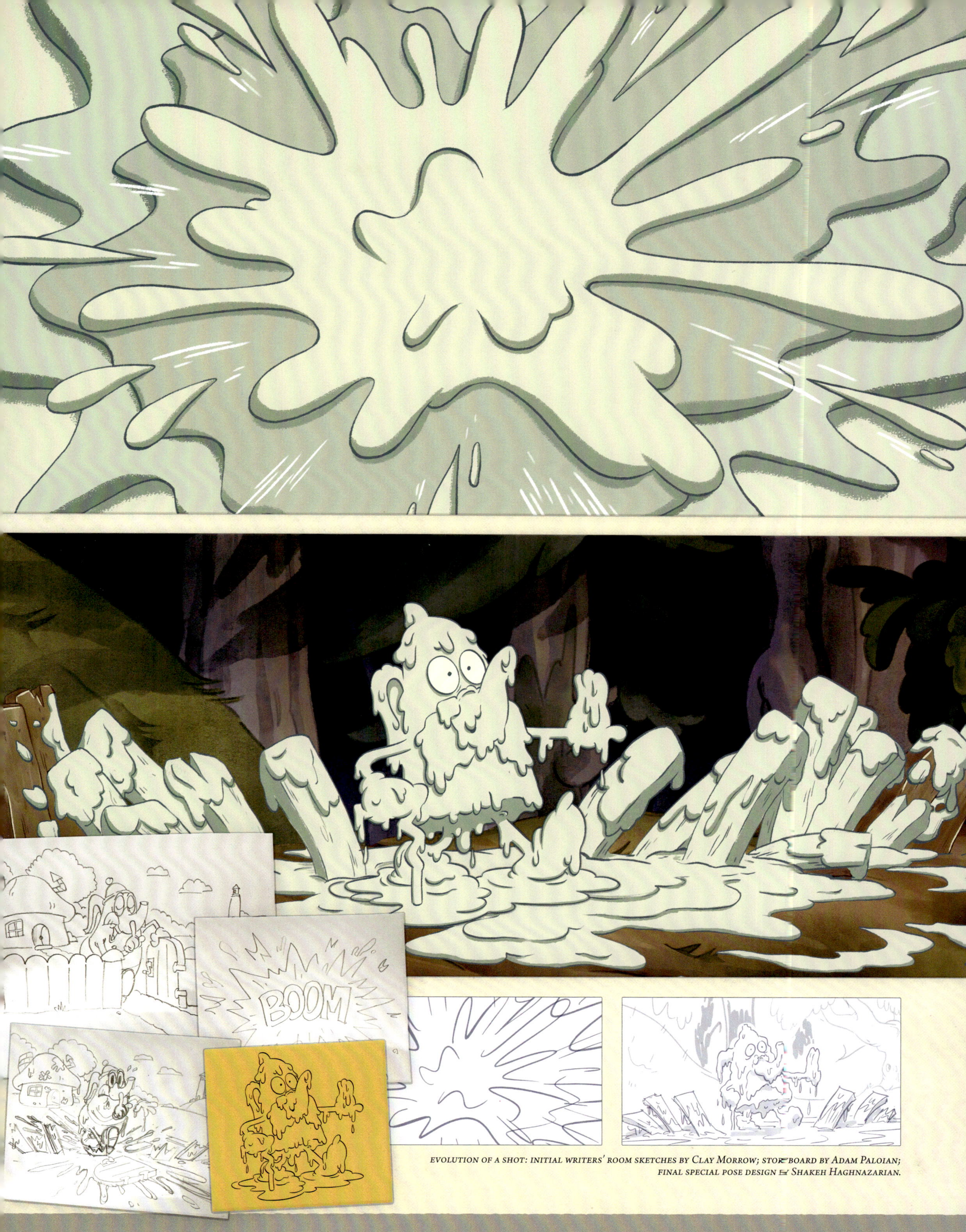

Evolution of a shot: initial writers' room sketches by Clay Morrow; storyboard by Adam Paloian; final special pose design by Shakeh Haghnazarian.

Background design by Laisay Bond; painting by Mallory Carlson.

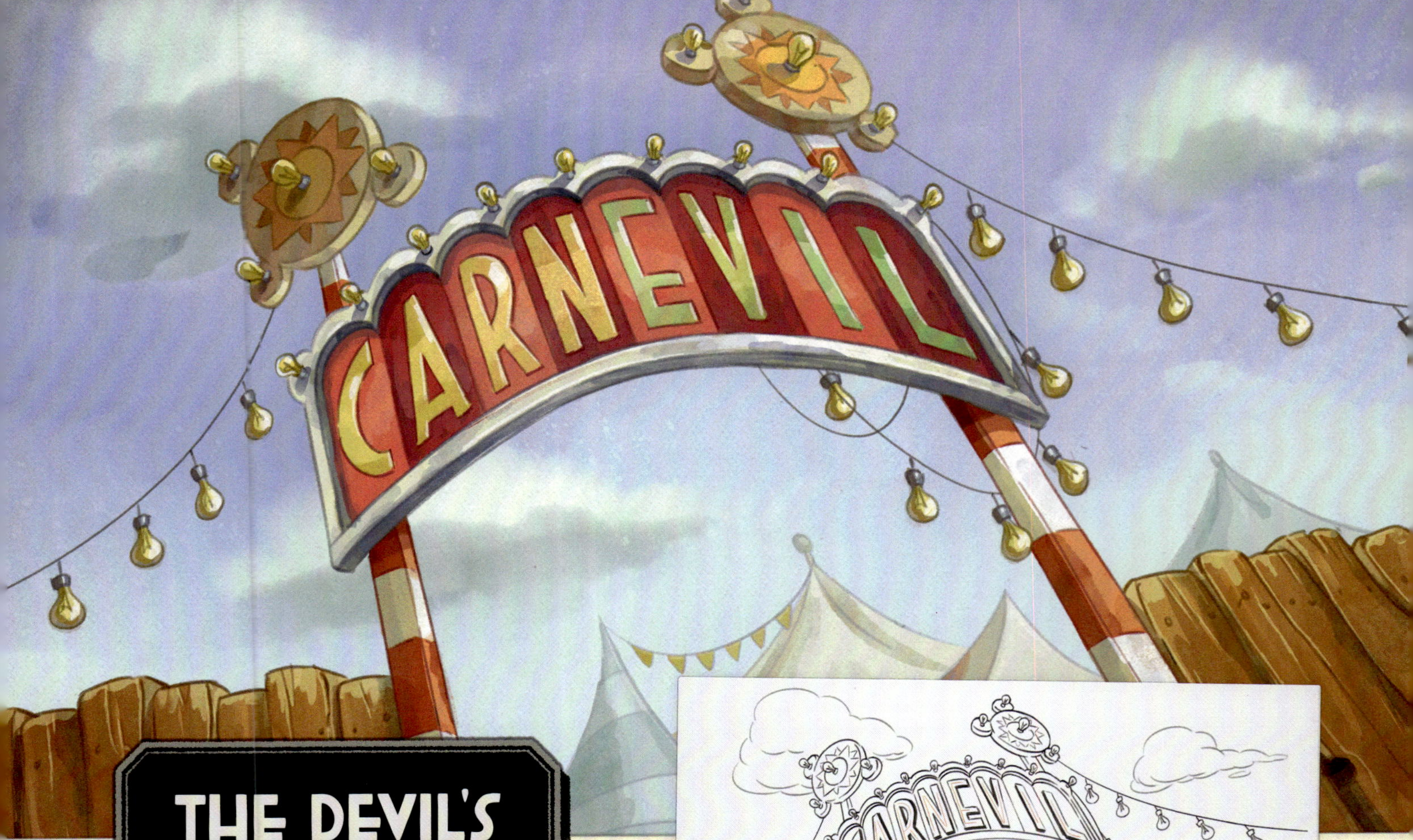

THE DEVIL'S CARNIVAL

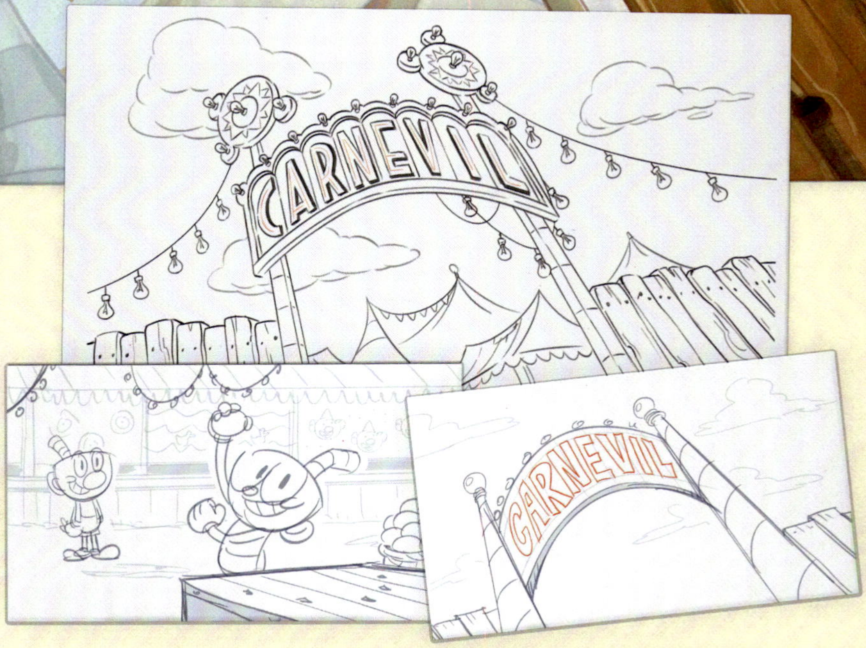

→ **ANDREA:** From a color standpoint, "Carn-Evil" was the hardest episode. If I want to stay *Snow White* at the beginning of the episode, how do I get to surreal insanity by the end of the episode? It was already hard to figure out the episode's naturalistic palette at the cottage, and then we had to switch to the carnival. The first of *many* palette switches . . .

Storyboard panels by Adam Paloian; color keys by Ivan Aguirre.

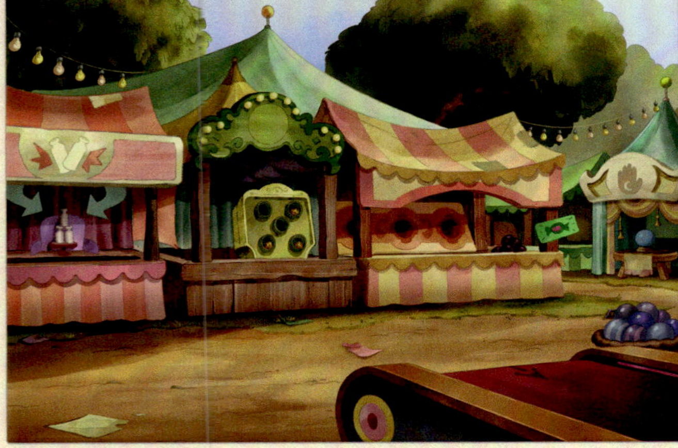

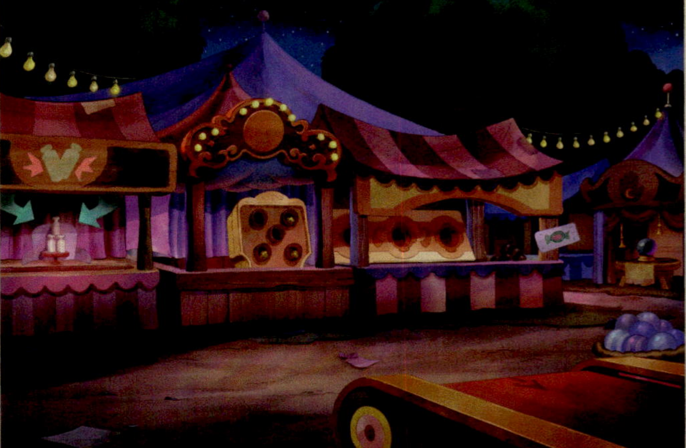

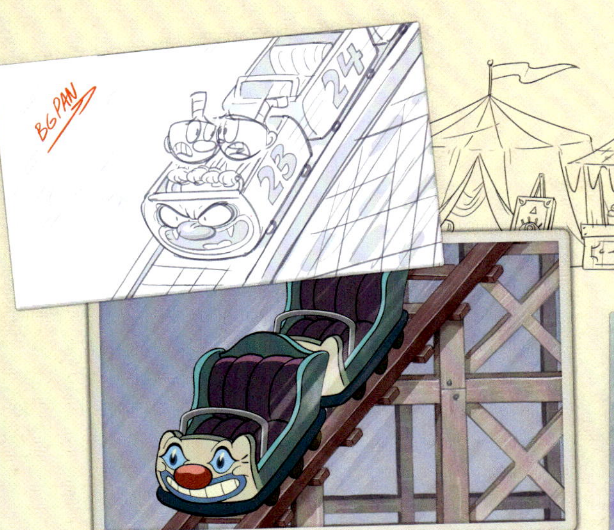

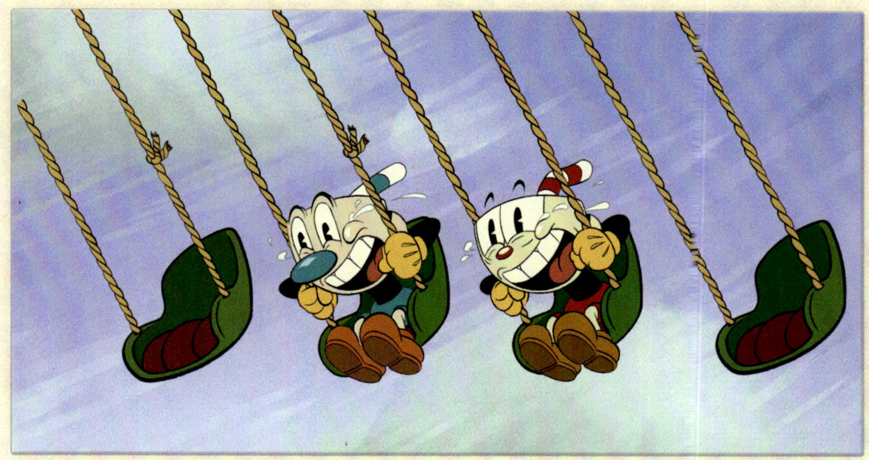

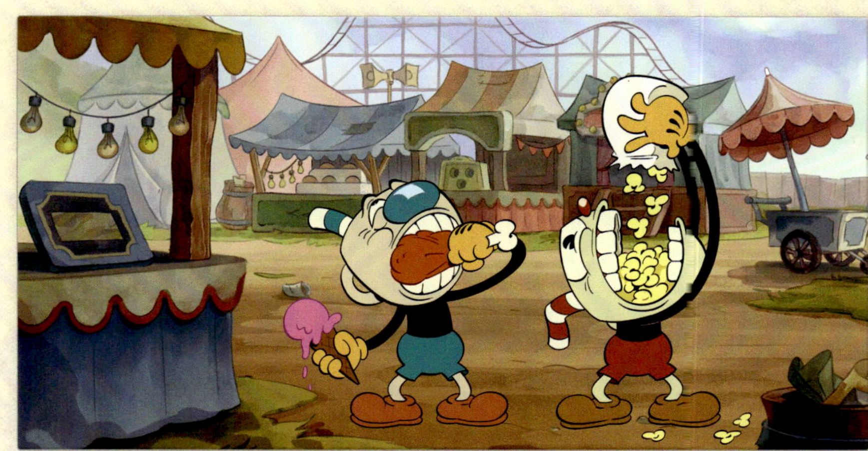

→ **DAVE:** Netflix was a little squeamish about doing a casino, so a carnival seemed like a great parallel idea—like a kid's version of a casino. Carnivals seem fun—they're so bright and lit up—but there's danger under the surface, so it felt like *of course* the Devil would be behind an operation like that. Talking in the story room, we elaborated on those ideas: we decided the carnival was just one of many things the Devil does to get souls.

DEEKI: The minute we decided it would be the Devil's carnival, we each had fifteen questions about how his whole operation works. Ideas start flying around, and you have to read the room to get a sense of what's lighting up the hive mind.

Storyboard panel by Adam Paloian; background designs by Lauren Duda and Laisay Bond; paintings by Michelle Thies and Mallory Carlson; incidental hot dog enthusiast—soulless, then soulful; special pose designs by Jim Soper.

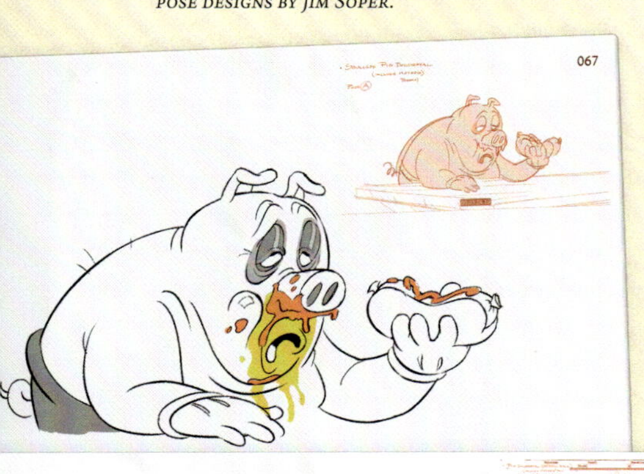

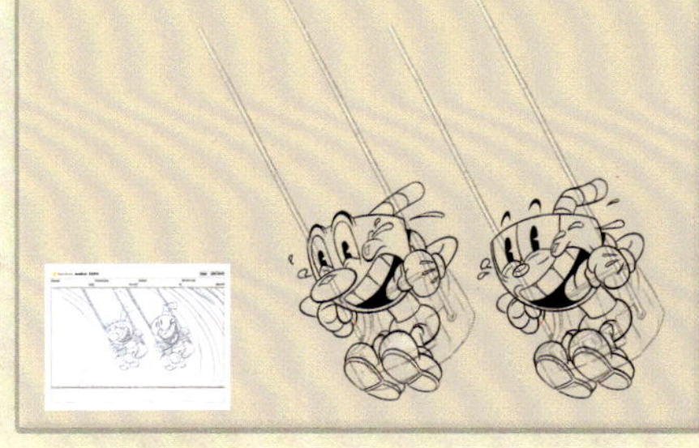

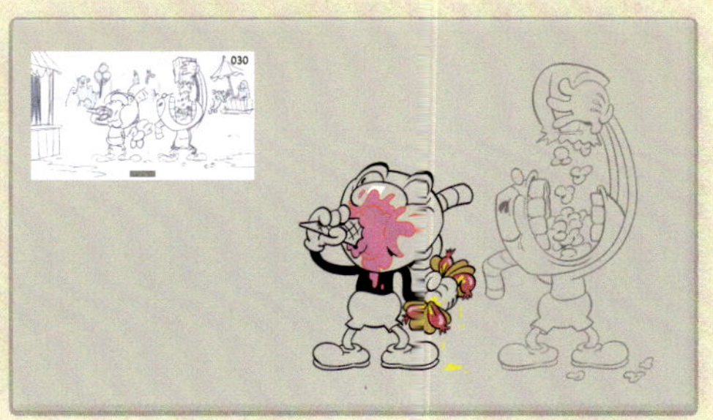

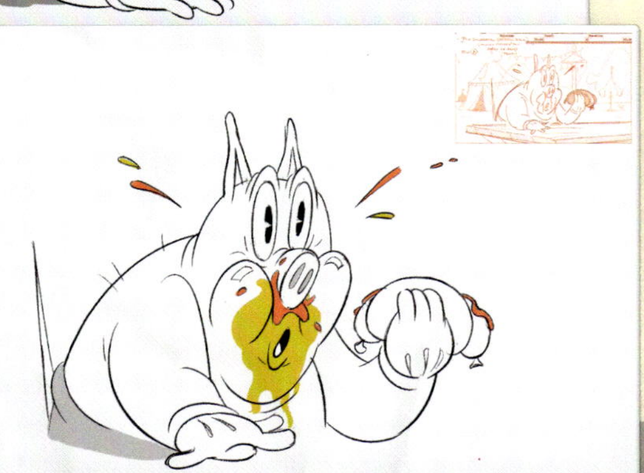

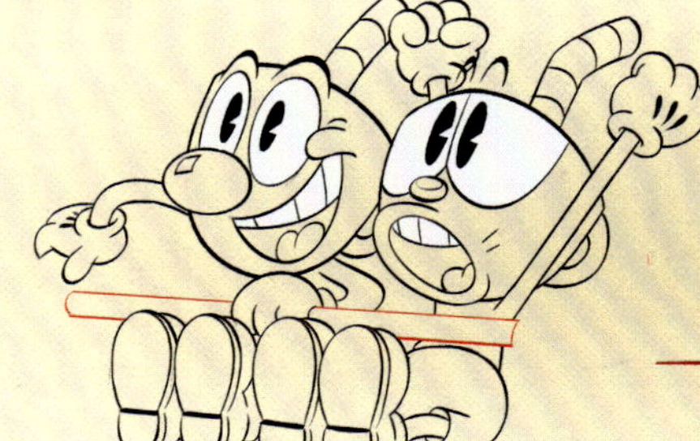

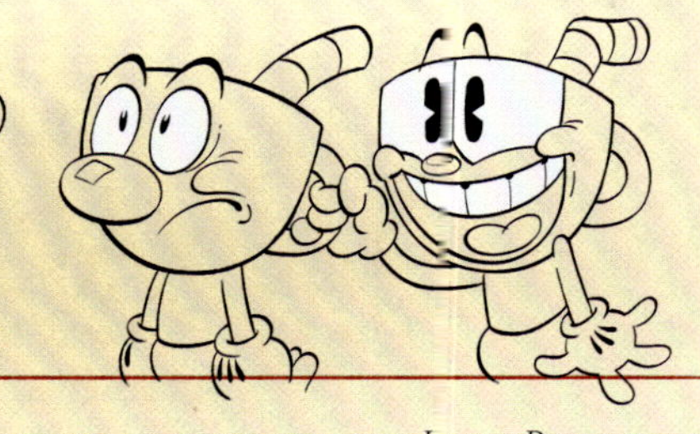

Carnival background designs by Lauren Duda; special pose designs by Shakeh Haghnazarian.

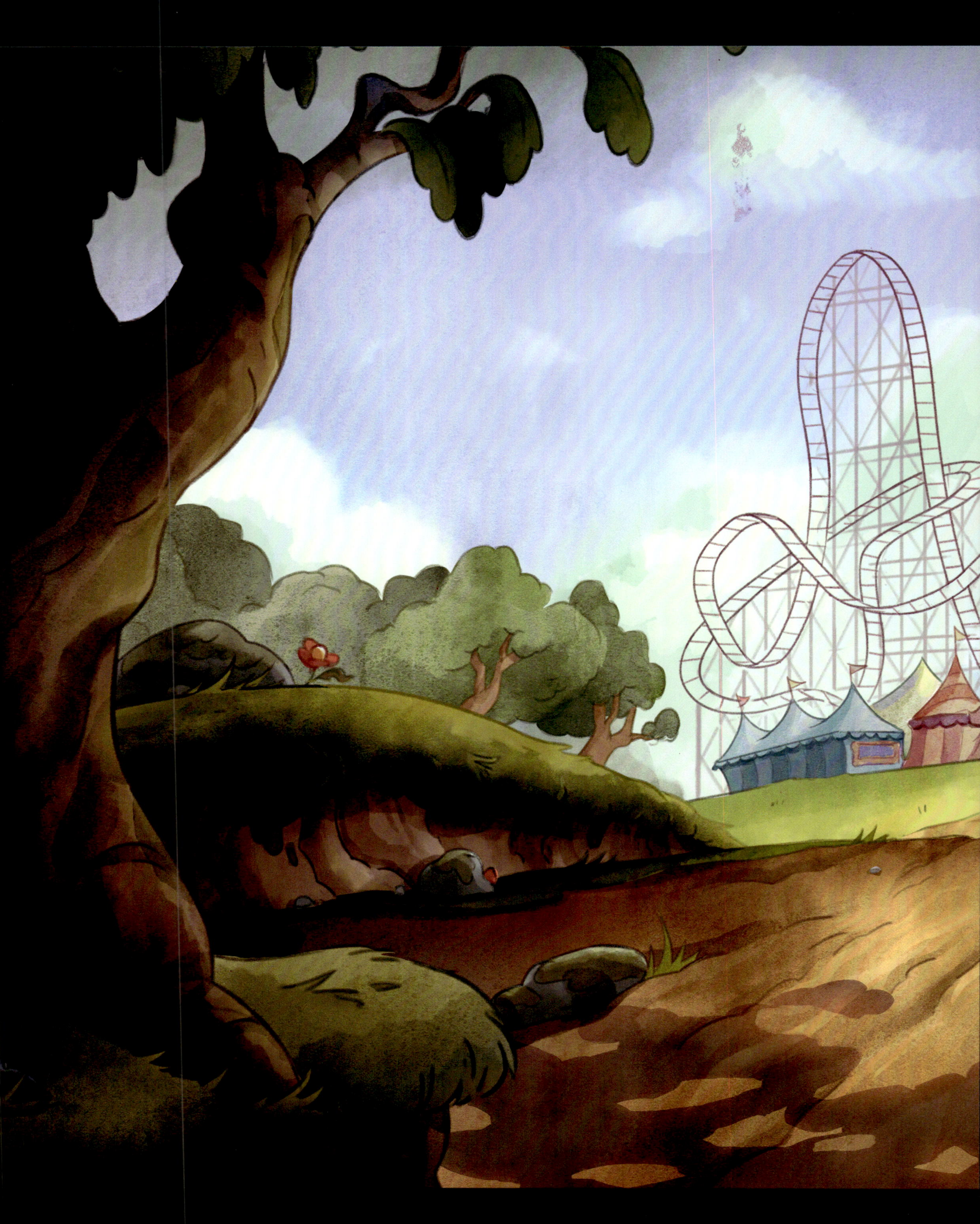

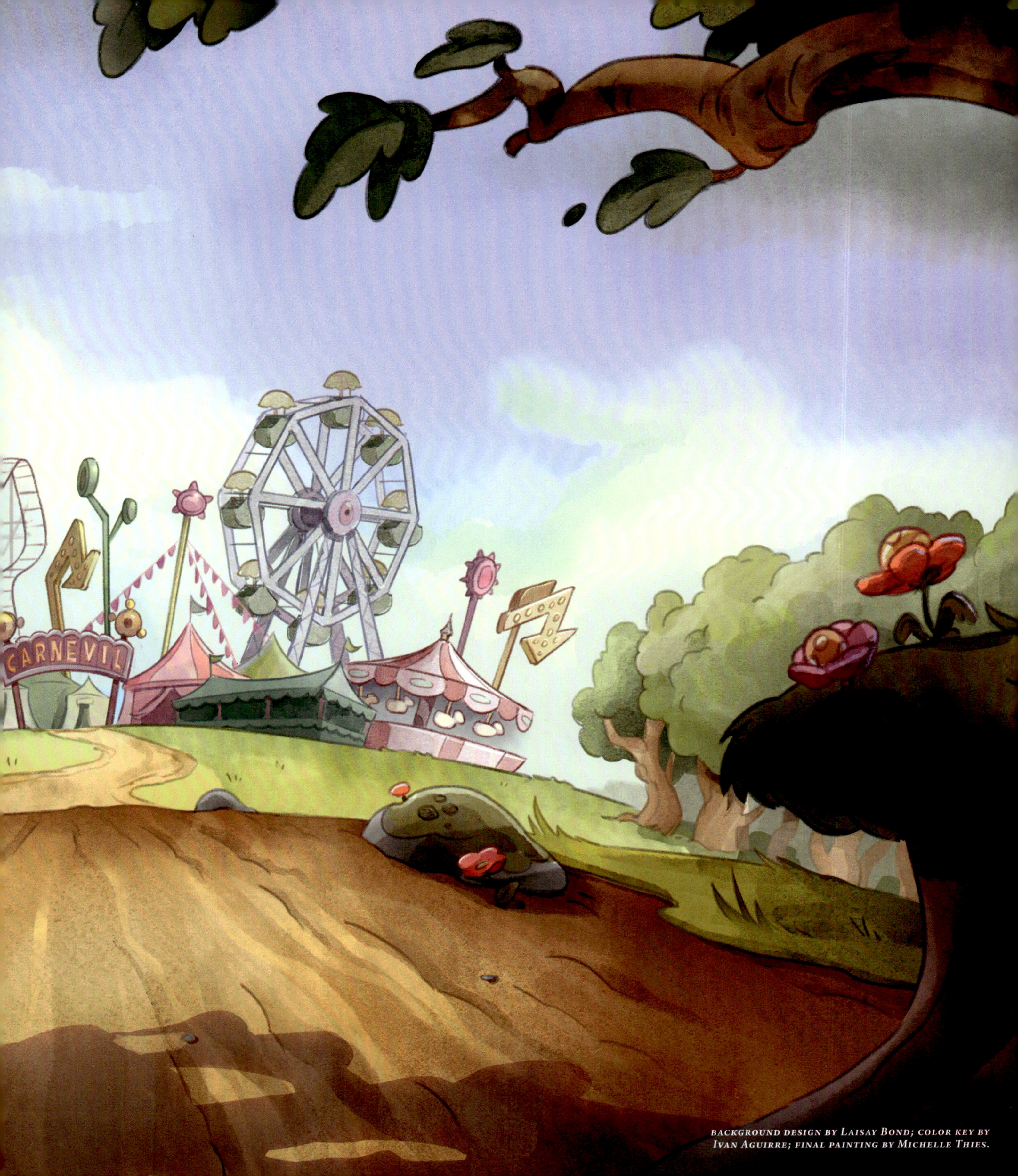

BACKGROUND DESIGN BY LAISAY BOND; COLOR KEY BY IVAN AGUIRRE; FINAL PAINTING BY MICHELLE THIES.

ADAM P: Soul Ball has giant signage and looks like the most important machine. I kept adding flashing lights and pointing fingers to make it as ridiculous and eye catching as possible.

ANDREA: The Soul Ball machine gets the strongest hues, it gets the most contrast, and everything around it is really subdued. We sucked the color out of its surroundings, so it feels like it's the most important thing in this carnival.

Soul Ball machine previs by Cosmo Segurson; final design by Laisay Bond; painting by Ivan Aguirre.

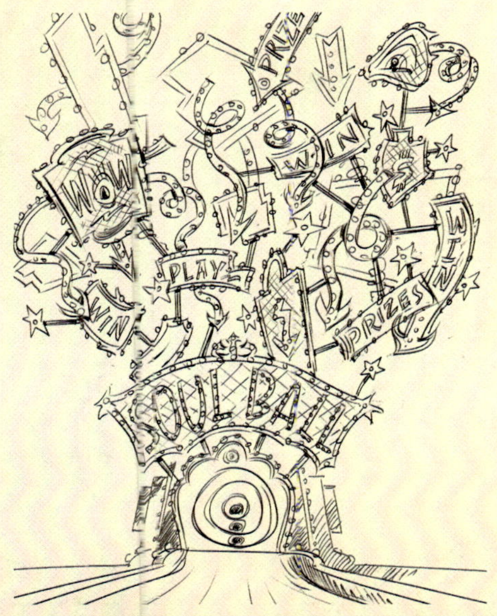

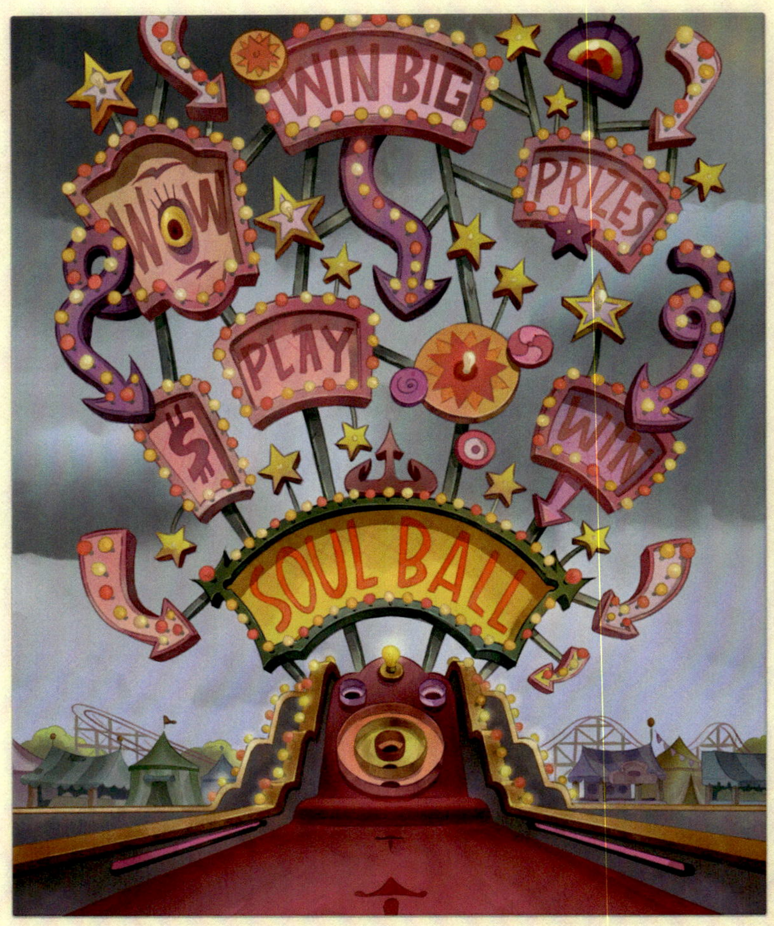

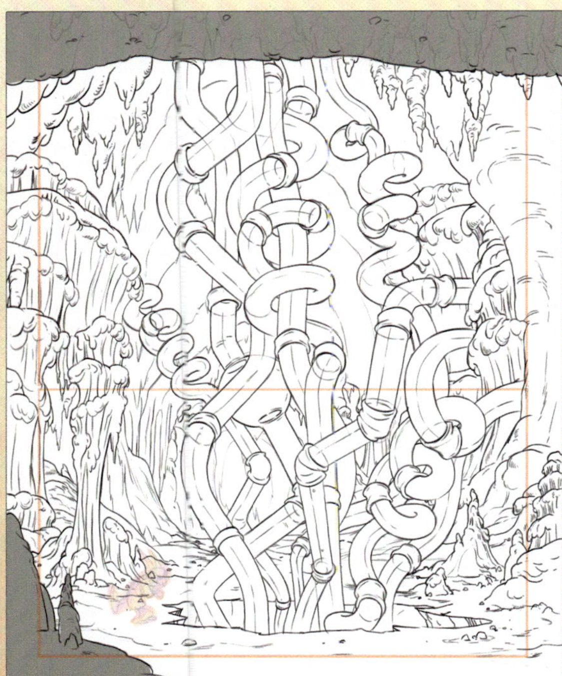

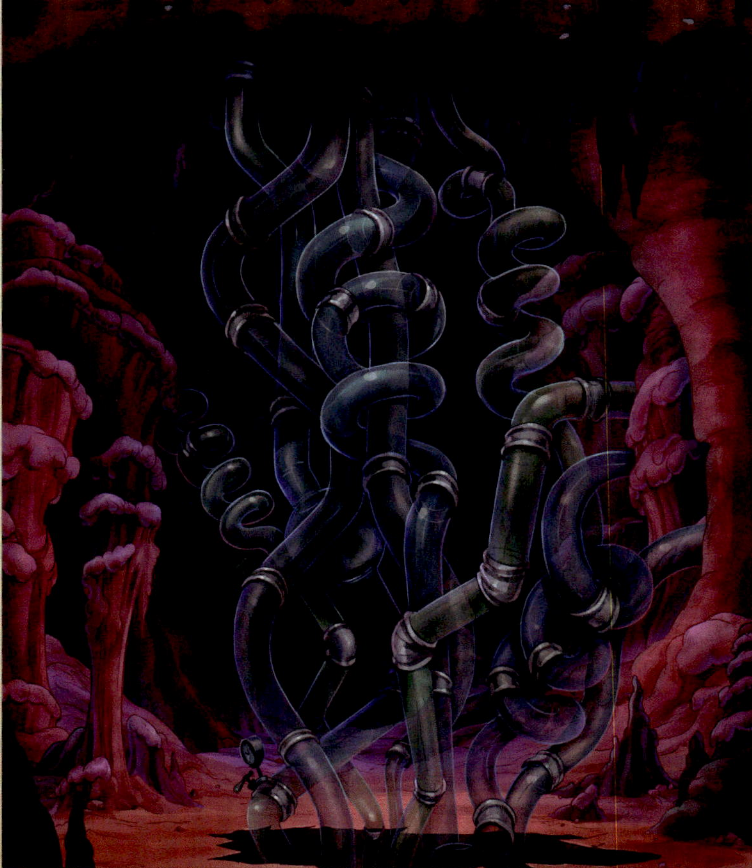

ADAM P: The pan down to the Devil's HQ tells you everything in one shot: the Soul Ball machine, Telephone's soul getting sucked into it, the tubes constantly collecting souls, and at the end of the pan, we reveal the Devil.

Background designs by Jessica Hong; painting by Michelle Thies.

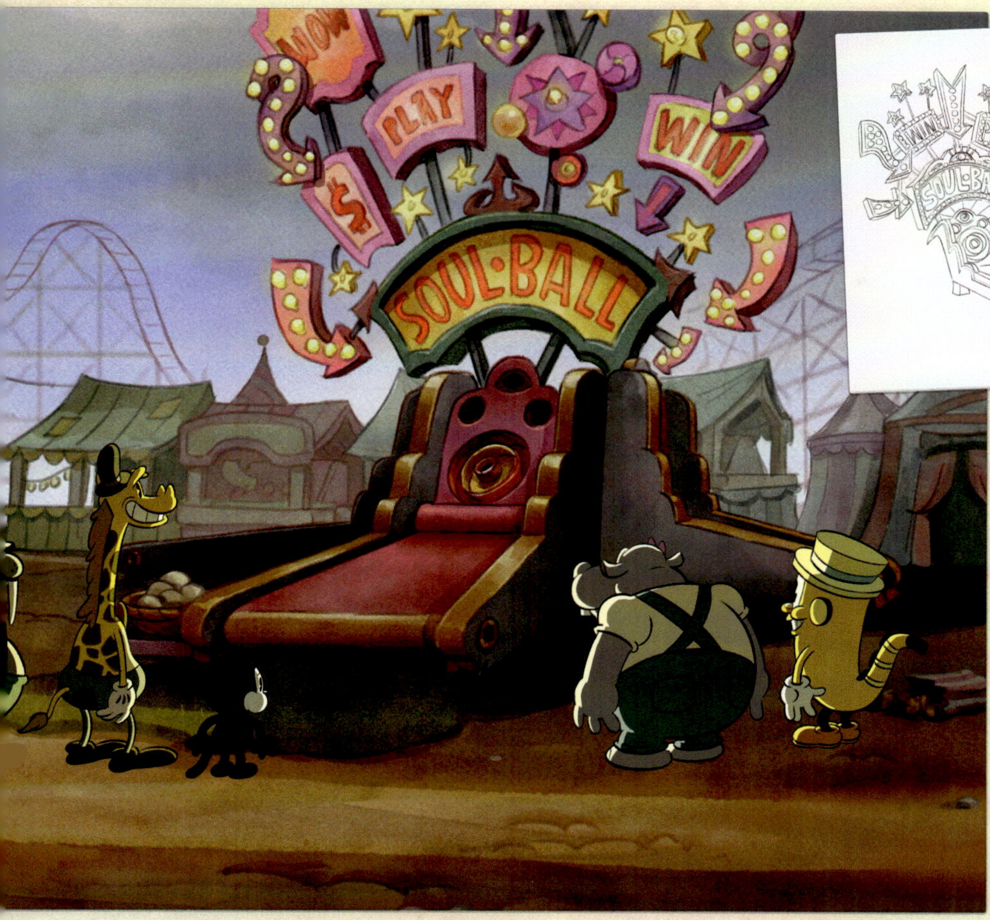

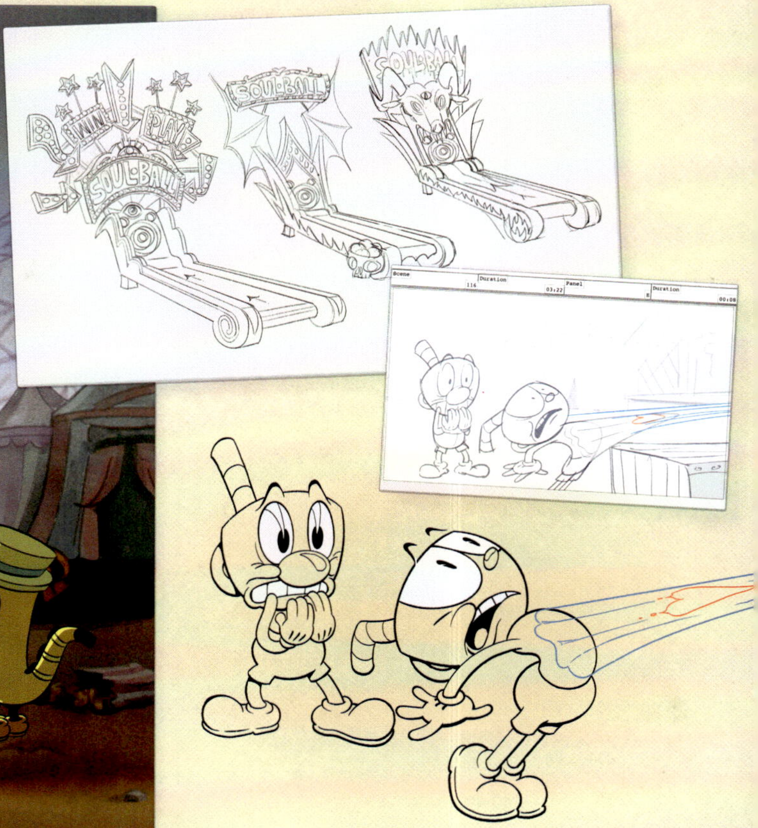

storyboard panel by Adam Paloian; background designs by Lauren Duda; special pose designs by Shakeh Haghnazarian.

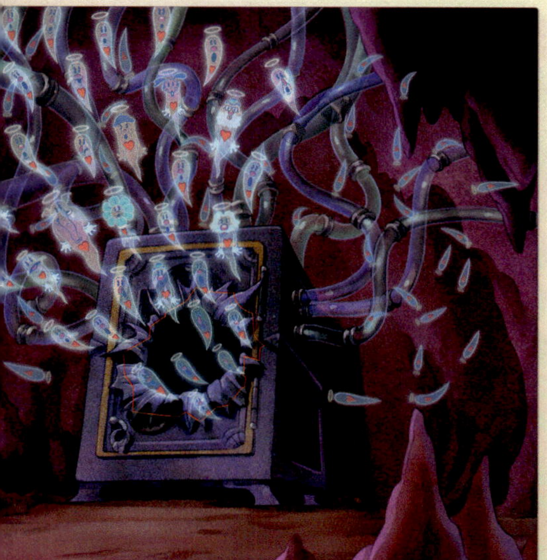

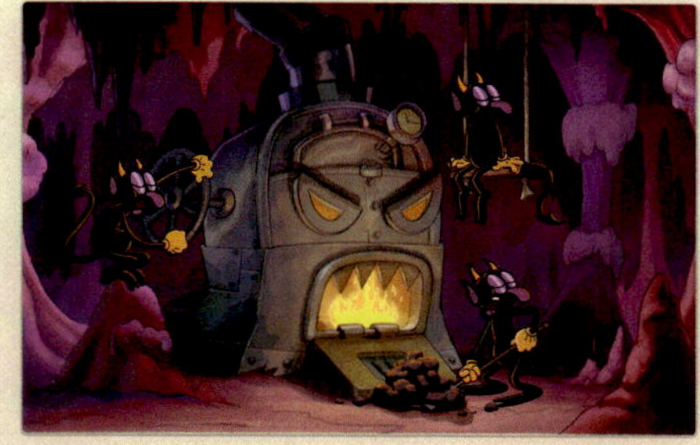

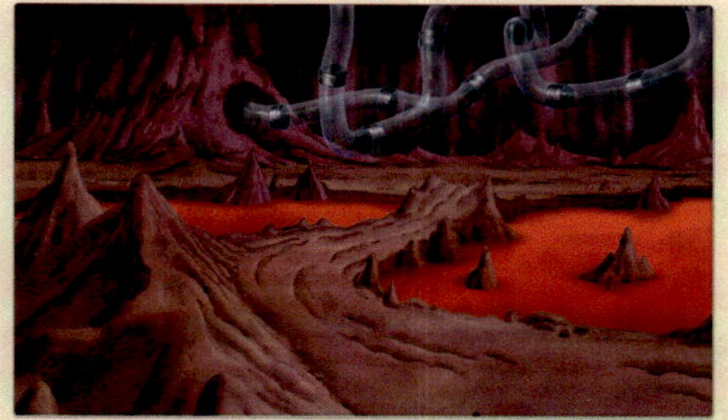

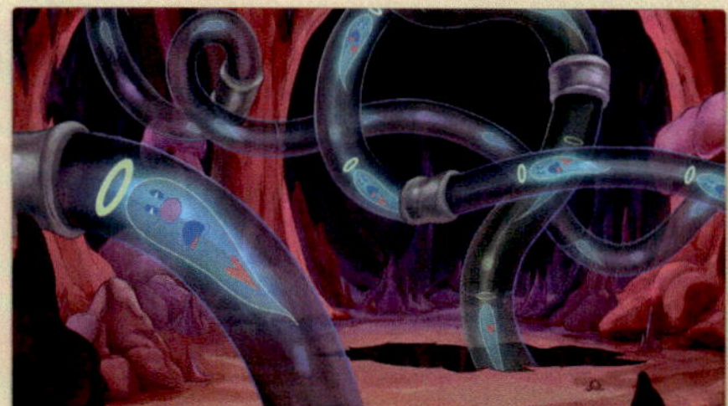

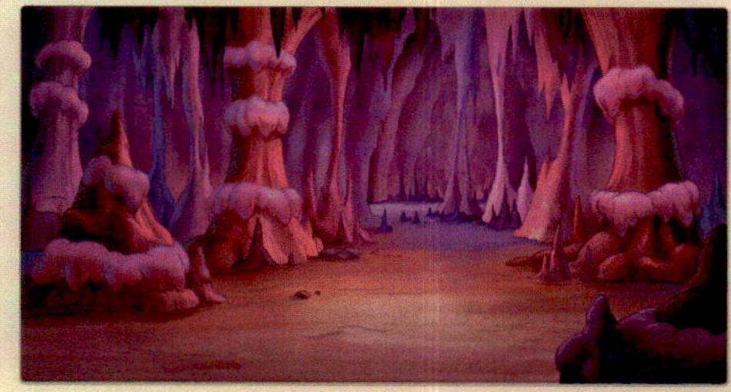

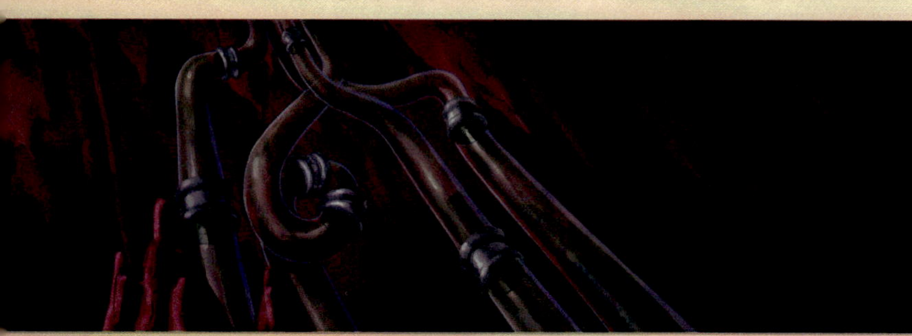

→ **ANDREA:** The first episode was giving me the sweats. The team was all learning how to paint similarly to one another, we were having to figure out tons of new locations in that episode, as well as making definitive color changes to shift the mood from this happy daytime naturalistic palette to this more sinister, weird, whimsical feel. It was a huge learning curve for all of us.

background designs by Jessica Hong; color keys by Ivan Aguirre; paintings by Mallory Carlson and Ivan Aguirre.

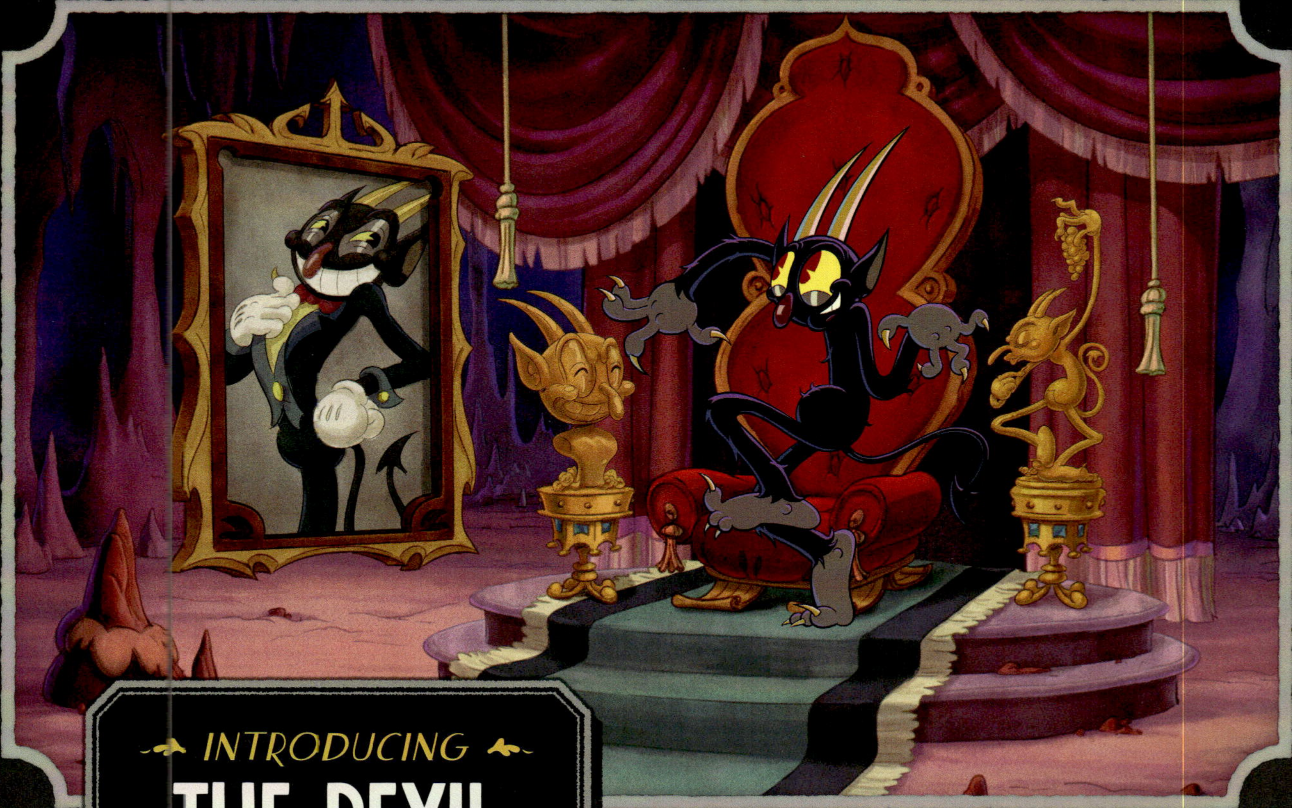

INTRODUCING
THE DEVIL

(voiced by Luke Millington-Drake)

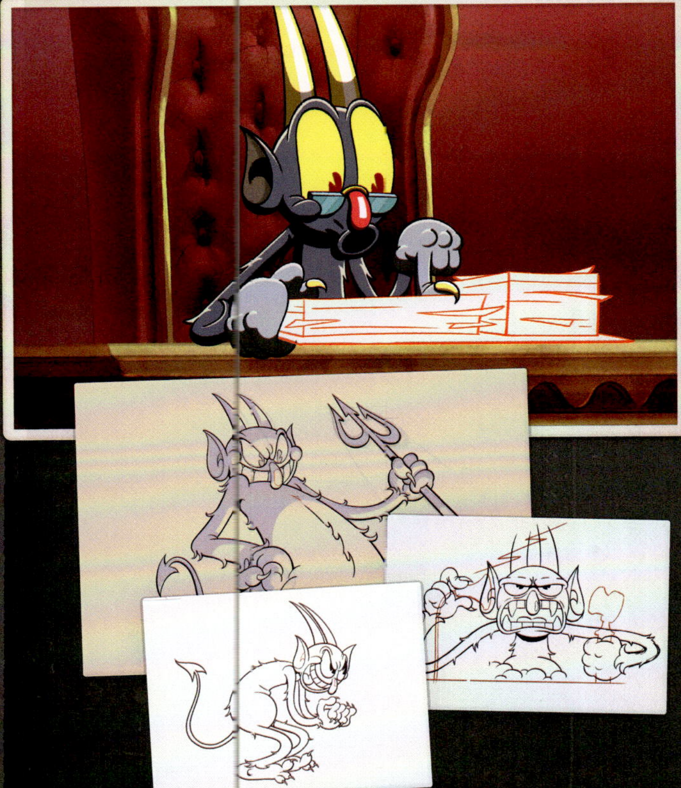

Special pose designs by Adam Paloian, Tapan Gandhi,

DAVE: Any great hero needs a great villain, and you can't do better than the Devil.

COSMO: It would have been easy to make the Devil just "the devil" we know from legend. Devil characters in movies are always really interesting, but they're usually not very funny—they don't have idiosyncrasies or an ego about themselves.

DAVE: We liked the idea that, in the beginning, before the Devil meets Cuphead, things are going great for him—he's having a ball, it's easy for him to pick off marks, he's collecting tons of souls—and then he meets Cuphead, and that starts to change the Devil's life pretty radically.

CLAY: The Devil is such a fun character, because he's so high and mighty that he can only go down.

DAVE: He's so self-involved. He's really arrogant. He's only interested in his own pleasures and boasting and feeling good about his own situation.

DEEKI: He's the ultimate theater kid.

CLAY: The characteristics that we gave him . . . It's like all the things that make him the Devil are also the things that make him weak—his ego, his hubris, his sense of vengeance. He's so petty and shallow and always showing off—there's so many ways to get at him.

MEGAN CASEY, CONTENT EXECUTIVE, NETFLIX: The thing I love about the Devil is how incredibly insecure he is. All his acting out and big emotions and self-congratulating—he's just trying to build himself up, and I think it's really endearing and funny. He has so many facets, which allows him to be devilish but also sad and sweet and charming, and you do root for him at times. He can be scary, but he's not this "dark overlord."

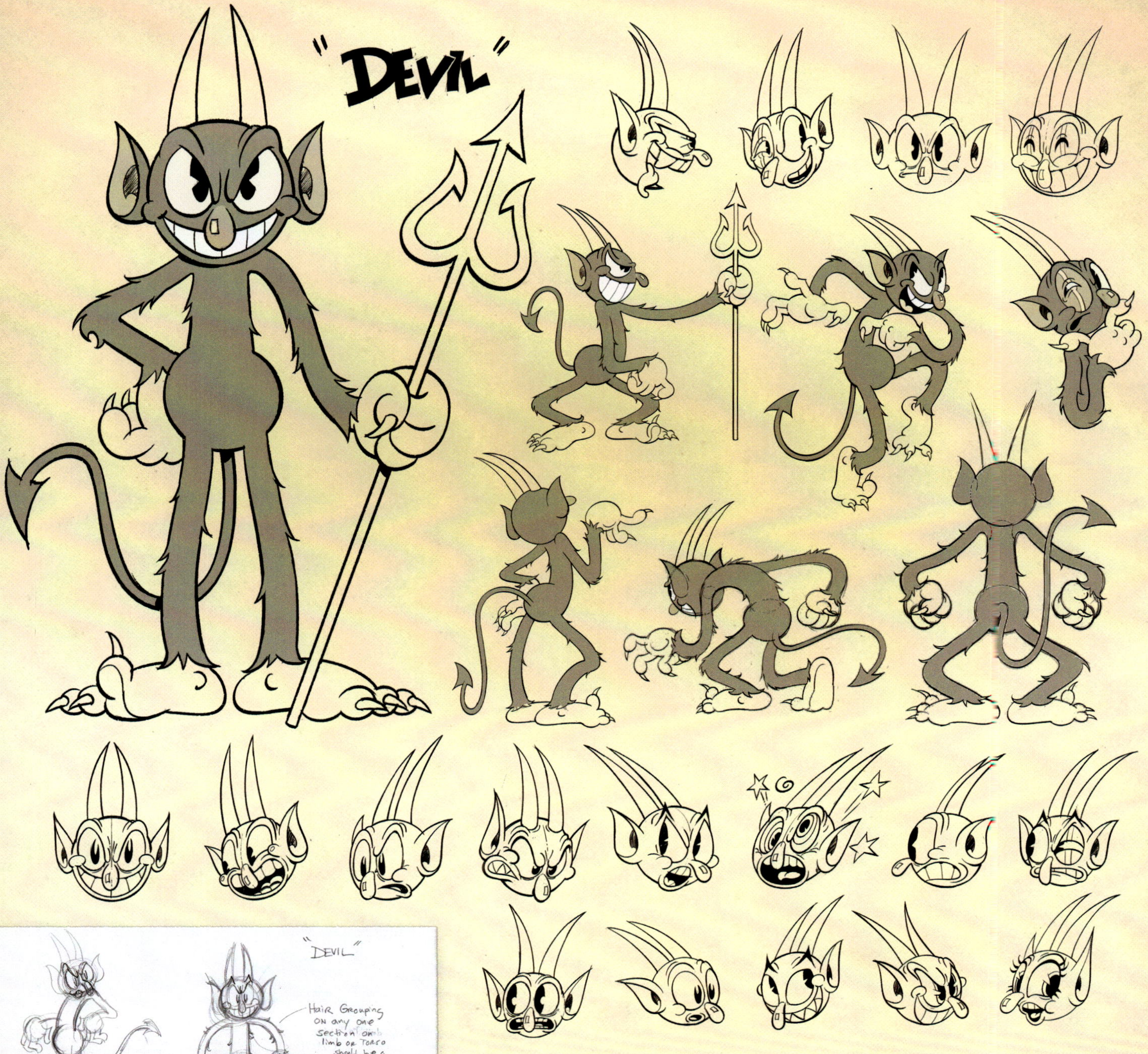

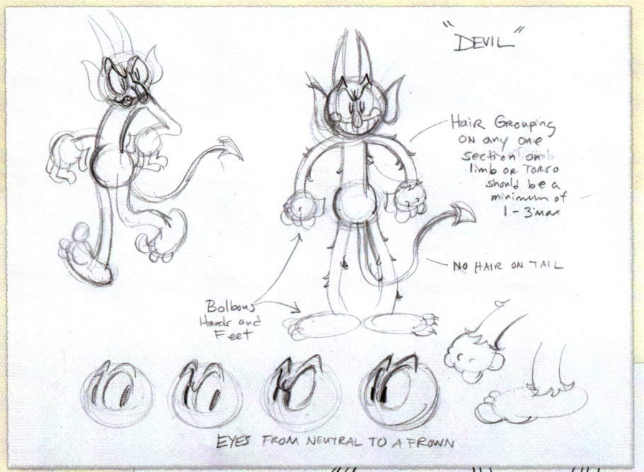

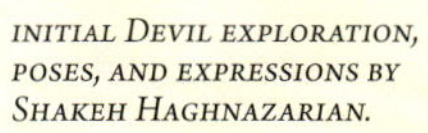

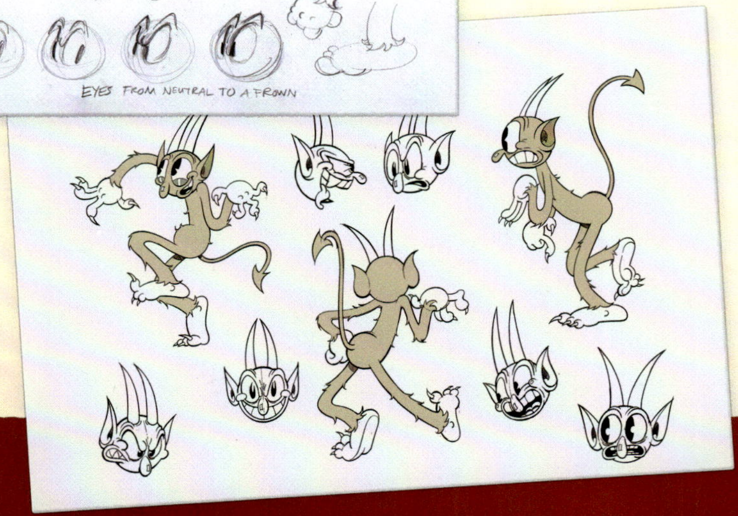

INITIAL DEVIL EXPLORATION, POSES, AND EXPRESSIONS BY SHAKEH HAGHNAZARIAN.

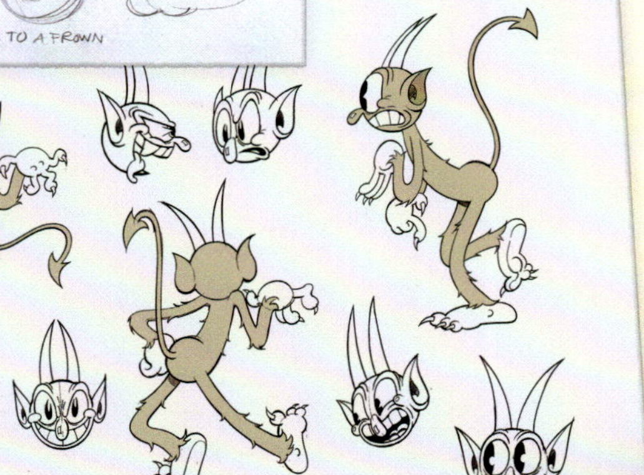

→ **SHAKEH:** I wanted to add just a smidge of goofiness to him. He's got these big hands and feet attached to lanky limbs with this silly nose. I was looking at a character from *Davy Jones' Locker* [1934] and *Hell's Fire* [1934] by Ub Iwerks when I was doing my exploration designs of him, and those shorts really sparked something in me when I was working on his poses and expressions.

CLAY: The way the Devil behaves, it's clear he's missing something; otherwise he wouldn't be trying so hard and posturing and posing like he does. He's very needy.

DAVE: The Devil shares with Cuphead that longing for more. He also thinks he deserves more than he gets, so he's kind of a big spoiled baby.

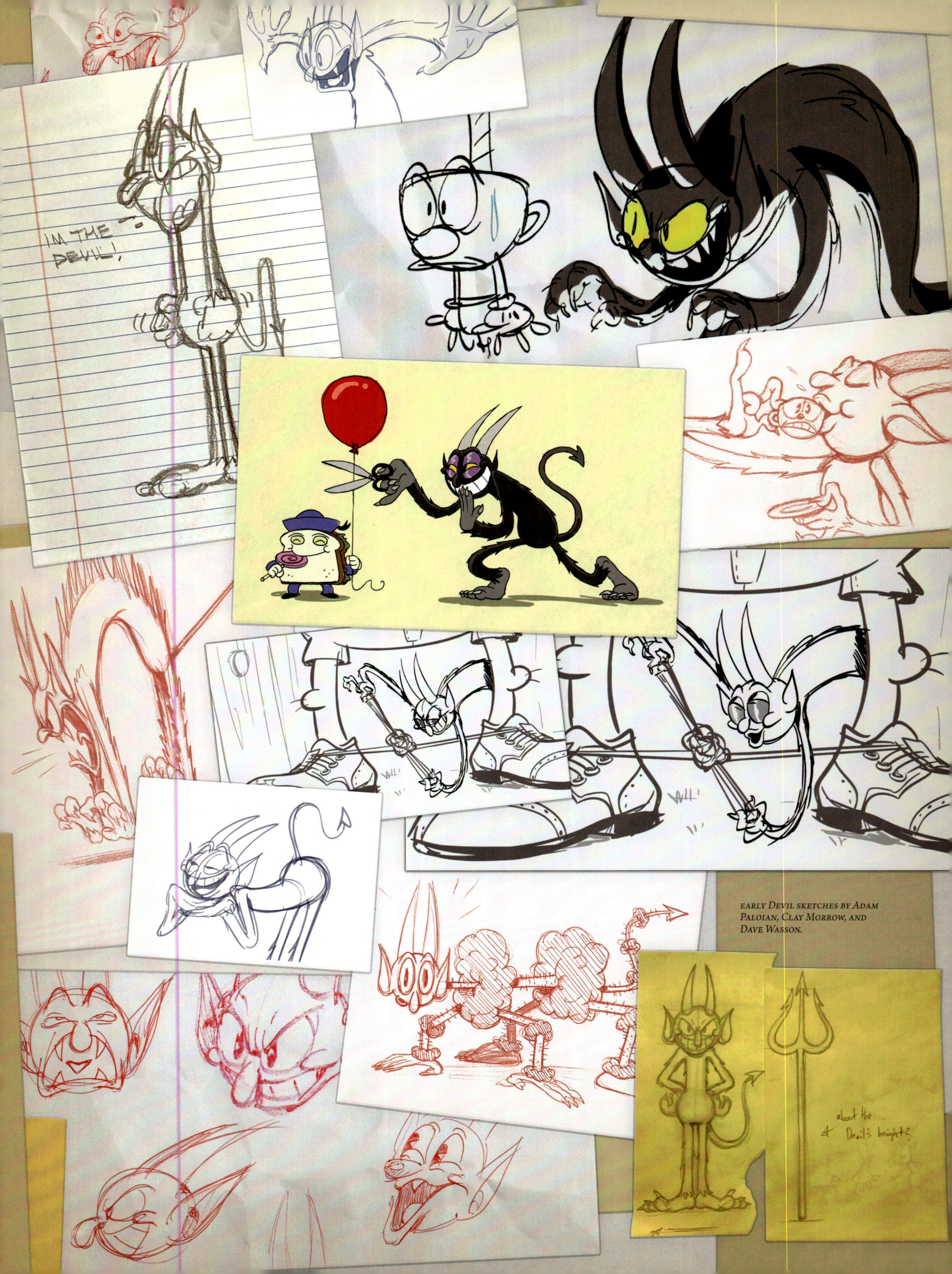

early Devil sketches by Adam Paloian, Clay Morrow, and Dave Wasson.

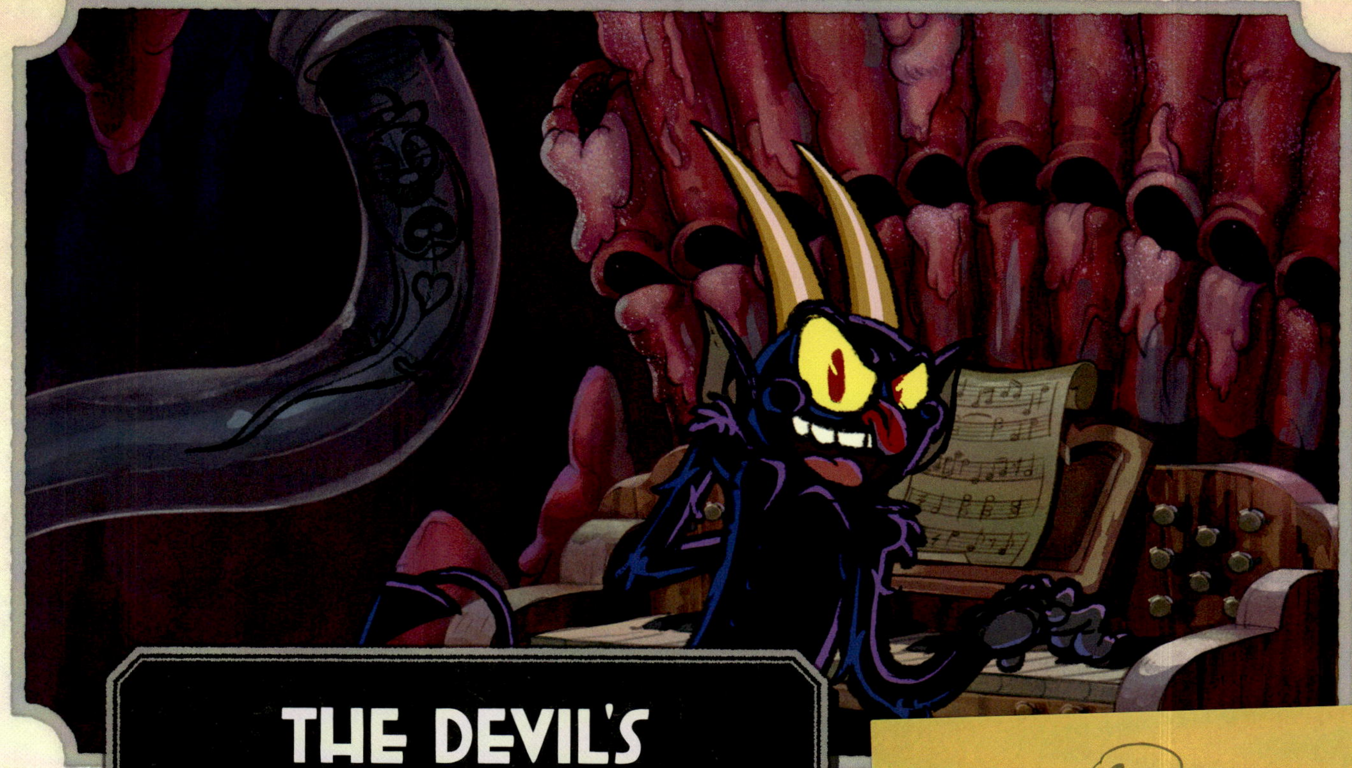

THE DEVIL'S OPENING NUMBER

DAVE: We knew we wanted to have songs. I thought a great way to introduce the Devil to the series would be with a song. Ego and I worked on that together. That was the very first piece of music we did for the entire series.

EGO PLUM, *THE CUPHEAD SHOW!* COMPOSER: I love the Devil's sensibility, and working with his voice and the jazzy style of a 1930s song was a dream come true. I was like a kid in a candy store.

DAVE: I had worked with Ego before, so we had a great working relationship. We have a kind of musical shorthand, and he's incredibly gifted when it comes to enhancing the mood of the story.

EGO: Imagine there's a gentle piano, but some of the notes are just a little off key. And you don't know *why* it's wrong, but you can *feel* something is wrong. That's my job: to make things feel like they're cute and innocent, but then something's a little off.

ADAM P: I was given an audio track that Dave and Ego put together, with Dave on temp vocals. I listened to it over and over, trying to block it out mentally. Dave and I worked closely on this section, and he'd act out poses for me as we'd brainstorm ways to improve it.

Early Devil sketches and poses by Adam Paloian.

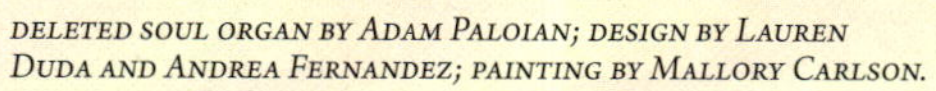

Deleted soul organ by Adam Paloian; design by Lauren Duda and Andrea Fernandez; painting by Mallory Carlson.

ADAM P: Before we came up with the idea of the soul tubes, I wasn't quite sure what the rules were on how souls functioned. I thought it might be visually fun to have the souls come out of the Devil's organ pipes and sing the backup "hoddely-hoddely-hoo" in his song.

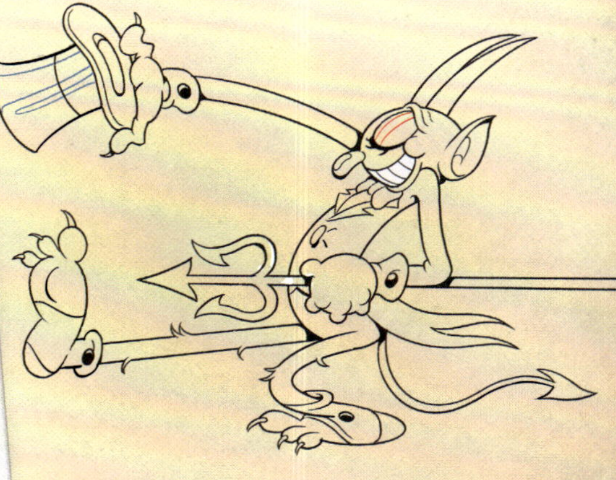

Devil sketches by Adam Paloian; special pose designs by Shakeh Haghnazarian.

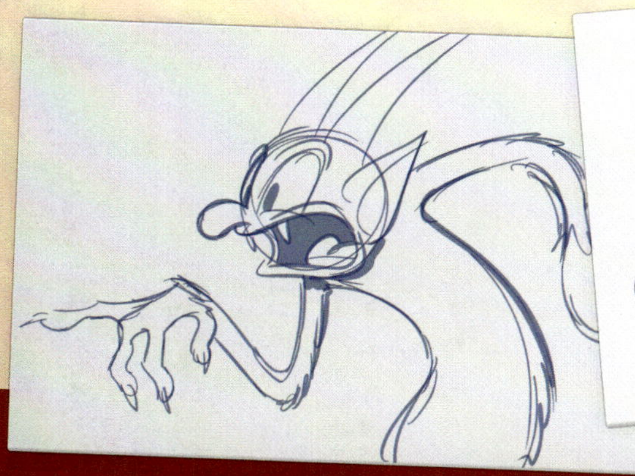

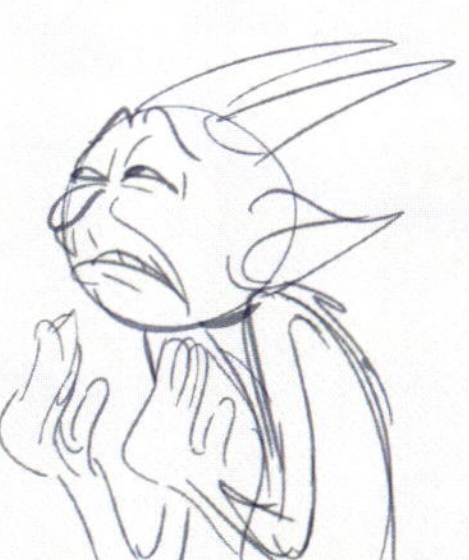

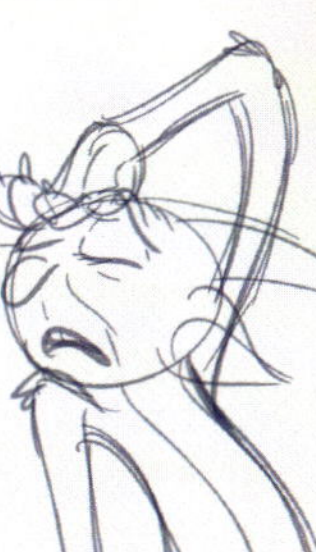

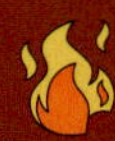

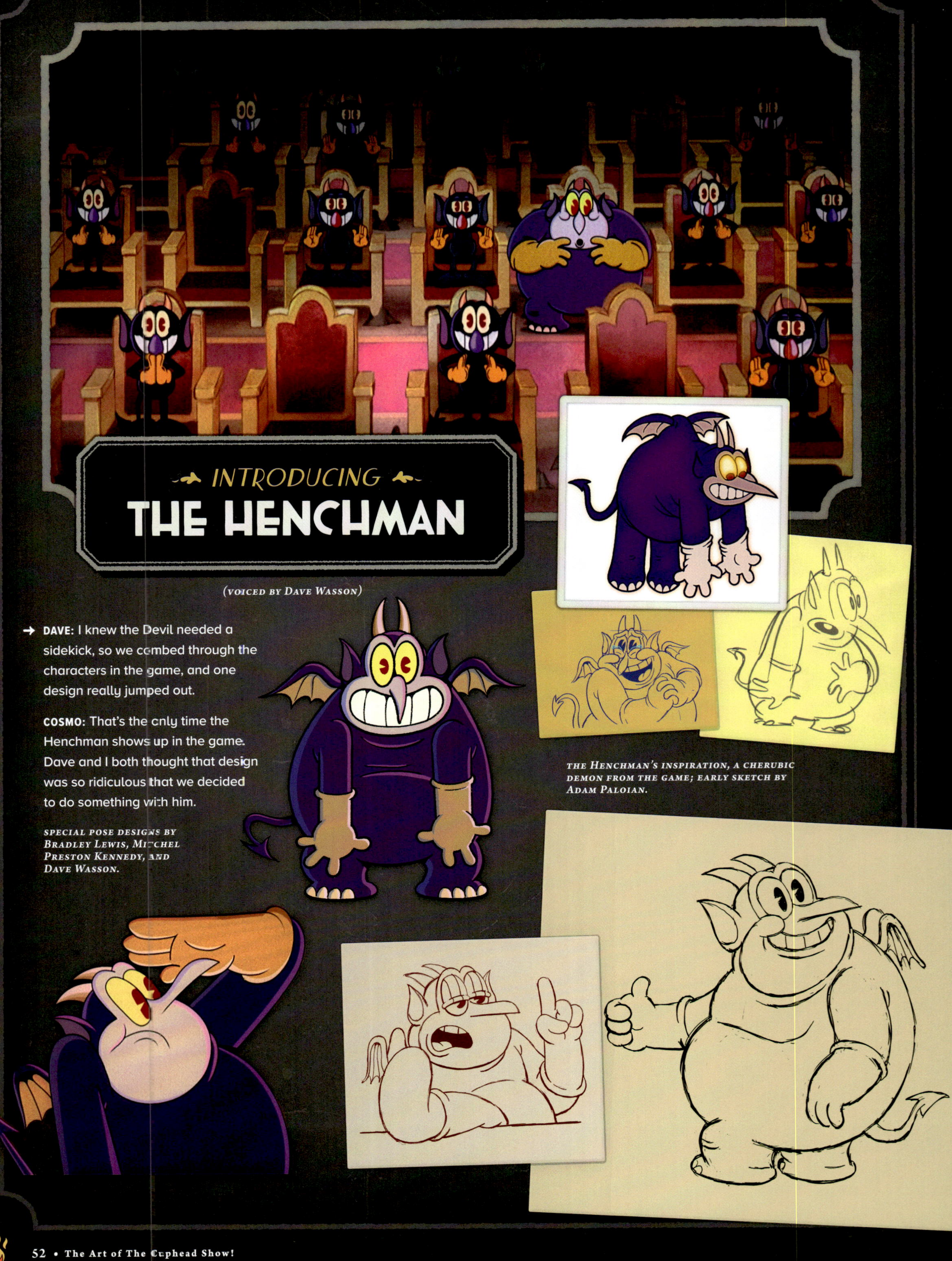

INTRODUCING THE HENCHMAN

(VOICED BY DAVE WASSON)

DAVE: I knew the Devil needed a sidekick, so we combed through the characters in the game, and one design really jumped out.

COSMO: That's the only time the Henchman shows up in the game. Dave and I both thought that design was so ridiculous that we decided to do something with him.

Special pose designs by Bradley Lewis, Mitchel Preston Kennedy, and Dave Wasson.

The Henchman's inspiration, a cherubic demon from the game; early sketch by Adam Paloian.

DAVE: The Henchman is a sweet, lovable but not too bright servant character, somebody the Devil can complain to and yell at when things aren't going his way. The Henchman is pretty unshakable in that role. He's probably the sweetest character in the entire series.

MEGAN C: The Henchman is the Devil's anchor, his security blanket, the person he feels the most open with—the Devil knows the Henchman will always be there. He's the constant companion. Even though he's not very smart, he's more mature than the Devil in a lot of ways.

CLAY: He's morally sophisticated—unlike most characters in the show.

DAVE: His personality really came into sharp focus for me once I was doing his voice. That contrast between the Devil's British sophistication and the Henchman's slow-witted sincerity just made them feel like a classic comedy duo.

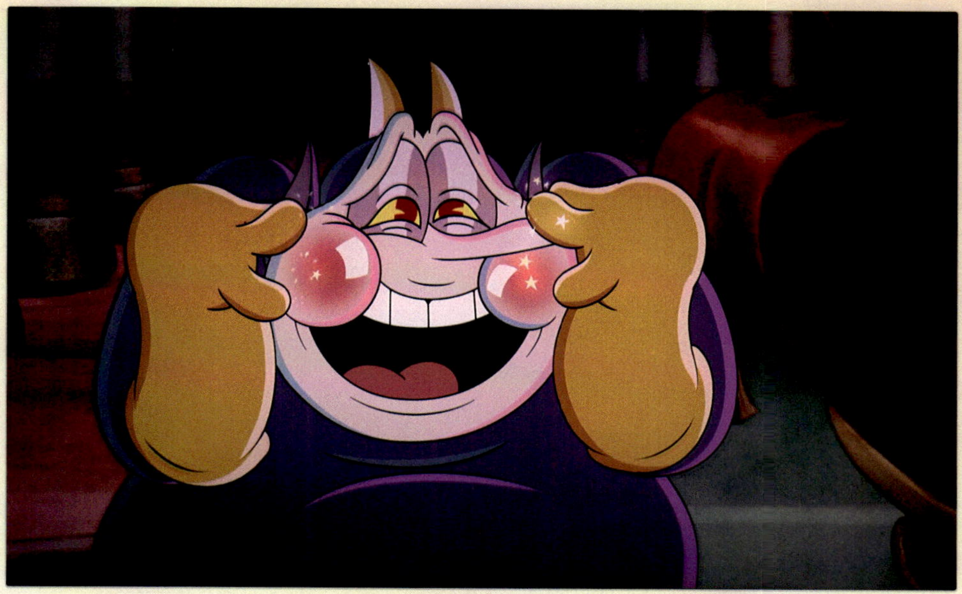

SPECIAL POSE DESIGNS BY ADAM PALOIAN AND ADAM FAY.

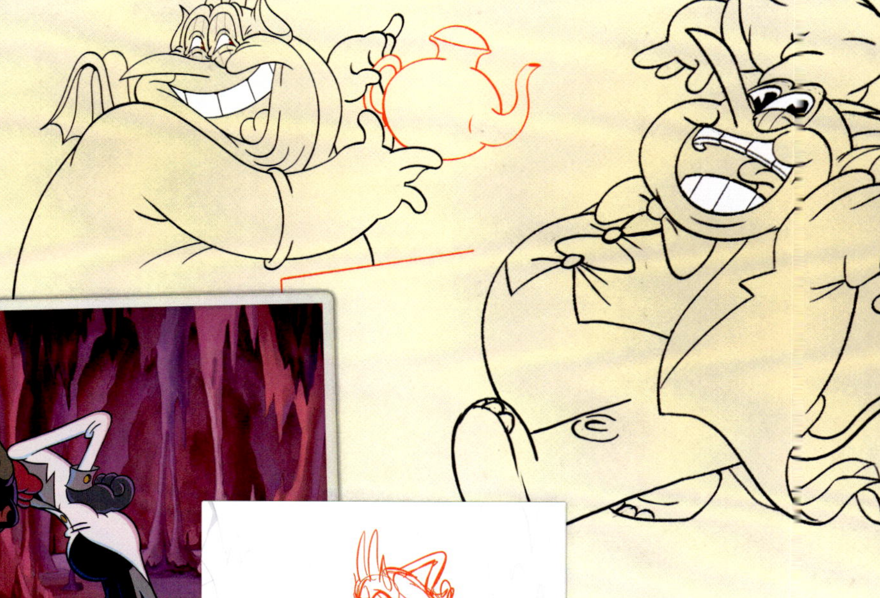

CLAY: Deeki and I always imagined that part of the Devil envies the bond between Cuphead and Mugman.

DEEKI: Cuphead humiliates the Devil in public and always escapes with his soul intact. That's motivation enough for a villain, but it's another level if he also envies Cuphead for having a best friend who's always there for him.

CLAY: The irony is that the Devil already has that in the Henchman. It's so funny and sad, but to me it explains on a subconscious level why the Devil has this hang-up. There's something he's missing.

SPECIAL POSE DESIGNS BY BRADLEY LEWIS AND DAVE WASSON.

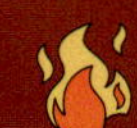

THE DEVIL'S FUNHOUSE

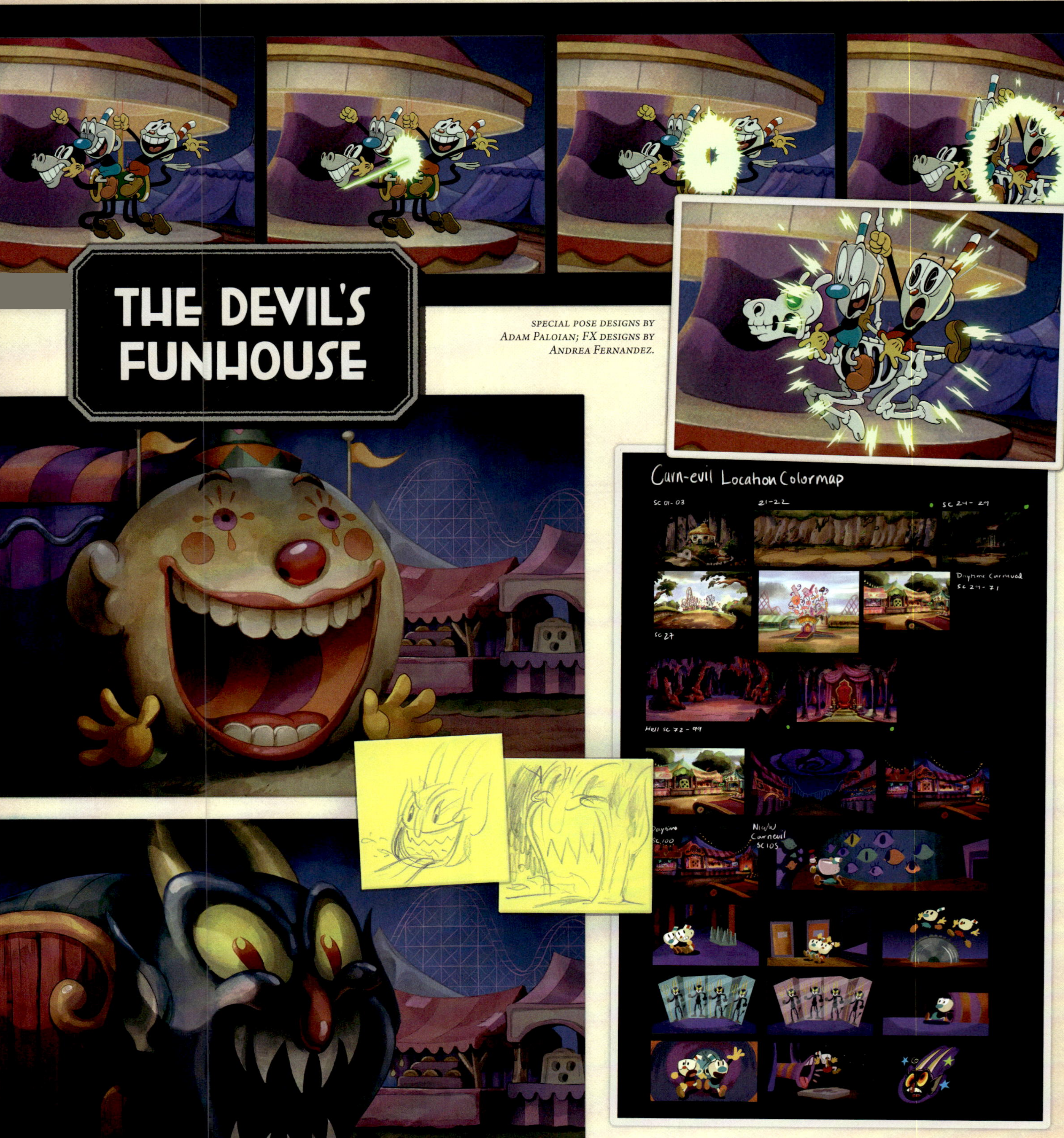

SPECIAL POSE DESIGNS BY ADAM PALOIAN; FX DESIGNS BY ANDREA FERNANDEZ.

THUMBNAIL SKETCHES BY COSMO SEGURSON; BACKGROUND DESIGNS BY LAUREN DUDA; PAINTINGS BY MALLORY CARLSON.

→ **ANDREA:** It is much harder on a show like this to switch palettes and still have it all feel cohesive and like it's from that same era. We had to hit the ground running and figure out how to do it in episode 1.

COLOR KEYS BY ANDREA FERNANDEZ, MICHELLE THIES, AND IVAN AGUIRRE.

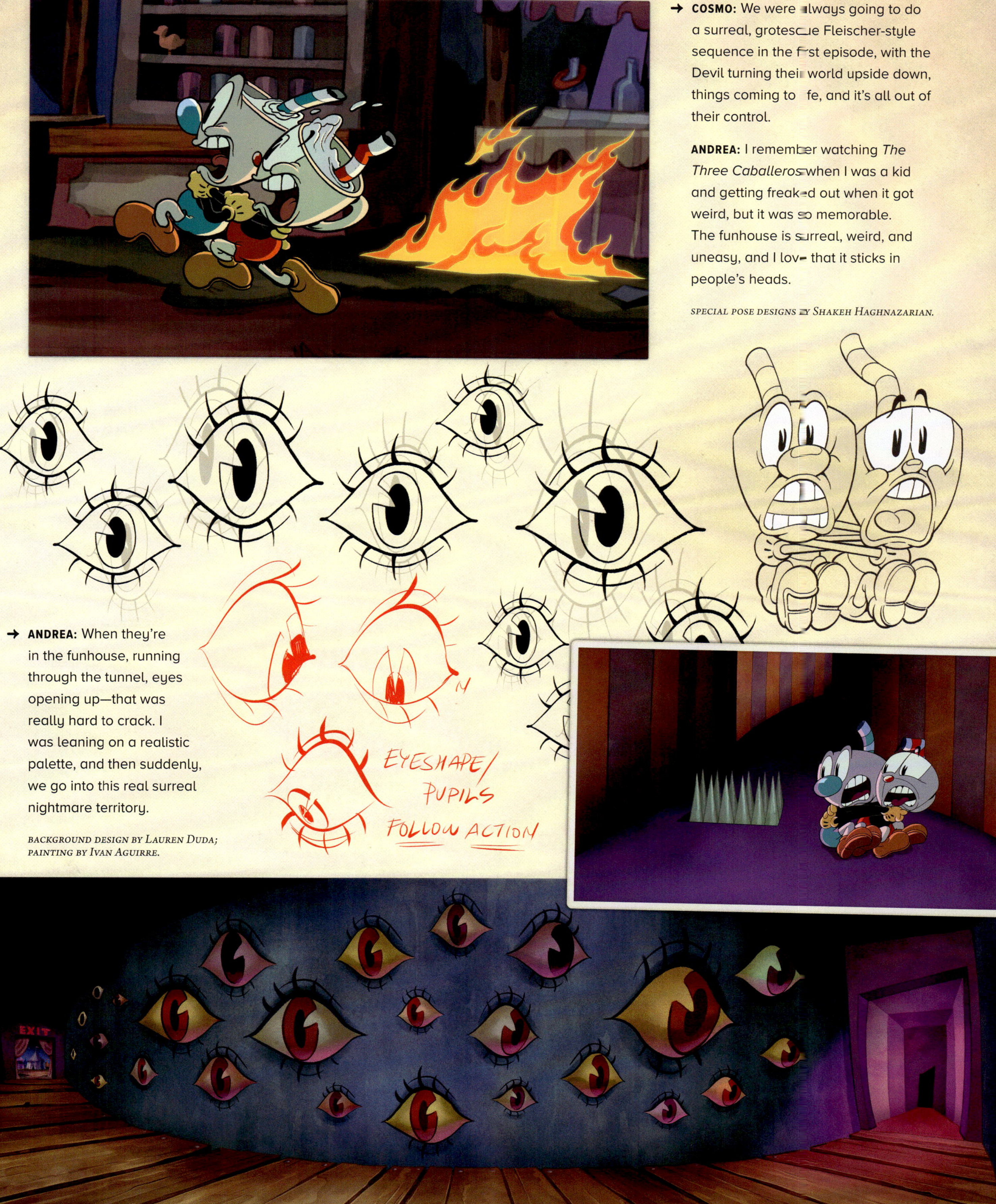

→ **COSMO:** We were always going to do a surreal, grotesque Fleischer-style sequence in the first episode, with the Devil turning their world upside down, things coming to life, and it's all out of their control.

ANDREA: I remember watching *The Three Caballeros* when I was a kid and getting freaked out when it got weird, but it was so memorable. The funhouse is surreal, weird, and uneasy, and I love that it sticks in people's heads.

SPECIAL POSE DESIGNS BY SHAKEH HAGHNAZARIAN.

→ **ANDREA:** When they're in the funhouse, running through the tunnel, eyes opening up—that was really hard to crack. I was leaning on a realistic palette, and then suddenly, we go into this real surreal nightmare territory.

BACKGROUND DESIGN BY LAUREN DUDA; PAINTING BY IVAN AGUIRRE.

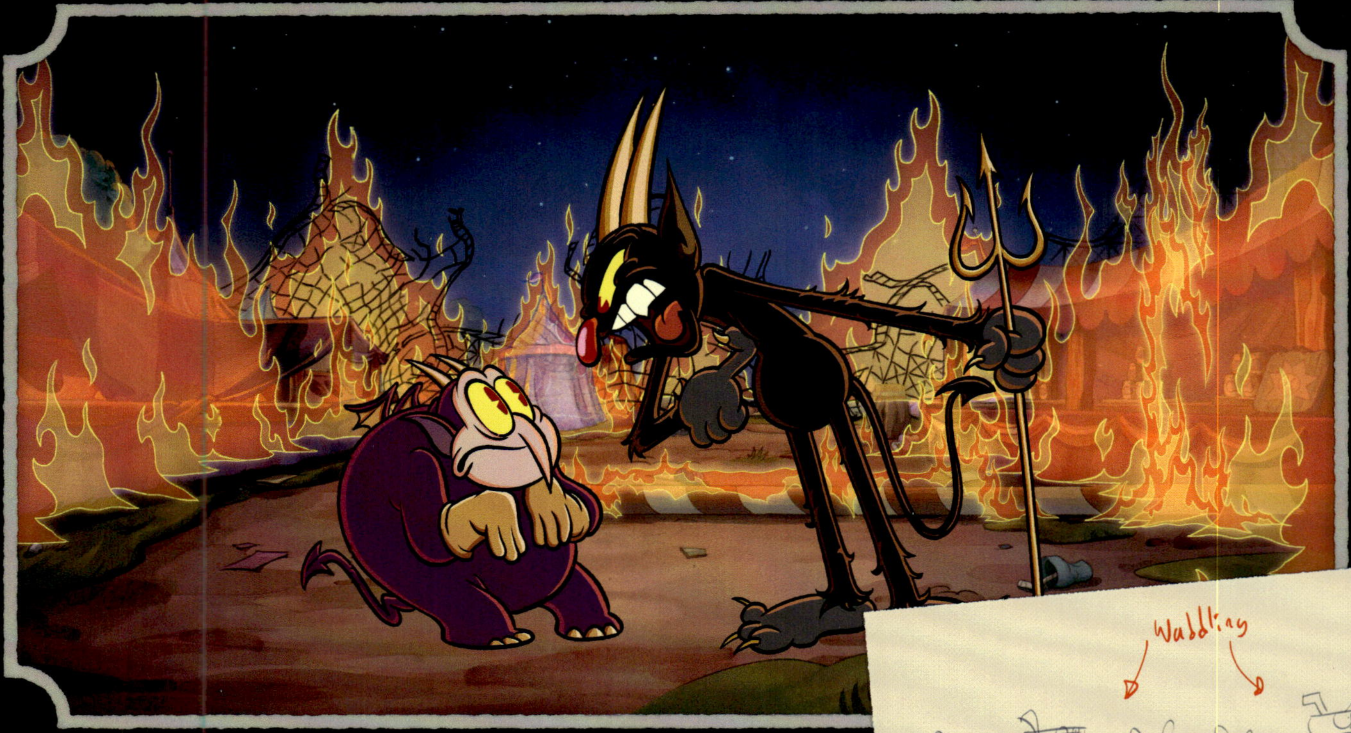

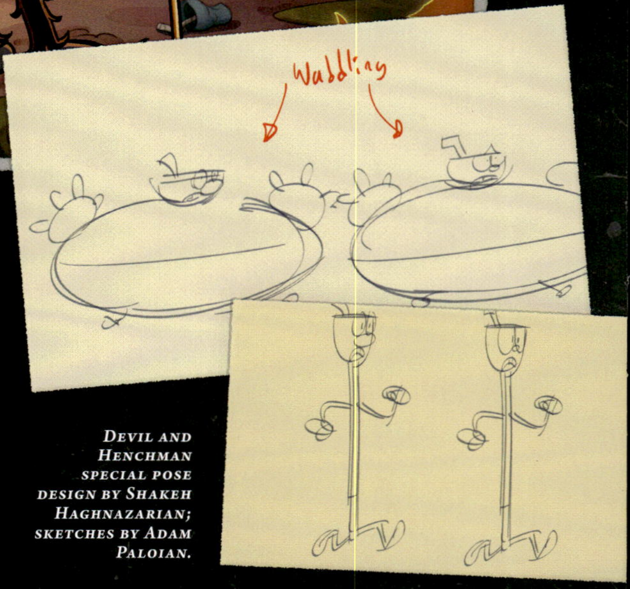

• STORYBOARD SPOTLIGHT •

DELETED FUNHOUSE SCENES

→ **ADAM P:** Originally, there was a whole hall of mirrors sequence in the funhouse. At one point, Cuphead and Mugman got separated. I had a shot where Mugman is surrounded by his own reflections. There was a part where they fell into a rotating tube; they keep falling over each other. We cut all that out, because it slowed down the pacing of the chase.

Deleted storyboard scenes by Adam Paloian.

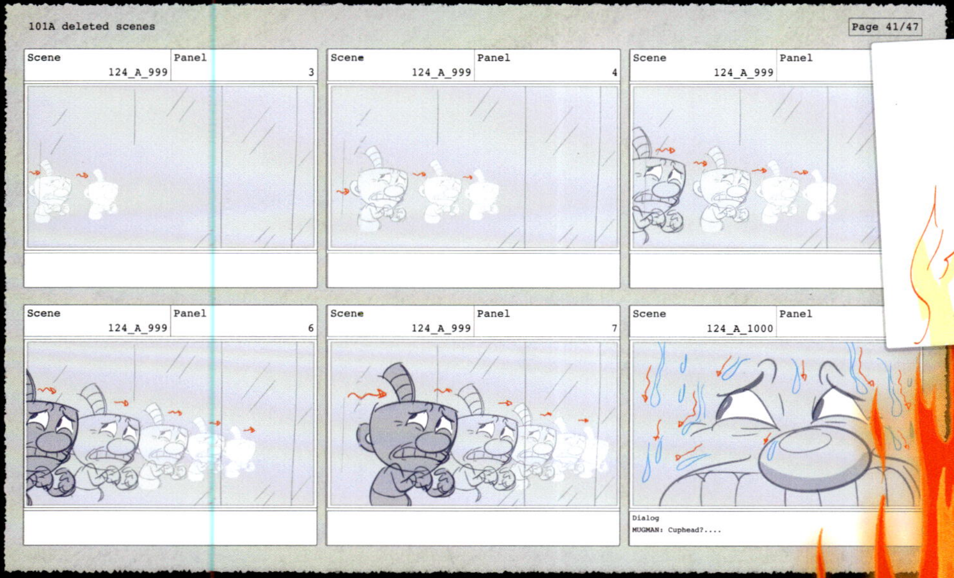

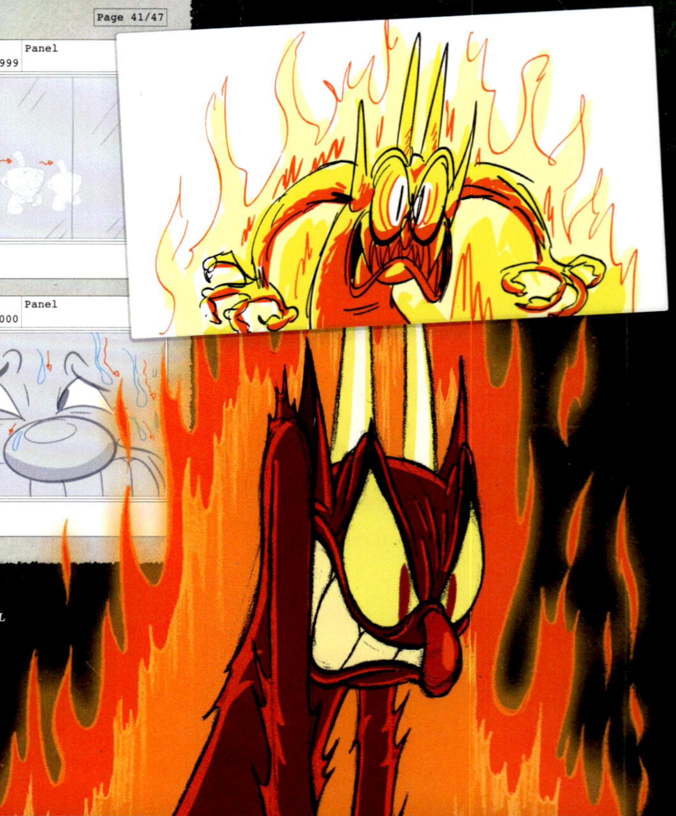

Waddling

Devil and Henchman special pose design by Shakeh Haghnazarian; sketches by Adam Paloian.

101A deleted scenes

Page 41/47

Scene	Panel
124_A_999	3
124_A_999	4
124_A_999	
124_A_999	6
124_A_999	7
124_A_1000	

Dialog
MUGMAN: Cuphead?....

Devil on fire storyboard panel by Adam Paloian; special pose design by Dan Haskett.

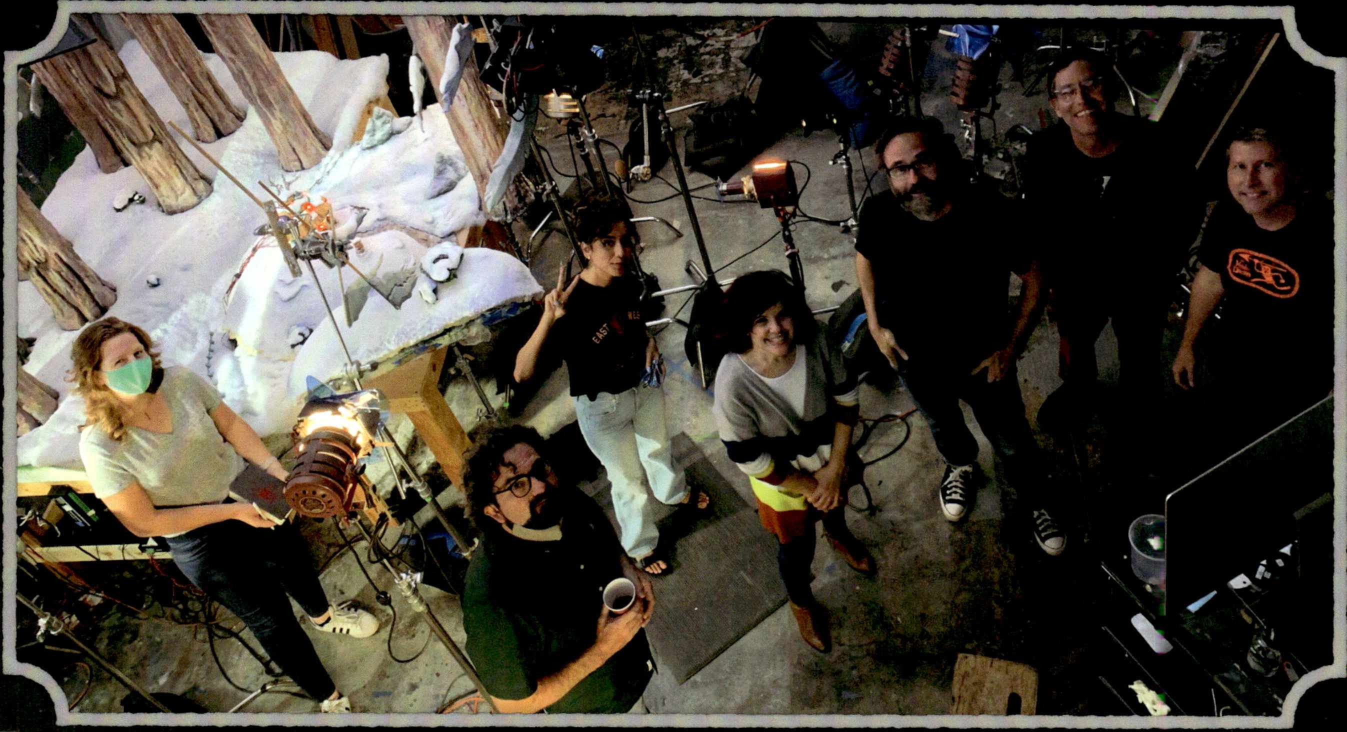

• STOP-MO SPOTLIGHT •

INTRODUCING SCREEN NOVELTIES

→ **COSMO:** We were lucky enough to get Screen Novelties involved. We've been using a technique from early Fleischer cartoons which is sometimes called the stereoscopic process, where you have a stop-motion set and 2D characters within the same frame.

DAVE: It was immediately clear from interviewing Screen Novelties that they were the right fit. They completely understood what we were going for. They were huge Fleischer fans and had been dying for an opportunity to re-create the stereoscopic process their whole careers.

MARK CABALLERO, COFOUNDER, SCREEN NOVELTIES: Cosmo and Dave knew we were huge nerds for this. We've been wanting to do a show like this for twenty-five years.

SEAMUS WALSH, COFOUNDER, SCREEN NOVELTIES: The Fleischers are part of the fabric of what we love about animation. Those Fleischer color classics are integral to our animation education.

MARK: Everybody has their own unique style. When you're adapting your style for a series, that style needs to maintain itself not just from the production art but into the stop-motion art as well. We got our crew together and played Fleischer cartoons so everyone knew what we were going for. We've established a rapport with them, so when we say we want something chalky or chunky or floopy, they understand our shorthand. Seamus and I oversee the build and launch everybody on their jobs. John Joyce built all the sets. Normally, we all work together in the same room, but because of the pandemic in 2020, John just started building sets out of his garage.

COSMO: Alicia Ellsworth painted all the sets. Aaron Wise was the photographer, and he had two people helping him out to light the sets. Then they would click and animate, click and animate. It was a small crew, and a very tight crew.

FROM LEFT TO RIGHT: CASEY FOLLEN, CHRIS FINNEGAN, ANDREA FERNANDEZ, MEGHAN CAPORALI, DAVE WASSON, COSMO SEGURSON, AND SEAMUS WALSH.

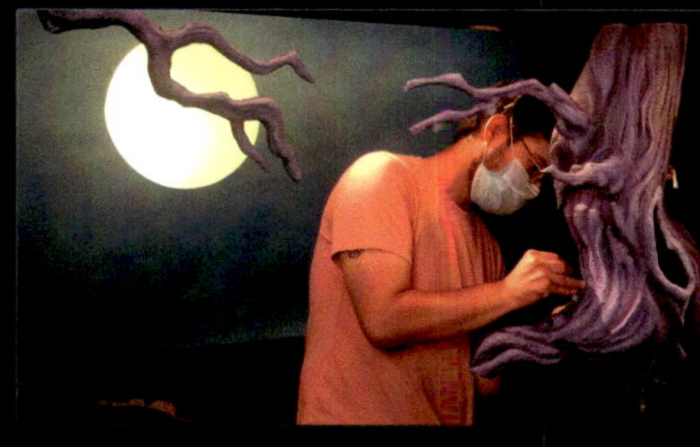

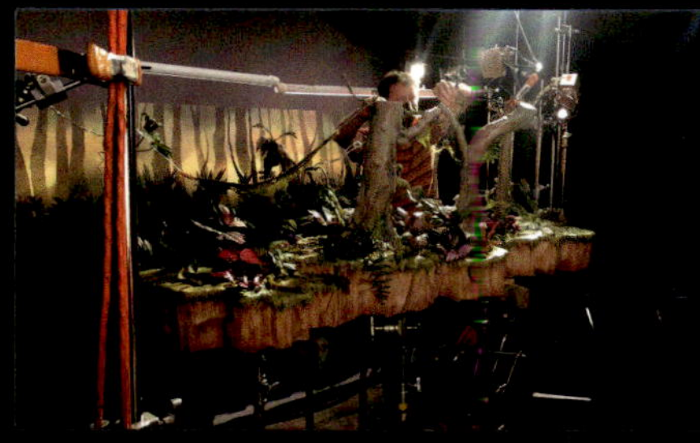

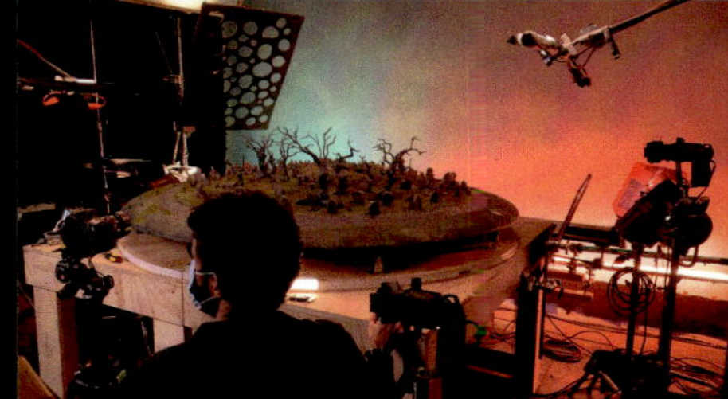

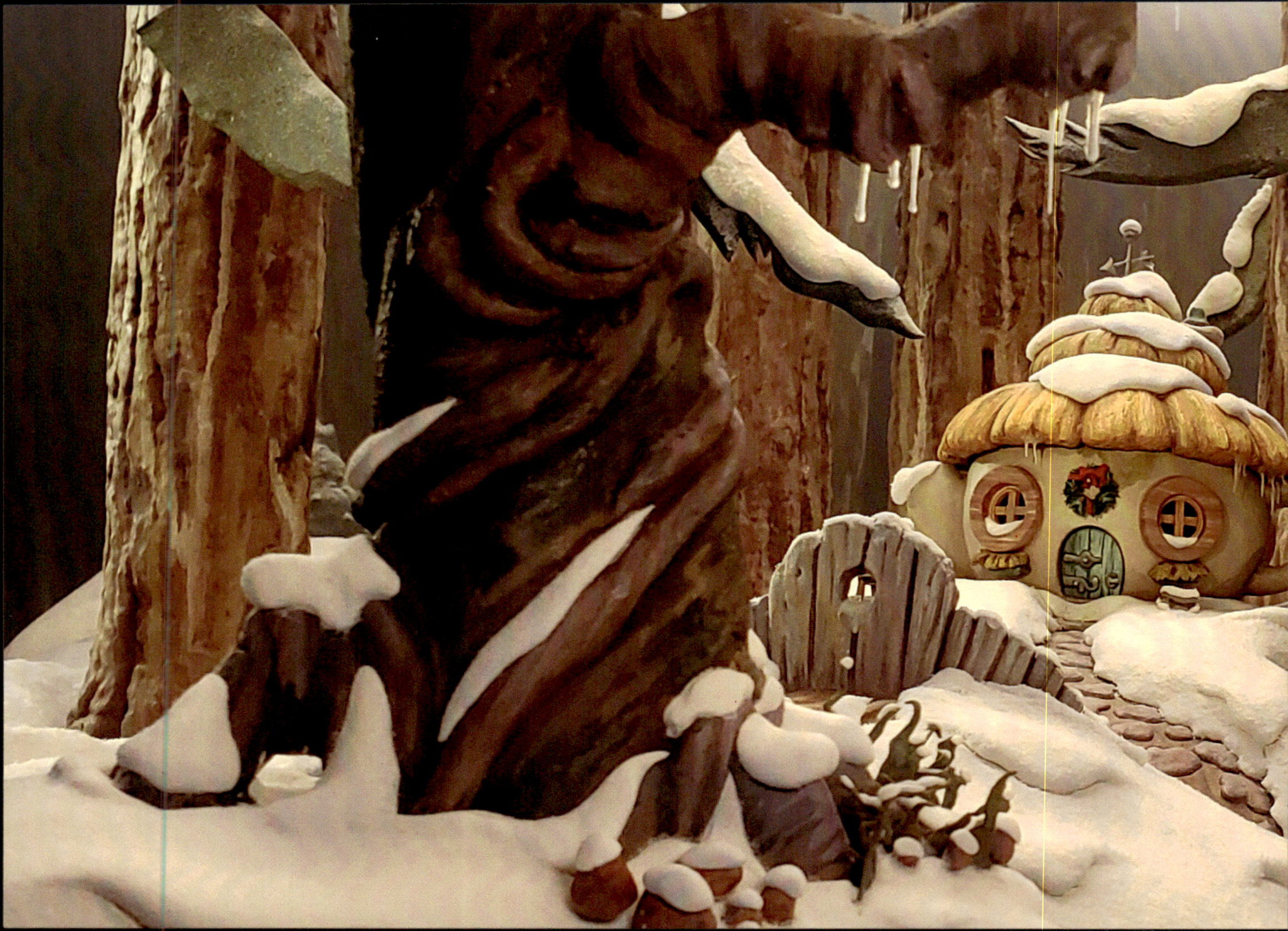

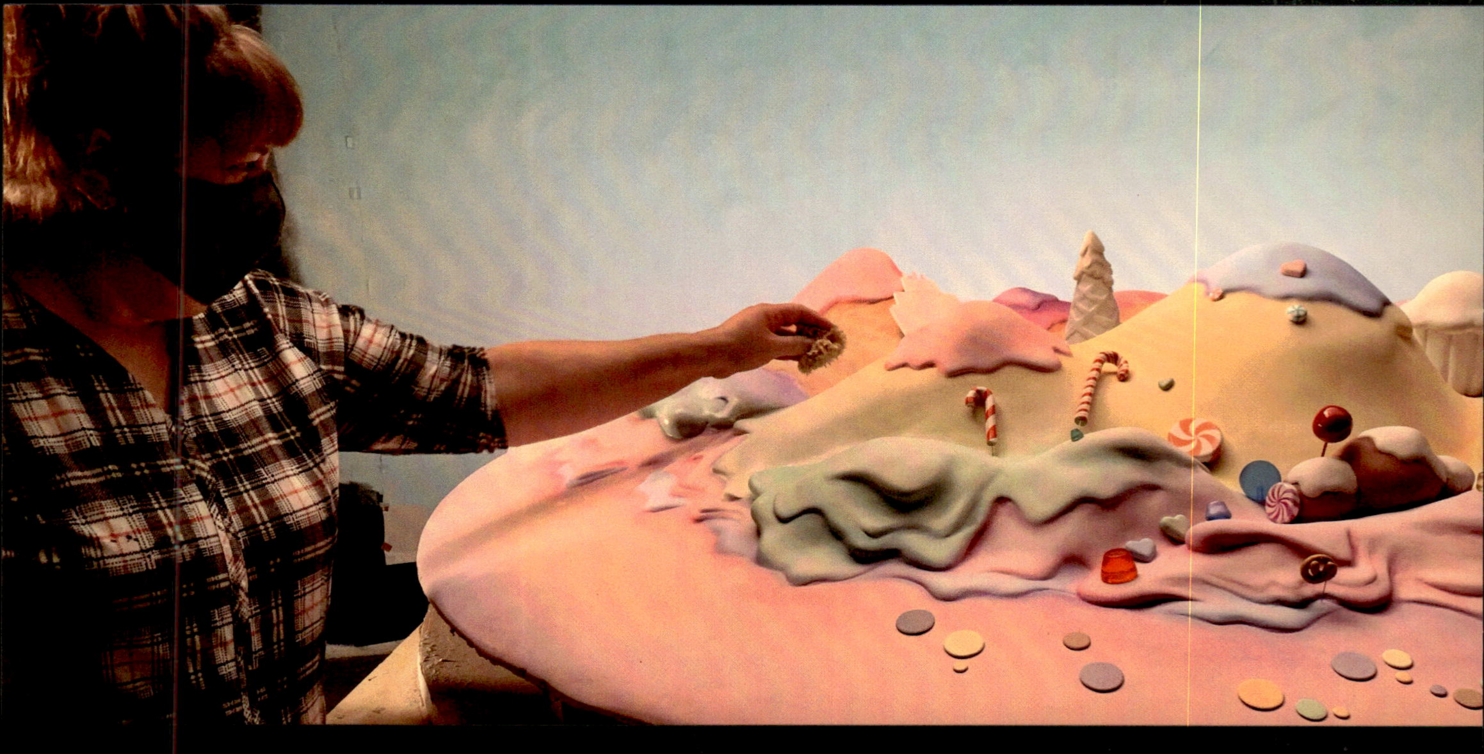

PRODUCTION STILLS OF STOP-MO SETS BY SCREEN NOVELTIES.

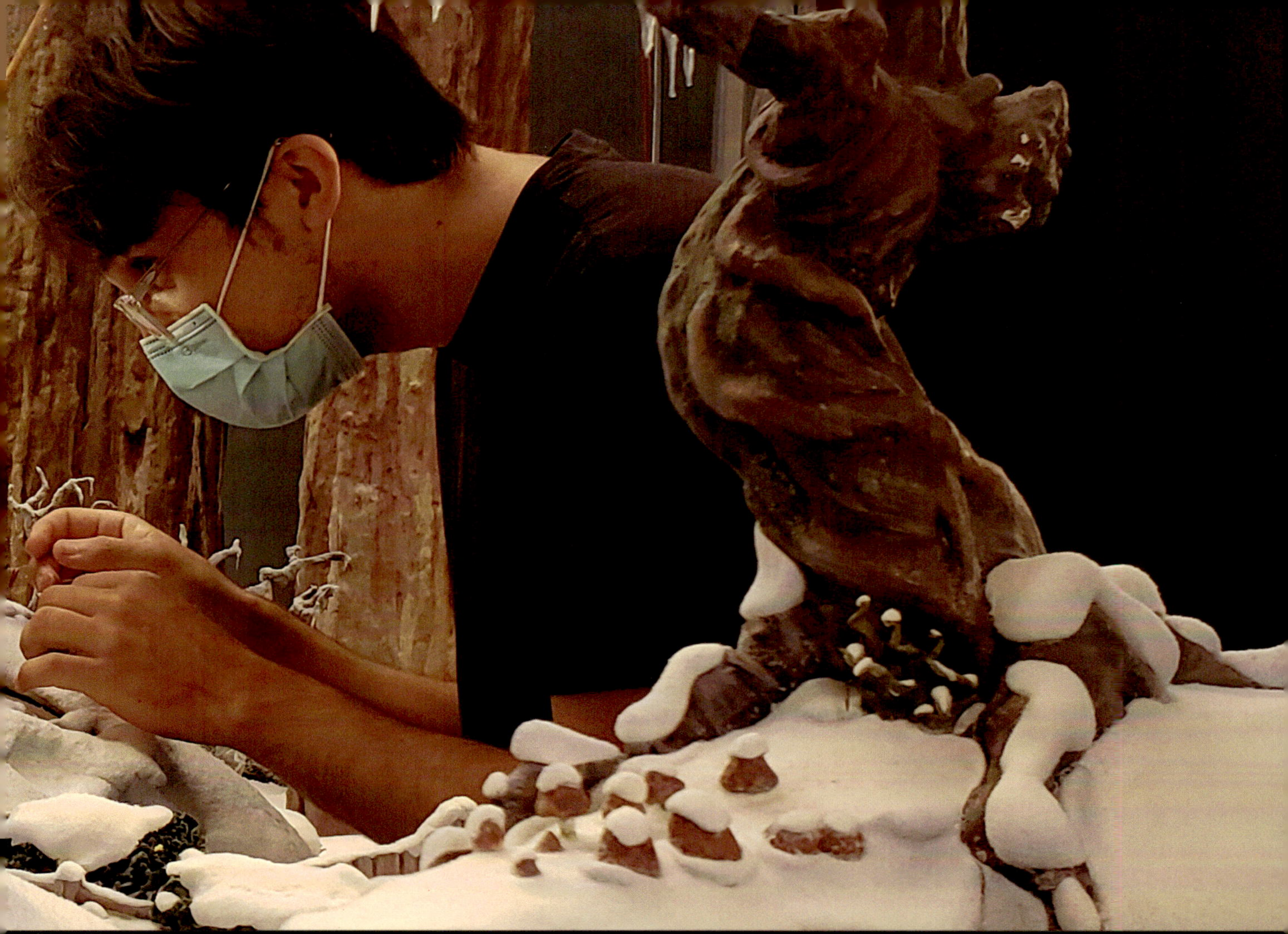

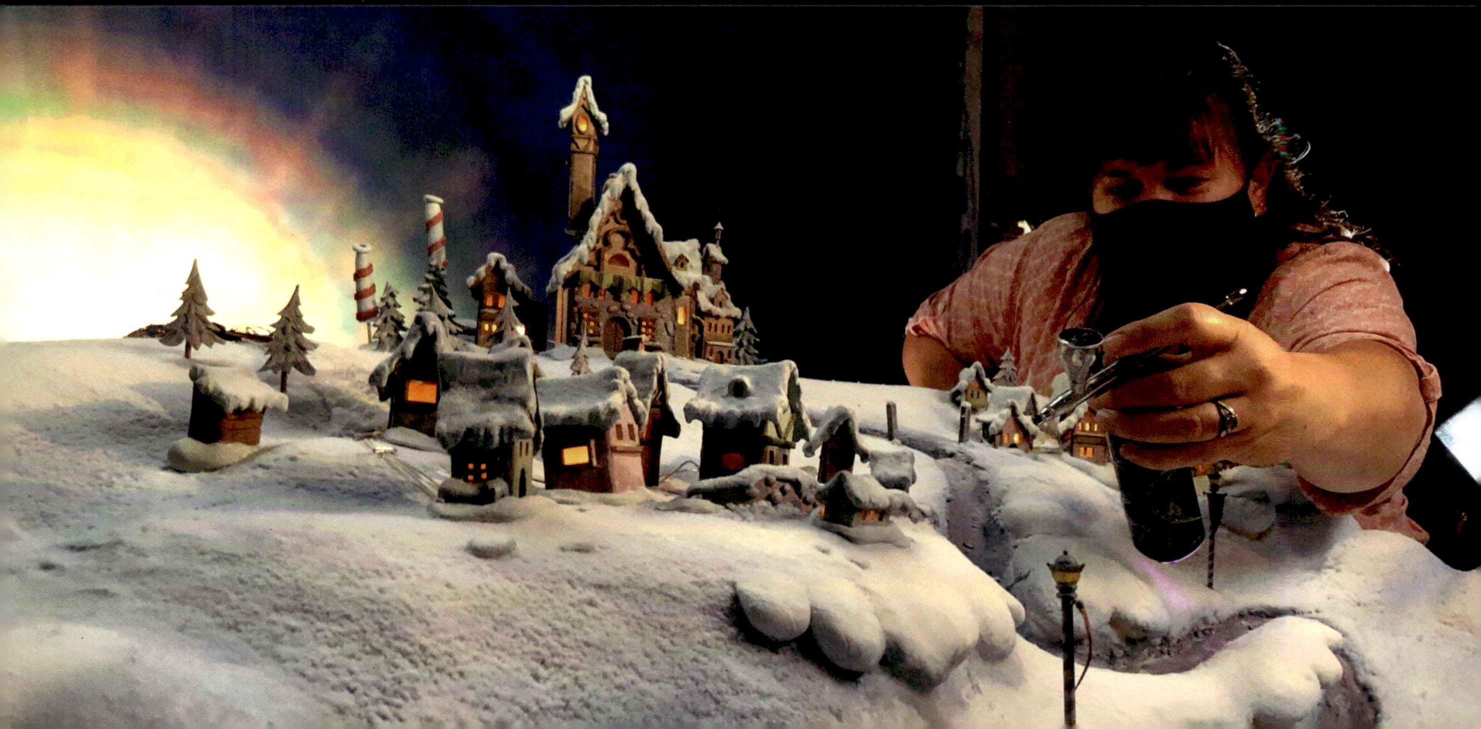

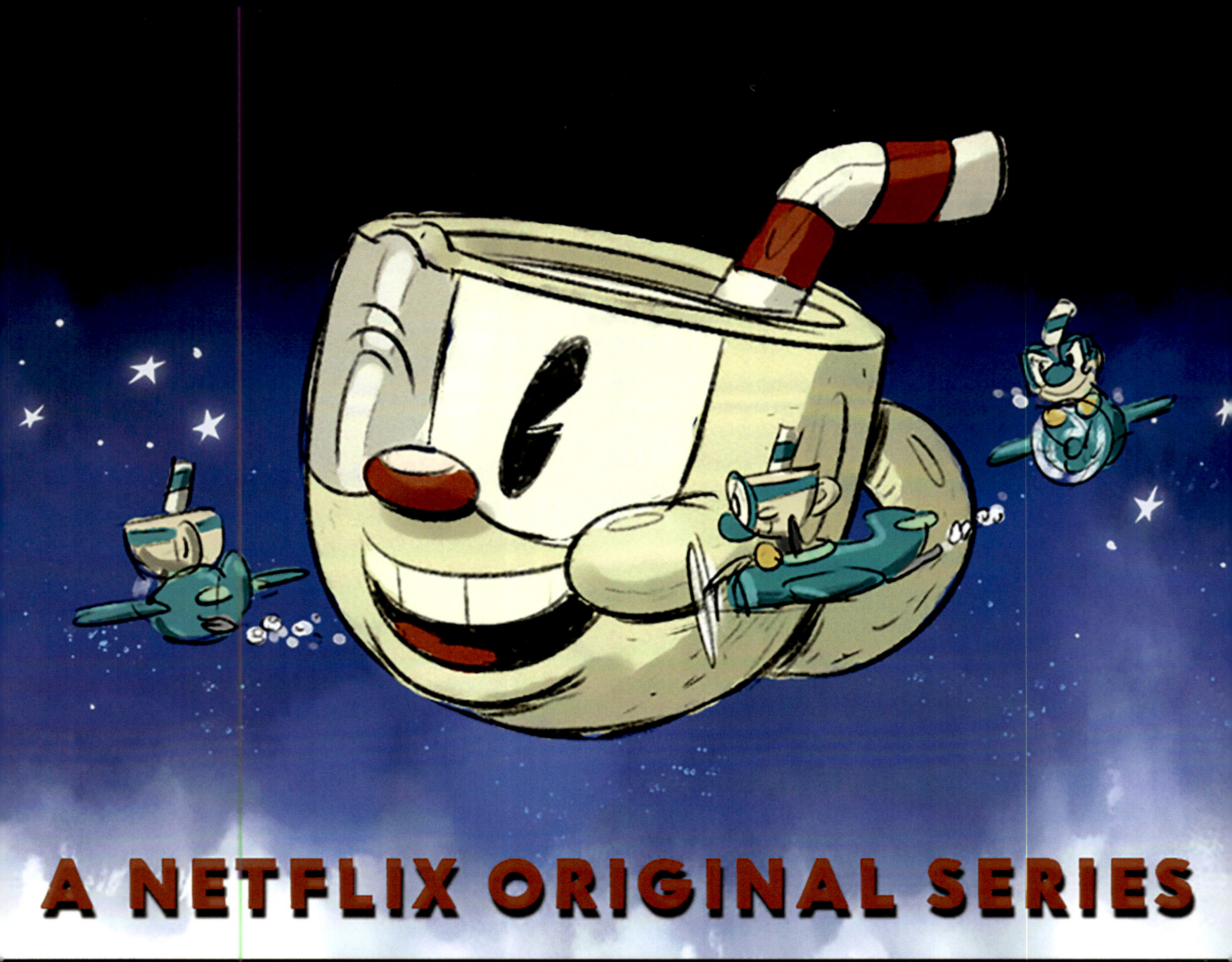

A NETFLIX ORIGINAL SERIES

STOP-MO VS. DIGITAL

→ **COSMO**: Screen Novelties doesn't have enormous spaces to create these environments, so they had to build in a lot of forced perspective within the painting of those sets. It's all about scale with stop-motion sets: when things are further back, you paint them with less detail; the things that you know will be closer to the foreground you paint with more detail, knowing that you'll capture that detail in the photography.

MARK: Even if the viewer doesn't realize what they're seeing, you can tell when there's a practical shot being done in camera as opposed to a digital shot.

COSMO: There's something special about real objects in real space with real light in front of a lens that's so difficult to re-create digitally. Looking at real objects in front of the camera lets your mind walk around in those spaces. In stereoscopic miniatures, it's no longer a painting, it's a real place: you're seeing that world change perspective at the same time as the 2D characters. It's a magical alchemy when that happens onscreen.

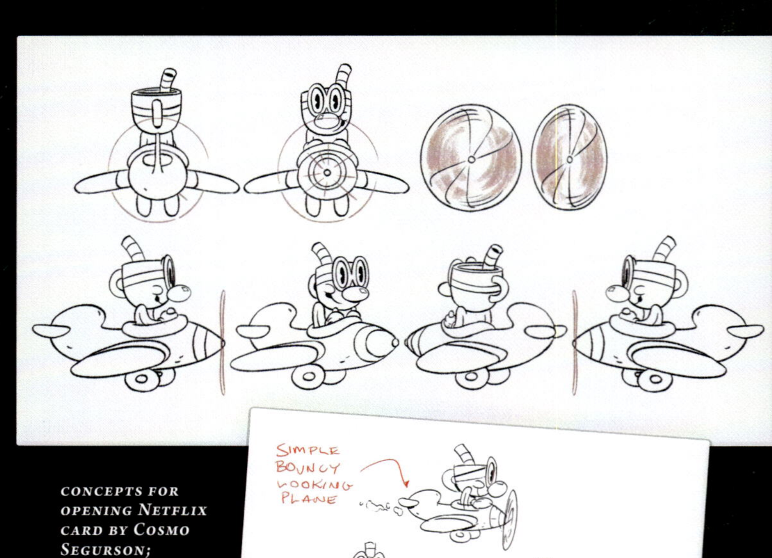

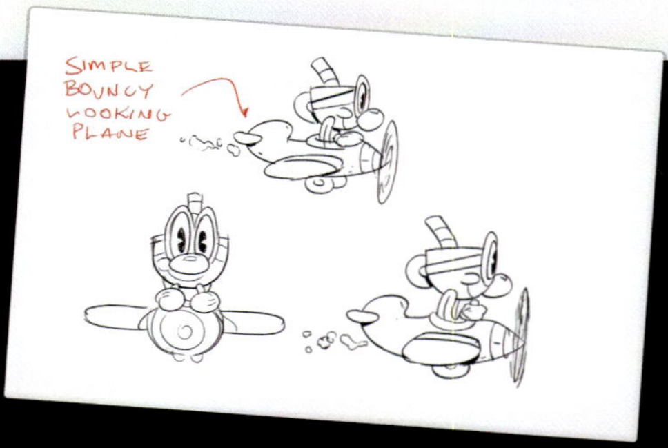

Concepts for opening Netflix card by Cosmo Segurson; character designs by Tapan Gandhi and Dave Wasson.

SEAMUS: I think part of that magical, intangible quality you get from practical effects is in the imperfections. With physical objects there's this built-in anarchy about it, and there's all these imperfections. If you go digital, math dictates everything, so in order to get that same feeling, you have to work all those imperfections into a mathematical digital model. I think that's why digital re-creations feel cold: it's too perfect.

MARK: The Fleischer brothers built a twelve-foot steel disk that weighed four tons, and it could be horizontal and vertical. When you see their stuff, you can tell that it's all handmade.

SEAMUS: We love the hands-on element. You build a thing, paint it, light it, and animate it, rather than just work on a computer all day. We actually get to play with all these materials.

MARK: If you're doing stop motion and you phone it in, you're wasting your time. It takes so long anyway; you might as well put in the effort to make it look good.

SEAMUS: It's very labor intensive.

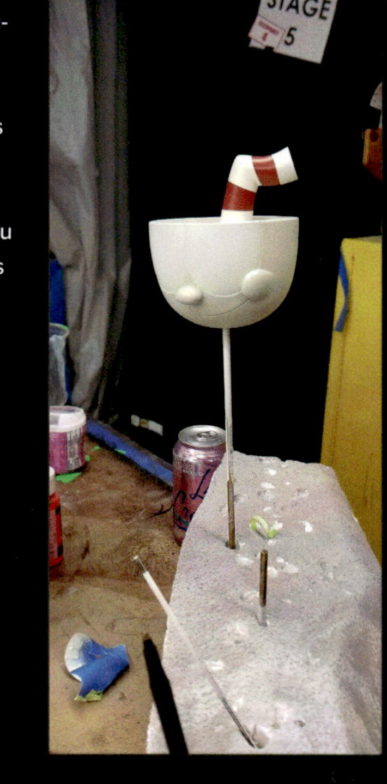

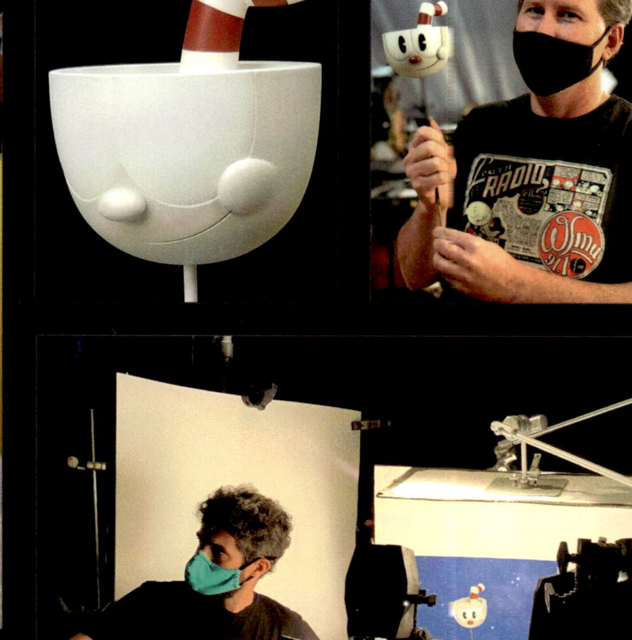

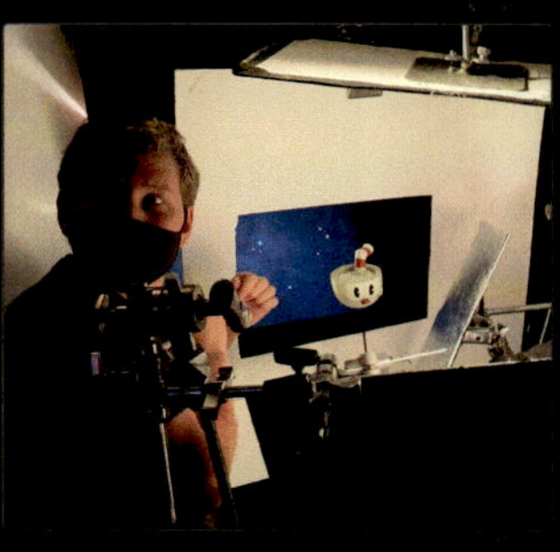

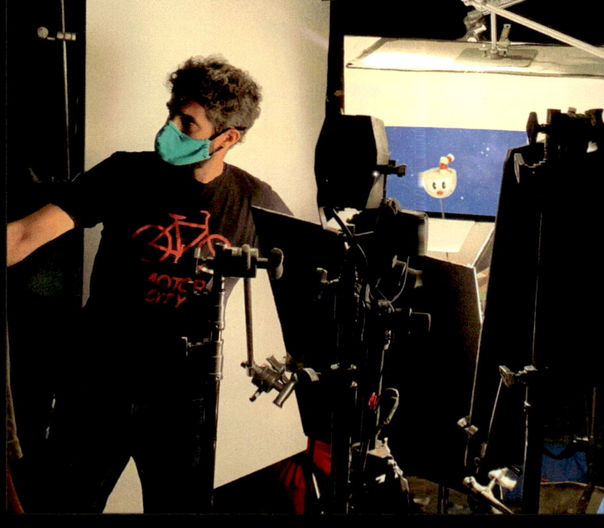

PRODUCTION PHOTOS OF OPENING NETFLIX CARD AT SCREEN NOVELTIES.

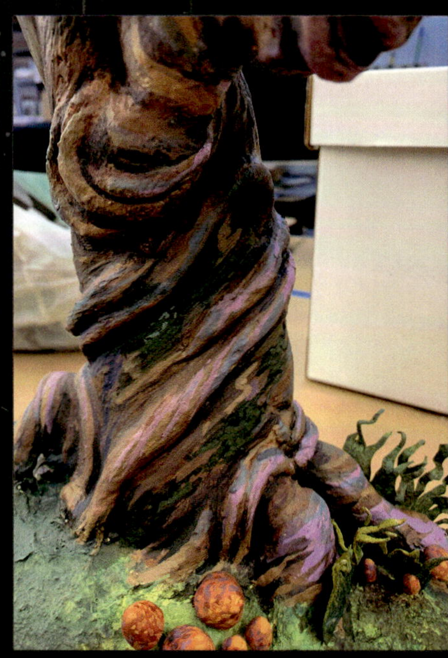

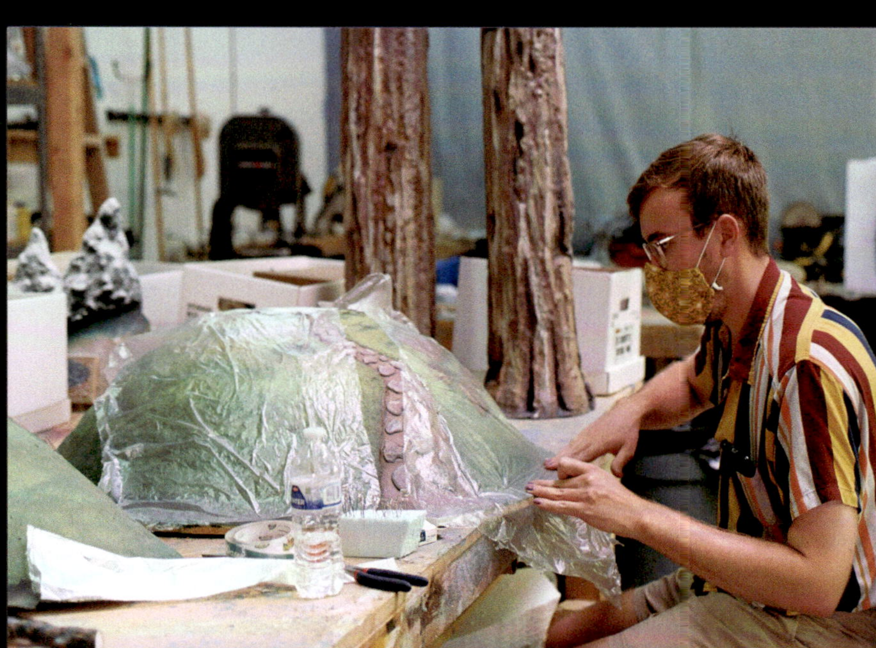

COSMO: It's all based on the paintings that Andrea's team provide. Screen Novelties interprets that in 3D. First, they build a foam core model of the set, and they put it in front of the lens to make sure they get the proportions right. They end up building the model out of foam and cardboard and all their magical materials.

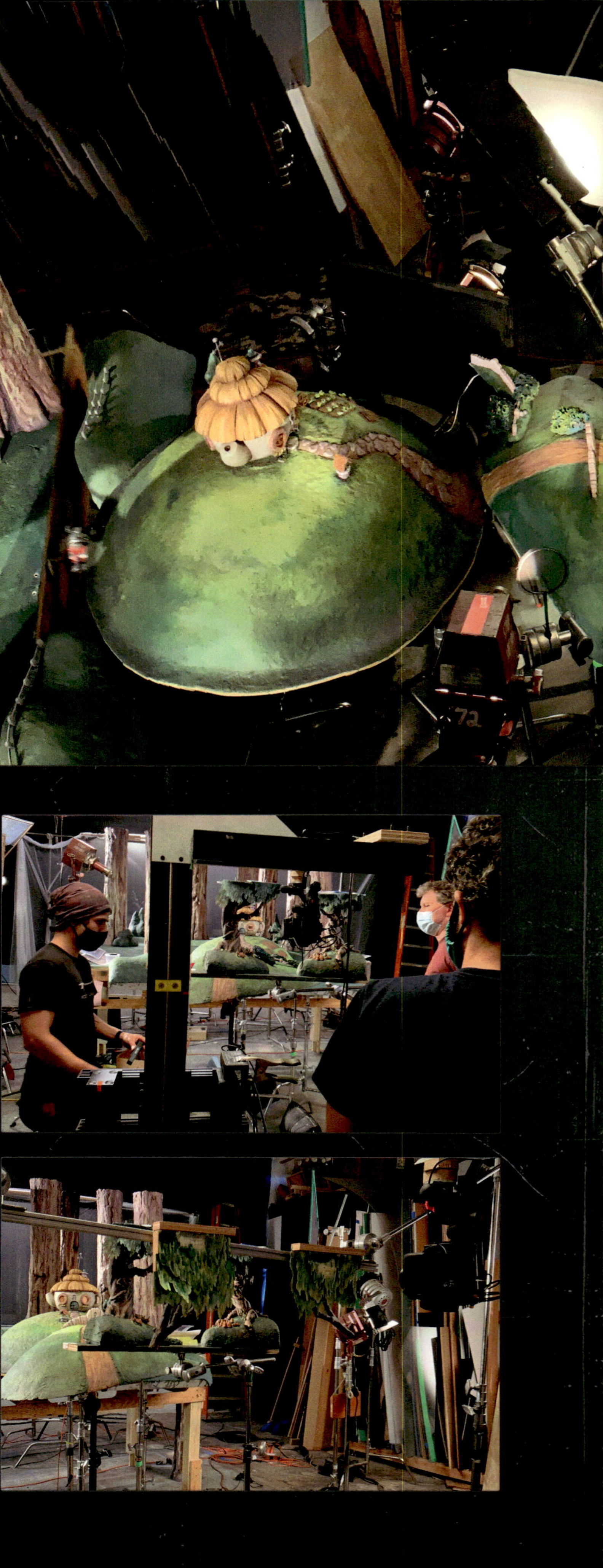

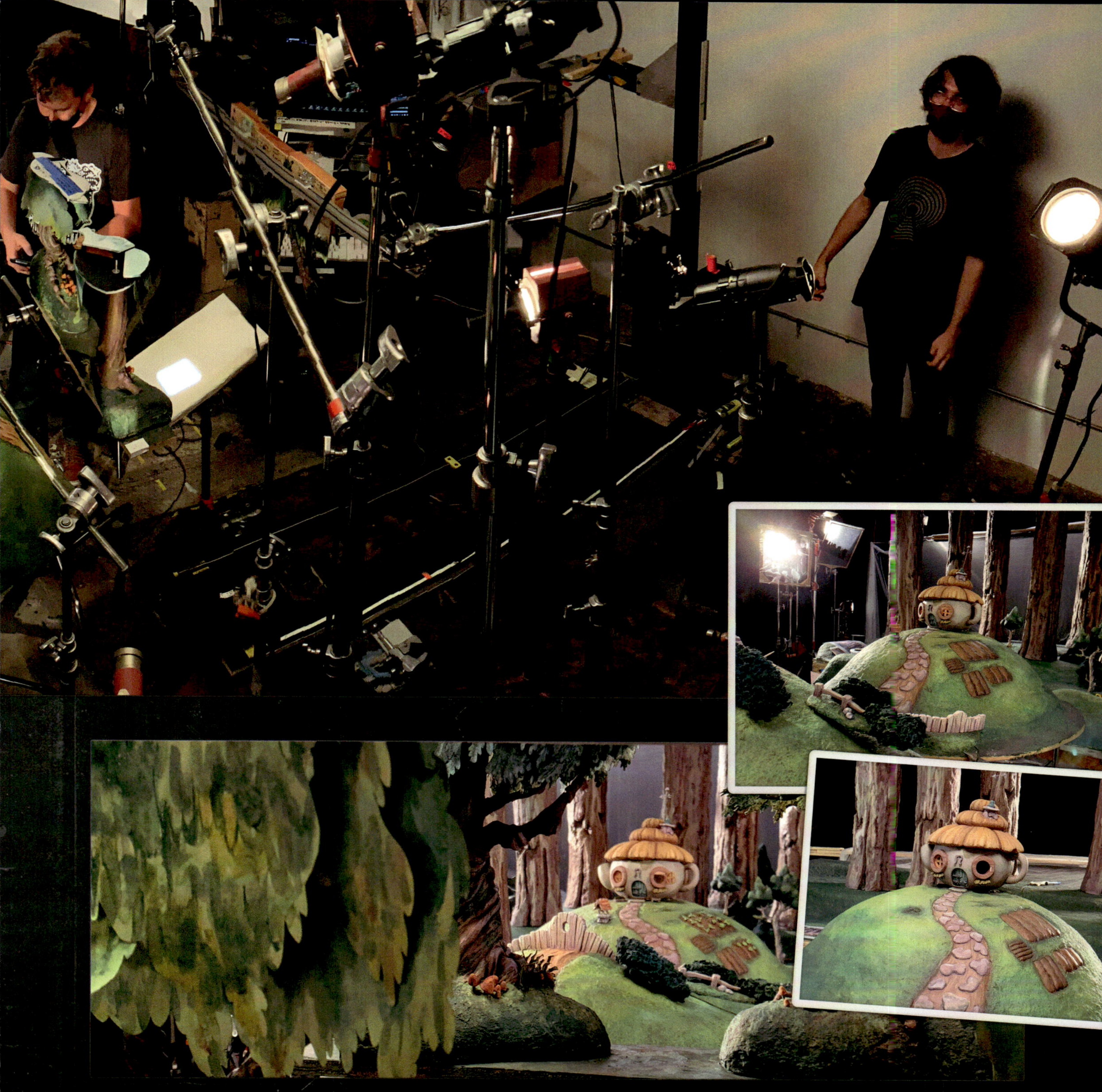

→ **COSMO:** When we see the cottage, the furthest-back trees are painted on a backdrop, like a theatrical set, but then between that mural and the physical trees, Screen Novelties hung a huge scrim of wedding veil material between the layers of sets.

MARK: For that cottage shot, we knew we wanted to create atmosphere in the forest. If you take the bridal veil and stretch it out, you can light it and shape it into a conical shape, like a "god light."

SEAMUS: The bridal veil serves two purposes: you're using it to create atmospheric perspective, like in a painting where things get grayer as they go back in space. We're faking that through forced perspective on our stages. The stage is only about ten feet deep. The veil helps gray out the layers as they get further back, which in painting would be known as atmospheric perspective. But then also it acts as a diffusion material, so light passes through the veil and dapples the [scenery] to get this nice soft quality so you're not working with hard lights bouncing off every surface.

COSMO: They lit the veil material from the side, so it really gives it an atmosphere of depth, like beams of light. It's beautiful.

ANDREA: When this stuff started coming in, I almost started crying. I've never seen anything that I've done actually get sculpted like this, and it was just a major highlight. I couldn't ask for more care and love to go into a set than this.

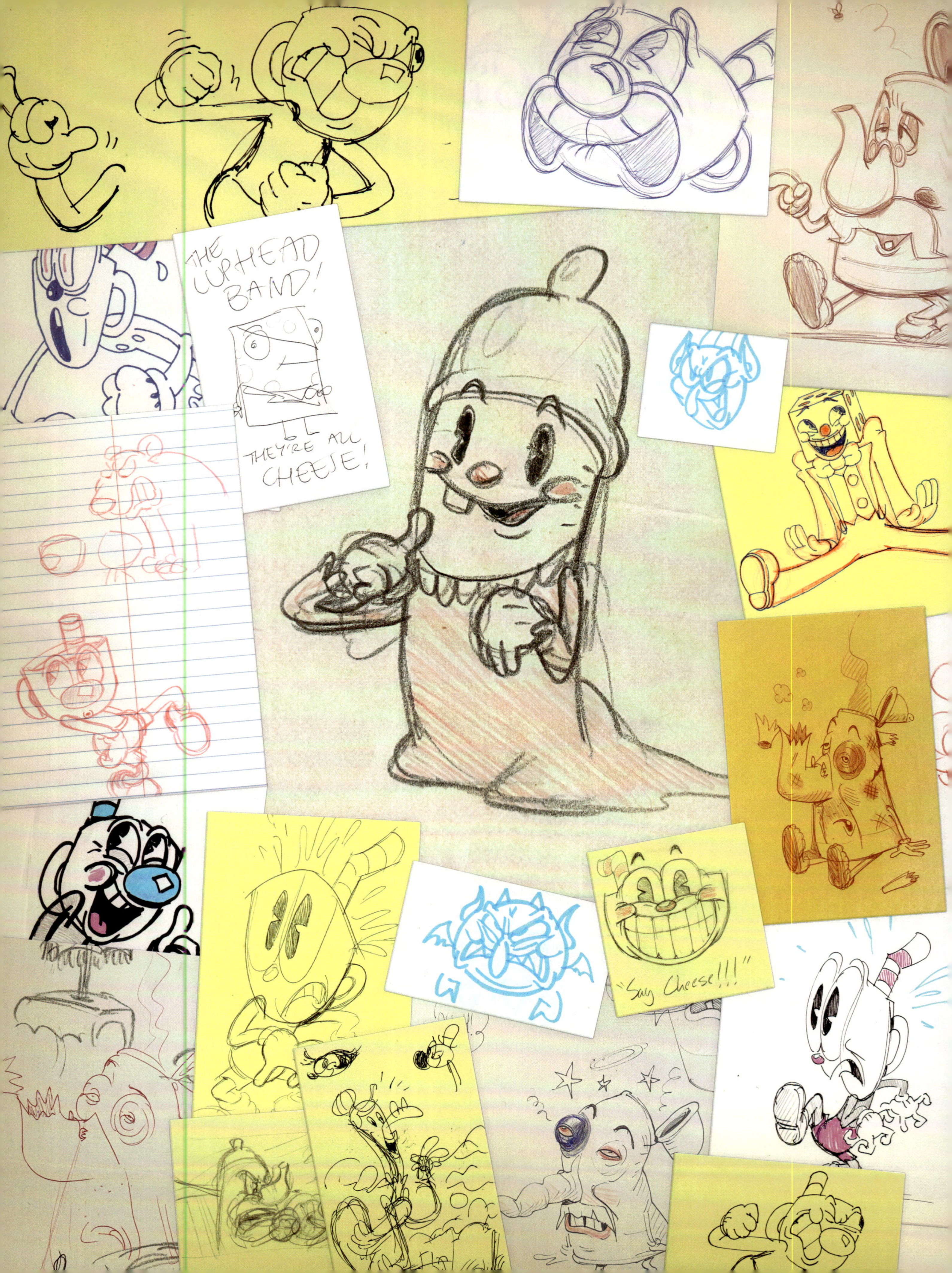
THE CUPHEAD BAND!
THEY'RE ALL CHEESE!
"Say Cheese!!!"

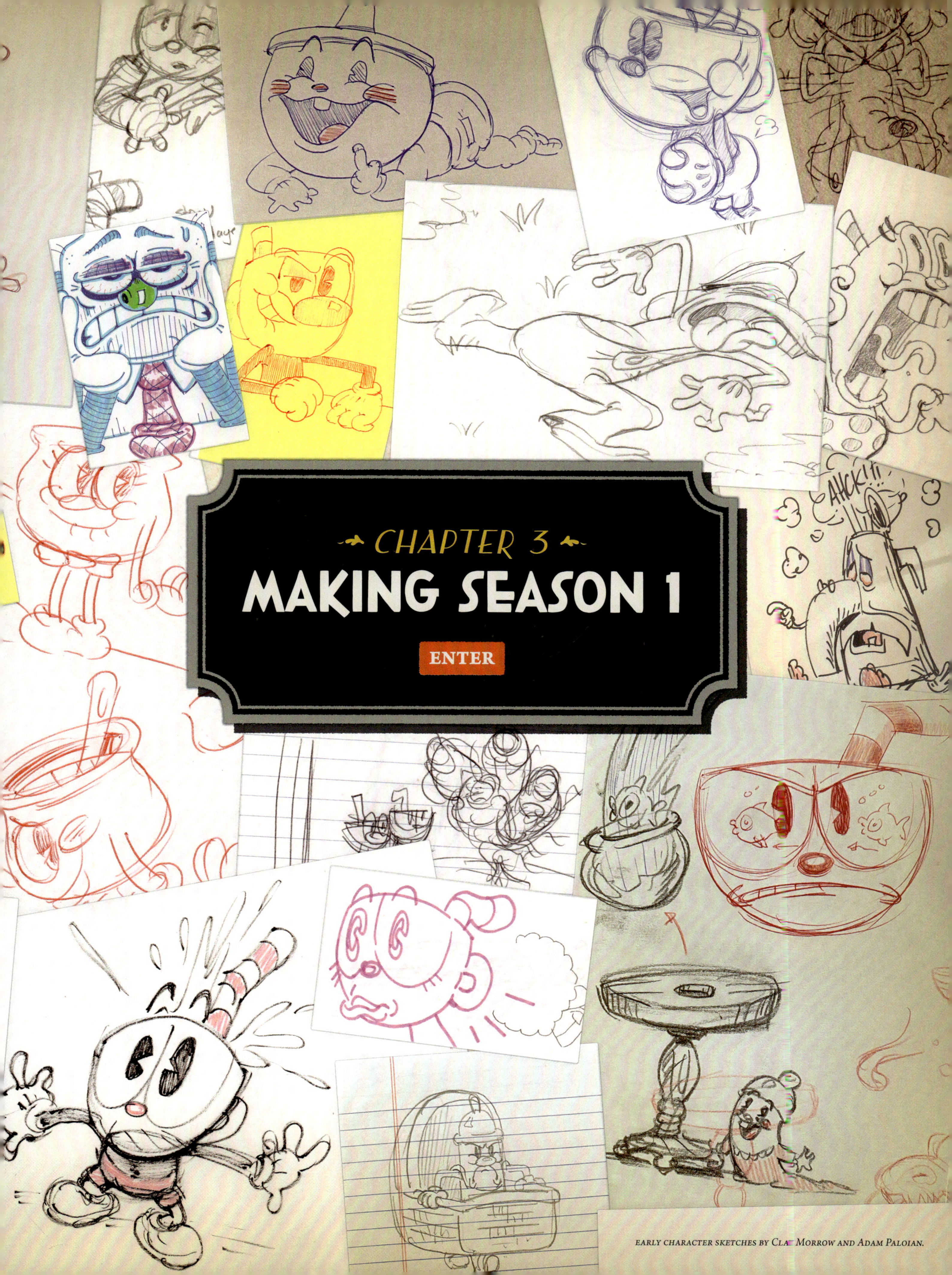

Chapter 3
Making Season 1

Enter

Early character sketches by Clay Morrow and Adam Paloian.

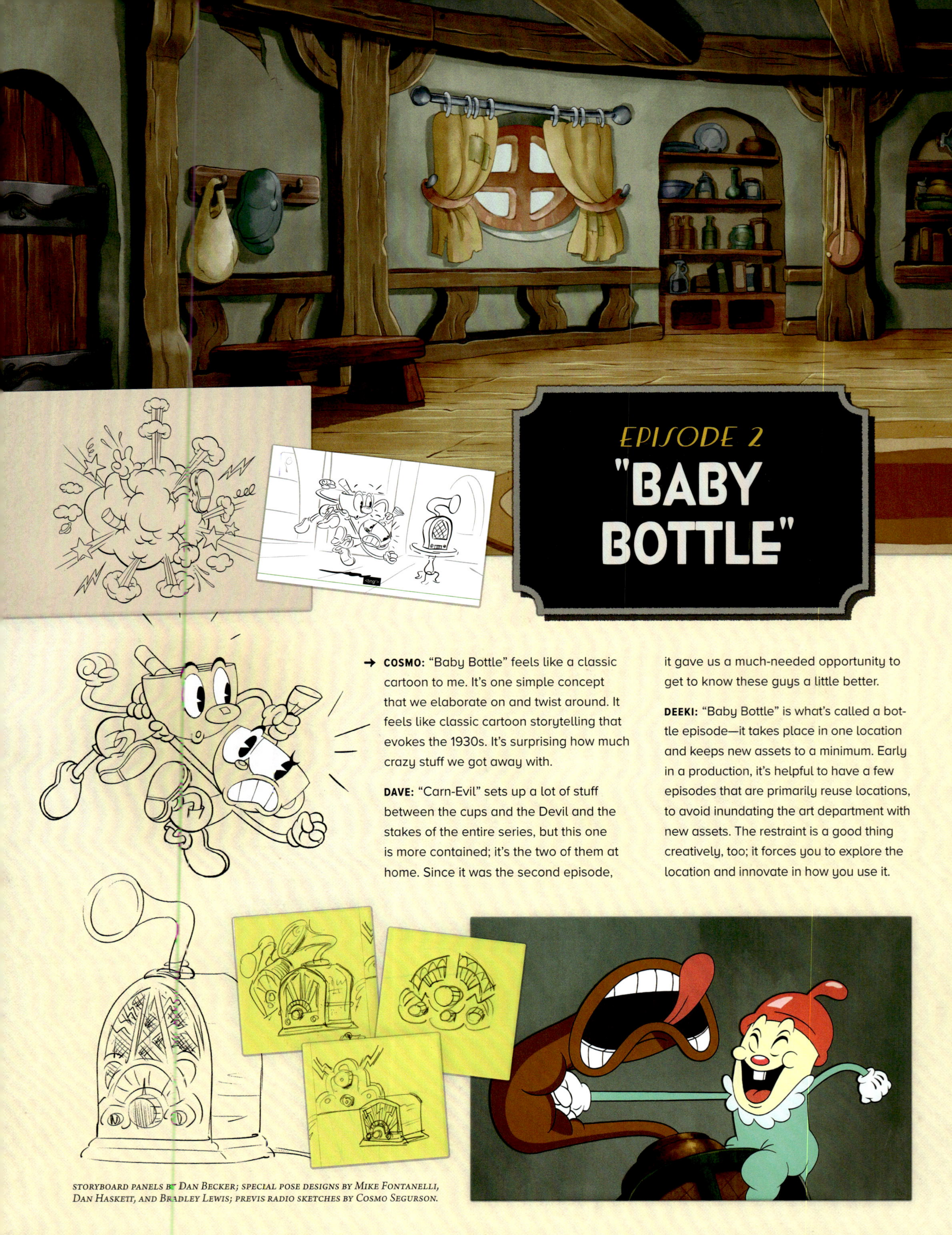

EPISODE 2
"BABY BOTTLE"

→ **COSMO:** "Baby Bottle" feels like a classic cartoon to me. It's one simple concept that we elaborate on and twist around. It feels like classic cartoon storytelling that evokes the 1930s. It's surprising how much crazy stuff we got away with.

DAVE: "Carn-Evil" sets up a lot of stuff between the cups and the Devil and the stakes of the entire series, but this one is more contained; it's the two of them at home. Since it was the second episode, it gave us a much-needed opportunity to get to know these guys a little better.

DEEKI: "Baby Bottle" is what's called a bottle episode—it takes place in one location and keeps new assets to a minimum. Early in a production, it's helpful to have a few episodes that are primarily reuse locations, to avoid inundating the art department with new assets. The restraint is a good thing creatively, too; it forces you to explore the location and innovate in how you use it.

STORYBOARD PANELS BY DAN BECKER; SPECIAL POSE DESIGNS BY MIKE FONTANELLI, DAN HASKETT, AND BRADLEY LEWIS; PREVIS RADIO SKETCHES BY COSMO SEGURSON.

Background design by Jessica Hong; background painting by Michelle Thies.

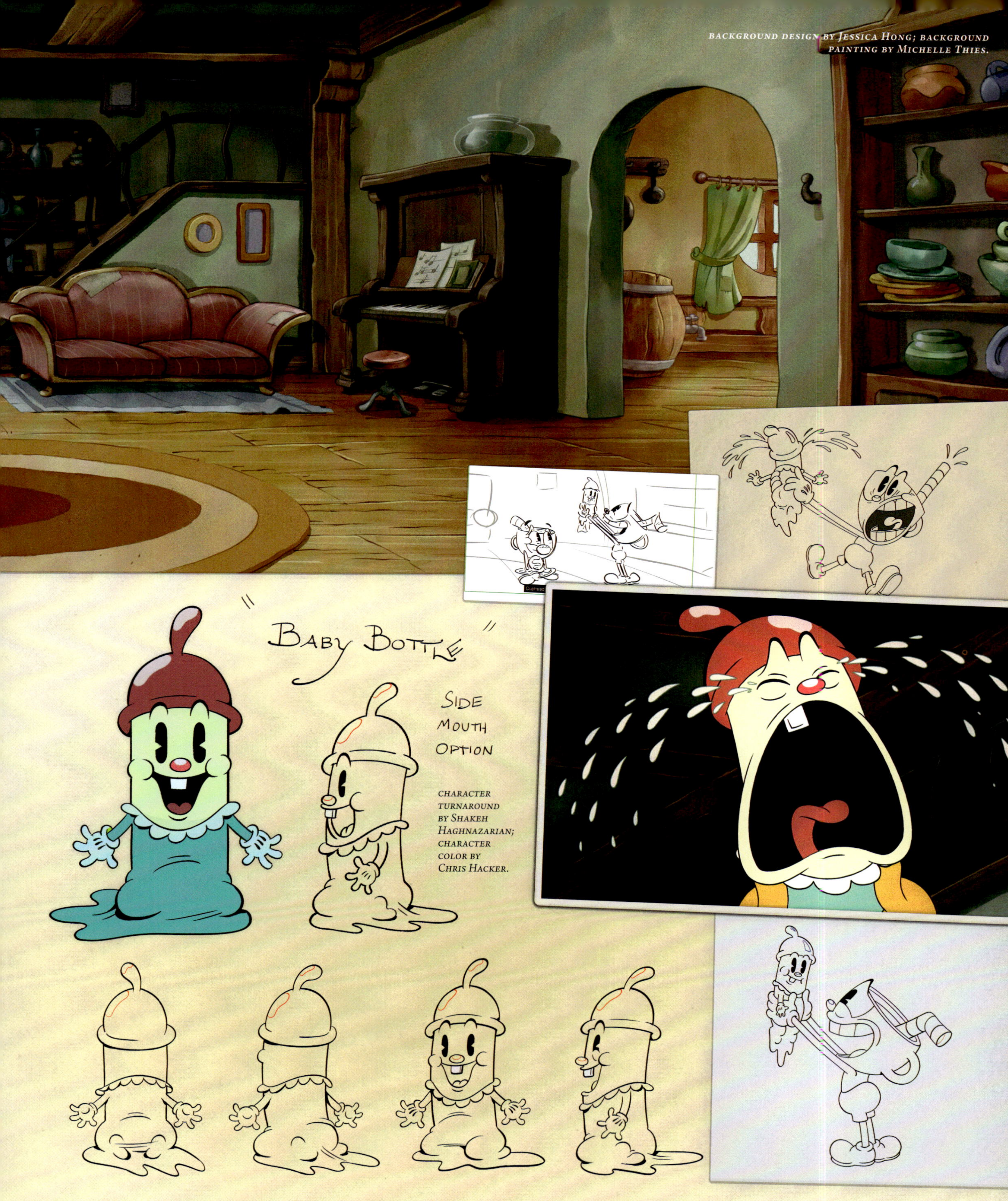

Character turnaround by Shakeh Haghnazarian; character color by Chris Hacker.

Storyboard panels by Dan Becker; special pose designs by Mike Fontanelli and Bradley Lewis.

➜ **SHAKEH:** I loved drawing that bottle. He was kind of like an evil Swee'Pea from *Popeye*, especially his expressions. All our designers did a great job with all the special poses on that one.

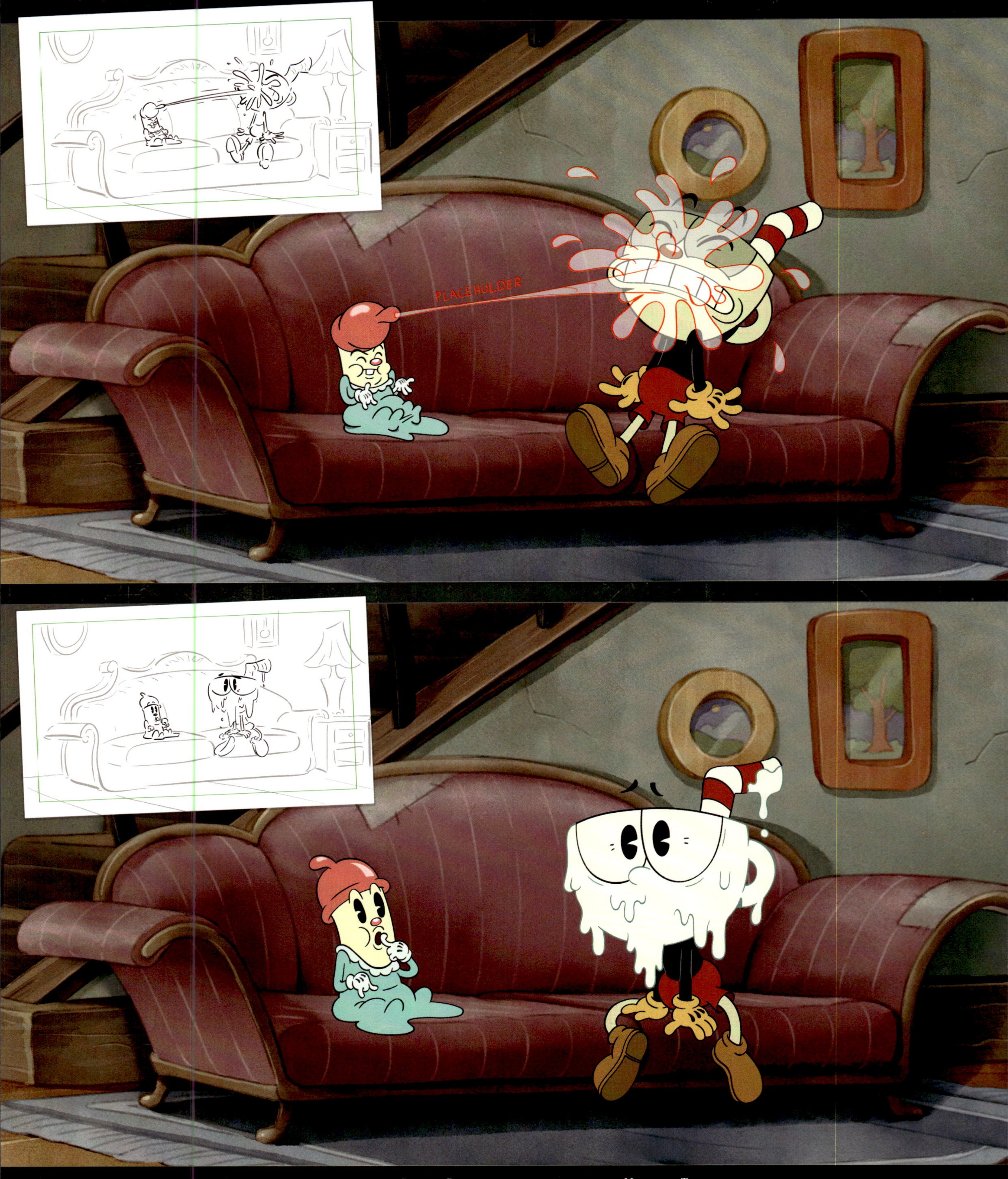

Dan Becker, background design by Lauren Duda, background painting by Michelle Thies

→ SHAKEH: You want to make it as sweet and saccharine as possible. You don't want to give away any surprises. There needs to be an element of shock.

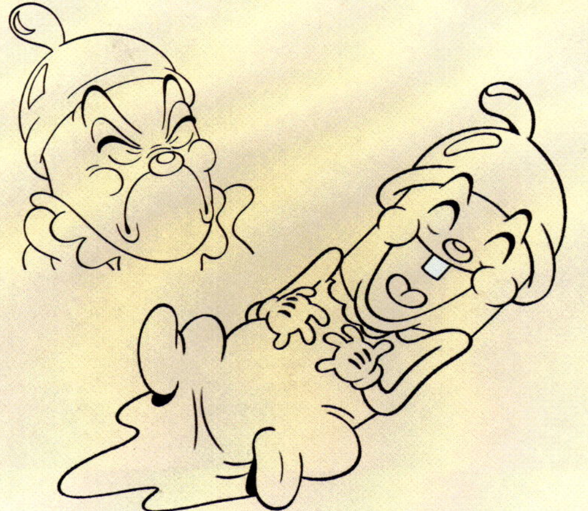

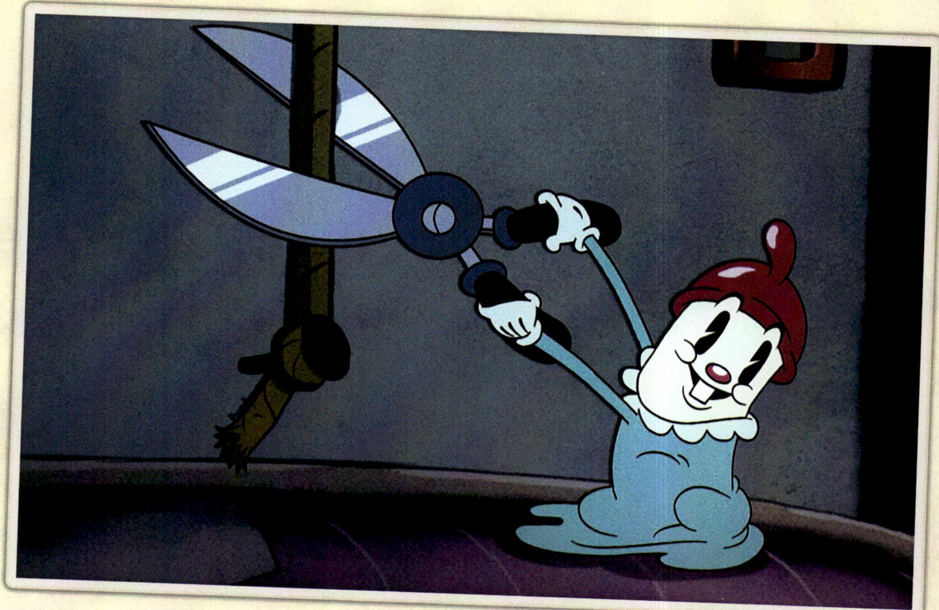

→ DEEKI: Another benefit of a bottle episode is that by putting your characters in a single location and dialing up some form of pressure, you're forced to explore character-based conflict and jokes that come from their flaws.

ADAM P: We found a temper for Mugman. It was a whole other aspect to him.

CLAY: It was pretty satisfying to get to that point and start to see who Mugman really is. There's some flaws to unravel. From there, we gained confidence to push him and get into some Mugman-focused episodes. He definitely became capable of supporting an entire episode.

COSMO: He became easier to write for the more we got to know him.

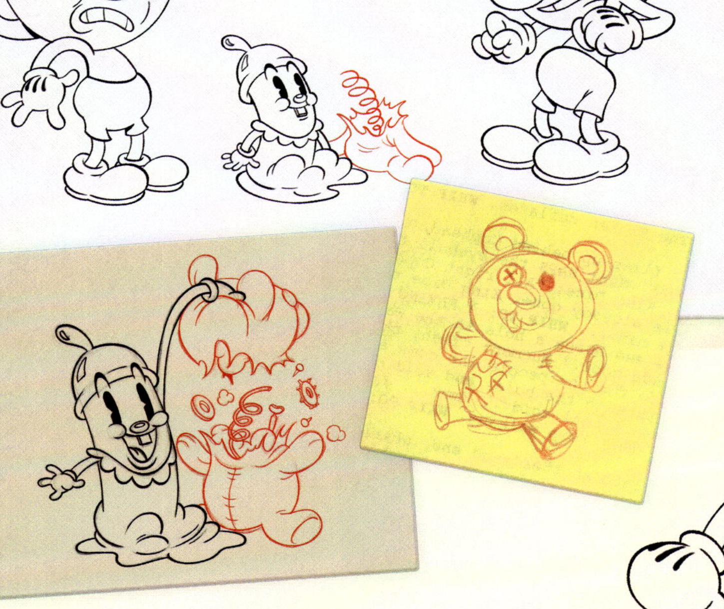

Initial sketch of Mugman's teddy bear on the back of the "Baby Bottle" outline by Shakeh Haghnazarian.

Special pose designs by Mike Fontanelli, Dan Haskett, Bradley Lewis, and Dave Wasson.

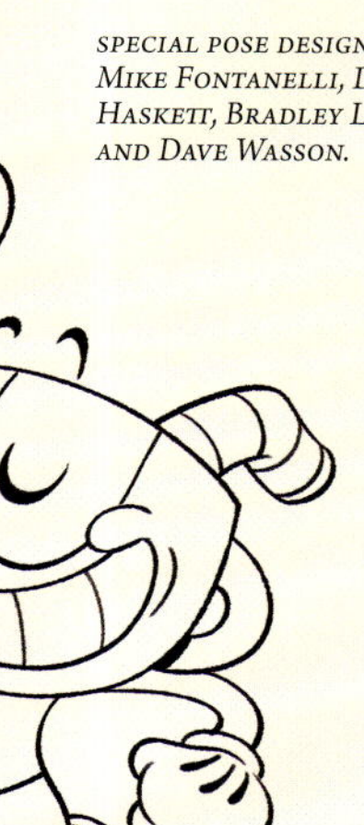

→ DAVE: Despite being in just one location, it plays fast and funny and the action is all character driven. That's when it hit us—whoa, this is actually working. That was a real breakthrough episode for us.

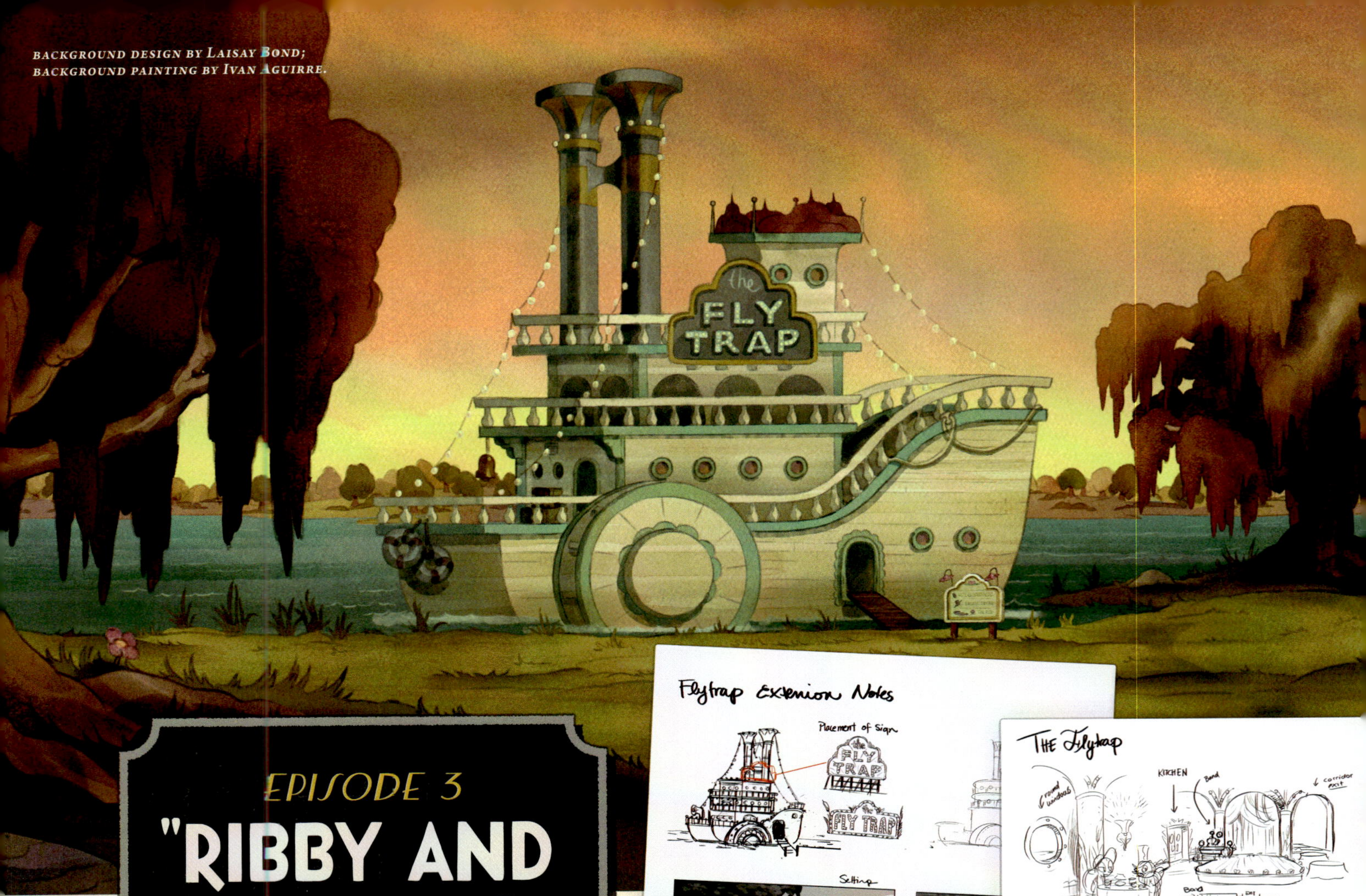

BACKGROUND DESIGN BY LAISAY BOND;
BACKGROUND PAINTING BY IVAN AGUIRRE.

EPISODE 3
"RIBBY AND CROAKS"

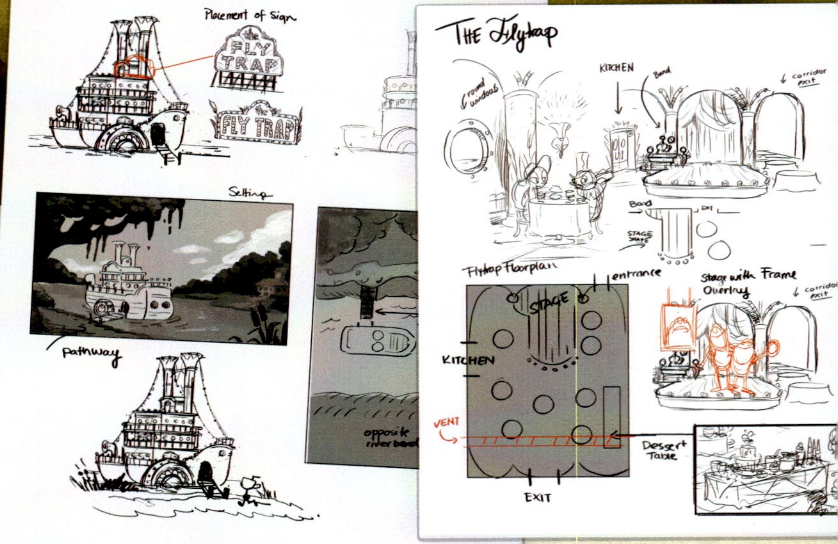

PREVIS FLY TRAP SKETCHES BY COSMO SEGURSON; RIBBY AND CROAKS TURNAROUNDS BY TAPAN GANDHI, ADAM PALOIAN, AND SHAKEH HAGHNAZARIAN.

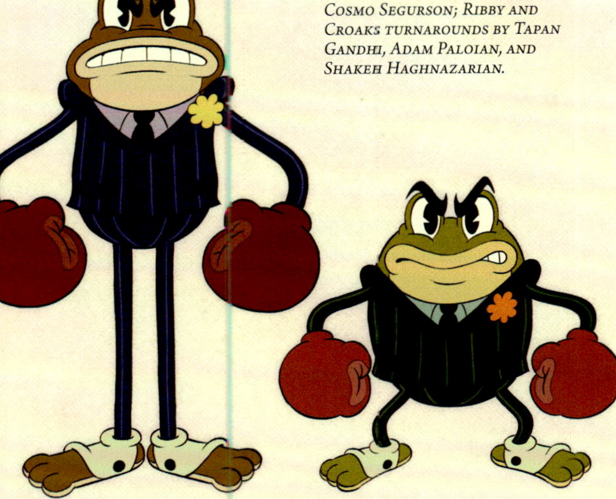

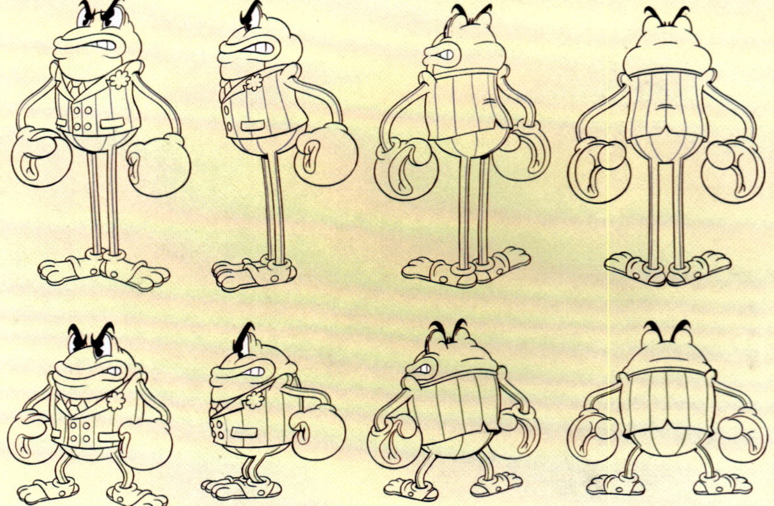

→ **COSMO:** Before the storyboard artists and designers bring the episode to life, we do a handout where we work up "previs," or previsualization. The idea is to get everybody aligned on the geography of where the story's taking place.

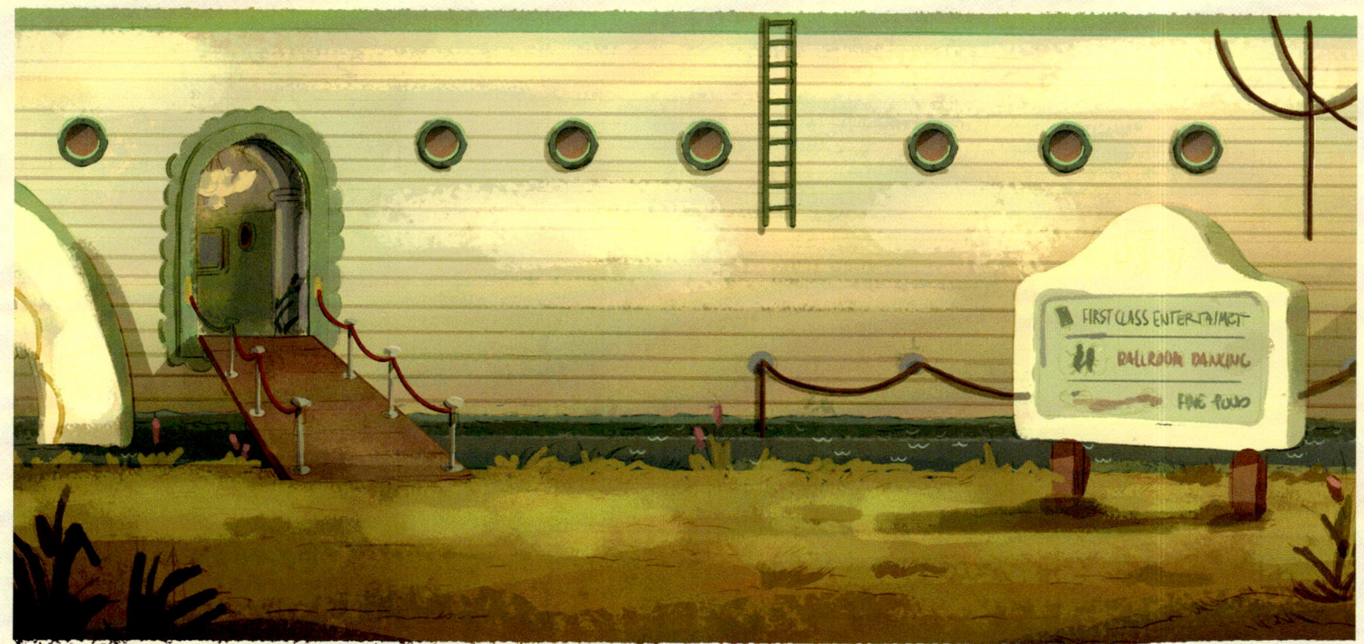

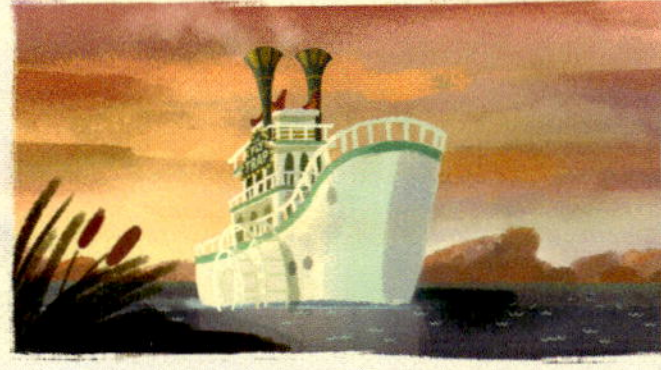

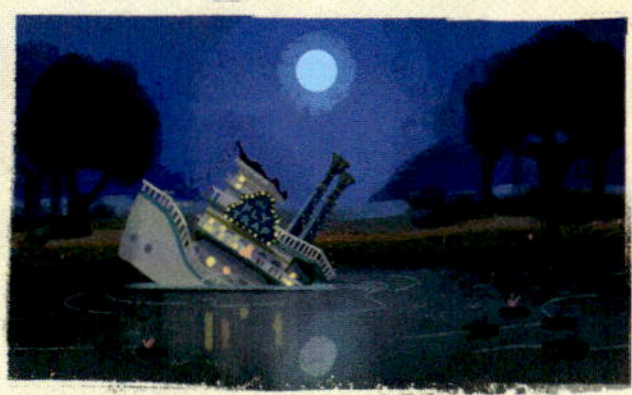

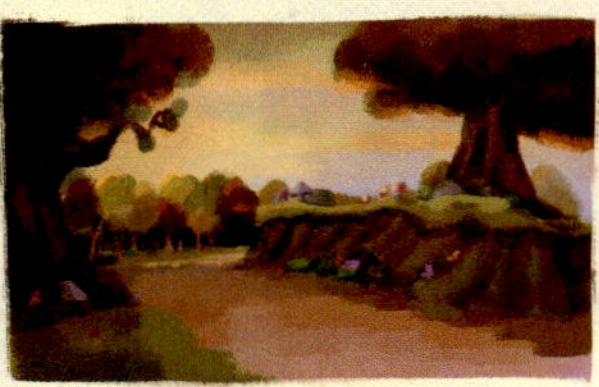

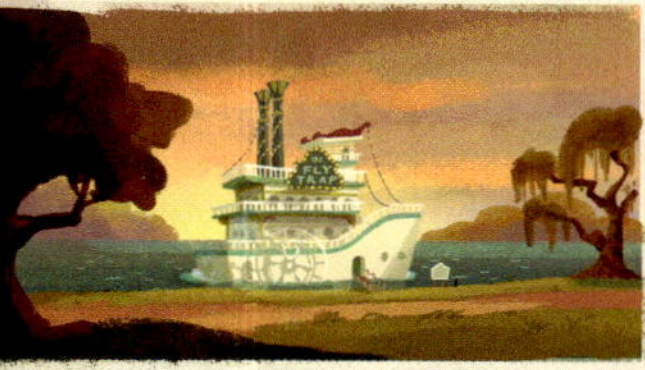

→ **ANDREA:** Every time we jumped into a new location or we had to do color shifts, we'd almost "mini color script" the episode, and then they would all jump in together and paint it all together.

COLOR KEYS BY IVAN AGUIRRE; STORYBOARD PANELS BY IAN VASQUEZ.

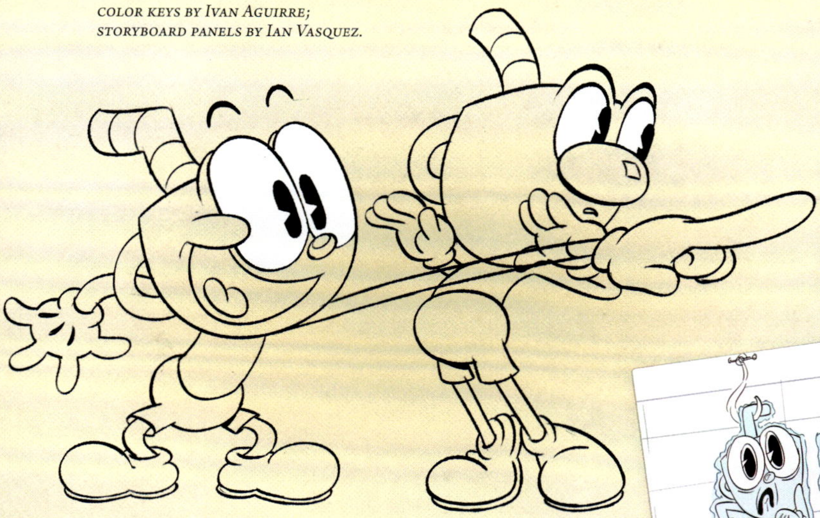

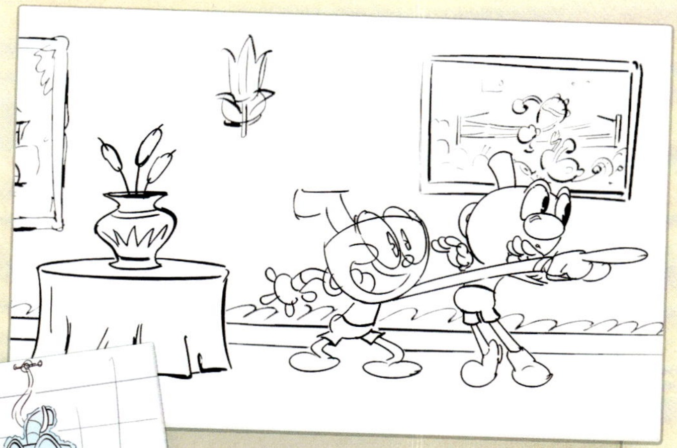

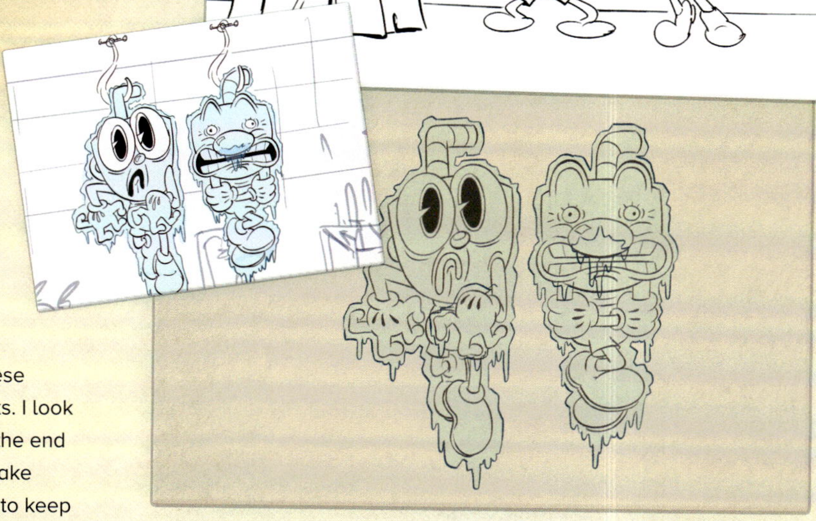

→ **ANDREA:** Design follows board, so design uses the storyboard as their guide.

TAPAN: The storyboards really come in handy for us designers, because they have the hard job of framing these scenes and making sure the scale of the characters works. I look at the storyboard front to back, make sure I'm getting to the end of the scene so when I'm designing a character, I don't make something visible that needs to be a reveal later on. I try to keep all that in mind so the joke lands.

SPECIAL POSE DESIGNS BY TAPAN GANDHI.

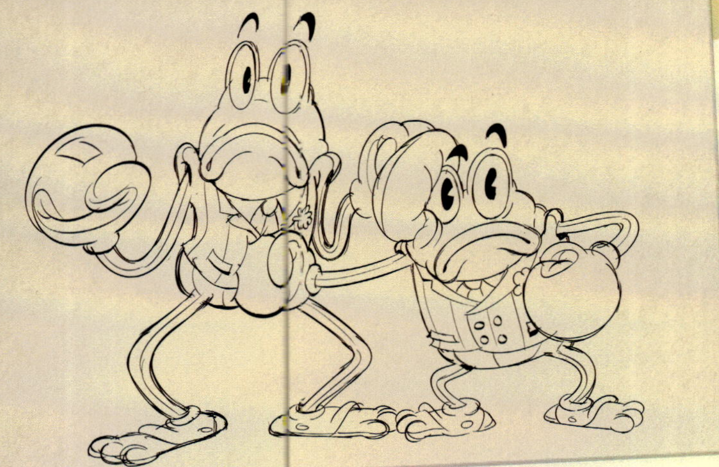

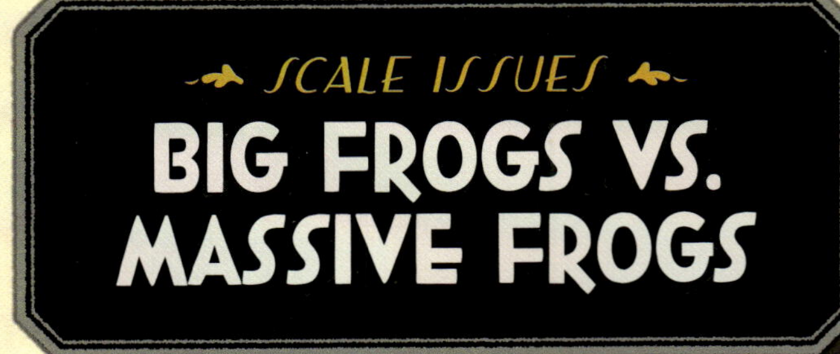

SCALE ISSUES

BIG FROGS VS. MASSIVE FROGS

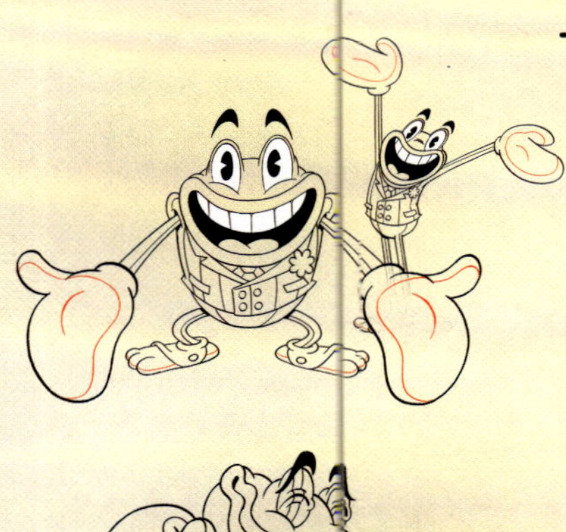

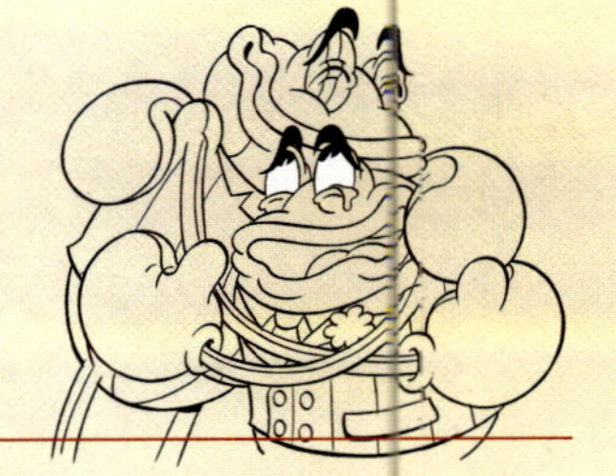

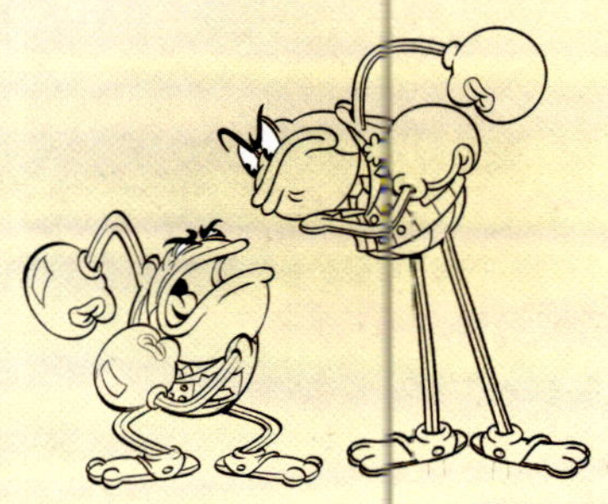

SPECIAL POSE DESIGNS BY TAPAN GANDHI AND ADAM PALOIAN.

→ **CLAY:** I never considered being loyal to the sizes of the characters. If we needed to alter that for a story, we could just make it something practical. I totally respect the game, but the game is not TV storytelling. If you want to present an effective visual means of story, you'll have to change the scale sometimes—it's not a big deal.

ANDREA: When it comes to assets, what usually presents a lot of problems for production are scale issues. When characters are much larger than Cuphead and Mugman, that means I have to consistently design backgrounds for two different scales, and that's super hard to do. We have that problem with Ribby and Croaks, where Dave is like, "But they're supposed to be massive!"

DAVE: In terms of scale, Cuphead and Mugman were the baseline—they're pretty much the scale they were in the game. For other characters, we made adjustments. It's all sort of by feel. But in the case of Ribby and Croaks, I wanted them to be huge. Massive. Like in the game.

ANDREA: I think Dave in his mind saw Ribby and Croaks as giants, and everyone else saw them as big frogs. There were huge scale issues in design because of that.

LAUREN: Our cast of characters is so wildly different in size; trying to hit that middle ground was a challenge.

ANDREA: Scale is relative to character, so we make the character feel big by making everything around it feel small, or vice versa. Character scale is very dependent on its surroundings. So if anything was insanely large in size, it would be double the backgrounds. On top of that, they're inside a club for insects. Figuring out how to make it work was breaking everyone's brain.

LAUREN: How do you get a table that doesn't feel tiny for the frogs or enormous for Cuphead and Mugman?

ANDREA: Dave wanted the bugs to be tiny, and Cuphead and Mugman to be bigger than the bugs, and the frogs are supposed to be massive.

DAVE: Massive, like in the game. Huge. Just . . . massive!

ANDREA: That episode never got to Dave's ethereal place of scale. I think it's pretty successful given the constraints of all the characters' sizes and having to follow a board that was already set. They feel big—maybe not as big as they do in the game, but still satisfying.

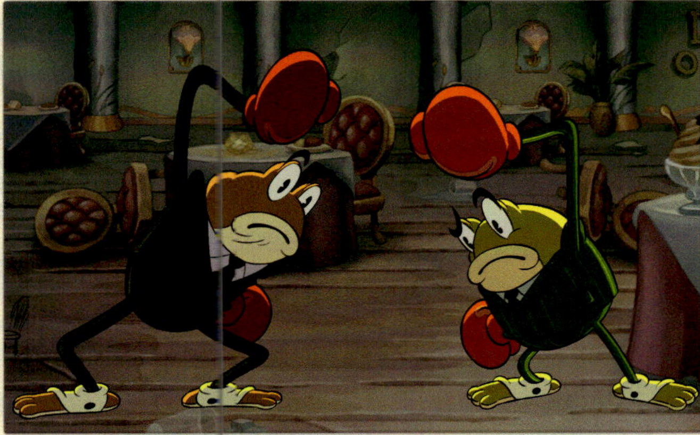

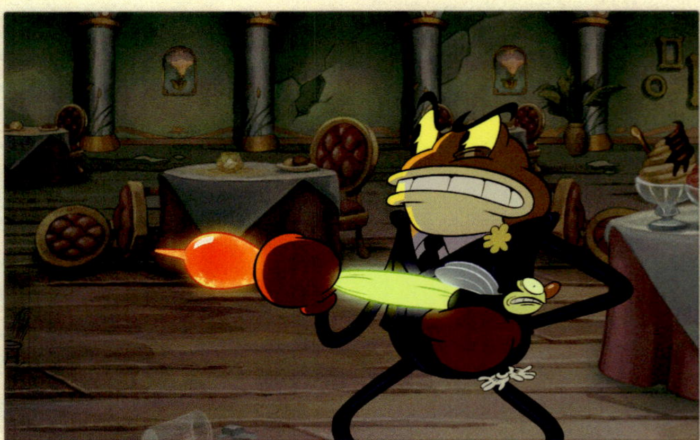

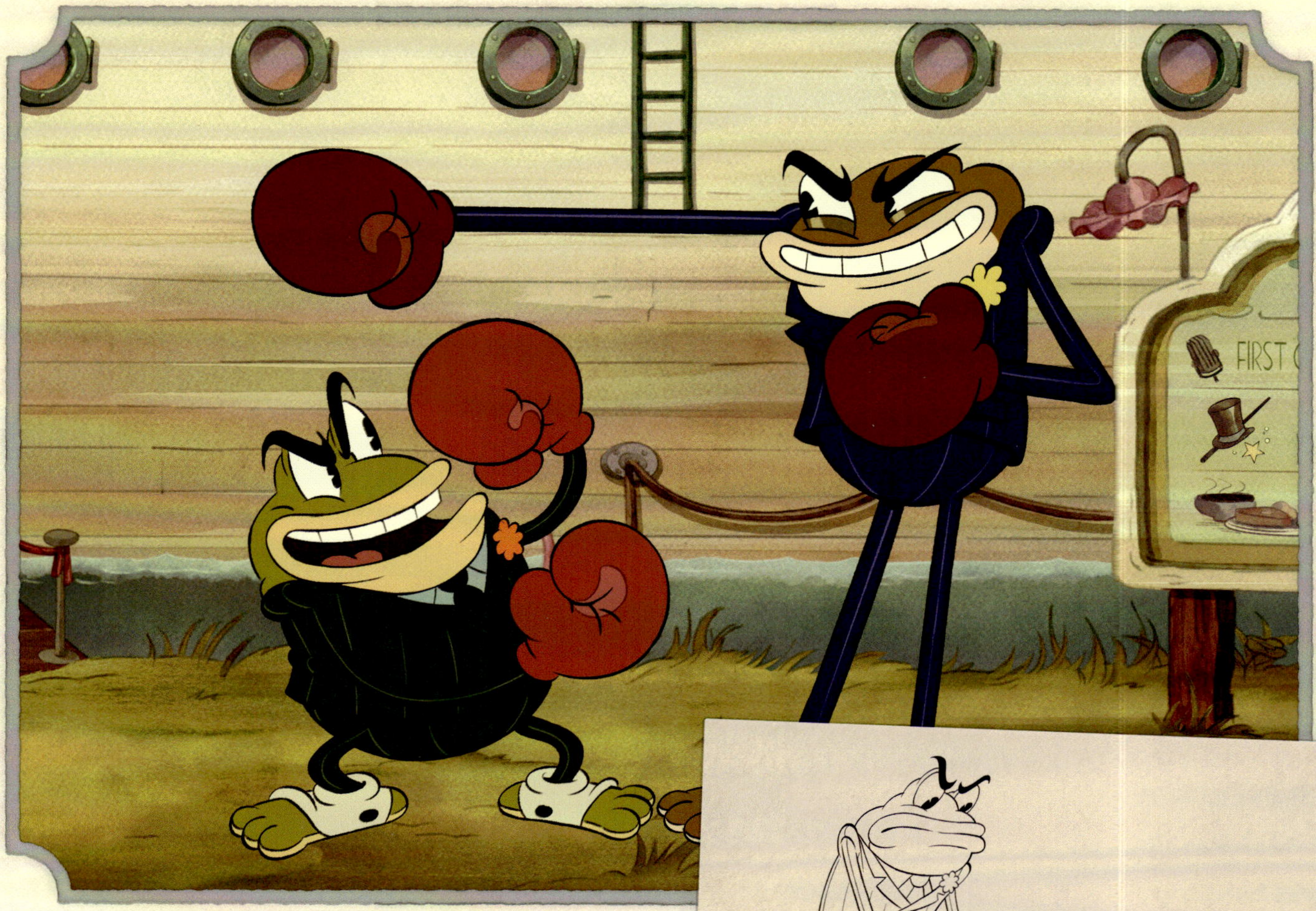

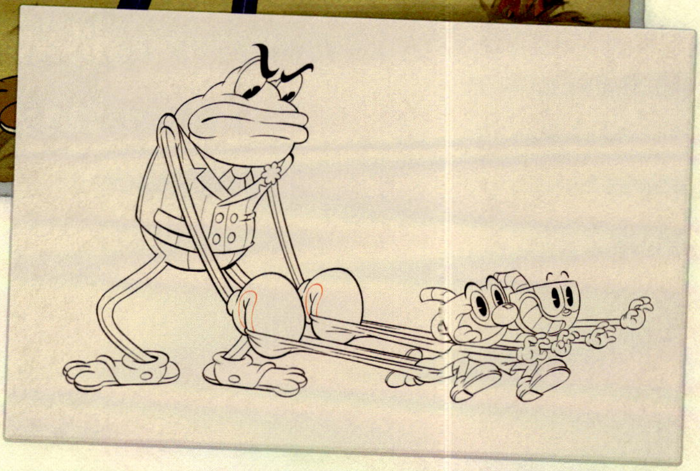

→ **DAVE:** Ribby and Croaks are the first to pick a fight with Cuphead and Mugman, and they pay the price for it. The boys just wanted ice cream. They weren't trying to get revenge on Ribby and Croaks. That's just the way it unfolded.

SPECIAL POSE DESIGNS BY *ADAM PALOIAN* AND *TAPAN GANDHI*; STORYBOARD PANELS BY *IAN VASQUEZ*.

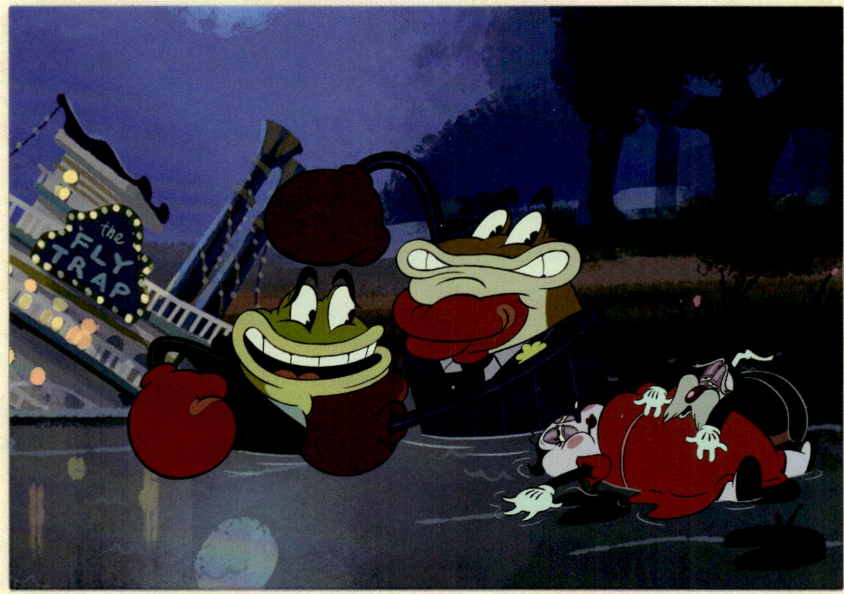

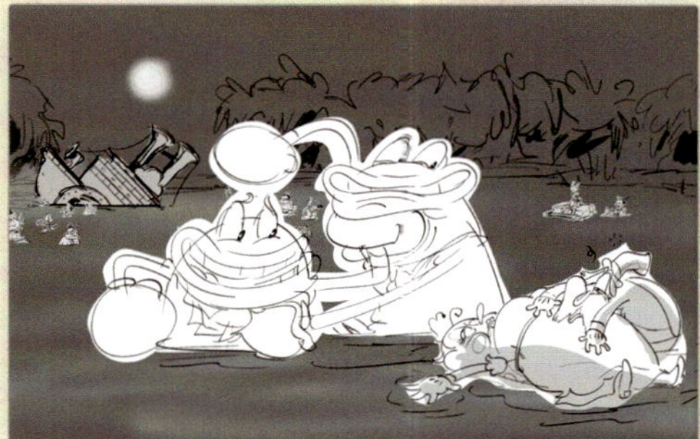

→ **DAVE:** At some point it became a conscious decision that every time Cuphead and Mugman came up against somebody, they totally screwed up their lives. People trying to harm Cuphead and Mugman always come out the worse for wear. They'd never destroy someone's life on purpose. They're not even aware it's happening.

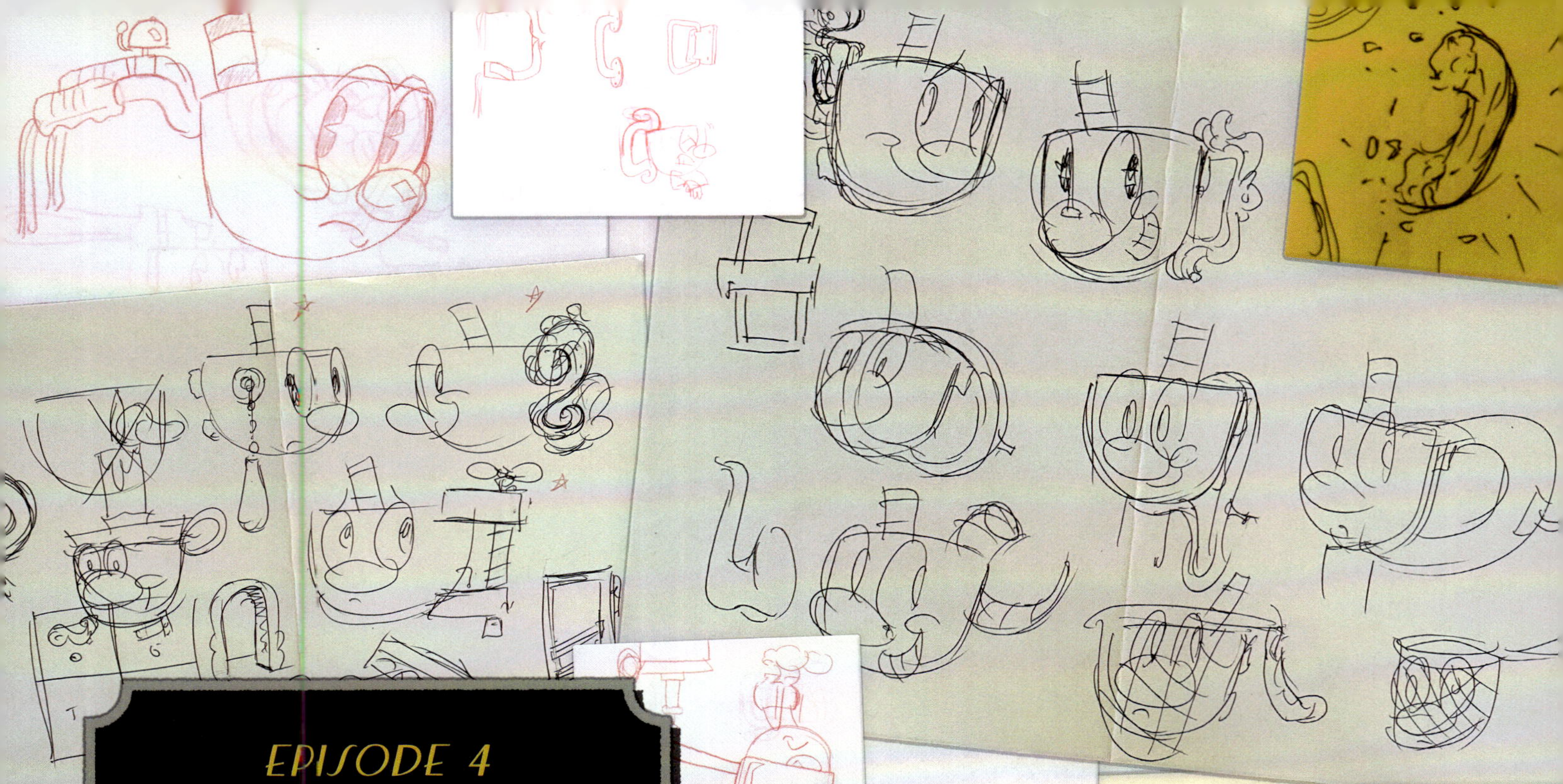

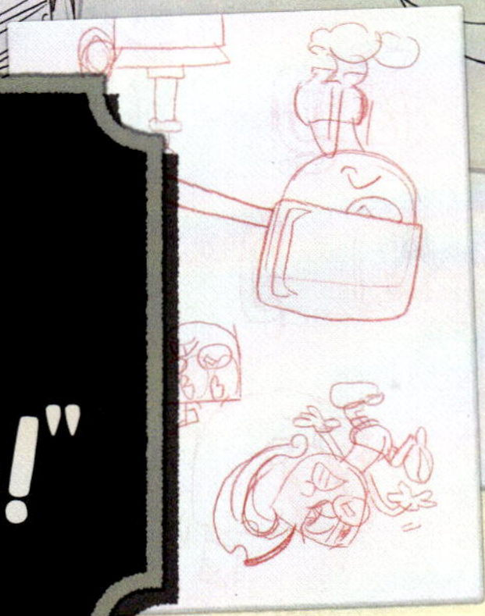

STORY ROOM SKETCHES BY COSMO SEGURSON; STORYBOARD PANEL BY DAN BECKER.

EPISODE 4

"HANDLE WITH CARE!"

→ **DEEKI:** We had the title before we knew whose story it was, but very quickly it became clear that this would be a truly disruptive event for Mugman.

CLAY: In "Handle," what happens to Mugman is so specific to him. If that happened to Cuphead, it'd be met with a shrug.

DEEKI: If you asked Mugman before the episode what his handle means to him, he'd have no opinion. But once it's broken, it's a problem that upends his world.

CLAY: Cuphead wouldn't care. Mugman cares, so he has to be punished.

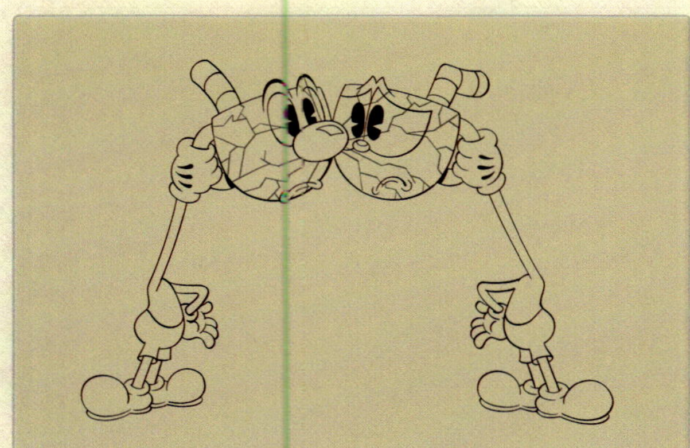

SPECIAL POSE DESIGNS BY MIKE FONTANELLI AND DAVE WASSON.

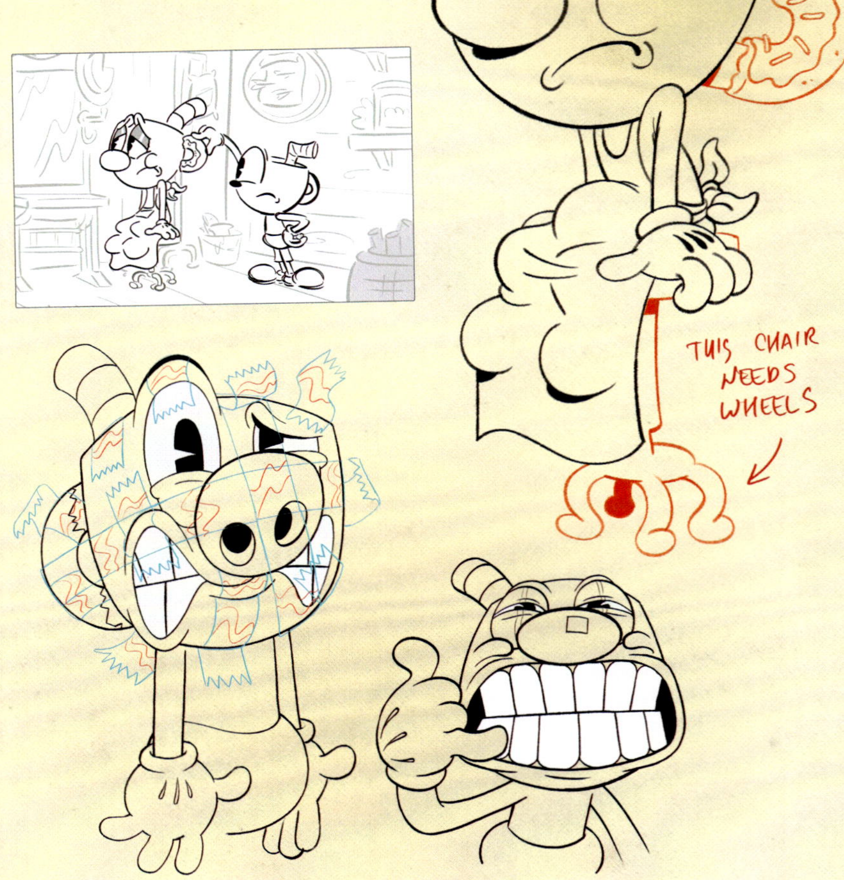

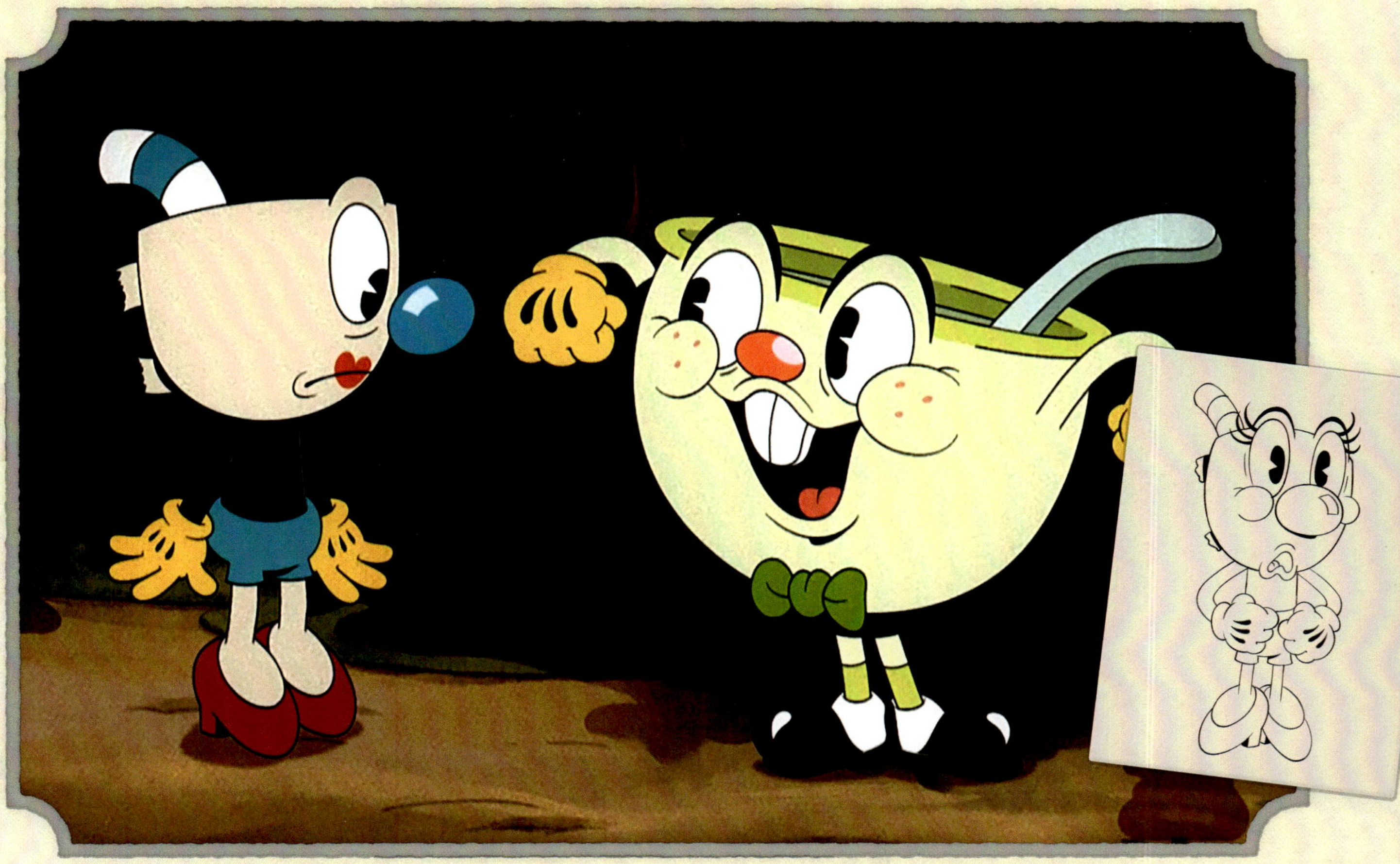

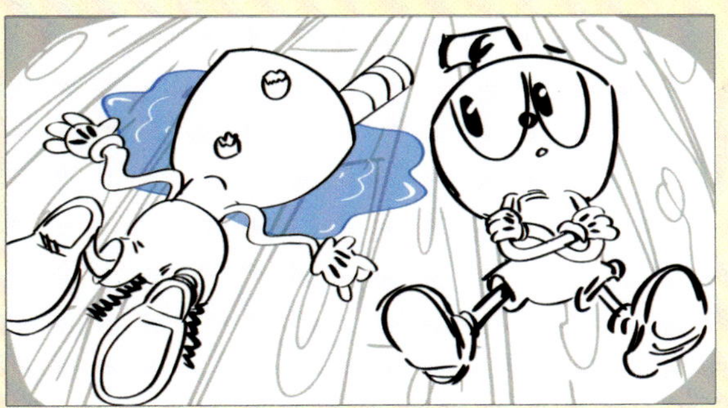

STORYBOARD PANEL BY KENNEDY TARRELL.

→ **KENNEDY TARRELL, *THE CUPHEAD SHOW!* STORYBOARD ARTIST:** This could only have been a Mugman reaction. We wouldn't necessarily bring Cuphead to that level of despair.

CLAY: Mugman has a way of letting it unravel who he is and what he stands for.

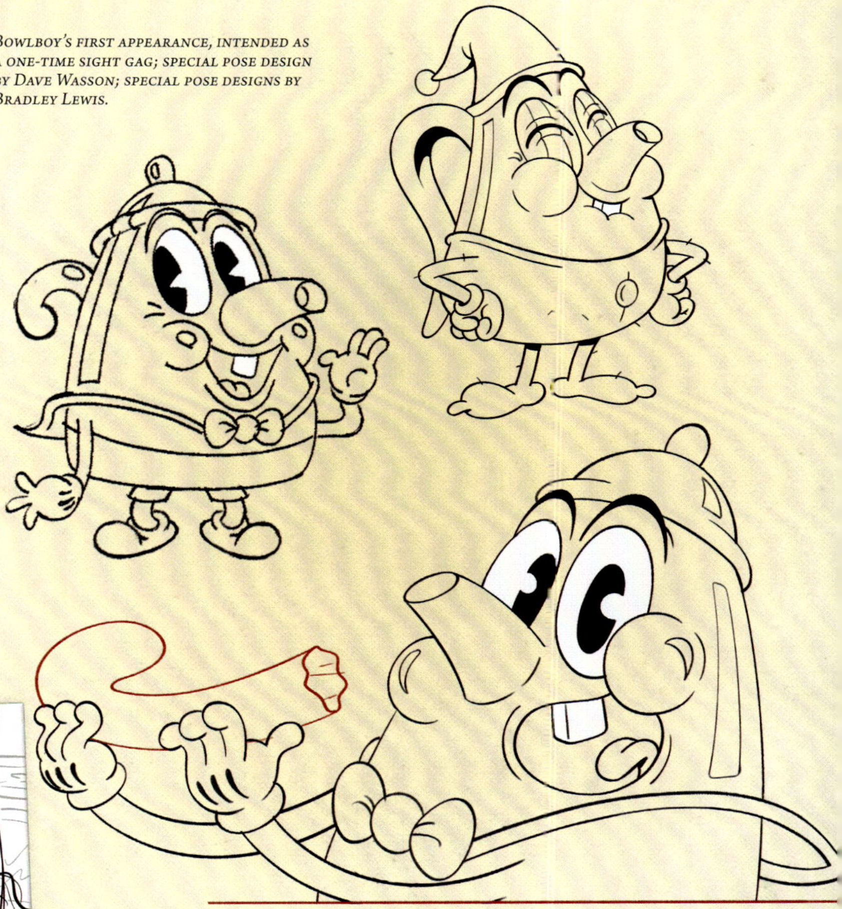

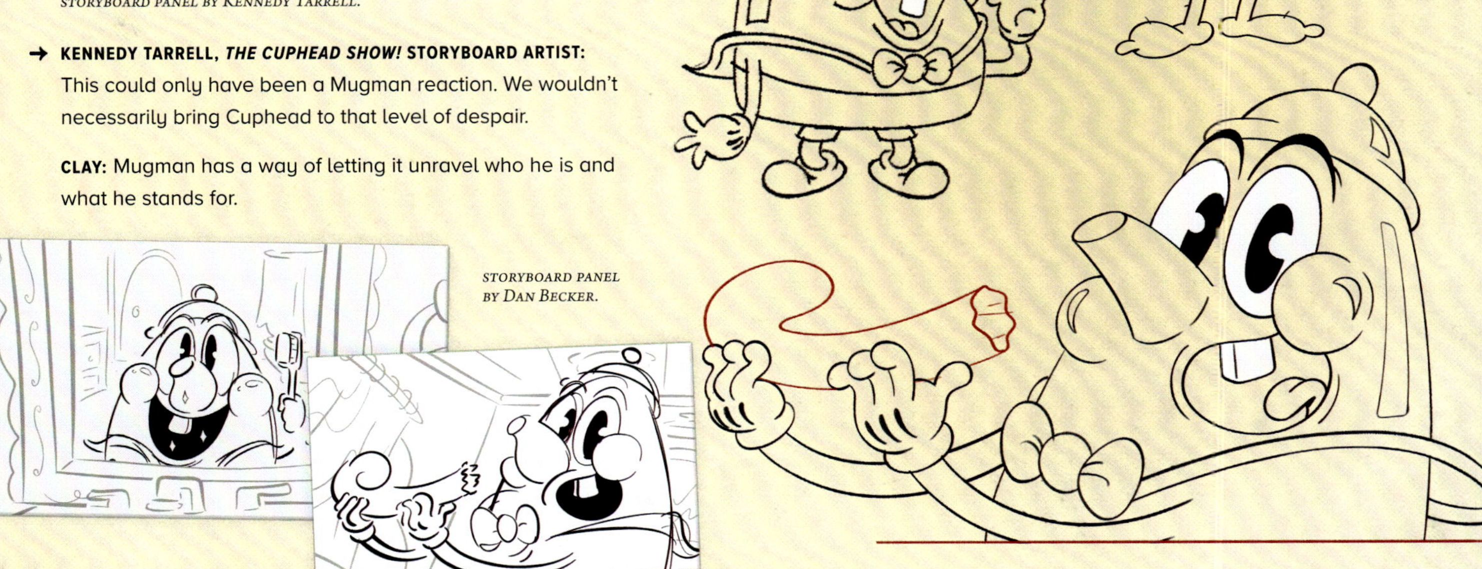

STORYBOARD PANEL BY DAN BECKER.

BOWLBOY'S FIRST APPEARANCE, INTENDED AS A ONE-TIME SIGHT GAG; SPECIAL POSE DESIGN BY DAVE WASSON; SPECIAL POSE DESIGNS BY BRADLEY LEWIS.

INTRODUCING
PORKRIND

(VOICED BY COSMO SEGURSON)

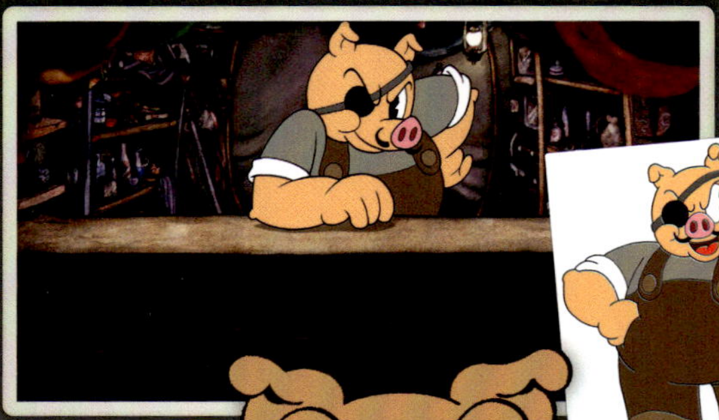

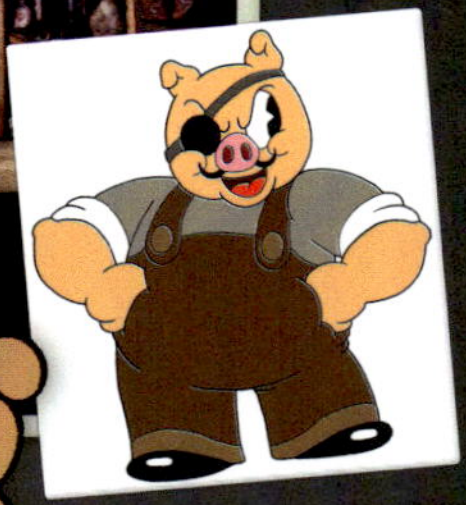

→ **DAVE:** It's always good to have someone who runs counter to Cuphead and Mugman. If you've got them being really loud and idiotic, you want that rubbing against someone who'd be super irritated by it.

CLAY: Early on, we discovered Porkrind as someone to torture. As soon as Cuphead and Mugman walk into the store, they're under his skin. It was so immediately satisfying.

COSMO: Cuphead and Mugman have no business being around him at all, which makes it fun to see his frustration. He's always just trying to get rid of them.

DAVE: He's no nonsense, and he's kind of mercenary. We knew he'd be this guy that could get you stuff, like black-market goods. He doesn't really care what you use the stuff for—that's not his problem. He just gets the stuff; he ain't asking no questions.

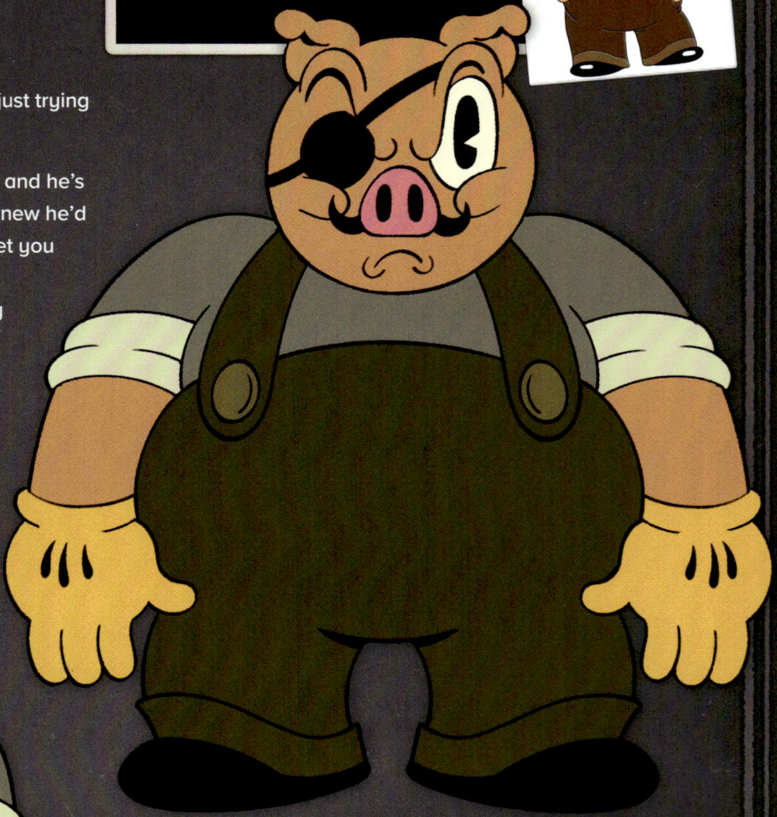

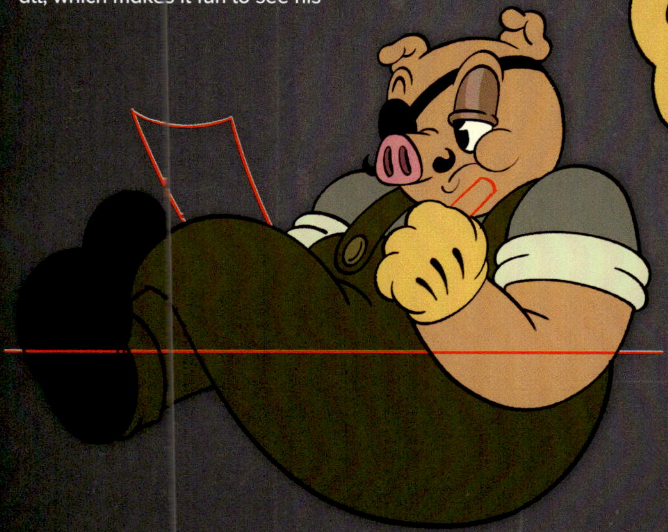

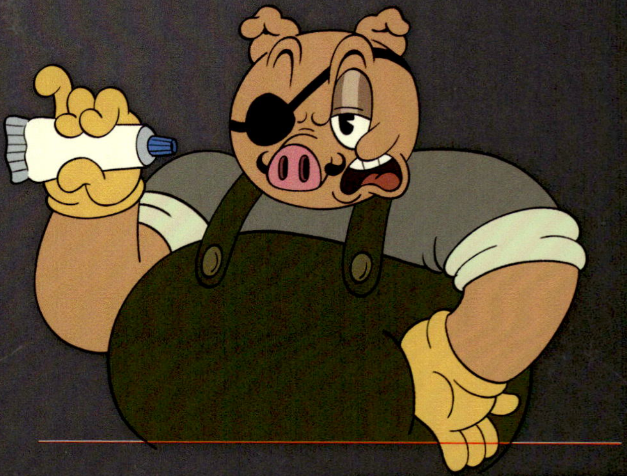

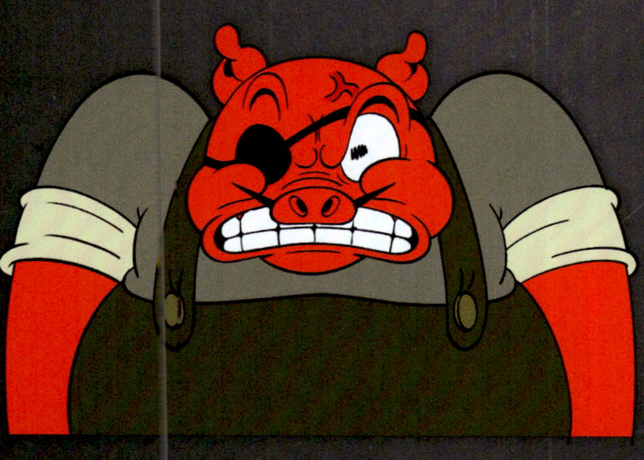

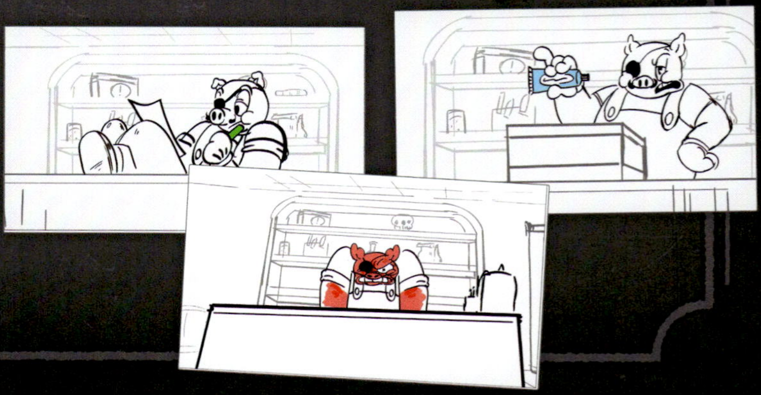

TOP: PORKRIND'S DESIGN FROM THE CUPHEAD GAME. SPECIAL POSE DESIGNS BY MIKE FONTANELLI AND BRADLEY LEWIS; STORYBOARD PANELS BY ZOË MOSS AND AUSTIN FABER; CHARACTER COLOR BY CHRIS HACKER.

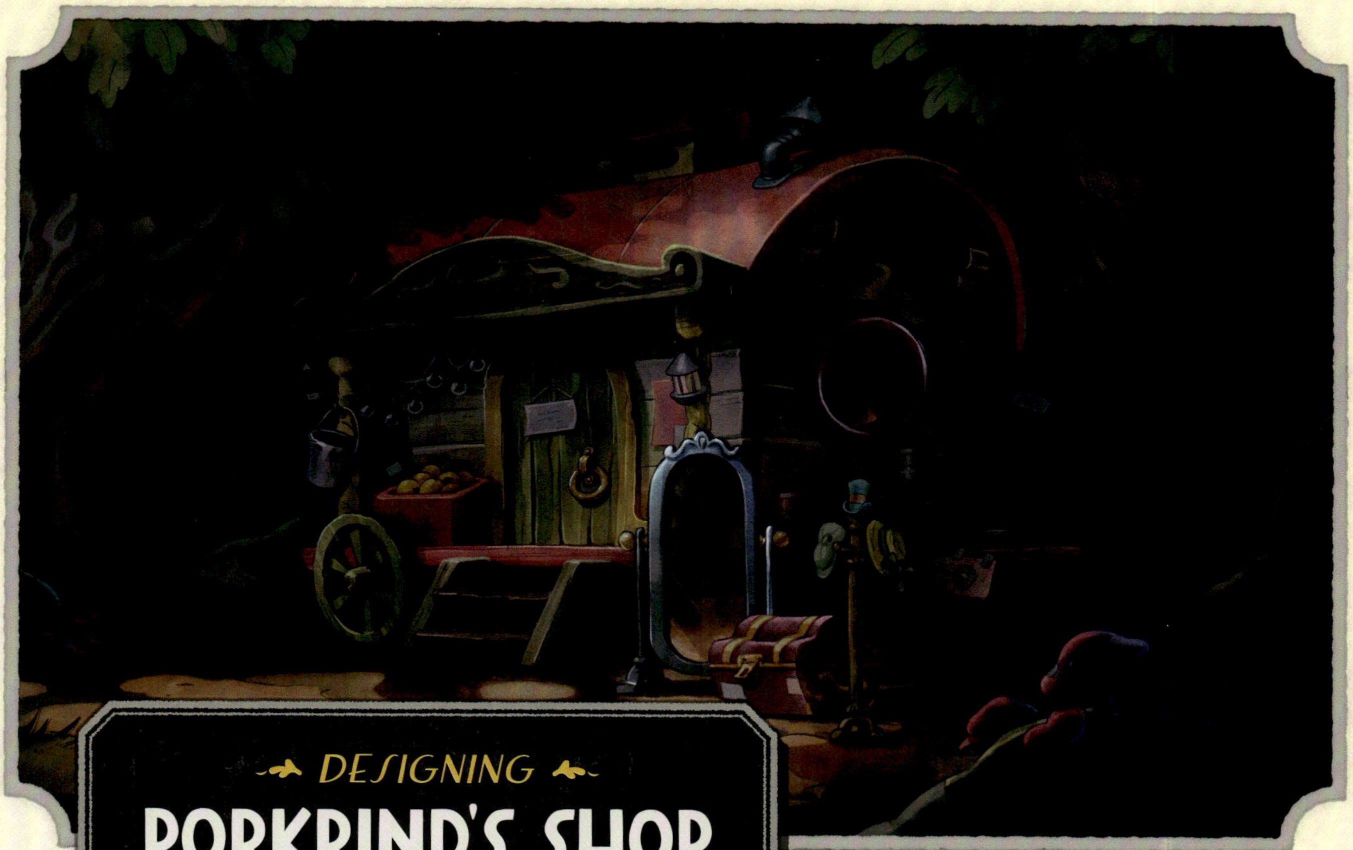

DESIGNING PORKRIND'S SHOP

BACKGROUND LAYOUT BY ANDREA FERNANDEZ AND LAISAY BOND; PAINTING BY MALLORY CARLSON.

→ **JESSICA HONG, *THE CUPHEAD SHOW!* BACKGROUND DESIGNER:** The highlight of the entire show for me was working on Porkrind's store—that's my jam, one hundred percent. It's my favorite part of the game. My favorite part of games in general is the item store component, so I was beyond thrilled that I got to do that.

DAVE: In the game, the store was mainly about magic, different potions and elixirs—like a magical 7-Eleven. But for the show, we wanted a world that felt more grounded; if Cuphead and Mugman could pop in and get any magic thing they wanted to solve any problem, that wouldn't feel as satisfying.

JESSICA: We had a lot more stuff in there originally. I was basically told to chill, because I might have gone a little too crazy. There were bird skulls, there were gas masks for a horse, a jar of weird eyeballs, some kinda monster's head . . .

ANDREA: There's a big chicken foot in a jar that I really like. There's a wall full of shoes in one episode—we don't know why he has a rack of shoes. The human skull is also kind of weird and perplexing—why does he have a human skull in there?

LAUREN: That's why that space is so fun—whatever we need it to be, it can be. It poses more questions than it answers.

ANDREA: And we have cartoony producers who are okay with it. If people don't have that cartoony mindset, they might think it needs to be a real space—but it doesn't. Your eye accepts what it accepts. In the world of *Cuphead*, we can do that. The design is rooted in realism, but the way we play with it is very cartoony from shot to shot.

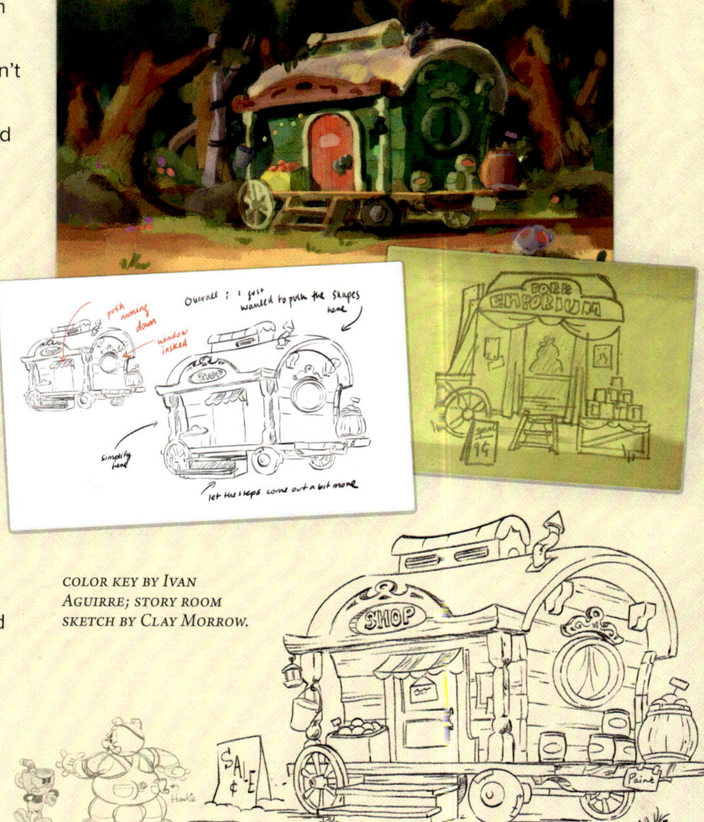

COLOR KEY BY IVAN AGUIRRE; STORY ROOM SKETCH BY CLAY MORROW.

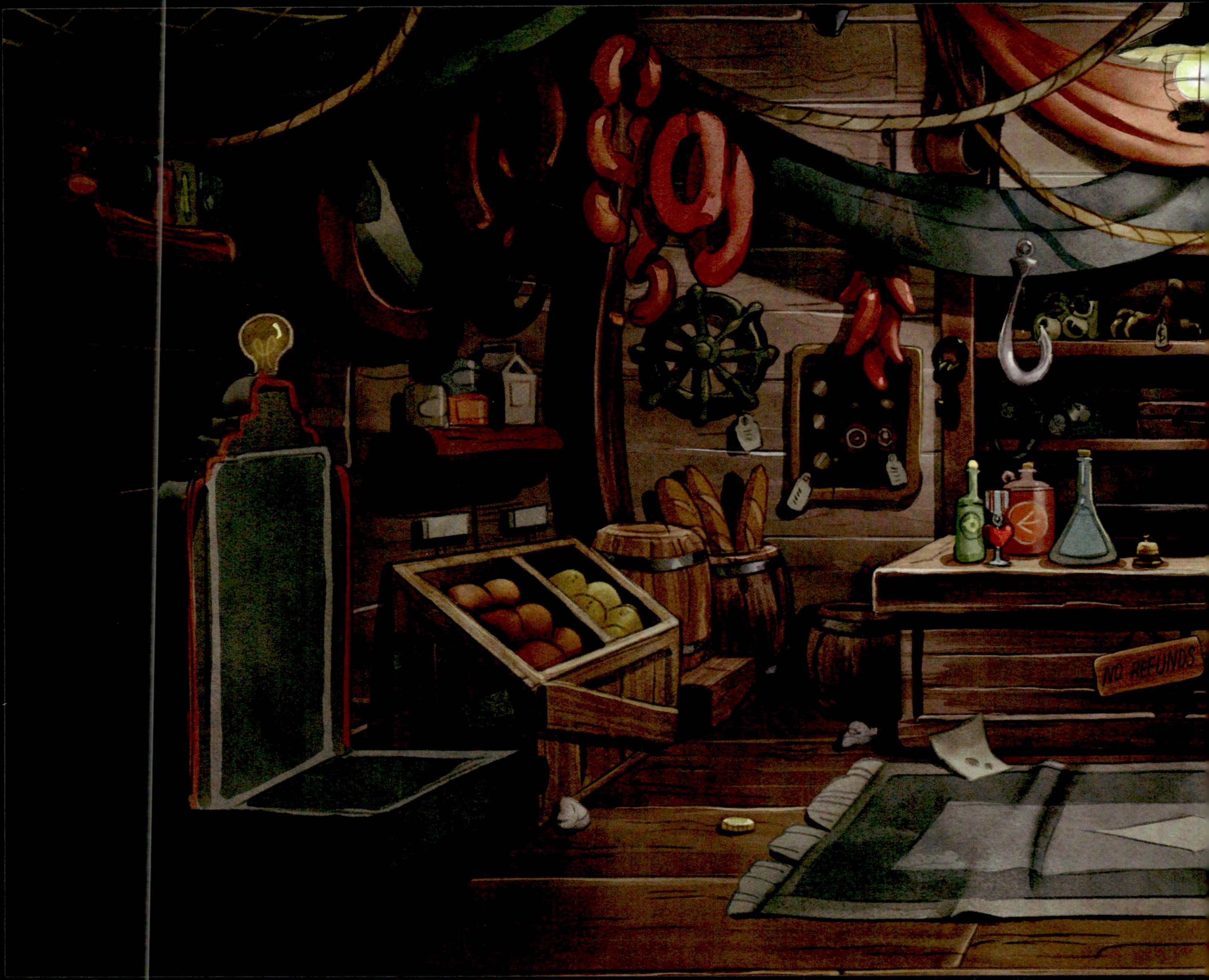

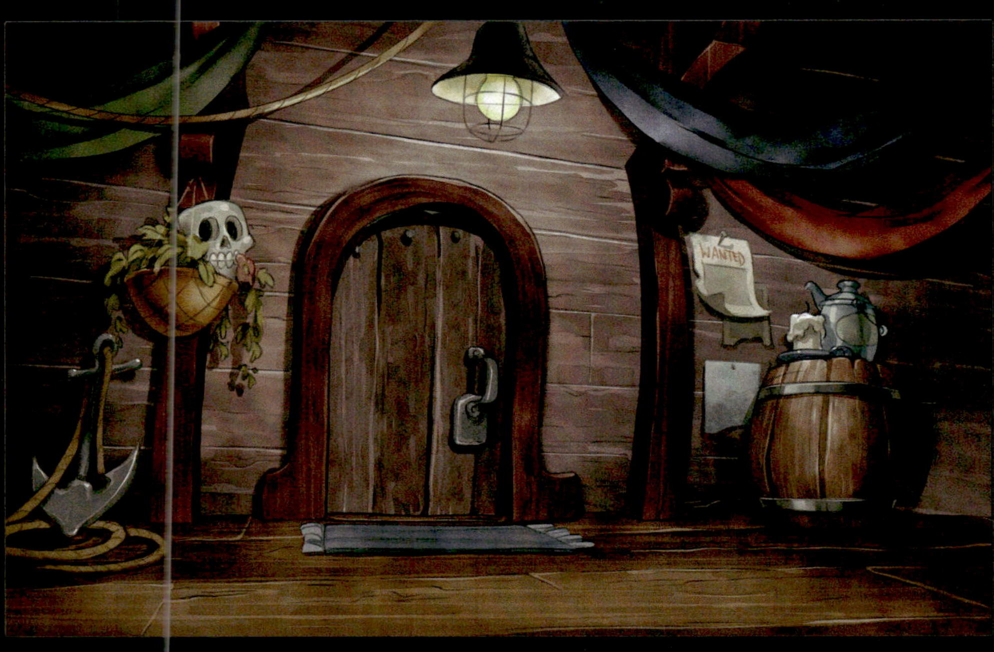
WANTED

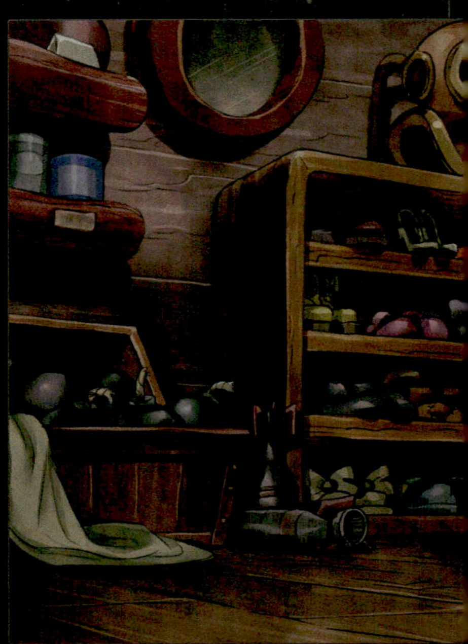

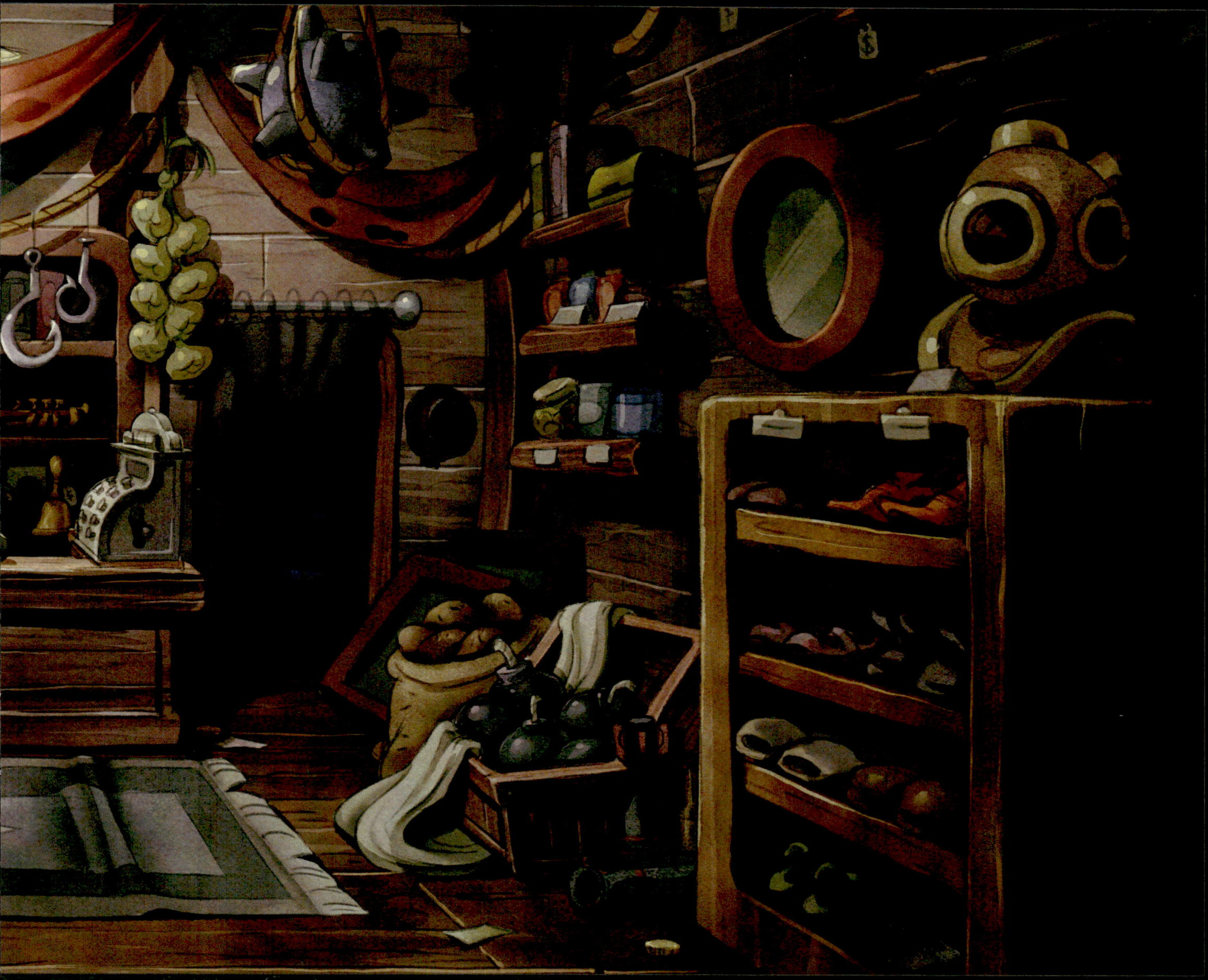

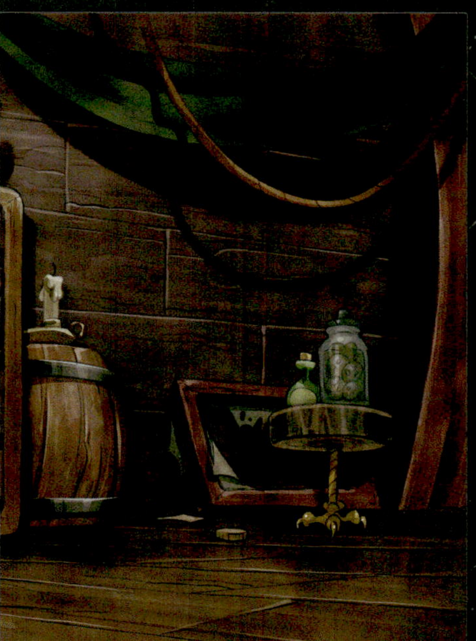

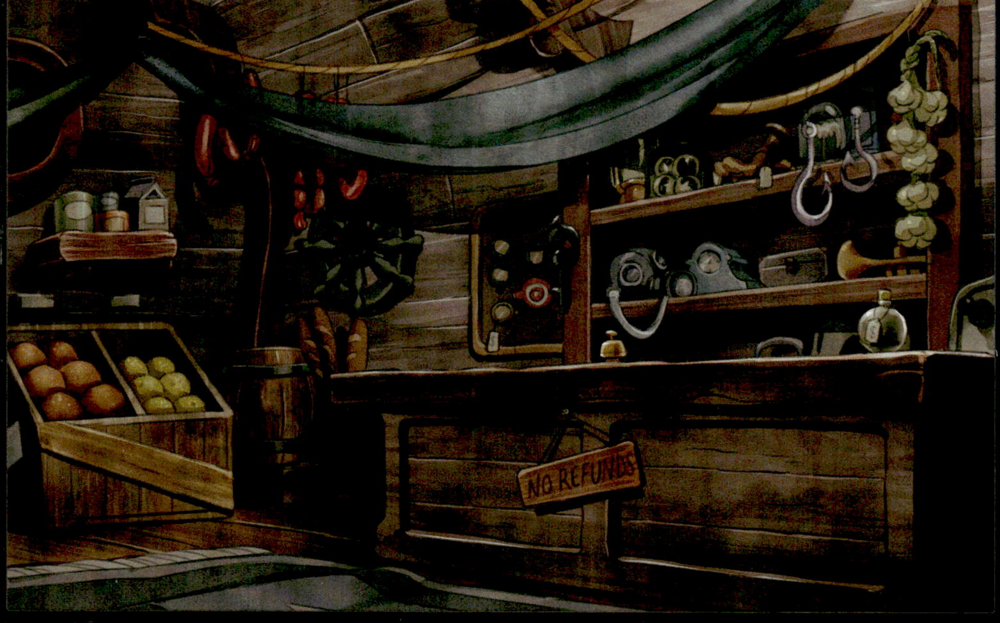

BACKGROUND DESIGNS BY *JESSICA HONG*; PAINTINGS BY *MICHELLE THIES*.

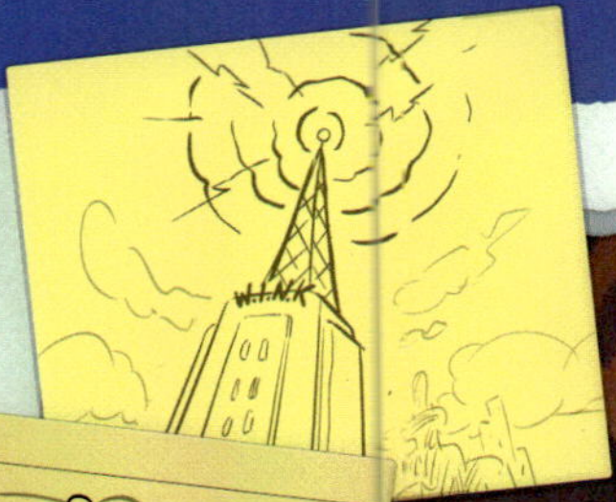

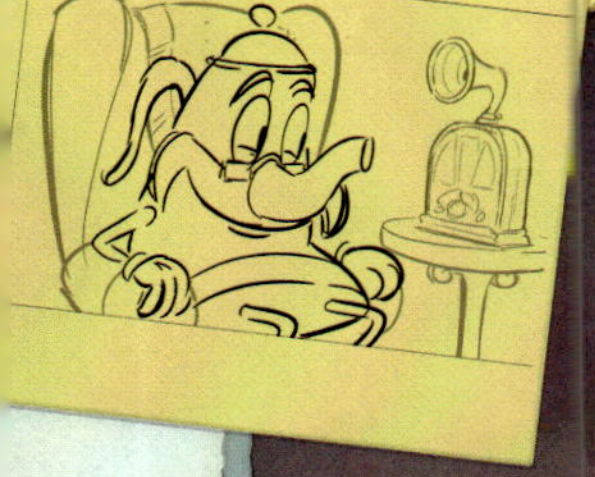

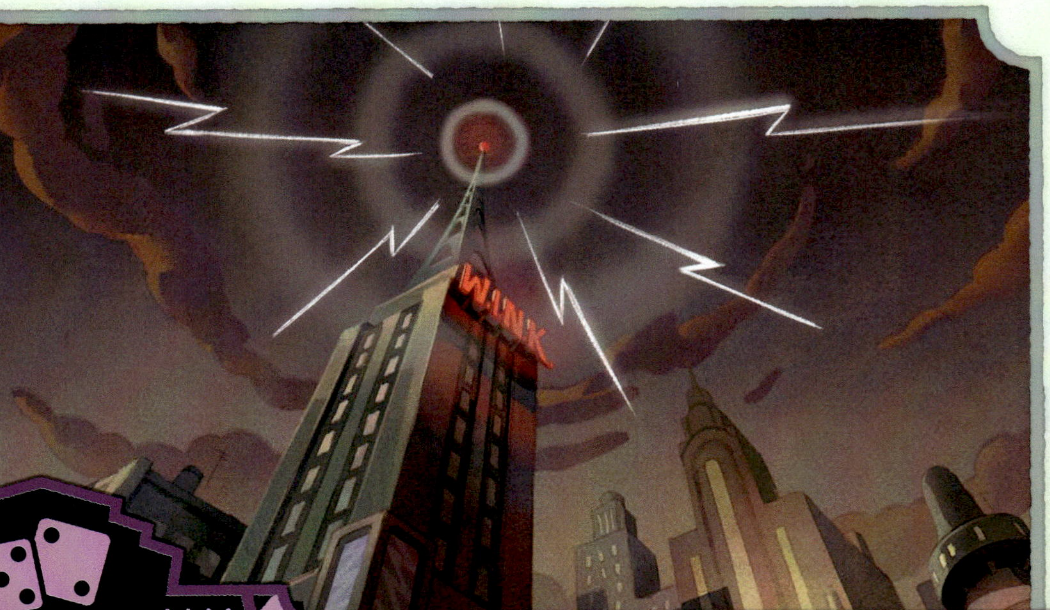

EPISODE 5

"ROLL THE DICE"

DEEP DIVE

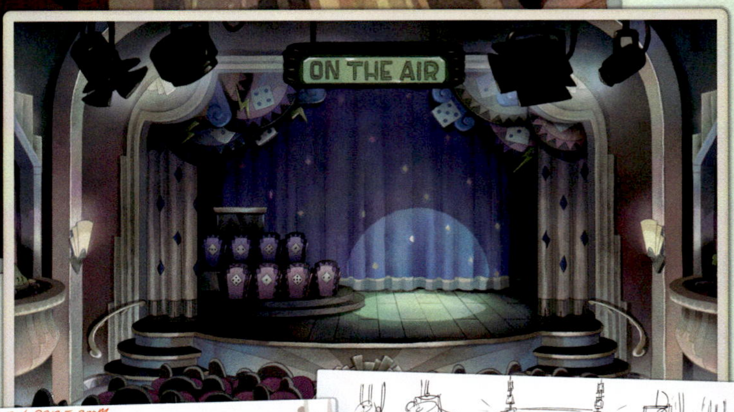

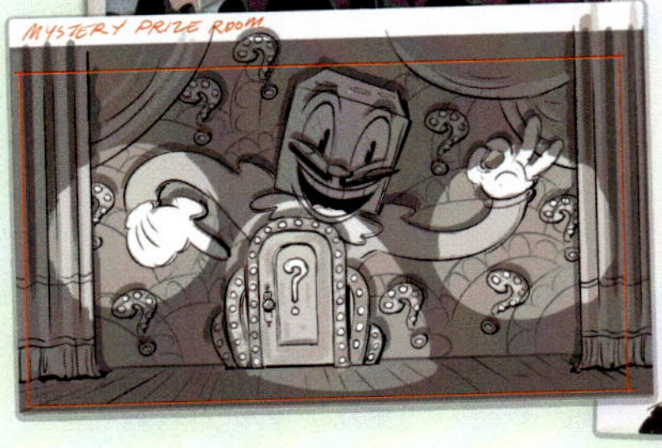

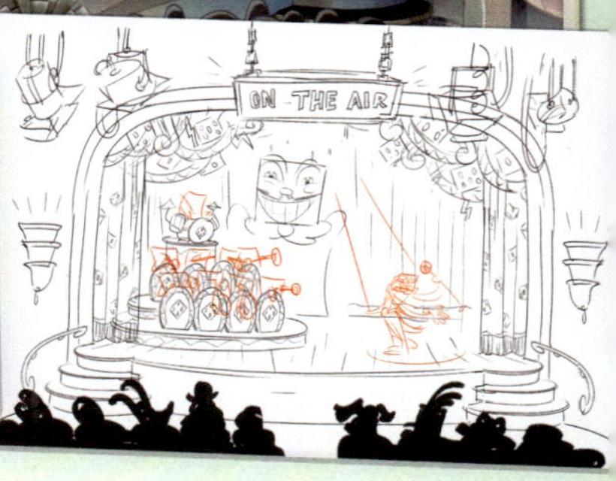

→ **ANDREA:** I could give Mallory an image and tell her the vibe that I want, like, "Let's try to achieve something that's nostalgic yet different," and she would immediately get on that wavelength.

MALLORY: I really like "Roll the Dice" a lot. Pretty much every piece was fun to do. The stage for King Dice's show is something I'm particularly proud of.

ANDREA: She had a really particular palette that just fit this show so well, and that really came out in "Roll the Dice."

Post-it sketches by Benjamin Arcand; previs sketch by Cosmo Segurson.

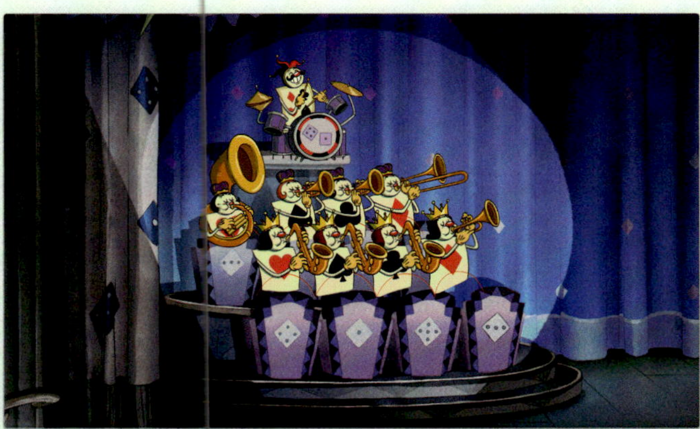

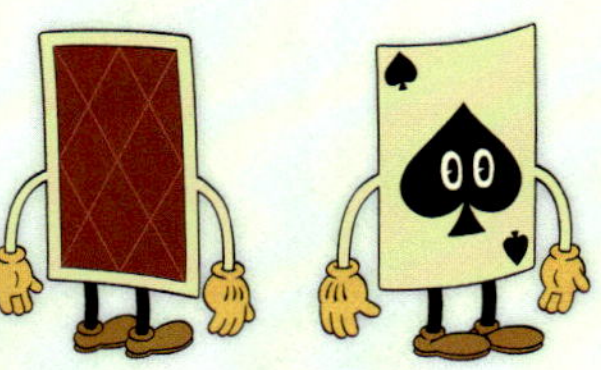

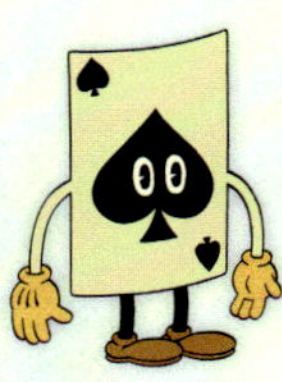

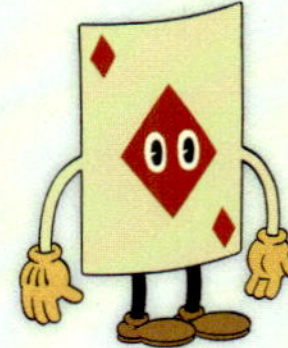

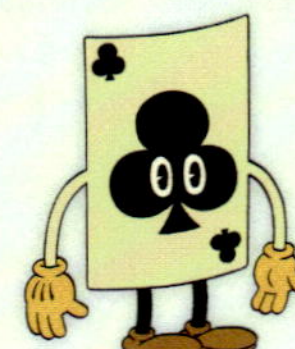

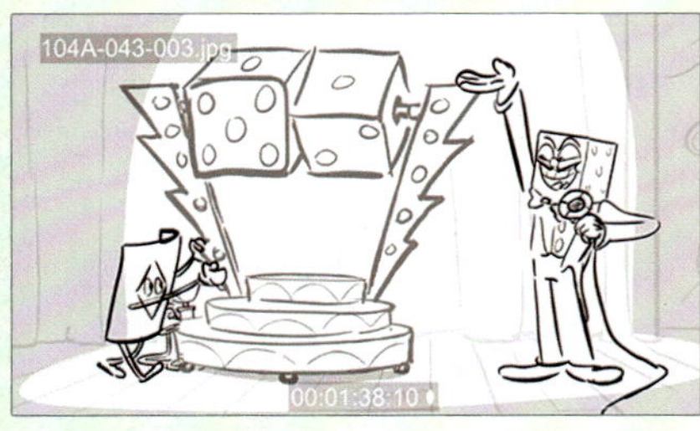

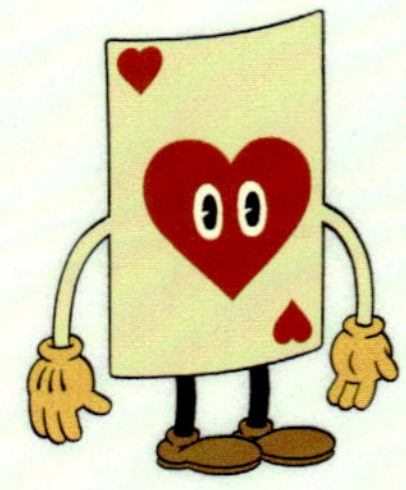

Storyboard panels by Benjamin Arcand; special pose designs by Tapan Gandhi and Adam Paloian; final background paintings by Mallory Carlson.

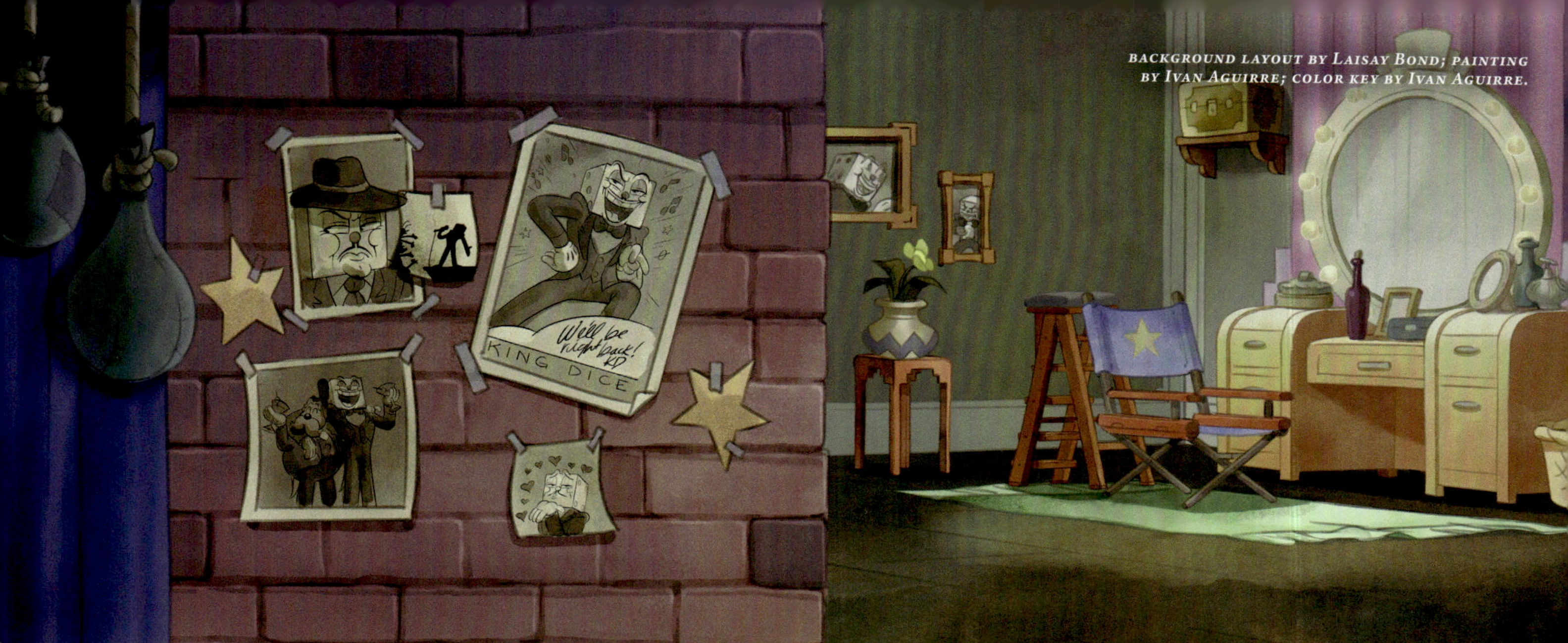

Background layout by Laisay Bond; painting by Ivan Aguirre; color key by Ivan Aguirre.

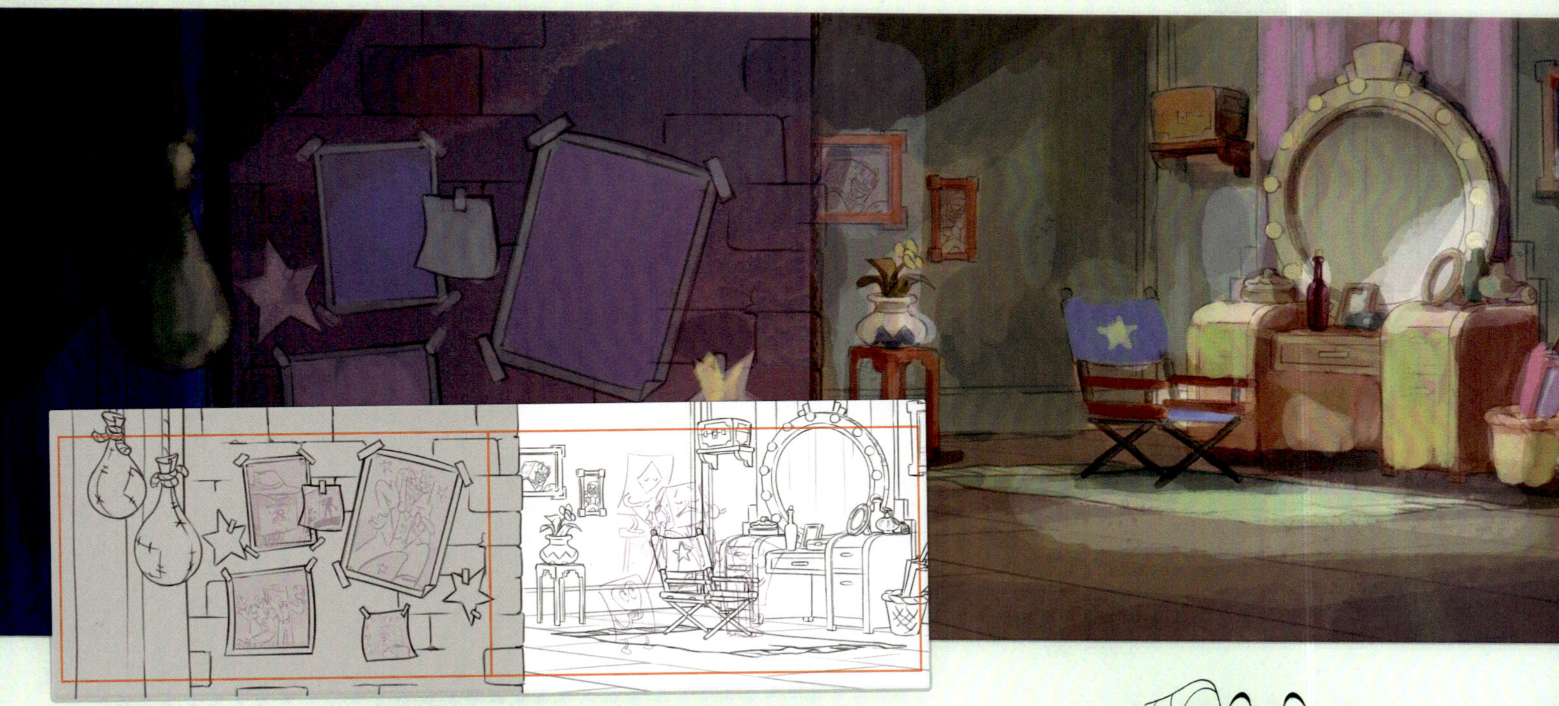

→ **DEEKI:** After focusing on Mugman in "Handle," we needed to put the spotlight on Cuphead. How does a Cuphead story feel different from a Mugman story? At the same time, we all wanted to introduce King Dice as soon as possible.

Storyboard panel by Benjamin Arcand.

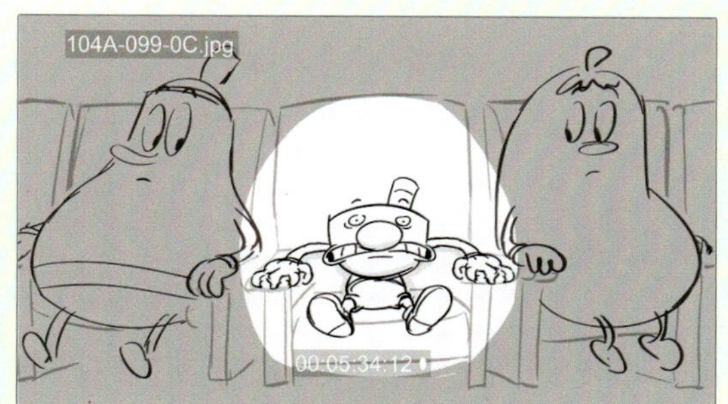

Special pose designs by Tapan Gandhi and Adam Paloian.

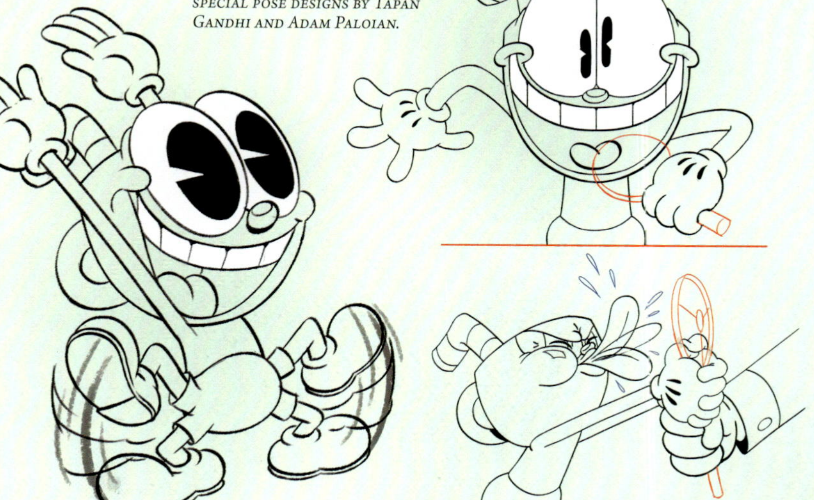

♦♠ INTRODUCING ♥♣
KING DICE

(VOICED BY WAYNE BRADY)

→ **ADAM P:** We didn't know much about King Dice from the video game, except that he's a villain, he worked for the Devil, he's smooth . . .

DAVE: King Dice and the Devil are both very dramatic and grandiose. So our problem became: how do we make them distinct from one another?

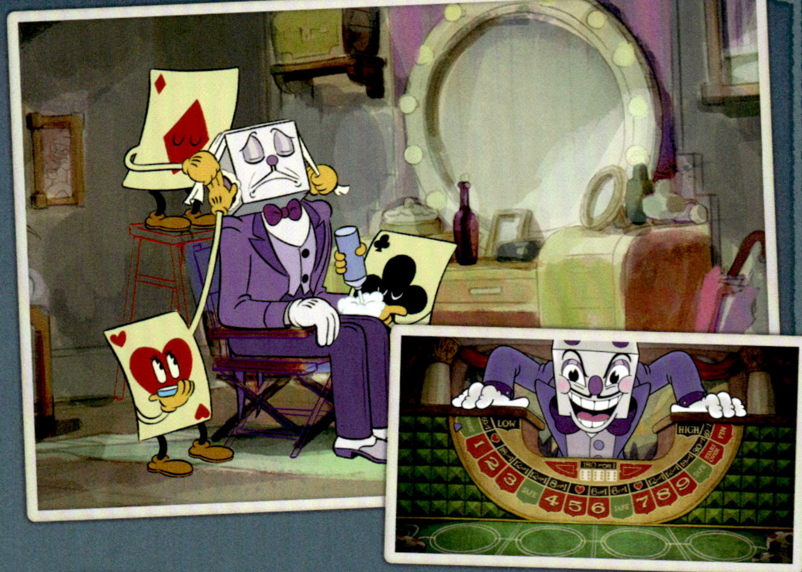

King Dice from Cuphead: Don't Deal with the Devil.

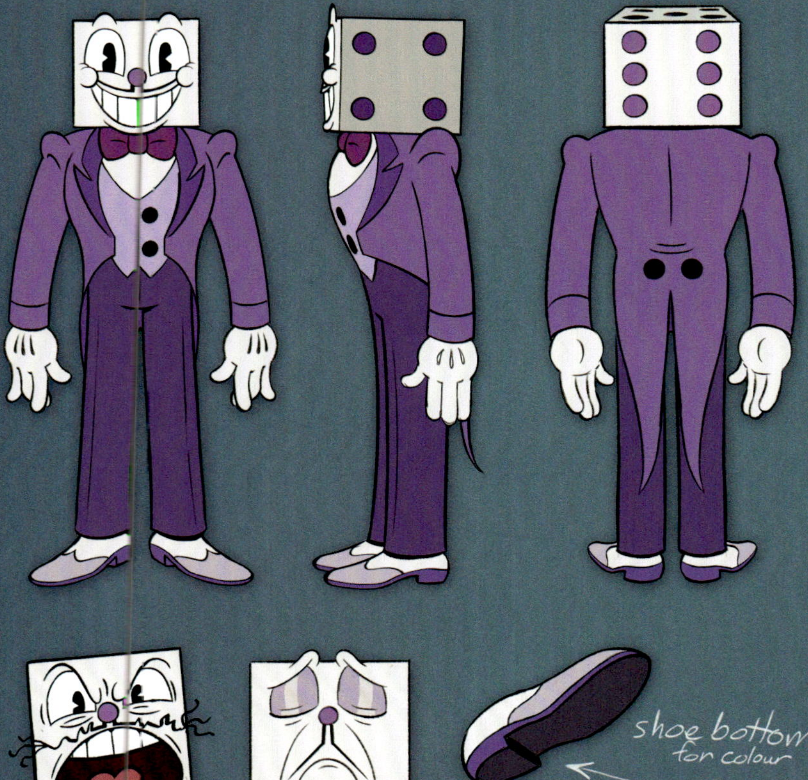

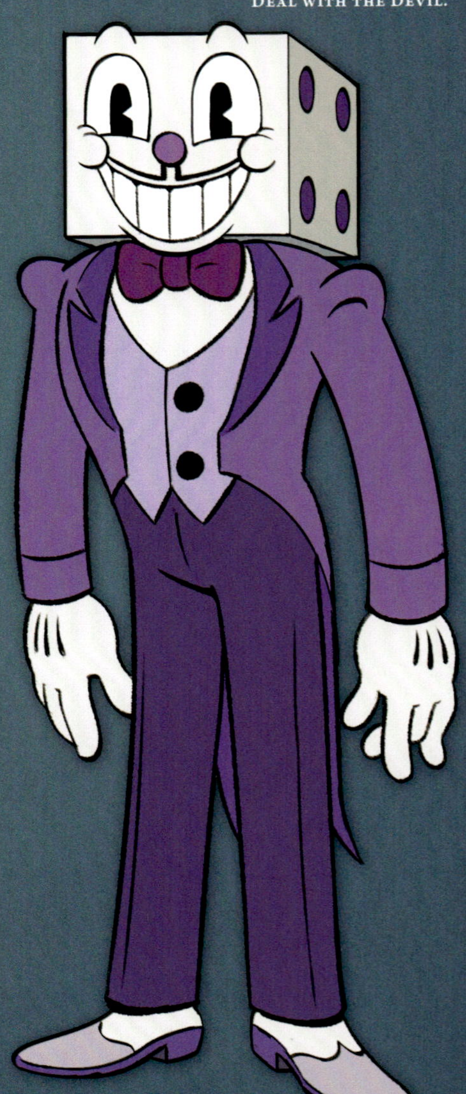

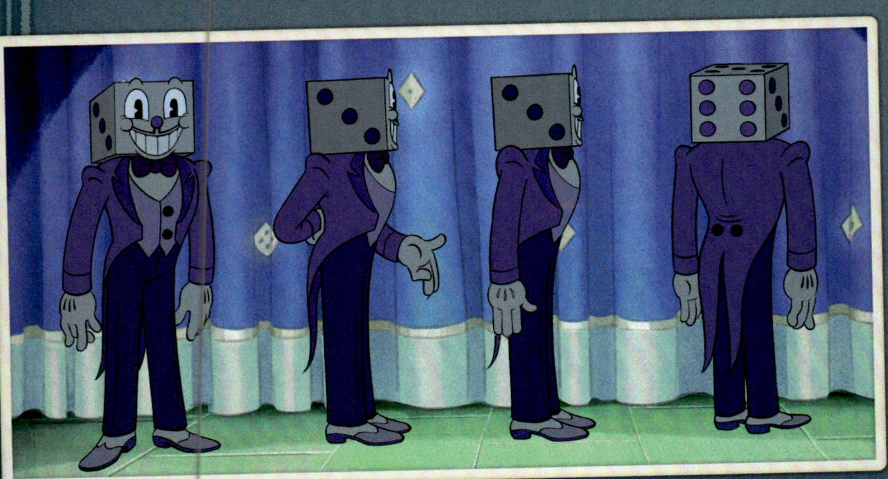

King Dice turnarounds by Tapan Gandhi and Adam Paloian; color design by Chris Hacker.

→ **DEEKI:** The Devil is impulsive and emotional, and King Dice is more conniving and calculating.

DAVE: King Dice is very slick, but ultimately, we couldn't let him succeed: that'd mean he captures Cuphead, the Devil wins in episode 5, and then we don't have a show.

DOS AND DON'TS BY ADAM PALOIAN.

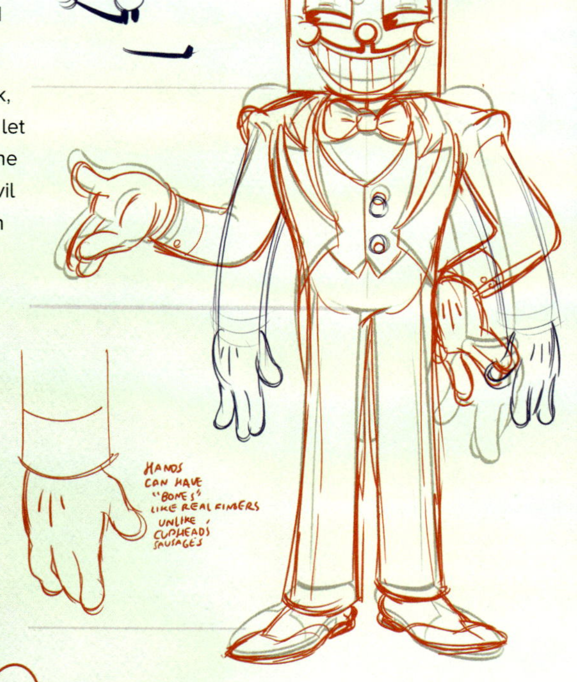

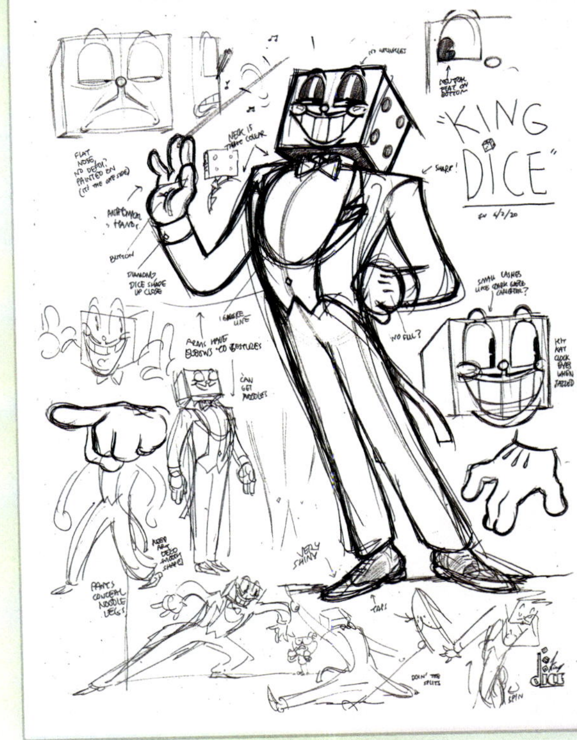

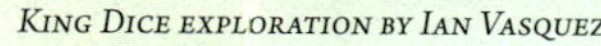
KING DICE EXPLORATION BY IAN VASQUEZ.

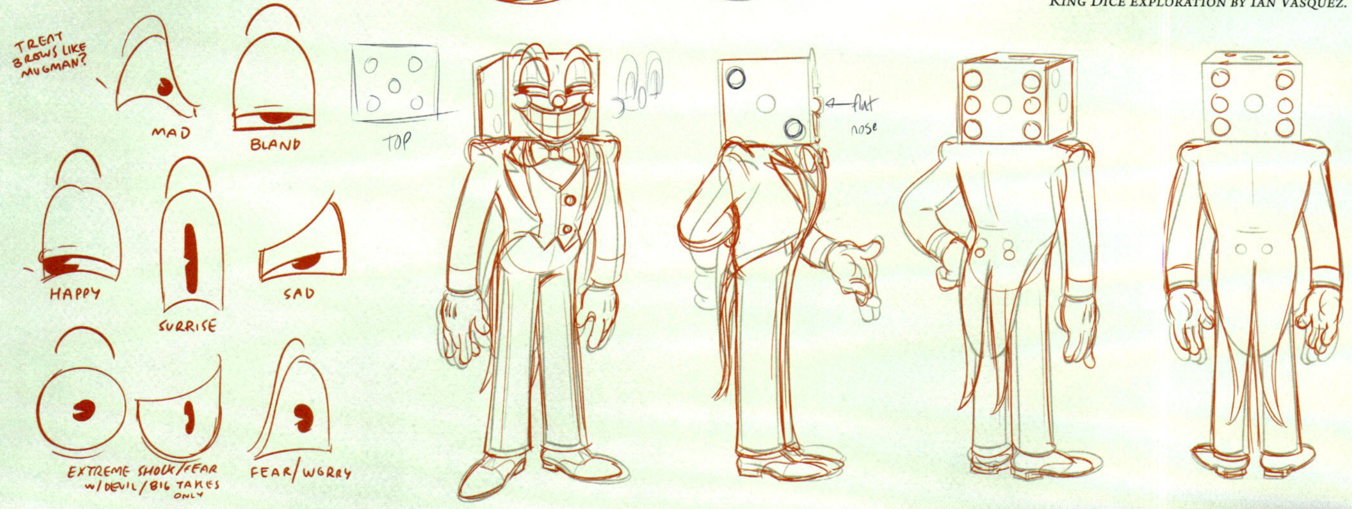

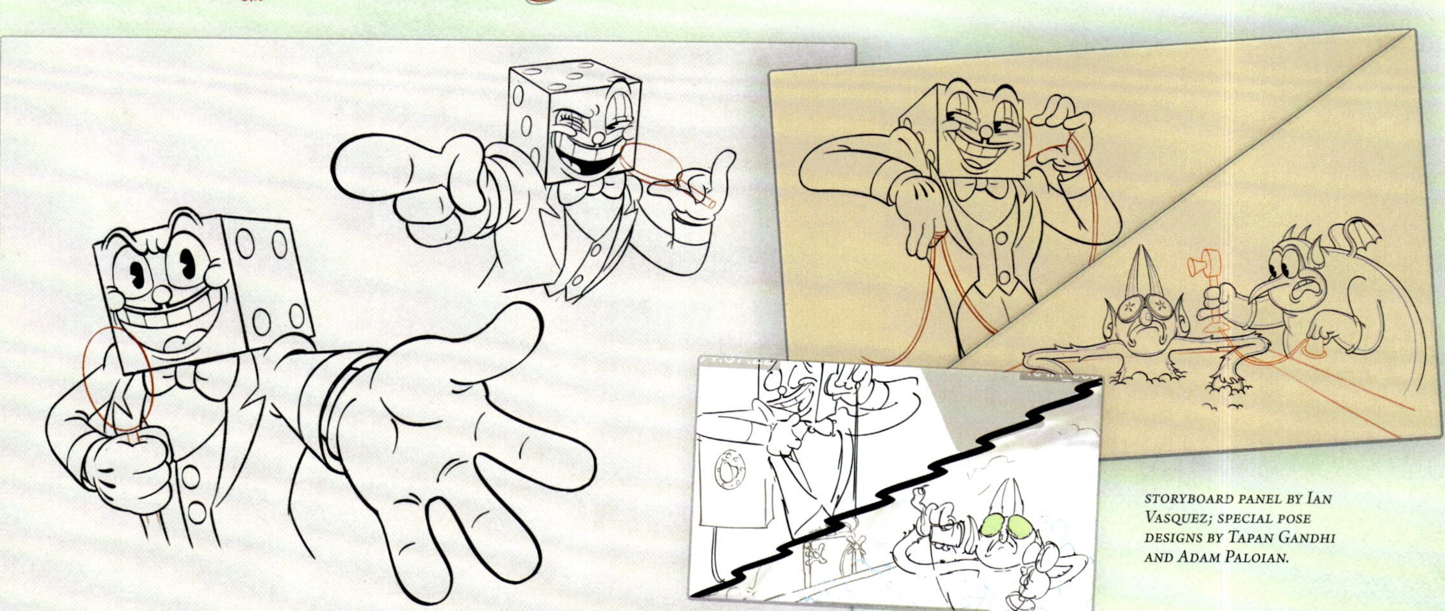
STORYBOARD PANEL BY IAN VASQUEZ; SPECIAL POSE DESIGNS BY TAPAN GANDHI AND ADAM PALOIAN.

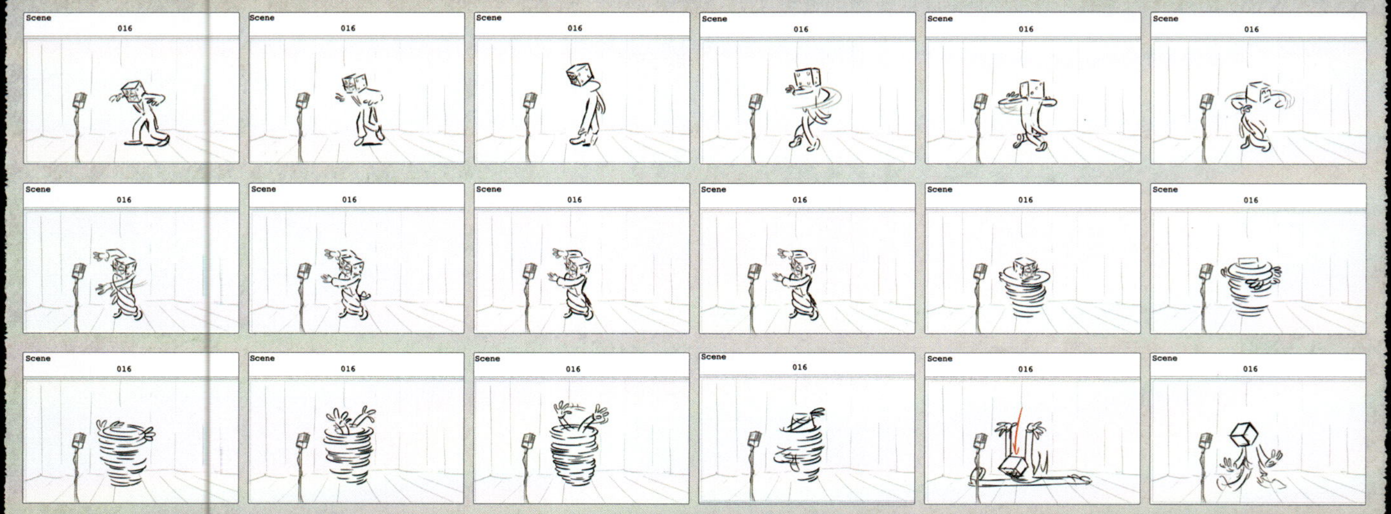

◆ STORYBOARD SPOTLIGHT ◆

AN HOMAGE TO ROTOSCOPE

DAVE: When we were first talking about King Dice, there was a thought that he'd be the one character who'd be rotoscoped. I thought we were going to have to film someone.

ADAM P: We were looking at Fleischer, where they did rotoscoping of dances, like in the old *Betty Boops*. That's how we wanted to introduce King Dice.

COSMO: Max and Dave Fleischer invented rotoscoping. They would bring a performer into a soundstage, hang up some curtains, and film them doing their moves. Then they'd project it onto a screen from below and trace over the live action frame by frame. Originally, it was a way to save time. But then it had such a unique look that they exaggerated the movements of the performers and stylized them into totally surreal creatures. I think that it went out of style because a lot of people within animation thought that was cheating. But to me it gives it another surreal edge that really messes with your mind as you look at it.

ADAM P: We wanted King Dice's entrance to feel as close to rotoscope as possible. Our board artist Benjamin did some really posed-out animation that evoked the feeling of that style.

COSMO: He overposed them, so when the animation comes back, it feels like rotoscope.

BENJAMIN ARCAND, *THE CUPHEAD SHOW!* STORYBOARD ARTIST: When I was doing the board, it was on twos or sometimes on fours—it was more key posing. There were in-betweens too, since it was a complex entrance.

DAVE: I couldn't believe how perfectly Benjamin executed it. It felt so authentic; I was blown away. I thought we'd get close, but I didn't think it'd be that spot on. It was everything I could have hoped for.

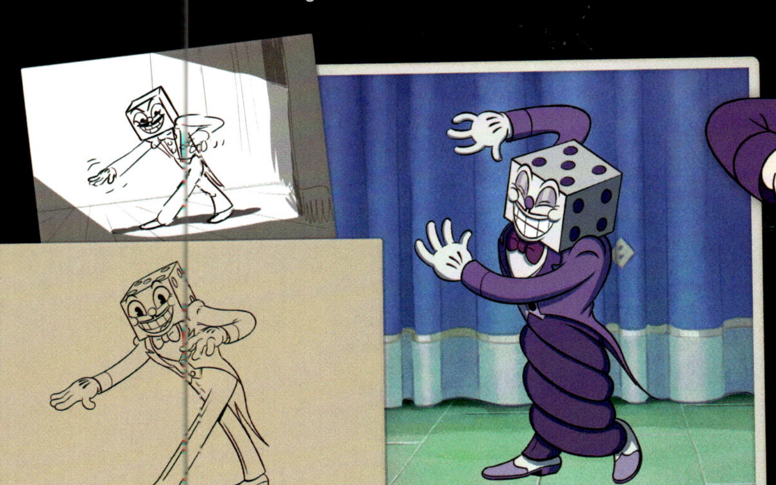

SPECIAL POSE DESIGN BY DAVE WASSON.

STORYBOARD PANELS BY BENJAMIN ARCAND; SPECIAL POSE DESIGNS BY TAPAN GANDHI.

→ **ANDREA:** I remember working on King Dice with Tapan and Adam [Paloian]. He had so many expression changes, and those 1930s expressions are so vital to the way characters look. Now, everything is a rig, so you're shuffling through a certain set of expressions. King Dice had so many of them that one of the suggestions I gave Tapan and Adam was to make just one head chart for him. He animated beautifully because of that.

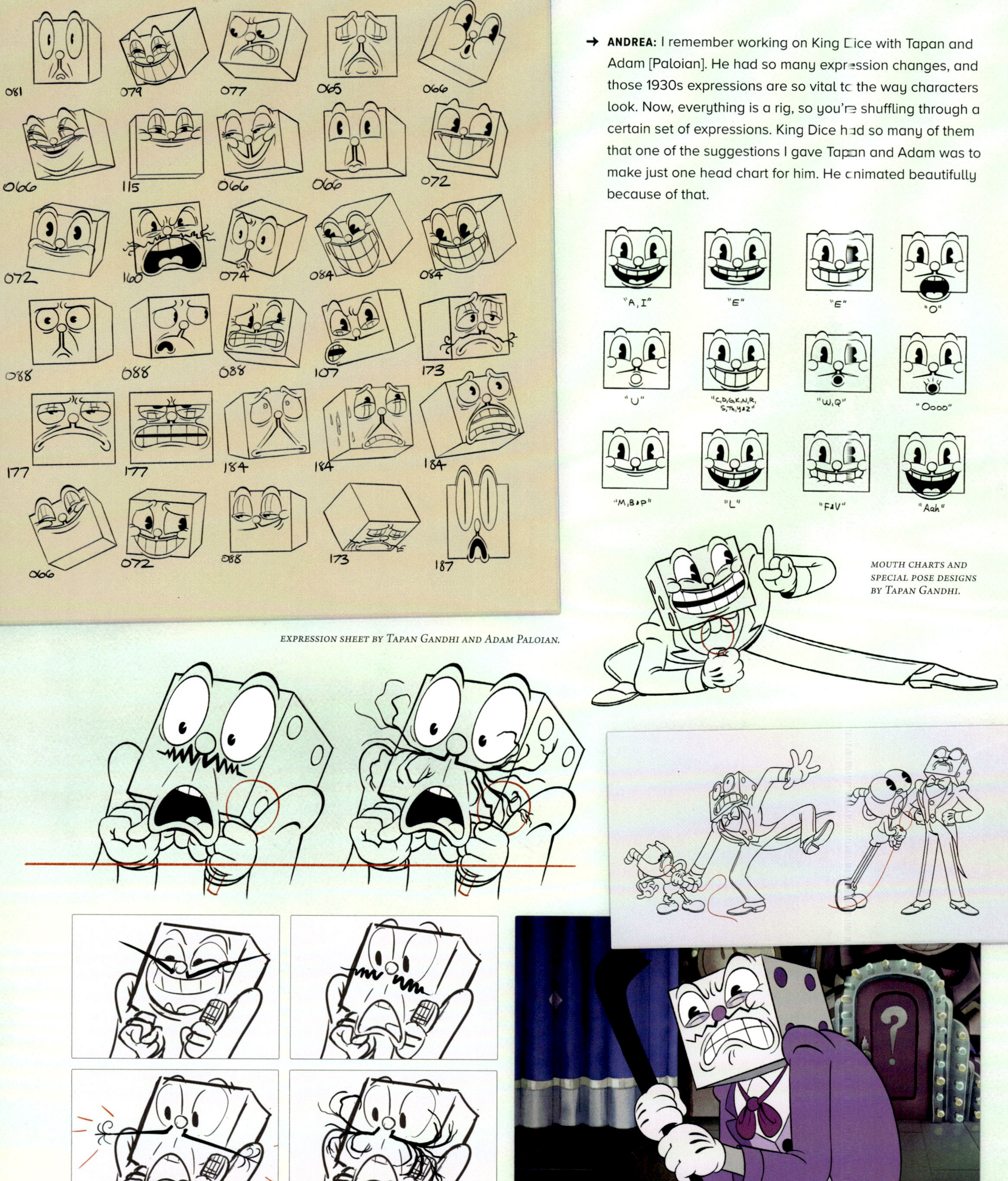

Expression sheet by Tapan Gandhi and Adam Paloian.

Mouth charts and special pose designs by Tapan Gandhi.

Storyboard panels by Benjamin Arcand.

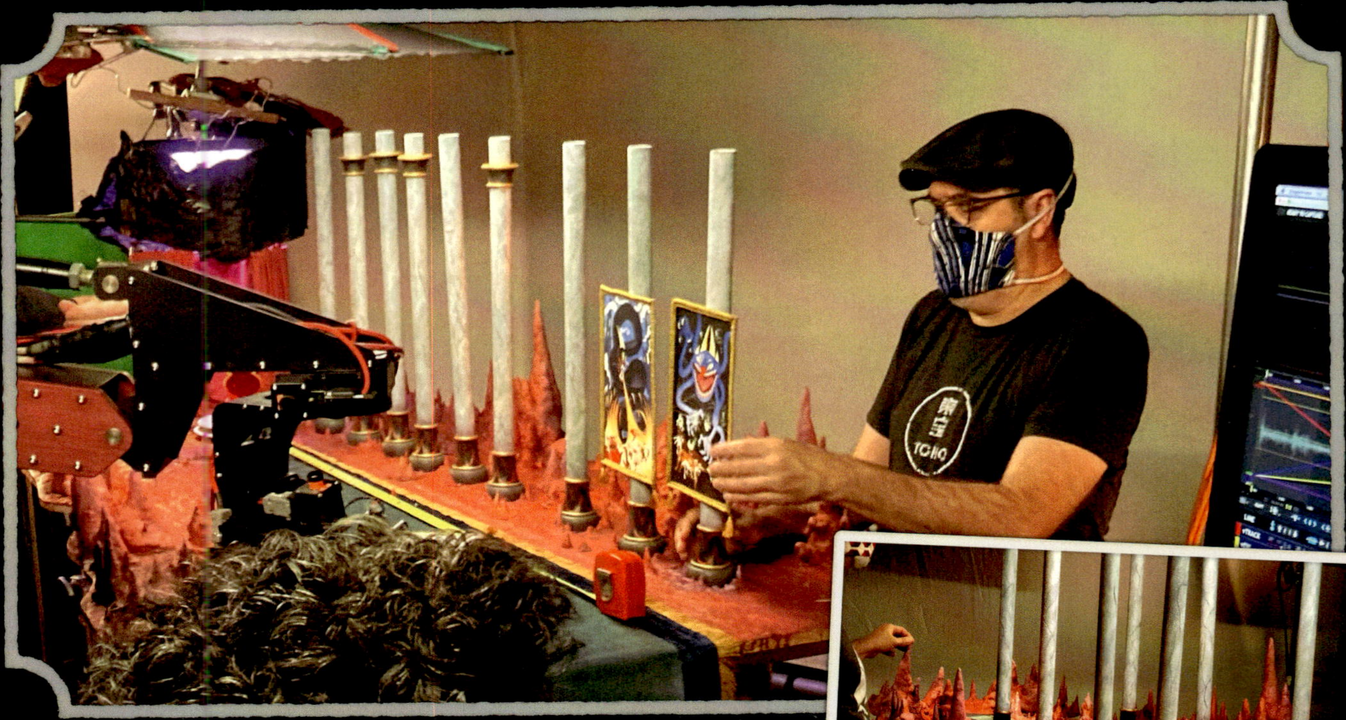

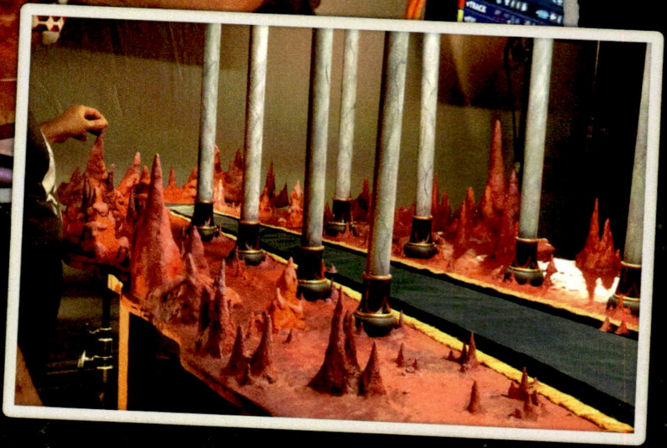

◆ STOP-MO SPOTLIGHT ◆

THE THRONE ROOM

SEAMUS: For King Dice's entrance into the throne room, we had to do multiple passes with the camera—it can't just be relegated to the background, because you need a foreground pass so King Dice can walk behind the column. You have to have multiple passes of things so characters can move through, which means lots of compositing. It's a weird combo of low tech and high tech.

MARK: We've done so many iterations of fire. Sometimes we'll shoot underneath a fan with ribbon attached, and the ribbon catches the light. Whenever possible, we try to shoot everything practical. Aaron Wise is our DP [director of photography], and he's a genius, helping us figure out the techy stuff that we don't always get. It was a combo of old and new school to make it work.

SEAMUS: We made some wheels with different fire colors. You take a little wheel of wire and cut out pieces of colored glass or lighting gels—get the most saturated ones you can and cut out organic shapes and test them out. You start to find color combos and intensity combos that give the feeling of a light flicker.

COSMO: There are happy accidents when two different components come together. Like when Screen Novelties puts that filter on the Devil's throne room set, where it looks like there's fire flickering on the columns, but there's obviously no 2D fire when they're filming it. But somehow, the 2D fire having its own pattern and the stop-motion set having its own flickering effect line up so beautifully—it's like magic, and it tricks your eye into thinking that light is coming from that fire.

SEAMUS: There's fire flicker in the 2D footage, so a certain amount of that is your brain: if we just insert a flicker into our lighting, your brain will put those two things together, so you can actually get away with quite a bit.

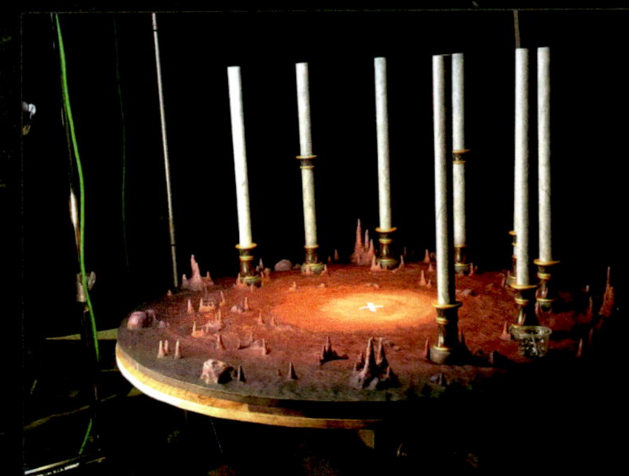

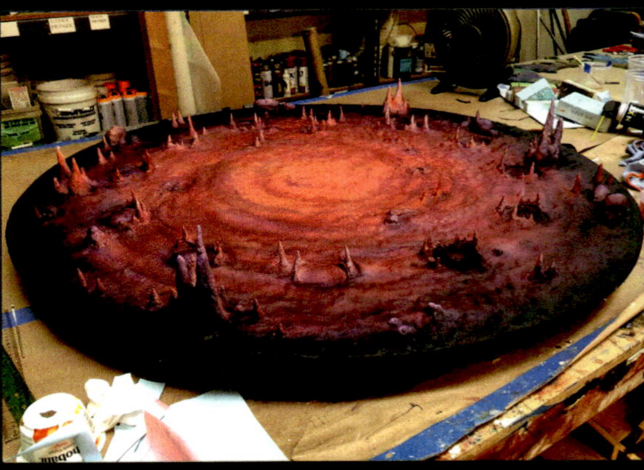

PRODUCTION STILLS OF STOP-MO GRAVEYARD SET BY SCREEN NOVELTIES.

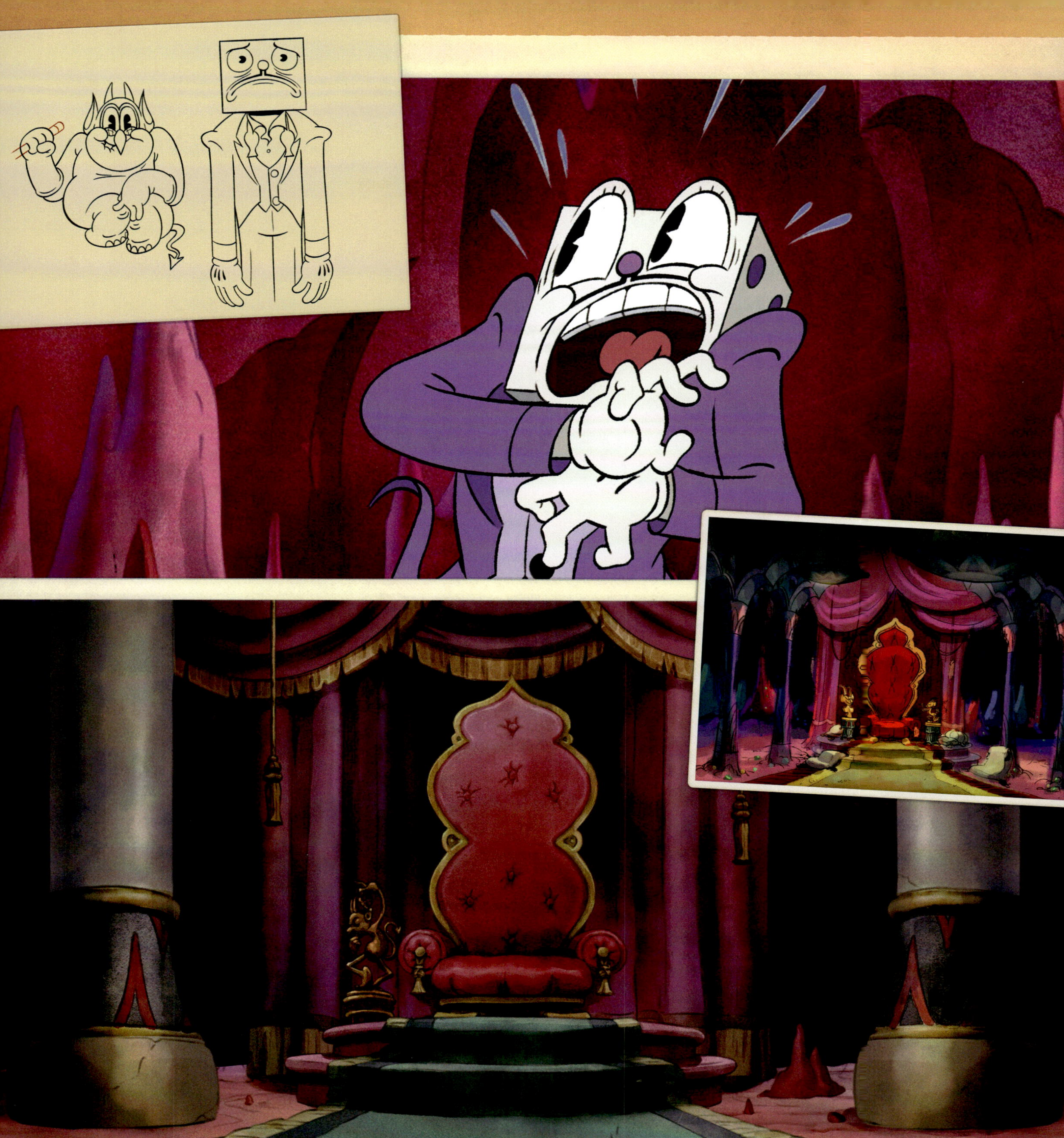

→ **ANDREA:** King Dice was one of our more successful characters, because we actually went in there and took those expressions from the board—beautiful drawings to begin with from Adam and Benjamin—and then [we were] creating it for a pipeline that's not friendly to this amount of drawings in a rig, but doing it in a way that the overseas team could access it. We were trying to streamline that process so you could actually see all those expressions onscreen.

Special pose designs by Tapan Gandhi; throne color key by Ivan Aguirre; final background design by Lauren Duda; painting by Ivan Aguirre.

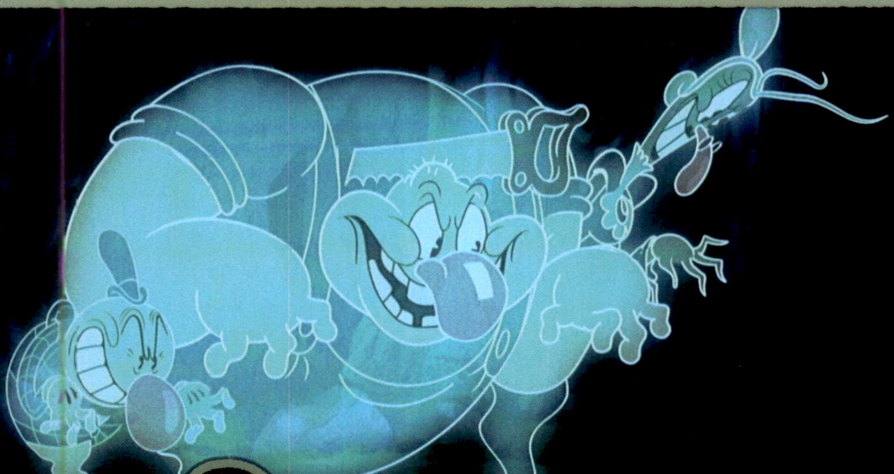

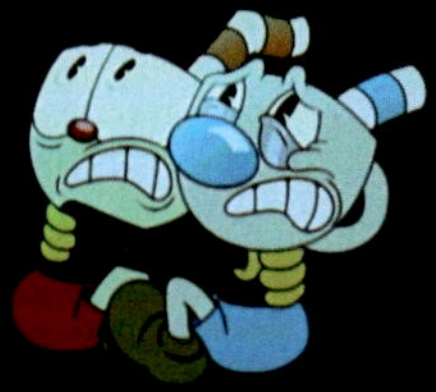

EPISODE 6
"GHOSTS AIN'T REAL!"

DEEP DIVE

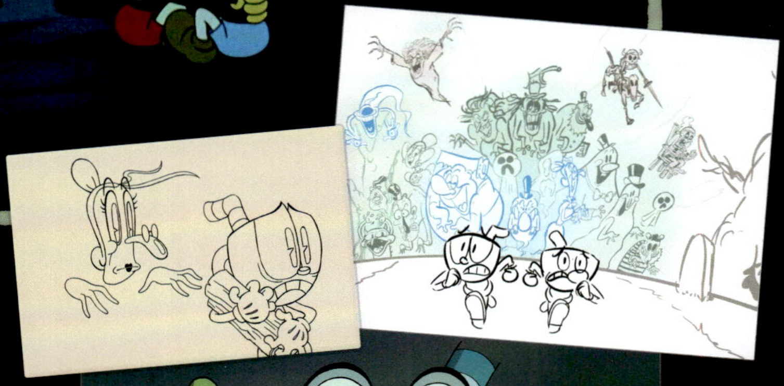

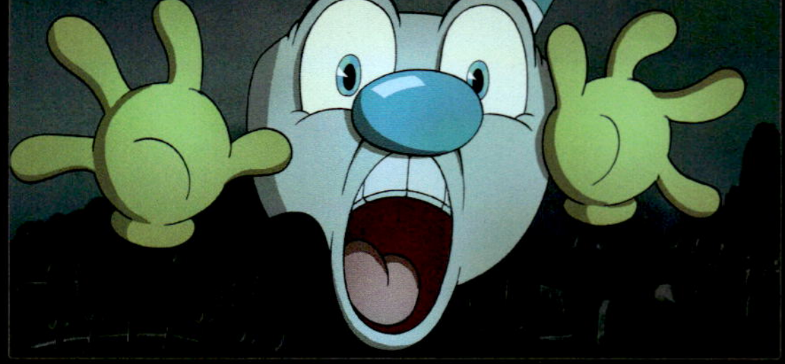

→ **ANDREA:** When the episodes are an event, when they create their own little world—like "Ghosts Ain't Real!"—that's awesome, because it gives me so much freedom to go wild.

LAISAY: "Ghosts Ain't Real!" was my favorite episode to work on. We really pushed the style in that one.

DAVE: This episode is one that every member of the team gave a bit extra on. Adam and the board team, Andrea and the whole art team, everybody at Screen Novelties, the animators at Lighthouse, and everyone else who touched it.

Special pose designs by Tapan Gandhi, Adam Fay, Adam Paloian, and Dave Wasson.

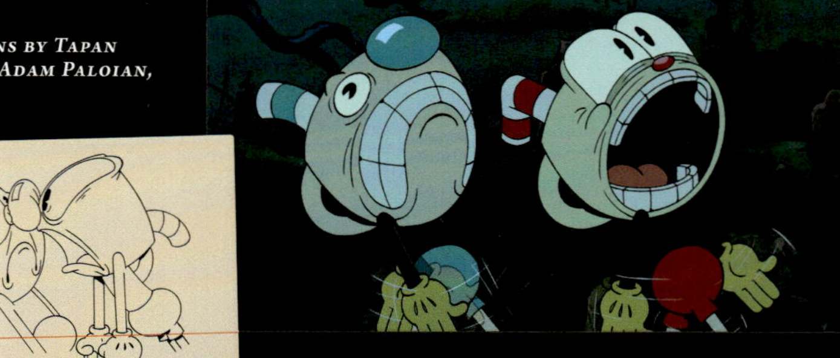

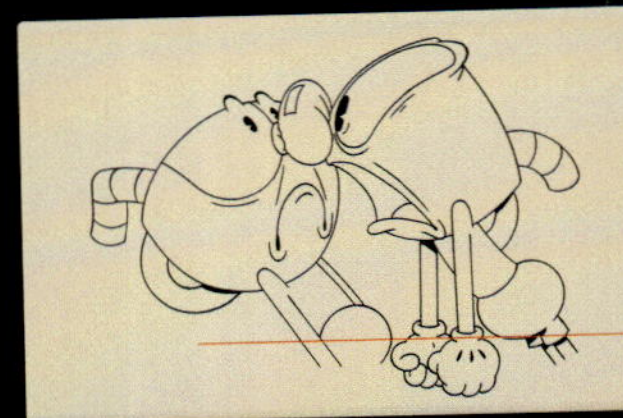

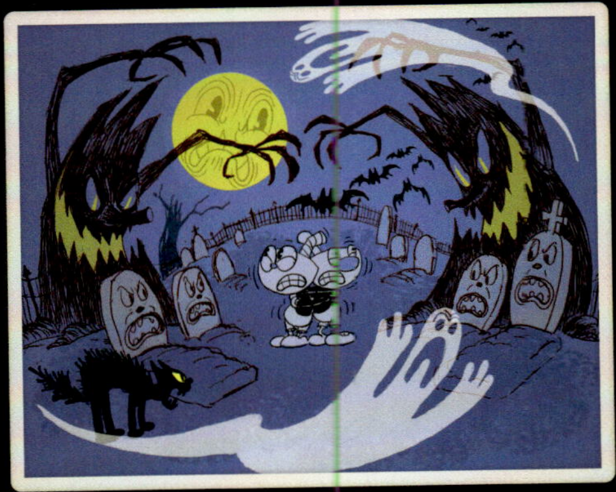

Dave Wasson's very first Cuphead drawing ever.

→ **DAVE:** When I was auditioning for the job, I did a few drawings to demonstrate the kinds of ideas we could explore for stories. The very first drawing I ever did was Cuphead and Mugman in a graveyard surrounded by bats and ghosts. I thought if we're going to do a cartoon series that looks like it was made in the 1930s, one of them has to have spooky stuff. That was such a prominent theme of cartoons from that era.

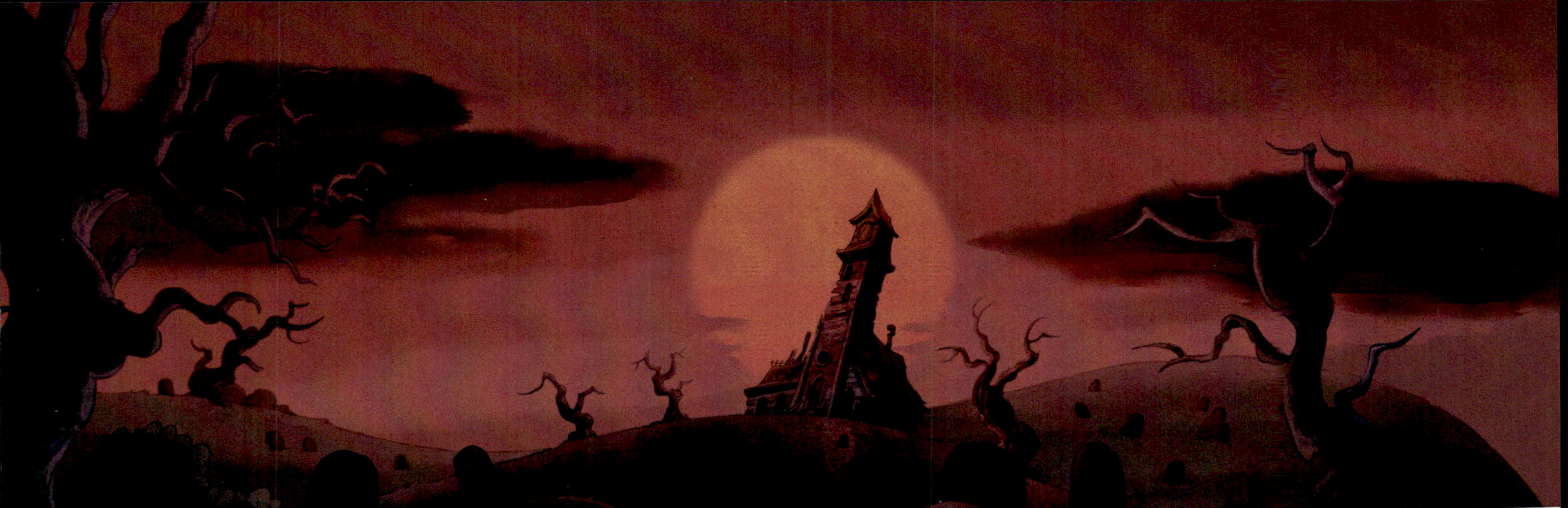

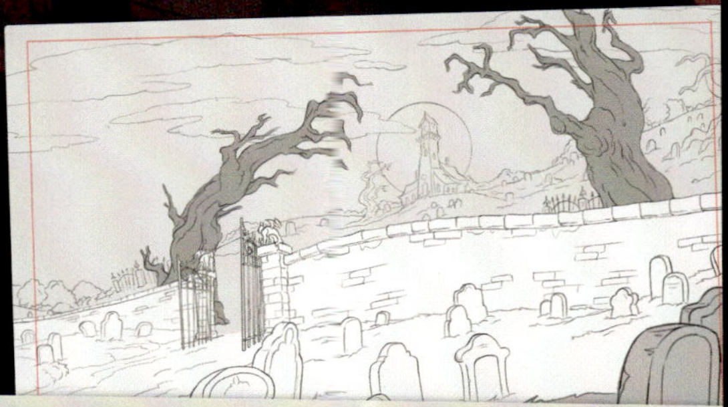

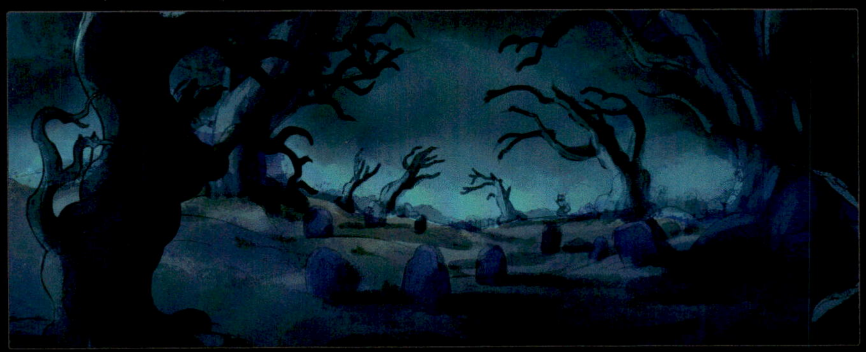

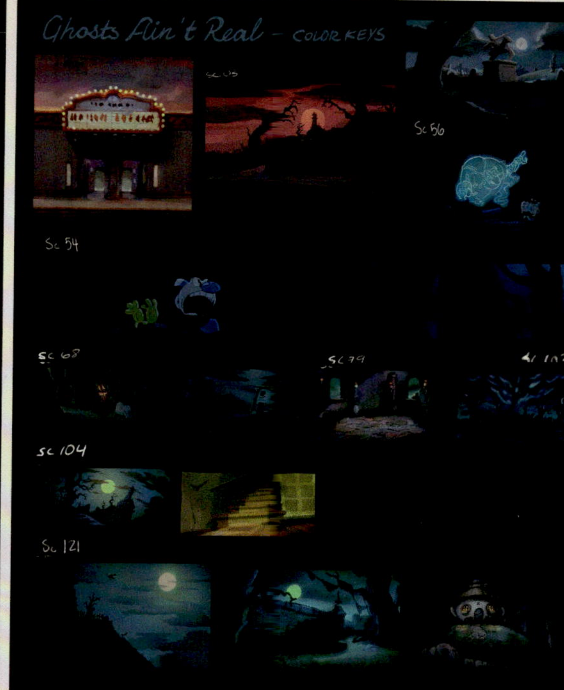

→ **COSMO:** Back in the 1930s, it was part of the culture to poke fun at death. It goes as far back as "London Bridge Is Falling Down"—a lot of those cutesy kids' songs are about death.

CJ: Early on, Cosmo and Dave spent a lot of time with the team, having everyone watch old cartoons so they could understand the history and the style of the golden age of animation, get the vibe, and learn about the ethos of that era. That was enormously valuable to the authenticity and reverence of the entire series.

CHAD: One of my earliest memories as a kid is watching *The Skeleton Dance* [1929] on an old VHS tape—it's monstery and fun but still has a dark and creepy edge to it that was unlike anything else available for kids our age at the time.

JARED: That's the kind of stuff we were steeped in, really, because we didn't even have cable! We had three channels and a VCR. So when it came time to watch something, we had to dive into our parents' collection of tapes—these classic, eerie, quirky cartoons sort of became our default TV channels in a way.

COSMO: There was a *Popeye* cartoon they'd show on TV called *Shiver Me Timbers* [1934], and I was always waiting for that one. It had such anarchy with the ghosts—and the ghosts don't really have much character in that one. There's some bizarre moments that really twist your mind. I remember thinking, "Where is this going?! How on earth is this going to wrap up?!"

BACKGROUND DESIGNS BY LAISAY BOND; PAINTINGS BY GREGORY MILLER AND IVAN AGUIRRE.

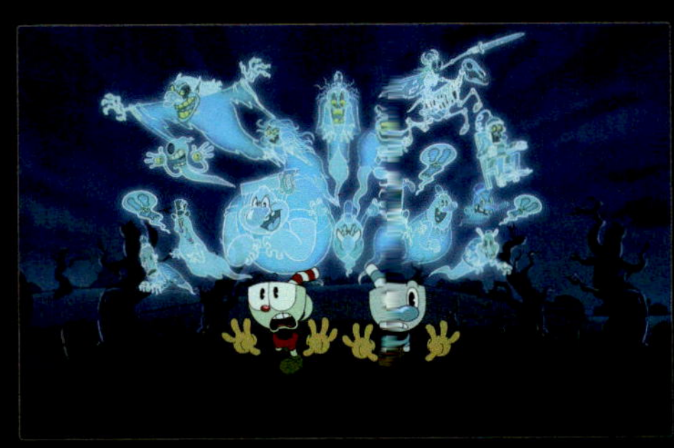

SPECIAL POSE DESIGNS BY ADAM PALOIAN AND DAVE WASSON.

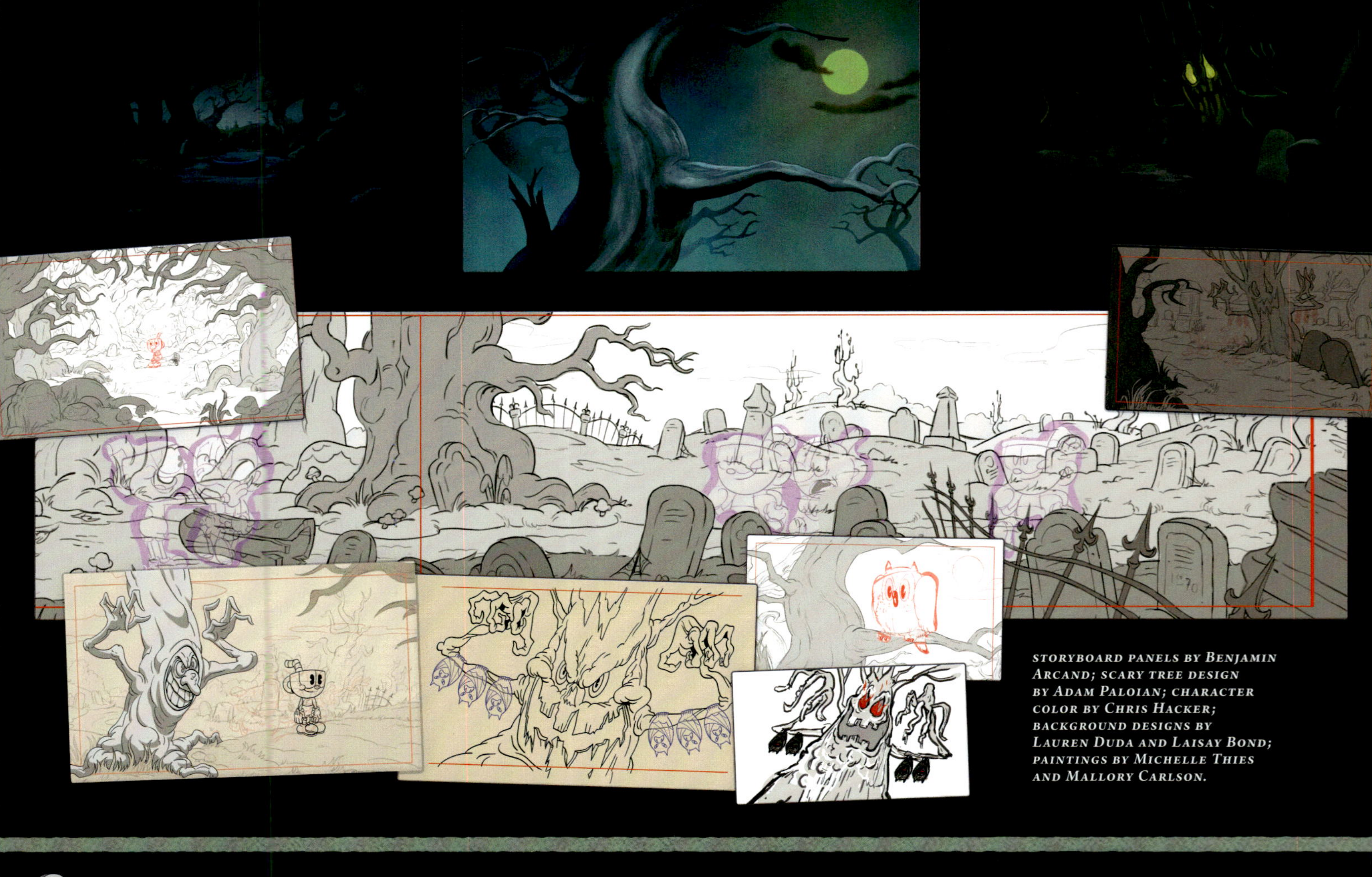

Storyboard panels by Benjamin Arcand; scary tree design by Adam Paloian; character color by Chris Hacker; background designs by Lauren Duda and Laisay Bond; paintings by Michelle Thies and Mallory Carlson.

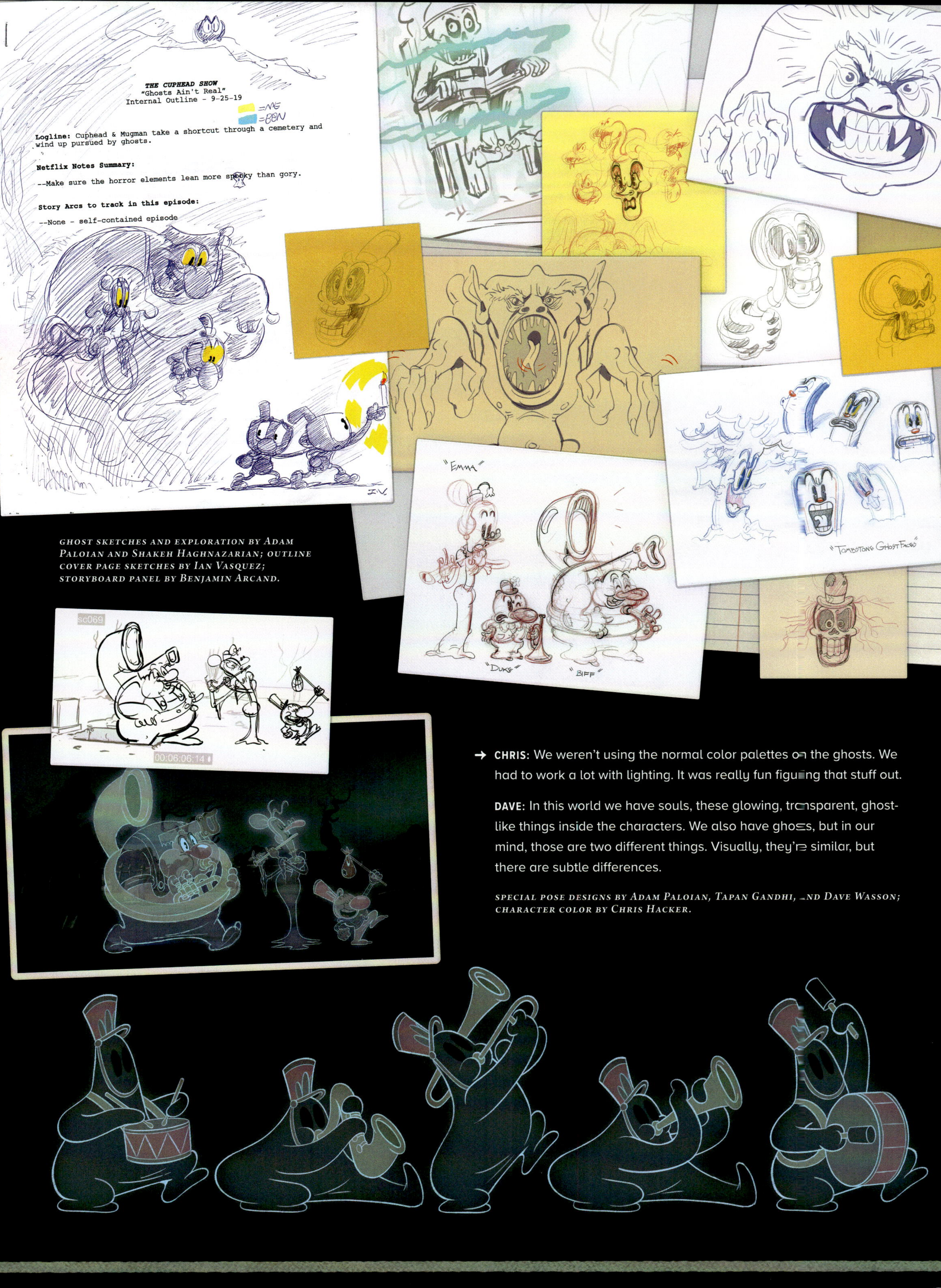

THE CUPHEAD SHOW
"Ghosts Ain't Real"
Internal Outline - 9-25-19

Logline: Cuphead & Mugman take a shortcut through a cemetery and wind up pursued by ghosts.

Netflix Notes Summary:

--Make sure the horror elements lean more spooky than gory.

Story Arcs to track in this episode:

--None - self-contained episode

Ghost sketches and exploration by Adam Paloian and Shakeh Haghnazarian; outline cover page sketches by Ian Vasquez; storyboard panel by Benjamin Arcand.

→ **CHRIS:** We weren't using the normal color palettes on the ghosts. We had to work a lot with lighting. It was really fun figuring that stuff out.

DAVE: In this world we have souls, these glowing, transparent, ghost-like things inside the characters. We also have ghosts, but in our mind, those are two different things. Visually, they're similar, but there are subtle differences.

Special pose designs by Adam Paloian, Tapan Gandhi, and Dave Wasson; character color by Chris Hacker.

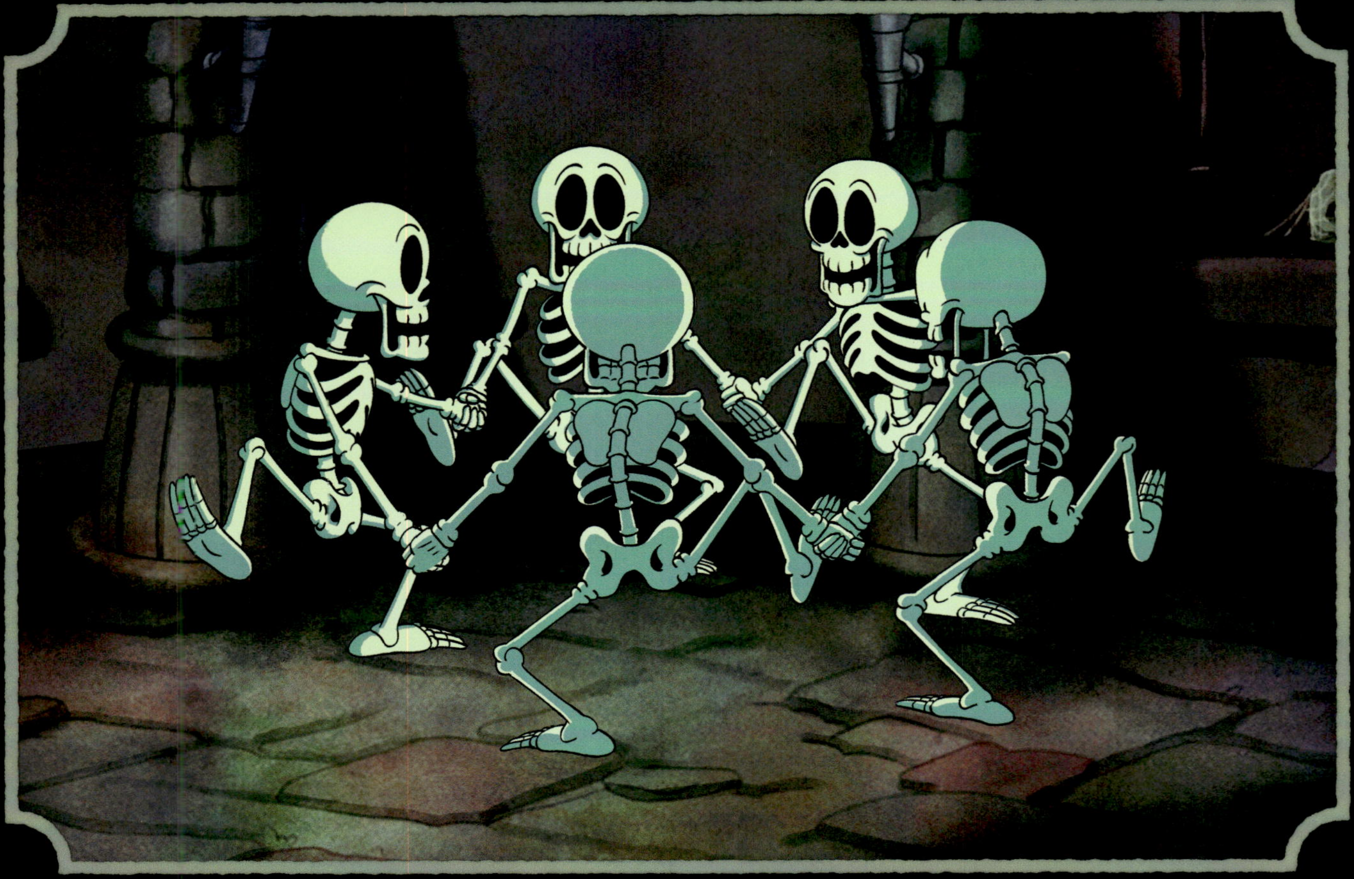

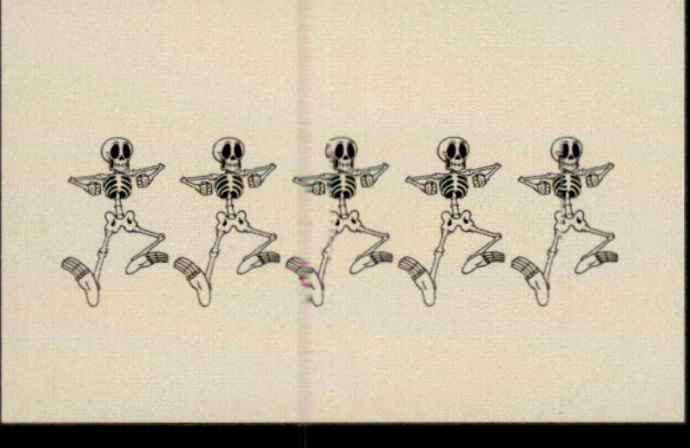

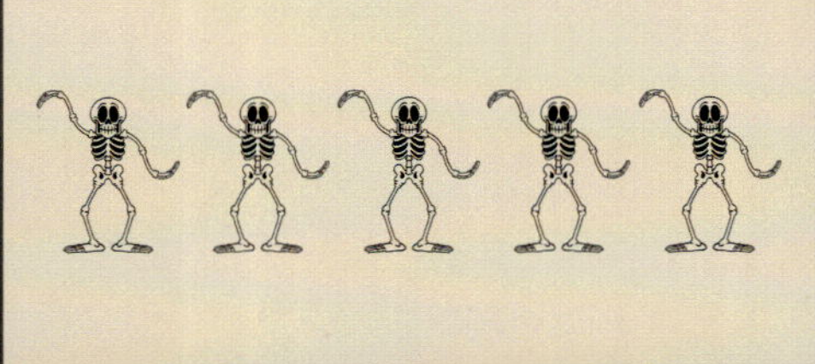

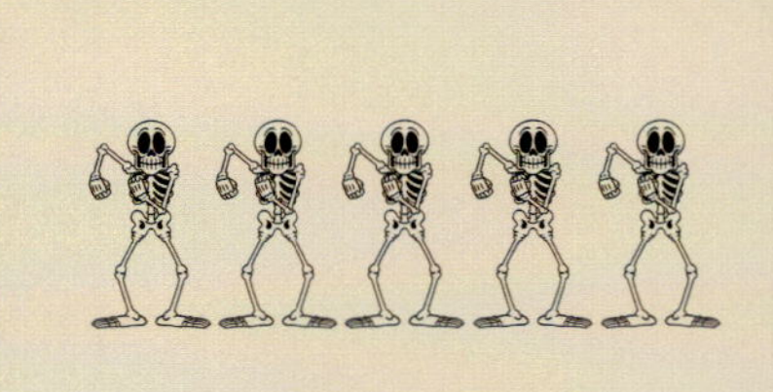

→ **COSMO:** I was thinking about *The Skeleton Dance*. There is no story whatsoever—it's pure atmosphere and sight gags set to music through this macabre lens.

DEEKI: The story had to be very simple. The goal is just to escape with their lives. This isn't a character-driven episode as much as it's a character-infused episode driven by the visuals.

DAVE: A lot of those cartoons from the 1930s are really just crazy fever dreams, where it wasn't really a story—it was more just a series of events that you're watching.

DEEKI: They'd have incredible images, great music, stunning animation, and mind-melting surreal gags—but the endings were usually pretty abrupt, without any real payoff. We wanted to evoke the feeling of a 1930s-style spooky chase, but we also wanted things to get real. The clock tower felt like the right setting for that kind of climactic moment.

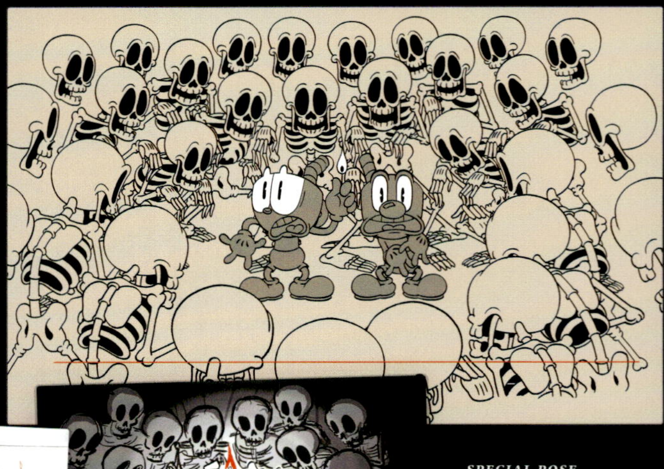

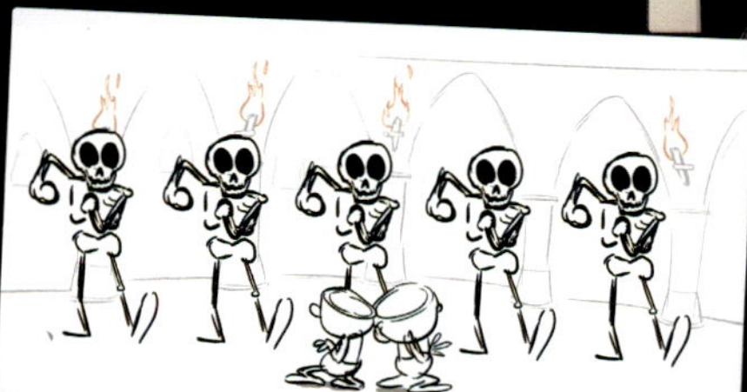

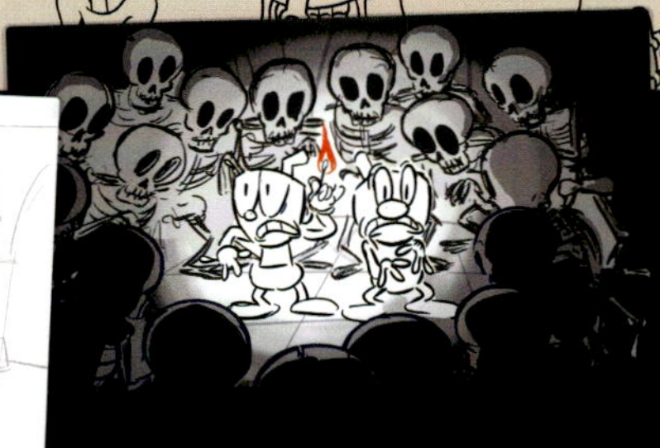

Special pose designs by Adam Fay and Dave Wasson; storyboard panels by Benjamin Arcand.

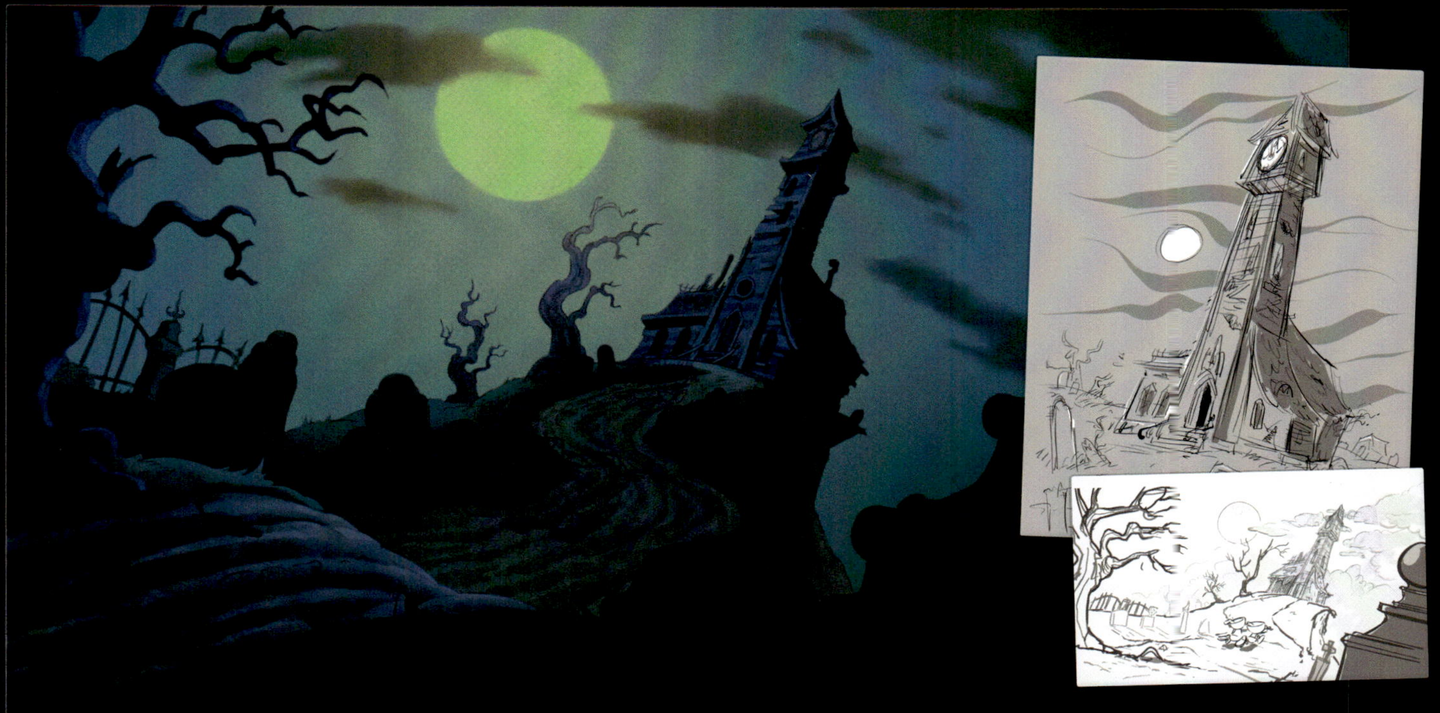

Clock tower previs by Cosmo Segurson; color script by Mallory Carlson.

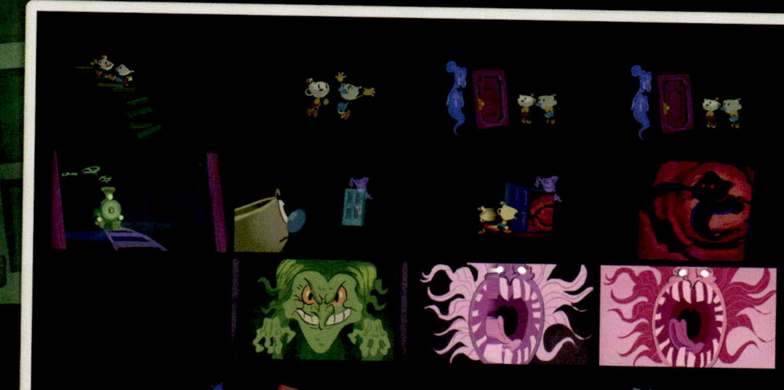

→ **LAISAY:** The clock tower layout in particular was really fun. I did one of a path leading up to the clock tower, and it kind of gives me the creeps. Sometimes it's fun to creep yourself out.

COSMO: The clock tower became a focal point within the architecture of the cemetery. I liked the idea that when the clock strikes midnight, something is going to happen. That was a subconscious idea, but it gave us a literal clock, and we instinctively sense that something will change at midnight.

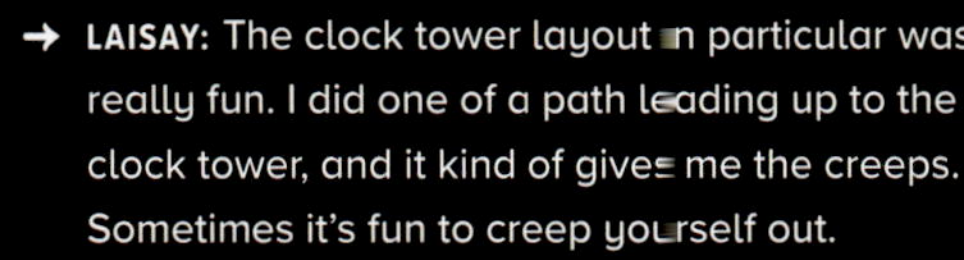

Storyboard panels by Benjamin Arcand; background designs by Laisay Bond; paintings by Gregory Miller and Ivan Aguirre.

BACKGROUND DESIGN BY LAUREN DUDA; PAINTING BY MALLORY CARLSON.

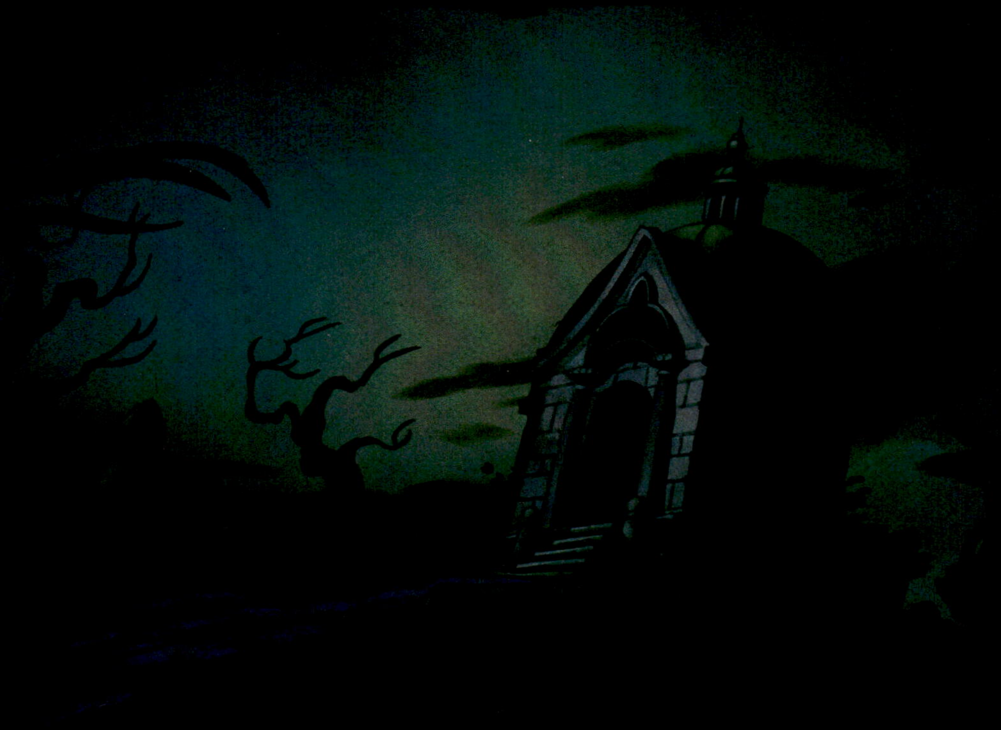

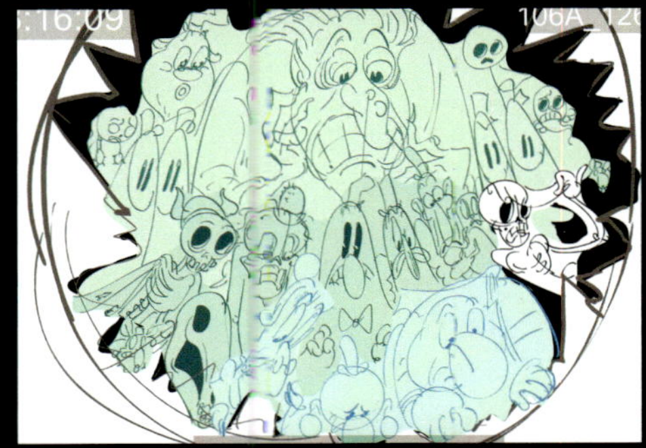

→ **COSMO:** Deeki pitched an ending that I found terrifying, where the ghosts chase Cuphead and Mugman to the top of the clock tower; they smash through the glass and then fall to their deaths. The ghosts actually think that Cuphead and Mugman died! I was surprised we got away with that.

DAVID "BABY DAVE" FONSECA, *THE CUPHEAD SHOW!* PRODUCTION ASSISTANT: I remember saying, "Oh wow, we're getting away with that—amazing!" And everyone whispering, "Yeah, we *are* getting away with that, don't bring it up, just go with it!"

COSMO: The anthropomorphic stylization of the characters let us push the boundaries. If they were human children, I do not think we'd be able to show them pretending to be dead in a graveyard at the end of a silly romp. The fact that they have cups and mugs for heads . . . We can get away with a lot more.

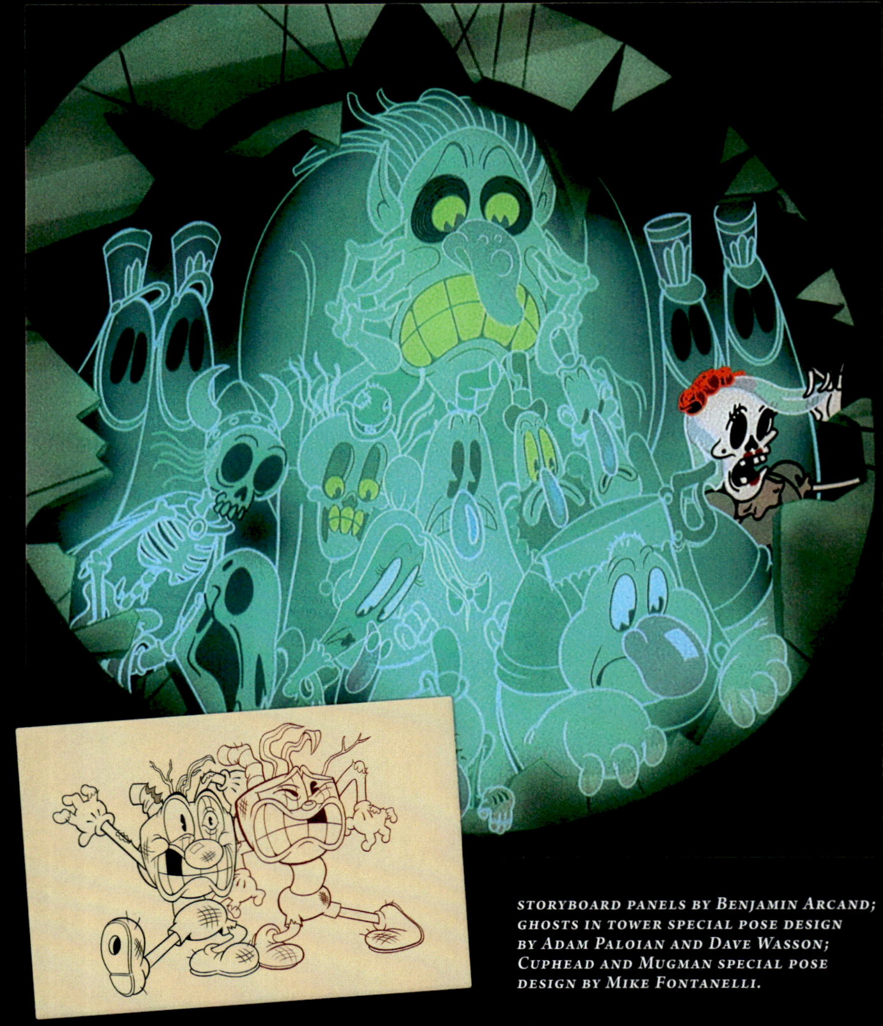

STORYBOARD PANELS BY BENJAMIN ARCAND; GHOSTS IN TOWER SPECIAL POSE DESIGN BY ADAM PALOIAN AND DAVE WASSON; CUPHEAD AND MUGMAN SPECIAL POSE DESIGN BY MIKE FONTANELLI.

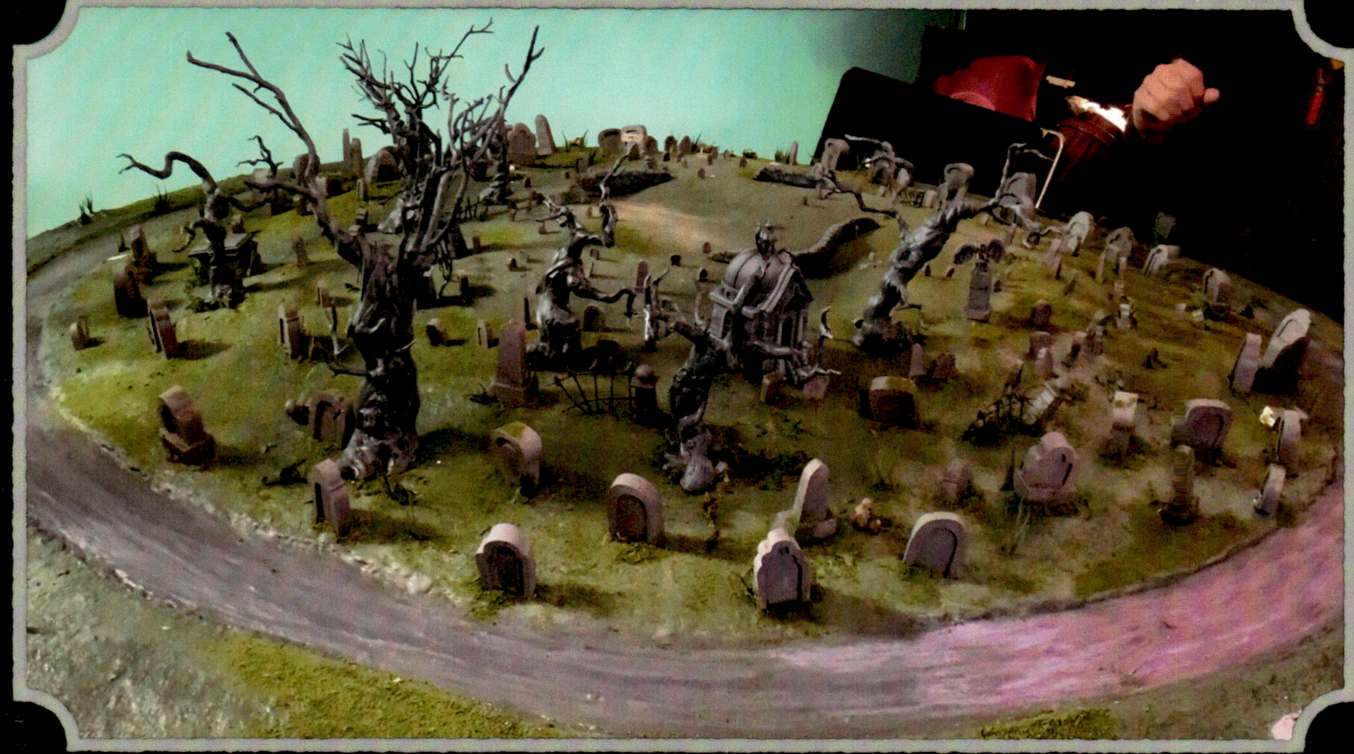

COSMO: Those headstones are only about an inch tall, but they feel so much larger when Screen Novelties shoots them a certain way with a certain lens.

DEEKI: The "gradually accelerating run" scene came from Clay's pitch in the story room.

DAVE: When Clay first acted out the idea of them trying to play it cool, walking faster and faster but getting more freaked out, we were laughing out loud. We kept it exactly the way he first pitched it.

DEEKI: It's a timing joke, in both dialogue and physicality, which is enough of a challenge.

COSMO: And on top of that, there's a 3D stop-motion background that's moving at the same speed.

DAVE: It was a big effort to get the vocal performances to build in united momentum, especially since it was the height of the pandemic, and we weren't able to record the actors together. On top of that, the walk cycles go from a normal walk to almost sprinting, and it's all happening in one shot.

STOP-MO SPOTLIGHT

THE GRAVEYARD

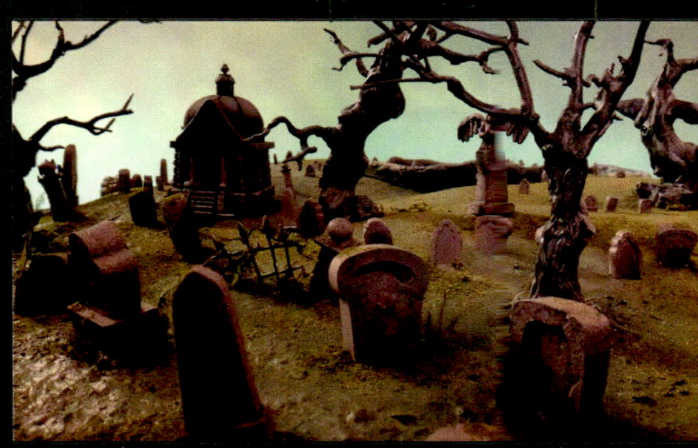

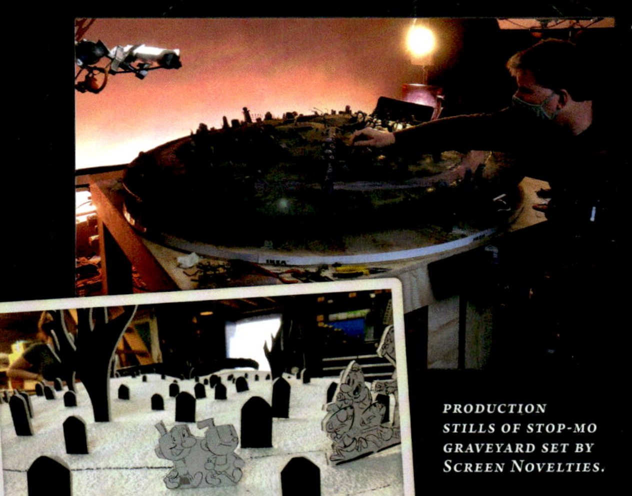

PRODUCTION STILLS OF STOP-MO GRAVEYARD SET BY SCREEN NOVELTIES.

COSMO: In the 1930s, the Fleischers used a technique where they'd build a miniature set on a disk and put the camera in front of it to make it feel like the landscape is going by, right to left.

MARK: We built the graveyard on a motorized disk, so we were able to increment it slowly. We can skip increments if we need to, to make it feel like it's moving faster. Dave actually graphed out the speed for us, and we started testing it. The other added challenge is the lighting.

SEAMUS: Within the shot, the lighting changes from peach [illegible] sunset orange into turquoise at night. And that was all done in camera, meaning without digital assistance.

ADAM P: There were so many moving parts with this episode, but when you see it all come together, it's totally worth the stress and the overtime.

DAVE: In the end we were all so proud of this episode. To me, this felt like a cartoon I'd been waiting to make my whole career.

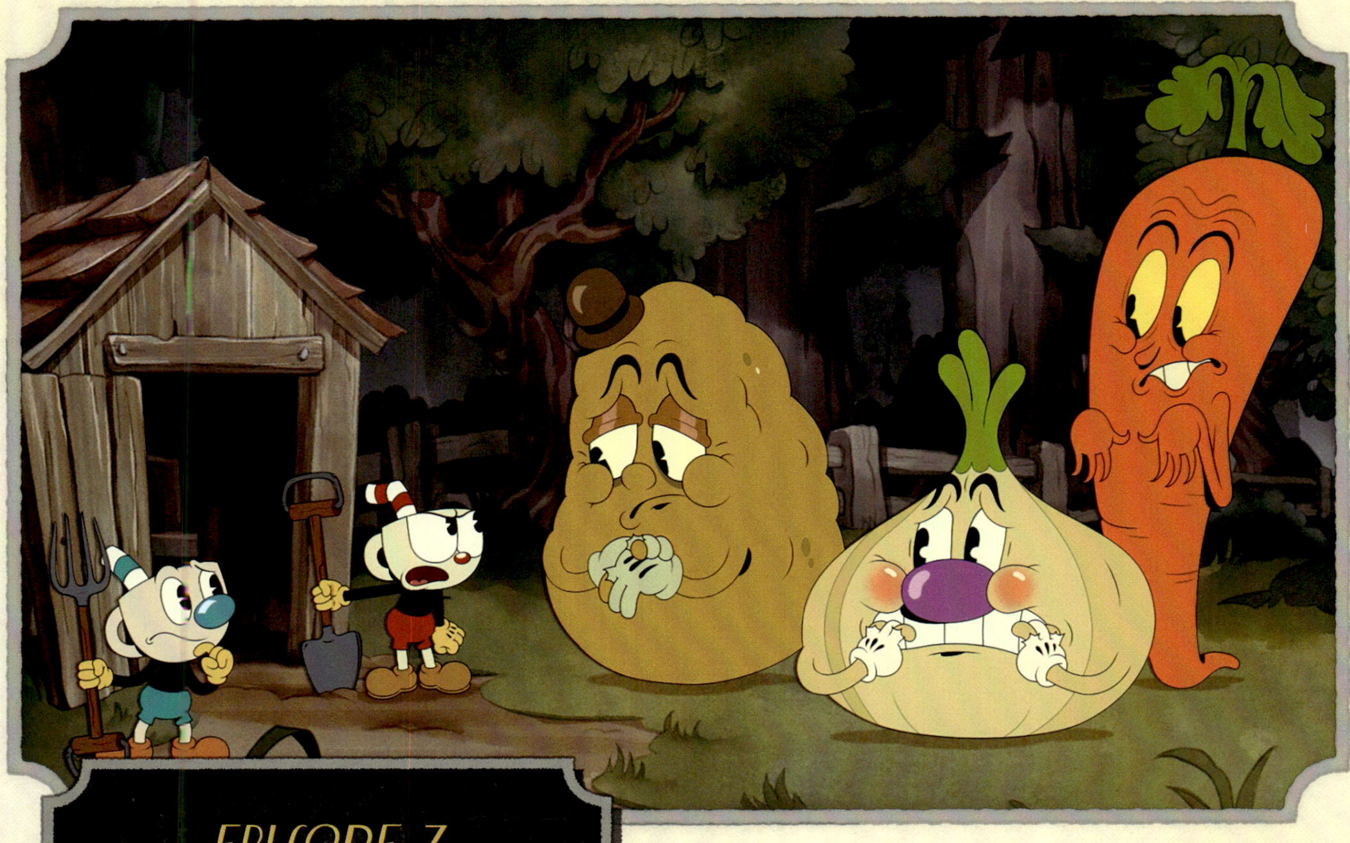

EPISODE 7 "ROOT PACKED"

BACKGROUND DESIGN BY LAUREN DUDA; PAINTING BY MICHELLE THIES; SPECIAL POSE DESIGNS BY MIKE FONTANELLI AND BRADLEY LEWIS.

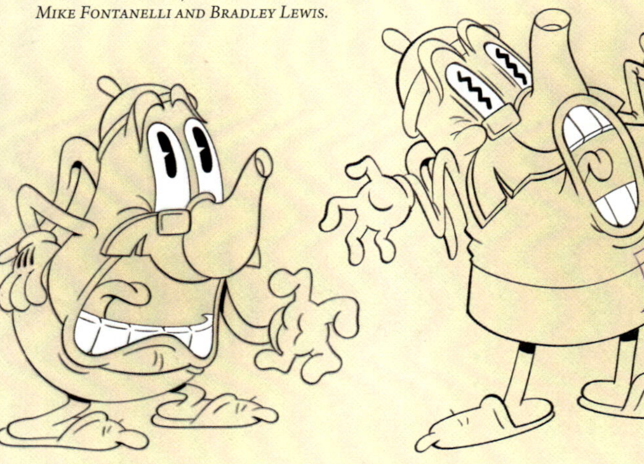

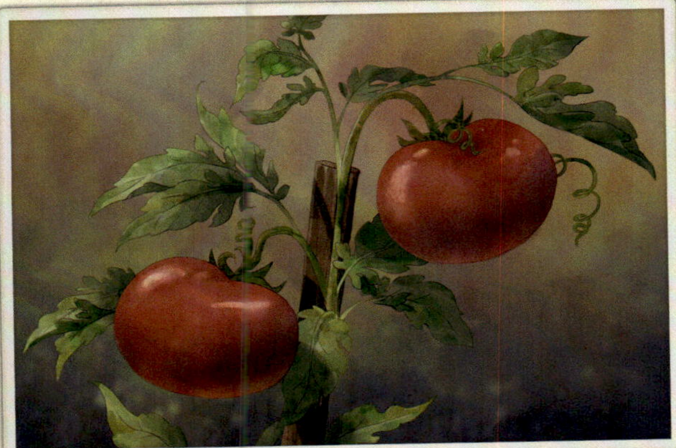

→ **GREG:** Something about the tomato plant in "Root Packed" was just so much fun for me. I loved the simplicity of it. That tomato plant, man . . . I love that thing.

BACKGROUND DESIGN BY LAISAY BOND; PAINTING BY GREGORY MILLER.

→ **DEEKI:** "Root Packed" was the first episode we wrote after "Carn-Evil." We saw them leave the cottage and meet a character from the game, so we tried the opposite—having characters from the game show up at the cottage.

DAVE: When we started working on that story, we gave Kettle a vegetable garden—a lot of these ideas are built out from the situations we would need in order to introduce certain characters and generate a story. It seemed right that he'd love his garden.

DEEKI: His babies.

DAVE: The first day we started editing the animatic, Clay said, "It would be great if Elder Kettle had a song to set up his garden." At first, I tried to talk him out of it, because I knew it'd be a lot of work, but later I went home and wrote the song "I Love My Little Veggies."

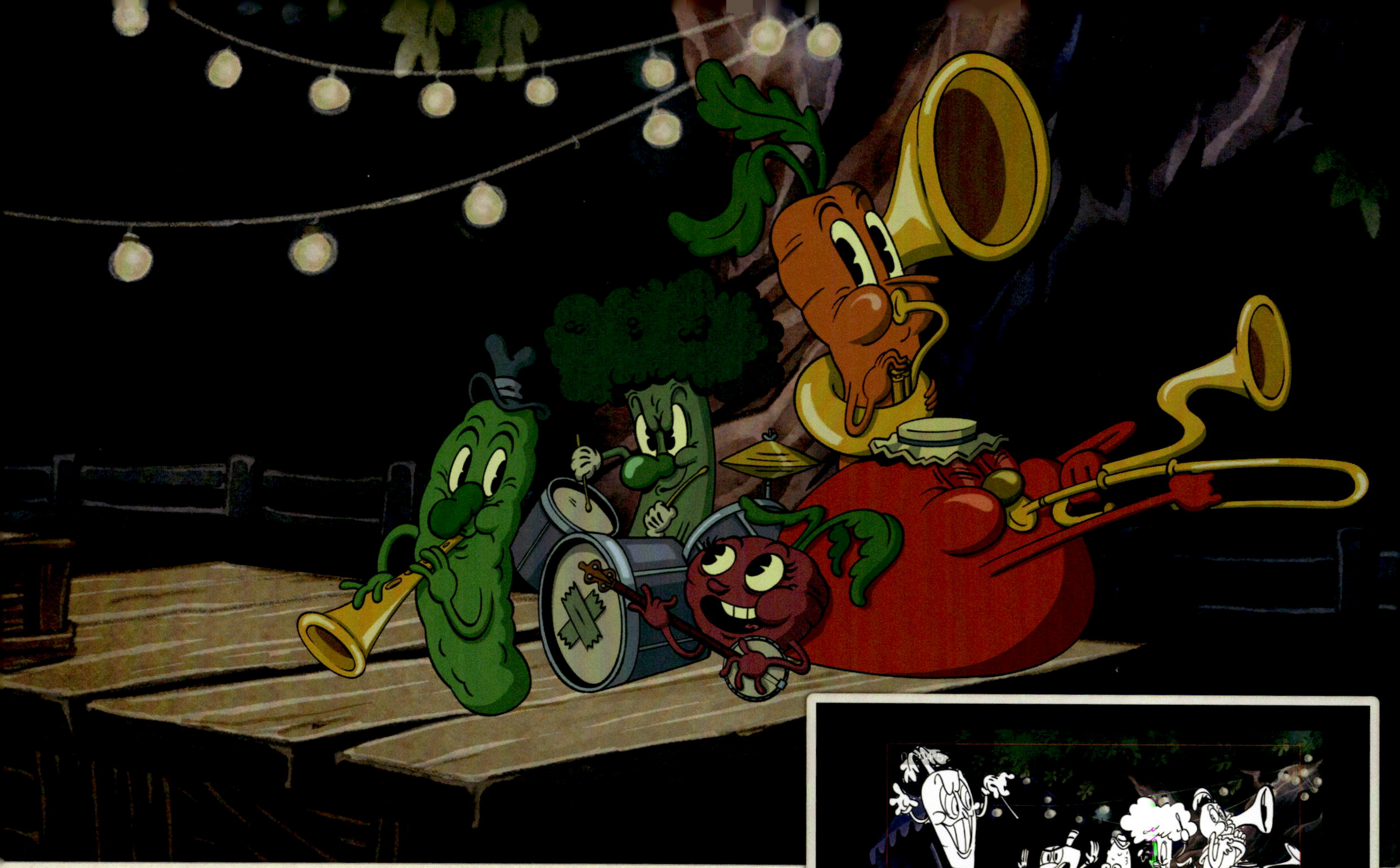

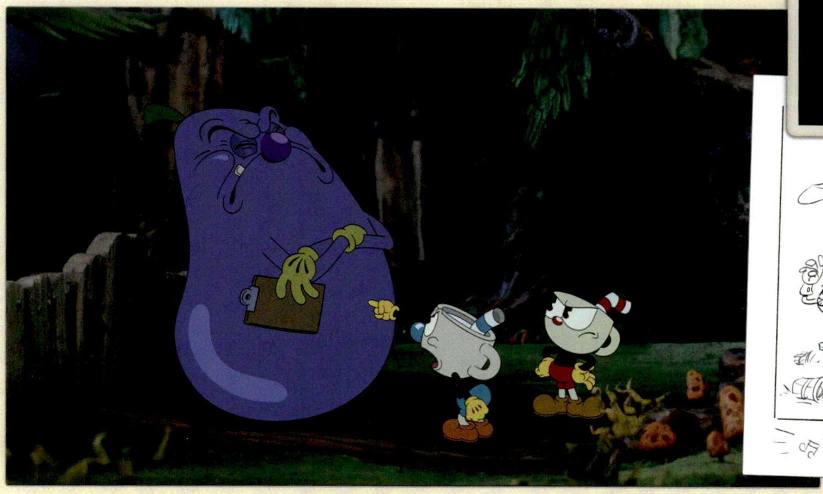

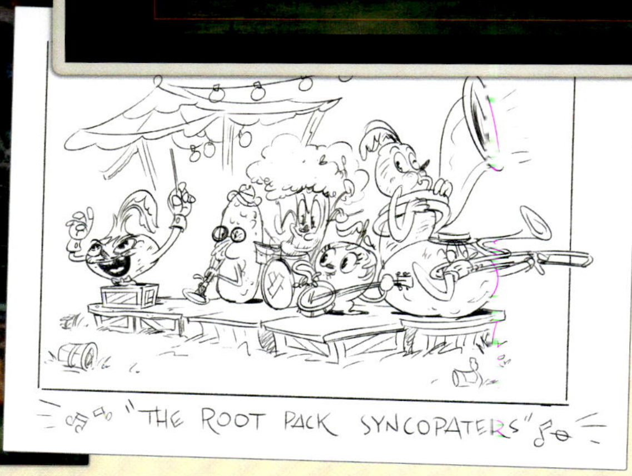

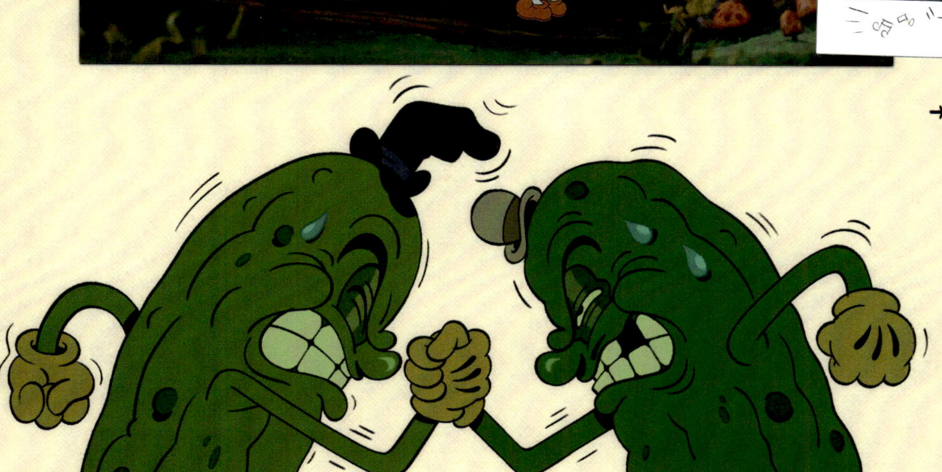

→ **CLAY:** "Root Packed" has this big pan across the party, and it took a while to get right. Sometimes you want things like that to go slower, but if you go *too* slow, it starts to feel . . . odd.

COSMO: One of the most difficult shots we did in the whole series is at the party in "Root Packed." All those characters needed to line up on the cottage front lawn and on the little stage in a very precise way, or the illusion would be ruined.

STOP-MO SET BY SCREEN NOVELTIES; BACKGROUND DESIGN BY LAUREN DUDA; BACKGROUND PAINTING BY MICHELLE THIES; VEGGIE BAND PREVIS BY COSMO SEGURSON.

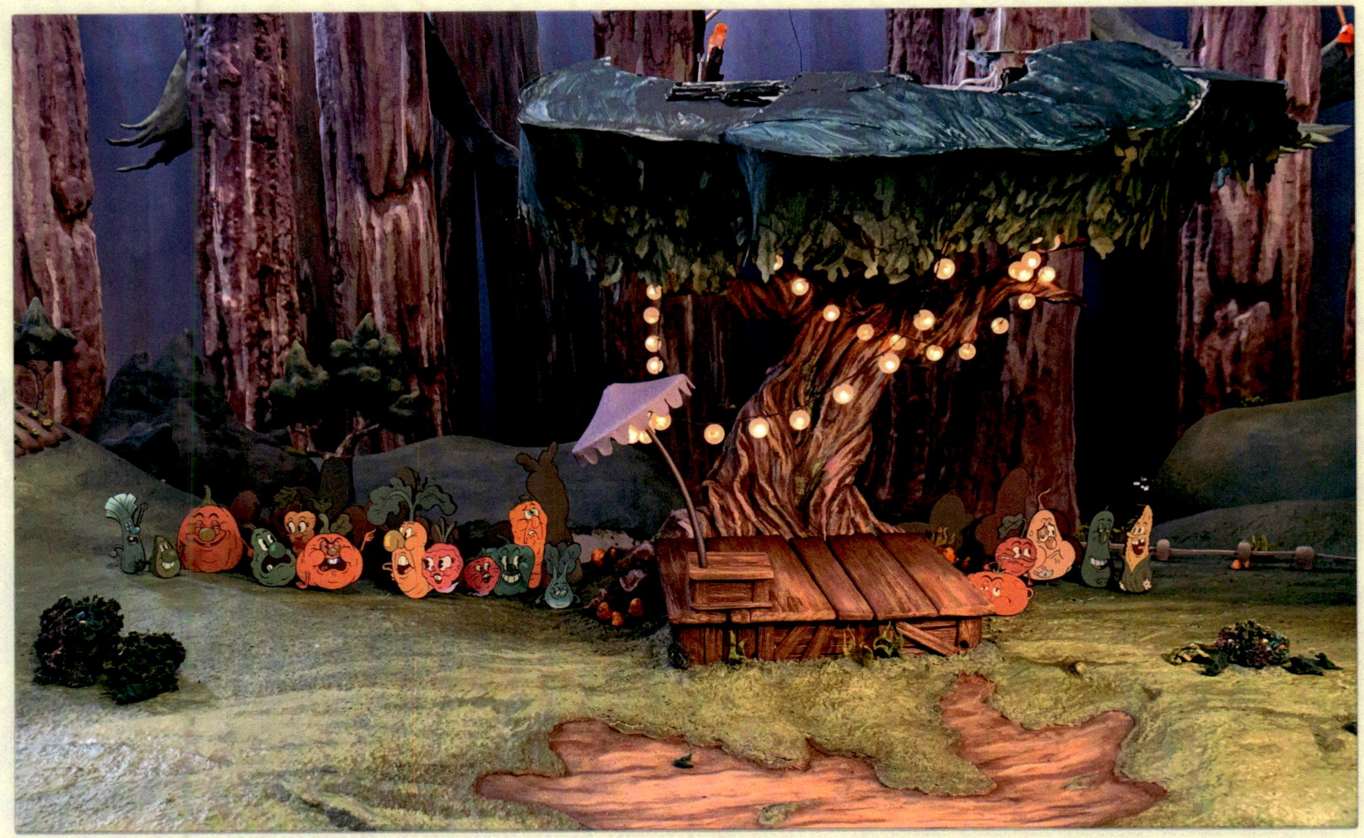

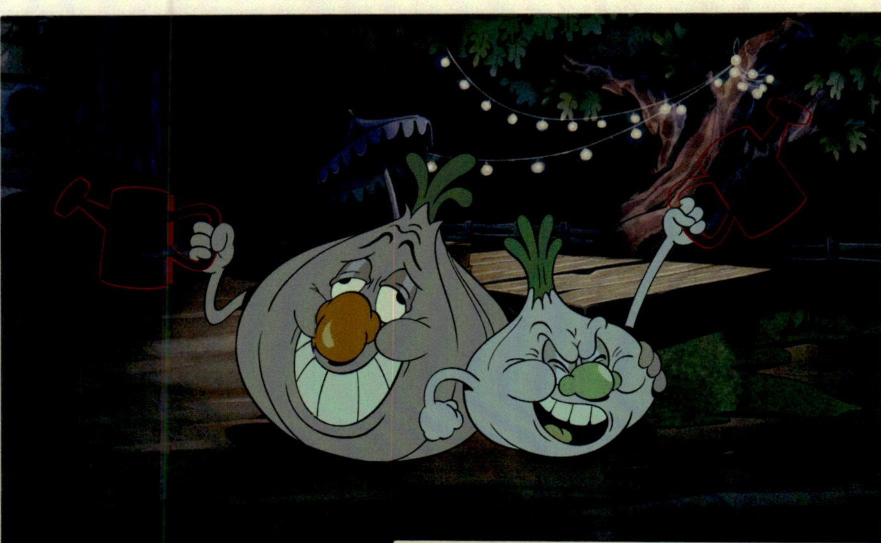

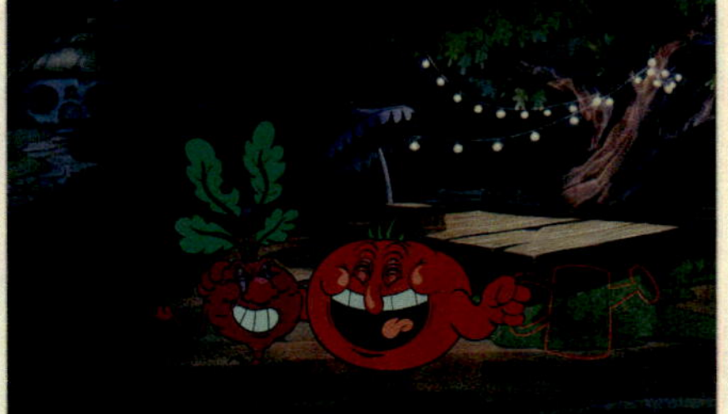

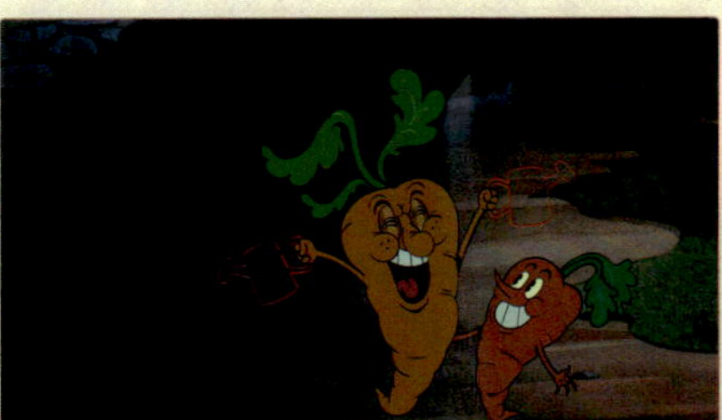

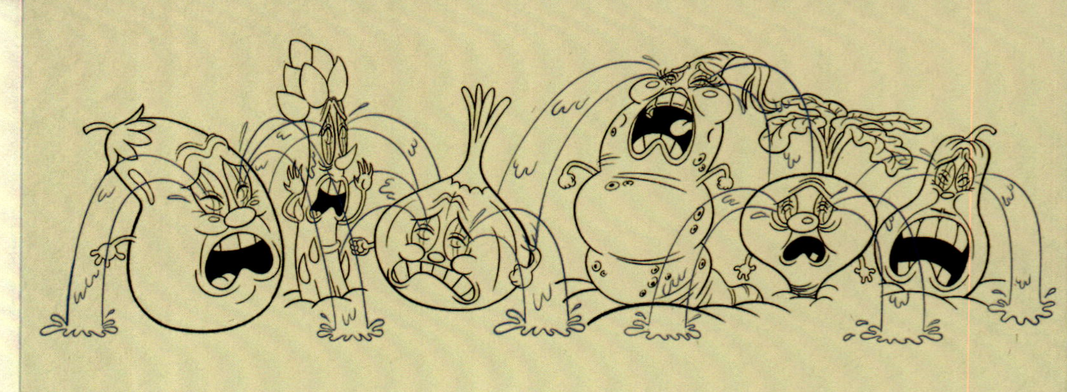

AUSTIN FABER, *THE CUPHEAD SHOW!* STORYBOARD REVISIONIST: I was on "Root Packed" storyboard revisions for two months. There was a crowd shot where I had to change certain expressions, or add more vegetables, or change certain designs, over and over. At the end of it I thought, "I never want to see vegetables again."

STOP-MO SET BY SCREEN NOVELTIES; SPECIAL POSE DESIGNS BY CRAIG KELLMAN AND BRADLEY LEWIS; BACKGROUND DESIGNS BY LAUREN DUDA; PAINTINGS BY MICHELLE THIES.

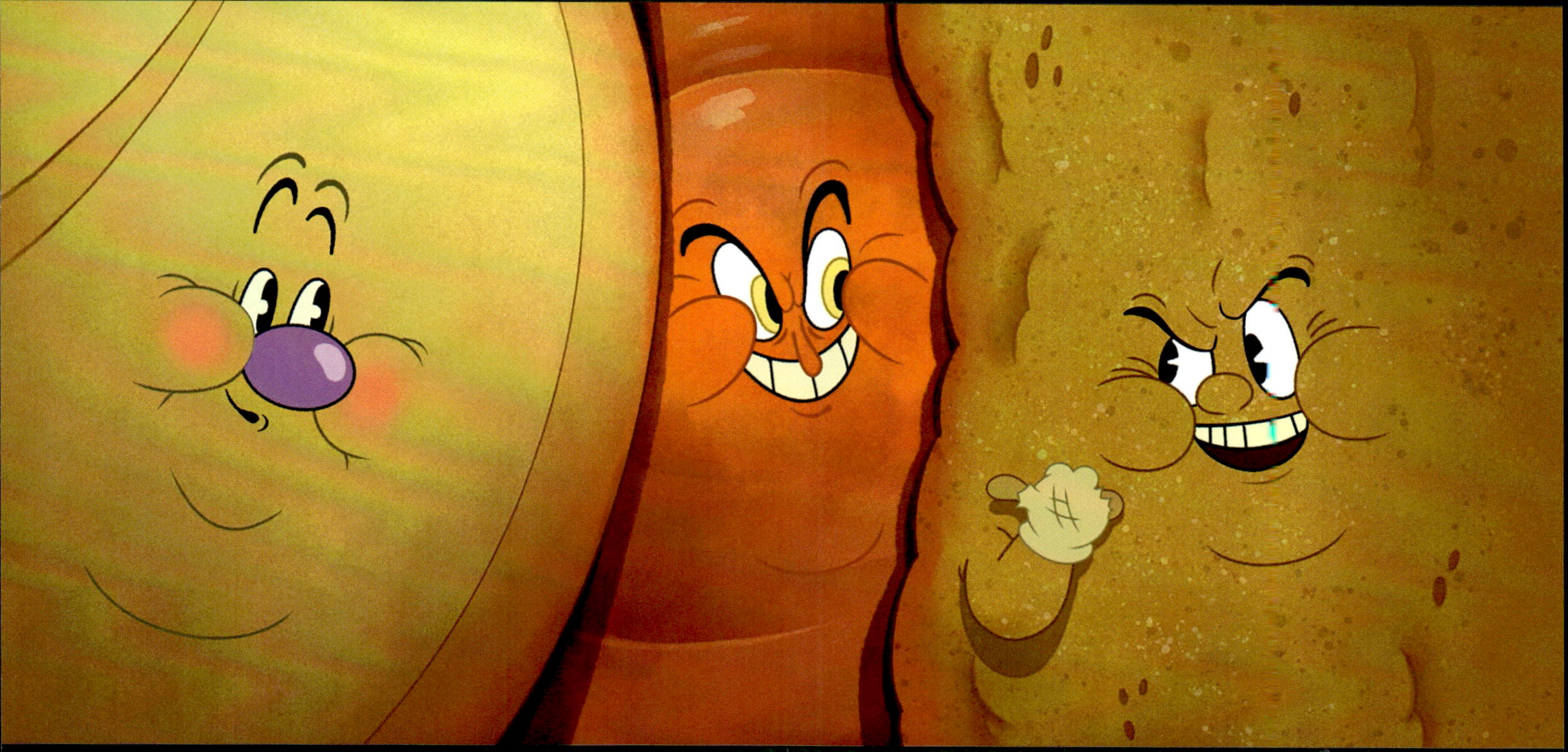

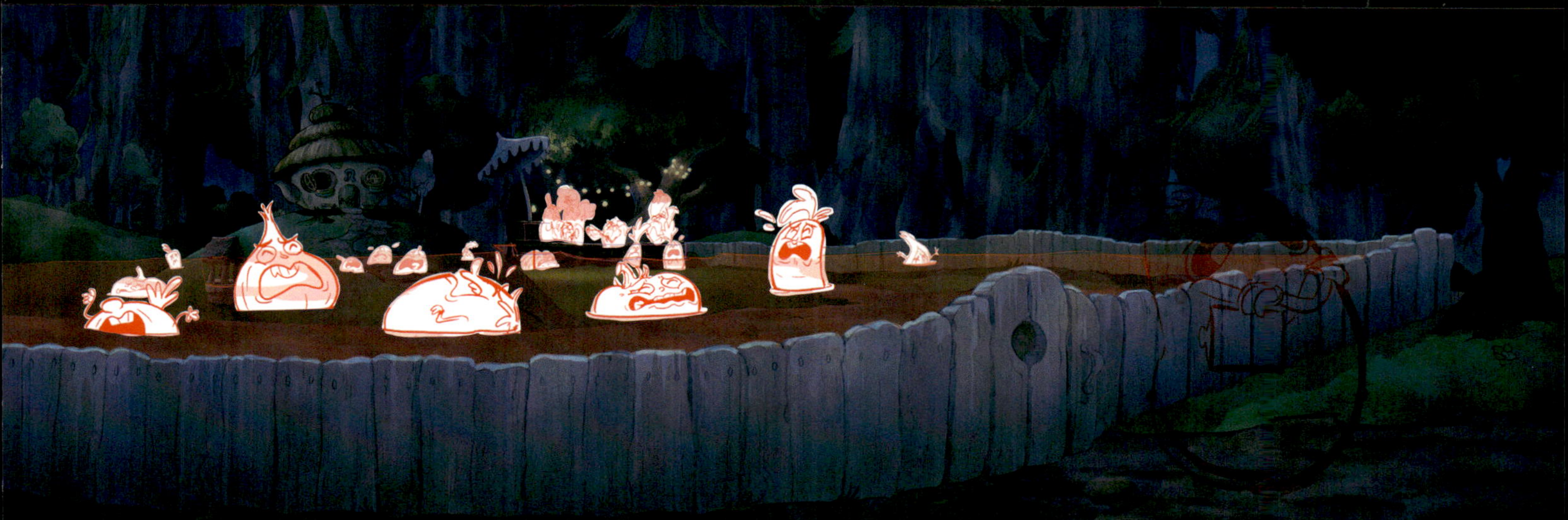

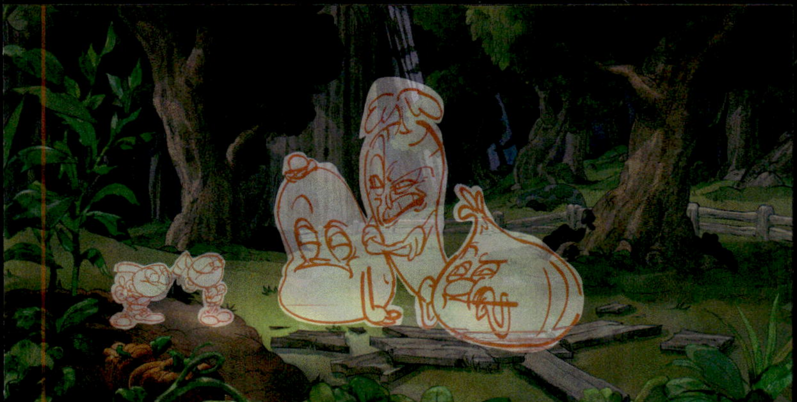

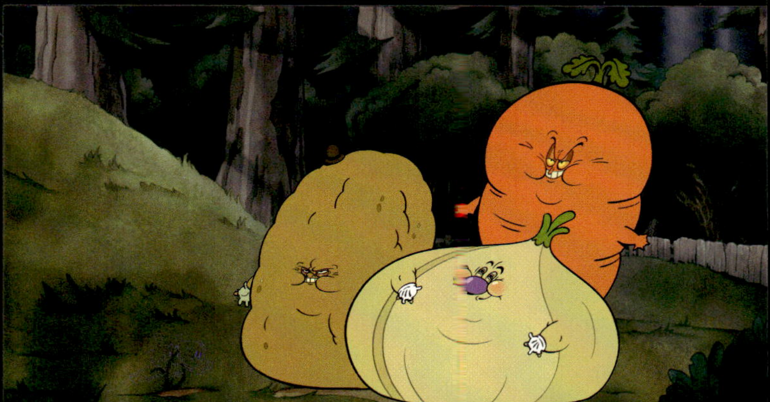

Root Pack faces and fat versions by Bradley Lewis; background designs by Jessica Hong and Lauren Duda; paintings by Mallory Carlson and Gregory Miller.

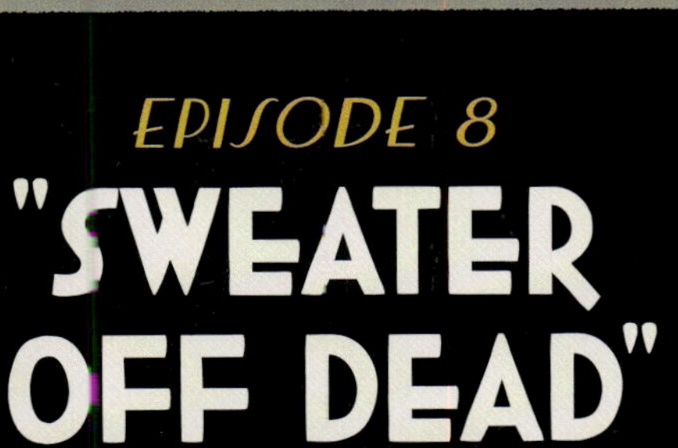

EPISODE 8
"SWEATER OFF DEAD"

→ **MEGAN BOYD, *THE CUPHEAD SHOW!* STORYBOARD ARTIST:** One of only two episodes where I drew Elder Kettle was "Sweater Off Dead," with the nightmare where he turns around and he's a skeleton and his head falls off. It's pretty unsettling and disturbing.

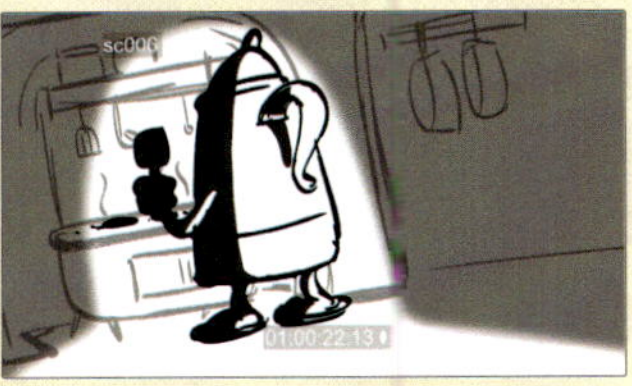

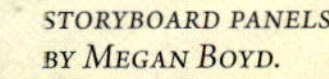

STORYBOARD PANELS BY MEGAN BOYD.

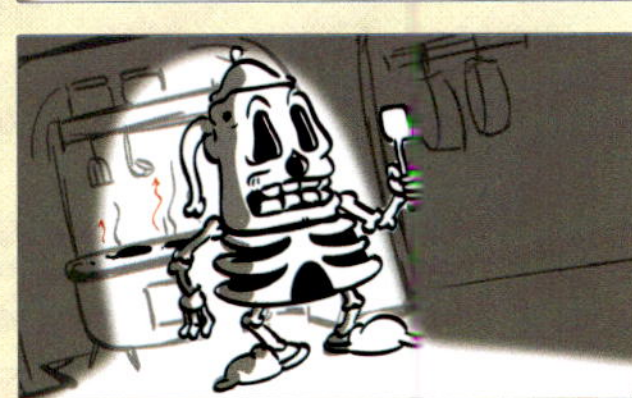

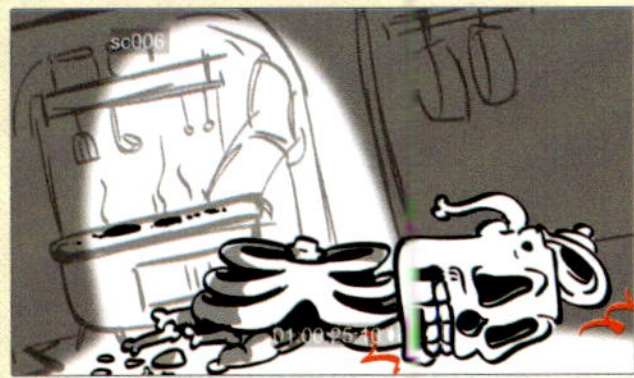

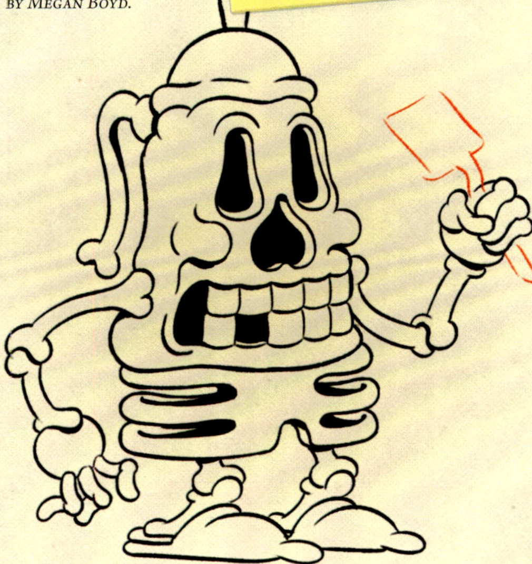

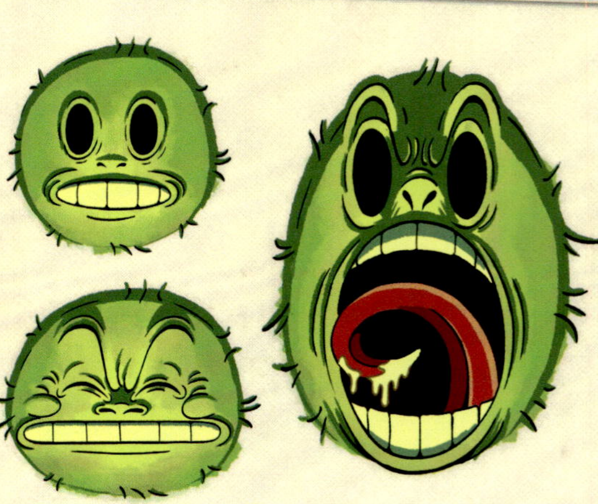

SPECIAL POSE DESIGNS BY TAPAN GANDHI; POST-IT SKETCH BY SHAKEH HAGHNAZARIAN.

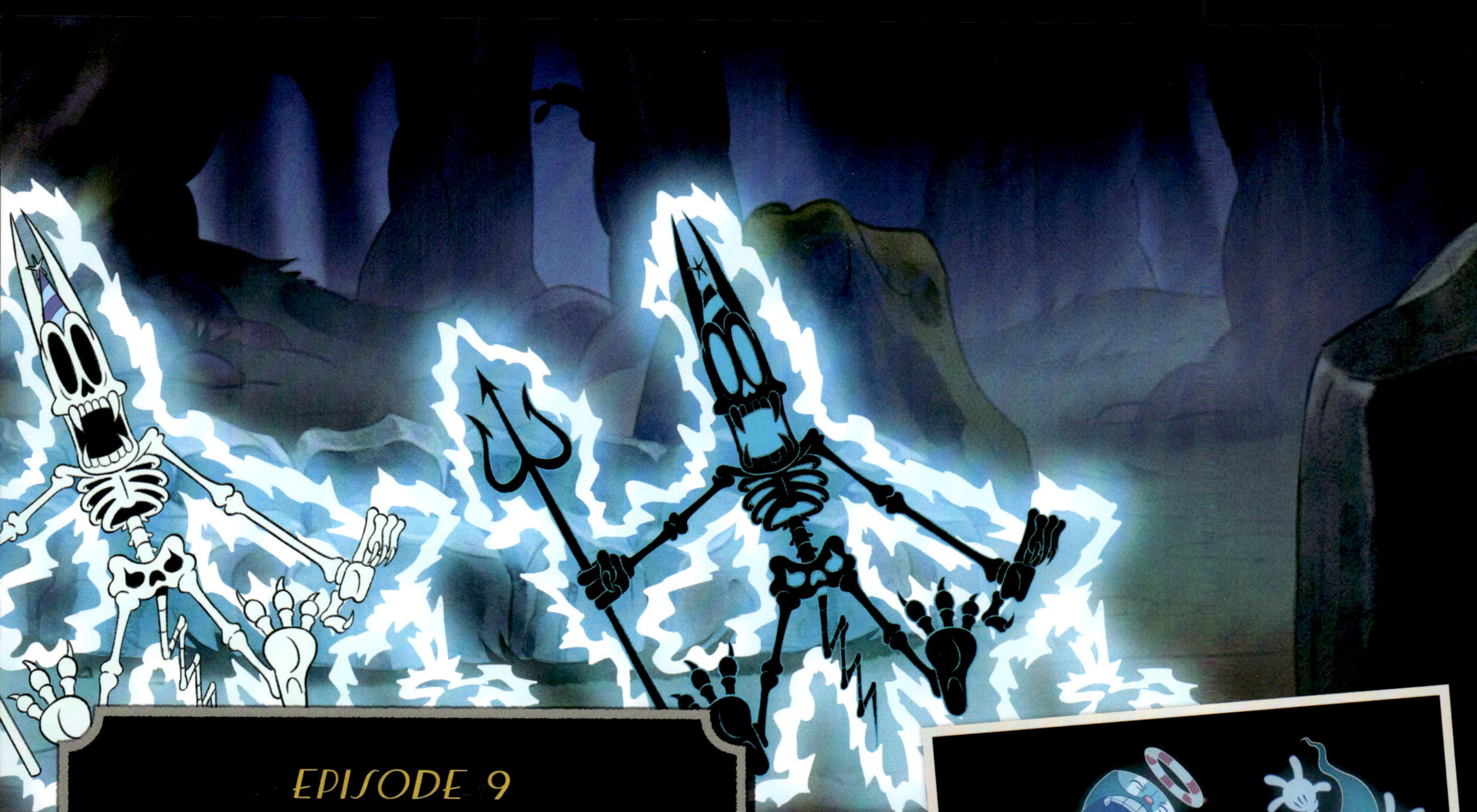

EPISODE 9

"SWEATER LUCK NEXT TIME"

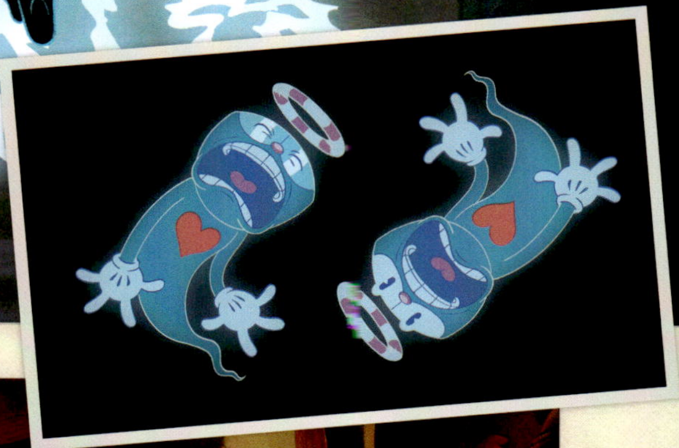

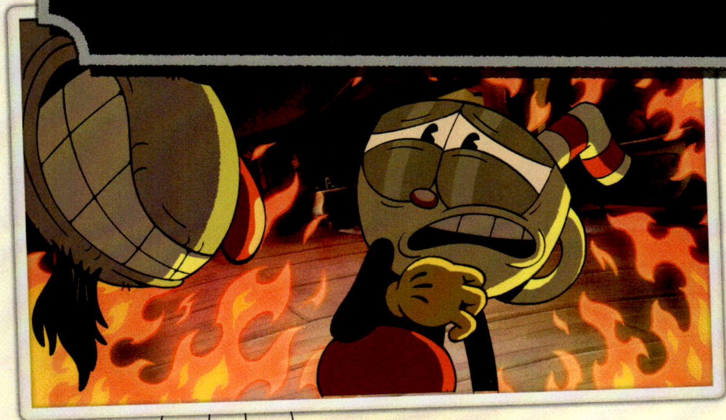

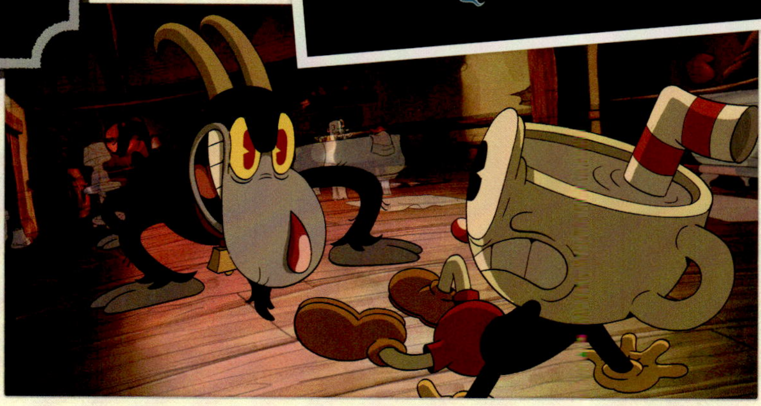

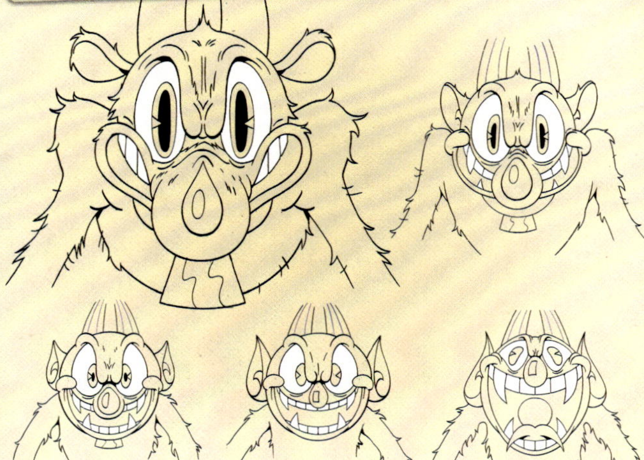
STORYBOARD PANEL BY MEGAN BOYD; SPECIAL POSE DESIGNS BY ADAM PALOIAN.

→ **ANDREA:** The more seriously I treat the backgrounds, the funnier the comedy becomes—and the bigger the contrast when things get scary. When it flips from the serene world that we know, and suddenly there's a horrific goat Devil, I love that—it freaks people out and makes them laugh at the same time.

ADAM P: The first time we did something truly scary was in "Sweater Off Dead." We wanted to remind people that the Devil is a real threat. Deeki originally had the goat's mouth split open, and a little head came out. But we dialed it back, because it was scarier than it needed to be.

MEGAN B: My favorite characters are always the villains, so I love the Devil. He's a villain, but you still empathize with him. the Devil has this controlled, elegant rage to him. It's below the surface. He *does* explode, and it's cool, but he doesn't do it all the time. There's a controlled, fluid movement, and that was hard to draw, because I'm not that personality at all—I *do* just explode and get angry!

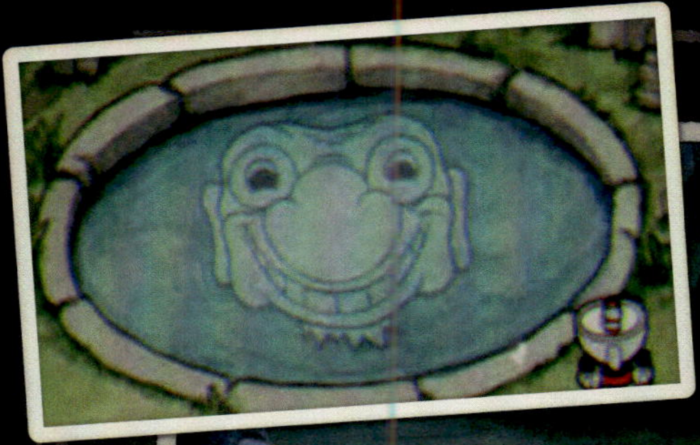

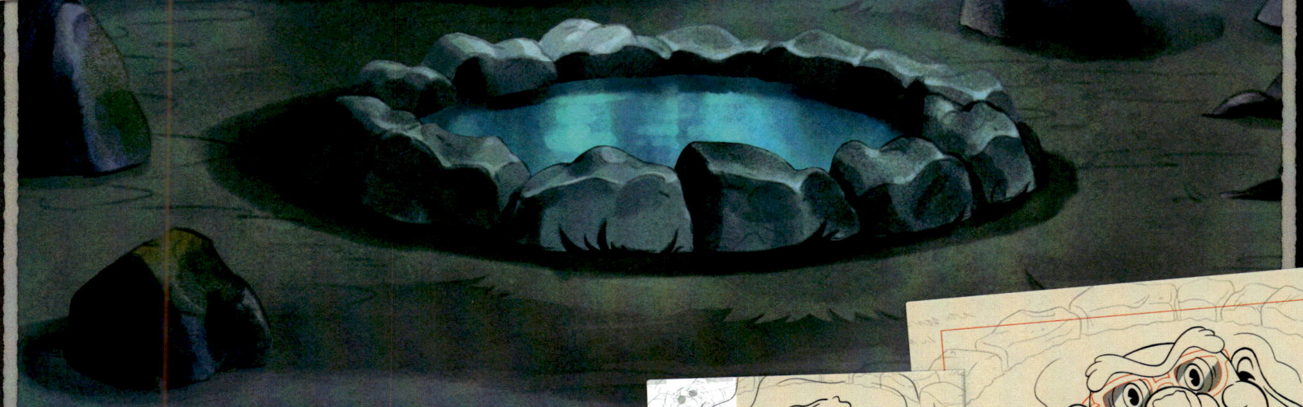

INTRODUCING
QUADRATUS

(voiced by Gary Anthony Williams)

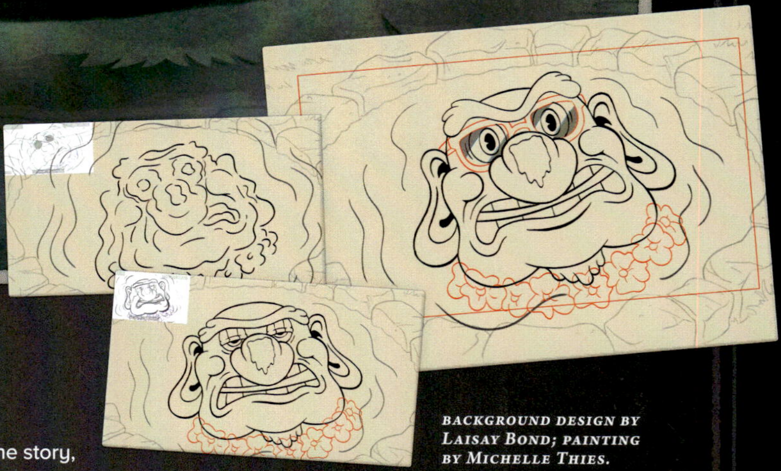

Background design by Laisay Bond; painting by Michelle Thies.

DAVE: In the game, Quadratus is someone you click on, and he gives you a little word balloon with advice. That felt like a really good device that we could take advantage of. When Cuphead and Mugman find themselves in a situation where they don't know how to deal with the Devil, they go to Quadratus—he appears in this pool and gives them advice.

CLAY: I resist being forced to take something seriously. I refuse to accept fantasy at face value. There's certain rules I accept. I accept gravity. But a fortunetelling all-knowing spirit in a pool of water? We'll see about that.

DEEKI: Early on, Clay tends to question and poke and prod—which I saw as a way to exercise the story, to make sure it's working.

CLAY: It's more of a defense mechanism against finding myself in a space where I just don't know where the information is coming from. I was probably trying to steer us to more grounded stuff.

DAVE: In a world like this, it's helpful to have a sage figure who gives you information that you couldn't possibly get any other way. Quadratus is a mysterious creature who knows everything, but the way he shares it is not always easily digested. That kind of character has always appealed to me.

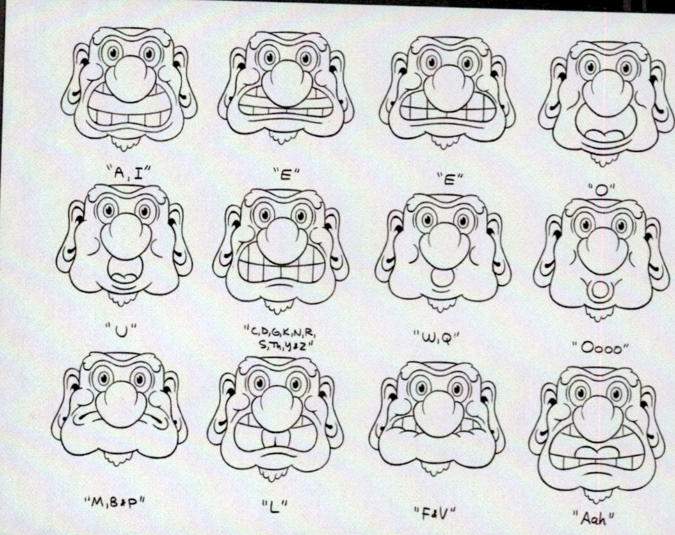

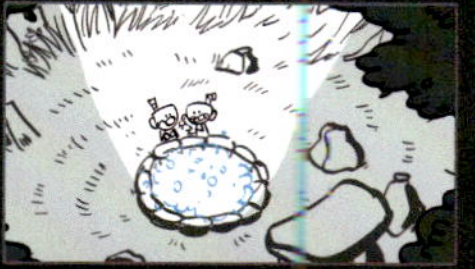

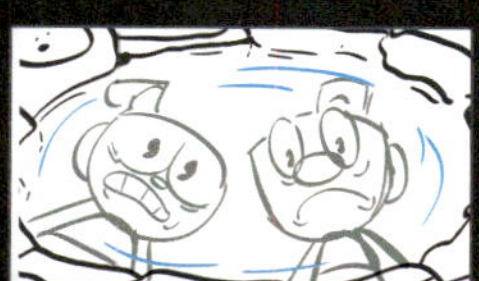

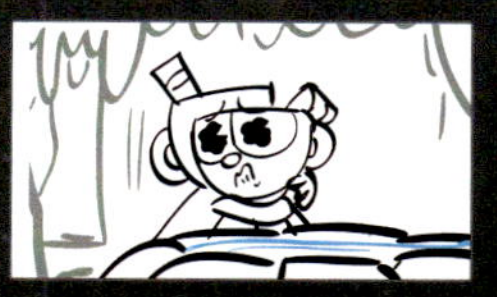

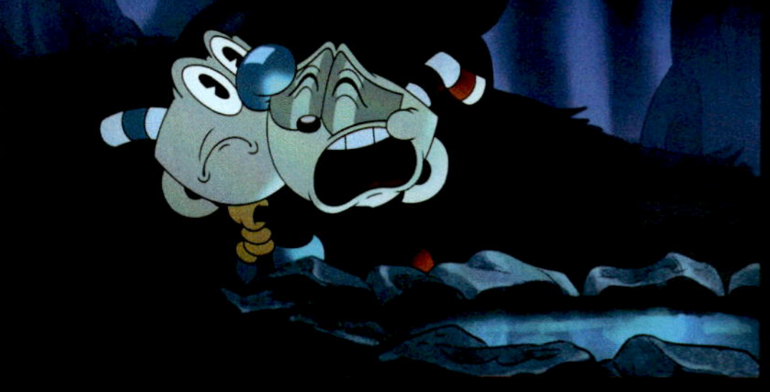

Upper left: Quadratus's game design. Special poses and mouth chart by Tapan Gandhi; storyboard panels by Megan Boyd.

PROPS & EFFECTS

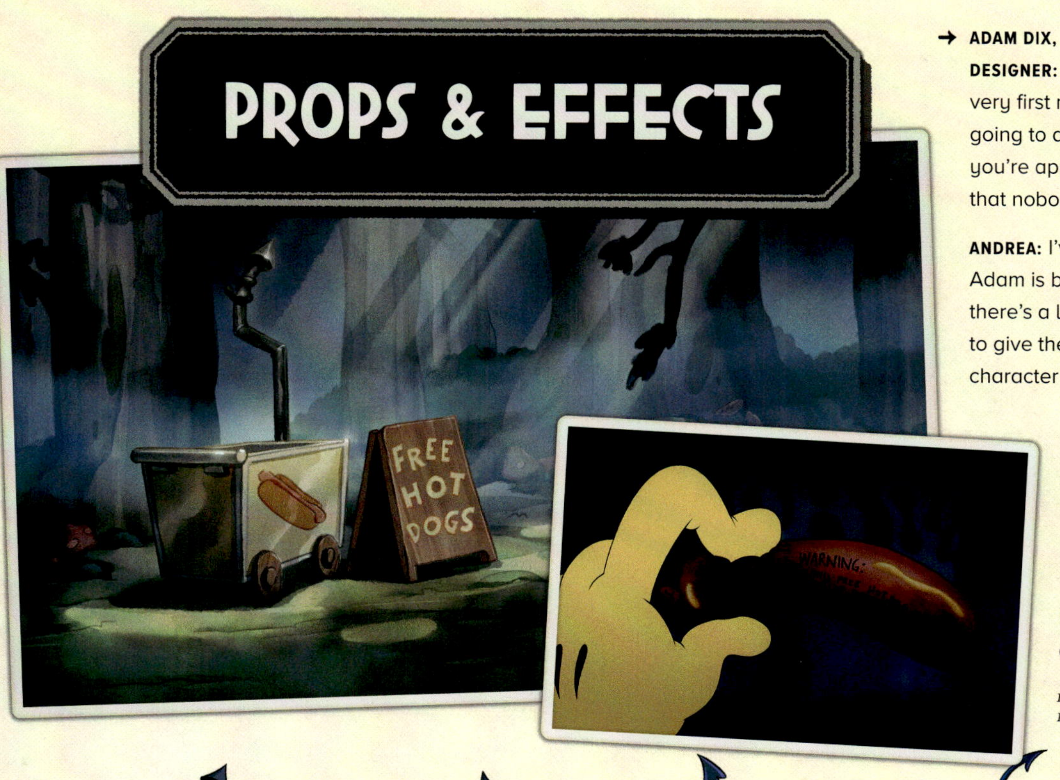

→ **ADAM DIX, *THE CUPHEAD SHOW!* PROPS AND EFFECTS DESIGNER:** When I first started on the show, the very first note Andrea gave me was "You're going to design this prop, but keep in mind that you're approaching it from such an early era that nobody had designed for animation before."

ANDREA: I've always wanted to work with Adam. Adam is by vocation a character designer, but there's a lot of props on this show, and I wanted to give them the attention usually reserved for character designs.

ADAM D: She said, "Imagine you're coming at it from the perspective of being an illustrator having to work in animation for the first time, having to find simplifications." That was one of the best notes she ever gave me in terms of understanding how to achieve the style.

Background design by Pat Marconett; painting by Michelle Thies.

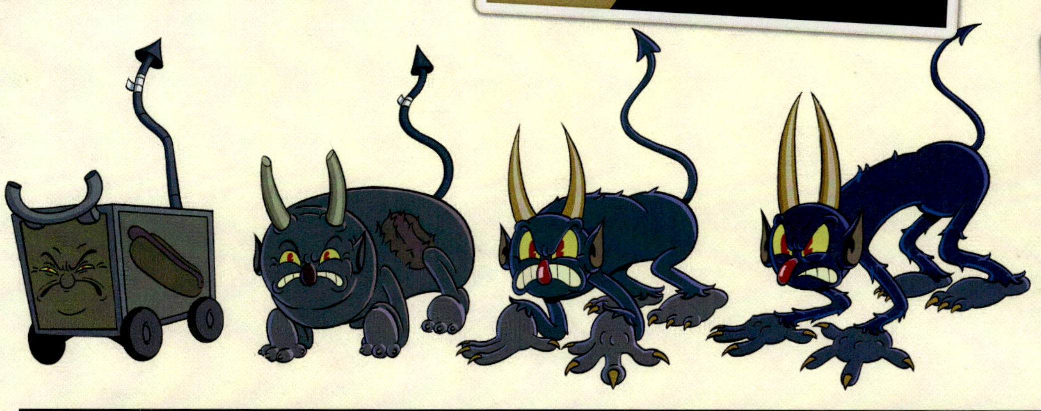

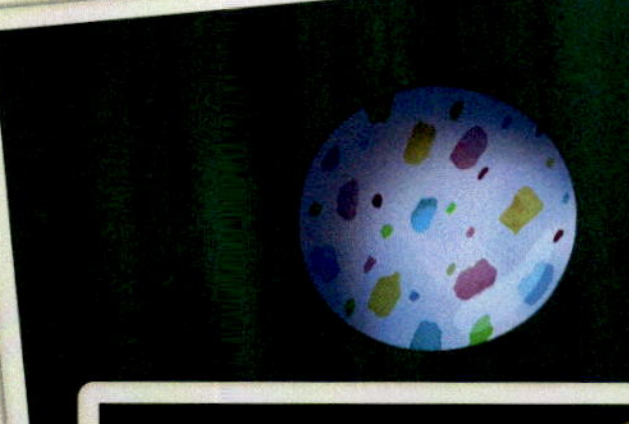

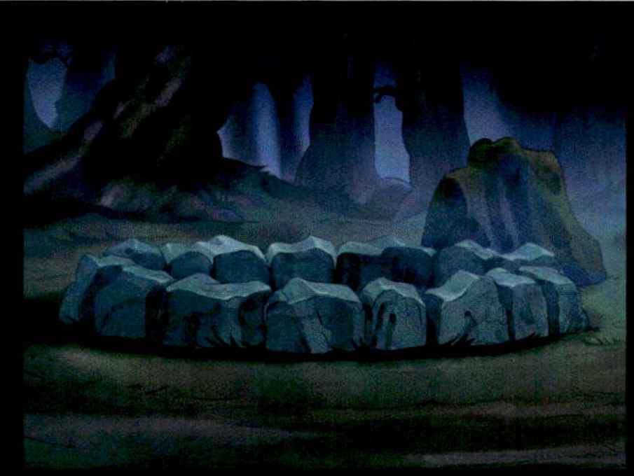

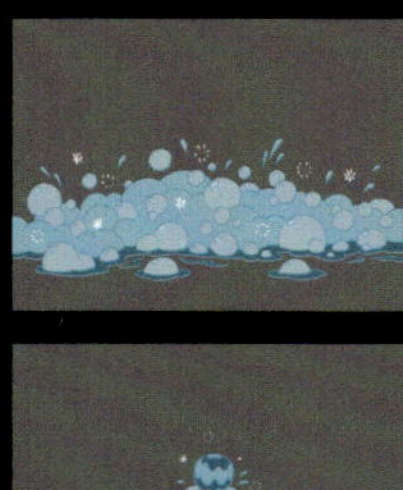

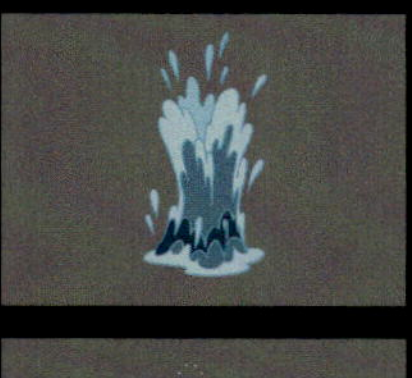

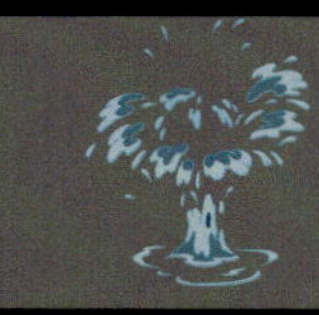

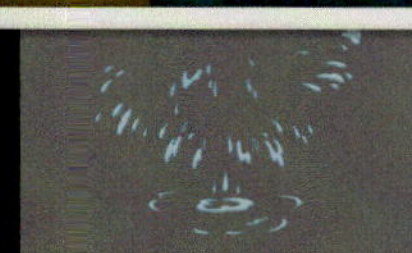

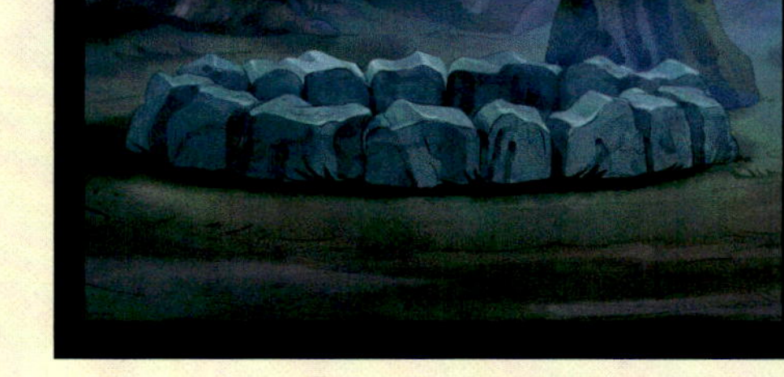

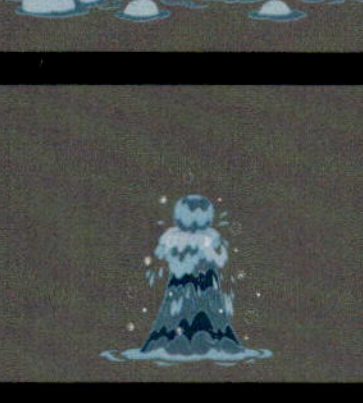

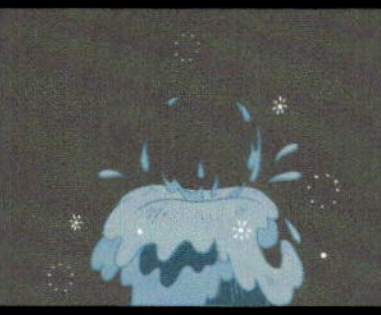

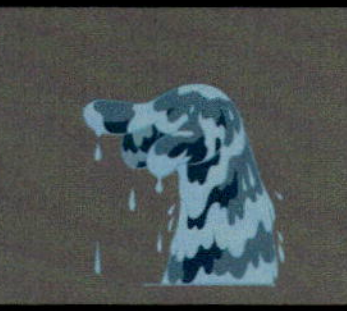

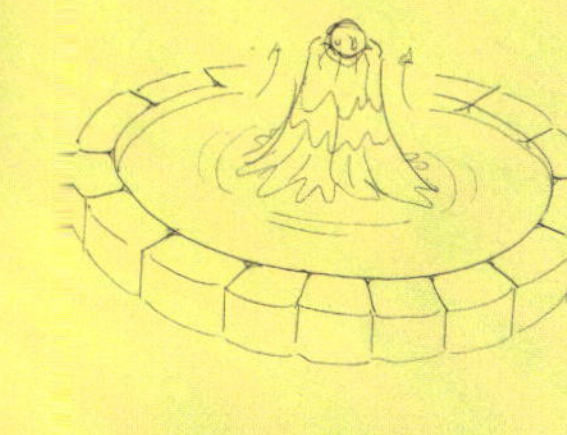

Special pose designs by Tapan Gandhi and Adam Paloian; water effects by Ed Skudder; story room sketch by Clay Morrow.

→ **ANDREA:** This was Adam's first props and effects gig. For some reason, they make props and effects the same person, so I had to also work with Adam on the effects.

ADAM D: The way Andrea phrased it was "I need somebody who can do squash and stretch," and I asked, "In props or in effects?" and she just said, "Yes."

ANDREA: Effects have been quite the headache on the show. They are such a huge part of figuring out the balance between the 1930s style and more modern, dynamic animation. That was a brain buster for both of us: getting 1930s-style effects is really difficult on such a high-action show. Effects in the '30s are really soft and funny, but cartoons were not action packed in the '30s, so there's not a lot of fireballs and explosions. Adam was instrumental in helping to figure that out.

ADAM D: It was a huge learning curve with the effects. It was like going back to animation school.

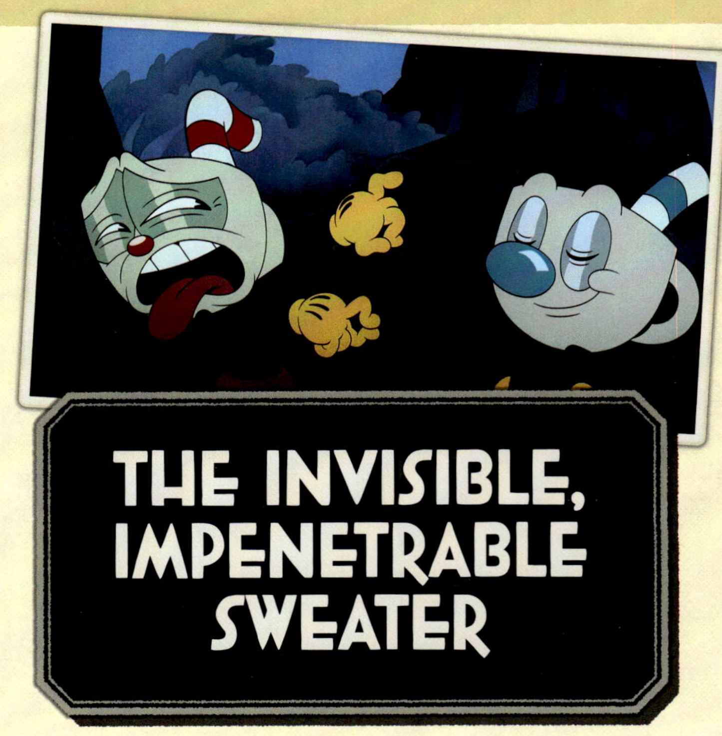

THE INVISIBLE, IMPENETRABLE SWEATER

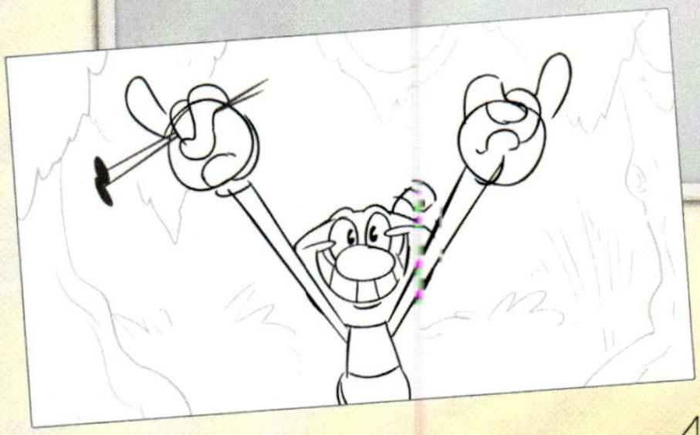

Above: Final design for the Invisible, Impenetrable Sweater.

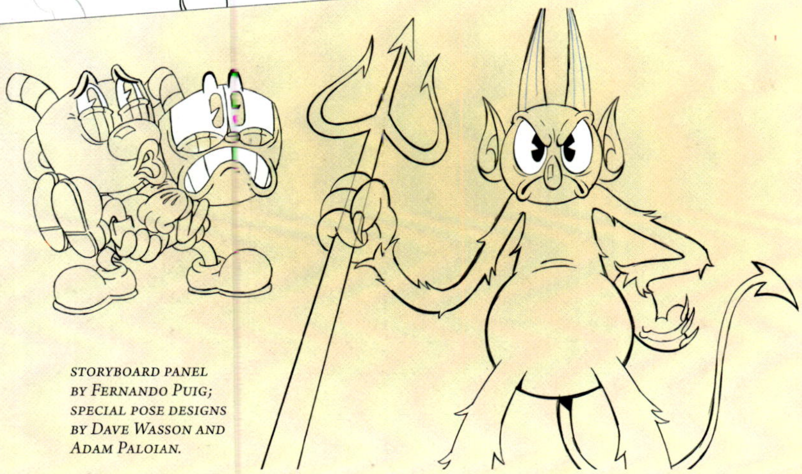

Storyboard panel by Fernando Puig; special pose designs by Dave Wasson and Adam Paloian.

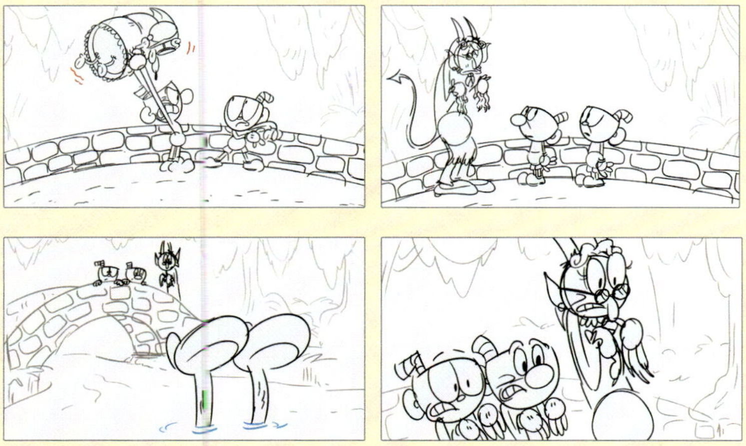

→ **DAVE:** Now that Cuphead had lost his soul at the carnival, the Devil should be able to just reach in and pull out Cuphead's soul. We needed some reason why the Devil and Cuphead could be together in the same place and have a scene together without the Devil just immediately ripping out Cuphead's soul. The invisible sweater evolved out of that necessity, but not everyone was onboard at first.

MEGAN C: I wrestled with that story in the beginning, mainly because of the conceit of an invisible sweater in animation—I wasn't sold. How is this really going to work? Then the whole journey to Quadratus—his name's weird, the idea's weird . . . There's a lot of weird stuff in that story! I had some doubts, but it all came together. I usually lean against sap and sentimentality, but I think the way it played out is lovely—the love between the two brothers totally works and feels super authentic.

DAVE: The sweater had to be impenetrable AND invisible. That way Cuphead would be protected but the devil wouldn't be able to see if he was wearing it or not. I knew we could get some good comedy out of that.

COSMO: It says a lot about Mugman, making the sweater without questioning it. Cuphead owes him forever after that—Mugman really saved Cuphead's soul. I feel like him making the sweater is the moment he becomes the rock that Cuphead really needs in his life, so he doesn't lose his soul.

DEEKI: You can't actually see the thing that visually represents their brotherly love. What you do see is Mugman once again carrying Cuphead's weight, doing whatever he can to save his brother's soul.

DAVE: Then you've got Cuphead, who's super irresponsible—he'd be the only one who would ever possibly take the sweater off. Which, of course, he does.

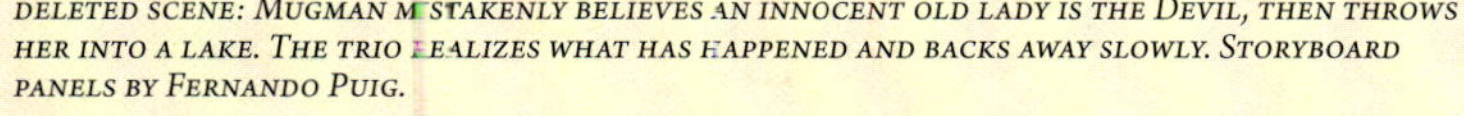
Deleted scene: Mugman mistakenly believes an innocent old lady is the Devil, then throws her into a lake. The trio realizes what has happened and backs away slowly. Storyboard panels by Fernando Puig.

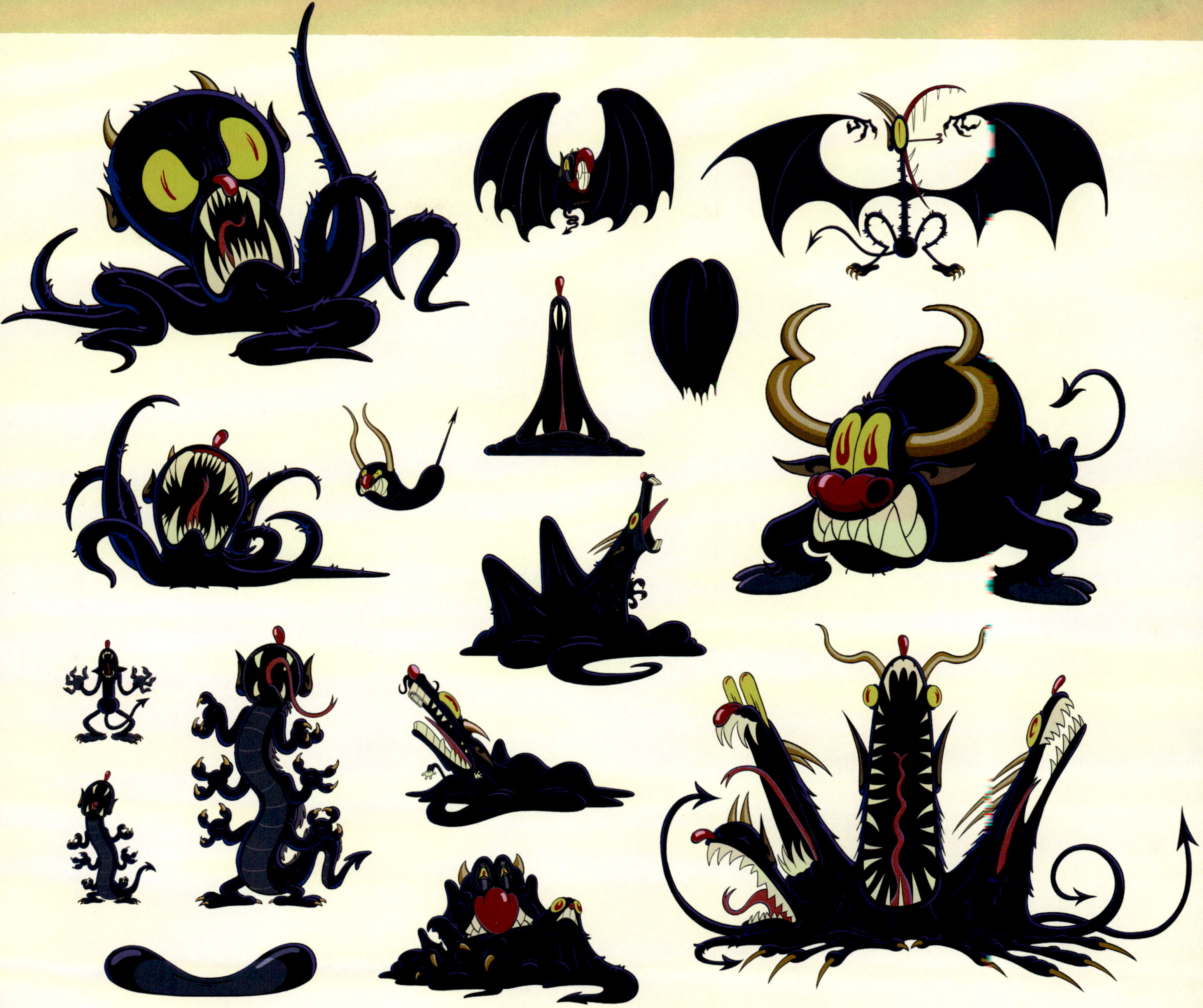

Devil transformation designs by Adam Paloian and Tapan Gandhi; color design by Chris Hacker.

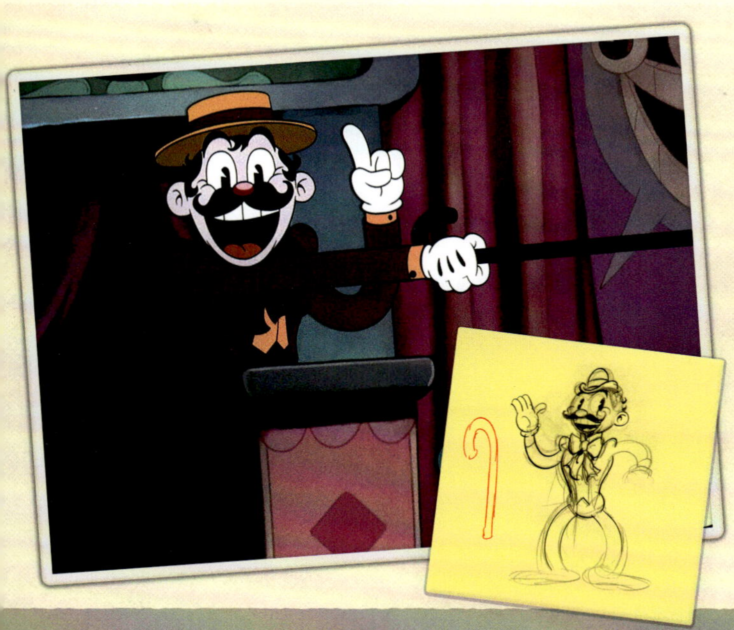

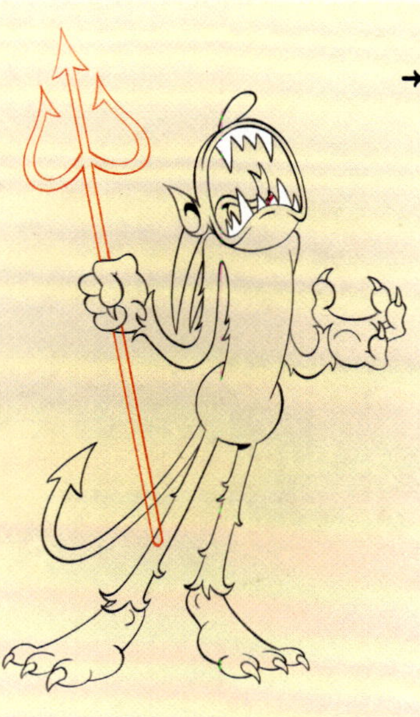

→ **COSMO:** One thing we lifted directly from the game was that he's a shape shifter.

CLAY: The first "Sweater" episode is much more serious, in terms of the scale and the ending. Between us two directors, Adam definitely had to do a lot heavier lifting in terms of selling the epicness, the fantasy, and the drama. The second "Sweater" is my preferred zone—high expectations followed by a rug pull. [*Laughs*]

Special pose designs by Mike Fontanelli and Dave Wasson; Devil barker sketch by Adam Paloian.

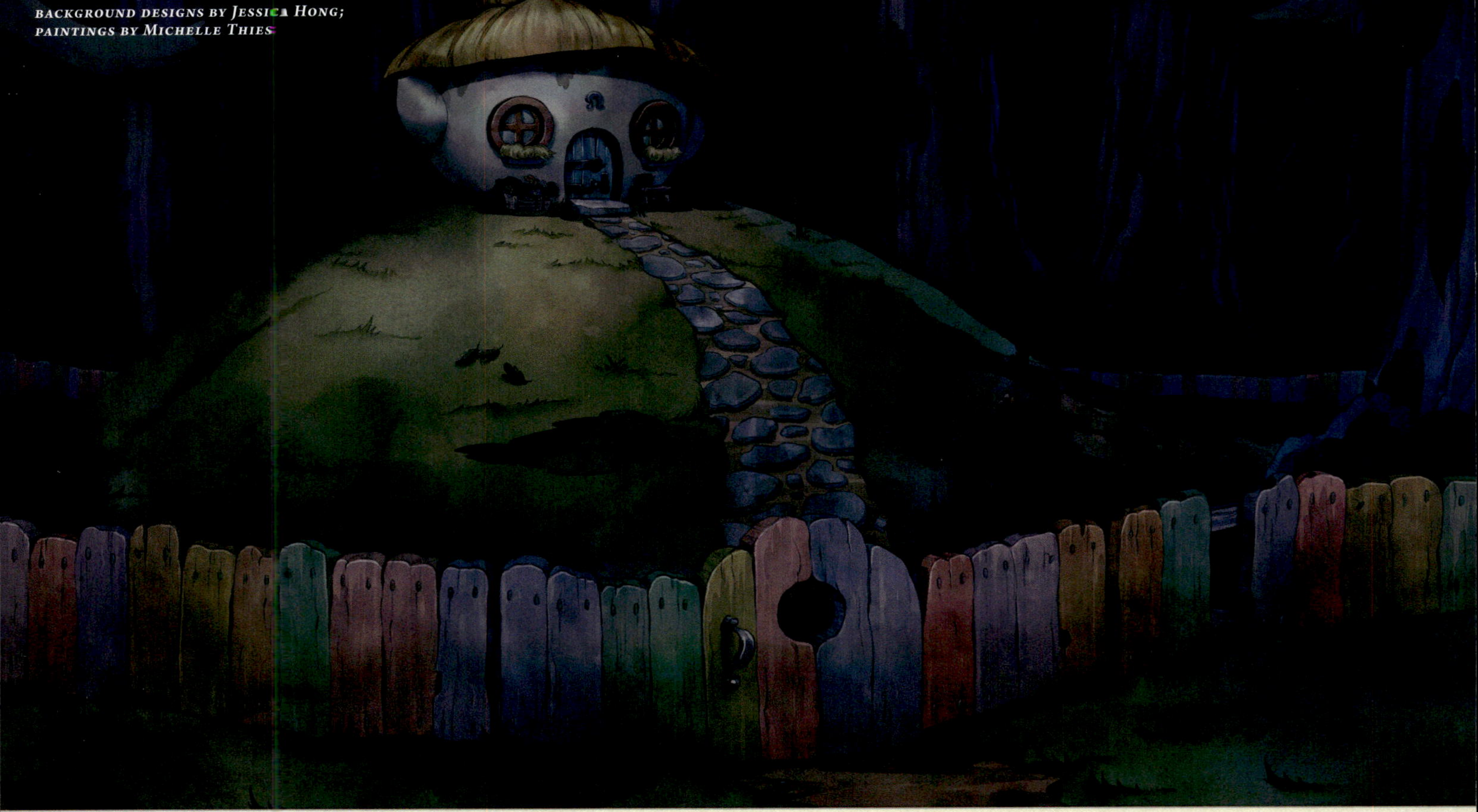

Background designs by Jessica Hong; paintings by Michelle Thies

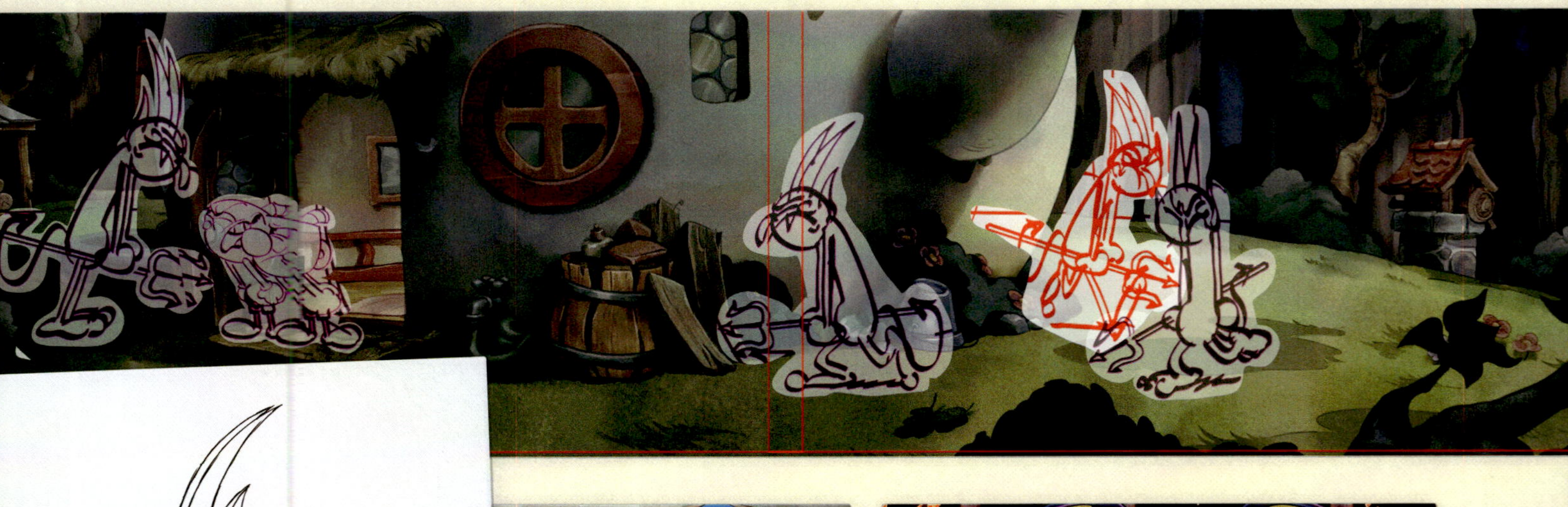

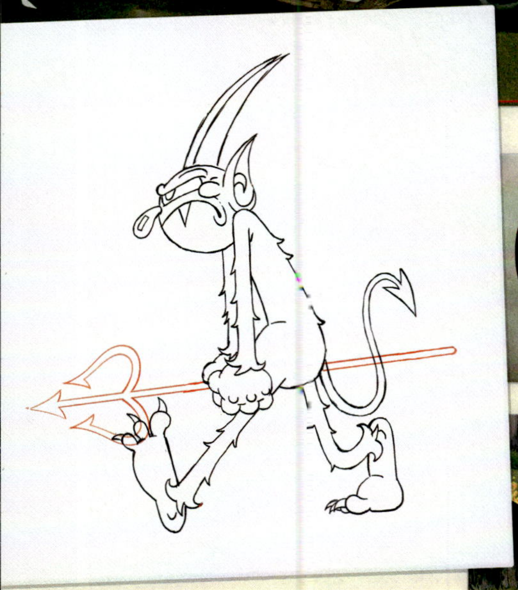

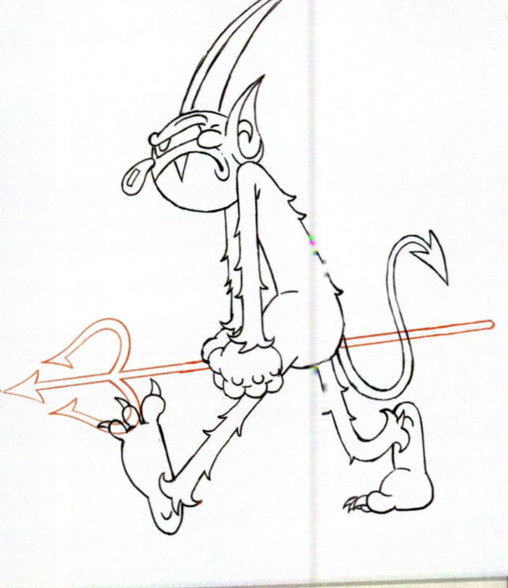

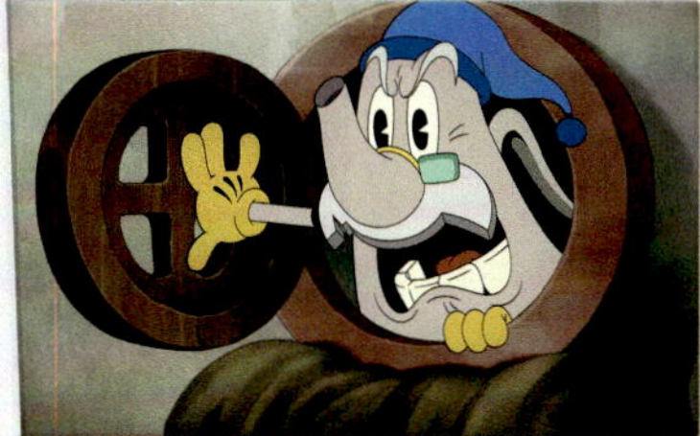

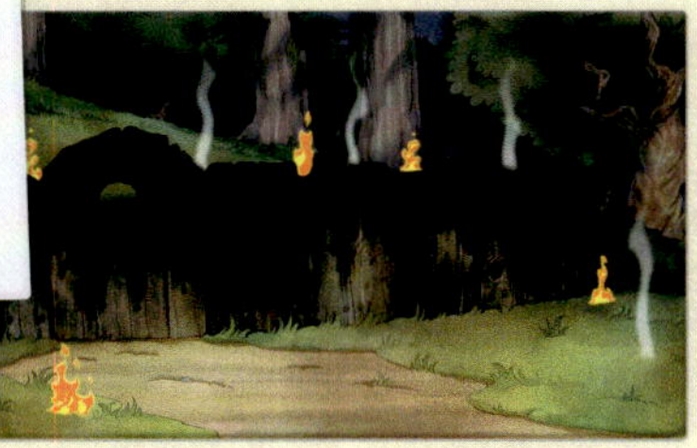

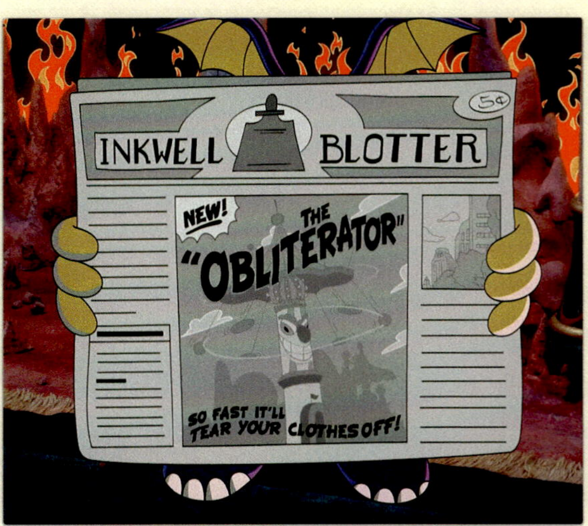

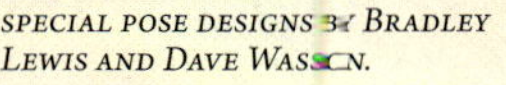

Special pose designs by Bradley Lewis and Dave Wasson.

DAVE: Even early on, that second "Sweater" was packed full of amazing stuff.

CLAY: We've got the Devil right where we want him. It's trackable for the audience—they'll be able to follow how we got him from the king of the underworld to having him go to their house, interact with them, and catch himself going, "I can't believe this is happening to me." Not only is it funny, but it's a lot of ground to cover—and I remember thinking how fast we got there, and it still felt believable.

DEEKI: Despite just barely escaping the Devil in the last episode, Cuphead disregards the stakes and the threat to his mortal soul in favor of his own comfort, and he takes the sweater off.

DAVE: And then he can't remember where he left it—we got a ton of great material out of that.

CLAY: Dave and I have said this many times—almost every time Deeki pitched an episode where we were making headway in both character and the overall story, we said, "It's not THIS, it can't be THIS," and when Deeki was done and we were thinking about it, we said, "It *is* THAT! I can't believe it's THAT!" It's shocking at first, then when you go through the mechanics you say, "No, this is what it is," and you just get so excited about how punishing it is for the Devil.

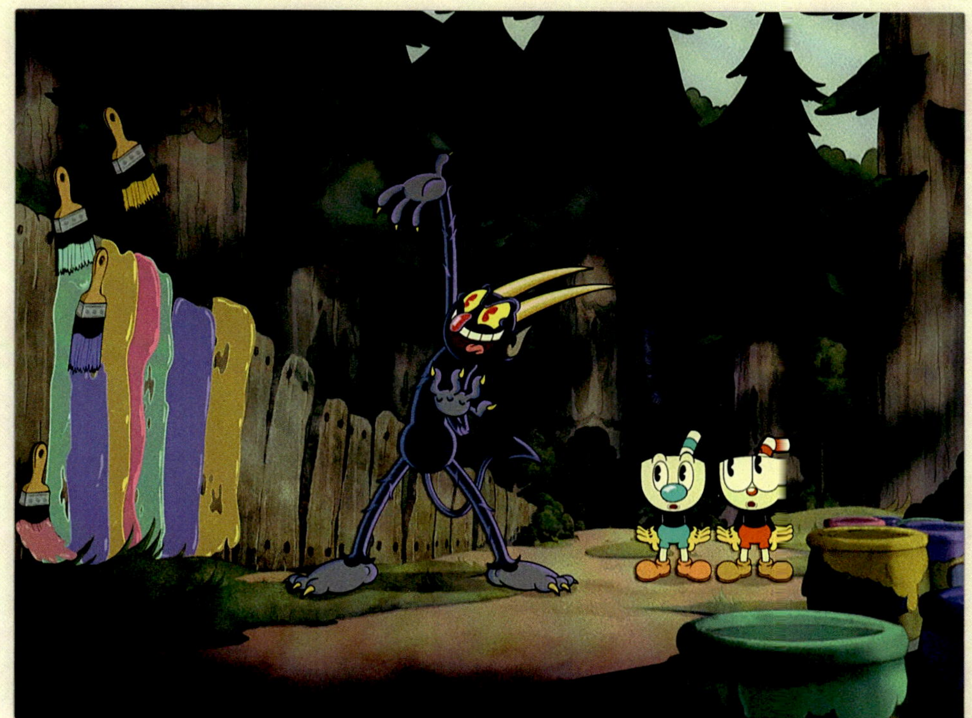

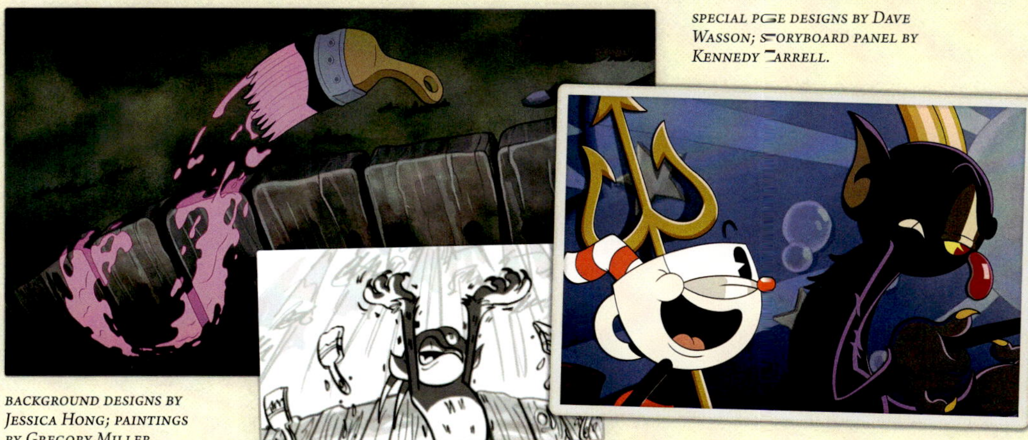

SPECIAL PAGE DESIGNS BY DAVE WASSON; STORYBOARD PANEL BY KENNEDY TARRELL.

BACKGROUND DESIGNS BY JESSICA HONG; PAINTINGS BY GREGORY MILLER.

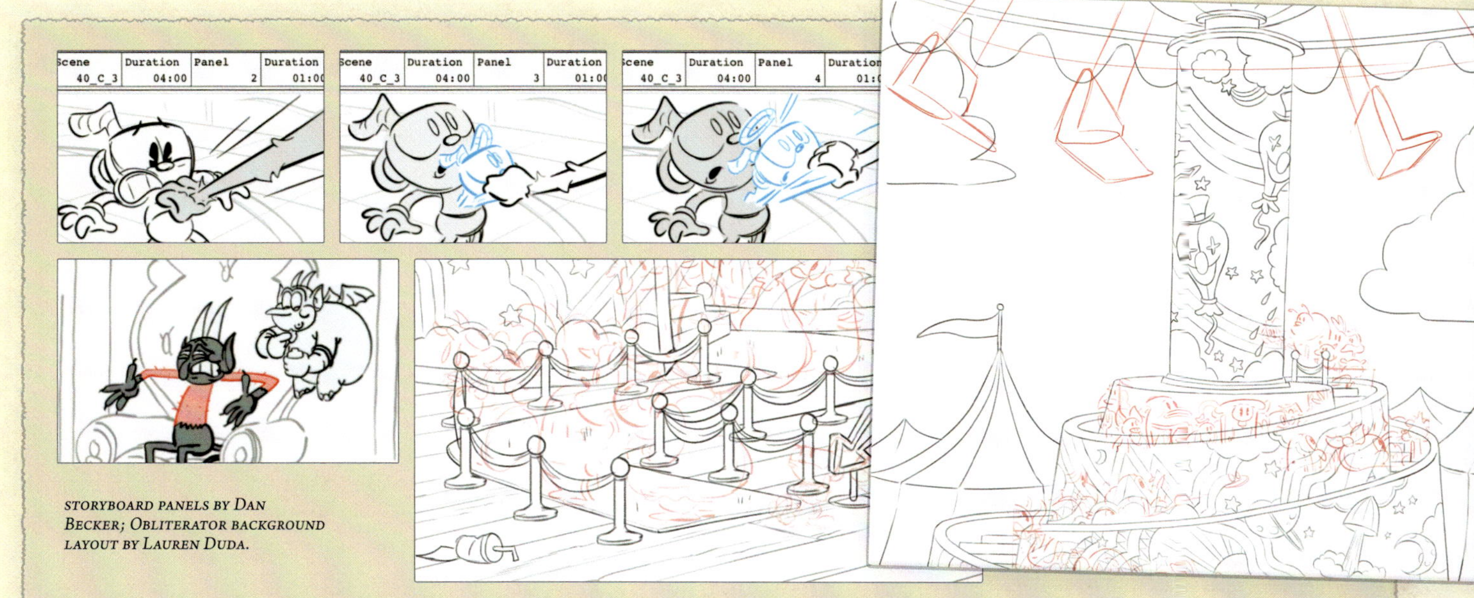

STORYBOARD PANELS BY DAN BECKER; OBLITERATOR BACKGROUND LAYOUT BY LAUREN DUDA.

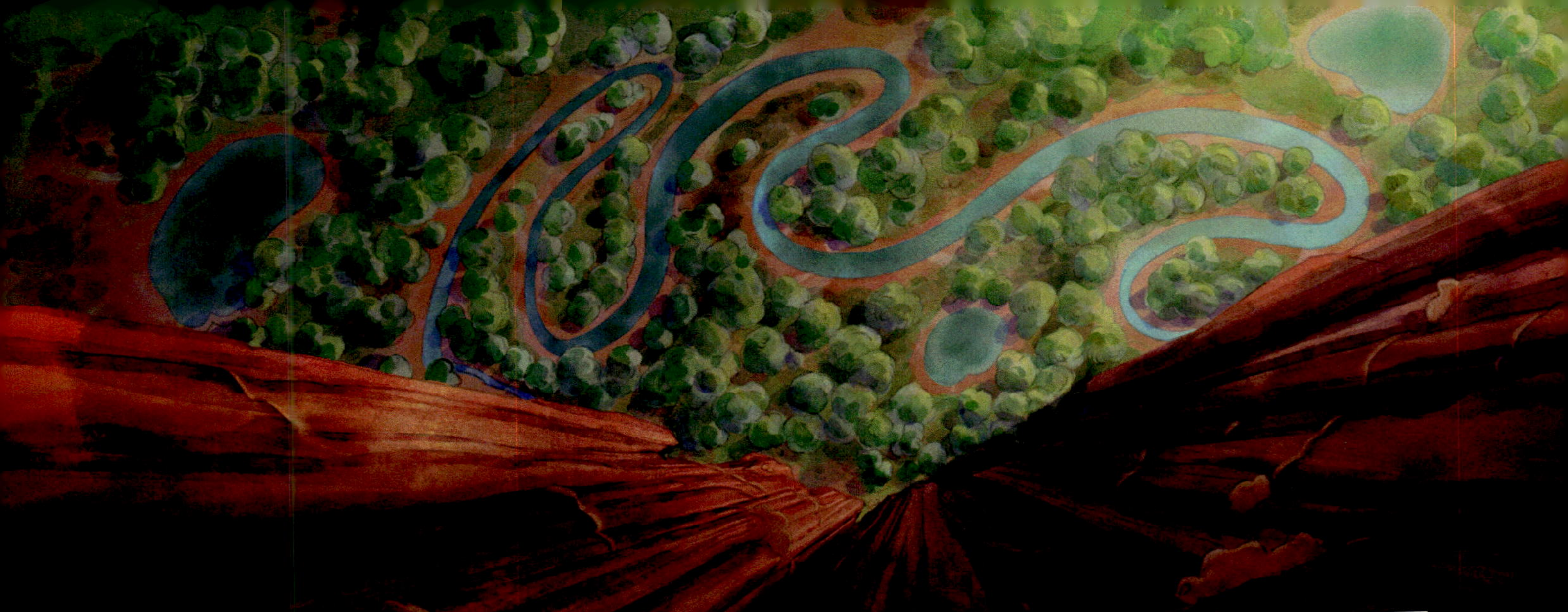

EPISODE 10

"DANGEROUS MUGMAN"

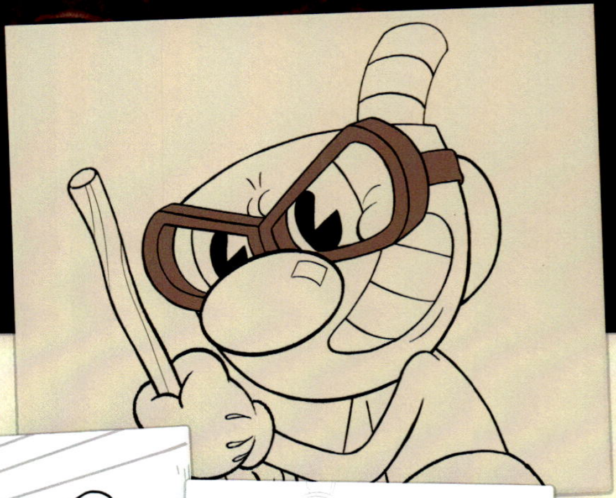

MICHELLE: The whole design team is so strong. I felt like each painting I did improved just by seeing the work everyone else was doing.

ANDREA: It's Michelle's fault that the painting is so complex on the show. When she came in and did Porkrind's, we said, "Can you make it look as beautiful and as painterly as *Snow White*?" And she said, "Okay." And it came out absolutely perfect.

DAVE: That might be my favorite painting in the whole show.

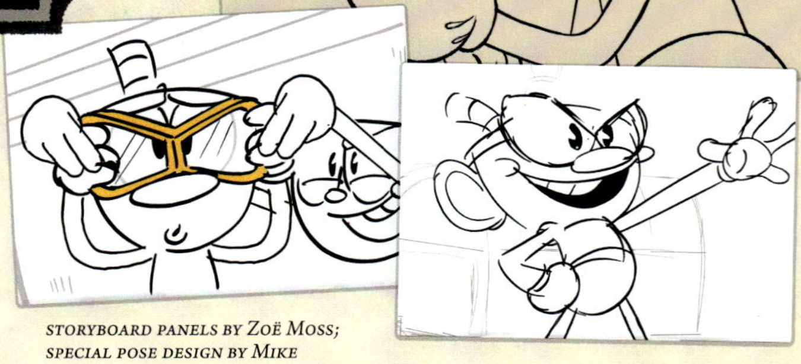

Storyboard panels by Zoë Moss; special pose design by Mike Fontanelli.

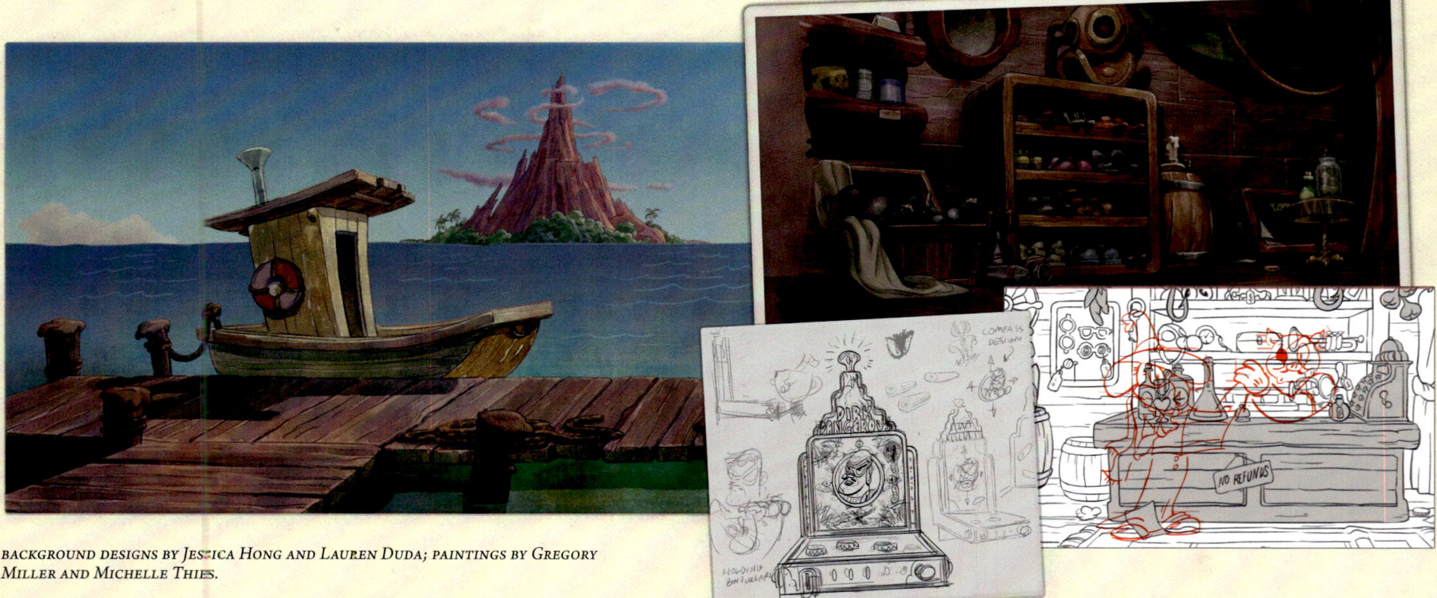

Background designs by Jessica Hong and Lauren Duda; paintings by Gregory Miller and Michelle Thies.

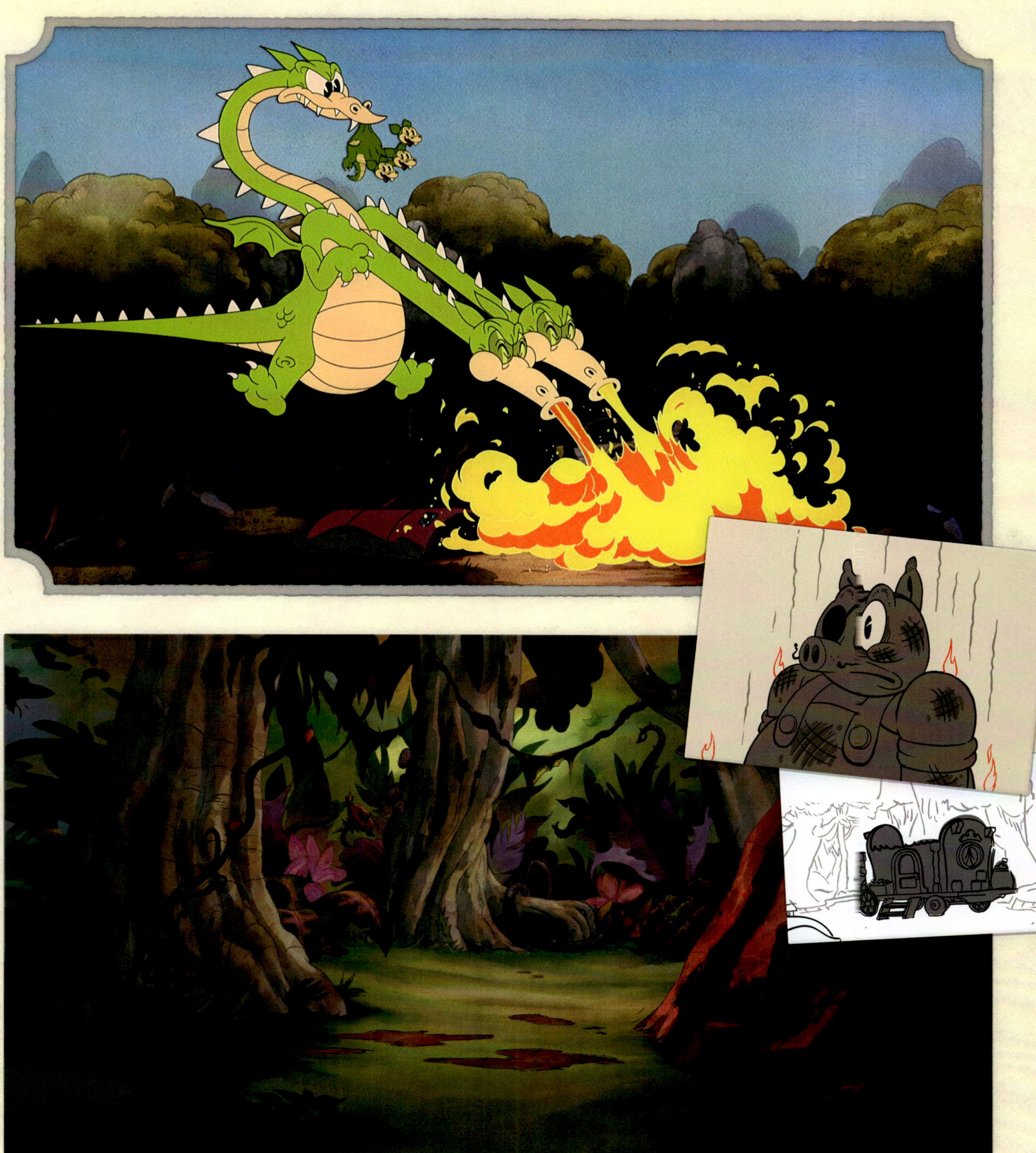

→ **ANDREA:** Greg Miller did this painting, and it just knocked everybody out.

GREG: I had been wanting to get onto a watercolor show for, like, twenty years. I used to be an illustrator, and I did watercolors. When I started this show, it felt like this is what I should have been doing for a while now.

ANDREA: Greg is a phenomenal watercolorist, so it was awesome getting him on this show. When we saw his first painting, the whole team went, "What the?!" He blew it out of the water. Just came in all nonchalant—laid down incredible watercolor like it was nobody's business—and I just said, "Whoa, take it easy, rock star."

STORYBOARD PANEL BY ZOË MOSS; GRIM MATCHSTICK AND BURNED-UP PORKRIND SPECIAL POSES BY DAVE WASSON; BACKGROUND DESIGN BY JESSICA HONG; PAINTING BY GREGORY MILLER; JUNGLE BACKGROUND DESIGN BY ANDREA FERNANDEZ; PAINTING BY GREGORY MILLER.

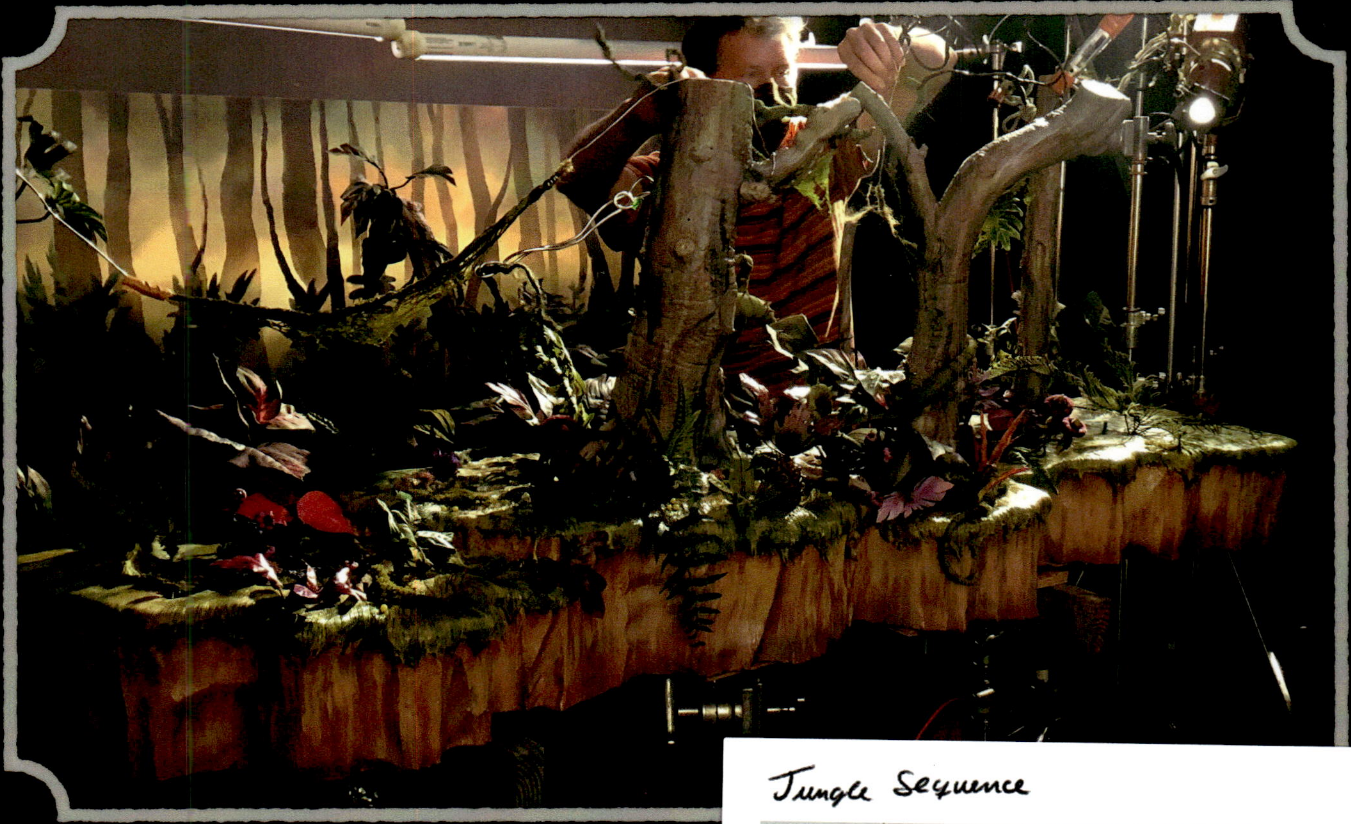

◆ STOP-MO SPOTLIGHT ◆

THE JUNGLE

COSMO: I really love the "Dangerous Mugman" sets. Screen Novelties took what Andrea's team imagined as this really lush, overgrown, moss-covered, purple-orange, very colorful jungle, and they were able to realize it in three dimensions. It's really beautiful. I could just live in that little world they made.

LAUREN: My favorite part was designing sets that got turned into stop-motion elements. It was such a unique experience to this show. It's always great seeing your backgrounds get painted, but this was a whole different level. Screen Novelties stuck to our backgrounds. They took exactly what I drew and modeled it. Screen Novelties just knocked it out of the park.

ANDREA: The stereoscopic stuff is pretty amazing to see come together.

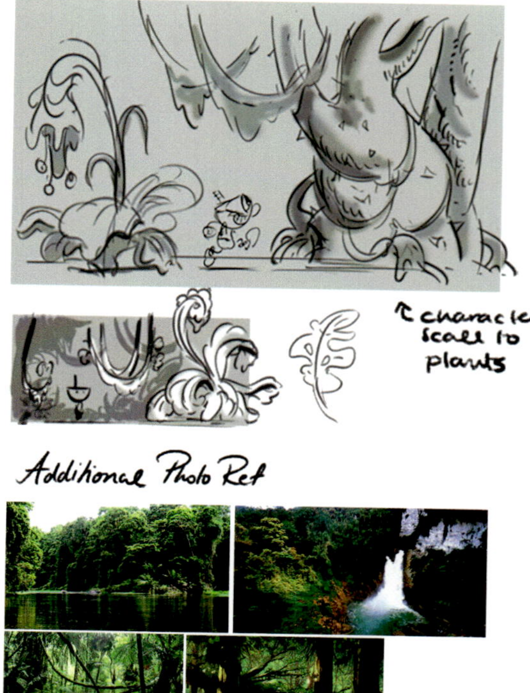

BACKGROUND PREVIS AND REFERENCE BY COSMO SEGURSON AND FINISHED DESIGN USED BY SCREEN NOVELTIES TO CREATE THE JUNGLE SET.

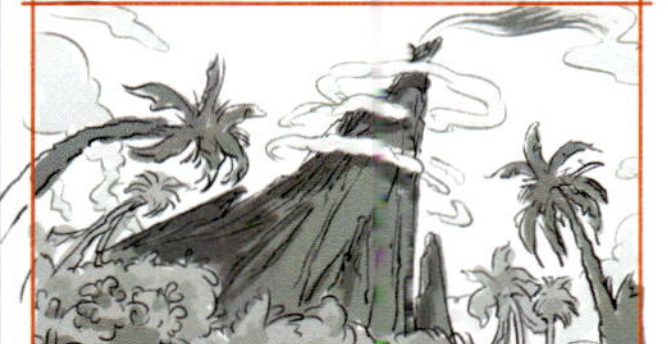
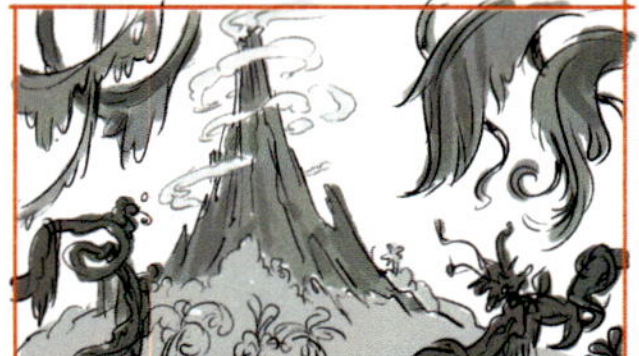
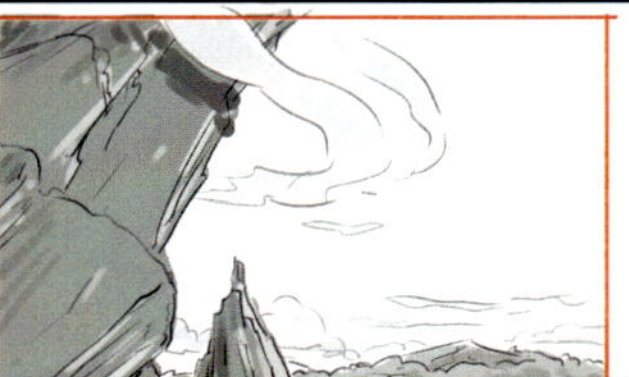
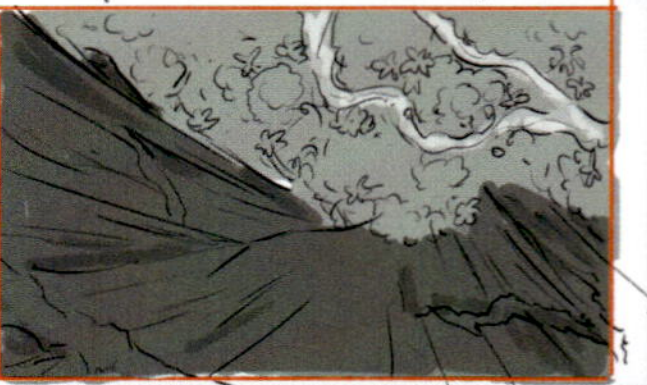

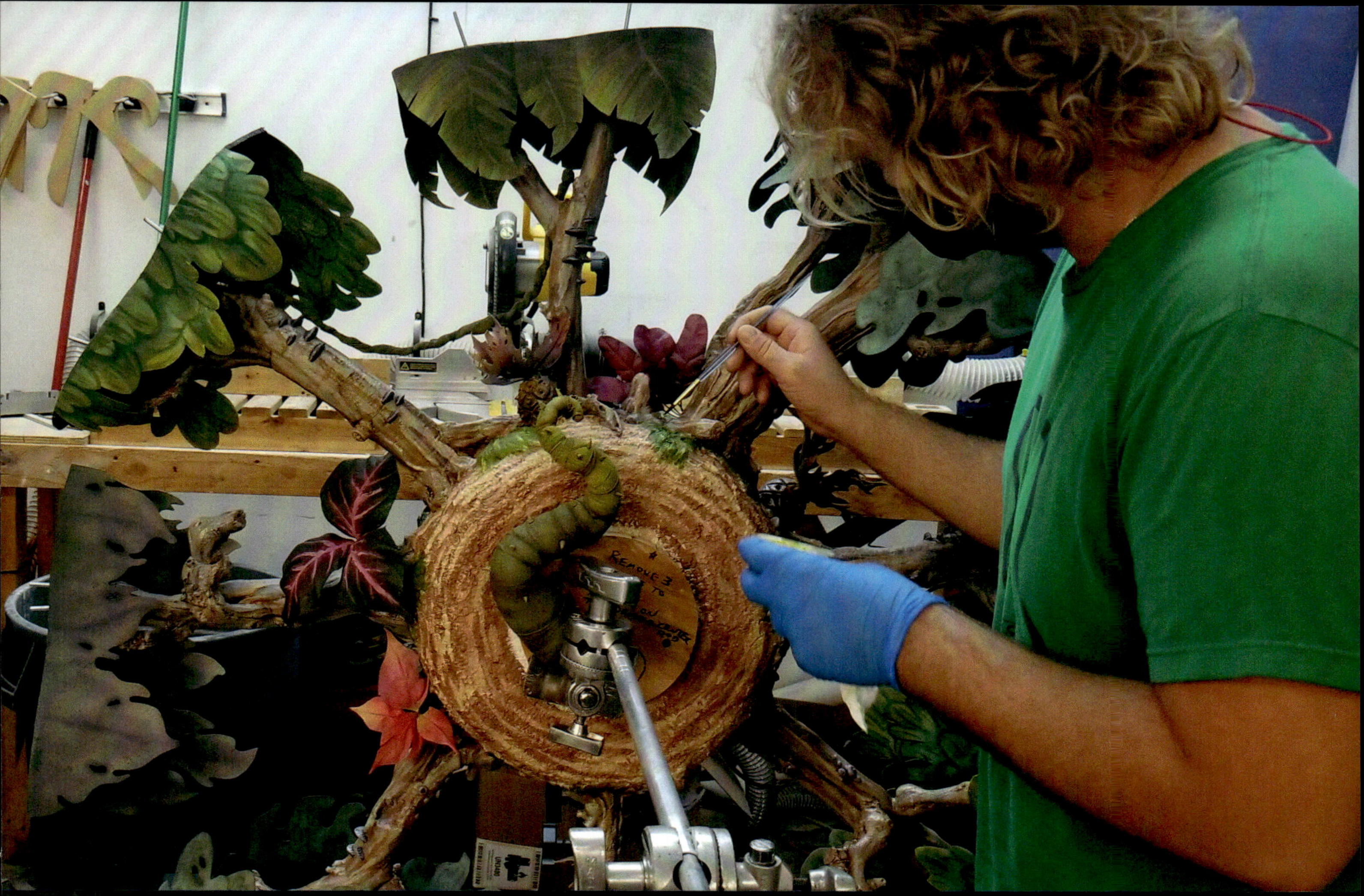

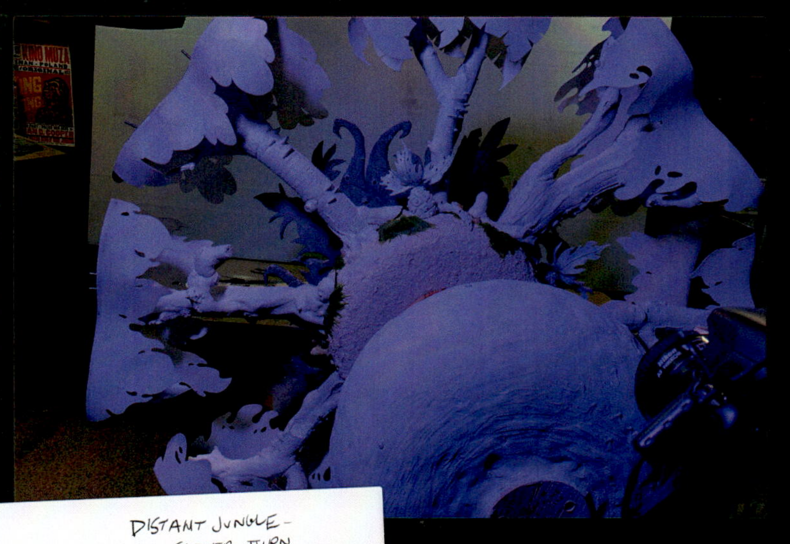

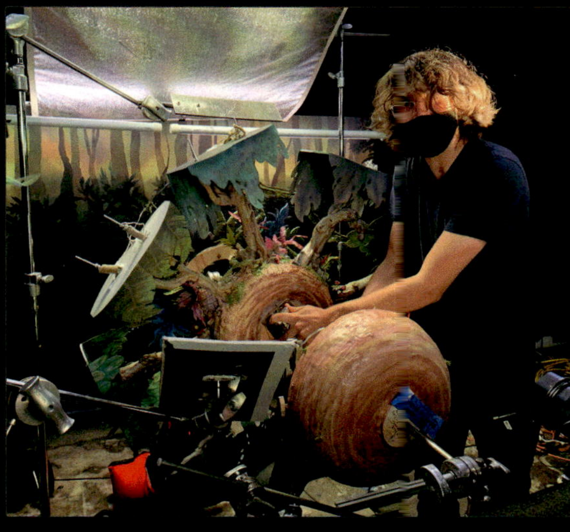

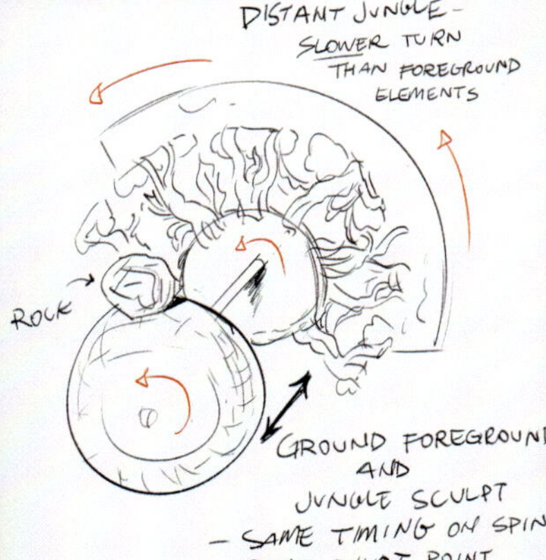

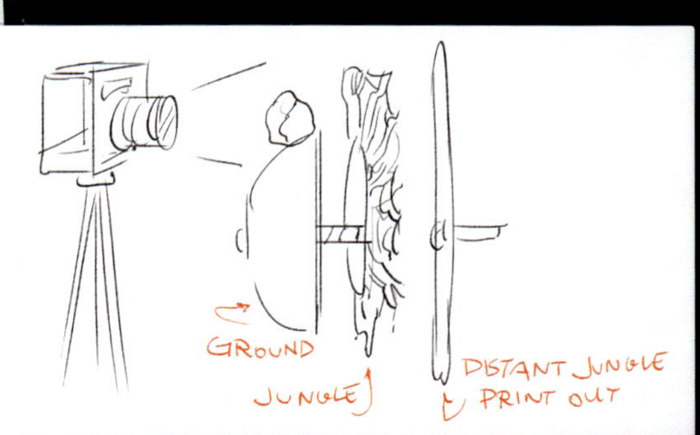

→ **ANDREA:** That episode in particular was really interesting—it has seven or eight stop-motion shots. Getting all the animation to line up with the matte paintings being done by Greg on our team was a challenge, but it's so worth it when it all comes together.

Previs by Cosmo Segurson; jungle set production stills by Screen Novelties.

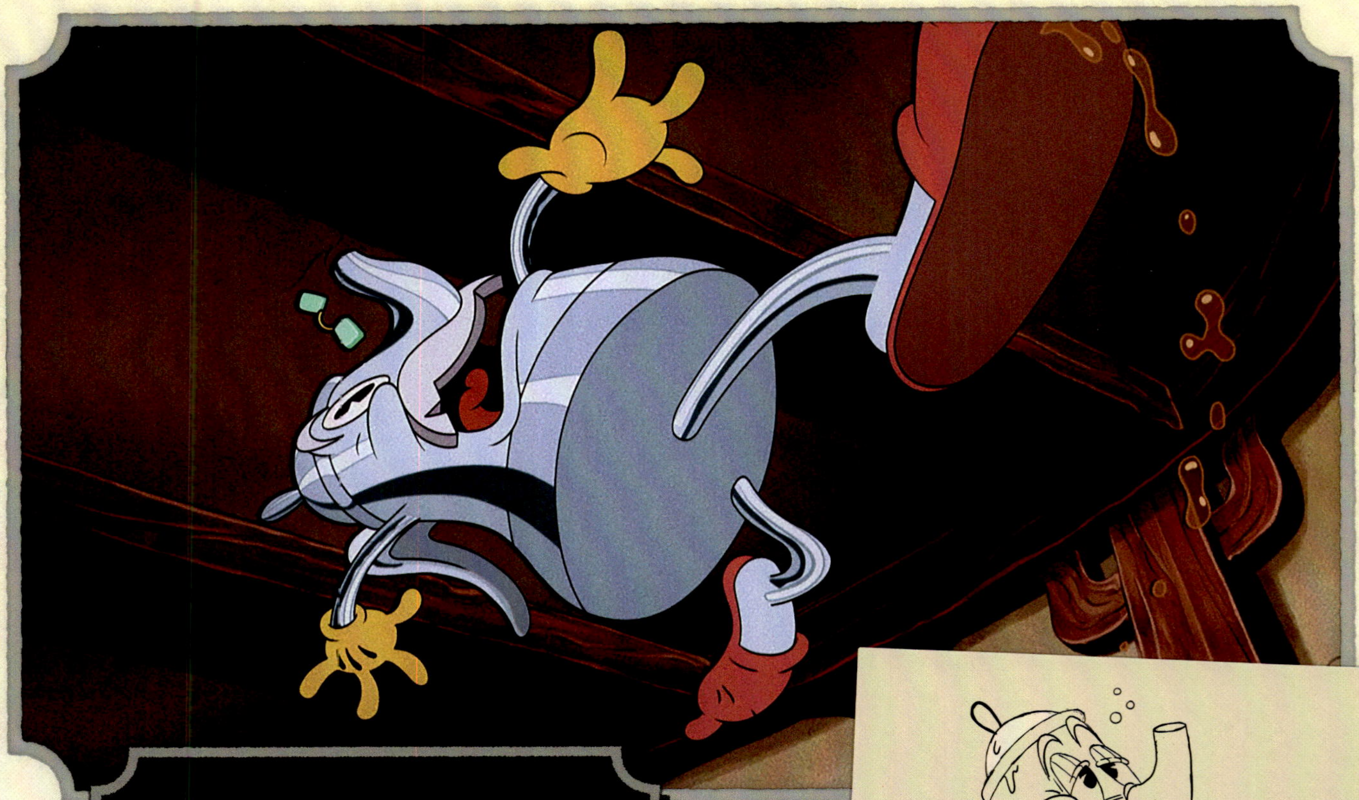

EPISODE 11

"DIRT NAP"

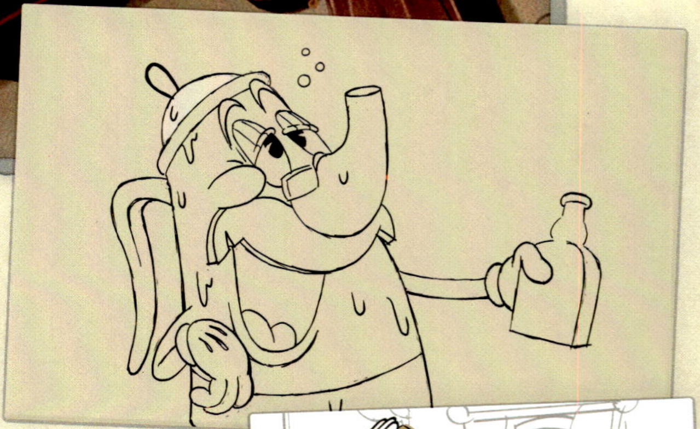

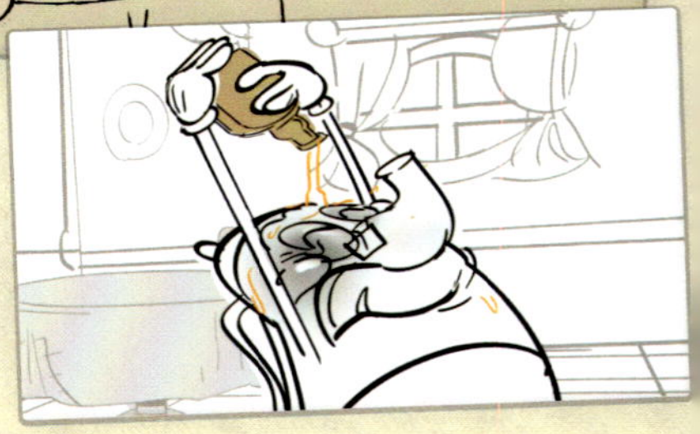

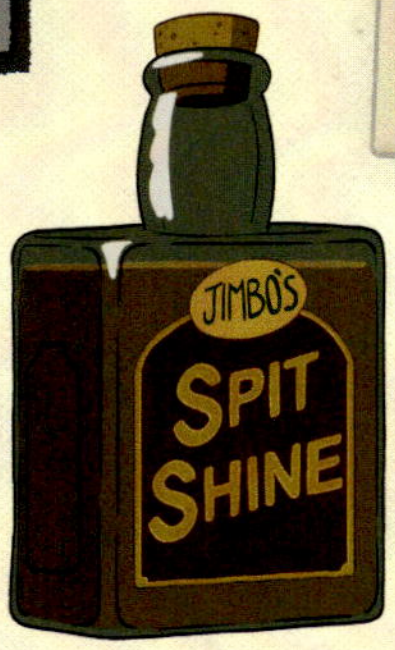

STORYBOARD PANEL BY KARL HADRIKA; PROP DESIGN BY ADAM DIX.

DAVE: We knew we wanted a story that focused on Elder Kettle. That was in the back of our minds when we were in the middle of breaking all that invisible-sweater stuff and figuring out all the rules and story beats. We were about to break for the day, and I said, "Wouldn't it be great if we had a story where Elder Kettle thought the boys were trying to kill him?" We beat that story out in, like, fifteen minutes—it just flowed out of us, and we were laughing our heads off.

KARL HADRIKA, *THE CUPHEAD SHOW!* STORYBOARD ARTIST: "Dirt Nap" is so inherently funny—when the log line is funny, it always makes for a great episode.

DEEKI: There are phases to that episode, and they build off one another and escalate—Kettle hears their compliments, then their concern, their pity, and finally what he believes is their intention to put him out of his misery.

KARL: There's a lot of internal agony. You see a darkness in his eyes when he thinks the boys are planning to kill him. It makes it so much funnier, because it's cups and a teakettle.

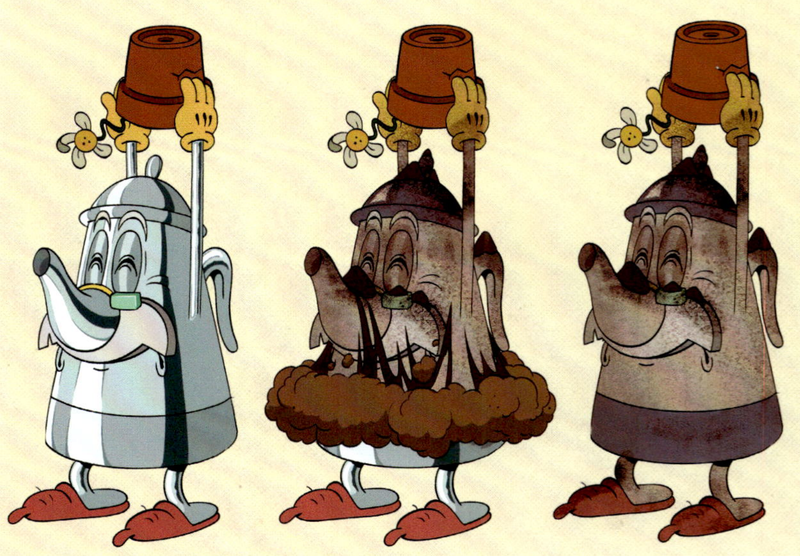

SPECIAL POSE DESIGNS BY MIKE FONTANELLI AND DAVE WASSON; COLOR DESIGN BY CHRIS HACKER; FX DESIGN BY ADAM DIX.

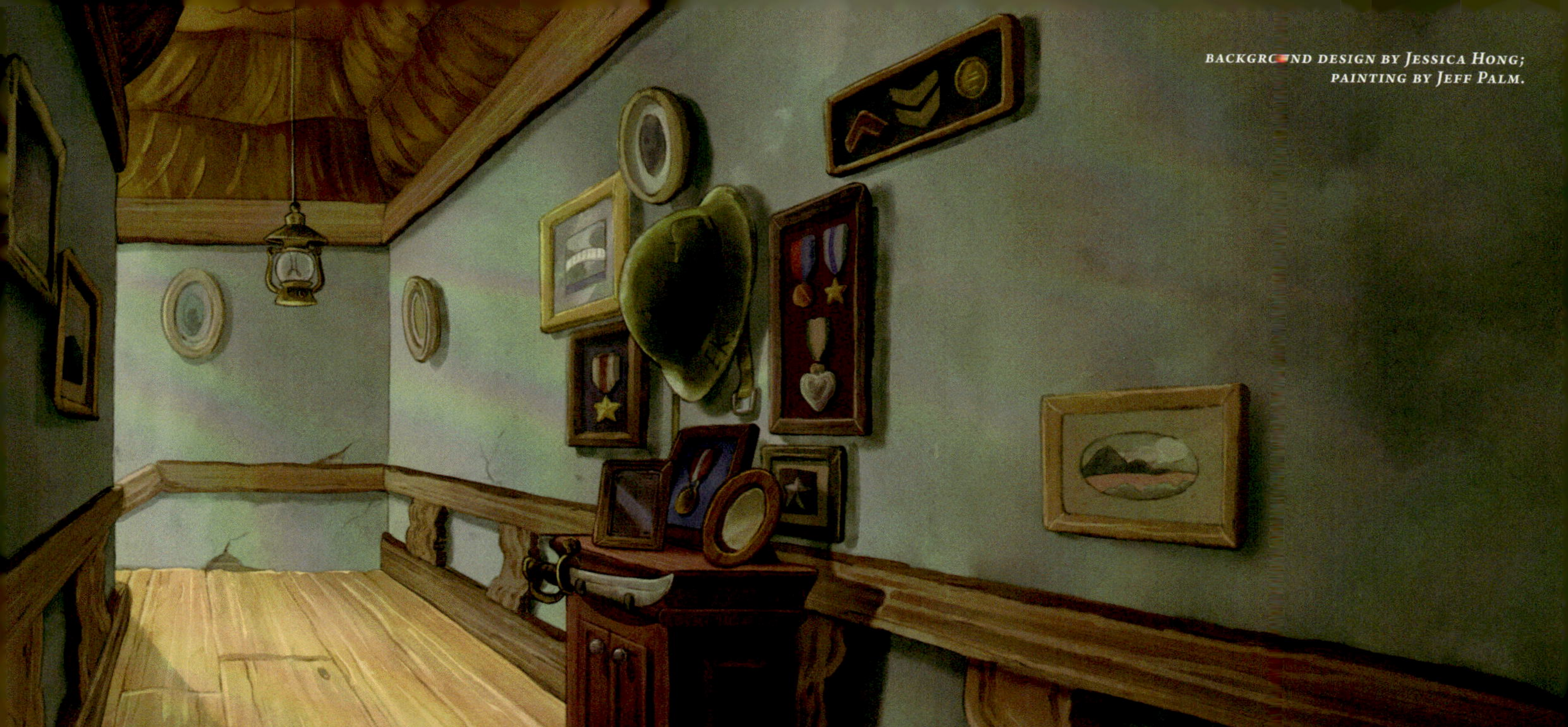

Background design by Jessica Hong; painting by Jeff Palm.

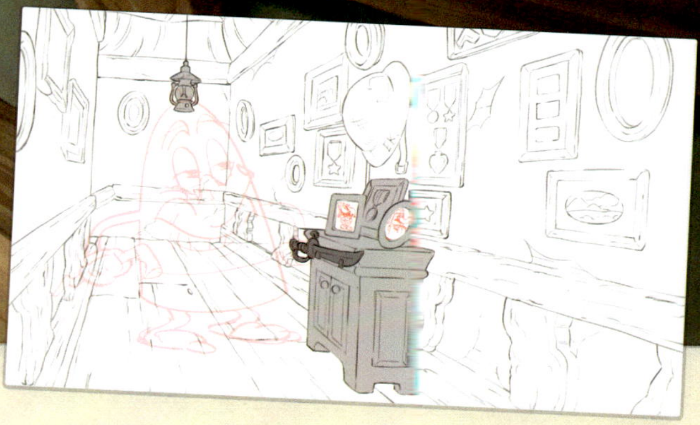

→ **ELI:** The little medals and swords on the wall in the game became the basis for this really rich, hilarious veteran persona that Elder Kettle takes on in the show.

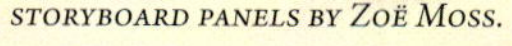

Storyboard panels by Zoë Moss.

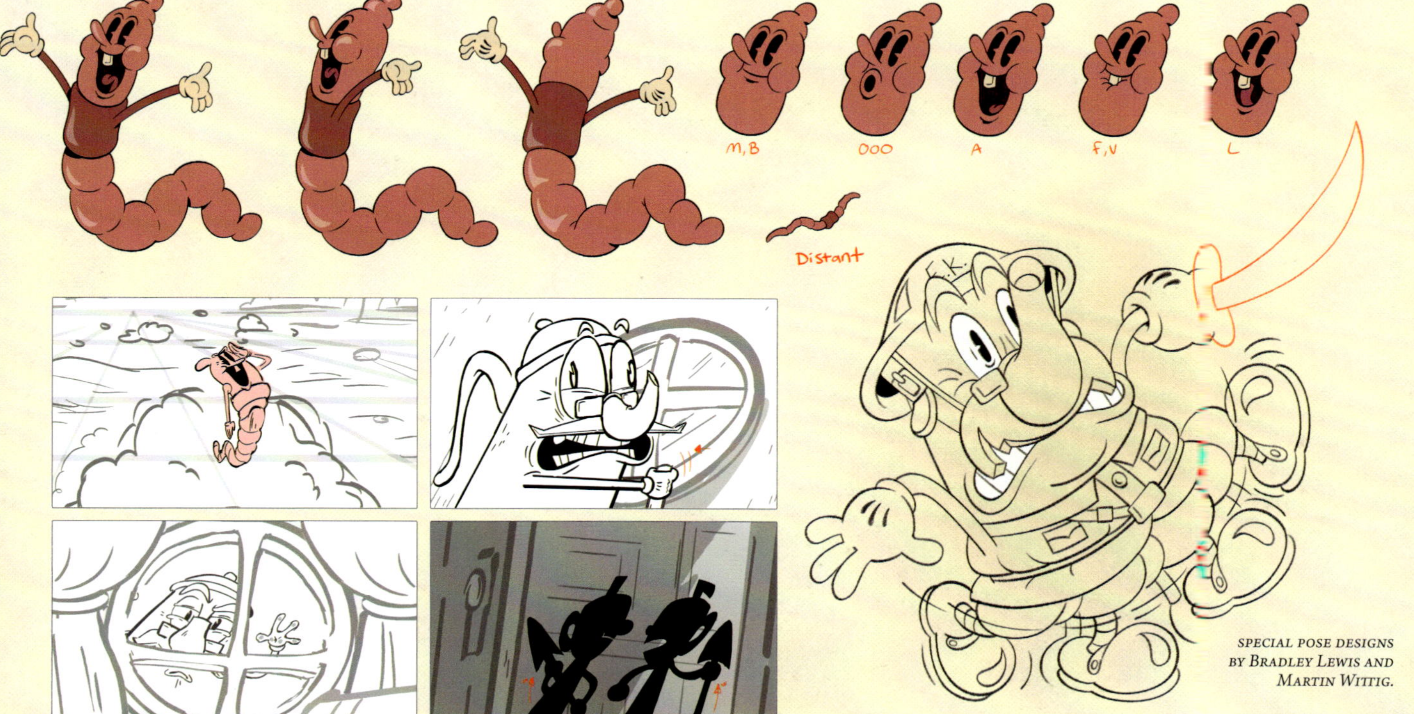

Special pose designs by Bradley Lewis and Martin Wittig.

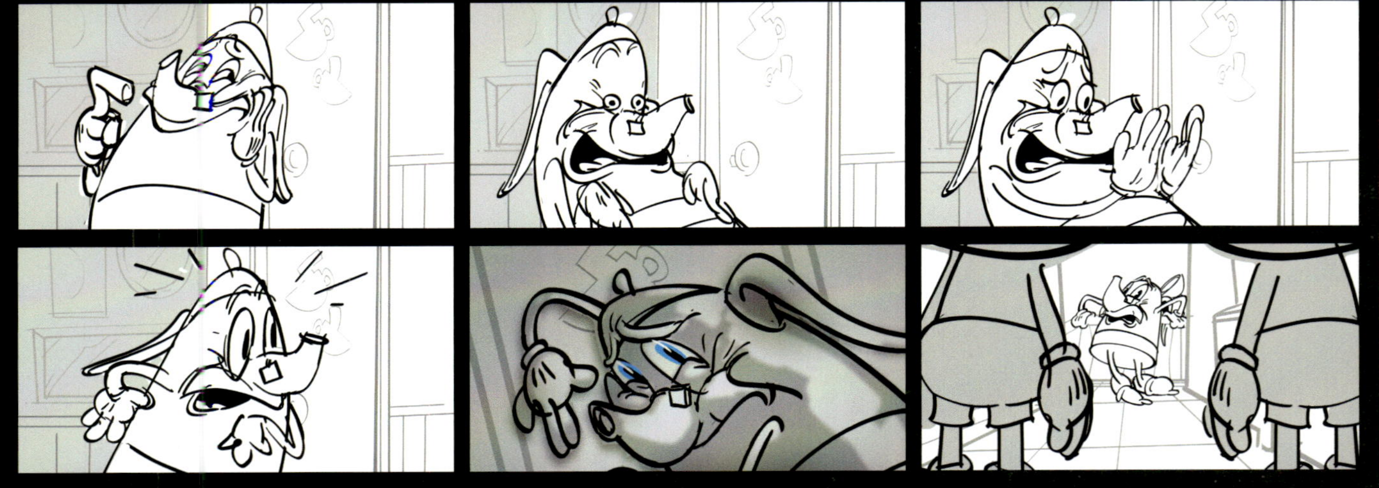

◆ STORYBOARD SPOTLIGHT ◆

REFLECTIVE KETTLE

→ **KARL:** Kettle fearing for his life yields really funny kinds of contortions. He's wrathful and paranoid. It's fun to draw those kinds of emotions.

CLAY: I always like the most basic, clear staging for visual comedy. Unless we were setting something up, it was mostly clear, straightforward staging—which is kind of what comedy filmmaking was like in the '30s anyway. Not a lot of complicated camera work going on in the Three Stooges. An episode like "Dirt Nap" is funniest when there's restraint in the staging, so you can savor the character moments. Karl's Elder Kettle expressions you absolutely want to savor.

KARL: Elder Kettle has a big placard of a face with little tube arms and legs. That was a great opportunity to zero in on some of his funny expressions.

SHAKEH: Karl made the best storyboard pitches with his Elder Kettle voice. He had Elder Kettle down. The timing, the way he pitched the boards—he was hilarious.

KARL: It does require spending time looking in the mirror and making faces at yourself, challenging yourself to make the most horrible, unflattering faces possible, and then saving them to use later.

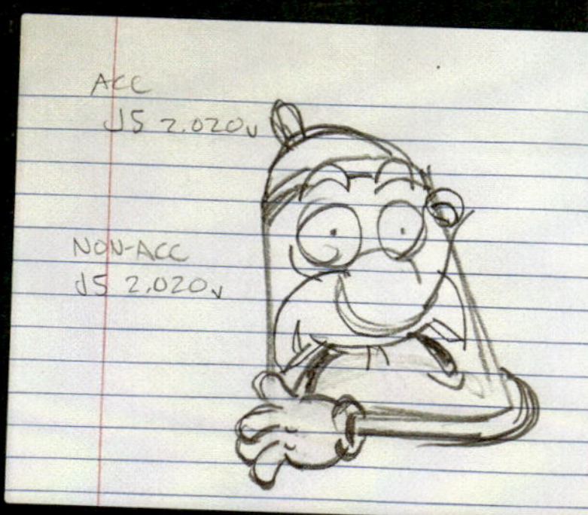

STORYBOARD PANELS BY KARL HADRIKA; STORY ROOM SKETCH BY CLAY MORROW.

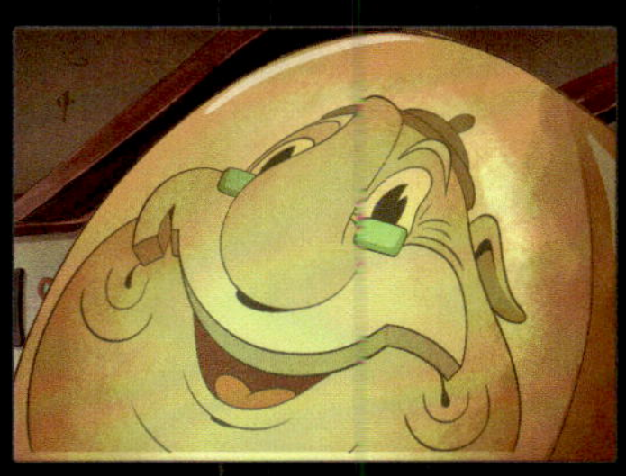

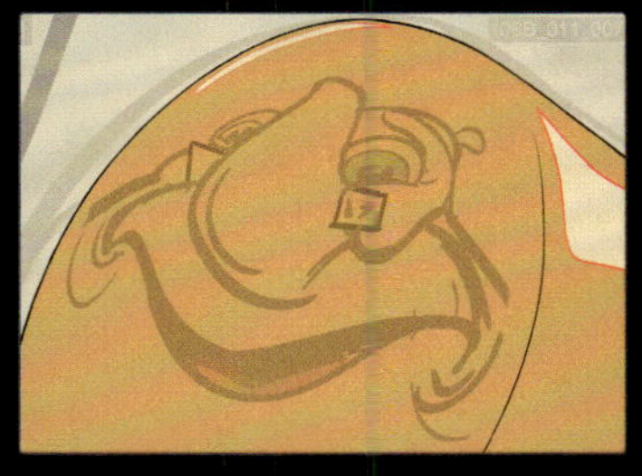

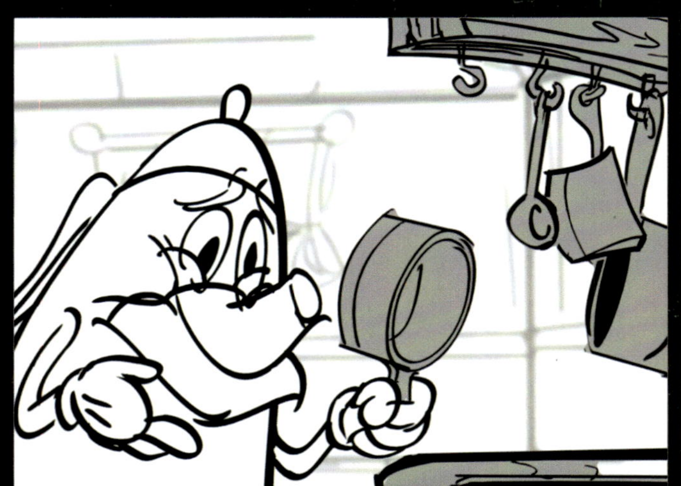

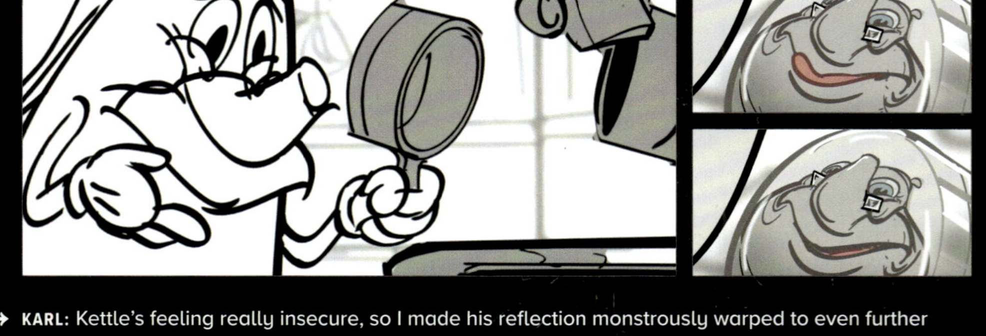

STORYBOARD PANELS BY KARL HADRIKA; SPECIAL POSE DESIGN BY BRADLEY LEWIS.

→ **KARL:** Kettle's feeling really insecure, so I made his reflection monstrously warped to even further magnify his insecurity. It's never flattering to look at your face from below, like when you accidentally turn your phone camera and see yourself. It literally magnified the sadness and the hurt in his eyes. It was a reflection of what he thought of himself.

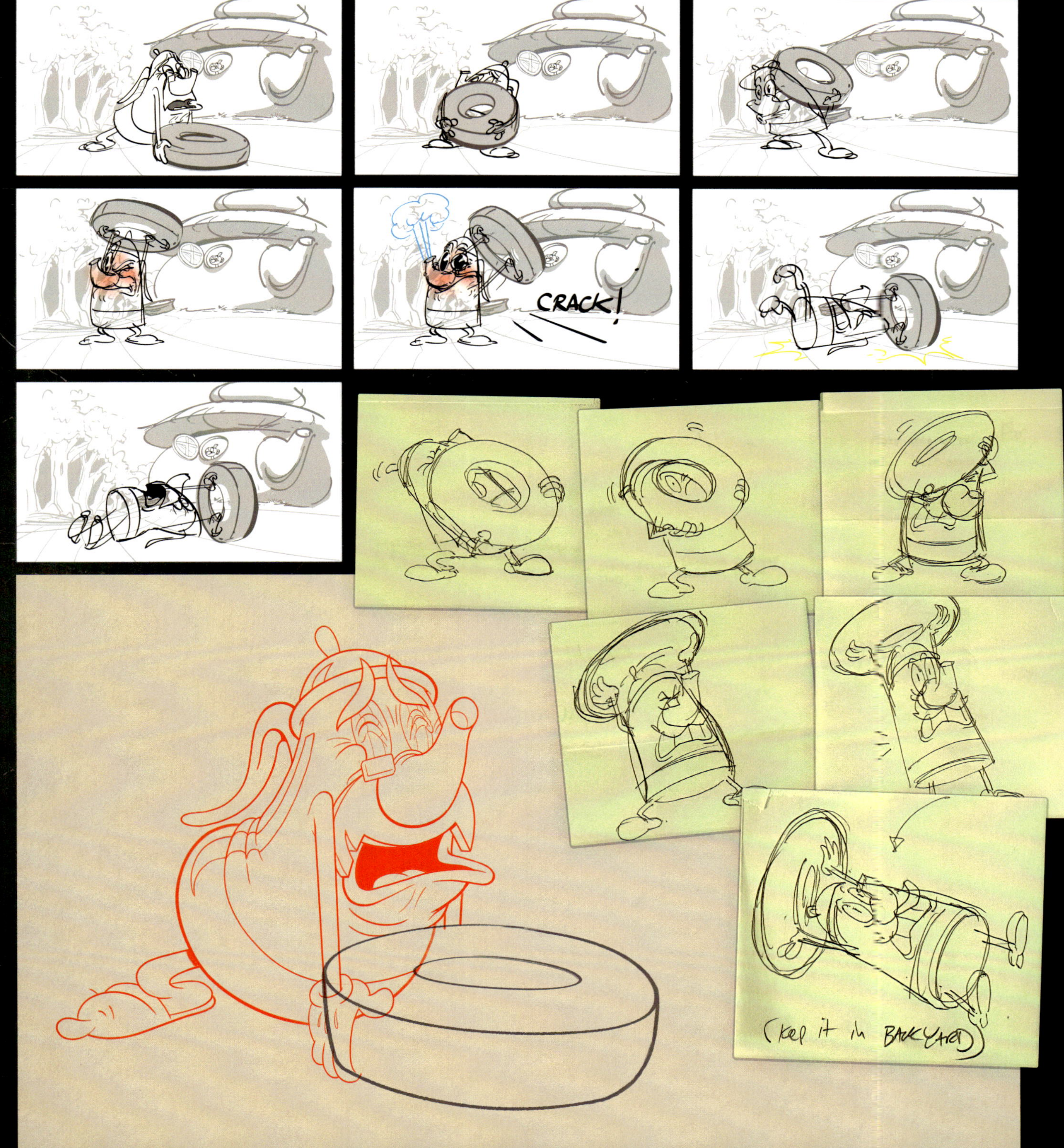

STORYBOARD PANELS BY KARL HADRIKA; STORY ROOM SKETCHES BY CLAY MORROW; SPECIAL POSE DESIGN BY MIKE FONTANELLI.

→ **KARL:** Elder Kettle trying to pick up a tire was one of those things where I had to think about how I would act it out. There's an added hesitation where he holds it up, and he tries to speak, but he has a throat spasm, and no air comes out. I love nuance like that. More often than not, in TV animation, a lot of those nuances don't make the cut. *Cuphead* is one of those shows where we knew our work was in good hands.

CLAY: Adam Paloian is super ambitious, and he wants to direct the legacy episodes. I don't care as much about that. I feel like some of the board artists picked up on that and were disappointed when they didn't get one of the epic ones. Until we saw "Dirt Nap," and they understood that with great character personalities, you can do more with less. You can create something pretty great—you don't have to go to the moon and back or introduce a new character.

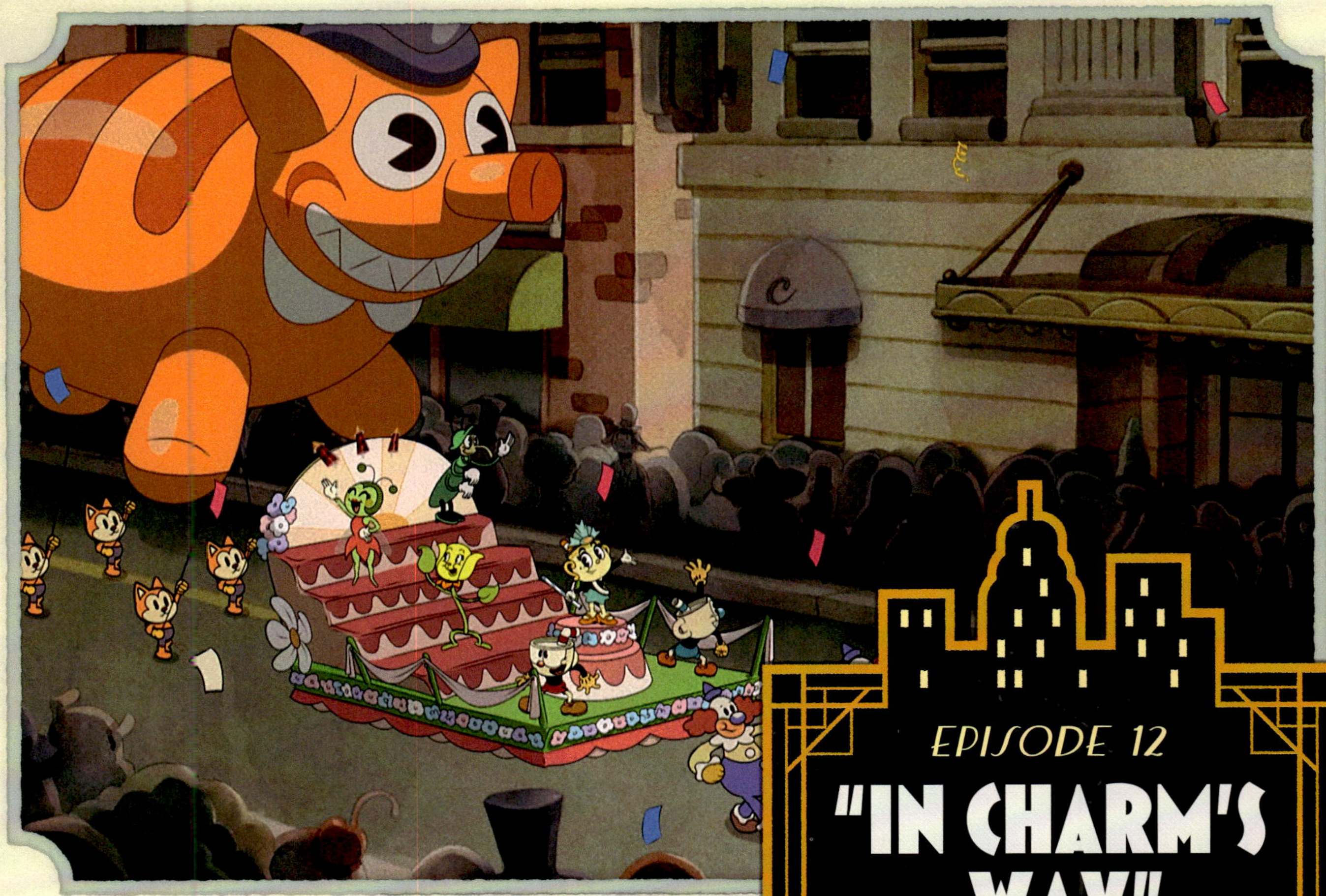

EPISODE 12

"IN CHARM'S WAY"

DEEP DIVE

DESIGNING INKWELL CITY

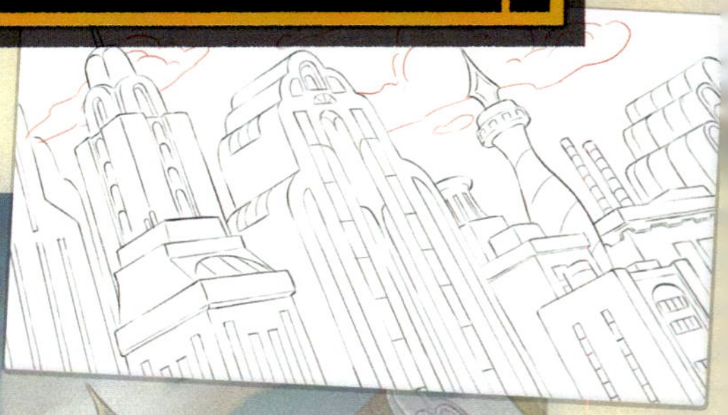

→ **ANDREA:** Inkwell City wouldn't be what it is if it weren't for Chalice: I wanted to make the city a stage for her. I was so excited about Chalice that I think "In Charm's Way" ended up being one of our strongest episodes visually. We placed real structures alongside whimsical structures. That gives the audience the signal that it's not just Fleischer inspired—it's something new based on those aesthetics.

JESSICA: It's a pretty distinct shape language—but we try to mix and match stranger, more fantastical elements. We have giant ballpoint pens or giant ink droppers, something that tells you this is not an average city for humans; it's more fun and fantastical. Art deco has such interesting, sometimes organic, shapes, so it's easy to combine those two elements and make something fun looking.

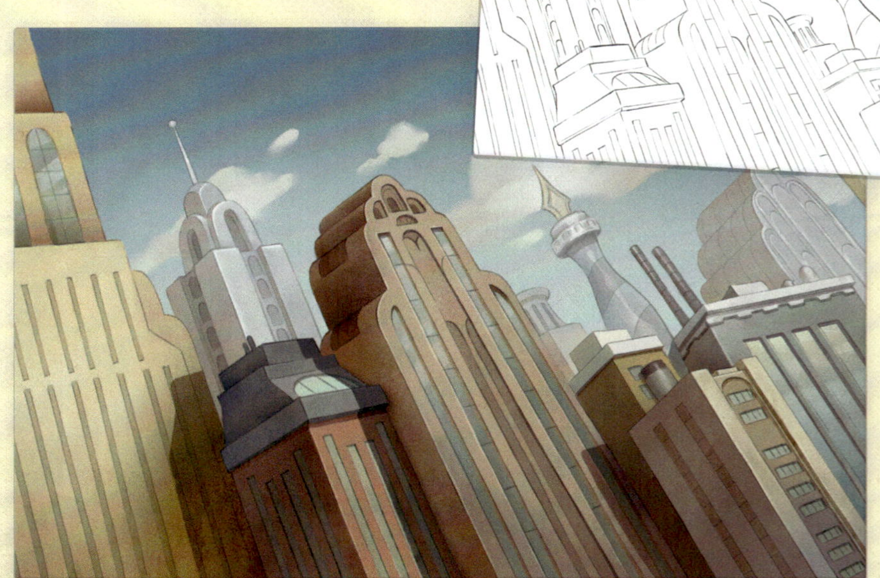

STORYBOARD PANELS BY *MEGAN BOYD*; BACKGROUND DESIGN BY *LAUREN DUDA*; PAINTING BY *MALLORY CARLSON*.

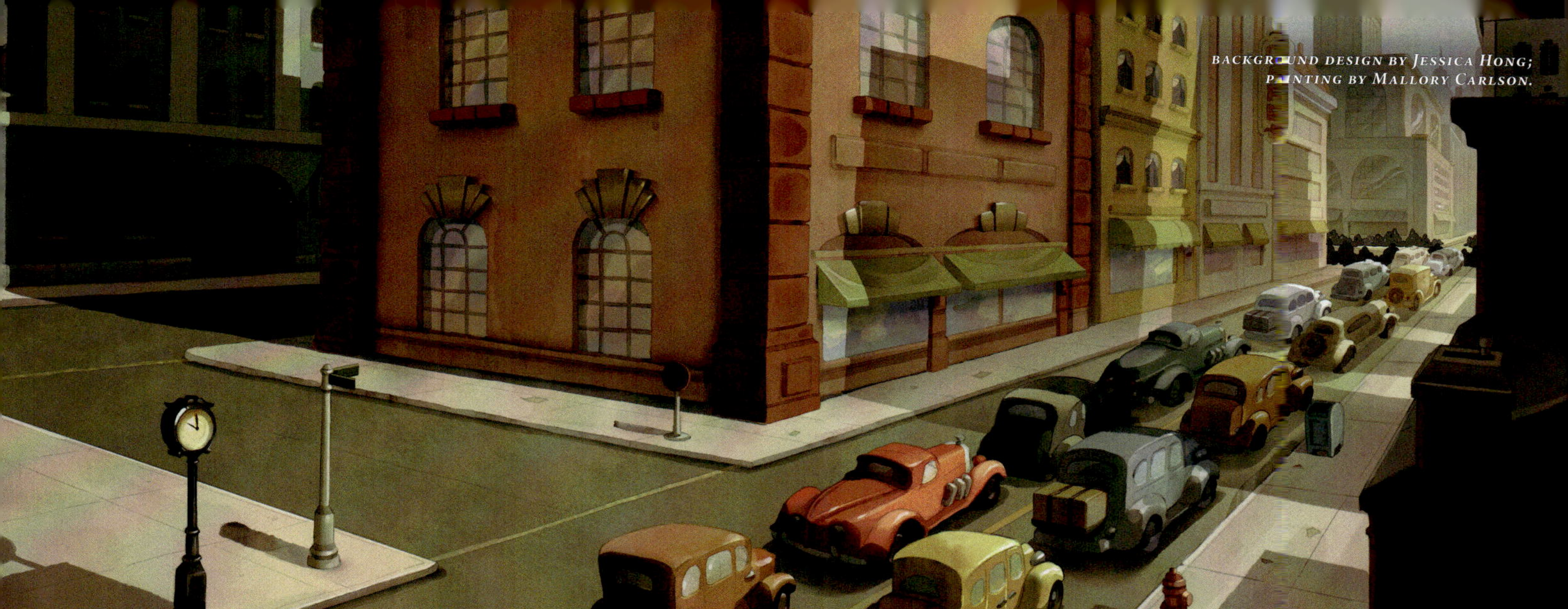

Background design by Jessica Hong; painting by Mallory Carlson.

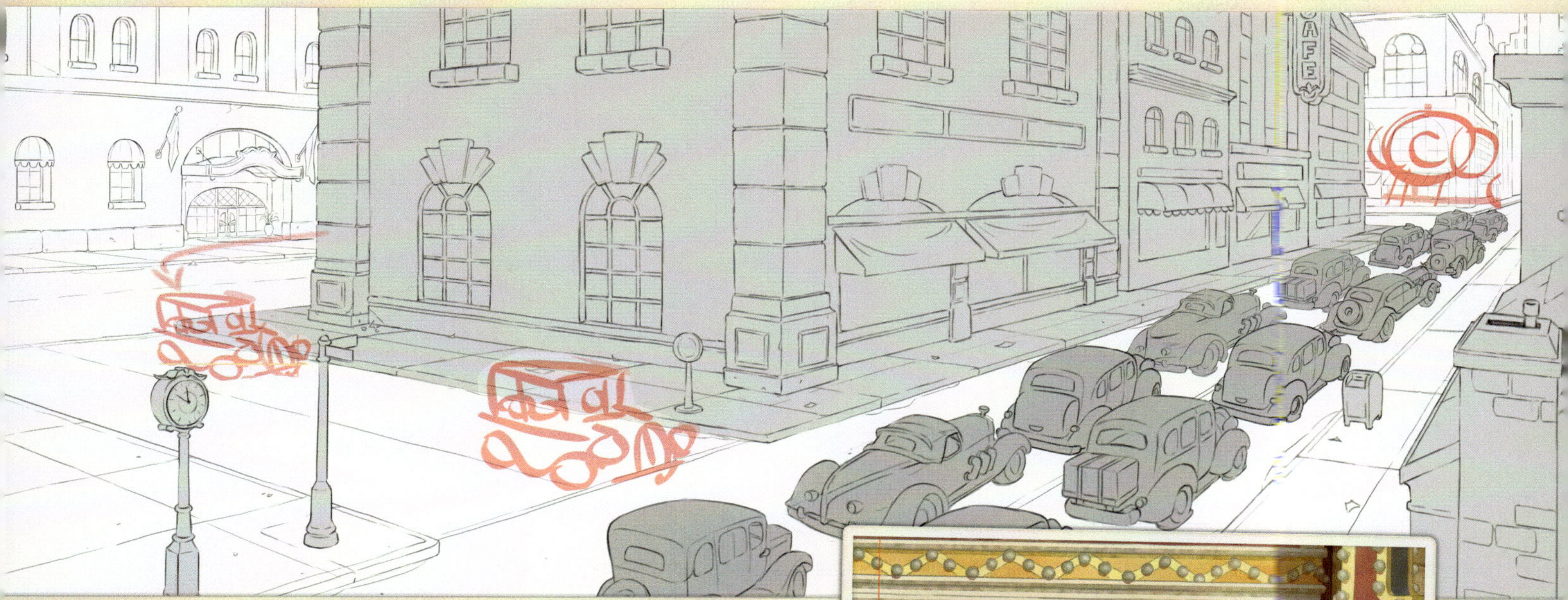

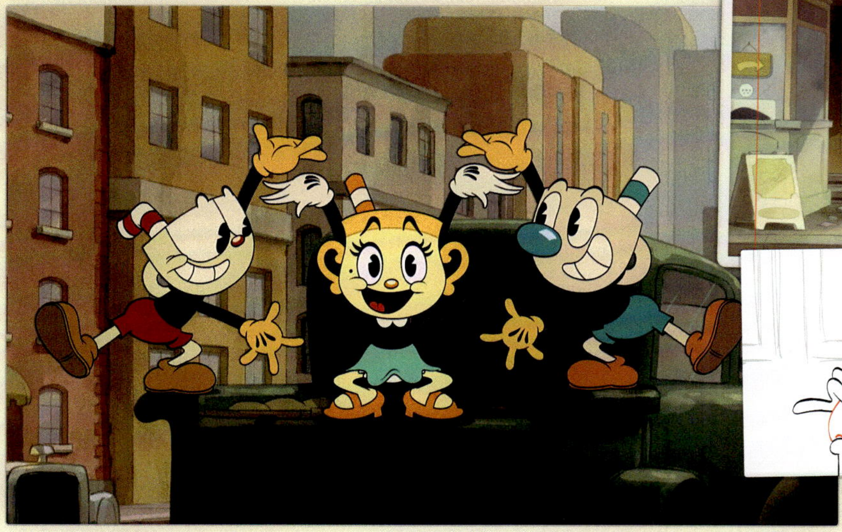

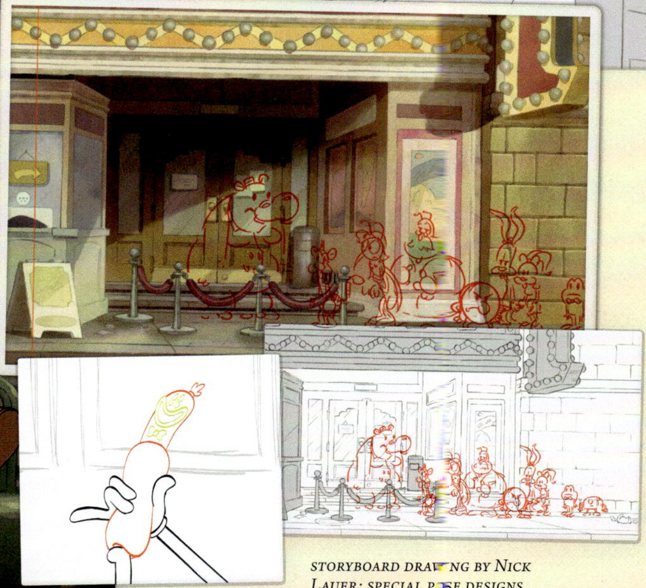

Storyboard drawing by Nick Lauer; special pose designs by Tapan Gandhi

→ **ANDREA:** Jess was pretty instrumental in building out the city. She's like the resident urban planner for Inkwell City. She draws so well; a lot of the conversations were about dialing it back. For those city scenes that were so Fleischer inspired and really difficult to execute—I think a lot of designers would have difficulty with these locations.

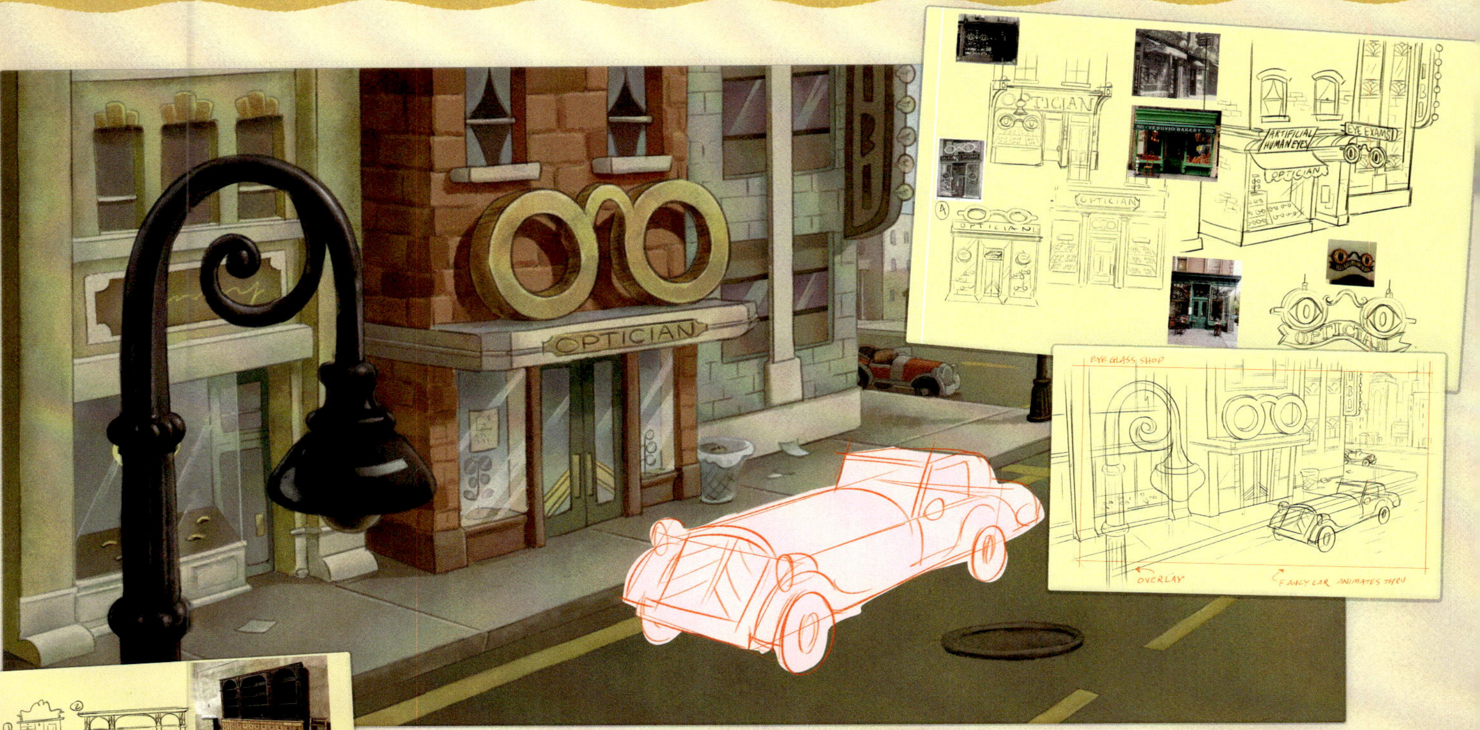

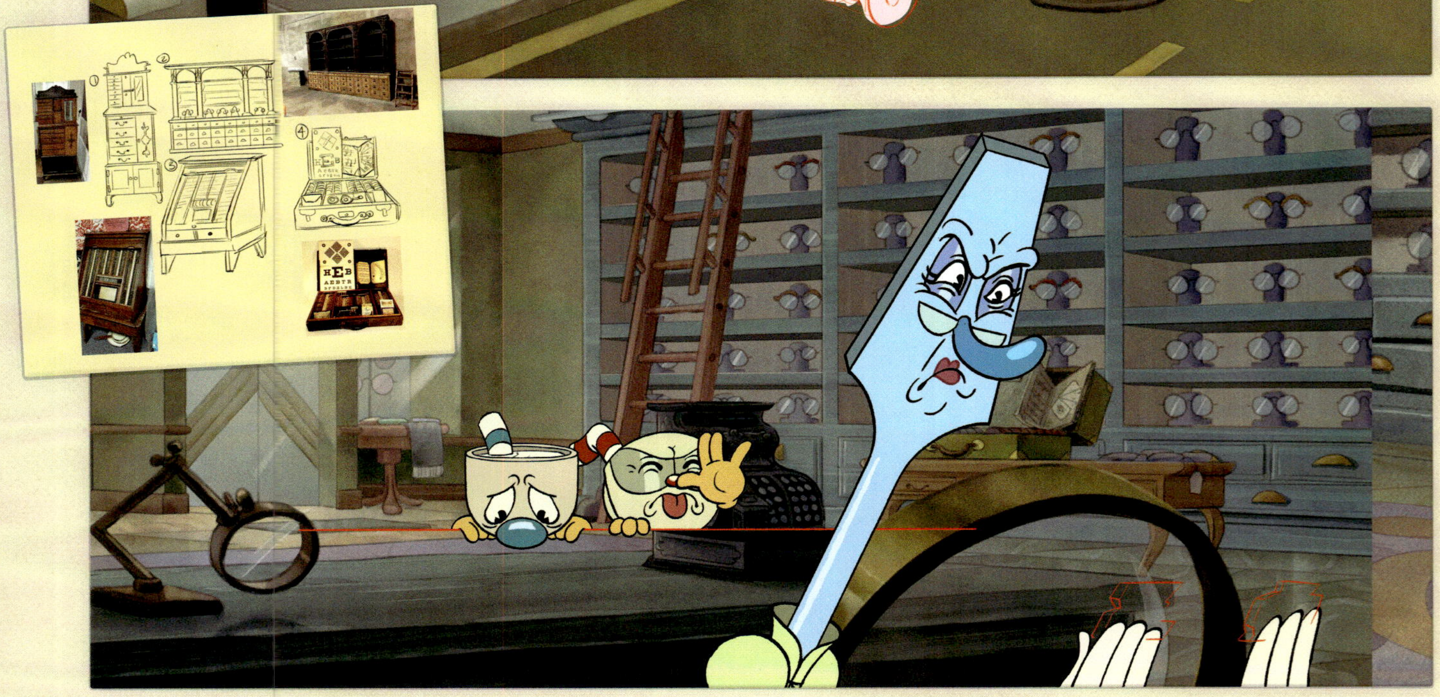

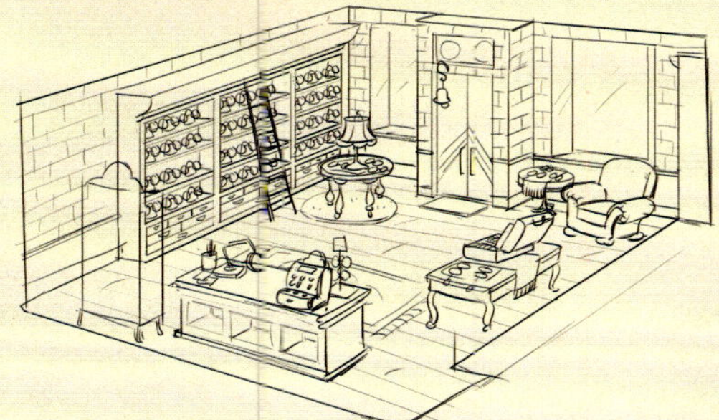

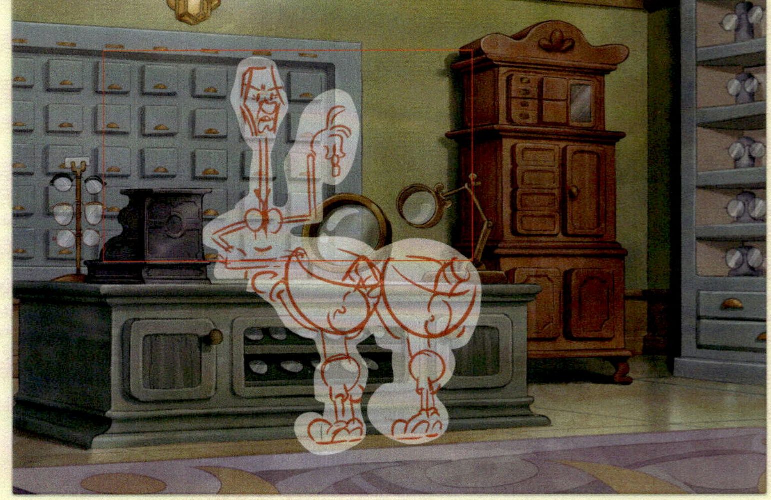

→ **JESSICA:** I really have to credit Laisay—she has the ability to keep things structural but also keep them cartoony and fun.

ANDREA: Getting there took a lot of torturing Laisay, but it totally paid off!

previs by Cosmo Segurson; background designs by Lauren Duda; paintings by Michelle Thies.

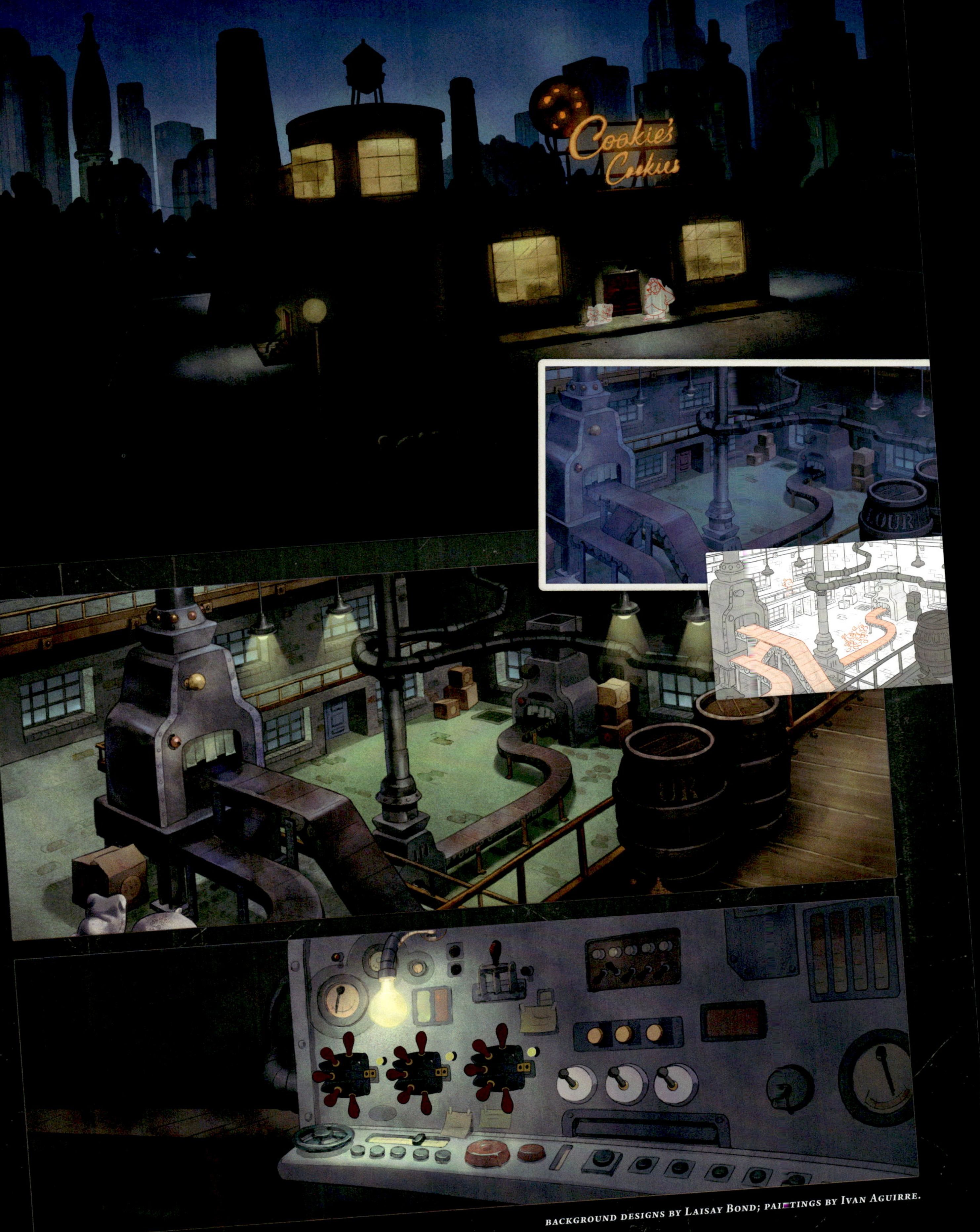

Background designs by Laisay Bond; paintings by Ivan Aguirre.

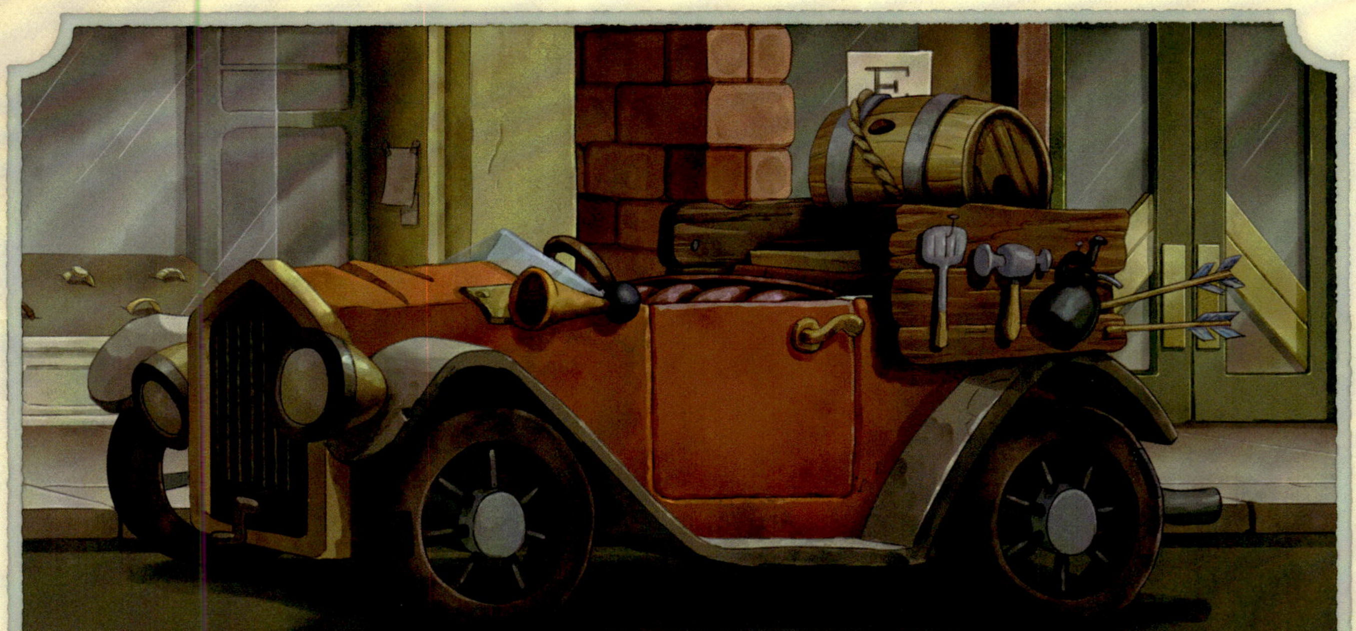

VEHICLE DESIGN

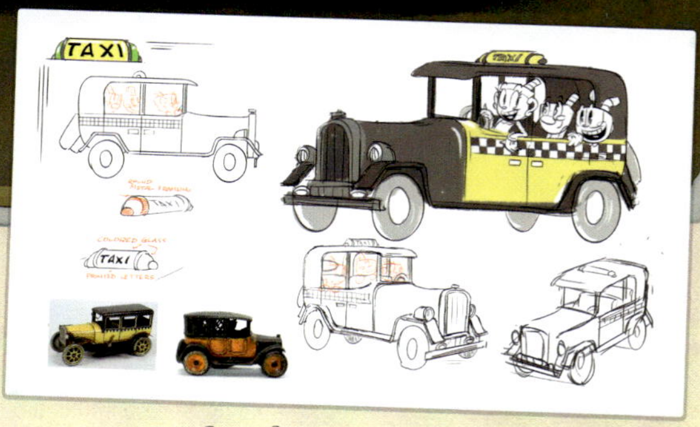

PREVIS BY COSMO SEGURSON.

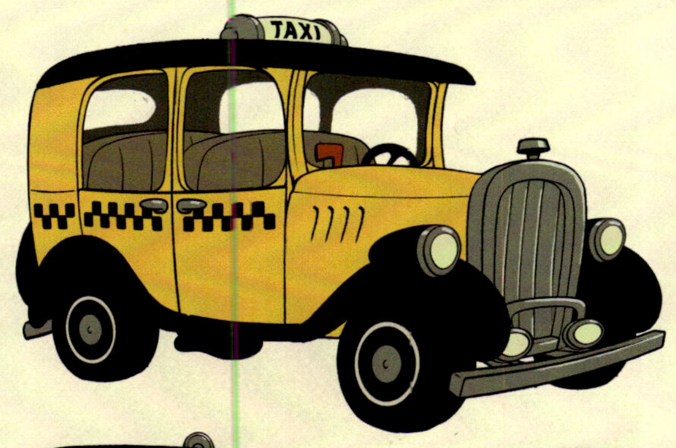

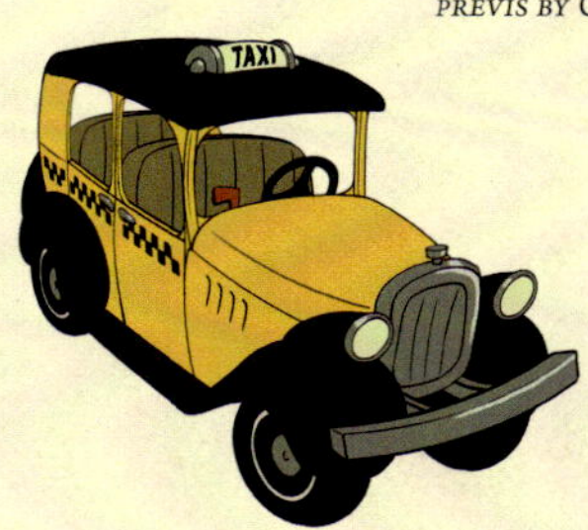

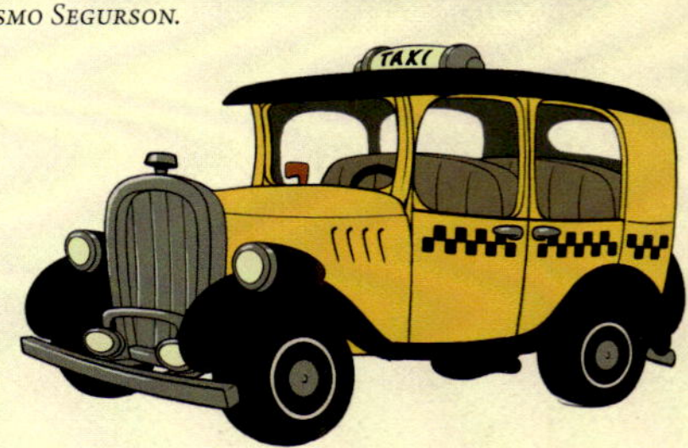

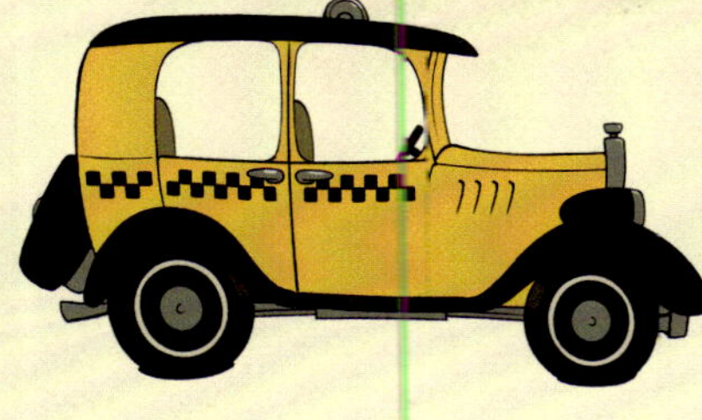

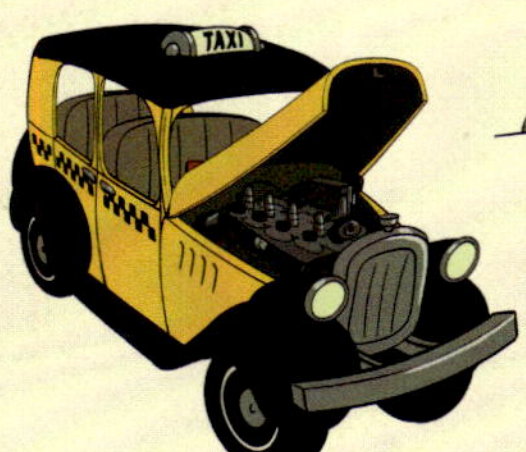

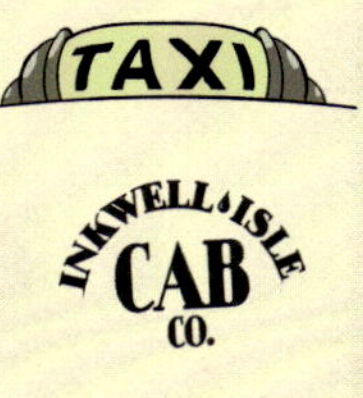

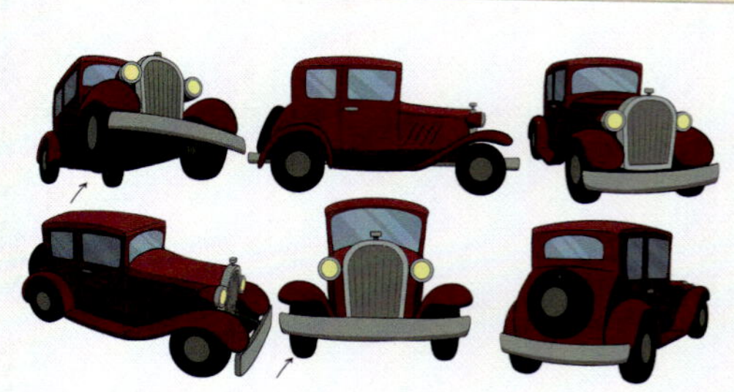

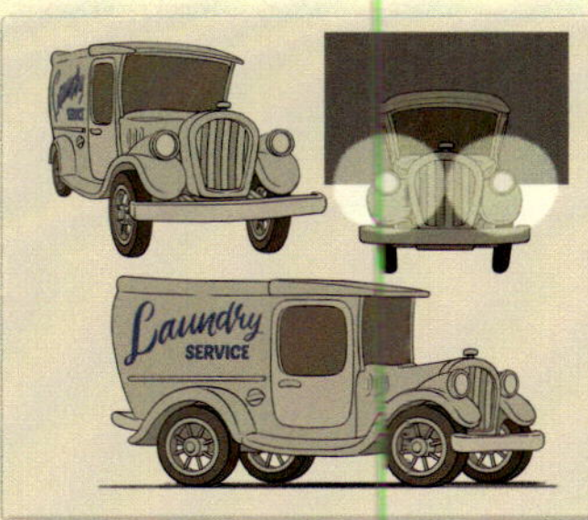

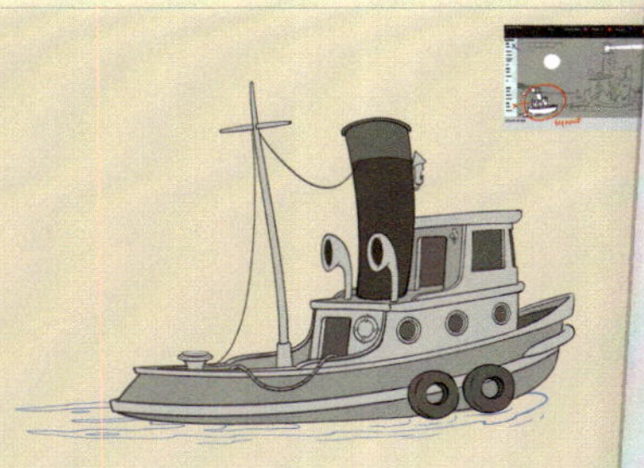

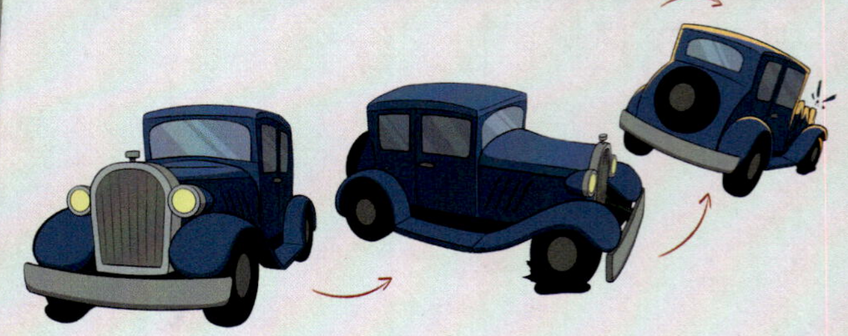

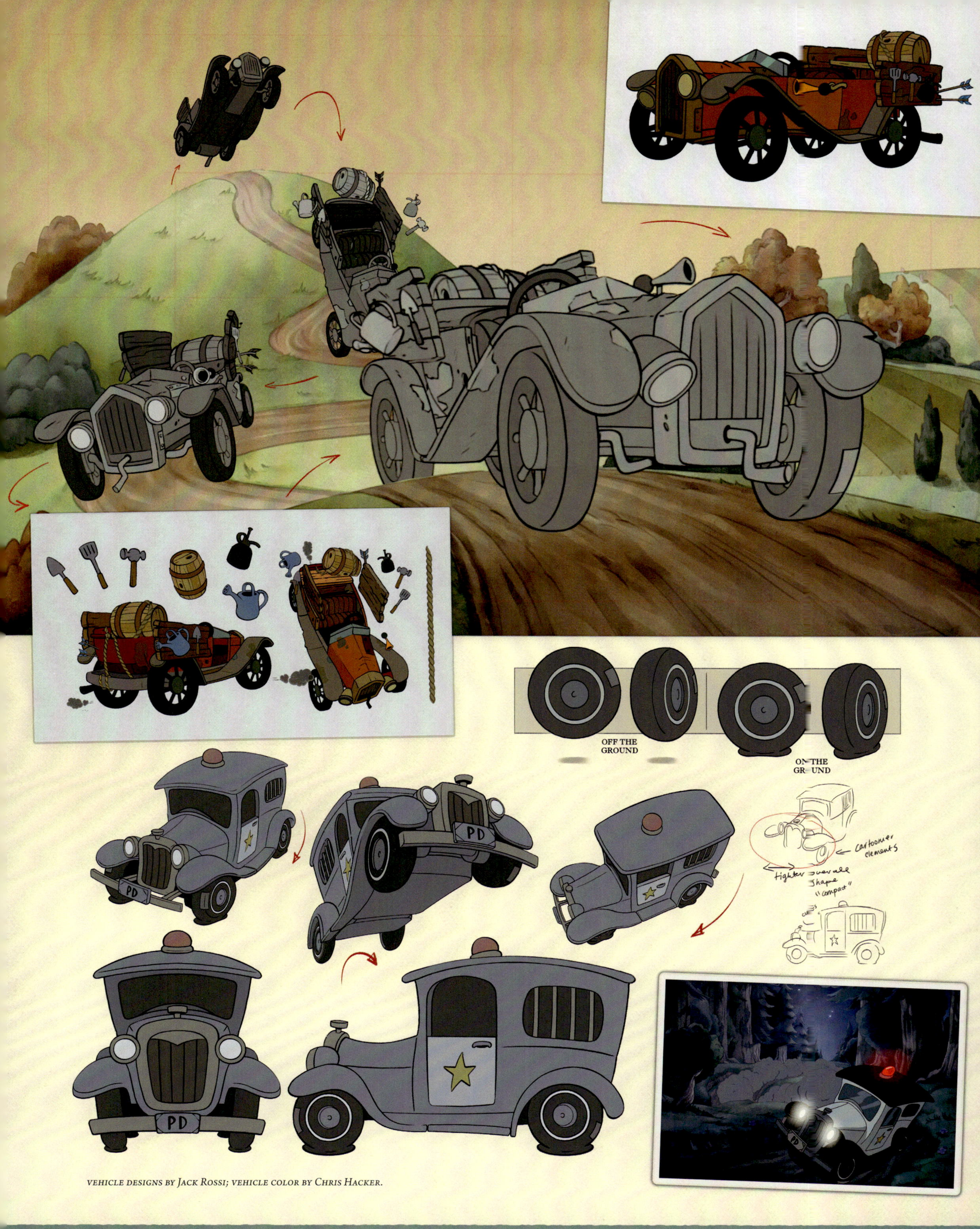

Vehicle designs by Jack Rossi; vehicle color by Chris Hacker.

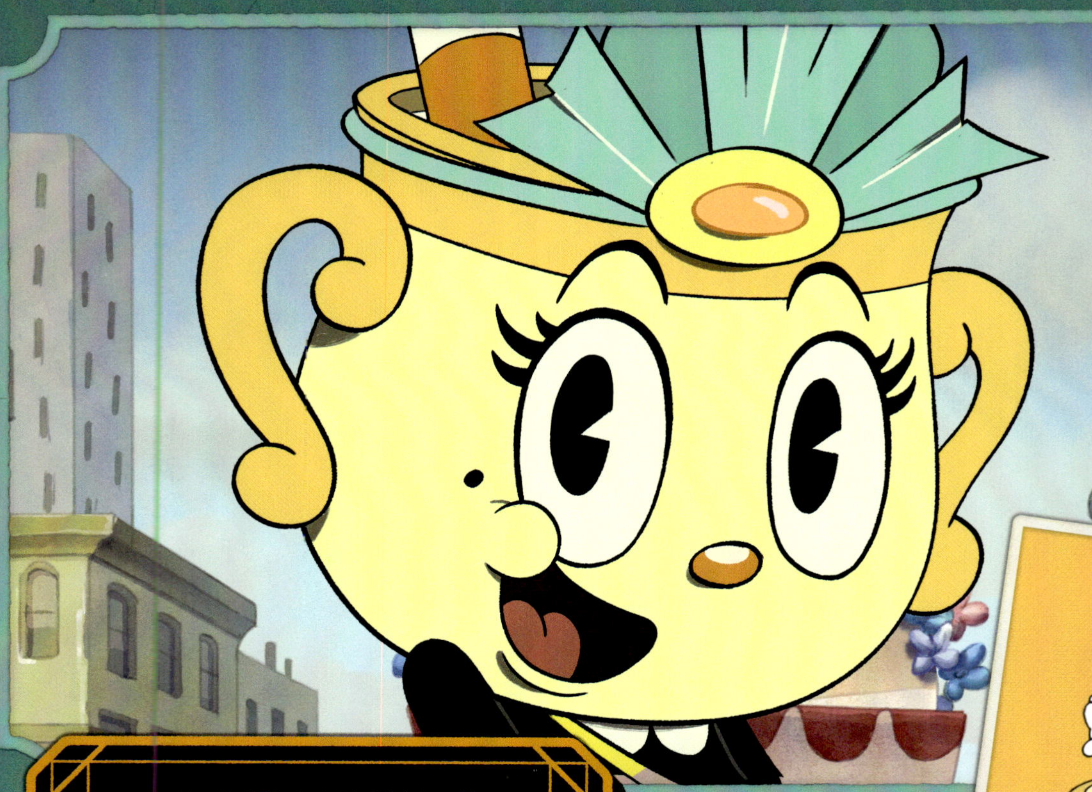

(voiced by Grey DeLisle)

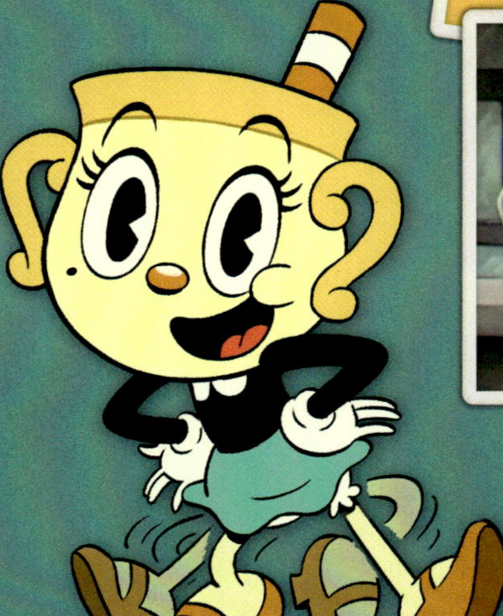

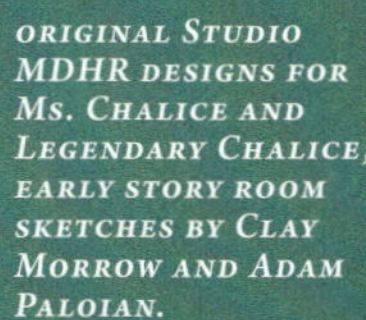

CJ: There was a lot of back-and-forth initially on her role in the series and her relationship to Cuphead and Mugman. She came to life early in the development process as the charming, magnanimous friend that is game for any adventure.

DAVE: The key to making her work for the show was figuring out her personality. A lot of the female characters in 1930s [cartoons] are damsels in distress. We thought it'd be fun to take her in the opposite direction.

MAJA: We knew from the get-go that we didn't want to see her in situations where she was a princess waiting to be saved or where she was a love interest to fight over.

Original Studio MDHR designs for Ms. Chalice and Legendary Chalice; early story room sketches by Clay Morrow and Adam Paloian.

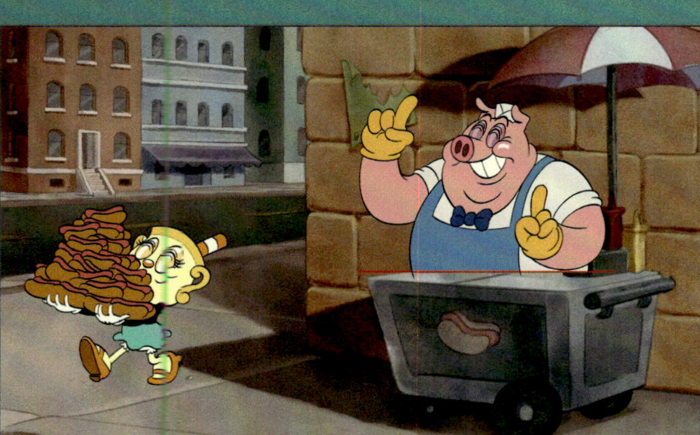

Special pose designs by Tapan Gandhi.

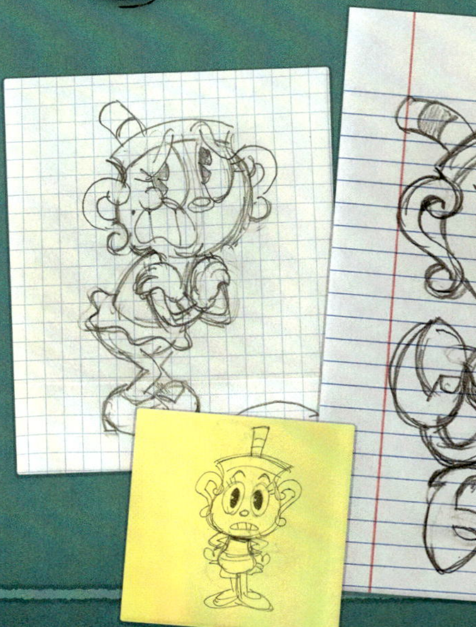

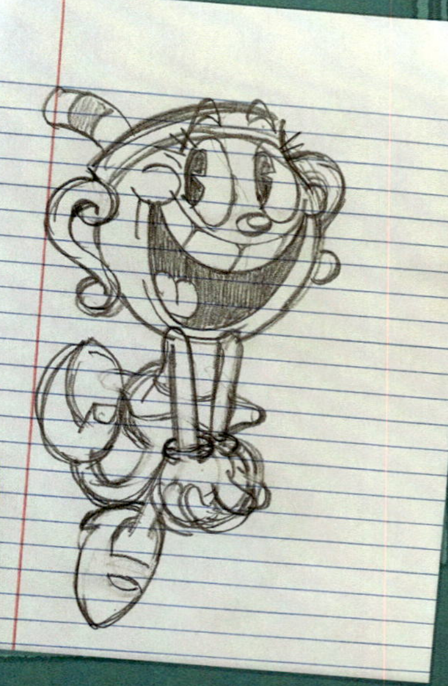

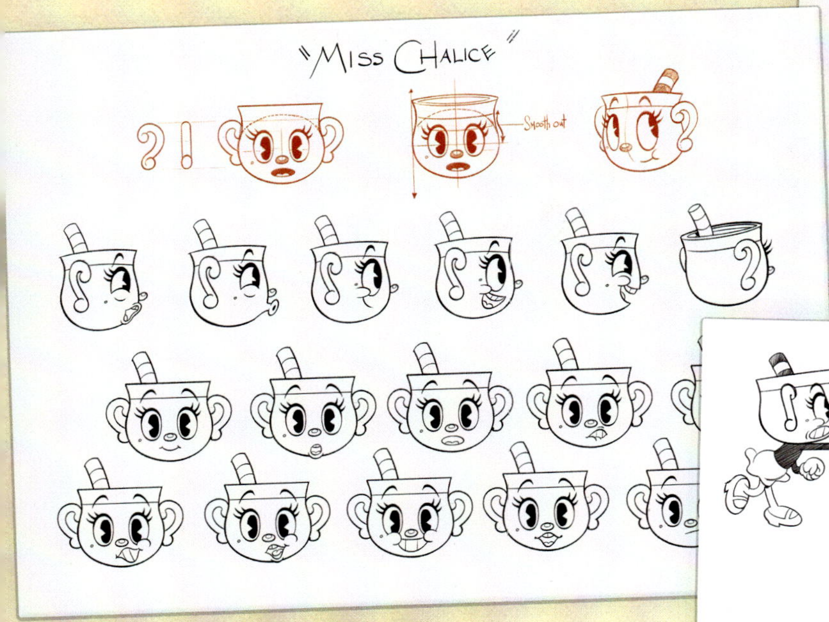

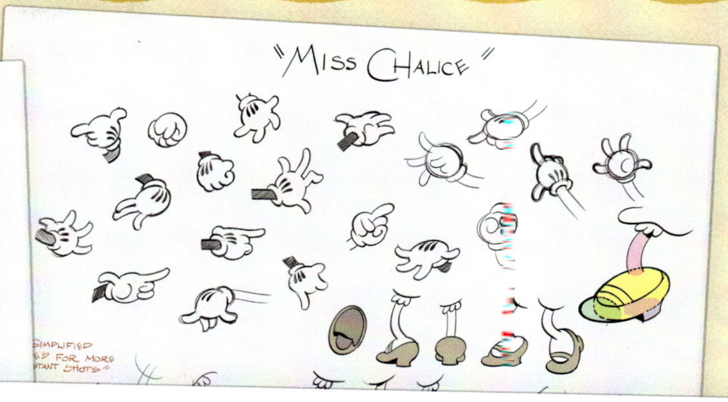

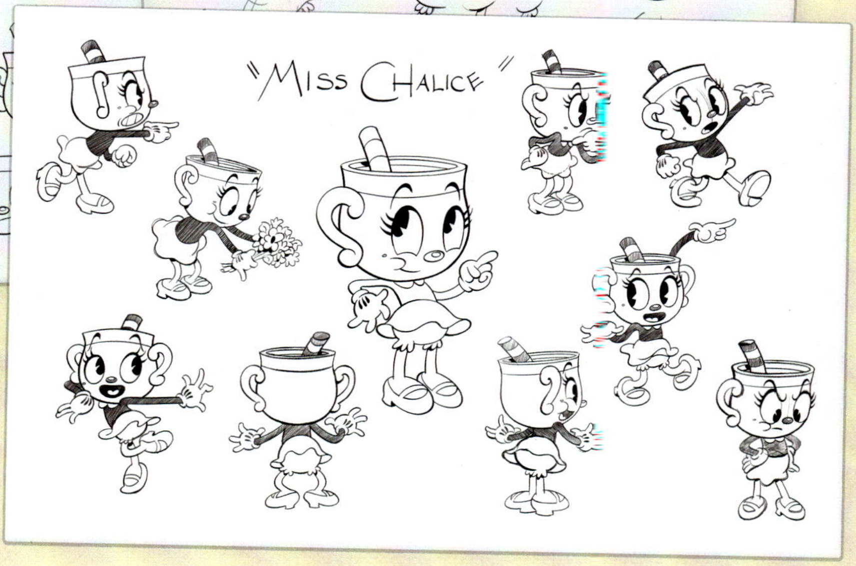

Ms. Chalice early designs and guidelines by Shakeh Haghnazarian.

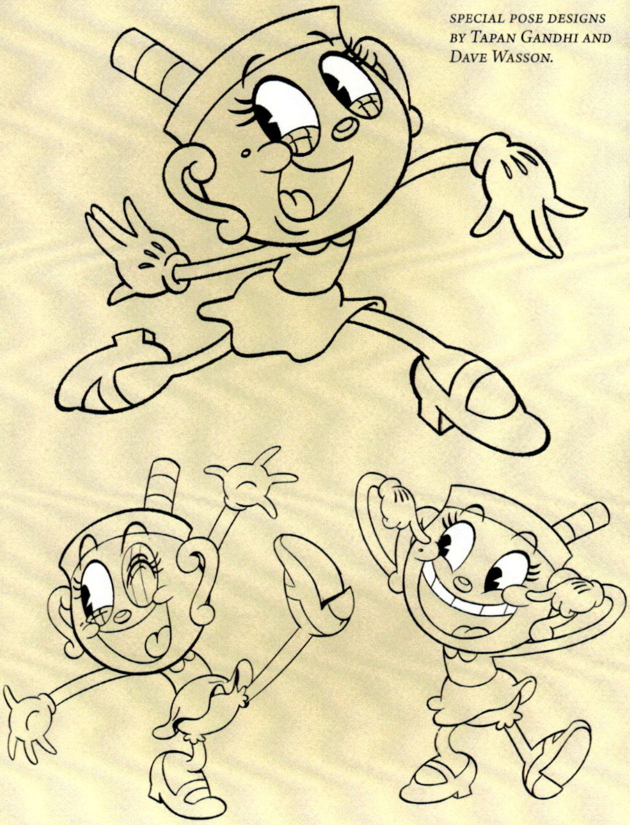

Special pose designs by Tapan Gandhi and Dave Wasson.

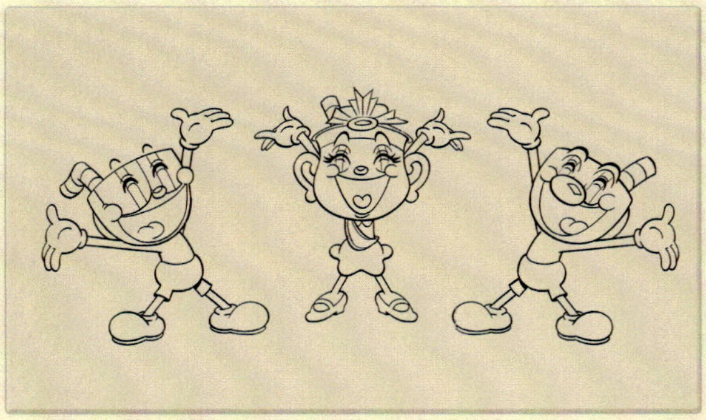

→ **MEGAN C:** I wanted Ms. Chalice to be like Katharine Hepburn in *Bringing Up Baby*. She should be flawed; she should be a chaos creator but also completely lovable and charming. She doesn't just get stuff for herself—she gets stuff for everyone around her, too. She shares the wealth.

CJ: We were nervous that getting her demeanor right was going to be tricky, but in fact she wound up becoming the character who completes the circle.

MAJA: We had always conceptualized her as rounding out a real trio and complementing Cuphead and Mugman with a vibrant personality of her own.

SHAKEH: Female characters from that era were typecast as either the Minnie Mouse, Betty Boop, or Olive Oyl type. With Chalice it was important for me to keep her appealing and cute, following the few designs we'd seen of her from the game promo art. It's nice to be simple in design sometimes and not get too loud with it and instead let the writing and direction give her depth and spunk.

COSMO: Shakeh did some amazing work to give Ms. Chalice more appeal. She's really adorable—you can't help but fall in love with her.

SHAKEH: She's not like Minnie Mouse—she's grittier, and she's got more dimension.

DAVE: It seemed like it'd be fun if she were a little smarter, quicker, and more streetwise than Cuphead and Mugman. She was on her own and surviving in the city, so she had to be sharp.

ANDREA: She's super cute and charming but has a mischievous streak. Out of all the characters on the show, I find myself the most entertained by Chalice. She's so sweet and cute, but she's also a little badass. She's definitely my favorite character.

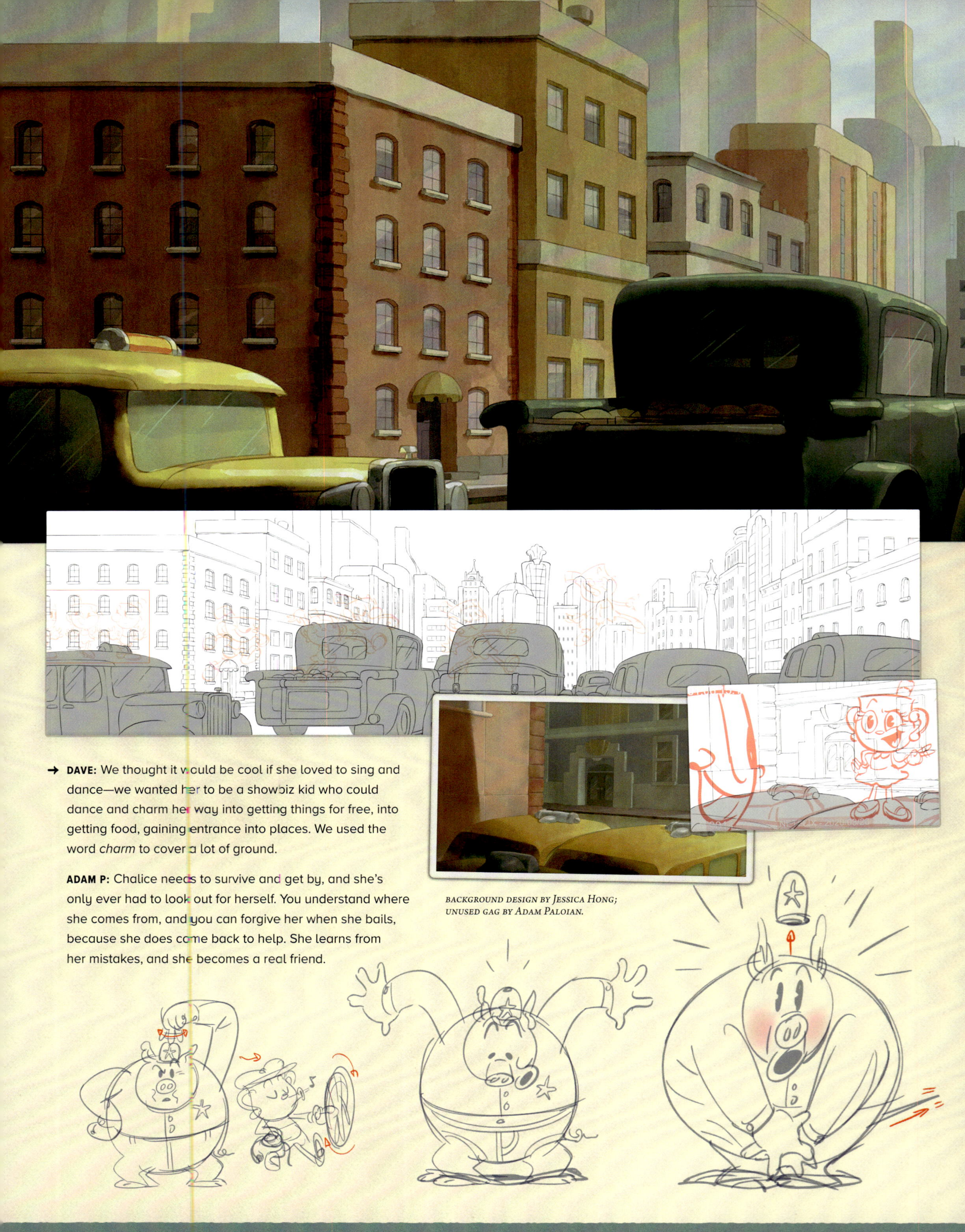

→ **DAVE:** We thought it would be cool if she loved to sing and dance—we wanted her to be a showbiz kid who could dance and charm her way into getting things for free, into getting food, gaining entrance into places. We used the word *charm* to cover a lot of ground.

ADAM P: Chalice needs to survive and get by, and she's only ever had to look out for herself. You understand where she comes from, and you can forgive her when she bails, because she does come back to help. She learns from her mistakes, and she becomes a real friend.

BACKGROUND DESIGN BY *JESSICA HONG*; UNUSED GAG BY *ADAM PALOIAN*.

Background painting by Gregory Miller and Jeff Palm.

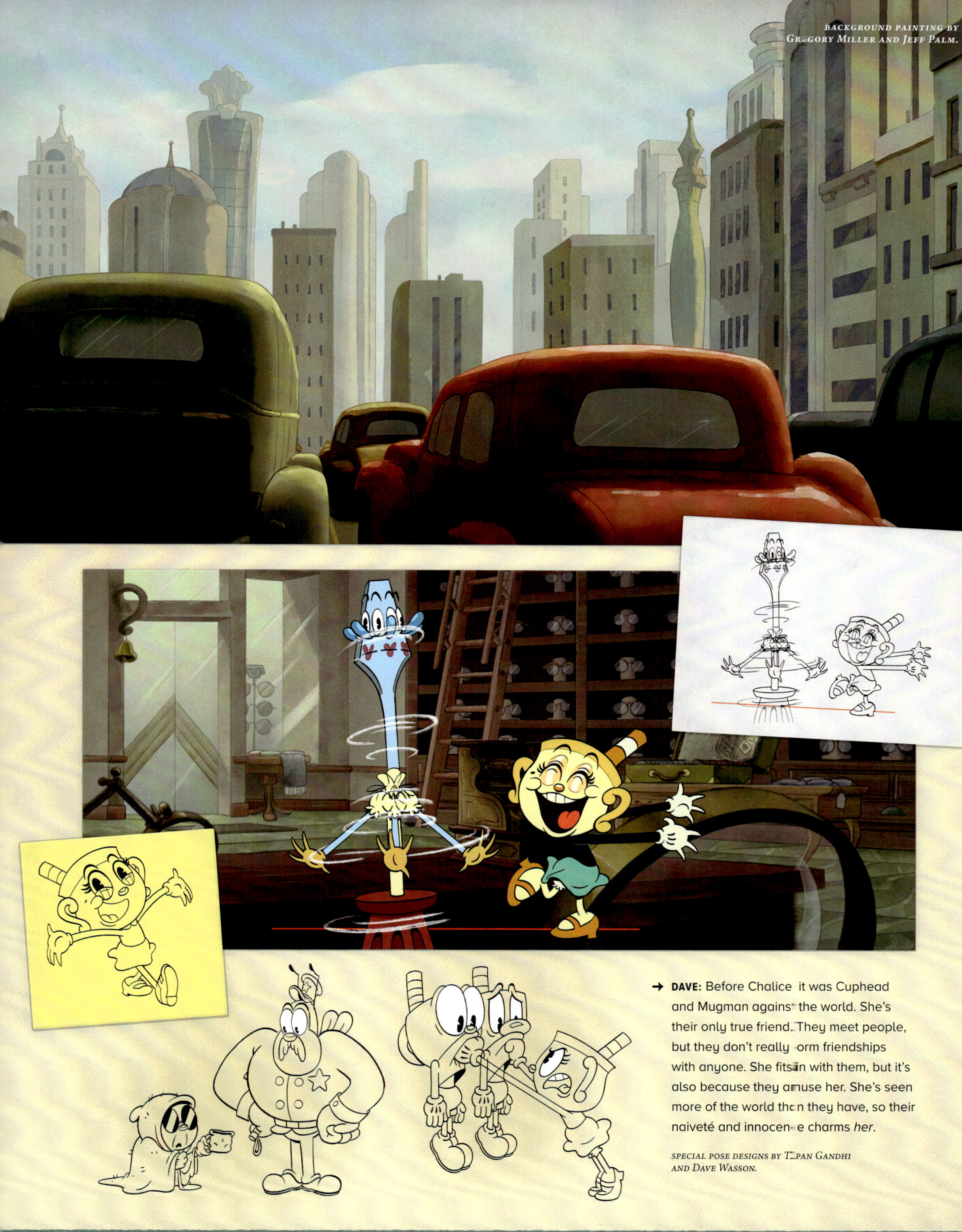

→ **DAVE:** Before Chalice, it was Cuphead and Mugman against the world. She's their only true friend. They meet people, but they don't really form friendships with anyone. She fits in with them, but it's also because they amuse her. She's seen more of the world than they have, so their naiveté and innocence charms *her*.

Special pose designs by Tapan Gandhi and Dave Wasson.

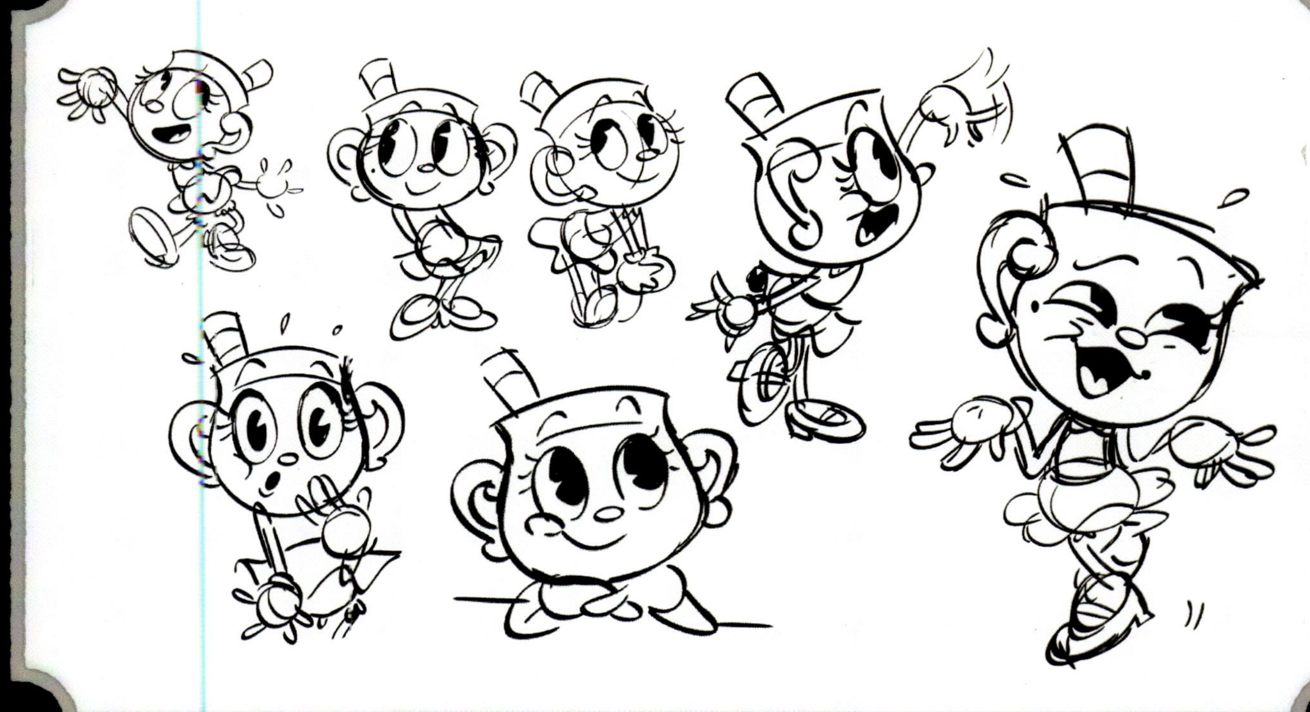

• STORYBOARD SPOTLIGHT •

STORYBOARDING MS. CHALICE

MEGAN B: I just loved Chalice's energy. At first glance she's cute, she's charming, but then it's revealed that she has a dark past and comes with all this baggage. I was trying to keep a level of charm, but not generic cutesy charm—something behind it almost makes you ask, "Is she messing with me?"

DAVE: Chalice is a really good performer, and in almost every situation, she's controlling what's happening, she's very much in charge, and I think Megan's acting and posing reflects that really well.

MEGAN B: She's feisty, she tortures Cuphead and Mugman a couple times, she gets them into trouble, she bails on them—she's not perfect, and I love her for that. She genuinely likes Cuphead and Mugman, but she's also looking out for herself, too. She feels real; it's not just like Minnie Mouse: "Oh, Mickey, I love you, and I'll always be here for you!" That's so one-dimensional. But with Chalice, you never really know—she can be anything.

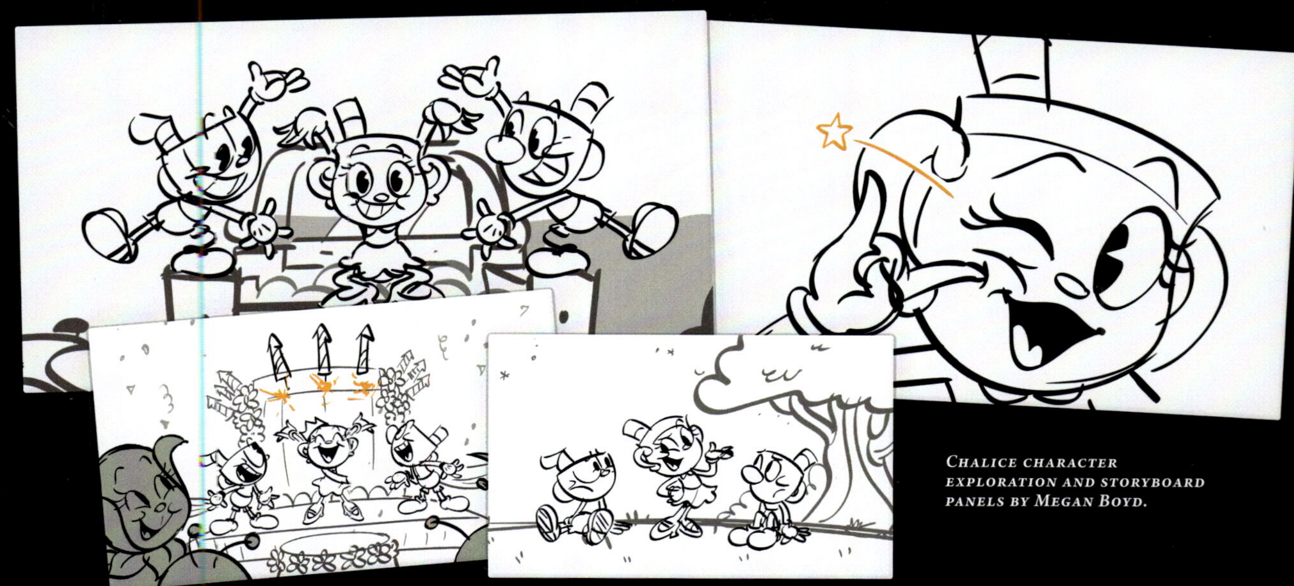

Chalice character exploration and storyboard panels by Megan Boyd.

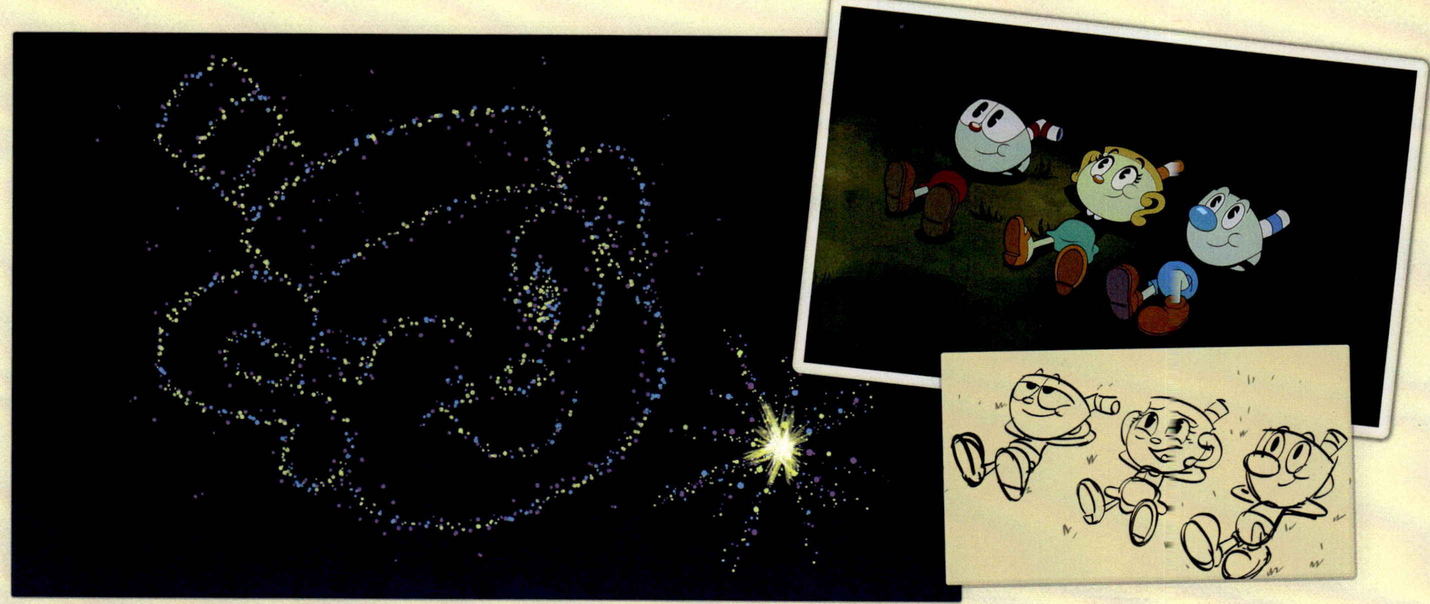

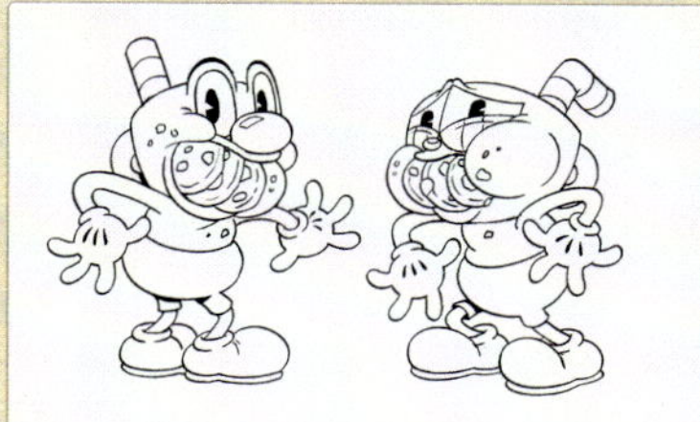

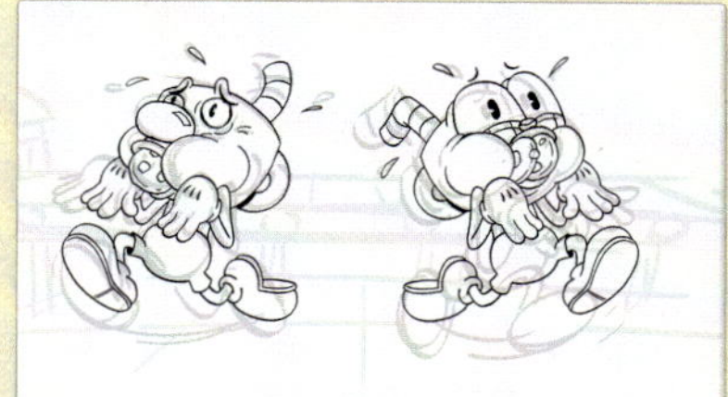

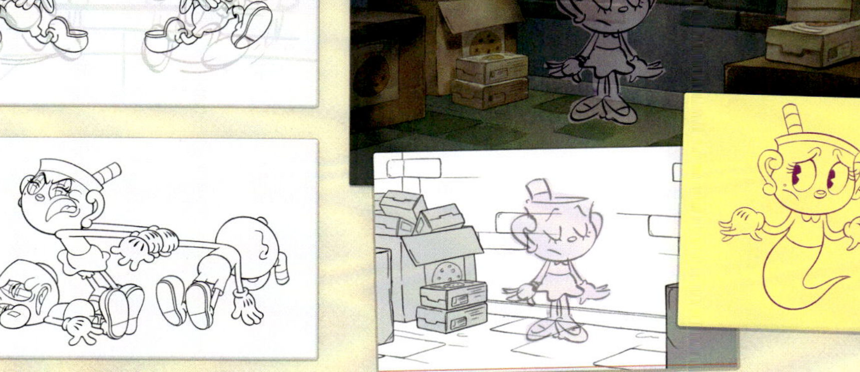

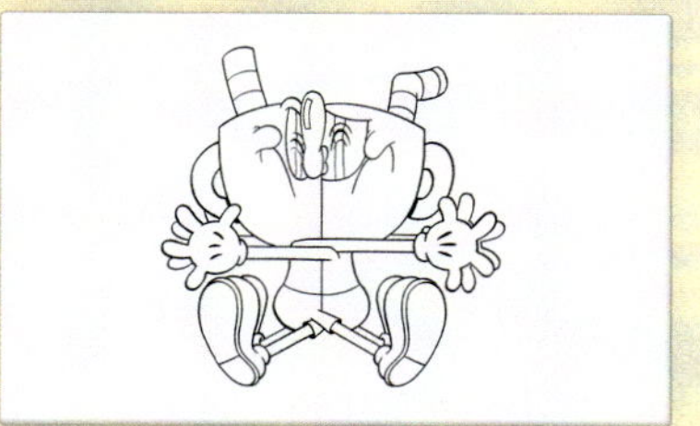

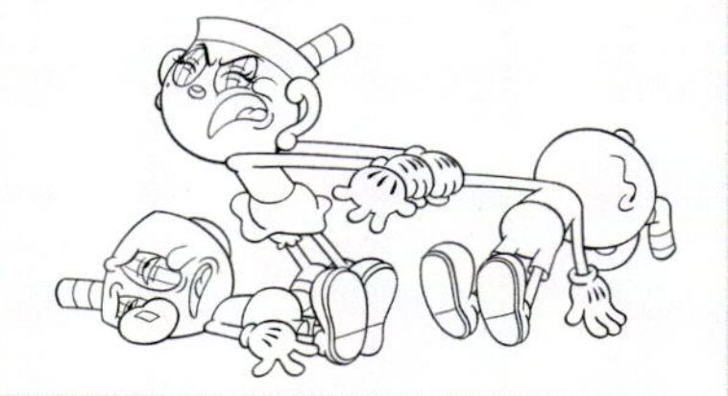

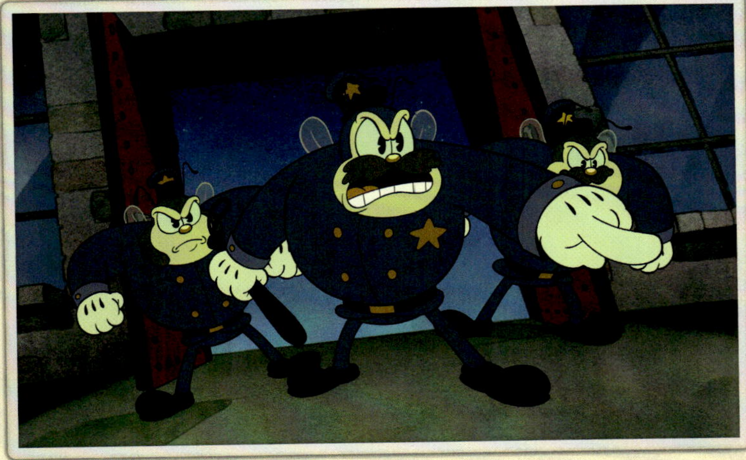

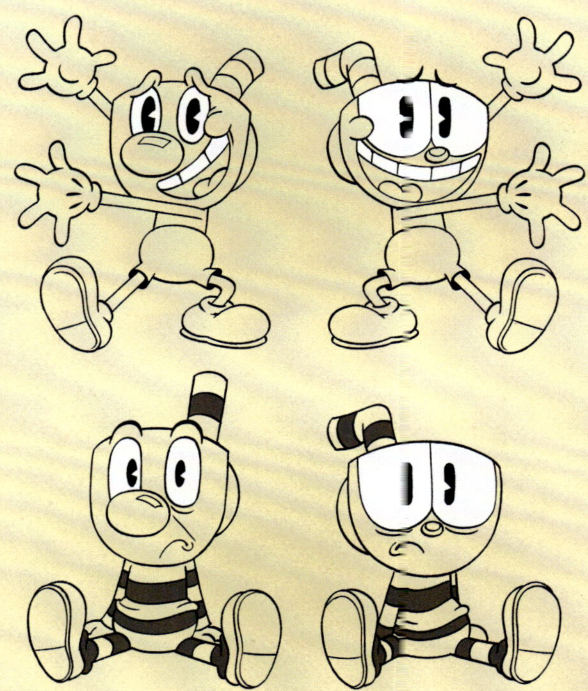

→ **DAVE:** She knows how to do stuff and make things happen, and that's really exciting for Cuphead and Mugman. Particularly for Cuphead: he and Chalice share a kindred spirit, a lust for adventure and going out and shaking things up and making stuff happen. Mugman's just along for the ride—he likes Chalice and trusts her.

Special pose designs by Tapan Gandhi and Dave Wasson; background design by Pat Marconetti; painting by Michelle Thies; FX design by Ed Skudder.

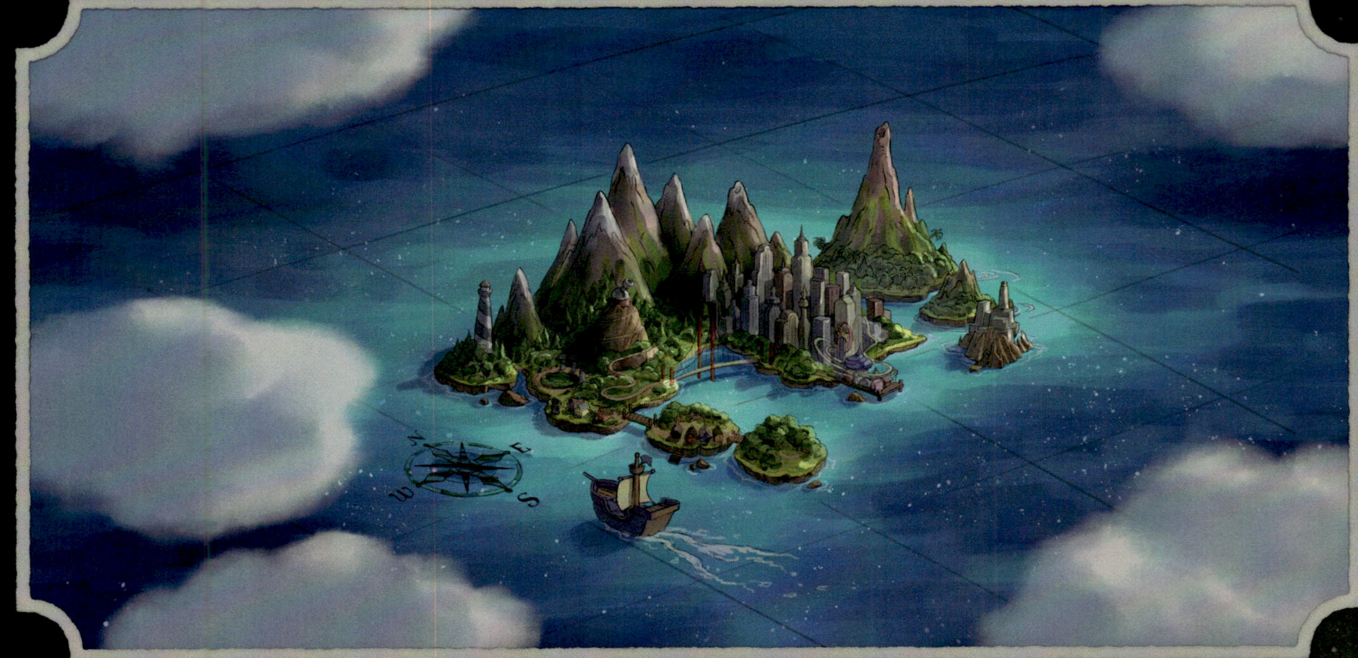

◆ MAIN TITLE SPOTLIGHT ◆

THE MAKING OF THE MAIN TITLE

→ **DAVE:** There was some discussion that since we were making this for streaming, maybe we didn't need a title sequence. I felt strongly that we *had* to have one. When I think back on the most memorable series—*The Bugs Bunny / Road Runner Show*, *SpongeBob SquarePants*, *Pee-wee's Playhouse*—they all have great title sequences with super-catchy theme songs. Those songs stay embedded in your brain for life.

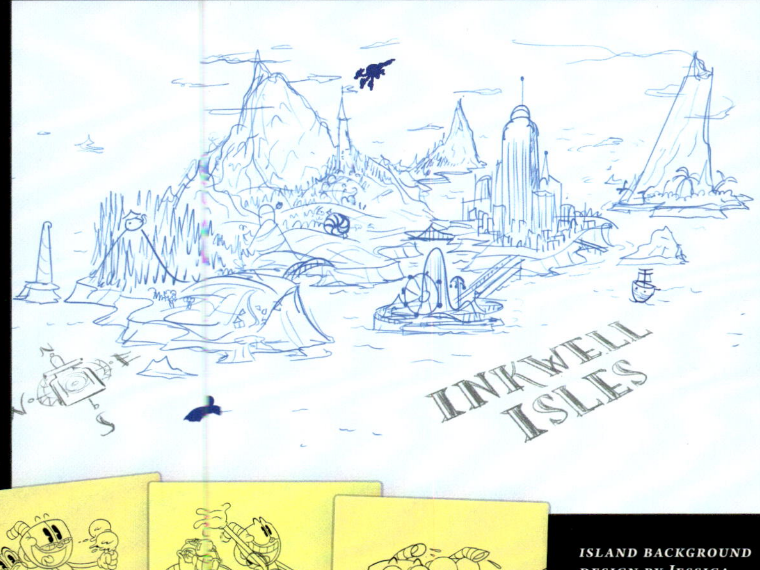

ISLAND BACKGROUND DESIGN BY JESSICA HONG; PAINTING BY GREGORY MILLER; SPECIAL POSE DESIGNS BY ADAM PALOIAN, TAPAN GANDHI, AND DAVE WASSON.

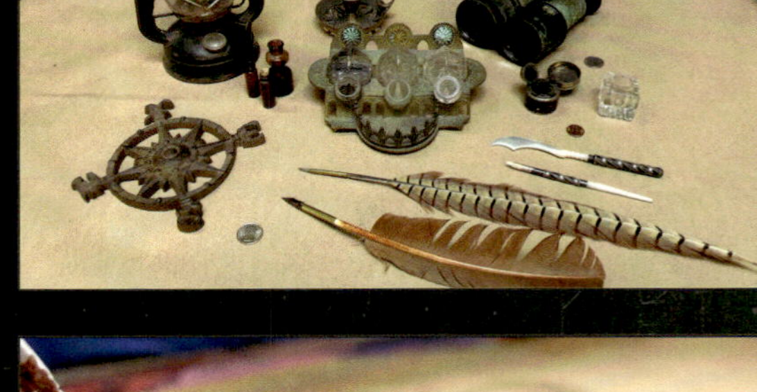

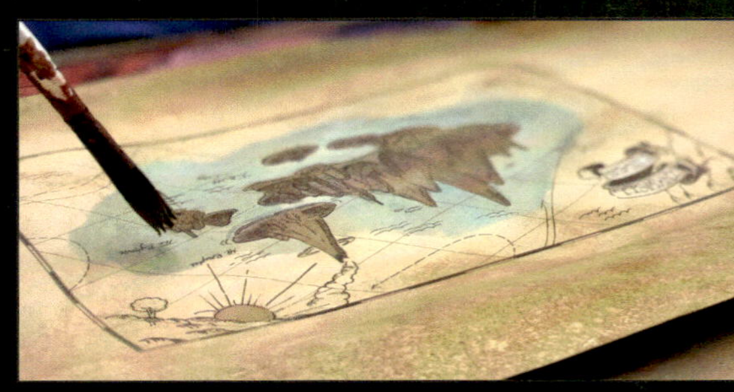

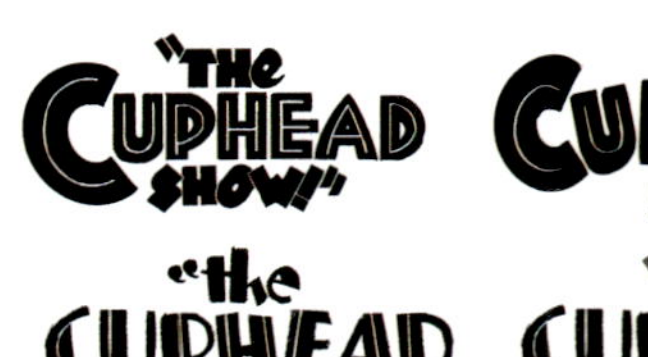

MAIN TITLE STOP-MO PRODUCTION BY SCREEN NOVELTIES; ORIGINAL LOGO CONCEPTS BY COSMO SEGURSON.

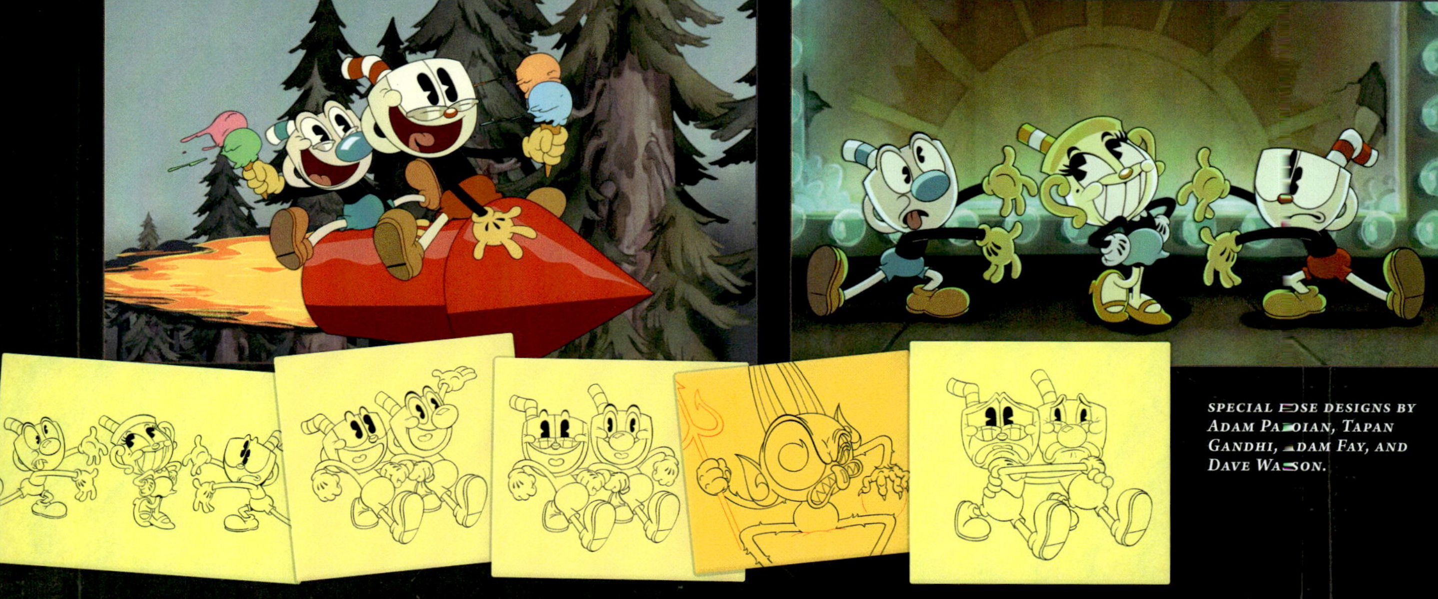

Special pose designs by Adam Paloian, Tapan Gandhi, Adam Fay, and Dave Wasson.

→ **COSMO:** The opening song is sort of like two songs. There's the first one that sets up the atmosphere, and the second one that sets up the characters.

DAVE: We wanted to get as much setup as we could into that opening song, and also convey the tone of the show.

EGO: I had this vision before we started that we'd all come into my studio and be in the same place when we record, but everything changed when the pandemic hit. I had to come up with completely new ways to do the whole thing. Now we have a brass section that's spread across the country, and you've got to combine it and mix it so it sounds like it's all happening in the same room. There's a lot of "magic of Hollywood" tricks that we do to make it feel like an old-time jazz recording. Hopefully people imagine there's this cool studio with one microphone in the center, these guys in suits playing. That's not what's happening, but that's the atmosphere we aspire to create.

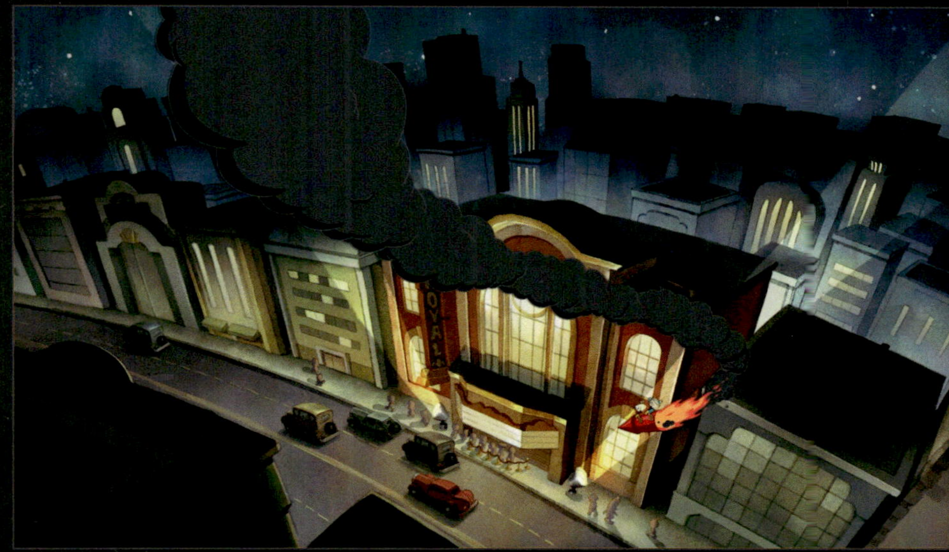

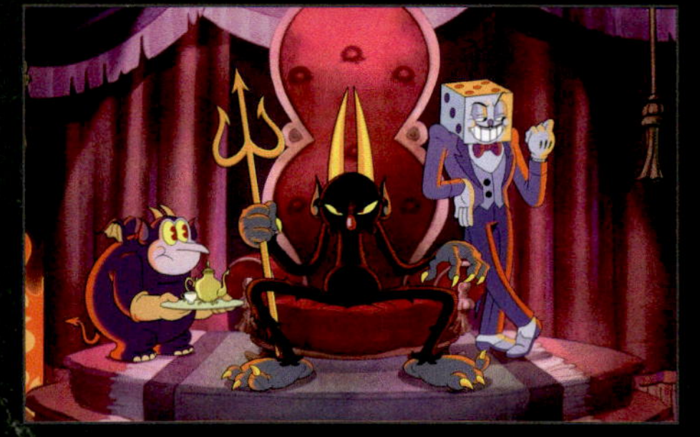

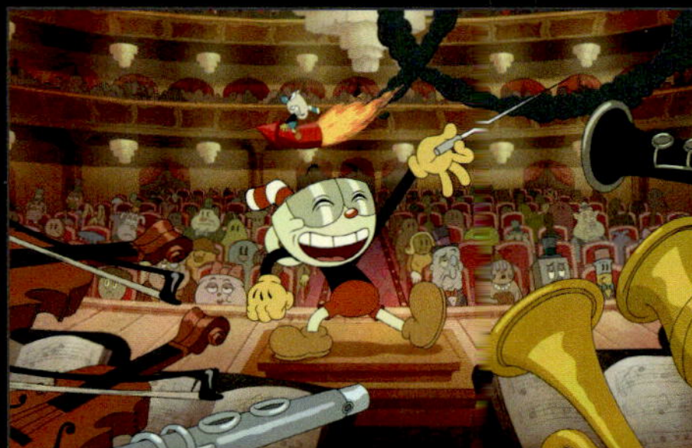

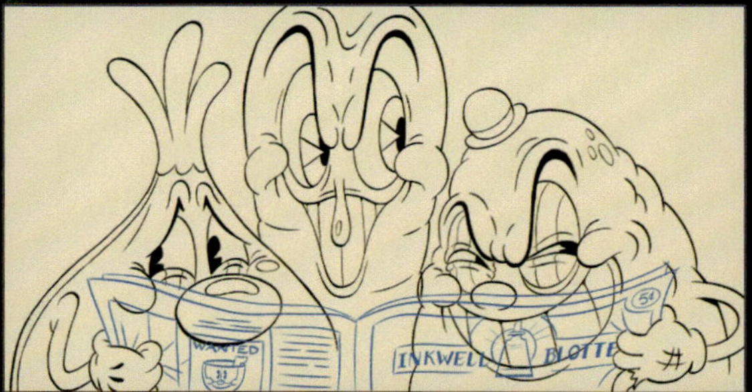

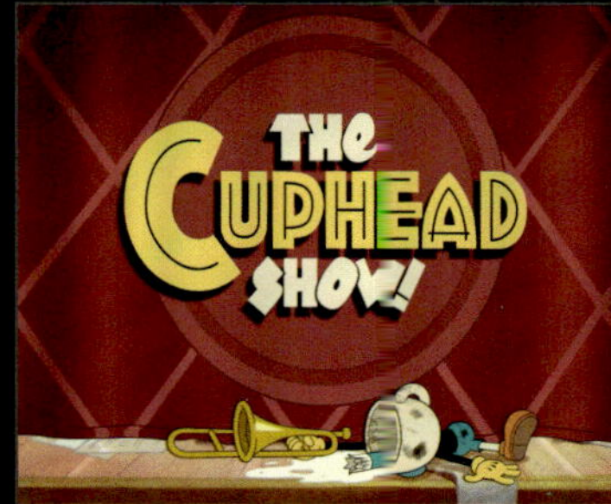

Background design by Benjamin Anderson, Laisay Bond, and Lauren Duda; paintings by Michelle Thies, Mallory Carlson, and Ivan Aguirre; character color by Chris Hacker.

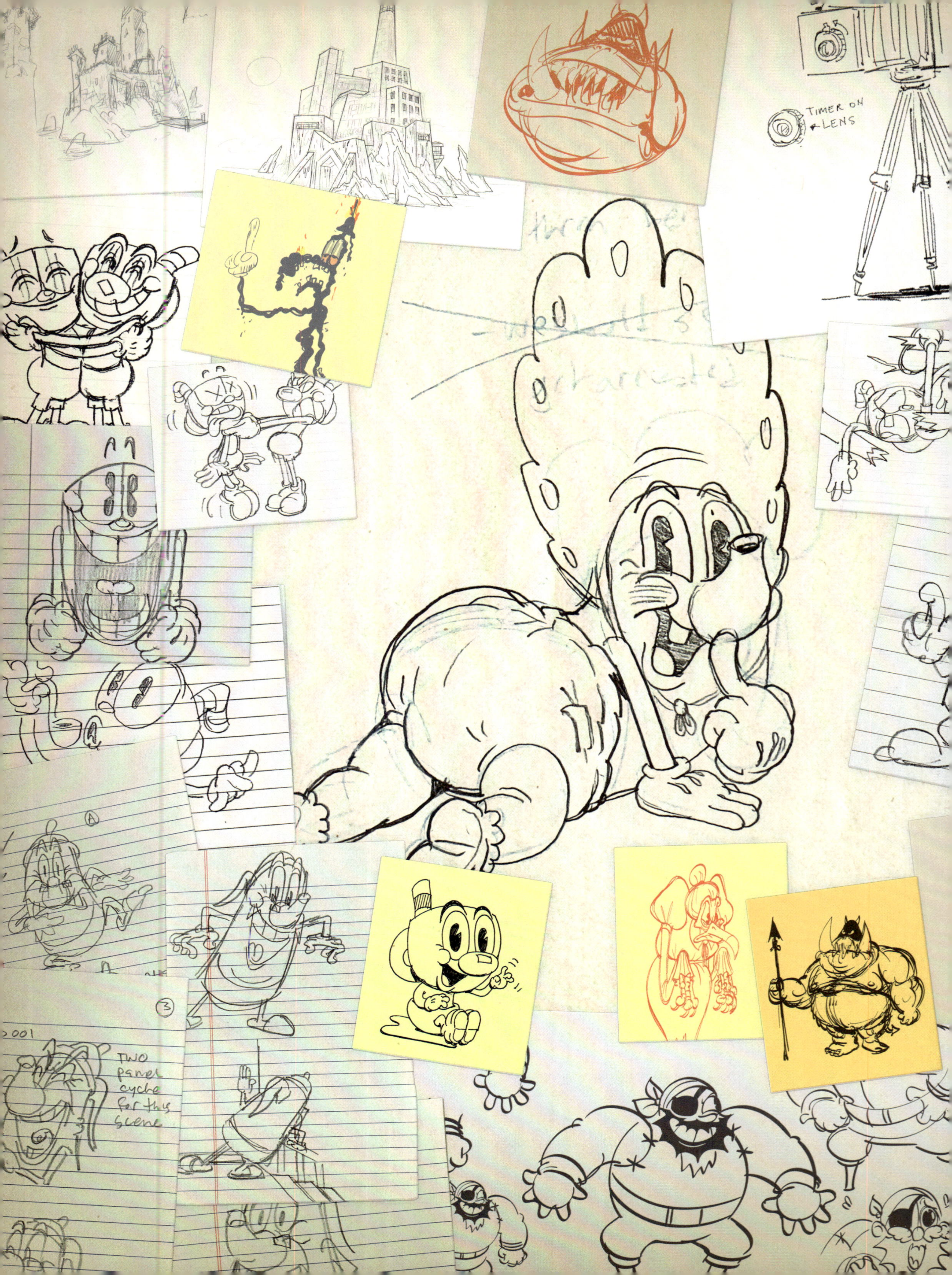
TIMER ON
←LENS
TWO
panel
cycle
for this
scene

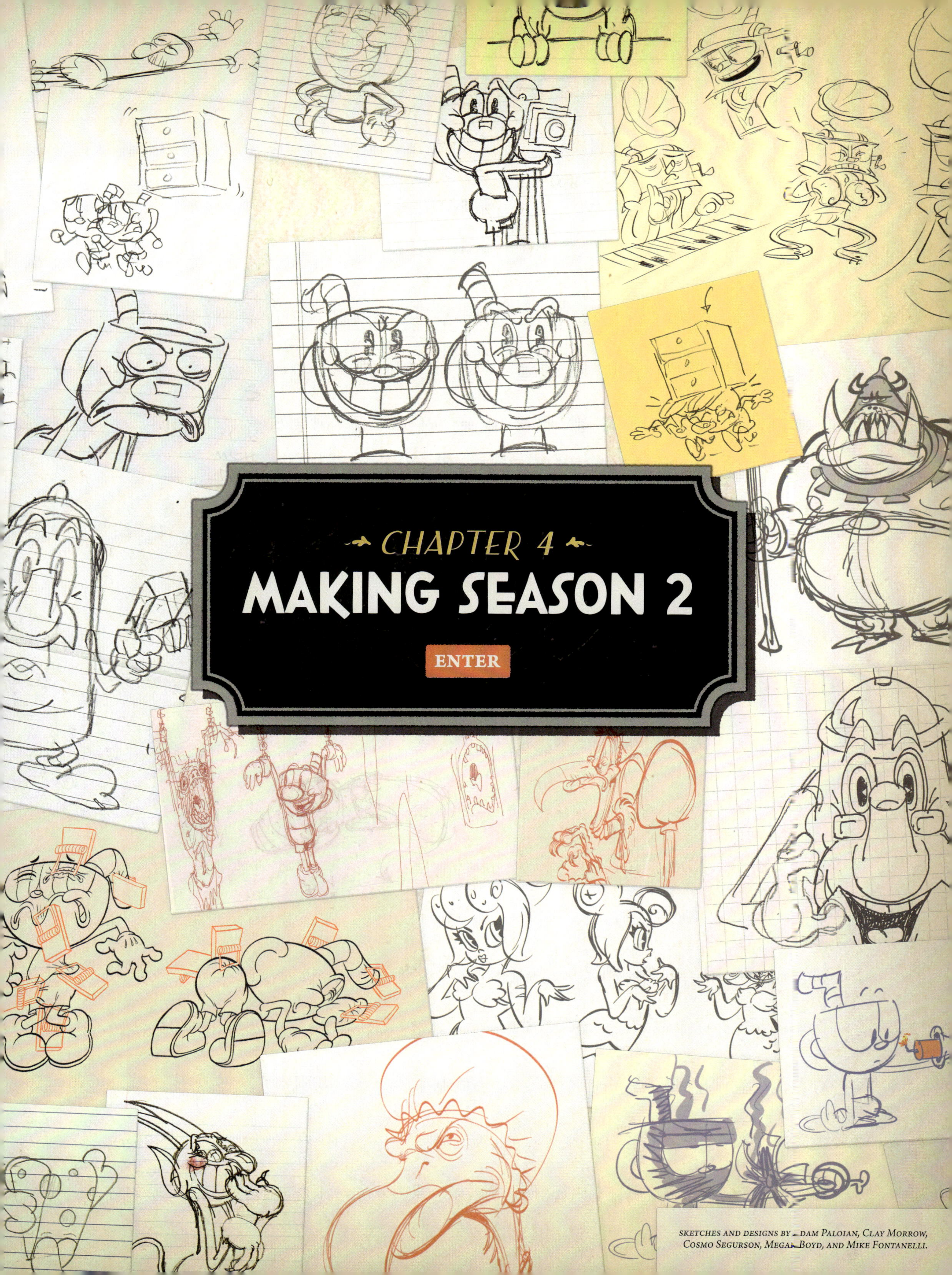

CHAPTER 4
MAKING SEASON 2

ENTER

Sketches and designs by Adam Paloian, Clay Morrow, Cosmo Segurson, Megan Boyd, and Mike Fontanelli.

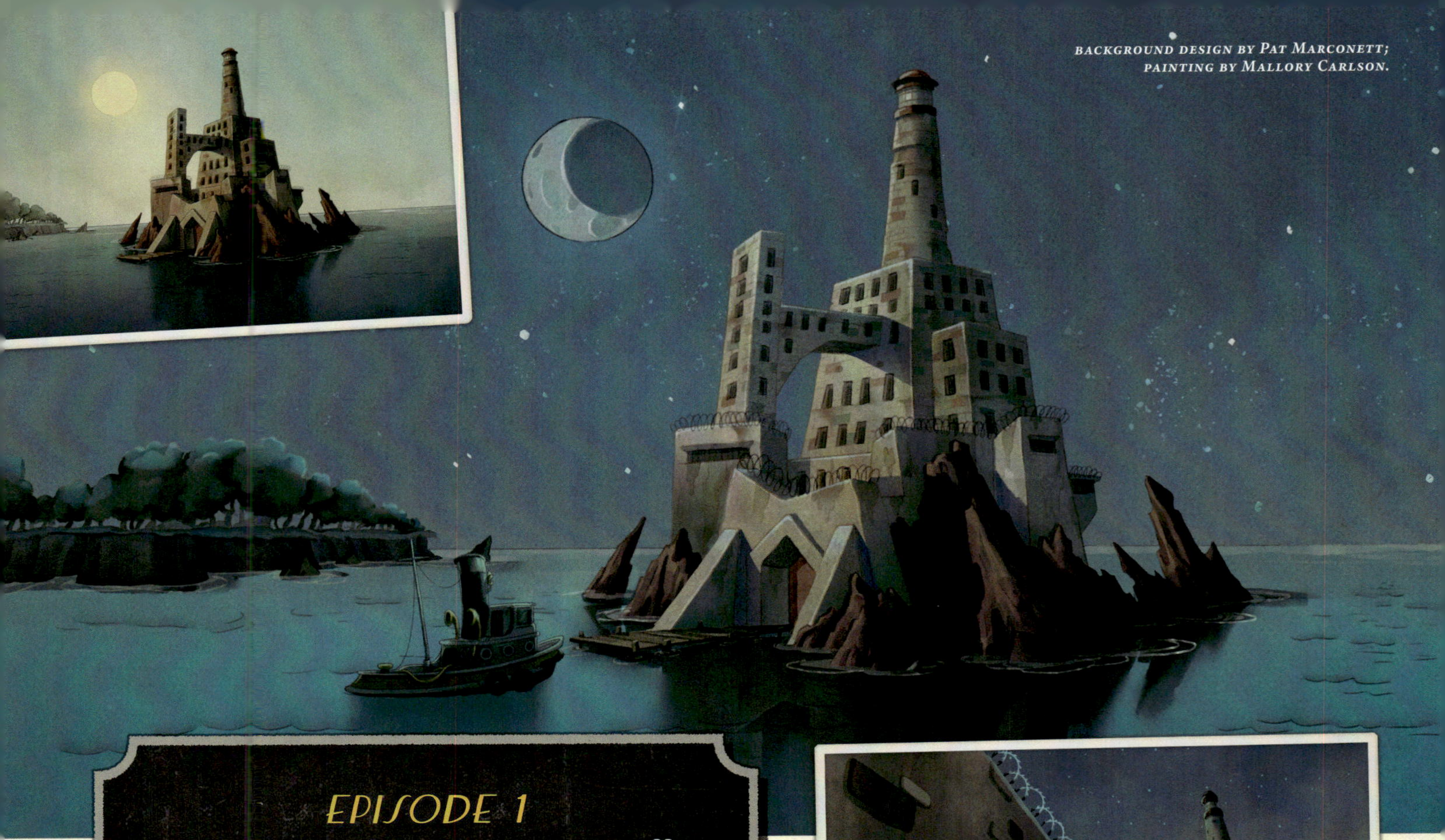

Background design by Pat Marconett; painting by Mallory Carlson.

Episode 1
"Jailbroken"

ADAM P: Cosmo has a really good sense of atmosphere with some of the locations. The prison exterior in "Jailbroken" is one of Cosmo's babies. It's a little German expressionist.

COSMO: There's a Buster Keaton short set in prison called *Convict 13* [1920] that operates in a similar way—trying to escape, making buddies, getting beat up by bigger inmates, and it's a nightmare. There's something really fun to play with in that contrast, to have a couple of innocents in a real world of danger.

ANDREA: There were some real brain busters on that episode. It's a location we had never really seen before in an older cartoon, and yet it had to *look* like an older cartoon.

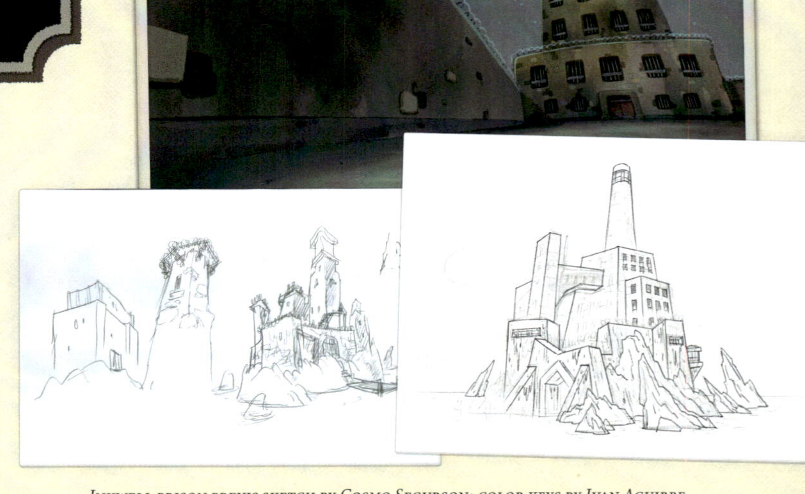

Inkwell prison previs sketch by Cosmo Segurson; color keys by Ivan Aguirre.

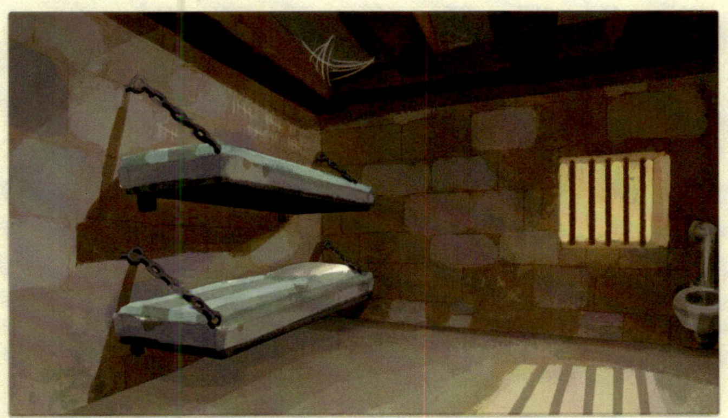

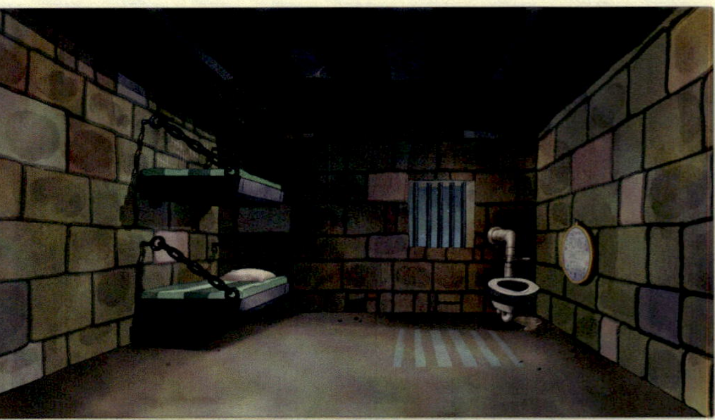

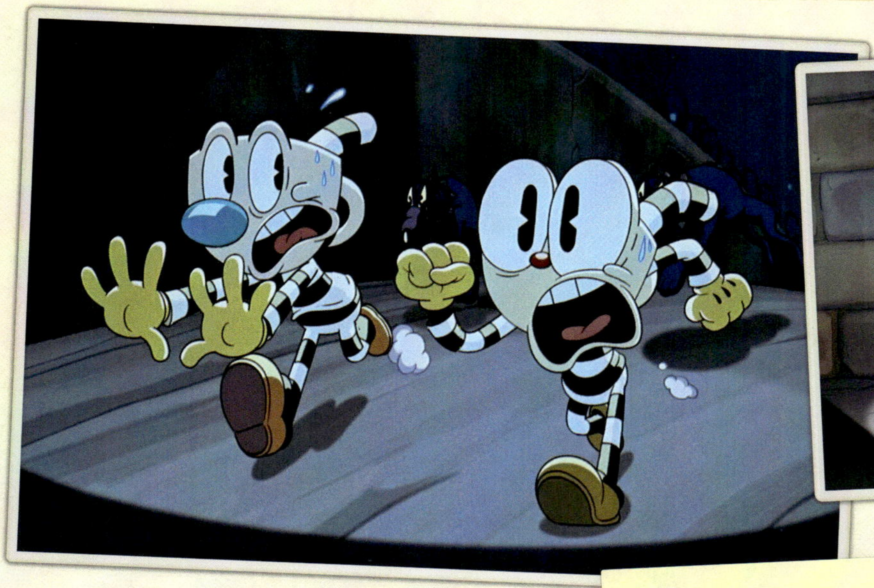

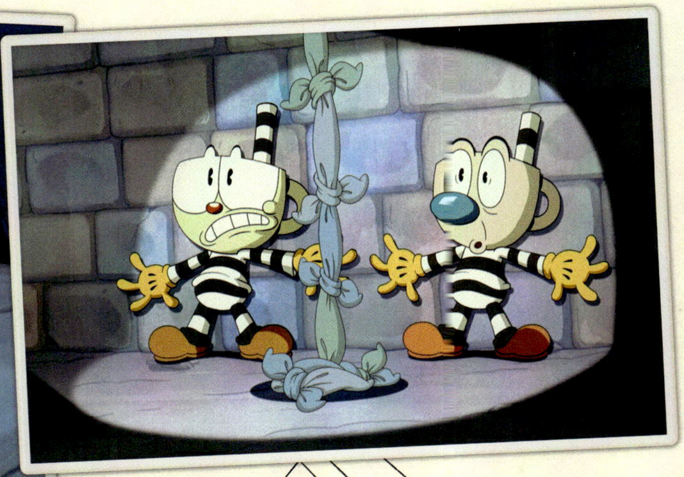

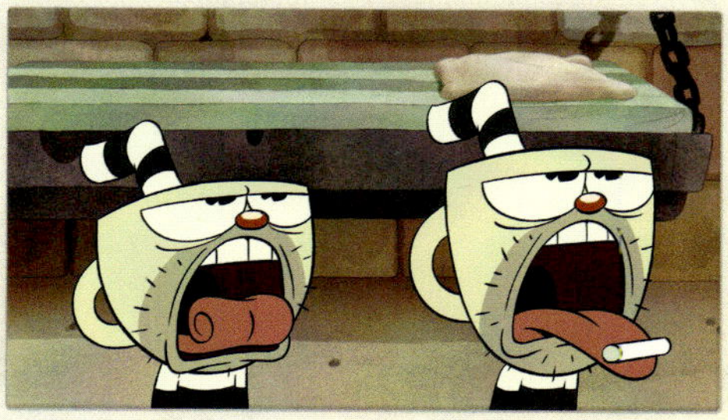

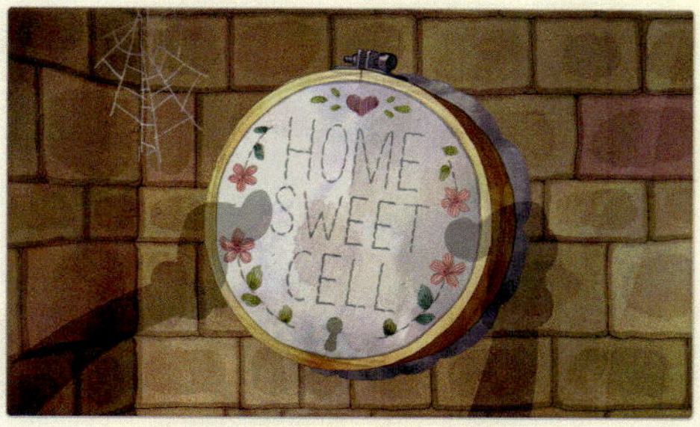

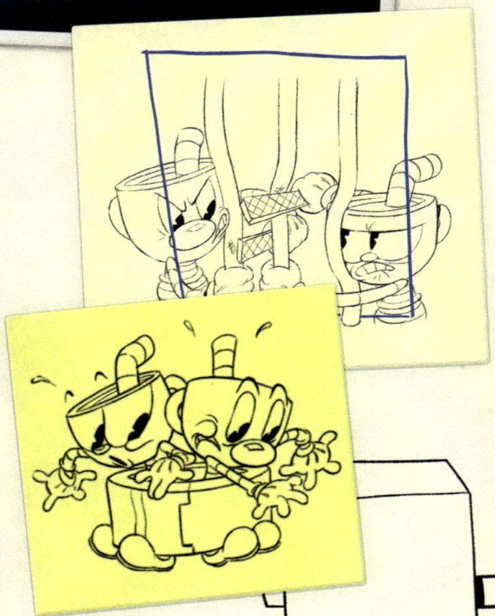

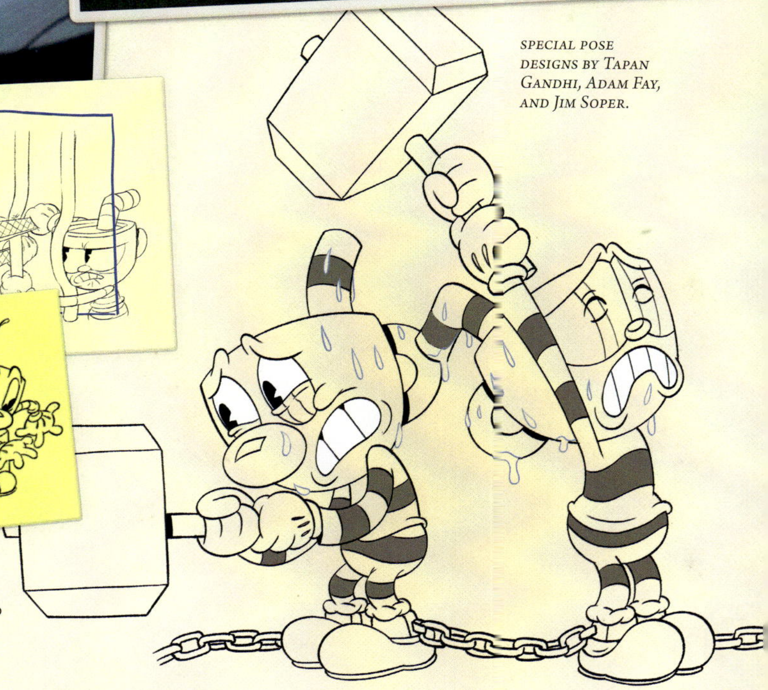

Special pose designs by Tapan Gandhi, Adam Fay, and Jim Soper.

Color key by Ivan Aguirre; background design by Pat Marconeti; painting by Ivan Aguirre.

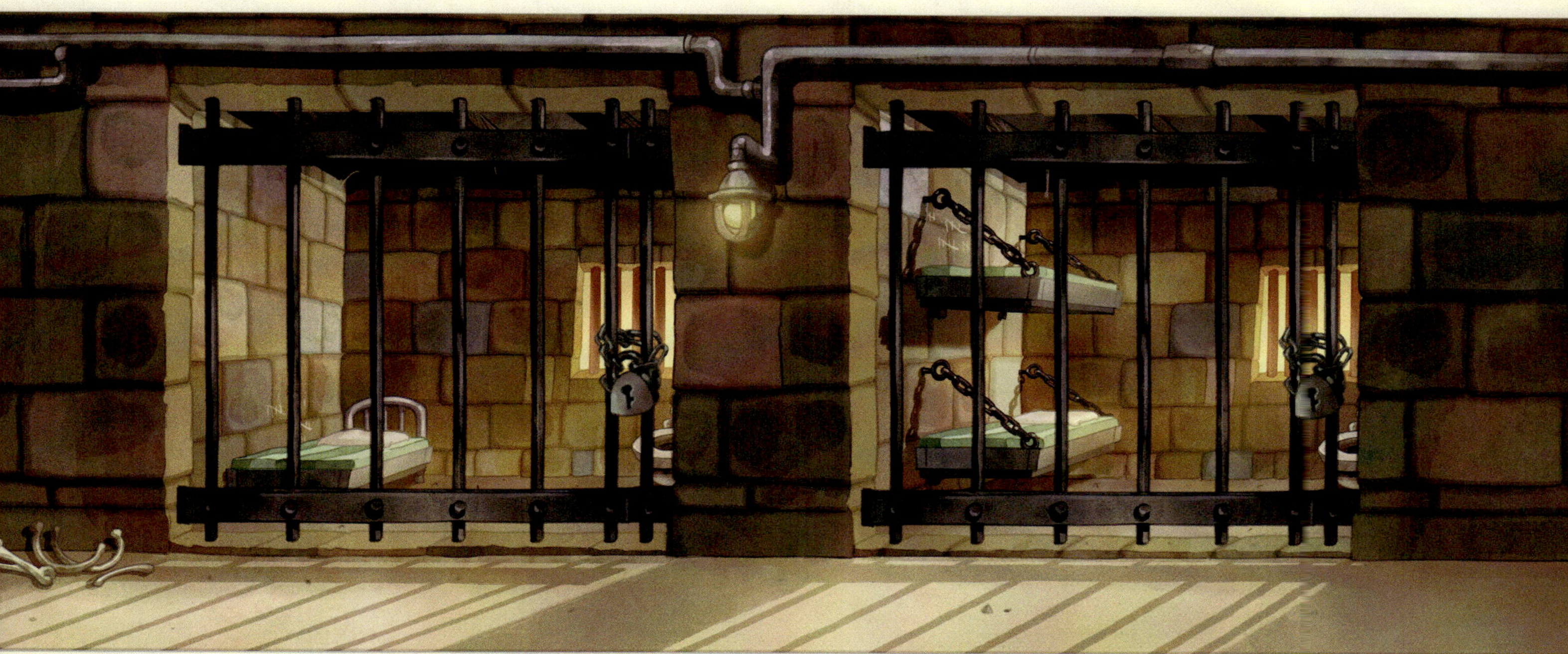

INCIDENTAL INMATES

→ **TAPAN:** My prompt for that episode was to go wild with animal species and objects that would be intimidating and scary. The trick was making them cartoonishly bigger than Cuphead and Mugman. There were some incidental inmates that weren't looking 1930s enough. I wondered why they didn't look like they belonged in this world. And it was literally just eye placement—I made them too focused. So I just separated the eyes a little bit while not making them completely walleyed, and it brought them to a happy medium.

Prisoner designs by Tapan Gandhi, Adam Fay, and Jim Soper; storyboard panel by Fernando Puig; character color by Chris Hacker.

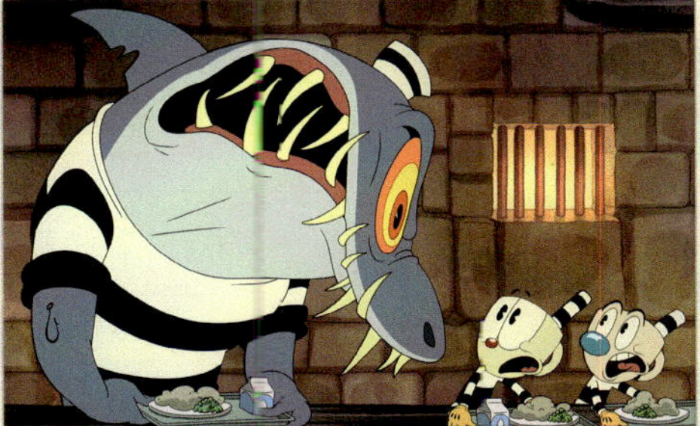

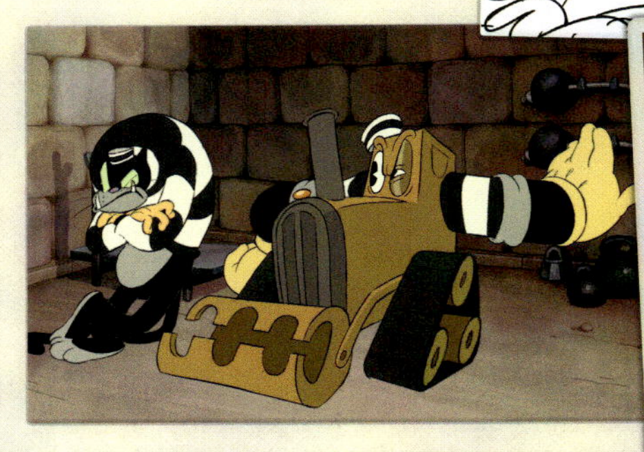

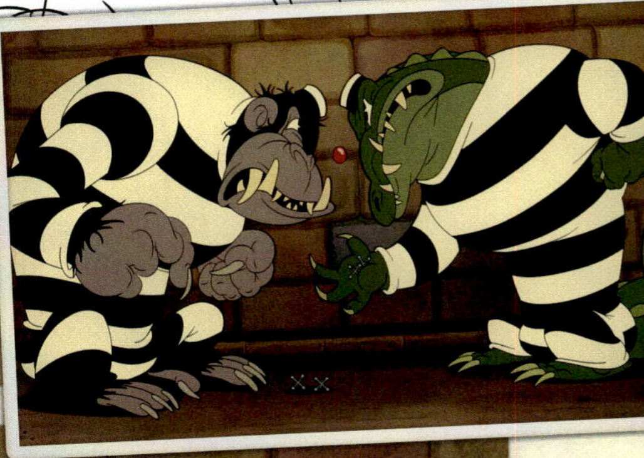

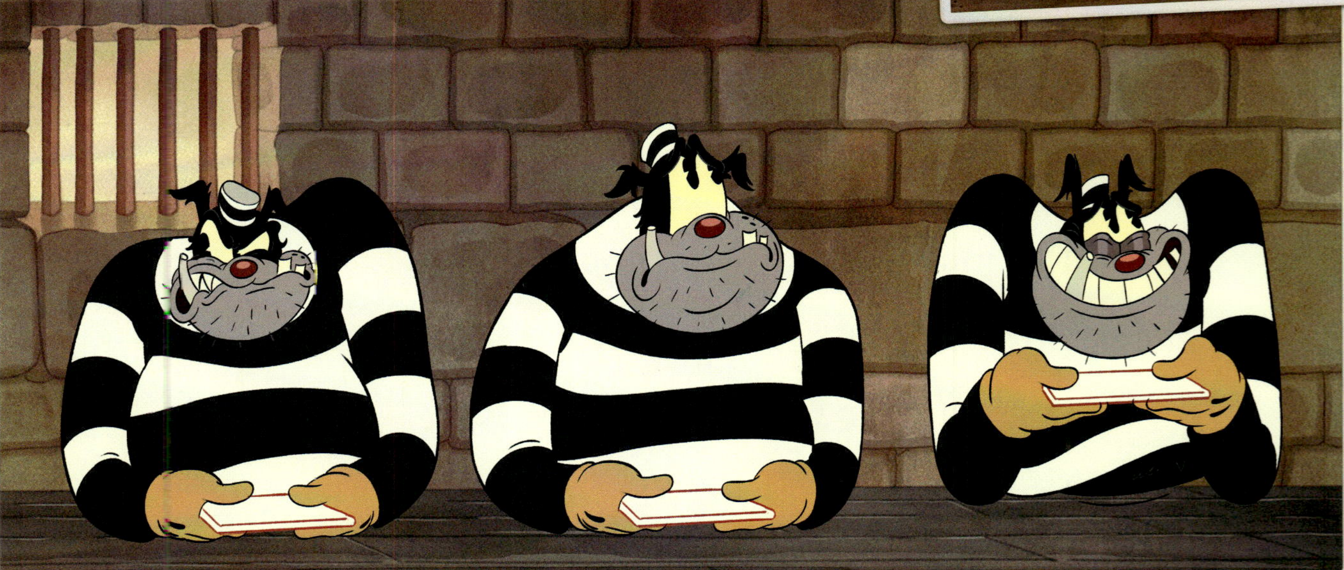

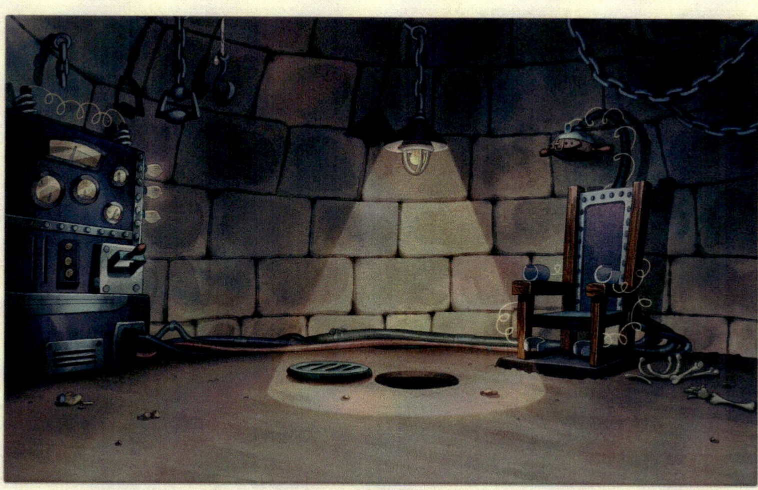

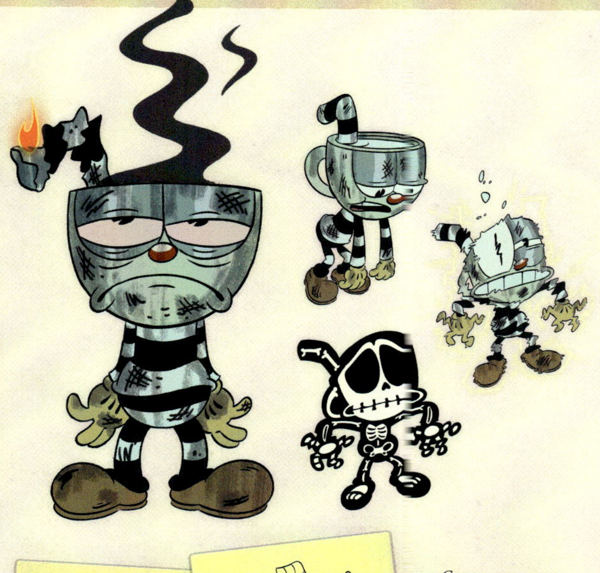

BACKGROUND DESIGN BY PAT MARCONETT; PAINTING BY MALLORY CARLSON.

→ **ANDREA:** Pat was instrumental in "Jailbroken"—he's got a creepy sensibility that maybe he's not entirely aware of . . .

PAT: The electric chair was one of my favorites.

ANDREA: He was just perfect for getting a weird vibe out of this jail—it was cartoony and fun, but it also had to be scary, and Pat totally delivered.

PAT: I remember we had so much back-and-forth about how many bones we were allowed to have throughout the jail.

ANDREA: Dave thought Pat was a secret serial killer. He said, "Why does Pat keep adding bones?!" I said, "That's just his vibe, man!"

PAT: I love weird, creepy, broken-down stuff—it's always my favorite.

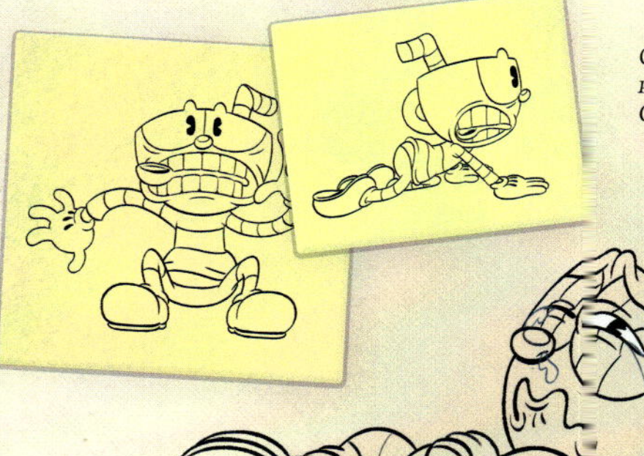

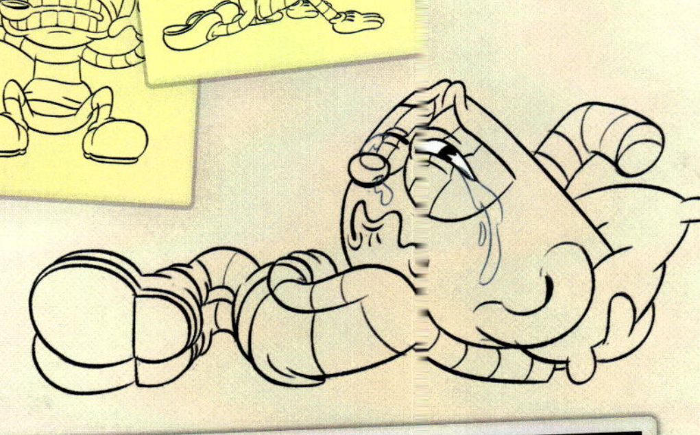

CUPHEAD SPECIAL POSES BY TAPAN GANDHI.

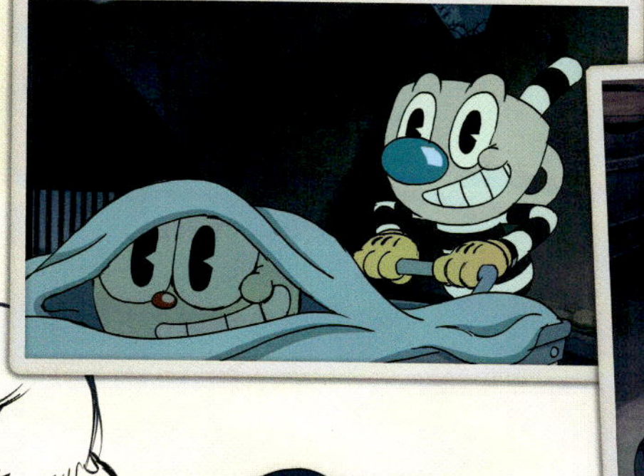

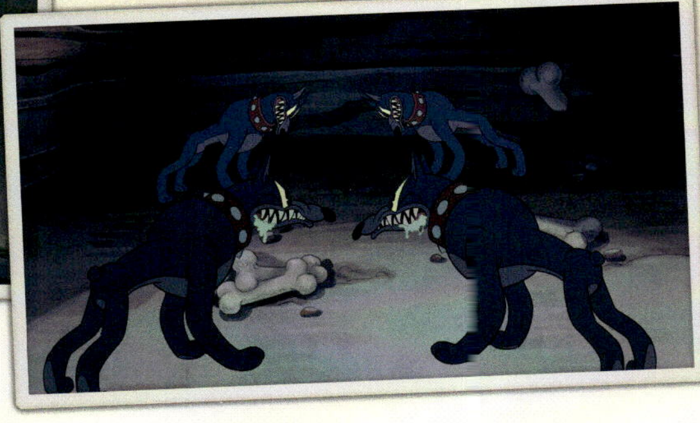

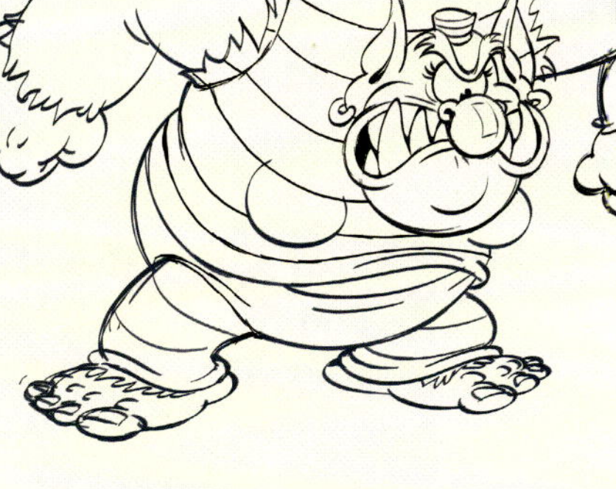

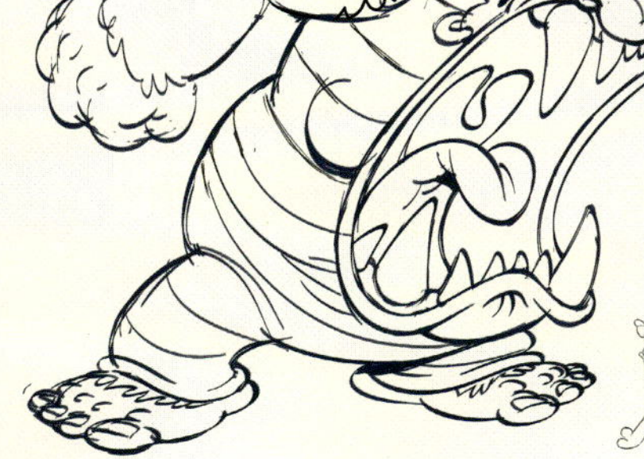

MISS CYCLOPS SPECIAL POSES BY ADAM PALOIAN.

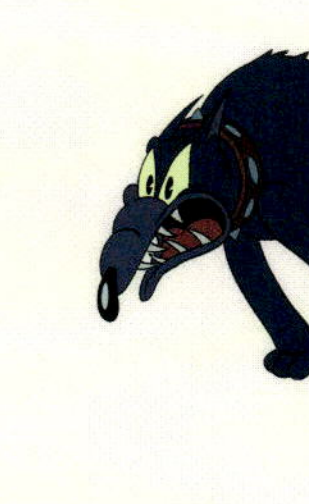

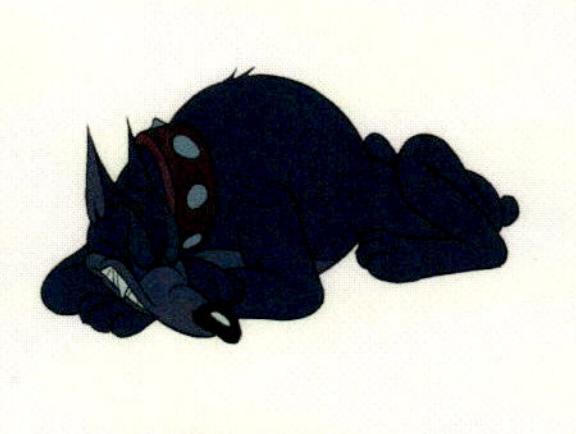

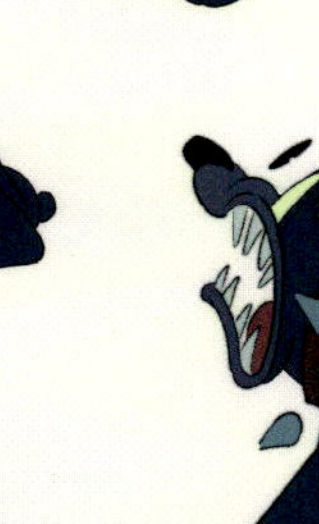

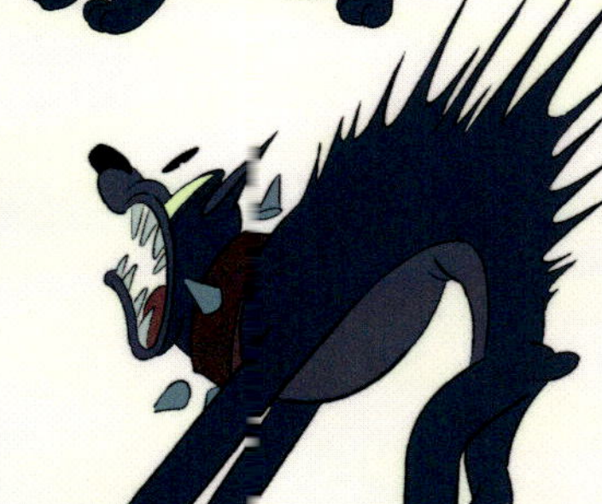

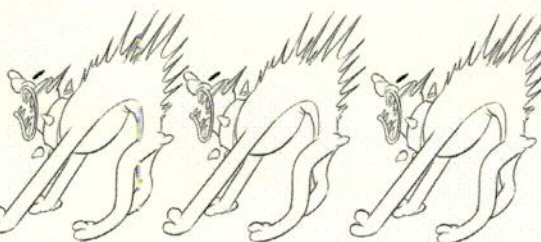

GUARD DOG SPECIAL POSES BY JIM SOPER.

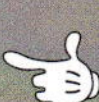

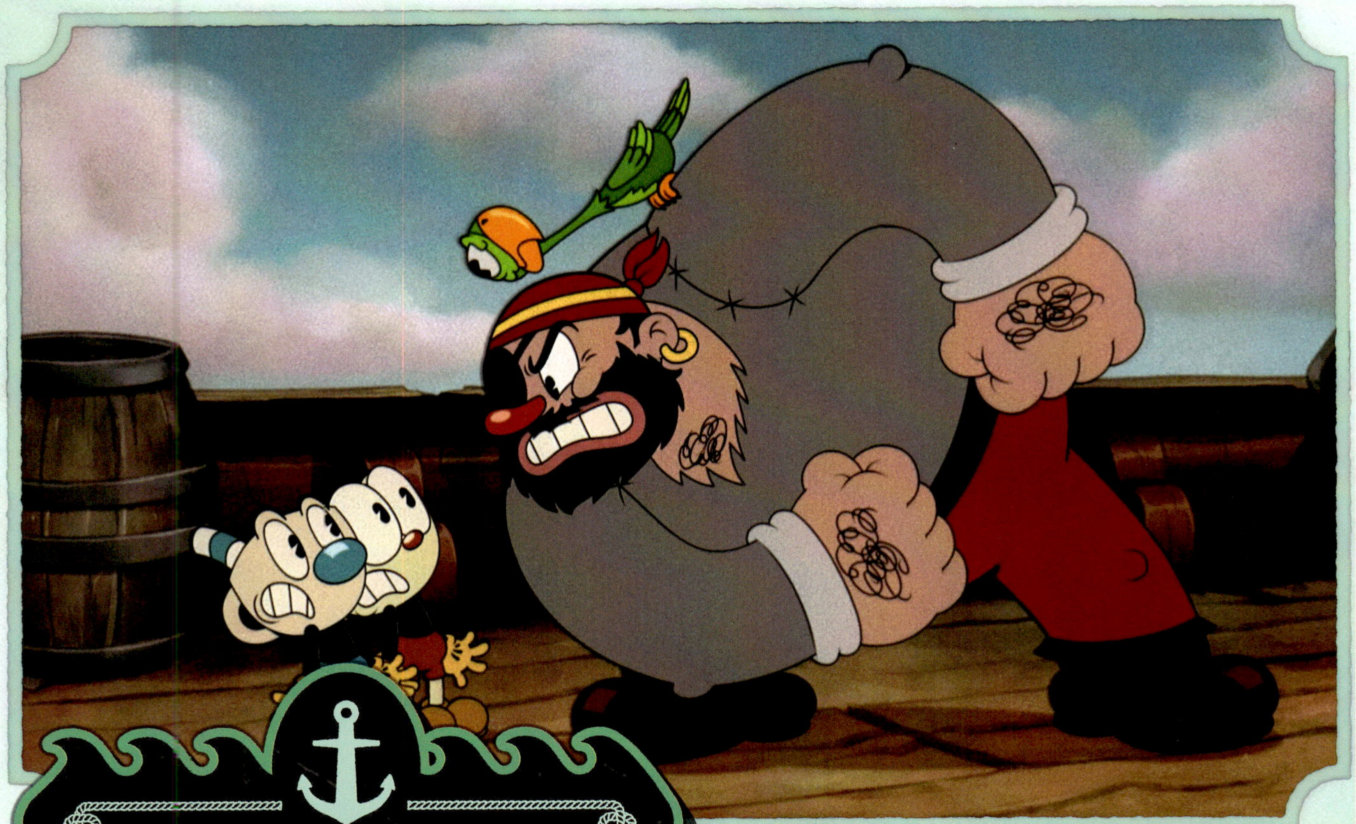

EPISODE 2

"A HIGH SEAS ADVENTURE!"

DEEP DIVE

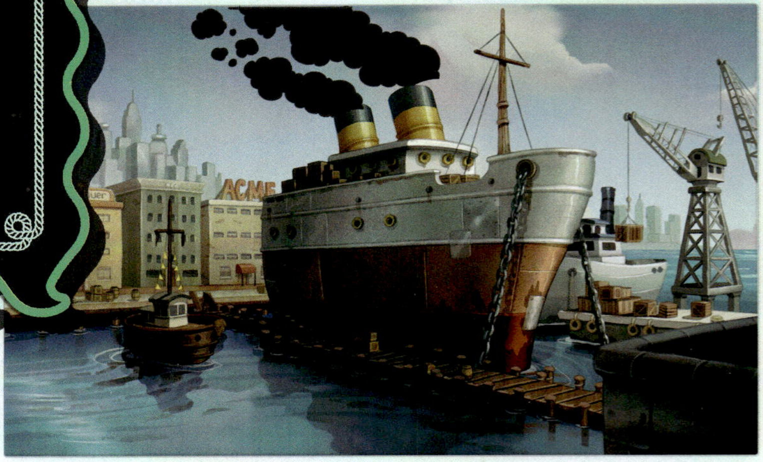

→ **ADAM P:** The first part has a lot more comedy—there's no real jeopardy yet. Moodwise, we were saving up for something more threatening.

ANDREA: It's blue skies and they're on a dock, then they're on a ship at sea and it gets cloudy, then it gets dark, then they're inside a cave, then they're inside a grotto . . . You have to develop a lot of different looks, and the challenge is that everyone has to simultaneously start painting and get in the same groove. The sheer amount of looks the team has to develop in a single episode can be incredibly challenging sometimes.

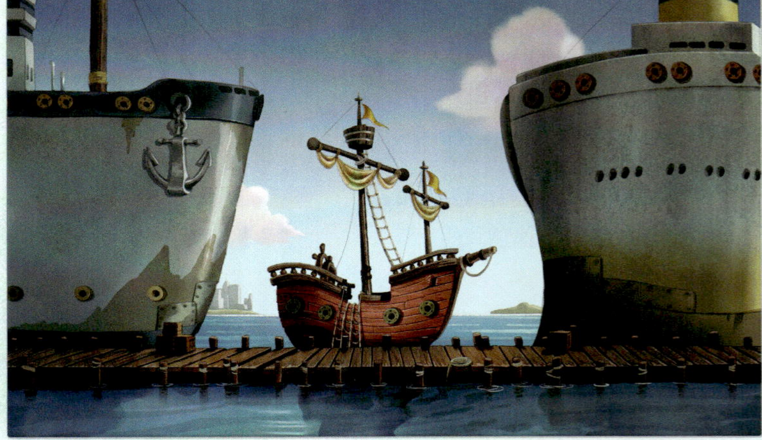

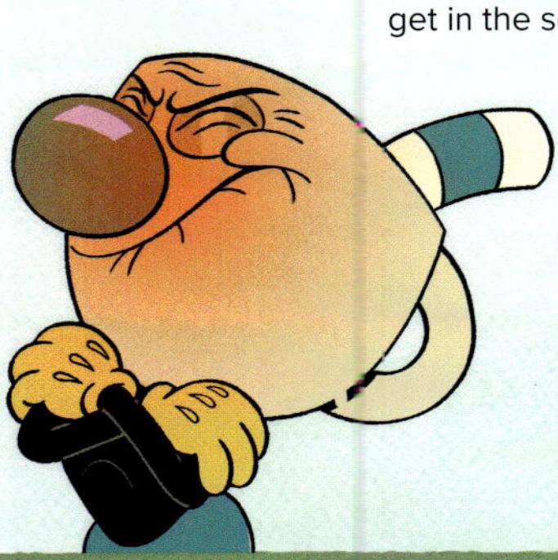

BACKGROUND DESIGNS BY LAUREN DUDA AND JESSICA HONG; PAINTINGS BY MALLORY CARLSON; MUGMAN SPECIAL POSE BY TAPAN GANDHI.

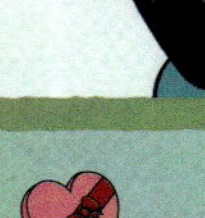

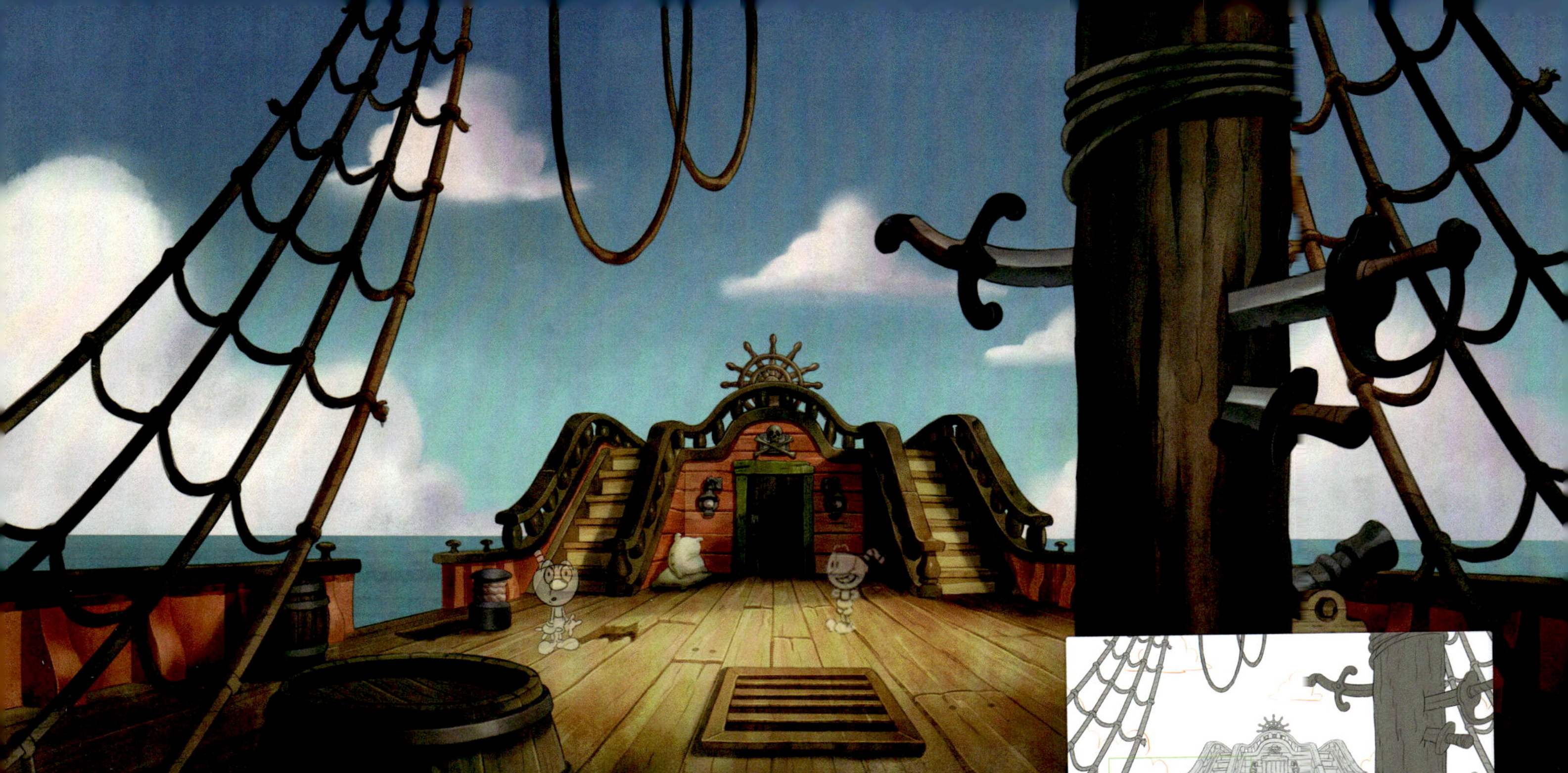

CAPTAIN BRINEYBEARD'S SHIP

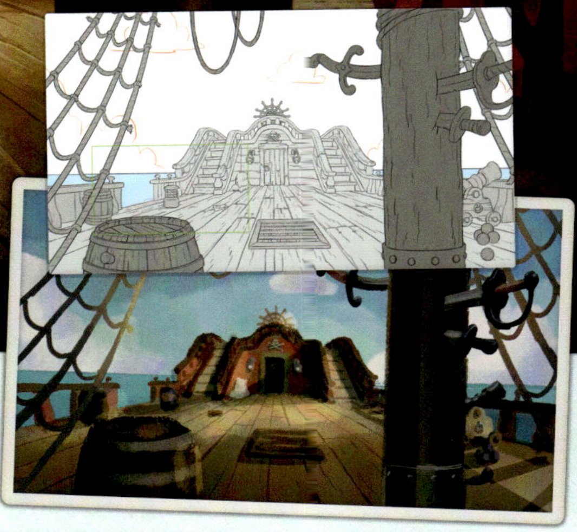

→ **LAUREN:** The ship design combines our reference from *Popeye* with elements from the *Cuphead* game. Captain Brineybeard is such a specific character and had such a specific ship in the game. The shapes were really fun. I got to hang out in the concept phase a little longer.

ANDREA: Ivan has a really good feel for naturalistic wood tones, so I knew he'd be great on the ship.

IVAN: Once someone has a key painting in the location, it's easier to look at that painting and see how they did it, and then we can start using the same textures, and that gets us on the same page.

Background designs by Benjamin Anderson; paintings by Ivan Aguirre.

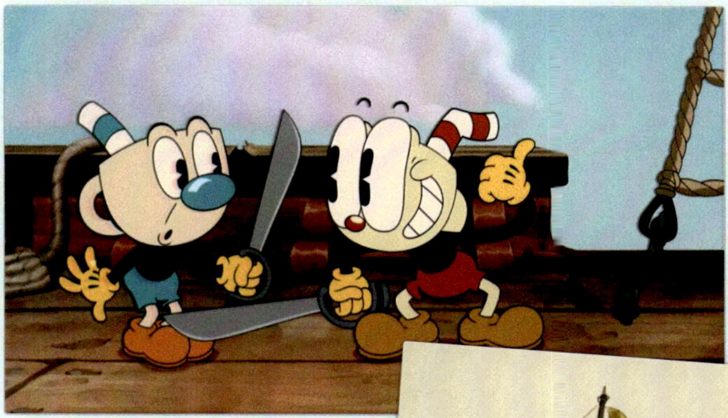

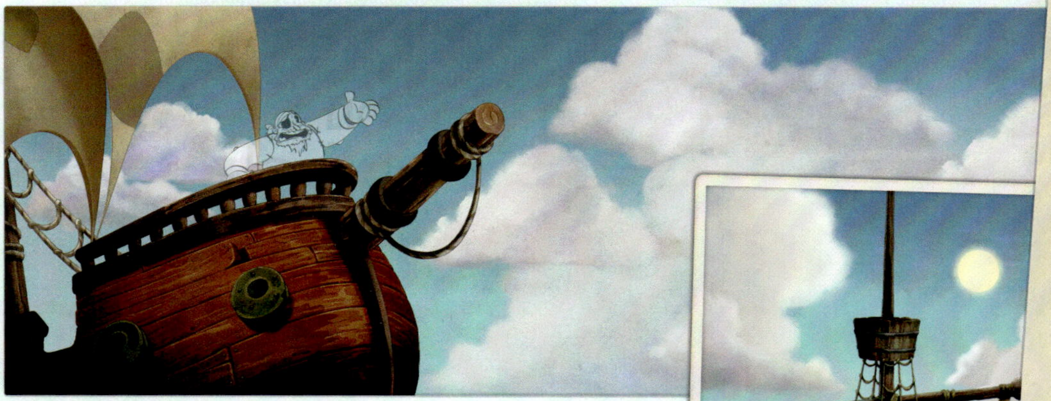

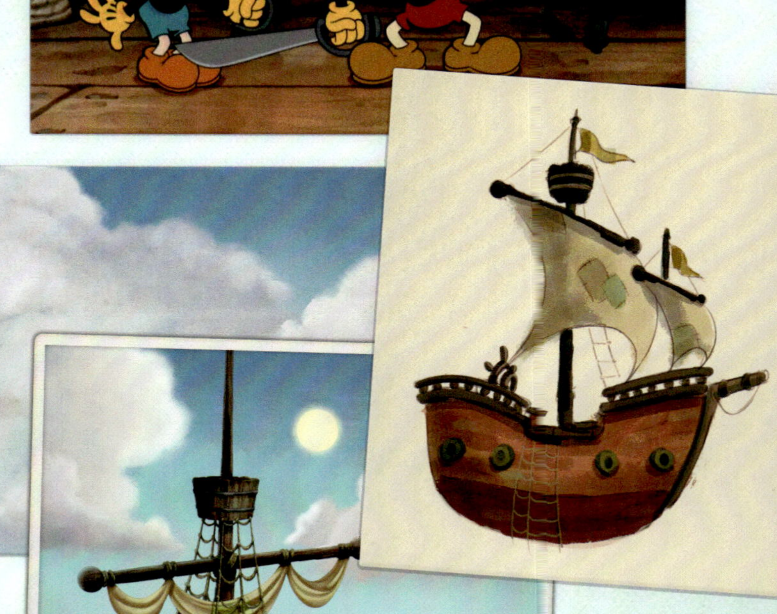

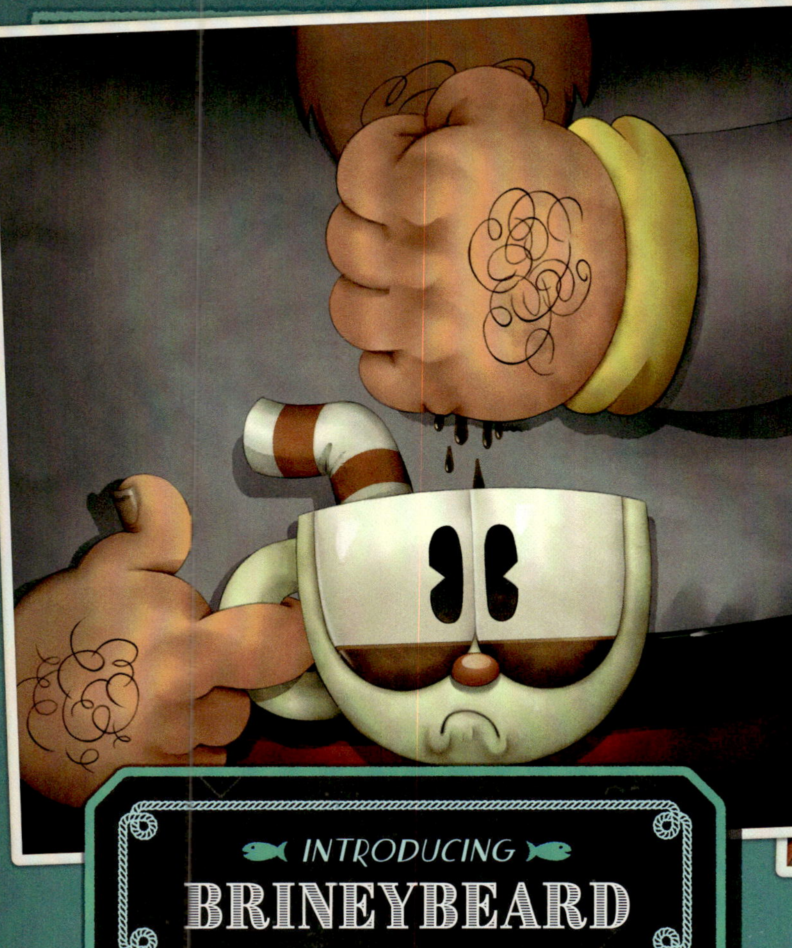

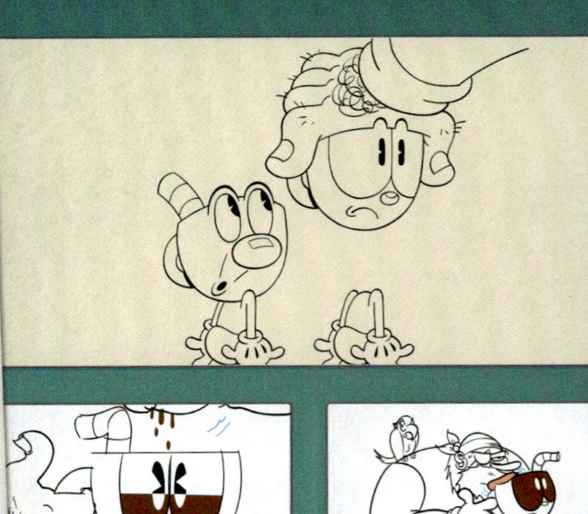

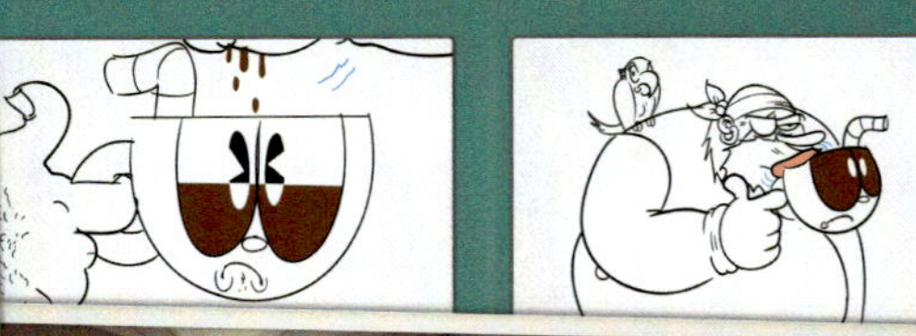

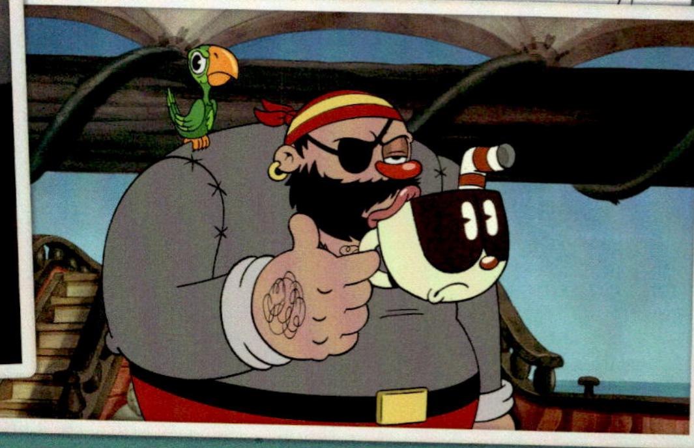

BACKGROUND DESIGN BY ADAM FAY; PAINTING BY MALLORY CARLSON; STORYBOARD PANELS BY FERNANDO PUIG.

INTRODUCING BRINEYBEARD

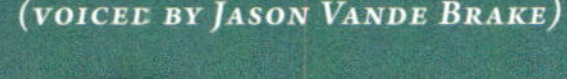

(VOICED BY JASON VANDE BRAKE)

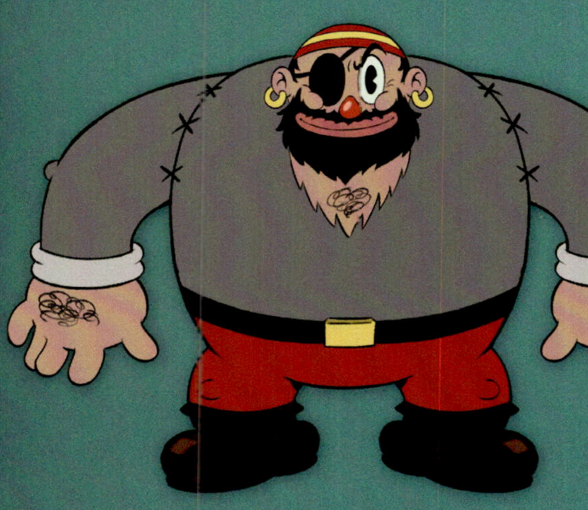

CHARACTER DESIGN AND SPECIAL POSE BY TAPAN GANDHI AND ADAM FAY.

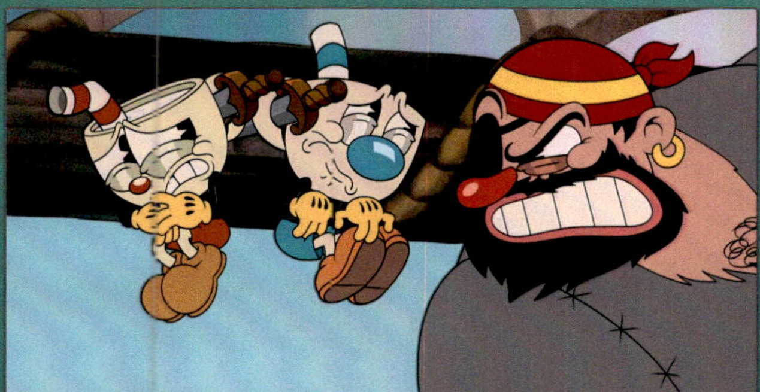

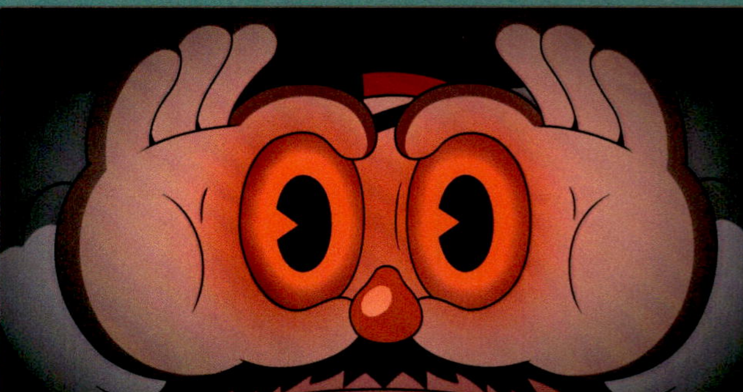

CHARACTER COLOR BY CHRIS HACKER.

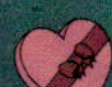

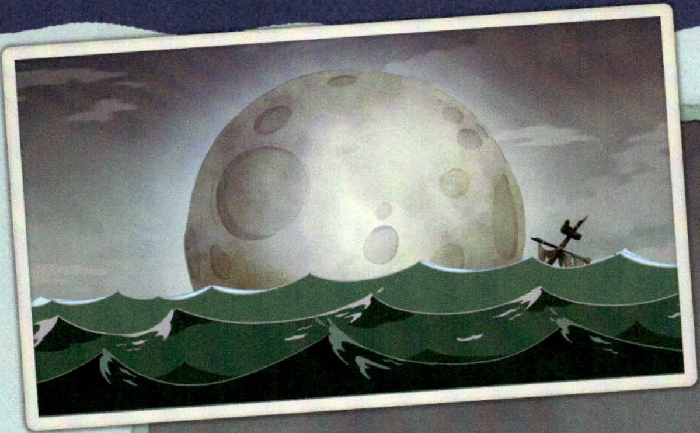

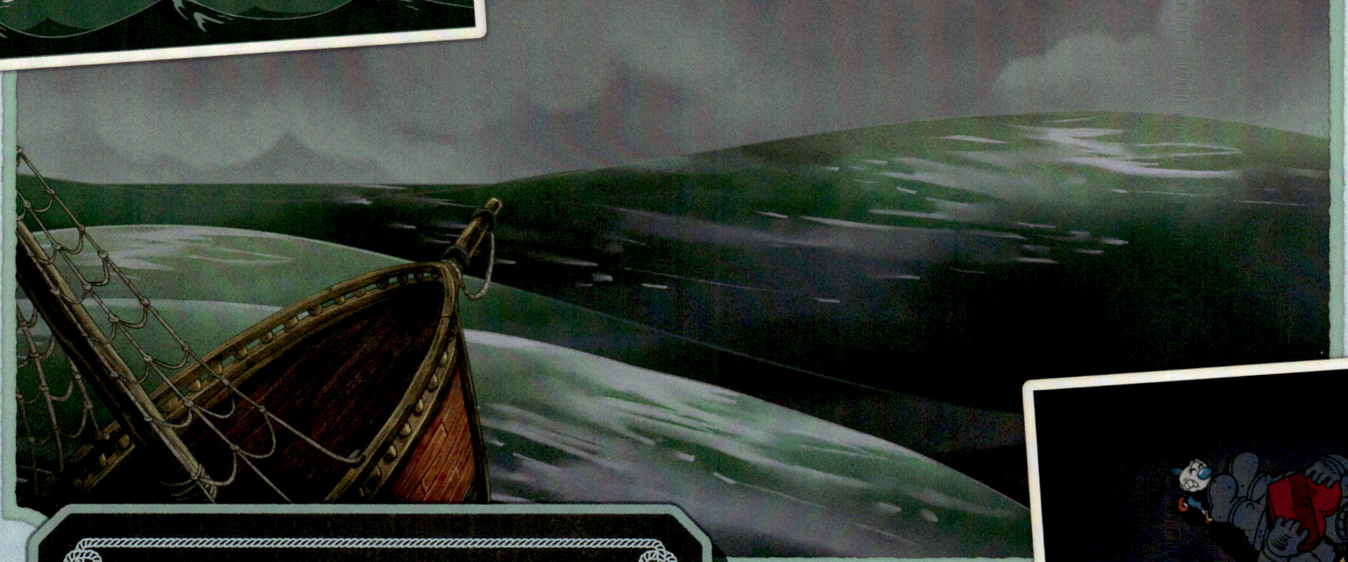

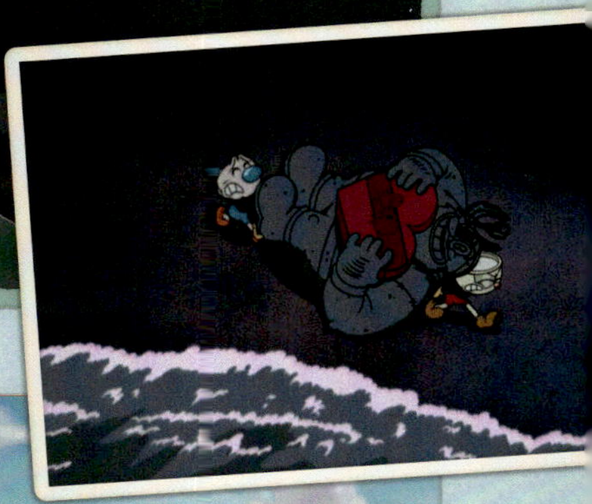

WATER EFFECTS

ADAM D: We had to spend quite a bit of time on water effects.

ANDREA: The water is inspired by *Popeye*, but you never see water react this way in *Popeye* cartoons. In the Fleischer shorts, the water is more graphic, and the design language is more like a comic book. A lot of stuff has to come together for an effect like that.

ADAM D: We scrubbed through countless different libraries, noticing things like "Look at how they're doing bubbles here" and "Look at how the water drops are a little bit fatter over here—do we want to go that fat?" We started talking about viscosity and physics—it got real brainy.

ANDREA: In this episode, there's so much mobility in the water that it almost becomes like a character. We have these big rolling hills of water, so you have to really think of it in terms of how it would work, not just from an aesthetic perspective but also physically how that water would react and move. We had to figure it out all over again every time—it's not textbook.

BACKGROUND DESIGN BY LAUREN DUDA; PAINTING BY MALLORY CARLSON.

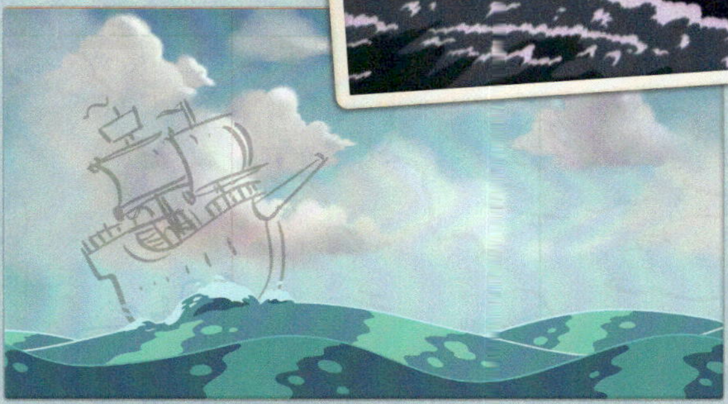

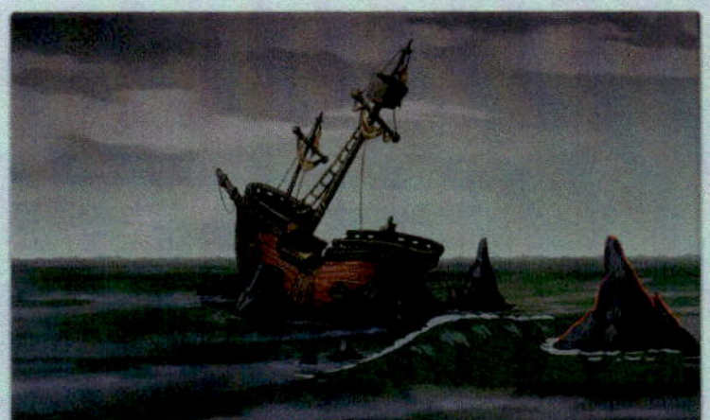

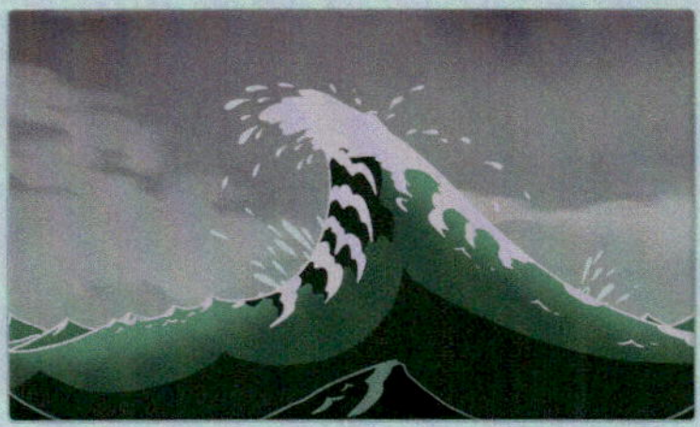

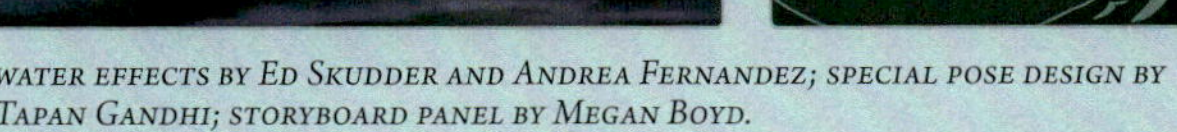

WATER EFFECTS BY ED SKUDDER AND ANDREA FERNANDEZ; SPECIAL POSE DESIGN BY TAPAN GANDHI; STORYBOARD PANEL BY MEGAN BOYD.

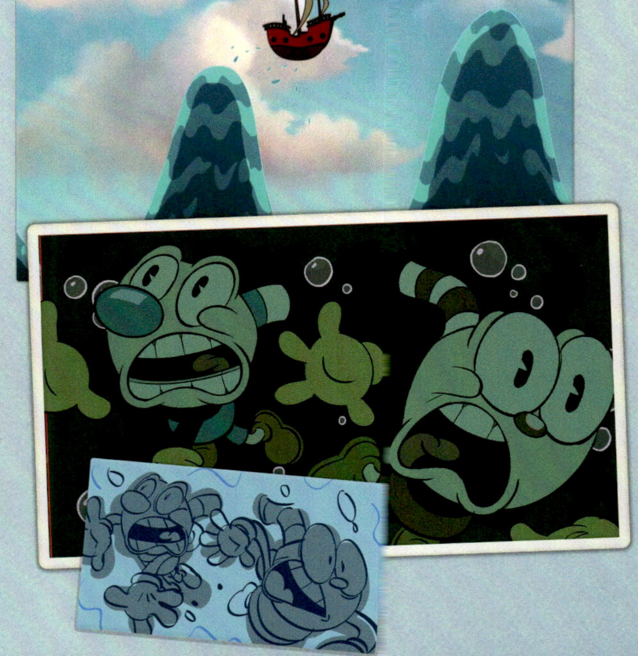

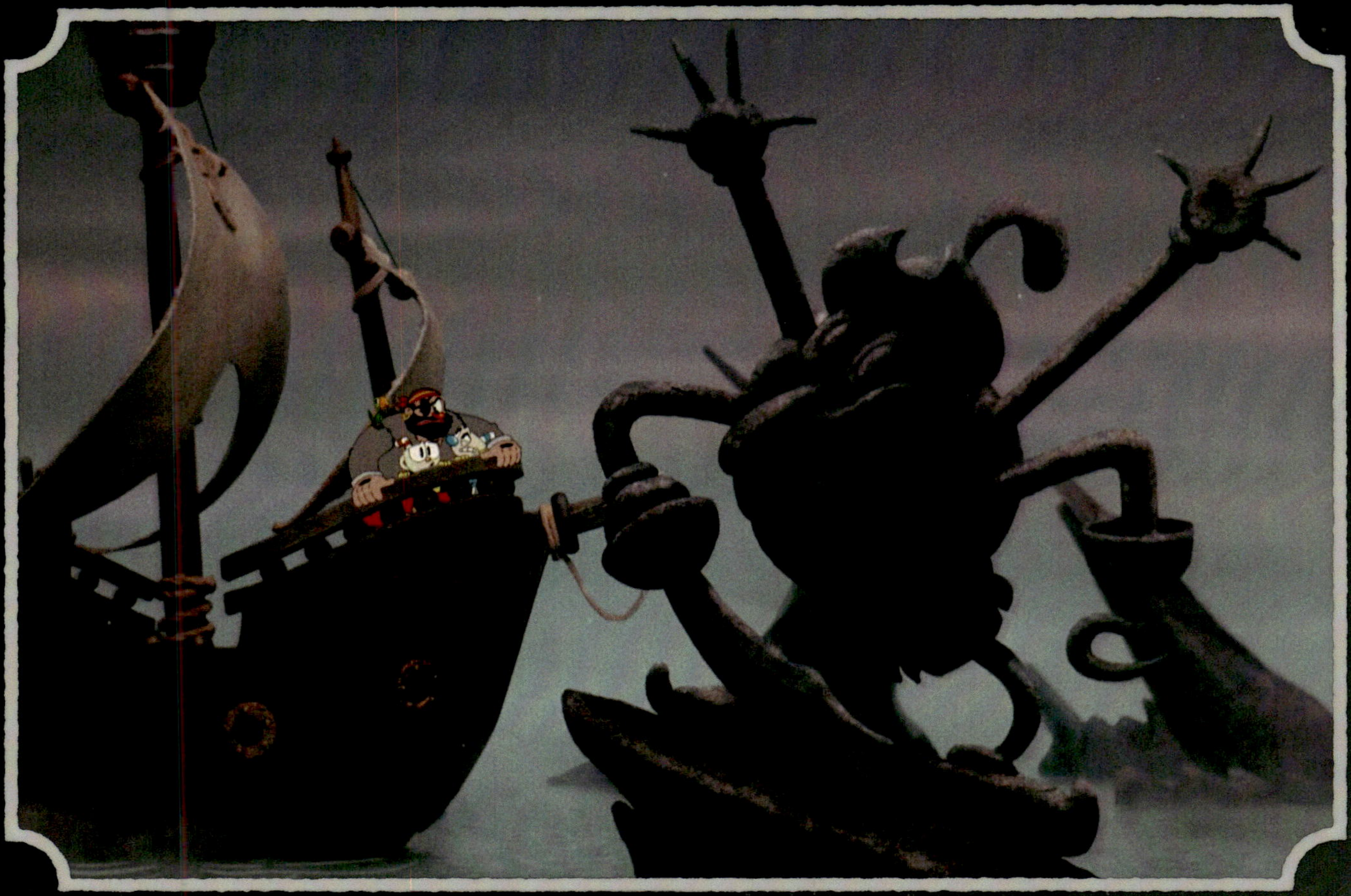

• STOP-MO SPOTLIGHT •

JOURNEY TO CALA'S CREEPY COVE

→ **COSMO:** Once we get into Cala Maria's cove, it transforms into this really spooky three-dimensional pirate ship graveyard.

ADAM P: I wanted the bones of a ship to look like a whale carcass, and as they pass through it, there's frozen pirates made of stone . . . The scenery starts to gradually immerse you in creepiness. The stop-mo captures that feeling really well.

DAVE: Screen Novelties really delivered on that set beyond our wildest expectations.

Petrified pirates design by Tapan Gandhi; painting by Gregory Miller; previs drawings and paintings by Andrea Fernandez.

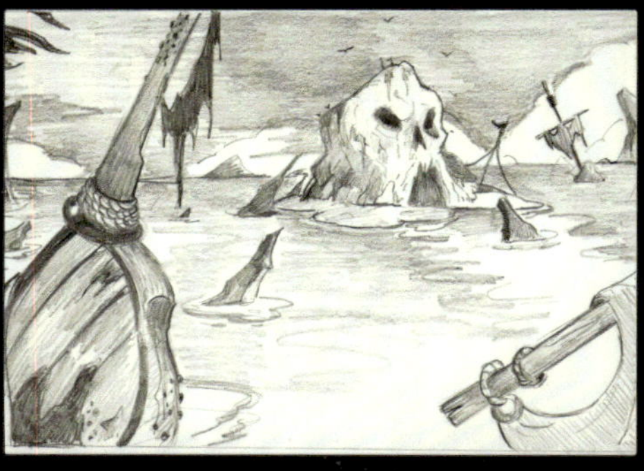

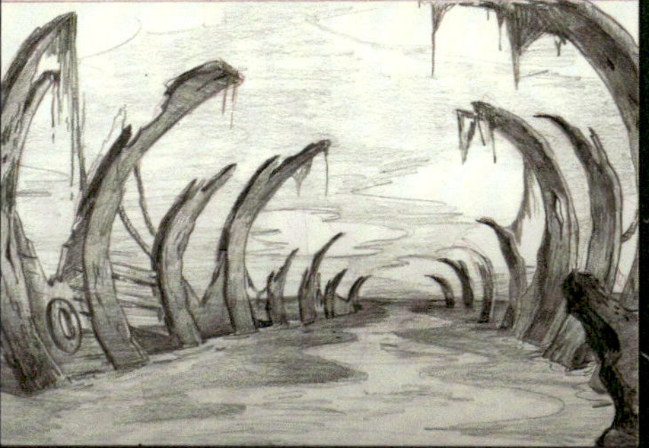

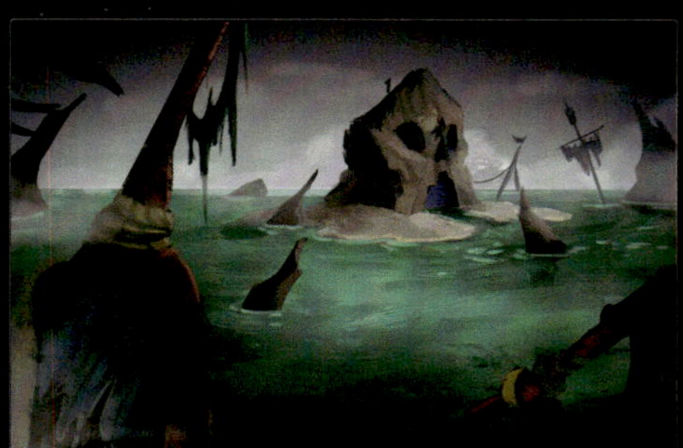

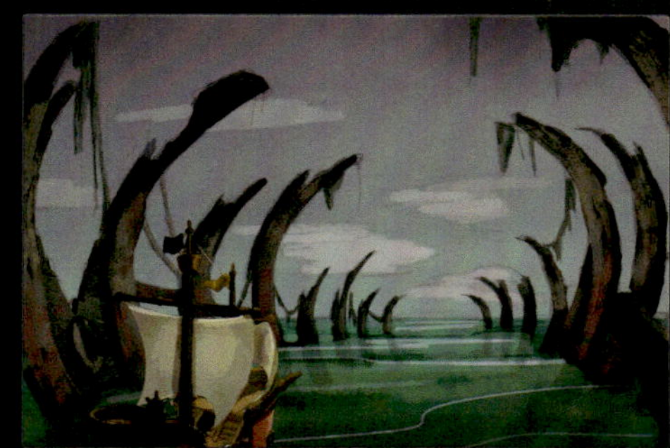

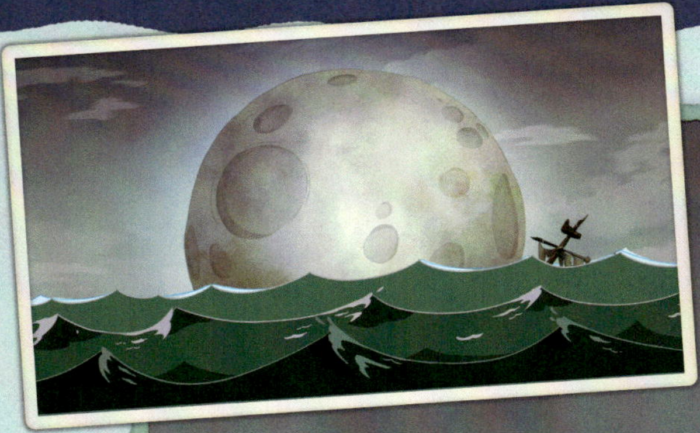

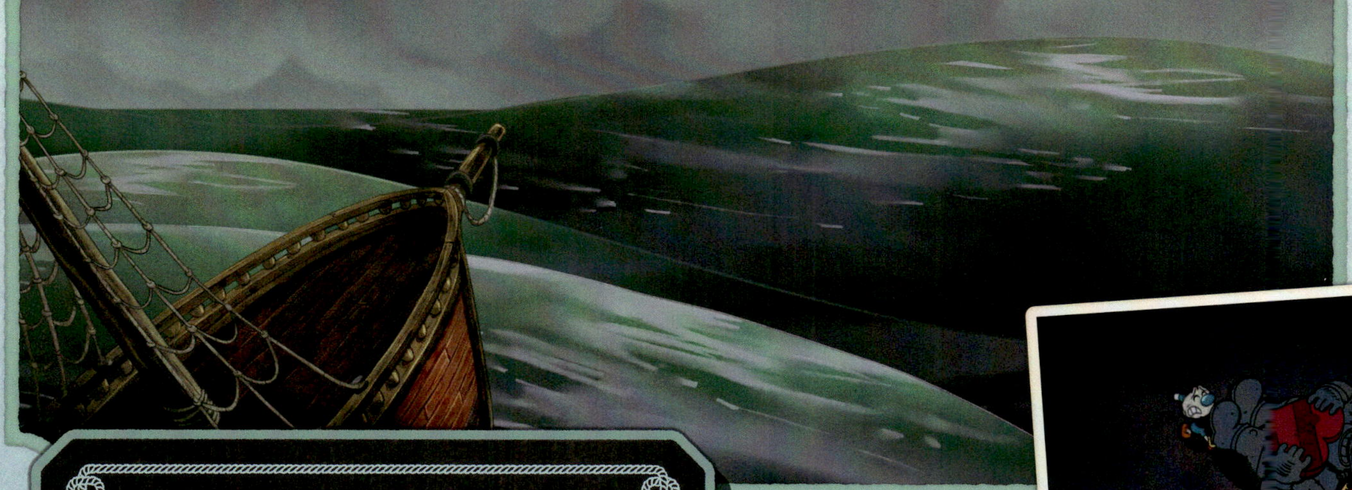

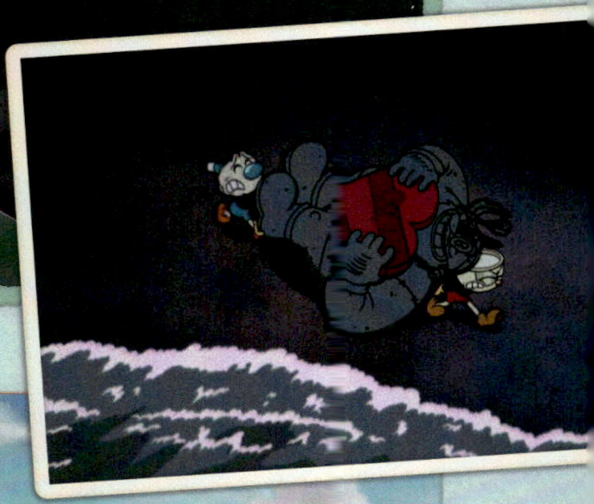

WATER EFFECTS

→ **ADAM D:** We had to spend quite a bit of time on water effects.

ANDREA: The water is inspired by *Popeye*, but you never see water react this way in *Popeye* cartoons. In the Fleischer shorts, the water is more graphic, and the design language is more like a comic book. A lot of stuff has to come together for an effect like that.

ADAM D: We scrubbed through countless different libraries, noticing things like "Look at how they're doing bubbles here" and "Look at how the water drops are a little bit fatter over here—do we want to go that fat?" We started talking about viscosity and physics—it got real brainy.

ANDREA: In this episode, there's so much mobility in the water that it almost becomes like a character. We have these big rolling hills of water, so you have to really think of it in terms of how it would work, not just from an aesthetic perspective but also physically how that water would react and move. We had to figure it out all over again every time—it's not textbook.

BACKGROUND DESIGN BY LAUREN DUDA; PAINTING BY MALLORY CARLSON.

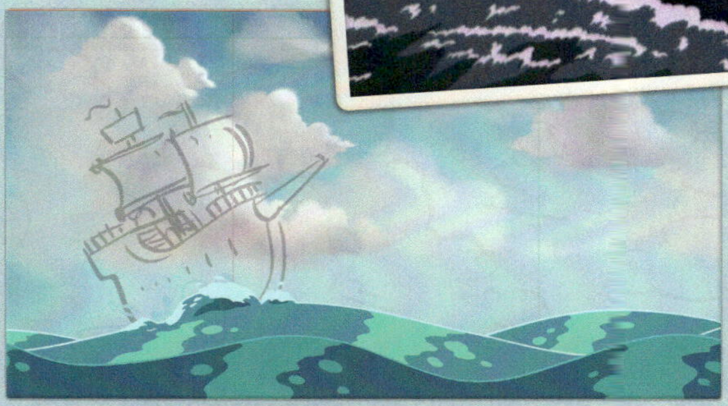

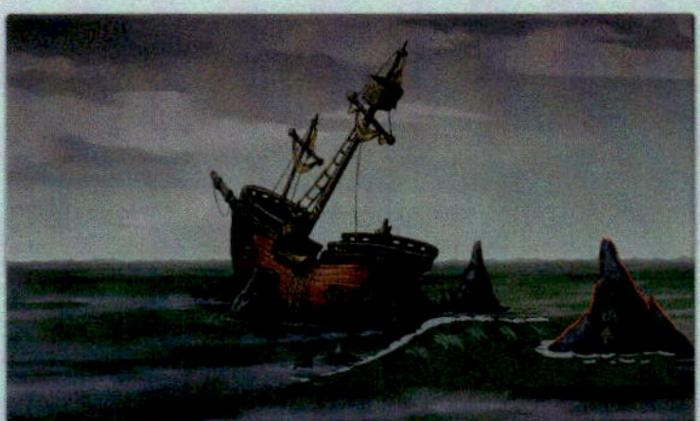

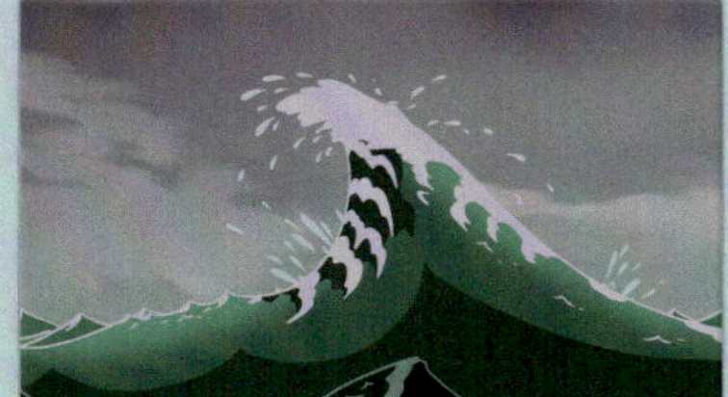

WATER EFFECTS BY ED SKUDDER AND ANDREA FERNANDEZ; SPECIAL POSE DESIGN BY TAPAN GANDHI; STORYBOARD PANEL BY MEGAN BOYD.

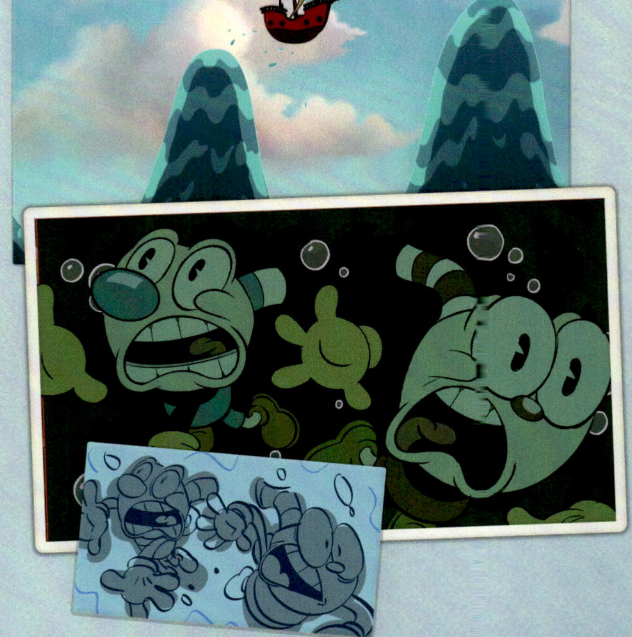

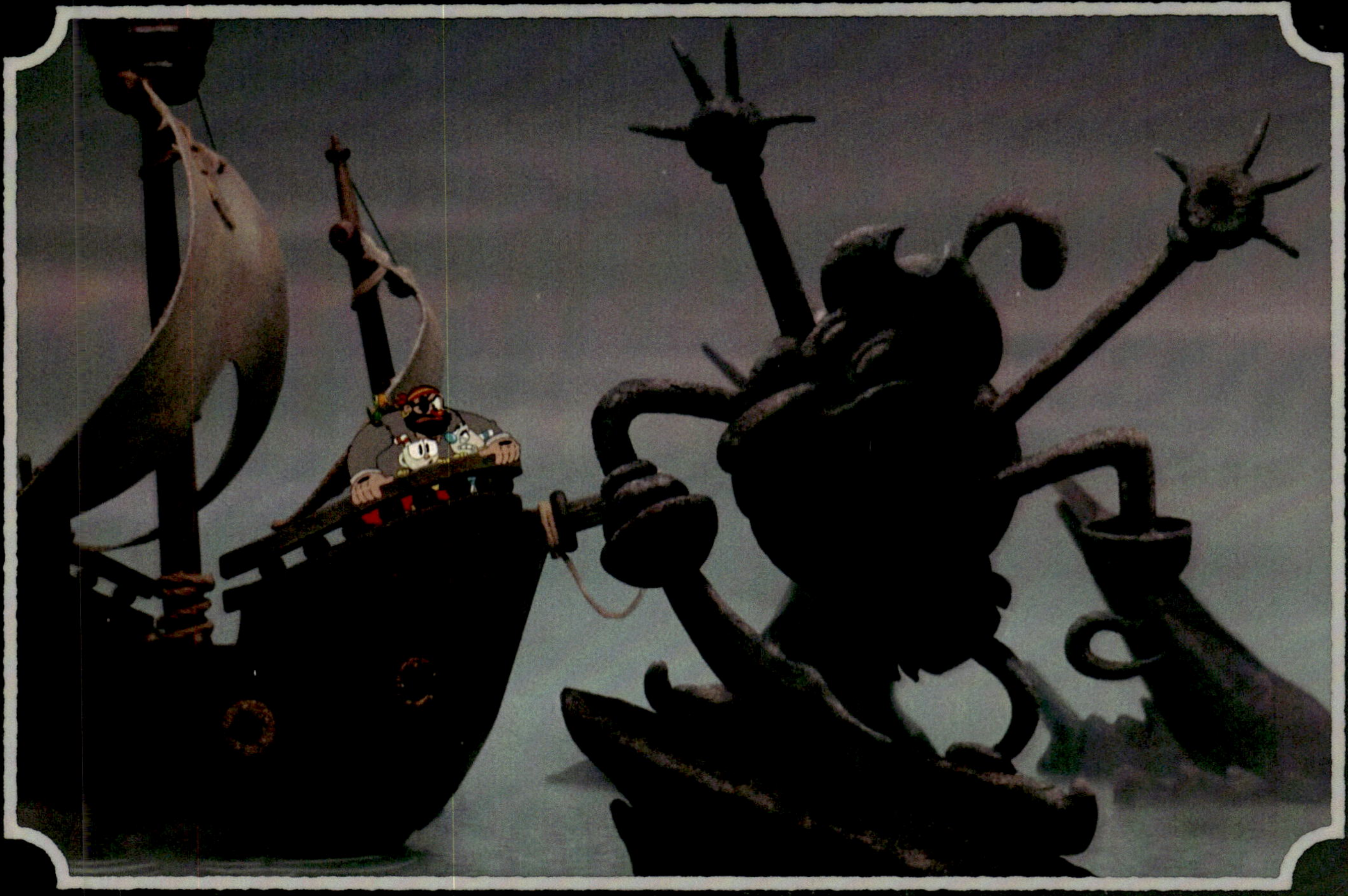

◆ STOP-MO SPOTLIGHT ◆

JOURNEY TO CALA'S CREEPY COVE

→ **COSMO:** Once we get into Cala Maria's cove, it transforms into this really spooky three-dimensional pirate ship graveyard.

ADAM P: I wanted the bones of a ship to look like a whale carcass, and as they pass through it, there's frozen pirates made of stone . . . The scenery starts to gradually immerse you in creepiness. The stop-mo captures that feeling really well.

DAVE: Screen Novelties really delivered on that set beyond our wildest expectations.

Petrified pirates design by Tapan Gandhi; painting by Gregory Miller; previs drawings and paintings by Andrea Fernandez.

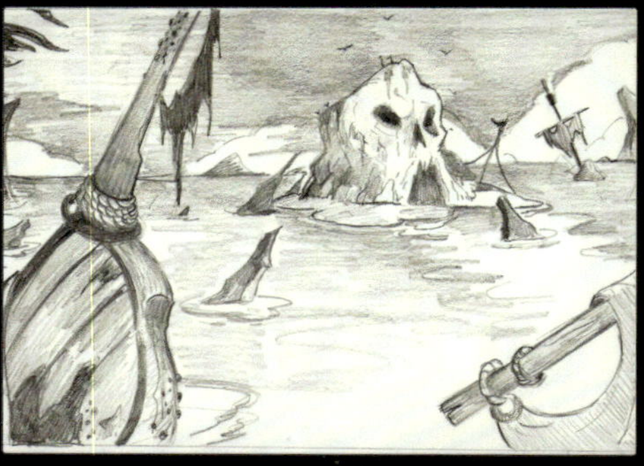

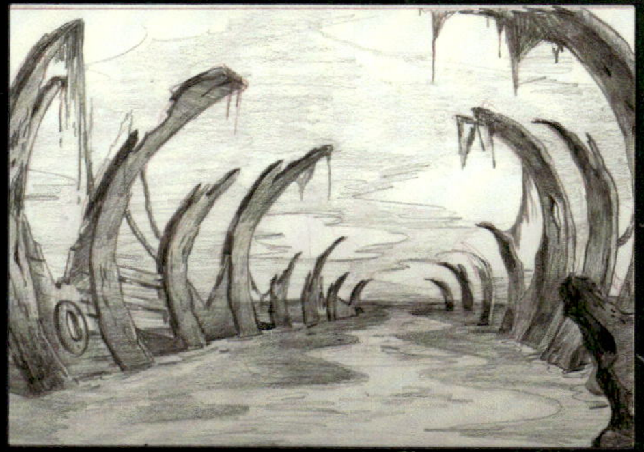

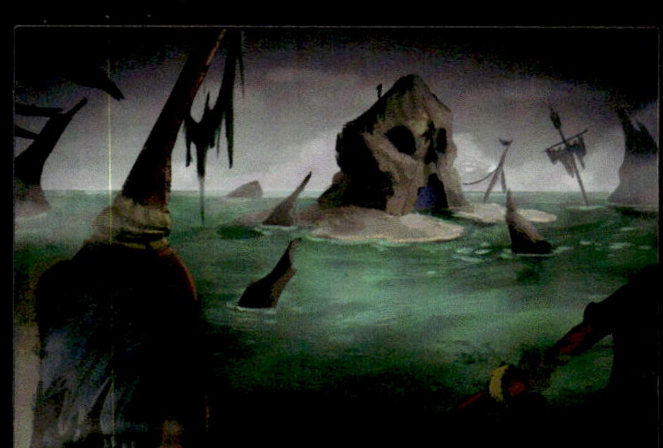

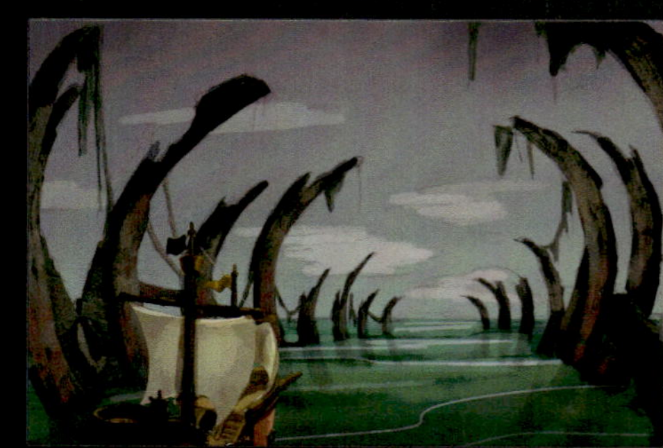

SEAMUS: In the background, there were all those sunken ships with the tattered sails draping down.

MARK: Initially, it was just going to be cutouts of the wrecked boats printed on paper.

SEAMUS: But if you just use a cutout, it comes off as a little bit stiff onscreen, and it doesn't react well to light.

MARK: We wanted to give it more dimension, so we added the sails. It's an old trick we learned years ago making our very first film.

SEAMUS: We cut off the sails and made new sails out of pieces of paper towel that we dredged in a glue-and-water solution. They get that blooming light quality that sails get when light hits them from behind. That type of effect is exactly why you do a dimensional set—you want the light and the texture and the color to all form into this perfect storm of an atmosphere.

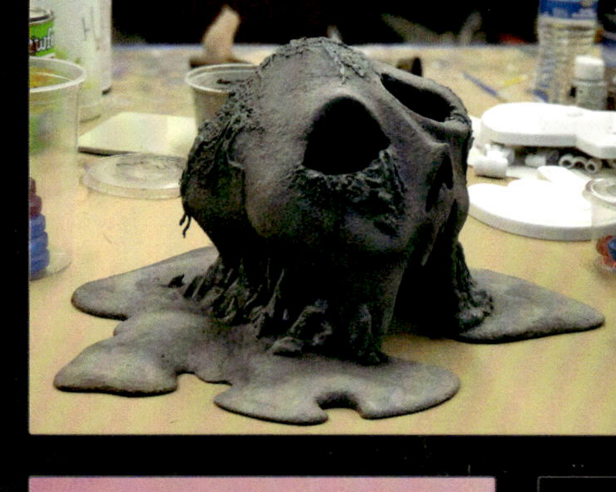

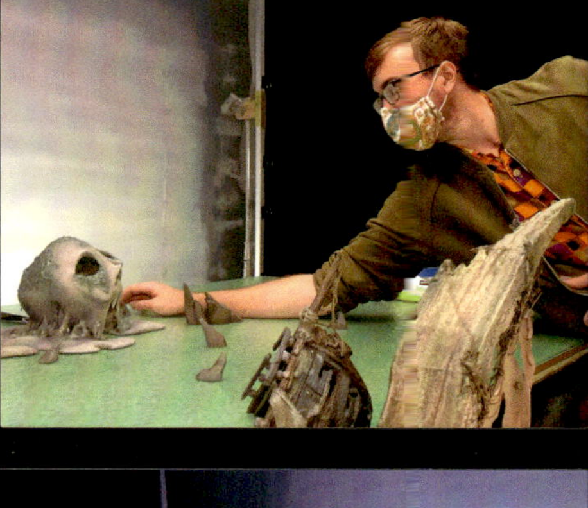

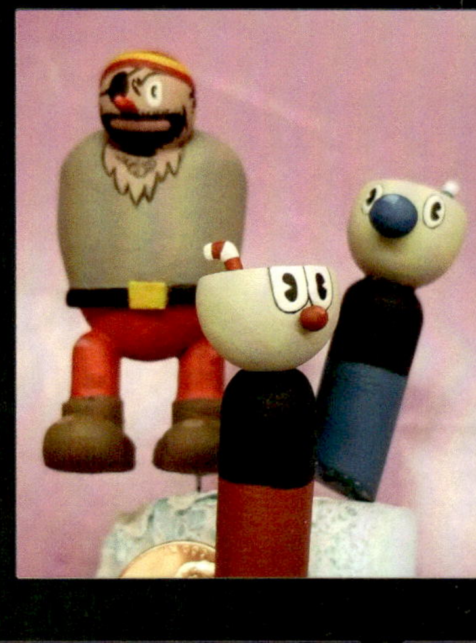

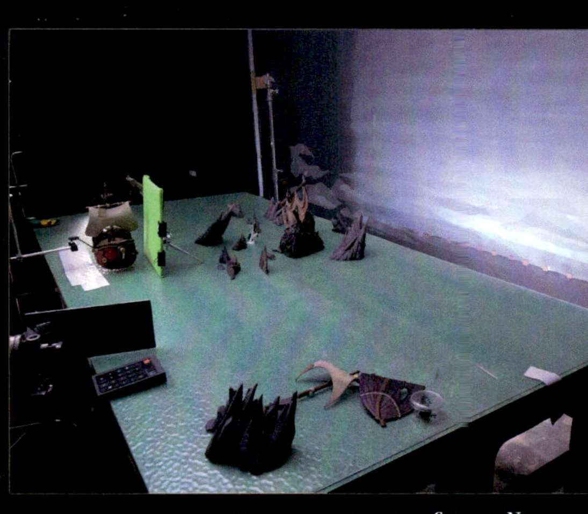

STOP-MO PRODUCTION AT SCREEN NOVELTIES.

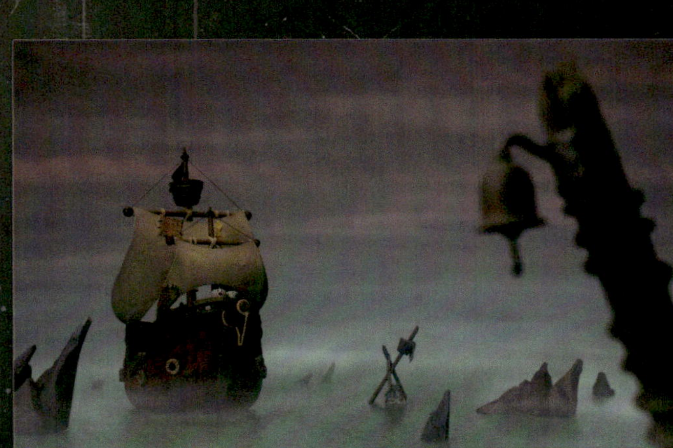

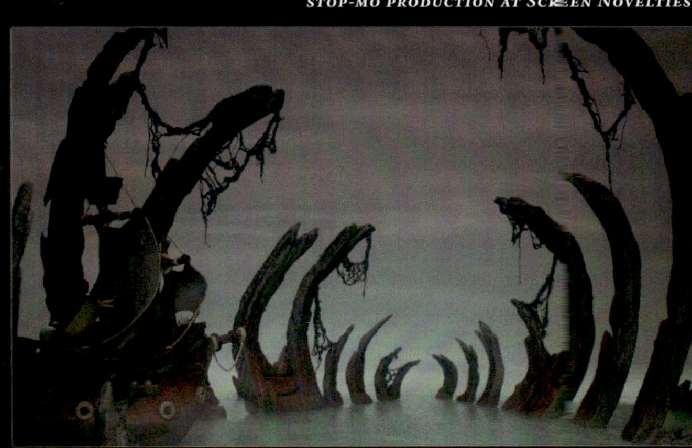

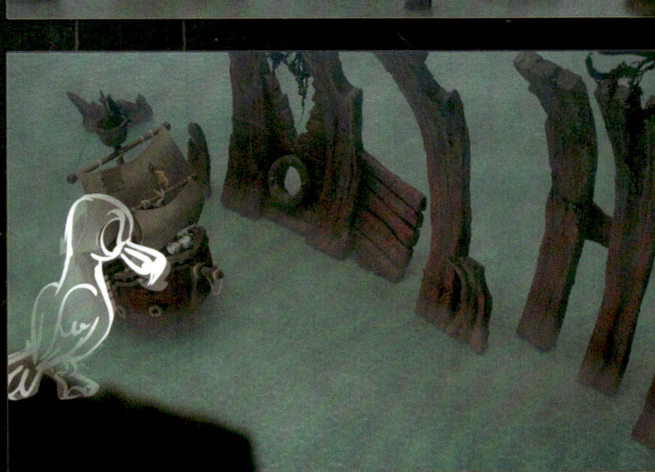

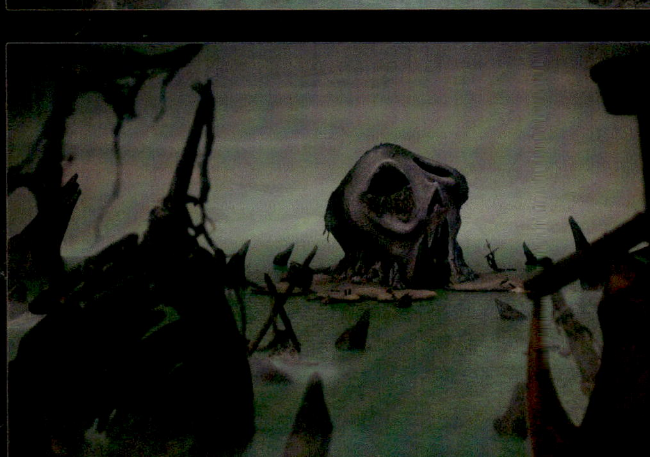

COSMO: Once they shot it, Mark and Seamus knew we were supposed to put our 2D characters on the model of their ship, bu they tried something and showed us footage: they built these minuscule models of Cuphead, Mugman, and Brineybeard and put them in the ship, so they're actually in the physical prop during the stop motion.

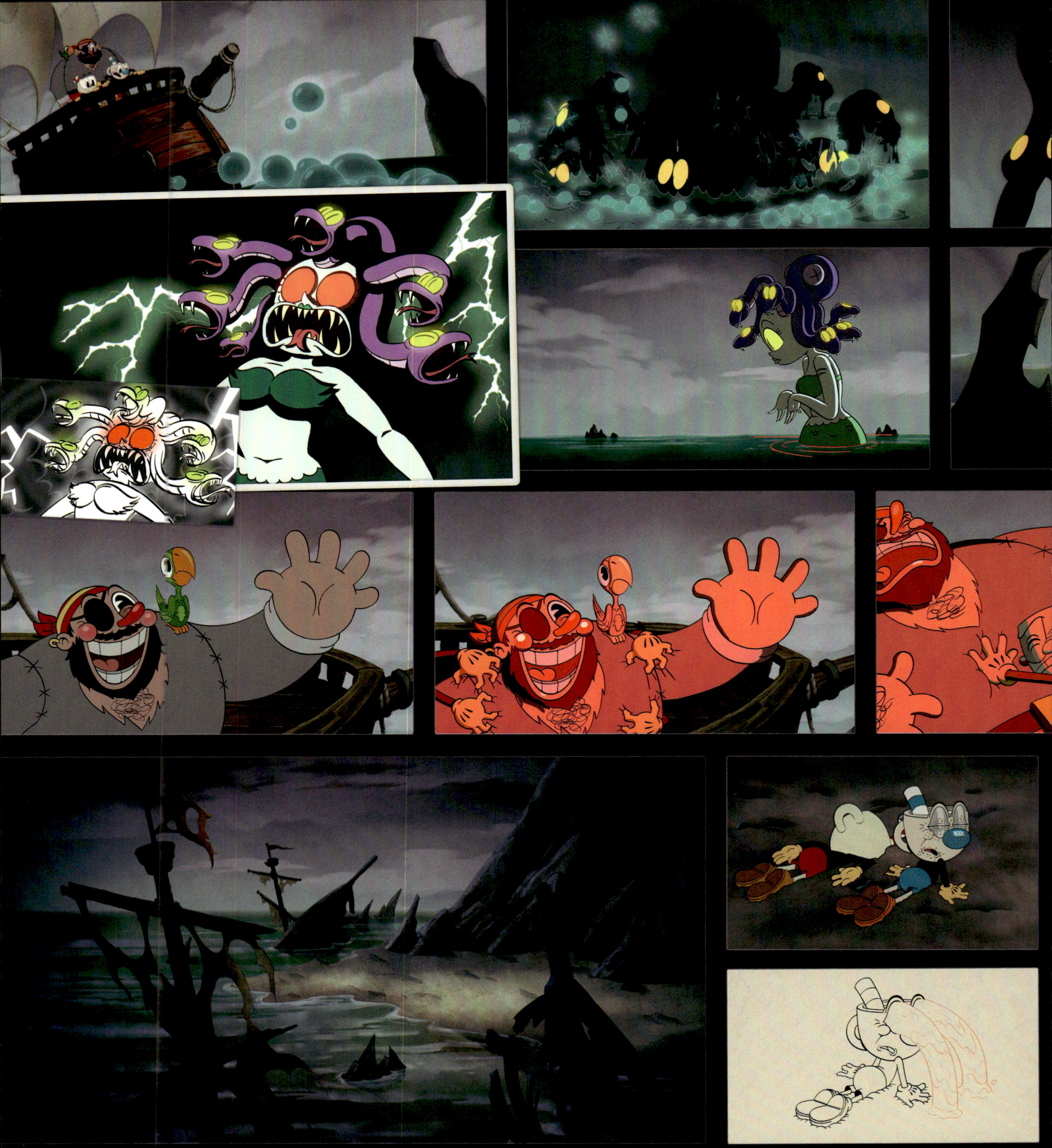

Background designs by Lauren Duda, Jessica Hong, and Pat Marconett; paintings by Gregory Miller, Michelle Thies, and Leah Chun; special pose designs by Tapan Gandhi, Adam Fay, and Adam Paloian; storyboard panels by Megan Boyd and Fernando Puig.

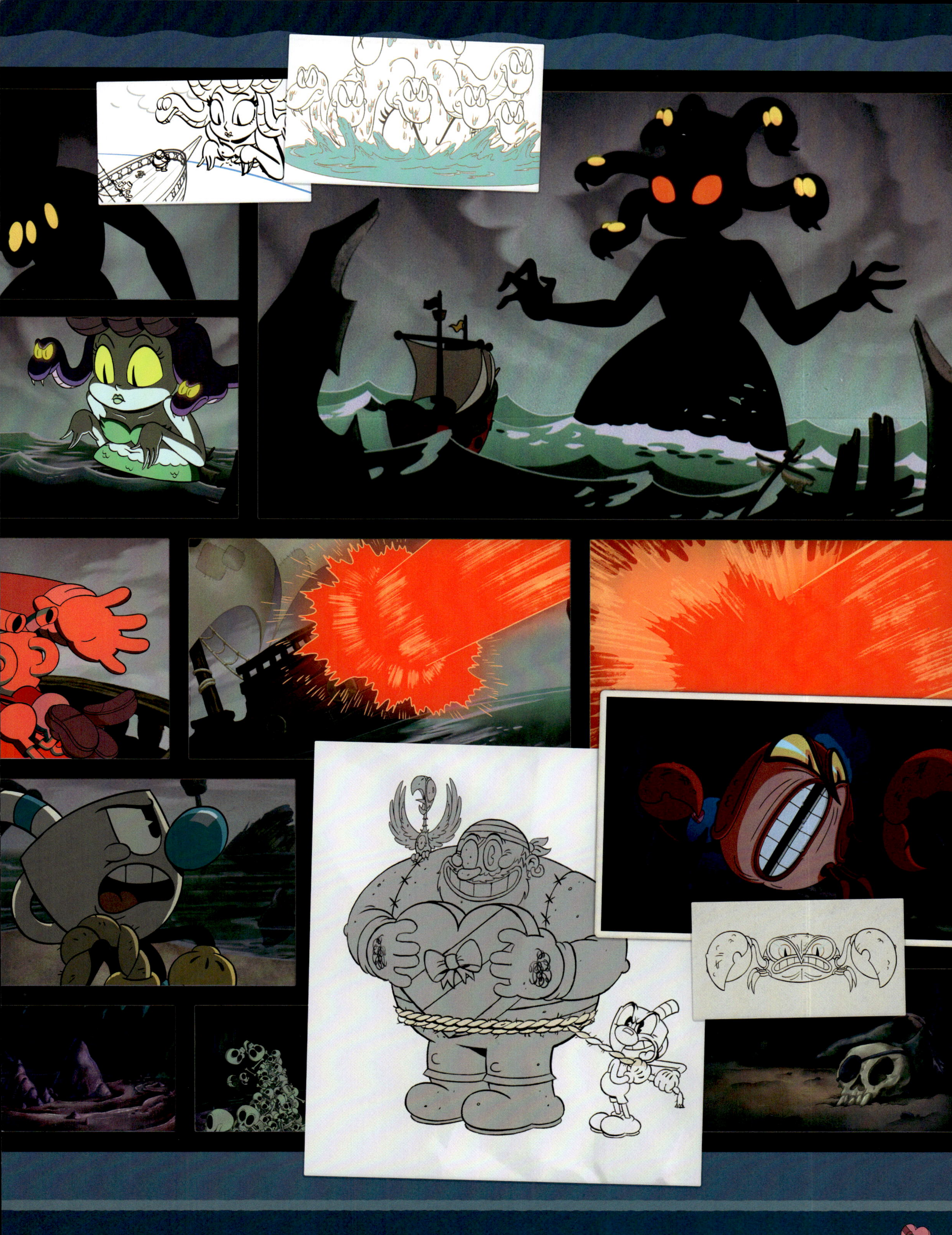

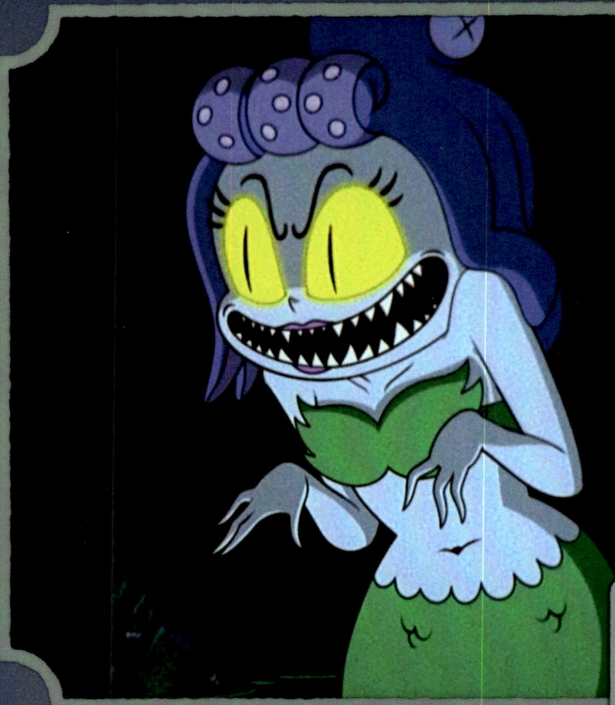

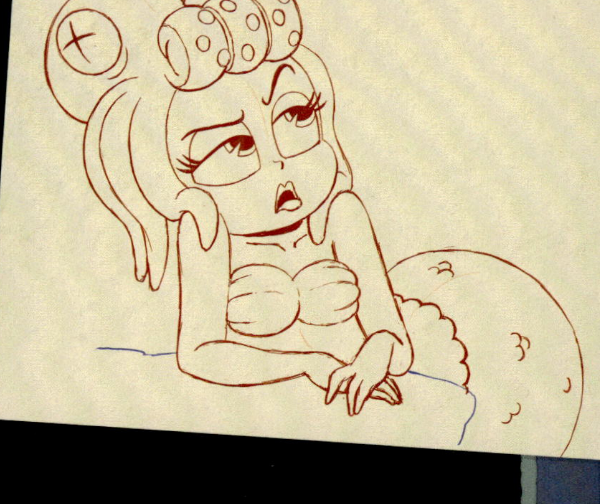

DESIGNING CALA MARIA

(voiced by Natasia Demetriou)

Special pose designs by Adam Paloian, Mitchel Preston Kennedy, and Dave Wasson.

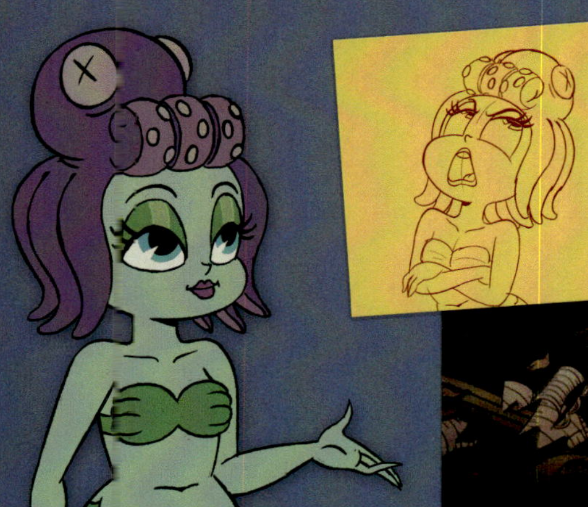

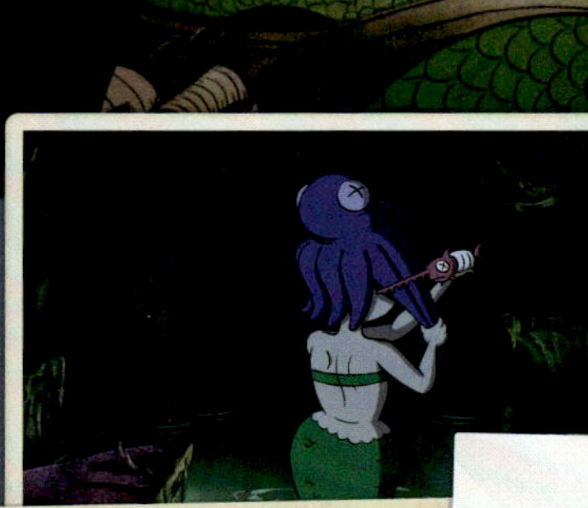

Cala model sheets and special pose designs by Tapan Gandhi and Adam Paloian; background designs by Lauren Duda; paintings by Michelle Thies.

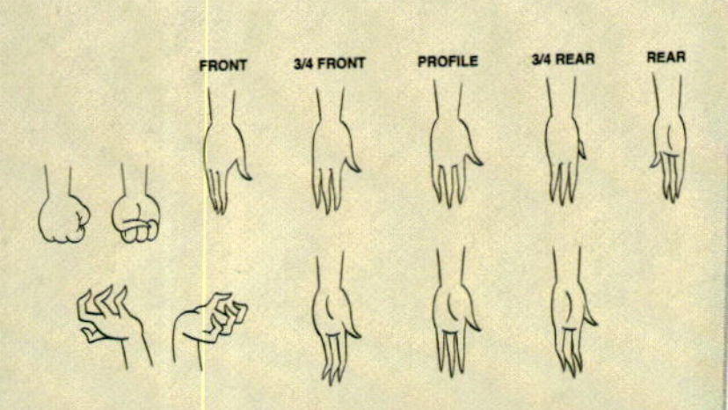

CALA MARIA (BEAST)
Mouth Chart

FOR LH - NOTE
Keep number of teeth consistent in a scene when Cala talks or sings

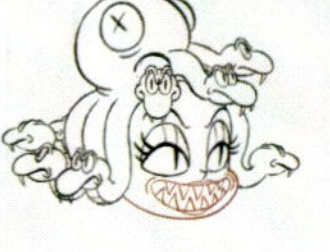
A,I

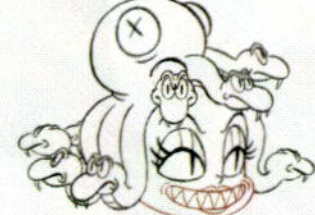
E

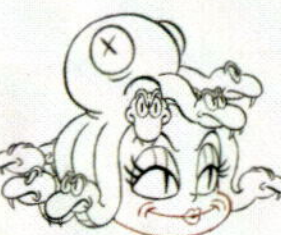
O,U

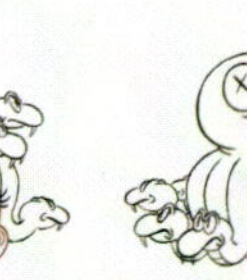
L

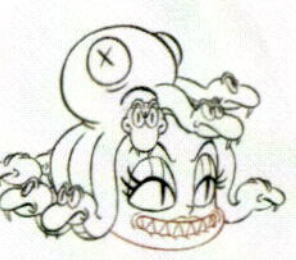
F,V

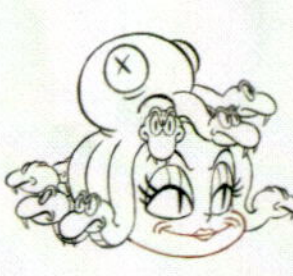
M

BRINEYBEARD'S PEGS

➜ **DEEKI:** In the rough card pitch, after Brineybeard is turned to stone, I put in a joke where Cuphead and Mugman drop him, and his legs get shattered.

DAVE: They rip the legs off a table and stick them on, and now he has pegs.

DEEKI: Dave thought our executive Megan would never go for it, so he cut it preemptively. After the card pitch, Megan had one note . . .

MEGAN C: I asked for the origin story of his peg legs. I wanted to see 'em get shattered.

DAVE: She totally surprised us sometimes. It's the opposite of how we thought she'd react.

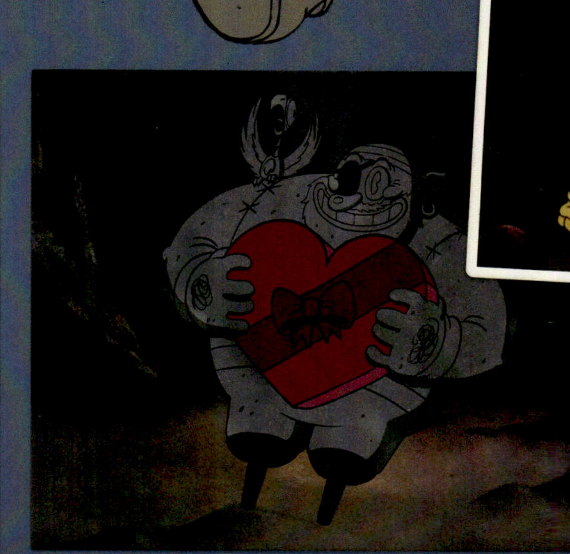

Special pose designs by Adam Paloian, Tapan Gandhi, and Adam Fay; character color by Chris Hacker.

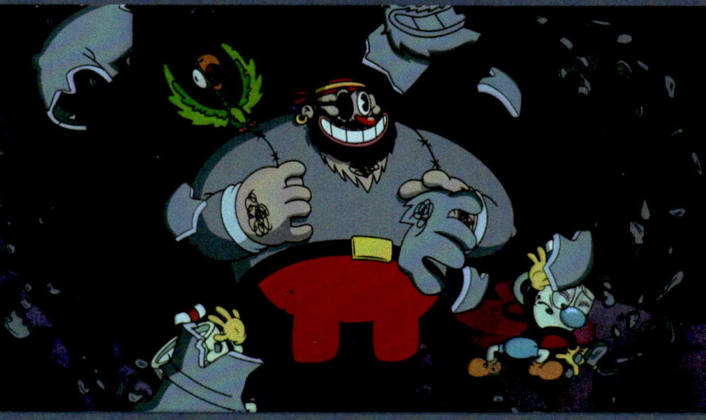

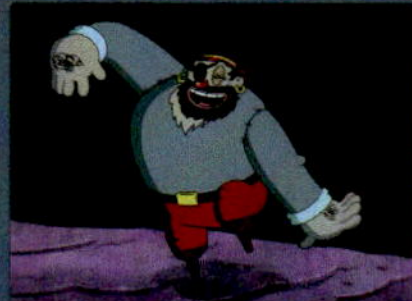

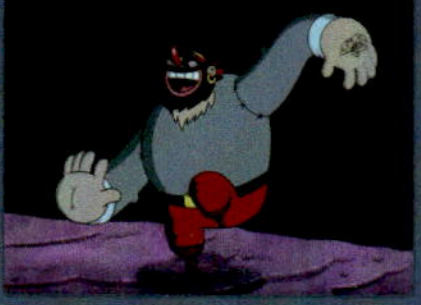

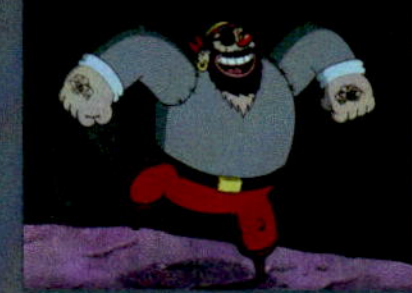

➜ **MEGAN C:** As an executive, it was great having the creative team be so open and collaborative in that space. Sometimes you challenge an idea, sometimes you pitch an idea, but at the end of the day it's all about trusting each other. I think that's what a good creative/executive relationship is built on.

DEEKI: Dave still wasn't sold. He was concerned about Brineybeard being revived and reacting badly to his missing legs.

DAVE: It's a horrifying thing to wake up to!

DEEKI: Then, in that same meeting, he suddenly lit up with an idea . . .

DAVE: Brineybeard's instantly thrilled that his legs are *two* pegs—he's like, "Most pirates just have *one* peg!"

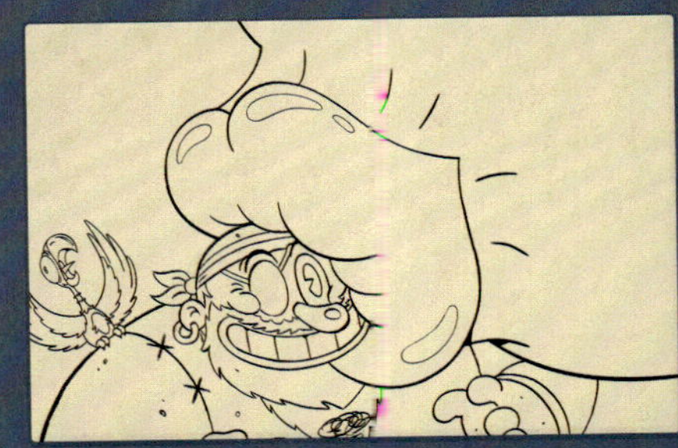

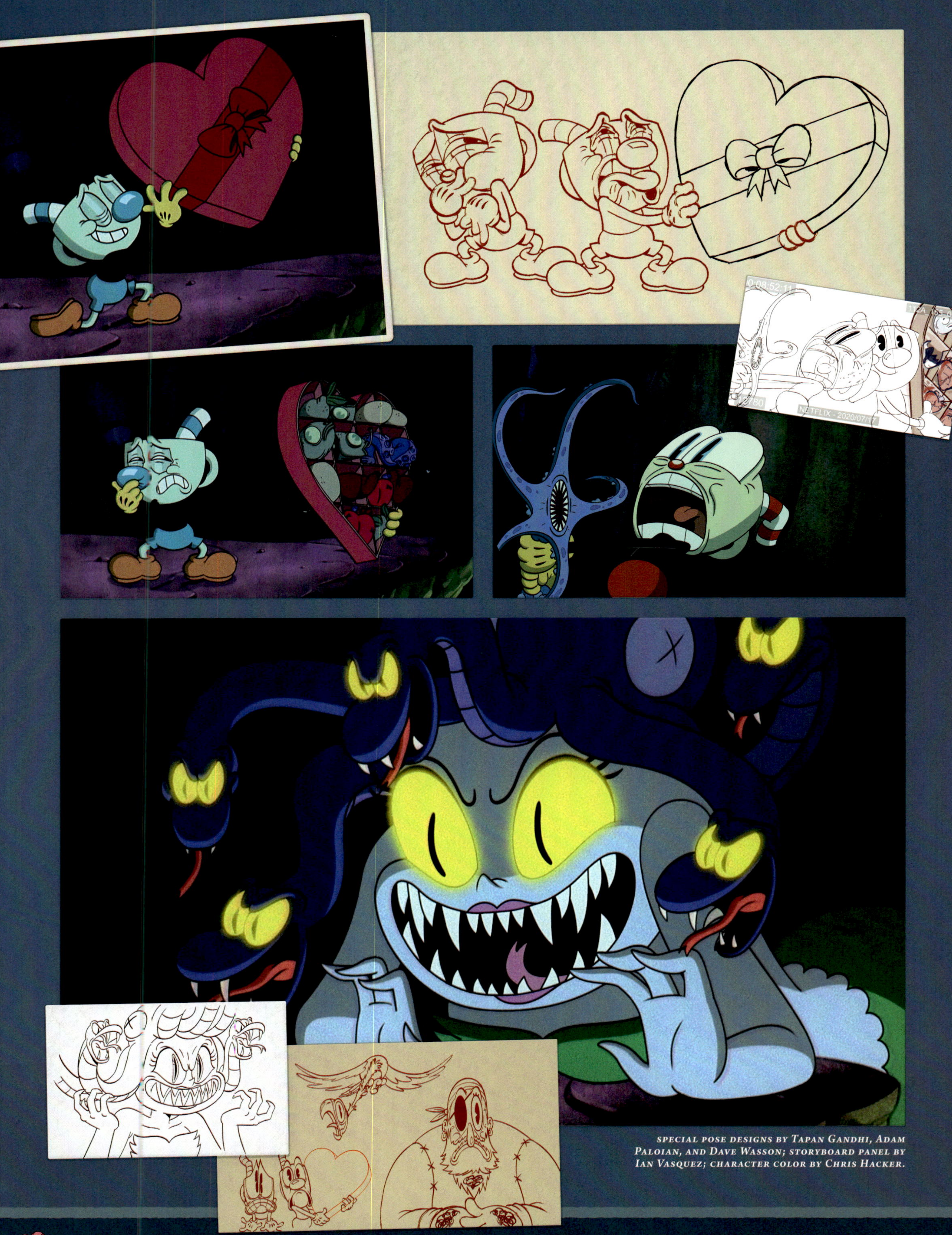

SPECIAL POSE DESIGNS BY TAPAN GANDHI, ADAM PALOIAN, AND DAVE WASSON; STORYBOARD PANEL BY IAN VASQUEZ; CHARACTER COLOR BY CHRIS HACKER.

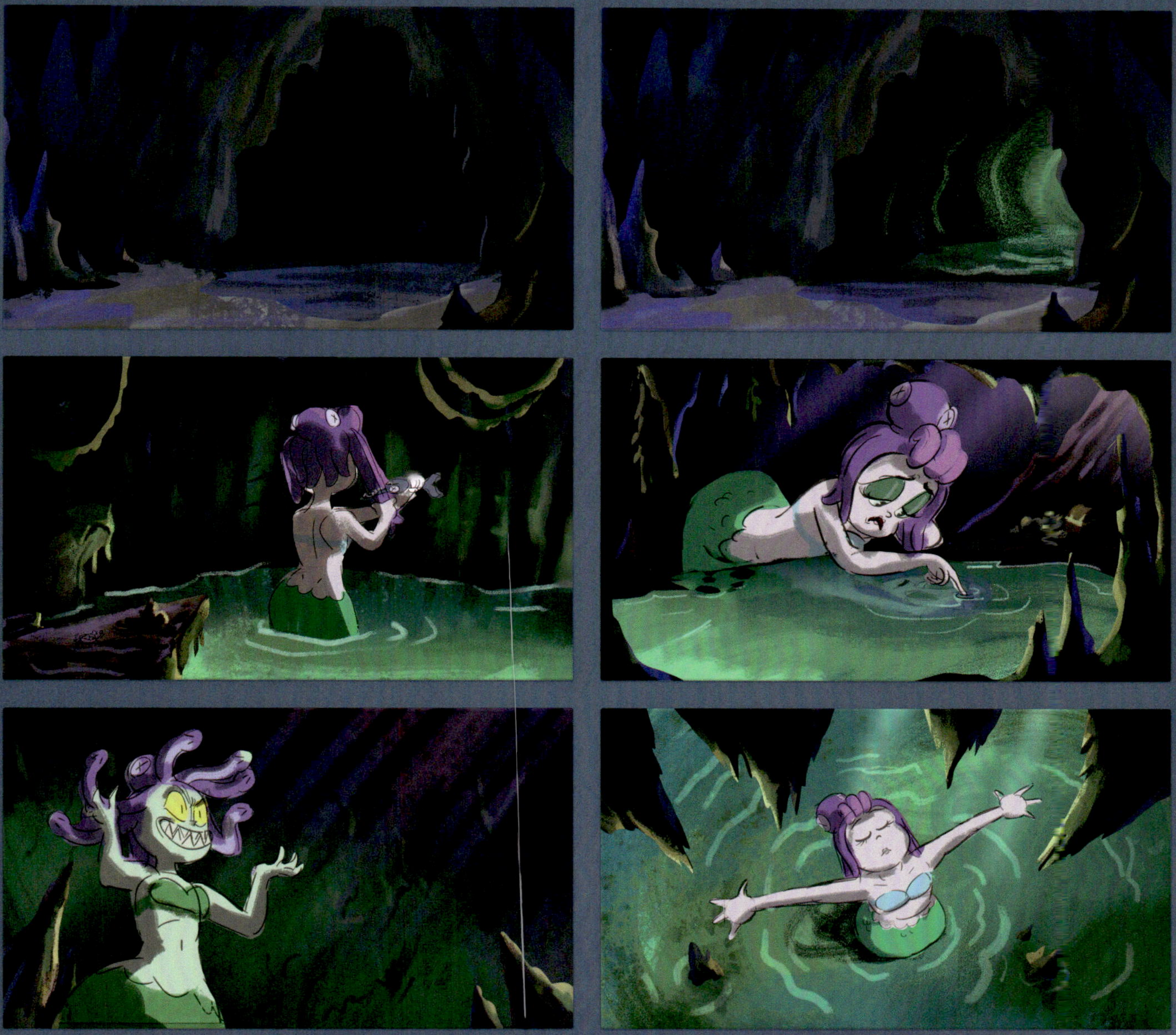

Color script for Cala Maria's cave by Michelle Thies.

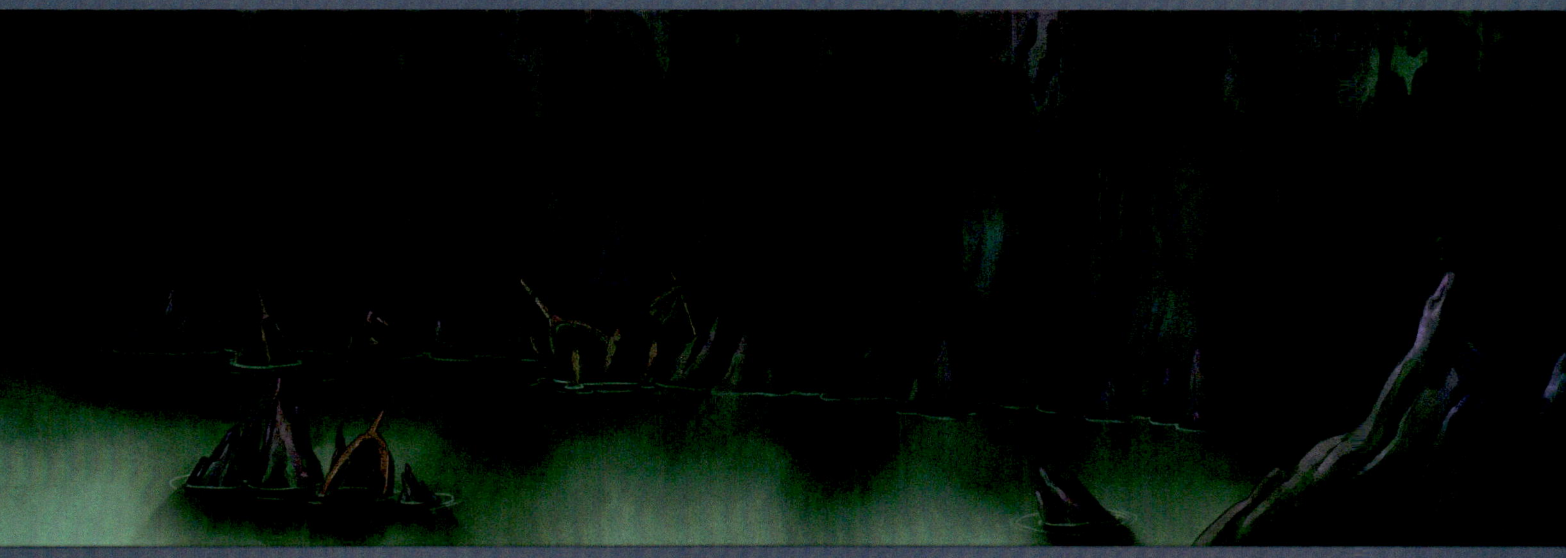

Design by Jessica Hong; painting by Michelle Thies.

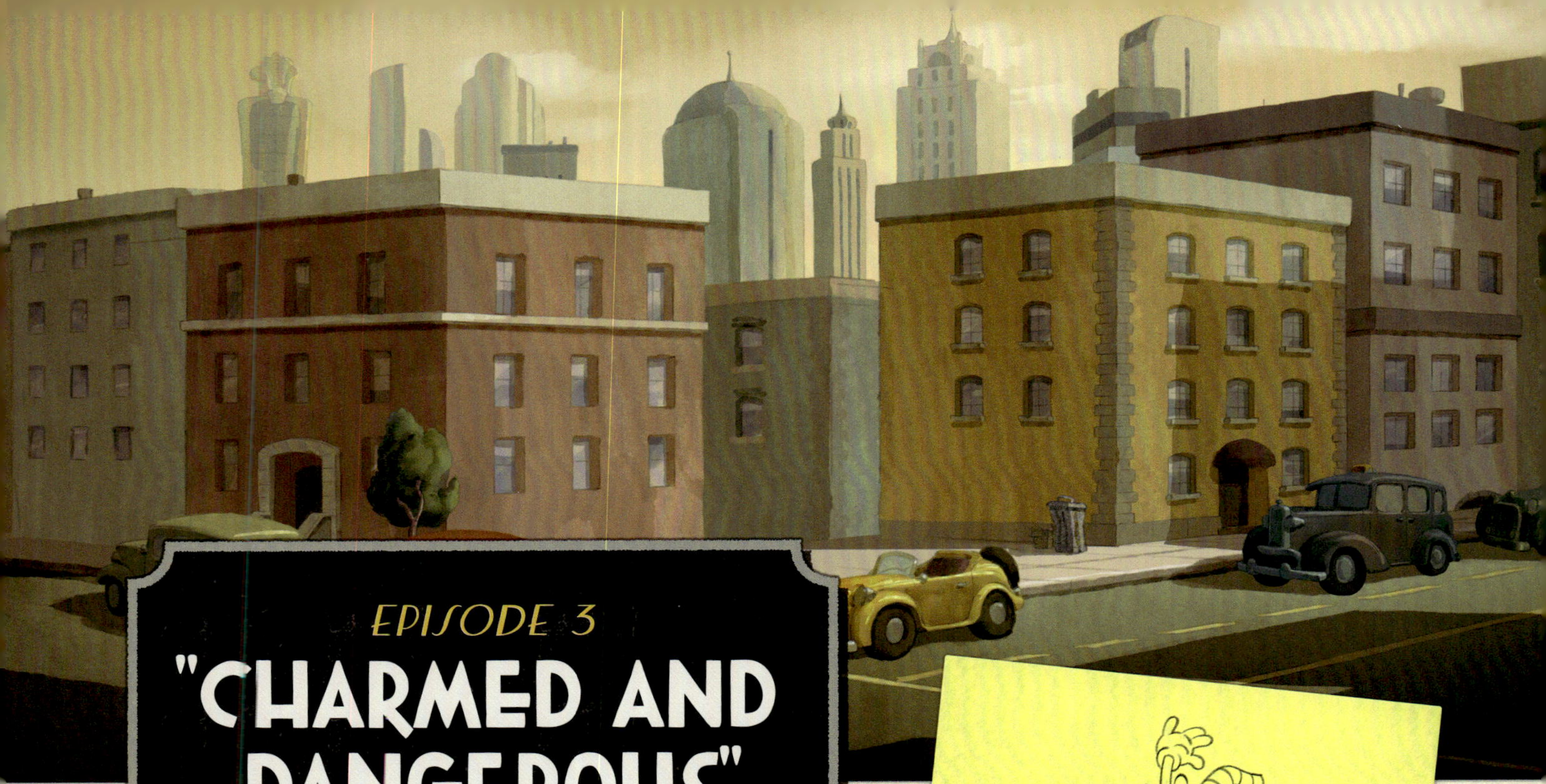

Episode 3

"Charmed and Dangerous"

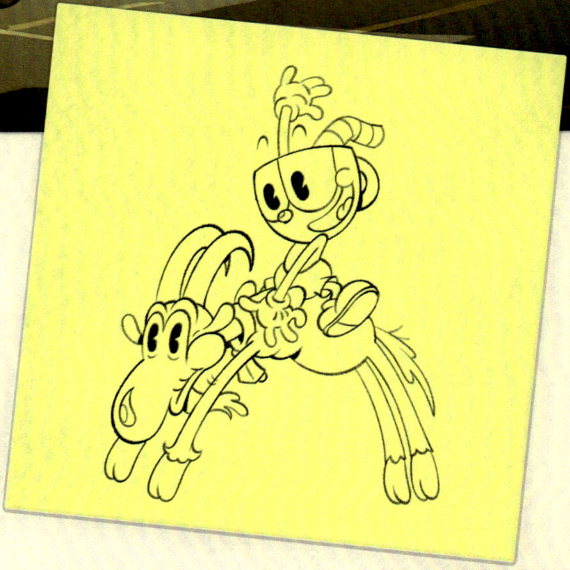

→ **KENNEDY:** In general, Chalice episodes tend to have more back-and-forth dialogue. She's a fast talker and usually trying to manipulate the boys. Cuphead and Mugman have such a strong dynamic as a two-person team; it does feel a little off balance when you bring Chalice in—I think in a fun way.

CLAY: There was an instinct for people to make her Minnie Mouse that we fought sometimes. She's "cute," but only when she needs to *use* "cute."

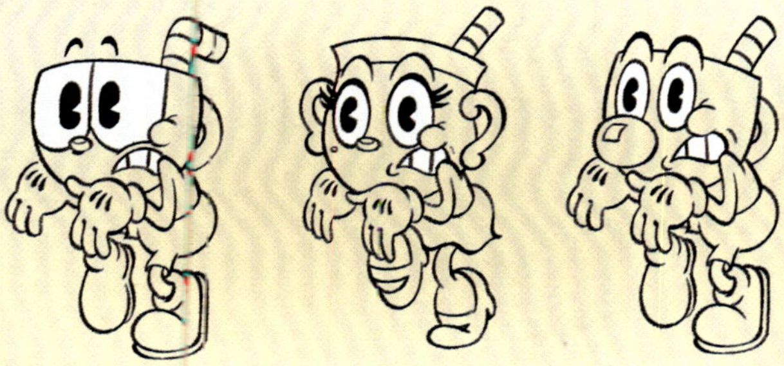

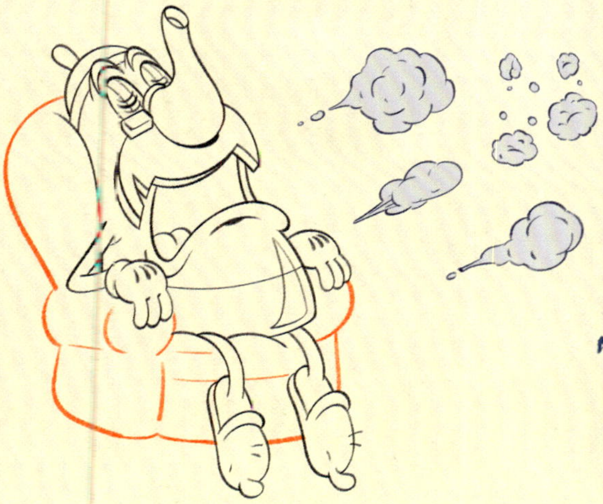

Car and steam designs by Adam Dix and Jack Rossi.

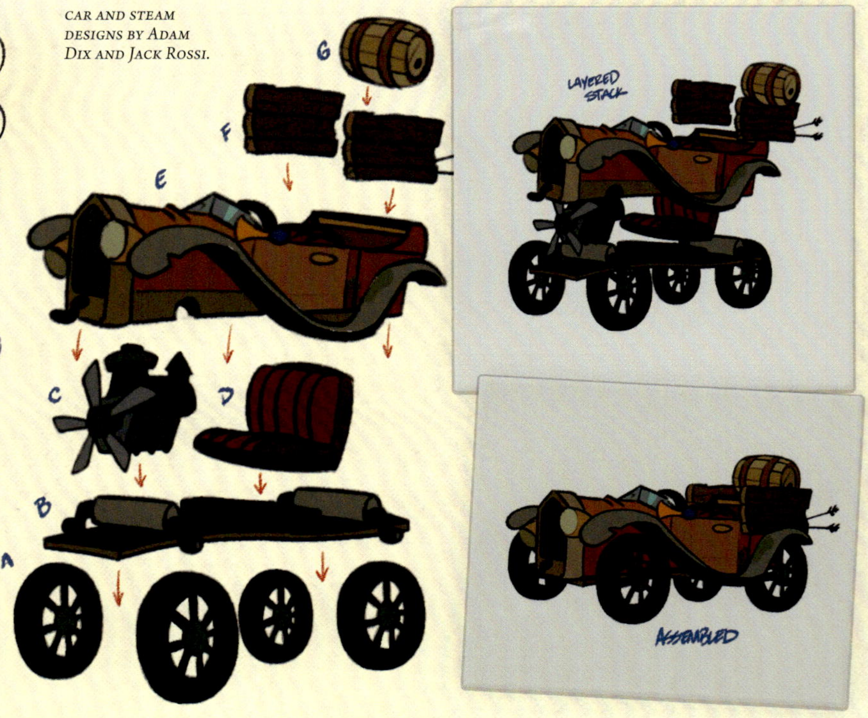

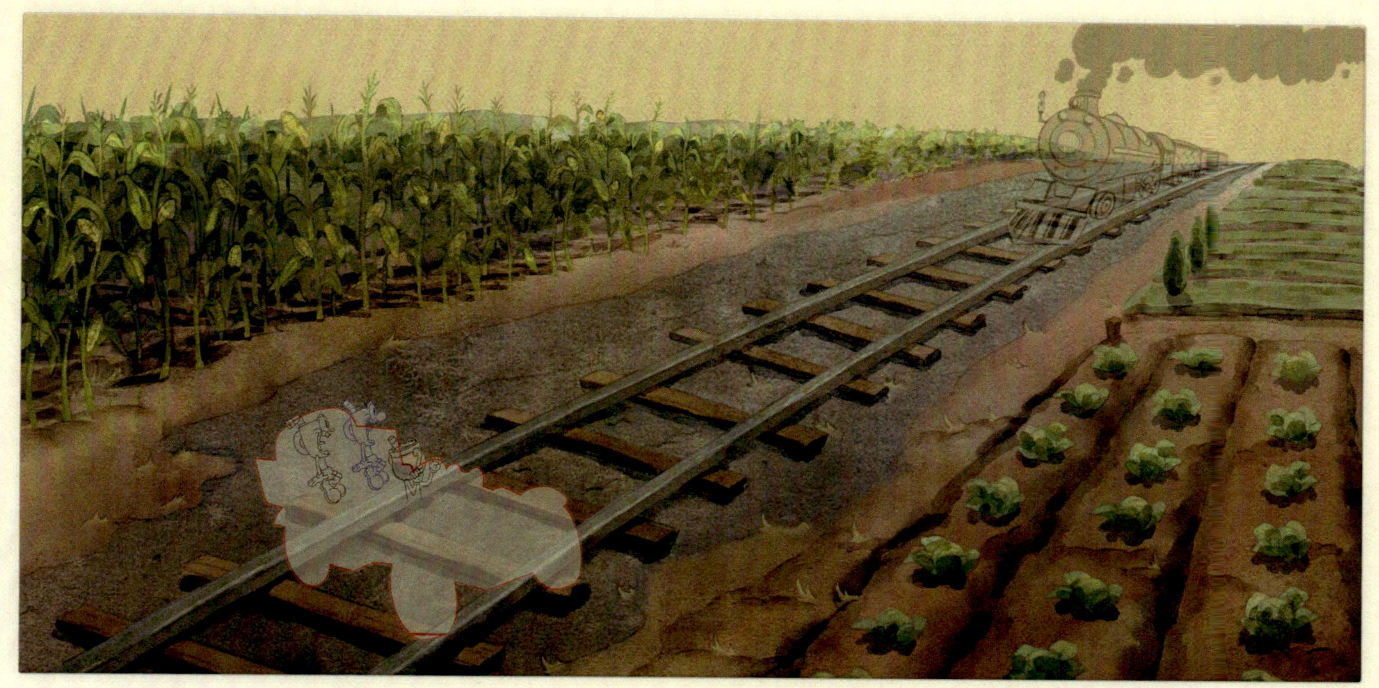

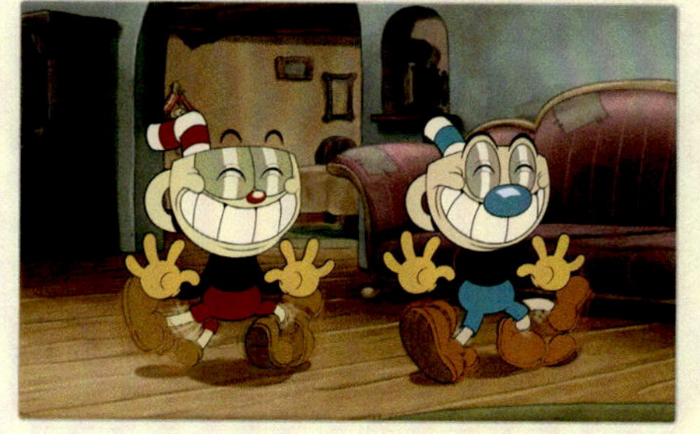

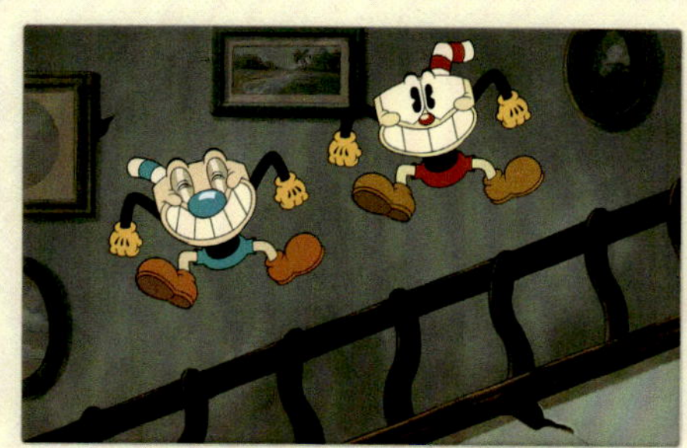

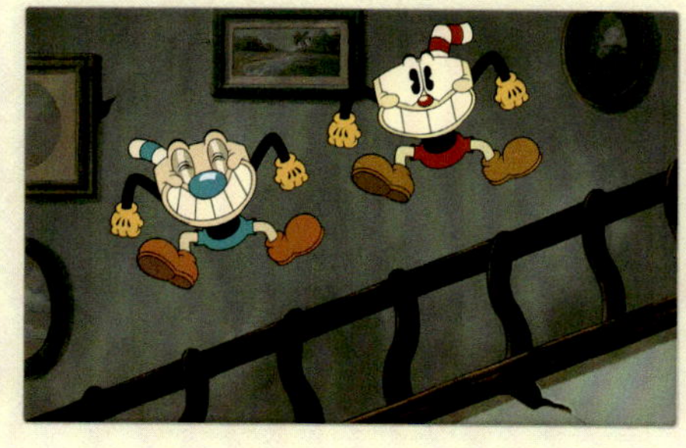

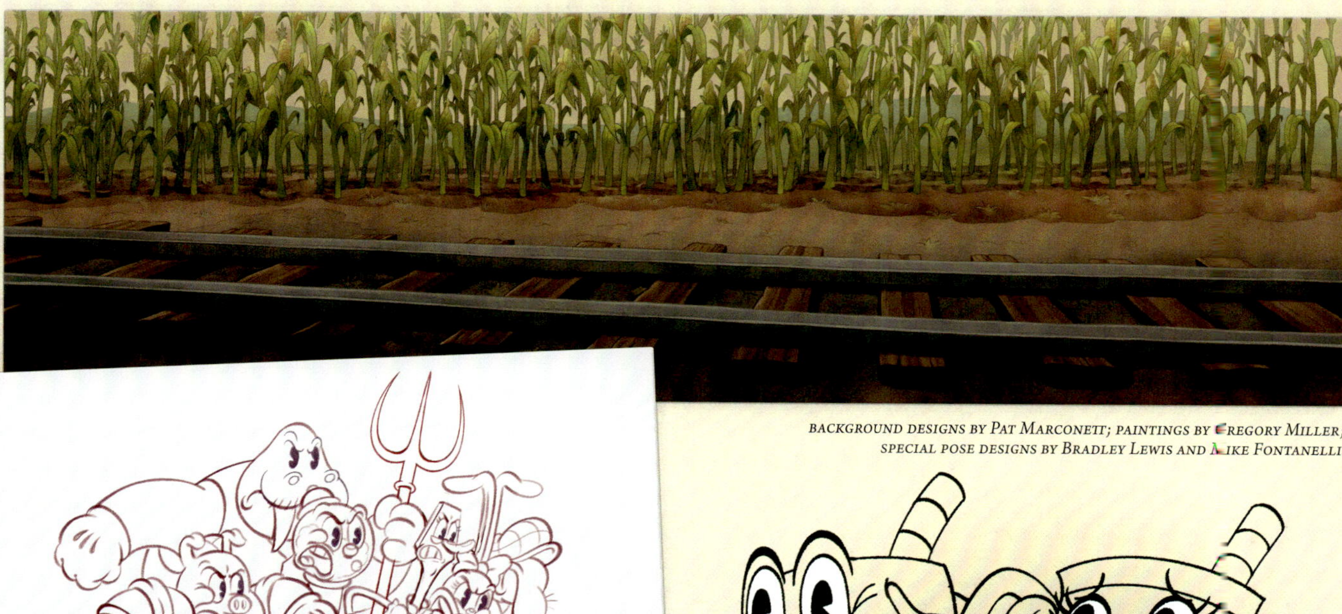

BACKGROUND DESIGNS BY PAT MARCONETT; PAINTINGS BY GREGORY MILLER; SPECIAL POSE DESIGNS BY BRADLEY LEWIS AND MIKE FONTANELLI.

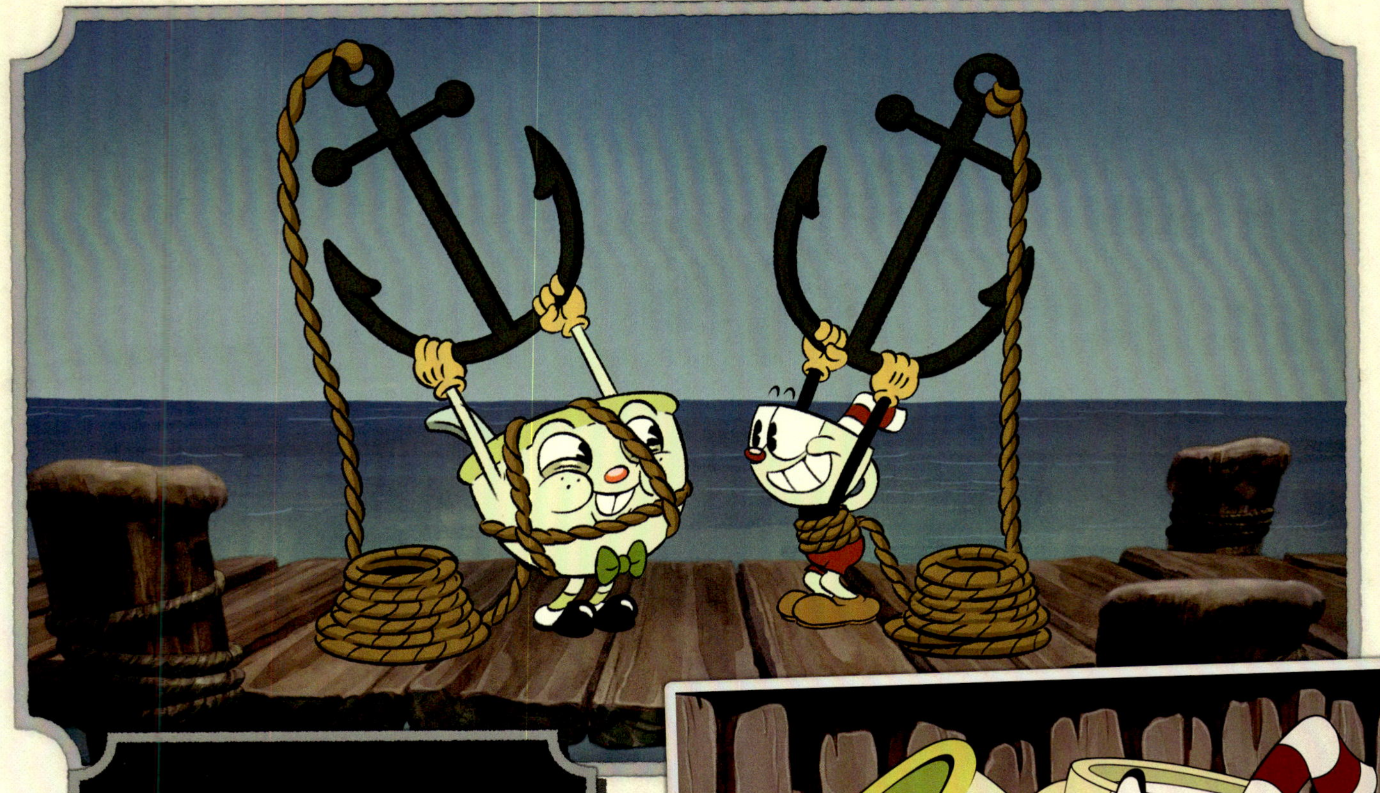

EPISODE 4 "ANOTHER BROTHER"

ELI: The amount of time in our personal life when my wife and I just randomly pop into Bowlboy . . . He's become a meme in my household.

DAVE: We had this idea floating around the story room for a while where Cuphead would trade in Mugman for a more reckless brother. Initially he was going to be a daredevil plate that takes things too far and gets shattered at the end.

DEEKI: Clay said if someone gets shattered, it should be someone who deserves it.

DAVE: That's when Deeki and Kennedy added a stroke of genius: Bowlboy.

KENNEDY: Bowlboy is terrifying. And a force of nature. Looking back on when Deeki and I wrote the card pitch for that episode, I don't really know when the moment was where Bowlboy flipped, when he went into scary land. But I love that about him. At first it was about how can we use Bowlboy to get under Mugman's skin, and he basically turned into a poltergeist.

DEEKI: When I rehearsed the card pitch with Kennedy, my advice was to be unafraid of making yourself look stupid. Kennedy was put to the ultimate test when I said, "You'll be pitching all the Bowlboy lines."

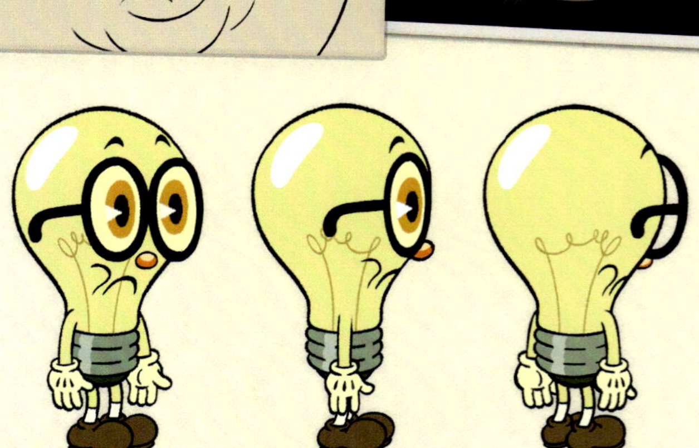

SPECIAL POSE DESIGNS BY TAPAN GANDHI AND MIKE FONTANELLI; LIGHT BULB TURNAROUND BY TAPAN GANDHI; CHARACTER COLOR BY CHRIS HACKER; BACKGROUND DESIGN BY JESSICA HONG; PAINTING BY GREGORY MILLER.

→ **ADAM P:** Clay was describing the mailman as having a mouth kind of like Sam the Eagle from *The Muppet Show*. It fit so perfectly. We were trying to match the voice Deeki did in the pitch. We tried to give him a heavy brow. And that flapping mouth really captured the monotone, and the stiff rigidness of the pencil—it was like, that's the guy! And that came from being in the room collaborating with everybody.

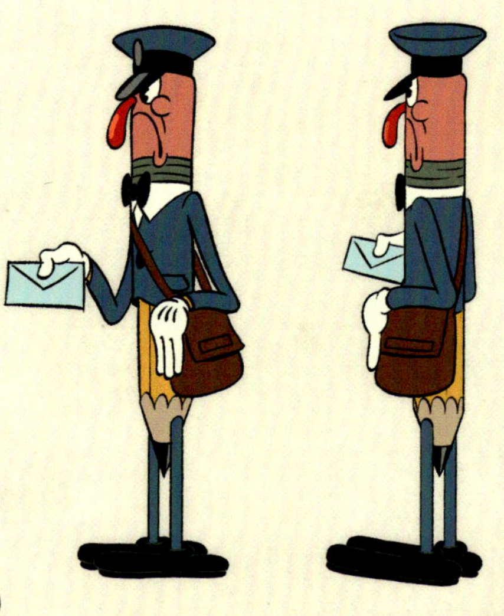

STORYBOARD PANELS BY FERNANDO PUIG; POSES FROM CHARACTER TURNAROUNDS BY TAPAN GANDHI.

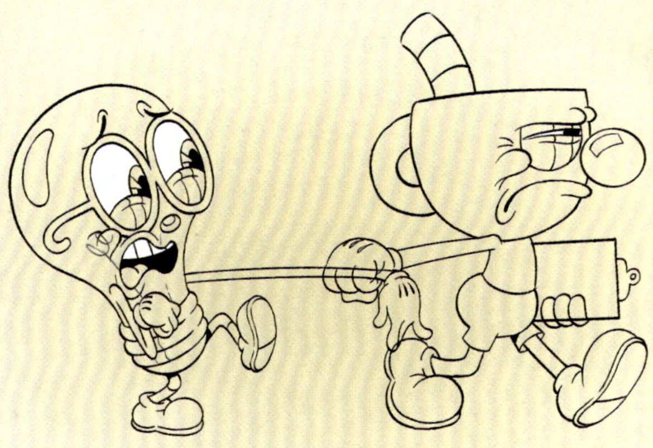

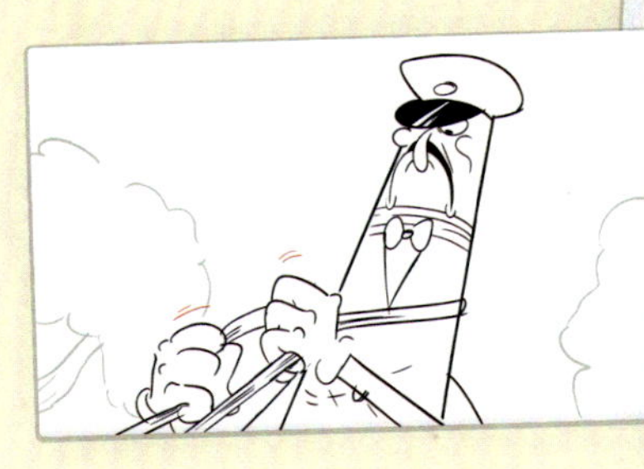

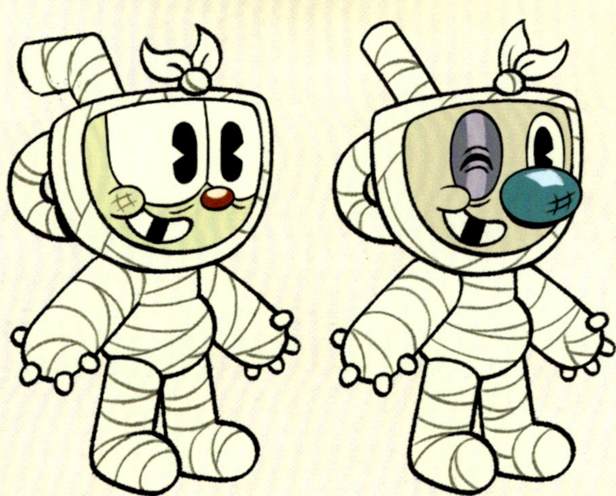

SPECIAL POSE DESIGNS BY MIKE FONTANELLI AND TAPAN GANDHI; CHARACTER COLOR BY CHRIS HACKER.

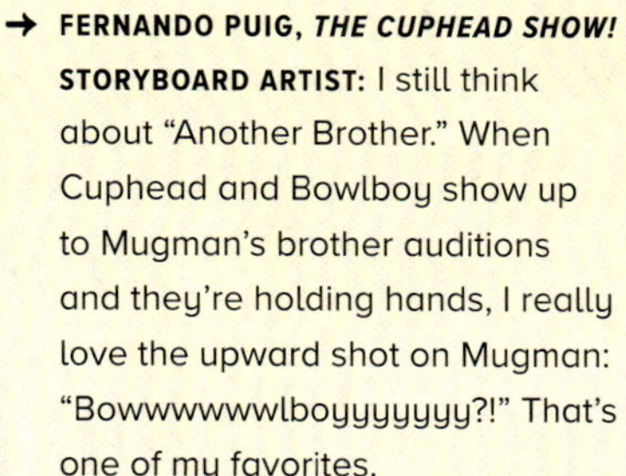

→ **FERNANDO PUIG, *THE CUPHEAD SHOW!* STORYBOARD ARTIST:** I still think about "Another Brother." When Cuphead and Bowlboy show up to Mugman's brother auditions and they're holding hands, I really love the upward shot on Mugman: "Bowwwwwwwlboyyyyyyy?!" That's one of my favorites.

ADAM P: Bowlboy doesn't need crazy expressions, because his voice is already telling you a lot. If you have crazy acting on top of a crazy personality on top of a crazy voice, then it's too much. He's more reserved

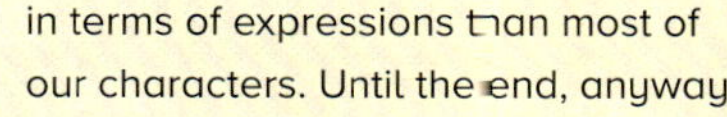

in terms of expressions than most of our characters. Until the end, anyway.

COSMO: I feel like the episode is a total tragedy for Bowlboy—he really wanted to be Cuphead's buddy, but he was too overzealous. He can't stop himself from doing everything he wants to do. Cuphead has a similar problem. Bowlboy is like Cuphead on steroids.

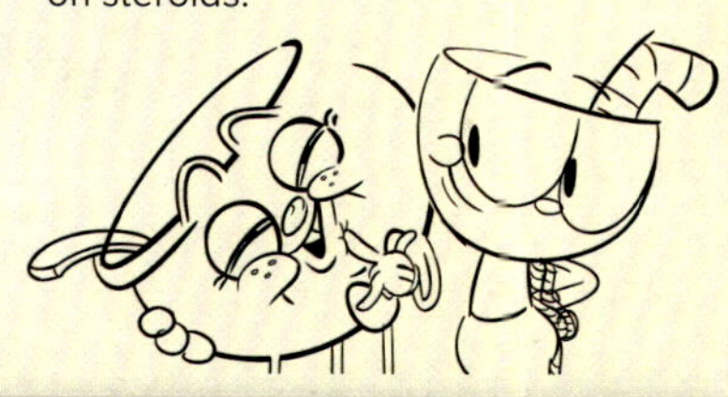

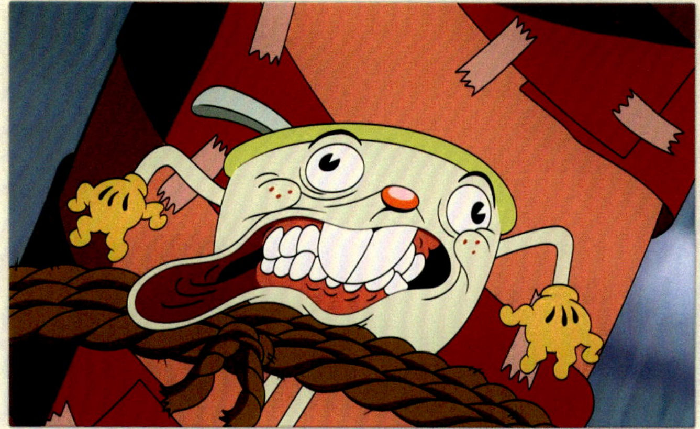

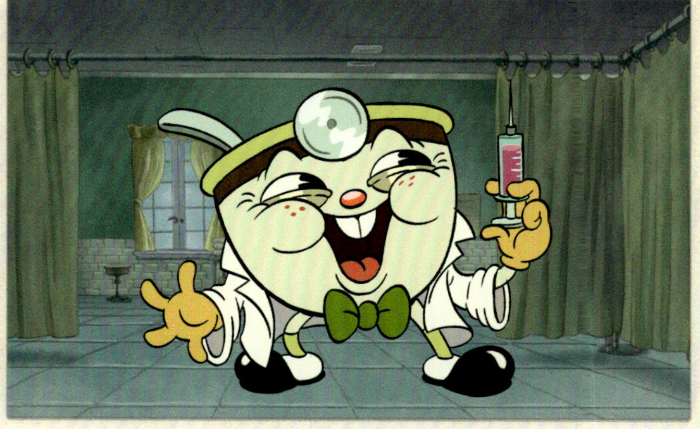

HOSPITAL BACKGROUND DESIGN BY PAT MARCONETT; PAINTING BY JEFF PALM.

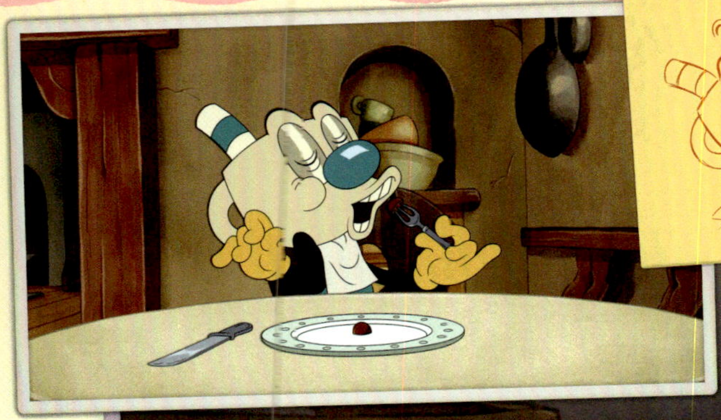

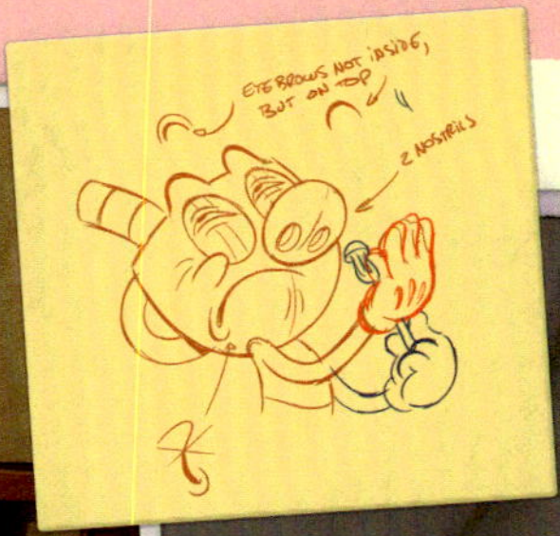

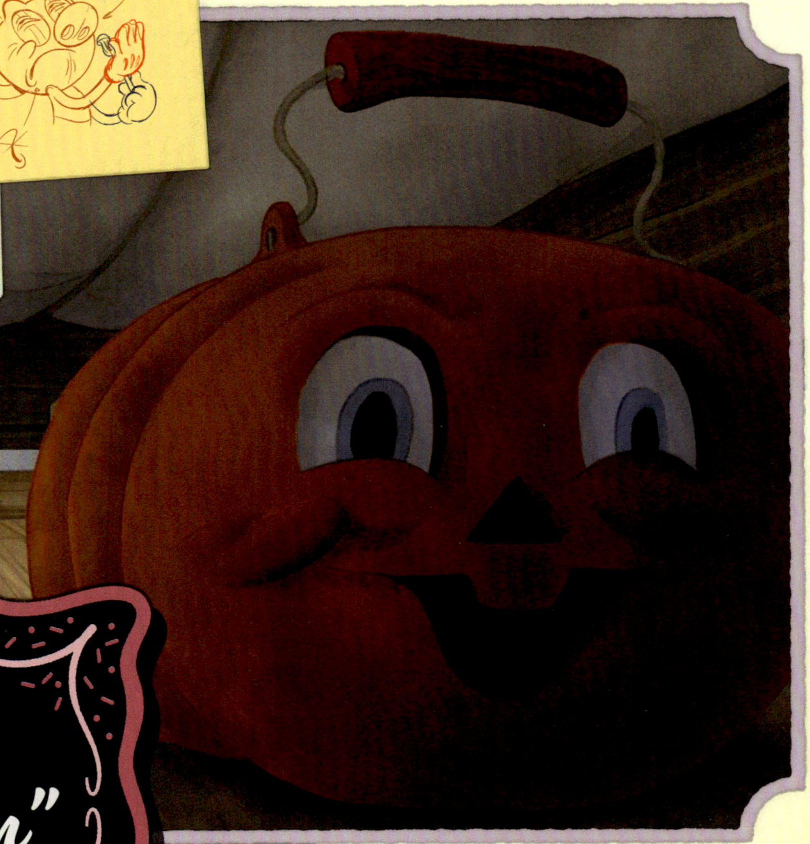

EPISODE 5
"Sweet Temptation"

DEEP DIVE

BACKGROUND DESIGN BY PAT MARCONETT; PAINTING BY JEFF PALM.

ADAM D: My favorite episode is "Sweet Temptation." I grew up loving the game Candyland, and this was like that but with terrifying characters.

MALLORY: I love the visual candy of the Baroness von Bon Bon episode. It's so magical. And when you think about it, it's also pretty disturbing!

COSMO: There was a Fleischer cartoon called "Somewhere in Dreamland" [1936] about these two poor kids who dream of a land made of candy and sugary sweets that has a nightmarish, surreal look to it. "The Cookie Carnival" [1935] was another big influence. And even some of those early illustrations for the Candyland board game came into play, where it's oozing with icing and a lot of pink and birthday cake colors.

ANDREA: One of the cool things about world building on this show is that we have great source material in the game. We then have to figure out how those incredible elements can be integrated into our show, our color theory on characters, and how the characters are moving in the space.

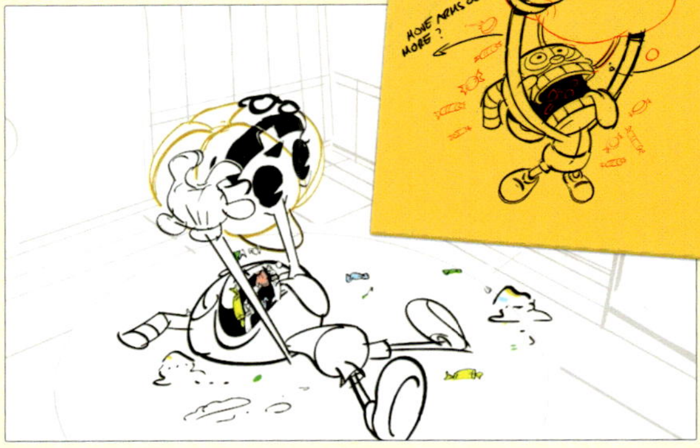

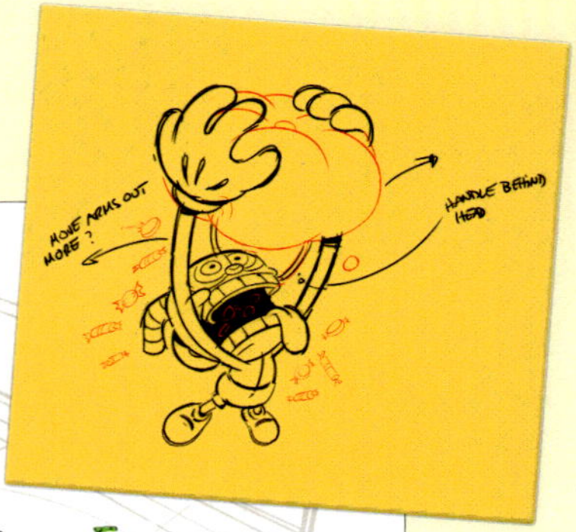

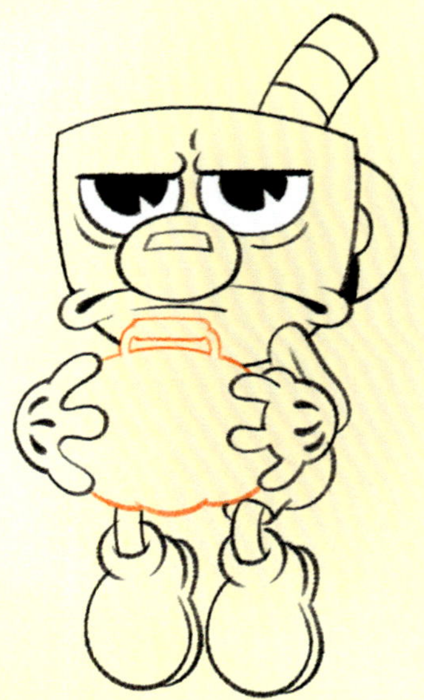

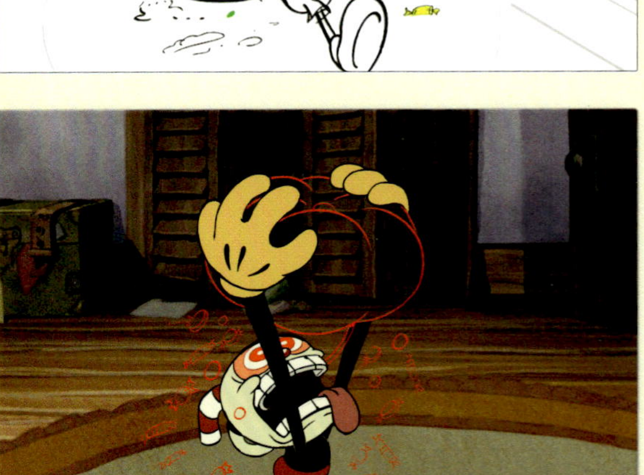

SPECIAL POSE DESIGNS BY BRADLEY LEWIS AND MIKE FONTANELLI; DIRECTOR'S NOTES BY CLAY MORROW; STORYBOARD PANEL BY KARL HADRIKA.

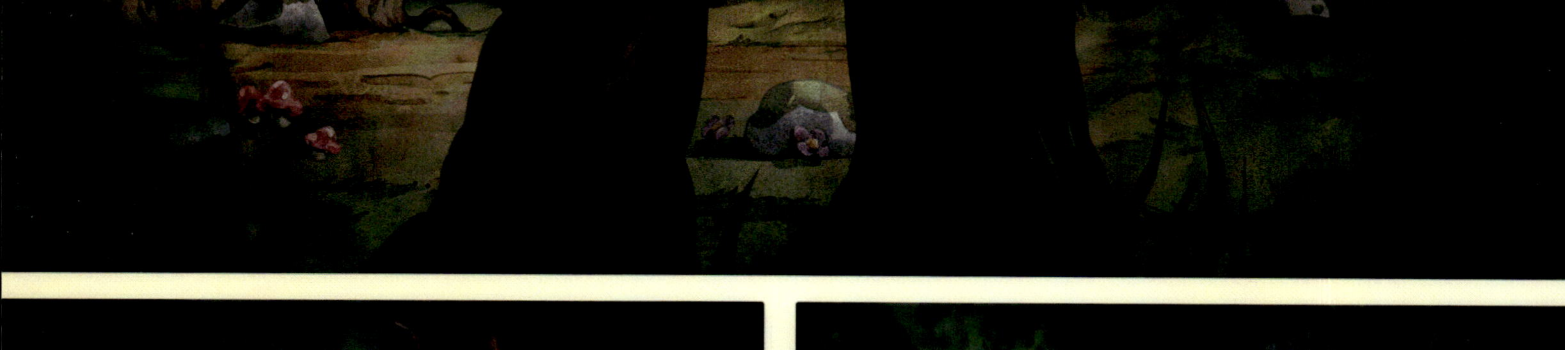

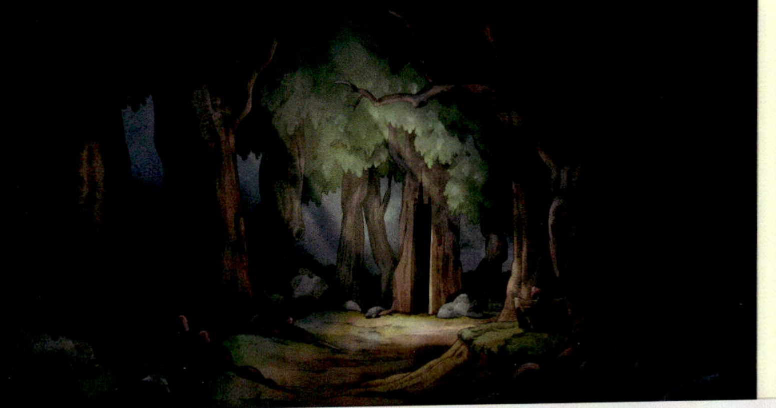

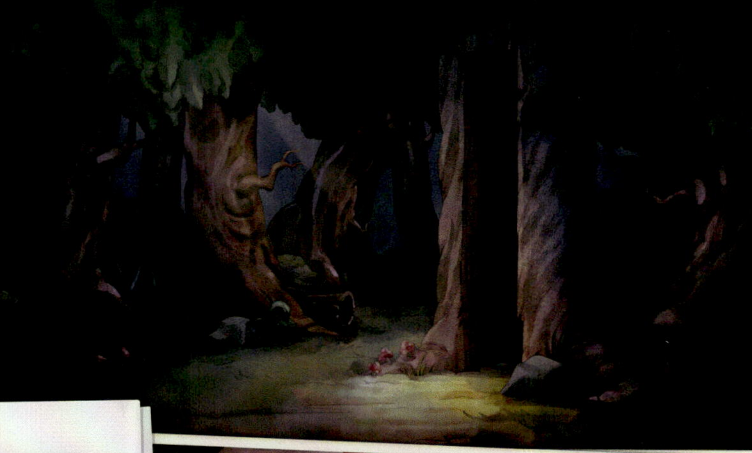

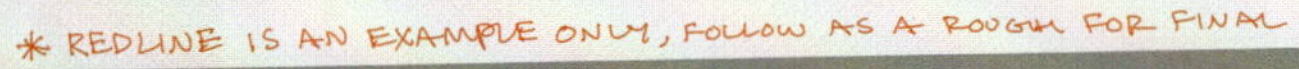

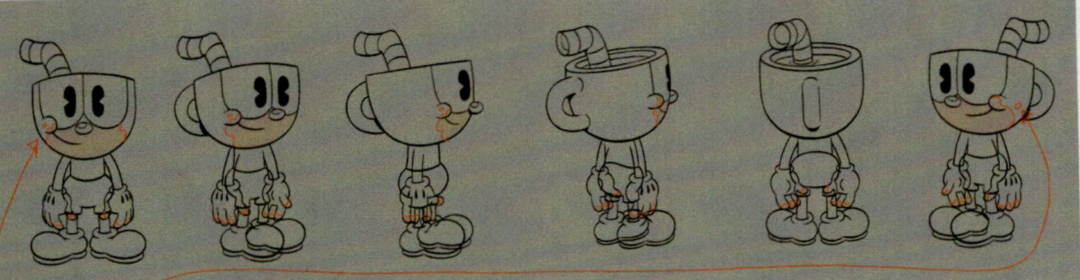

• TURNAROUND OF CUPHEAD TO SOLITIFY WHERE THE CHOCOLATE IS ON HIS FACE AND HANDS TO KEEP IT CONSISTANT ACROSS SCENES 29, 31, 32, 35, 36, 37, 40, 41. USE EXISTING APROVED SPECIAL POSES AS REFRENCE FOR THIS TURN SO THAT WE DONT HAVE TO OPEN THEM BACK UP AND MATCH THEM TO THIS TURN.
CLAY

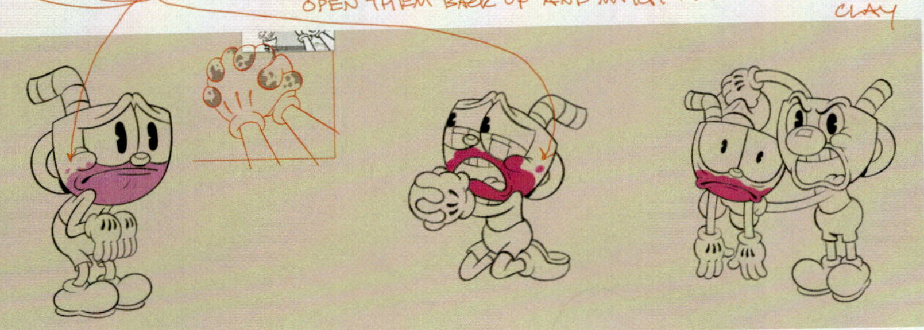

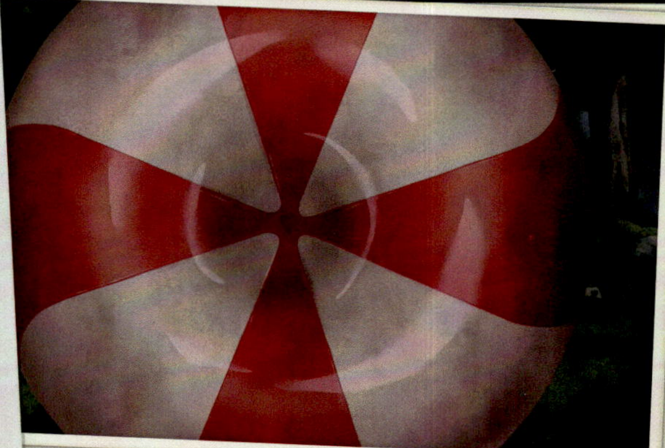

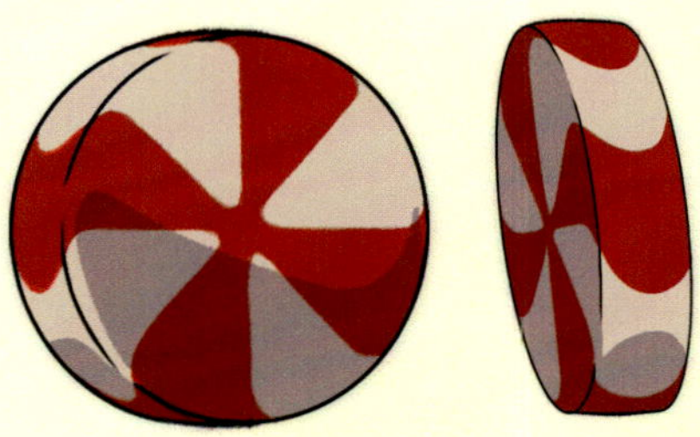

PEPPERMINT DESIGN BY ADAM DIX; TURNAROUNDS AND SPECIAL POSE DESIGNS BY BRADLEY LEWIS AND MIKE FONTANELLI.

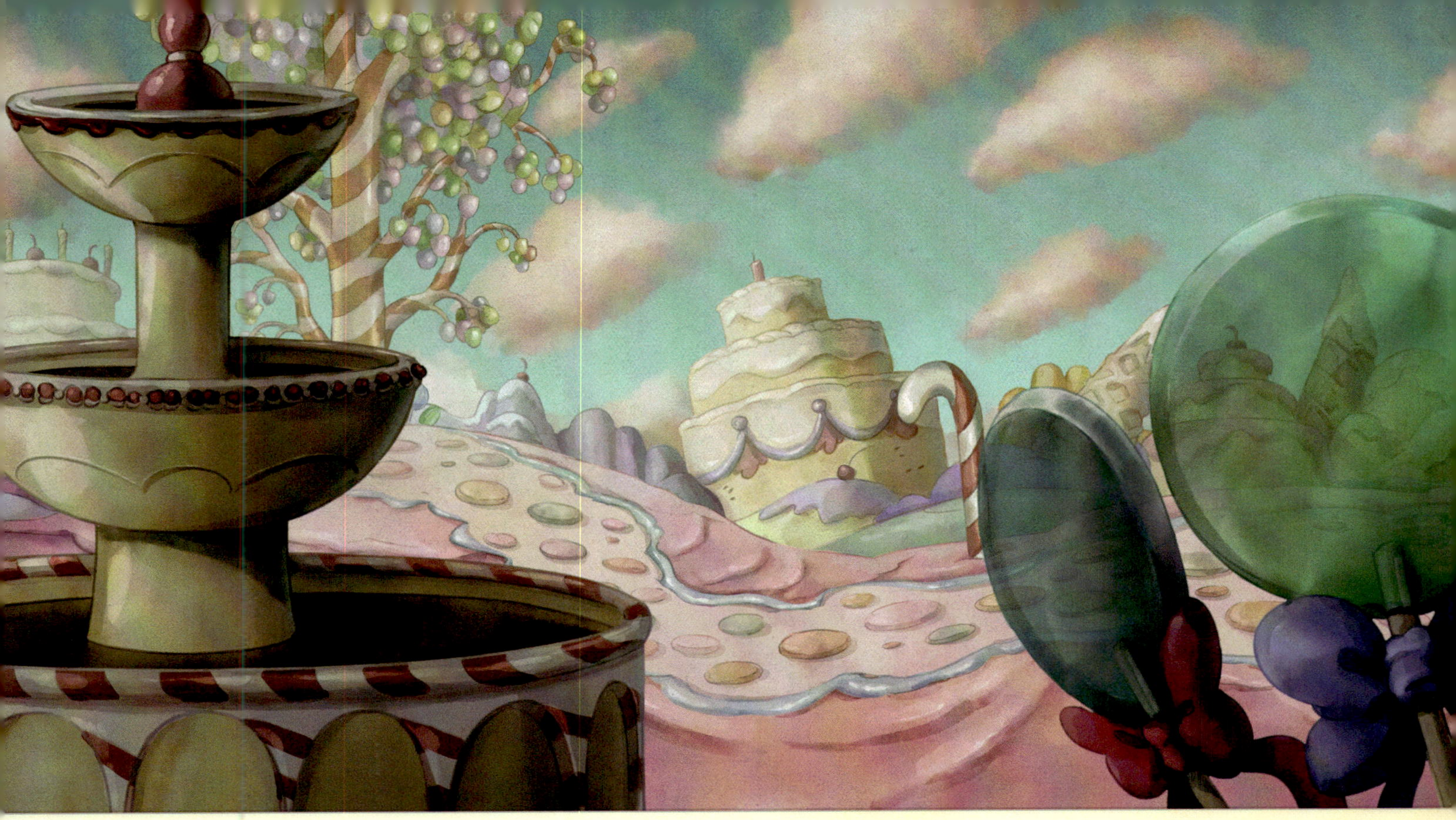

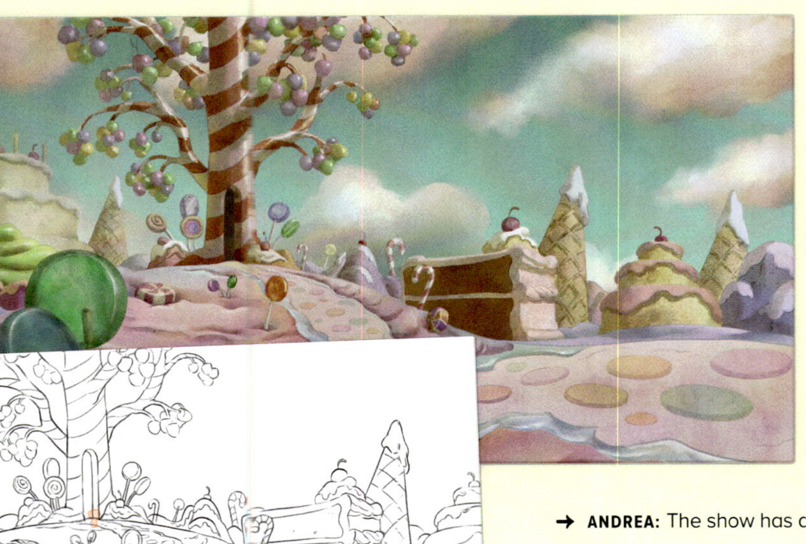

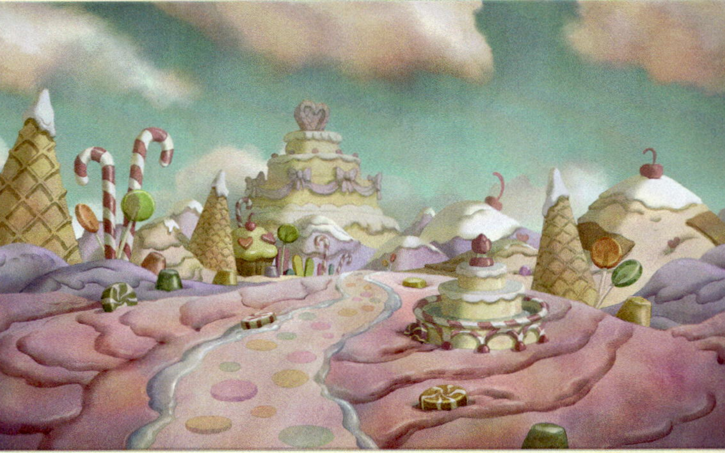

ANDREA: The show has a lot of world building, which is very hard from a design perspective, but what's exciting is I can change aesthetics easily. We can have an episode that feels like "Sleepy Hollow," and right next to it is an episode that feels like a *Silly Symphony*. But it feels a little weird if you switch palettes too much. For example, going from a graveyard to Sugarland in the same episode—we don't do that in the show. It takes you out of the immersion. We try to not jar the audience visually. You have to feel out the story in terms of mood and tone to find the right balance.

DEEKI: In the story room, you go on the adventure and play it out, then you start the next one. For the art team, sometimes they're juggling multiple adventures at the same time.

JESSICA: We were usually working on four episodes at any point in time. It was such constant whiplash.

ANDREA: I definitely felt some whiplash. "High Seas Adventure" and "Sweet Temptation" were running at the same time. They were such different aesthetics, and I only had a tiny bit of time to decide what I wanted them to look like. The production is constantly moving forward. We're not making movies, we're making episodes: in a series, it's a marathon.

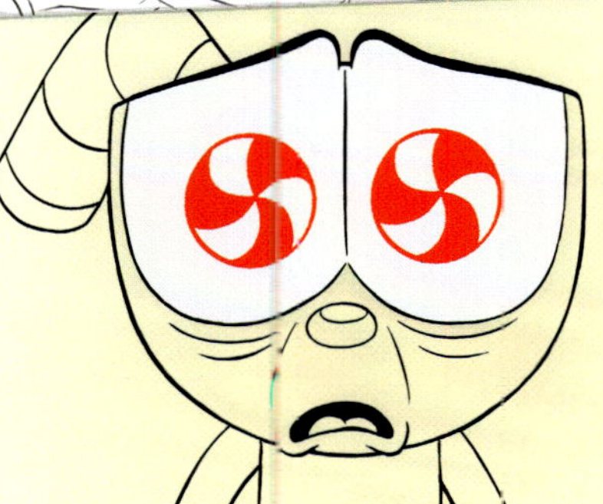

Special pose designs by Mike Fontanelli.

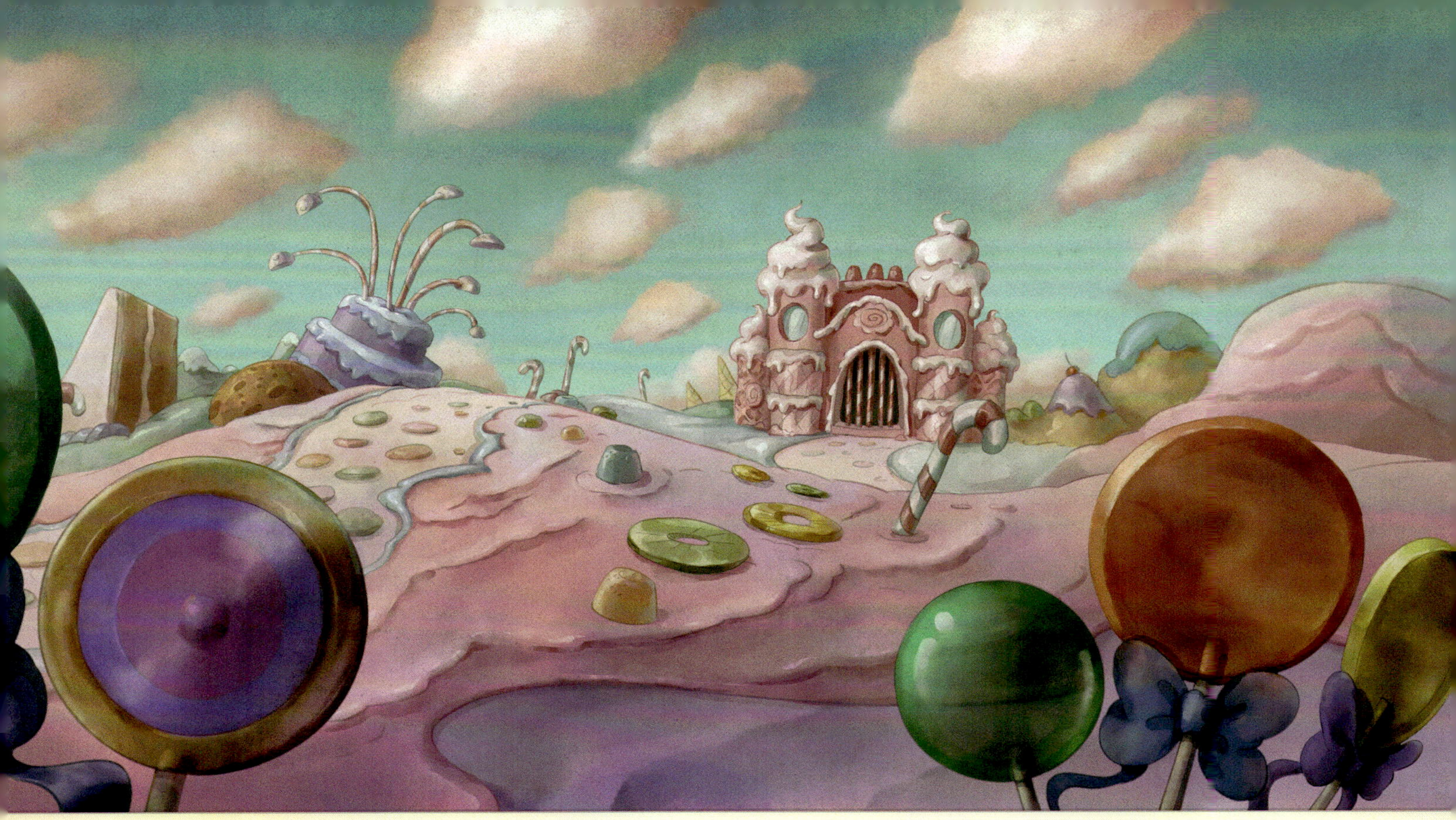

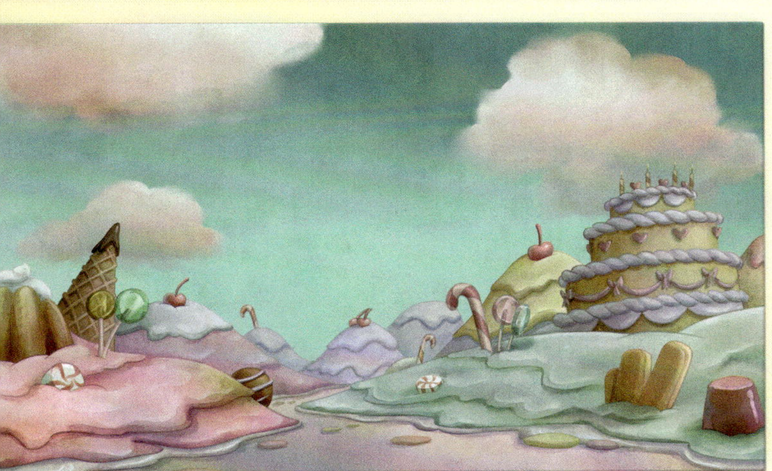

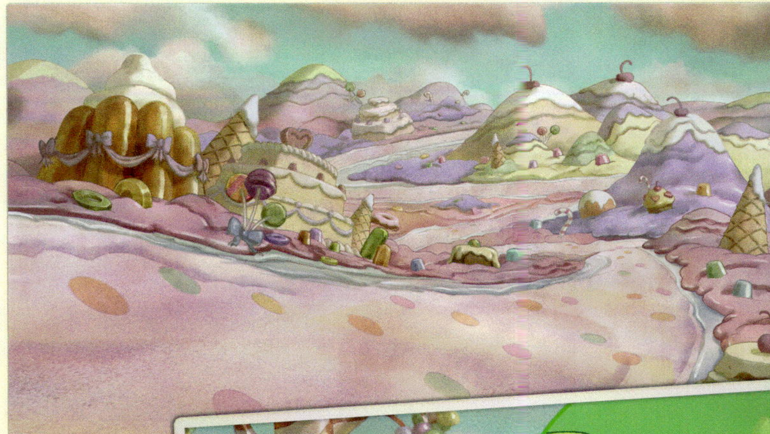

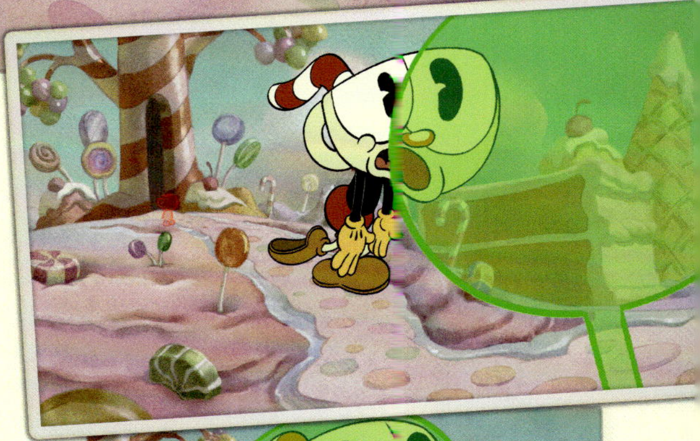

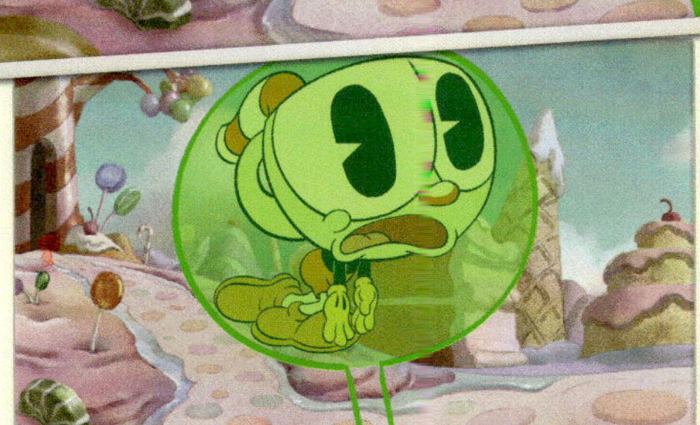

COSMO: Trying to re-create the golden era of animation is almost an impossible task under the best of circumstances, but trying to re-create it on a TV schedule is total insanity.

JACKIE WATSON, *THE CUPHEAD SHOW!* PRODUCTION MANAGER / ASSOCIATE PRODUCER / LINE PRODUCER: We say all the time, "This is why we don't produce art like this anymore for a TV series."

COSMO: The real challenge is the sheer amount of drawings in this kind of animation. It is *a lot* of drawings!

CAROLYN: The volume of artwork, and the quality that each piece had to achieve . . . the fact that the team was able to get it to that place on a TV schedule is a miracle.

ANDREA: The painting is so complex that, literally, the computers will not paint more. They can't handle the amount of information in those files.

JACKIE: The skill to make watercolor backgrounds digitally and make it look traditionally watercolor is a feat alone. On top of that, the file sizes are enormous because it's layers and layers of paint to achieve this traditional style.

Background designs by Andrea Fernandez and Jessica Hong; paintings by Michelle Thies and Gregory Miller; *Cuphead* special pose designs by Mike Fontanelli.

STOP-MO SPOTLIGHT

BUILDING SUGARLAND

MICHELLE: Seeing the stop-motion sets has been so inspiring, how they're incorporating the look of what we do into the set. Whenever I see them, I feel really inspired in a way that you kind of lose in the day to day of painting.

LAUREN: The work coming out of Screen Novelties is so impressive. They never cease to amaze me.

JESSICA: The Sugarland sets looked legitimately delicious.

MARK: Seamus had to say, "Would you stop touching that set?!"

SEAMUS: But you did not stop touching.

MARK: I kept touching. I'll be honest with you—I wanted to eat that thing.

DAVE: Here's a fun fact: the Sugarland set was built on top of the graveyard set from "Ghosts Ain't Real!," so it's definitely haunted.

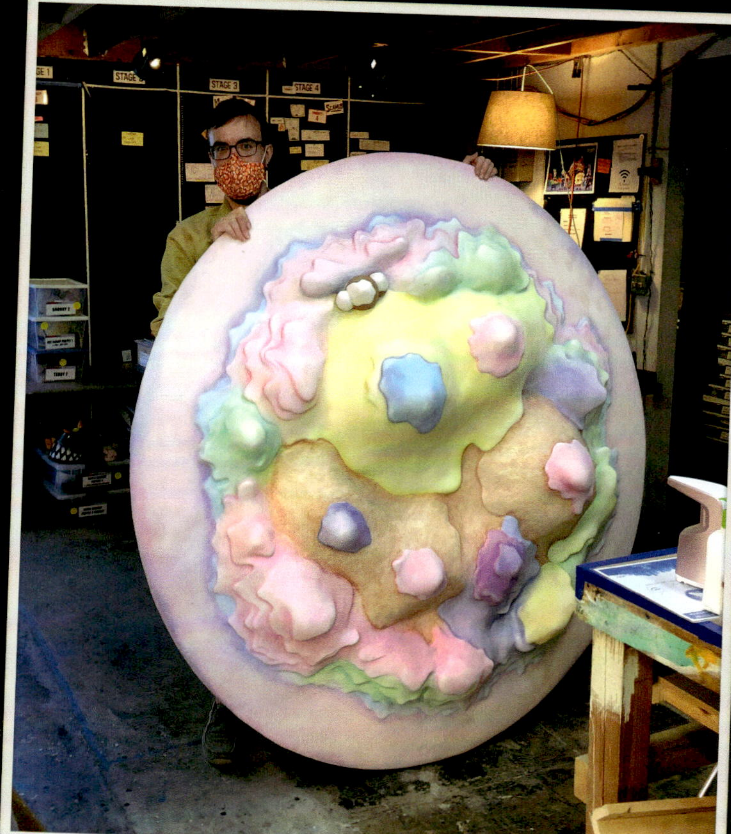

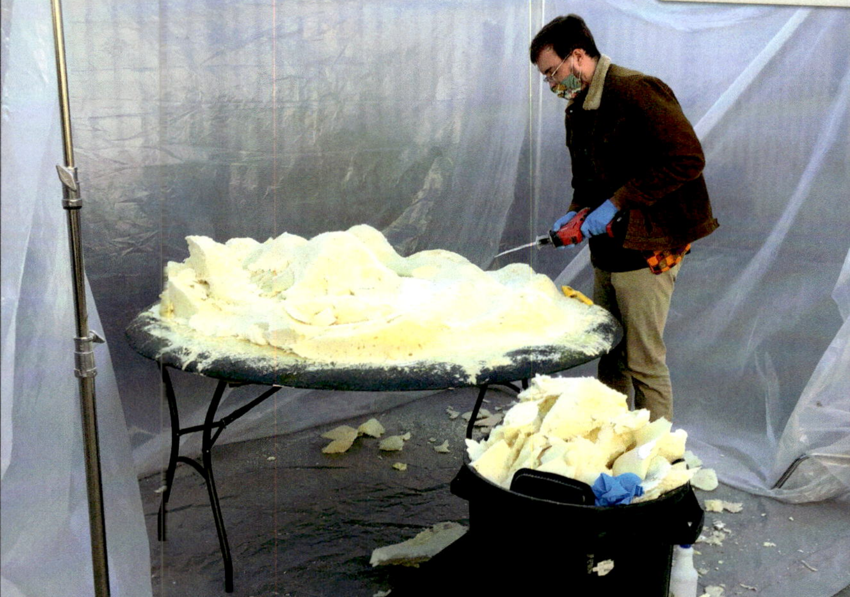

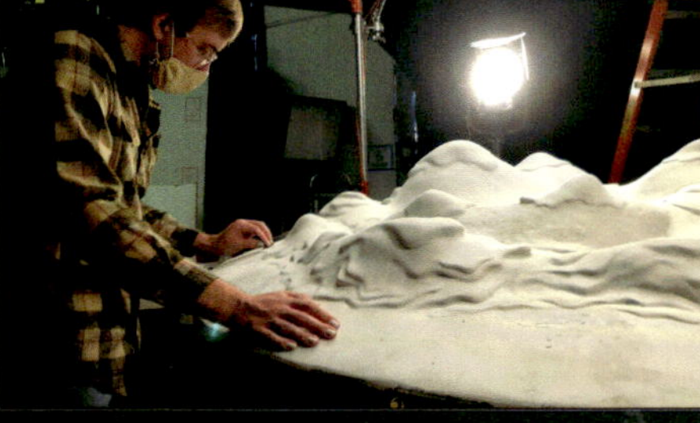

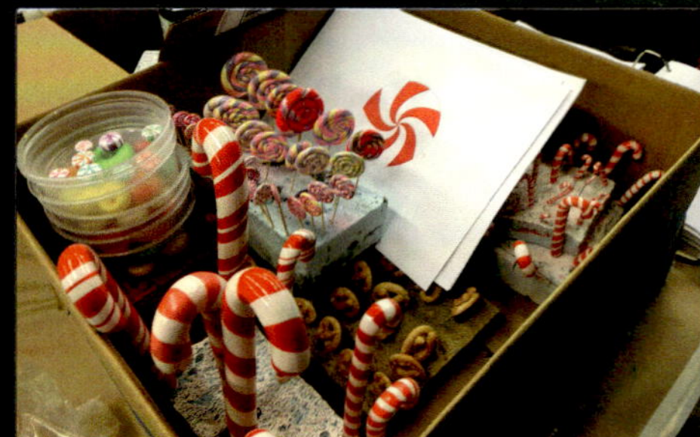

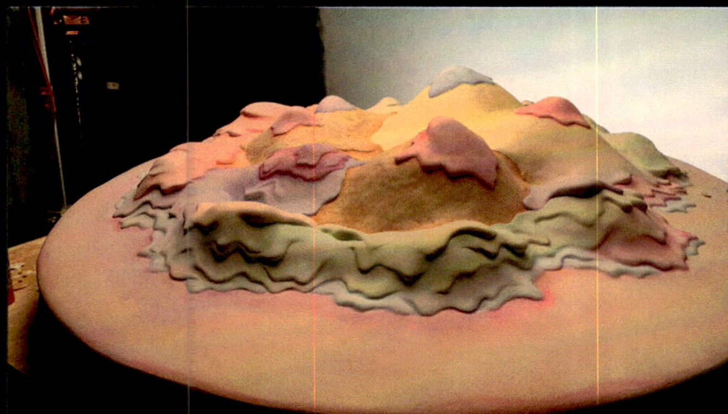

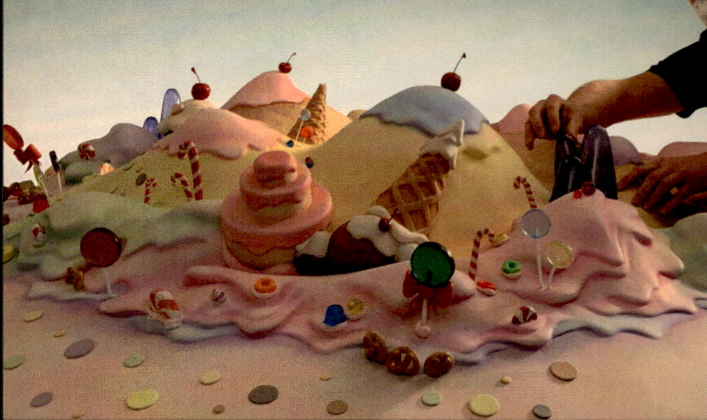

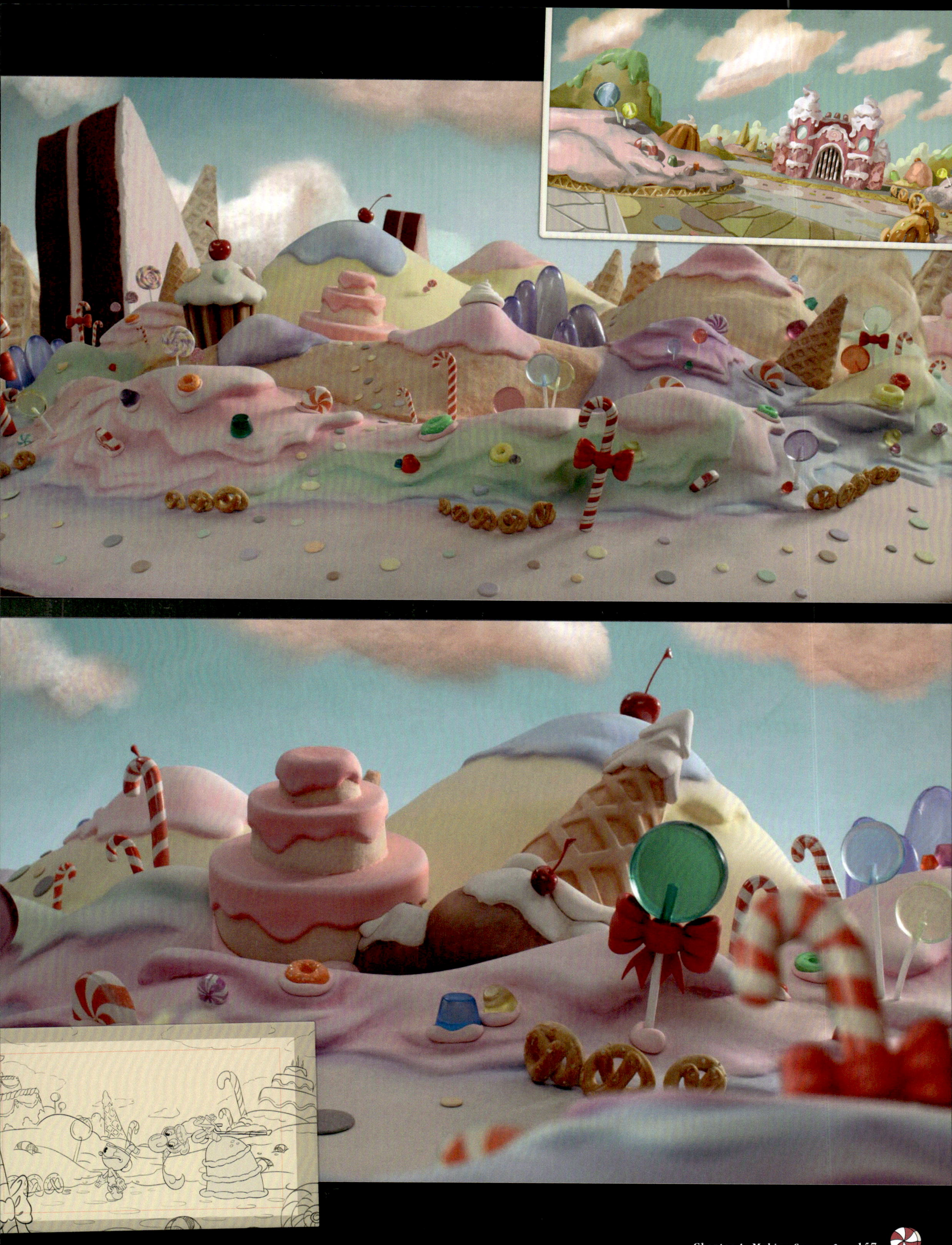

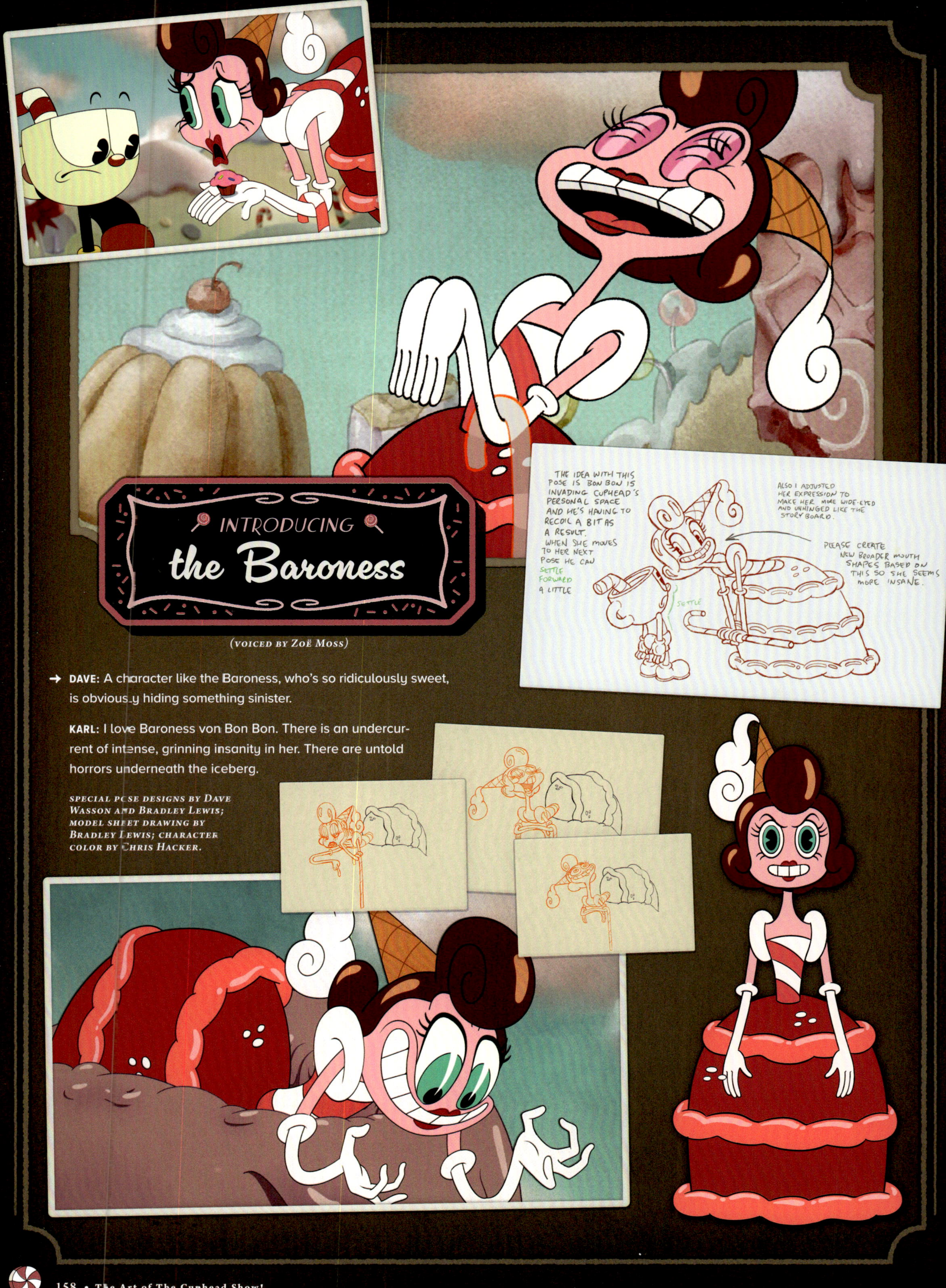

INTRODUCING the Baroness

(VOICED BY ZOË MOSS)

→ **DAVE:** A character like the Baroness, who's so ridiculously sweet, is obviously hiding something sinister.

KARL: I love Baroness von Bon Bon. There is an undercurrent of intense, grinning insanity in her. There are untold horrors underneath the iceberg.

SPECIAL POSE DESIGNS BY DAVE WASSON AND BRADLEY LEWIS; MODEL SHEET DRAWING BY BRADLEY LEWIS; CHARACTER COLOR BY CHRIS HACKER.

→ **ZOË MOSS, *THE CUPHEAD SHOW!* STORYBOARD ARTIST:** Having the opportunity to play up the scary stuff was so much fun. You get to combine the best of Cyndi Lauper with an evil, sharp-toothed monster. I knew what to do with her, because she's just a really fun weirdo who can turn on a dime. That episode just fits my DNA.

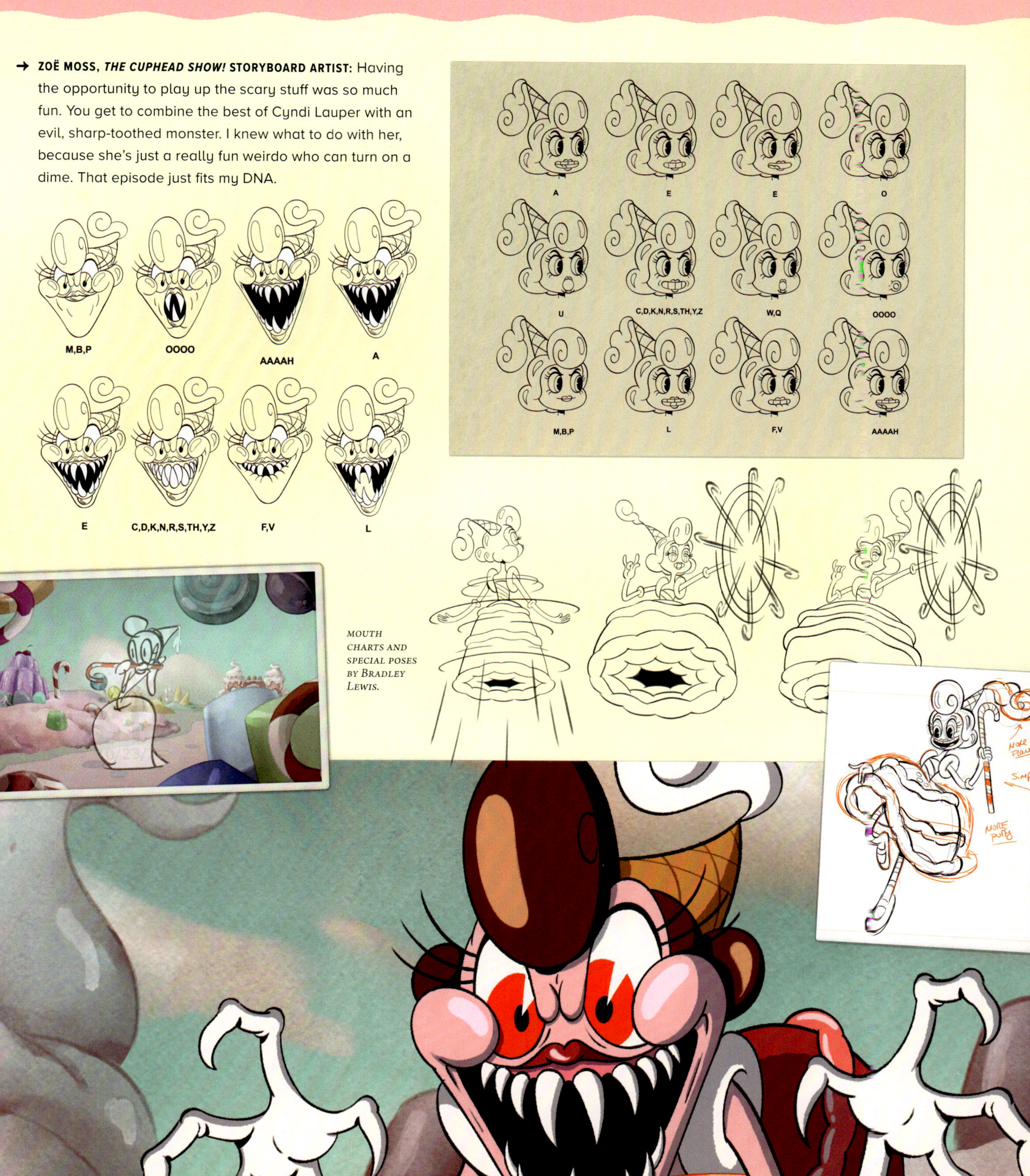

MOUTH CHARTS AND SPECIAL POSES BY BRADLEY LEWIS.

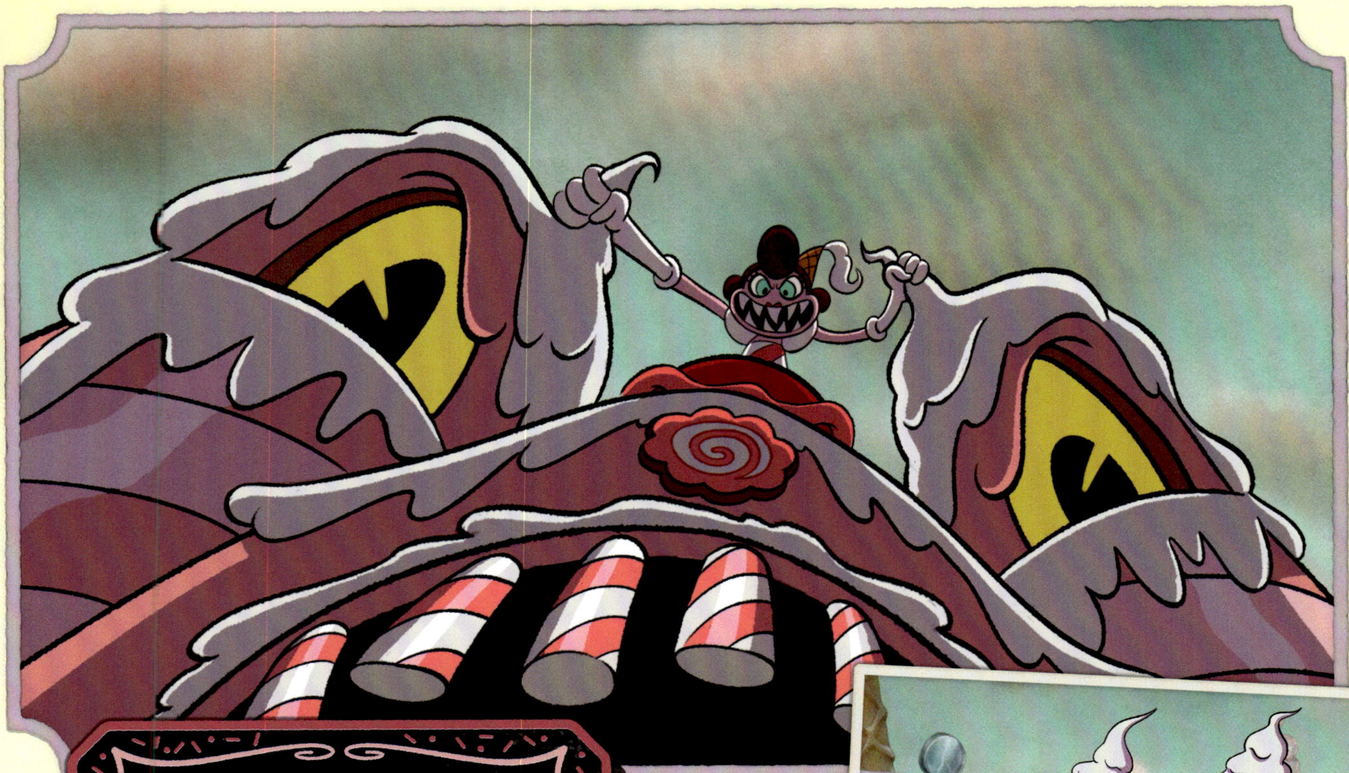

The Castle

→ **ANDREA:** I try to avoid huge anthropomorphic characters, like a building that also comes to life and moves around—for example, the castle in "Sweet Temptation." It's super difficult to pull off. In this case, we did it because *obviously* we need to go to Sugarland, we need to see Bon Bon, and we need to see that castle running around.

DAVE: When it comes to scale, may have lost Ribby and Croaks, but I'm getting that castle. And it has to be huge. Like in the game!

ANDREA: Getting it fully animated and at the right scale—it's a headache.

DAVE: Just . . . massive!

ANDREA: We had to pick and choose when we were willing to give ourselves headaches. For me, that castle is absolutely worth all the headaches.

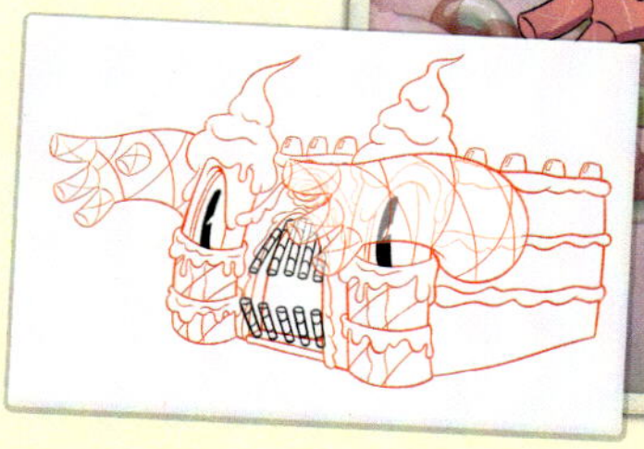

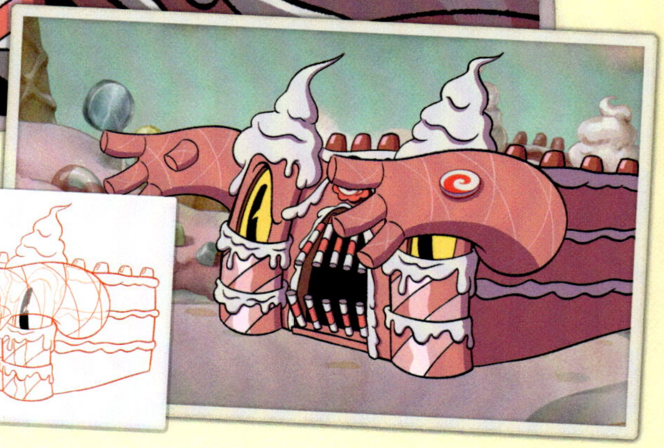

SPECIAL POSES FOR CASTLE MONSTER BY MIKE FONTANELLI.

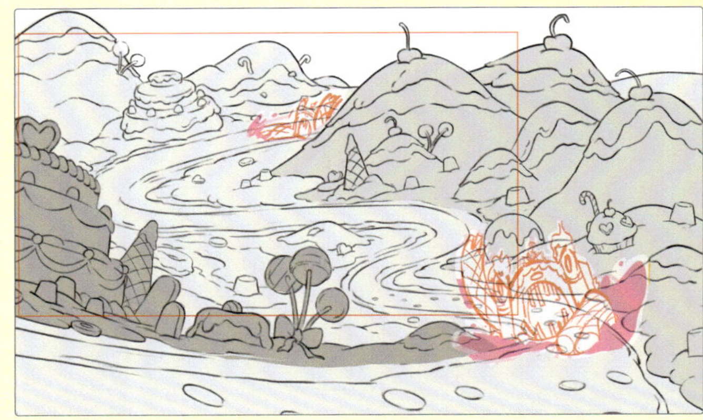

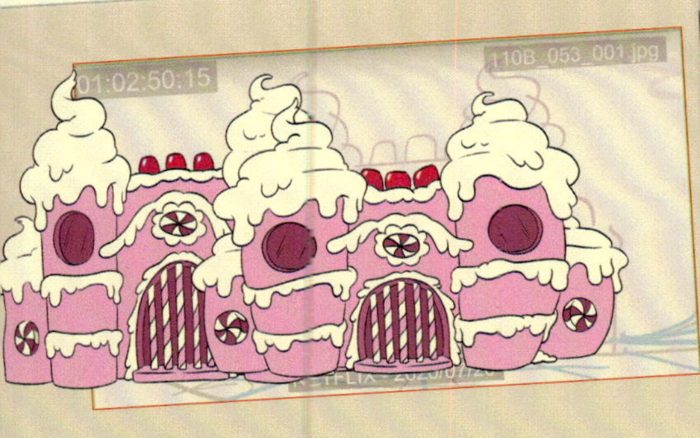

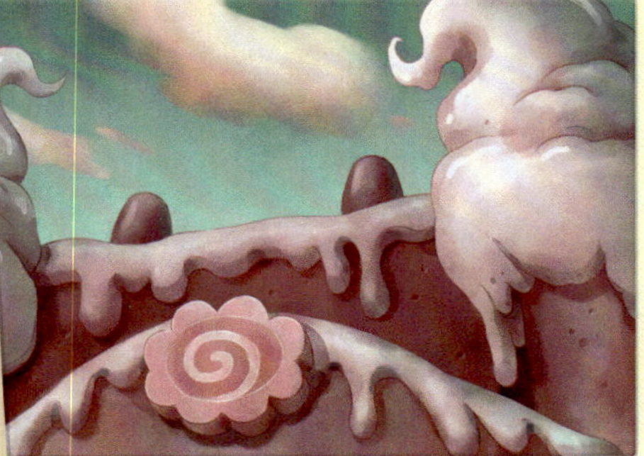

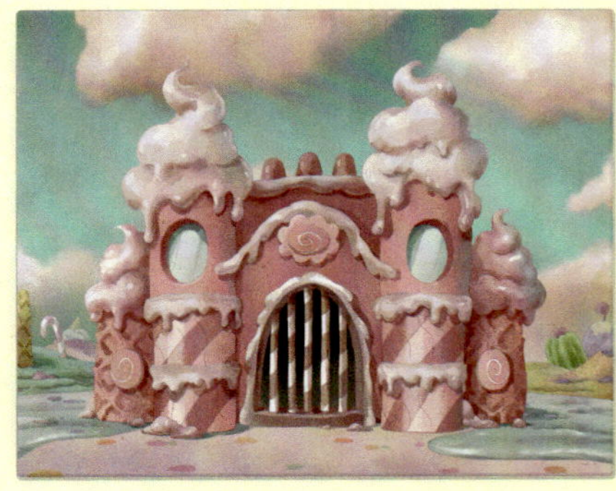

BACKGROUND DESIGNS BY JESSICA HONG, LAISAY BOND, AND PAT MARCONETT; PAINTINGS BY MICHELLE THIES AND GREGORY MILLER.

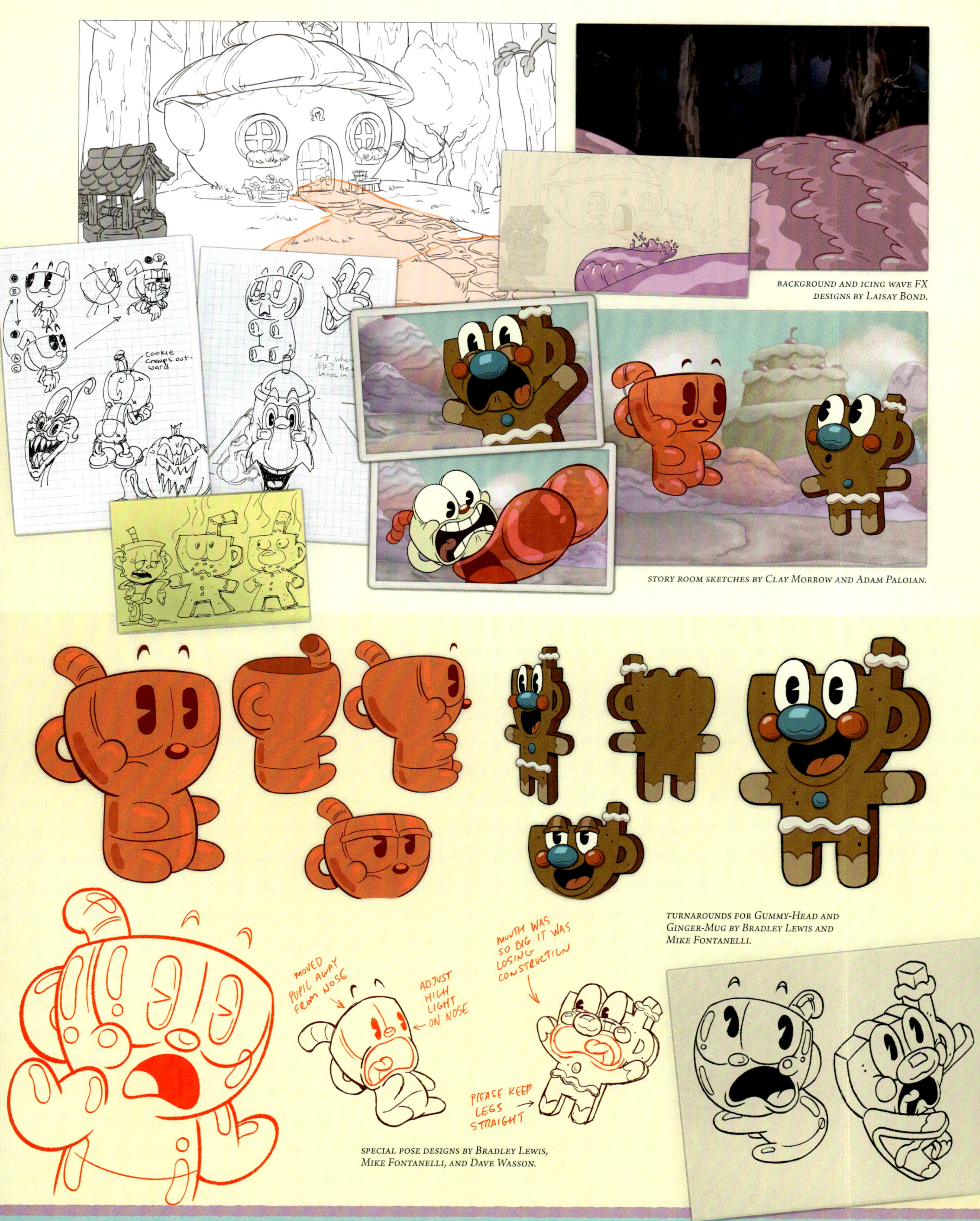

Background and icing wave FX designs by Laisay Bond.

Story room sketches by Clay Morrow and Adam Paloian.

Turnarounds for Gummy-Head and Ginger-Mug by Bradley Lewis and Mike Fontanelli.

Special pose designs by Bradley Lewis, Mike Fontanelli, and Dave Wasson.

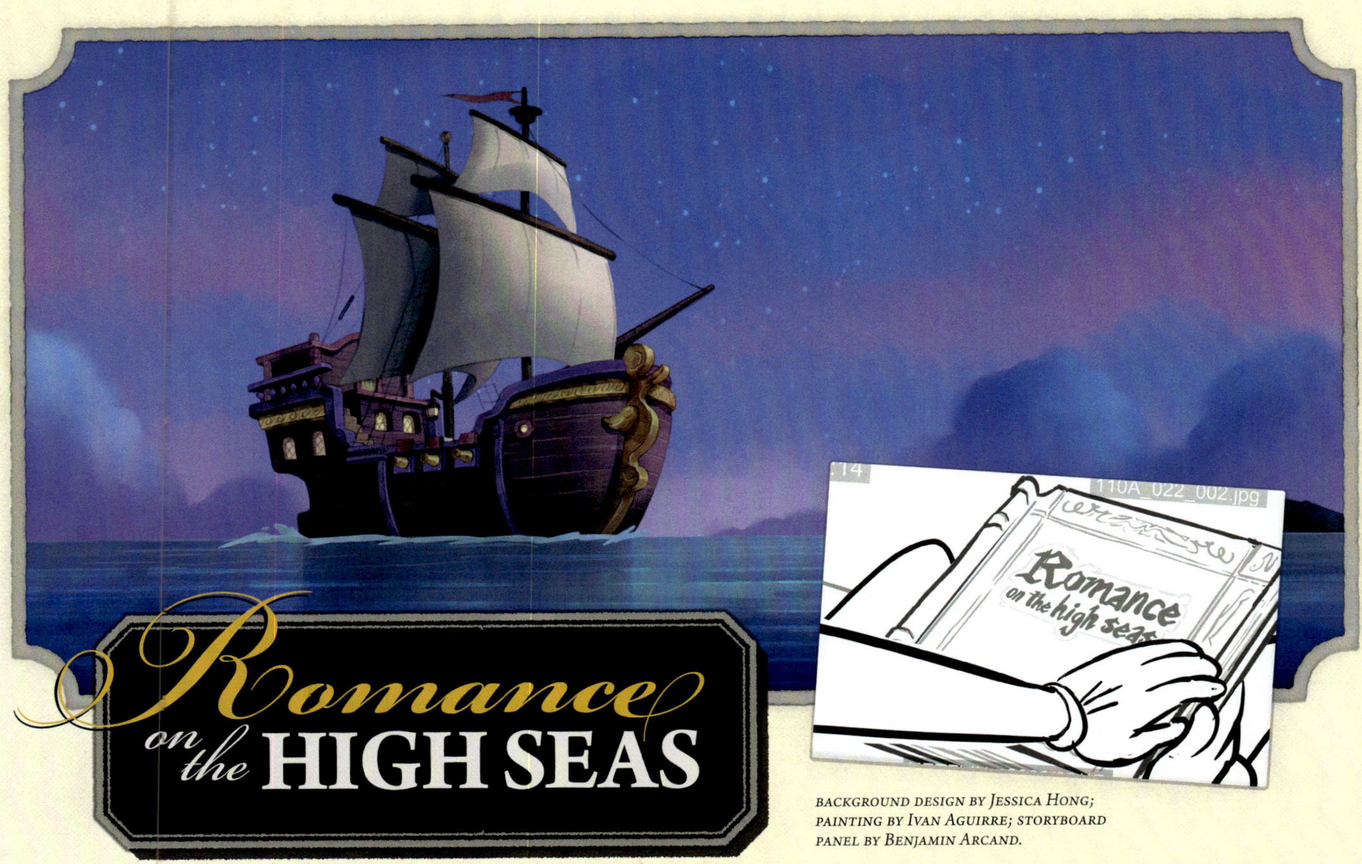

Romance on the HIGH SEAS

BACKGROUND DESIGN BY JESSICA HONG; PAINTING BY IVAN AGUIRRE; STORYBOARD PANEL BY BENJAMIN ARCAND.

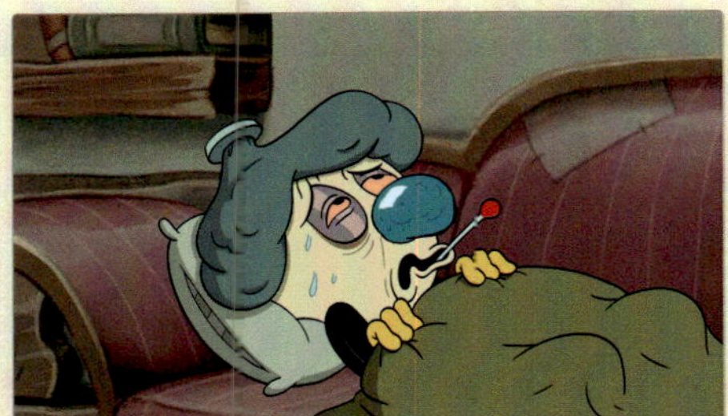

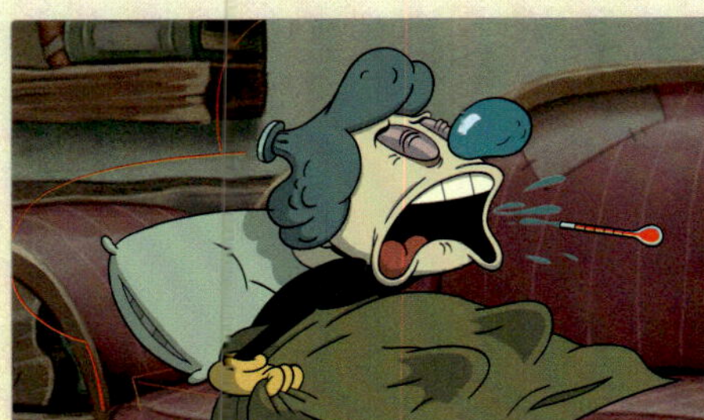

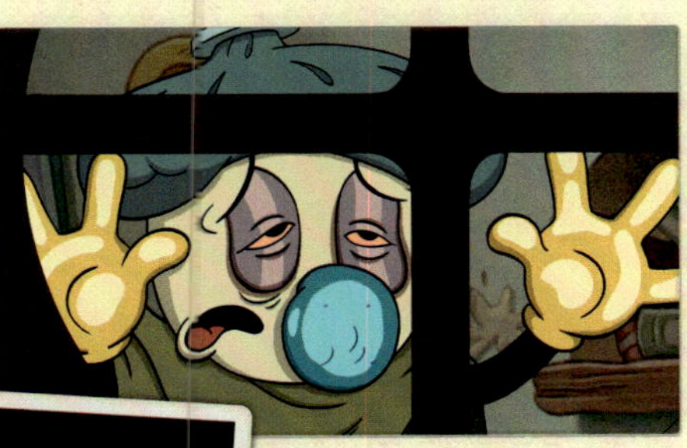

SPECIAL POSES BY TAPAN GANDHI AND MARTIN WITTIG; BACKGROUND DESIGNS BY LAUREN DUDA; PAINTINGS BY LEAH CHUN AND JEFF PALM.

→ **COSMO:** Mugman pretends to be so ill that he can't run errands with them. And he clearly loves running errands, so we *know* it must be important if he's skipping them.

DAVE: He needs to maintain his secret that he loves romance novels. Presumably, he's doing it to save face—he knows he'd be teased mercilessly by Cuphead *and* Elder Kettle. It's like he's doing it out of self-preservation, sneaking around reading his romance novels.

COSMO: That episode is like an onion where we learn more and more about Mugman, starting with a lie, a secret, then going into his fantasy, and then pure violence to keep the romance going and to keep the secret.

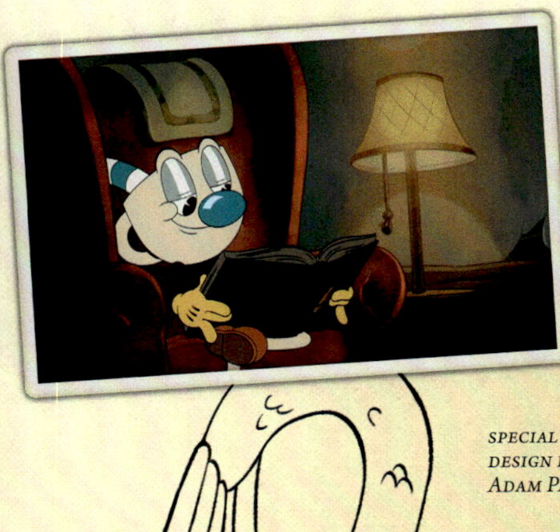

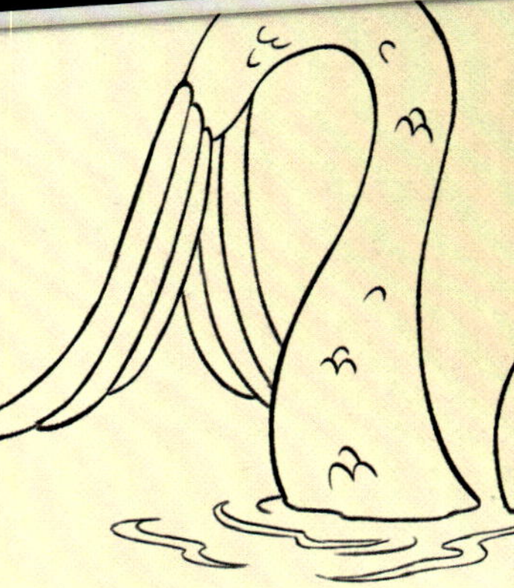

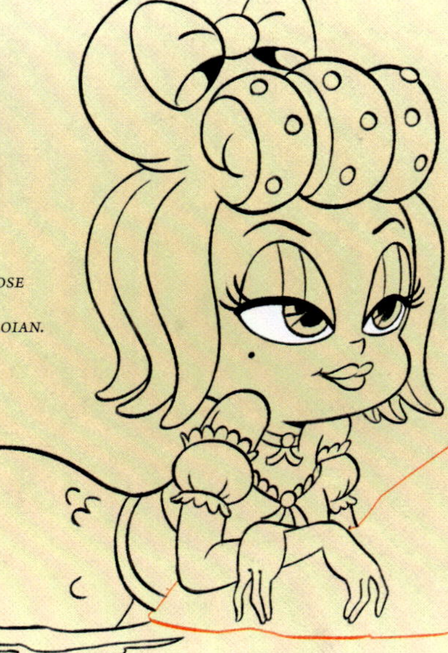

SPECIAL POSE DESIGN BY ADAM PALOIAN.

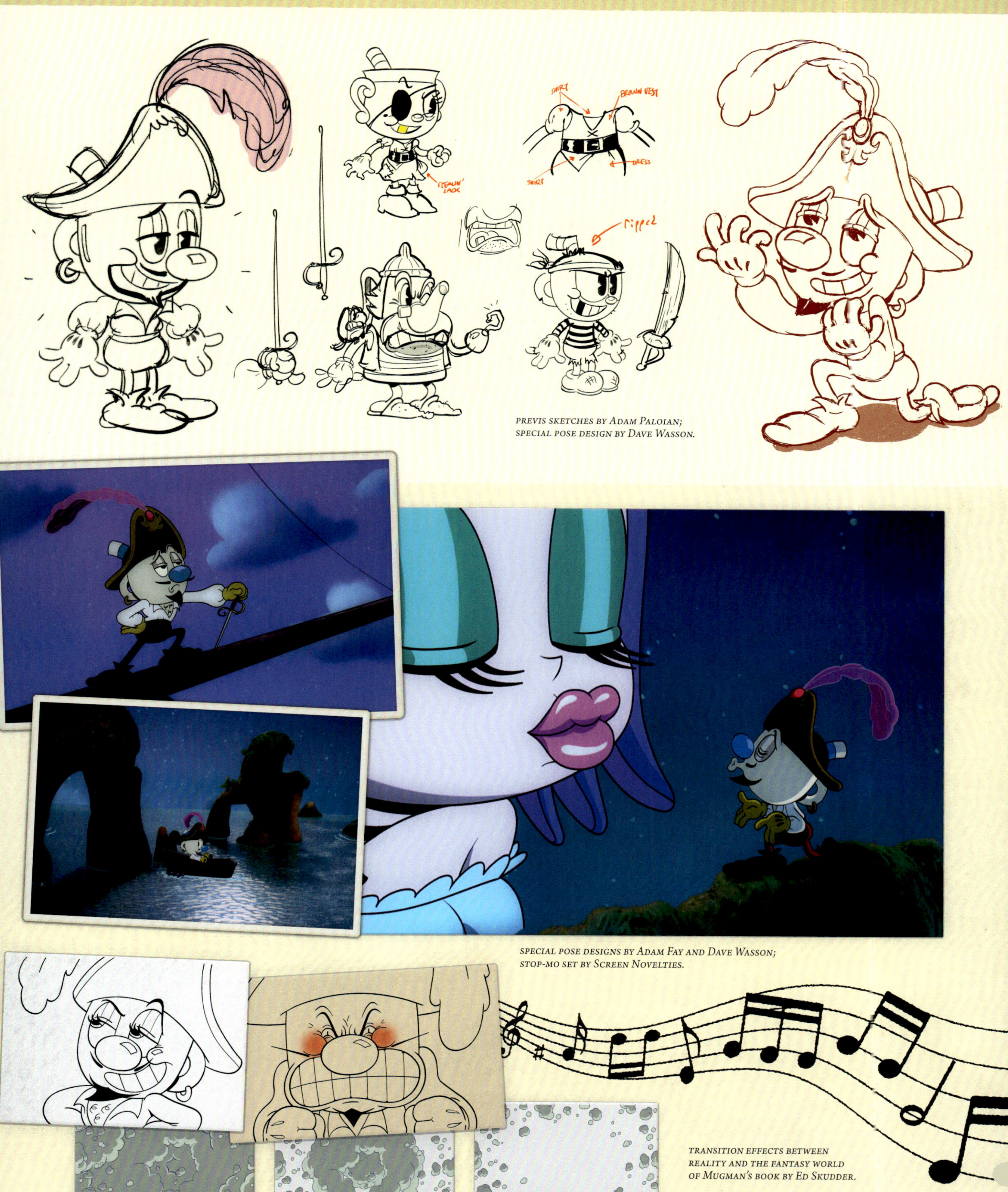

PREVIS SKETCHES BY ADAM PALOIAN; SPECIAL POSE DESIGN BY DAVE WASSON.

SPECIAL POSE DESIGNS BY ADAM FAY AND DAVE WASSON; STOP-MO SET BY SCREEN NOVELTIES.

TRANSITION EFFECTS BETWEEN REALITY AND THE FANTASY WORLD OF MUGMAN'S BOOK BY ED SKUDDER.

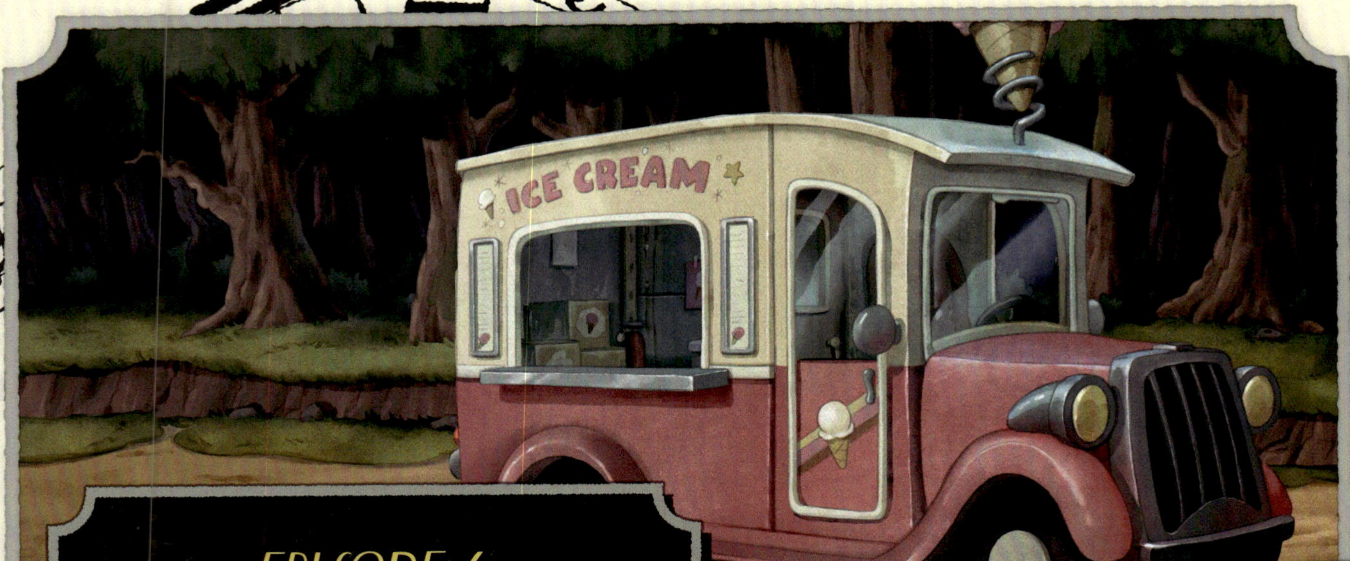

EPISODE 6

"THE I SCREAM MAN"

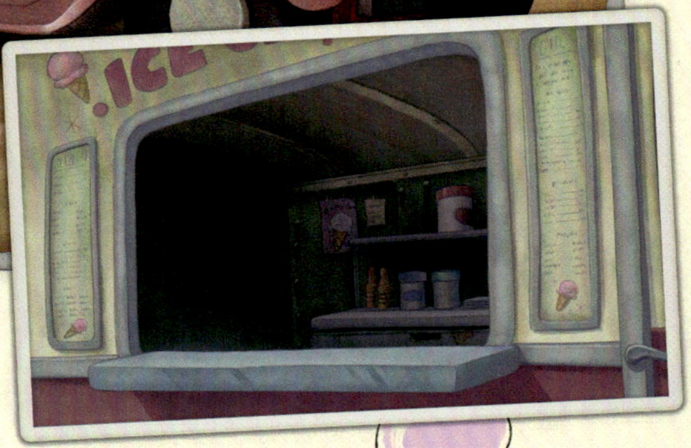

→ **DAVE:** This story was inspired by actual events.

ADAM P: The ice cream man in my neighborhood started off as a minor nuisance and became the bane of my existence. He would play "Turkey in the Straw" on a loop, full blast. It sounded like there was an ice cream truck in my living room.

CLAY: Once we were working from home, we could hear the ice cream man's music from Adam's apartment.

ADAM P: Eventually I was forced to be confrontational and hunt down the ice cream man and ask him to lower the volume.

DEEKI: One day Adam came in telling us this story in a frothing rage. It was clear that he did not find any of it funny. Which made it hilarious.

ADAM P: Months go by, and we have peace—I don't hear him at all, I figured maybe he forgot about me. Then he comes back with a vengeance, louder than ever, so I rented one of those electric scooters and chased after him, but I fell and hurt my leg. And in response to me getting injured, he blasted the music even louder. When I told this story to Deeki, he came in a couple days later with an episode about my torment from the ice cream man. It was the greatest gift of my life.

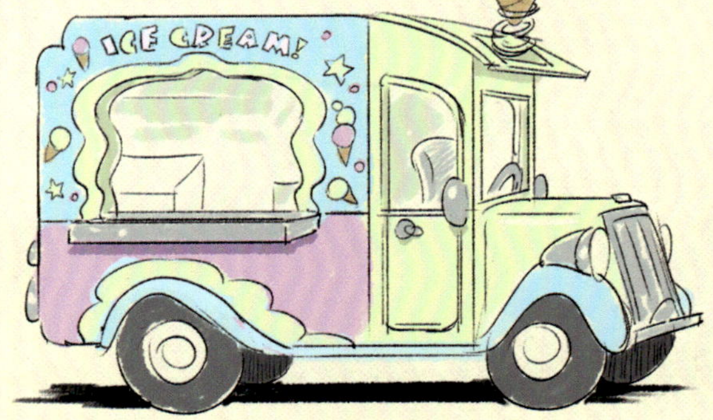

BACKGROUND DESIGNS BY BENJAMIN ANDERSON AND LAUREN DUDA; PAINTINGS BY MALLORY CARLSON; ICE CREAM TRUCK PREVIS BY COSMO SEGURSON.

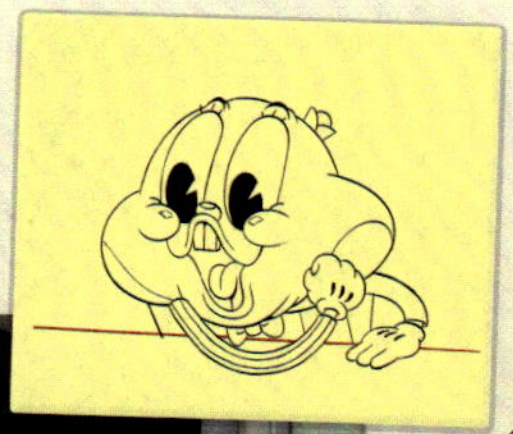

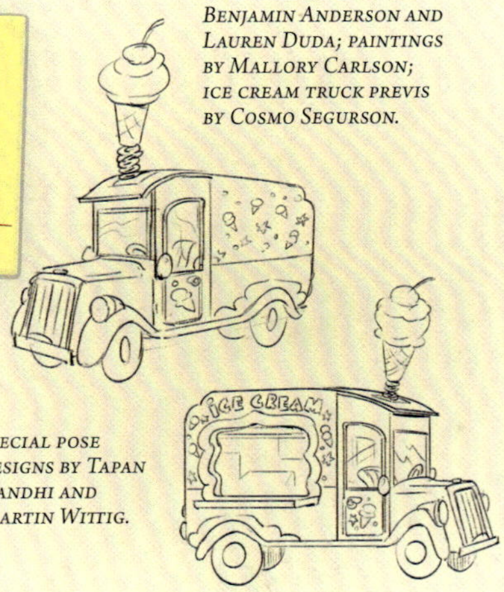

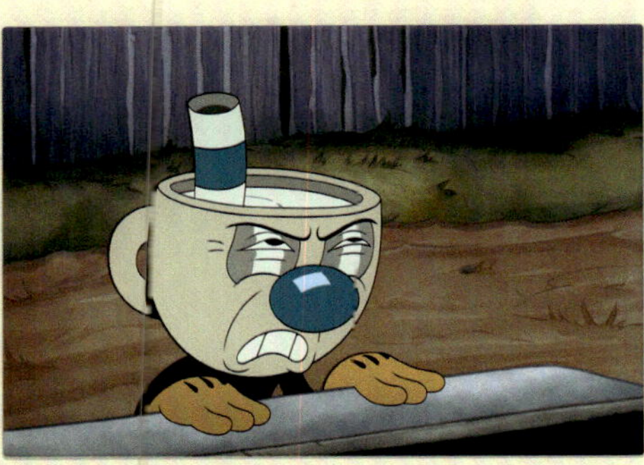

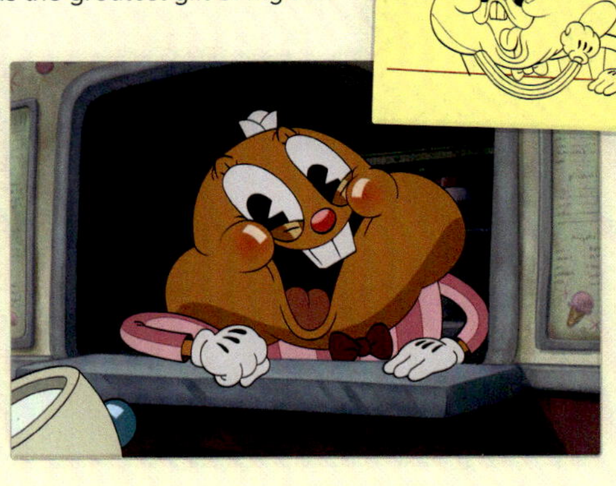

SPECIAL POSE DESIGNS BY TAPAN GANDHI AND MARTIN WITTIG.

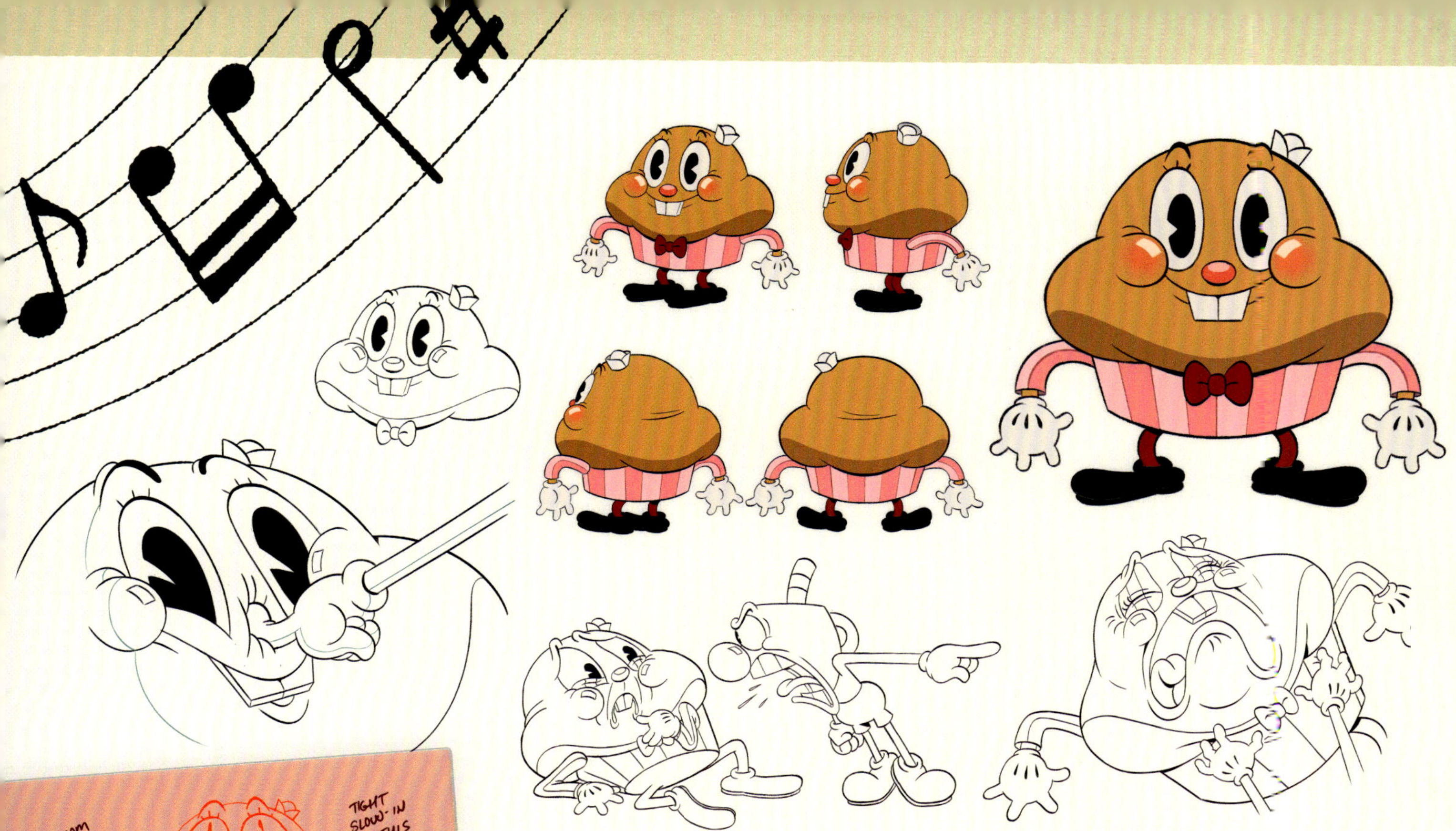

Ice cream man turnaround by Adam Paloian and Tapan Gandhi; special pose design by Tapan Gandhi, Adam Paloian, and Dave Wasson.

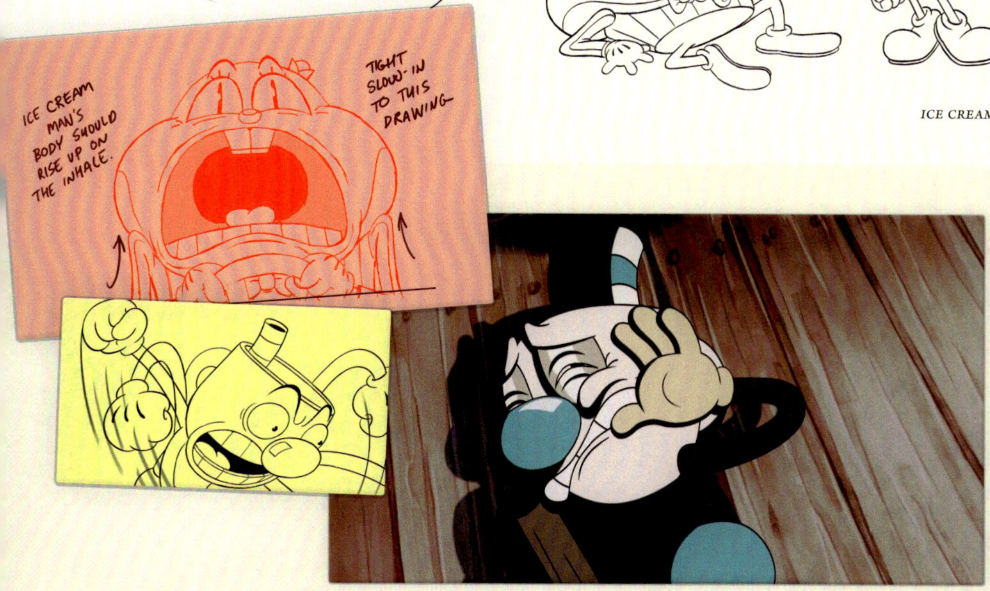

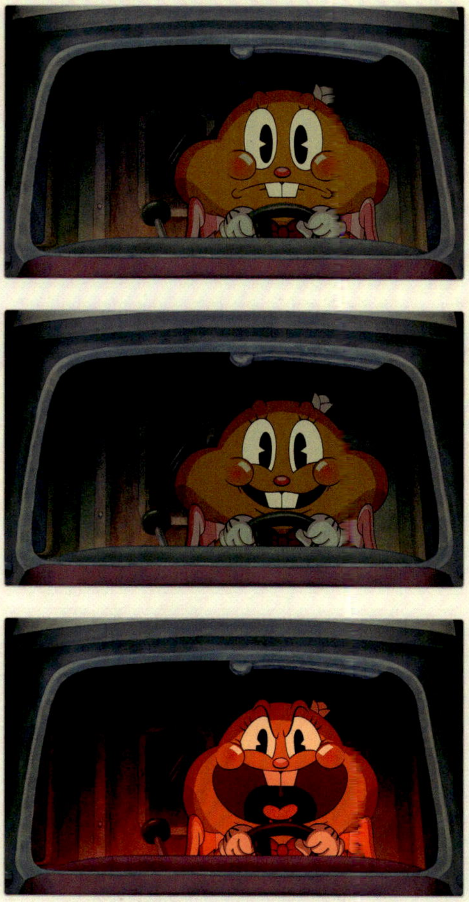

COSMO: He's a dopey, honest, hardworking, upbeat guy who loves his job. He's unflappably optimistic—and you just want to kill him.

ADAM P: In the beginning Mugman is polite, but his patience is tested, and he eventually snaps. He's not just an archetype of "the timid guy"—there are other aspects to his character. He can get to a place of rage. If you can get to a place where Mugman can snap, it's satisfying and shocking.

CLAY: Mugman prides himself on being rational, thinking things through, giving people a chance, doing the right thing—but it feels so satisfying to take him from that high-and-mighty place to this place of "I'll kill someone and won't feel bad about it." That kind of an episode is amazing.

DAVE: That story forced us to reveal a lot about Mugman—when you don't have Cuphead to lean on, you just have Mugman's psychosis. In that episode, you start realizing how weird Mugman is when you get him by himself. There's a lot going on under the surface. He's very caring and loving and the voice of reason—but there's a lot of weird stuff going on in that kid's head.

CLAY: When the stakes are high, they're so much higher for Mugman than they are for Cuphead. Some things get under Cuphead's skin, but for the most part, Mugman is way more susceptible to unraveling.

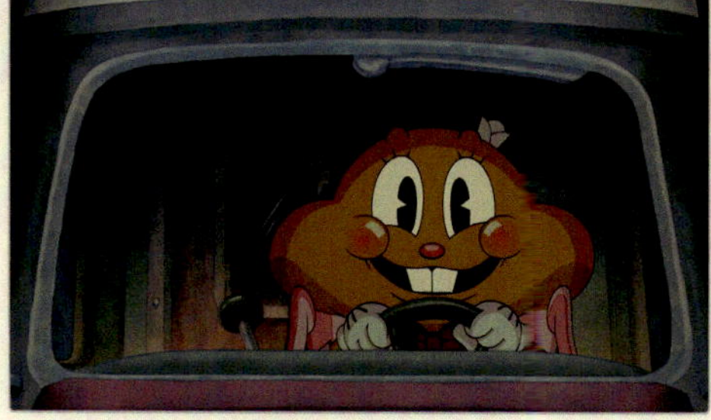

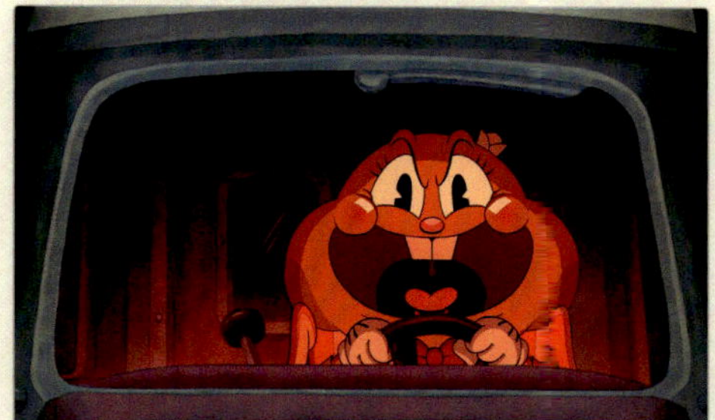

Background design by Pat Marconett; painting by Jeff Palm.

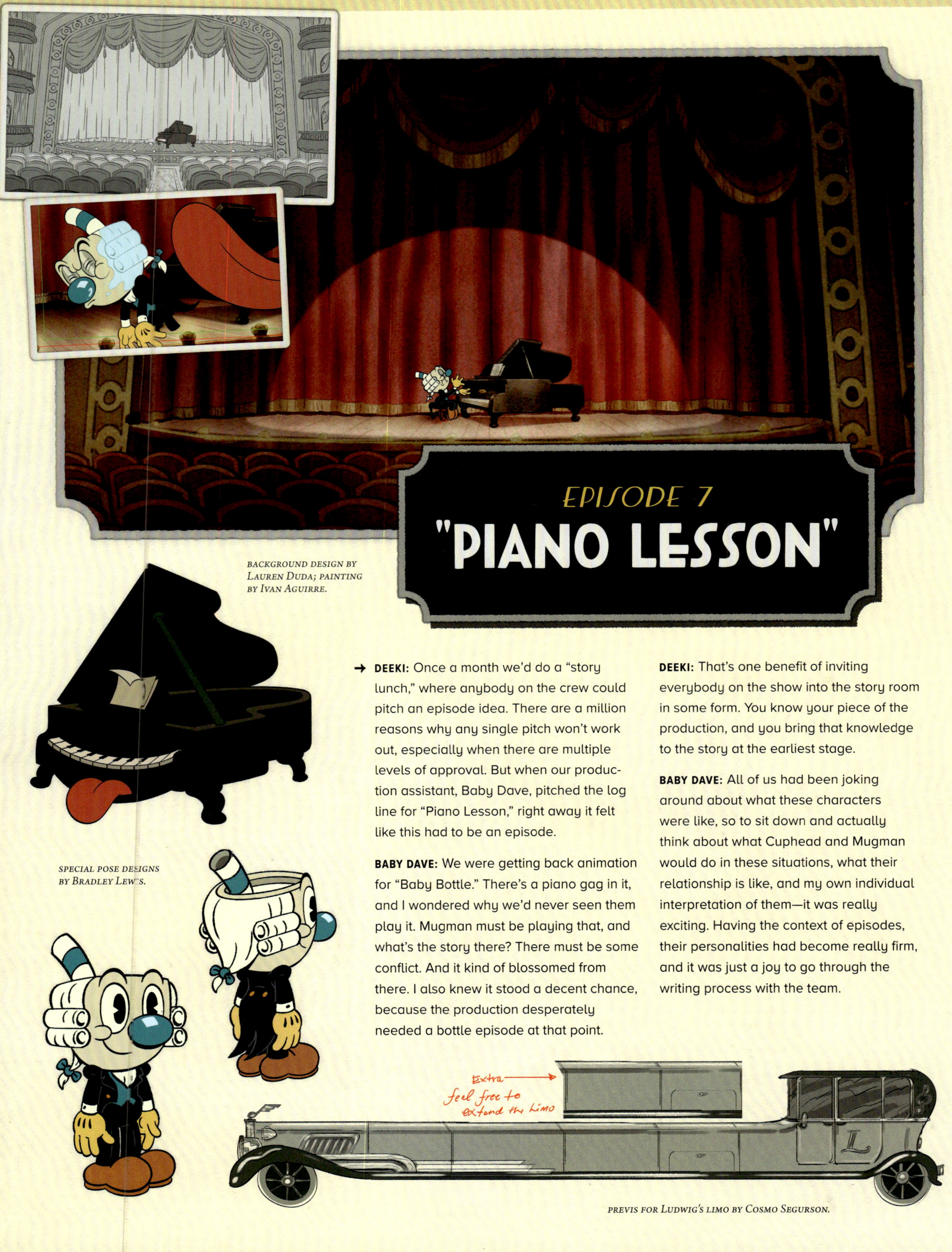

BACKGROUND DESIGN BY LAUREN DUDA; PAINTING BY IVAN AGUIRRE.

SPECIAL POSE DESIGNS BY BRADLEY LEWIS.

PREVIS FOR LUDWIG'S LIMO BY COSMO SEGURSON.

EPISODE 7

"PIANO LESSON"

→ **DEEKI:** Once a month we'd do a "story lunch," where anybody on the crew could pitch an episode idea. There are a million reasons why any single pitch won't work out, especially when there are multiple levels of approval. But when our production assistant, Baby Dave, pitched the log line for "Piano Lesson," right away it felt like this had to be an episode.

BABY DAVE: We were getting back animation for "Baby Bottle." There's a piano gag in it, and I wondered why we'd never seen them play it. Mugman must be playing that, and what's the story there? There must be some conflict. And it kind of blossomed from there. I also knew it stood a decent chance, because the production desperately needed a bottle episode at that point.

DEEKI: That's one benefit of inviting everybody on the show into the story room in some form. You know your piece of the production, and you bring that knowledge to the story at the earliest stage.

BABY DAVE: All of us had been joking around about what these characters were like, so to sit down and actually think about what Cuphead and Mugman would do in these situations, what their relationship is like, and my own individual interpretation of them—it was really exciting. Having the context of episodes, their personalities had become really firm, and it was just a joy to go through the writing process with the team.

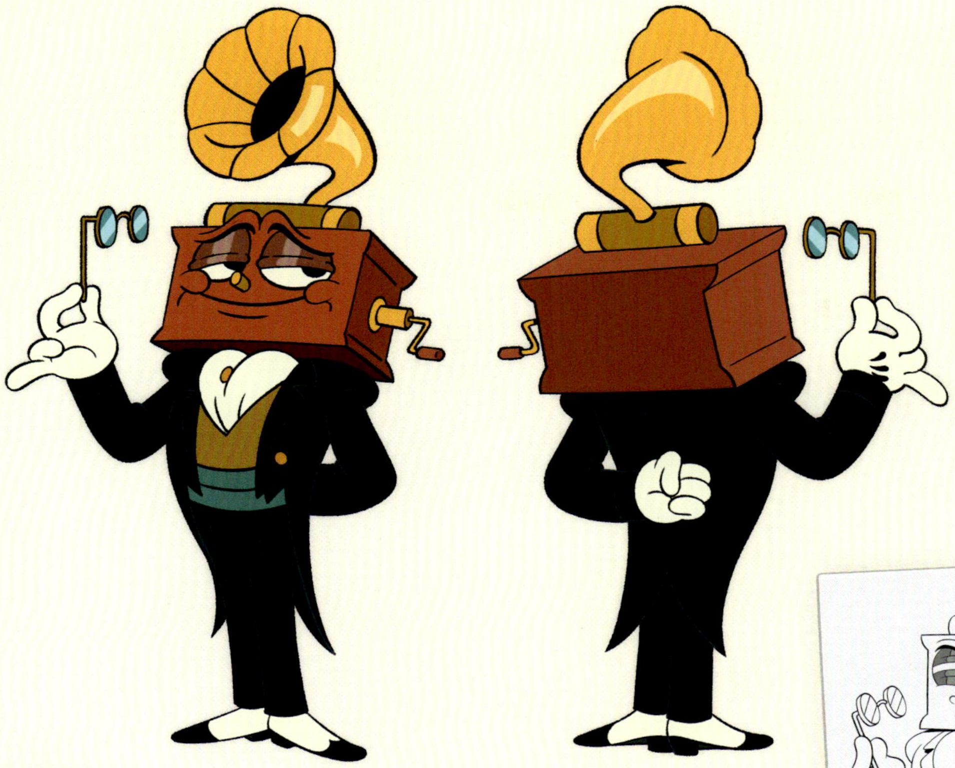

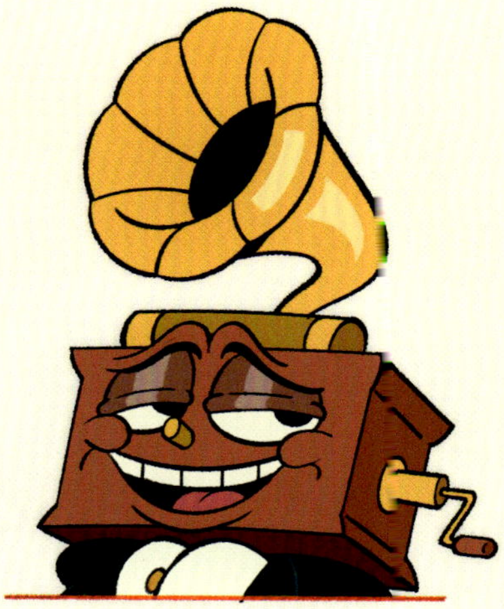

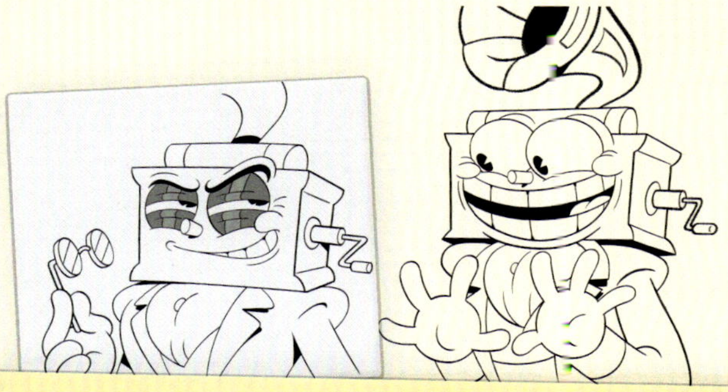

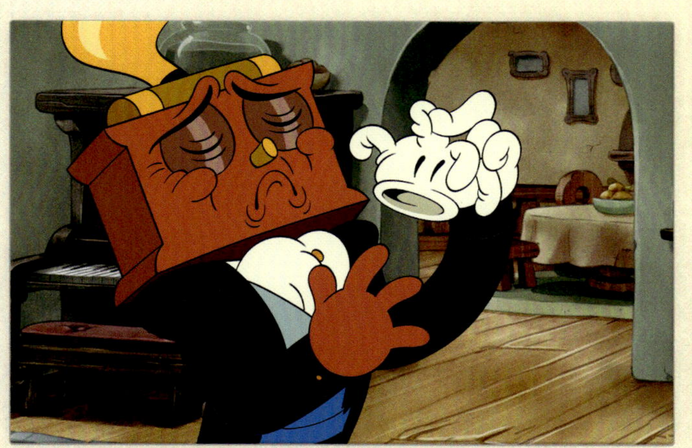

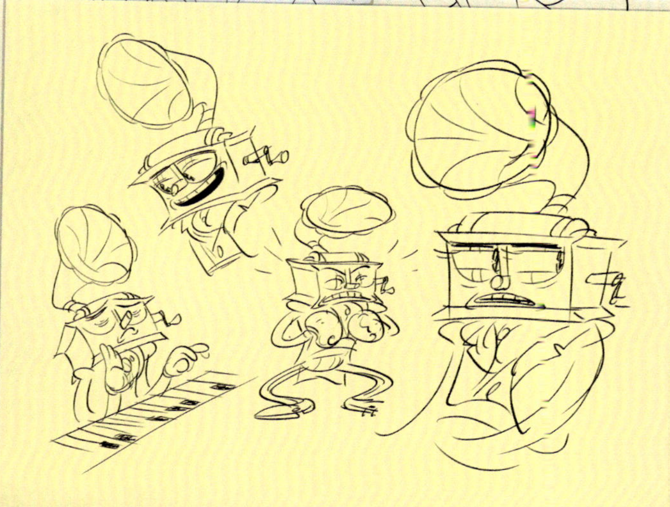

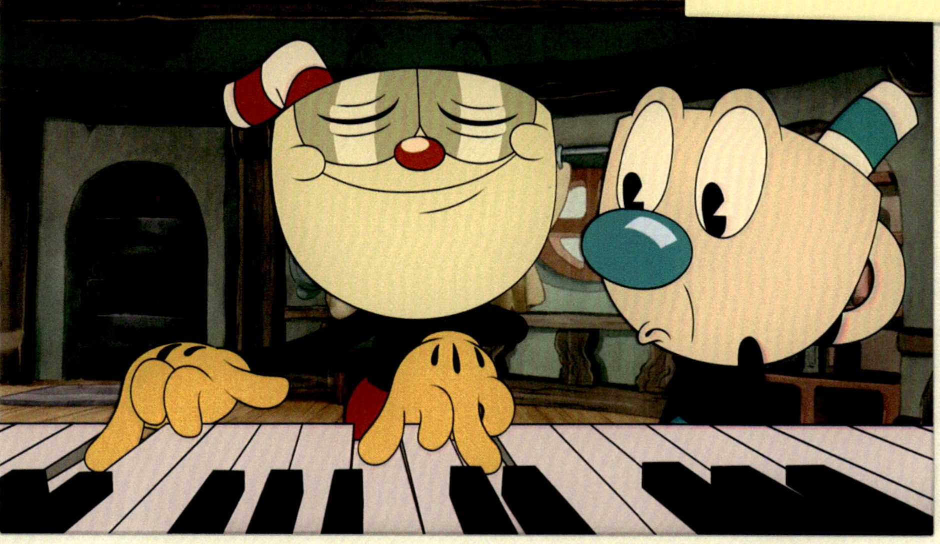

→ **COSMO:** Mugman wants to be an adult and wants to be more cultured.

KENNEDY: He thinks he's the classy one. And it's so fun to see Cuphead succeed at being cultured, and it just crushes Mugman. He's at his funniest when he's jealous or despairing.

CLAY: So many of our stories involve a breaking point or a meltdown. Nobody does those better than Mugman.

Previs for Ludwig by Cosmo Segurson; special pose designs and turnaround by Bradley Lewis.

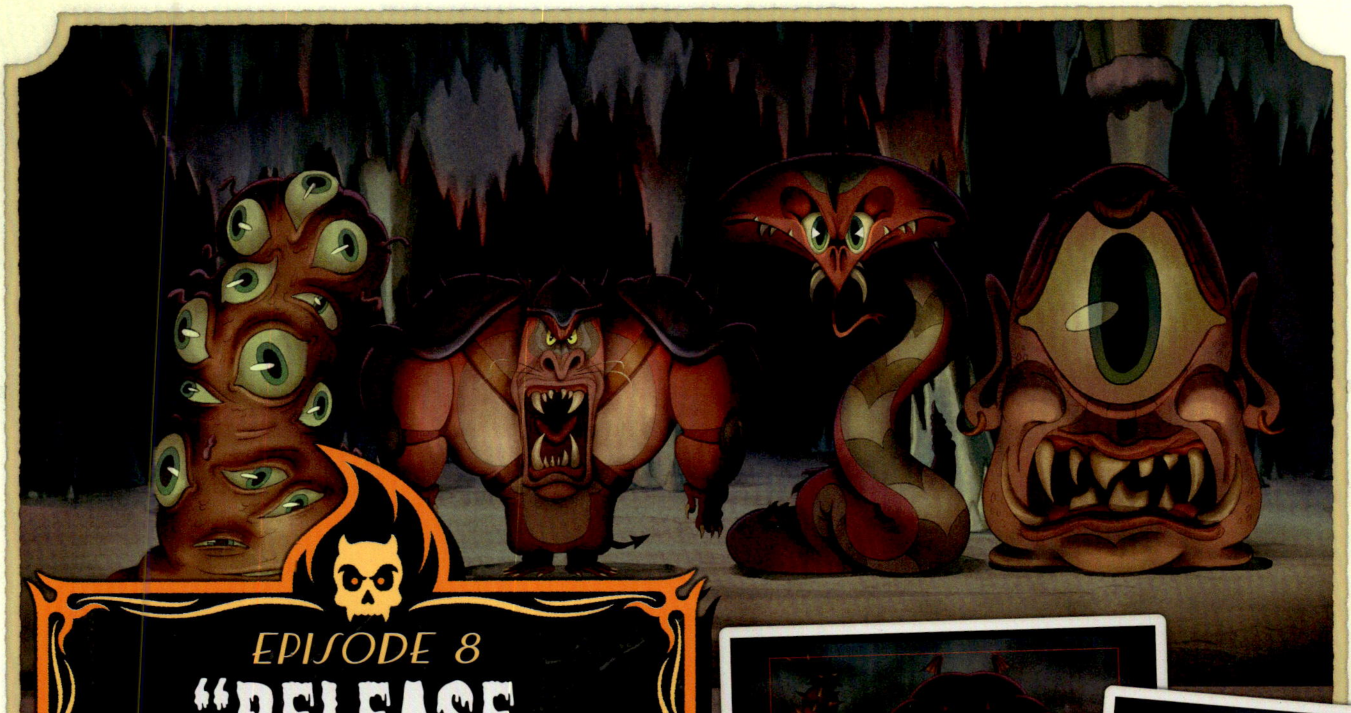

EPISODE 8

"RELEASE THE DEMONS!"

DEEP DIVE

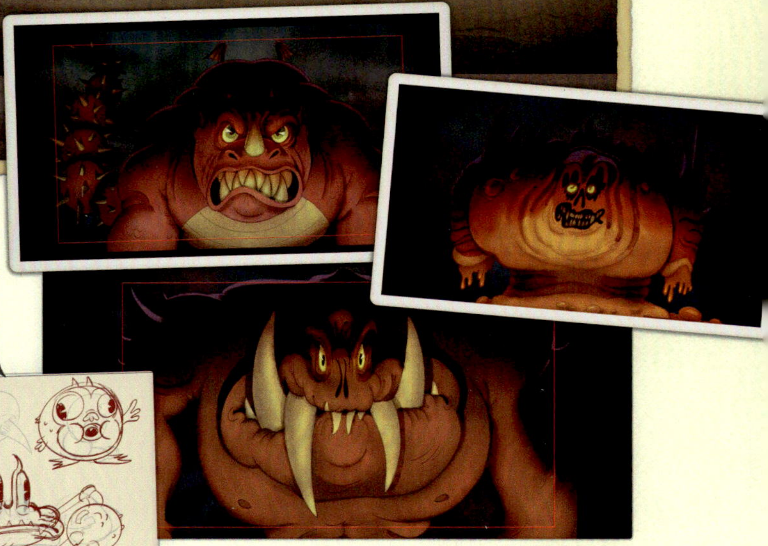

BACKGROUND DEMON DESIGNS BY ADAM PALOIAN; PAINTINGS BY MALLORY CARLSON.

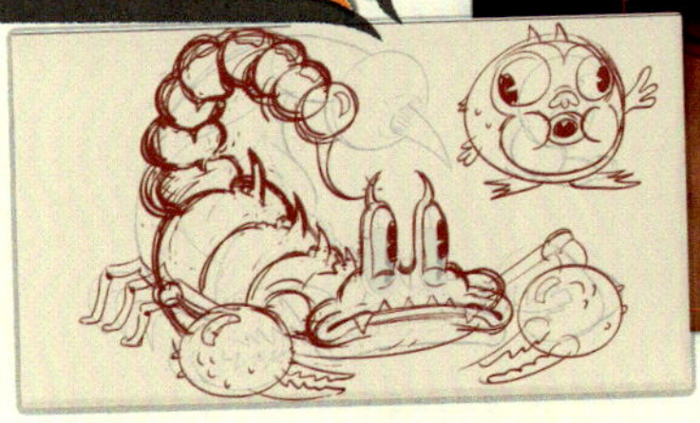

→ **DAVE:** Oh man, this one was a doozy—we really pulled out all the stops.

ADAM P: Originally, we were going to use all the little identical demons from "Sweater Off Dead." And then Deeki came in with this surprise pitch.

DEEKI: The Devil is so enraged about Cuphead that he keeps accidentally incinerating his finest demons.

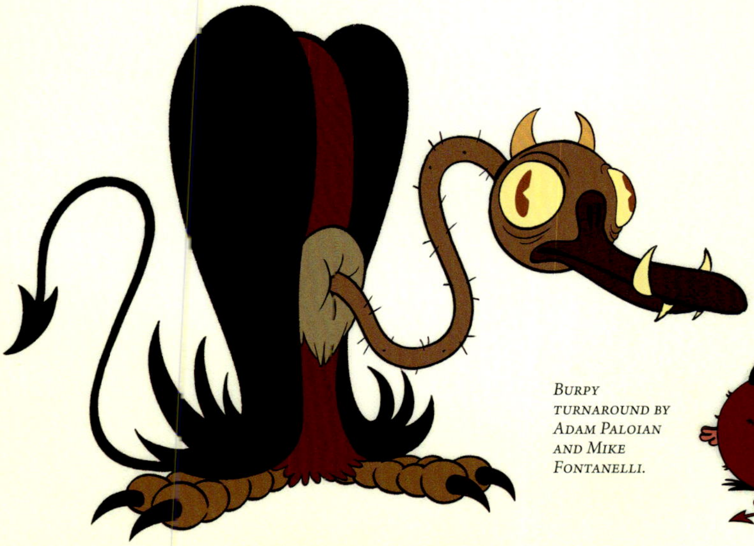

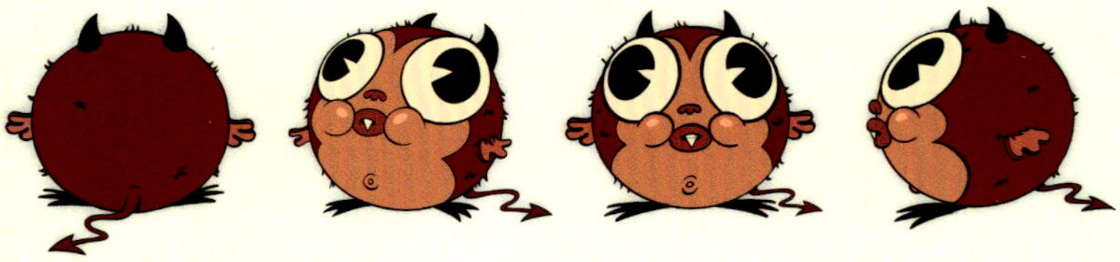

PREVIS SKETCH BY SHAKEH HAGHNAZARIAN.

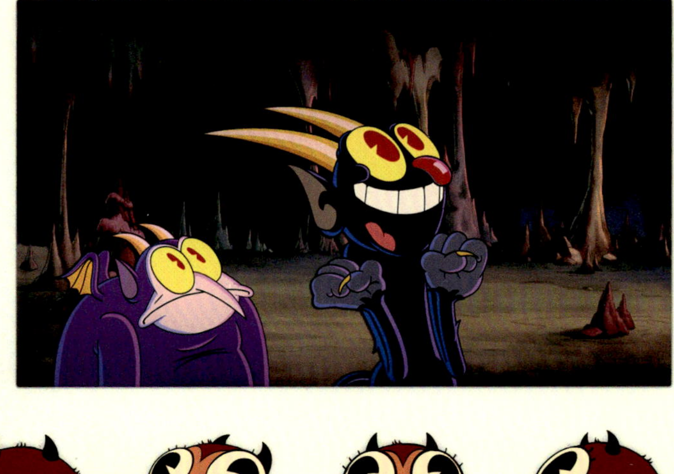

BURPY TURNAROUND BY ADAM PALOIAN AND MIKE FONTANELLI.

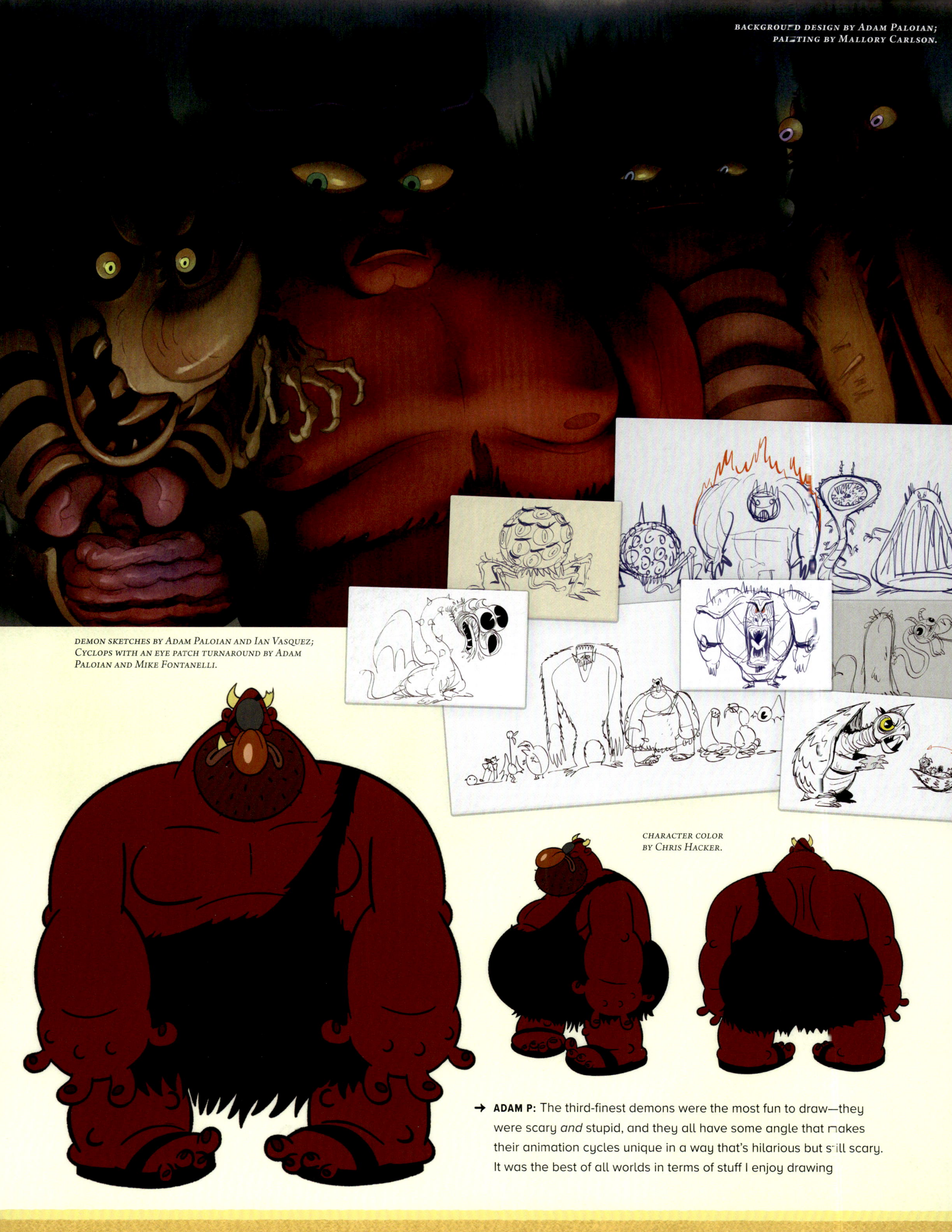

BACKGROUND DESIGN BY ADAM PALOIAN; PAINTING BY MALLORY CARLSON.

DEMON SKETCHES BY ADAM PALOIAN AND IAN VASQUEZ; CYCLOPS WITH AN EYE PATCH TURNAROUND BY ADAM PALOIAN AND MIKE FONTANELLI.

CHARACTER COLOR BY CHRIS HACKER.

→ **ADAM P:** The third-finest demons were the most fun to draw—they were scary *and* stupid, and they all have some angle that makes their animation cycles unique in a way that's hilarious but still scary. It was the best of all worlds in terms of stuff I enjoy drawing

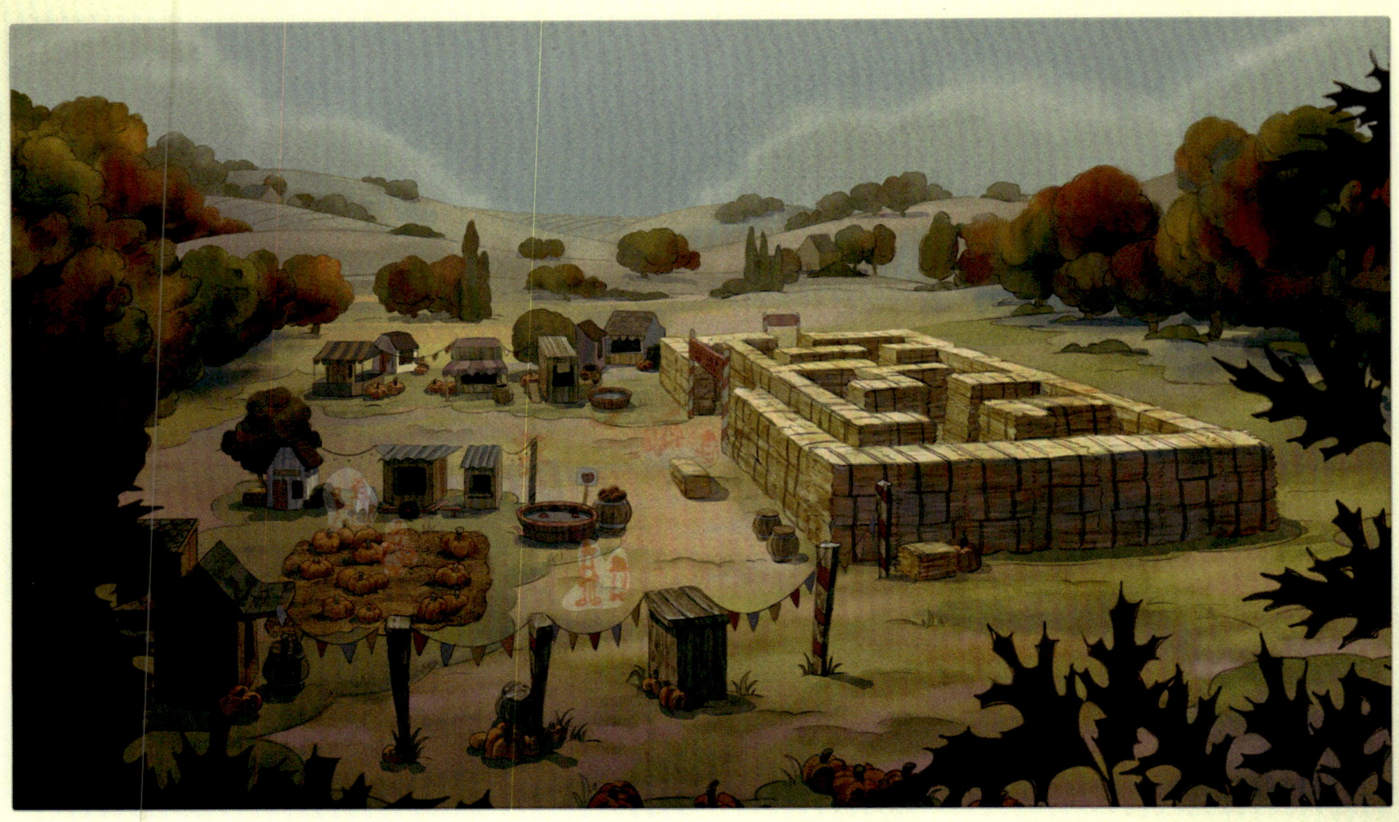

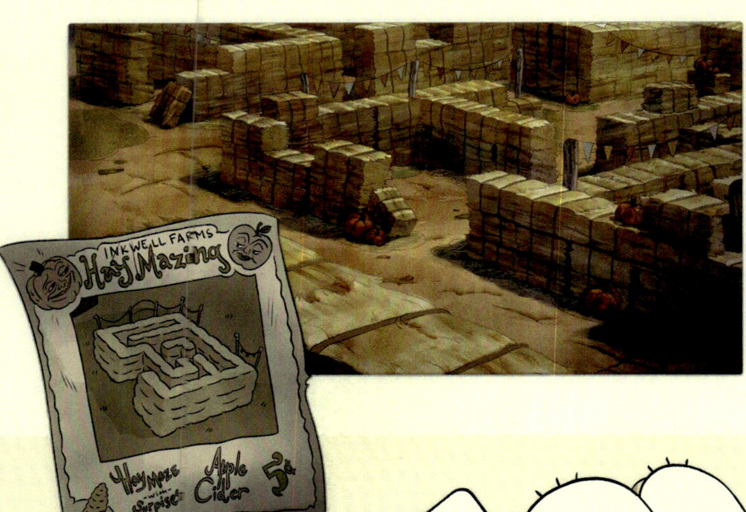

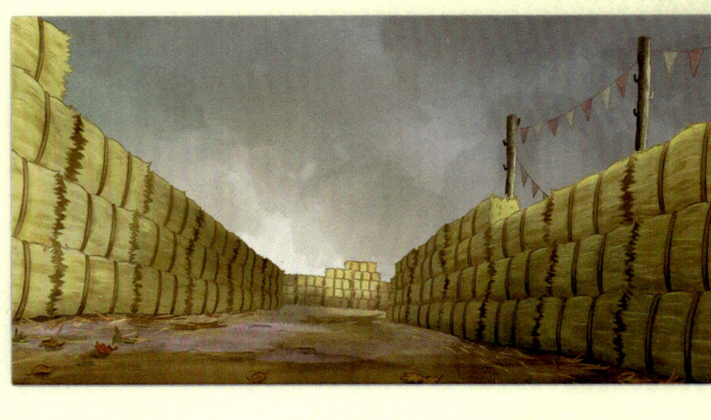

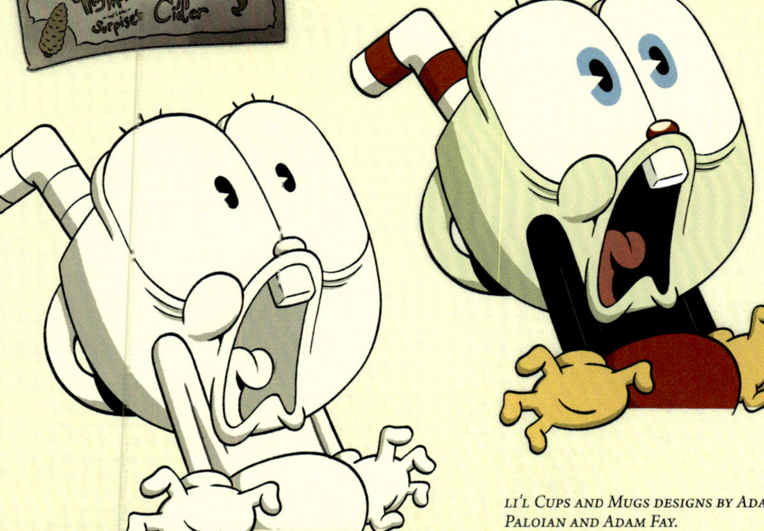

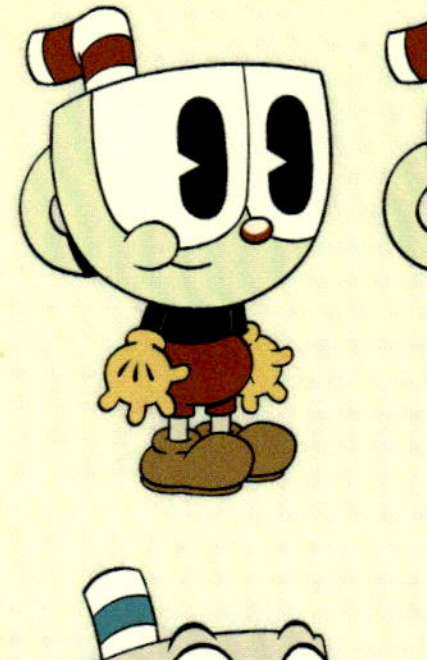

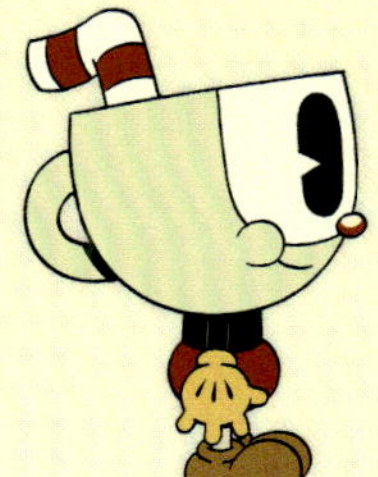

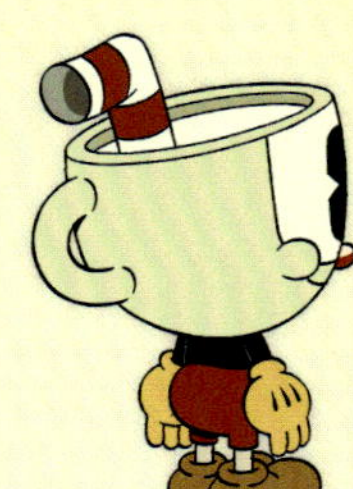

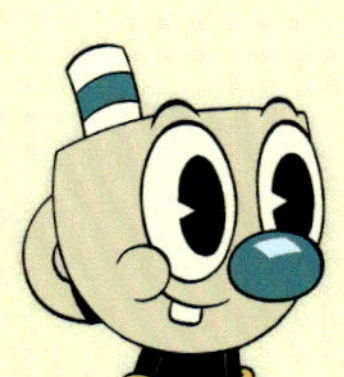

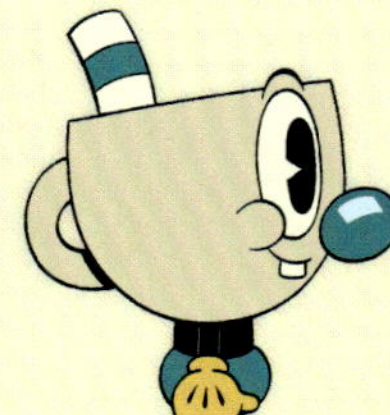

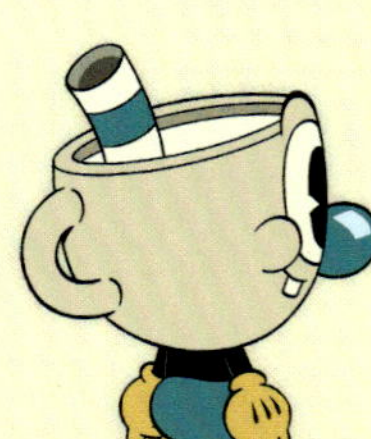

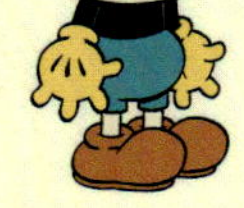

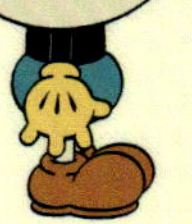

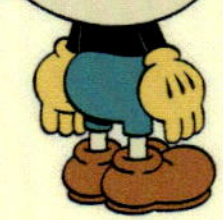

LI'L CUPS AND MUGS DESIGNS BY ADAM PALOIAN AND ADAM FAY.

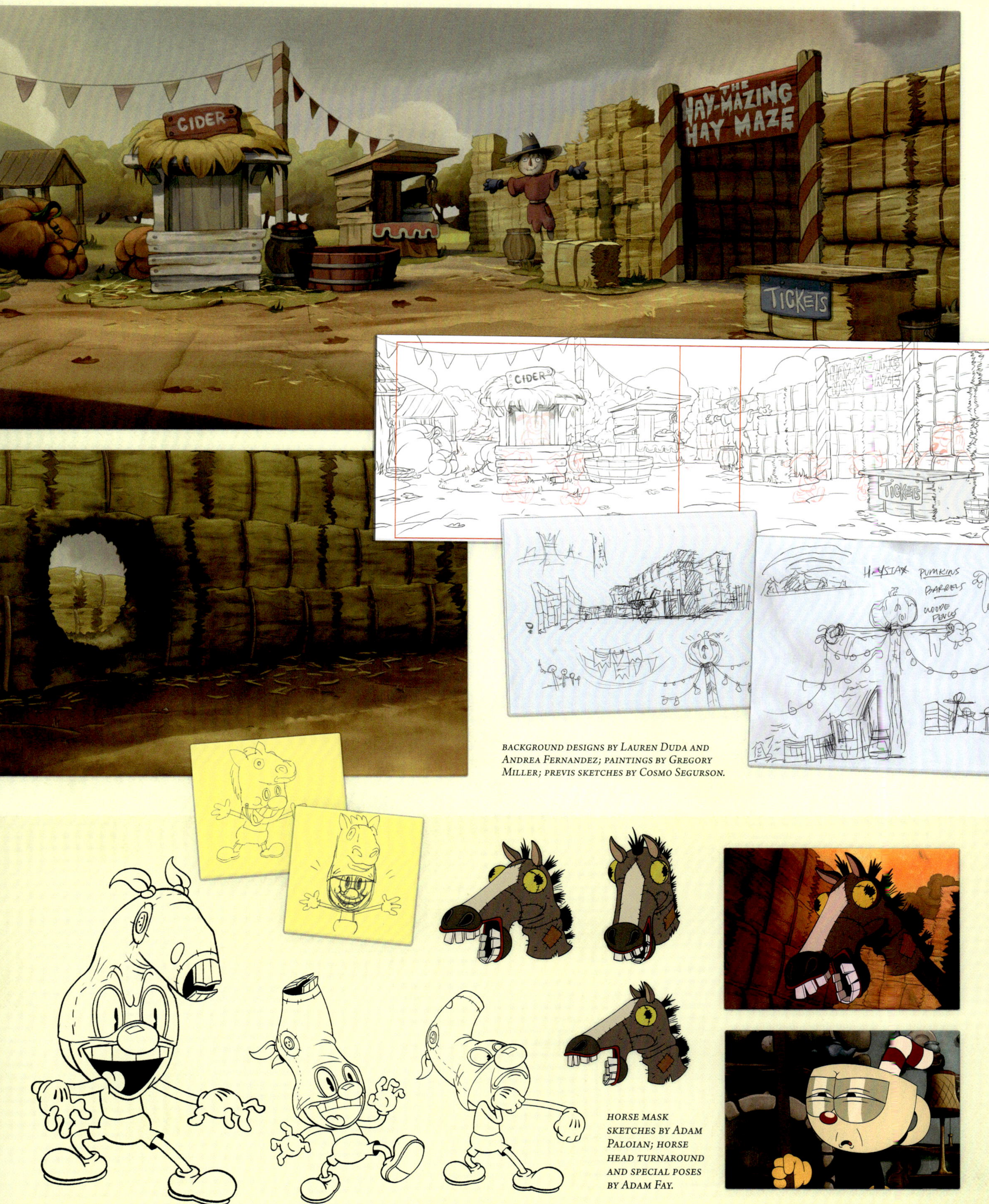

Background designs by Lauren Duda and Andrea Fernandez; paintings by Gregory Miller; previs sketches by Cosmo Segurson.

Horse mask sketches by Adam Paloian; horse head turnaround and special poses by Adam Fay.

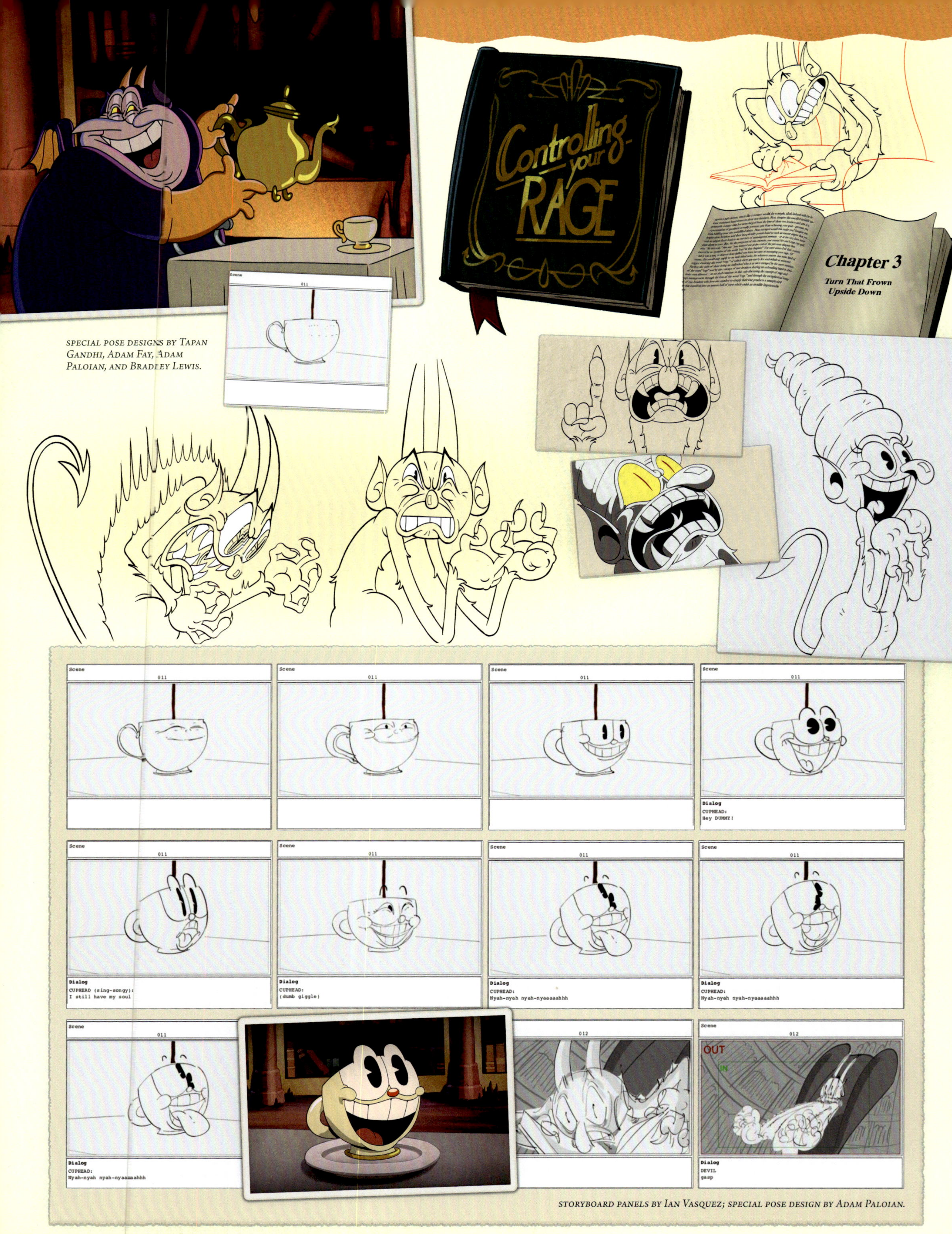

Special pose designs by Tapan Gandhi, Adam Fay, Adam Paloian, and Bradley Lewis.

Storyboard panels by Ian Vasquez; special pose design by Adam Paloian.

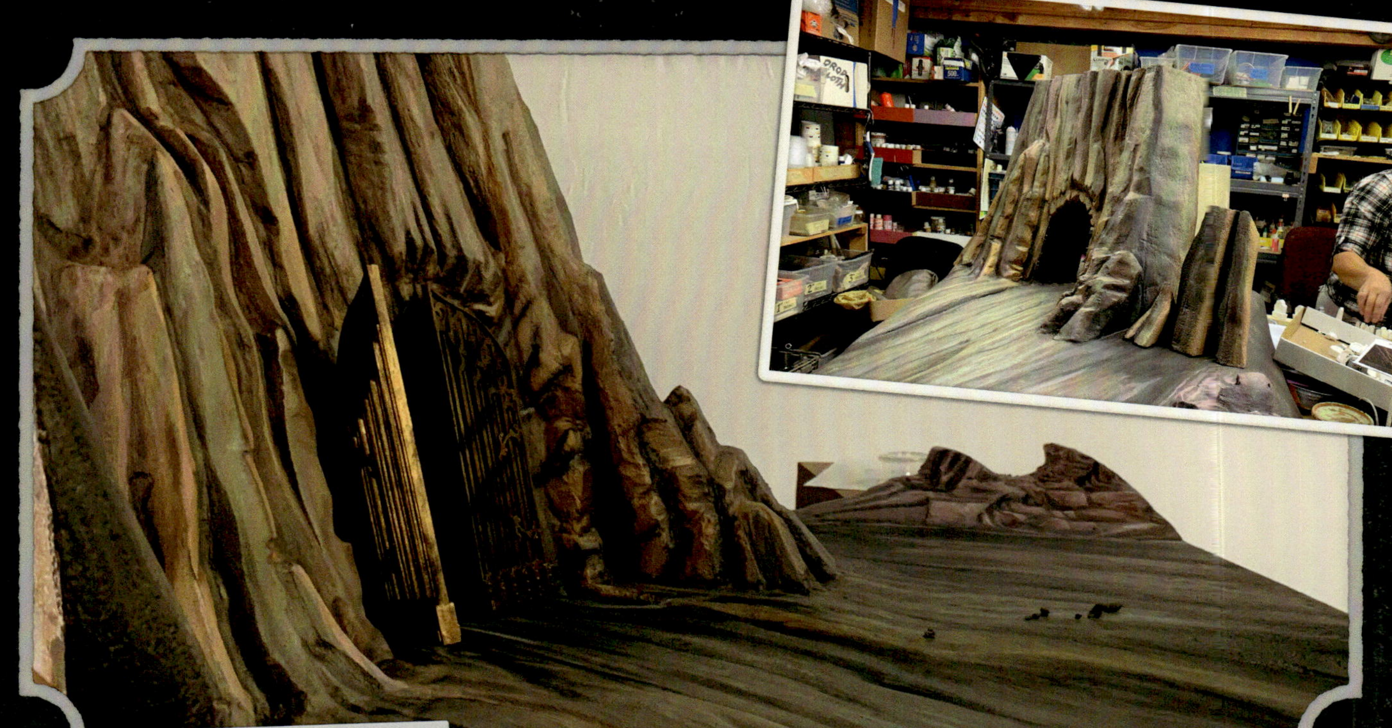

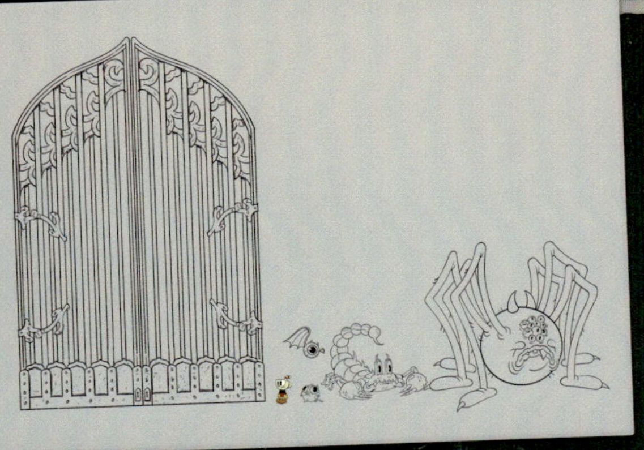

GATES OF HELL DETAIL BY COSMO SEGURSON; STOP-MO PRODUCTION BY SCREEN NOVELTIES.

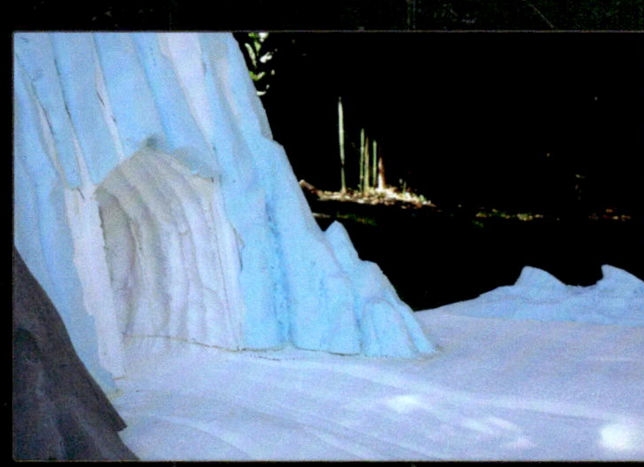

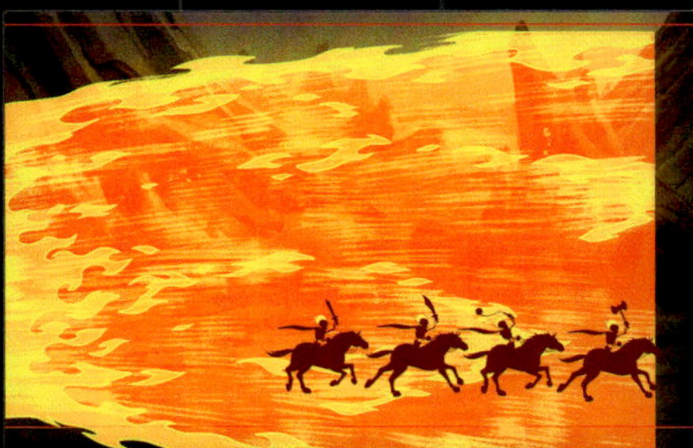

◆ STOP-MO SPOTLIGHT ◆

THE GATES OF HELL

→ **ANDREA:** Screen Novelties is so amazing. Sometimes we can just send them a color key, and they nail it. Other times, we need the set to track more closely with the characters, and we really need a meet-up between the background that's painted and the 3D elements. We're also doing matte paintings to fill in some of the blanks. In this case, all they needed was a color key.

MARK: We knew we had to switch out the gates when they crashed open. What you don't see behind the scenes is all these little balls of wax and wire hidden out of the camera's view to hold the gates open. We realized the hinges were loose. The scrappy animator in me said, "Use whatever you can to make it stick!" At the back end of the gate, where the camera's not seeing it, I would take little pieces of wax to get just the tiniest bit of increment.

SEAMUS: That stiff wax is great, because if you can hide it from the lens, you can get those nice little increments. You don't always need technology to solve every problem.

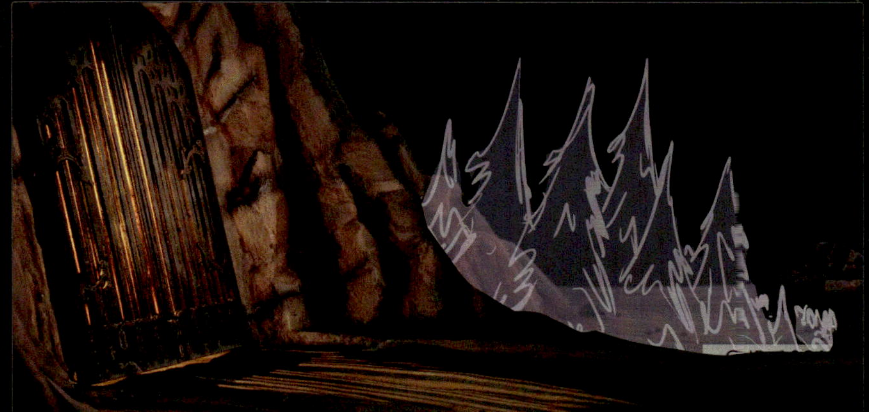

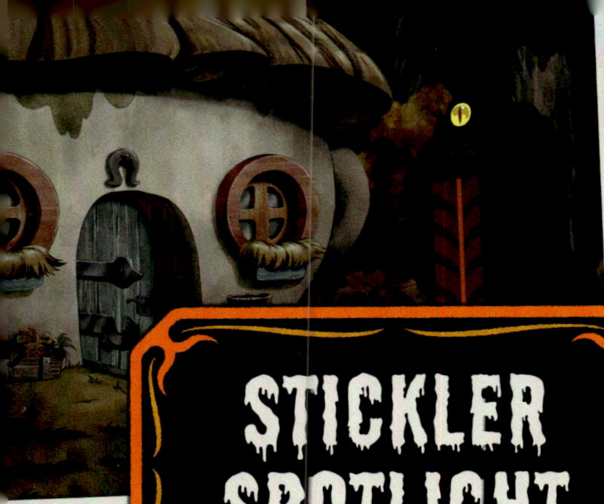

STICKLER SPOTLIGHT

(voiced by Andrew Morgado)

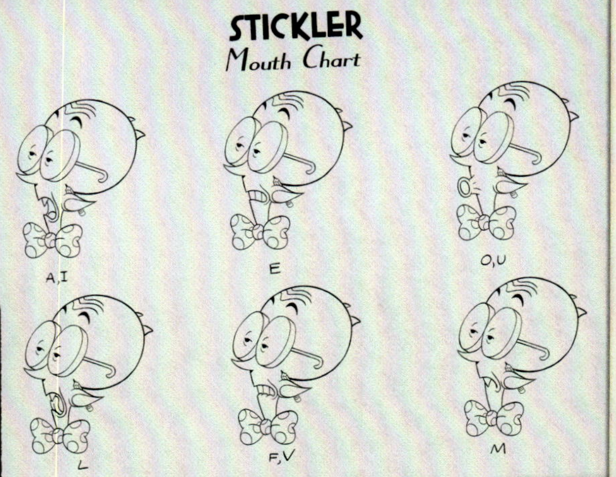

STICKLER
Mouth Chart

A,I
E
O,U
L
F,V
M

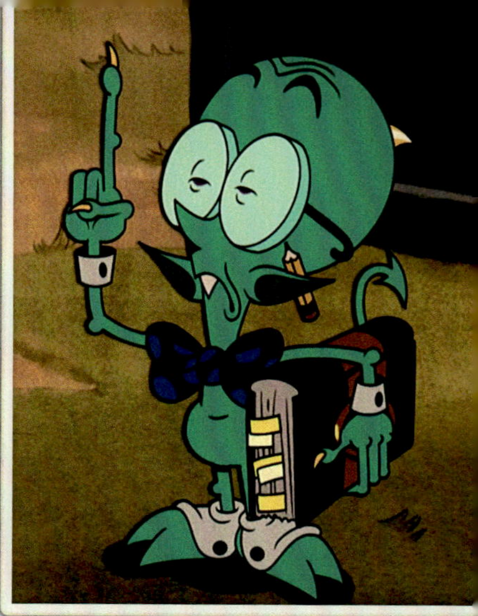

Stickler mouth chart and special pose designs by Adam Paloian.

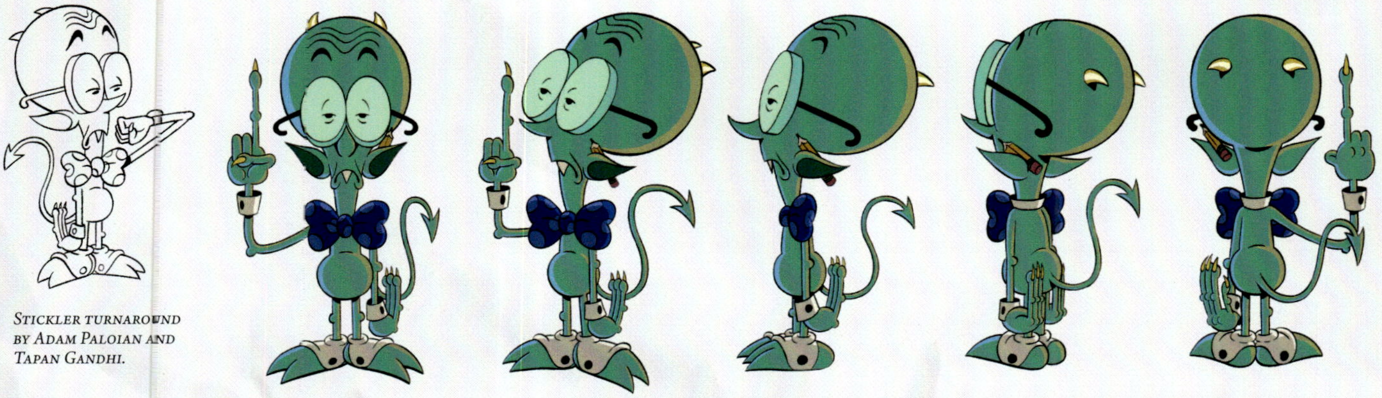

Stickler turnaround by Adam Paloian and Tapan Gandhi.

→ **DAVE:** Stickler is one of our best characters. Other than Cuphead, he's the character that irritates the Devil the most. He was Deeki's creation, and his personality seemed fully formed the moment we met him. That character added a whole other flavor to the Devil's story.

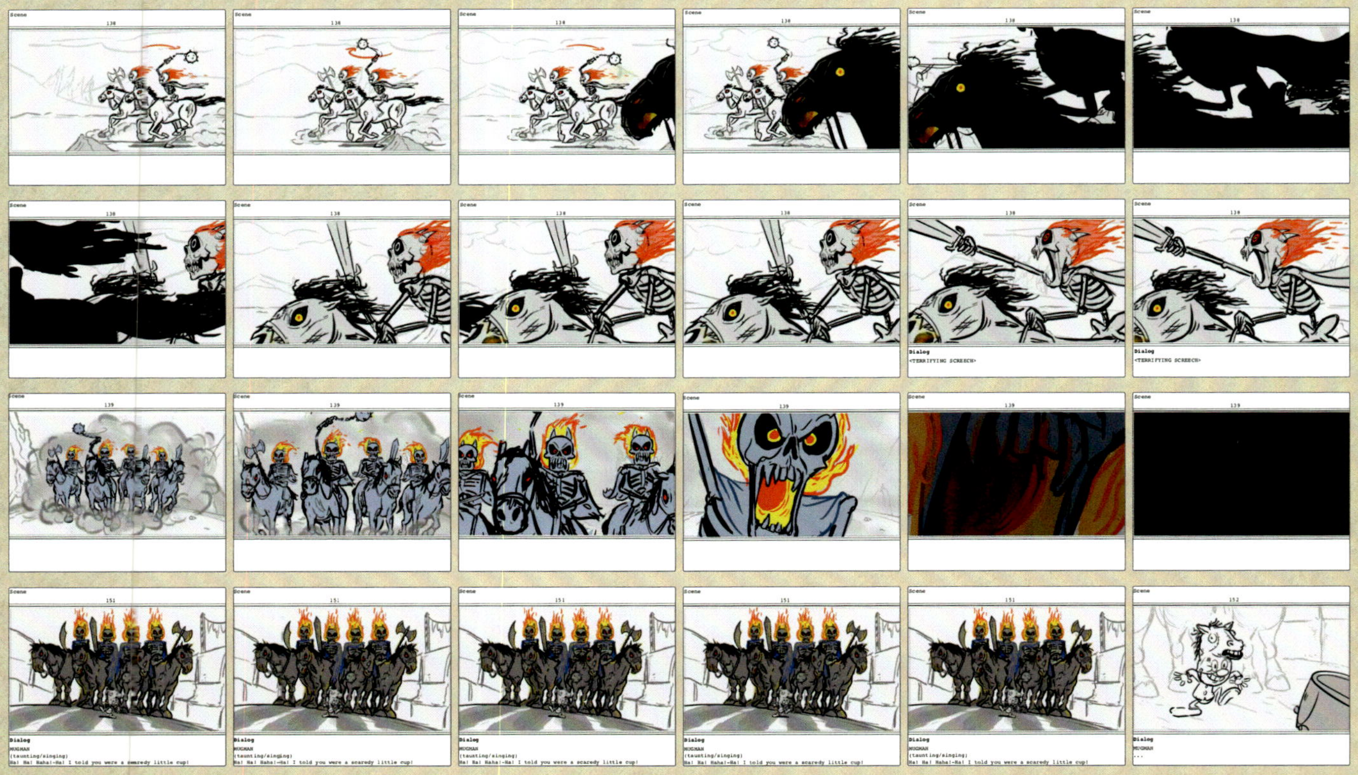

Storyboard panels by Benjamin Arcand.

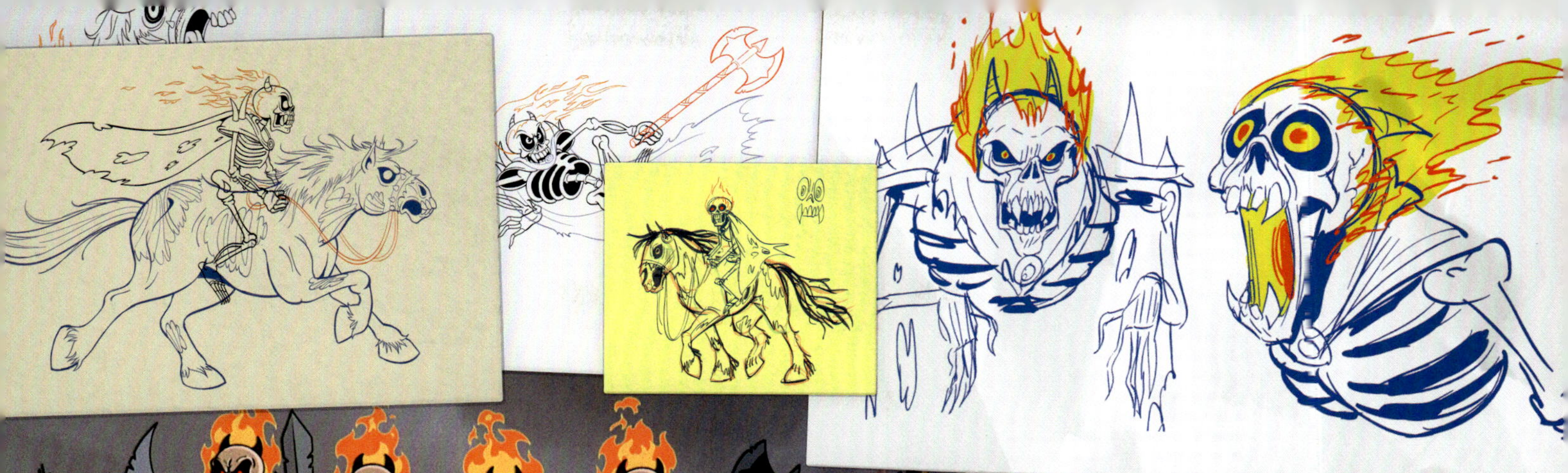

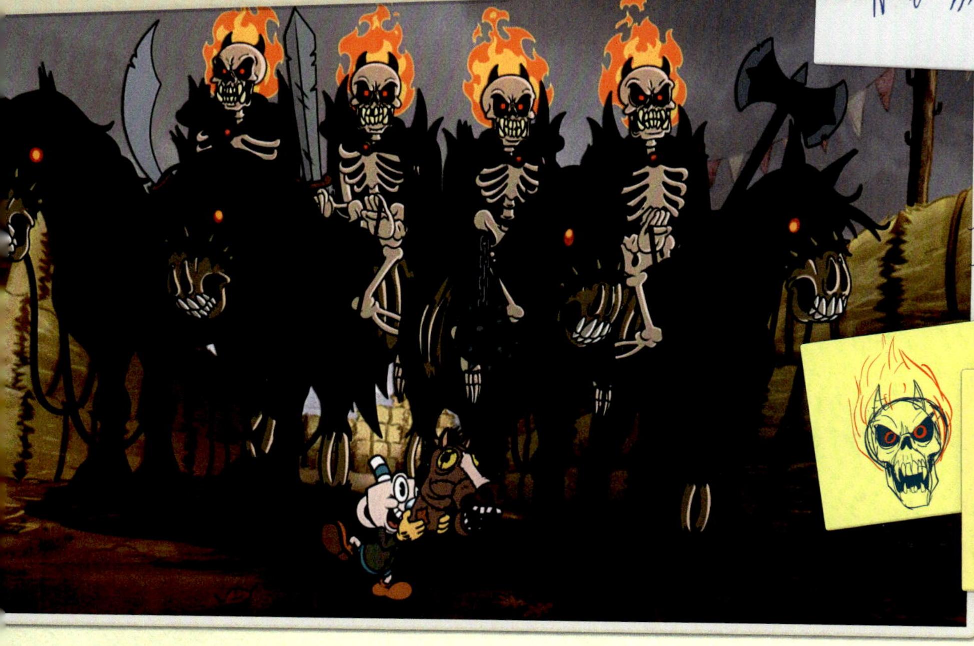

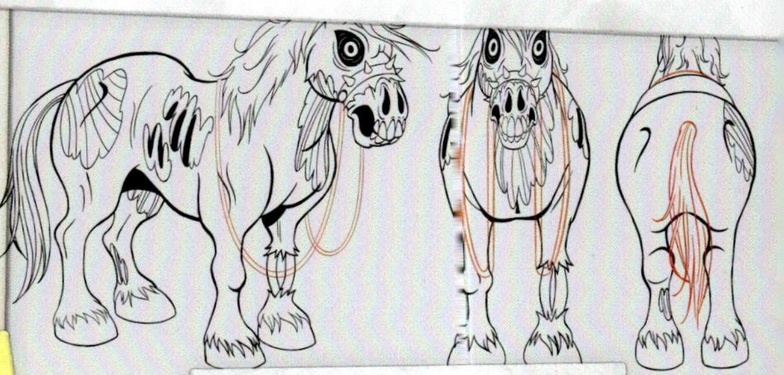

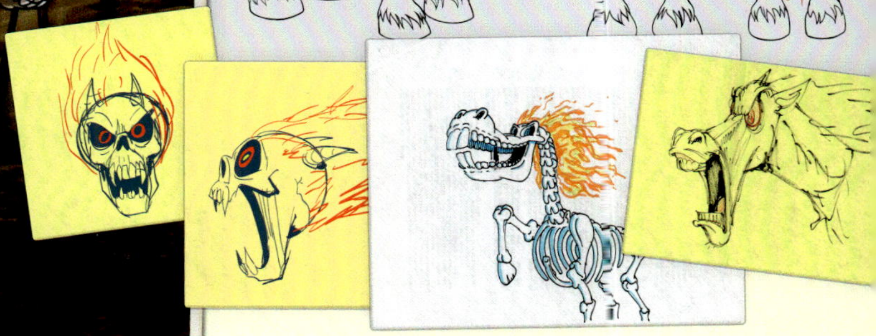

Story room sketches of the Four Horsemen by Adam Paloian and Clay Morrow.

Horseman and horse turnarounds and special poses by Adam Paloian and Mike Fontanelli.

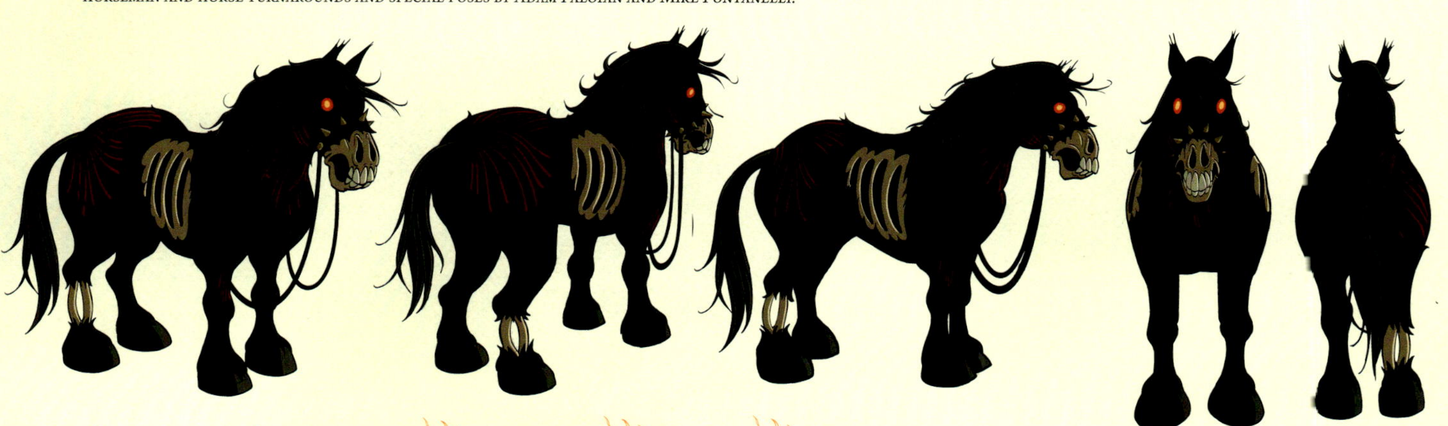

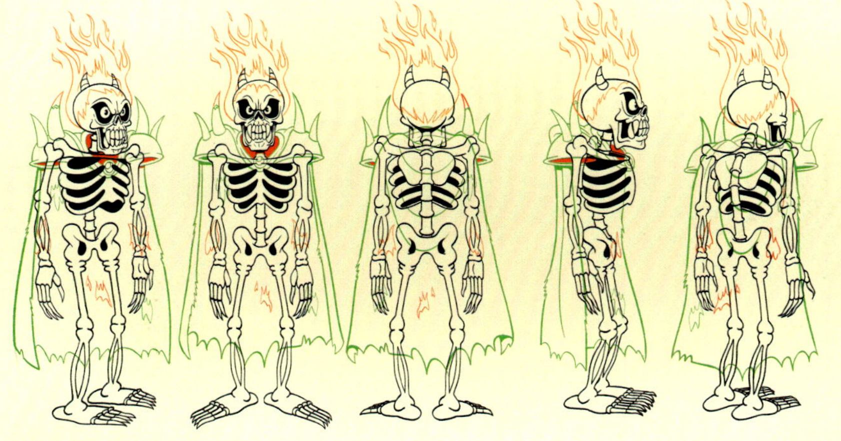

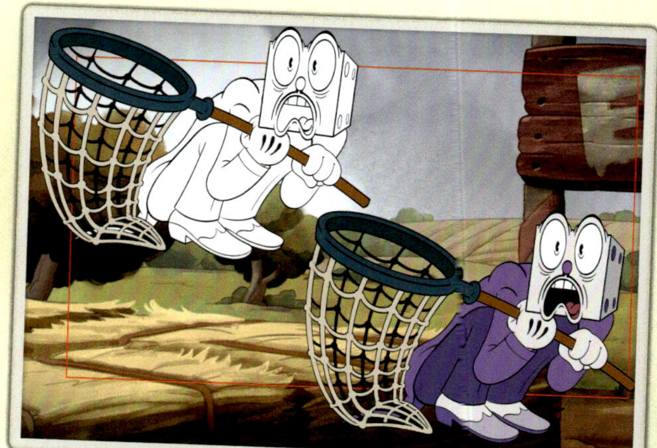

King Dice special pose by Bradley Lewis.

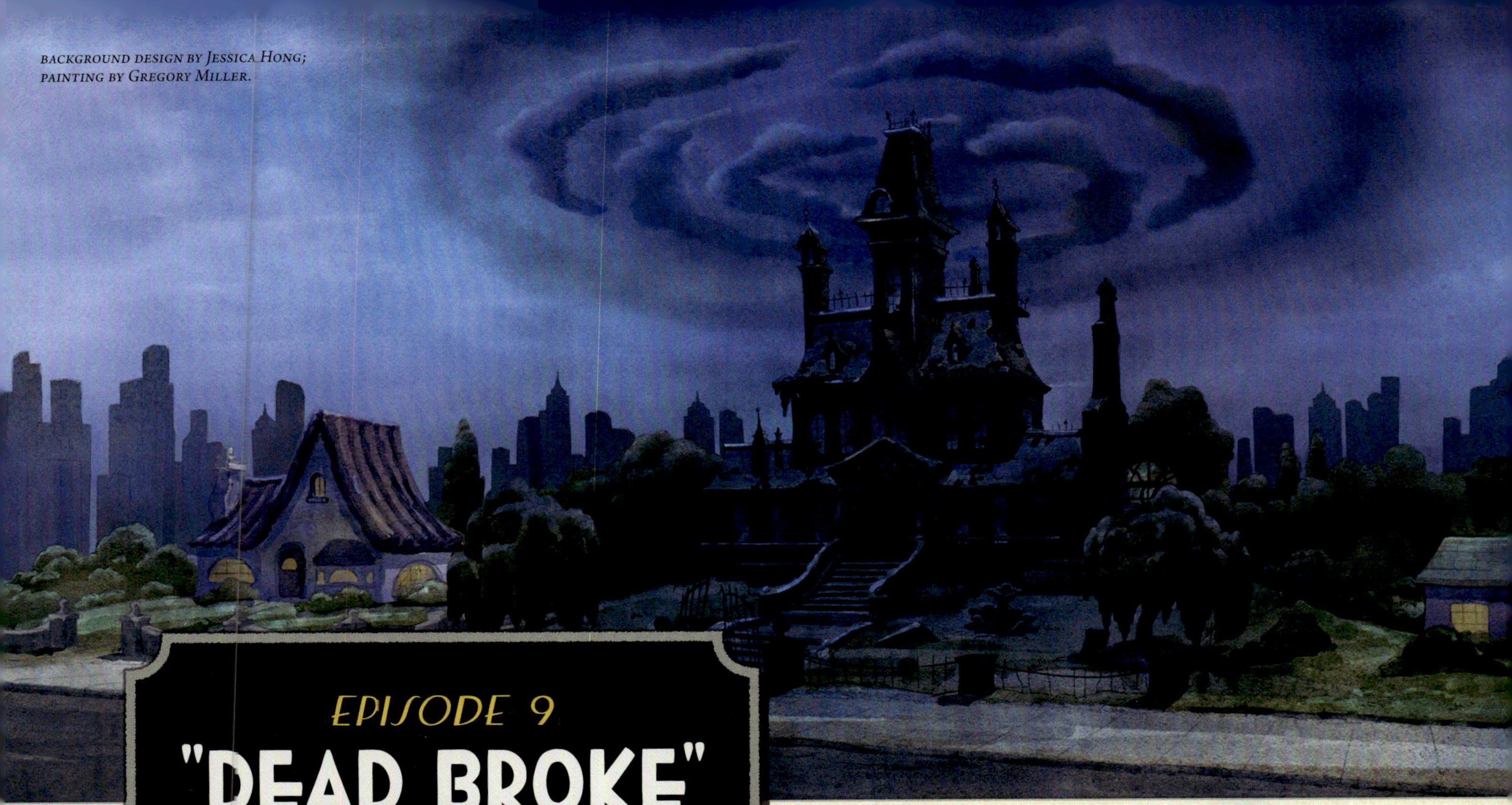

BACKGROUND DESIGN BY JESSICA HONG; PAINTING BY GREGORY MILLER.

EPISODE 9

"DEAD BROKE"

→ **ANDREA:** This episode happened because during a production meeting, I begged for a smaller episode to lighten the load on the design team. I also asked for a Chalice episode—not for the design team, just because I like Chalice.

DEEKI: I pitched a ghost-hunting episode with one hundred percent reuse. Instead of a mansion, it was the grand reopening of the Fly Trap, with ghosts scaring away the customers. Dave wasn't feeling it and suggested a mansion inhabited by four ghost sisters. I said, "No problem, but you have to tell Andrea."

ANDREA: At ten a.m. it was one hundred percent reuse, and at ten thirty there was a mansion and four new characters. Frustrating? Yes. Worth it? *Also* yes. I love this episode.

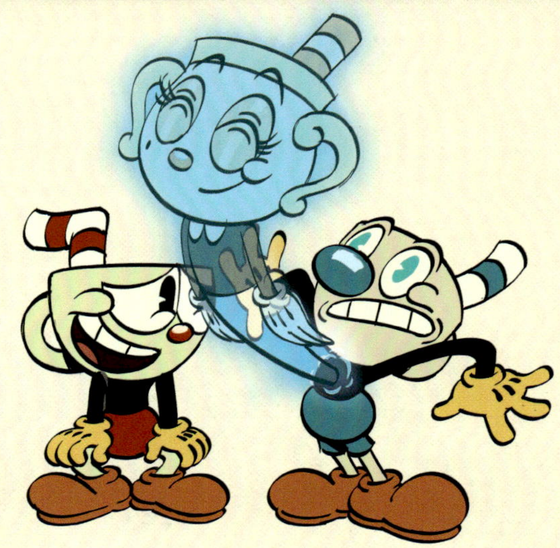

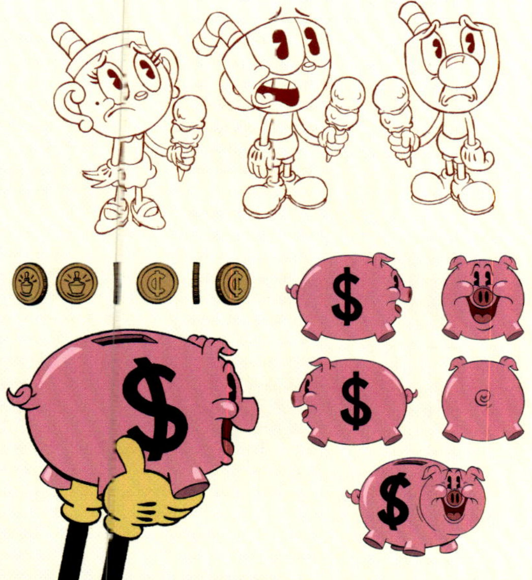

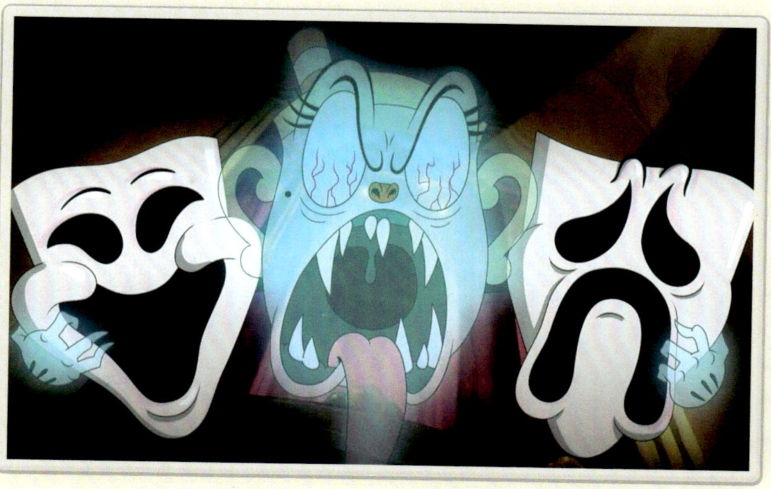

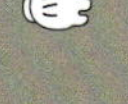

PIGGY BANK TURNAROUND BY MARTIN WITTIG; SPECIAL POSE DESIGNS BY MARTIN WITTIG, DAVE WASSON, AND ADAM PALOIAN.

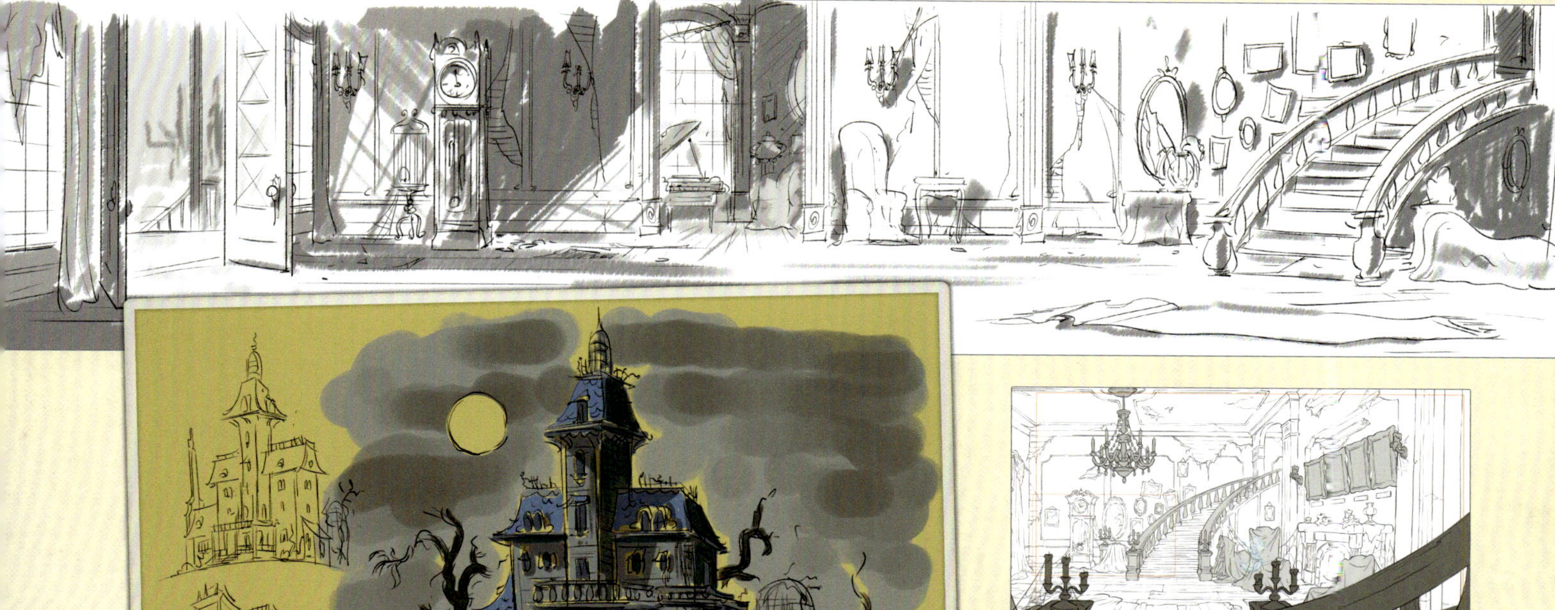

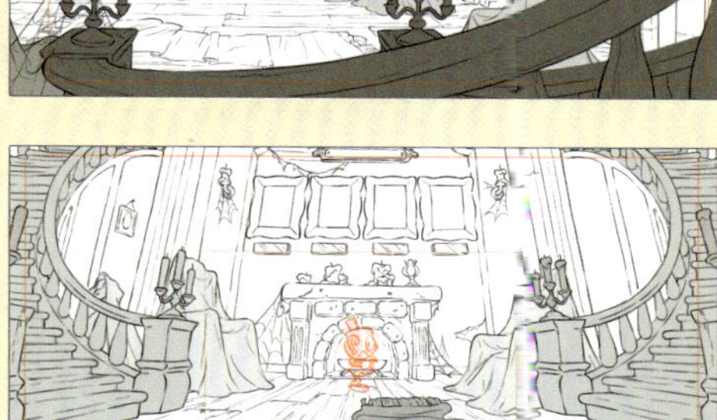

→ **ANDREA:** Everyone had a different idea of what a mansion should look like. Was it going to have a Georgian sensibility? Was it Haunted Mansion–style Southern gothic? Or something like Cruella de Vil's mansion, which is more English countryside? It was tricky to get everyone to sign off on an aesthetic.

Previs sketches by Cosmo Segurson; background designs by Jessica Hong.

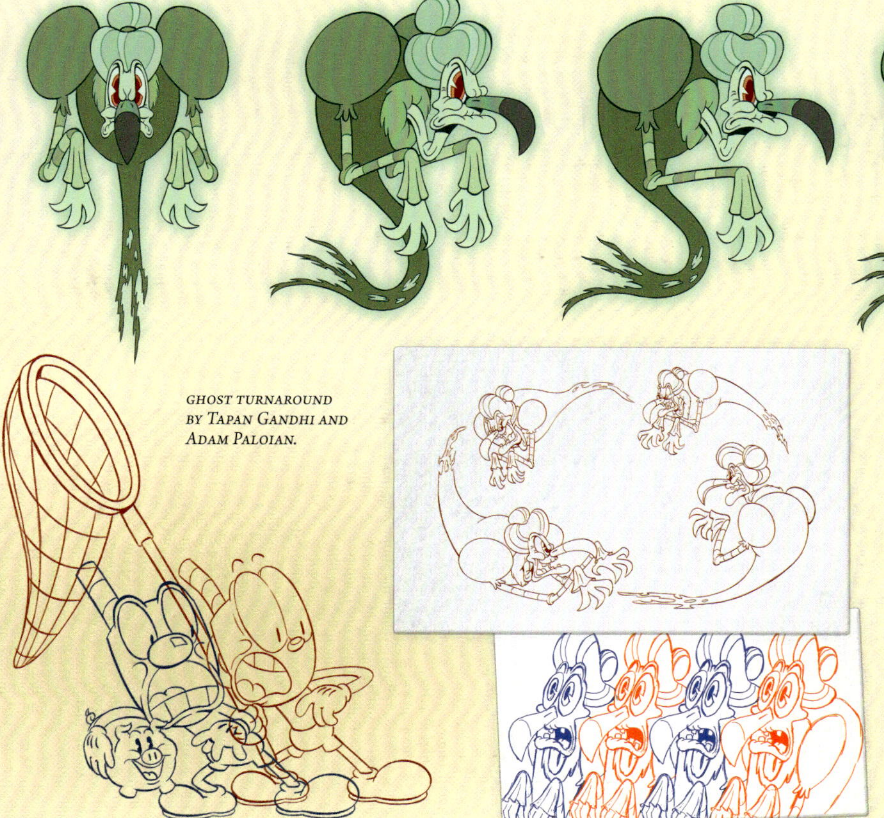

Ghost turnaround by Tapan Gandhi and Adam Paloian.

→ **ADAM P:** We leaned into a lot of the tropes of cartoon horror from the 1930s, like a flying dresser and levitating objects. It's funny when Chalice does it, but the ghosts are more of a threat, because they actually want to trap them in these paintings. It was a nice, safe version of horror where no one's going to die—they're just eternally trapped in a painting.

Special pose designs by Tapan Gandhi and Dave Wasson.

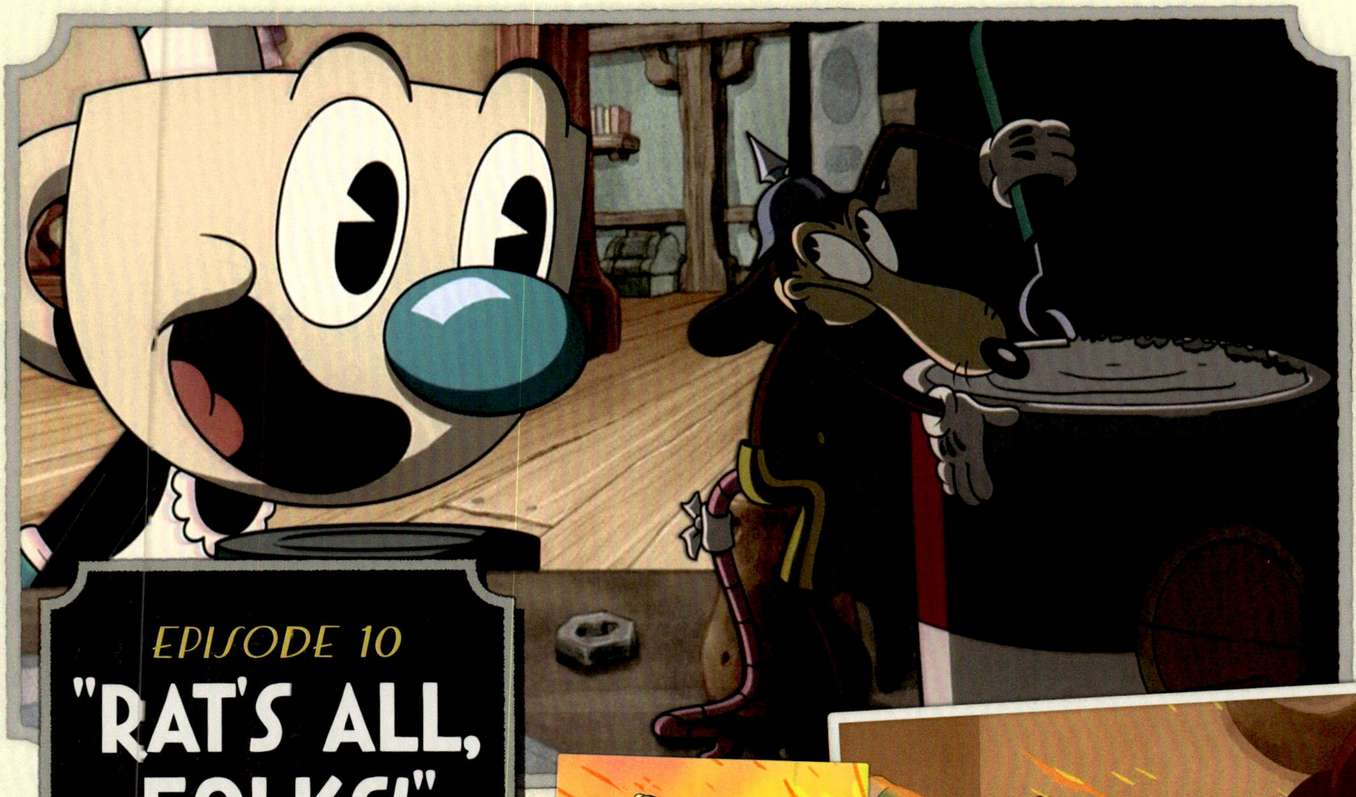

EPISODE 10

"RAT'S ALL, FOLKS!"

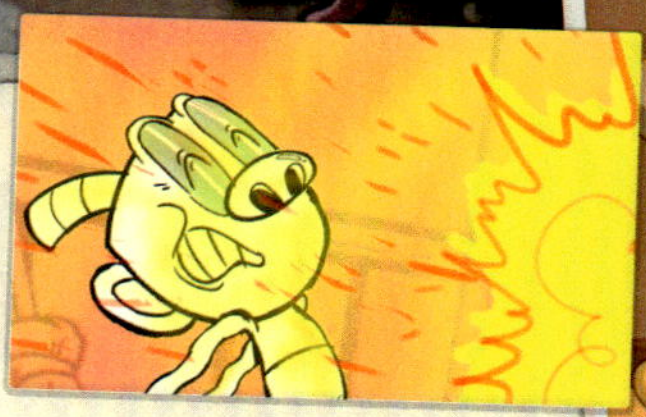

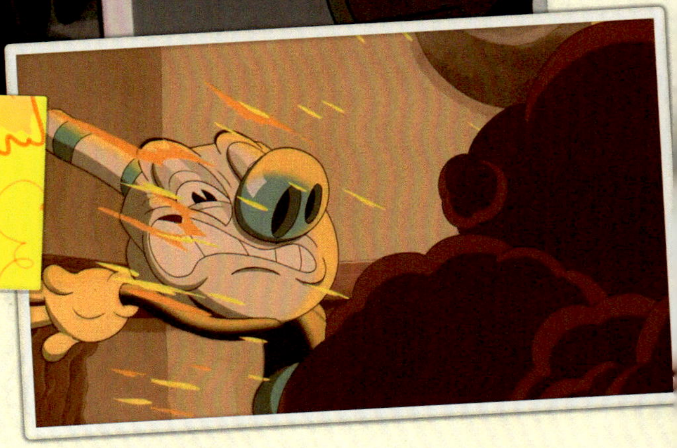

→ **FERNANDO:** Werner needed to have an episode. I love that character. He's probably my favorite boss from the game.

NICK LAUER, *THE CUPHEAD SHOW!* STORYBOARD REVISIONIST: Fernando asked me if I wanted to help him with an idea to pitch at a story lunch. I didn't know anything about writing a story, so we started out way too big. The cottage was going to turn inside out and have gears and conveyor belts everywhere.

FERNANDO: Initially we thought Werner could be an enemy to Elder Kettle, because he's from a war, and Elder Kettle's a veteran. We thought of an episode where he's their new neighbor and just wants to live a peaceful life, but Elder Kettle doesn't trust him because of the war. But then Cosmo had the idea that Werner should be rat sized.

NICK: We talked to Deeki about it and figured out how to not complicate it so it could actually be made. That was really fun: to come up with an episode and go through the writing process and see it evolve. I'd never done that before, and I learned a ton by doing that. The Werner episode taught me how to construct a satisfying story.

BACKGROUND DESIGN BY PAT MARCONETT; PAINTING BY MICHELLE THIES; STORYBOARD PANEL BY ZOË MOSS; SPECIAL POSE DESIGNS BY MIKE FONTANELLI.

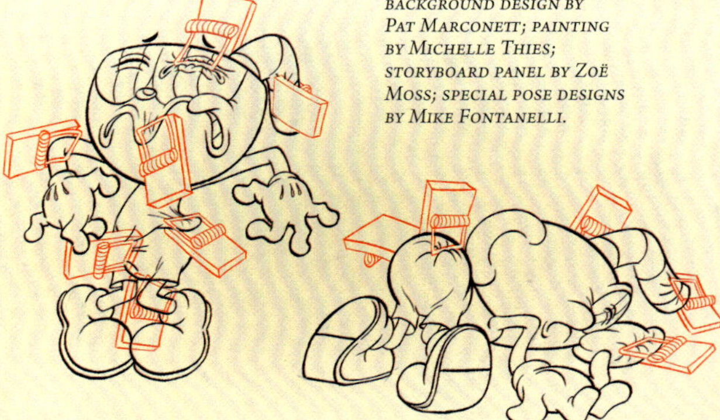

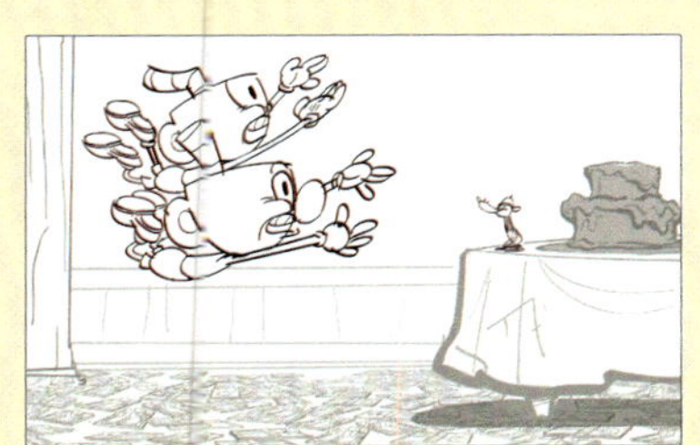

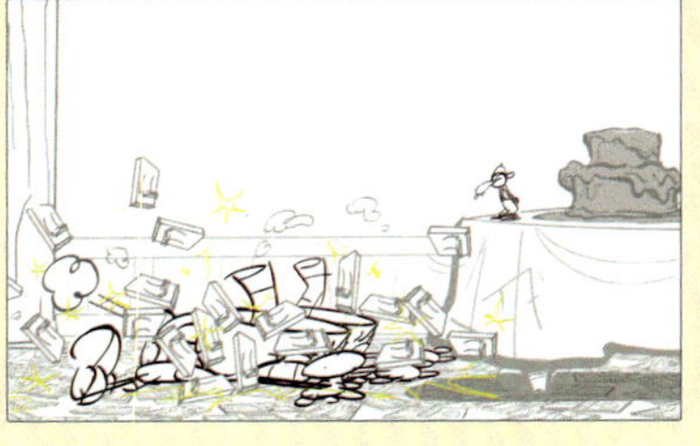

STORYBOARD PANELS BY KARL HADRIKA.

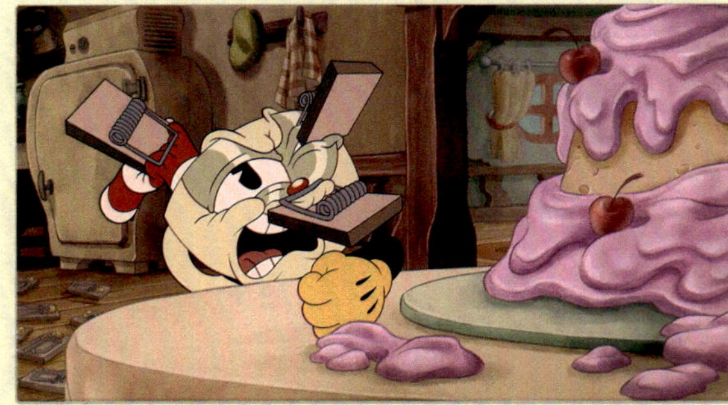

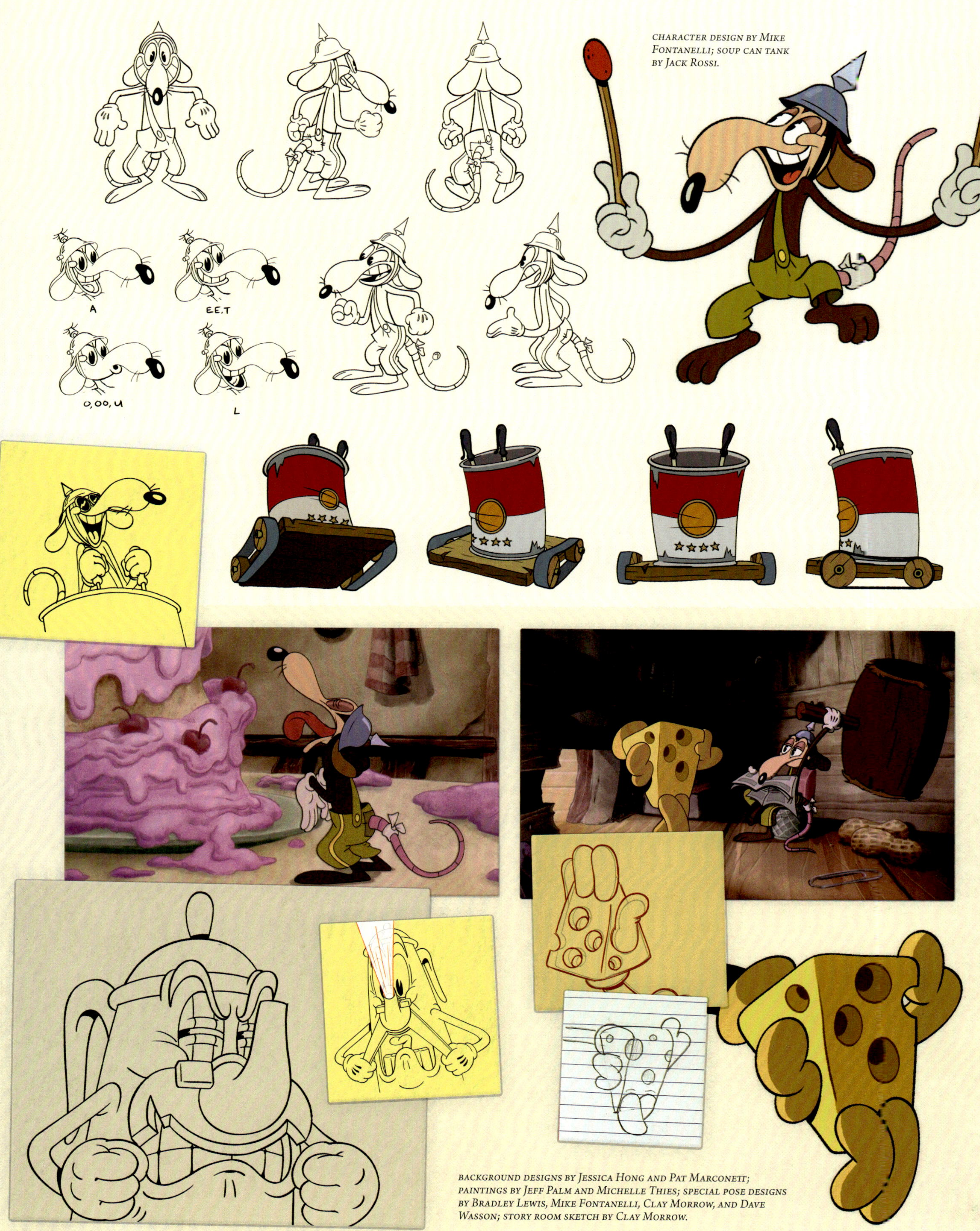

Character design by Mike Fontanelli; soup can tank by Jack Rossi.

Background designs by Jessica Hong and Pat Marconett; paintings by Jeff Palm and Michelle Thies; special pose designs by Bradley Lewis, Mike Fontanelli, Clay Morrow, and Dave Wasson; story room sketch by Clay Morrow.

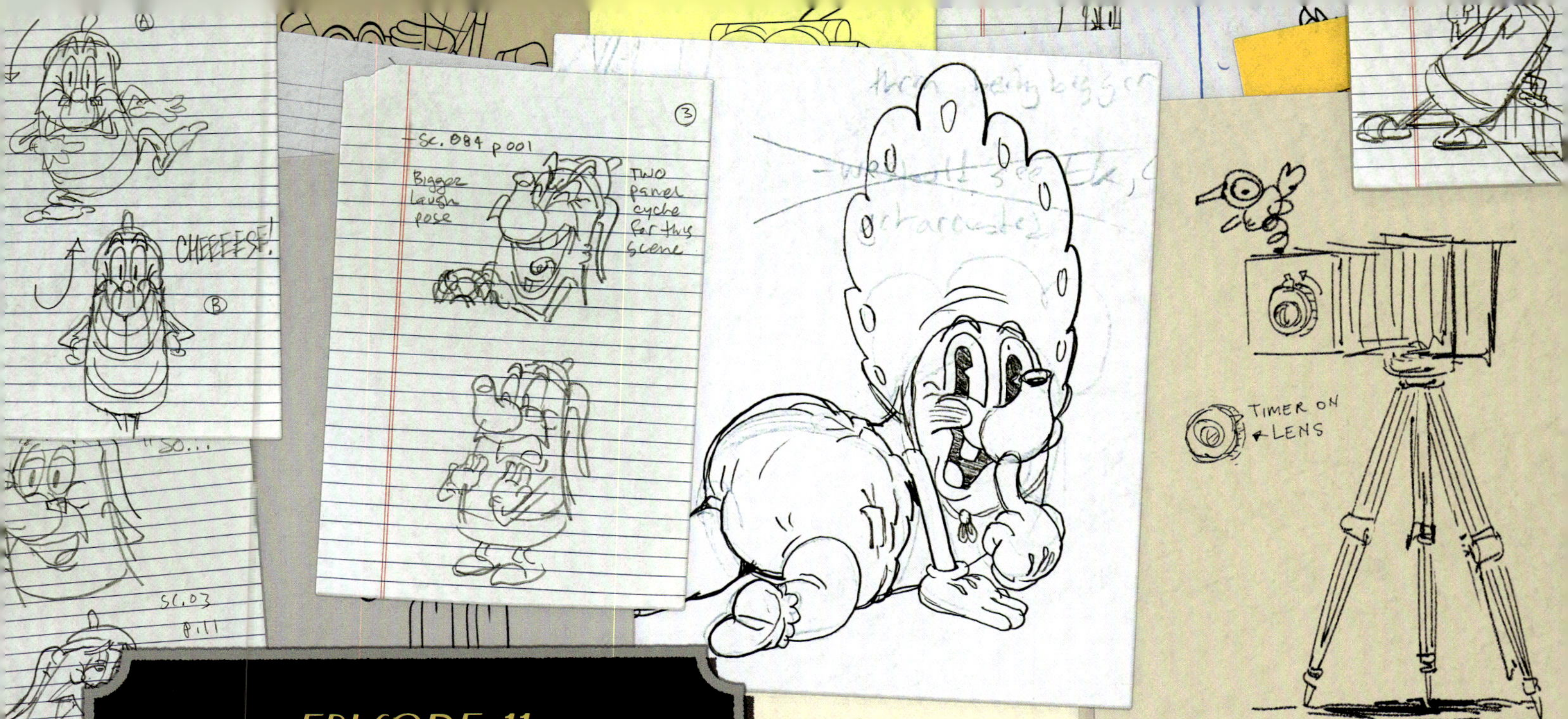

DIRECTOR'S THUMBNAIL SKETCHES BY CLAY MORROW; DIAPER BABY STORY ROOM SKETCH BY ADAM PALOIAN.

EPISODE 11

"SAY CHEESE!"

→ **DAN BECKER, *THE CUPHEAD SHOW!* STORYBOARD ARTIST:** My favorite episode is "Say Cheese!," because I love Elder Kettle's complete insanity. He's sweet to Cuphead and Mugman, he cares about them, and yet he also tries to kill them on occasion.

DAVE: He loves the boys, and he values being the wise authority figure—but that doesn't make him invulnerable from sinking to their level. Very much like my own experiences in parenting.

CLAY: That episode started with a springboard that I did, with Cuphead and Mugman seeing Elder Kettle in an old advertisement. He does not handle it well.

KENNEDY: At the start, Kettle just wants a family photo, and it's very sweet. *That* Kettle is very different from *unhinged* Kettle, who's very different from cool young Kettle burning down billboards.

DAN: The contrast in tones makes it really inspiring to work on. Something dynamic and funny is always happening.

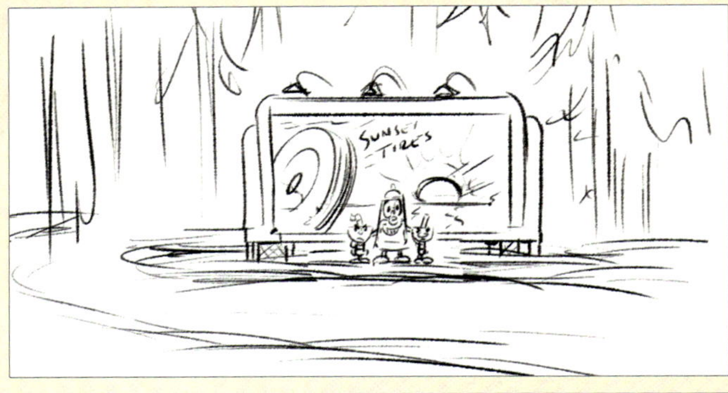

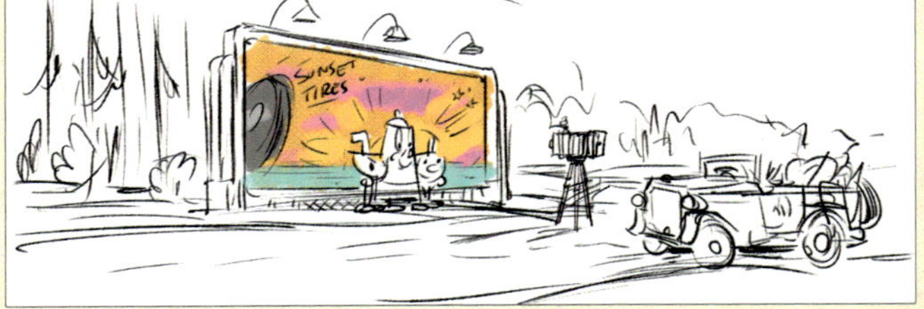

BILLBOARD AND CAMERA CONCEPTS BY COSMO SEGURSON; STORYBOARD PANELS BY DAN BECKER.

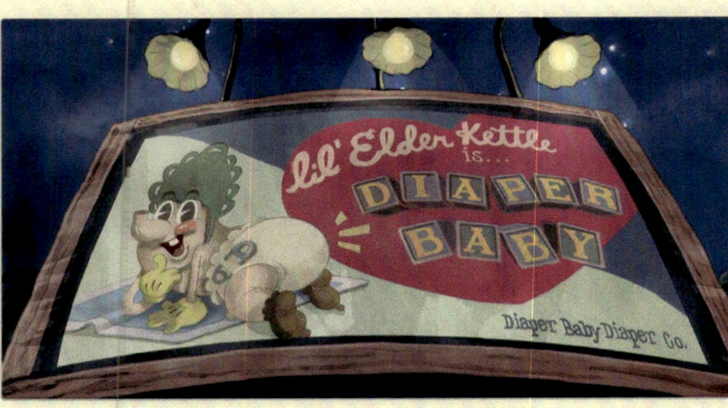

BILLBOARD LAYOUT BY LAUREN DUDA; PAINTING BY MALLORY CARLSON.

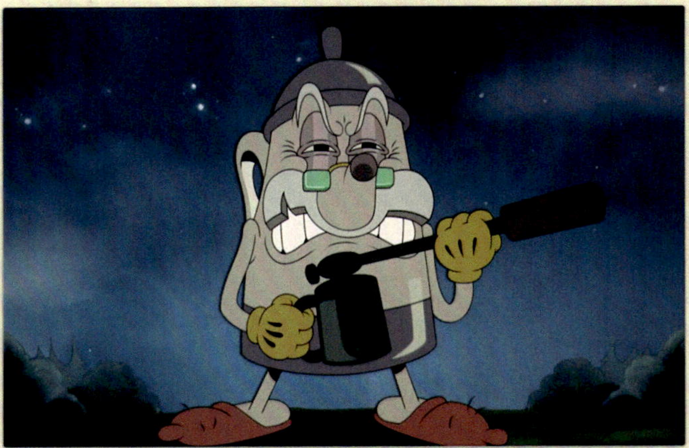

ELDER KETTLE WITH FLAMETHROWER SPECIAL POSE BY DAVE WASSON.

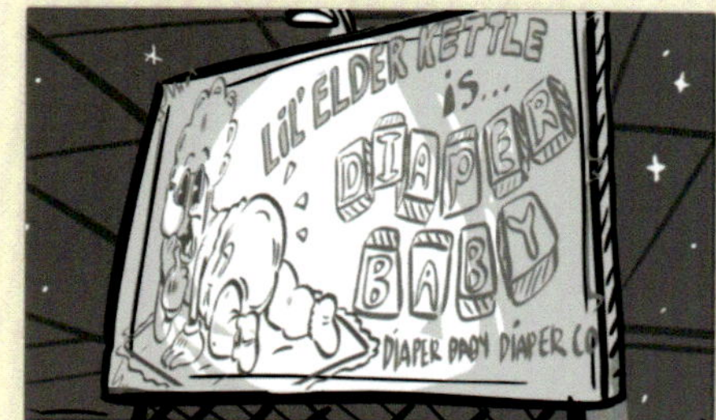

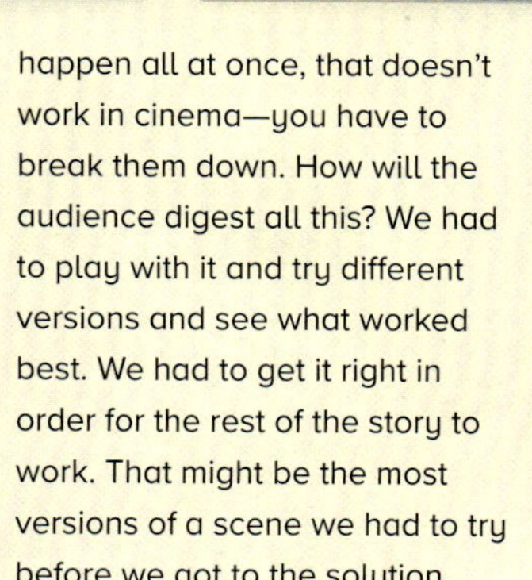

CLAY: Staging the billboard reveal was so difficult. It seems so obvious now, but the mechanics were tricky, because so much is happening all in one moment. In your mind, it plays, you accept that it happens. But when you're showing it visually, what is the order of the sequence of events? Whenever you have a bunch of things that would basically happen all at once, that doesn't work in cinema—you have to break them down. How will the audience digest all this? We had to play with it and try different versions and see what worked best. We had to get it right in order for the rest of the story to work. That might be the most versions of a scene we had to try before we got to the solution.

ABOVE: STORYBOARD PANELS BY KENNEDY TARRELL. LEFT AND BELOW: STORYBOARD PANELS BY DAN BECKER.

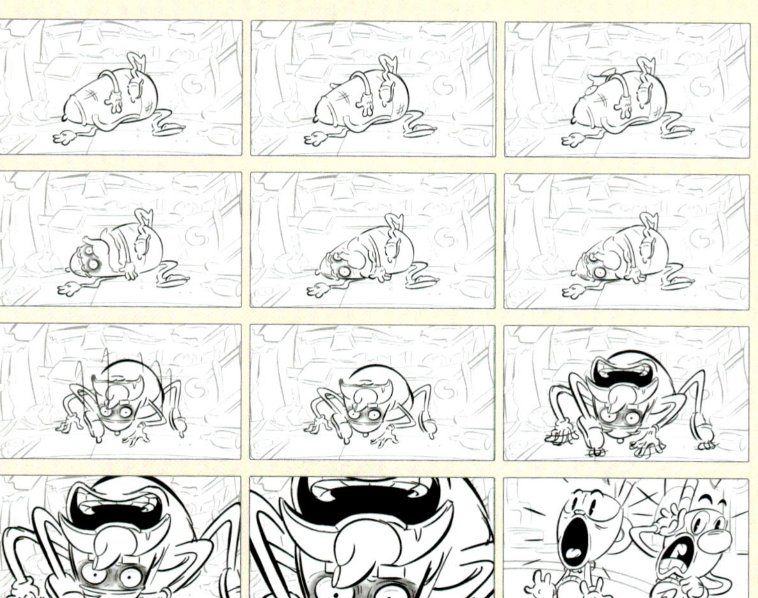

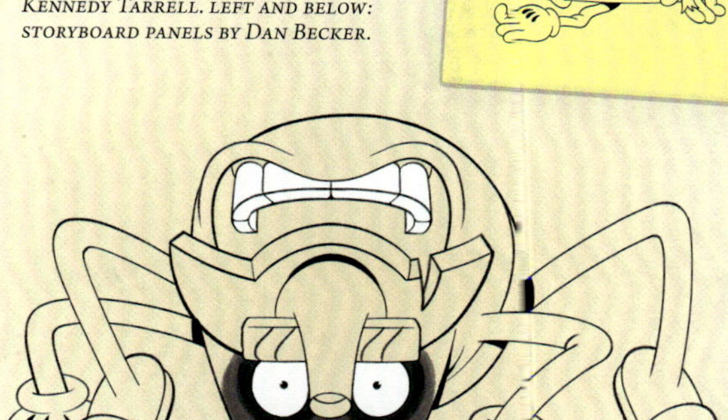

DAN: When I first heard Deeki's card pitches, I would latch on to the most inspiring things. In "Say Cheese!," as soon as I heard the "spider crawl," I started drawing—I always start with the thing that makes me laugh the most.

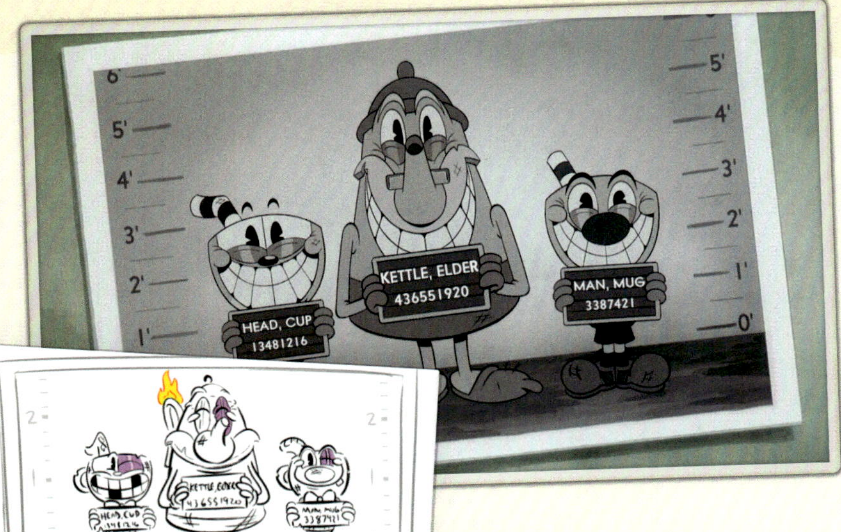

ELI: Mug shots and mayhem aside, the real through line of their relationship is the love they have for each other.

CLAY: Kettle is tearing up, he's finally got this thing he wanted, and he's not bothered by the fact that they're going to jail. That's the most satisfying kind of ending to me—when something like going to jail is a positive.

SPECIAL POSE DESIGNS BY BRADLEY LEWIS.

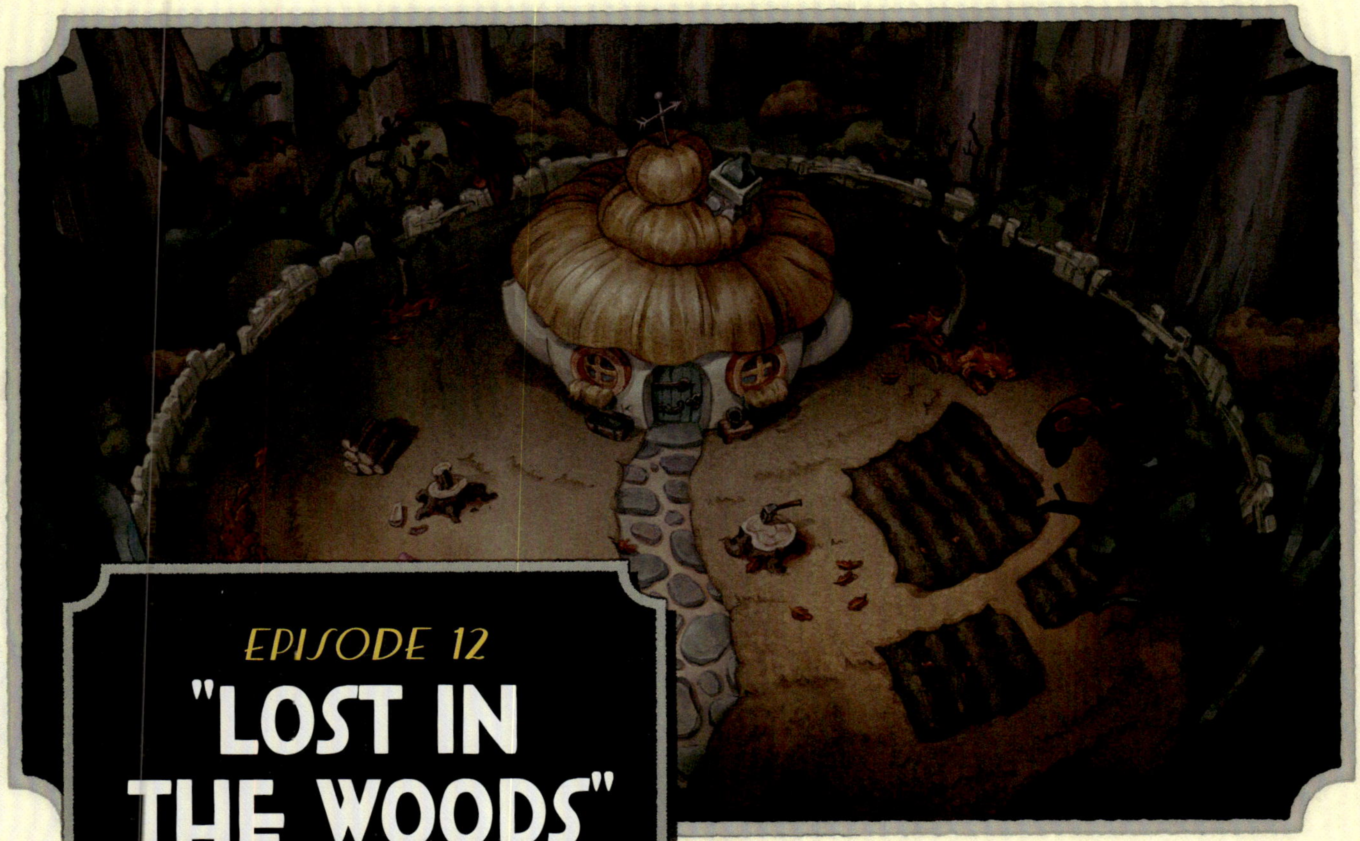

EPISODE 12

"LOST IN THE WOODS"

→ **PAT:** There were a ton of scenes in forests in this show, so depending on the episode, we had to find ways to make each location feel unique.

ANDREA: Sometimes it's autumn, sometimes it's deep winter, sometimes they're in Alpine-style setups, then it's a spooky forest or a cemetery forest . . . There's a surprising number of forests in the Inkwell Isles. Just in this one episode, we're in the forest across multiple seasons.

BACKGROUND DESIGN BY JESSICA HONG; PAINTING BY MICHELLE THIES; SQUIRREL TURNAROUND AND POSES BY MARTIN WITTIG.

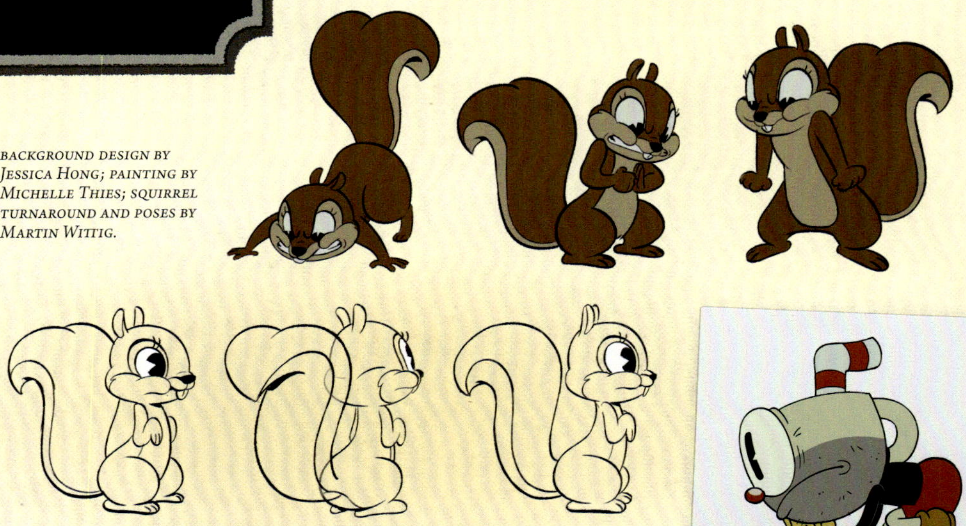

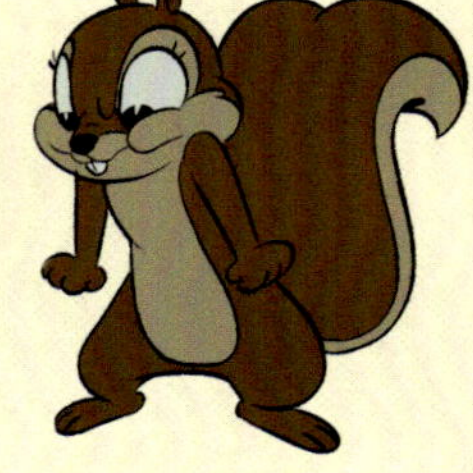

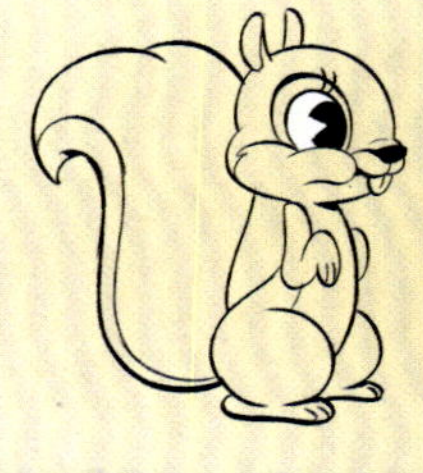

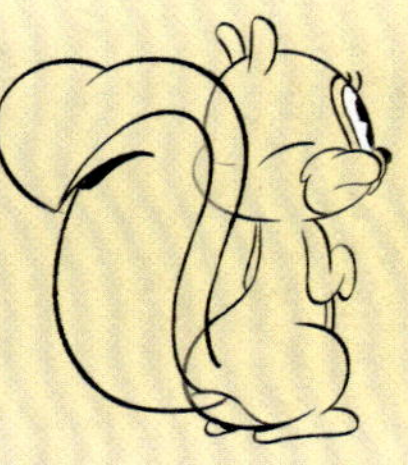

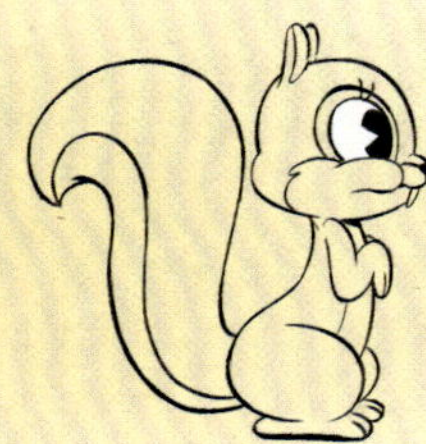

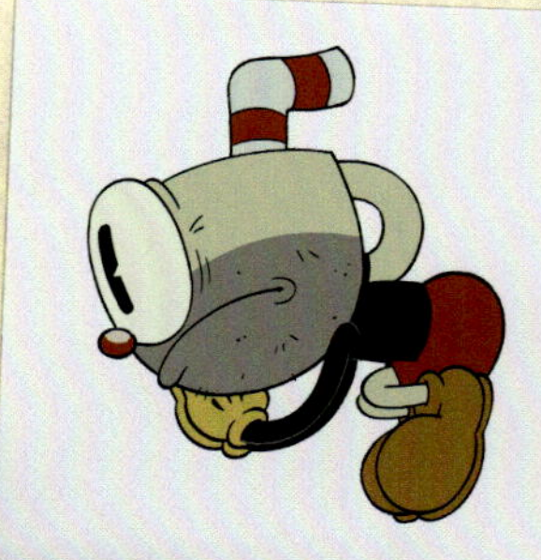

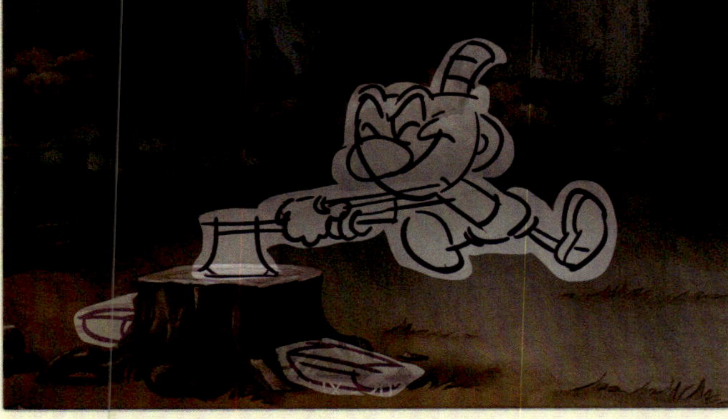

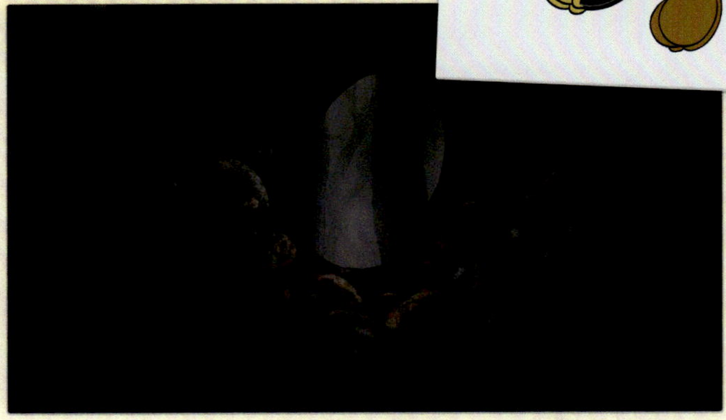

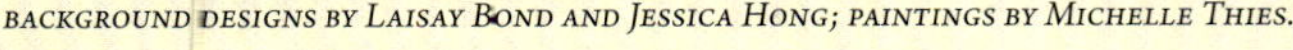

BACKGROUND DESIGNS BY LAISAY BOND AND JESSICA HONG; PAINTINGS BY MICHELLE THIES.

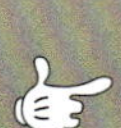

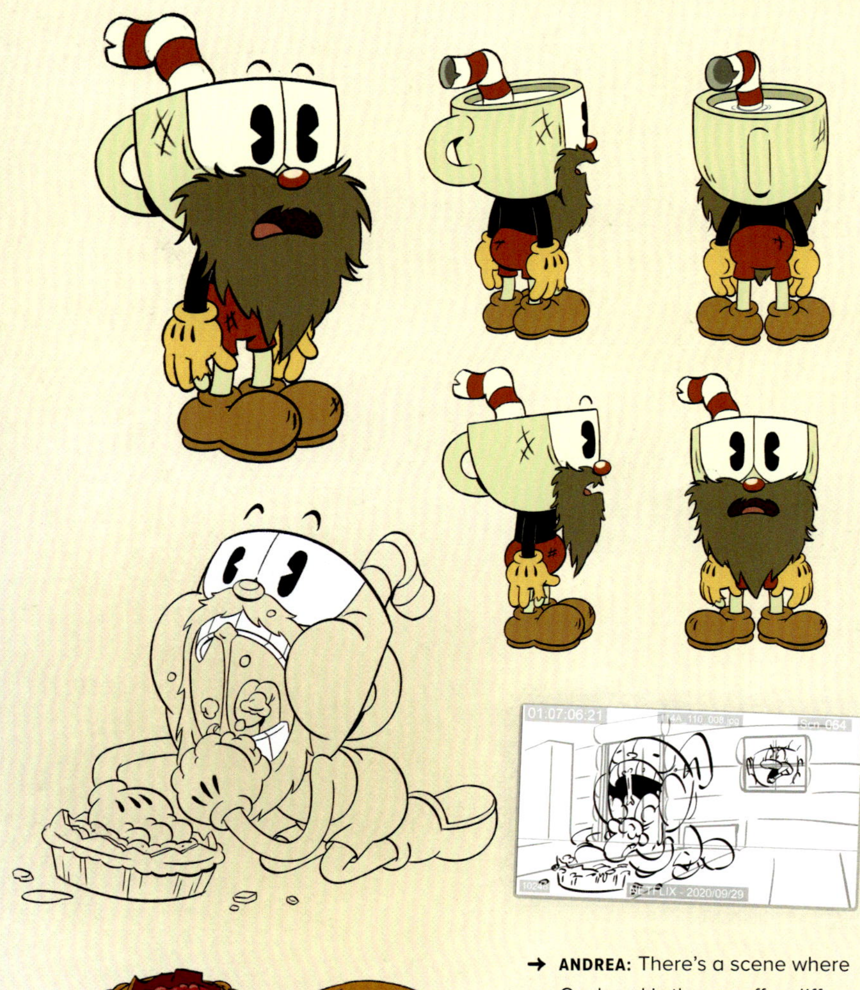

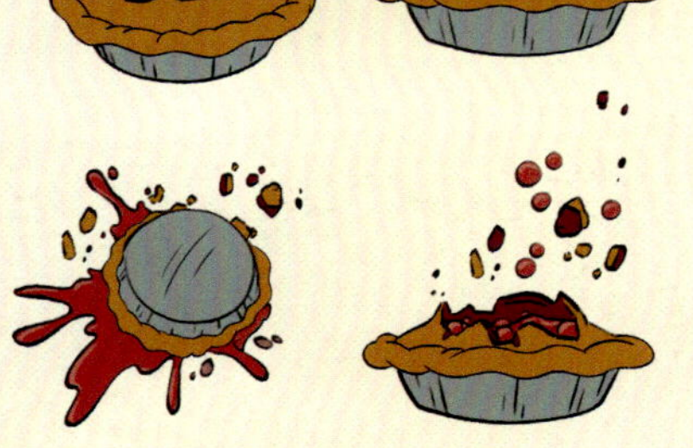

ANDREA: There's a scene where Cuphead is thrown off a cliff . . .

DAVE: . . . and he hits every branch on the way down. It goes on and on and on . . .

ANDREA: . . . and on and on and on for *ages*. And Dave kept saying . . .

DAVE: . . . "It has to be longer! He needs to fall *wayyyyy* longer."

ANDREA: I said, "No, I'm cutting you off at five fields. We're not going past five fields. We can't paint that much." And he said . . .

DAVE: . . . "Only five fields?! How is that possible?! No one gets injured falling only five fields!"

ANDREA: I said, "I don't know what to tell you. It's only five fields."

DAVE: In the end, I think I got six fields.

BEARDED CUPHEAD TURNAROUND BY TAPAN GANDHI; SPECIAL POSE DESIGNS BY MARTIN WITTIG; PIE DESIGNS BY ADAM DIX; STORYBOARD PANEL BY JULES BRIDGERS; CHARACTER COLOR BY CHRIS HACKER.

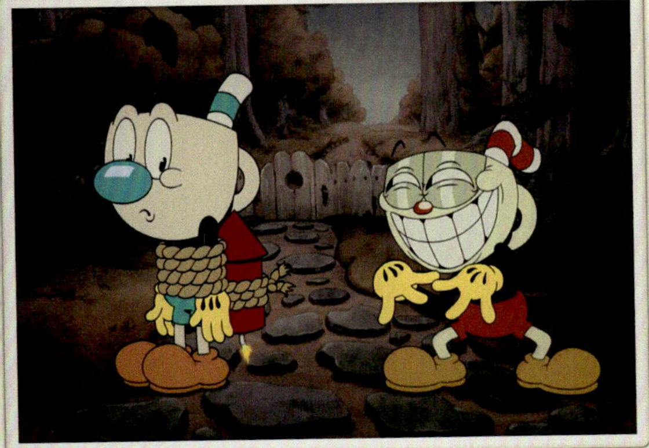

SPECIAL POSE DESIGN BY CLAY MORROW.

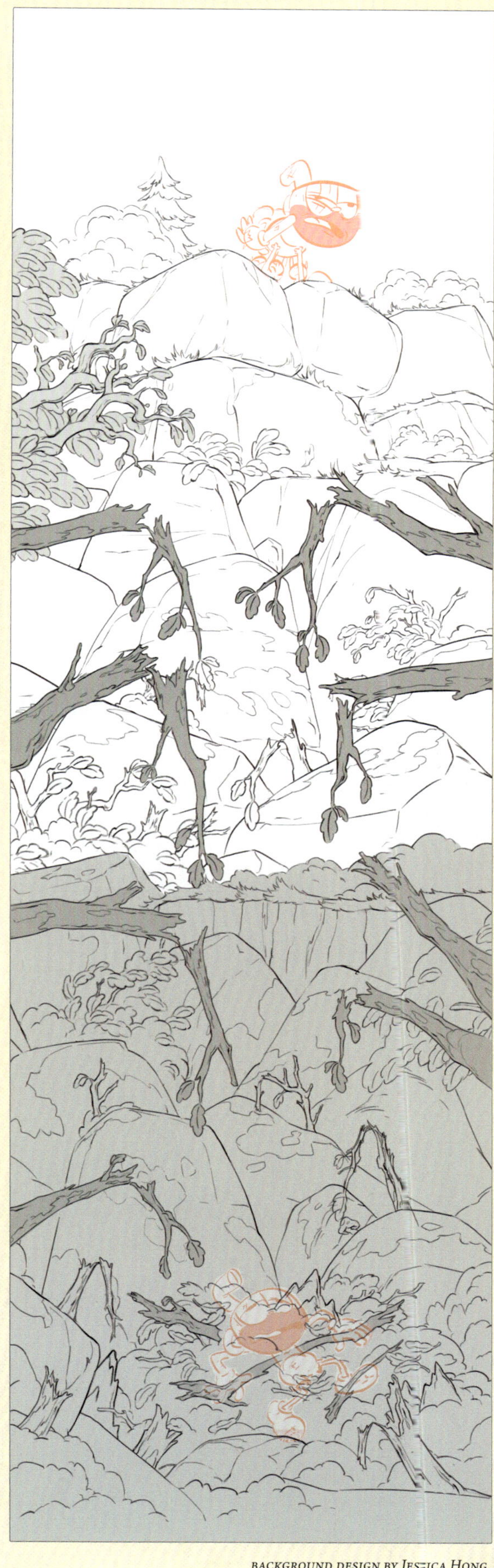

BACKGROUND DESIGN BY JESSICA HONG.

EPISODE 13

"THE DEVIL'S PITCHFORK"

• AND •

SEASON 3, EPISODE 1

"THE DEVIL'S REVENGE!"

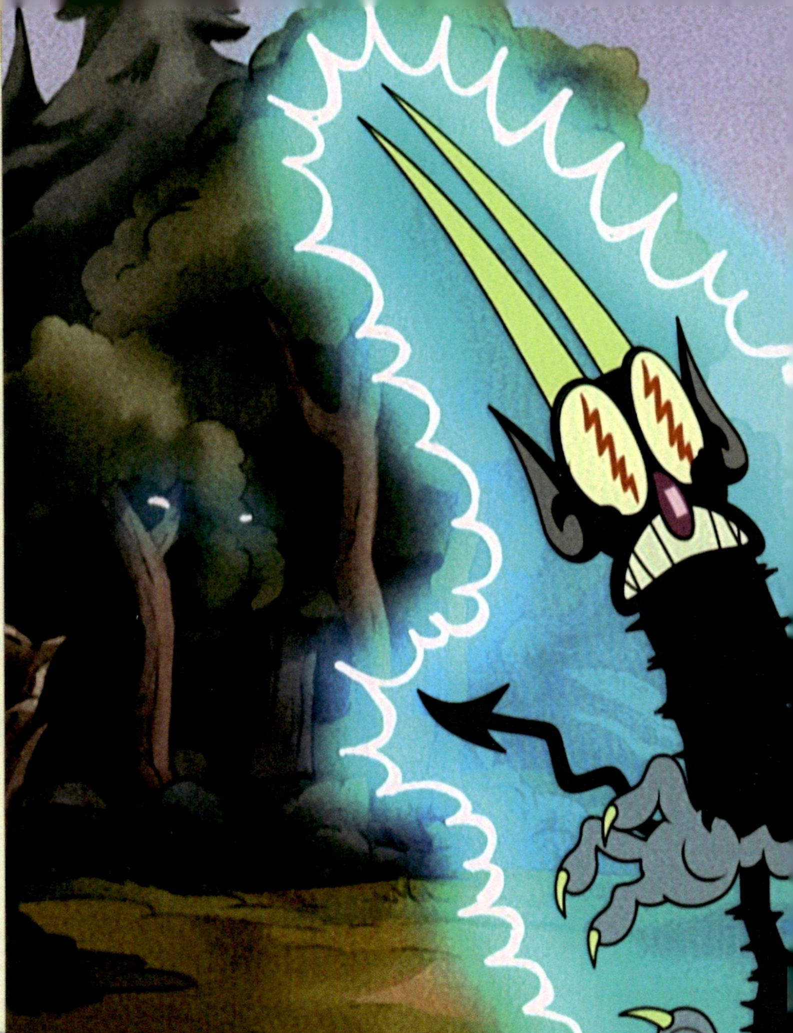

DAVE: When a villain is funny, it doesn't have to take away from what makes them a villain. That's what's so great about the Devil. One minute you're laughing, because he's whining and pathetic, but moments later he's genuinely terrifying.

MEGAN B: To me, Cuphead and Mugman are annoying kids. Part of me is always rooting for the Devil to kick their ass. It's fun to see the main characters get taken down a peg.

DAVE: Cuphead and Mugman are two weird, unconventional characters, and the Devil doesn't really know how to deal with them. They laugh at him. They don't take him seriously. They're not intimidated by him.

MEGAN B: Let's be honest: did the Devil *really* do anything wrong? I mean, Cuphead and Mugman are pretty annoying. I like the Devil. And he's got a cool pad.

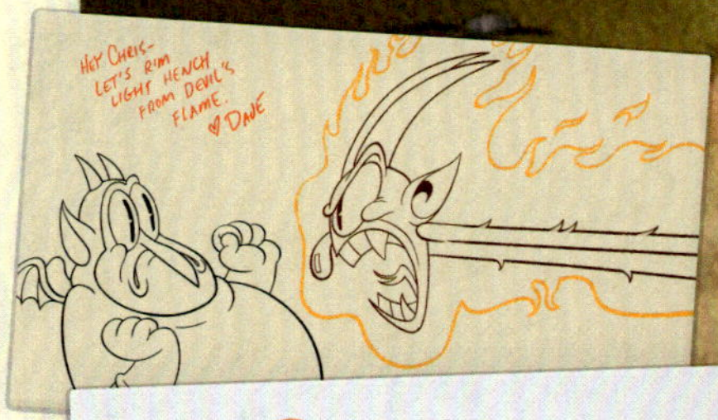

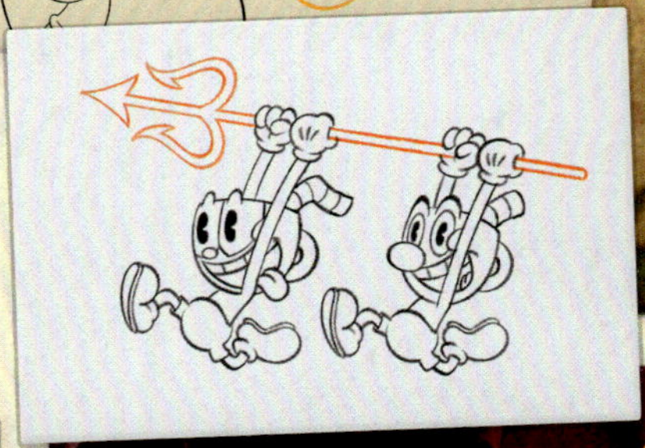

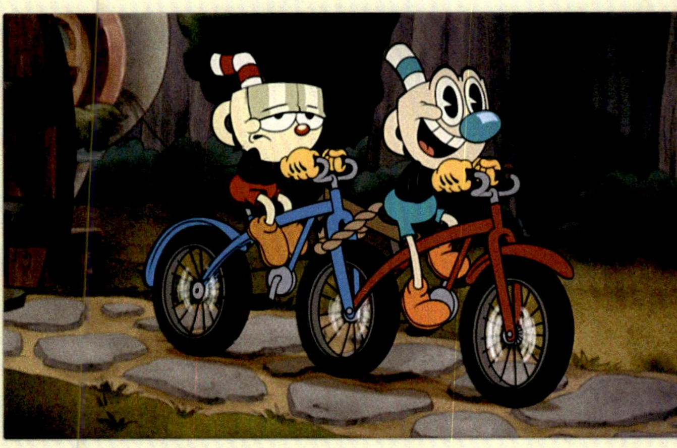

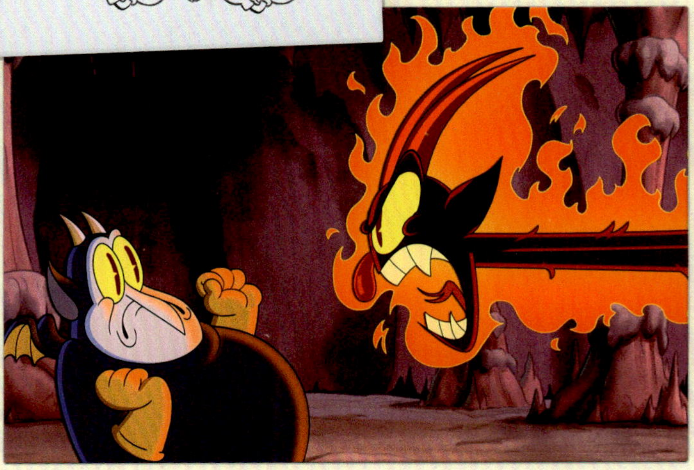

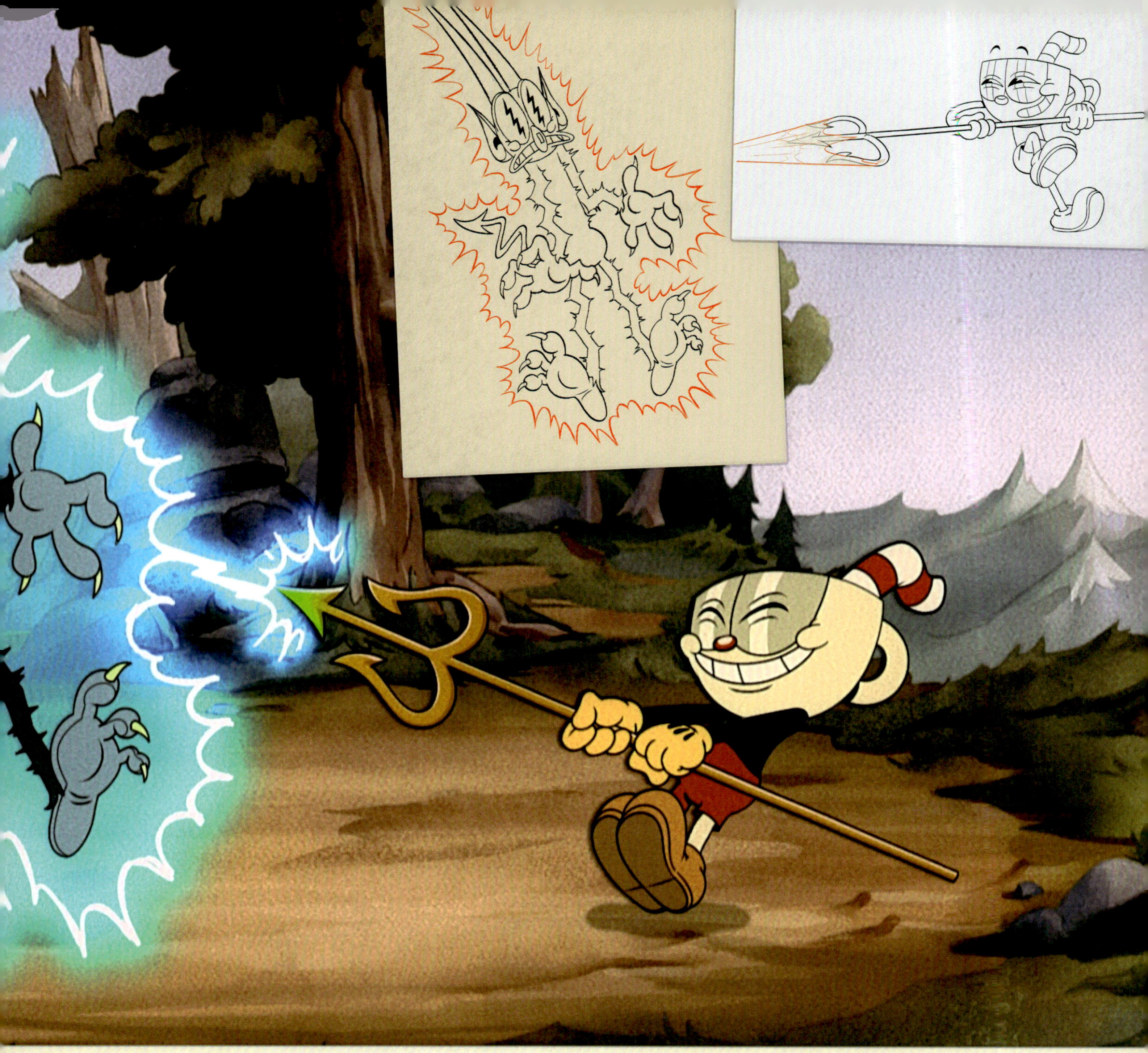

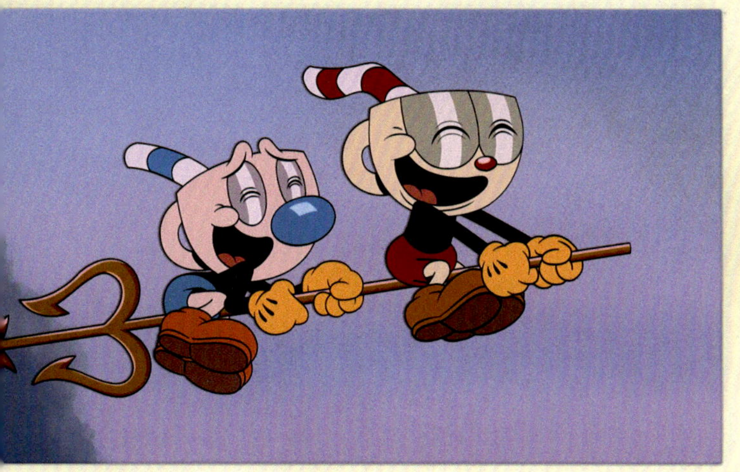

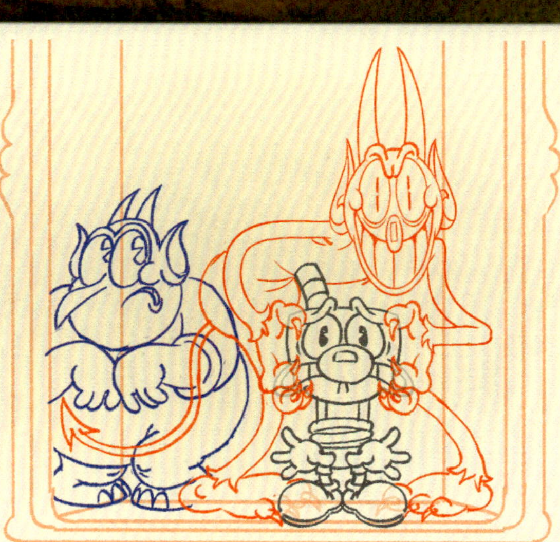

Special pose designs by Bradley Lewis, Mike Fontanelli, and Dave Wasson; character color by Chris Hacker.

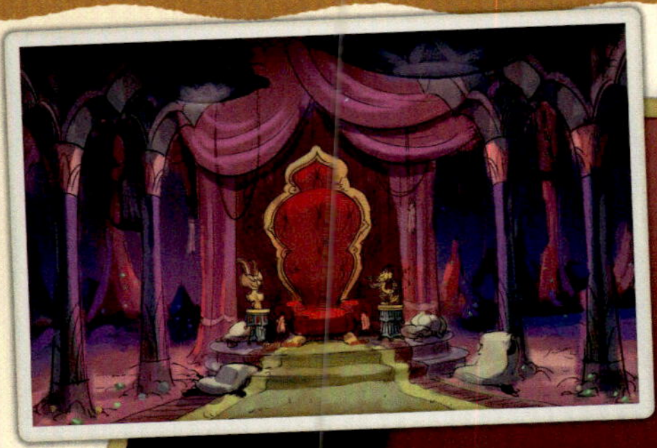

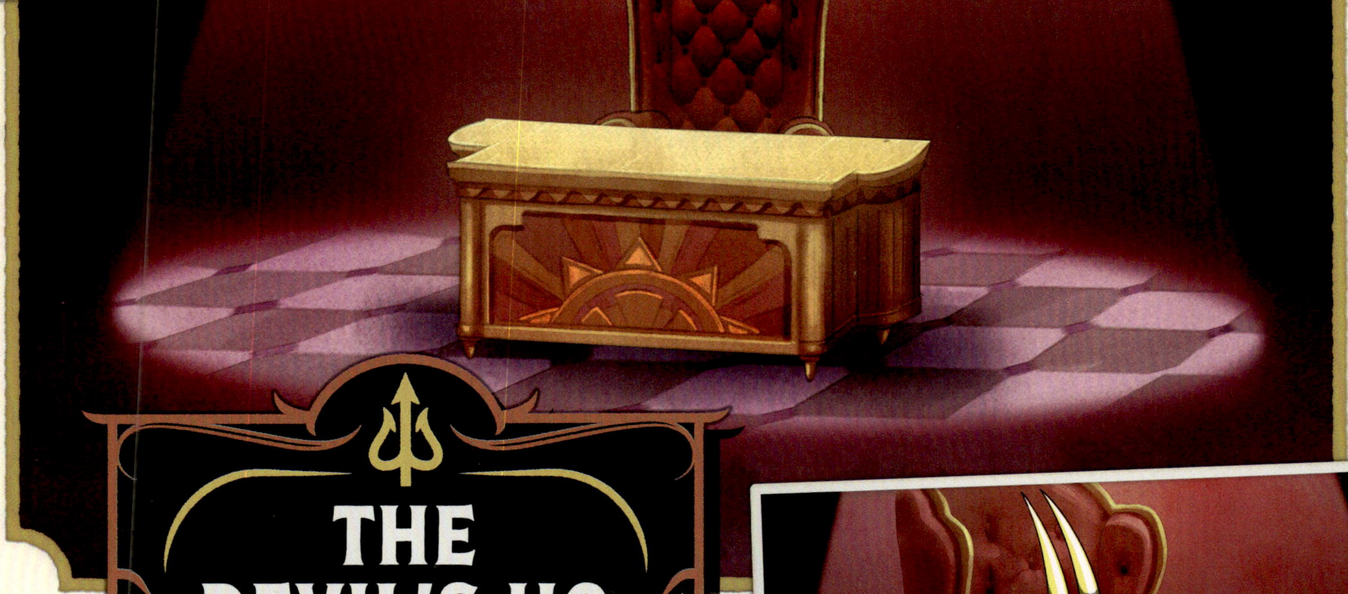

THE DEVIL'S HQ

DEEP DIVE

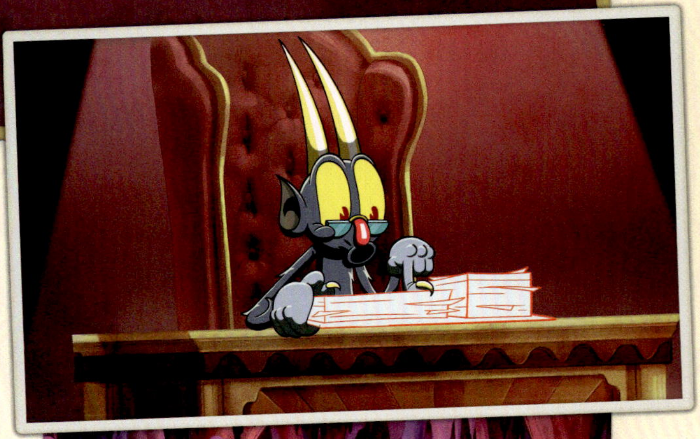

→ **ANDREA:** The loudest location is probably the Devil's HQ. Ivan has what I call "the juicy palette." He's got an inclination toward warm hues and purples and pinks, and he really helped develop the Devil's HQ. But we kept that palette only to HQ, so it'd feel really special compared to the surface. We only ever pushed those more fantastical hues in the places we wanted to feel otherworldly. The rest is very naturalistic and metered all the way through.

IVAN: In most of the backgrounds we're trying to go for a watercolor look. The HQ backgrounds get a little more opaque than we usually do. We tried to make it feel like it was a wash painting.

ANDREA: To get an entire team of painters to do the exact same feel over many paintings is very difficult, but it's even harder when it's organic materials, because there's so much variance in the end result. The Devil's HQ definitely gave us a lot of headaches in the beginning, but it was worth it.

DAVE: We watched a lot of early cartoons that depicted the underworld. There was a Willie Whopper Ub Iwerks cartoon [*Hell's Fire*, 1934] where he goes to hell . . . There's *Pluto's Judgement Day* [1935] where he goes to hell and is on trial for being mean to kittens. They've all got lots of stalactites, caves, fire, little demons shoveling coal into furnaces—that imagery is so fun and felt true to the period.

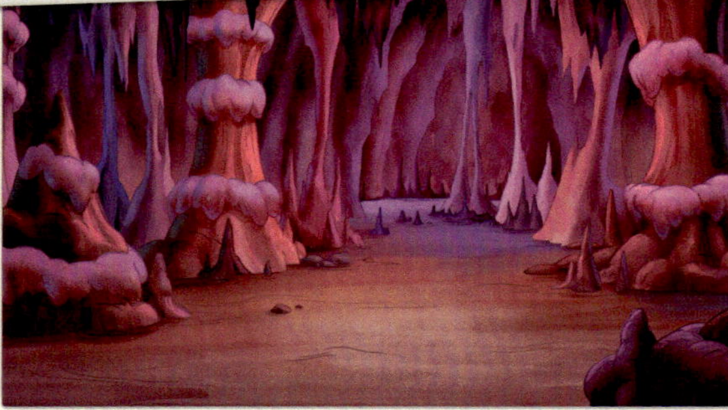

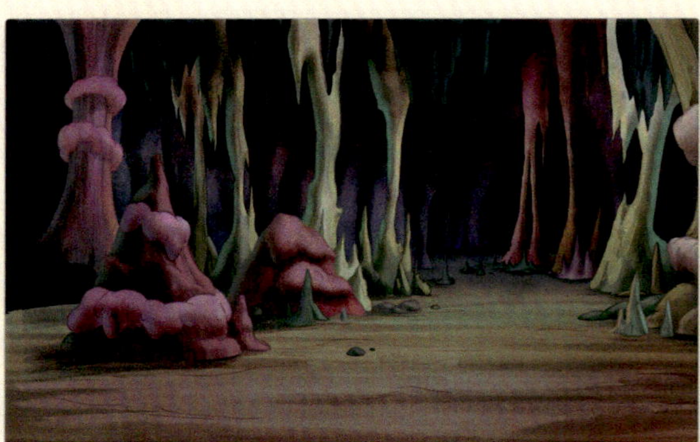

BACKGROUND DESIGNS BY LAISAY BOND, JESSICA HONG, AND COSMO SEGURSON; PAINTINGS AND COLOR KEYS BY IVAN AGUIRRE.

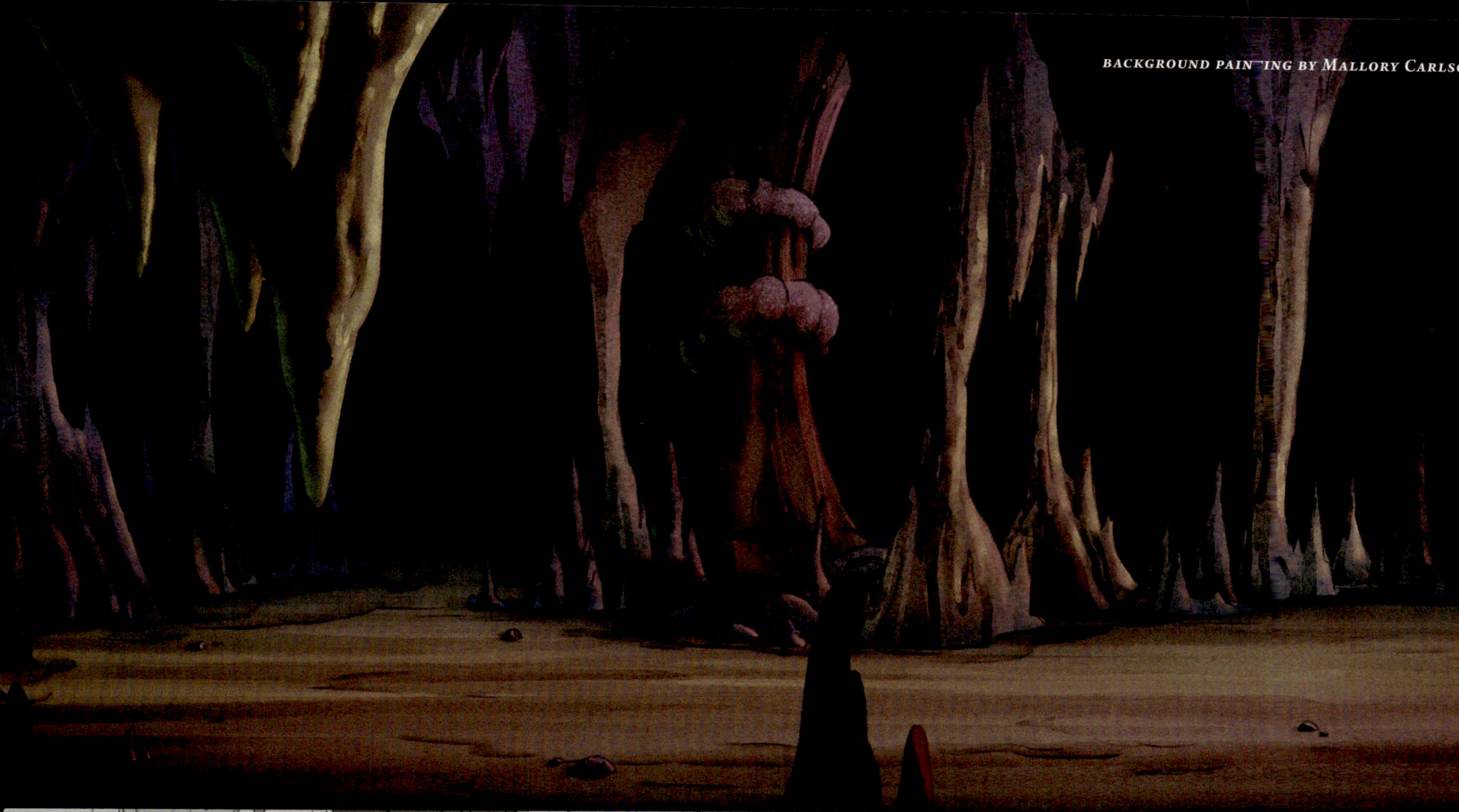

Background painting by Mallory Carlso

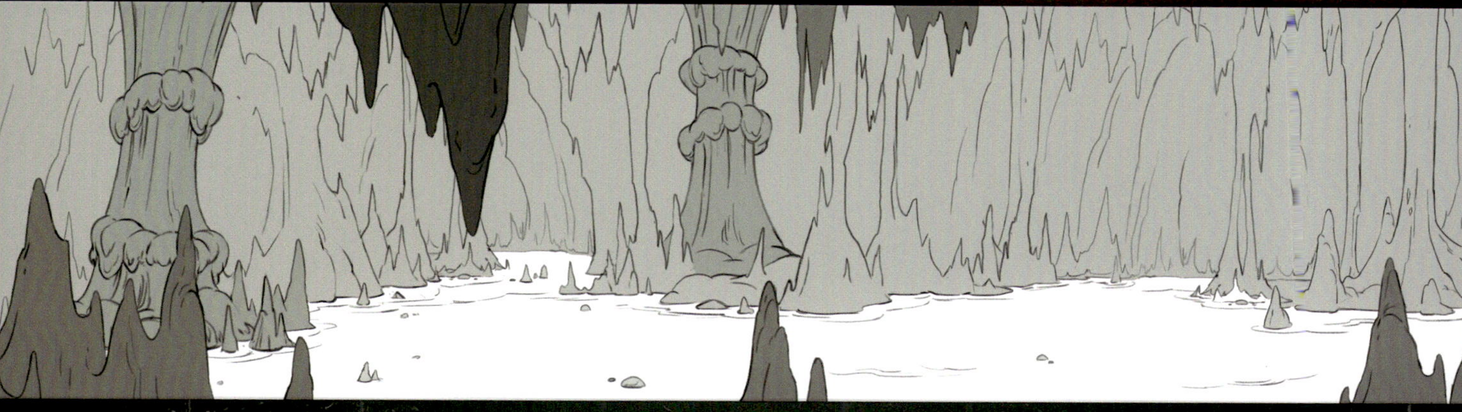

The Devil's Library

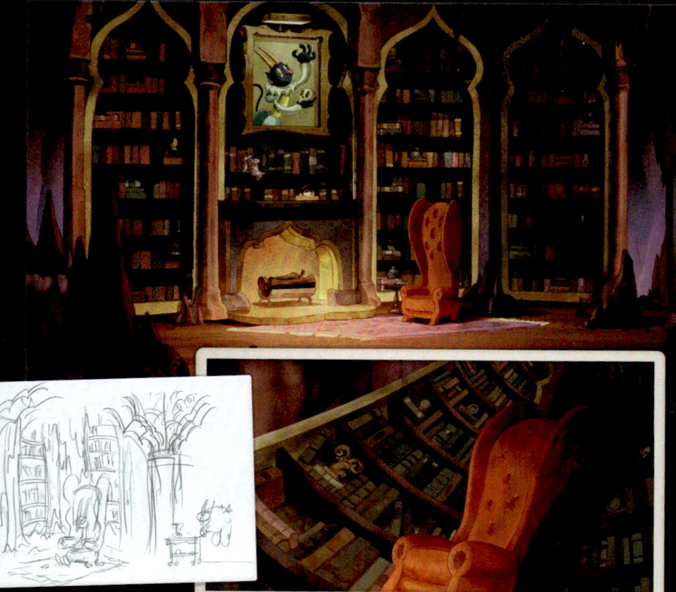

Devil's library sketch by Cosmo Segurson; color key by Ivan Aguirre; final painting by Mallory Carlson.

The Devil's War Room

Background design by Jessica Hong.

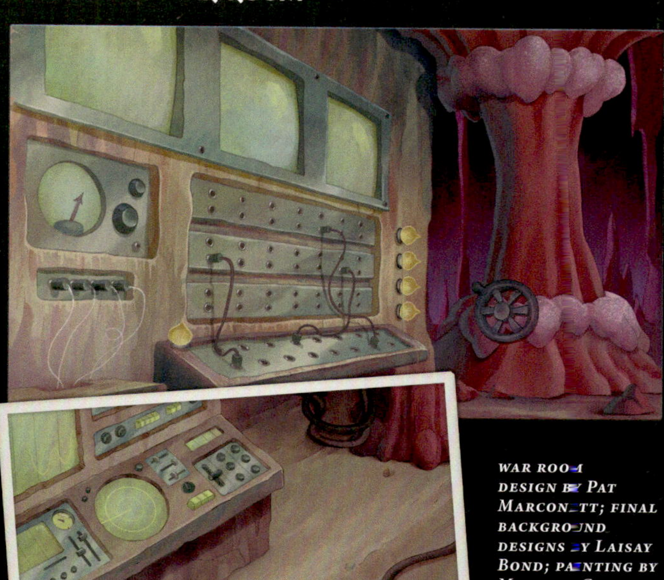

War room design by Pat Marconett; final background designs by Laisay Bond; painting by Mallory Carlson.

THE DEVIL'S DANCE CAVE

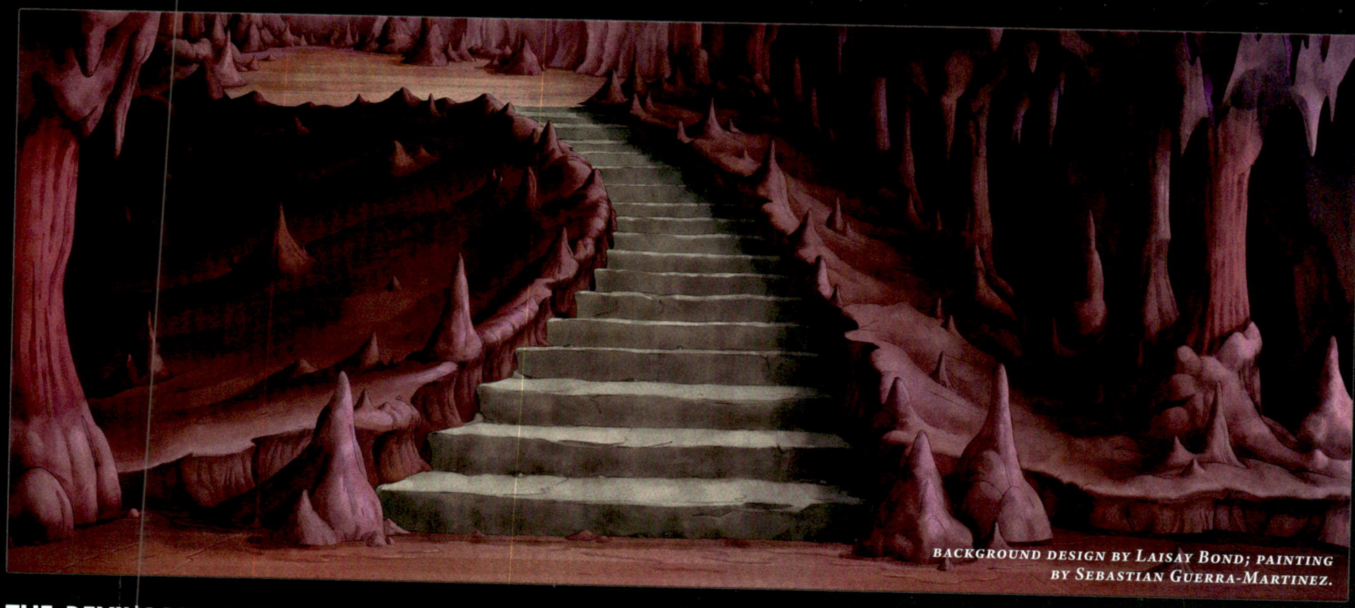

Background design by Laisay Bond; painting by Sebastian Guerra-Martinez.

THE DEVIL'S DUNGEON OFFICE

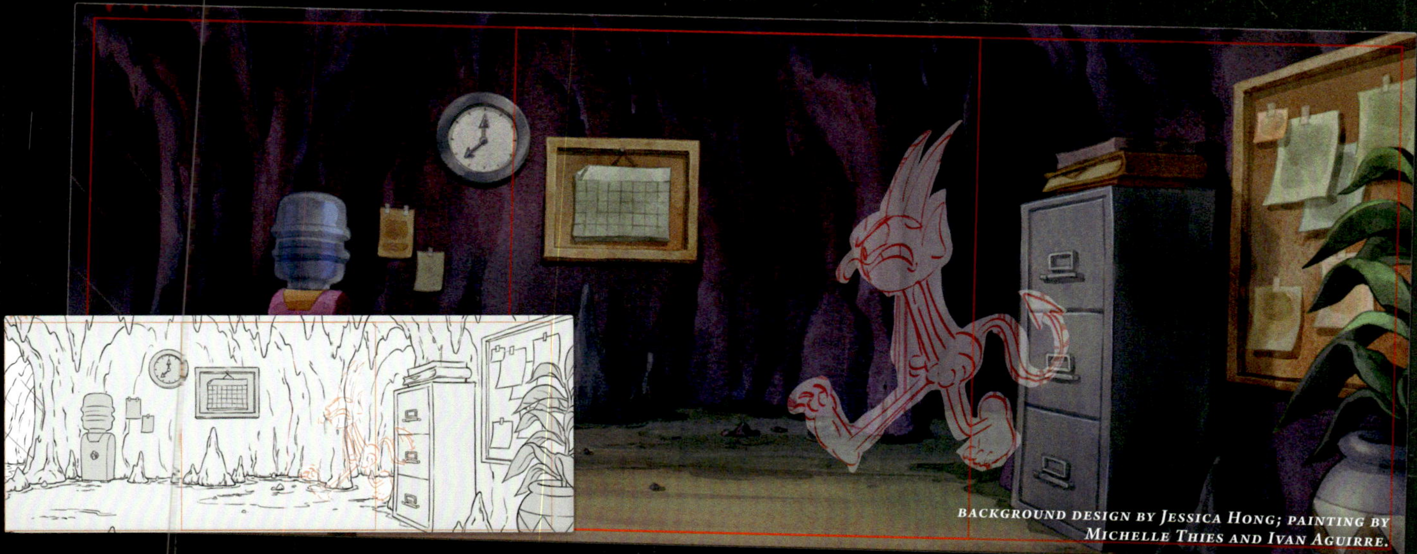

Background design by Jessica Hong; painting by Michelle Thies and Ivan Aguirre.

THE DEVIL'S BREAK ROOM

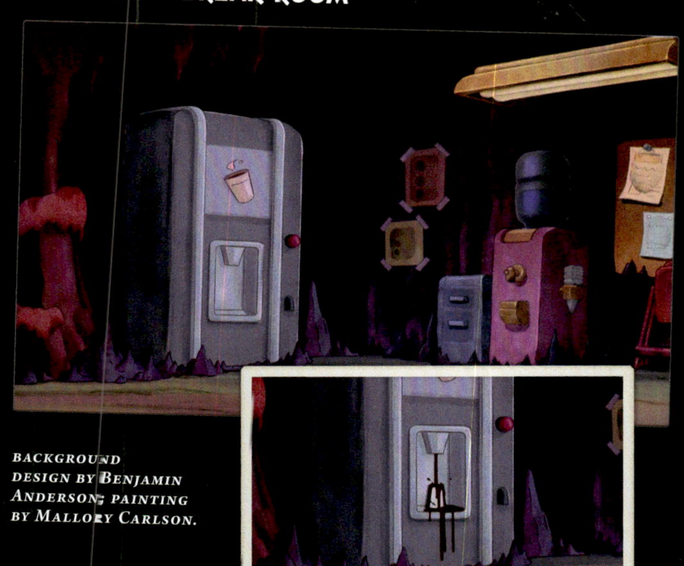

Background design by Benjamin Anderson; painting by Mallory Carlson.

THE DEVIL'S THEATER

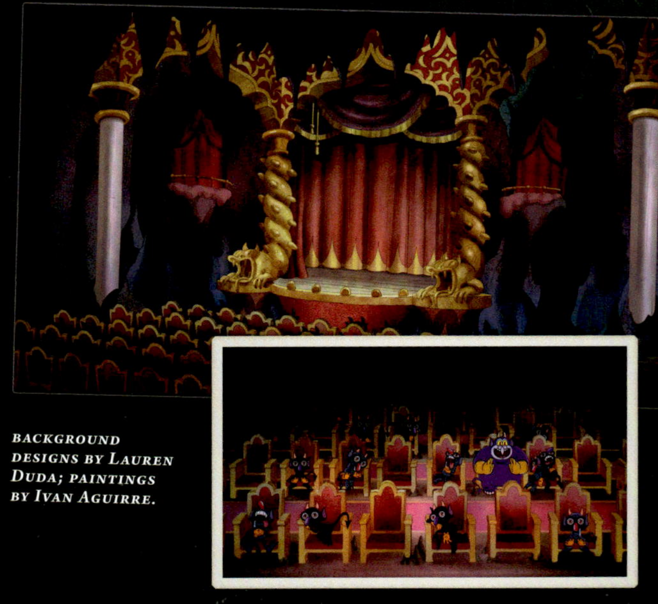

Background designs by Lauren Duda; paintings by Ivan Aguirre.

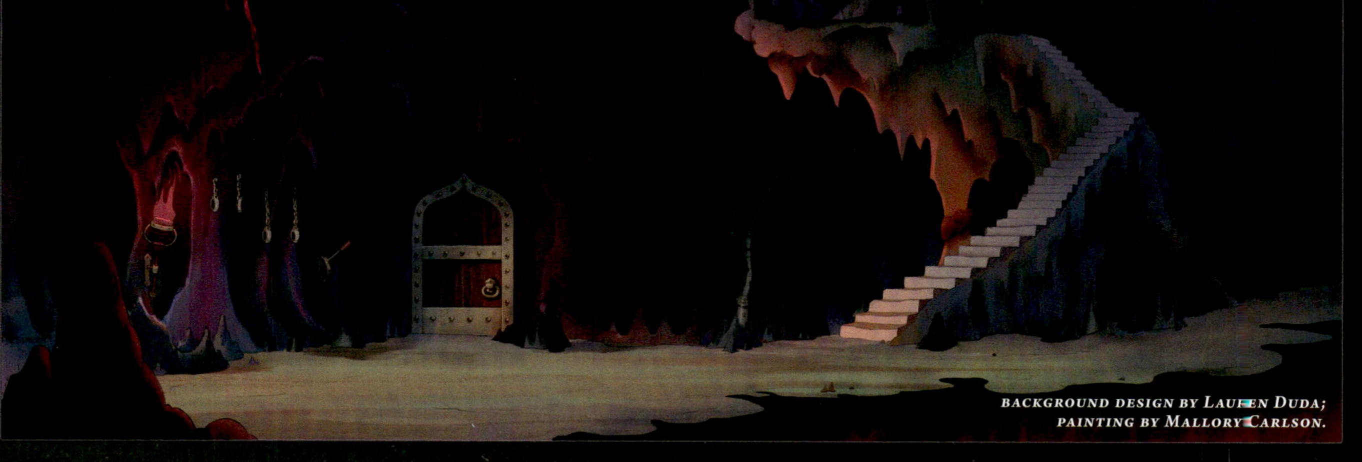

Background design by Lauren Duda; painting by Mallory Carlson.

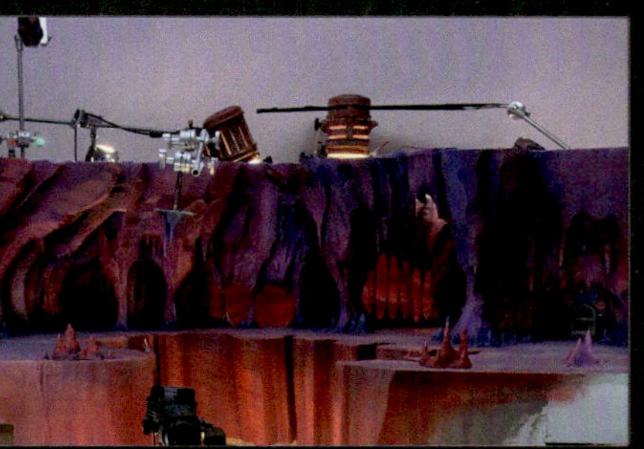

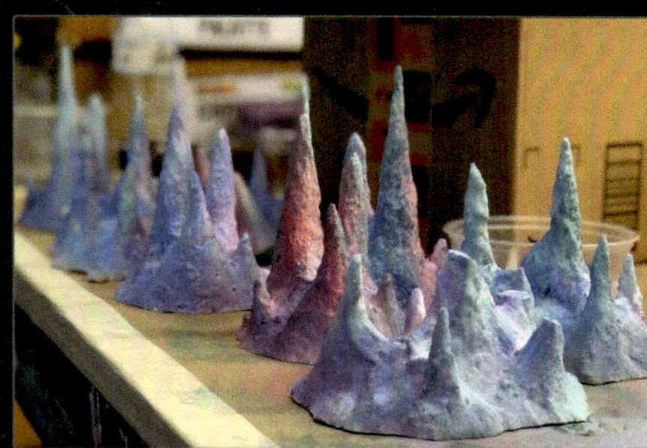

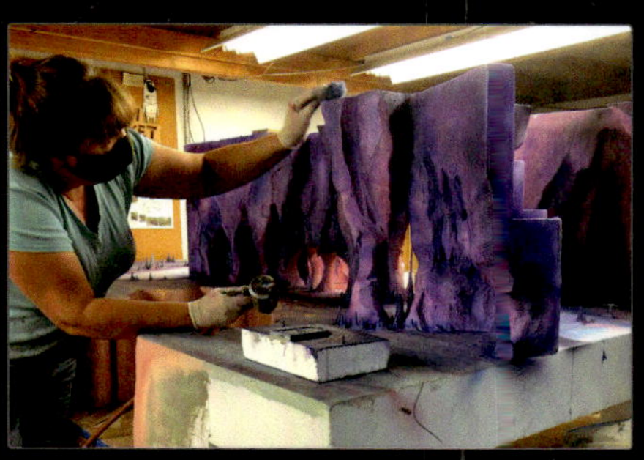

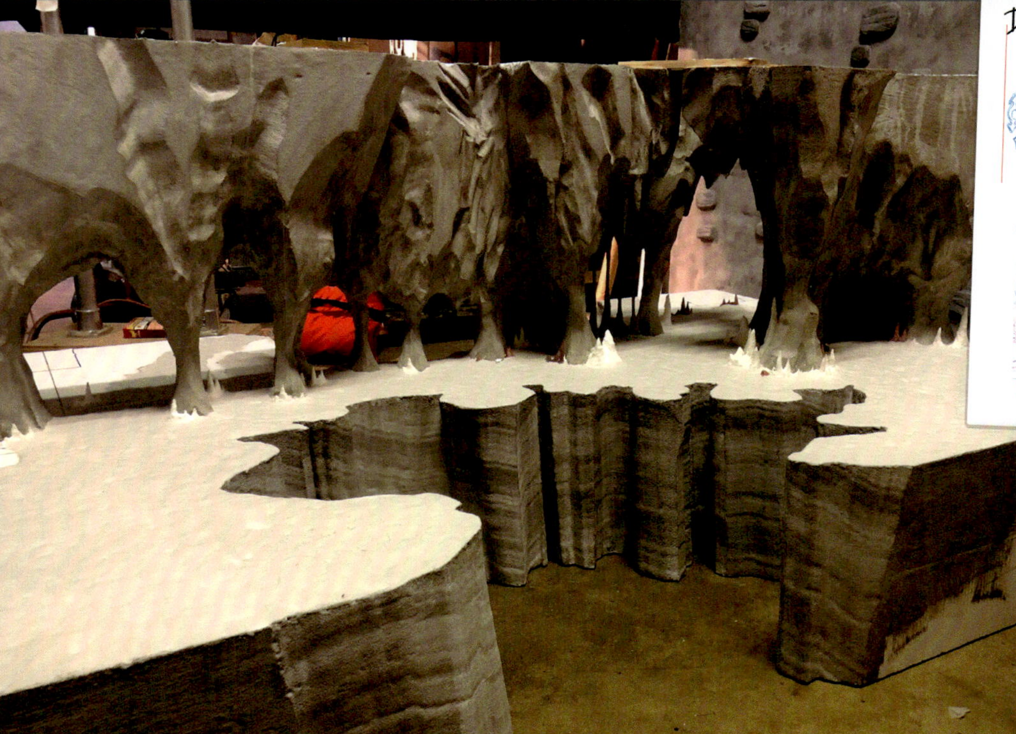

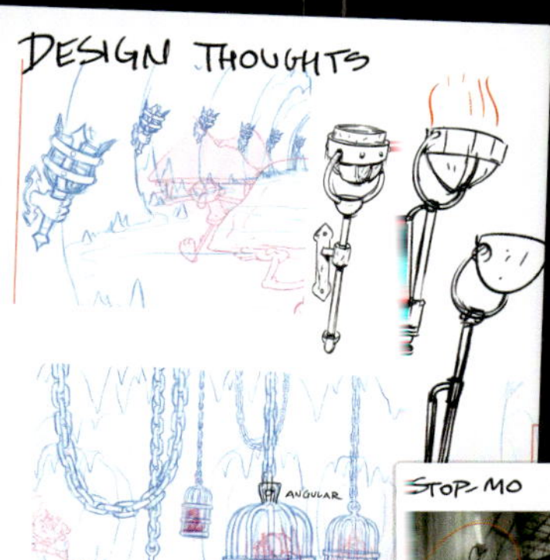

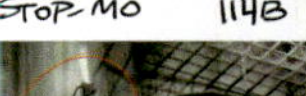

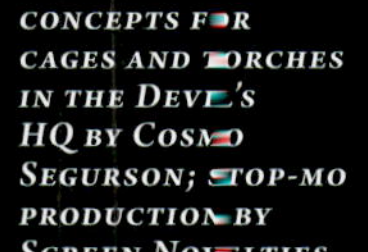

Concepts for cages and torches in the Devil's HQ by Cosmo Segurson; stop-mo production by Screen Novelties.

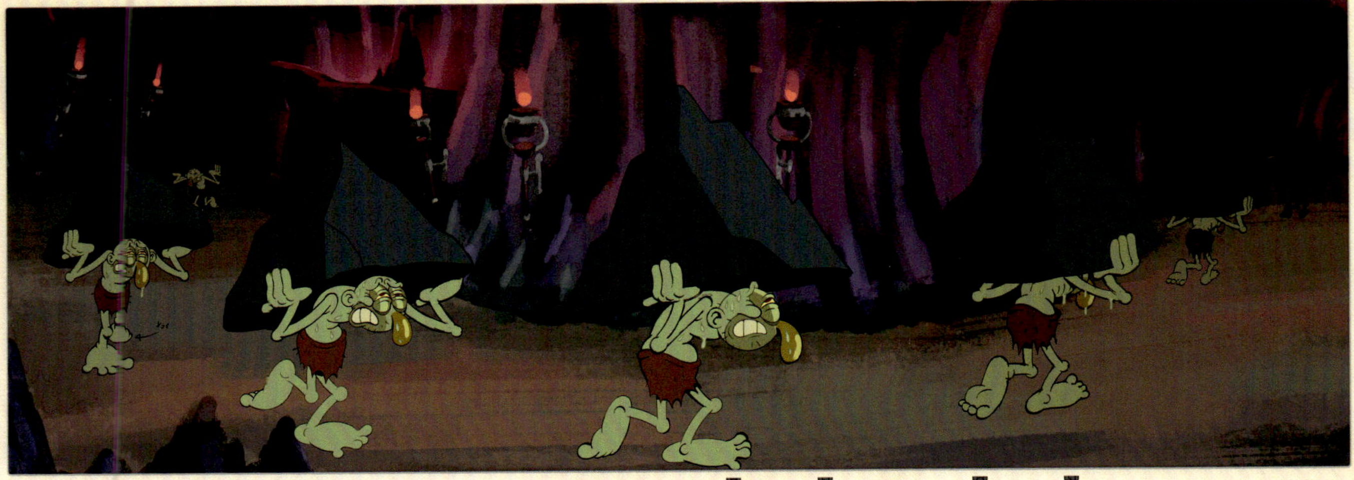

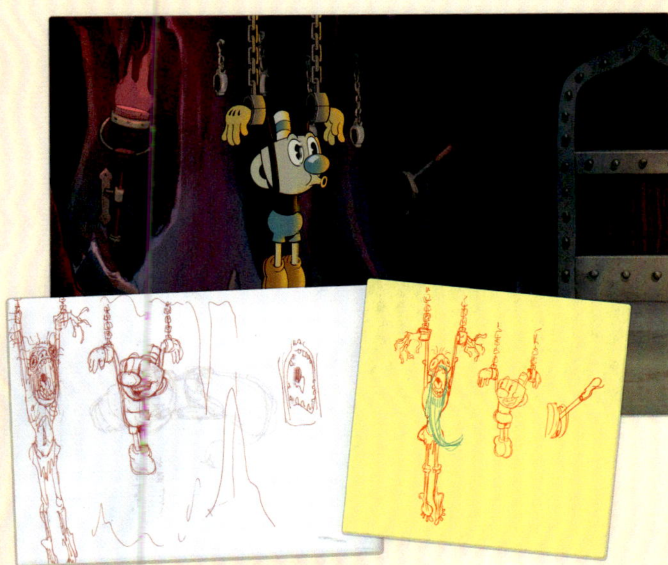

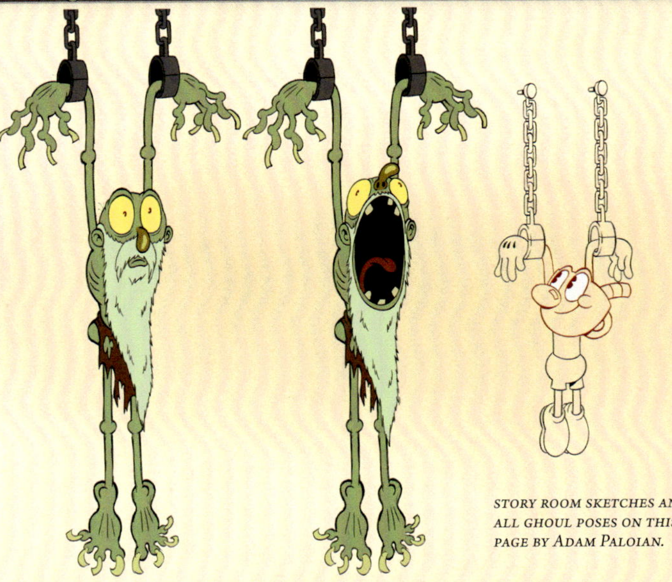

STORY ROOM SKETCHES AND ALL GHOUL POSES ON THIS PAGE BY ADAM PALOIAN.

→ **ADAM P:** In the writers' room, if an image got me excited about a scene, I'd try to draw it and preserve that inspiration for when we got to the storyboards. That bit in particular made me laugh so hard, and it was so exciting, because it was dark and it was a little bit adult, and it was such a great contrast: cute Mugman with his button nose next to this emaciated guy with long fingernails.

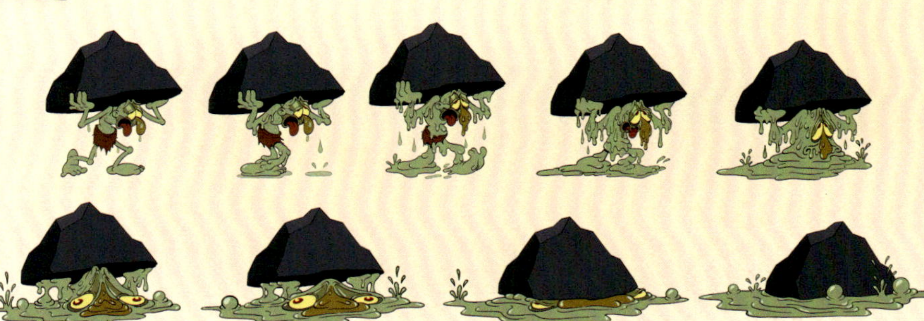

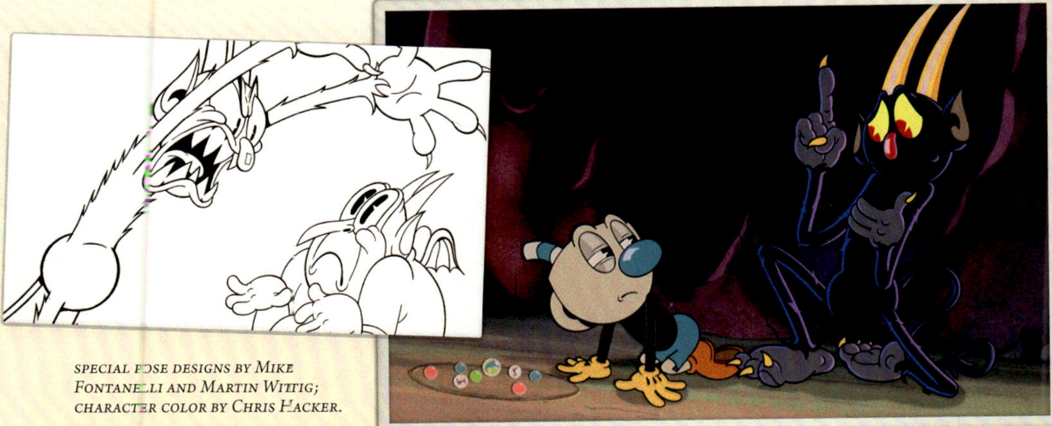

SPECIAL POSE DESIGNS BY MIKE FONTANELLI AND MARTIN WITTIG; CHARACTER COLOR BY CHRIS HACKER.

→ **MALLORY:** One of my favorite brother moments in the whole series is when Mugman is down below with the Devil, and the Devil is trying to trick him into thinking that Cuphead is long gone and is up in heaven, and Mugman says, "Yeahhhhh, I'm not buyin' it."

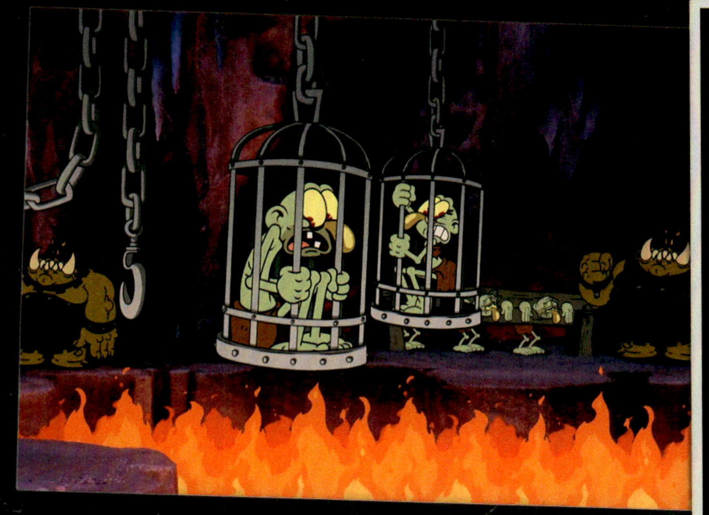

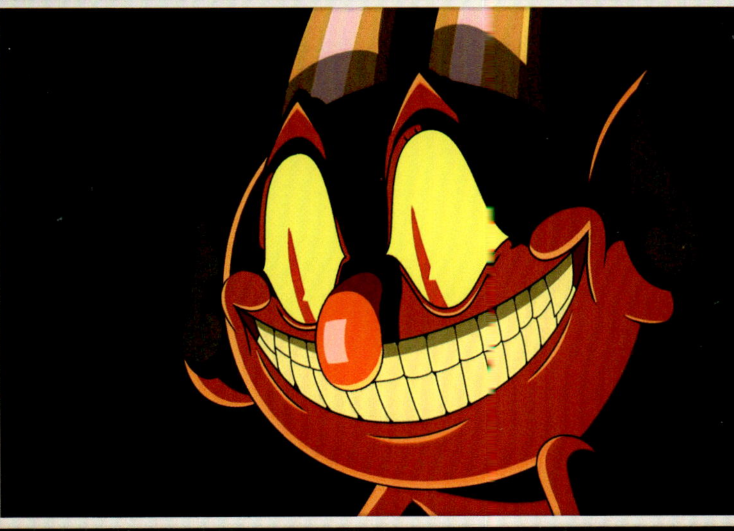

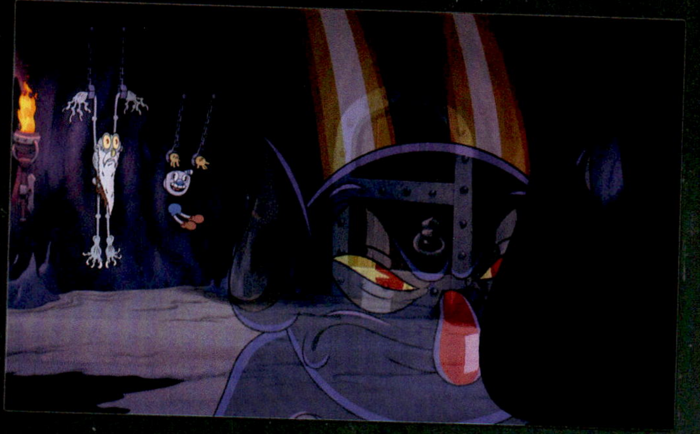

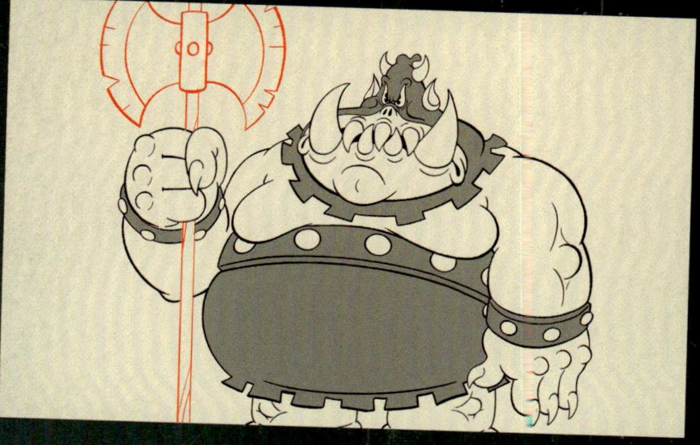

Special pose designs by Bradley Lewis, Dave Wasson, Adam Paloian, and Mike Fontanelli.

THE DEVIL'S THRONE ROOM

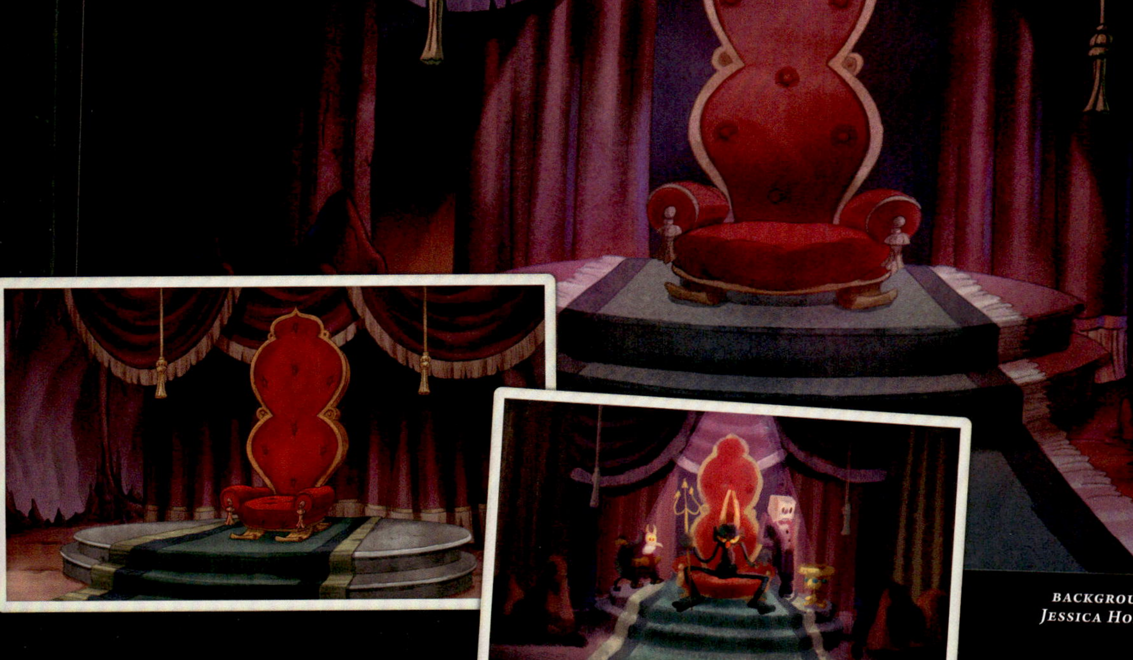

Background designs by Lindsay Bond and Jessica Hong; paintings and color key by Ivan Aguirre.

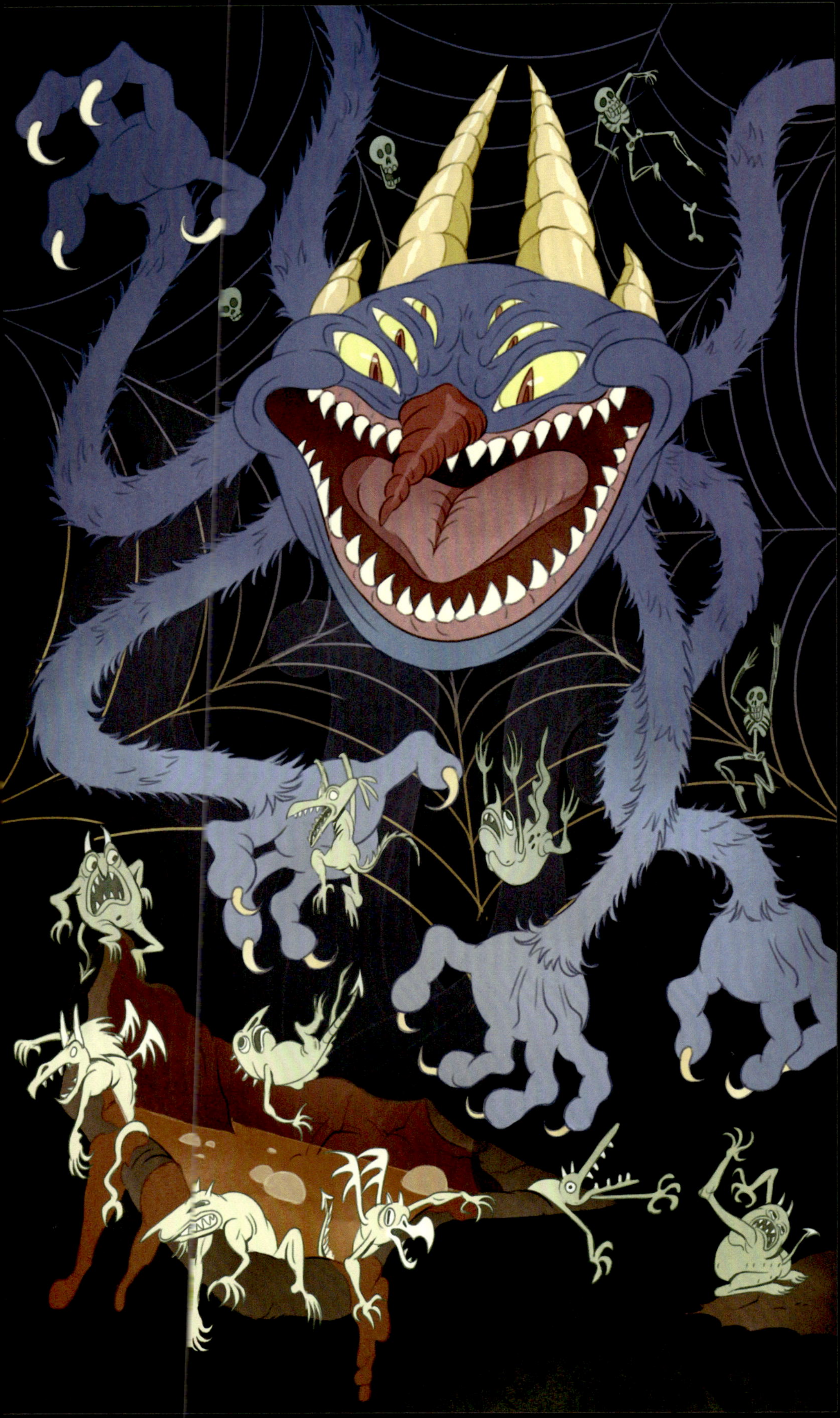

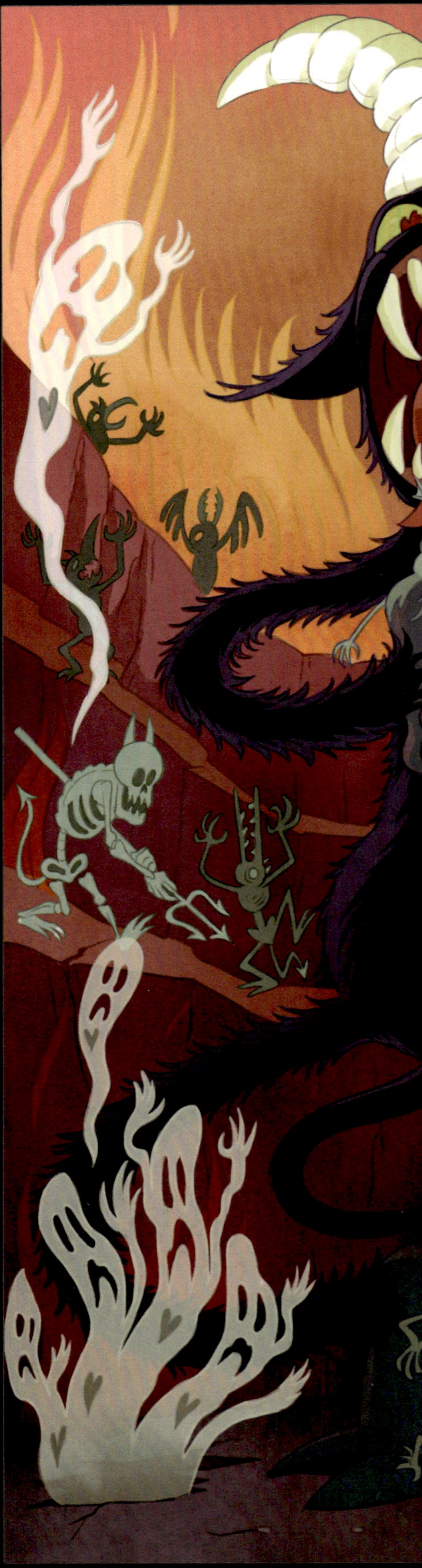

Devil's tapestry paintings by Michelle Thies.

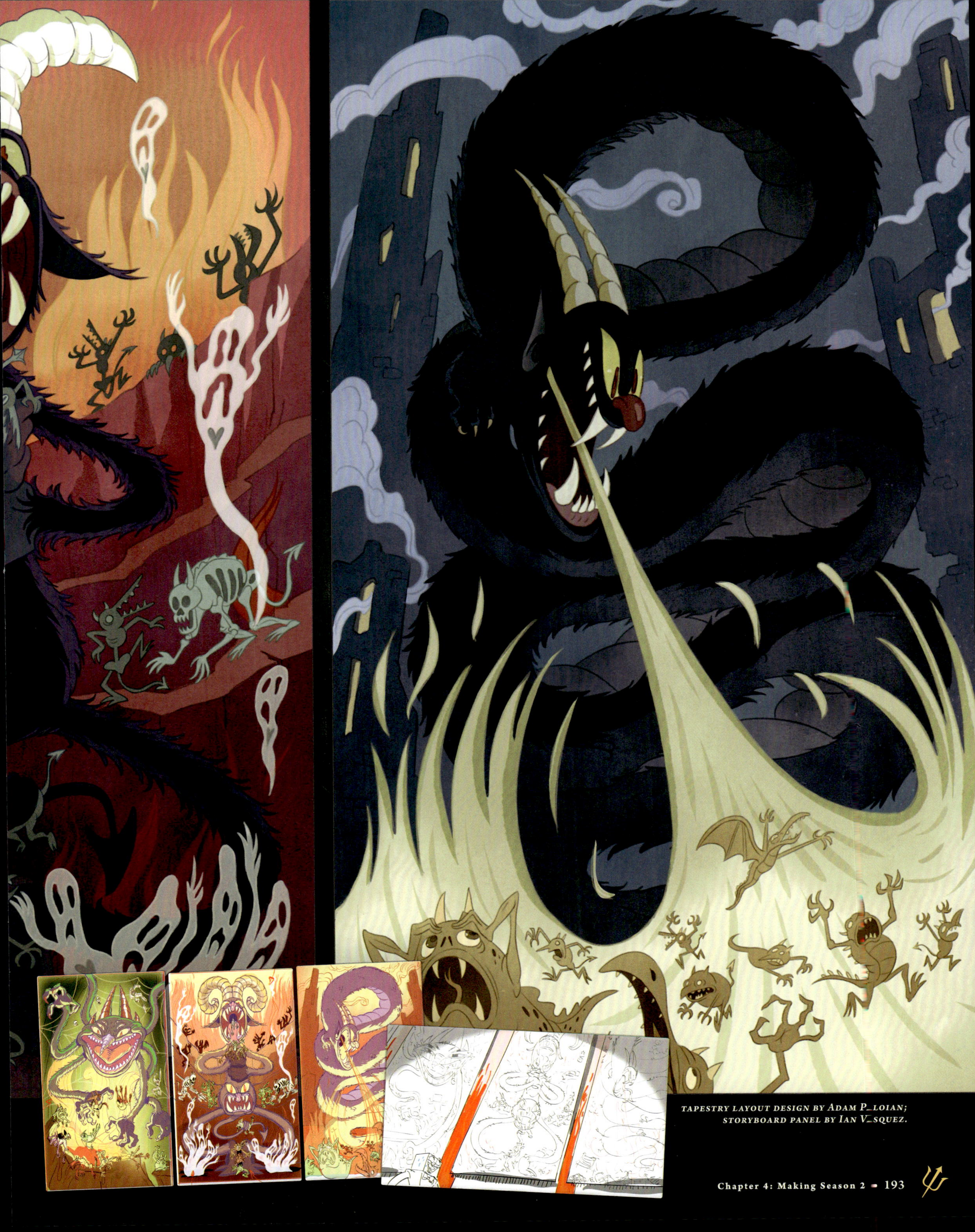

Tapestry layout design by Adam P_loian; storyboard panel by Ian V_squez.

THE DEVIL'S SOUL TUBES

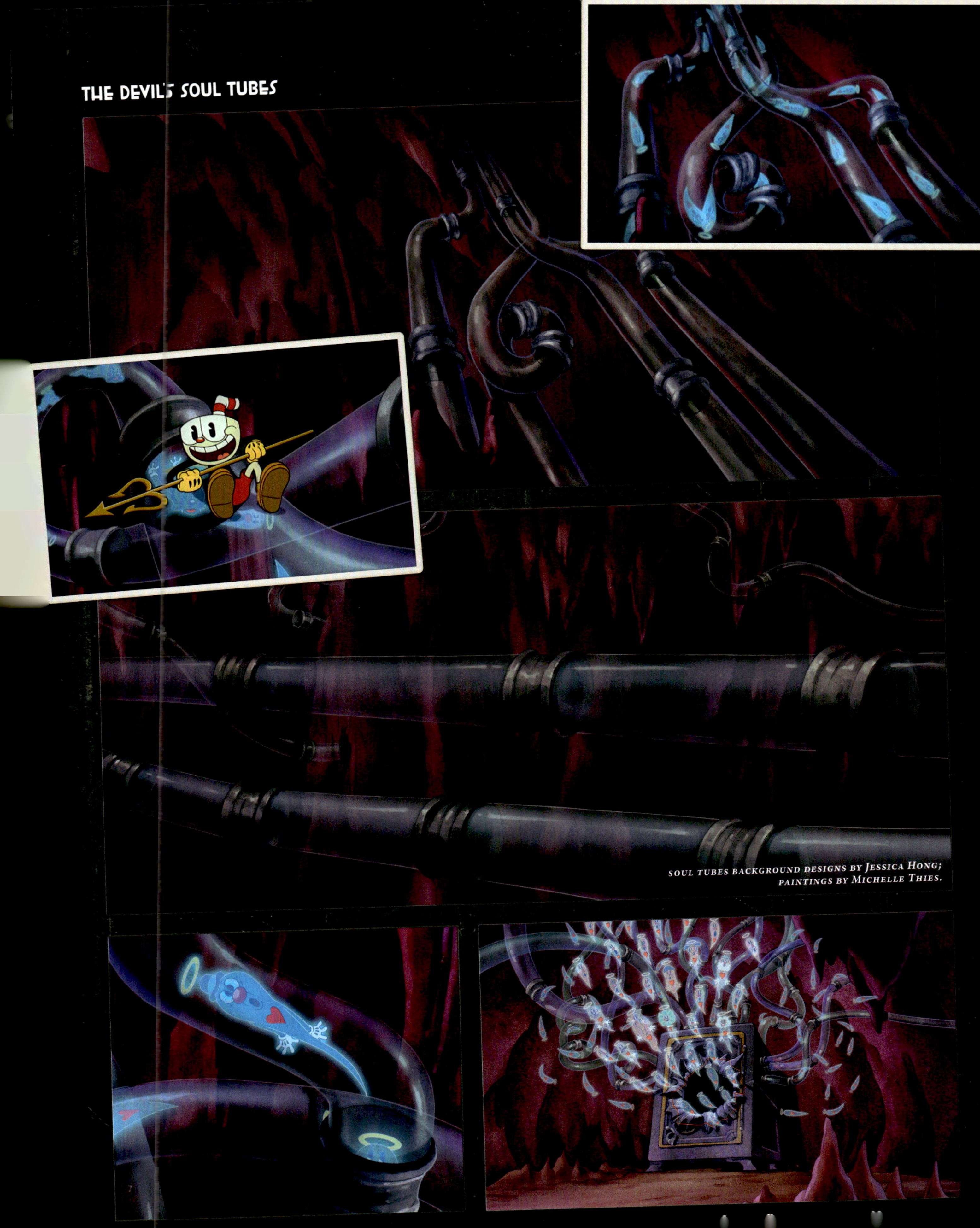

SOUL TUBES BACKGROUND DESIGNS BY JESSICA HONG; PAINTINGS BY MICHELLE THIES.

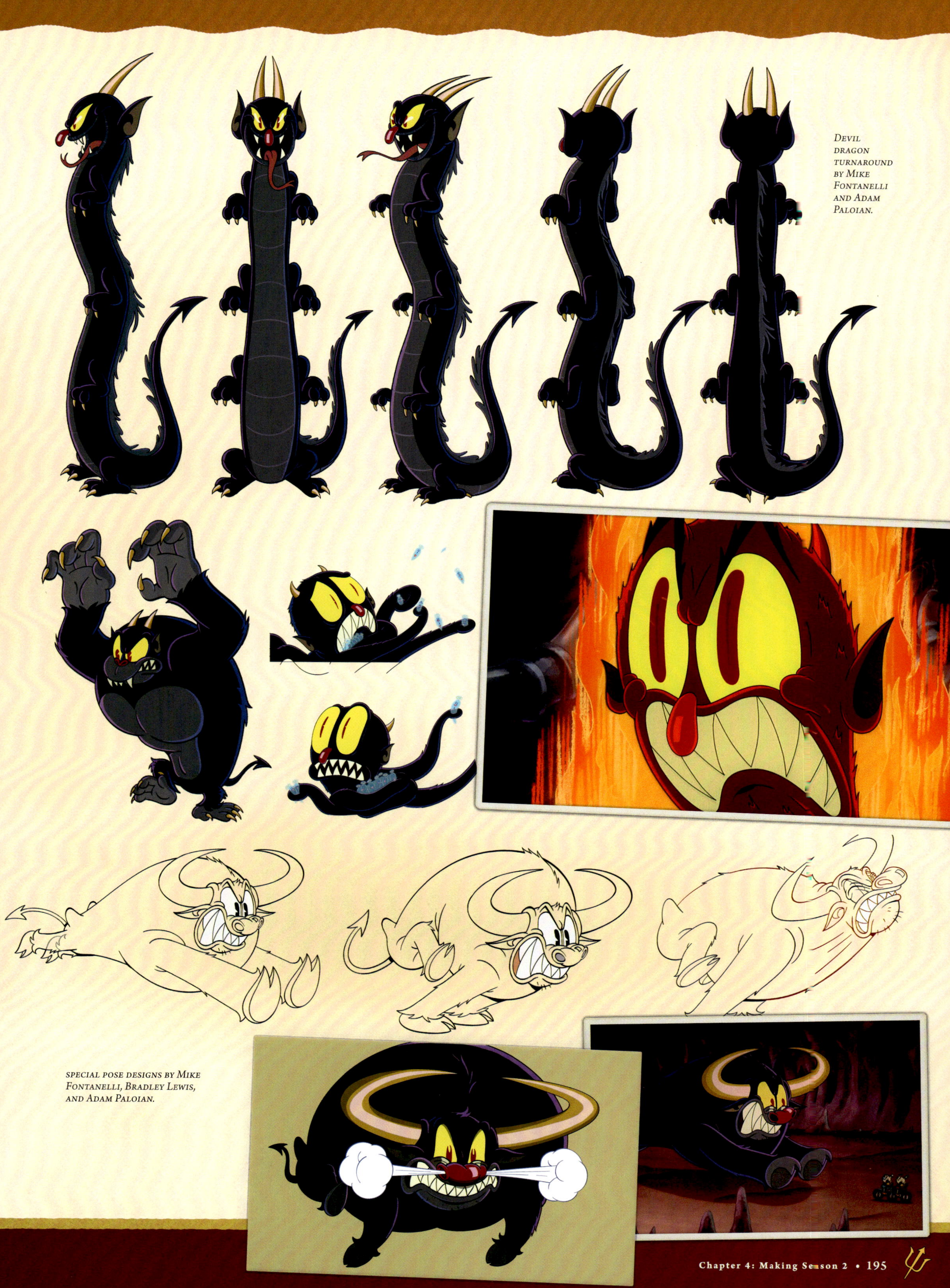

Devil dragon turnaround by Mike Fontanelli and Adam Paloian.

Special pose designs by Mike Fontanelli, Bradley Lewis, and Adam Paloian.

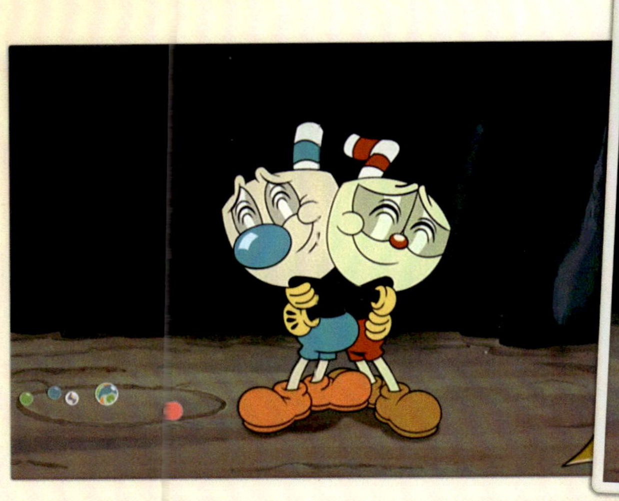

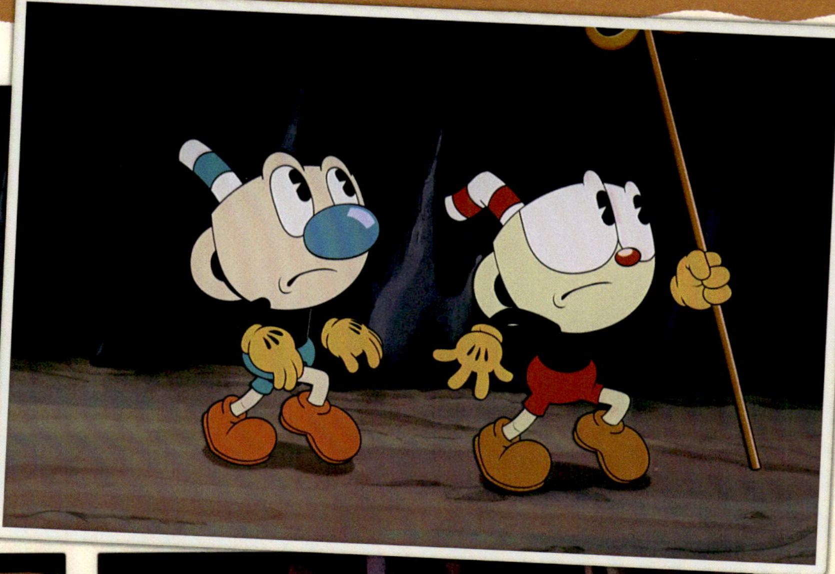

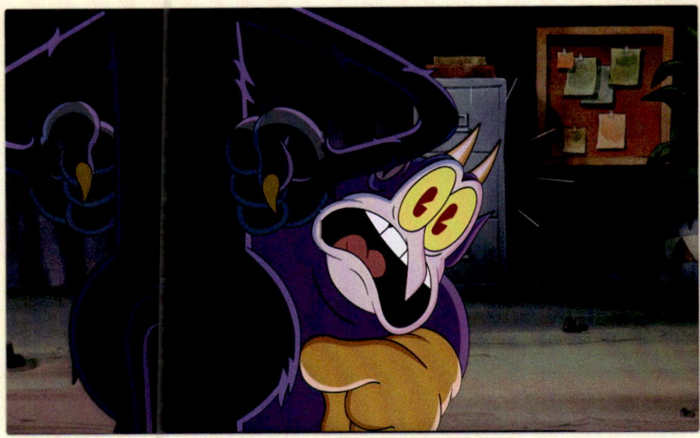

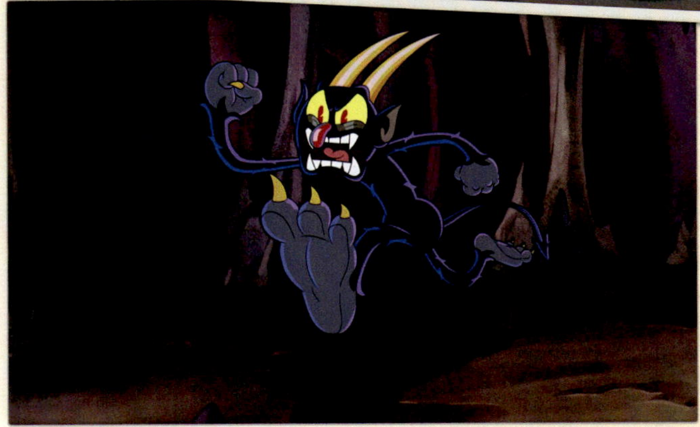

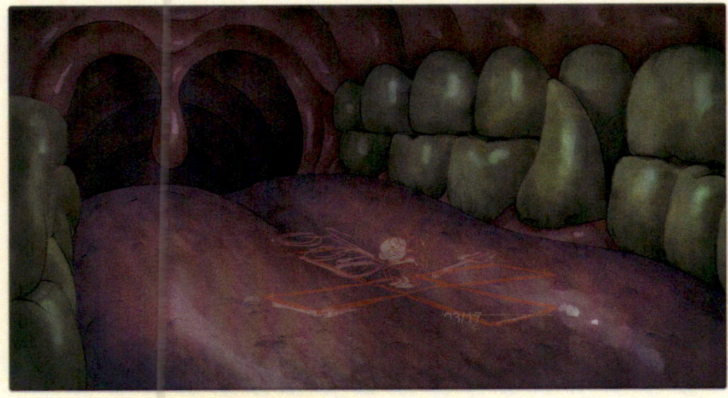

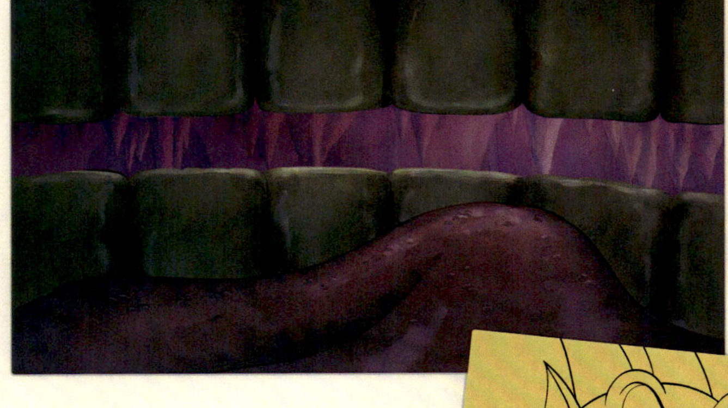

Devil's mouth background designs by Jessica Hong; paintings by Gregory Miller.

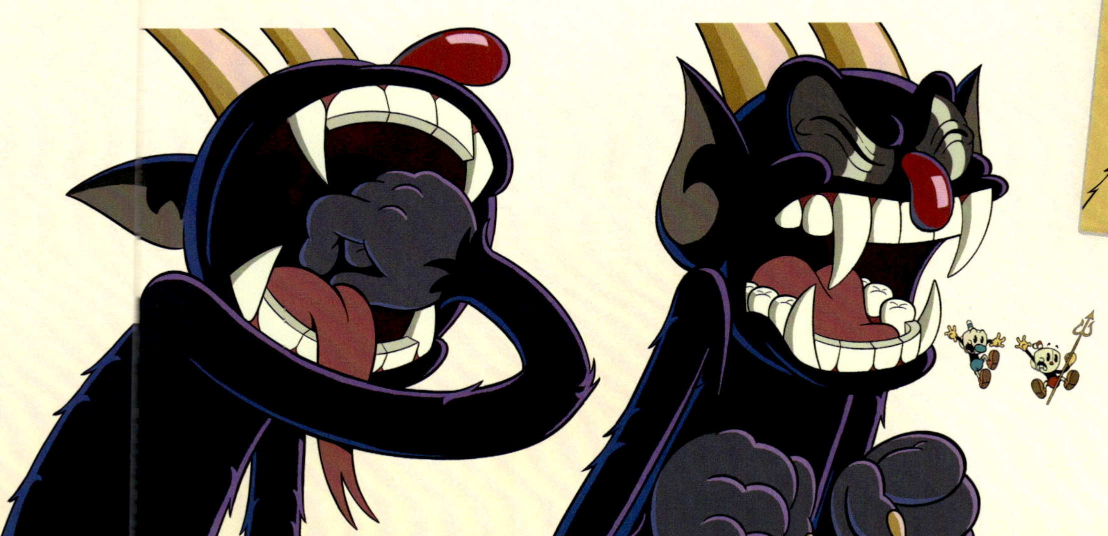

Special pose designs by Adam Paloian, Martin Wittig, and Bradley Lewis; character color by Chris Hacker.

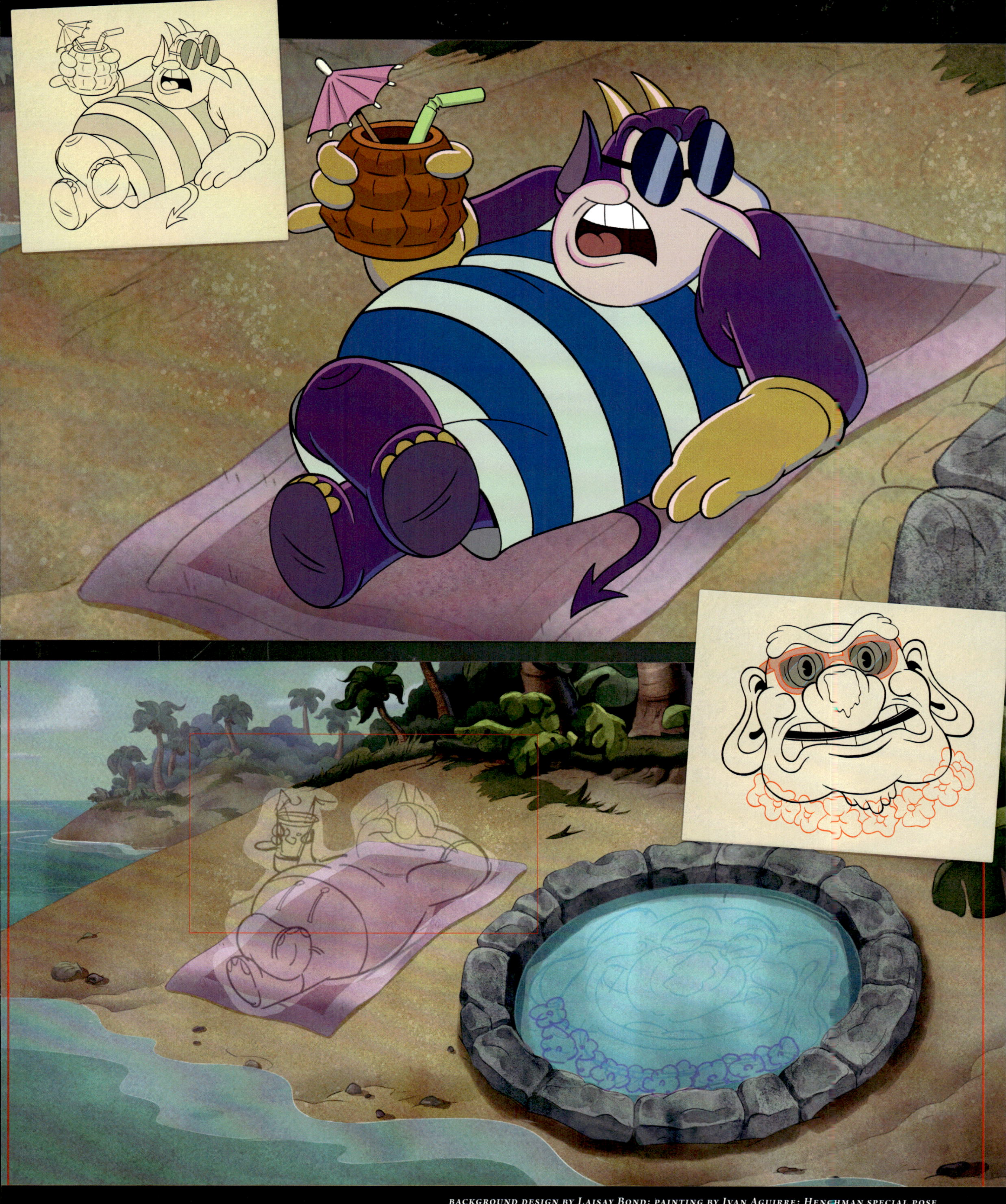

Background design by Laisay Bond; painting by Ivan Aguirre; Henchman special pose design by Dave Wasson; Quadratus special pose by Martin Wittig.

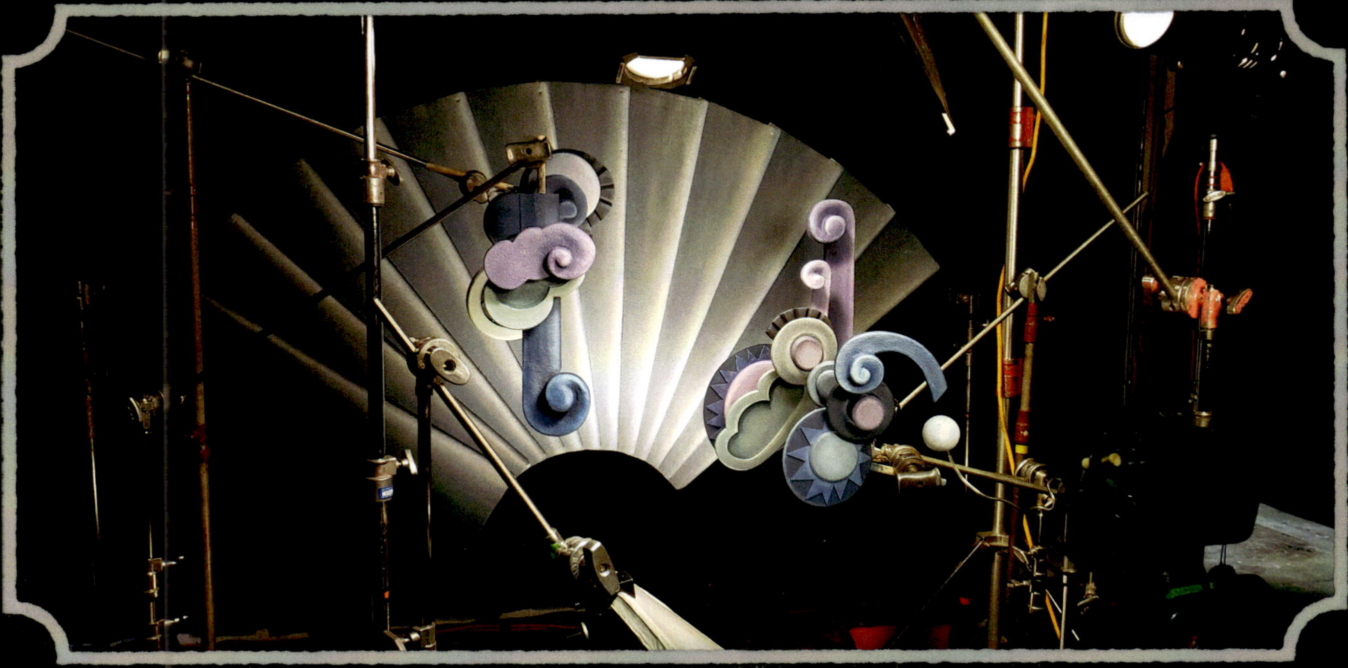

◆ MAIN TITLE SPOTLIGHT ◆

THE TITLE CARD

→ **COSMO:** When I watched *Popeye* cartoons as a kid, every time those doors opened and closed, I was very much ready to watch a *Popeye* cartoon. We wanted to give every episode a really exciting opening title sequence. Each one of them has a unique stop-motion element.

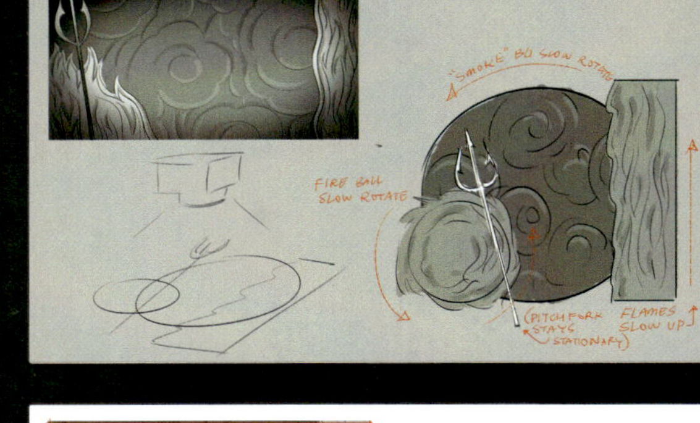

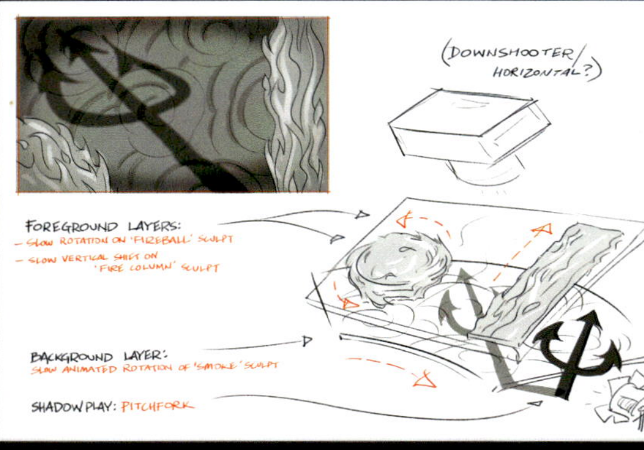

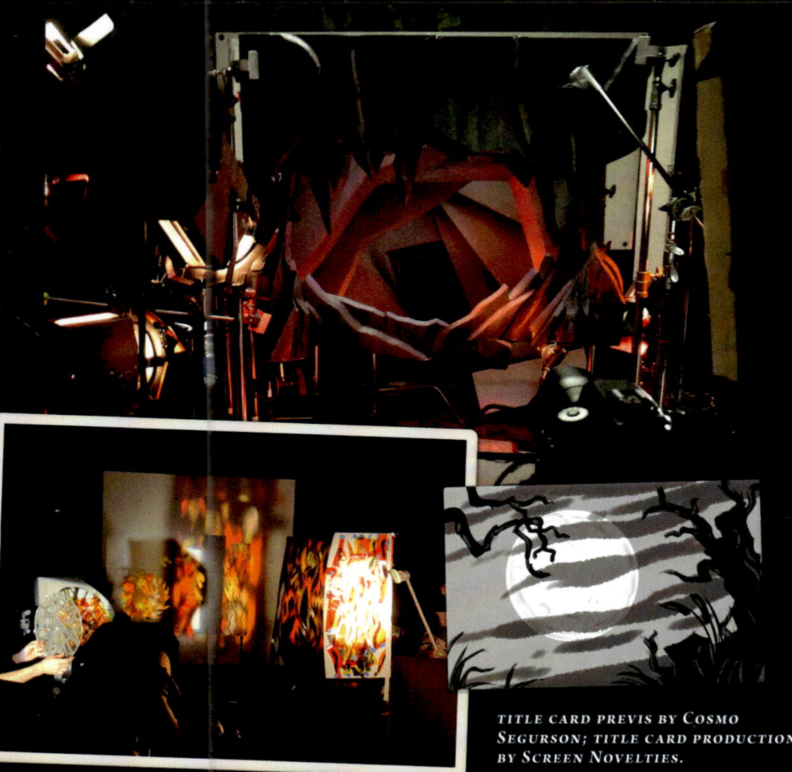

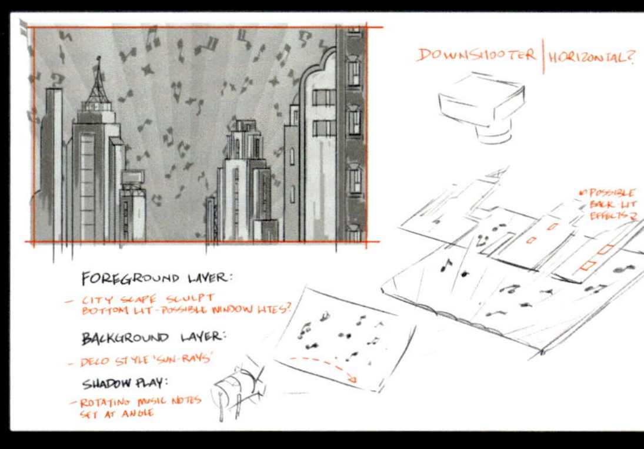

TITLE CARD PREVIS BY COSMO SEGURSON; TITLE CARD PRODUCTION BY SCREEN NOVELTIES.

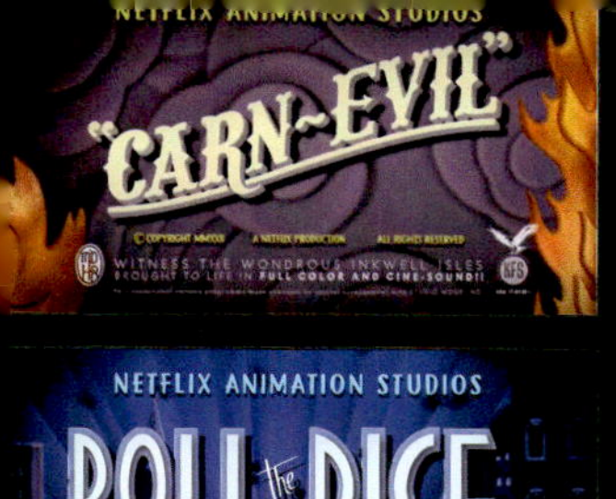

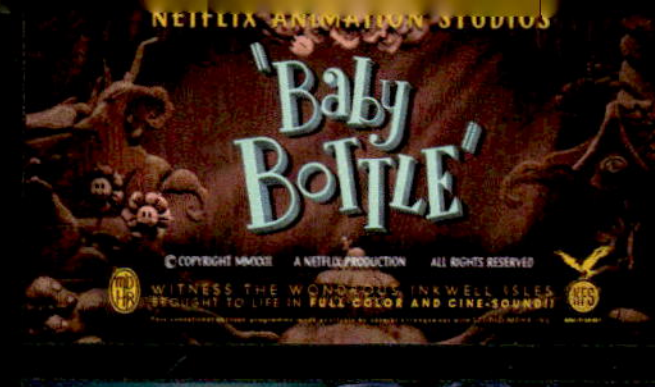

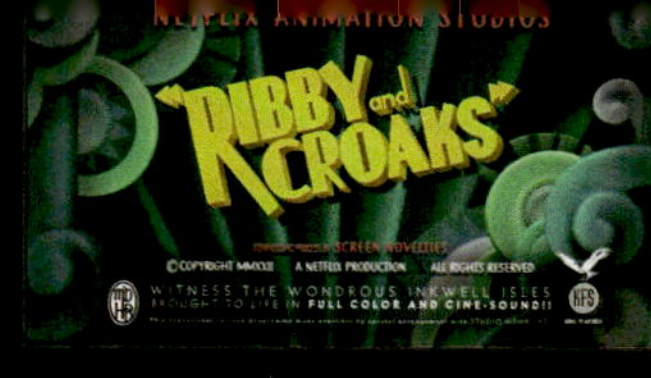

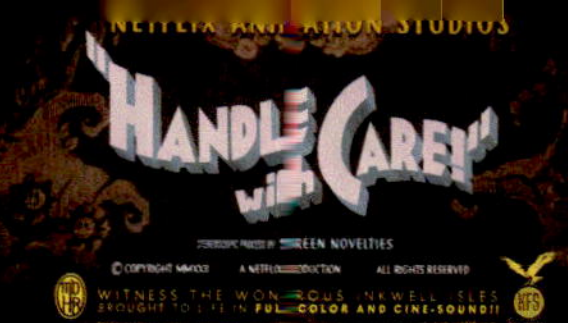

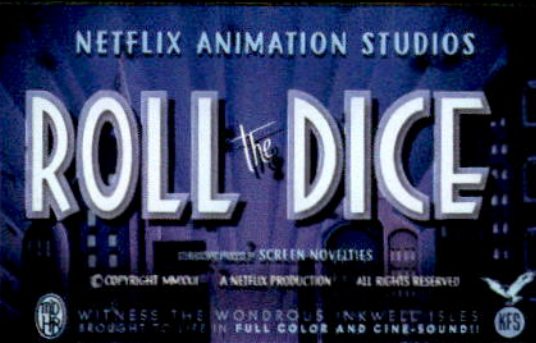

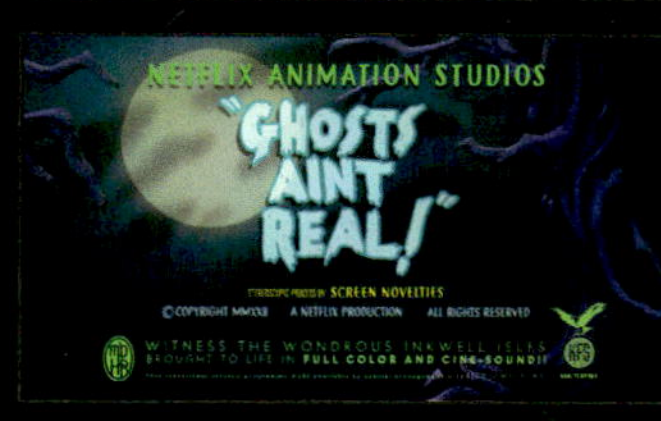

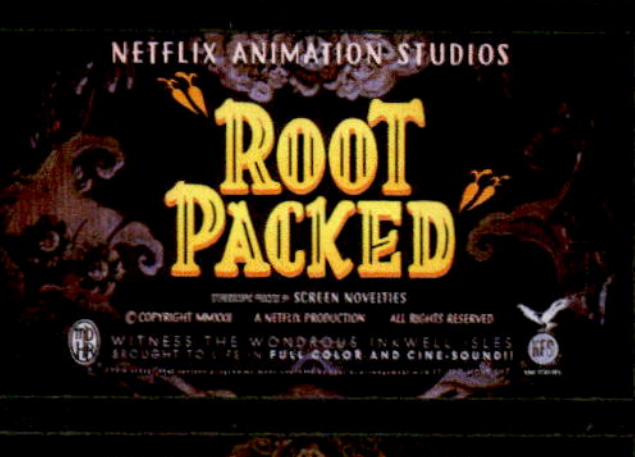

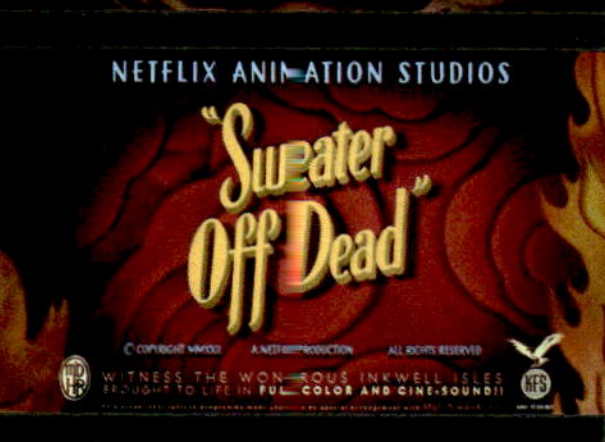

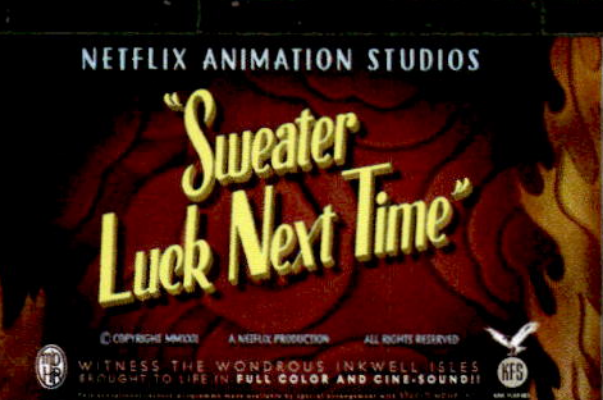

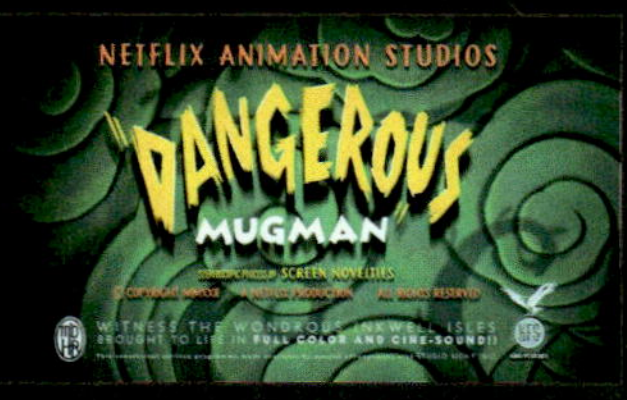

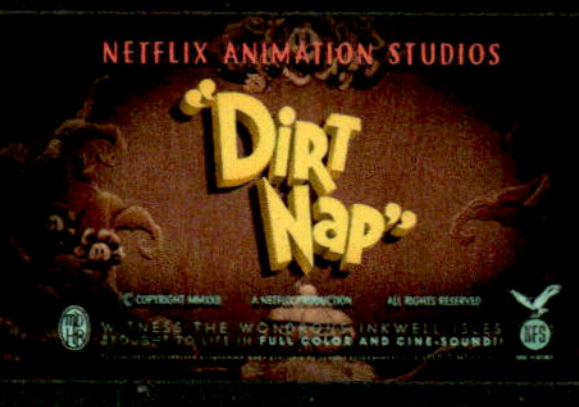

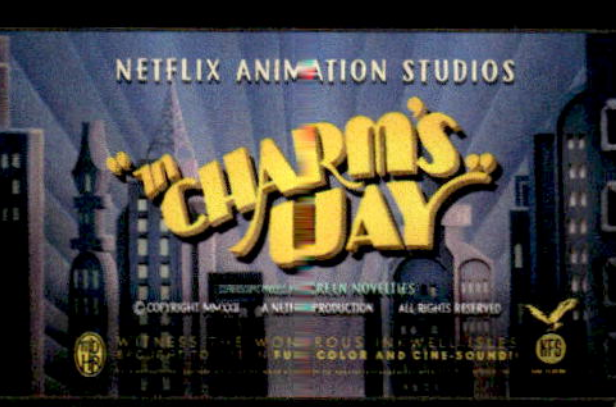

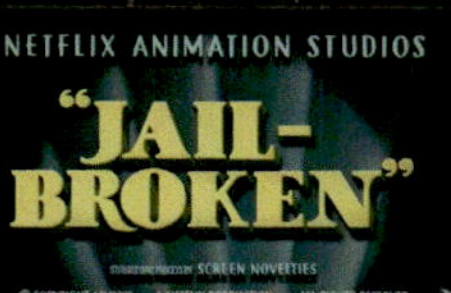

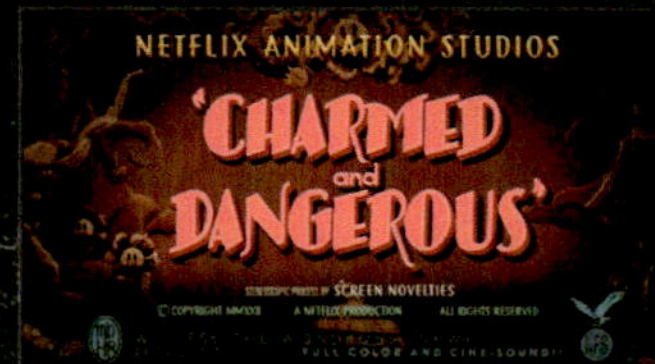

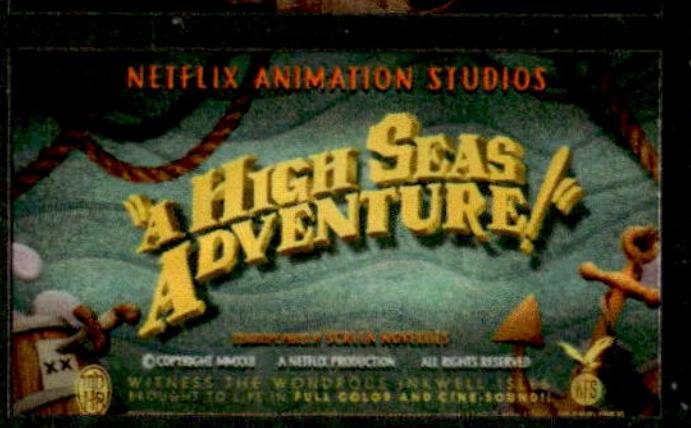

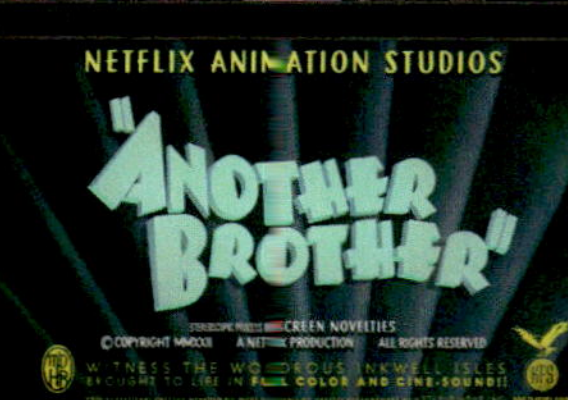

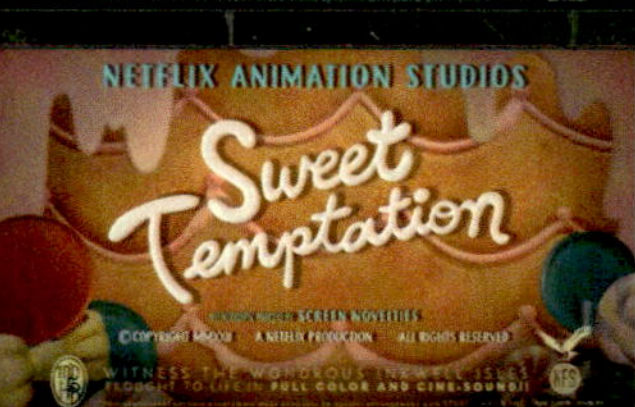

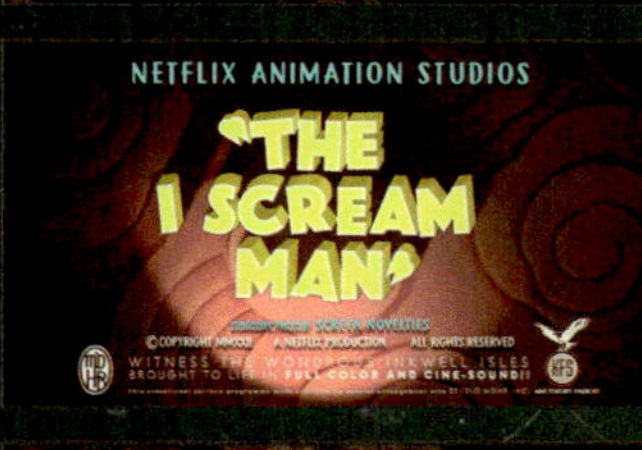

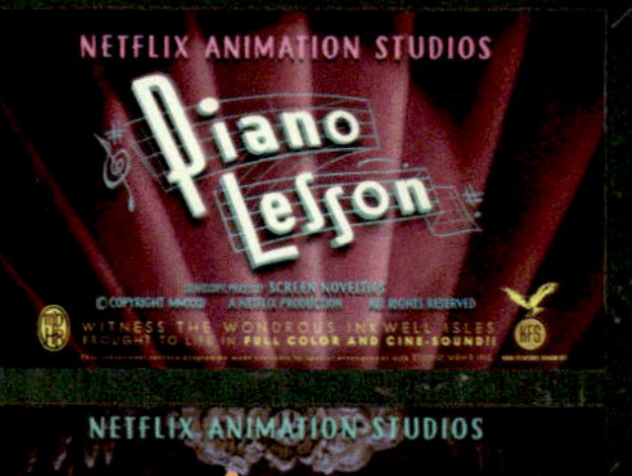

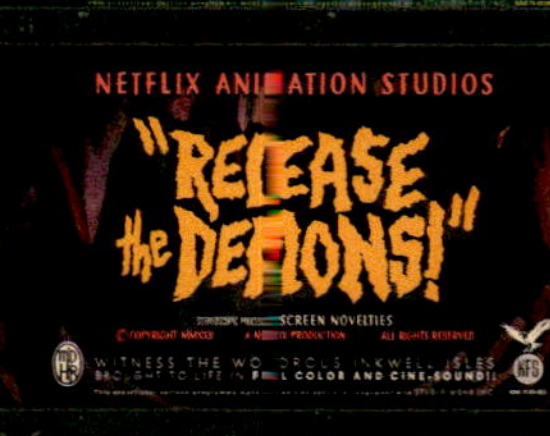

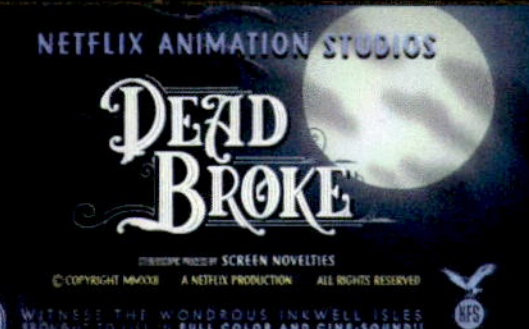

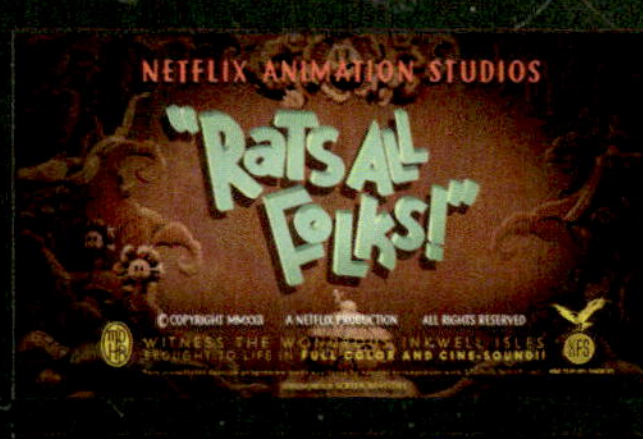

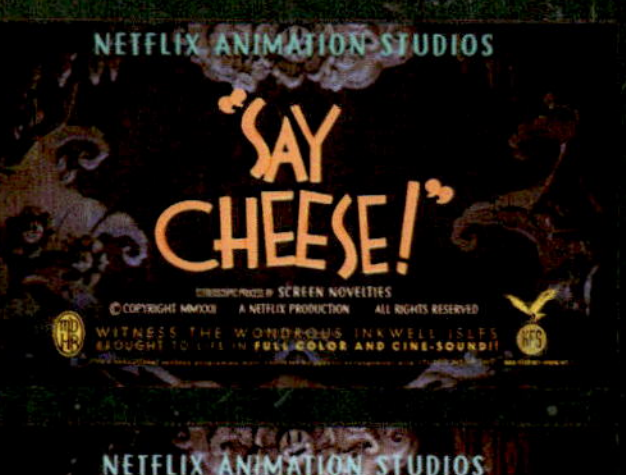

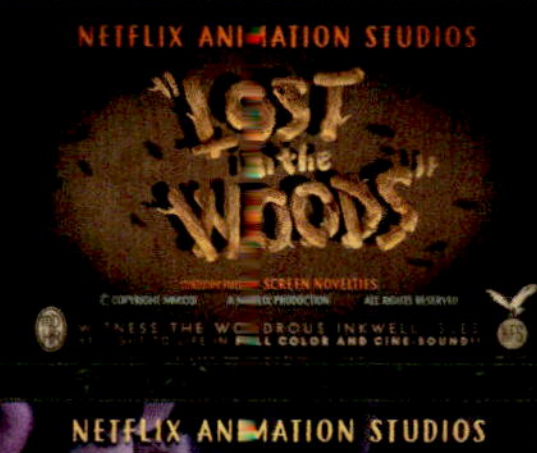

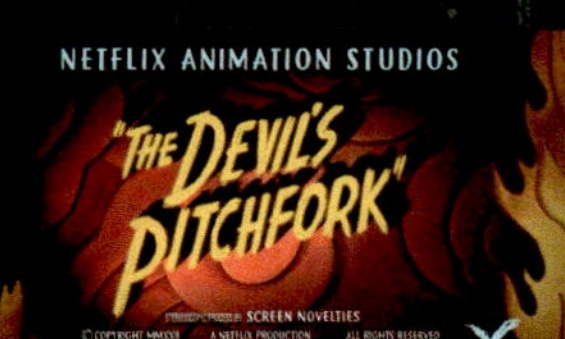

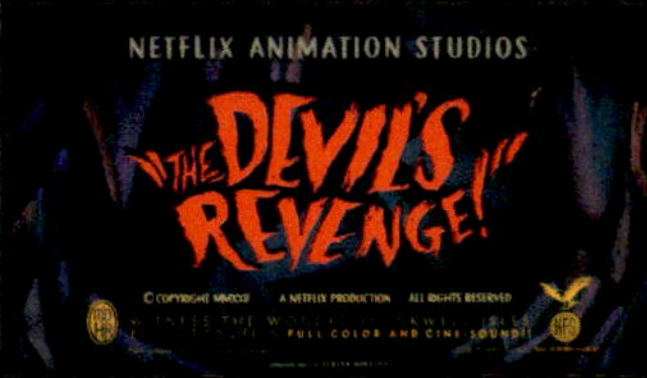

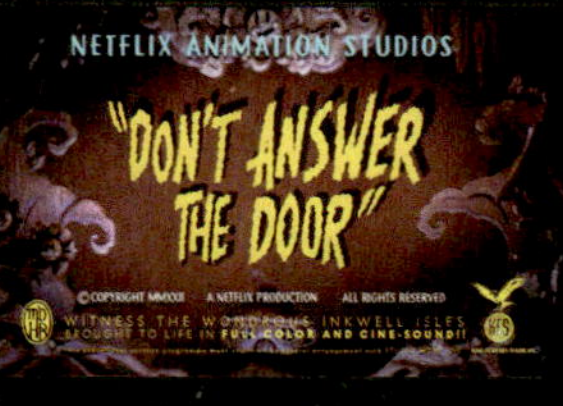

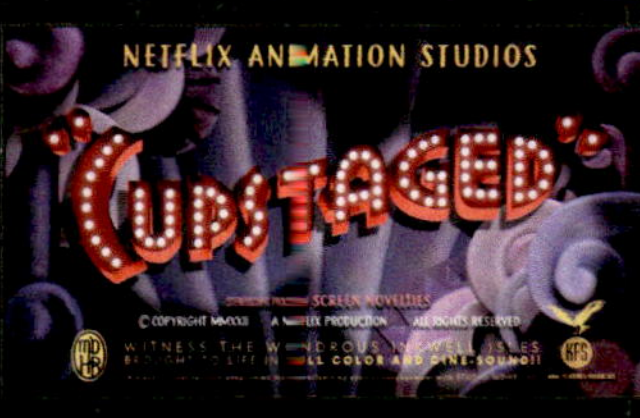

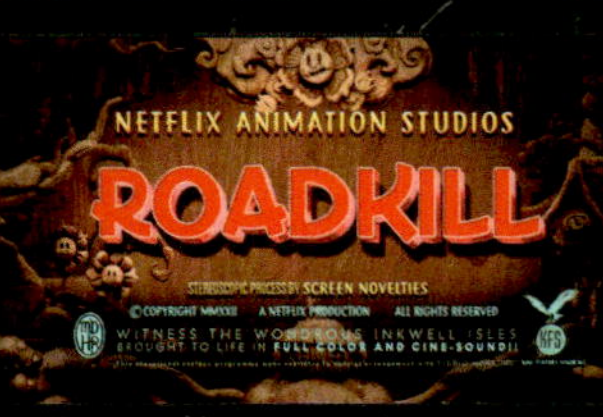

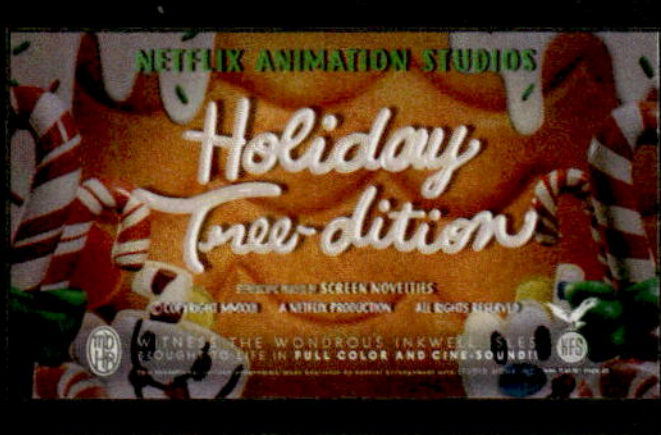

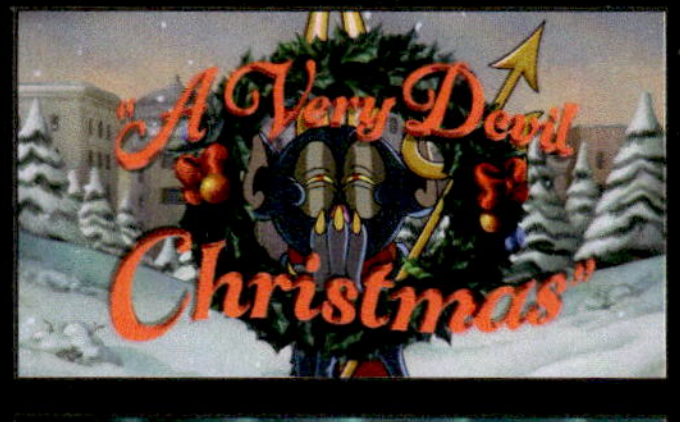

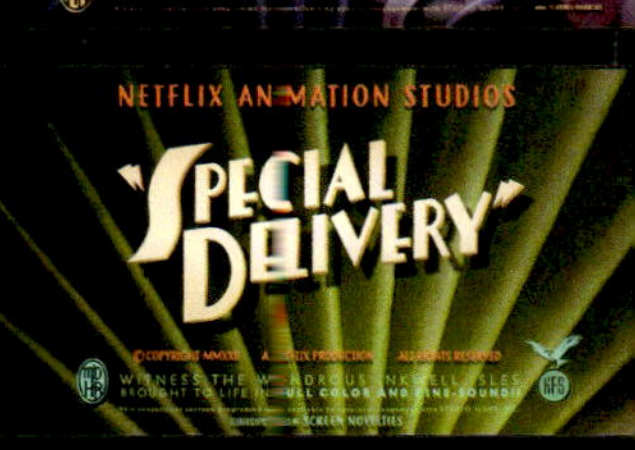

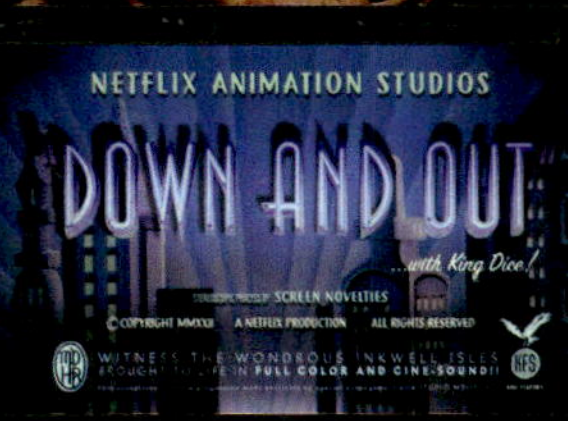

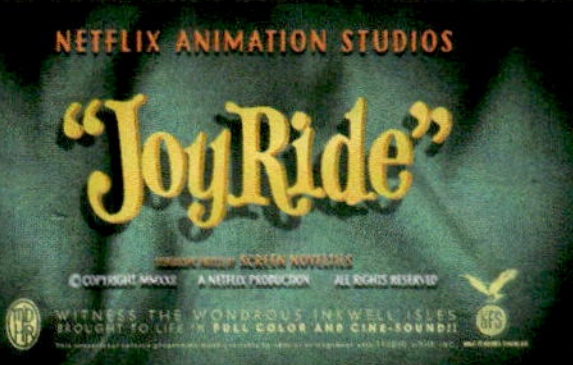

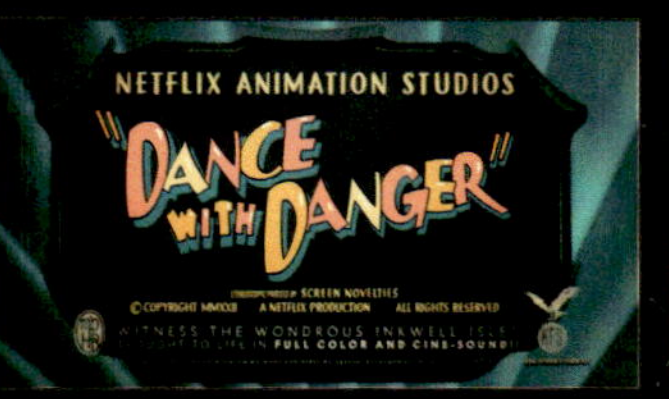

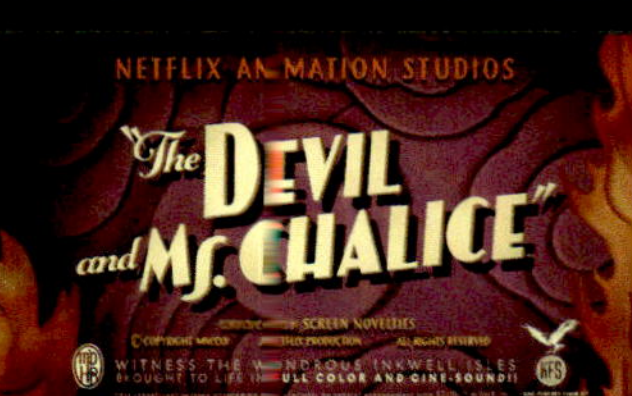

ALL TITLE CARDS: COLOR DESIGN BY ANDREA FERNANDEZ; LETTERING BY ANDREA FERNANDEZ, COSMO SEGURSON, AND TARAN GANDHI

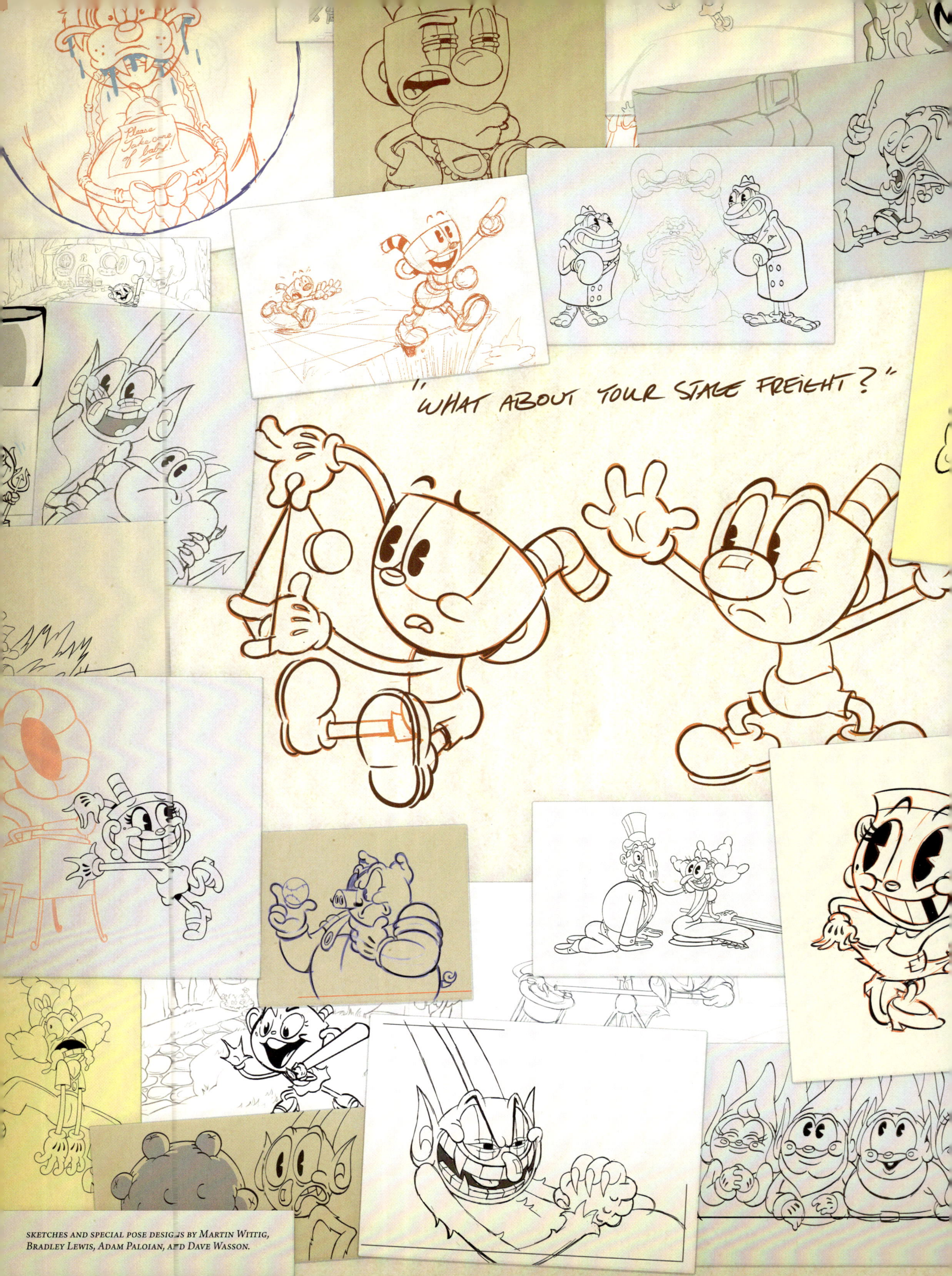

SKETCHES AND SPECIAL POSE DESIGNS BY MARTIN WITTIG, BRADLEY LEWIS, ADAM PALOIAN, AND DAVE WASSON.

CHAPTER 5
MAKING SEASON 3

ENTER

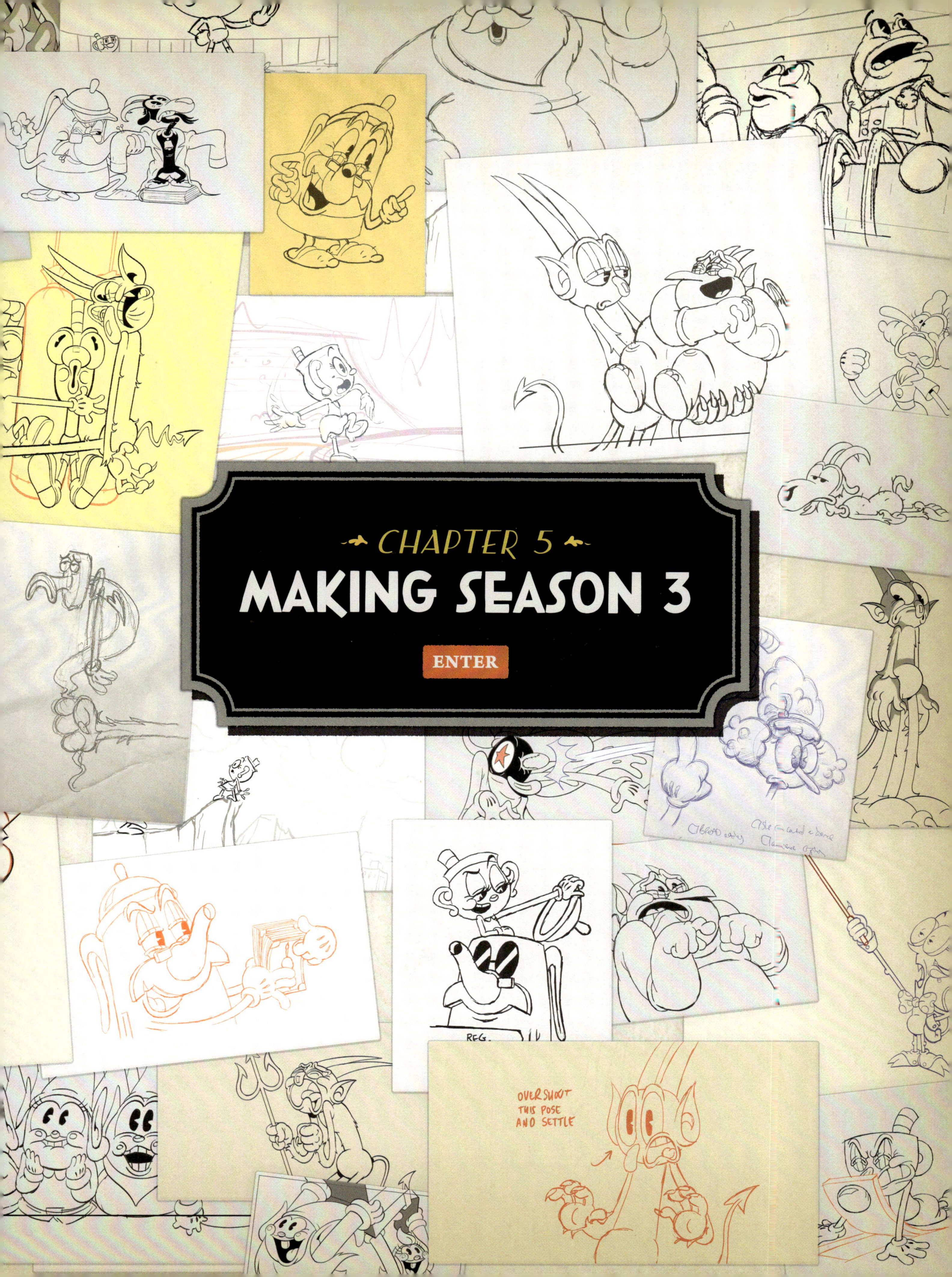

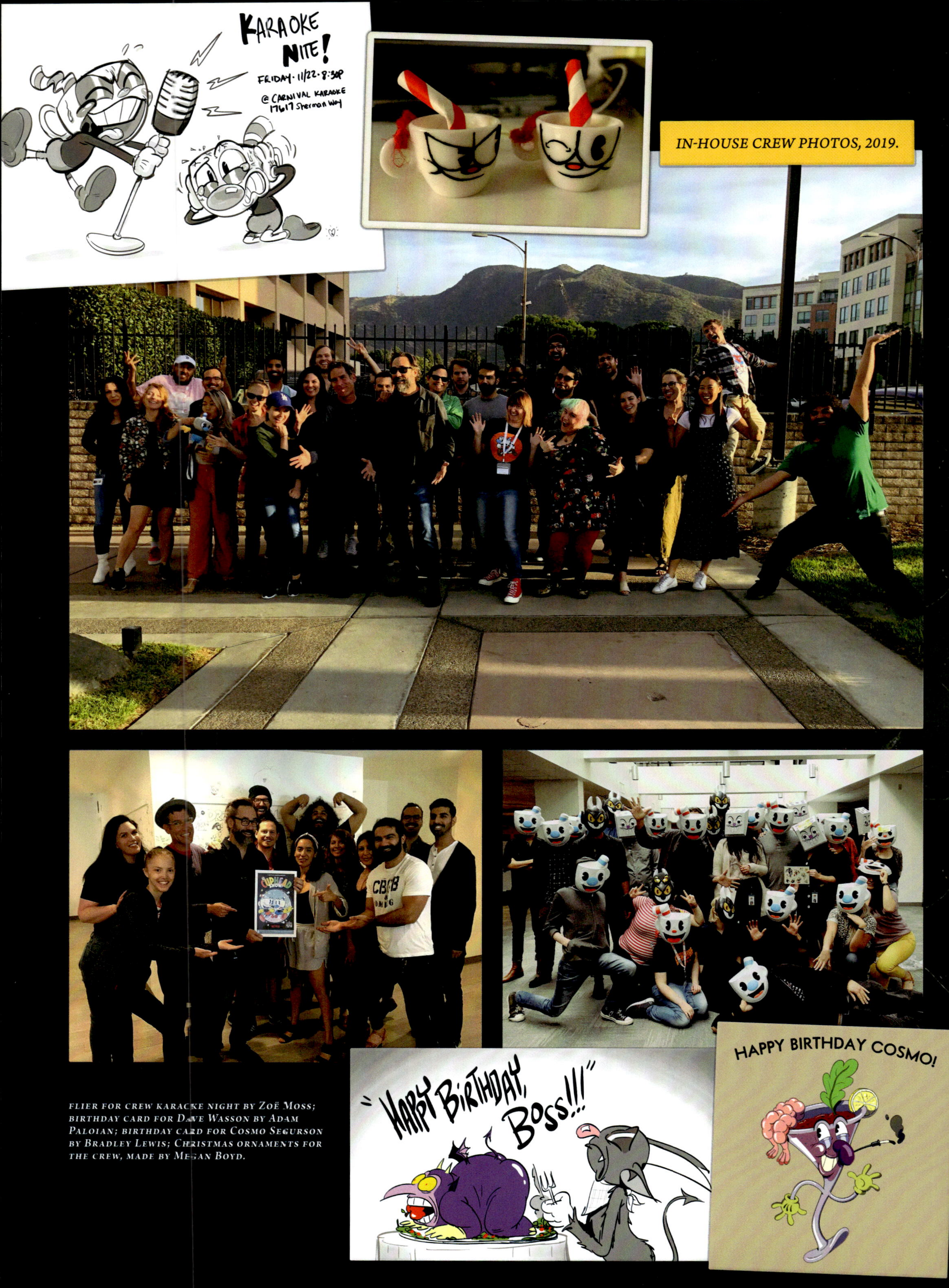

FLIER FOR CREW KARAOKE NIGHT BY ZOË MOSS; BIRTHDAY CARD FOR DAVE WASSON BY ADAM PALOIAN; BIRTHDAY CARD FOR COSMO SEGURSON BY BRADLEY LEWIS; CHRISTMAS ORNAMENTS FOR THE CREW, MADE BY MEGAN BOYD.

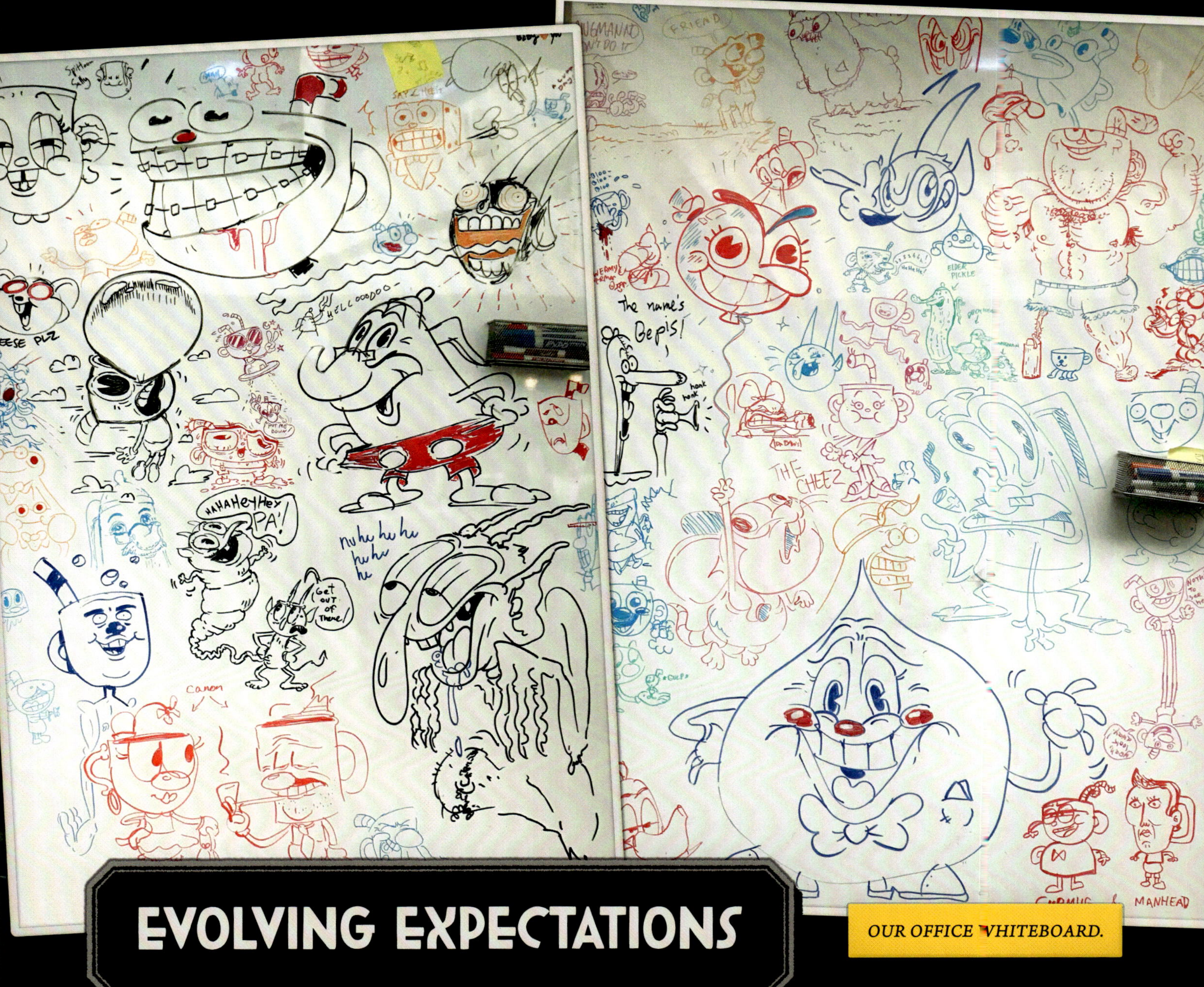

OUR OFFICE WHITEBOARD.

EVOLVING EXPECTATIONS

→ **ANDREA:** We did a bunch of awesome-looking paintings in-house, and when the paintings started coming back from overseas, I almost jumped out a window. I'm thinking it's a disaster and it's not going to work. It's really, really hard to get an entire group of people sitting right beside you to paint like they're the same person. And then you send that to new people overseas, and it's a whole different ball game. They haven't been privy to the experimentation and the conversations—they're not sitting with me day to day talking about the kinds of subtleties that are not needed for any other show. There was a point we hit with the paintings coming in from the overseas team—it became obvious it was going to be harder than we initially thought for them to hit the style that we developed in-house. We all pulled together, we made tutorials, and we sat there almost clinically with a chart of brushes. We had to go through, group each brush, explain what each brush did . . . It was so methodical, and the only reason it worked is because of the cohesion our in-house team developed in the beginning.

LAUREN: The earlier phases of concept design and sorting out the feel of it—you become really immersed, and when the production gets rolling and you have to switch gears more frequently, it gets a little harder.

ADAM P: I'm glad Clay and I shared an office. It was out of limitation, but if I were alone, I might have had a breakdown. This show was so hard—to have Clay there, we could just talk with the door closed and the most stressful times became funny.

CLAY: From day one, Adam and I just decided to support each other. It's such an ambitious show—we knew we needed that.

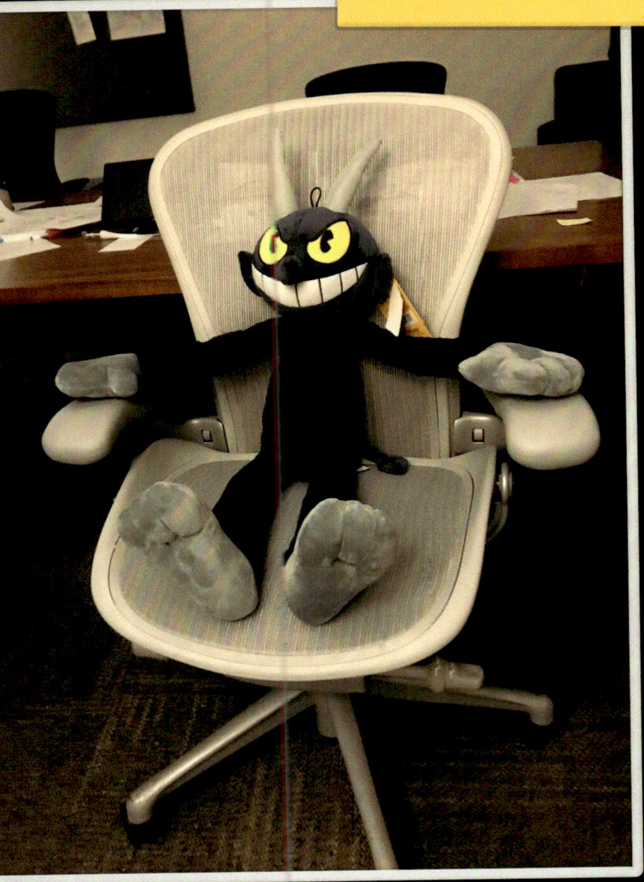

OUR OFFICE OVERLORD.

THE STORY ROOM

ADAM P: Being in the writing room destroyed all the anxiety of the day because we were just constantly laughing.

DAVE: The first season was really great because we could spend more time in the writers' room. And then as we got deeper into the various stages of production—we had storyboarding, design, editing, recording the actors, and music all happening at once—it was harder for us to find time to be in the writers' room. We were more involved with just trying to get the show executed.

DEEKI: The best scenario is a few early weeks of nothing but accumulating a table full of Post-its and notebook scraps with ideas, doodles, anything—even if it has nothing to do with the show. For example, "Adam's rivalry with the ice cream man." After the table gets covered with half-baked ideas, one day they come in and I've got index cards on the wall and stories start to take shape.

CLAY: We got to a place that I always aspire to, where you open the door and there's the character and the audience is already laughing. It's like on *Three's Company* when Mr. Furley shows up. Nothing has happened—he's not even making an expression yet. But just his presence tells the audience it's about to get fun. There's so many sitcoms where they do that. They open the door, and it isn't as powerful—and you're like, "Who cares?"

DEEKI: Sometimes Dave would ask, "What's the clearest version of this that someone watching will understand immediately?"

DAVE: You need to establish a normal baseline before you can show what's weird. You want to see how the world actually works before Cuphead and Mugman screw the whole thing up.

CLAY: People can't have a primal comedic reaction if they have to think too hard about something: that's "witty," or it's "clever," and the audience might be *appreciating* something—but that's not the same as a visceral reaction.

COSMO: We had a lot of stories to come up with, but once you factor in run time, it becomes about how you divide up the minutes. The grand total for the whole show is four hundred forty minutes.

DAVE: That is the number that has come to haunt us all.

MEGAN C: I love rubbing this in Dave's face. In the early days, he was saying they were going to be seven-minute cartoons. Then it was eight or nine. I remember telling him, "You're crazy, I think they're going to be longer than that." And he said, "No, no, the *Bugs Bunny* shorts were six minutes." But I think it grew into the right space organically. Because we weren't locked into needing it to hit a certain format, we had that latitude to adjust. The stories and the characters became so rich and so fun; it kept ballooning. Then it was ten minutes, then it was eleven, and then it was, "Oh wait, this one's fourteen!"

DEEKI: Usually, episode length is predetermined. This was the first time I ever heard a broadcaster say, "Make each one the length it should be." It's so wonderful and so rare to have that kind of flexibility in animation.

MEGAN C: If you don't have to cut a joke or think about when the commercial is going to come in, it should always be what's best for the story.

→ **MARGARET HOFFMAN, *THE CUPHEAD SHOW!* SCRIPT COORDINATOR:** Fun fact: the writers' room at Burbank Studios was called "the Devil's HQ," so we were literally conducting business in the Devil's office.

ADAM P: Deeki color-coded the wall of cards mapping out the season so you could visualize how the season felt. The Chalice episodes were on blue cards; the Devil was on pink cards. Throughout the season, you want all different colors and kinds of episodes.

DEEKI: Each of us wanted a character-driven comedy, but we all have different approaches. Dave likes comedy that's clear and primal; Cosmo likes strange and bizzare; Clay likes economical and punishment based; Adam likes ultraspecific neuroses against an epic backdrop. My role was putting all that into a blender and condensing it into a collective voice and tone, then framing the stories so they're producible.

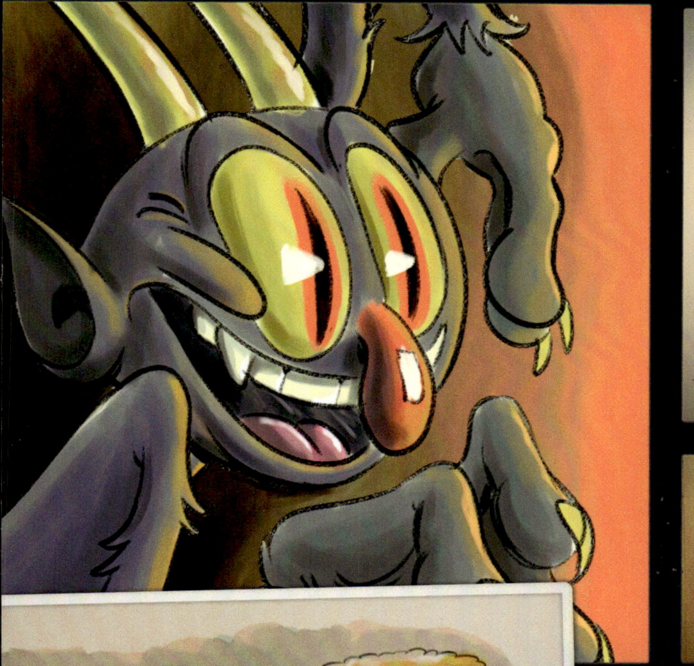
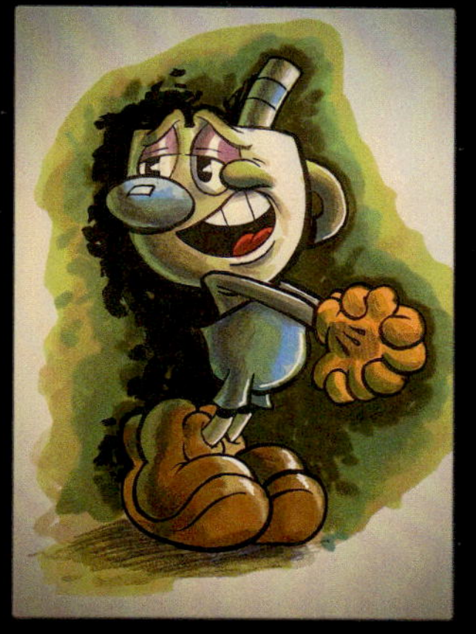
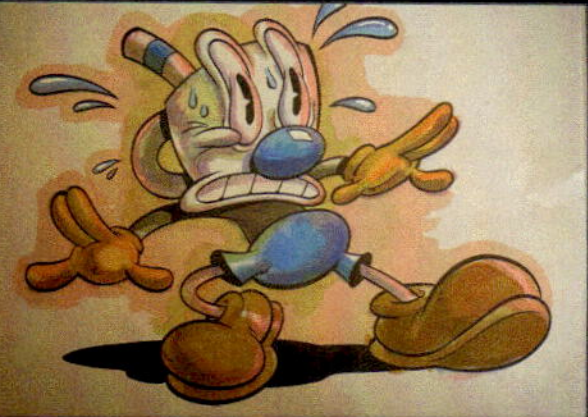
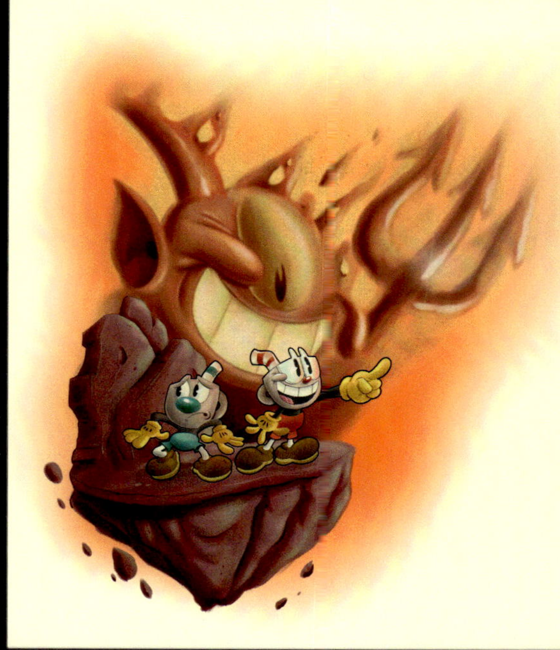

PAINTINGS AND SKETCHES BY JARED MORGAN.

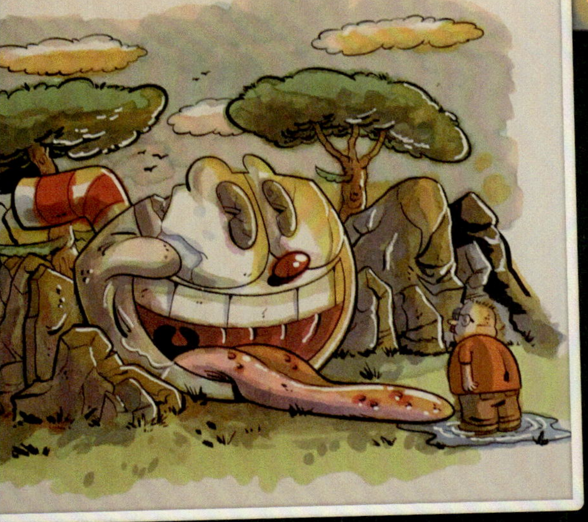
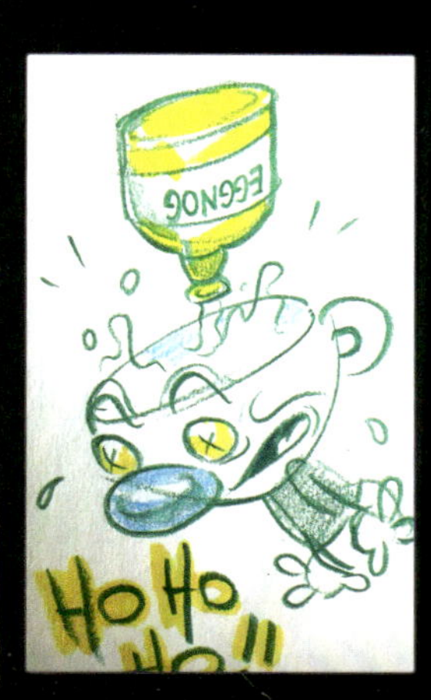

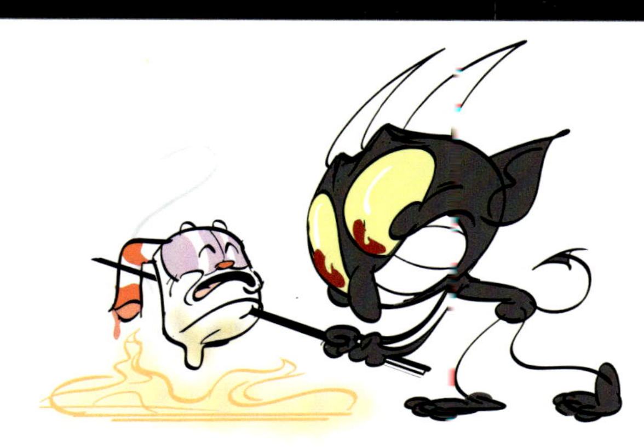

PAINTINGS AND SKETCHES BY KARL HADRIKA.

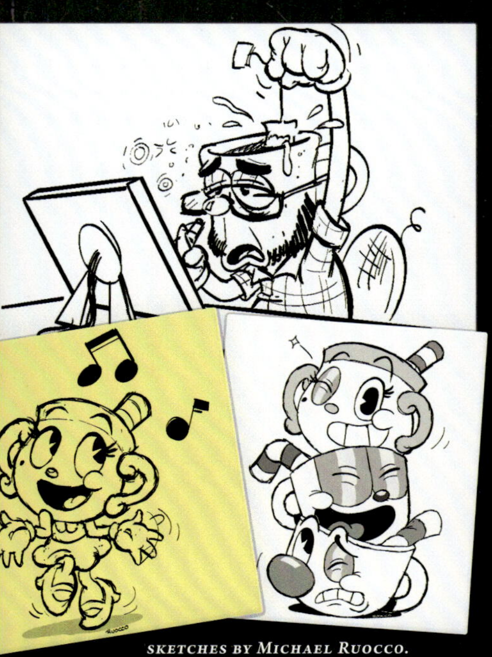

SKETCHES BY MICHAEL RUOCCO.

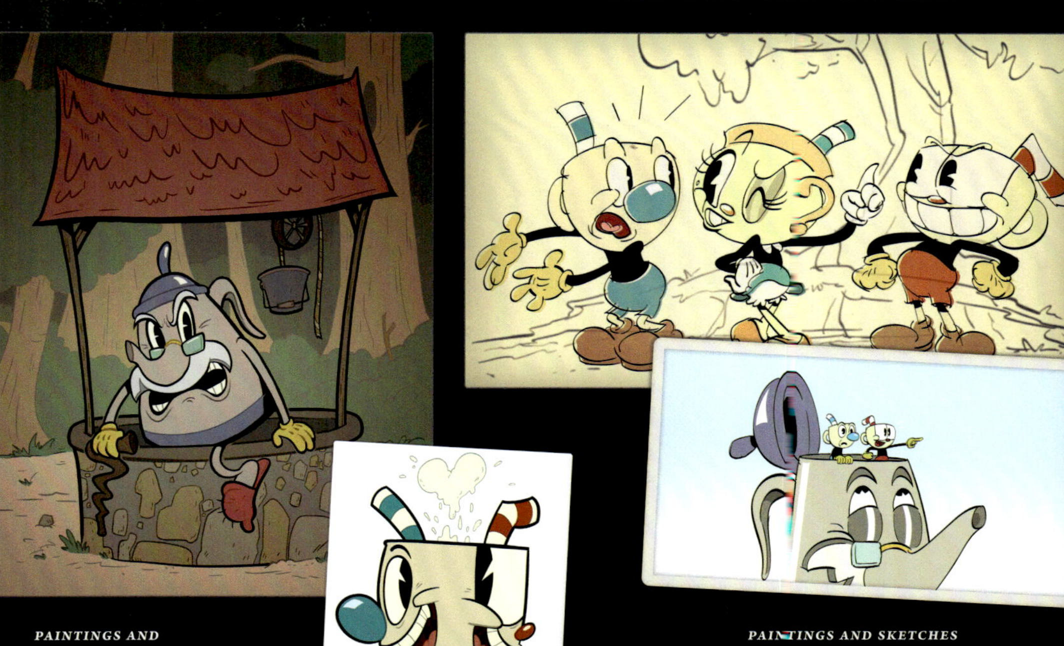

PAINTINGS AND SKETCHES BY ZOË MOSS.

PAINTINGS AND SKETCHES BY NICK LAUER.

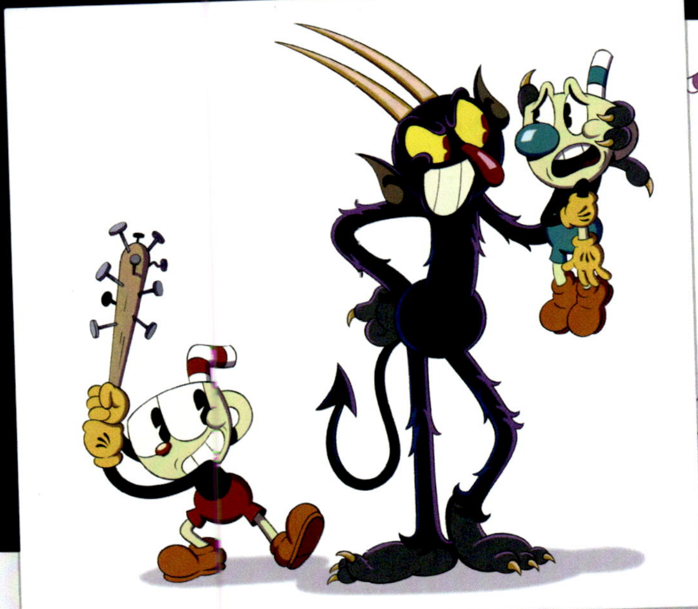

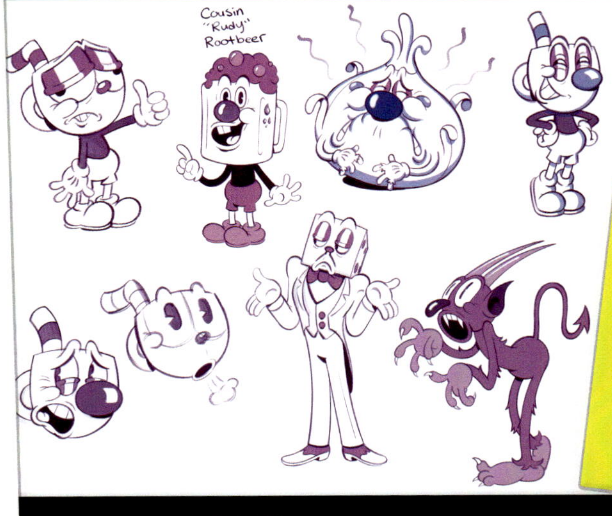

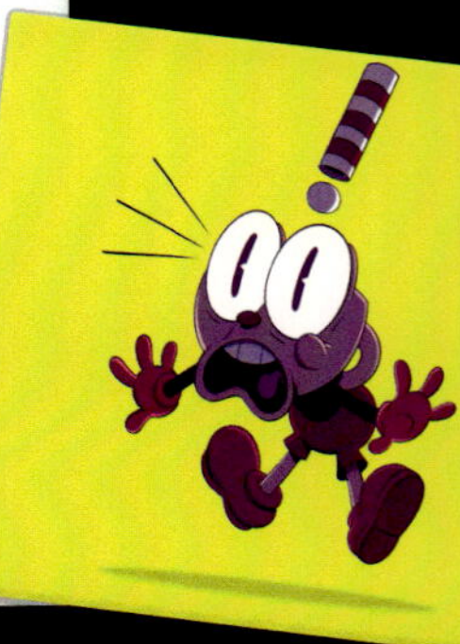

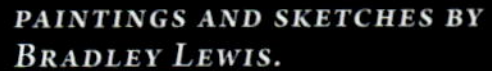

Paintings and sketches by Bradley Lewis.

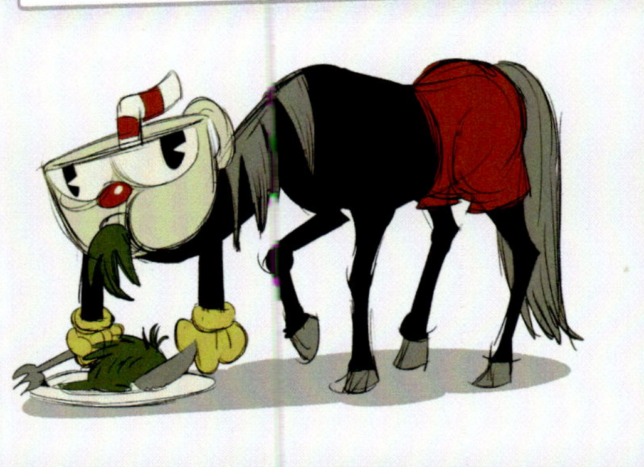

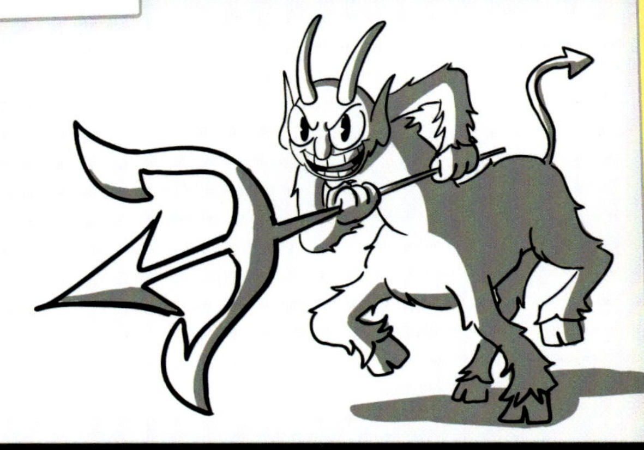

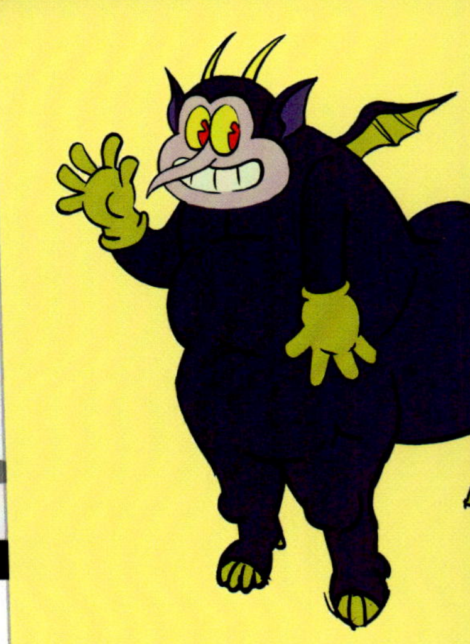

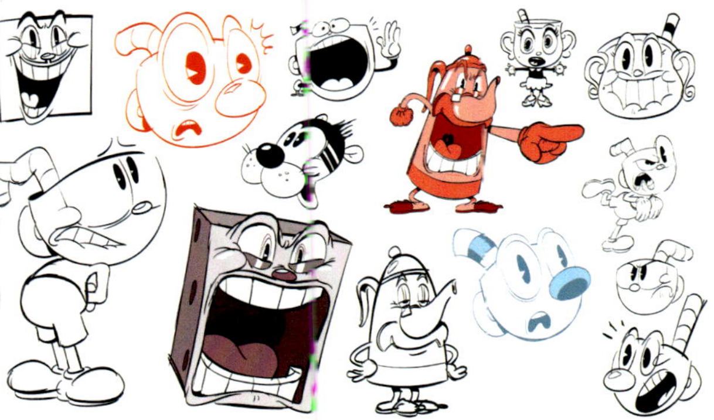

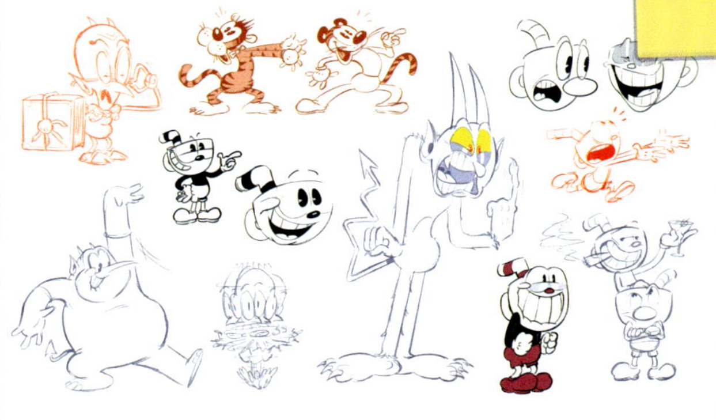

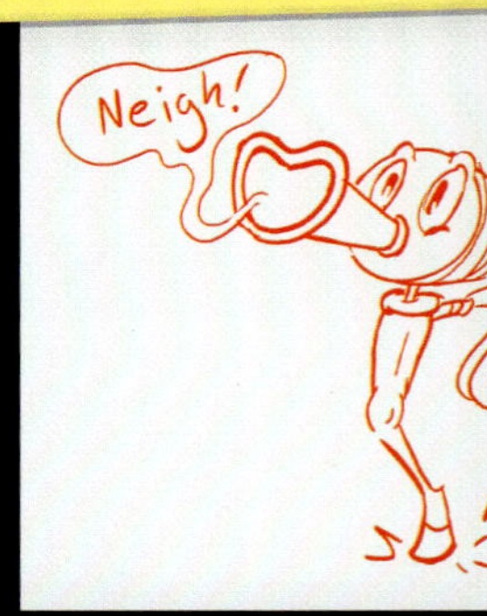

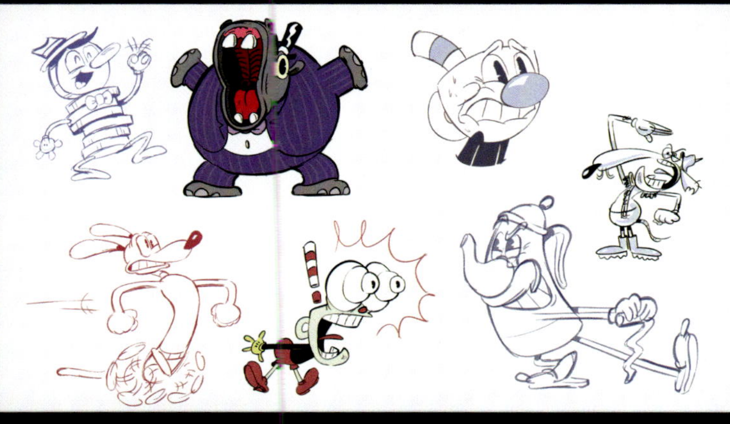

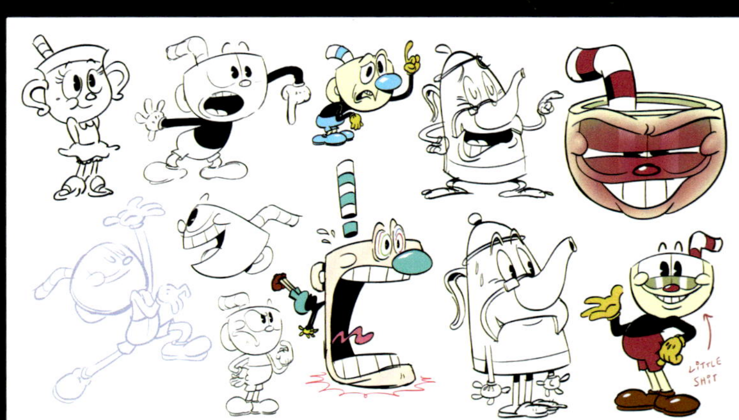

Paintings and sketches by Nick Lauer.

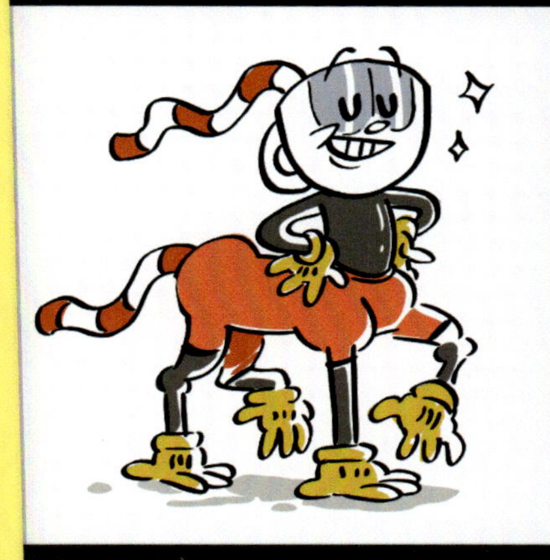

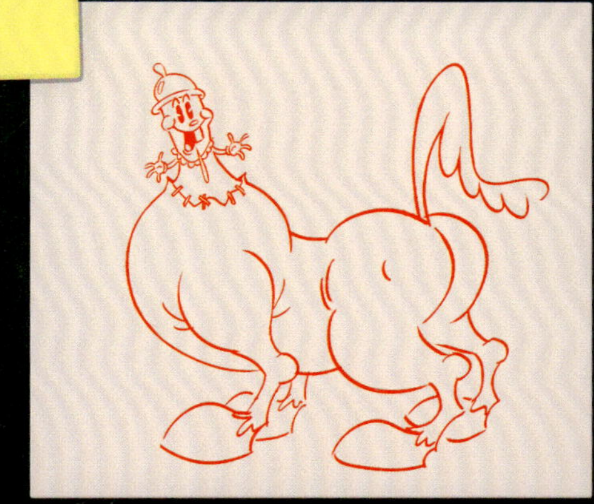

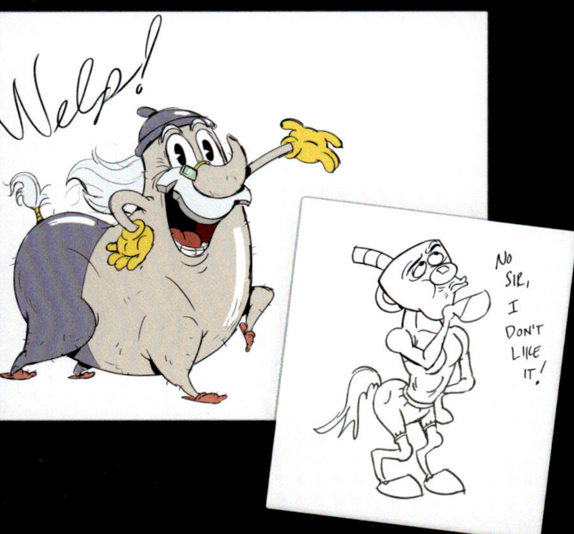

"Cup-taur" sketches by Adam Dix, Kennedy Tarrell, Mike Fontanelli, Allen Zhang, Thalia Nalapraya, Zoë Moss, Mike Fontanelli, and Adam Fay.

STORYBOARDING

DAVE: In boarding, you want somebody who has great draftsmanship skills. But it has to be a combination of a few things. It's better if they have a little bit of animation experience and know how things move. They also have to draw *funny*, and very expressively. *And* they have to hit a deadline. When you staff up, you're almost looking for unicorns.

ADAM P: We tried to cast the storyboards to the strengths of each board team—usually based on who's newer versus who's had more experience—and they can complement one another and help each other out. If we knew a particular board artist was especially good with a certain character, we always tried to give them that episode if it worked out in terms of schedule. We had a fantastic team, and everyone got a taste of something different.

DAVE: It's difficult enough finding the right board artists, but they've also got to work together in storyboarding teams. Their personalities and their work have to complement one another.

ADAM P: Fernando has a really specific sense of humor that's dry and underplayed, and Megan knows how to do everything with storyboarding—together they're this great comedic duo with different flavors that really complemented one another in the boards. It surprised me how well they matched up—they didn't even know each other, but they communicated a lot and worked so well together.

MEGAN B: I think Adam divided the episodes really well. He always played to our strengths. Fernando would get a lot of the comedy acting sections where they're bouncing off of each other, and I would get some of the more complex things, like the dances and the songs.

ADAM P: Benjamin and Ian worked on different ends of the continent—I had to be a middle man between them, but it was fun because I had already worked with both of them on *SpongeBob*. Ian is hilarious, with amazing character acting. Benjamin is a masterful board artist, and he can do anything with a scene.

BENJAMIN: You can't work with Adam and not bring your A-game. The fact that he trusts me is a huge confidence boost. He really brought the best out of me on this show.

ADAM P: Sometimes when you first read something, it feels really obvious how to execute it. But when you sit down to do the work, you start uncovering all sorts of problems you didn't initially notice. That's the most fun part of storyboarding—the problem solving.

MEGAN B: Our job is to make anything work. You're supposed to be able to take anything and elevate it and make it work.

DAN: We became a really close group. Everyone's work was so high quality—you'd see something from Ian and Benjamin and think, "I gotta step it up!"

ZOË: What made boarding on the show so special was that it felt intimate. You could learn from everybody else.

NICK: I was a revisionist for six or seven months before I got the promotion to storyboard artist, and I'm really glad I started there. Everything I learned as a revisionist comes in handy as a board artist. Dave brought me to editorial meetings and scratch records and showed me the process and how things work behind the scenes. It's good to know what happens to your stuff after you're done with it.

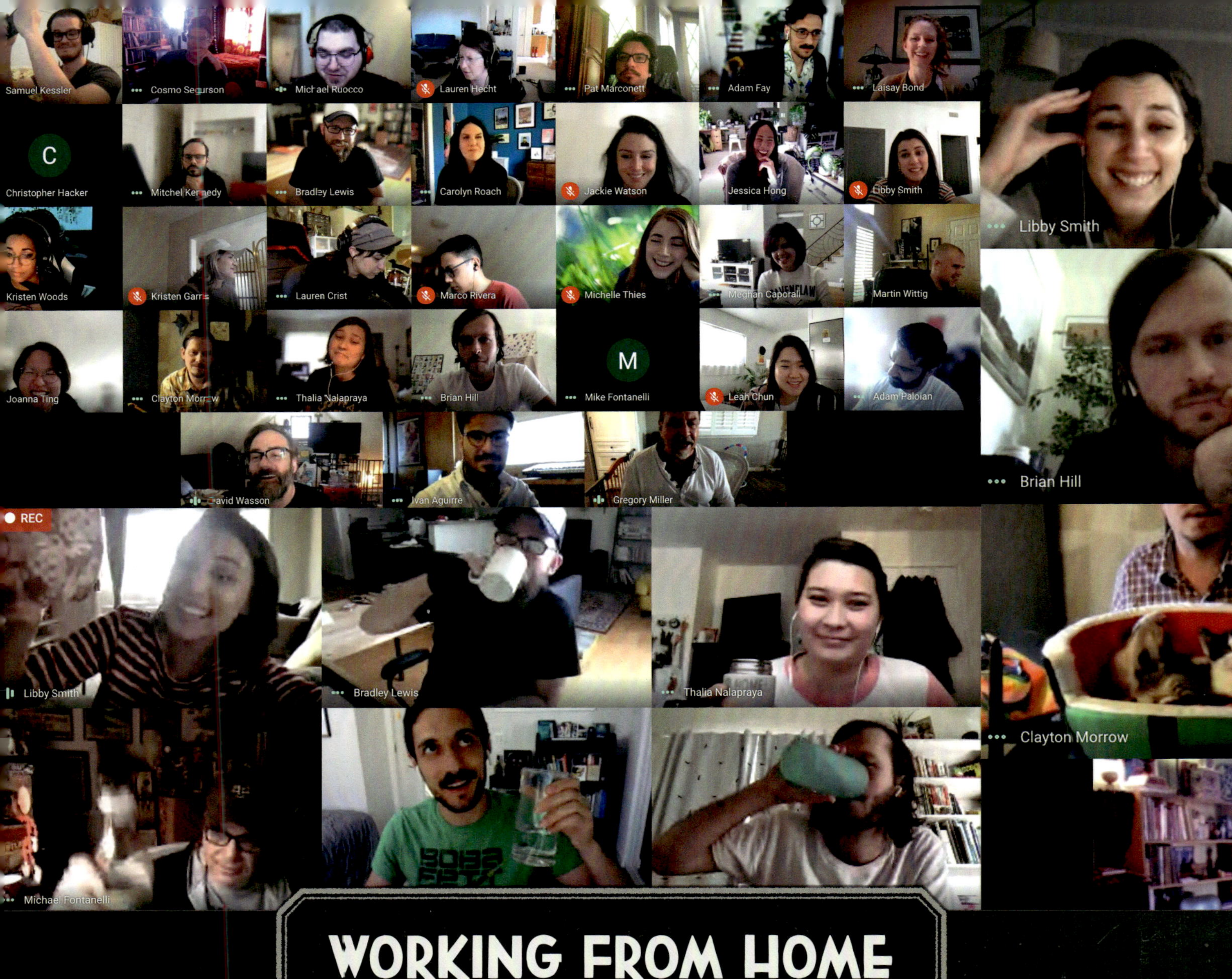

WORKING FROM HOME

→ **DEEKI:** We were an in-person crew for about the first year. Then in March 2020, the pandemic hit, and the world went into lockdown. We had to adjust to working from home and making the show remotely.

KENNEDY: We did digital drawing sessions—anything to keep hanging out. As a team, we had to figure out how to lean on one another without being there to physically lean on.

BABY DAVE: Working on the production in person was a tremendous pleasure. Working from home, a little less so. I found myself in my head a lot more, so I needed to learn how to be friendlier to myself. I was finding ways to interact with the crew in a more meaningful way. So I started baking!

DEEKI: One day, Baby Dave showed up to my house with freshly baked bread. It was delicious.

CLAY: Baby Dave's bread deliveries were definitely one of the few upsides of the global pandemic.

BABY DAVE: I really wanted that experience: to deliver bread to people, to share joyous creation. It felt like something we all desperately needed during that time.

ADAM P: Working from home, we were in meetings every minute of the day. It was not like that when we were in the office. Things got a lot busier when we were working from home.

IVAN: We were comfortable with the style of the show by the time we started working from home, so that helped. It would have

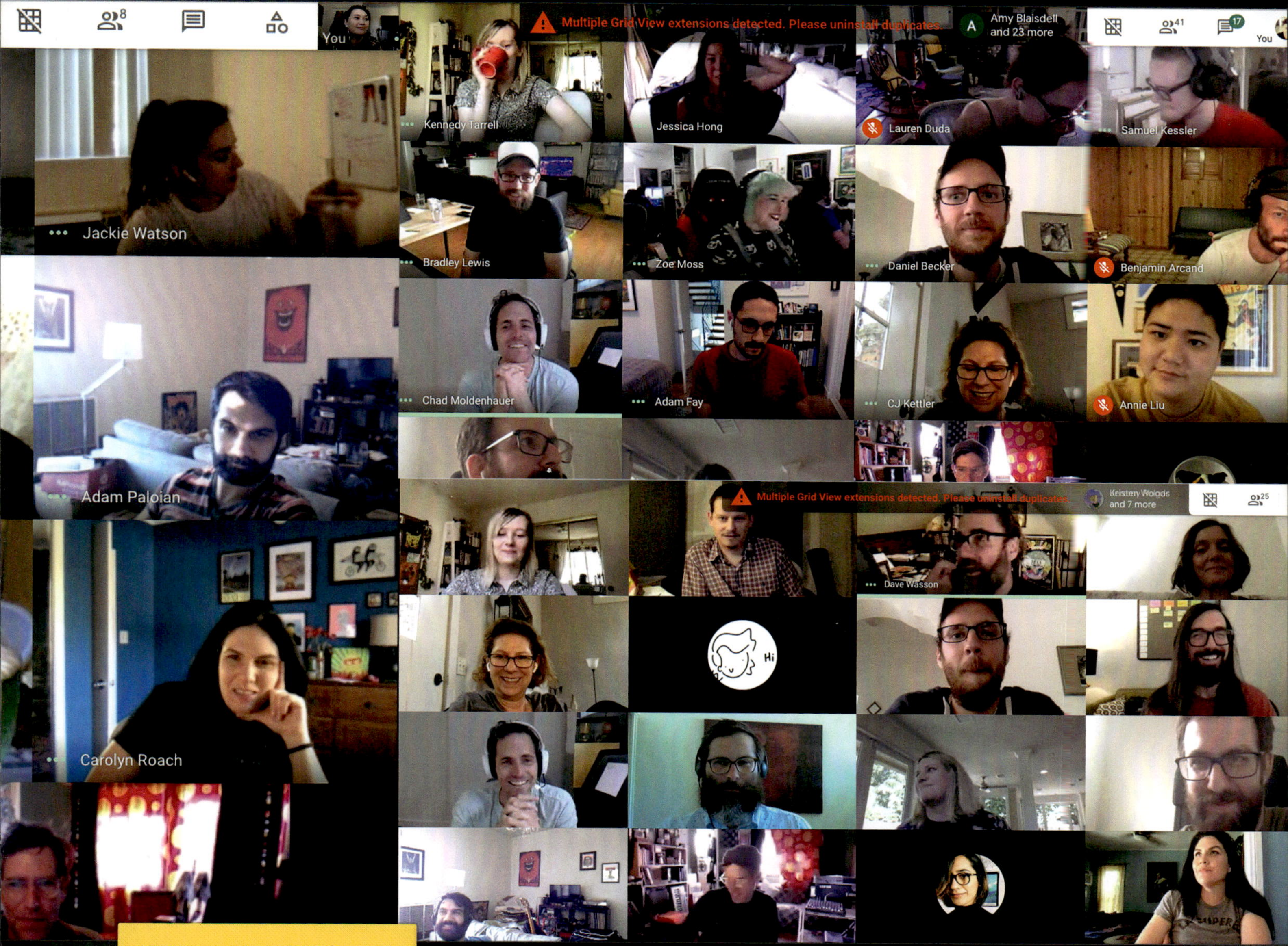

VIRTUAL COWORKERS, 2020.

been more difficult trying to learn this complex style without your peers around.

ANDREA: I am super grateful we got to be in house in the beginning to figure it all out. I don't think we would have achieved the look that we did had we not been in house initially to collaborate with one another in person.

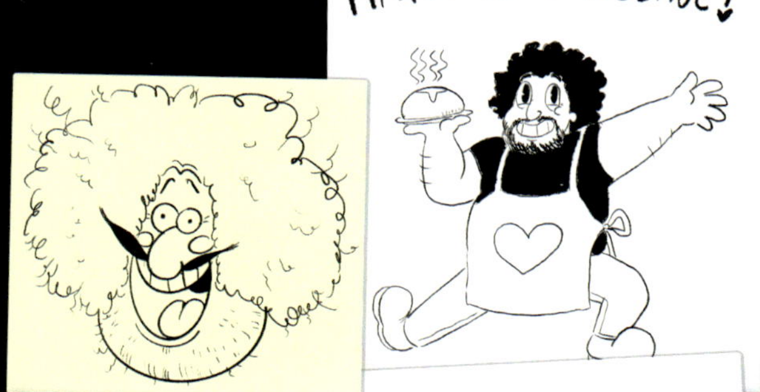

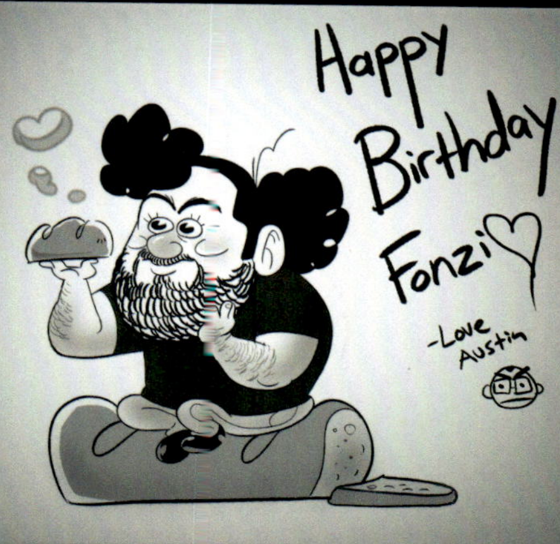

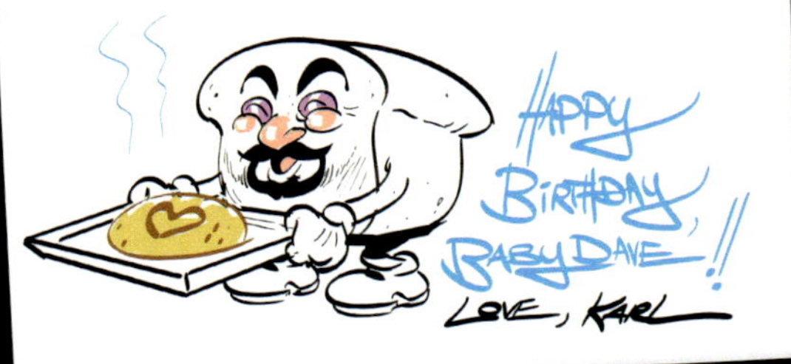

CREW ART FEATURING BABY DAVE AND HIS BREAD BY KARL HADRIKA, AUSTIN FABER, ALLEN ZHANG, DAN BECKER, AND FERNANDO PUIG.

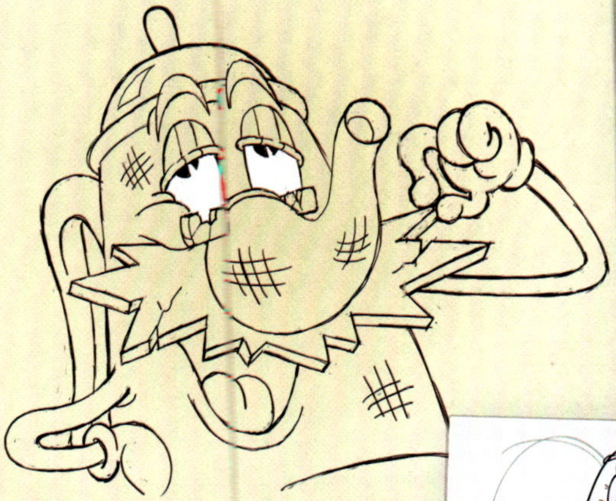

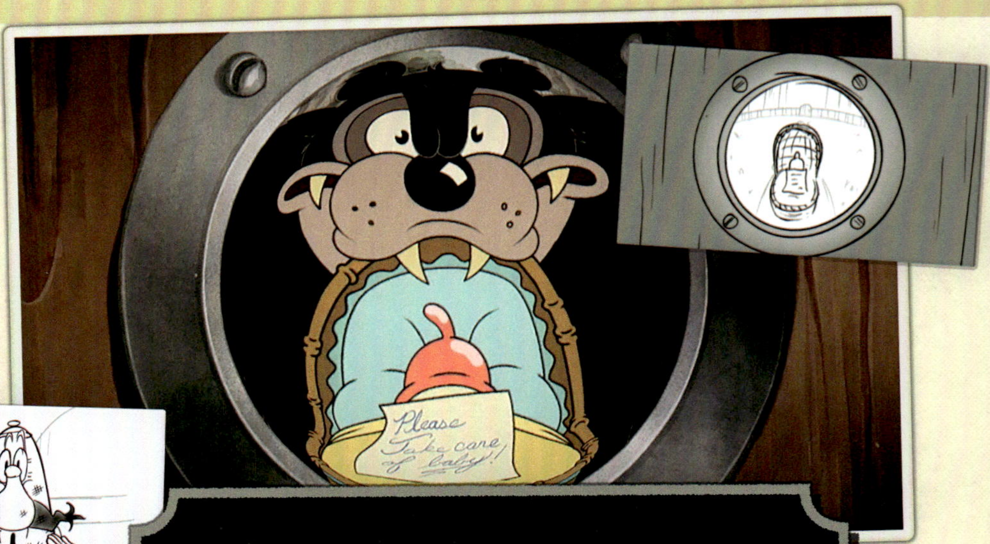

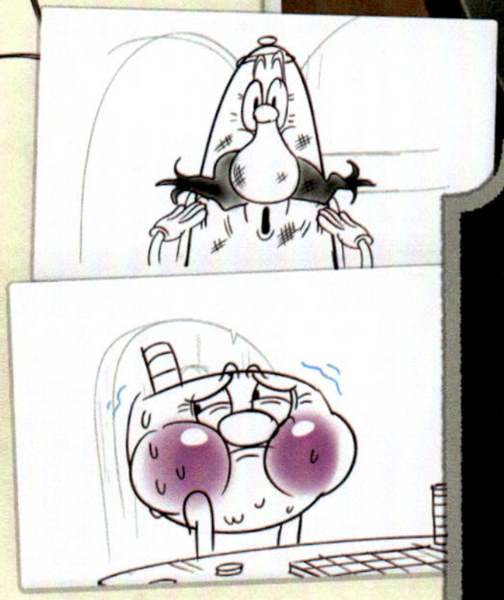

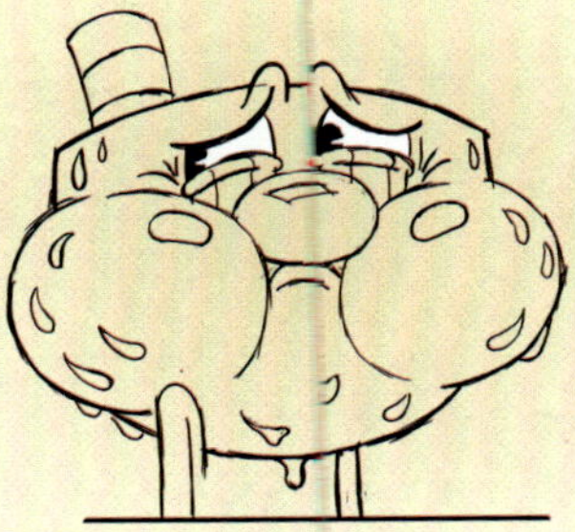

EPISODE 2

"DON'T ANSWER THE DOOR"

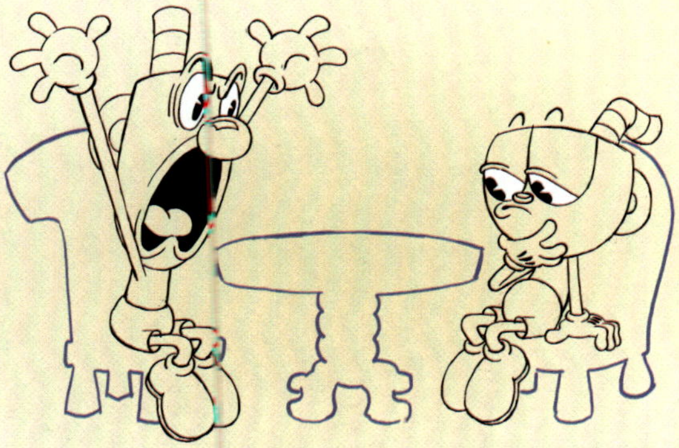

DEEKI: Every time you write a new story, you have to consider what's happening in the production. We knew this episode had to be lighter on new designs, and we knew it would be storyboarded by Fernando. We tried to give him a story that would play to his strengths.

FERNANDO: Working on an episode without a board partner was a challenge for sure. It was a lot of pressure. I needed to make the fact that they're inside the house and don't want to open the door something that's entertaining. The dialogue was so good and the pacing was so tight, I wanted the drawings to enhance what was already working so well.

DAVE: Fernando really made the most of all the ups and downs in that story.

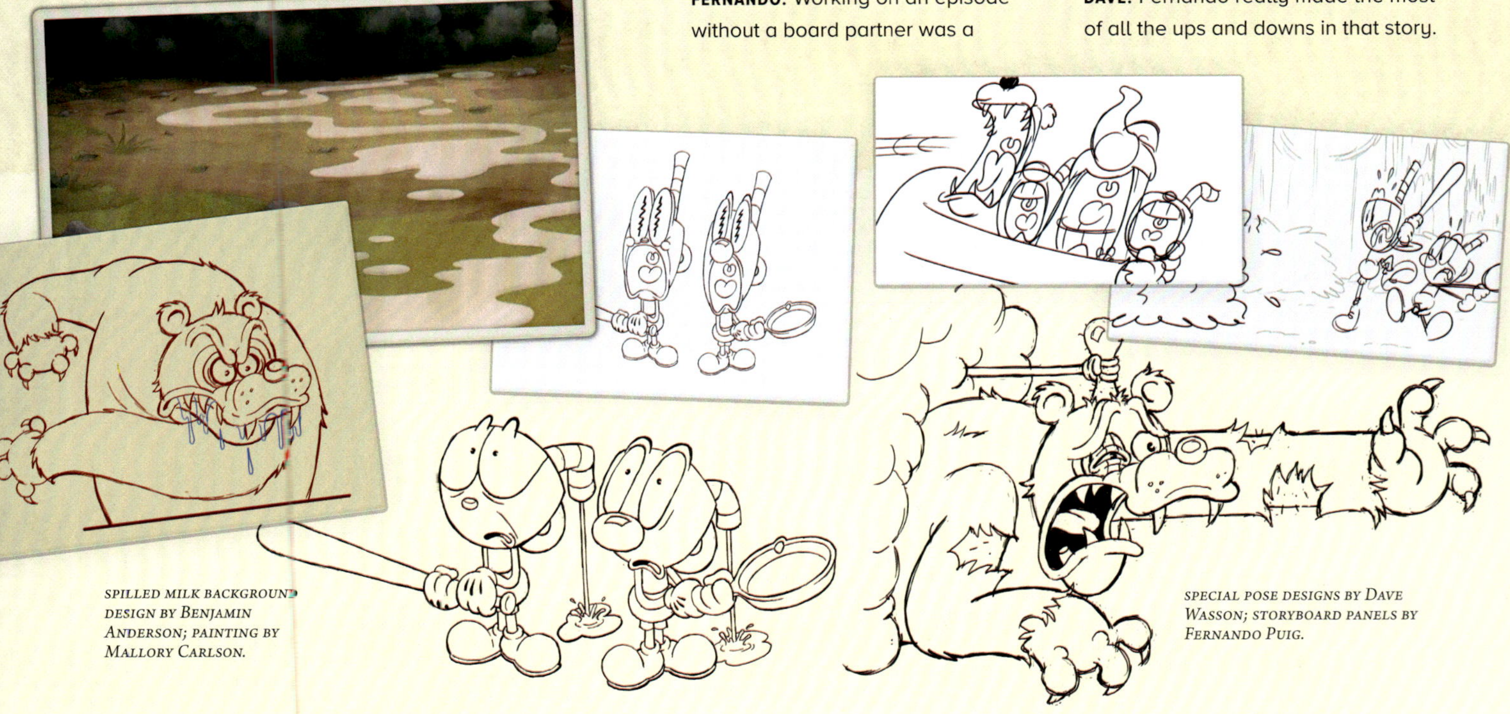

SPILLED MILK BACKGROUND DESIGN BY BENJAMIN ANDERSON; PAINTING BY MALLORY CARLSON.

SPECIAL POSE DESIGNS BY DAVE WASSON; STORYBOARD PANELS BY FERNANDO PUIG.

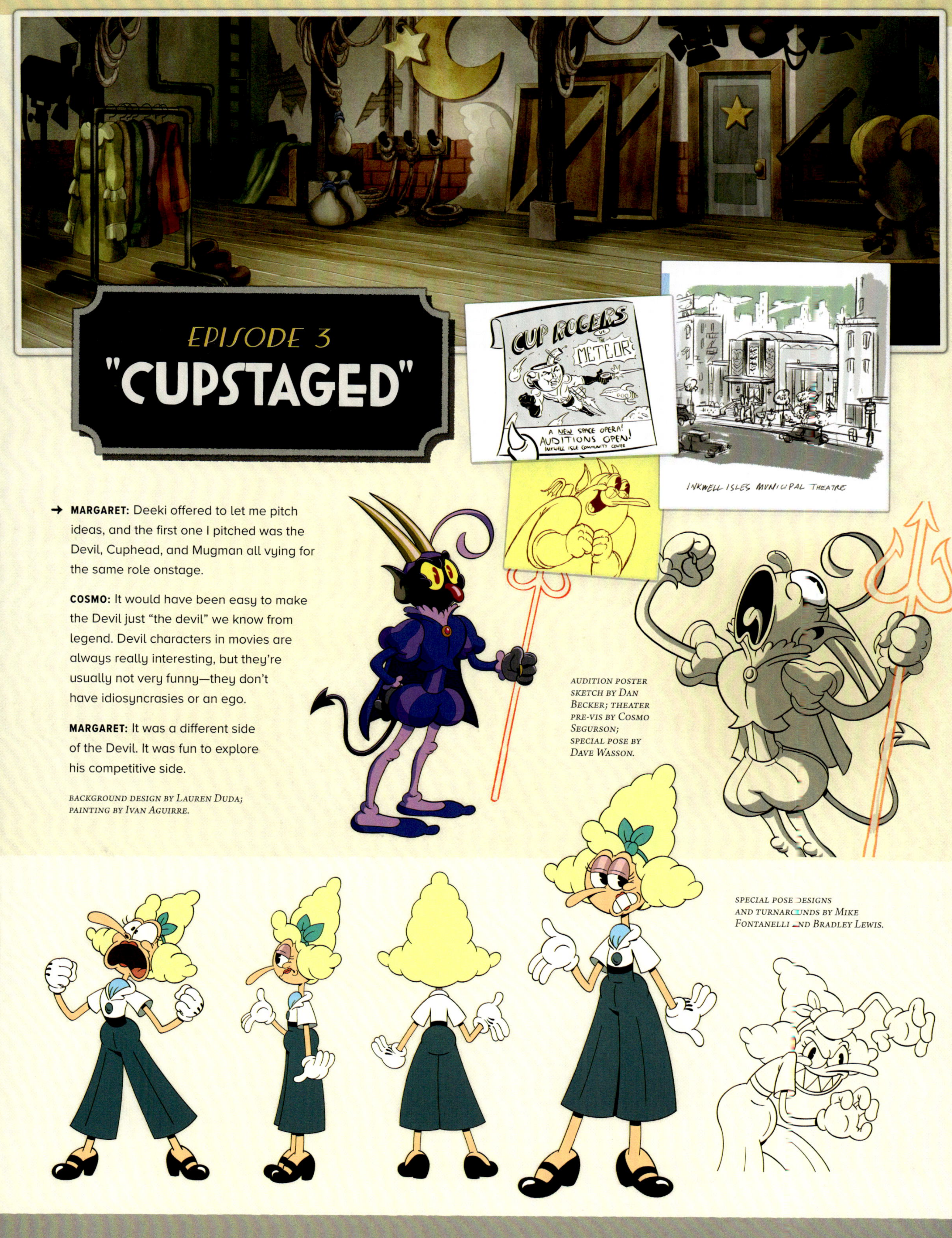

EPISODE 3

"CUPSTAGED"

→ **MARGARET:** Deeki offered to let me pitch ideas, and the first one I pitched was the Devil, Cuphead, and Mugman all vying for the same role onstage.

COSMO: It would have been easy to make the Devil just "the devil" we know from legend. Devil characters in movies are always really interesting, but they're usually not very funny—they don't have idiosyncrasies or an ego.

MARGARET: It was a different side of the Devil. It was fun to explore his competitive side.

Background design by Lauren Duda; painting by Ivan Aguirre.

Audition poster sketch by Dan Becker; theater pre-vis by Cosmo Segurson; special pose by Dave Wasson.

Special pose designs and turnarounds by Mike Fontanelli and Bradley Lewis.

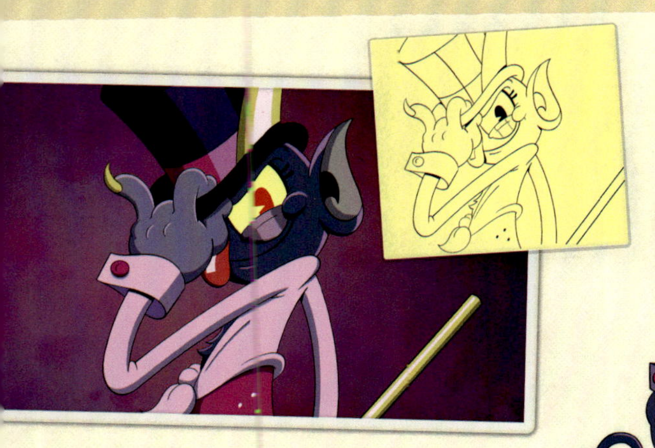

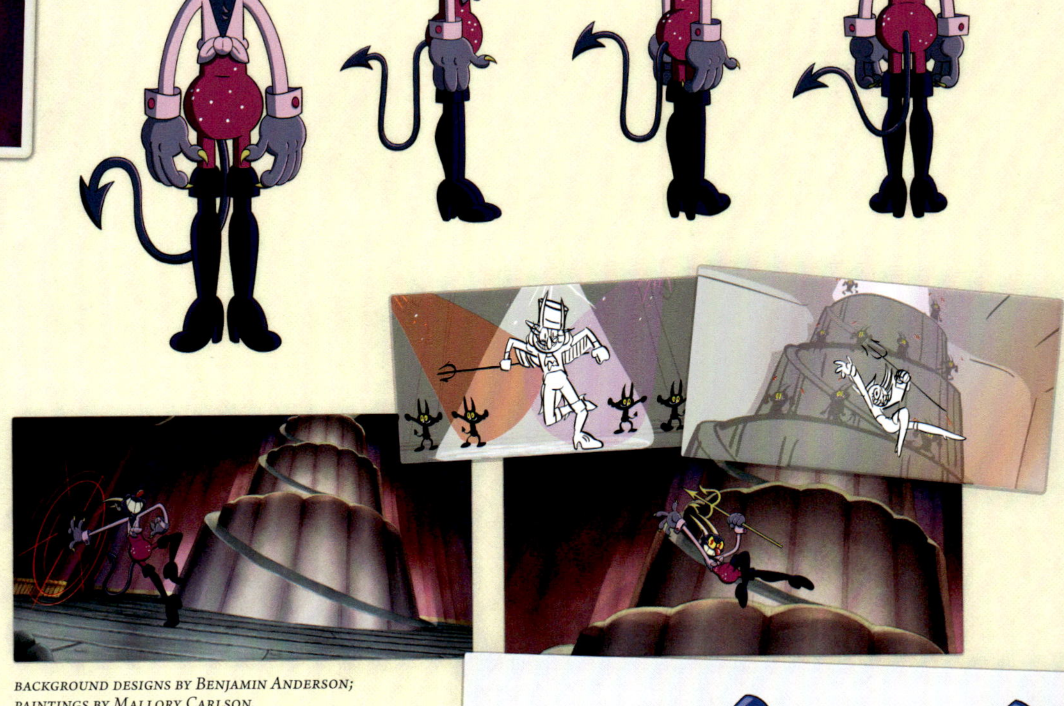

→ **KENNEDY:** Doing his musical number was an absolute mind trip. I was looking at *Cabaret* and RuPaul, and just pulling these really wild references. I did a doodle of the Devil in thigh-high boots, and I thought, "There is no way they'll let this through." So I showed it to the team and they said, "This is awesome, we should add fishnets." Any other show would have told me to check in with reality. Only on *Cuphead* do they tell you to add fishnets to the Devil.

Devil's costume change turnaround by Bradley Lewis.

Background designs by Benjamin Anderson; paintings by Mallory Carlson.

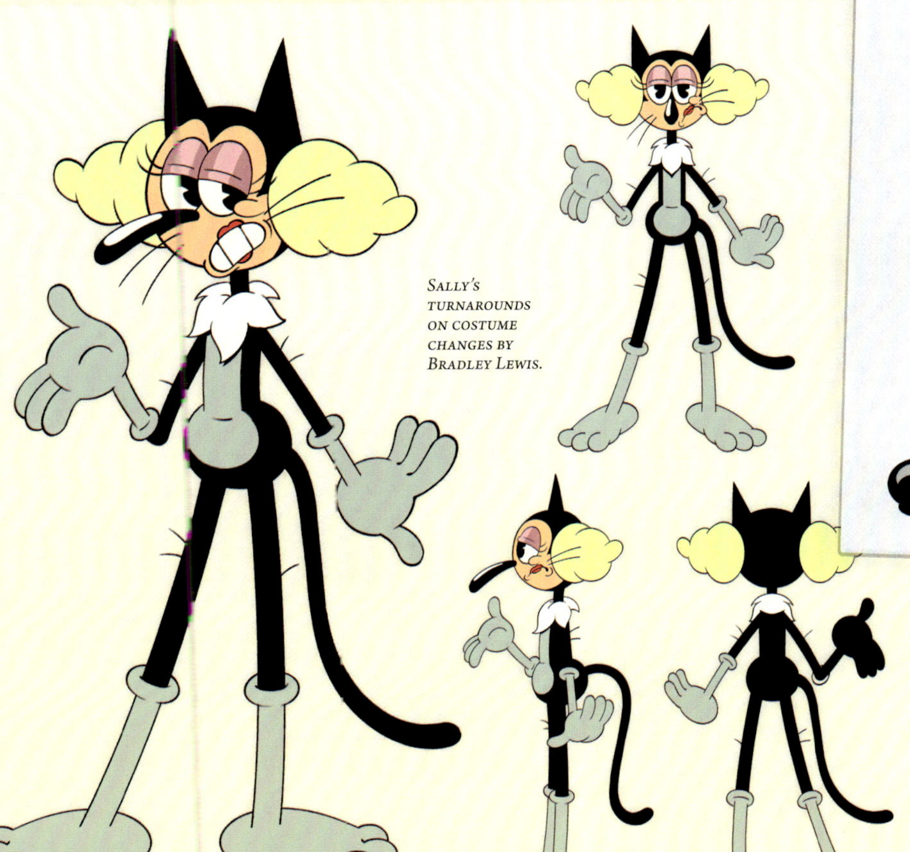

Sally's turnarounds on costume changes by Bradley Lewis.

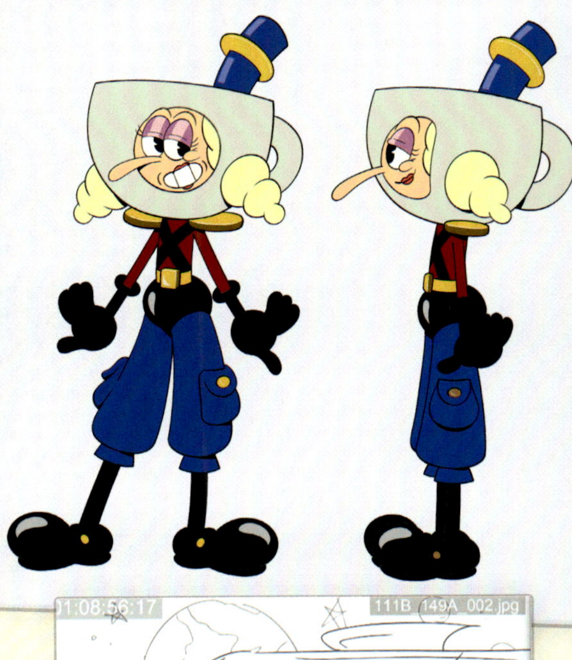

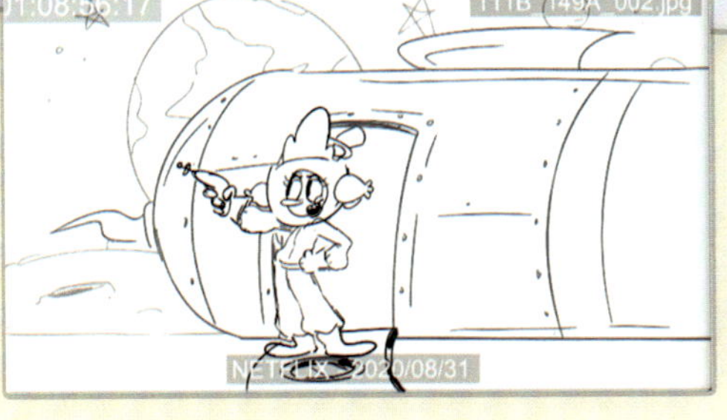

Storyboard panels by Kennedy Tarrell and Dan Becker.

EPISODE 4
"ROADKILL"

→ **MARGARET:** I was in the recording room with Dave and Cosmo. There was a line in "Sweater Luck Next Time" where Elder Kettle confused the Devil for a cat. Dave and Cosmo laughed so hard at that. I wondered, what if Elder Kettle took the Devil in as a cat? How would the Devil behave, and what would entice him to stay with Elder Kettle and deal with it?

DEEKI: Mugsy had a knack for coming up with premises that generated tons of funny character moments. Her original pitch had the Devil disguising himself as a cat and sneaking up to the cottage. It was really funny, but the Devil would never actively debase himself that much. I thought if he *woke up* in that situation, it could have a little more impact. So I added a literal impact.

NICK: I boarded Elder Kettle running over the Devil at sixty miles per hour, which is one of my favorite things I've ever gotten to draw. I love that Kettle is not super worried about who or what he hit—he's more concerned that nobody saw.

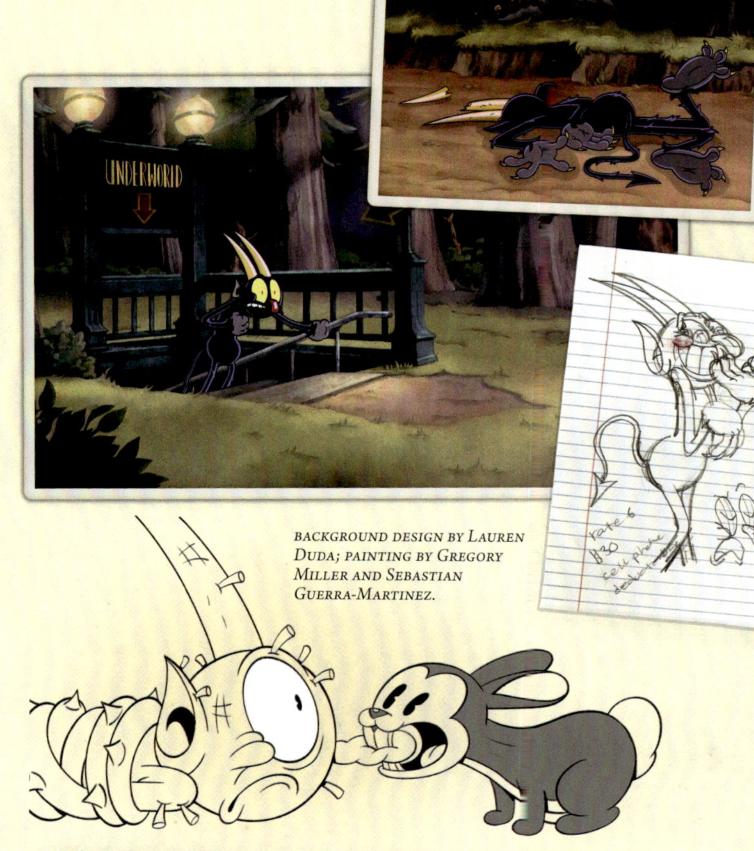

BACKGROUND DESIGN BY LAUREN DUDA; PAINTING BY GREGORY MILLER AND SEBASTIAN GUERRA-MARTINEZ.

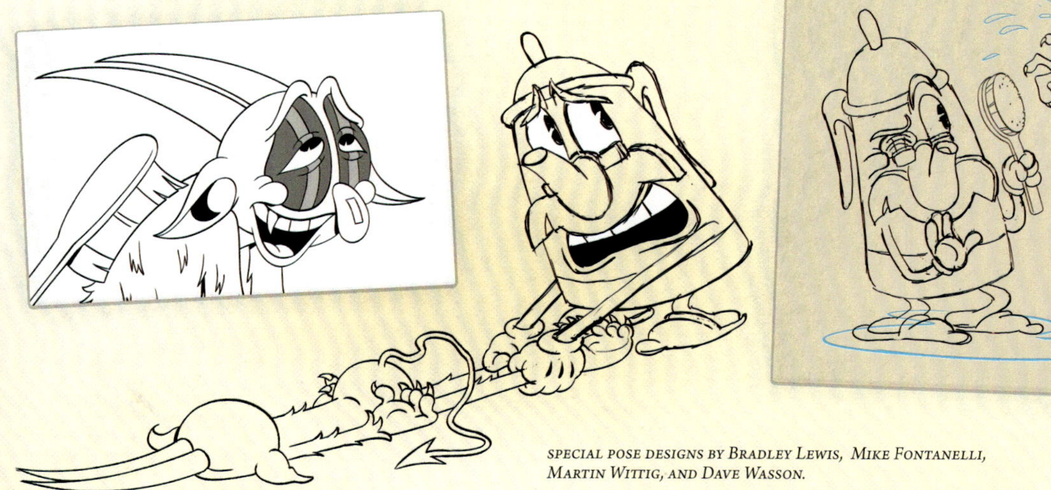

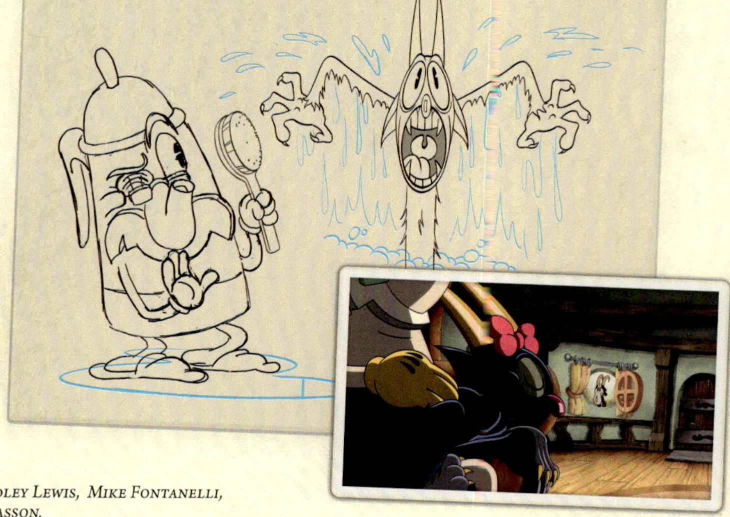

SPECIAL POSE DESIGNS BY BRADLEY LEWIS, MIKE FONTANELLI, MARTIN WITTIG, AND DAVE WASSON.

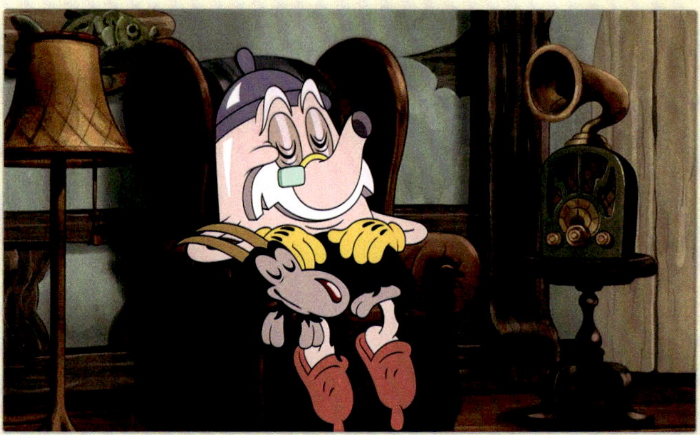

→ **MARGARET:** The Devil is just so on edge all the time—for him to go along with pretending to be a cat, there'd have to be a prize that makes it all worth it. For the Devil, that prize is always going to be Cuphead's soul.

AUSTIN: If nothing else, the Devil is a really motivated character. In "Roadkill," his primary motivation is "I will do whatever it takes to get that cup." He's a little desperate. He has some of that Wile E. Coyote in him, where he's convinced there's no way his plan could possibly fail.

DAVE: This episode was one of our most absurd, with this ridiculous premise and so much slapstick comedy. But with the B-story between Elder Kettle and the goat, it also turned out to be one of our sweetest.

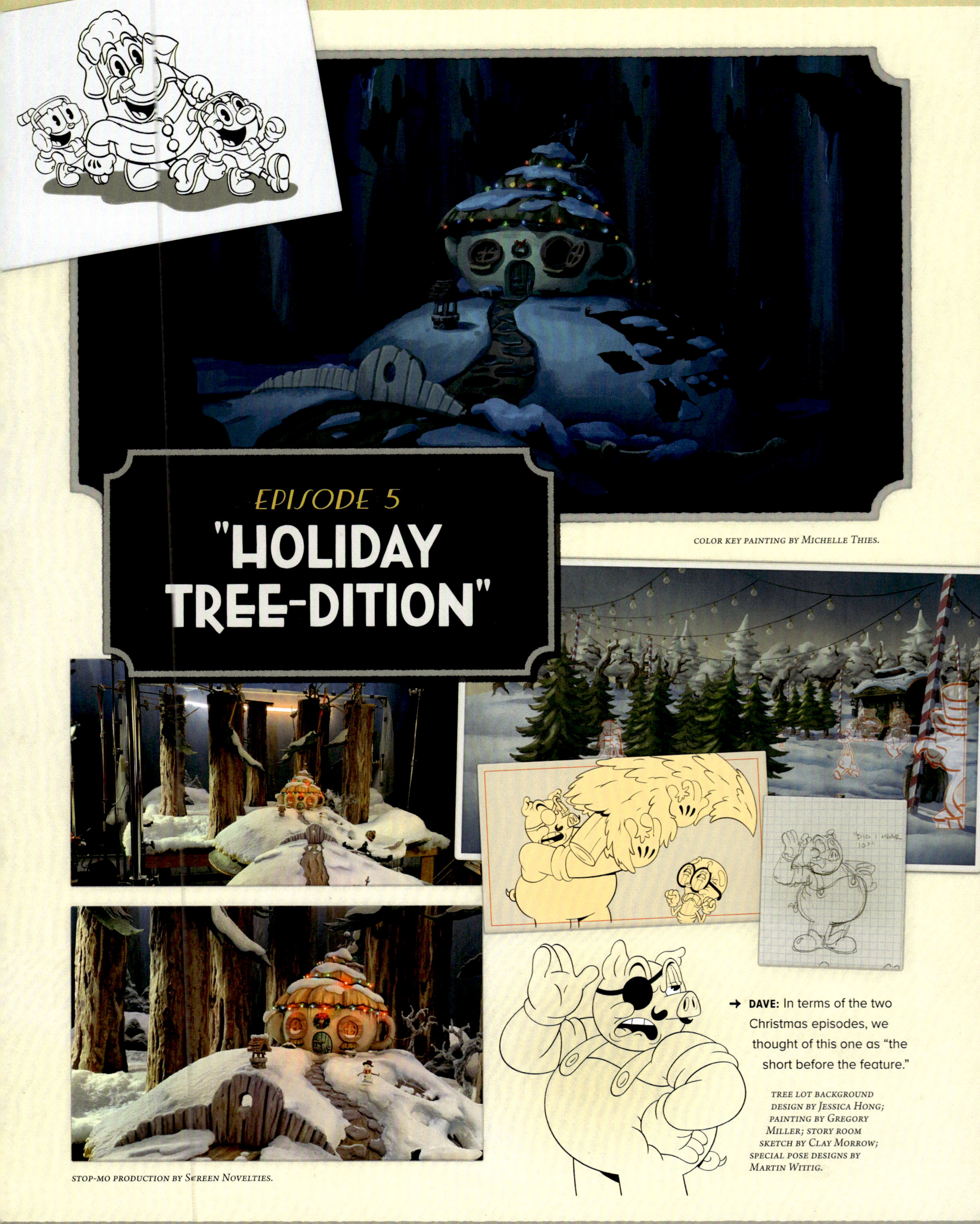

COLOR KEY PAINTING BY MICHELLE THIES.

EPISODE 5
"HOLIDAY TREE-DITION"

→ **DAVE:** In terms of the two Christmas episodes, we thought of this one as "the short before the feature."

TREE LOT BACKGROUND DESIGN BY JESSICA HONG; PAINTING BY GREGORY MILLER; STORY ROOM SKETCH BY CLAY MORROW; SPECIAL POSE DESIGNS BY MARTIN WITTIG.

STOP-MO PRODUCTION BY SCREEN NOVELTIES.

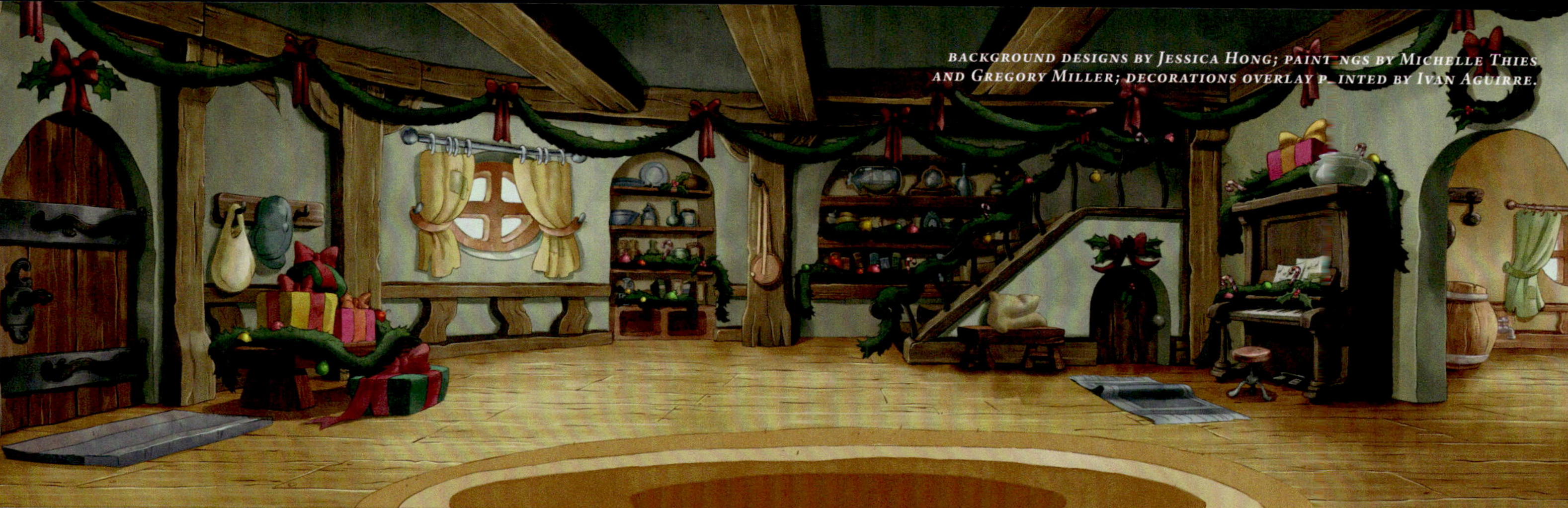

BACKGROUND DESIGNS BY JESSICA HONG; PAINTINGS BY MICHELLE THIES AND GREGORY MILLER; DECORATIONS OVERLAY PAINTED BY IVAN AGUIRRE.

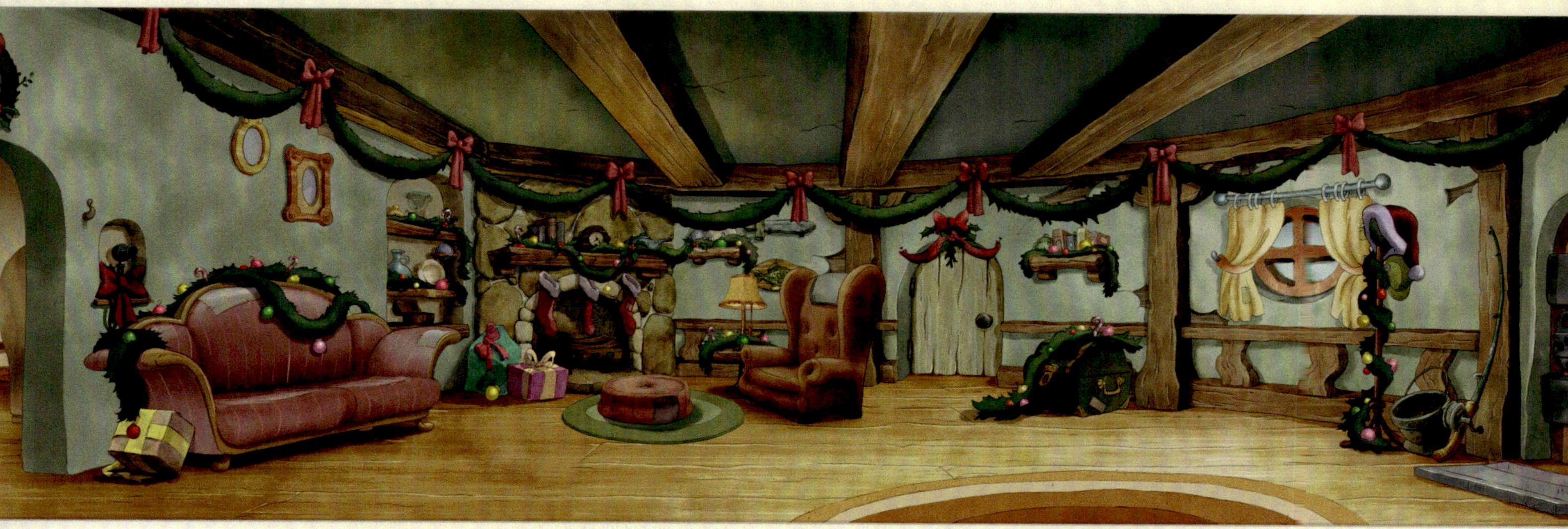

→ **JARED MORGAN, *THE CUPHEAD SHOW!* STORYBOARD ARTIST:** Clay always had a laser-focused solution for any little bit that was missing. In the tree farm scene, I had Porkrind posed and a little stoic—he's got one up on Mugman and he knows it. Clay gave me a great note—he said, "Let Porkrind rock on his feet a little." That little rock, just a few panels, it makes him so much more of an imposing force.

CLAY: You don't always need to go big. In TV production, it's all about economy—meaning no money, of course, but also the economy of your storyboarding. If you do it right, less is usually more. A small targeted fix can have a big impact.

JARED MORGAN: It's so great when a director gives you that bit of nuance that just elevates the whole scene. It really helps create a tapestry of character. Clay would throw something in, and you're like, "This is exactly what I was missing!"

CLAY: Porkrind-related solutions come real easy for me. I relate strongly to Porkrind, for better or worse.

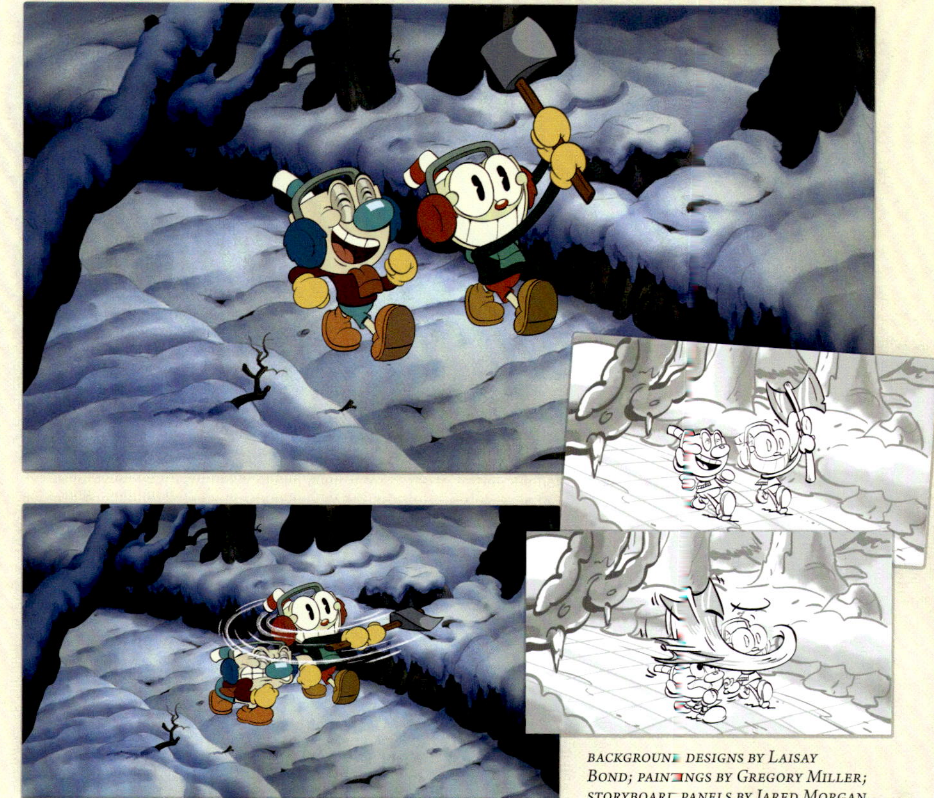

BACKGROUND DESIGNS BY LAISAY BOND; PAINTINGS BY GREGORY MILLER; STORYBOARD PANELS BY JARED MORGAN.

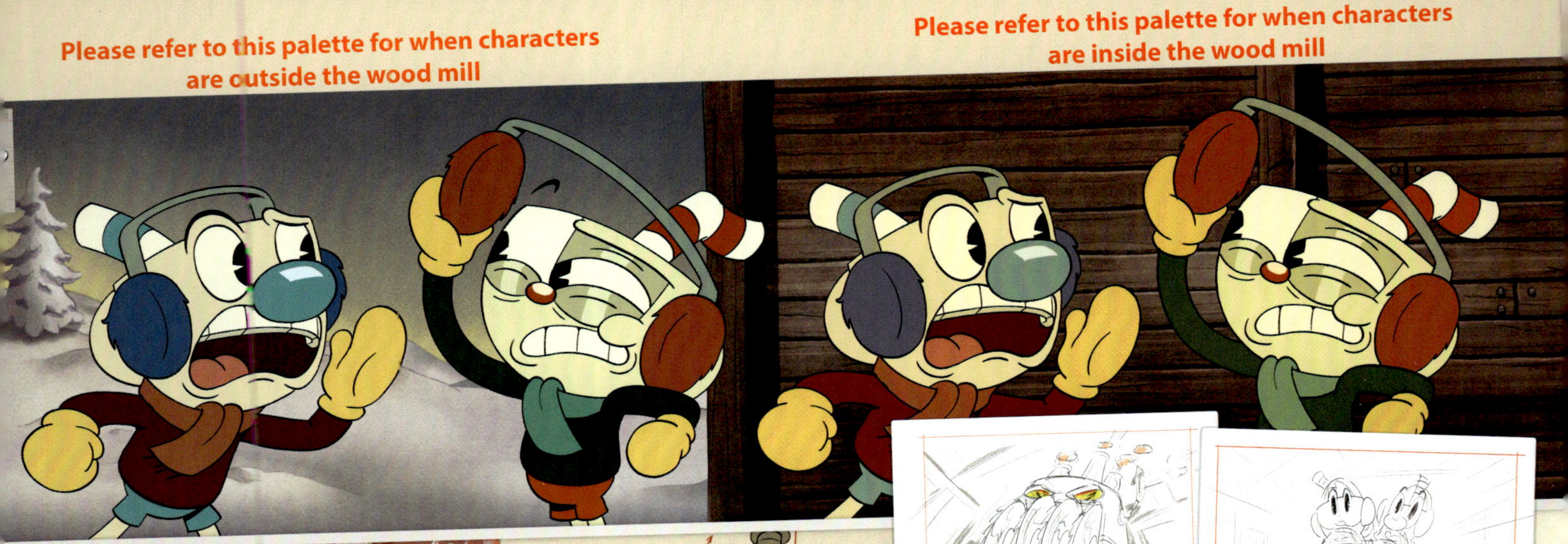

Please refer to this palette for when characters are outside the wood mill

Please refer to this palette for when characters are inside the wood mill

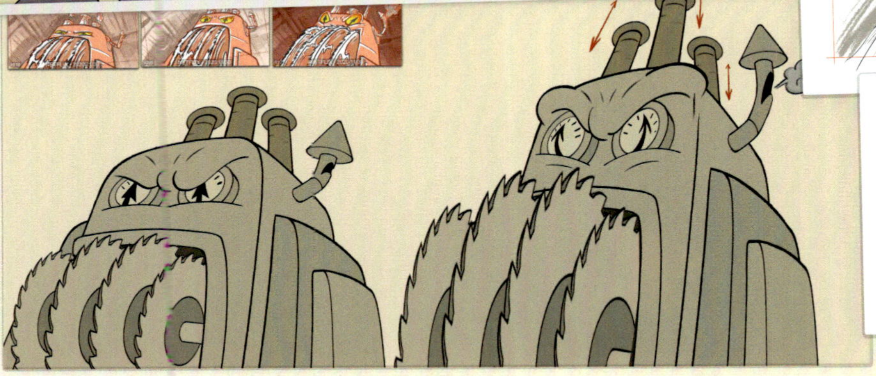

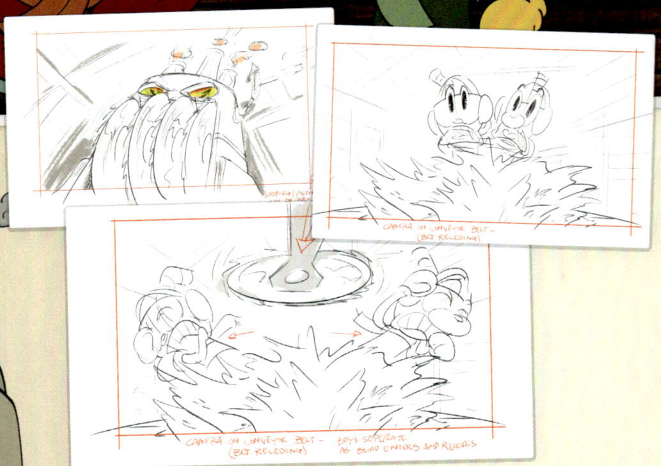

Sawmill previs by Cosmo Segurson.

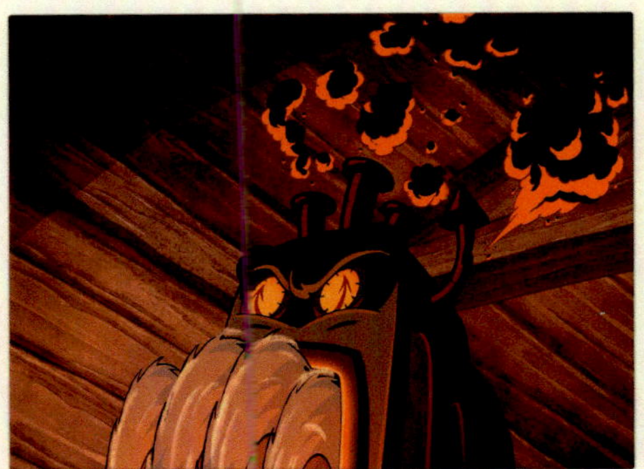

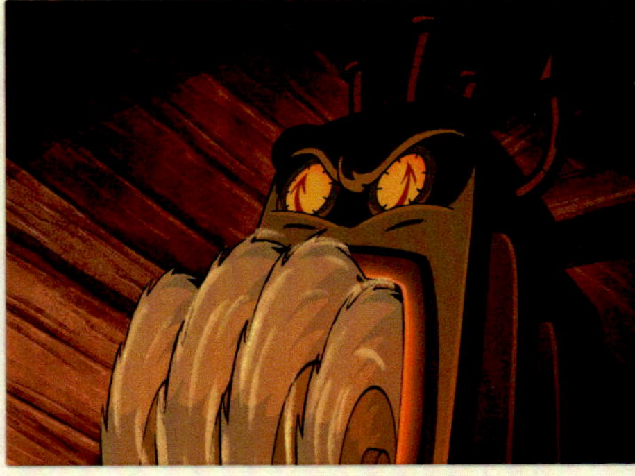

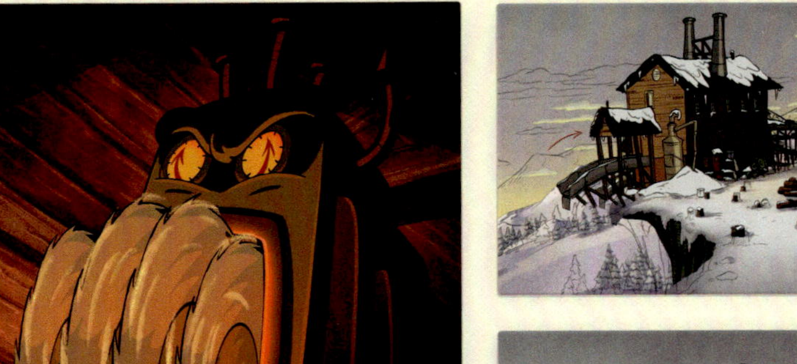

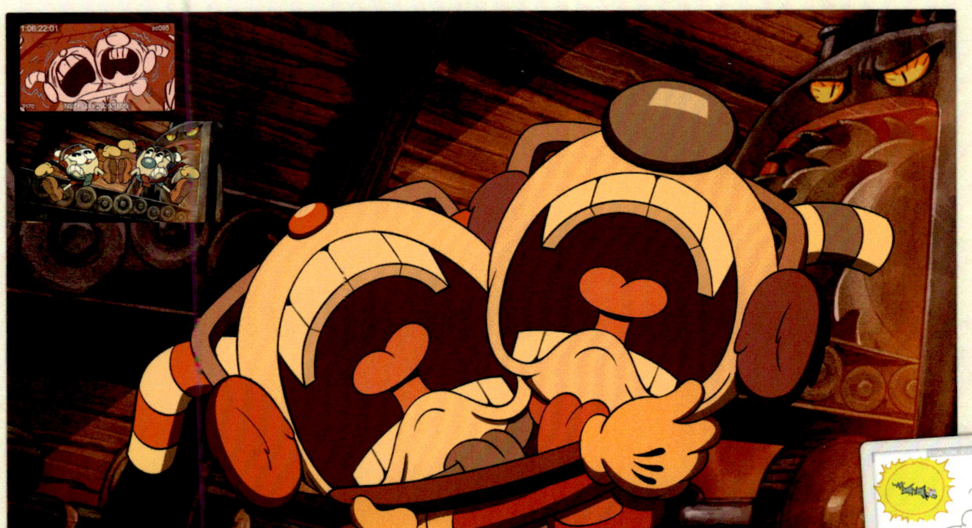

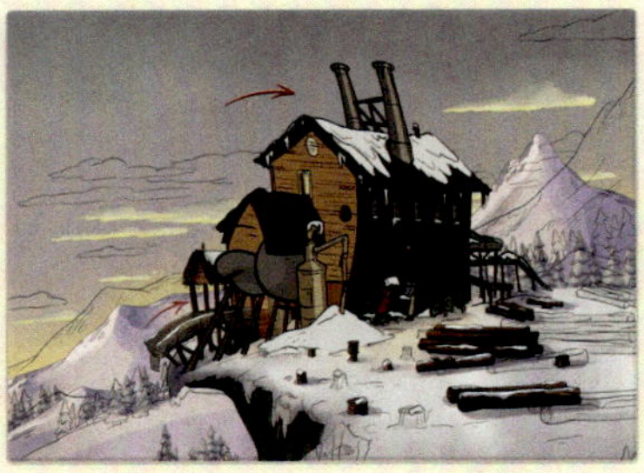

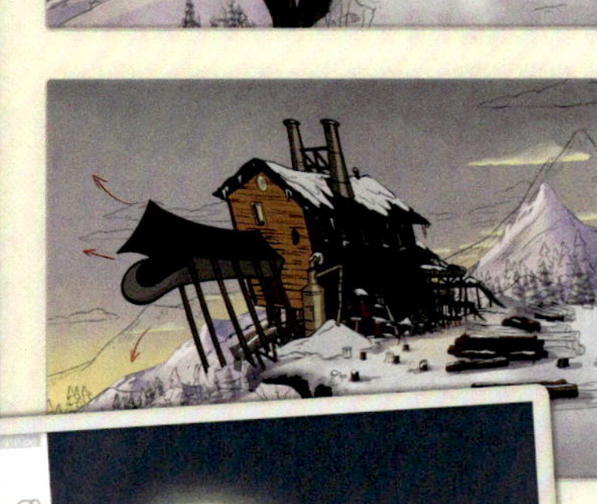

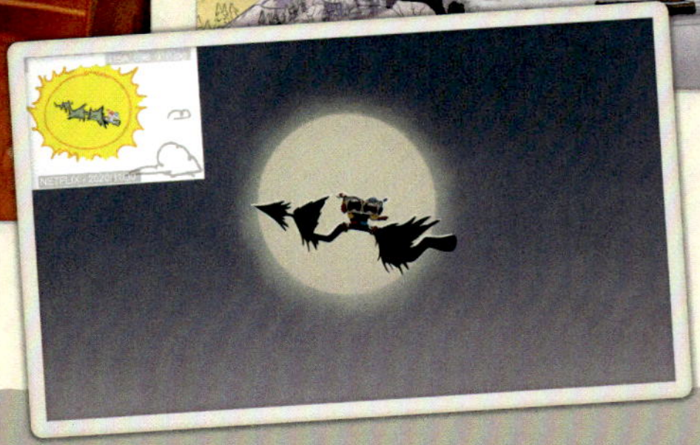

Storyboard panels by Zoë Moss; special poses by Adam Fay; background designs by Pat Marconetti; paintings by Ivan Aguirre and Sebastian Guerra-Martinez.

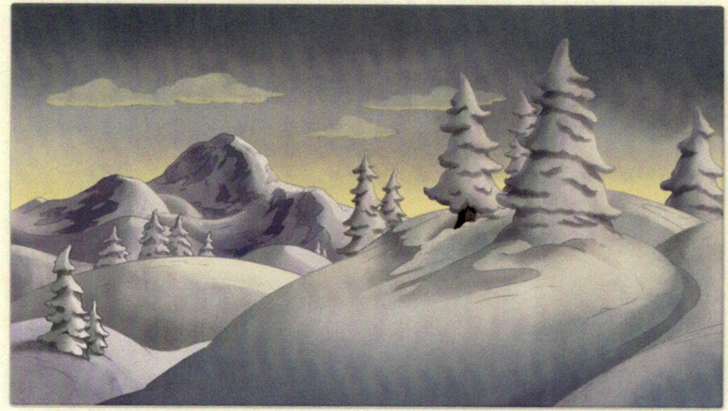

background design by Laisay Bond; painting by Ivan Aguirre.

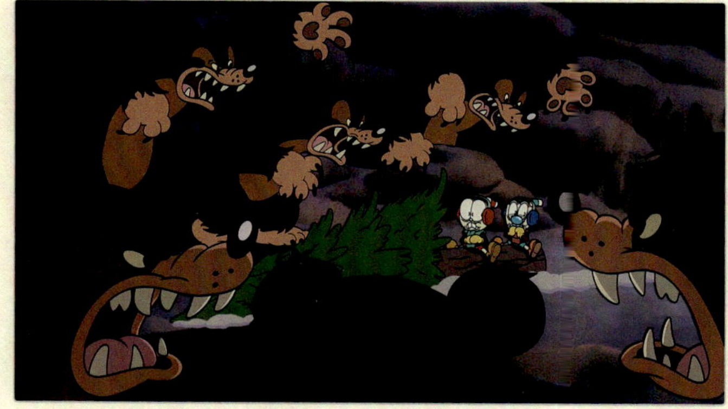

background design by Jessica Hong; painting by Gregory Miller.

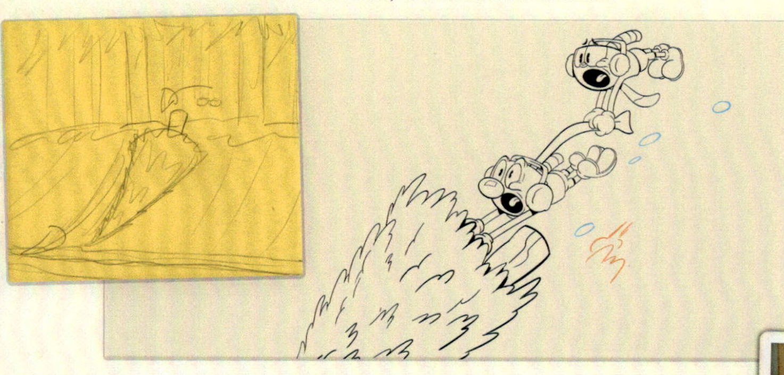

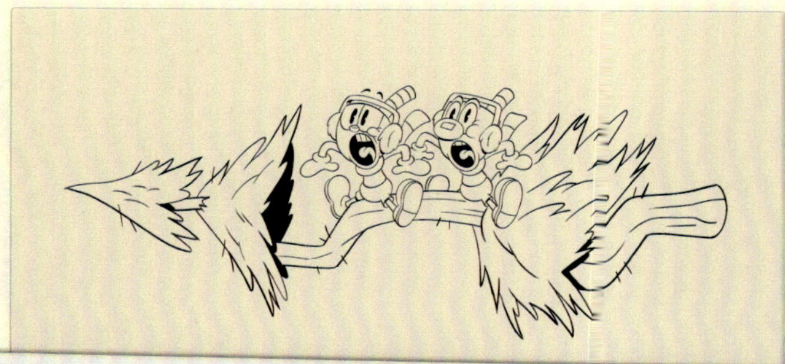

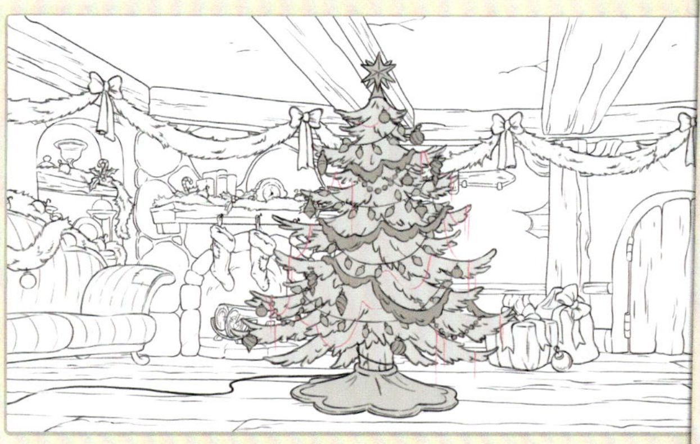

background design by Jessica Hong; painting by Ivan Aguirre.

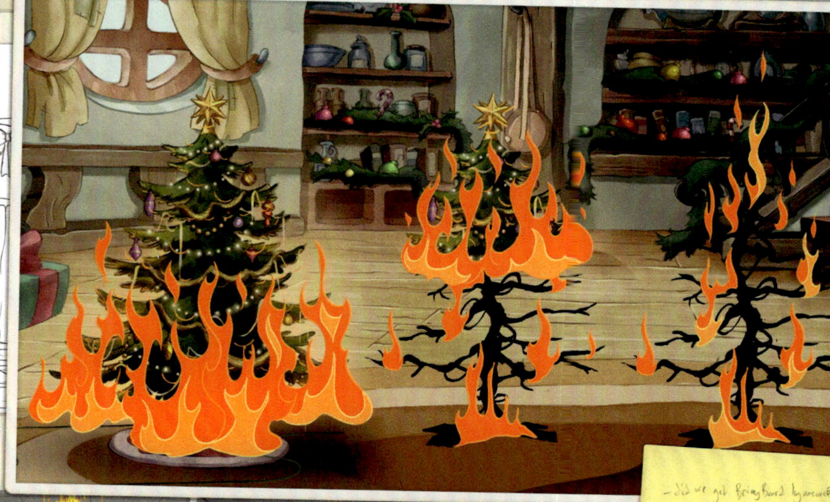

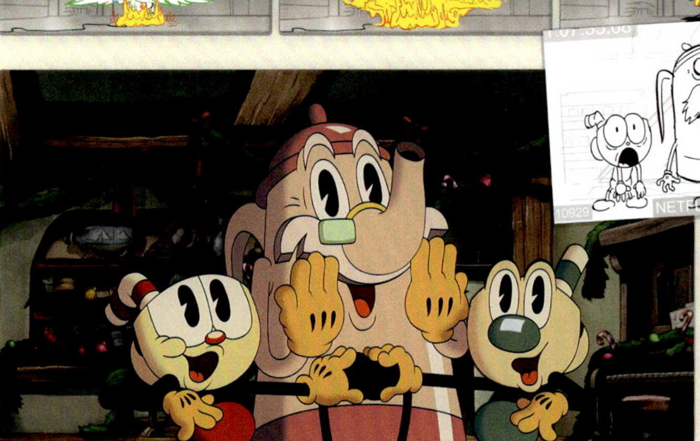

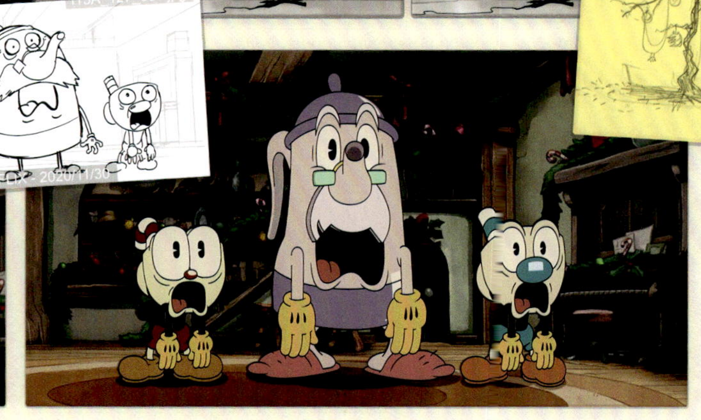

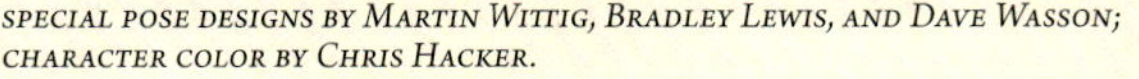

special pose designs by Martin Wittig, Bradley Lewis, and Dave Wasson; character color by Chris Hacker.

storyboard panels by Zoë Moss; story room sketch by Adam Paloian.

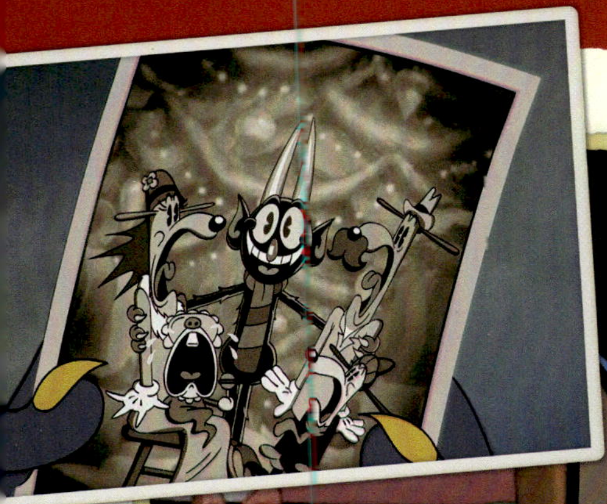

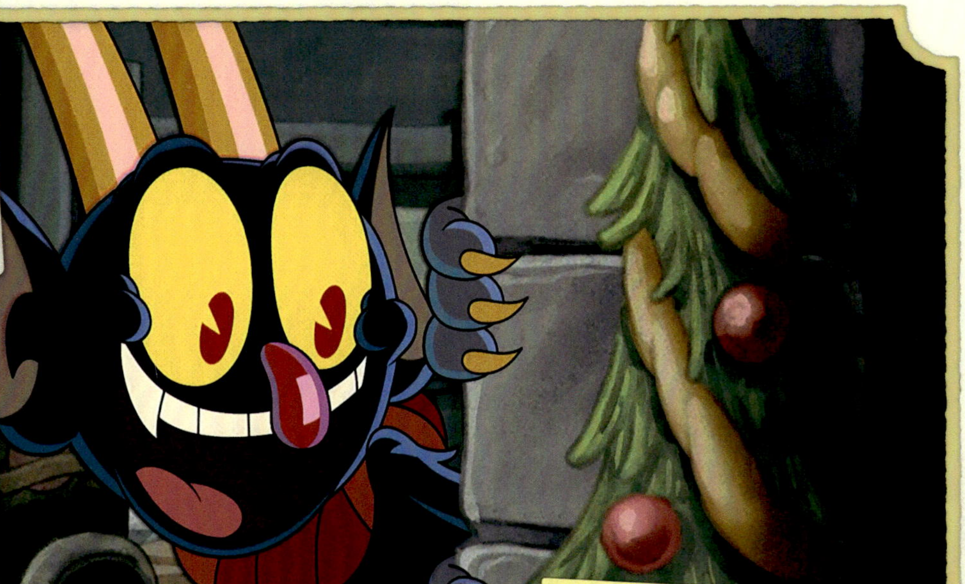

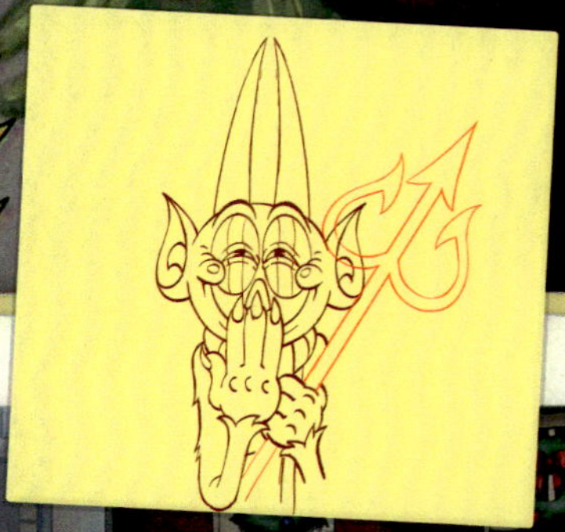

EPISODE 6

"A Very Devil Christmas"

DEEP DIVE

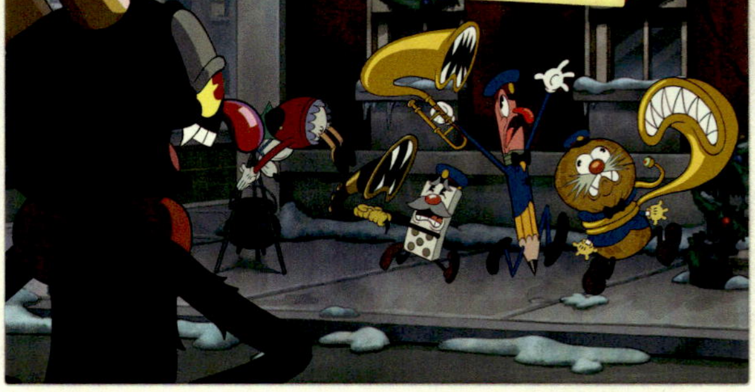

BACKGROUND DESIGN BY BENJAMIN ANDERSON; PAINTING BY SEBASTIAN GUERRA-MARTINEZ.

→ **CHELSEA JAUREGUI, *THE CUPHEAD SHOW!* COLOR DESIGNER:** I joined the production a little later. When I started, my first show was a three-part special, "A Very Devil Christmas." It was the perfect introduction to the show.

ANDREA: I love Christmas specials. I watch the same ones every year. I also had a weird video of bits of all these Christmas cartoons, and one of them was Disney's *Santa's Workshop* [1932]. I was obsessed with it as a kid. So when Deeki first pitched the Devil going to the North Pole, I immediately knew what I wanted Santa's workshop to look like.

DAVE: "A Very Devil Christmas" might be my favorite thing I've ever been a part of.

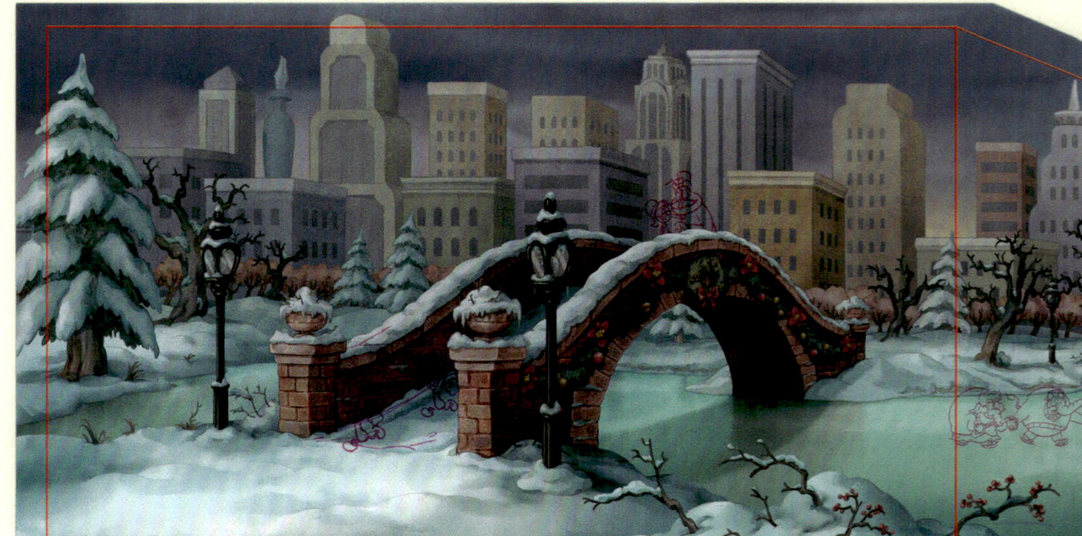

SPECIAL POSE DESIGNS BY CLAY MORROW, ADAM PALOIAN, AND MIKE FONTANELLI.

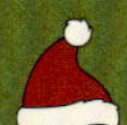

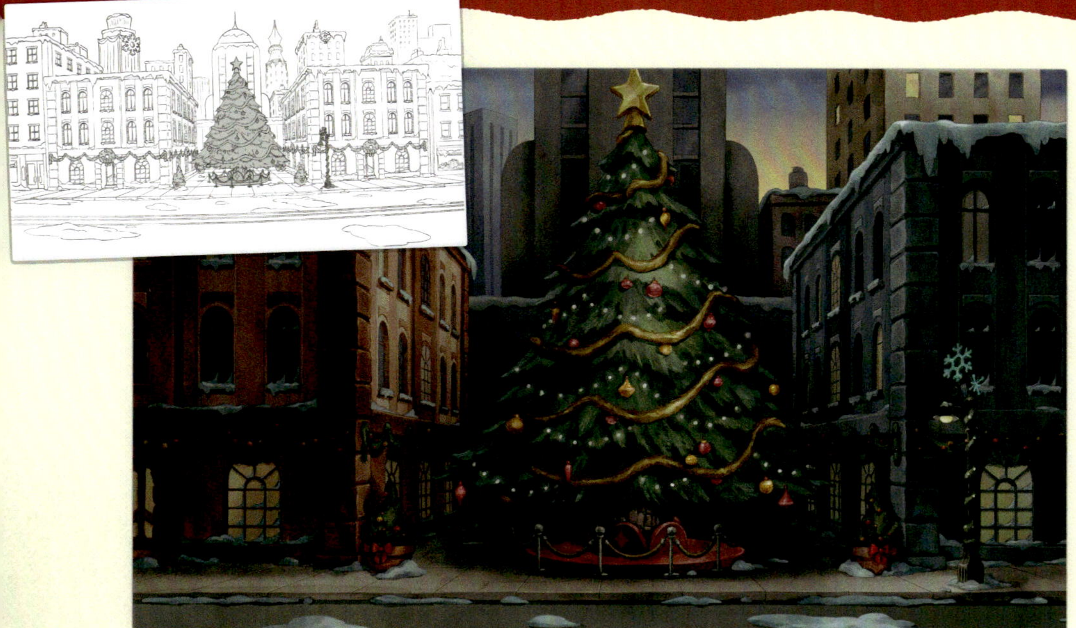

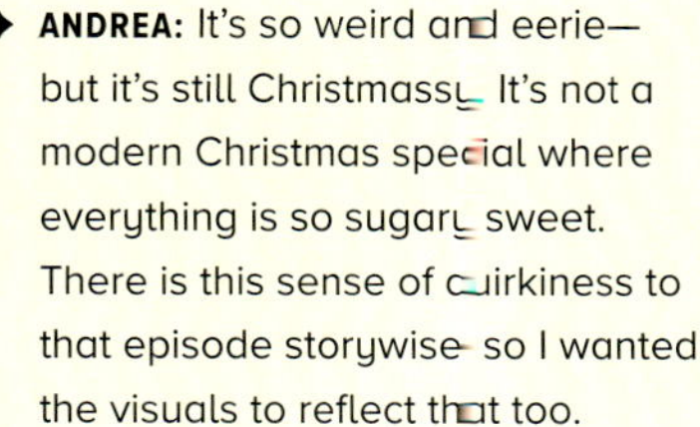

ANDREA: It's so weird and eerie—but it's still Christmassy. It's not a modern Christmas special where everything is so sugary sweet. There is this sense of quirkiness to that episode storywise so I wanted the visuals to reflect that too.

ADAM P: The Devil wants a gift—Henchman says he can just make a train out of thin air, but the Devil says it's not the same. It's not a gift unless someone else gives it to you.

CLAY: That's a defining trait for the Devil: he's not satisfied unless it works for him the way it works for everybody else.

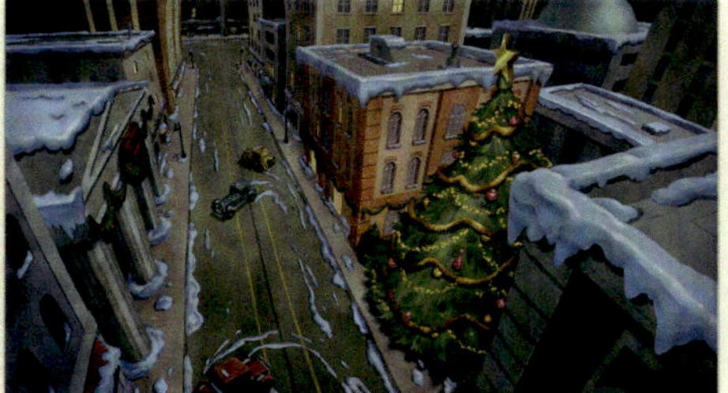

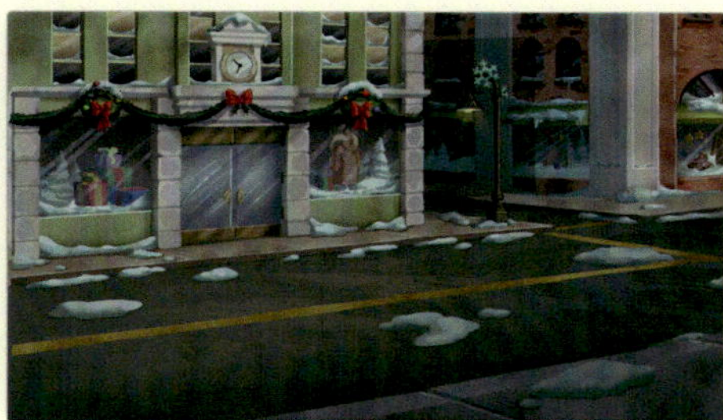

PREVIS BY COSMO SEGURSON; BACKGROUND DESIGNS BY LAISAY BOND, JESSICA HONG, AND LAUREN DUDA; PAINTINGS BY MICHELLE THIES, GREGORY MILLER, AND LEAH CHUN.

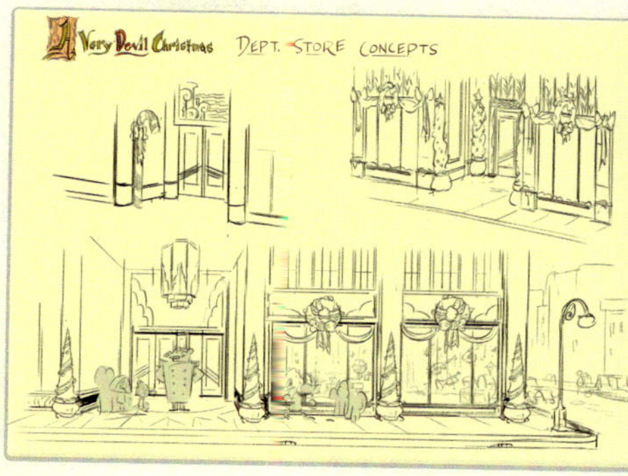

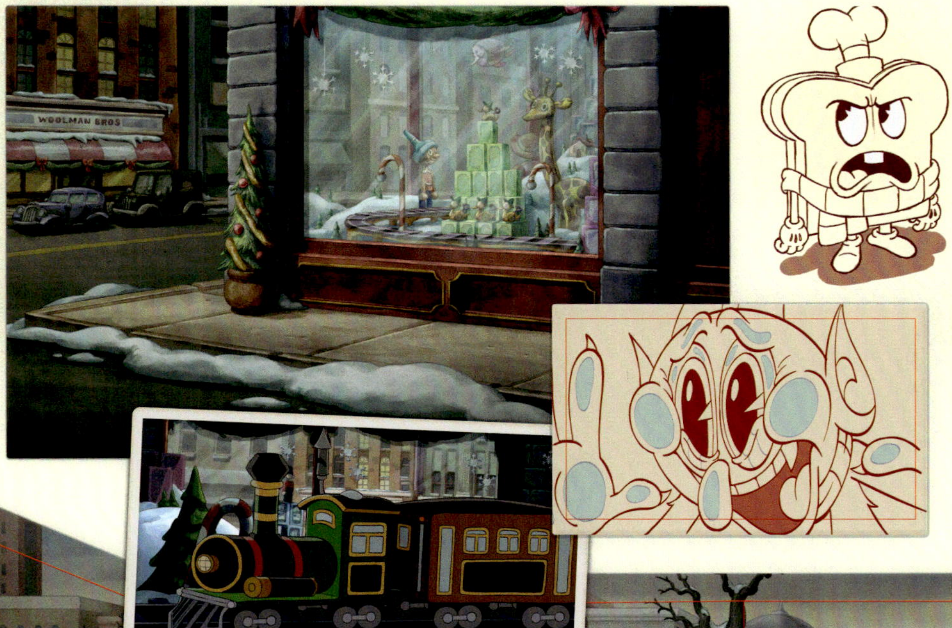

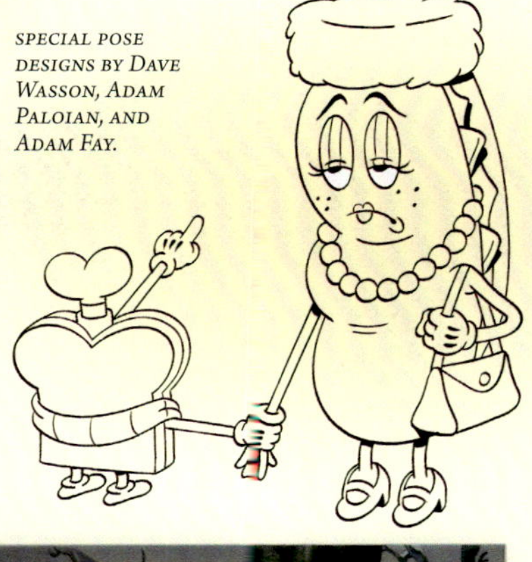

SPECIAL POSE DESIGNS BY DAVE WASSON, ADAM PALOIAN, AND ADAM FAY.

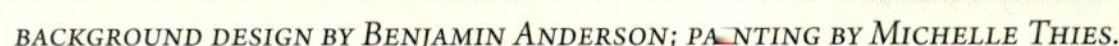

BACKGROUND DESIGN BY BENJAMIN ANDERSON; PAINTING BY MICHELLE THIES.

The North Pole

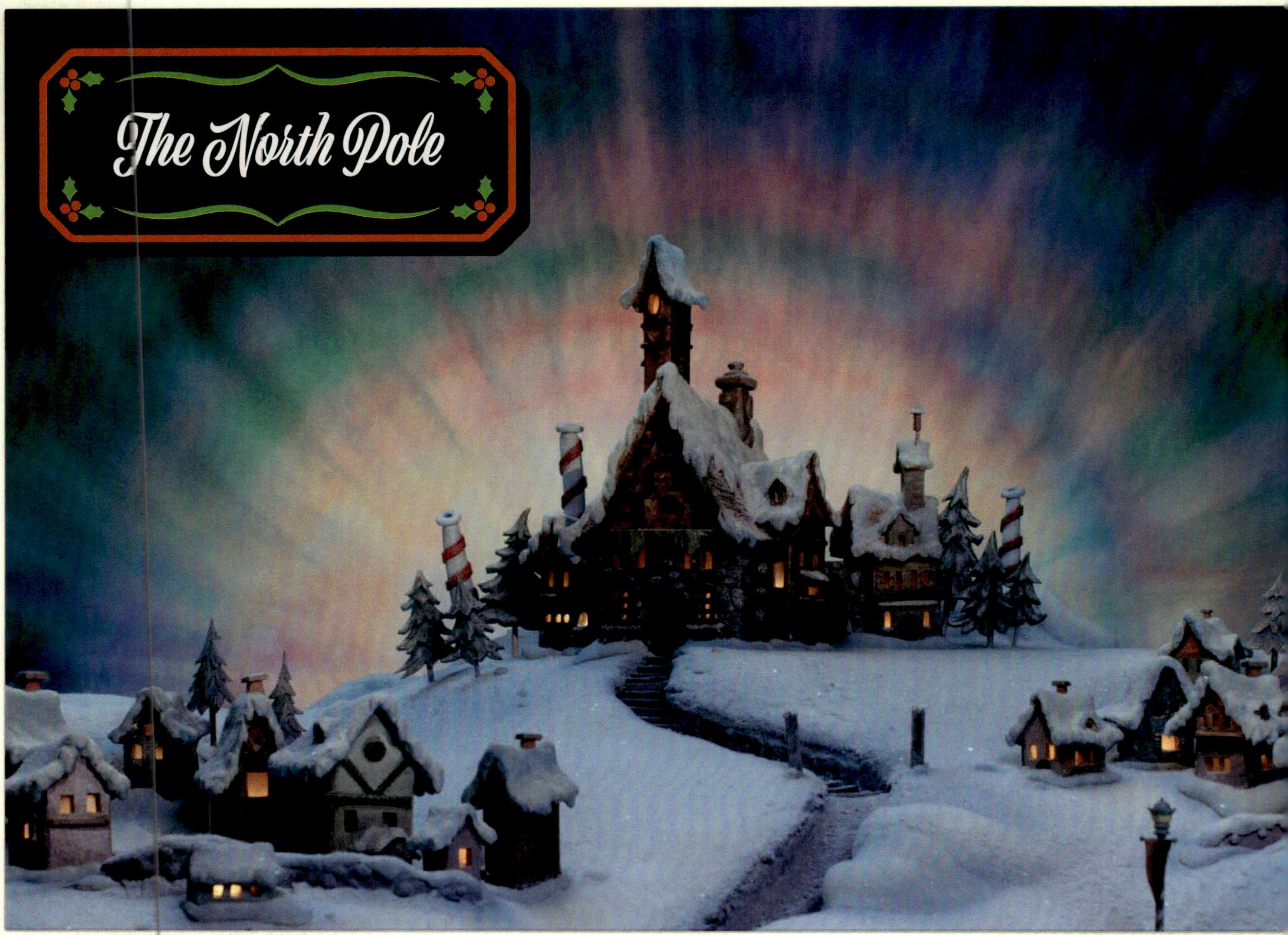

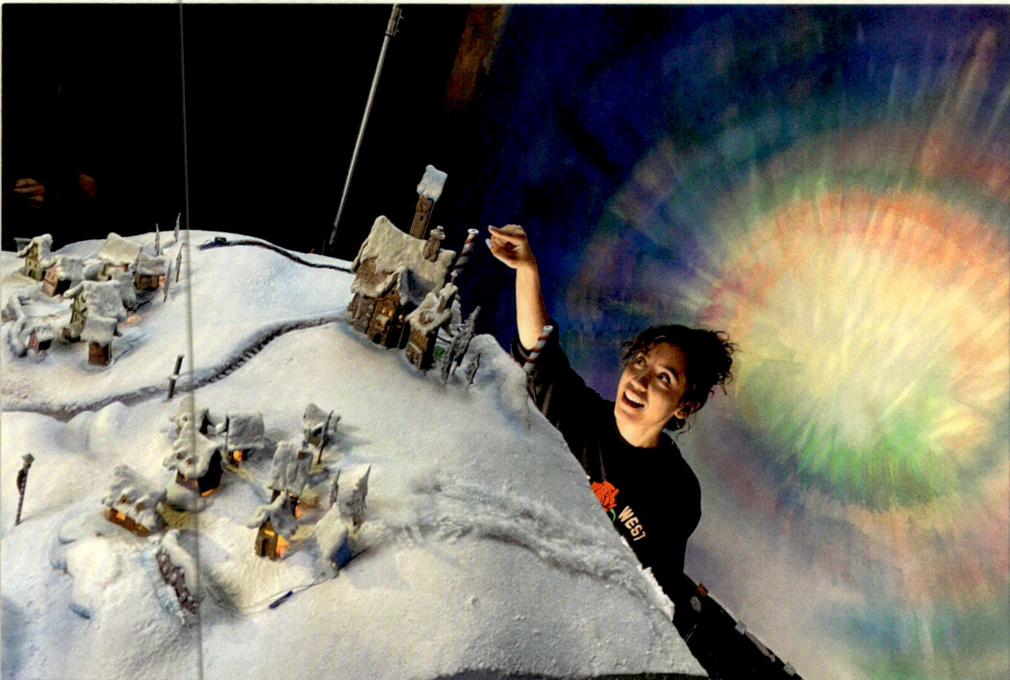

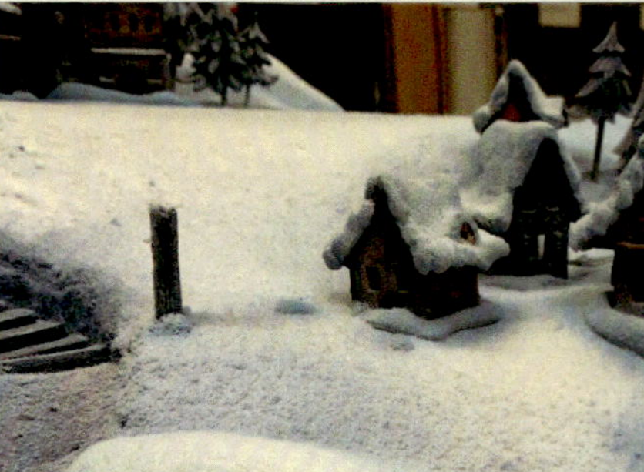

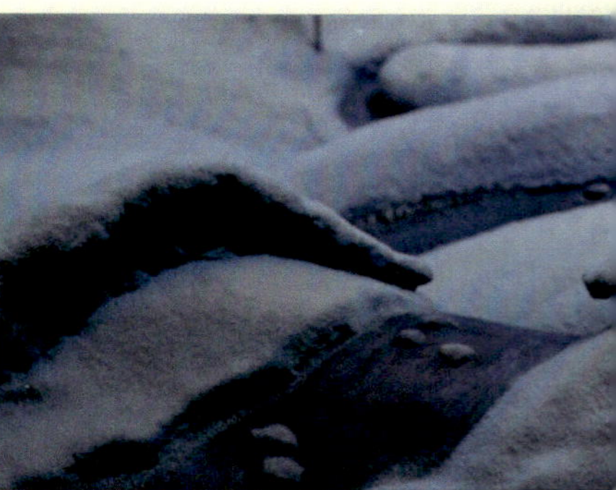

STOP MO SETS BY SCREEN NOVELTIES.

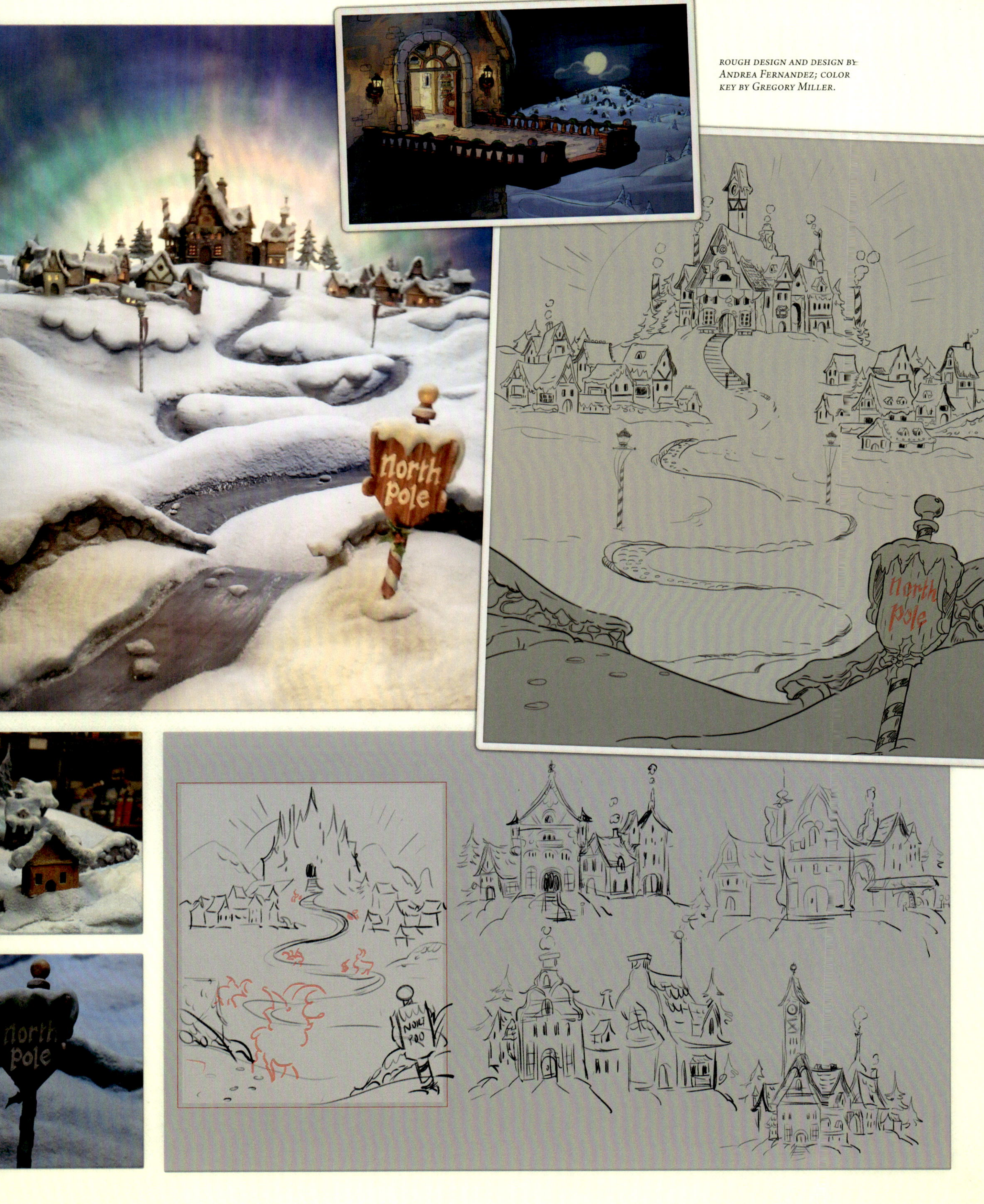

Rough design and design by Andrea Fernandez; color key by Gregory Miller.

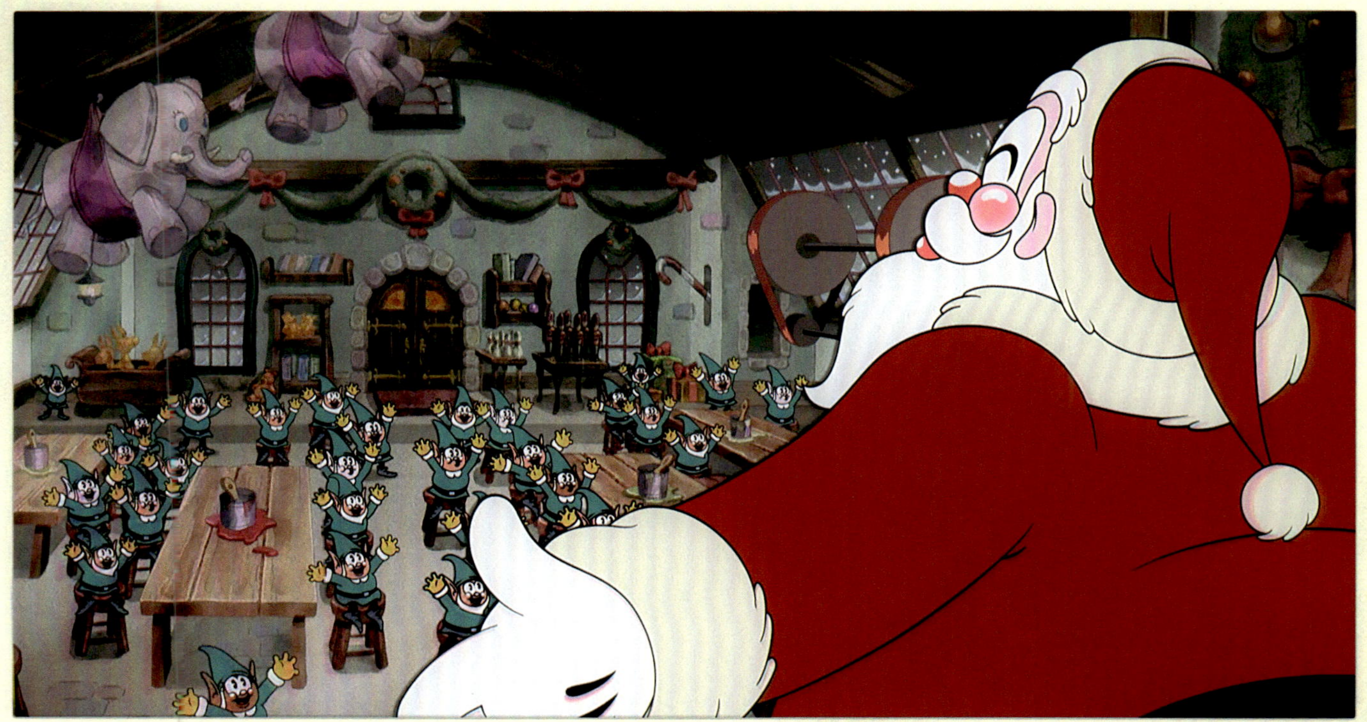

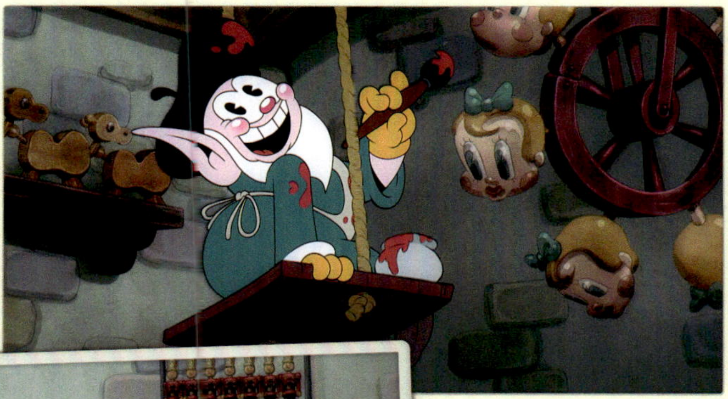

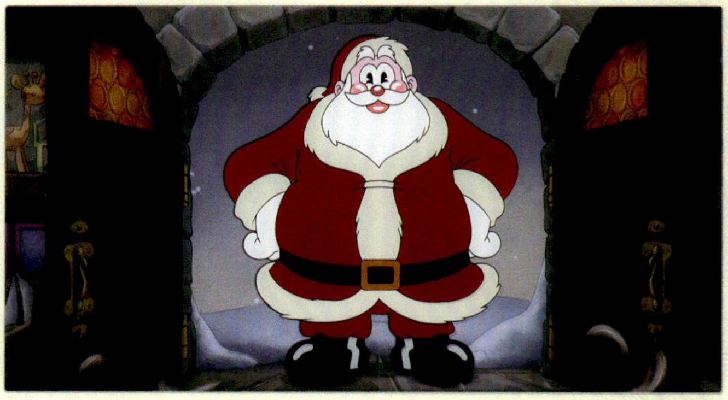

BACKGROUND DESIGNS BY LAISAY BOND AND LAUREN DUDA; PAINTINGS BY IVAN AGUIRRE AND SEBASTIAN GUERRA-MARTINEZ; SANTA SPECIAL POSE DESIGNS BY DAVE WASSON.

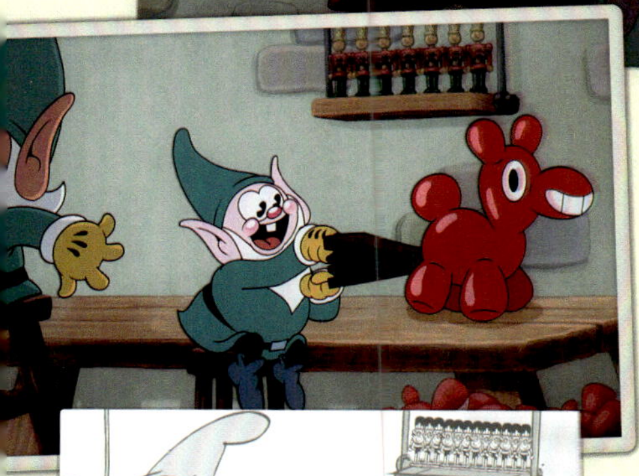

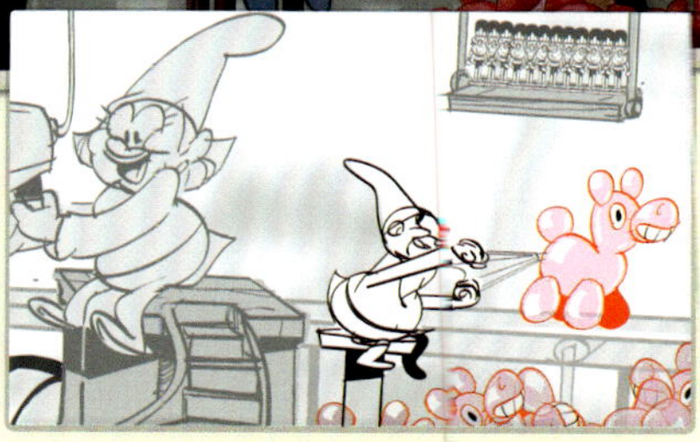

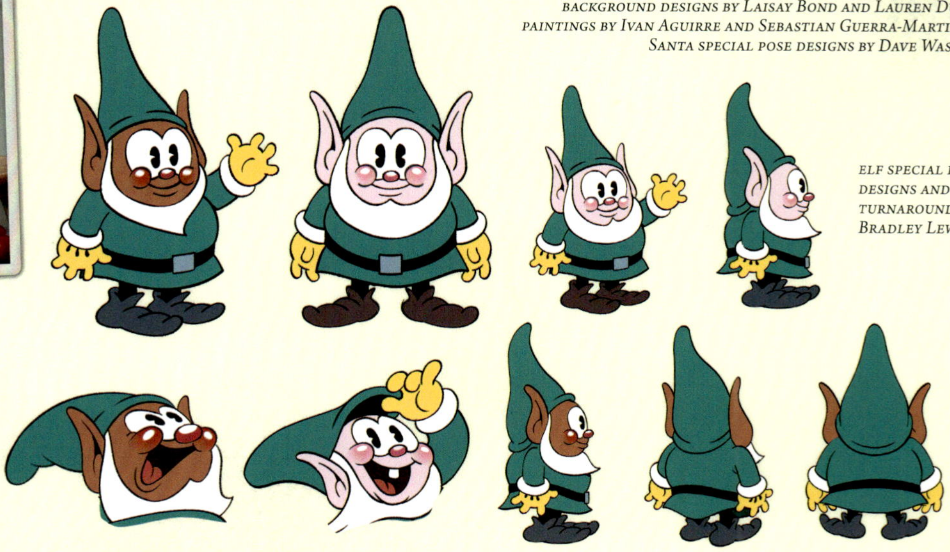

ELF SPECIAL POSE DESIGNS AND TURNAROUNDS BY BRADLEY LEWIS.

STORYBOARD PANEL BY KARL HADRIKA.

→ **CLAY:** One of the things I'm happiest about is how sincere our characters are. It gives a real grounding to all the other stuff that goes on in an episode to always be able to very quickly go right to the emotion, for the Devil, for Cuphead, for Mugman, for Henchman. As soon as you cut to a character, you get right to their emotions and you believe it, and that's not always the case in comedy. Even Bugs Bunny isn't always sincere with his emotions. That's why it's so satisfying when you see actual sincerity in a character like the Devil.

➜ **DAVE:** In our early brainstorm sessions, before we came up with "Holiday Tree-dition," we had the unexpected problem of having more Christmas ideas for the Devil than Cuphead and Mugman. We came up with several ideas: (1) The Devil wants to get on the nice list so he can get a present. (2) Something happens to the Devil, and he transforms like a werewolf into Santa. (3) For some reason, the Devil has to deliver all of Santa's presents. I thought we would have to choose one of those concepts and throw the other two away. Then Deeki went away with that material and had one of his truly inspired moments.

DEEKI: Every day after work, I'd take all my notes and ideas to the Corner Bakery to write the rough pitch. I was sitting there driving myself nuts because I loved all three concepts. And then it just clicked—it *is* all three. When I got to the moment the Devil gestures to Santa's lap like he wants to sit, I started laughing so hard that the other customers began to stare. I realized that if someone were to come over and glance at my notebook, they'd see "The Devil sits on Santa's lap," and it would just raise so many questions—and then I started laughing uncontrollably.

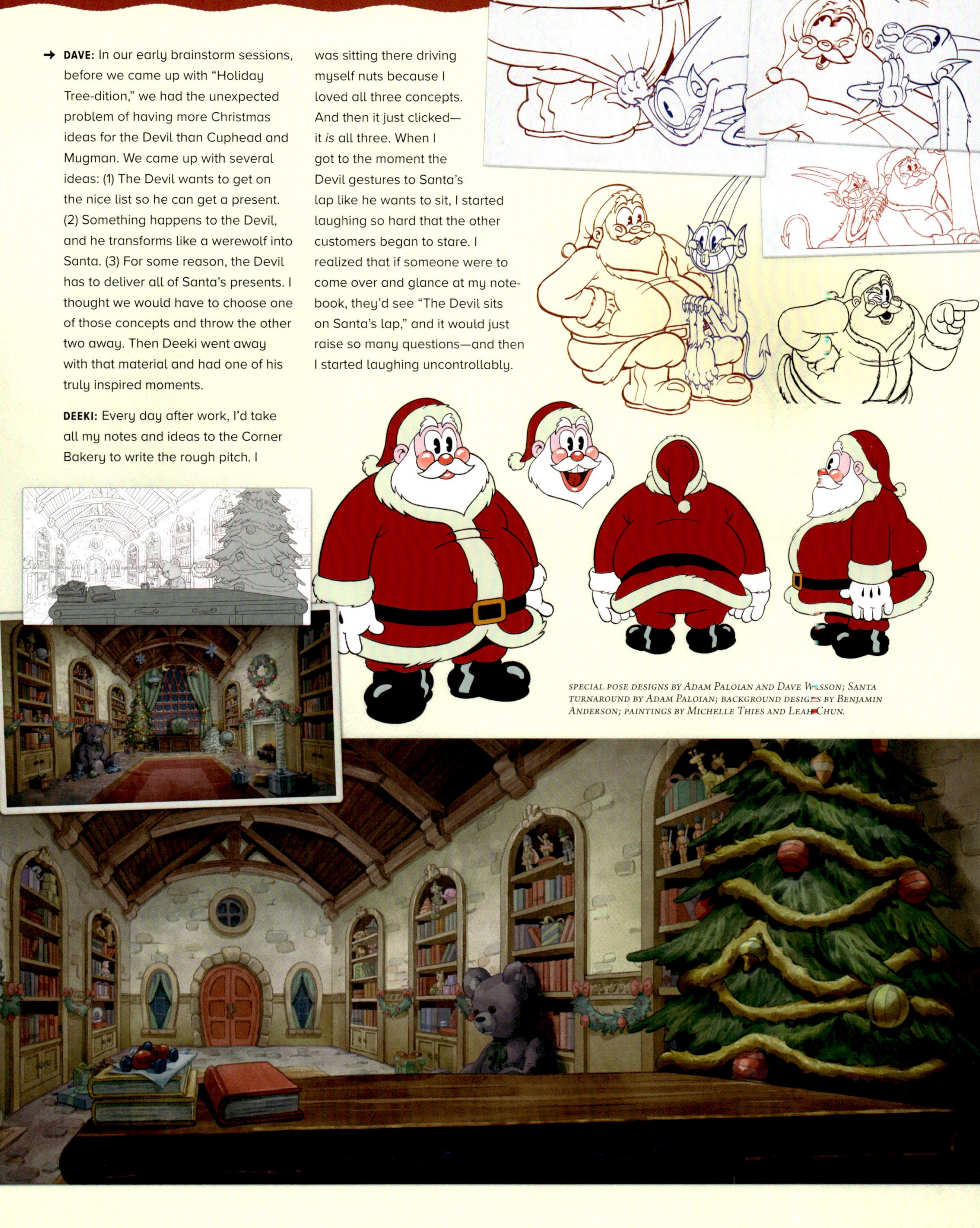

Special pose designs by Adam Paloian and Dave Wasson; Santa turnaround by Adam Paloian; background designs by Benjamin Anderson; paintings by Michelle Thies and Leah Chun.

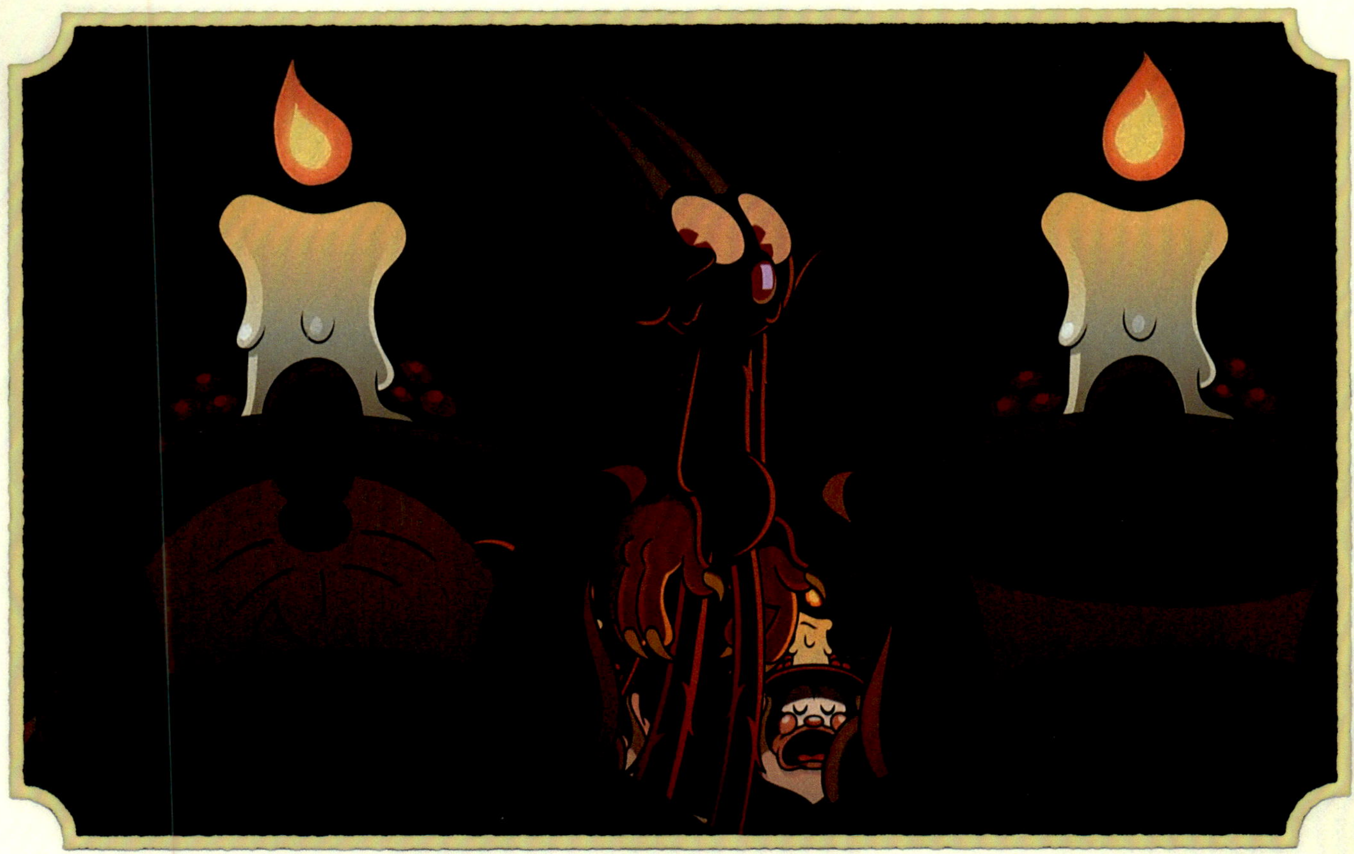

ABOVE: BACKGROUND DESIGN BY JESSICA HONG; PAINTING BY SEBASTIAN GUERRA-MARTINEZ.
BELOW: BACKGROUND DESIGN BY LAUREN DUDA; PAINTING BY GREGORY MILLER.

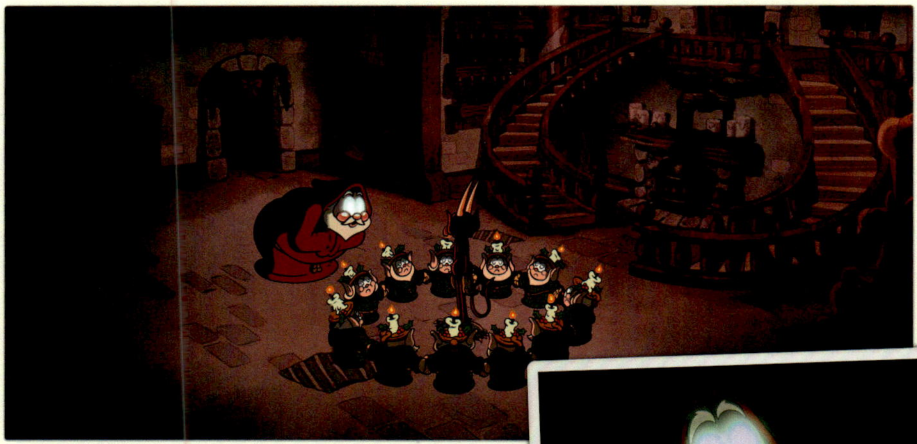

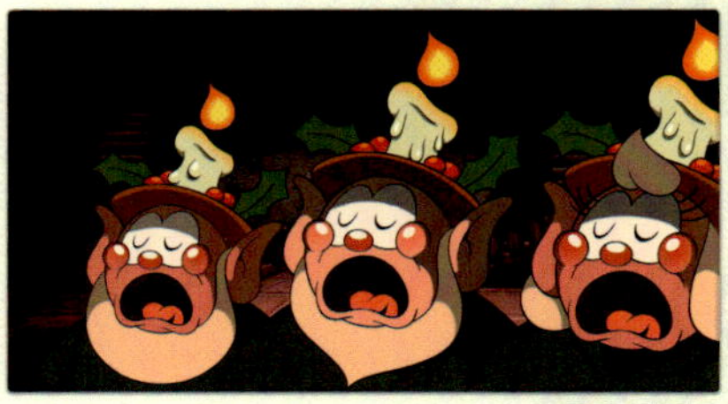

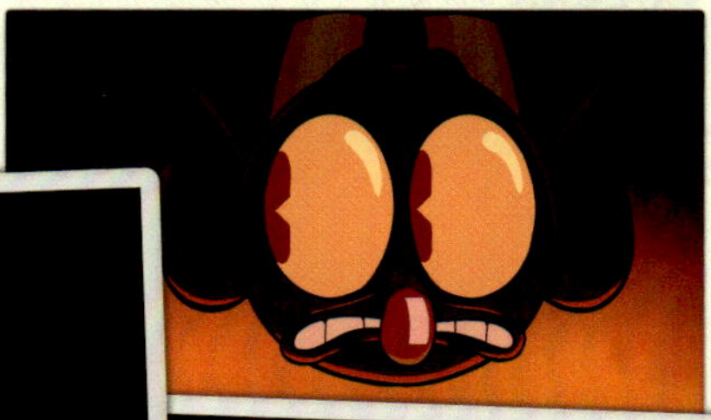

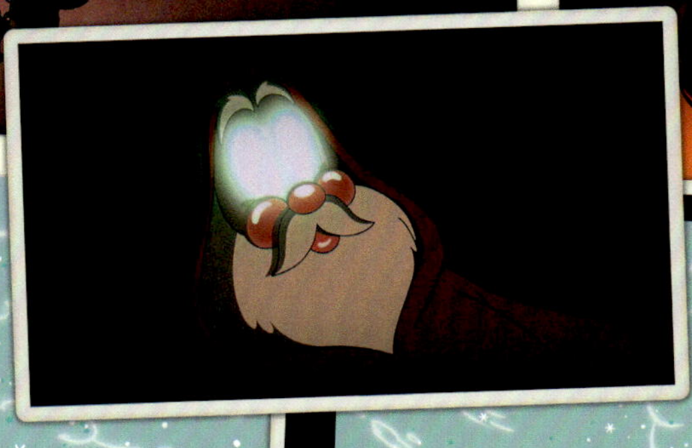

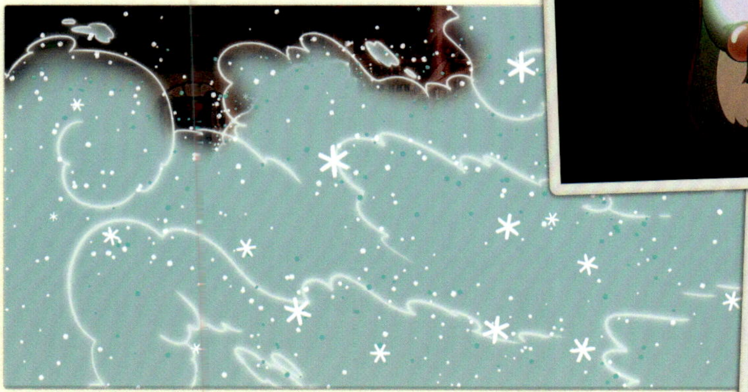

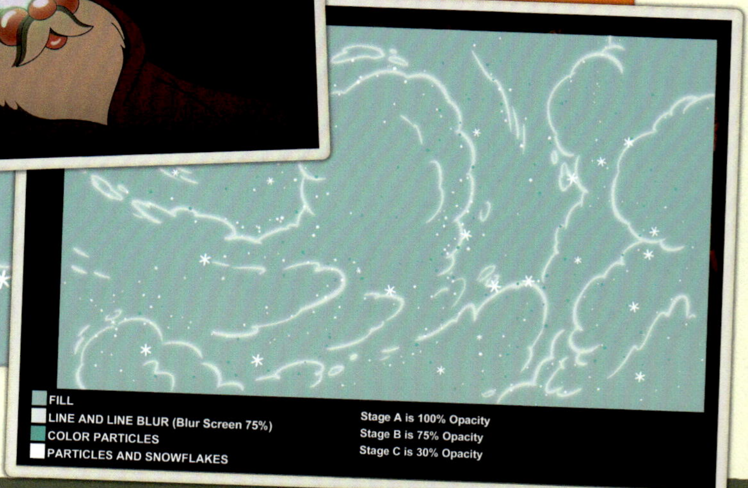

SPECIAL POSES BY BRADLEY LEWIS AND MIKE FONTANELLI; MAGIC WIND DESIGN BY ED SKUDDER; CHARACTER COLOR BY CHRIS HACKER AND CHELSEA JAUREGUI.

FILL
LINE AND LINE BLUR (Blur Screen 75%)
COLOR PARTICLES
PARTICLES AND SNOWFLAKES

Stage A is 100% Opacity
Stage B is 75% Opacity
Stage C is 30% Opacity

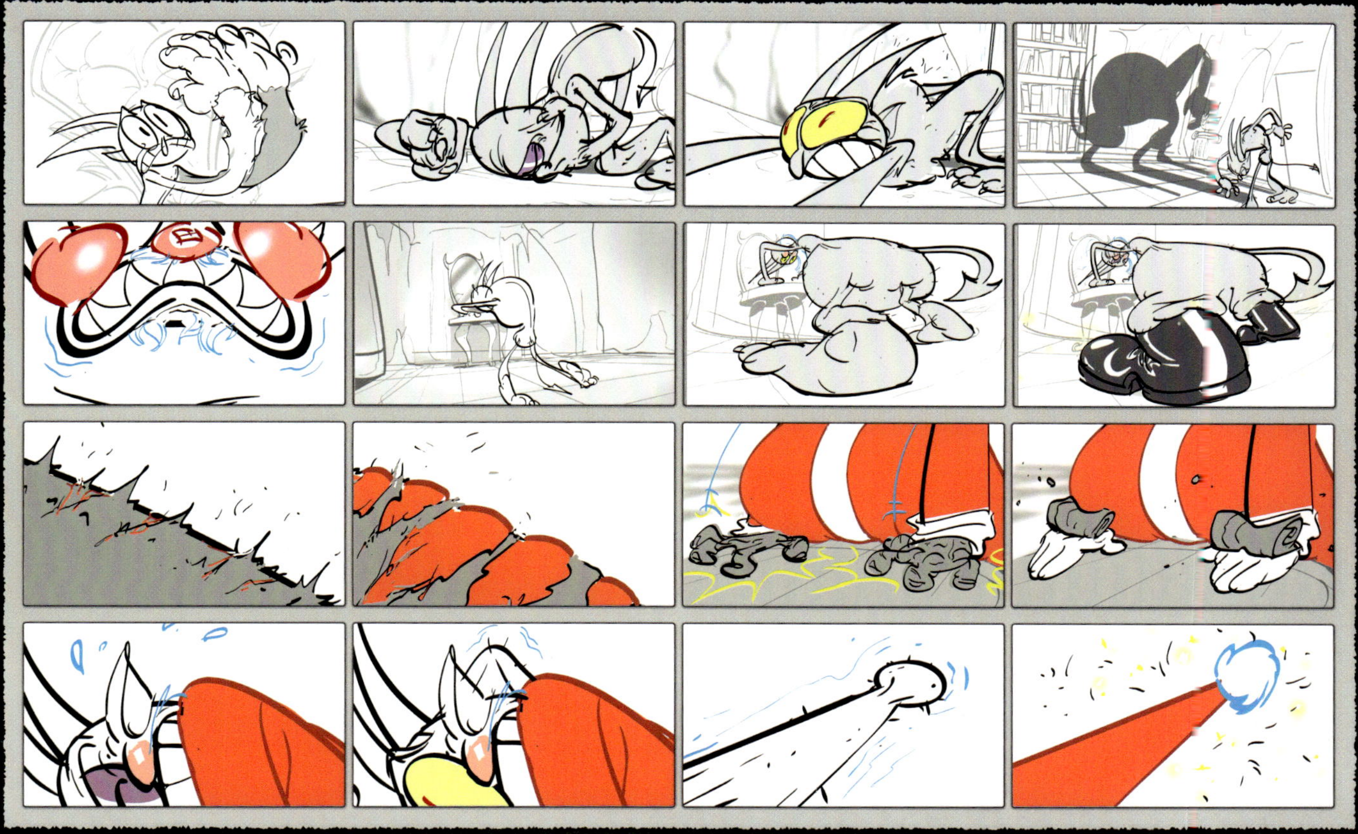

• STORYBOARD SPOTLIGHT •

A VERY DEVIL SANTA

→ **MICHAEL RUOCCO, *THE CUPHEAD SHOW!* STORYBOARD SUPERVISOR:** I would get so inspired looking at some of Karl's scenes. The Devil's Santa transformation in particular has a rawness to it. It's just so viscerally painful. Even before the painful sound effects, you could almost hear the sounds from Karl's drawings.

KARL: A big part of the horror in this sequence is the Devil having no idea what's happening to him.

ADAM P: It's some kind of curse, and all the Devil knows is he's powerless to stop it. It's rare that we've seen the Devil this panicked and upset. In terms of storyboarding, there was a lot to think about, and I knew I could trust Karl on that section.

KARL: I'm very proud of what I was able to do with the Devil transforming into Santa. That was a fun moment to put in some graphic, almost body horror stuff. It was an interesting marriage of the '30s cartoon aesthetic combined with a more modern, primal horror transformation.

MICHAEL: That sequence is like if the movie *The Santa Clause* with Tim Allen were a horror film.

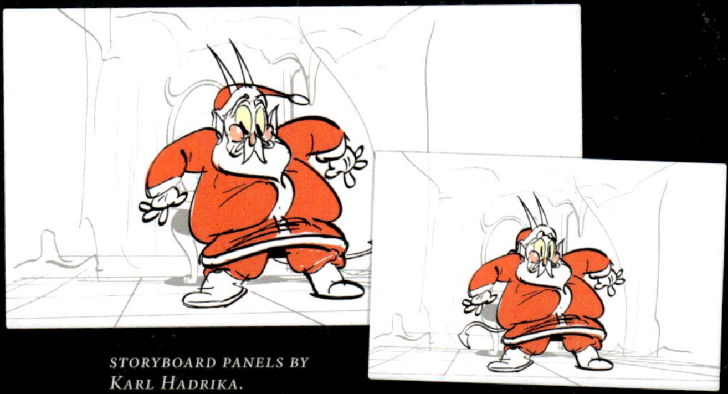

STORYBOARD PANELS BY KARL HADRIKA.

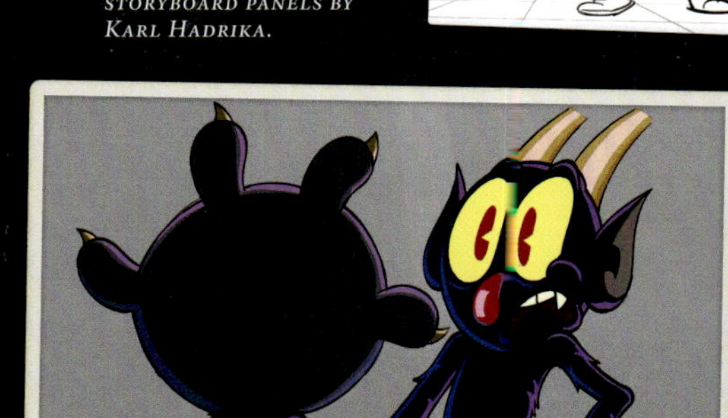

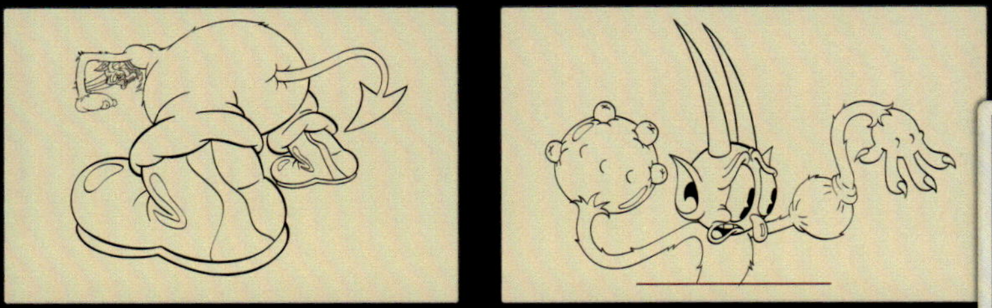

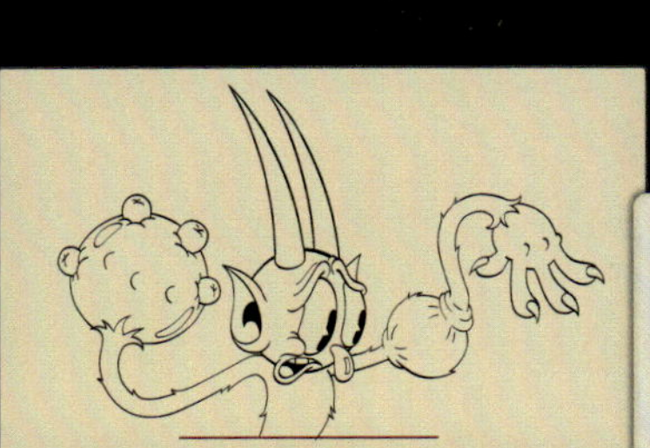

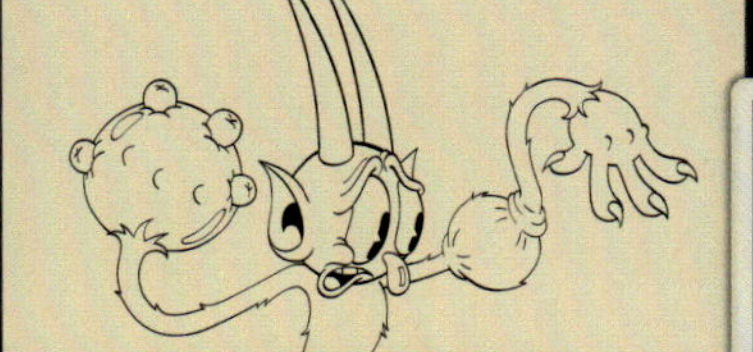

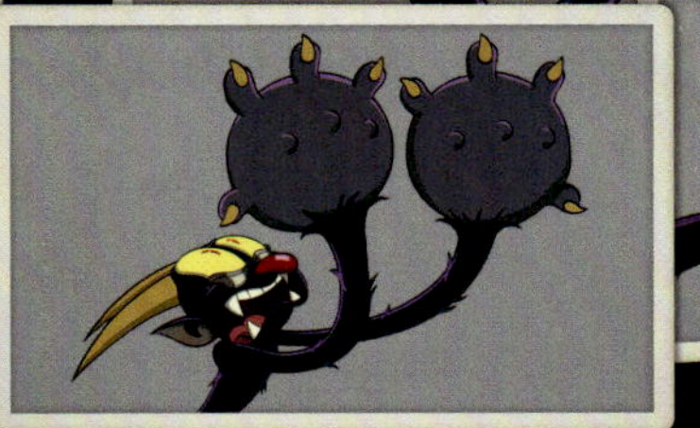

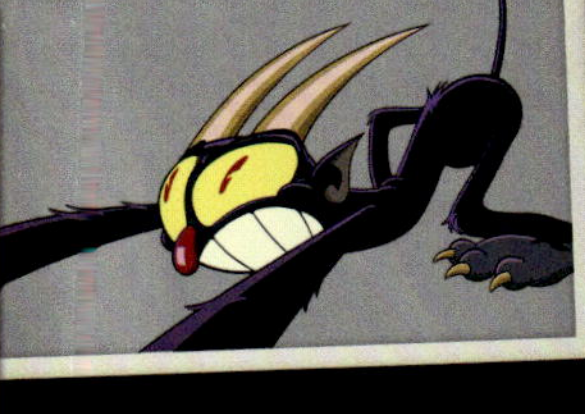

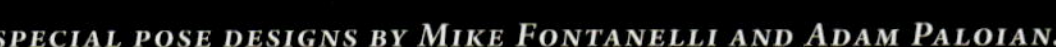

SPECIAL POSE DESIGNS BY MIKE FONTANELLI AND ADAM PALOIAN.

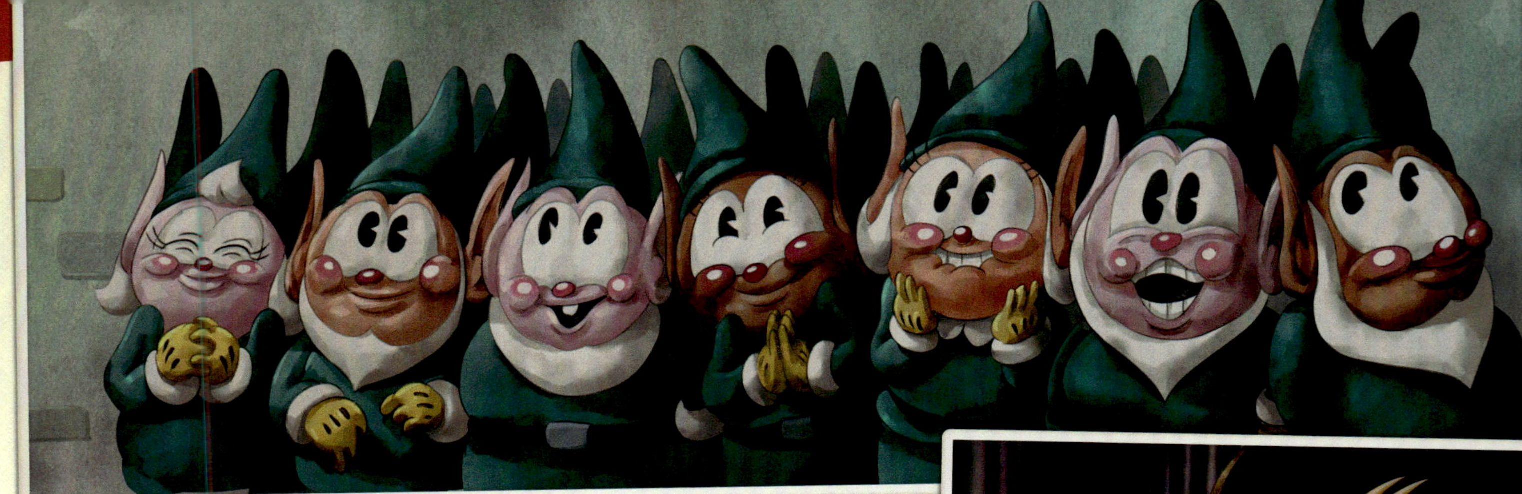

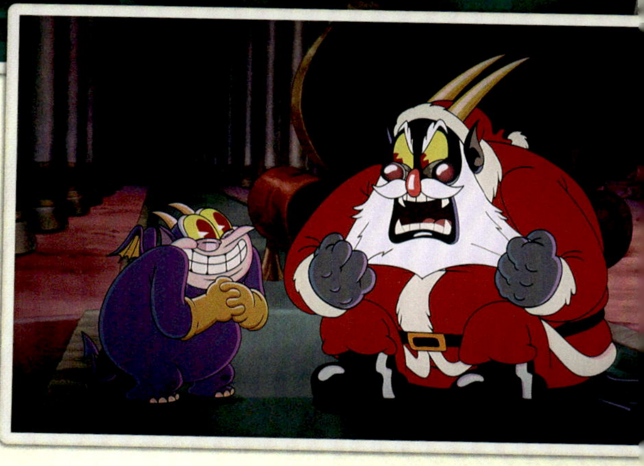

→ **DAVE:** After the storyboard stage, we build fairly elaborate animatics, where you time the storyboard panels, dialogue, music, and sound effects. It's this process that really tells you if you've got the goods or not, if the story and jokes are playing, and whether or not you still have a lot of work ahead of you. The animatic never lies.

ADAM P: All of them ran long, so we always had to cut it down. Trying to preserve jokes while you're cutting is always a challenge. With this episode, everything worked, every drawing was hilarious, so it was especially painful to make cuts. I was relieved it went from a two-parter to a three-parter. There was just too much incredible material.

DAVE: It's sort of like sculpting—you just know when it feels right. It's a series of constant refinements to the sculpture. When something doesn't look right, you carve it away, or you add a little something.

ADAM P: With experience, you realize killing some of your own ideas can end up making the overall idea that much better—and it's a strange feeling.

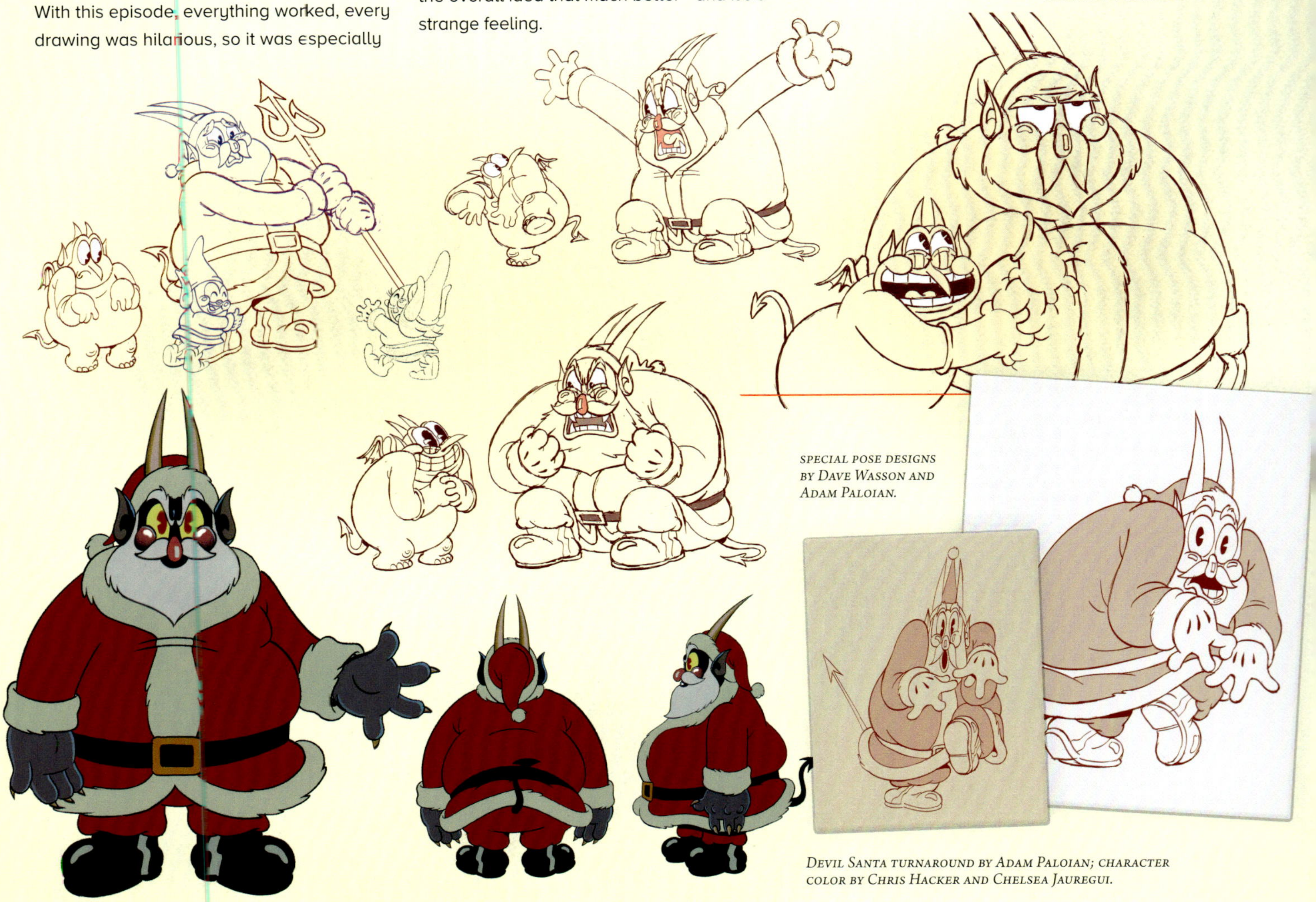

Background design by Adam Paloian; painting by Leah Chun.

Special pose designs by Dave Wasson and Adam Paloian.

Devil Santa turnaround by Adam Paloian; character color by Chris Hacker and Chelsea Jauregui.

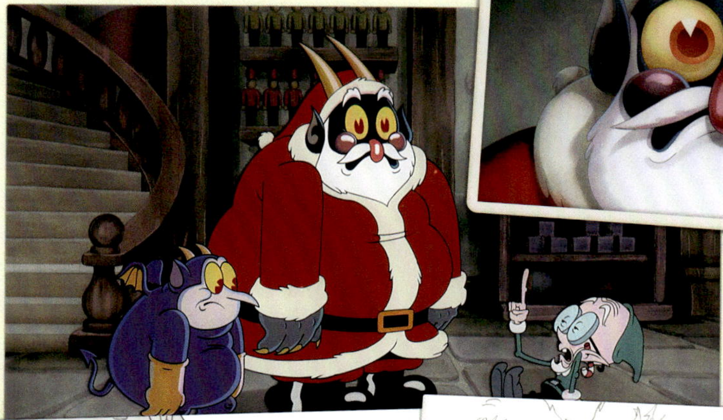

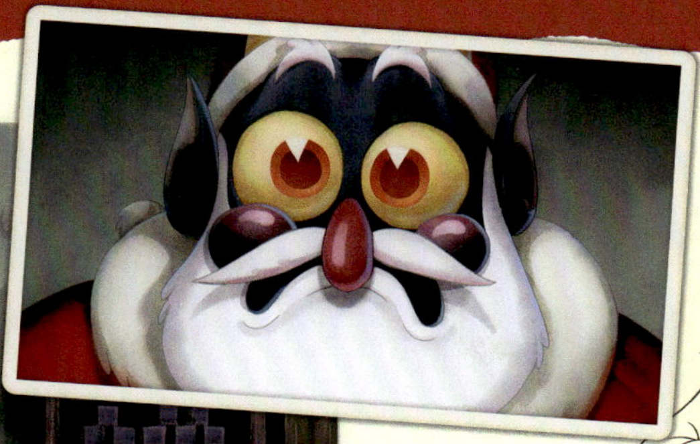

Freaked-out Devil Santa face design by Adam Paloian; painting by Mallory Carlson.

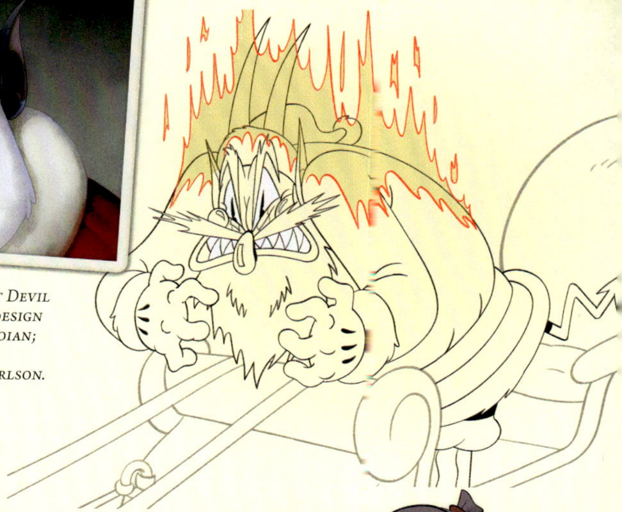

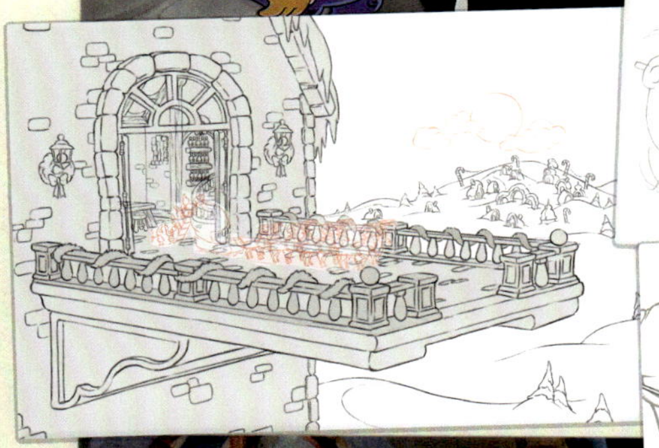

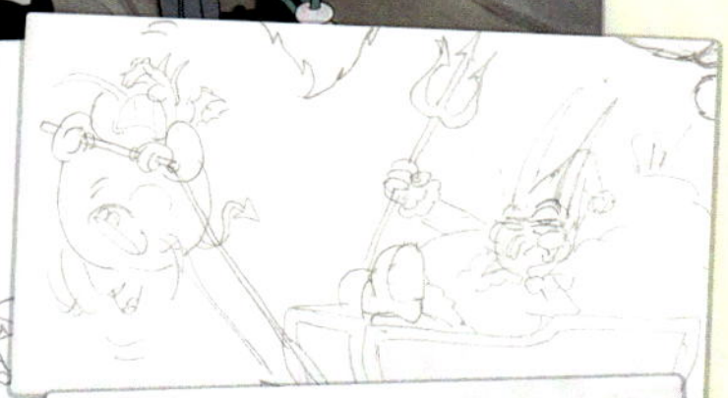

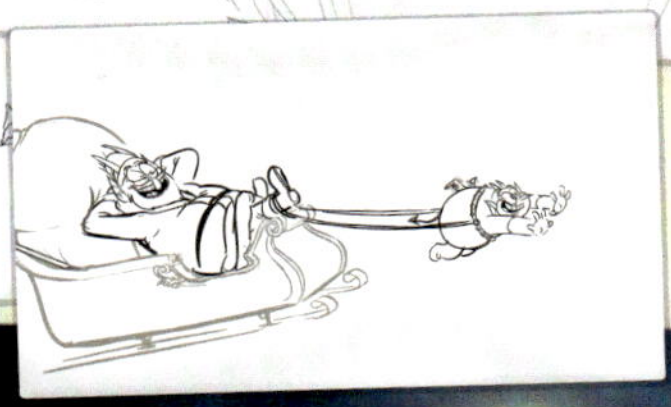

Background design by Jessica Hong; background painting by Gregory Miller; storyboard panel by Benjamin Arcand; story room sketch by Clay Morrow.

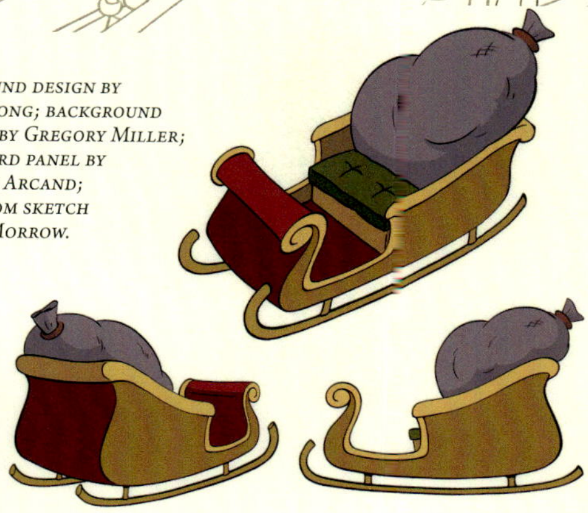

Special pose designs by Adam Paloian, Adam Fay, Bradley Lewis, Martin Wittig, and Dave Wasson; sleigh design by Jack Rossi.

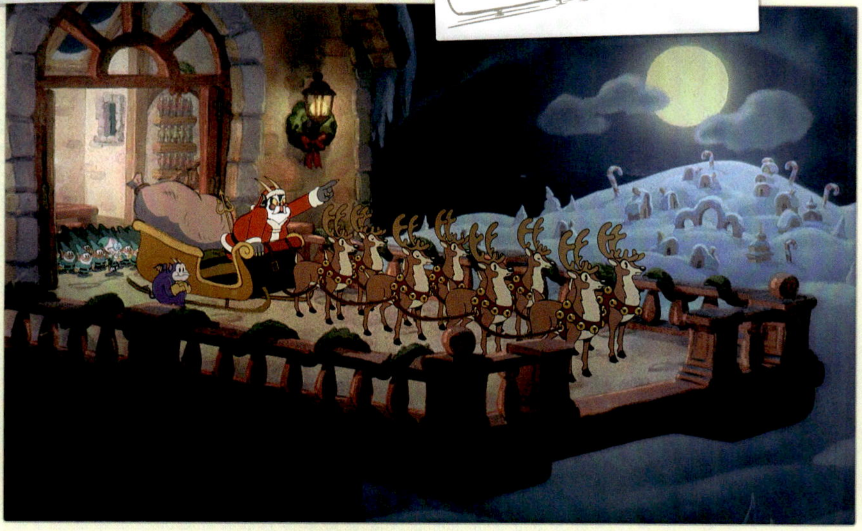

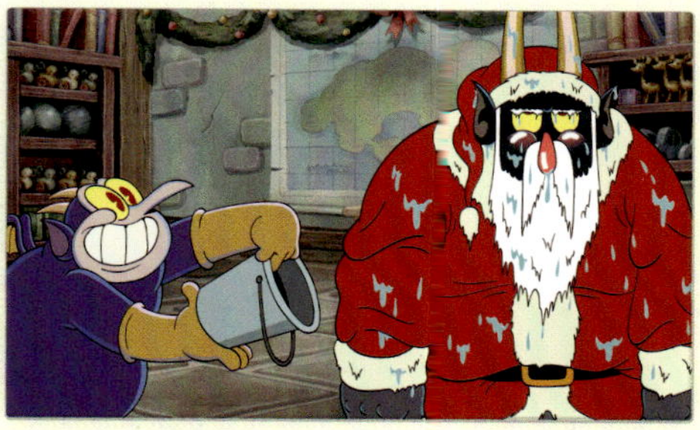

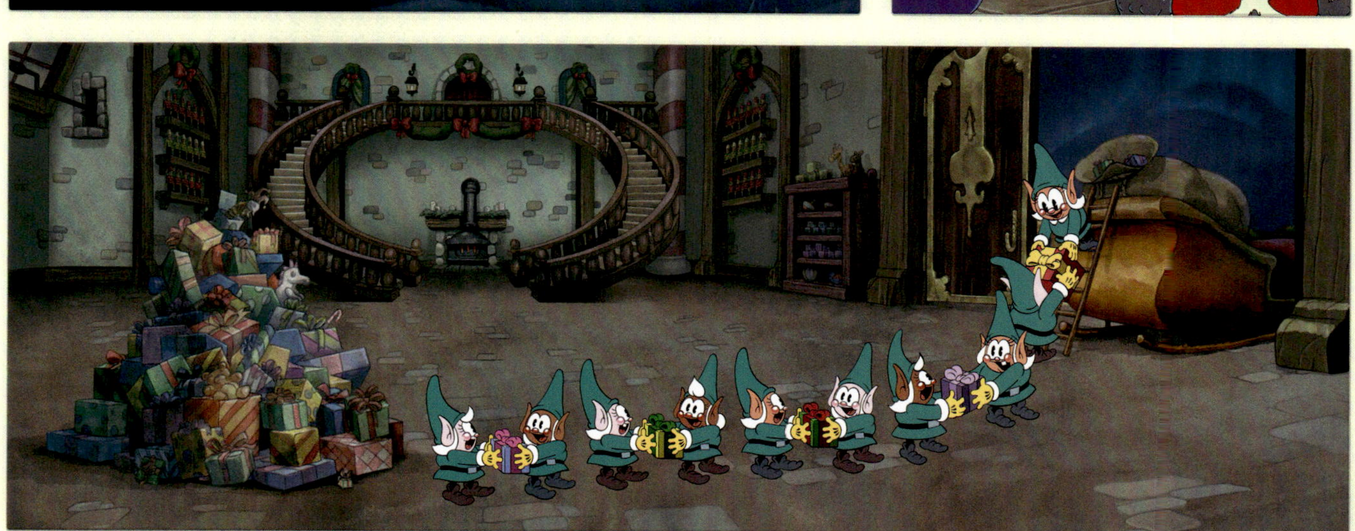

Reindeer and elves passing presents special poses by Bradley Lewis; background design by Pat Marconett; painting by Sebastian Guerra-Martinez.

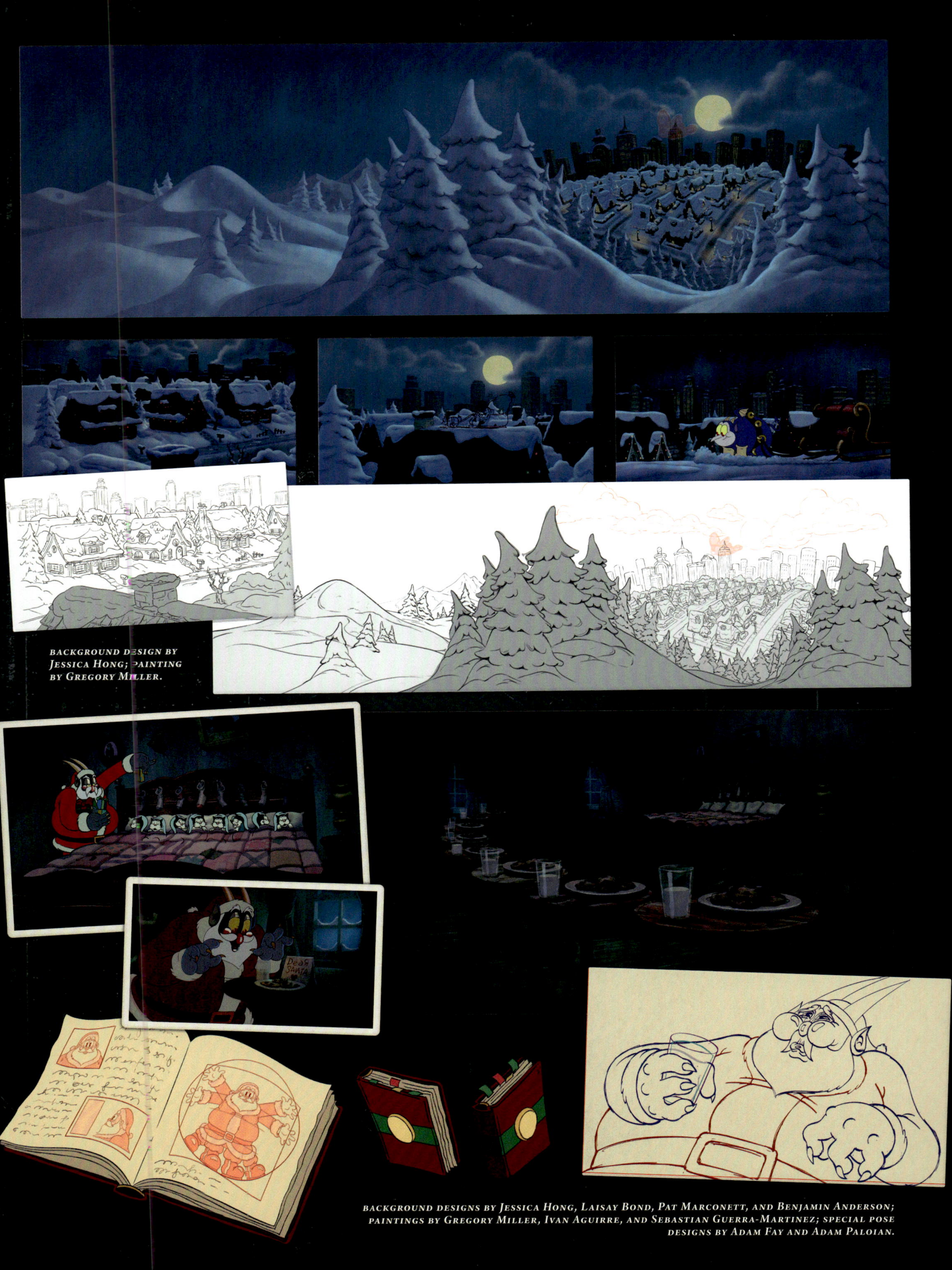

Background design by Jessica Hong; painting by Gregory Miller.

Background designs by Jessica Hong, Laisay Bond, Pat Marconett, and Benjamin Anderson; paintings by Gregory Miller, Ivan Aguirre, and Sebastian Guerra-Martinez; special pose designs by Adam Fay and Adam Paloian.

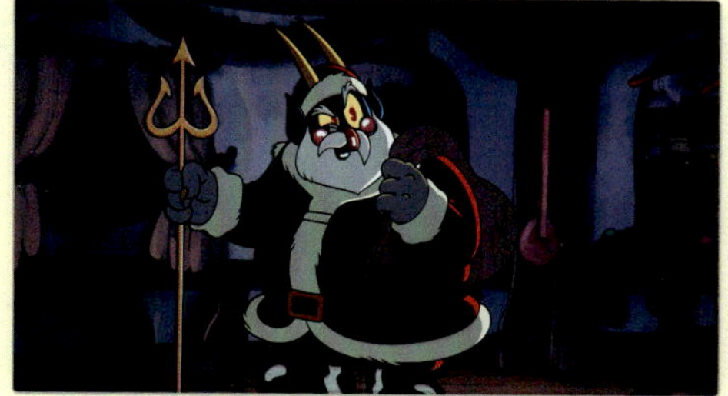

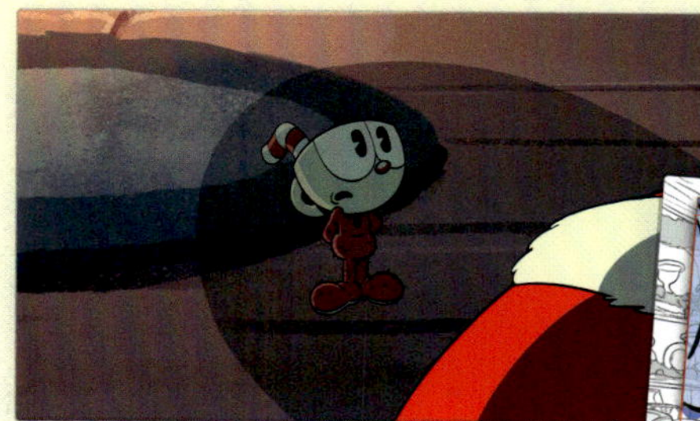

BACKGROUND DESIGNS BY PAT MARCONETI, ADAM PALOIAN, AND JESSICA HONG; PAINTINGS BY MICHELLE THIES AND VIVIAN WU.

→ **ADAM P:** In the cottage, when Cuphead interacts with Devil Santa, we needed to play that up a little bit more. It's a small scene, but a crucial one. We were stuck on it for a while as we were editing the animatic. I stayed up and pitched an idea to Dave, and he said, "That's it!" Dialogue is not my strength, but that moment felt so satisfying.

DAVE: This scene is Cuphead at his most sincere and vulnerable. It really felt nice to see this side of his personality.

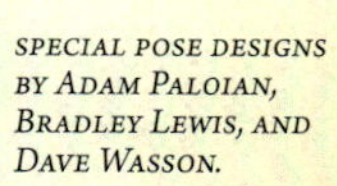

SPECIAL POSE DESIGNS BY ADAM PALOIAN, BRADLEY LEWIS, AND DAVE WASSON.

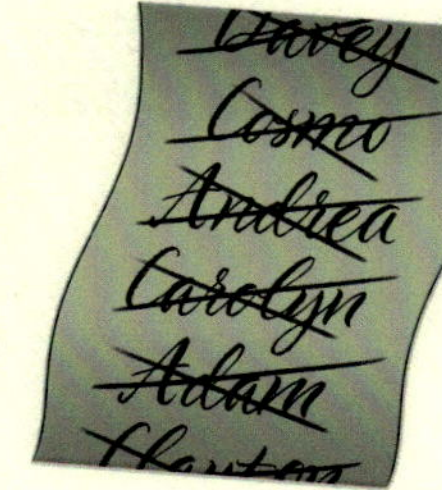

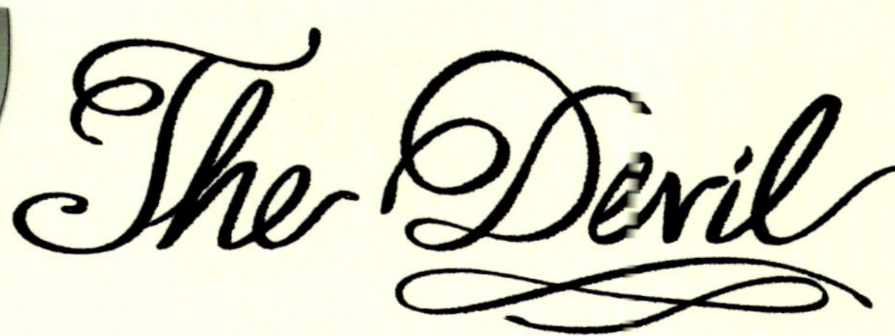

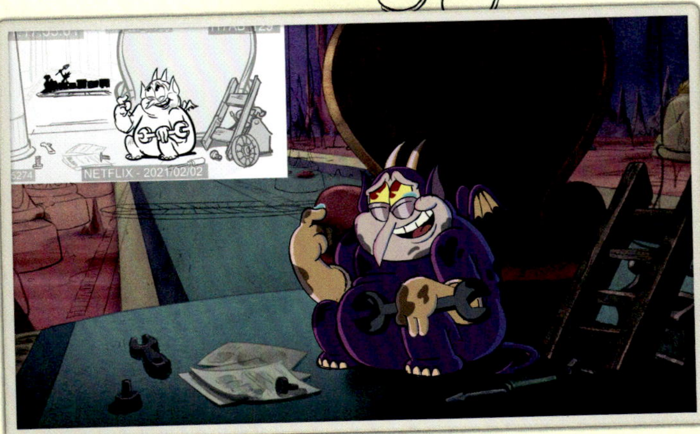

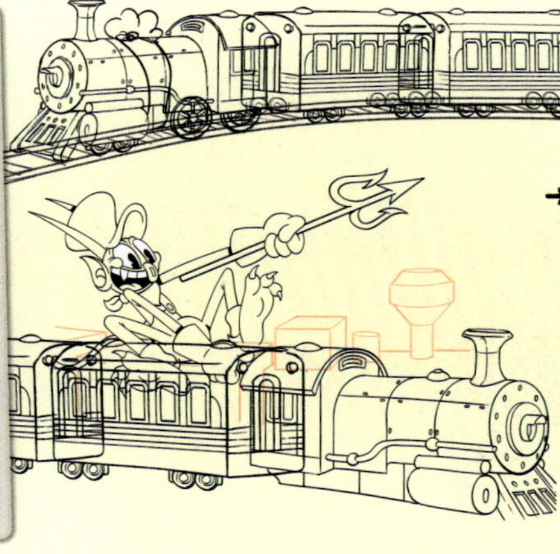

→ **DAVE:** On this episode, we pulled out all the stops. Everyone who touched it made it better. This is probably the best example of what this team could do.

THE DEVIL'S TRAIN CONCEPT BY COSMO SEGURSON.

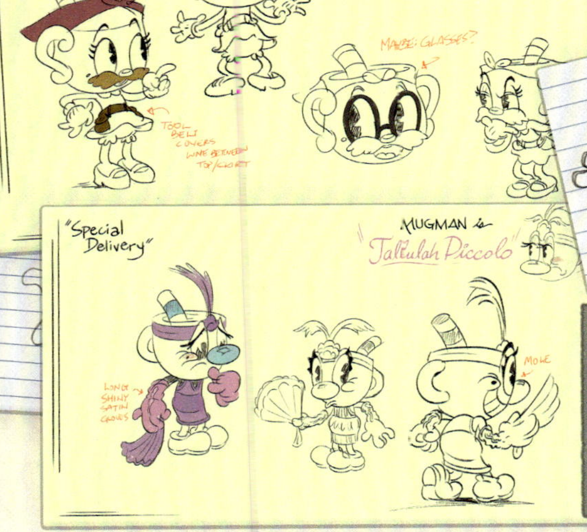

EPISODE 7
"SPECIAL DELIVERY"

PREVIS FOR "BIFF MACINTOSH" AND "TALLULAH PICCOLO" BY COSMO SEGURSON; MUGMAN AS TALLULAH SKETCHES BY CLAY MORROW.

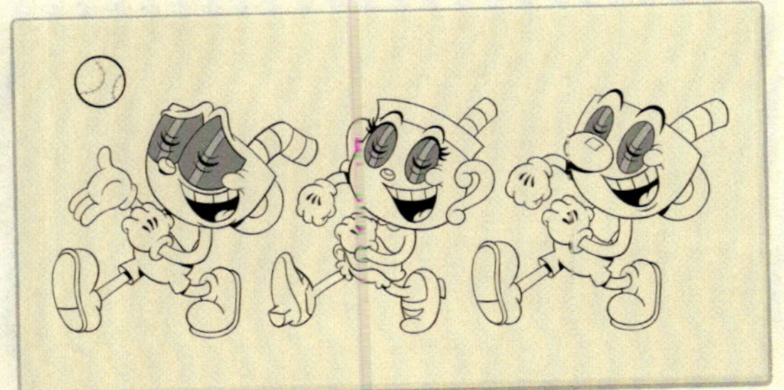

→ **CHRIS:** Yes, Cuphead and Mugman typically cause havoc and make problems—but they mostly undermine people who have it coming to them. Like a child-hating shopkeeper who makes them transport a bomb.

JARED MORGAN: Anytime you get to torture a character, it's always funny. Especially a character who's a jerk. So I love it when Porkrind is feeling guilty, and he's listening to the horse names, which are all horrifying.

DEEKI: In the story room, we were all pitching out disturbingly evocative horse names. Dave had the clear winner: "And here comes Charred Carcass!"

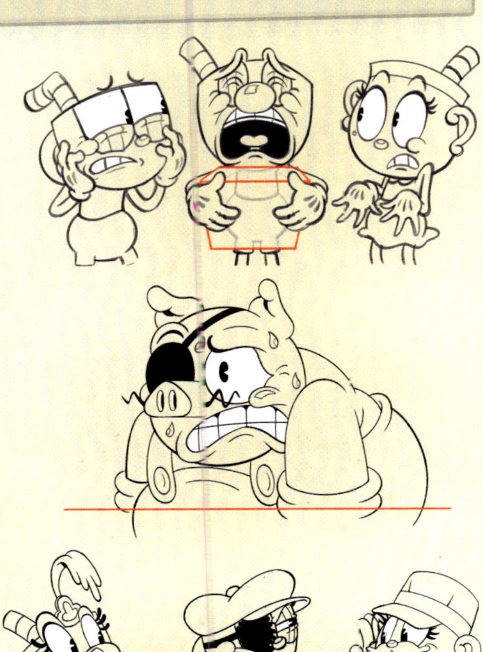

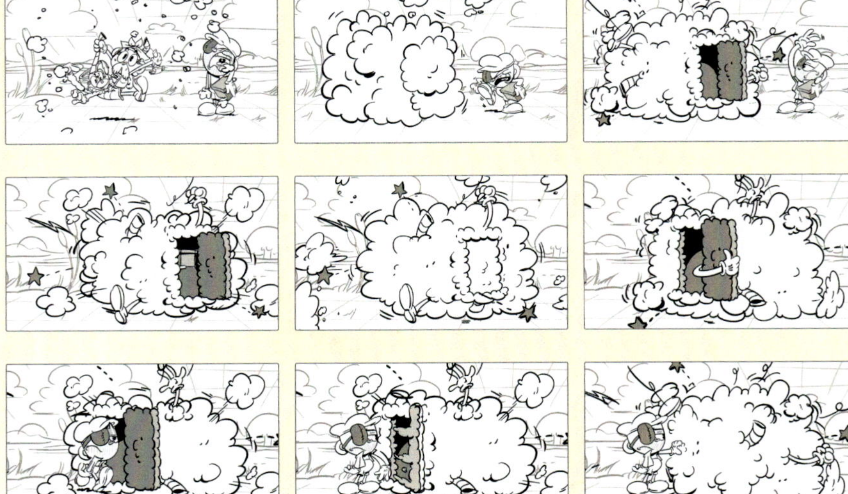

DELETED SCENE: FIGHT CLOUD SHORTCUT BY JARED MORGAN.

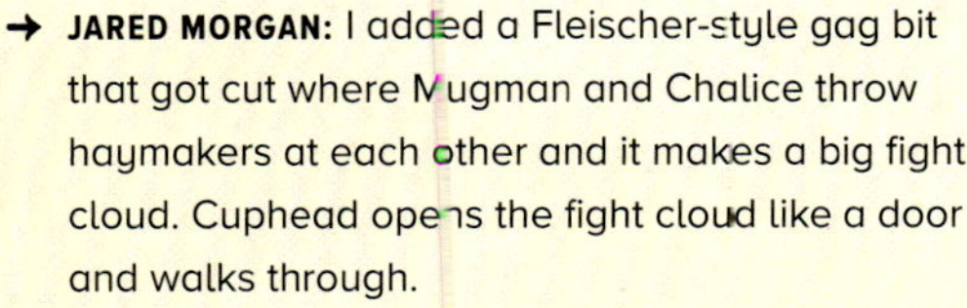

→ **JARED MORGAN:** I added a Fleischer-style gag bit that got cut where Mugman and Chalice throw haymakers at each other and it makes a big fight cloud. Cuphead opens the fight cloud like a door and walks through.

SPECIAL POSE DESIGNS BY BRADLEY LEWIS AND MIKE FONTANELLI.

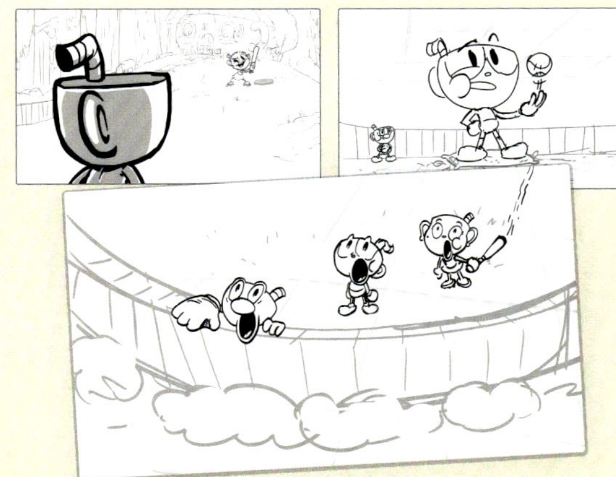

DELETED SCENE: ORIGINALLY, THE EPISODE OPENED WITH THE TRIO PLAYING BASEBALL AT THE COTTAGE, SHOWING THE BUILDUP TO THE MOMENT PORKRIND'S WINDOW SHATTERS. STORYBOARD PANELS BY ZOË MOSS.

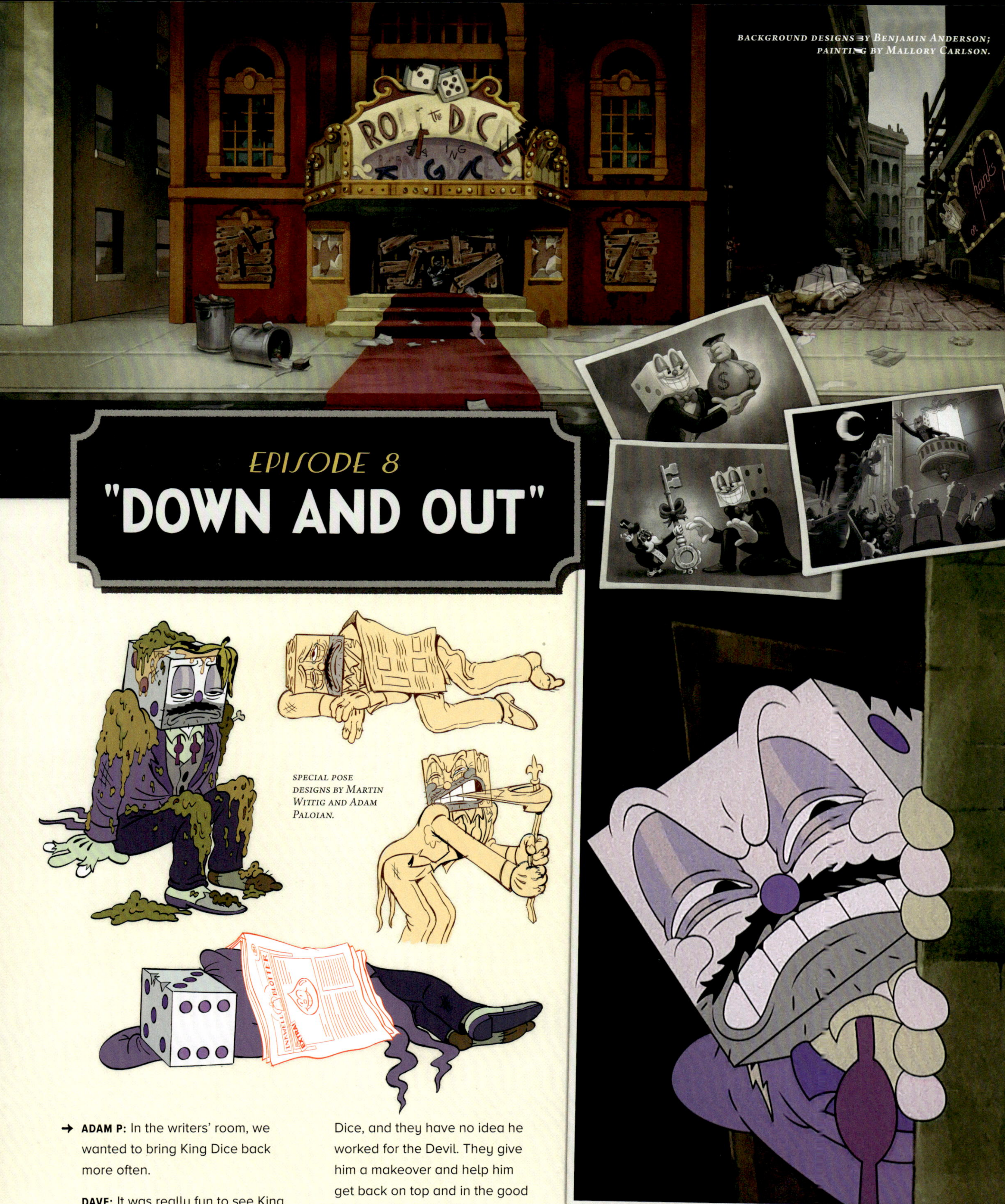

BACKGROUND DESIGNS BY BENJAMIN ANDERSON; PAINTING BY MALLORY CARLSON.

EPISODE 8
"DOWN AND OUT"

SPECIAL POSE DESIGNS BY MARTIN WITTIG AND ADAM PALOIAN.

LAYOUT DESIGNS FOR BLACK-AND-WHITE PHOTOS BY ADAM PALOIAN AND LAUREN DUDA. PAINTINGS BY RACHEL KIM.

→ **ADAM P:** In the writers' room, we wanted to bring King Dice back more often.

DAVE: It was really fun to see King Dice at such a low point. Cuphead and Mugman are big fans of King Dice, and they have no idea he worked for the Devil. They give him a makeover and help him get back on top and in the good graces of "the boss." I love a good comeback story.

➜ **DEEKI:** Zoë had a pitch where King Dice lives in the alley behind the theater. That image was irresistible. Unfortunately, her story was about King Dice becoming Mugman's piano teacher—just as we were doing the Ludwig story. Zoë heard Ian and Nick developing their own King Dice idea, where Cuphead and Mugman become like agents for King Dice. The three of them did a premise together and then I combined all our ideas into one pitch. The story for this episode was a true collaboration.

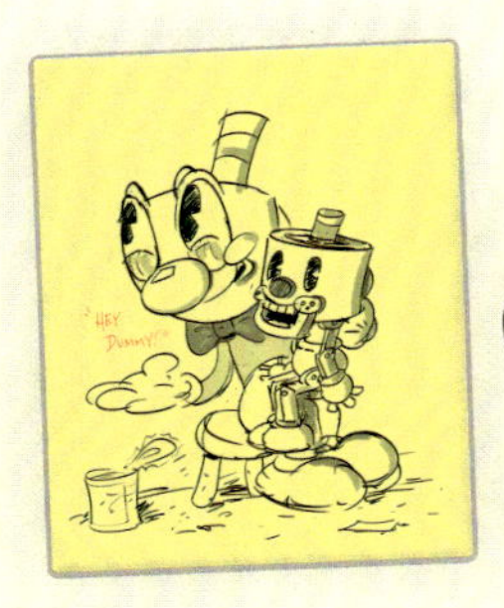

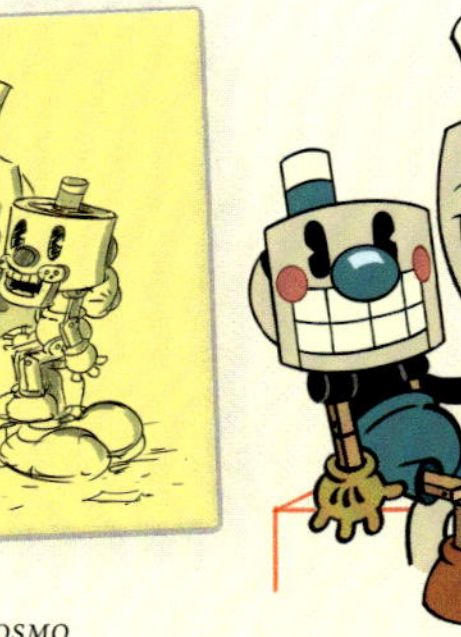

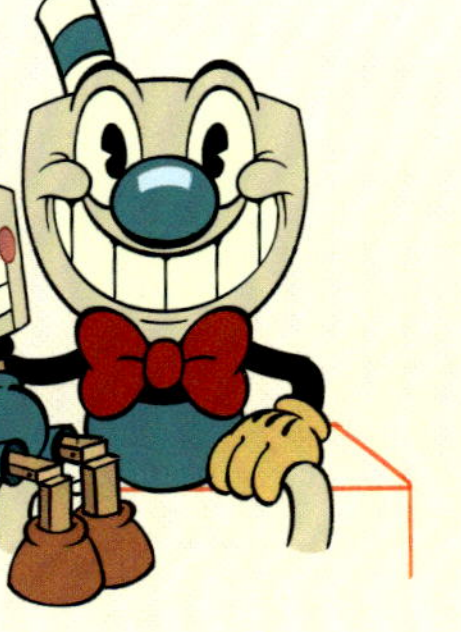

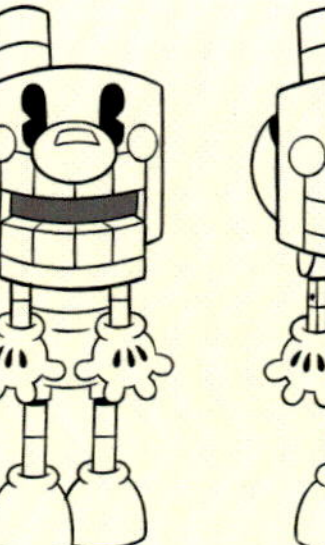

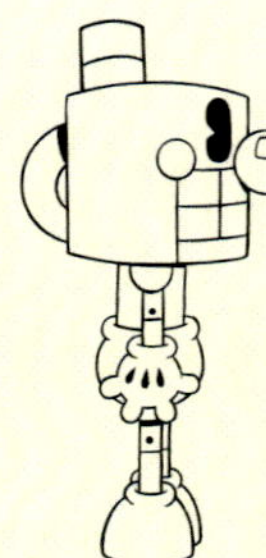

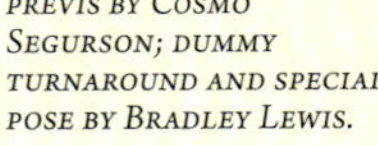

Previs by Cosmo Segurson; dummy turnaround and special pose by Bradley Lewis.

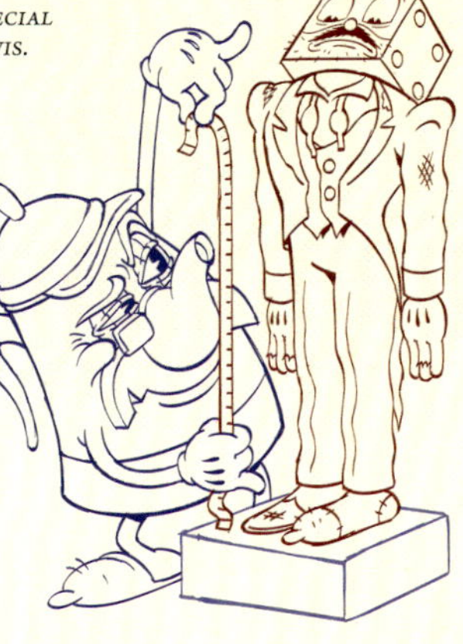

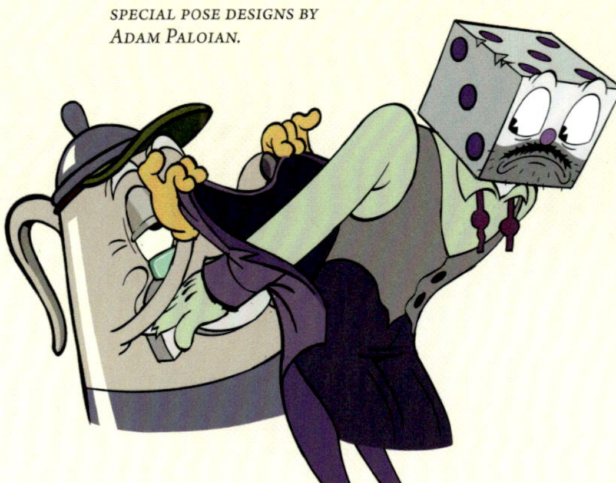

Special pose designs by Adam Paloian.

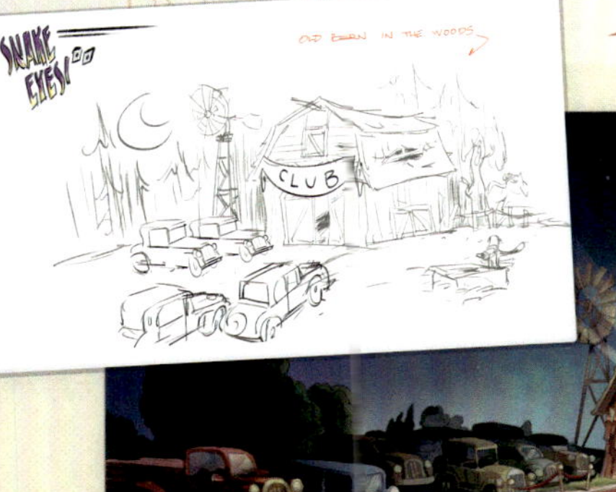

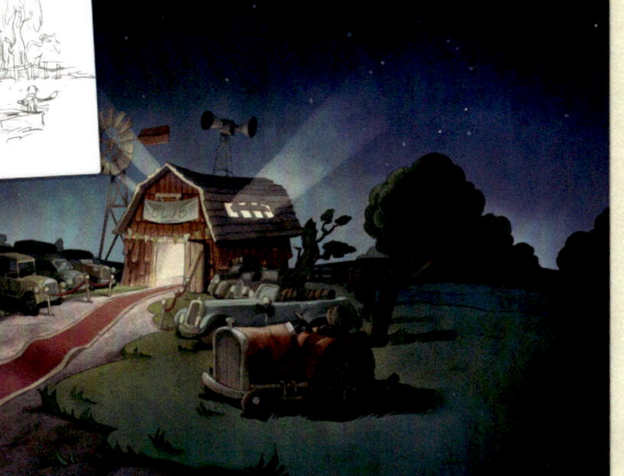

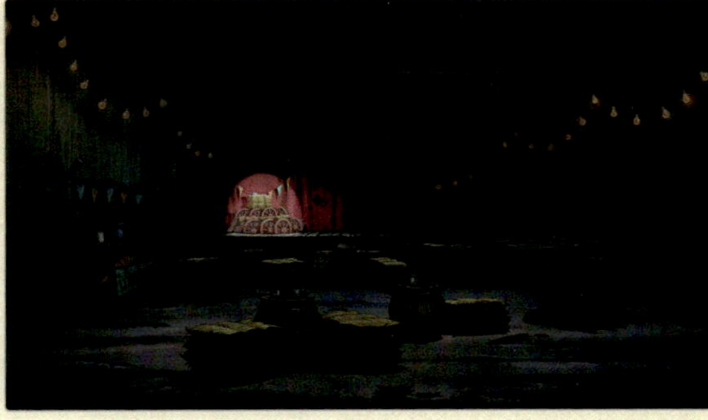

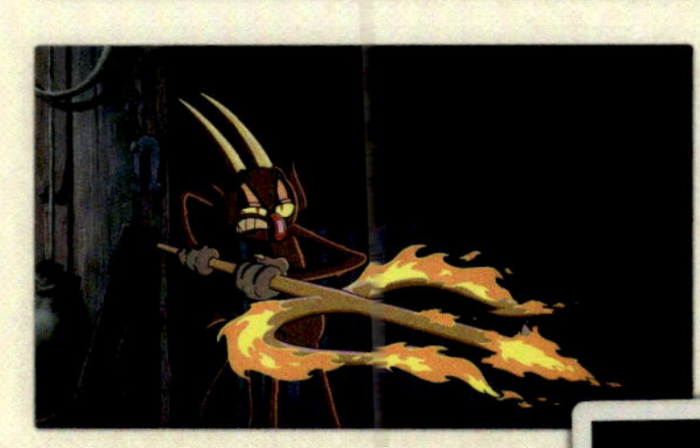

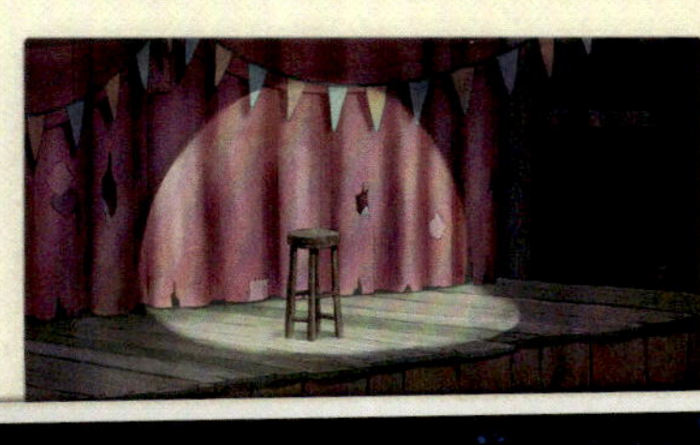

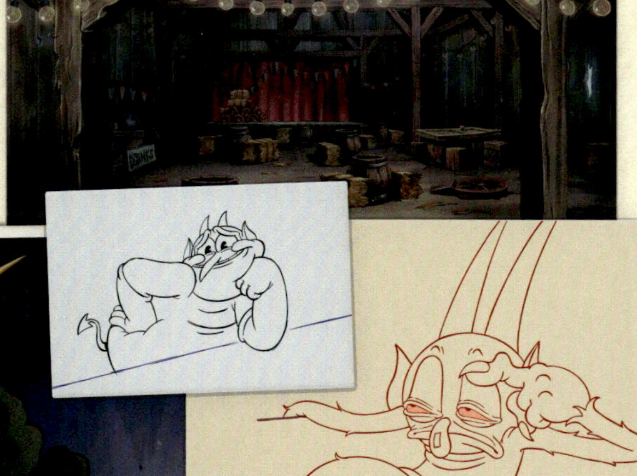

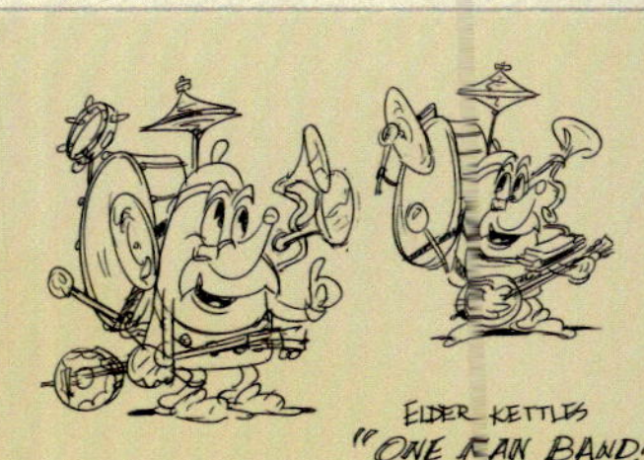

Deleted scene: originally, Elder Kettle kept showing up to audition for the club. Concept for Elder Kettle's one-man band by Cosmo Segurson.

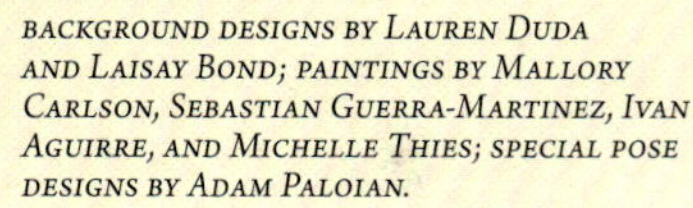

Background designs by Lauren Duda and Laisay Bond; paintings by Mallory Carlson, Sebastian Guerra-Martinez, Ivan Aguirre, and Michelle Thies; special pose designs by Adam Paloian.

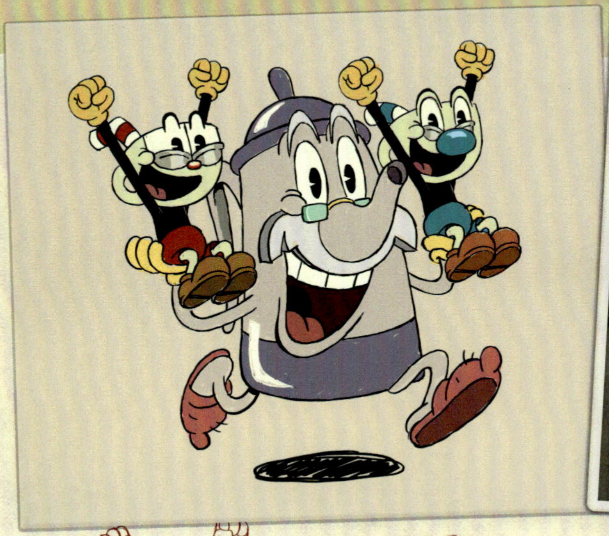

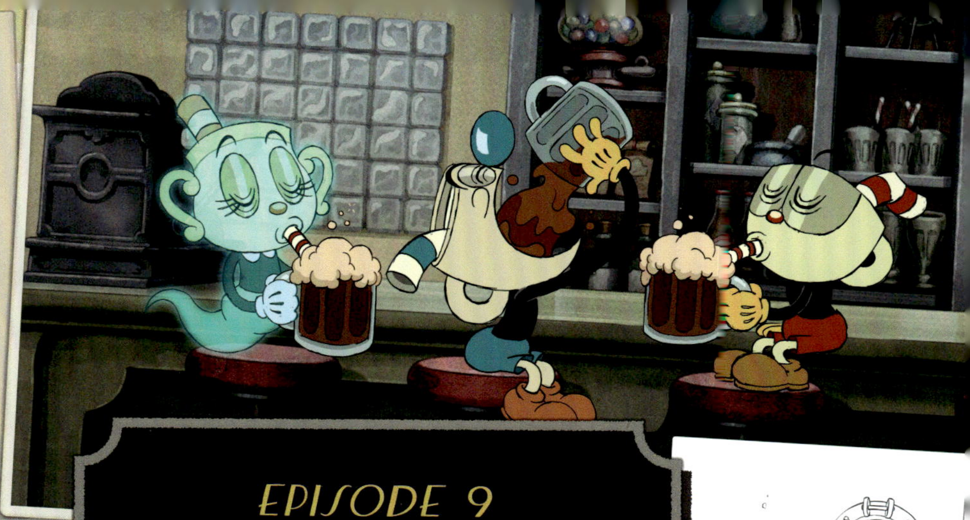

EPISODE 9
"JOY RIDE"

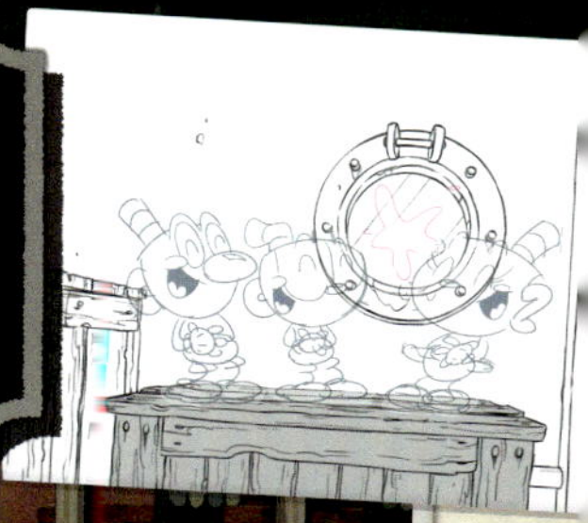

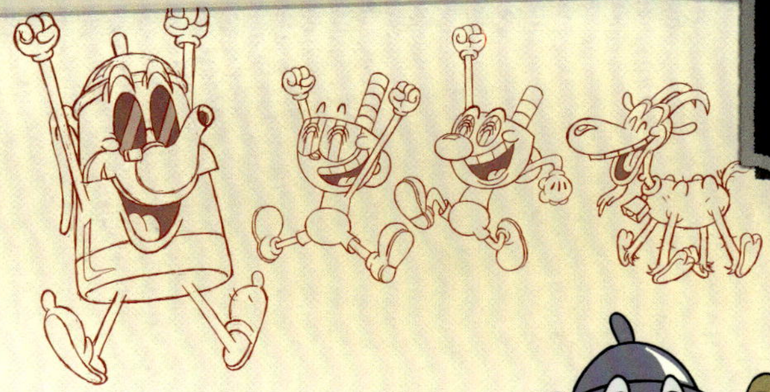

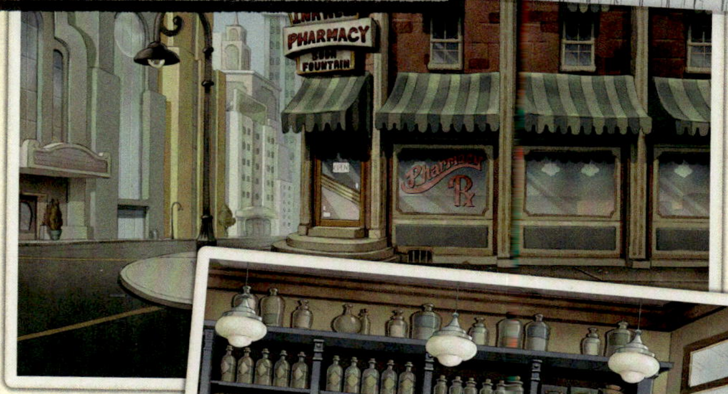

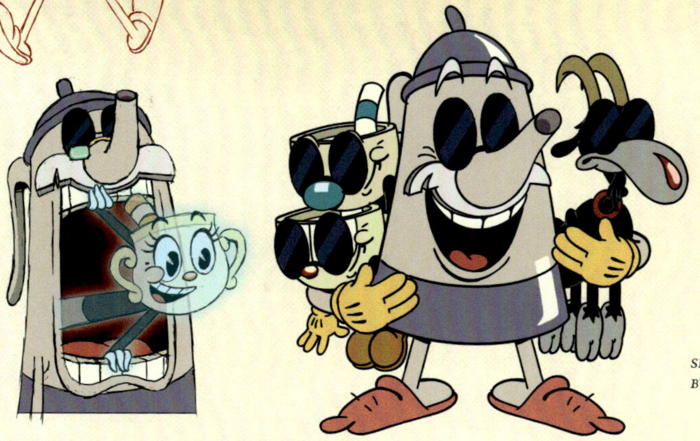

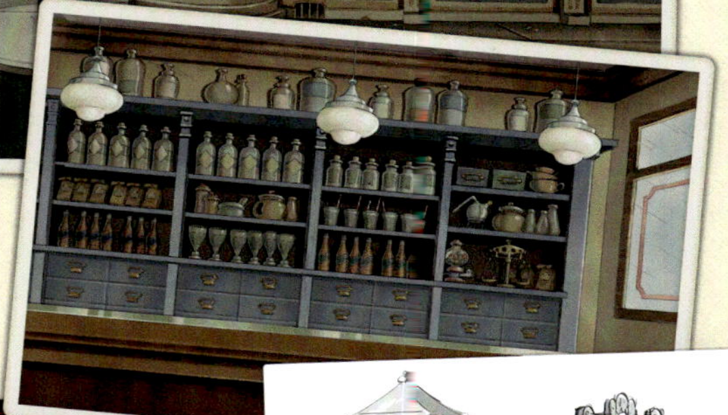

SPECIAL POSE DESIGNS BY DAVE WASSON.

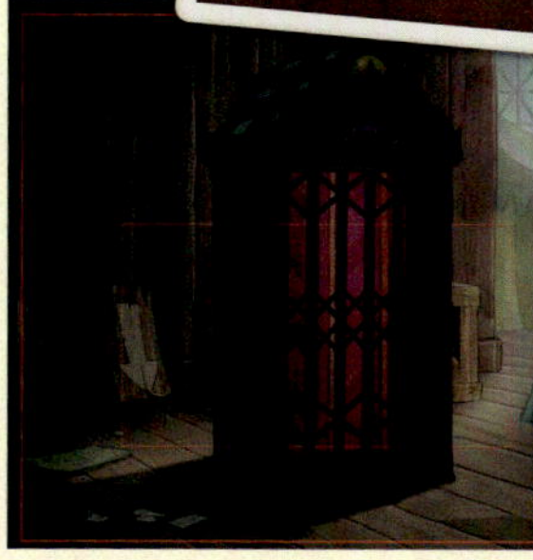

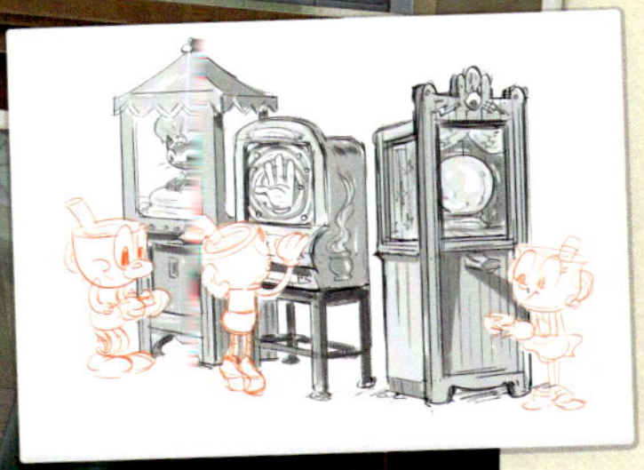

→ **DAVE:** To me, the whole reason to do this episode was the fun of having Kettle act like a maniac and seeing the boys completely baffled by his crazy behavior.

CLAY: "Joy Ride" is really just the one joke—Chalice possesses characters and does whatever she wants. There weren't any consequences—it was a romp, almost a montage. But it works really well as a deceptive buildup to the rug pull at the end—that ominous moment at the fortunetelling machines.

BACKGROUND DESIGNS BY LAUREN DUDA, JESSICA HONG, AND LAISAY BOND; PAINTINGS BY MICHELLE THIES, MALLORY CARLSON, AND IVAN AGUIRRE.

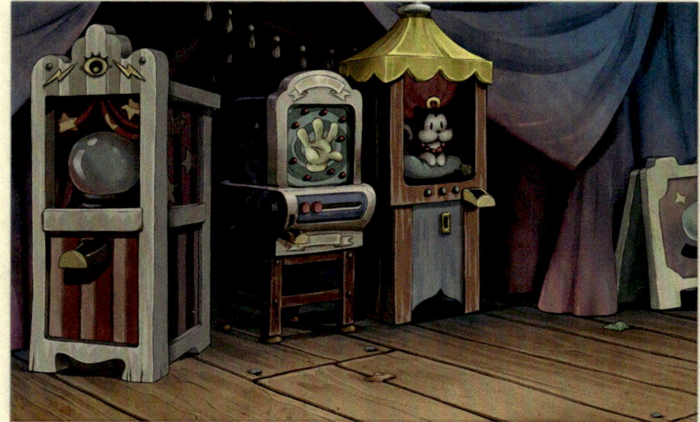

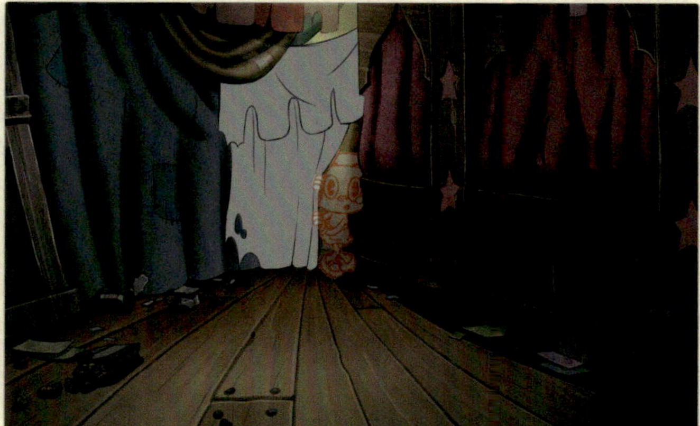

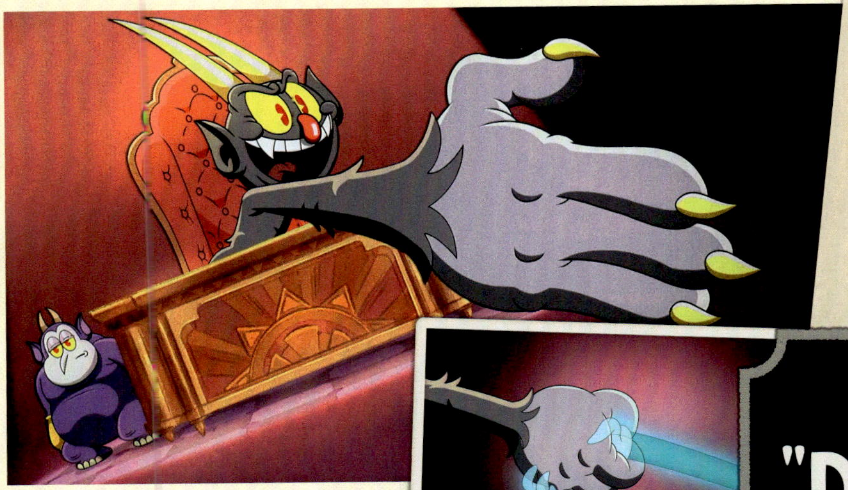

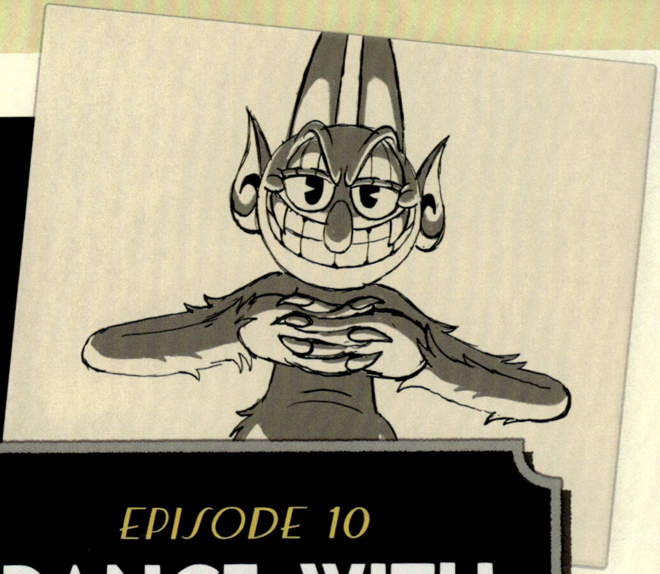

EPISODE 10

"DANCE WITH DANGER"

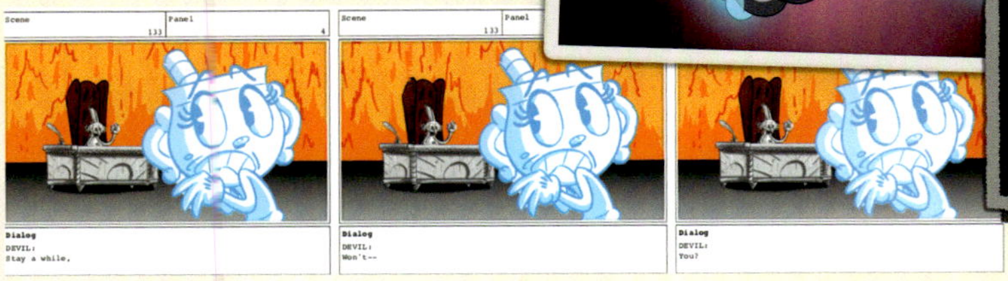

Background design by Cosmo Segurson; painting by Rachel Kim; storyboard panels by Jared Morgan.

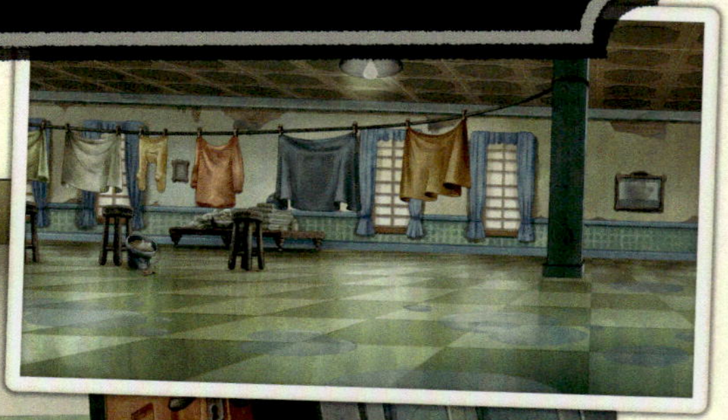

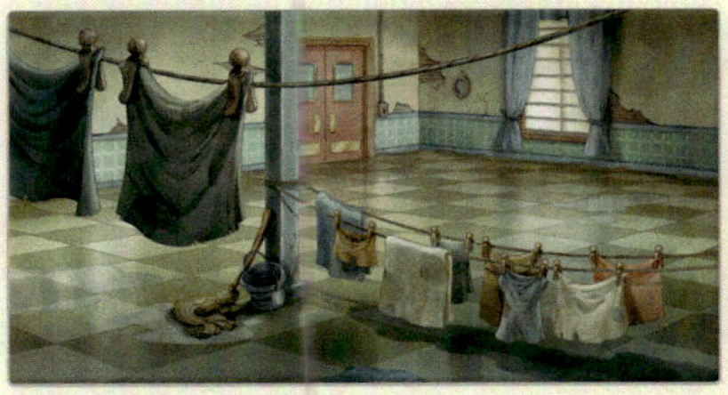

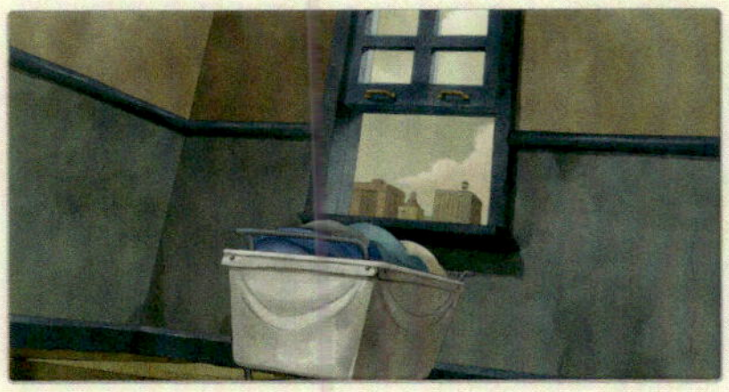

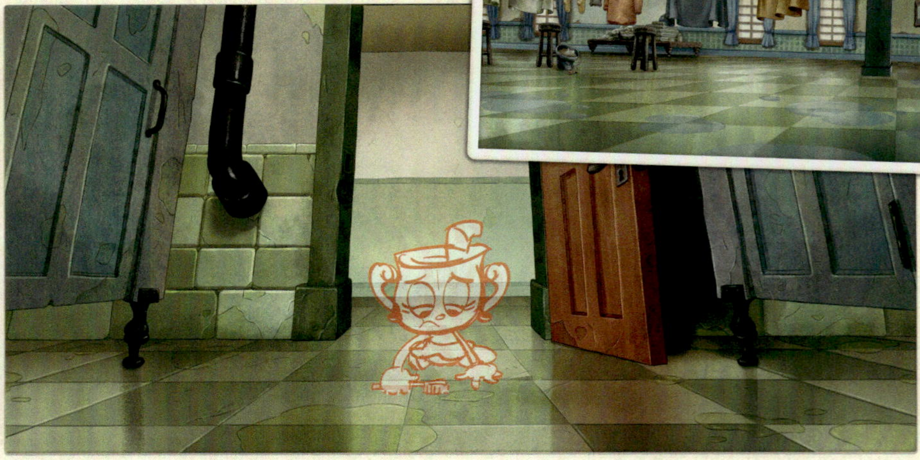

Background designs by Laisay Bond and Clarke Snyder; paintings by Michelle Thies and Ivan Aguirre.

→ **JARED MORGAN:** This episode gets real. Chalice dies, ends up in a nightmare realm surrounded by fire, and makes a deal with the Devil. It's such a high note of the series—and it's scary as hell!

COSMO: I love that we find out why she's conflicted with the Devil and what that relationship is. I love that it happens toward the end of the run, so when you look back on the earlier Chalice episodes, you have a deeper understanding of her and what's motivating her.

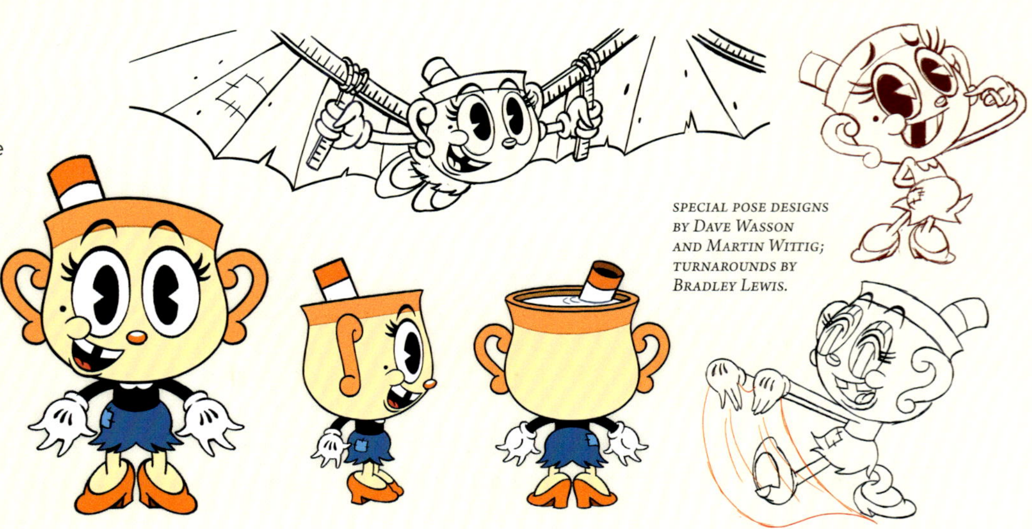

Special pose designs by Dave Wasson and Martin Wittig; turnarounds by Bradley Lewis.

→ **ADAM P:** At one point early on we thought maybe she had a ghost family in a graveyard. Or maybe she was a street urchin who was a little more rough looking, in tattered clothes, like maybe she's a thief—a little bit of a criminal on the run all the time. She became more clever. I remember when we landed on her using charm to persuade people. It felt like a good balance. People wanted her to remain looking like Chalice and being sweet, but we wanted her to be fun and a little deceptive.

COSMO: We always knew we wanted her to be a tap dancing freak. We had a bunch of different design ideas for how to show tap dancing without making our animation studio want to quit. It was going to be really hard to show every move. So we came up with multiples and drybrush on her legs and feet while her head and hands stay in one place. And as long as you hear the tapping sound, it feels like she's dancing a lot. It's a great visual trick and it keeps her energy high.

ANDREA: Chalice's personality and voice are so strong, you can get away with a trick like that. If she were a less dynamic character, I don't think we could have taken that shortcut.

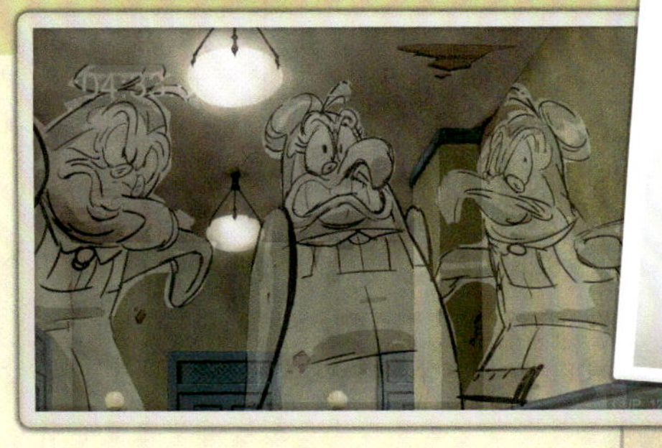

PENGUIN PREVIS BY COSMO SEGURSON; SPECIAL POSE DESIGN BY DAVE WASSON; PENGUIN TURNAROUND BY CLAY MORROW.

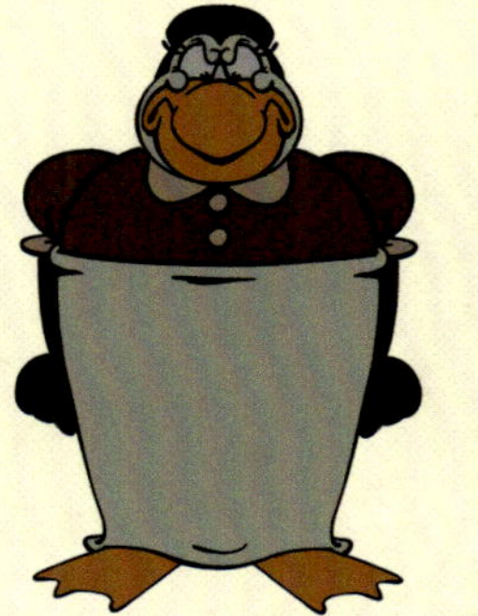

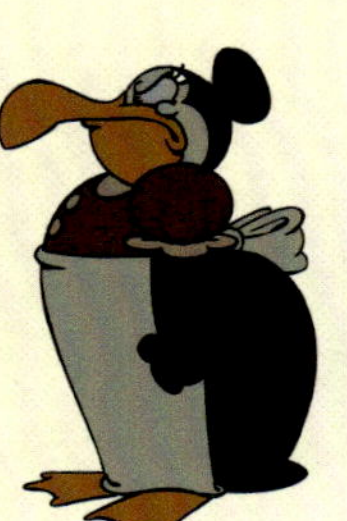

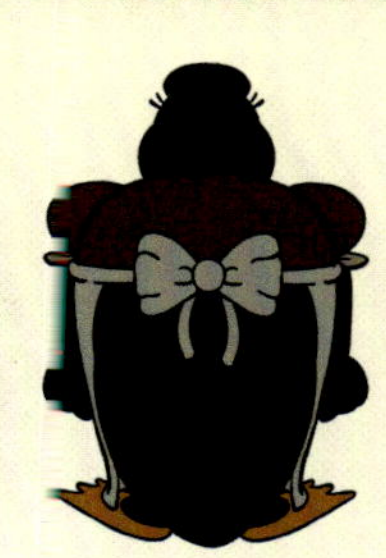

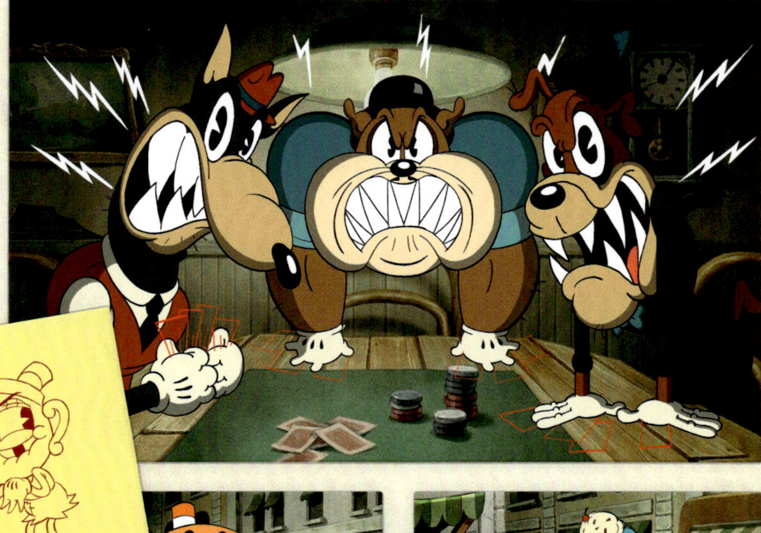

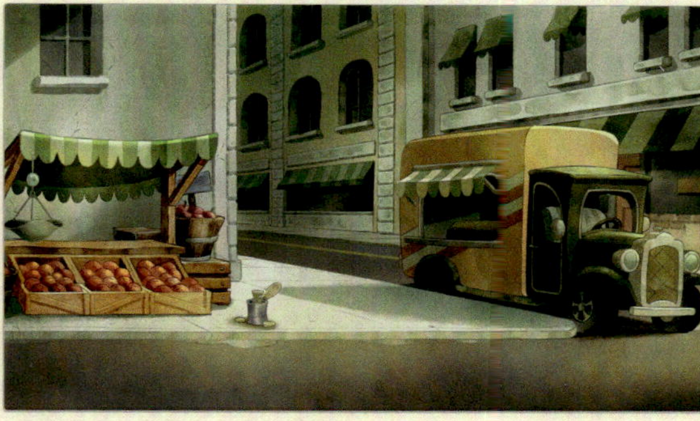

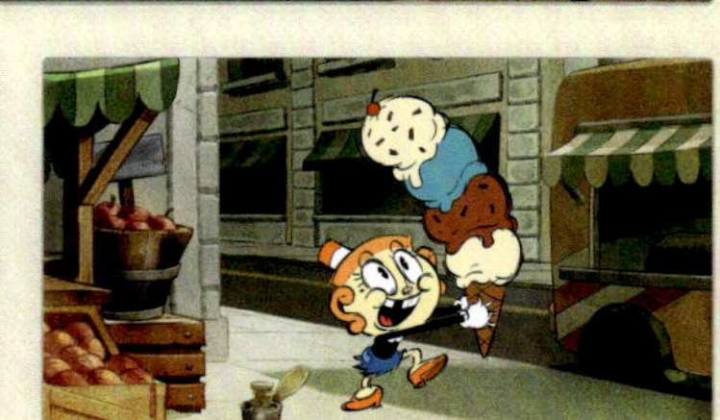

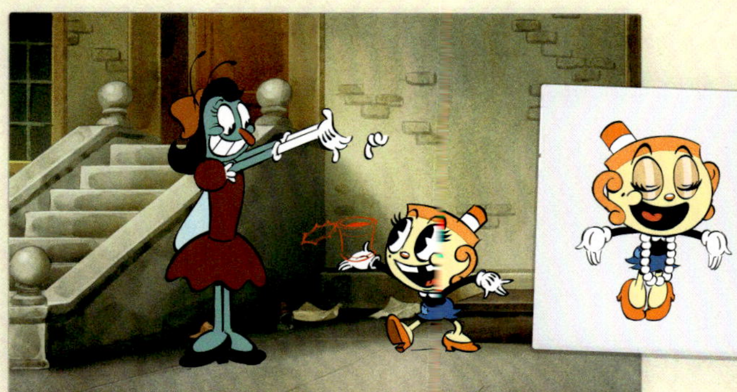

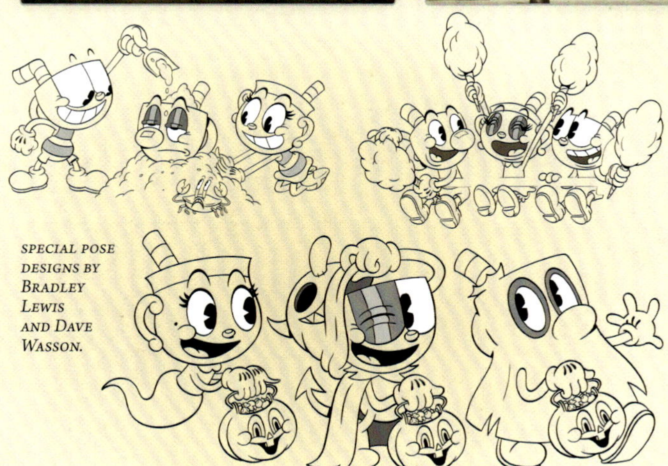

SPECIAL POSE DESIGNS BY BRADLEY LEWIS AND DAVE WASSON.

→ **ADAM P:** Chalice being a ghost was a challenge: how do you make it okay to laugh at a dead kid?

JARED MORGAN: She has this huge musical number—ta-da! Then, POW! She gets obliterated by a trolley. We've literally killed a character onscreen.

MARK: The Ms. Chalice backstory is definitely the episode we wrestled with the most, from a standards and practices perspective. Not only is she hit by a trolley—she goes into limbo and meets the Devil!

ADAM P: It's got a whole bunch of stuff that tests the limits of a kids' show. I think that makes it really exciting. As a kid you always want to see shows that are for a slightly older audience.

POKER DOGS SPECIAL POSES BY MIKE FONTANELLI; BACKGROUND DESIGNS BY LAISAY BOND AND JESSICA HONG; PAINTINGS BY MICHELLE THIES AND IVAN AGUIRRE.

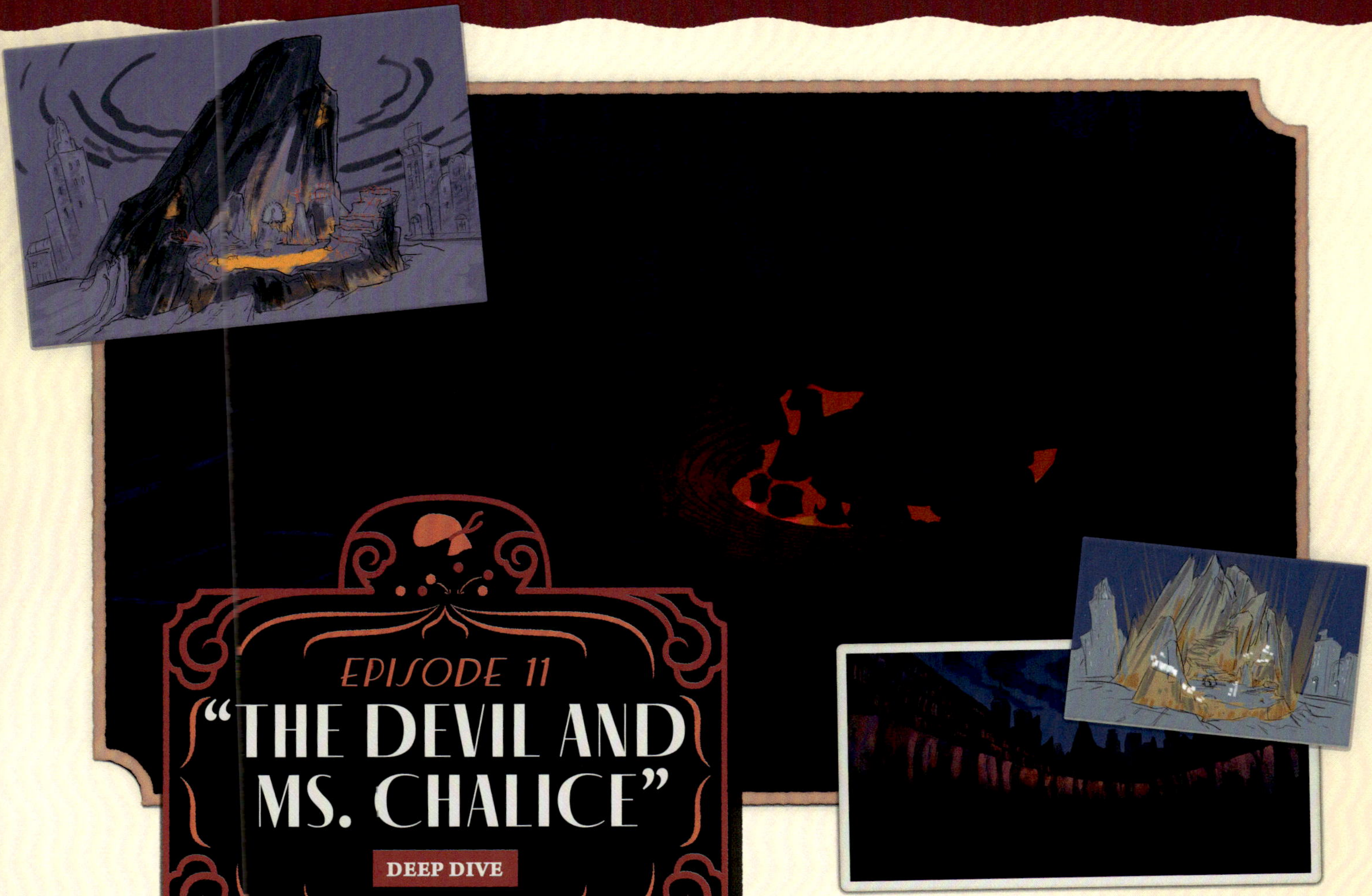

EPISODE 11
"THE DEVIL AND MS. CHALICE"
DEEP DIVE

BACKGROUND DESIGN BY LAISAY BOND; PAINTING BY GREGORY MILLER.

→ **ANDREA:** On this show, we've got to be a little more extra than other shows.

CLAY: Chalice being turned into a skeleton and then becoming a pile of dust was a key moment.

DAVE: Even though the Devil was often silly and whiny, this was one of those great opportunities to show that he could also be ruthless and terrifying.

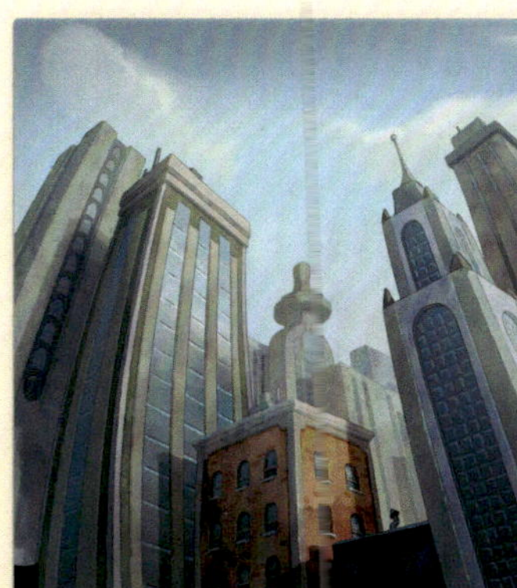

BACKGROUND DESIGN BY LAISAY BOND; PAINTING BY SEBASTIAN GUERRA-MARTINEZ.

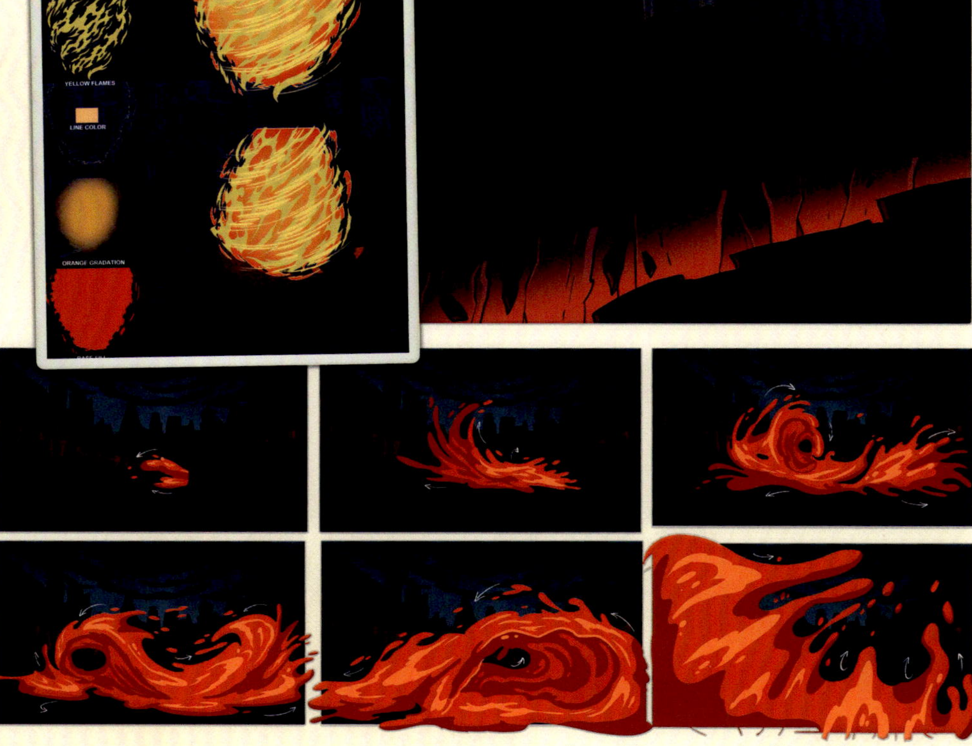

BACKGROUND DESIGN BY JESSICA HONG; PAINTING BY GREGORY MILLER; PREVIS BY COSMO SEGURSON; FIRE AND LAVA EFFECTS BY ED SKUDDER.

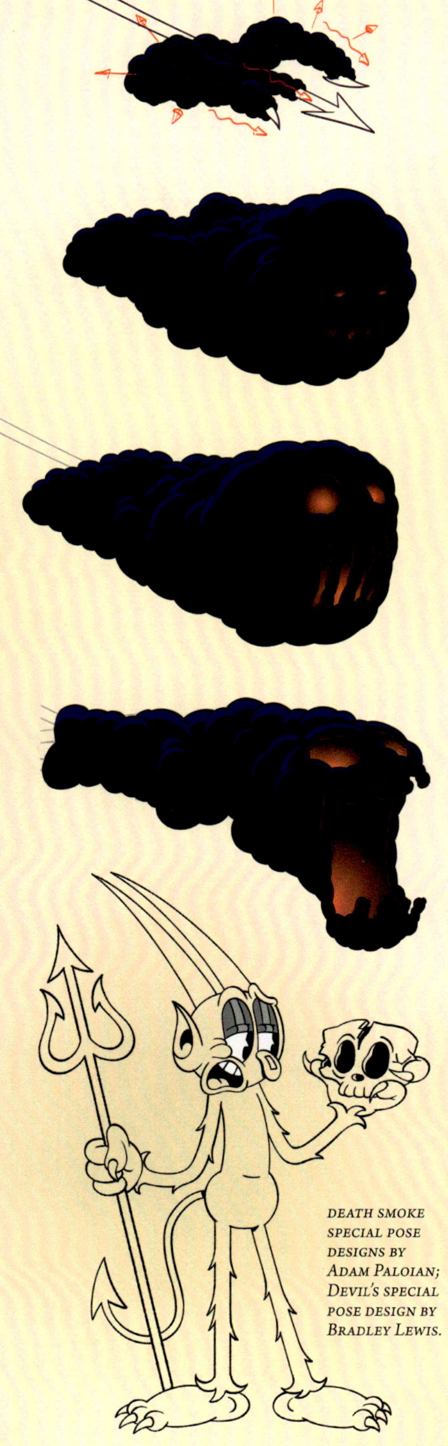

DEATH SMOKE SPECIAL POSE DESIGNS BY ADAM PALOIAN; DEVIL'S SPECIAL POSE DESIGN BY BRADLEY LEWIS.

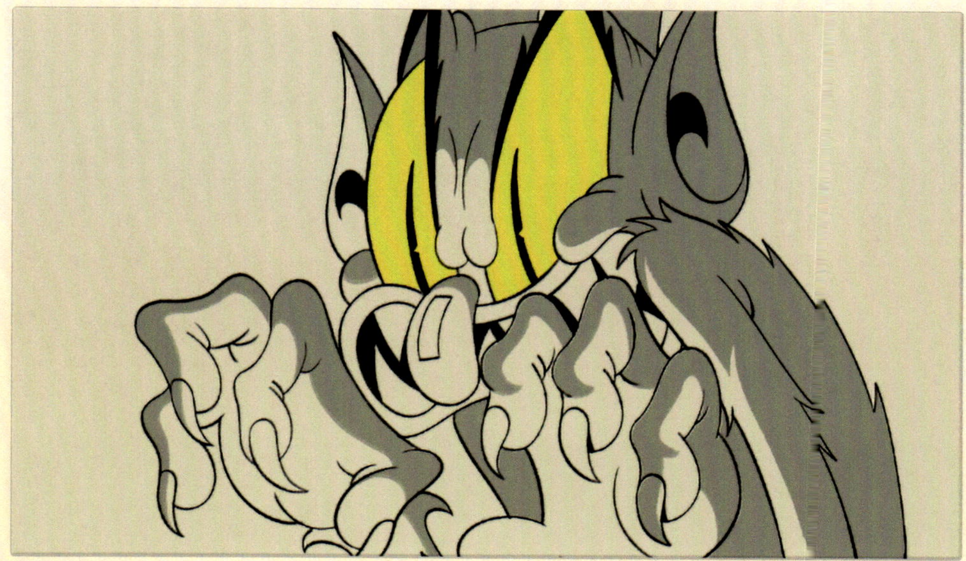

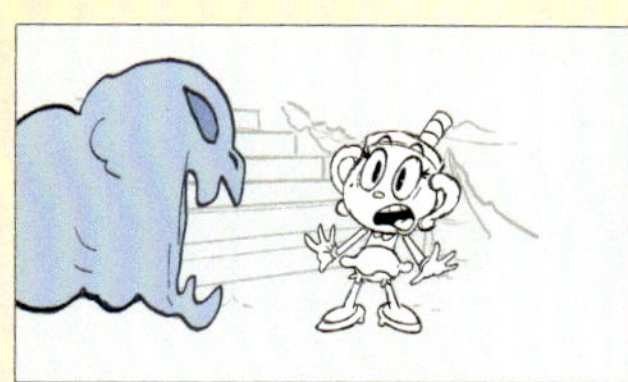

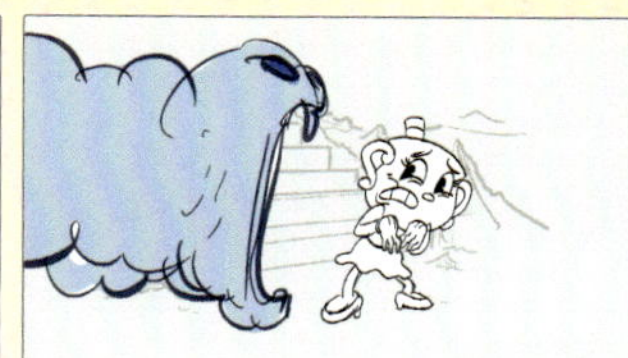

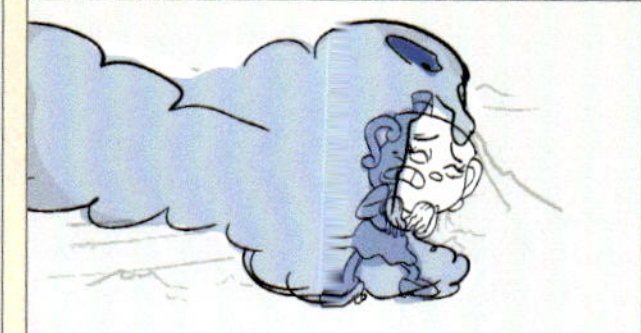

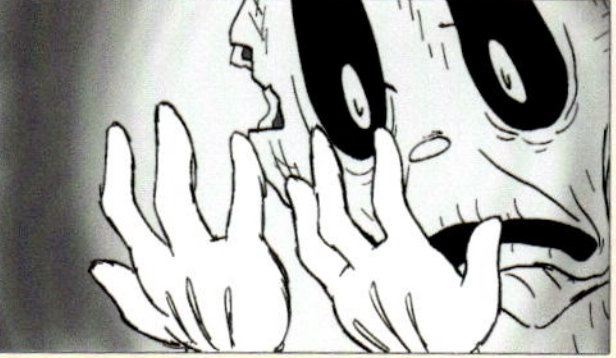

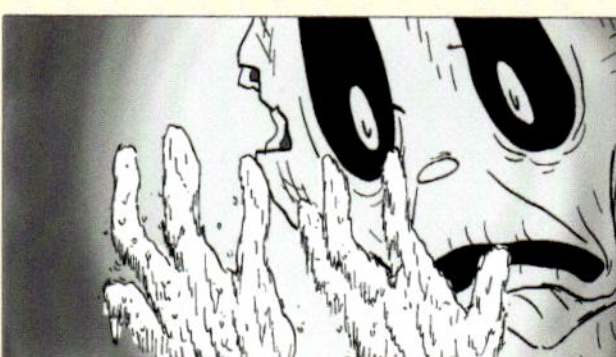

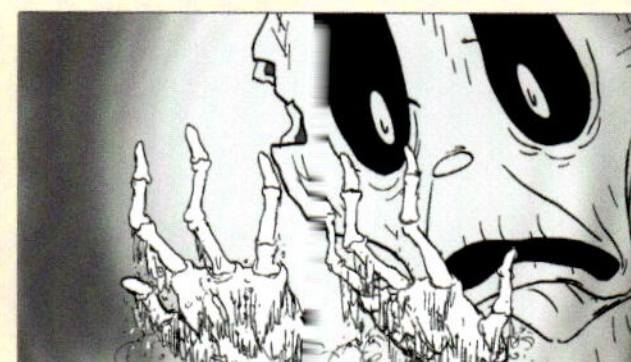

SPECIAL POSE DESIGN BY BRADLEY LEWIS; STORYBOARD PANELS BY MICHAEL RUOCCO.

→ **DEEKI:** In the first card pitch to the crew, you could feel the shock and unease—it was great!

MICHAEL: That big skull cloud encompasses her, and there's a moment where she stops and thinks she's okay—and then a crack starts to form down her forehead, and then it escalates. You think something bad is going to happen immediately, and then it's slow: things fall off, her handle falls off, her gloved hands turn to dust . . .

ADAM P: You physically see the result of what happens if they lose. It wasn't there just for shock value—it meant something.

CLAY: A lot of the '30s cartoons are moral tales, almost like *Grimm's Fairy Tales*: there are certain images that get seared into your mind. It's like biblical stuff—you remember what's at stake. There's no small or subtle.

MS. CHALICE TURNS TO DUST SPECIAL POSE DESIGNS BY ADAM PALOIAN.

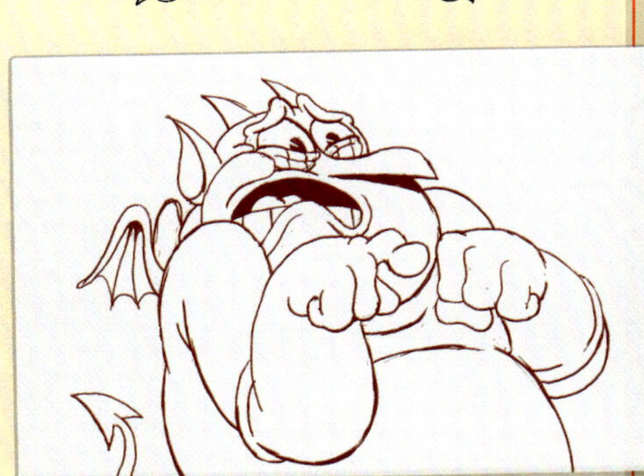

HENCHMAN'S SPECIAL POSE DESIGN BY DAVE WASSON.

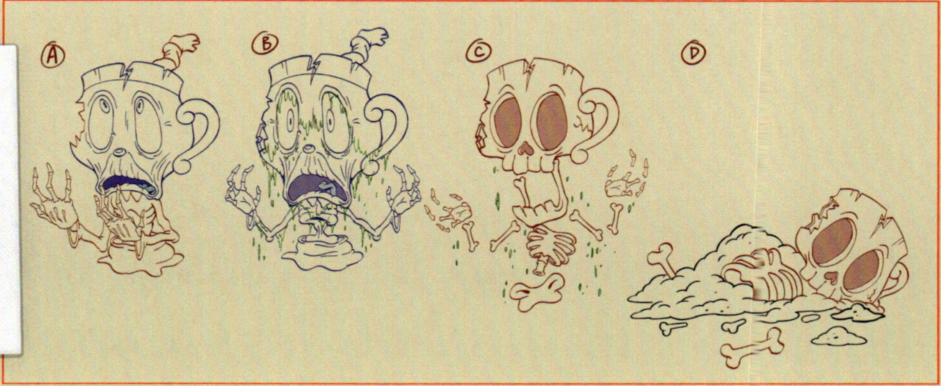

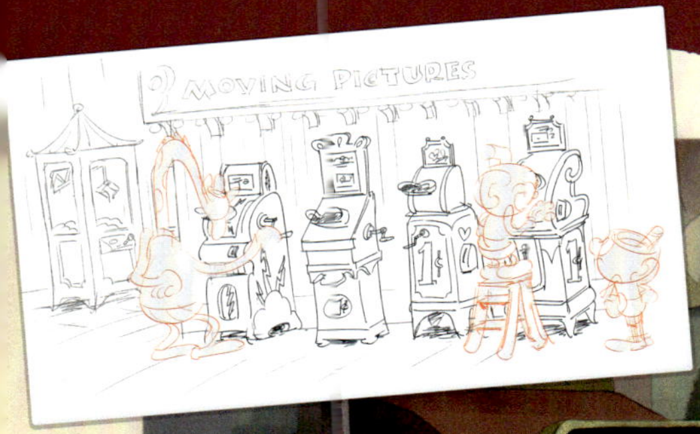

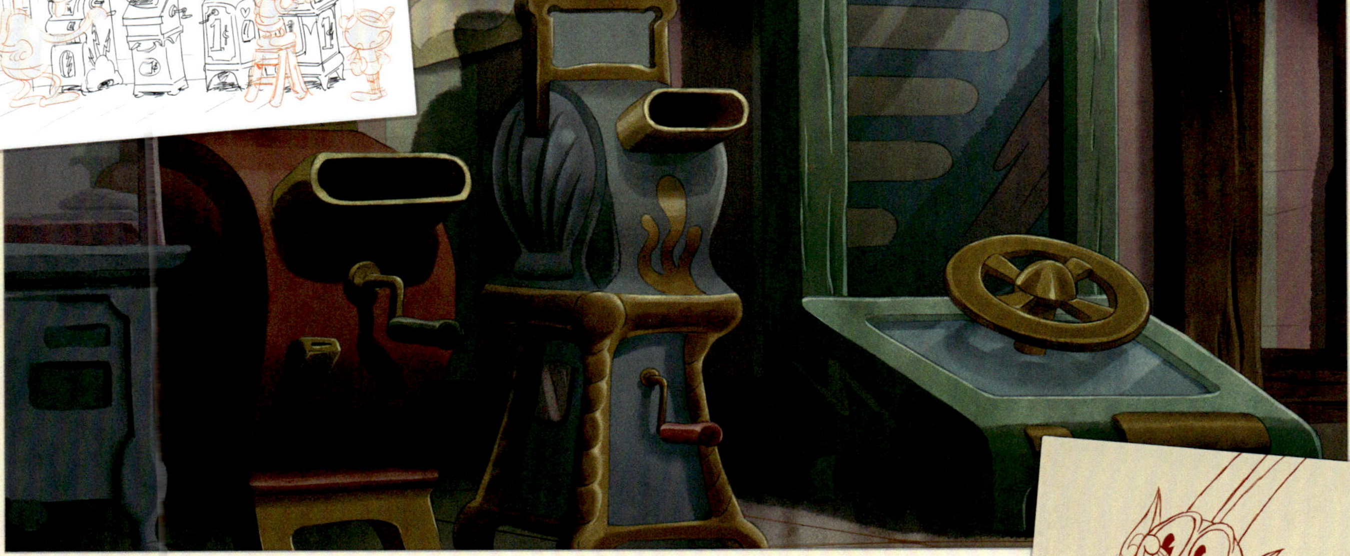

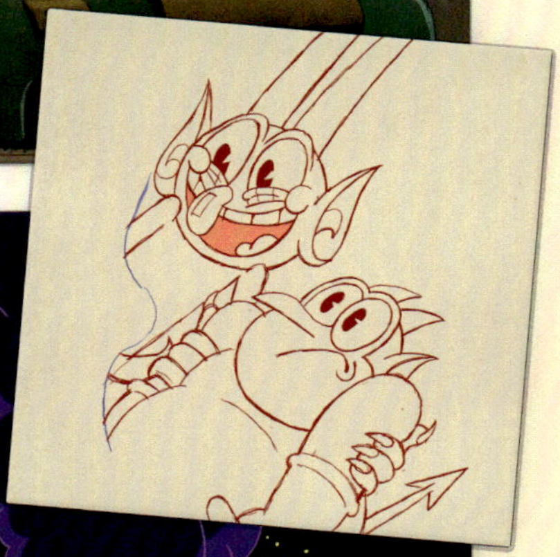

BACKGROUND DESIGN BY LAUREN DUDA; PAINTING BY RACHEL KIM.

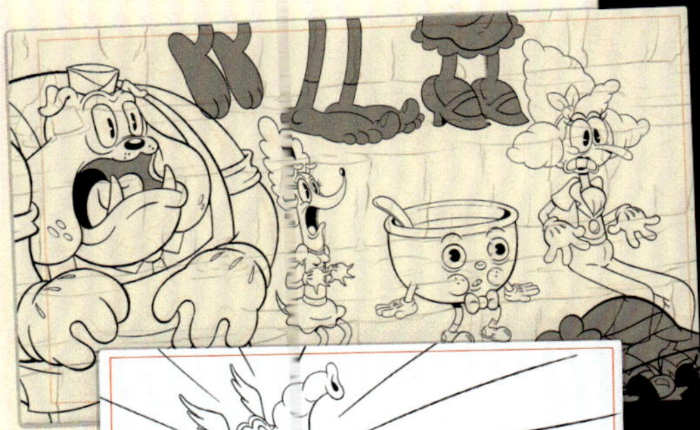

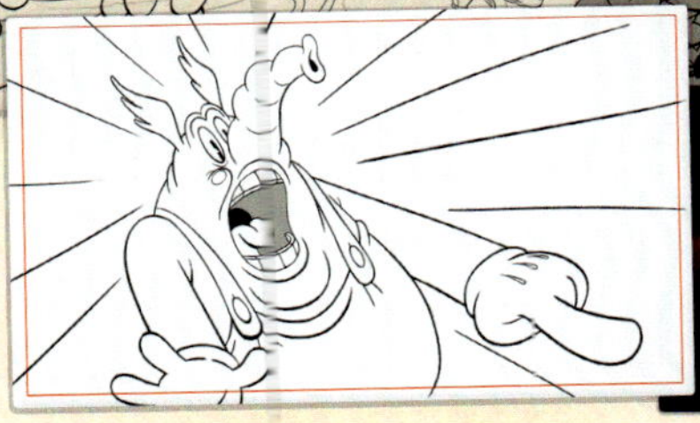

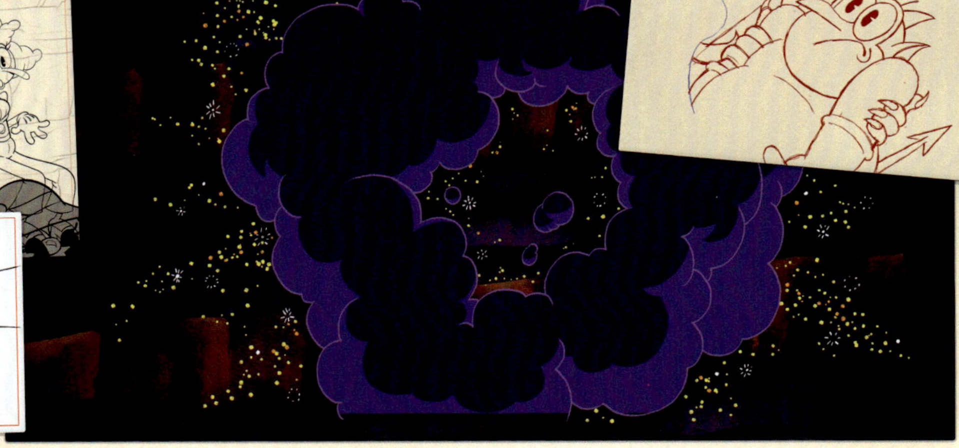

→ **MICHAEL:** I knew that was going to be a pain to track all those incidentals. Nobody likes drawing crowds and doing A/B poses on a crowd. Knowing that we're cutting back to the crowd for multiple reactions and angles, there are certain things you have to consider. You can't have all of them pump their arms in the air at once. They have to be offset or moving at different rates of speed so you're not having everybody do the same thing over and over again. It has to feel organic.

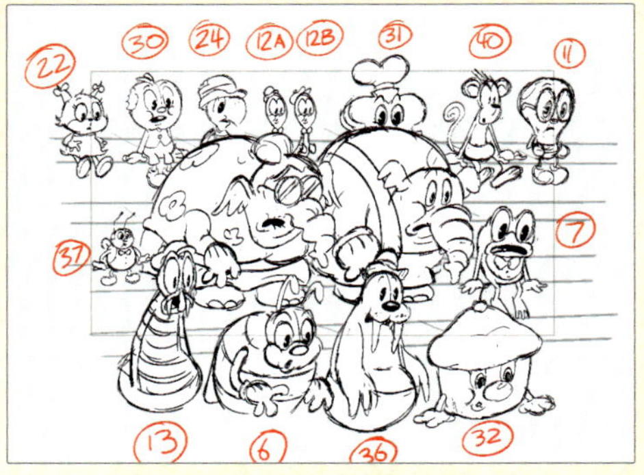

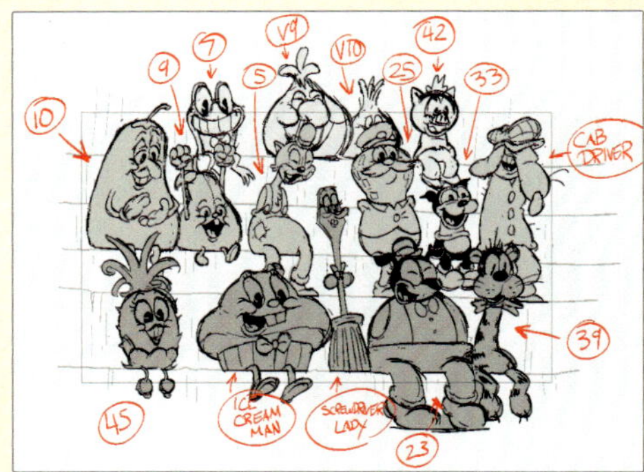

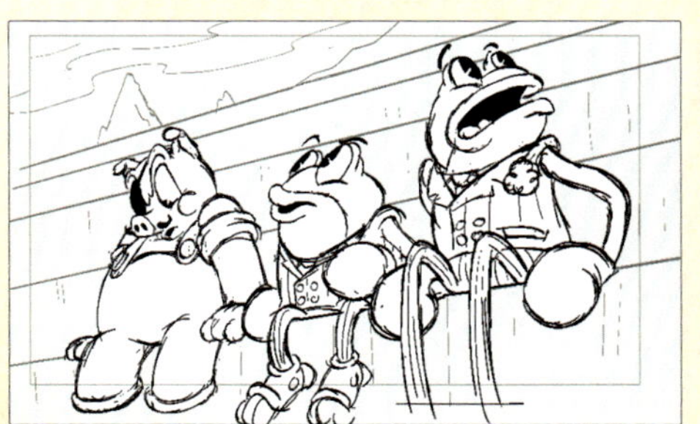

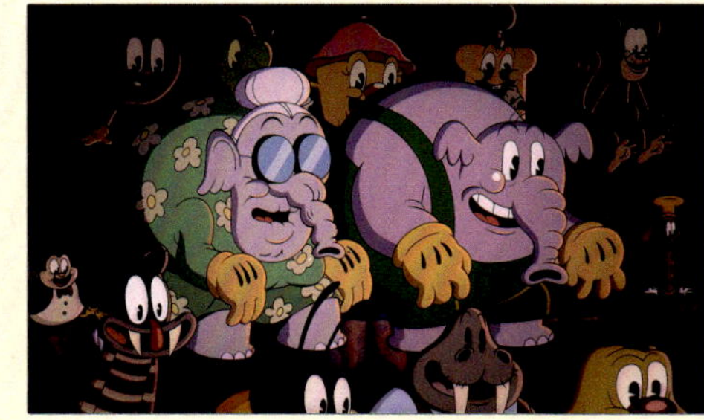

STORYBOARD PANELS AND INCIDENTAL TRACKING BY MICHAEL RUOCCO; SPECIAL POSES BY MIKE FONTANELLI, ADAM PALOIAN, AND DAVE WASSON; DEVIL'S TELEPORTING SMOKE DESIGN BY ED SKUDDER.

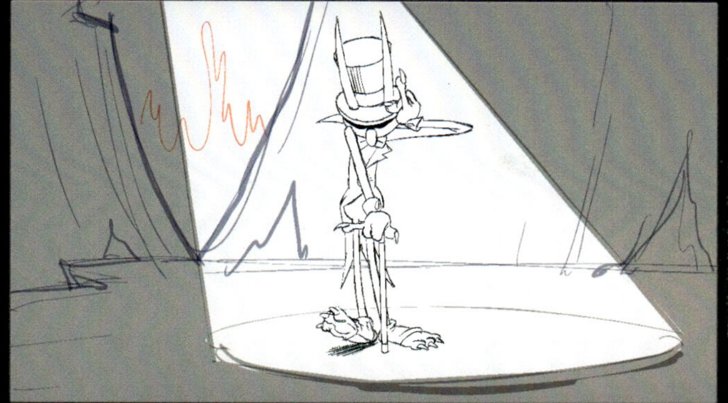
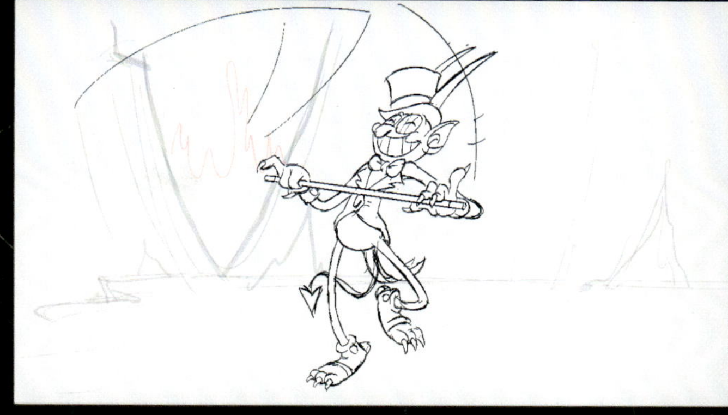
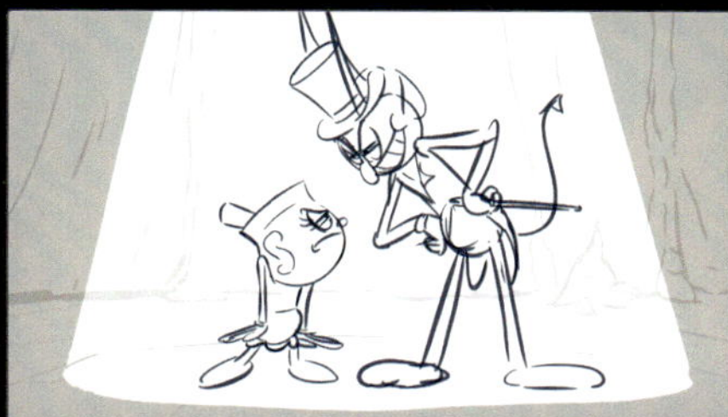
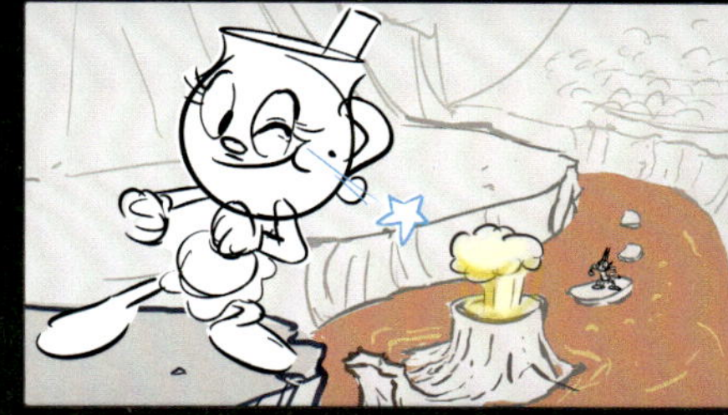
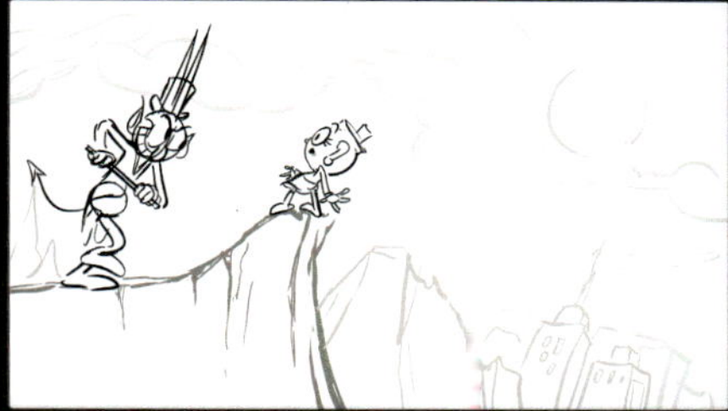

◆ STORYBOARD SPOTLIGHT ◆

DANCING WITH THE DEVIL

DAVE: Anytime you have characters dancing, that's about the most difficult thing you can animate. Normally I would avoid it at all costs. But then Adam, Benjamin, and Michael were all so up for the challenge that I said, "Okay, I think you guys are insane, but let's go for it."

MICHAEL: When I saw Benjamin's work for the first time, I knew right away I had to up my game. I wanted to just bow down before him. His drawings are so naturally full of life.

BENJAMIN: We had to figure out a lot of the dance moves and pretty much rough animate the episode. How can you storyboard dance moves without key posing them? It was a good challenge, and it flowed way better using this approach.

MICHAEL: Benjamin is phenomenal, and he goes to town with everything he does. Some of the poses he did are so outlandishly pushed, but they still feel of that era.

ADAM P: Michael is an incredibly talented animator. I wanted him to be a board supervisor, and I knew he was very adaptable and had done some work on the Chalice finale and I knew he could go above and beyond.

MICHAEL: I knew that my work would have to be animated by other people, so I went in and did more extra poses in this section. It's not fair to give the animator something really vague and assume they'll figure it out, so I storyboard as if I have to animate it myself. I think about where the foot is, how it turns, the antic on a pose . . .

CLAY: I don't know what we would have possibly done without Michael. He really saved us on that finale episode. Essentially, he was animating in-house on a truncated timeline that would make your skin crawl.

MICHAEL: It was a fun challenge to work in a style that I really admire, but it's one of those styles where you have to almost forget your training: there are certain sensibilities and techniques that wouldn't exist in the 1930s.

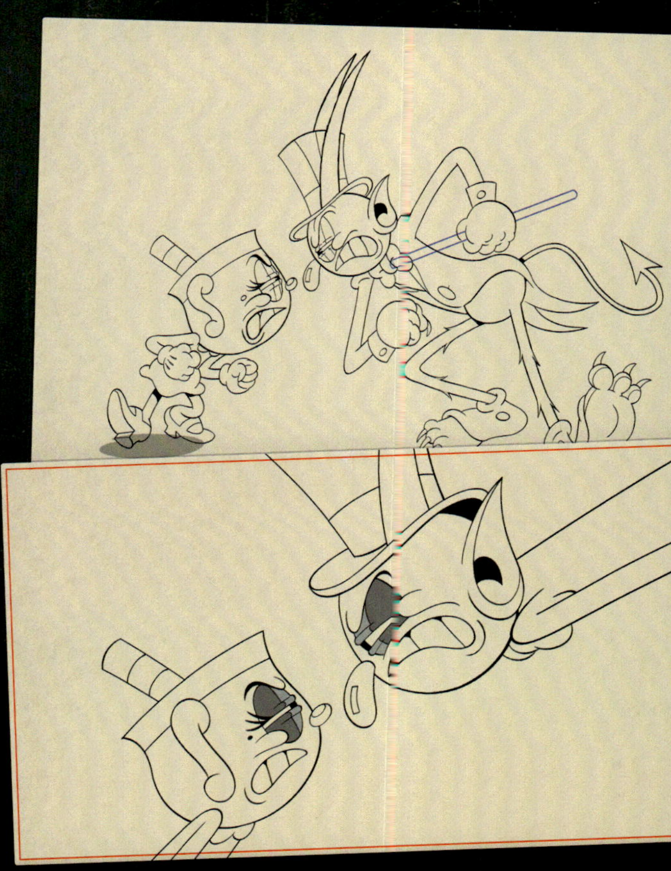

STORYBOARD PANELS BY BENJAMIN ARCAND; SPECIAL POSE DESIGNS BY BRADLEY LEWIS.

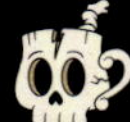

→ **MICHAEL:** She gets close to the edge, nearly falls into the lava, then reveals it's a fake-out. This is essentially a life-or-death dance battle: she needs to keep her cool and work through it. She's so in the moment—it shows that she's clever and she can work herself out of a jam. Whenever *I* got into a jam on the production, I was lucky I had two fantastic storyboard revisionists, Allen Zhang and Sam Kessler. They worked so hard on every episode, even reboarding whole sequences themselves. They really saved me on that production, especially as a first-time supervisor. I couldn't have had better revisionists on my team.

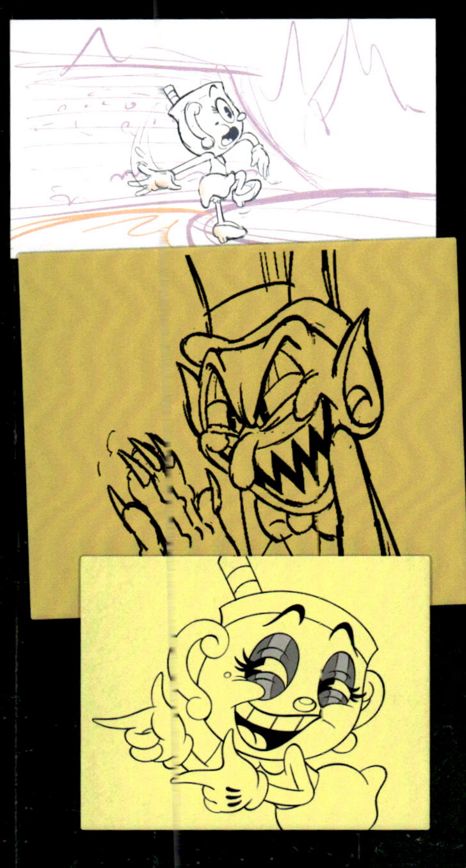

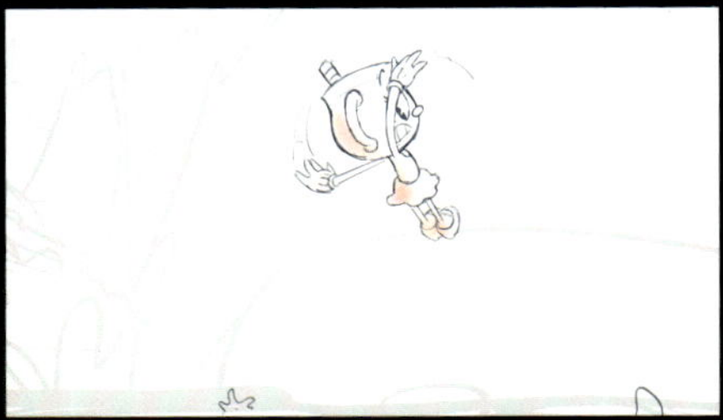

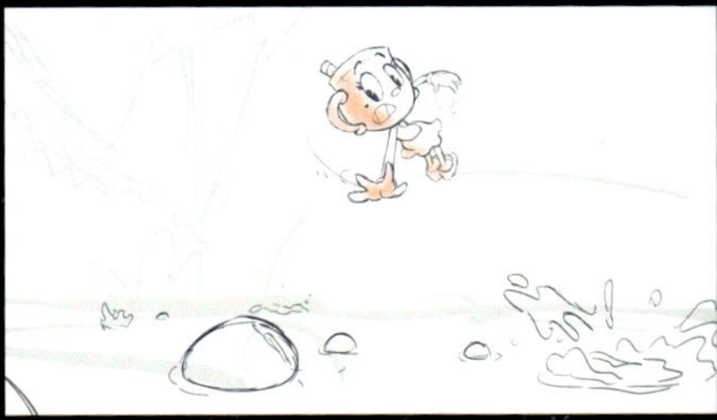

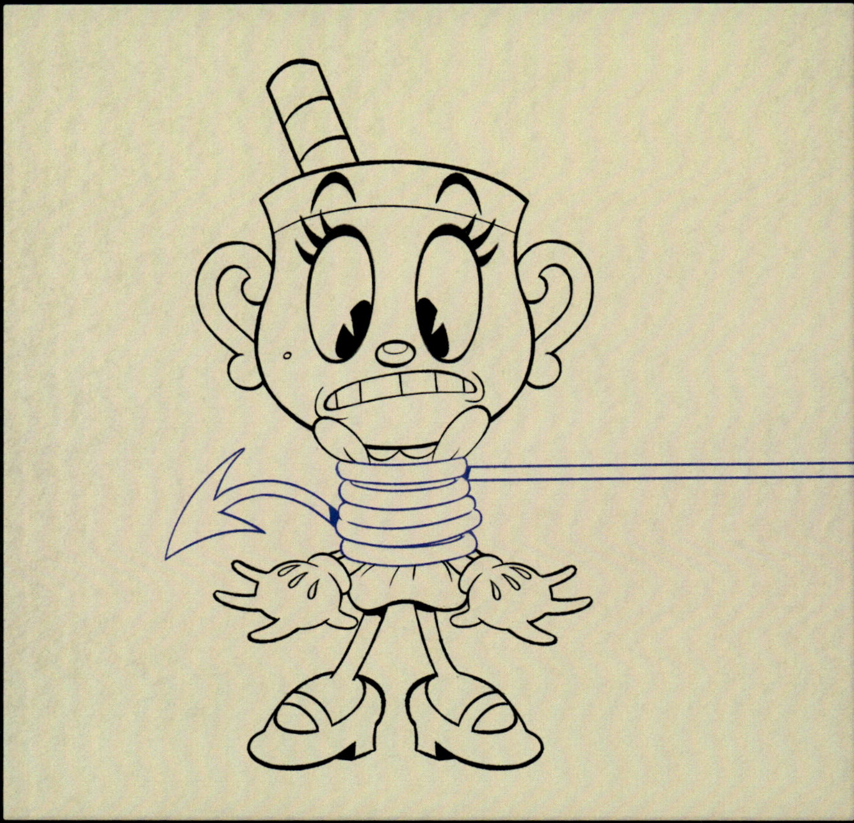

→ **MICHAEL:** The finale was my first time animating dancing. Since we storyboard before Ego does the music, we had to animate to a temp track. The music over my section was "Puttin' On the Ritz," and Ben's section was set to "Sing, Sing, Sing."

BENJAMIN: Working with a music track, you let the music, the beats, the accents inspire your work and even lead your decisions sometimes.

MICHAEL: In the temp track, there was a bit where the band is riffing and the music almost feels like it's rolling. I got a bolt of Fleischer-style inspiration and had the Devil pop off his own head and roll it down his arms toward camera.

DAVE: Michael's work on this whole episode was phenomenal. It's some of the best animation in the whole series.

MICHAEL: Sometimes you encounter a problem that winds up being a happy accident. As I started boarding it and posing it out, I remembered that he has horns. He can't roll his head with horns attached, so I attached the horns to his hat, then he just lifts the hat, rolls his head, and when it lands back on his shoulder, he puts his hat with the horns back on.

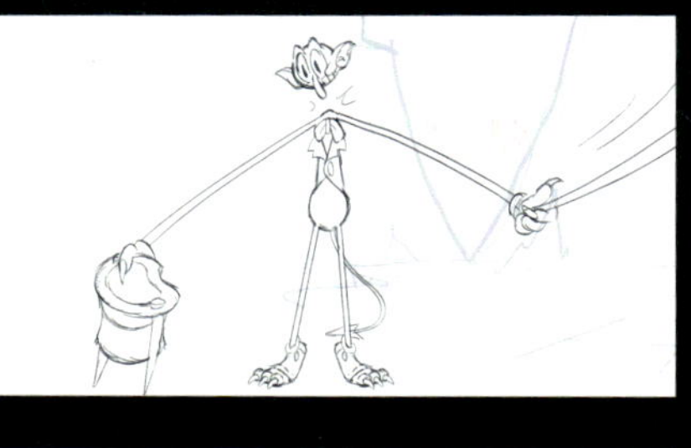

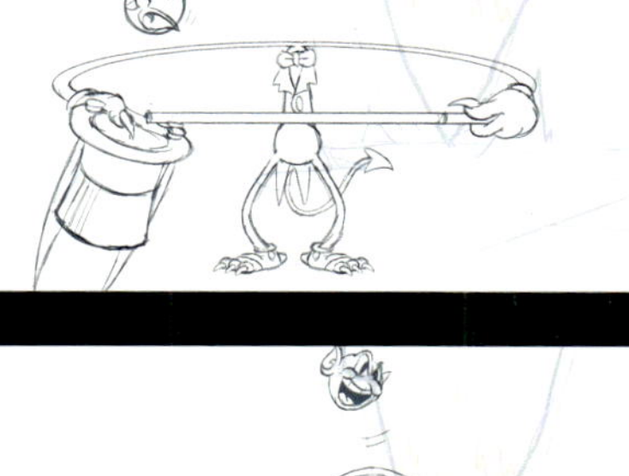

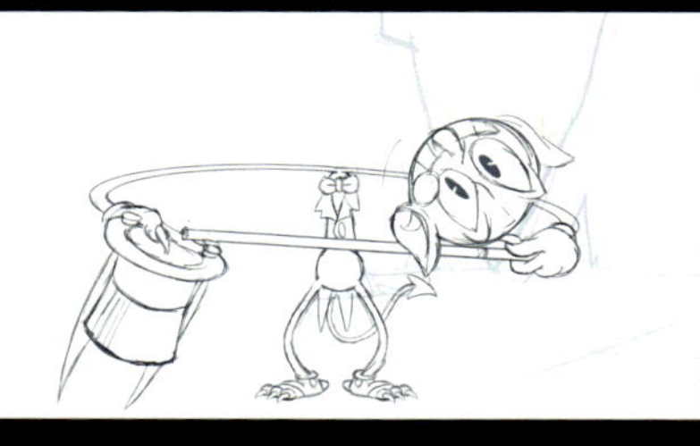

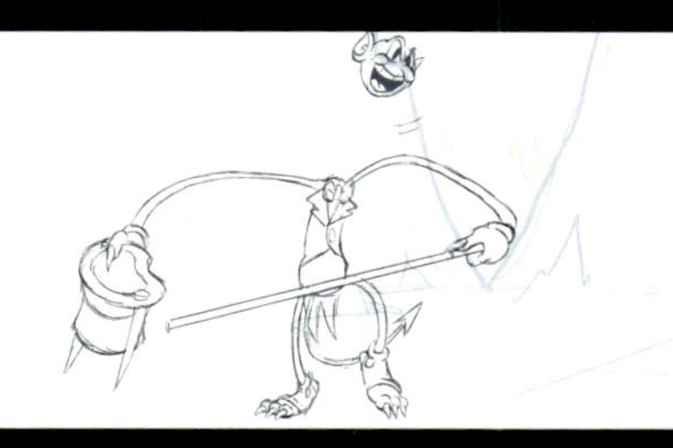

STORYBOARD PANELS BY MICHAEL RUOCCO; SPECIAL POSE DESIGNS BY MARTIN WITTIG.

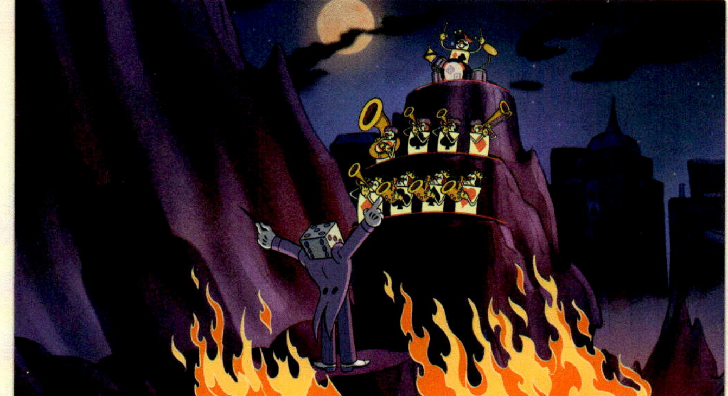

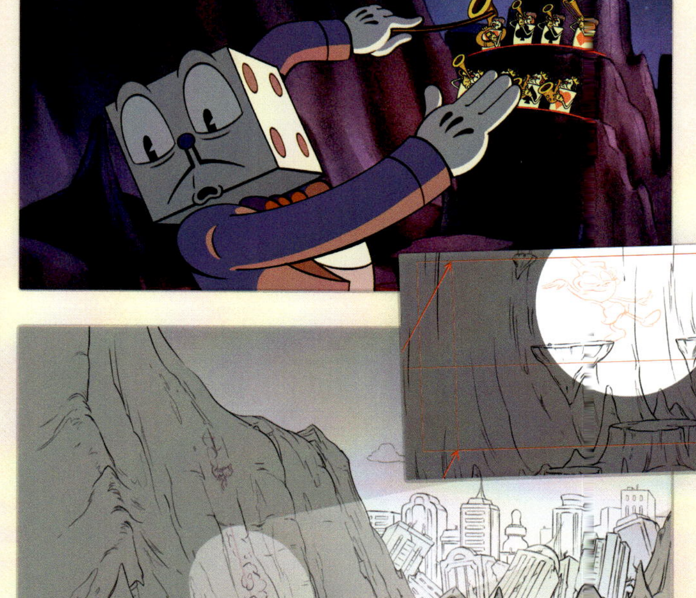

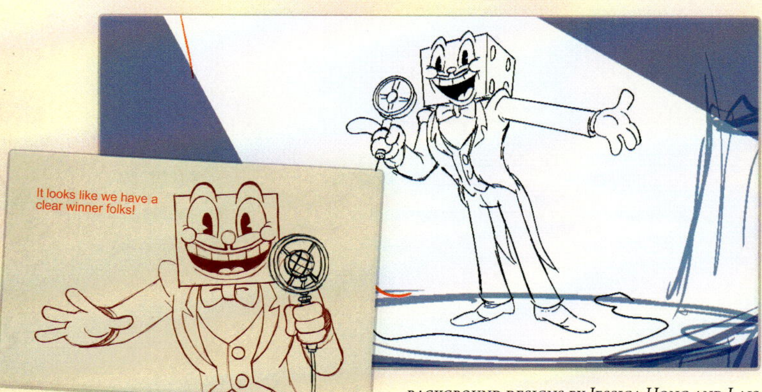

BACKGROUND DESIGNS BY JESSICA HONG AND LAISAY BOND; PAINTINGS BY IVAN AGUIRRE.

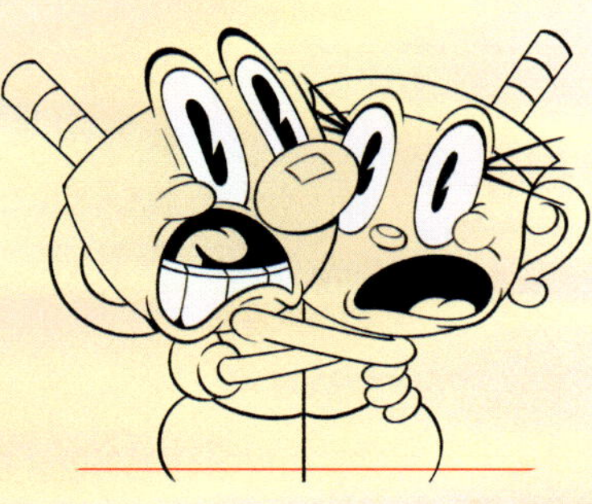

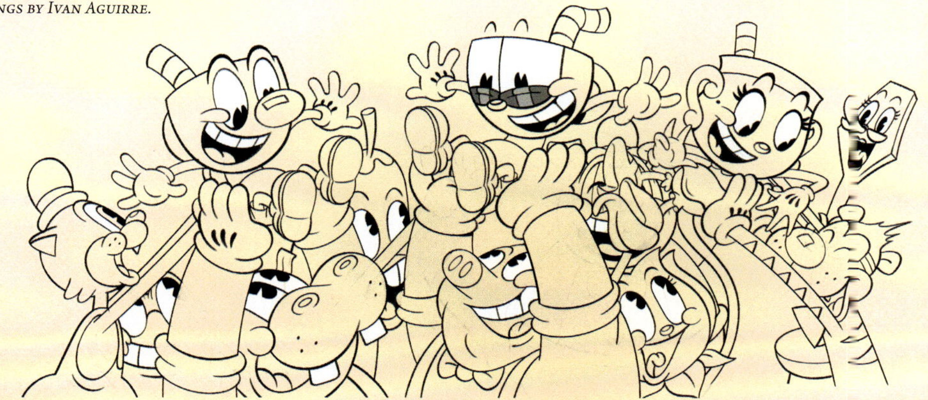

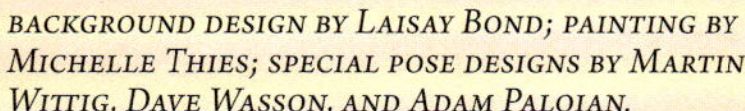

BACKGROUND DESIGN BY LAISAY BOND; PAINTING BY MICHELLE THIES; SPECIAL POSE DESIGNS BY MARTIN WITTIG, DAVE WASSON, AND ADAM PALOIAN.

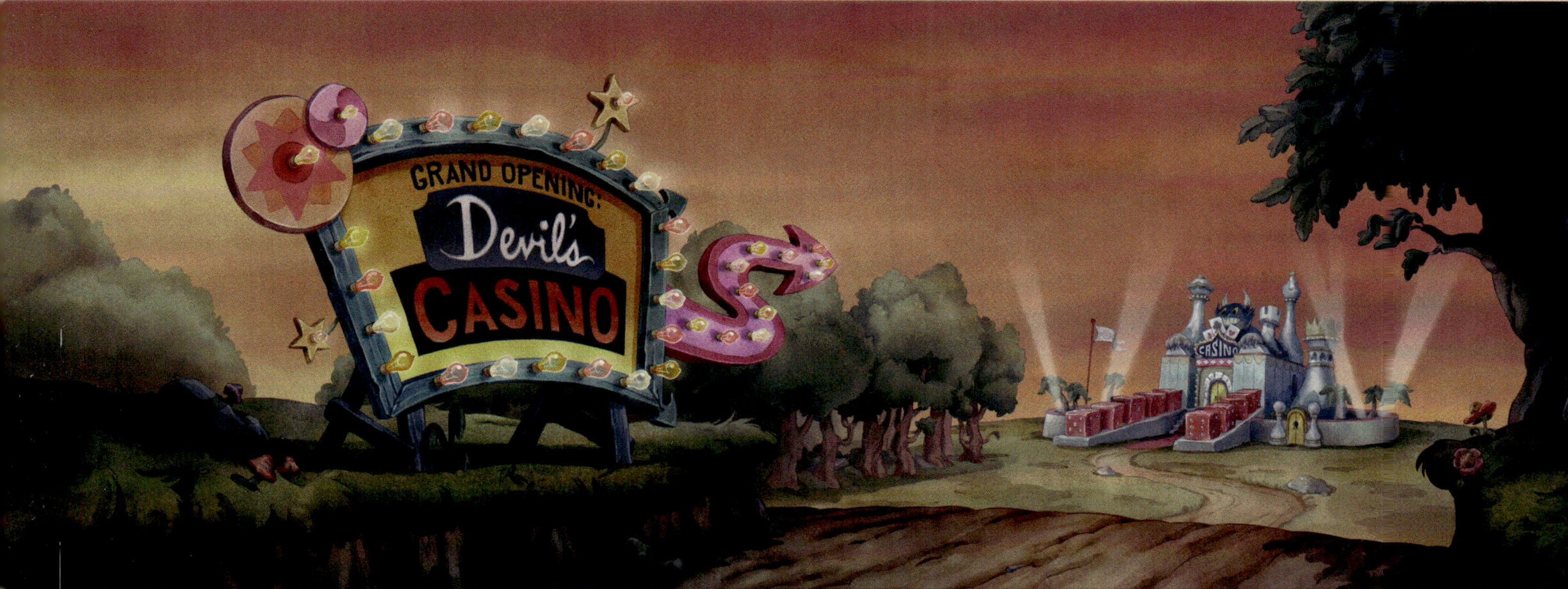

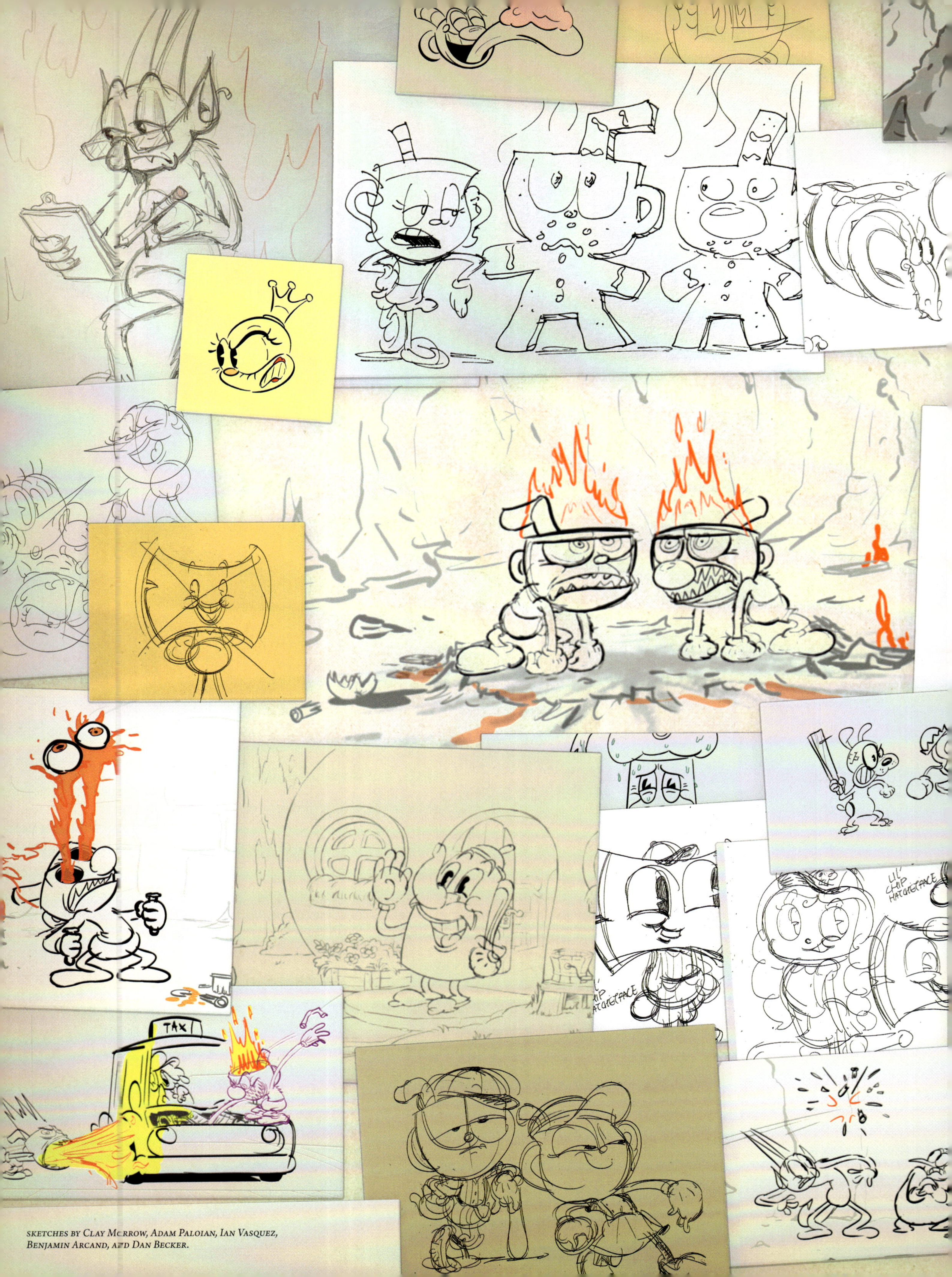

sketches by Clay Morrow, Adam Paloian, Ian Vasquez, Benjamin Arcand, and Dan Becker.

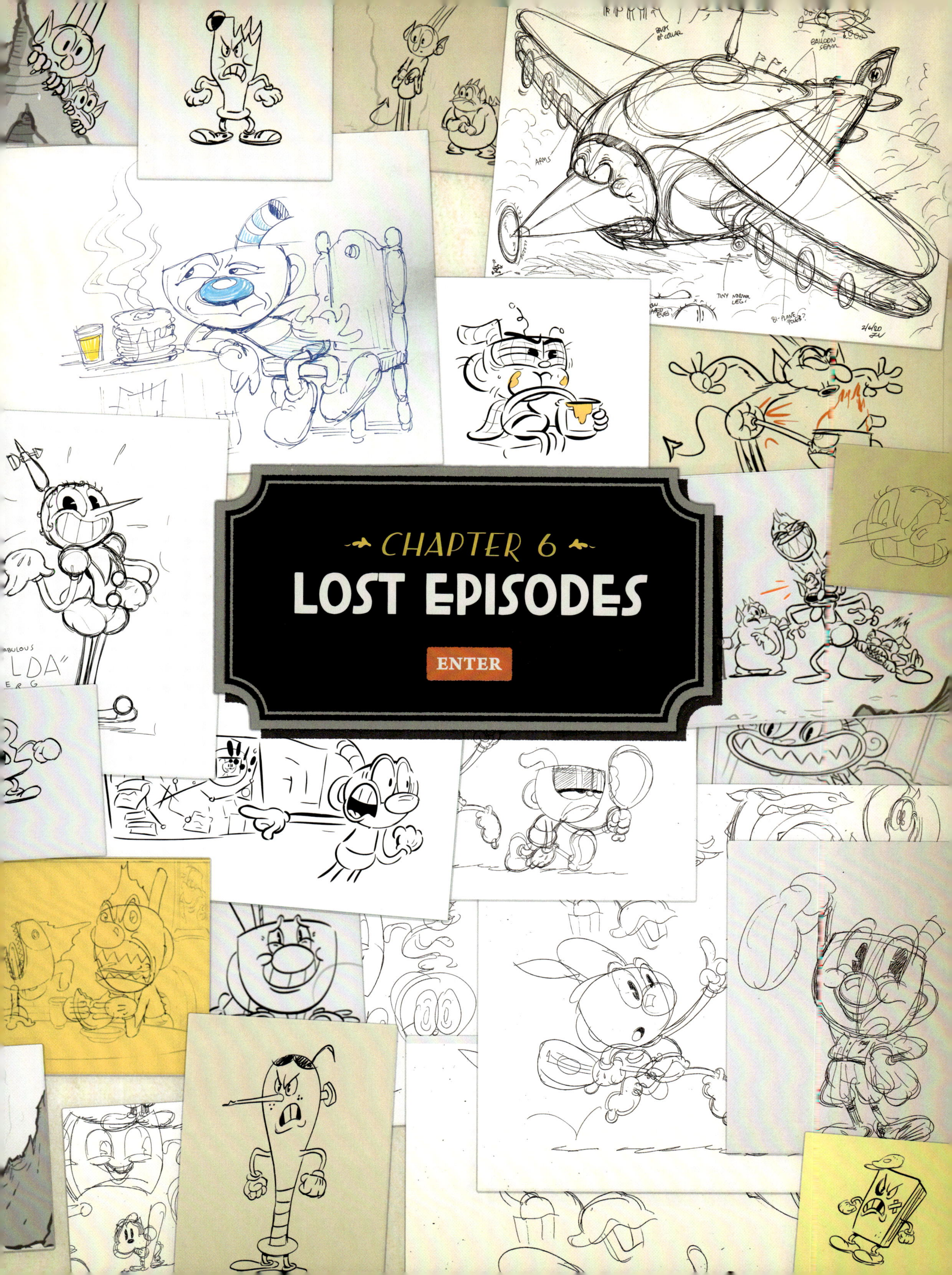
CHAPTER 6
LOST EPISODES
ENTER
ARMS

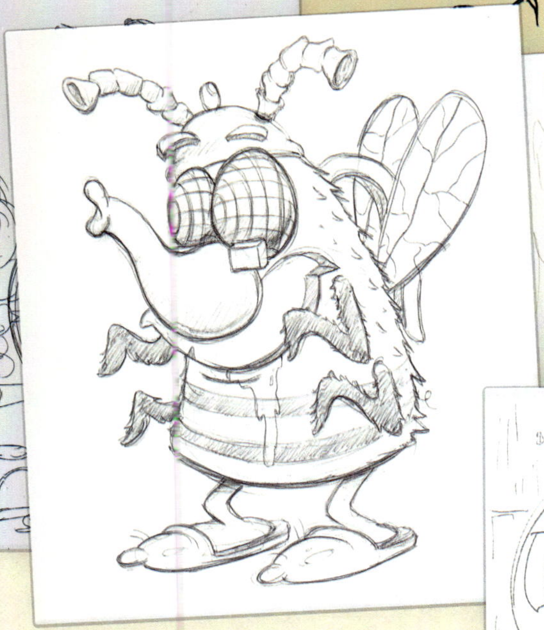

Goopy awaits the call that shall never come . . . sketch by Ian Vasquez.

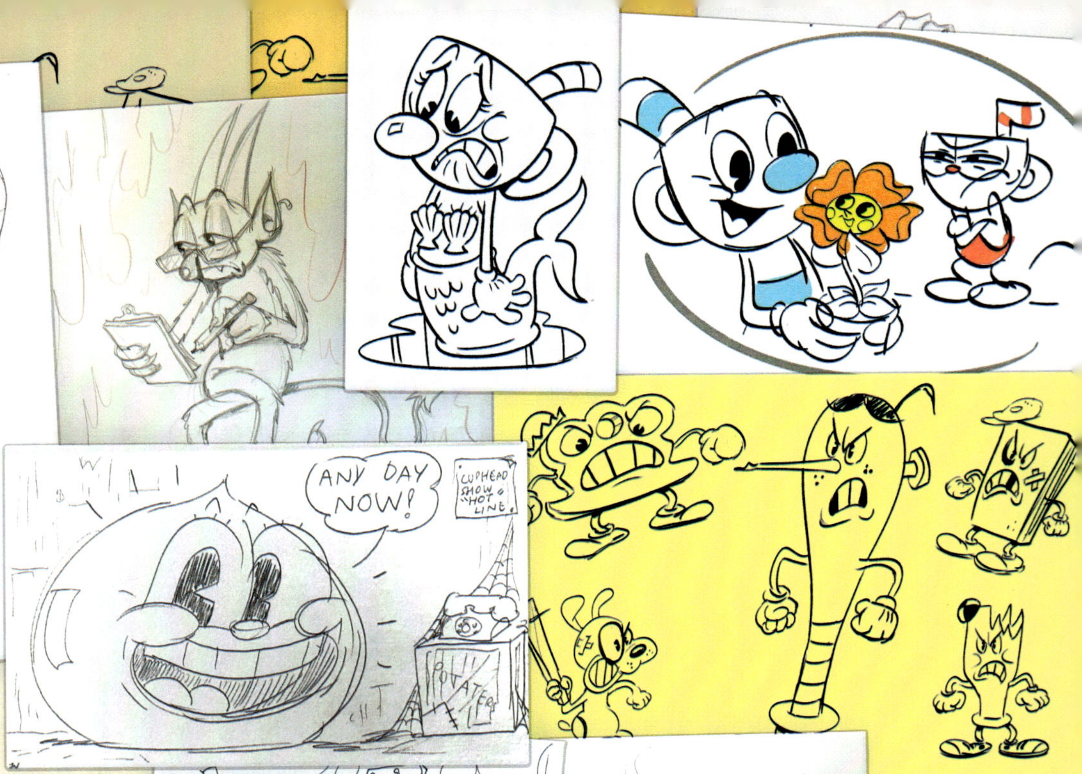

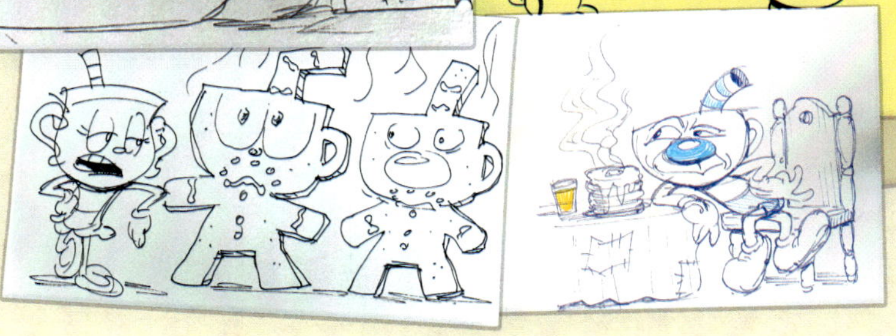

➜ **DAVE:** So, what happened was, there came a point in the production where we realized that we had way overwritten and overstoryboarded past what we were budgeted to produce. These stories weren't cut because they weren't good enough. We just didn't have the money or the resources to finish them.

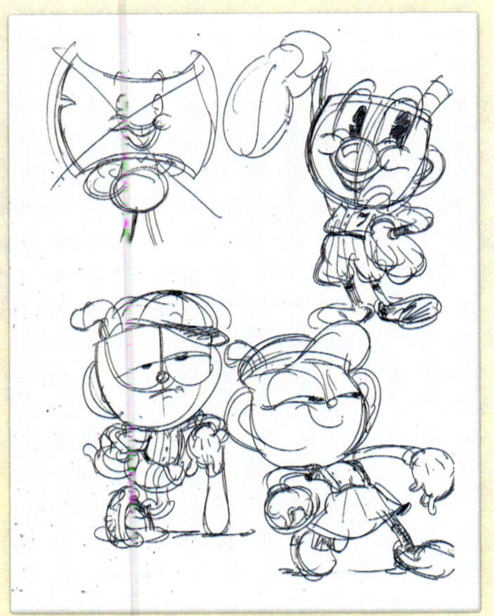

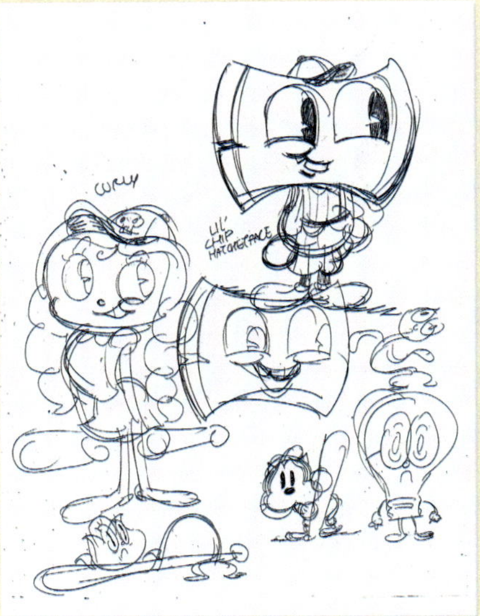

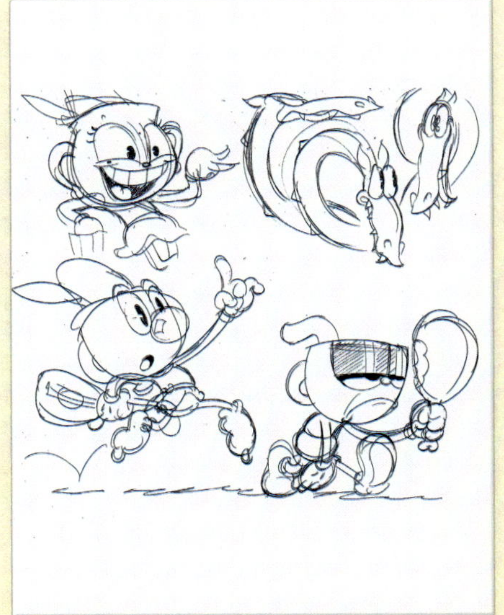

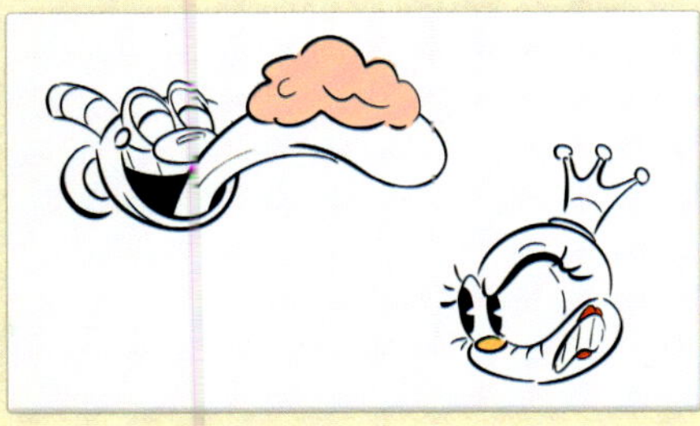

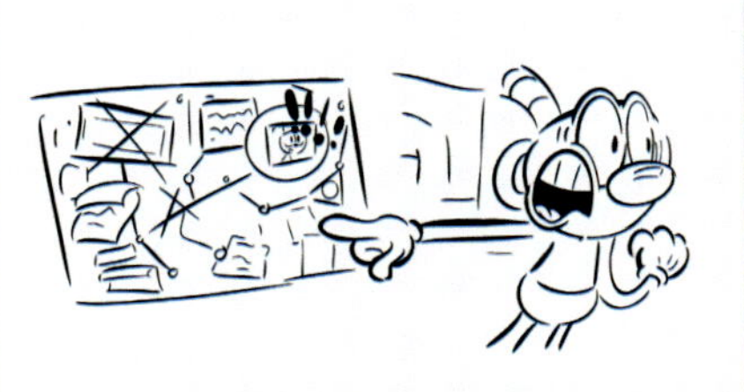

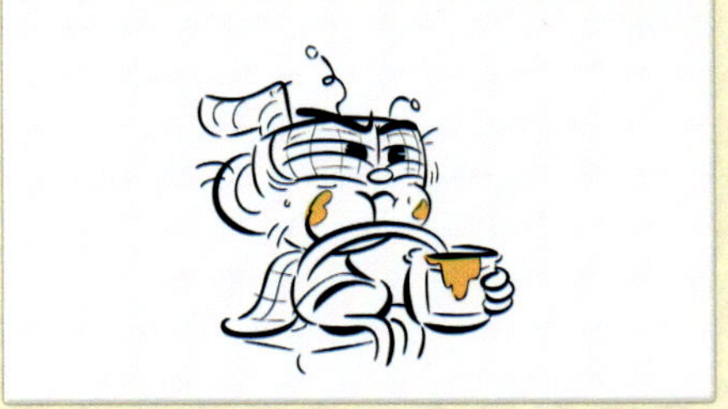

Crew premise pitches. Megan Boyd's Cagney Carnation origin story; "The Little Rat-Skulls" by Mike Fontanelli; Grim Matchstick episode by Ian Vasquez; "Chalice vs. Bon-Bon" by Adam Paloian; "The Legend of Cala Mer-Mug" by Mike Fontanelli; "The Kettle Flies at Midnight" by Dan Becker; "A Very Devil Diary" by Adam Paloian; "The Stinky Pancakes" by Adam Paloian; "Cupball" by Ian Vasquez; "Honey I'm Home" by Dan Becker.

"BEPPI BOOM"

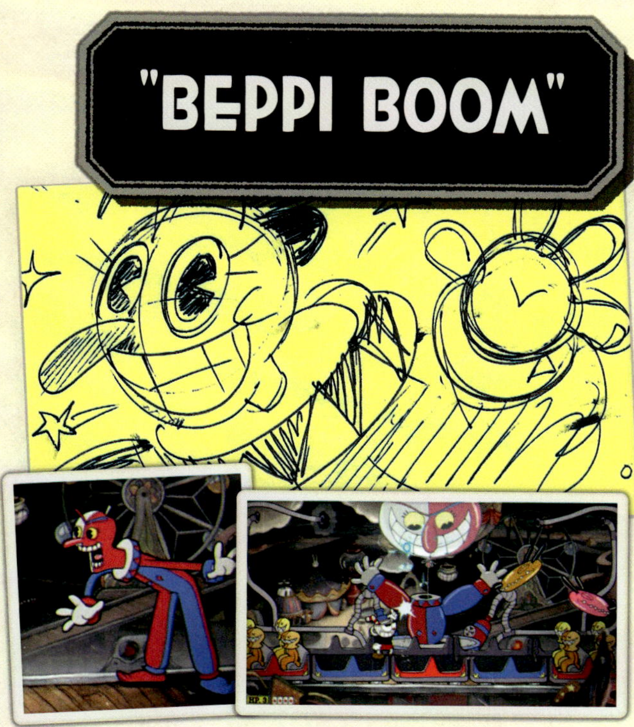

BEPPI SKETCH FOR PROPOSED EPISODE BY MEGAN BOYD. BELOW THAT: BEPPI FROM THE GAME.

→ **MEGAN B:** I just love Beppi. He's a clown, clowns are creepy—it's fun! I wanted to do a story about how he got to that insane point in the game, where he is completely unhinged and terrifying.

DEEKI: Megan's setup was that it's Kettle's birthday, and he's extremely sad. The boys resolve to cheer him up by hiring a clown.

MEGAN B: As a child, you don't have the maturity to realize, "Elder Kettle's old and that's why he hates birthdays—he's thinking about existential dread and death!" Cuphead and Mugman were genuinely just trying to do something nice for Elder Kettle.

DEEKI: Beppi keeps trying and failing to cheer up Kettle. Nothing works. Beppi grows enraged and ultimately gets so mad that he pops like a balloon—and *that* cheers up Elder Kettle. It was hilarious, but there are tons of factors that go into choosing episodes.

ANDREA: I just find Beppi visually awkward in terms of production design. I didn't understand how we could get him to animate on-screen and also be appealing. He works so well on a runner because he's flat and you never see different views of him. The scale in the game is very different from the scale in the show.

DEEKI: Production concerns aside, Megan wrote a great premise. The story got funnier as it unfolded and ended with a bang.

MEGAN B: I was so proud of that one. I felt like I hit a new point in my career, like, "Holy shit, I can write!" I've always been self-doubting about that aspect of myself.

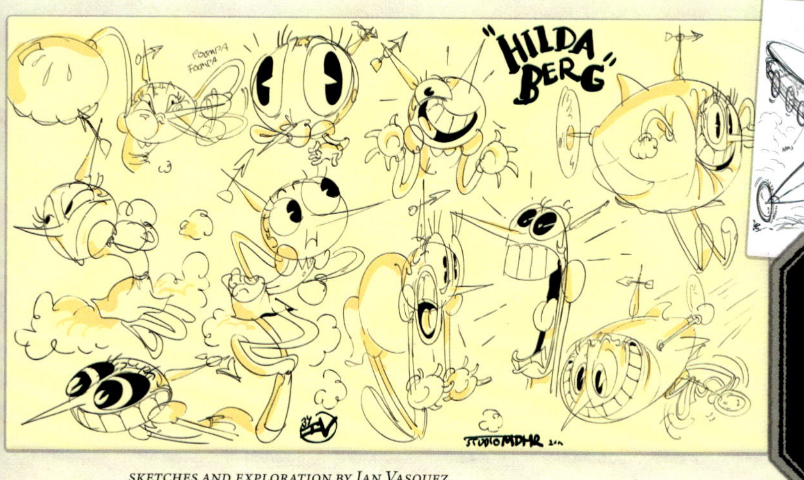

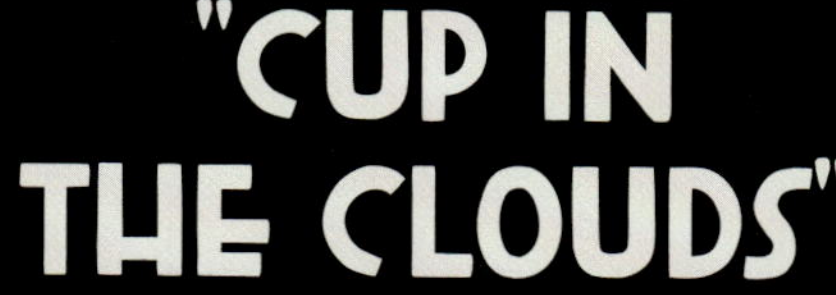

"CUP IN THE CLOUDS"

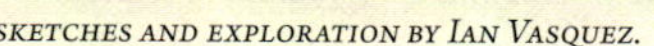
SKETCHES AND EXPLORATION BY IAN VASQUEZ.

→ **ELI:** For Hilda Berg in the game, rendering her as this almost Cuphead-sized character at the start of the fight doesn't constrain her to that size *during* the fight. She can transform into horoscope clouds, contort into a massive half-moon, and spit UFOs out of her mouth.

CHAD: Hilda is a great example of the challenges of translating a game to a show. She is by far one of the most beloved bosses in the game, and any episode that had her in it felt like it would have to be a sort of "kitchen sink" episode that captured it all at once.

DEEKI: Early on we talked about how to tackle a Hilda episode, but there were so many moving parts to consider that we didn't really dive into it until Ian wrote a great story called "Cup in the Clouds." It was everything you could possibly want from a Hilda episode.

CHAD: It was important to us that a Hilda episode hit some of the main aspects of what her character is—morphing with constellations, having multiple forms, being bigger than a regular citizen of the Inkwell Isles, for example.

DEEKI: Ian's idea would have delivered on all that, but considering the production realities at the time, the Hilda episode everyone wanted would have been impossible.

CLAY: A really important thing to me is to not be that precious with what's presented to you. It has to exist on its own and to make that feel like its own thing, you can't be bound to anything. Some of the game characters are so popular that inevitably they're going to come with a lot of baggage.

JARED: This is one of those places that the design constraints of the game—setting Hilda in the same replayable level—are really hard to replicate in an episode of television.

MAJA: In many ways, Hilda's celestial scope, her huge personality, and her massive fan affection all make her feel more suited to an epic movie rather than just an episode of a show.

"THE GREAT COOKIE WAR"

→ **KENNEDY:** I think bottle episodes only work on shows where you have really strong characters. Cuphead and Mugman just pull this madness out of each other, and Elder Kettle starts out kind of Machiavellian, but he ends up pulled into the madness. I just love the dynamic those three have.

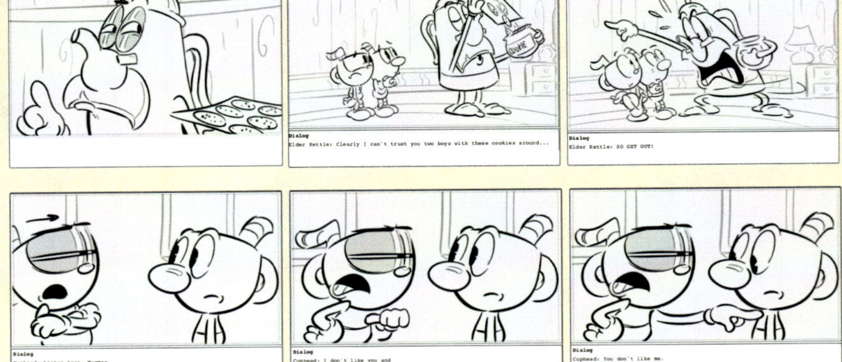

STORYBOARD PANELS BY DAN BECKER AND KENNEDY TARRELL.

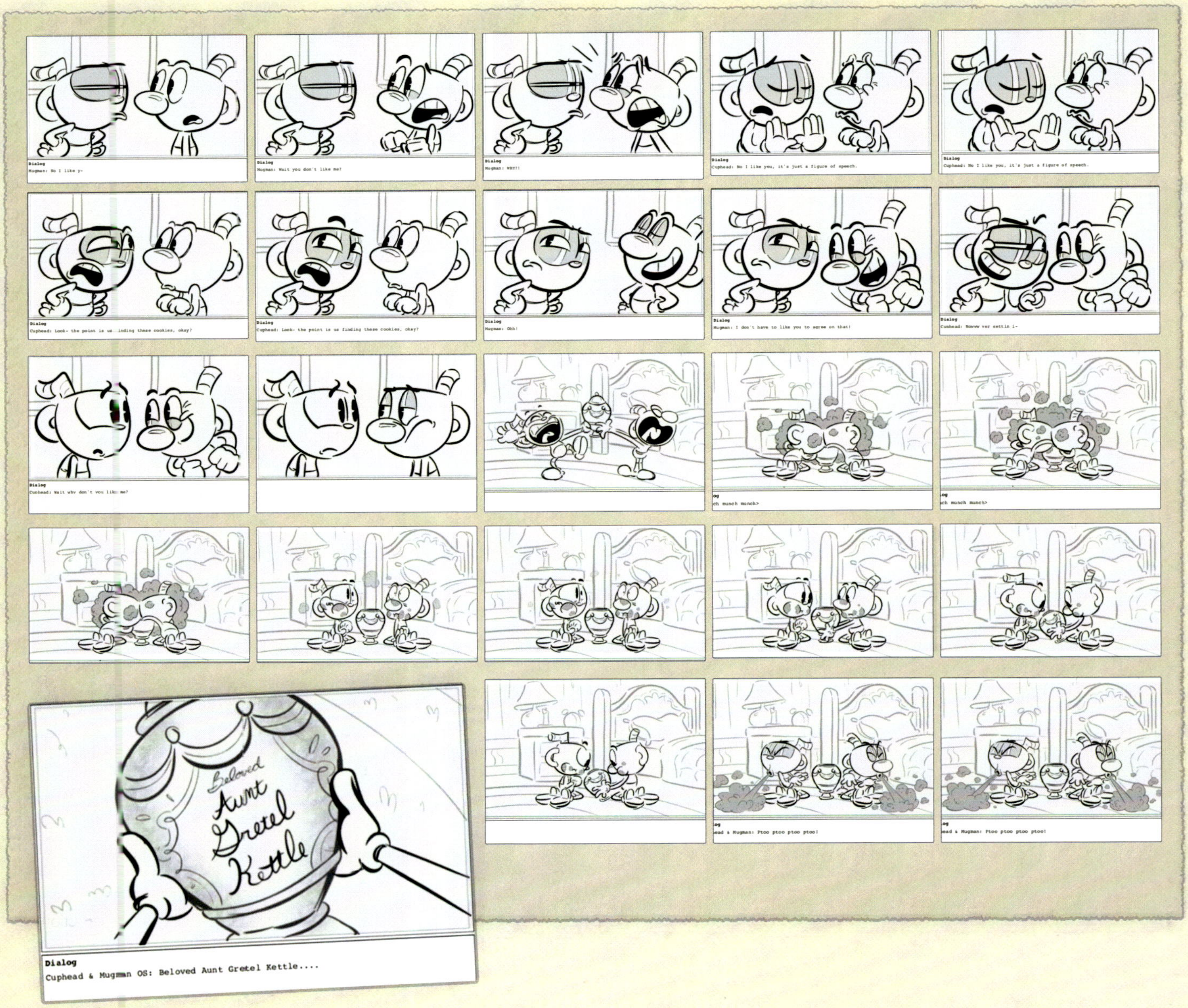

Dialog
Cuphead & Mugman OS: Beloved Aunt Gretel Kettle....

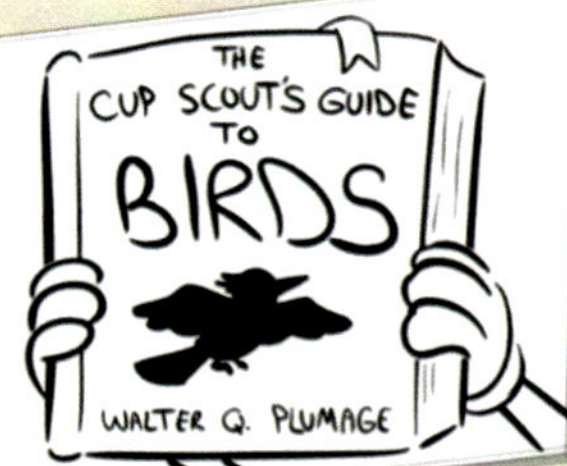

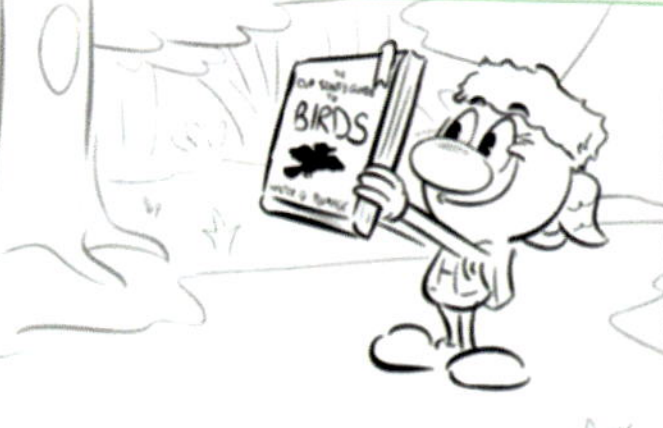

"BIRDWATCHERS"

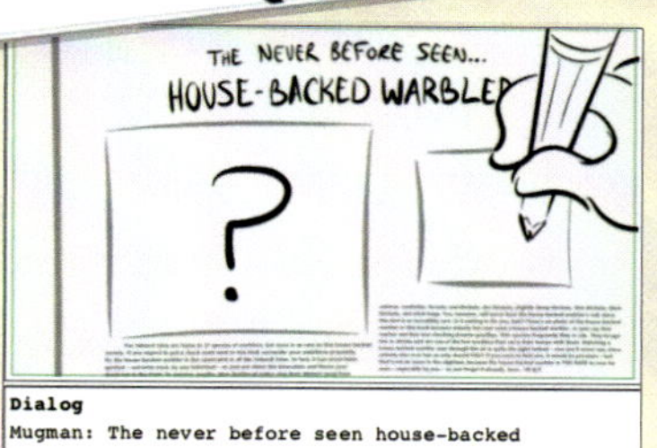

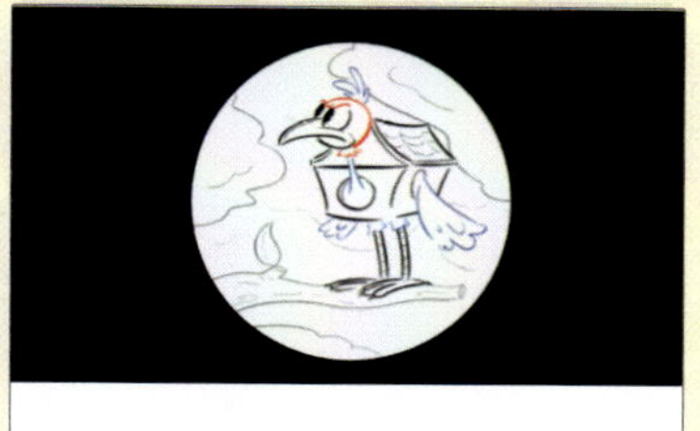

→ **KENNEDY:** "Birdwatchers" was my final episode, and the first episode where I finally drew the boys fully on model.

DAN: They're trying to get a photo of this elusive bird and are just punished mercilessly. Wally continually gets the better of them.

Story room sketch by Clay Morrow.

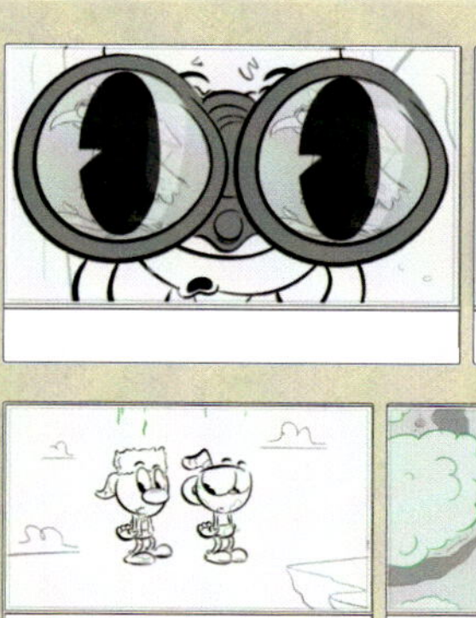
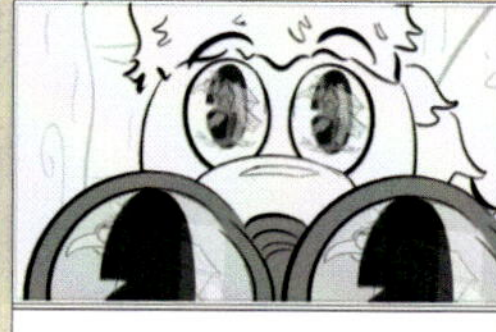
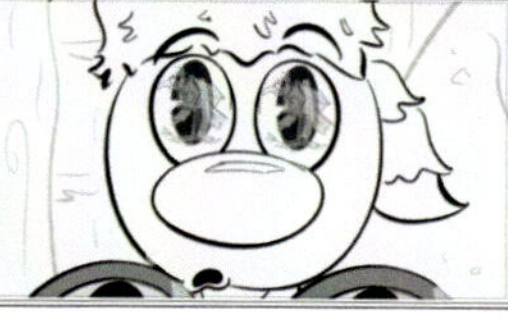
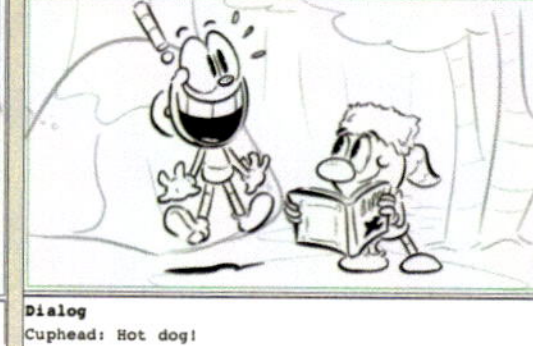

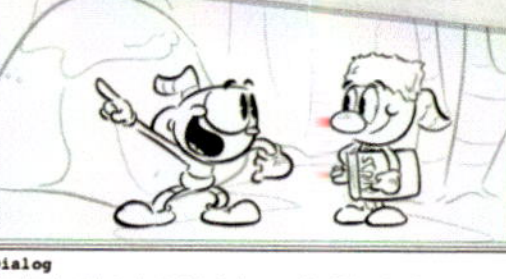

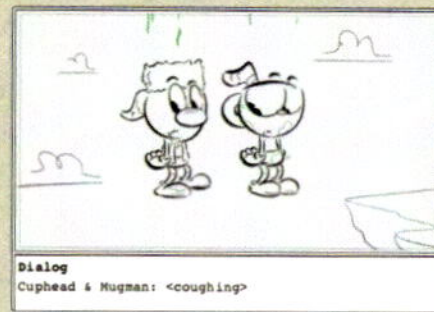

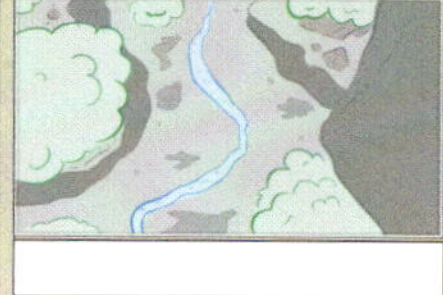
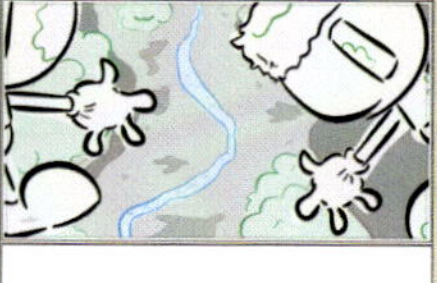
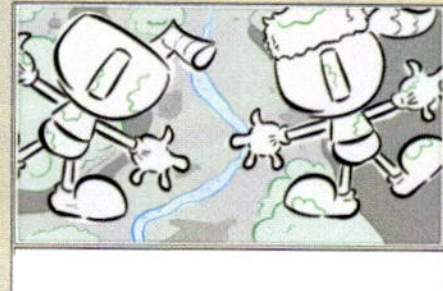
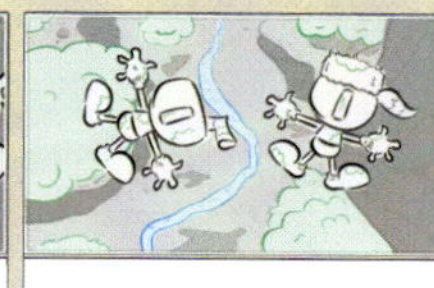
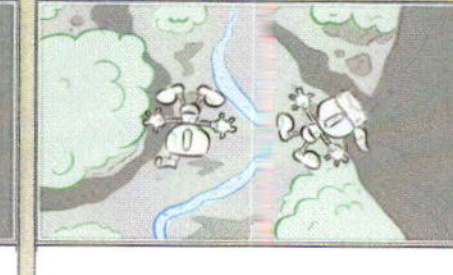
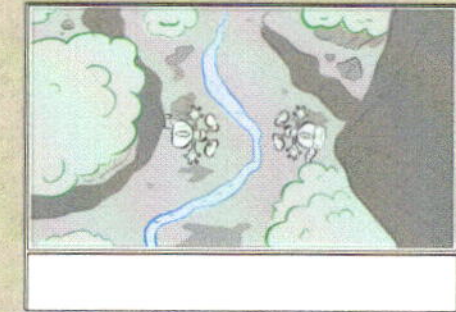
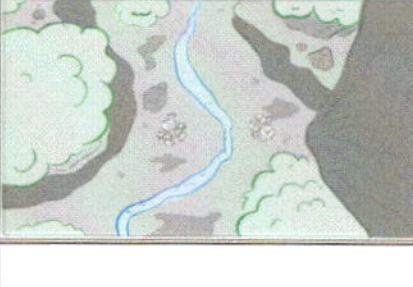
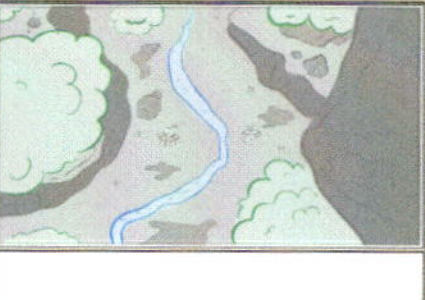
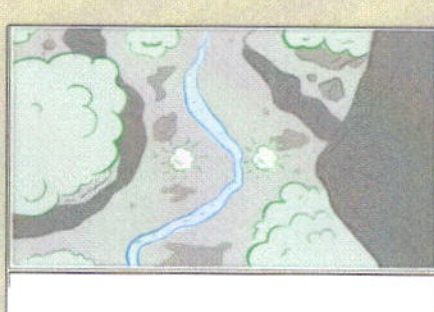
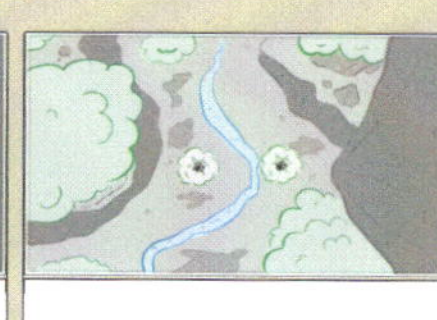
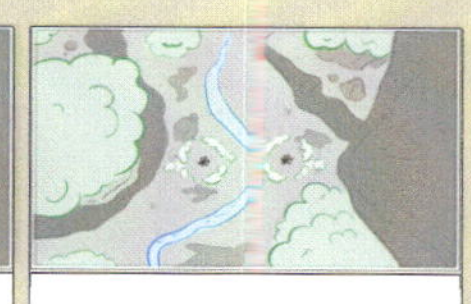
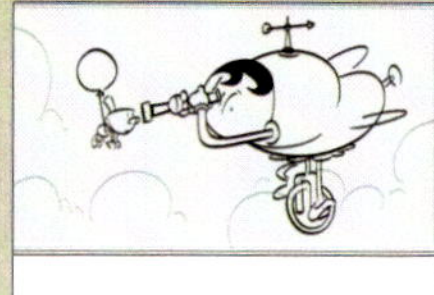
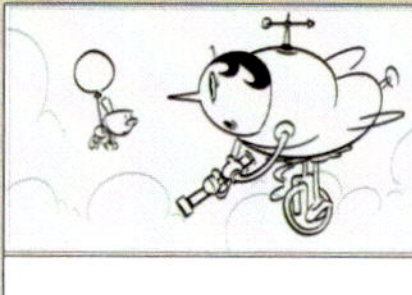
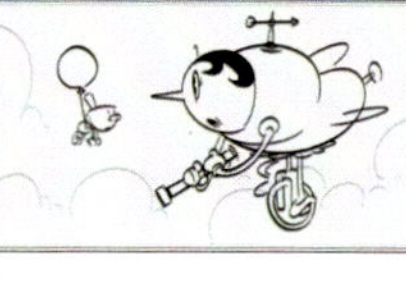
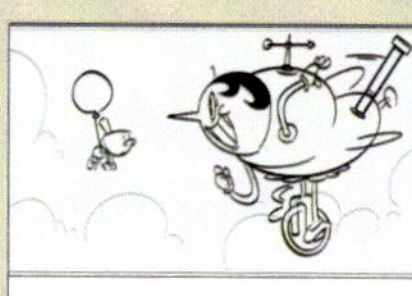
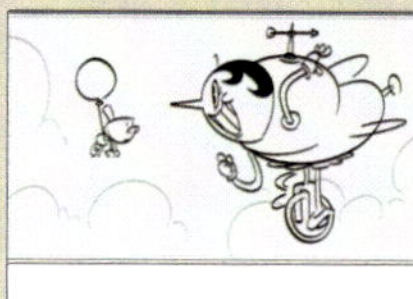
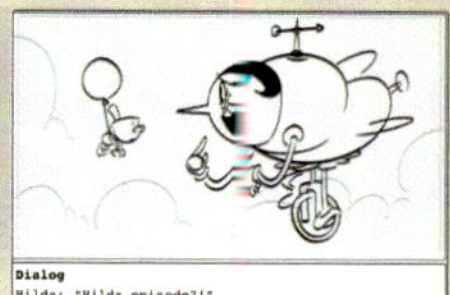

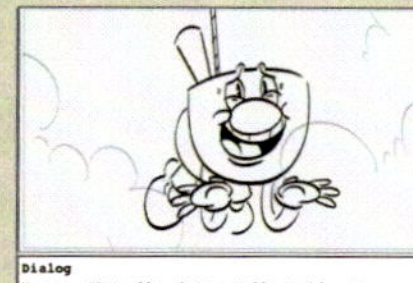

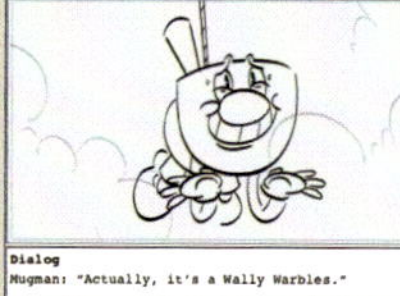

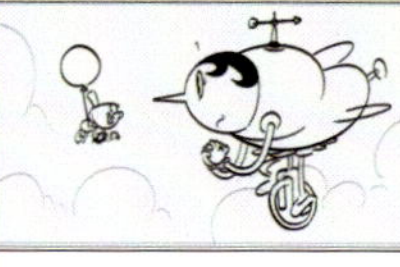
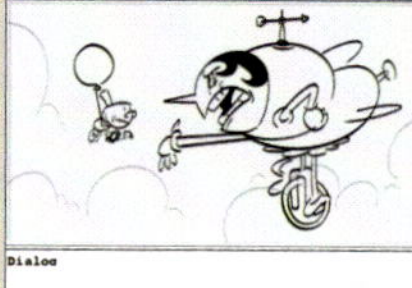

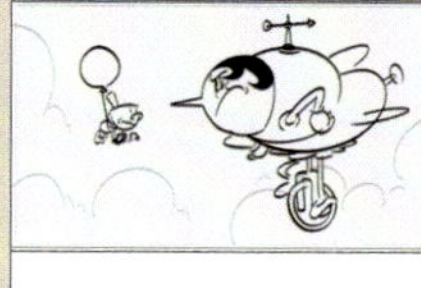
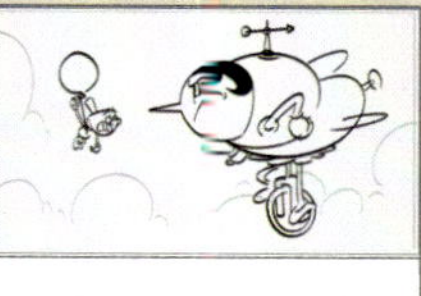
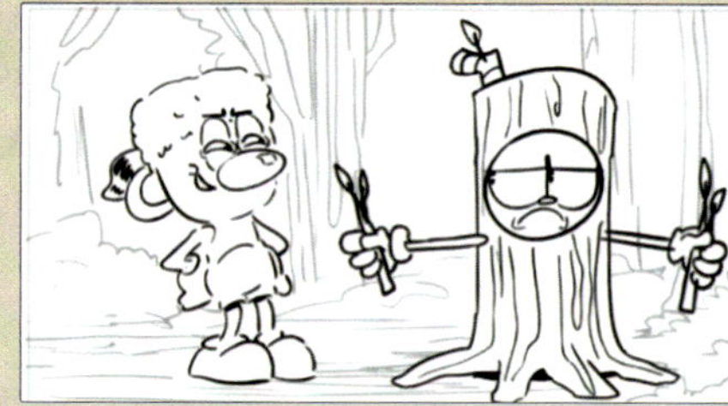
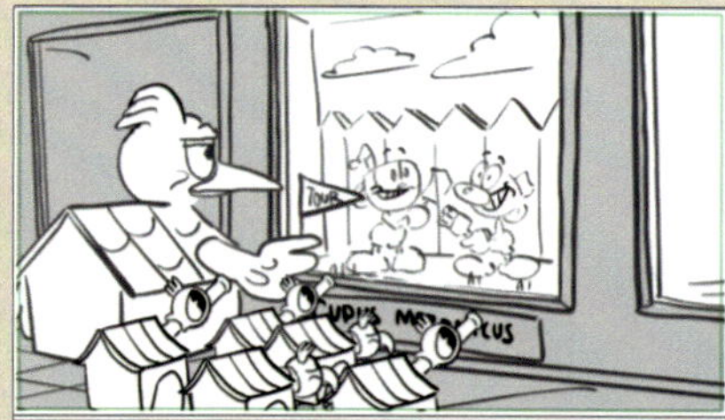
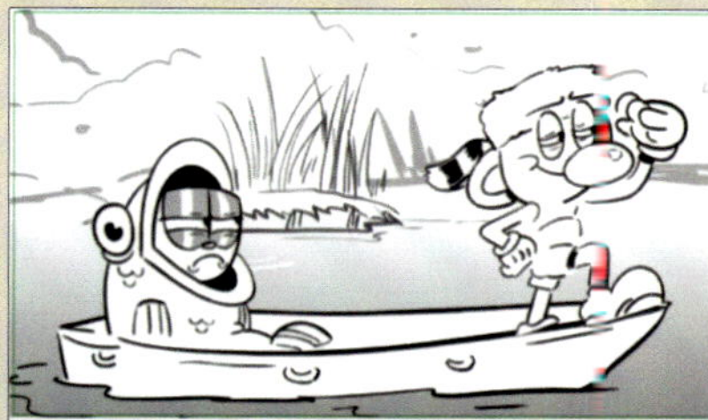

"RETURN TO SUGARLAND"

→ **KENNEDY:** They're listening to the radio, and they realize that Baroness von Bon Bon has been arrested. They look over and see a police van, and she's inside laughing maniacally. When Deeki did card pitches, the bar is raised really high, and it's really fun among the board artists to be like, "Okay, it worked once, so we can't blow it." I remember I was visiting home and I was practicing the Baroness's crazy laugh. My dad and sister were peering down at me like, "Hey, are you good?" And I'm like, "Oh yes, this is a thing I'm being paid to do."

Story room sketches by Clay Morrow; storyboard panels by Kennedy Tarrell and Dan Becker.

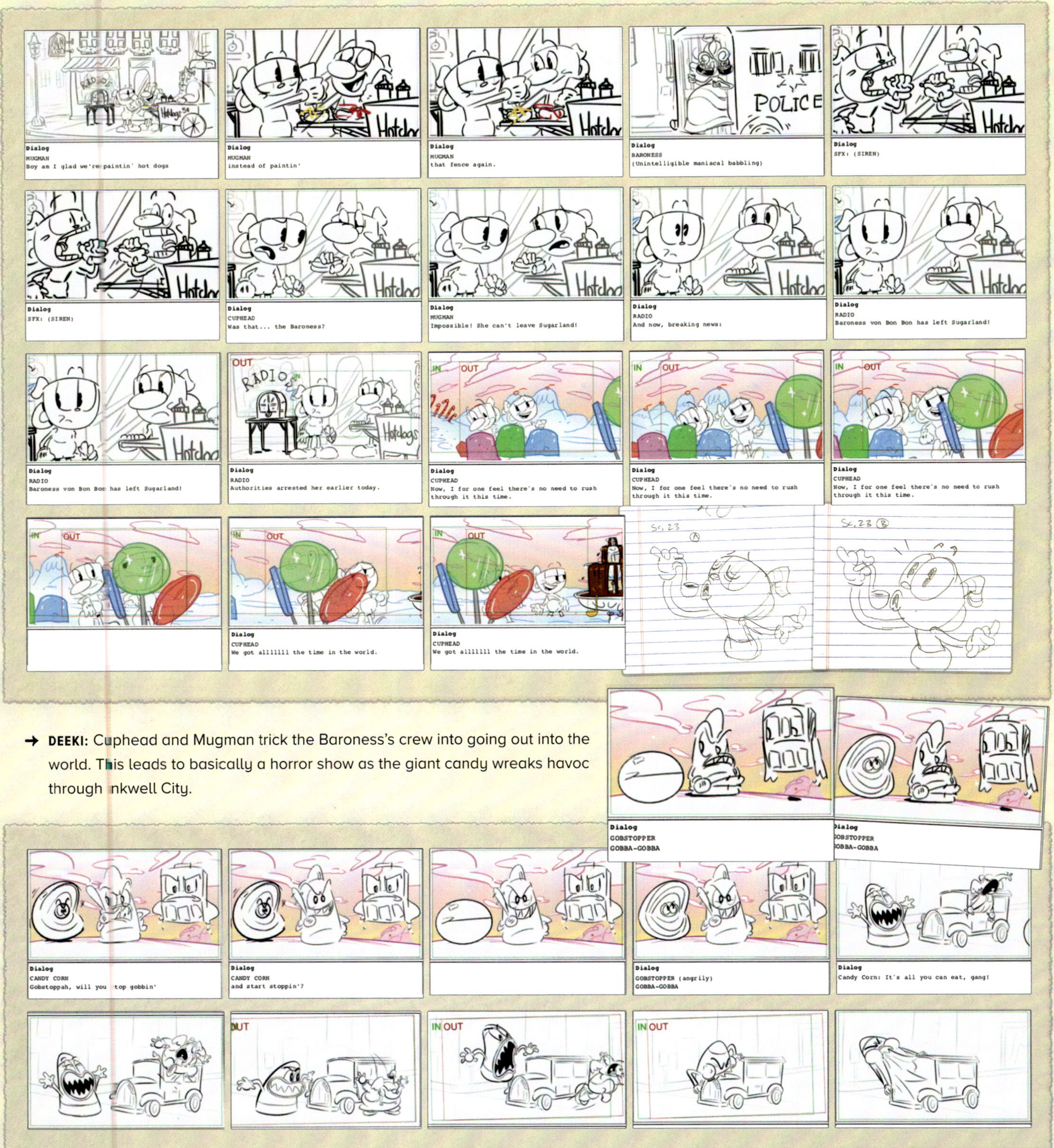

→ **DEEKI:** Cuphead and Mugman trick the Baroness's crew into going out into the world. This leads to basically a horror show as the giant candy wreaks havoc through Inkwell City.

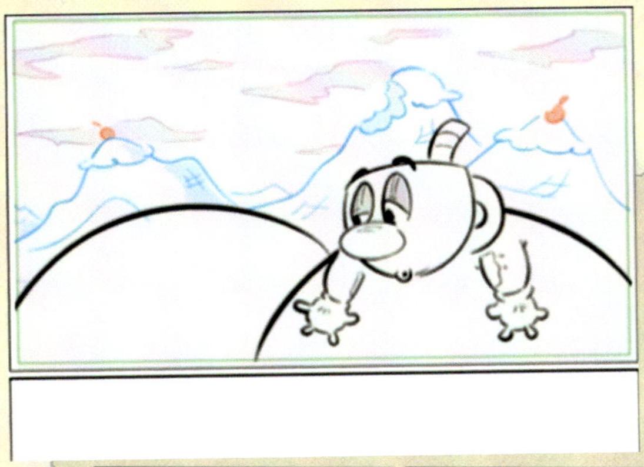

DAN: And it's all so Cuphead and Mugman can have their fill of candy in Sugarland.

KENNEDY: Clearly, they've learned nothing.

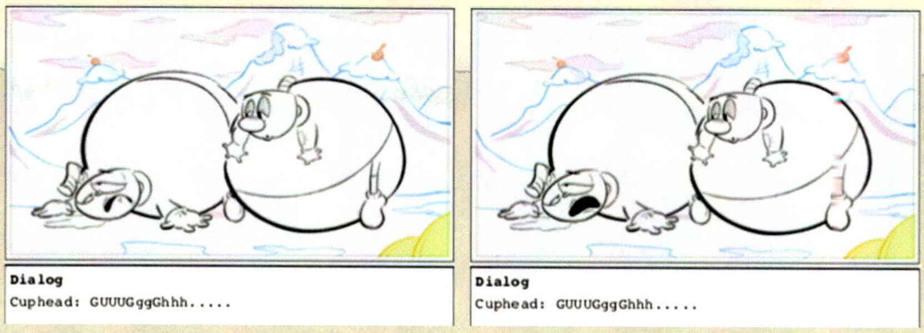

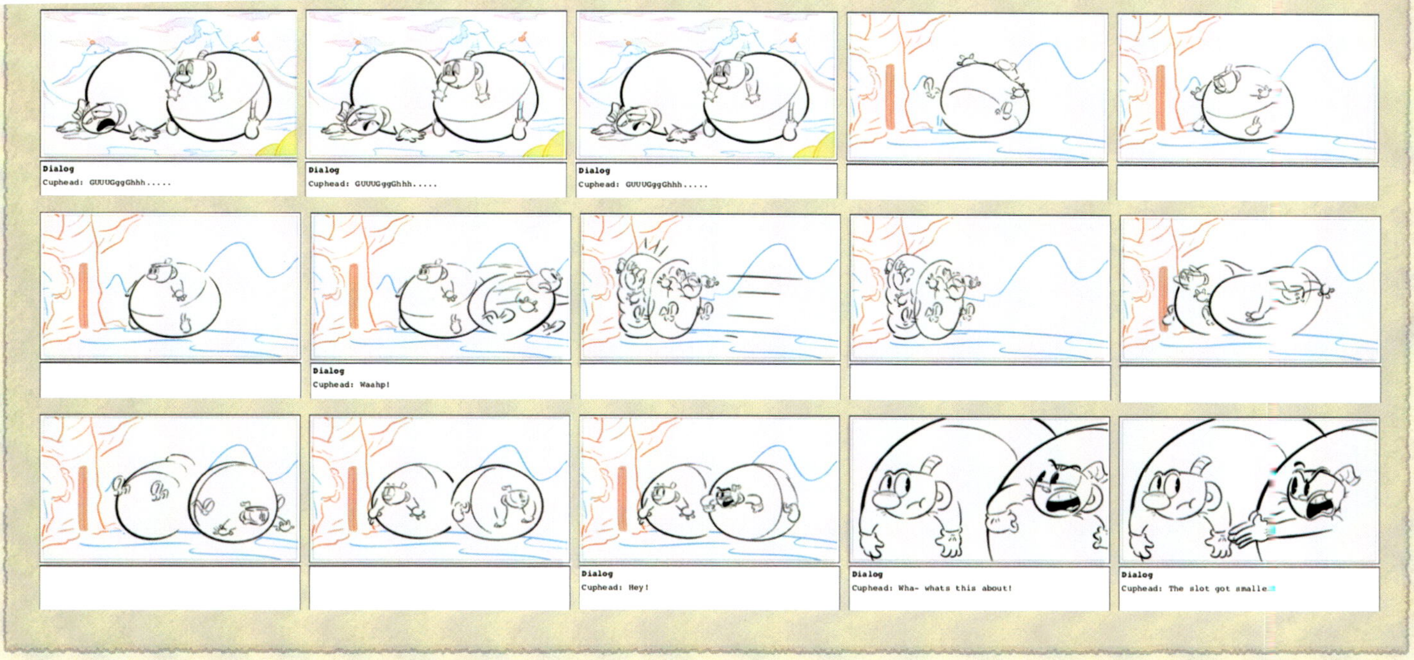

Dialog
Cuphead: GUUUGggGhhh.....

Dialog
Cuphead: GUUUGggGhhh.....

Dialog
Cuphead: GUUUGggGhhh.....

Dialog
Cuphead: GUUUGggGhhh.....

Dialog
Cuphead: GUUUGggGhhh.....

Dialog
Cuphead: Waahp!

Dialog
Cuphead: Hey!

Dialog
Cuphead: Wha- whats this about!

Dialog
Cuphead: The slot got smaller

DAN: The premise for this episode came together so quickly. During the pandemic, I was playing the game and I saw the candy corn character, which I thought was the coolest-looking character. I got the idea in the shower, wrote it up in fifteen minutes, sent it to Deeki, and everyone really responded to it. It was a great reminder to not overthink my first instincts.

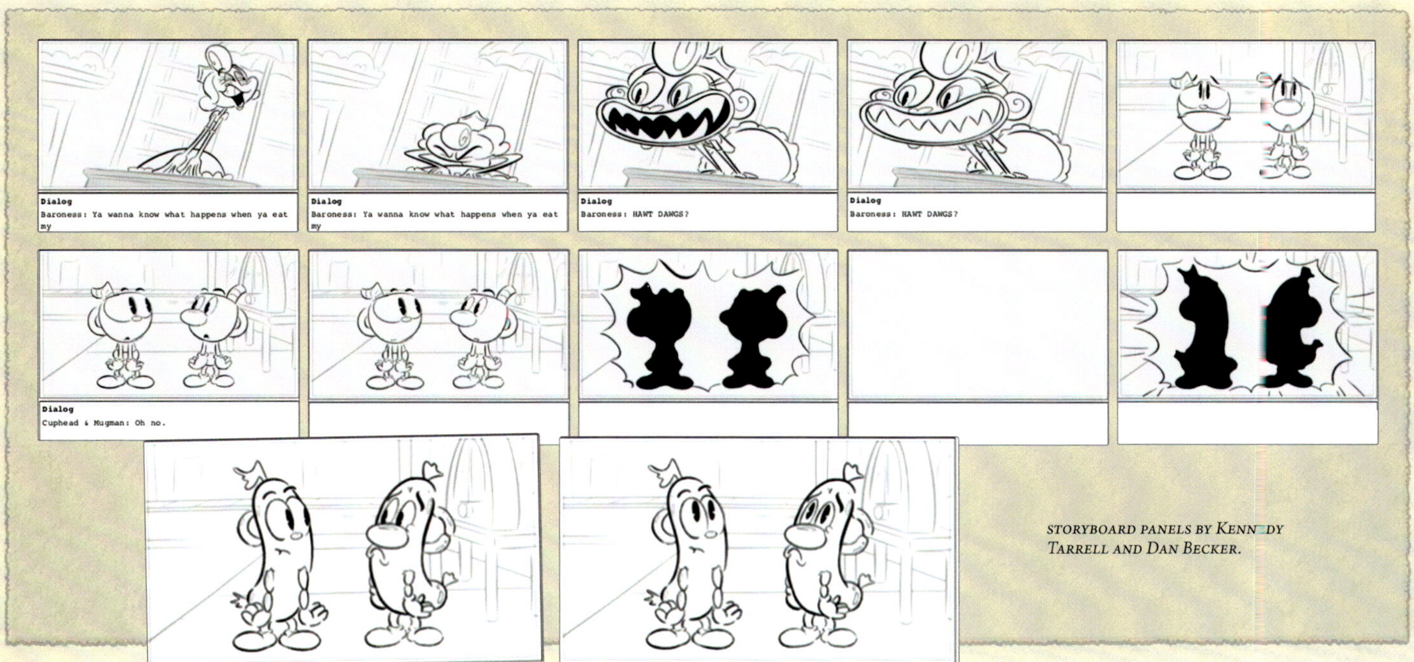

Storyboard panels by Kennedy Tarrell and Dan Becker.

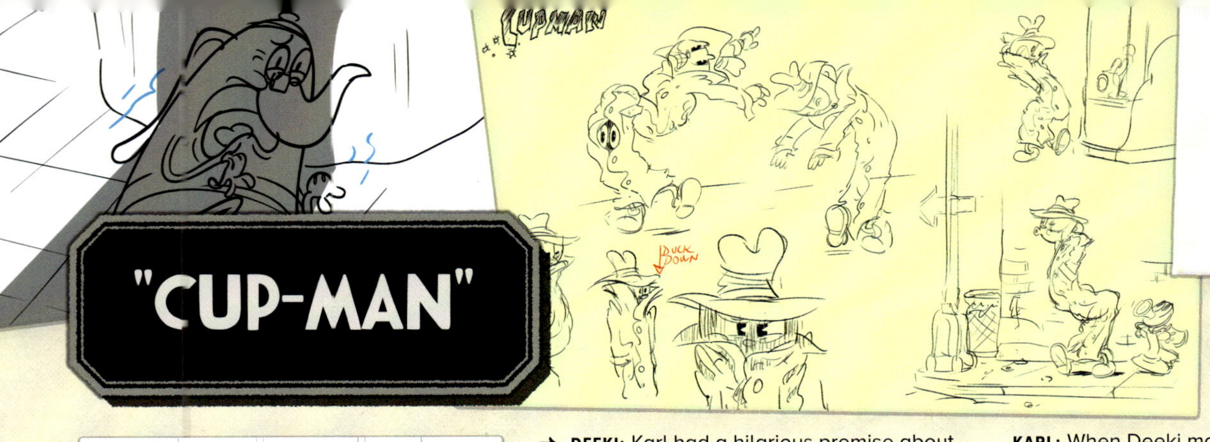

"CUP-MAN"

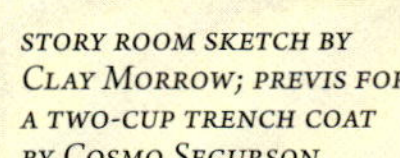

STORY ROOM SKETCH BY CLAY MORROW; PREVIS FOR A TWO-CUP TRENCH COAT BY COSMO SEGURSON.

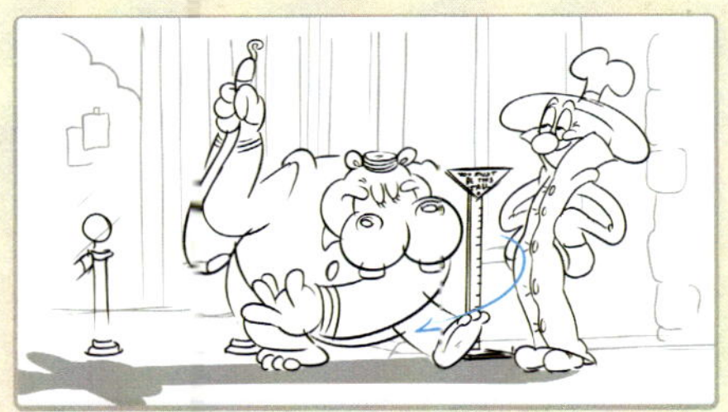

STORYBOARD PANELS BY FERNANDO PUIG.

→ **DEEKI:** Karl had a hilarious premise about Cuphead and Mugman wanting to see a gangster movie, so they stack on top of one another in a trench coat to get past the usher. They try out their getup on Elder Kettle, who believes they're an intimidating full-grown man. At the same time, we had a Cagney Carnation episode in progress. The two ideas seemed to work well together.

KARL: When Deeki married the "Cup-Man" idea to the Cagney story, it scratched another itch—to do more with the bosses—so it evolved into something I became even more excited for. I was happy that the seed of it still existed. In animation, things evolve, and the process works best when it's collaborative.

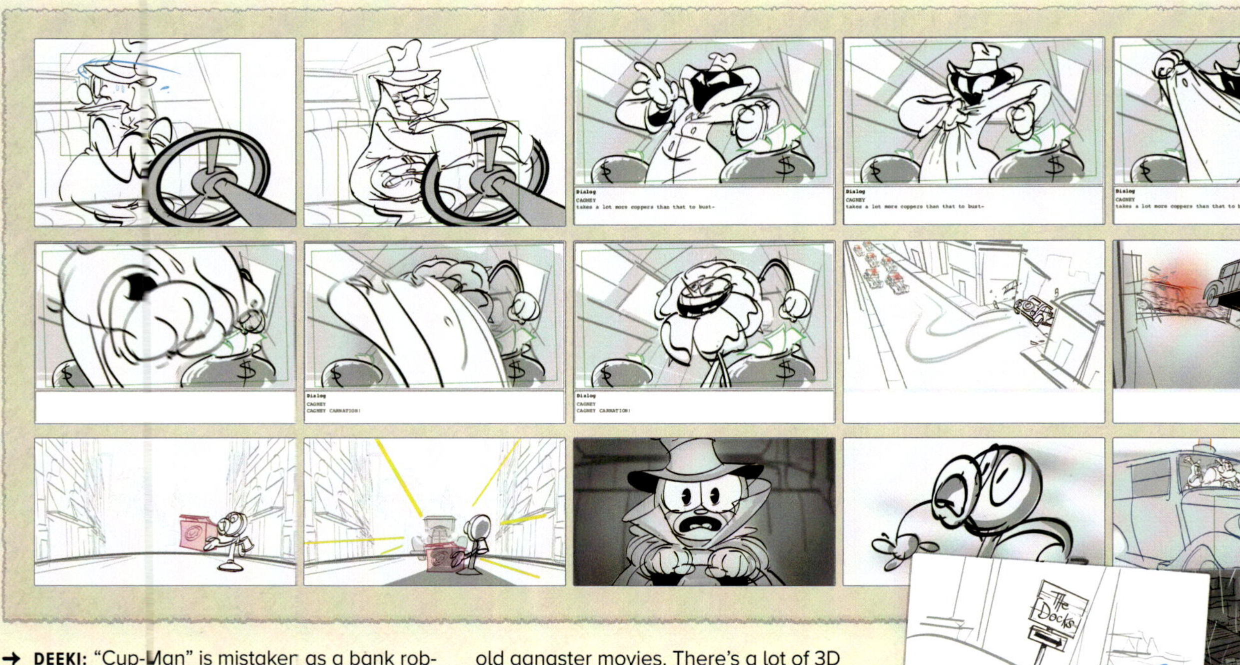

→ **DEEKI:** "Cup-Man" is mistaken as a bank robber's getaway driver. The cops give chase, and the robber is revealed to be Cagney.

KARL: I did a lot of research on the cars from *The Public Enemy*, *White Heat*, and other old gangster movies. There's a lot of 3D models you can toggle through online. It definitely helped inform that look. Cars are notoriously difficult to draw, and the cars of that era have a really specific shape.

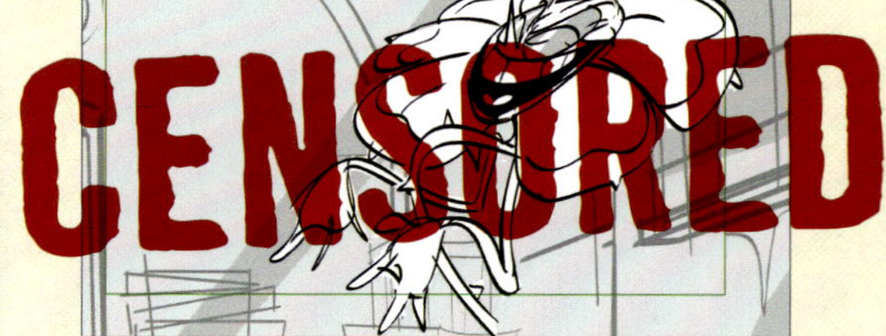

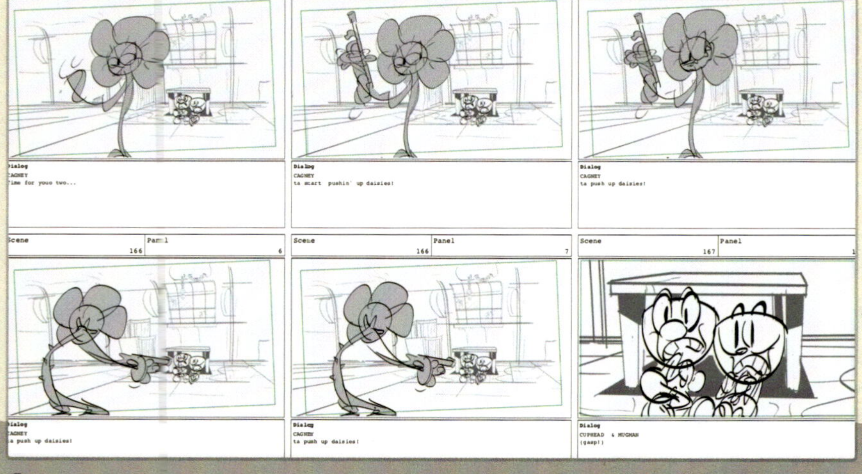

→ **DEEKI:** Cagney takes "Cup-Man" to his hideout at the docks. From there, things escalate to a place so intense that it's not suitable for a family publication.

STORYBOARD PANELS BY KARL HADRIKA.

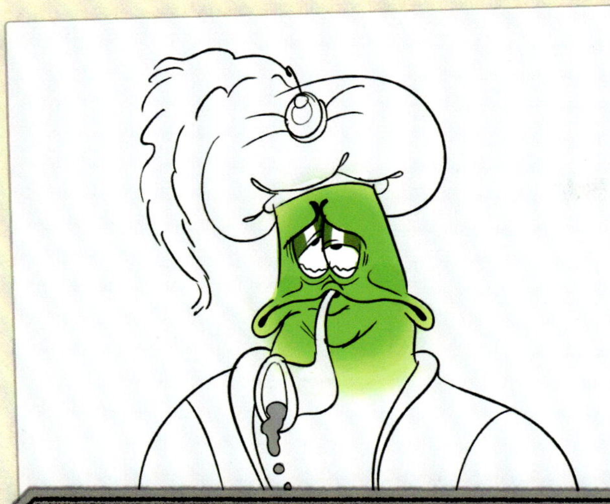

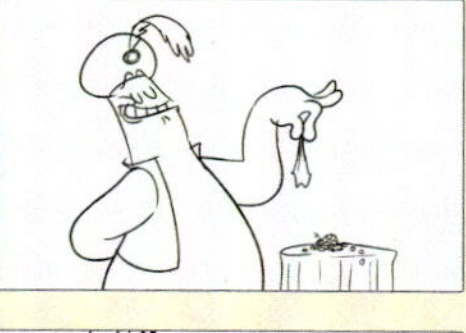

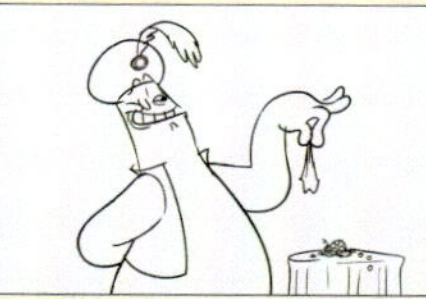

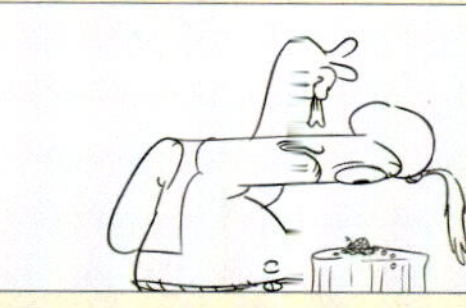

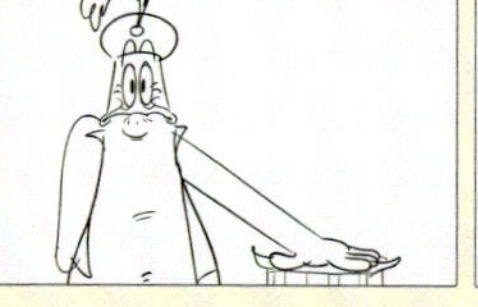

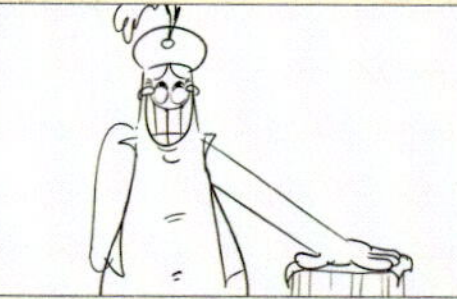

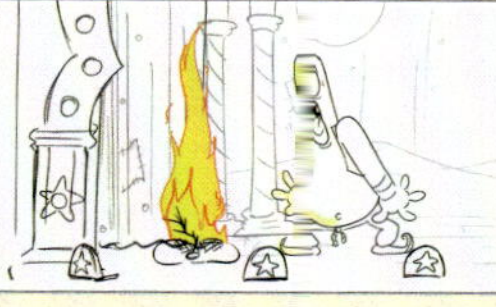

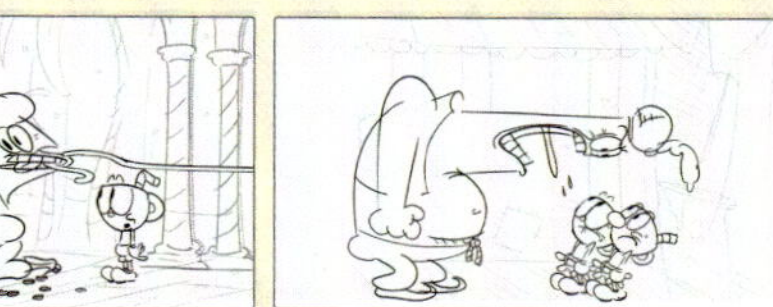

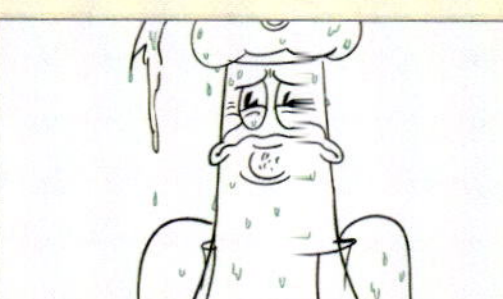

"STRANGE MAGIC"

→ **DEEKI:** Djimmi is basically the worst magician of all time. Cuphead and Mugman go to see his show, complain about him, and he winds up getting fired. Then he's confronted by a mysterious stranger who offers him a chance to have *actual* magic . . .

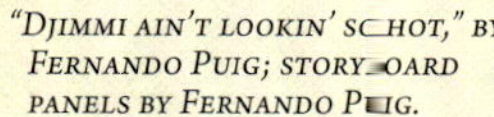

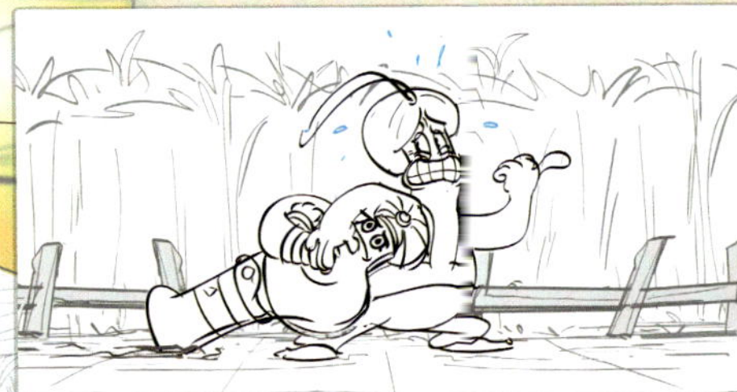

"Djimmi ain't lookin' so hot," by Fernando Puig; storyboard panels by Fernando Puig.

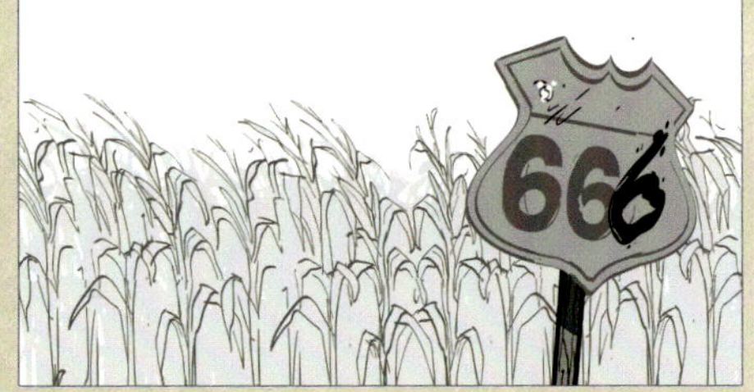

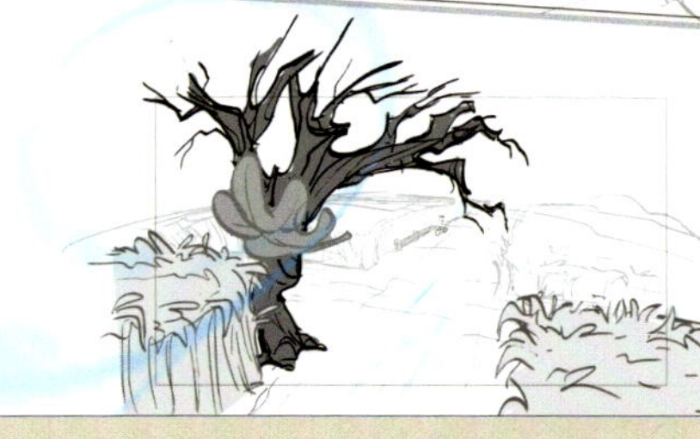

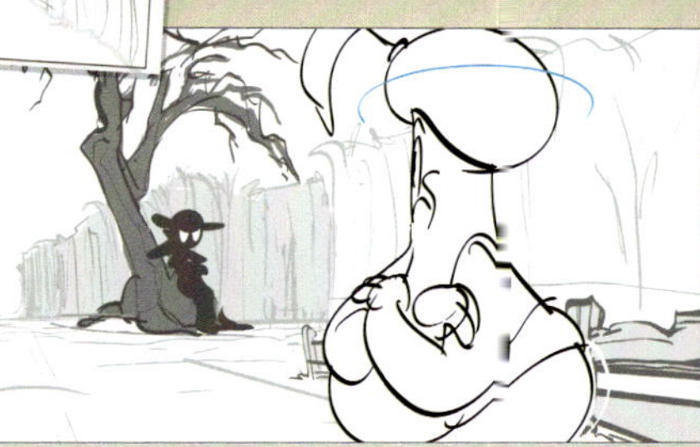

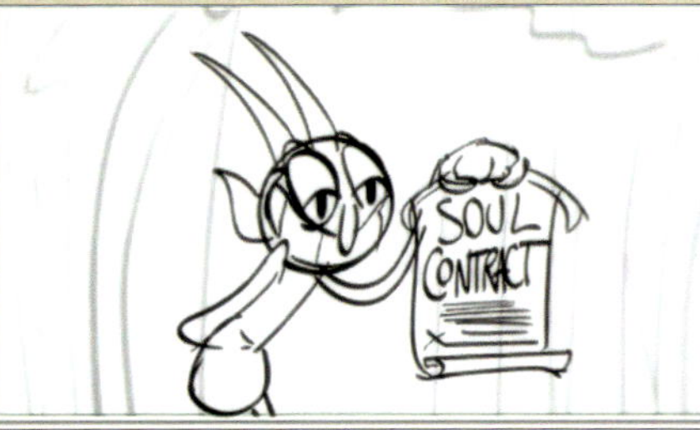

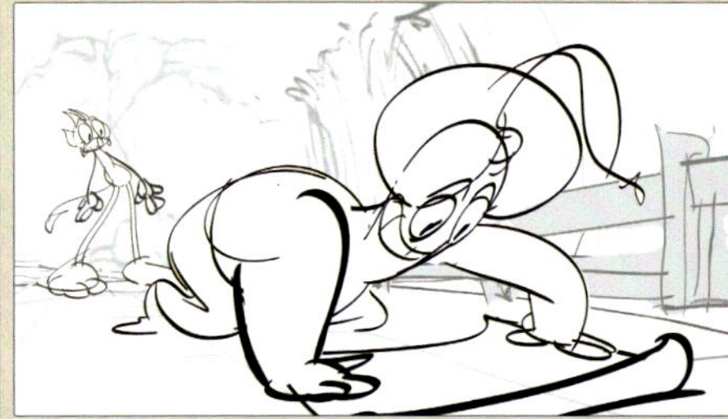

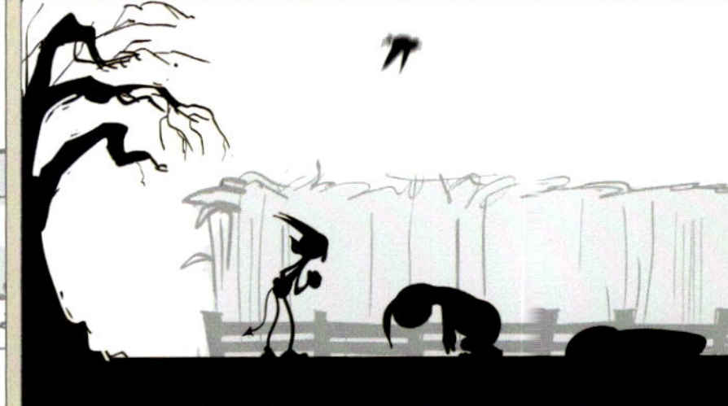

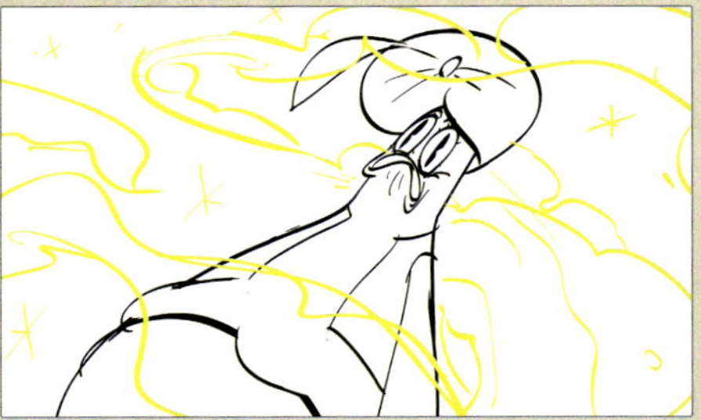

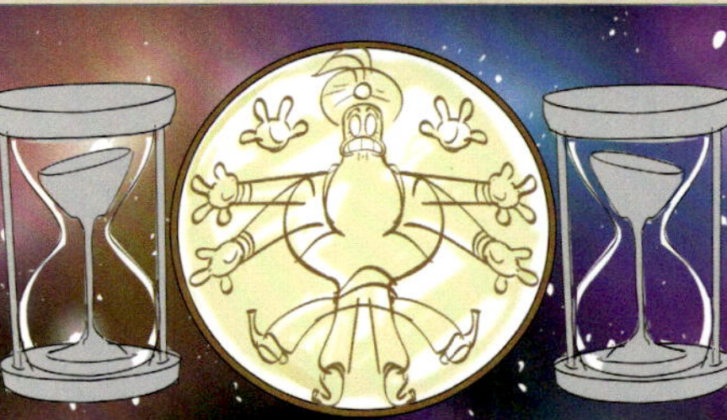

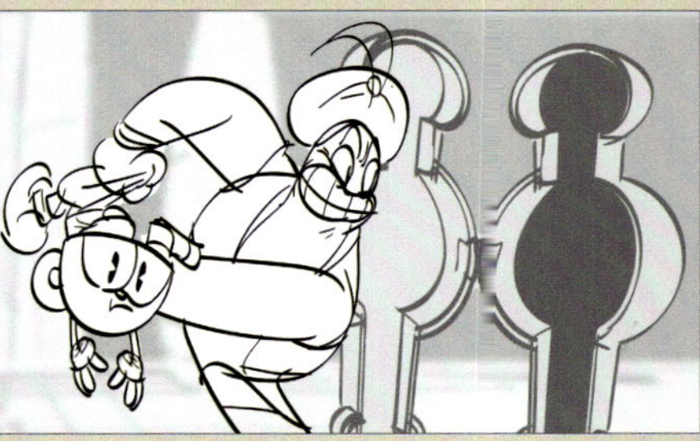

Storyboard panels by Karl Hadrika.

"EVIL & VILE"

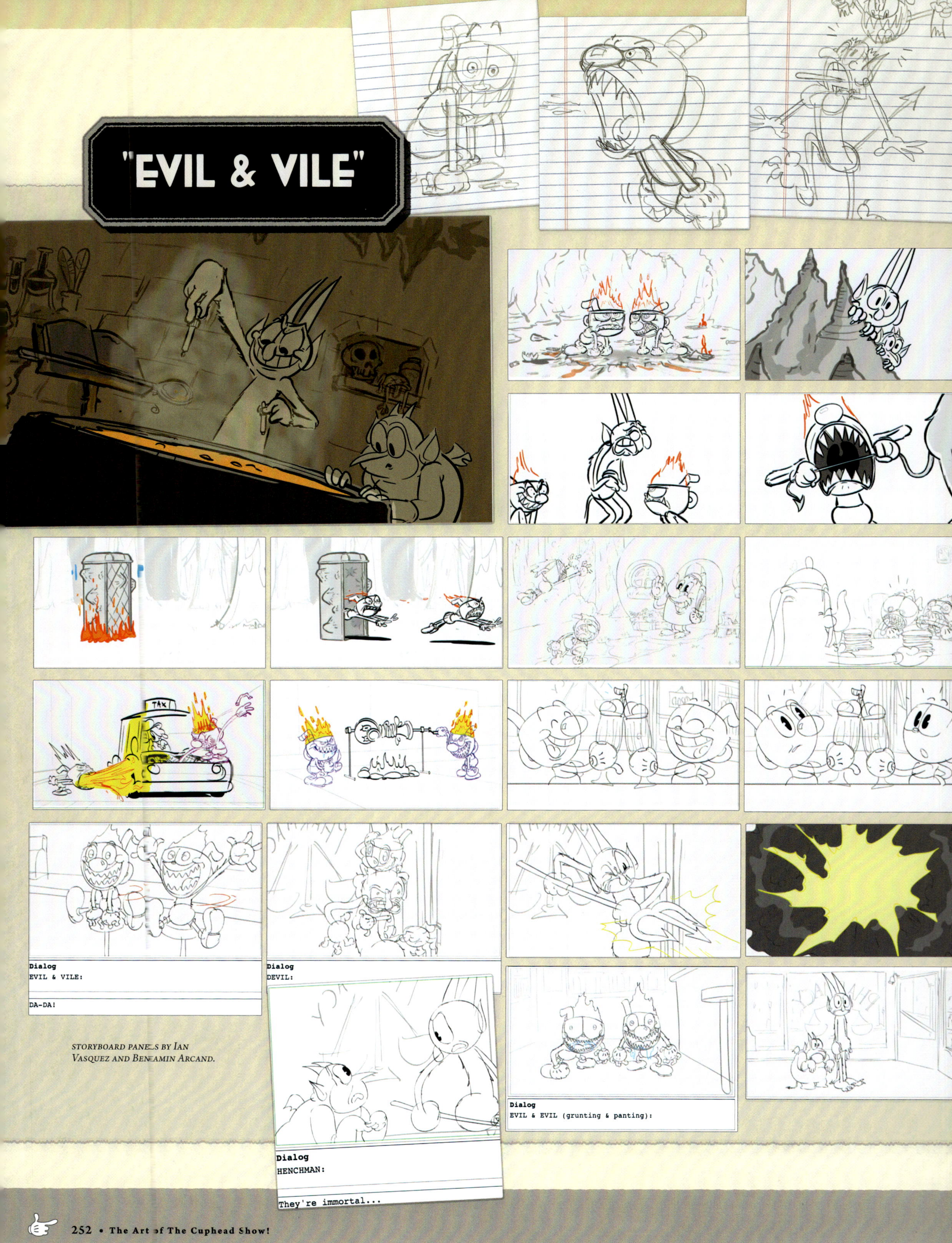

Storyboard panels by Ian Vasquez and Benjamin Arcand.

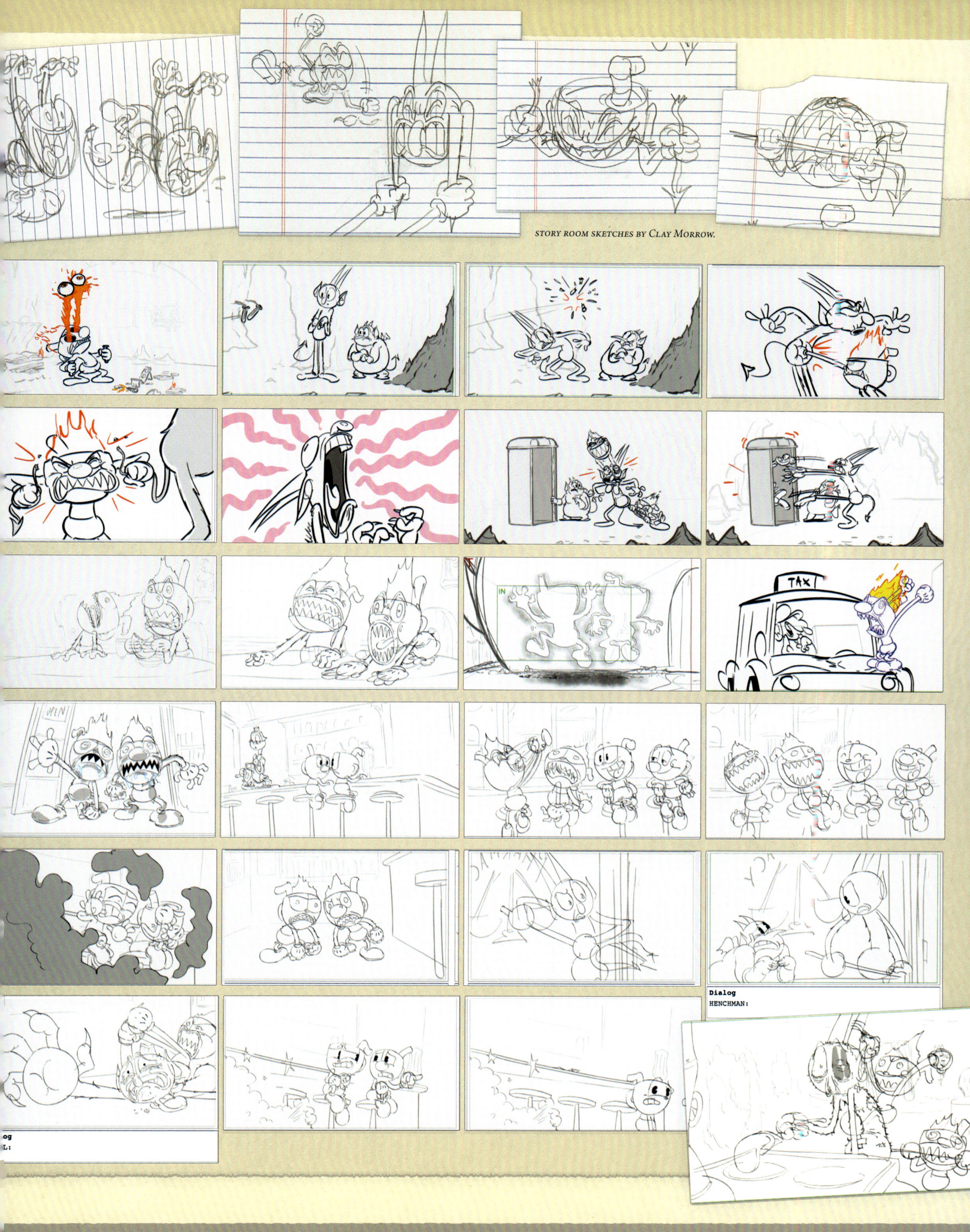

Story room sketches by Clay Morrow.

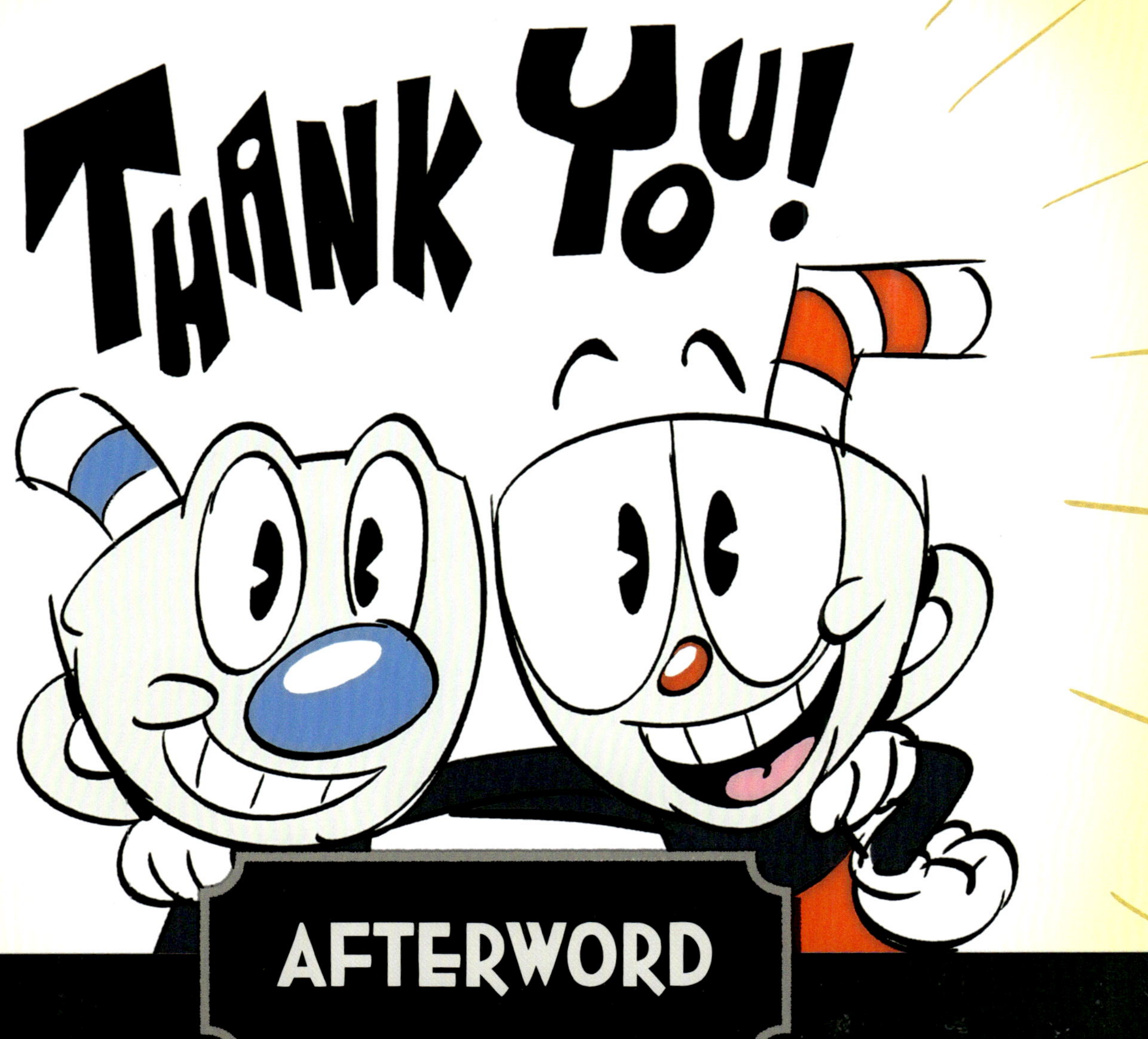

AFTERWORD

MAJA: I think that when you watch the show, it's clear that the creative team put so much love and care and attention into maintaining the things about the world of *Cuphead* that fans care about—it's a show that just feels like *Cuphead*, which is so much easier said than done.

ELI: The *Cuphead* universe is playful enough to sustain being twisted in all these different directions but still be recognizable as the *Cuphead* people love. It is the real test of the endurance of an IP and a world and a creative space that it can be given all these different treatments and still resonate with people universally.

CJ: The particular alchemy of this team was incredible: the show feels like a fast-paced, relentlessly funny modern cartoon, but infused with the spirit of the era that inspired it.

MEGAN C: From Deeki's pitches to the storyboards to the animatics to the final animation and Ego's beautiful score—it was a real career highlight seeing this show come together.

ANDREA: Every single person brought something incredibly special to the mix, and everyone was such a cheerleader for one another.

JARED MORGAN: It felt like everyone's work was pushing all the other departments to do their best. Seeing all this amazing work day after day, I was like, "I gotta do better!" It felt invigorating.

CLAY: The amount of talent on the crew was almost an embarrassment of riches.

COSMO: I'm so proud of the work we did, and so proud to have been a part of it.

ANDREA: This show looks awesome, and it's all due to the incredible work of the art team. The background design team is fantastic; our painters are incredible; our color stylist Chris Hacker goes above and beyond every time.

CHRIS: It's so much easier to work on a show when it's top-down good, like, the writing is funny, the designs are great, the storyboard is amazing. You feel more driven to make it look good when every step before you is kickass. You don't want to drop the ball—you want to make it look awesome.

ADAM P: As hard as the show was to make, it all feels really worth it. It turned out great.

KARL: It didn't matter that it could be difficult or challenging, because we all had that runner's high. Even when we got fatigued, we would see the next episode when Deeki did a card pitch for the crew, and we'd get all excited again. It was impossible not to be inspired.

ZOË: We did not look like we all came from the same place. You could tell we came from everywhere. Every artist had something special they brought.

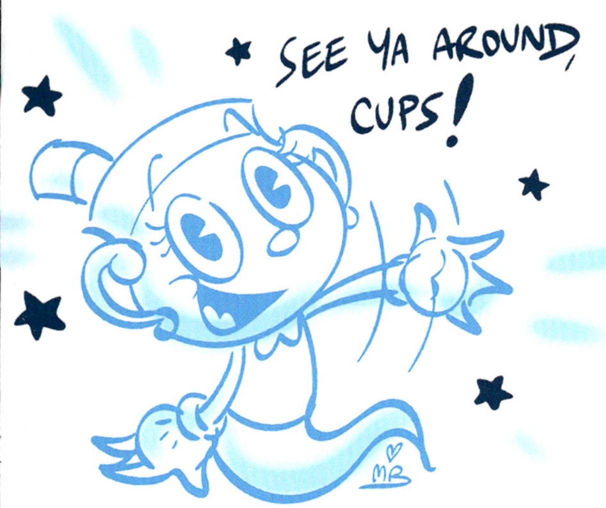

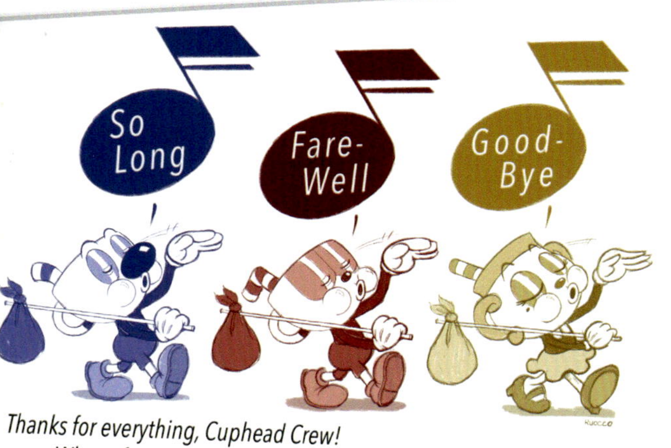

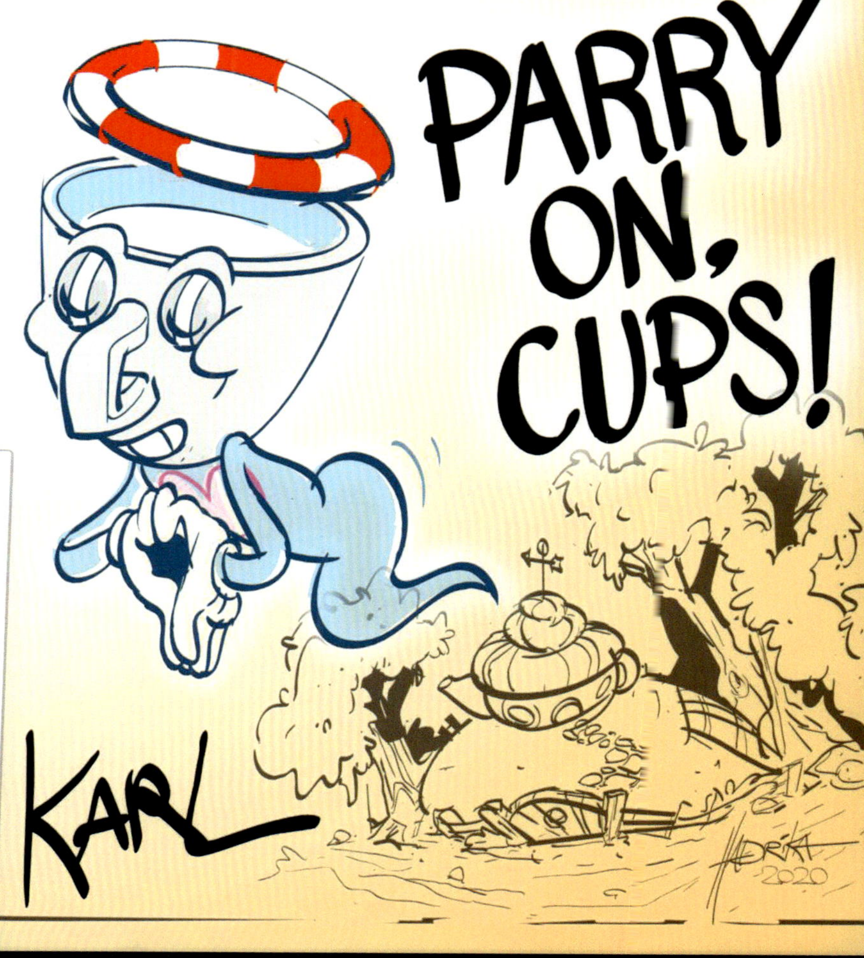

LAUREN: At every step of the process, you're one-upping and elevating the previous team. It's like, "You guys made an amazing script, then amazing boards, and now it's gonna be amazing designs," and everyone brings their A-game.

TAPAN: I always think of the endgame, which is seeing it onscreen, showing it to my nieces and nephews, showing it to my family and friends.

ADAM P: There's an arc to the whole show and little bits of continuity that make it work as a streaming show that just feel so satisfying. It was all planned; it wasn't a big accident.

DEEKI: This was the best creative experience of my career, and I've never worked with a more talented team. We had such momentum with the stories and so many awesome ideas. There could definitely be another three seasons.

ANDREA: I have to hand it to MDHR. I am so surprised at how hands off they were with the art, considering they had such an artistic property. Putting myself in their shoes, had I come up with this concept and people were riffing off it, I would be *insane* about babysitting it!

JARED: The vast amount of anything that can happen in the '30s, the style of the rubber hosing, and everything coming alive, but also anything can be nightmarishly weird. It's this unending fountain of creativity that the '30s brings, so it's exciting to see that all merge together.

CHAD: We brought this cartoon flair into a video game, and now this cartoon flair is coming back into the medium it's supposed to be in.

ANDREA: I am so thankful to MDHR because they trusted us. The amount of assets we had to produce and the amount of time we had to produce them in would have been near impossible if they didn't trust us. The wrong partners could have completely derailed the look of this show. It was so time consuming to achieve that if we had people who were stopping us to get their notes in, we would have had to water down the look. But we didn't have to because we had such trusting partners. We didn't have to spend time correcting—we spent our time creating, and that is a huge asset on a show like this.

DAVE: This show started off a love letter to a specific period in animation, but it wouldn't have been possible without the love that everyone put into it. I remember saying to each member of the team as they were hired, "A show like this only comes along once in a career. Let's make it count." Hopefully, we did.

Farewell cards by Adam Paloian, Michael Ruocco, Megan Bond, and Karl Hadrika.

THE END

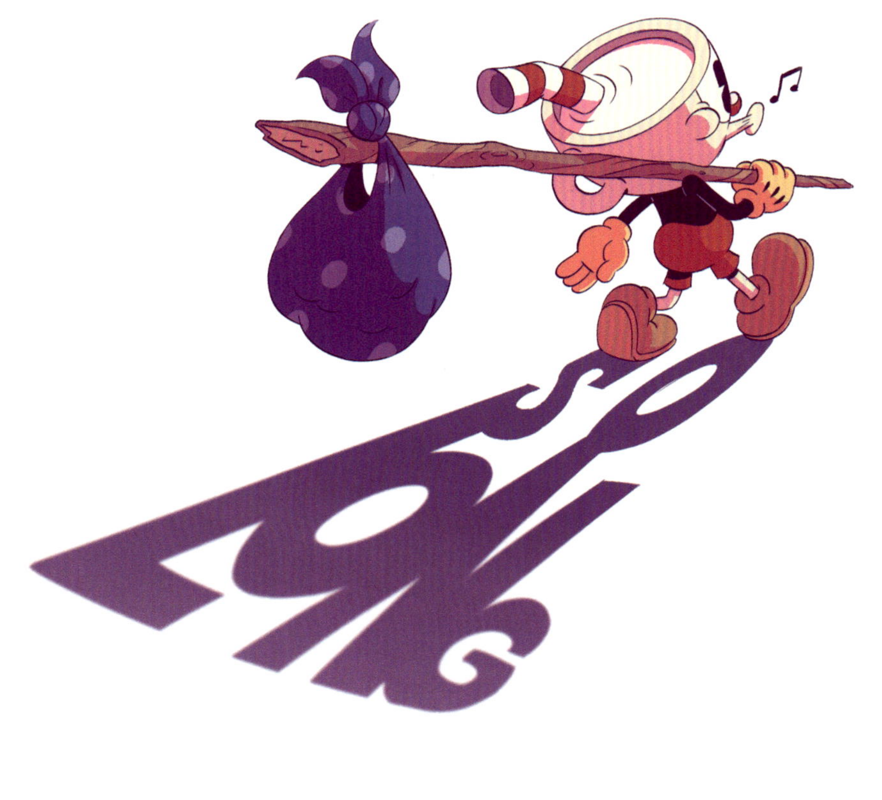

Farewell card by Bradley Lewis.

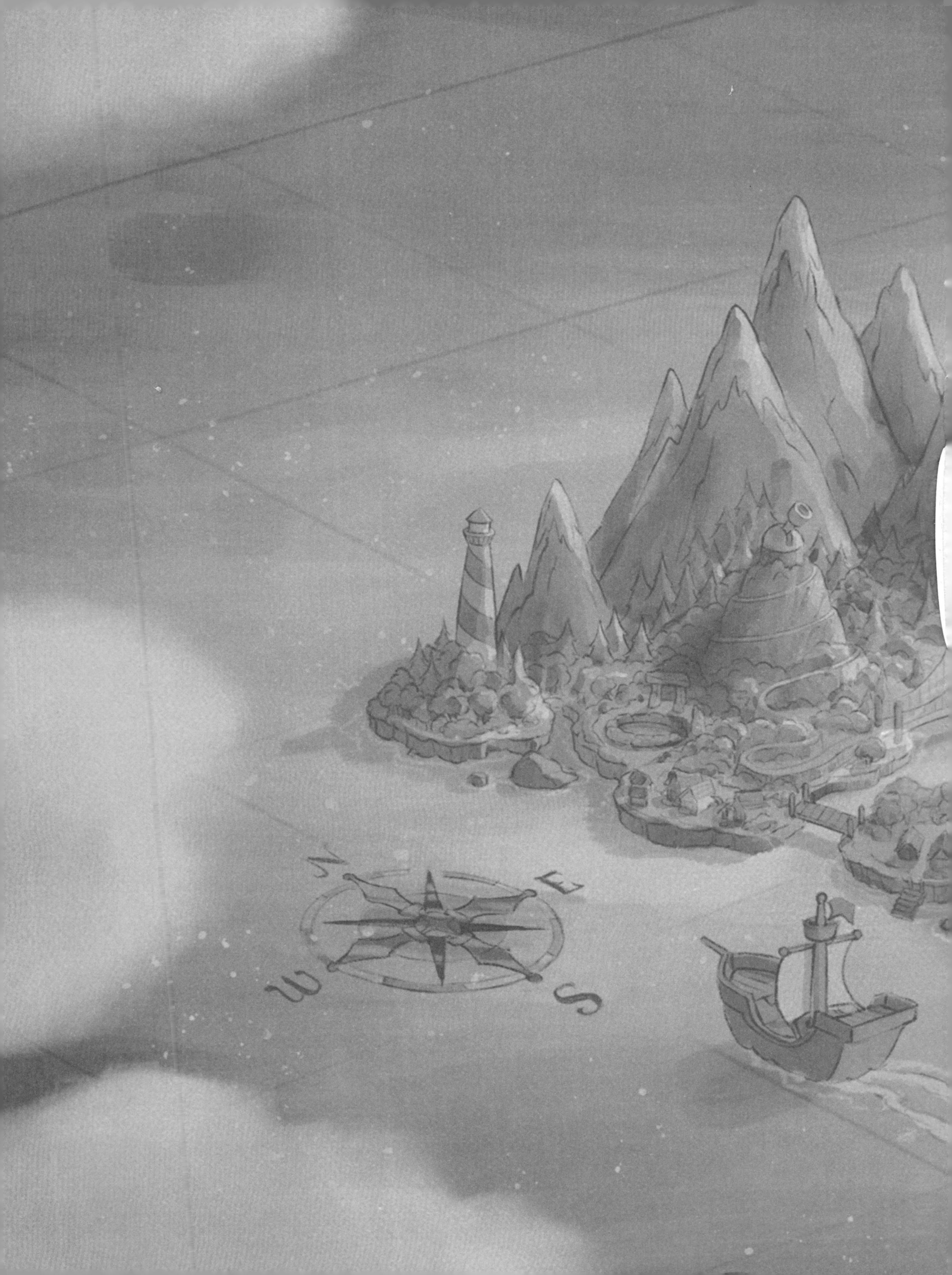
N
E
W
S

I3819626

NOTES FROM A DECORATOR'S LIFE

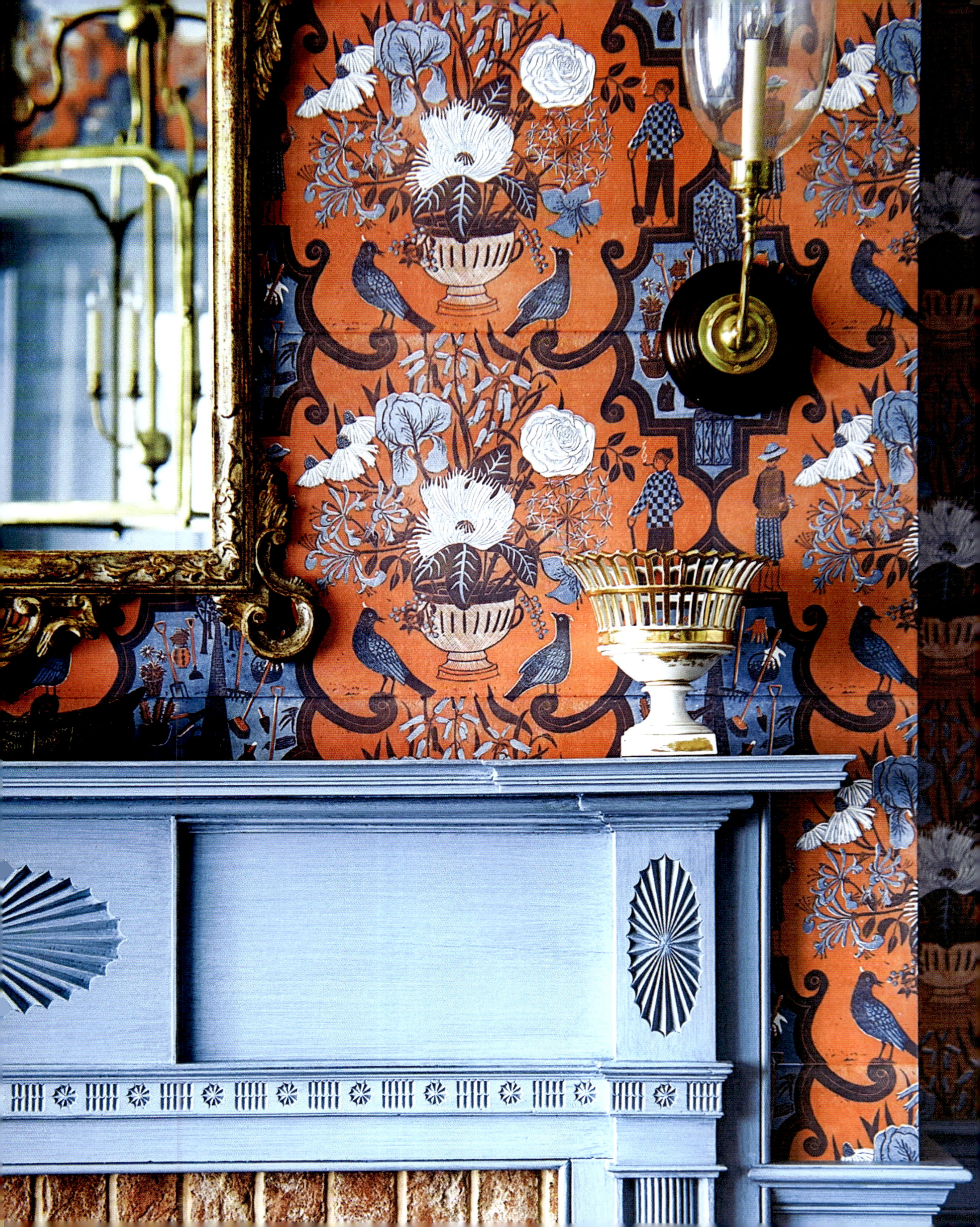

NOTES FROM A DECORATOR'S LIFE

LIBBY CAMERON

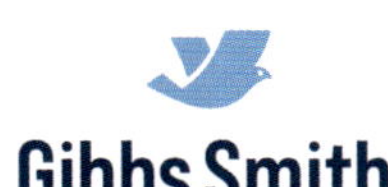

Gibbs Smith

First Edition
30 29 28 27 26 5 4 3 2 1

Photography credits: page 240

Published by
Gibbs Smith
570 N. Sportsplex Drive
Kaysville, Utah 84037
www.gibbs-smith.com

The authorized representative in the EEA is Simon and Schuster Netherlands BV, Herculesplein 96 3584 AA Utrecht, Netherlands, info@simonandschuster.nl

Designed by Rita Sowins | Sowins Design
Printed and bound in China

This product is made of FSC®-certified and other controlled material.

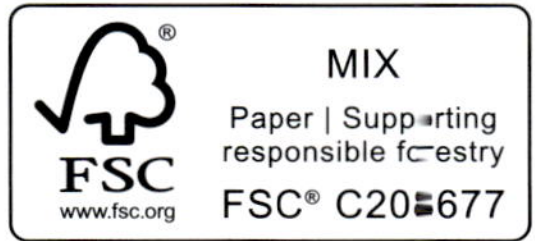

Library of Congress Control Number: 2025938811
ISBN: 978-1-4236-6789-6

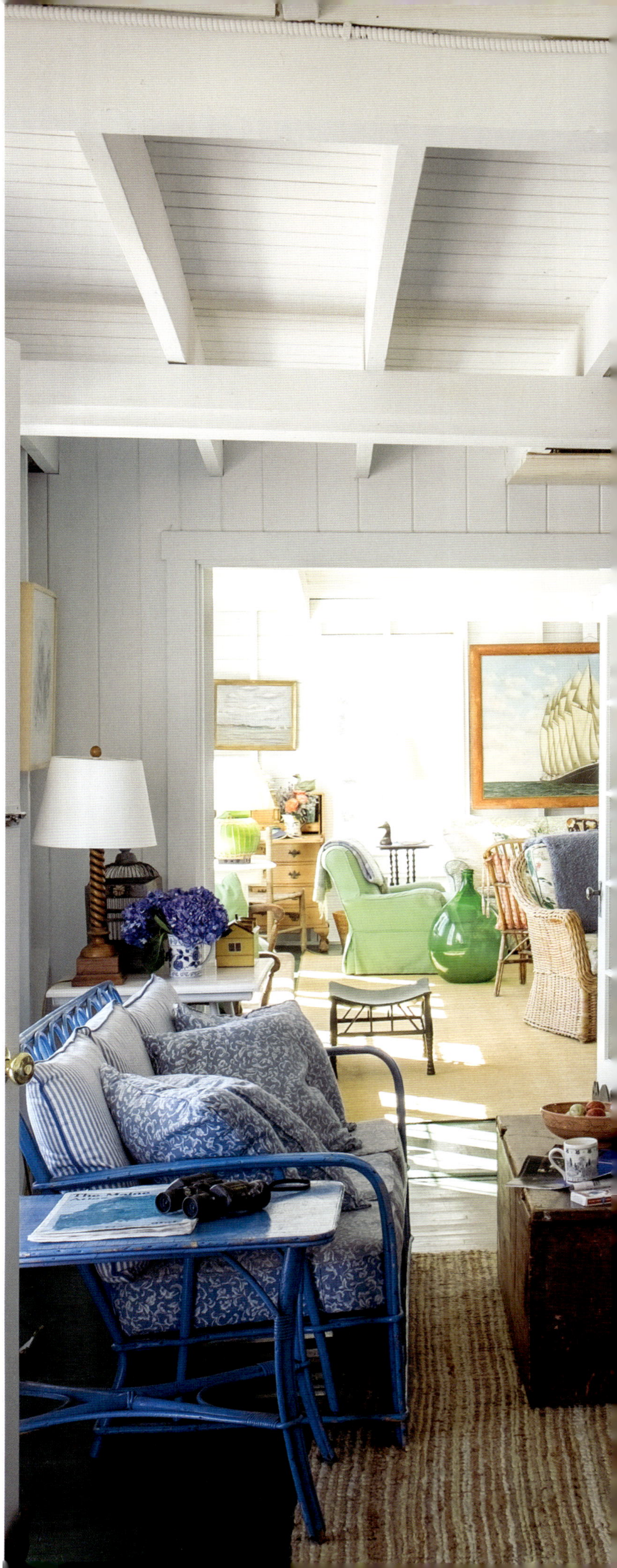

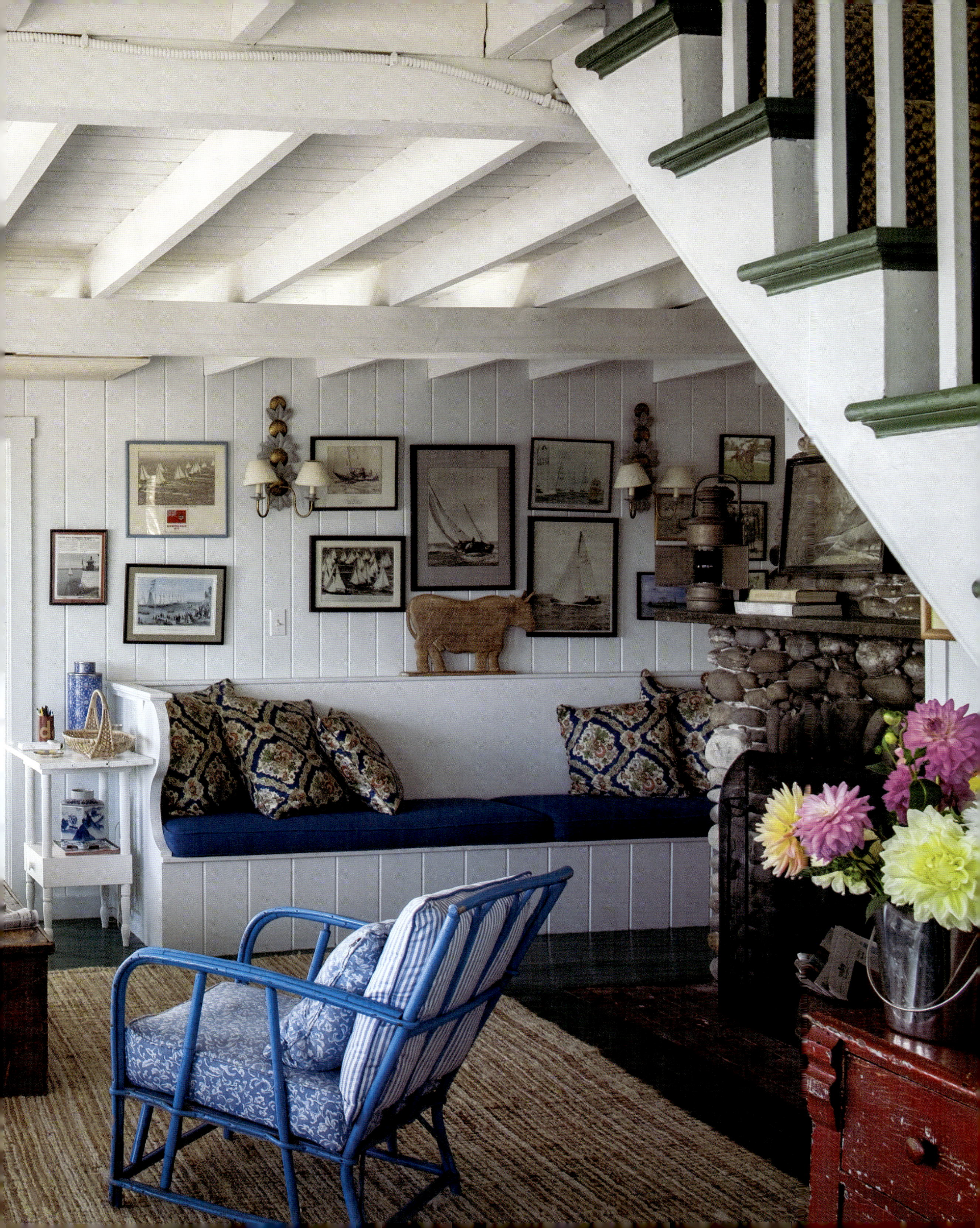

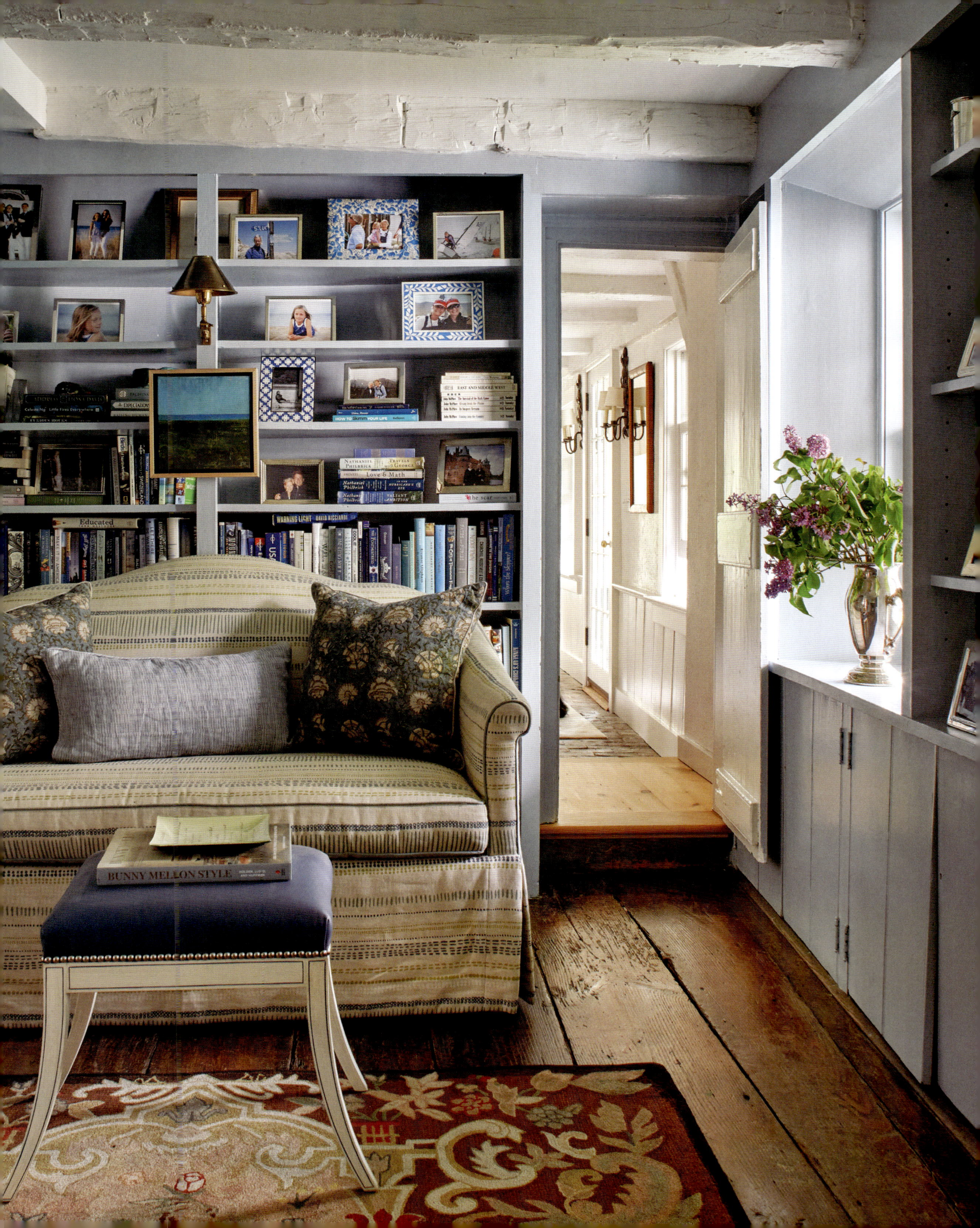

BUNNY MELLON STYLE
Educated
WARNING LIGHT
DAVID RICCIARDI
EAST AND MIDDLE WEST
Love & Math

CONTENTS

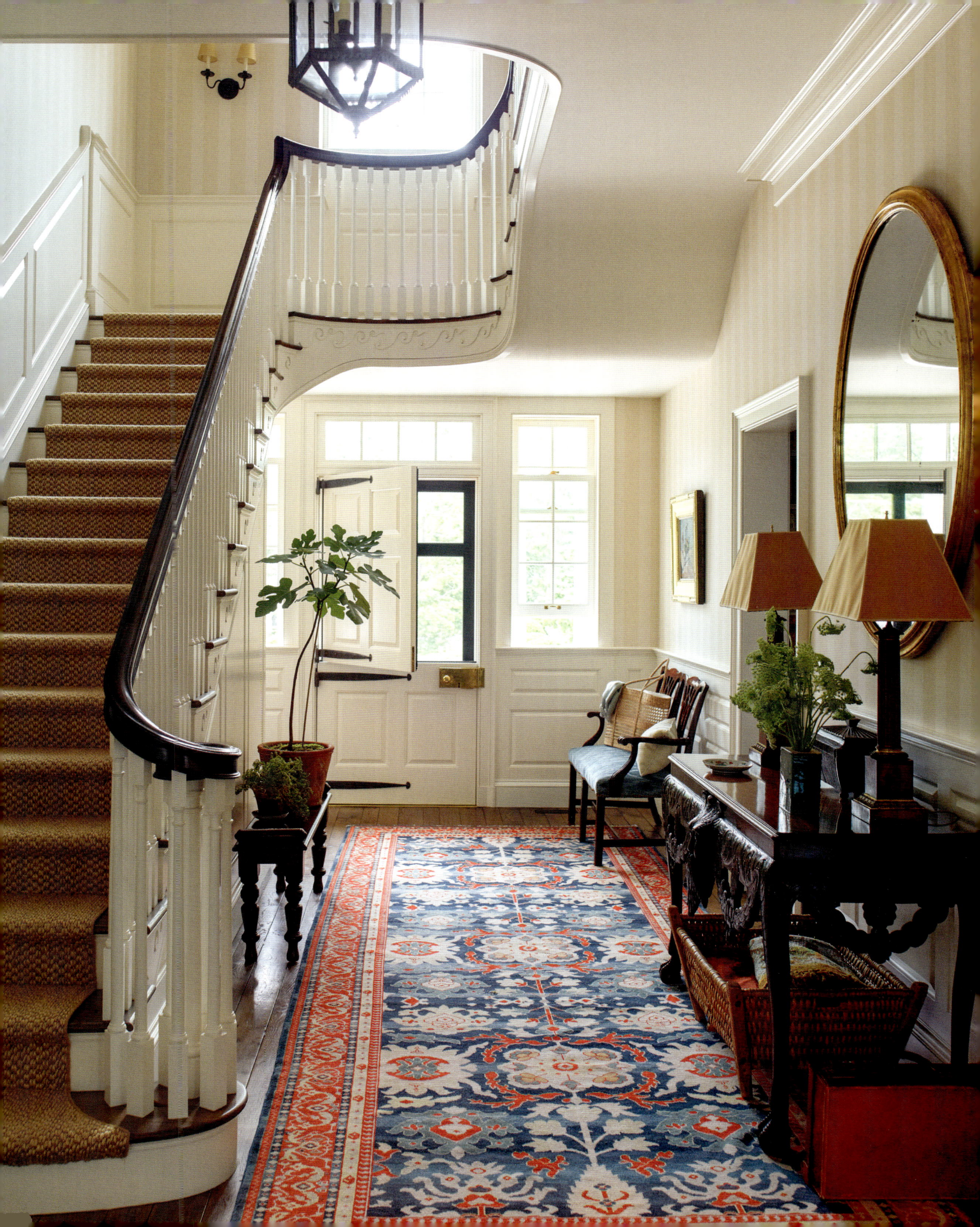

FOREWORD

I have known Libby Cameron for the greater part of my professional career as an antiques dealer.

I remember first meeting Libby back in the 1980s, while traveling with Sister Parish on our way to Boston for a lecture on decorating with antiques at the Boston Design Center. A very young and newly hired Libby was Mrs. Parish's assistant. I think it was our conversation about animals, specifically the dogs we loved, that cemented my fondness for her.

Over the next fourteen years as a designer at Parish-Hadley, Libby was a regular customer at my shop, John Rosselli Antiques and Decoration, sourcing accessories for her many projects. I was frequently intrigued by her selections, as the items she chose were often personal favorites of mine, which I had hoped to keep.

By 1995, Libby opened her eponymous design firm. Her training, passion for design, and creative abilities enabled her to hit the ground running.

Libby's success stems from her innate ability to understand her clients' personalities and lifestyle, thus creating livable interiors where comfort and function are paramount, ingredients that make a house into a home. Her creativeness, professionalism, and hard work have endeared her to both her clients and the design community.

For me personally, her devotion to her family and friends, and to her dogs, has made her a dear friend and a valued colleague.

—John Rosselli

ACKNOWLEDGMENTS

For years now I have dreamed of writing a book. I imagined that it would be a diary of stories and descriptions of what I have seen and learned. I would never have been brave enough to begin this project without the many people who have helped me and made it a reality. Thank you for your hard work, for believing in me, and for making it possible.

I want to thank Carolyn Englefield for her enthusiasm and input. She gave me the courage to begin. The direction of the book has changed since Carolyn and I first talked, and it became a different sort of reflection. I realized that instead of a coffee table book of pictures that I wanted to tell the stories of my experiences.

Howard Christian has been invaluable in steering me and believing that all of my words and pictures might actually add up to something. It was with his steady reasoning, edits, and suggestions that this book has come to be. He was able to remove the cobwebs that were in the way.

Jonathan Garguilo is a wonderful friend and has been so supportive and helpful. Thank you for your suggestions and guidance, and for your friendship over the last forty-odd years.

I have been lucky enough to have many wonderful clients who have provided me with the inspiration, fun, and challenge of making your house your home. Thank you for believing in me: I am very, very grateful.

Many, many thanks BJ Berti who has cheered me on and held my hand from the start. She is always at the end of a telephone line to answer my many questions and give me advice. So many thanks to Madge Baird and Jennifer Adams at Gibbs Smith for all their patience, hard work, and knowledge. And to Rita Sowins who has arranged and placed all of the pictures so well.

Thank you to the magazine editors over the years—Lou Gropp, Peggy Kennedy, Carolyn Sollis, Carolyn Englefield, Doretta Sperduto, Mitch Owens, Dara Caponigro, Clint Smith, Newell Turner, Barbara Plumb, Stephen Drucker—who commissioned stories on some of the projects I have worked on, and to the others who have featured my work, even if in some small way.

Thank you to all of the talented photographers who contributed to this book and for documenting so much of what I love.

I want to thank Neil Forster for so much of his time and for his infinite patience. I am eternally grateful for being bailed out over and over. When I honestly thought chapters and photographs had disappeared forever, he found them and brought me back from the brink several times.

Many, many thanks to Maggie McDonald for guiding me through the digital world and social media. You always have and always do make it seem effortless.

Elizabeth Flores is and always has been there for us all—I am so grateful for all that you do.

I want to thank my children: Flora for her thoughts and edits on the almost complete chapters and for her sage advice, and Charlotte and Bean, who have been so supportive and believed in this project form the start. I hope that my career has never gotten in your way, and that I have been able to show you that dreams can come true.

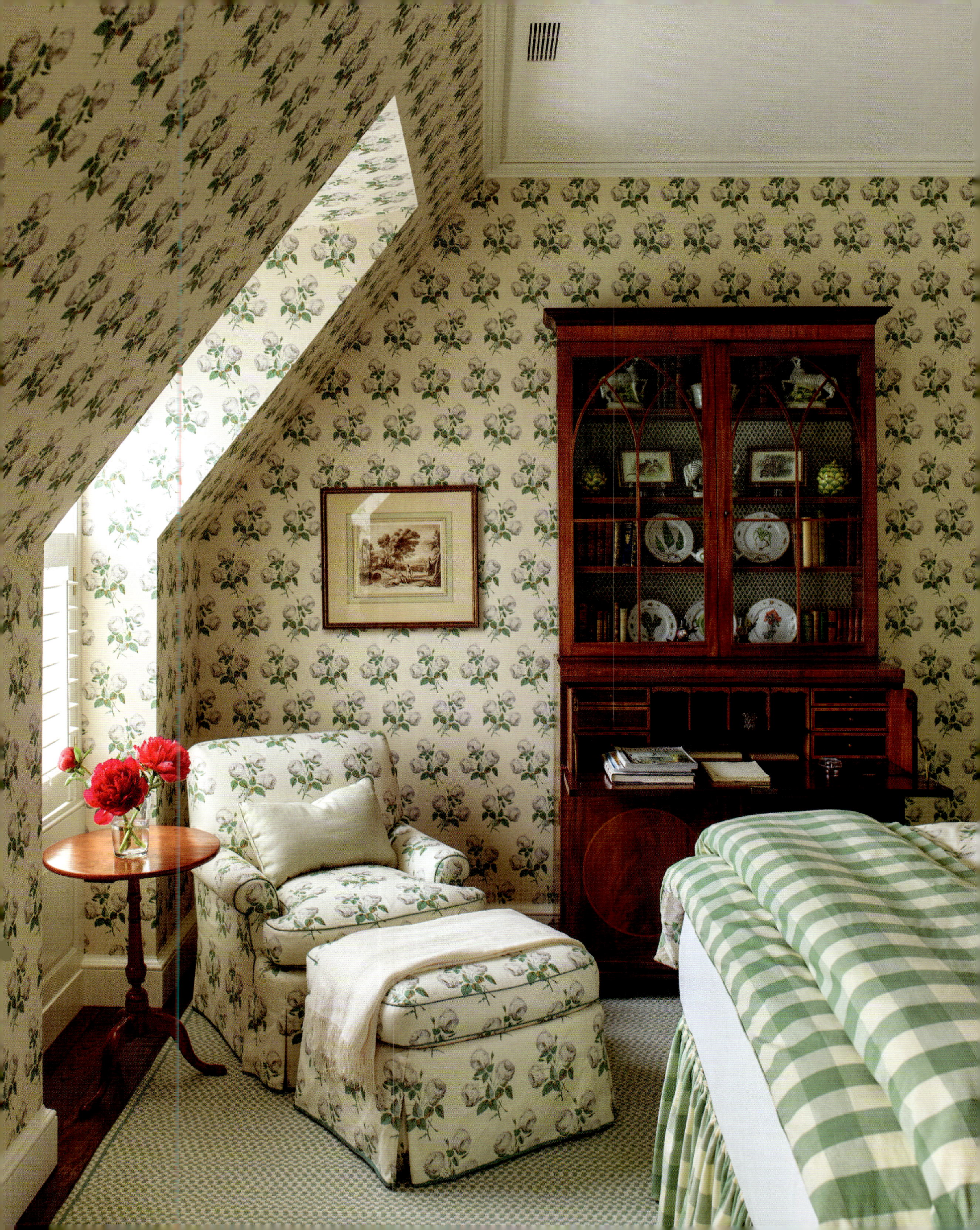

INTRODUCTION

Everyone's life is a story unto itself, and I feel so incredibly lucky to have had the life that I have had. I suppose that is what this book is: a memoir of a well-lived and full life. I have tried to step back and look at all of my life experiences up to this point to understand what has led me to where I am today. Many people have helped me get where I am. My grandfather always told me that we all need to be inspired in life, so to figure out what holds your interest and do what you love. My father always told me to follow my instincts and be brave. I have taken from each of them, and others, and that has enabled me to pursue what matters most to me.

Decorating houses for people can be your whole life, and your relationship with your clients is essential. Helping a client to find joy and comfort in their space is what I love the most about what I do. For me, it's not about wealth or fame or material things but about the thrill of working with people and the satisfaction that work can bring. I spend a great deal of time with my clients—I travel with them and get to know them very well. It is so important to have a good relationship with them, and trust is really the biggest part. People have to trust you—trust your judgment, your taste, and your sense of discretion. You also have to be transparent, and I have learned to wear my heart on my sleeve. We all are from such different places, but we come together with the goal of creating a suitable, comfortable, and comforting space in which to live.

The journey has been wonderful—and at times daunting—but I have landed on my feet. I've worked hard, and my work has given me purpose and meaning. To me that is a well-lived life. I'm extremely close to my three wonderful children and, as of now, four grandchildren. I have always prioritized what I believe matters most: simply enjoying life and what is around me by living in the moment. I've tried to instill the wonder and marvel of an ordinary life in my children, to show and teach them about the simple joys: the sound of a bird, the color of the leaves in autumn, the cat's whisker shape of a new moon, or the taste of summer tomatoes and corn. We cry together when pets and people die and find infinite comfort in something as simple as the touch of a hand. My children and my animals have kept me grounded and attuned to what is real and to what matters most. I believe life is about making the ordinary feel exciting and come alive, and something as simple as recovering a chair or moving furniture around in a room can be revitalizing. The extraordinary will take care of itself.

Our society and culture puts such an emphasis on striving to have an extraordinary life, filled with power and success. Many people find the extraordinary lives of others to be a source of much admiration, but in many ways, this compels us to justify our existence in the world and can lead to ignoring what matters most. If you work too hard, you can end up sacrificing playfulness and the joy that can be found around every corner.

I try to remember to live authentically and to enjoy every moment. As E. B. White wrote, "Hang on to your hat. Hang on to your hope. And wind the clock, for tomorrow is another day."

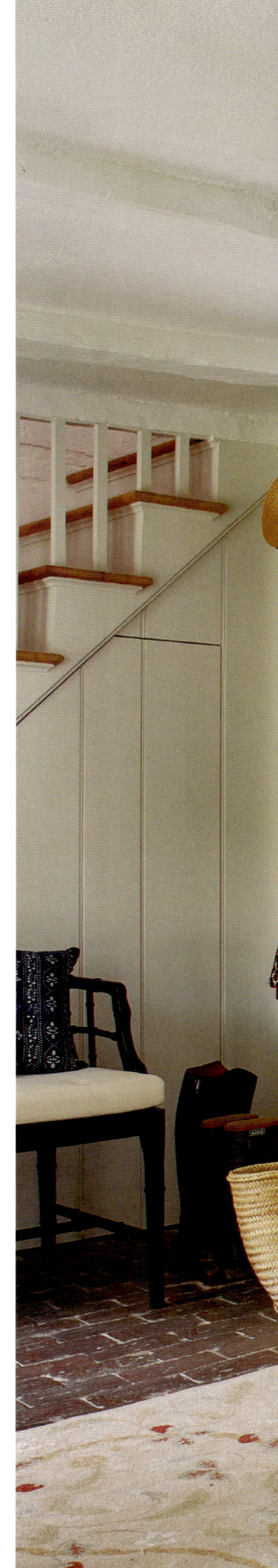

This front hall is in one of the oldest farmhouses in Greenwich and still retains its original wood siding, hardware, beams, and brick floor. The hatstand is from Meg Braff Designs; the demilune bone inlay table is from John Rosselli; the rug was made by Elizabeth Eakins.

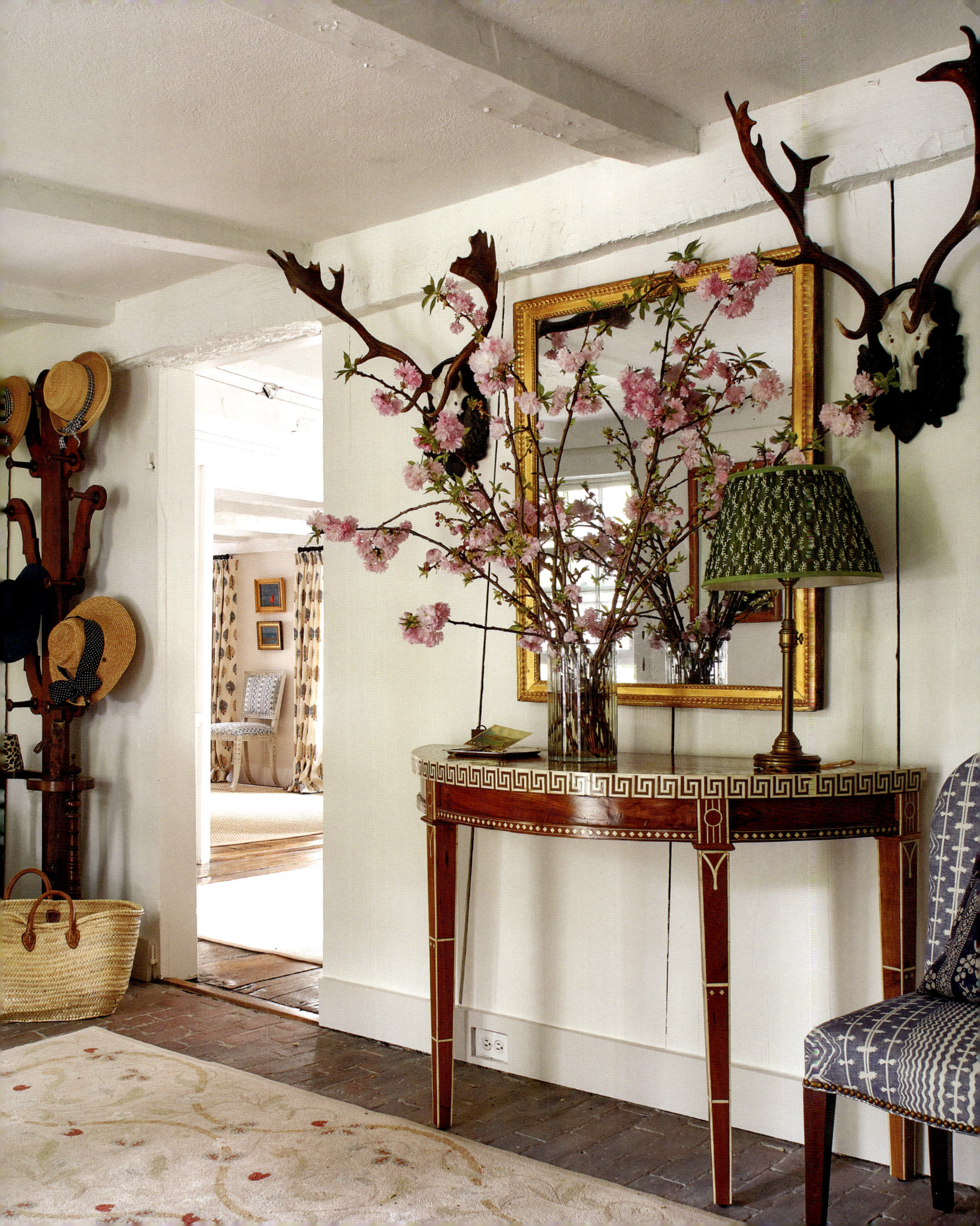

PARISH—

HADLEY

"I am lucky enough to have always lived in beautiful houses, and I suppose I grew up assuming that all houses are beautiful."

—LIBBY CAMERON

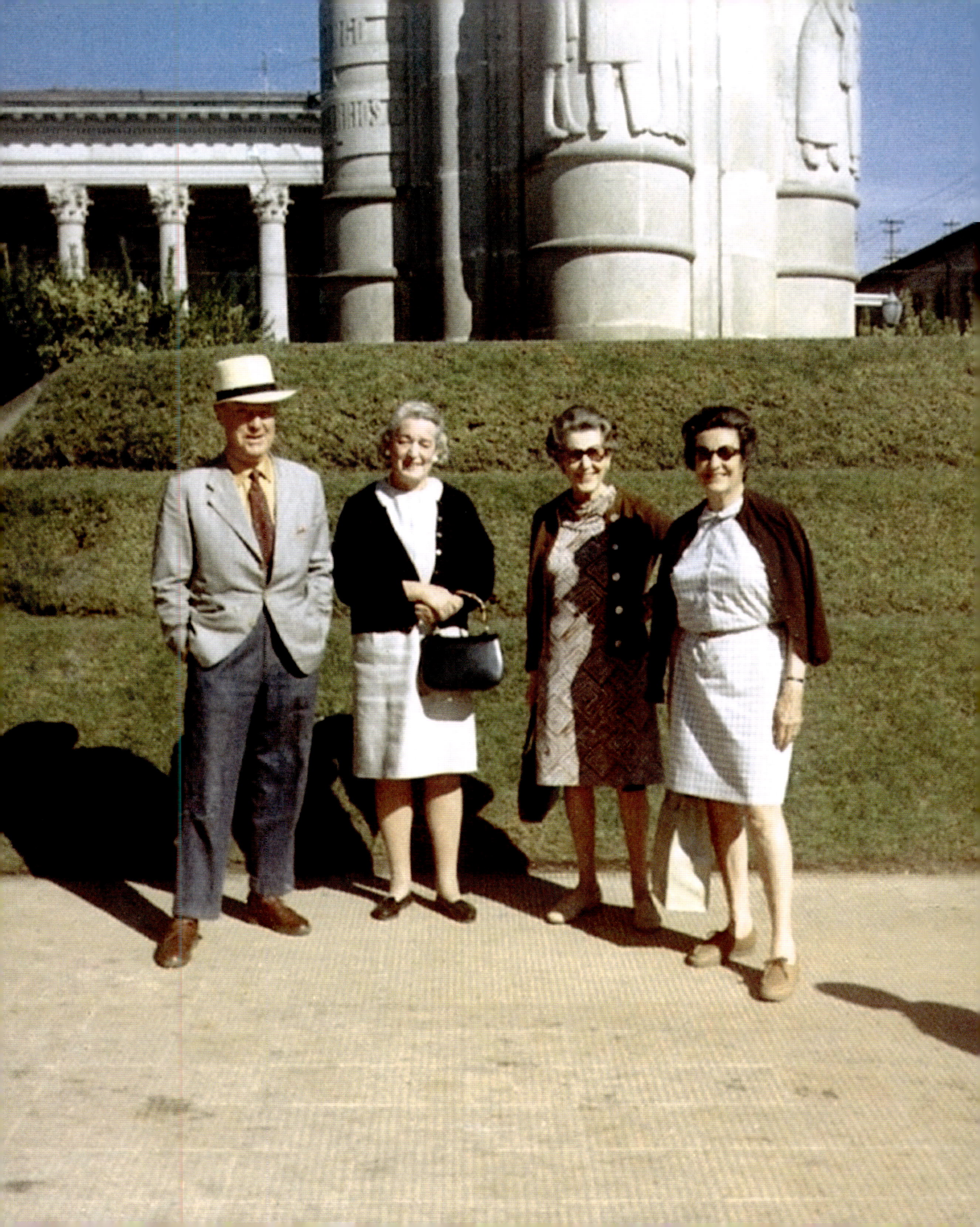

I am lucky enough to have always lived in beautiful houses, and I suppose I grew up assuming that all houses are beautiful. Although that is not always the case, it certainly can be, and it is wonderful to help people make their house into a home.

I never expected to work in the world of interior design or to have had the experience of working as a decorator for so many years. A slightly circuitous path led me to an internship at Parish-Hadley. It was absolutely the most wonderful experience on every level and it was a magical time in my life.

I knew of Mrs. Parish long before I met her. Sister Parish was a name that I had always heard growing up. I wondered about the name "Sister," but Granny had a few friends with unusual names like that: Boysie, Girlsie, Mac, Hillsy, Avis, and Fadden. Mrs. Parish was called "Sister" because her brothers called her that, not because she had ever wanted to be a nun.

My grandparents, and my grandmother's sister and her husband, were friends with Mrs. Parish. Parish-Hadley decorated my great-aunt's house on Coolidge Point on the North Shore of Massachusetts, as well as my grandparents' houses in Washington, DC, and Maine. My great-uncle, Jeff Coolidge, had an importing company based in Central America, so they all traveled there together. Mrs. Parish loved the textiles and weaving from that part of the world and was always on the hunt for new and beautiful things.

I grew up for the most part in Washington, DC, and spent summers in Maine, which was the best of all worlds—a perfect balance. Washington, DC, is terribly hot and humid in the summer, so it was wonderful to be able to go somewhere cool, to be on the water and have the freedom of Maine as a child. I love the sound and smell of water, and to this day, I still love to be near any body of water.

I come from a family of animal lovers. My father had the biggest soft spot for animals. I saw him cry for the first time as a child when he accidentally hit a mother porcupine in

Maine; her baby was nearby watching. He had a big heart and although he had a sometimes gruff, aloof exterior, when it came to animals he would always melt.

Animals have always been a huge part of my life and there have been many. We always had at least three dogs, a cat or two, many guinea pigs, mice, rabbits, and birds in our house. I had a naughty gray pony called Noodles, who would without fail immediately go down onto his knees when crossing a stream—with his saddle on and me in it—and roll with utter joy. Noodles would take off toward any lake or pond when we were close enough for him to smell it—clearly he loved the water as much as I did. At one point, I even had a pet pig named Annabel Lee. My sister saw a sign for "Piglets" while driving in Maine so, of course, being animal obsessed like I was, she got one and brought her to me. The piglet had red hair and was so adorable. She slept in my room at the foot of my bed. Her little pointed hooves looked like four tiny high-heeled shoes. She hopped, jumped, and twirled about like a baby goat does, dancing as she followed me around. By the end of the summer, she weighed sixty pounds and I was firmly told that she could not go back to Washington, DC, with us. She stayed in Maine with Arlene Brown, the milk lady, who had a small farm and was as besotted with Annabel Lee as I was. I had mice when I was little that ran up and down the piano keys while I practiced—perhaps that it why I never mastered the piano. We also had a mynah bird, who simply appeared one day flying in through my bedroom window. He stayed with us for a few years. He would imitate the sound of the telephone ringing, which drove my mother absolutely crazy.

Each summer, at the beginning of June, my mother, my two brothers, my sister, our nanny, Tatie, and I would all (quite literally) wedge into our yellow, wood-paneled Ford station wagon along with all of the animals. We left Washington, DC, for the summer with the menagerie in tow, each of us riding without a seat belt (no one wore seat belts in those days) and drove north. My father would come up to Maine on the weekends and would take us out on his boat. We would sail to nearby harbors for overnights, which I loved to do.

The first stop on the way to Maine was always my great-aunt Katherine Coolidge's house in Manchester-by-the-Sea on the North Shore of Boston. We would stay at the "farmhouse," a simple white clapboard house on Coolidge Point for a week or so and then drive on to Maine where we stayed until Labor Day. When the nights started to get colder

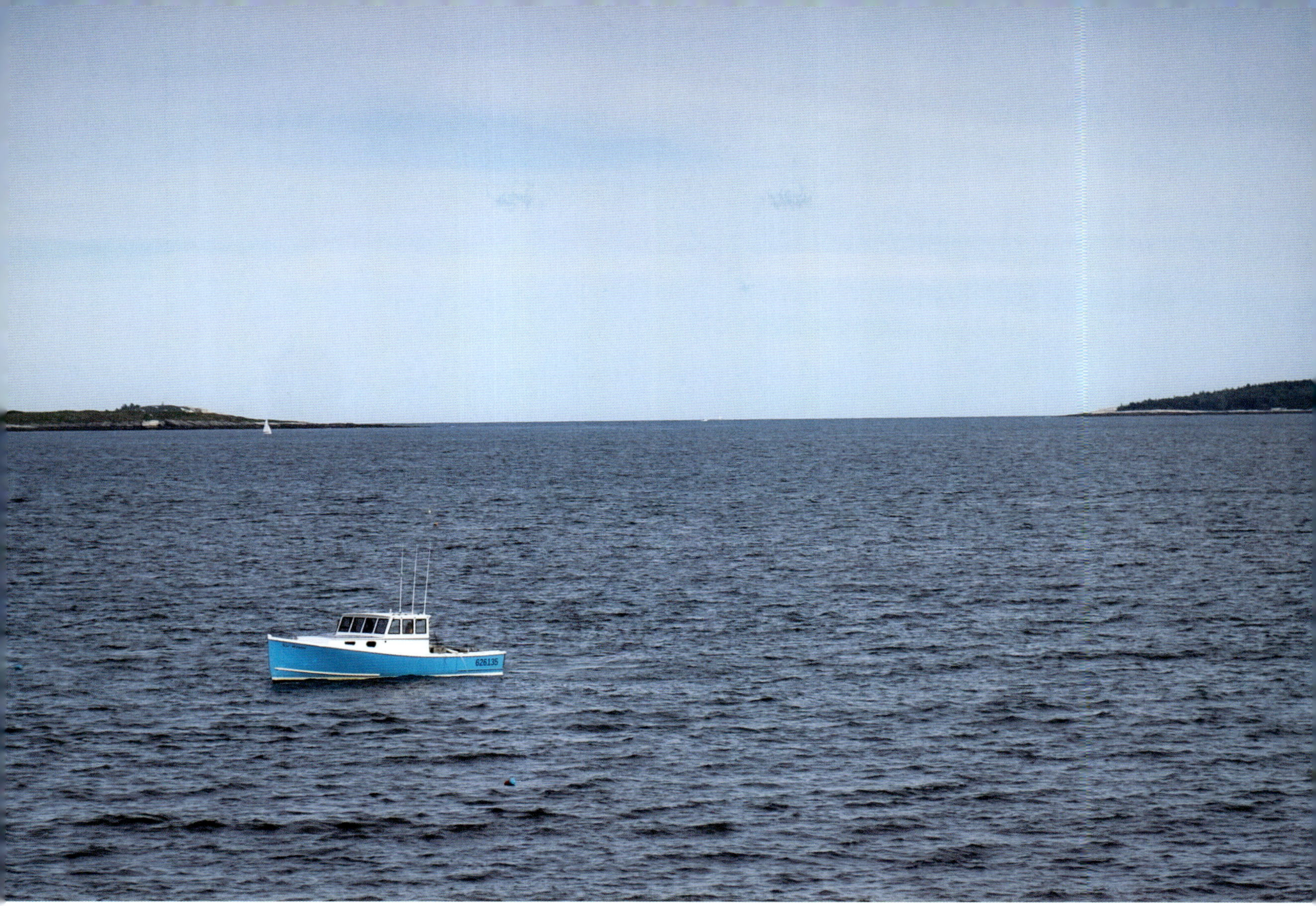

PREVIOUS PAGE: From left to right: My grandfather Bob Hooker, Sister Parish, Katherine Coolidge, my grandmother Dolly Hooker. Antigua, Guatemala, 1967.

ABOVE: The view from the house in Newagen facing east with Fisherman's Island beyond. The lobstermen put out their lobster pots in front of the house in Newagen and usually come early in the morning to check their traps.

RIGHT: My redheaded piglet, Annabel Lee, in Maine.

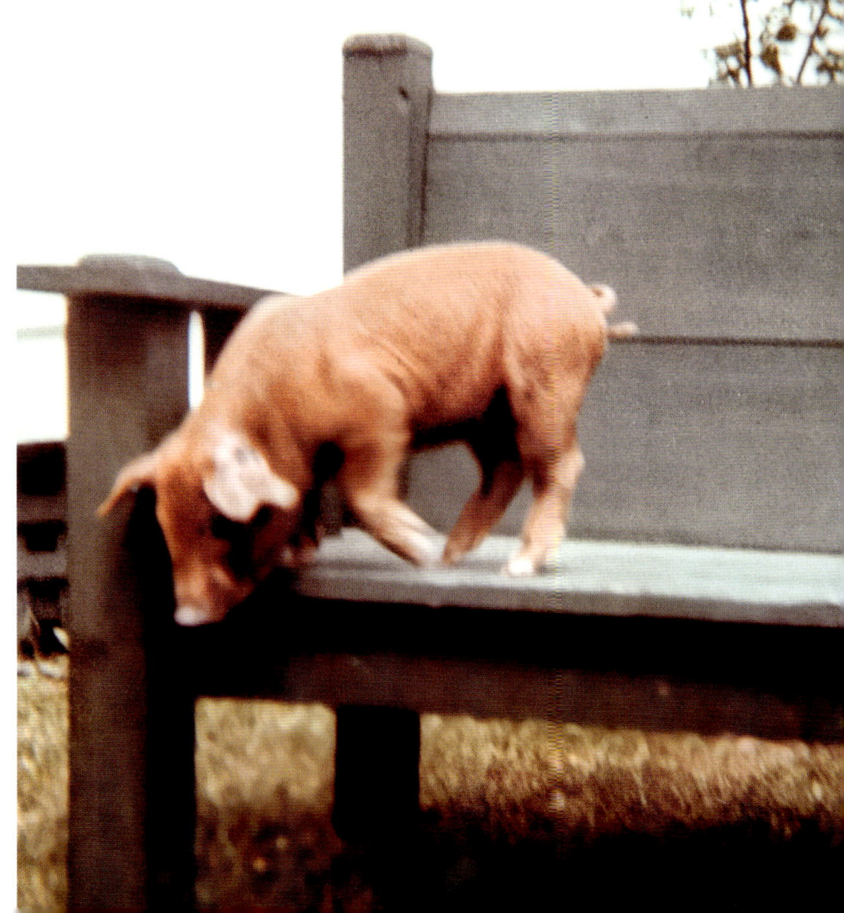

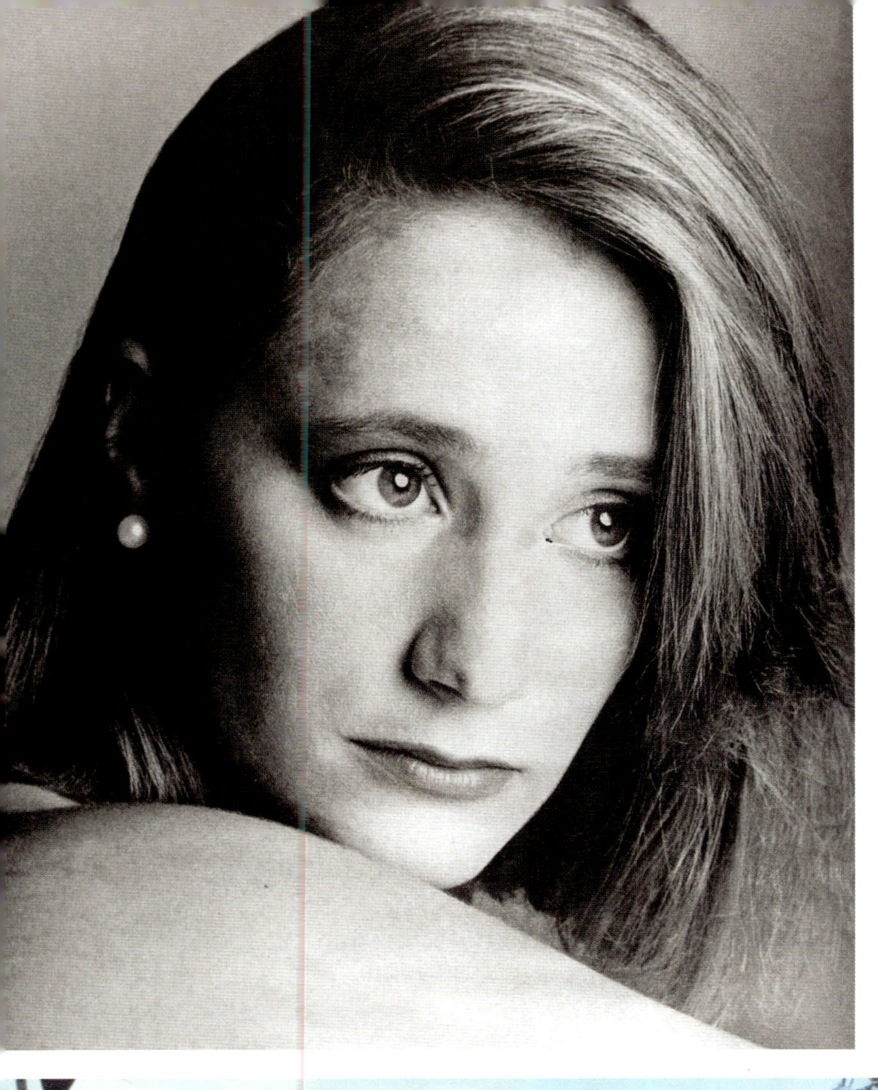

LEFT: This photo of me was taken for *Interview Magazine* in 1985.

BELOW: Rory Cameron at his house, Les Quatres Sources, in Ménerbes, France, in 1984.

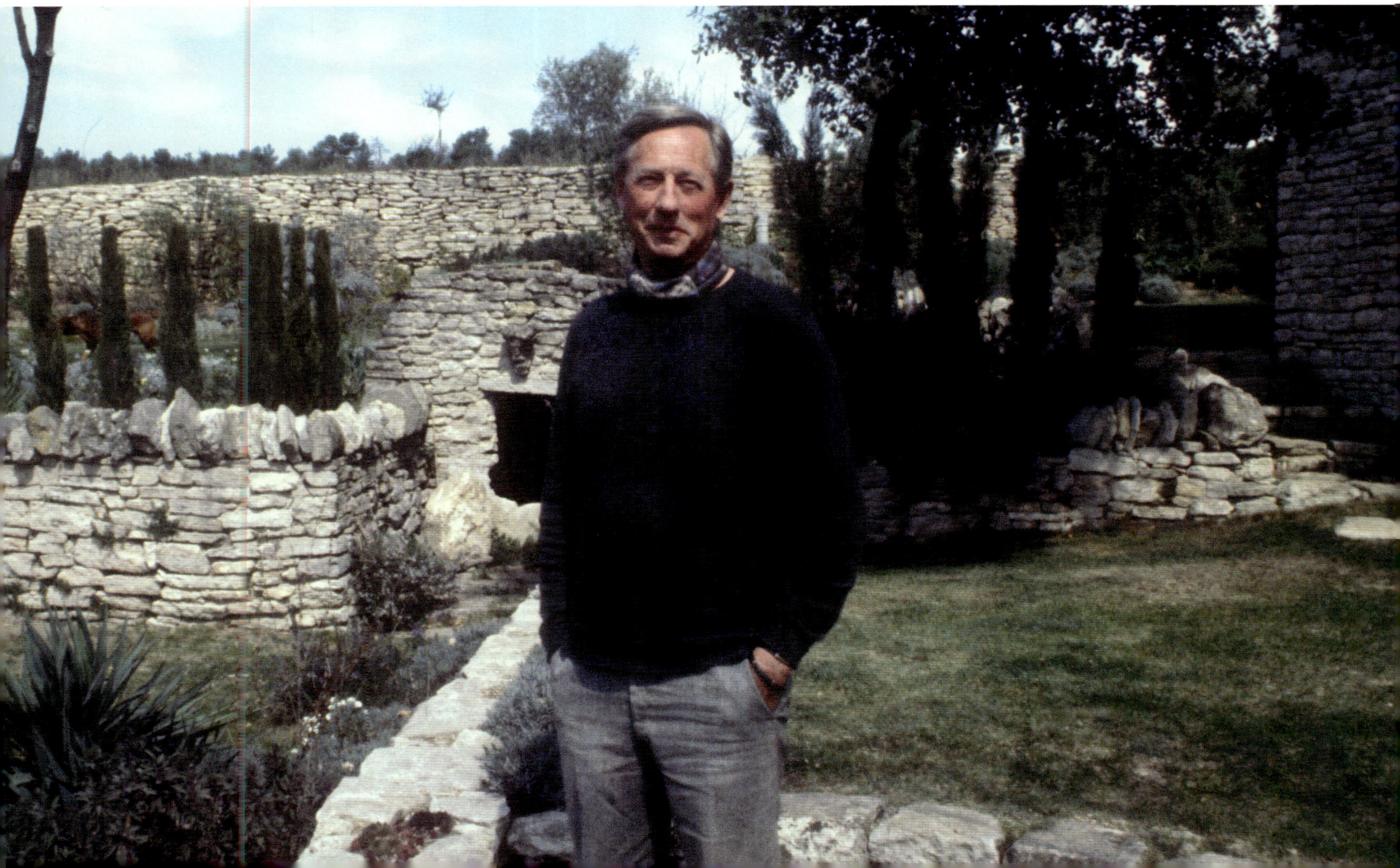

in August and the leaves just started to turn, my heart would sink knowing it was about time to leave and return to school.

I was convinced growing up that I wanted to be a veterinarian but science and medicine didn't come easily enough to me to make that my career. I still can remember the periodic table poster that was on the wall of my fourth-grade science classroom showing the abbreviations for the elements. That chemical chart never sank in—it always just looked like a jumble of letters, a blur, a language I couldn't learn.

During vacations and on weekends, I worked at veterinary hospitals and volunteered at the Washington National Zoo. Just after high school, I spent four months working at the Jersey Wildlife Preservation Trust, Gerald Durrell's zoo for endangered species on Jersey, one of the beautiful Channel Islands off the coast of France. It was a small and quite rustic zoo in those days. I was assigned to feed and take care of the tapirs, wallabies, and lemur monkeys, along with a variety of birds. There was a young and adorable striped baby tapir at the zoo when I first arrived who followed me everywhere, and a crowned pigeon who would run up to me, stop suddenly, and nod his head up and down while making a drumming sound. We became quite attached. Many mornings, I would head off at the crack of dawn with Martin, a native of Jersey and one of the longtime keepers at the zoo. We would drive in his van to pick up animals at neighboring farms that had just died, for whatever reason, and bring them back to the zoo to be fed to the larger cats and birds. It was necessary and critical for the survival of the carnivorous animals that lived in a zoo on an island where they could not kill what they needed to eat. I hated that part of working there, but it did help me to respect and understand the animal world in a way that I hadn't before.

There were two baby lowland gorillas who were amazingly smart and so fun to work with. They would play for hours and were fascinated with my work boots and shoelaces. They had long fingers and were quite dexterous; they figured out how to untie and then tie the shoelaces back up again albeit with a somewhat sloppy knot. I was in their enclosure with them one afternoon when a visiting family's child threw something in our direction, and those babies went crazy—climbing and chasing up and around and over the top of the cage, screaming and baring their teeth. They were obviously terrified. Those young gorillas probably weighed seventy pounds each. They climbed to the top of the cage and dropped down onto me again and again. It was not only very dangerous but also very scary. It took a while before peace and calm were restored. I was very lucky to have not been bitten or hurt during their frenzy. It was at that moment that I had a slight change of heart about spending my life working with wild animals. Nonetheless, my house is still somewhat of a zoo with my many Labrador retrievers.

I moved to New York City in 1981. Like any young person moving to New York right after college, the possibilities seemed endless.

My first job was working for a catering company owned by Donald Bruce White, organizing parties. I then went to work in the development office at the Central Park Conservancy to help with fundraising. It turns out asking for money is not one of my strengths. Neither job captivated me, and I was becoming quite discouraged. Shortly thereafter, I got married and realized how much I wanted a career and to find something that I really loved to do—something that was all my own before having children. Nothing I had tried seemed right or viable and I was at a loss.

I asked for life advice from my cousin, Rory Cameron, whom I was very close to. Uncle Rory (as I affectionately called him) was a bon vivant and the kindest man on earth. He was renowned for his beautiful houses. He lived in the south of France, and at one point had a house at the northern tip of Ireland in Donegal, where I was able to spend a summer with him. Rory came to New York often so I was able to spend time with him. He immediately took me under his wing and was so supportive and helpful. Rory had an enormous influence on me and really was the one who drew me into the world of design. I could not help but be influenced by his beautiful houses and his love of every facet of design. I remember a lunch that we had at an Indian restaurant at the top of the building next to the Paris Theater, next door to Bergdorf Goodman's. Kenneth Jay Lane, the creator of "Fabulous Fakes" jewelry joined us, and during that lunch we dreamed, schemed, and plotted my future. Rory and Kenny encouraged me to call Parish-Hadley and ask if I could meet with Mrs. Parish. It seemed to me like a leap of faith but I have always been brave when necessary. Rory said to wear a navy blue dress (not black) that came just to the knee in length. He said, "Soi-même": be your own self. Kenny Lane said I should wear a strand of pearls and simple kitten heels. After much discussion and laughter, I got up the nerve to call Parish-Hadley and ask if I could come and see Mrs. Parish. I was invited to tea.

When the appointed day arrived, I walked into this very beautiful office that had so much energy, and I was taken in at once. The walls were covered in overlapping squares of

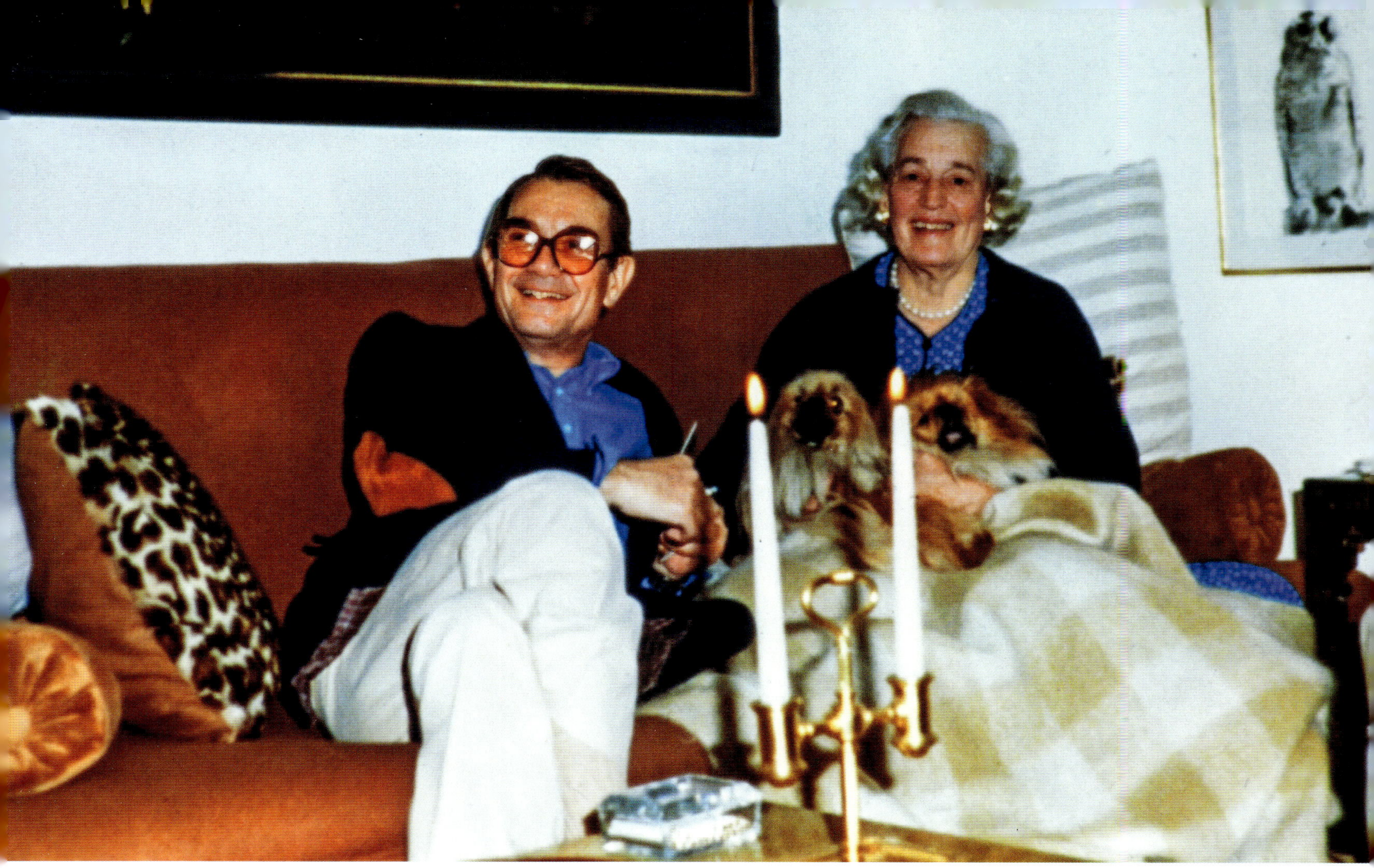

ABOVE: Albert Hadley and Sister Parish at Albert's house, Fort William, in Pocantico Hills, circa 1988, with Mrs. Parish's Pekingese dogs Nanny and Ricky.

RIGHT: Albert Hadley in his apartment's red hall. The texture of these walls was wonderful—they felt like corrugated cardboard that had been painted a shiny red.

FAR RIGHT: Albert Hadley and Sister Parish in front of their offices on East 69th Street.

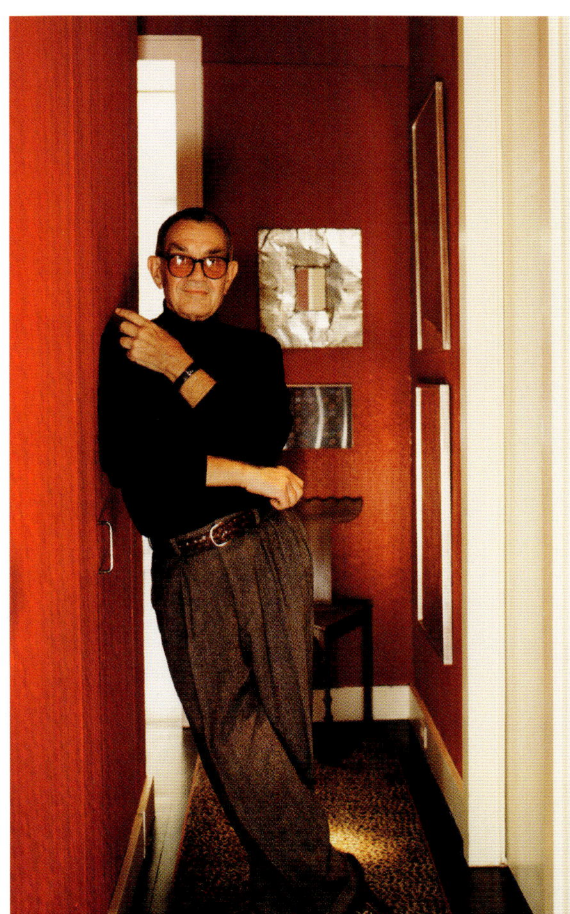

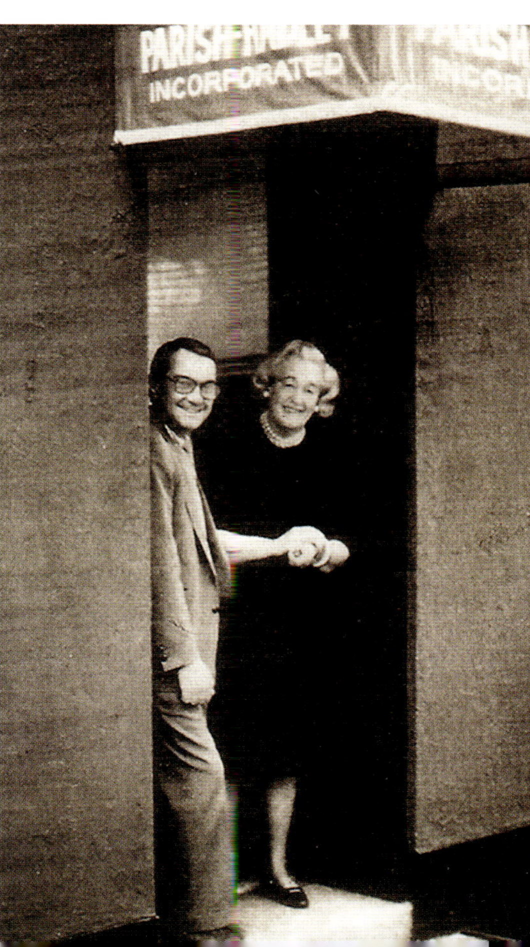

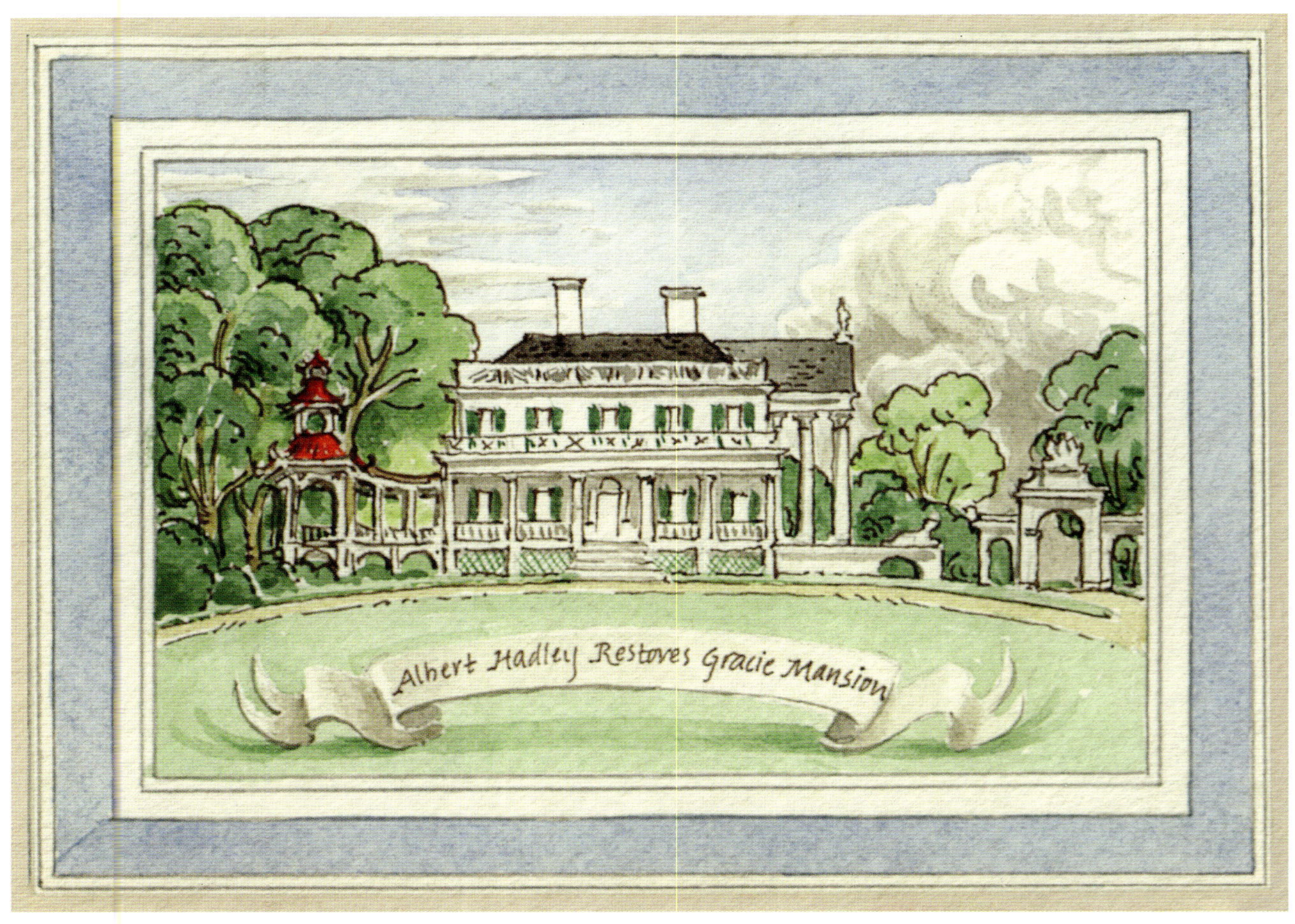

A watercolor of Gracie Mansion, painted and given to Albert Hadley by Mark Hampton in 1984.

silver tea paper. There were two incredibly comfortable upholstered chairs to sit on. There was a lovely, gilded mirror over a fireplace. I remember noticing how pretty the cream-and-gilt desk lamp on the receptionist's desk was. I don't know what I had expected, but something sparked in me. I loved the feel of the office and how pretty it was. I knew at that moment that this was it: I wanted to work there. At that point in my life, I knew absolutely nothing about interior decorating.

Mrs. Parish, as formidable a woman as she was, was always very kind and good to me. She had asked Mr. Hadley to join us that afternoon. I had not met him before. He was very gentle and kind and had many helpful ideas and suggestions. He told me that I should go to Parsons or to the Fashion Institute of Technology, and to visit every museum I possibly could. They hedged about any sort of work prospects and made it very clear that they did not hire the children of their clients. I had hoped a door would open for me and that a job would suddenly be there. I was crestfallen.

I met Uncle Rory later that day to tell him all about the meeting. He convinced me not to give up, told me to "keep at it," and suggested I call Parish-Hadley often to volunteer or help in any way possible just to get my foot in the door. I enrolled in some beginning level interior design courses at Parsons and called every week or so hoping that something might change. I think they were pretty sick and tired of me and my persistence, but it paid off. A call finally came. Would I be available to help with an apartment being installed and be at the apartment to accept deliveries every day? Needless to say, I jumped at the offer. What an experience that was watching that job on Beekman Place come together, and to see how it all really worked and what an installation entailed.

The apartment was in the final stages of being done; craftsmen were glazing walls, installing wallpaper, putting down carpeting, putting up lights, and hanging curtains before the furniture arrived. I was in heaven. I spent every day there for a month or so. Each day was different and it was so exciting to experience it all firsthand. The workmen were all very nice and interesting to talk to, and they were very patient with me. I asked a million questions, and they explained how they did what they did. I loved watching them work and seeing a room being glazed. I still do.

Pete from Weidl Painting glazed the living room walls. He knew absolutely everything about color and how to mix paint and texture surfaces. He used little blue cans of Japan paint that he would scoop out in small amounts with a plastic coffee spoon from a

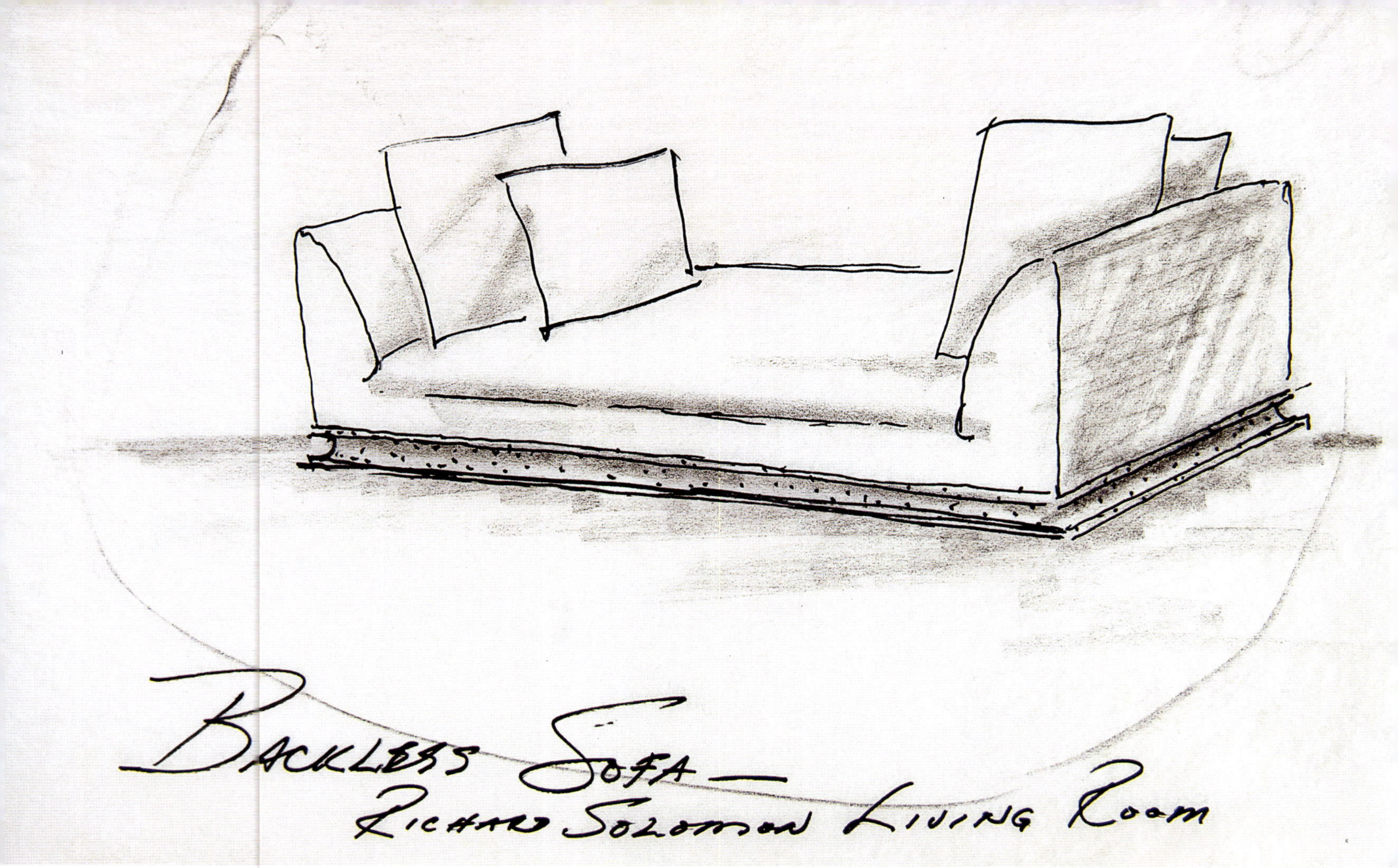

BACKLESS SOFA —
RICHARD SOLOMON LIVING ROOM

ABOVE: One of the many sketches Albert Hadley did for furniture he wanted made for clients.

RIGHT: Albert's sketch for an upholstered door. The detail shows the spacing of the nailhead bordered edge.

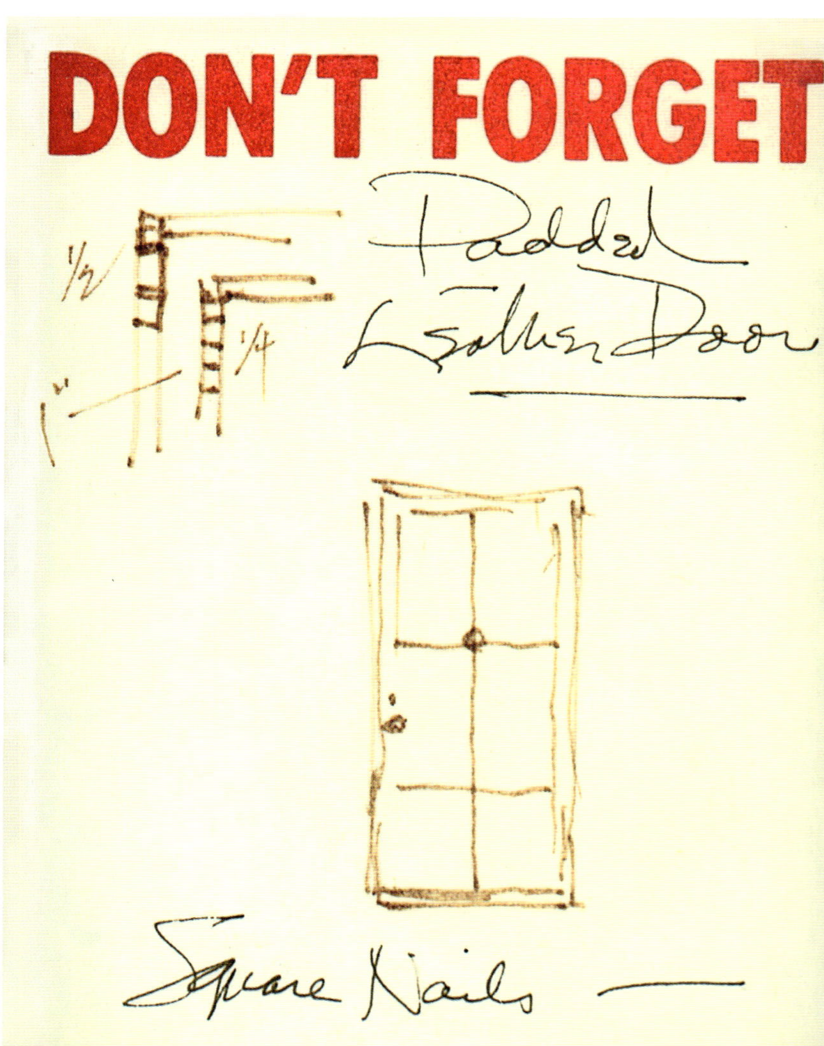

deli or with a painting knife. Then he would add the color to a glazing compound in a clean pot along with paint thinner and linseed oil to make a glaze, stirring in both directions over and over again to make sure that the color was completely mixed in. Pete could create the most beautiful colors and finishes on top of a mirror-smooth base color. He would use many different techniques—a stipple, a mottle or striae, a crosshatch with different sized brushes, sponges, rags, and steel wool. I have never been able to get the same level of quality and depth on my own that he did, but it still fascinates me to watch the process.

Six weeks later, after that apartment was done, I was offered a full-time job at Parish-Hadley, and I was absolutely over the moon. I started out in an office that was a converted closet. There were two small closets across from the sample room that were made into "offices" for Brian McCarthy and me. The desks were just about twenty-eight inches wide, and there was a small single drawer underneath. The desktop was on one side of the deep closet and there were upper shelves on the other side with a filing cabinet below. There wasn't enough space to have a door, so everything that went on in the office was right in front of us.

I was hired to be Albert Hadley's assistant for his newest project, the restoration of Gracie Mansion. Ed Koch was the mayor of New York City. Mr. Hadley had been asked to work on the original Gracie Mansion where Mayor Koch's private living quarters were. There was a different attached wing that was used for parties and events, and Mark Hampton was redecorating that portion of Gracie Mansion at the same time.

The restoration committee for Gracie Mansion had received several donations for the house: a lovely Zuber wallpaper for the dining room, "Les Jardins Francais," a handsome Duncan Phyfe settee for the living room, and a pretty set of antique American bamboo bedroom furniture. Mayor Koch was very tall and the bed was far too short to use as his own. Instead, a bed with an upholstered headboard was made for his room and the guest room got the bamboo furniture. The history of the original house—its architecture and furniture—was the starting point and set an appropriate direction.

We had meetings for the project very early in the morning before Mayor Koch had to leave for City Hall. He was quite funny, very jolly and friendly, but not particularly interested in the redesign of his house. And he certainly did not have to be—the decorating committee made all of the final decisions.

Working with Albert Hadley was the most extraordinary education I could ever have hoped for. He was the best teacher—patient, engaging, and always curious to hear others' opinions. He was humble and kind, a true Southern gentleman. Albert would walk me through a floor plan and say what he thought each room might look like, how the curtains might fall, and how the furniture should be arranged. I still have the curtain sketches he did for the rooms at Gracie Mansion.

This was all so new to me and it was a very different language to learn. I didn't know what a gimp or porphyry was, but I learned in no time. From the very first moment, it was exciting and challenging; each day was different and at times quite daunting.

At the end of the day, many of us would stay late just to have time with Mr. Hadley in a more relaxed setting. He asked that we call him Albert. But Mrs. Parish was always called Mrs. Parish. Without the phones ringing and constantly being interrupted, we would go over projects and discuss rooms. It was the best part of my day. Floor plans were drawn and reviewed in depth for every job. Albert used rolls of yellow trace paper, sketch pads, pencils, and black felt tip pens. He would transform two-dimensional floor plans into beautiful renderings of rooms. He sketched with ease and expressed his thinking through his drawings. Many mornings I would arrive to find a lovely pencil-and-ink rendering or watercolor on my desk that he had done overnight based on our conversation from the evening before. I have so many of his drawings on the little Don't Forget pads of paper that were all over the office. What worked, what was appropriate, what made a space better with everything functioning properly was always discussed at length and in depth. We discussed the logical order of a space: a front and a back, a top and a bottom, an important place and a less important place. All these things were taken into consideration when creating a design. Albert always stressed the importance of architecture, balance, and proportion. How a house worked and flowed was paramount. Coat closets, linen closets, slop sinks, and broom closets were also essential to every project.

Albert had an incredible ability to listen and to edit. He could distill all of the ideas and information, and then express them visually with such clarity. What was appropriate was always an overriding concern. He employed an unspoken rule of mixing things up—both old and new, the important with the less important pieces—which really is what the Parish-Hadley sensibility was all about. Parish-Hadley was a place where everything was made better, with everything working properly. The importance of architecture, balance, and proportion was always paramount.

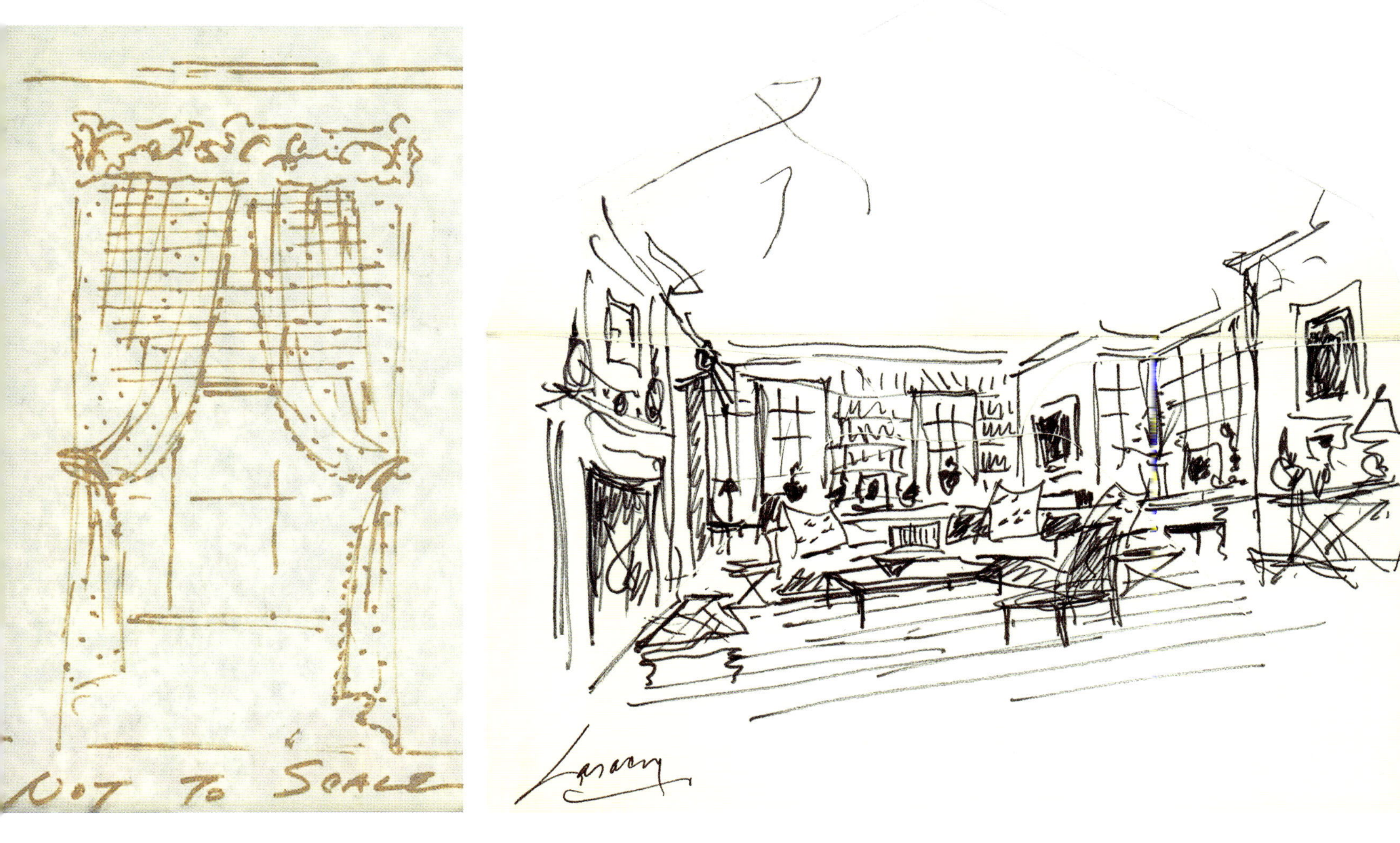

ABOVE LEFT: A sketch by Albert Hadley of his idea for curtains at Gracie Mansion.

ABOVE RIGHT: A quick sketch by Albert Hadley to suggest what a living room would look like.

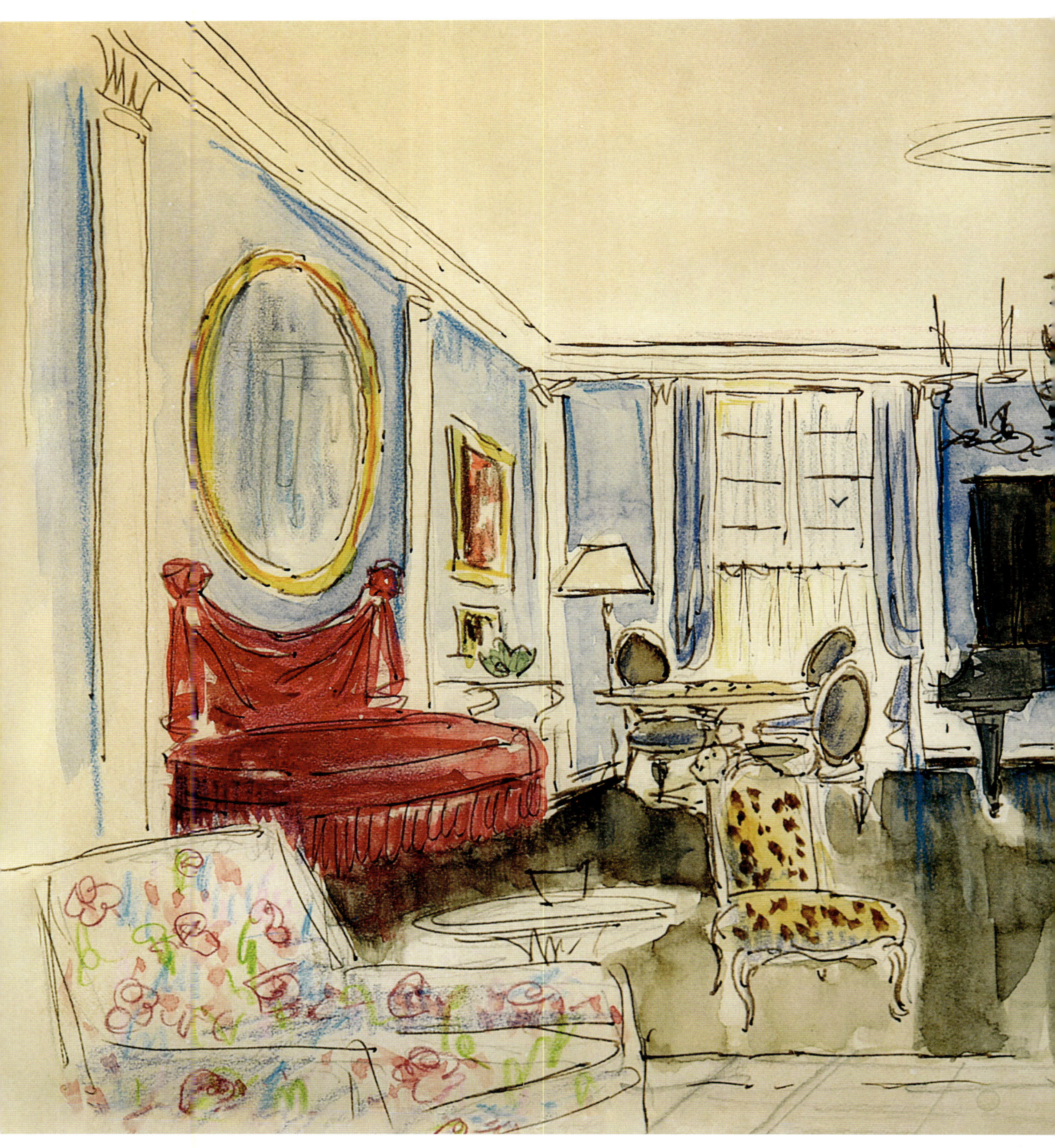

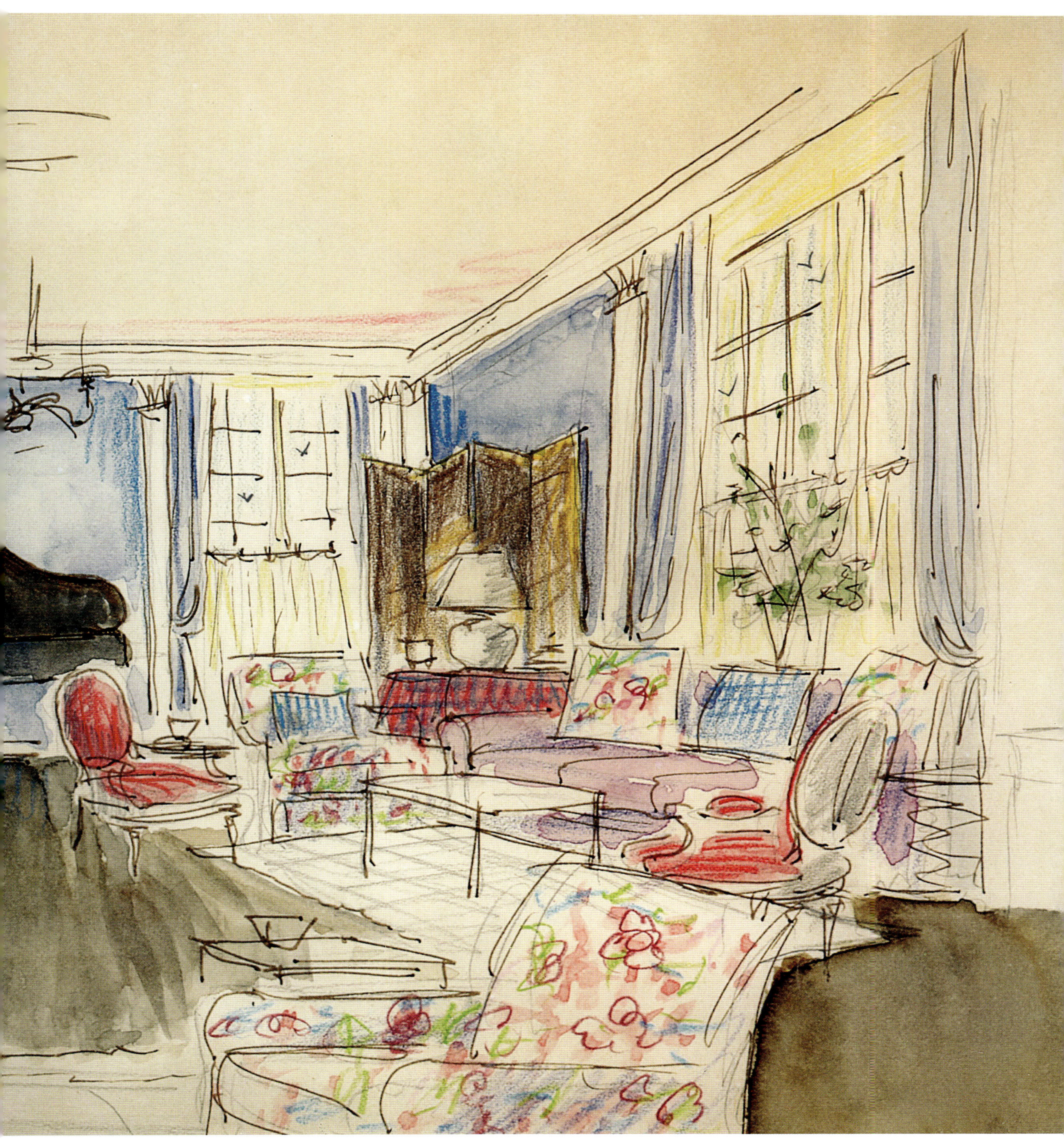

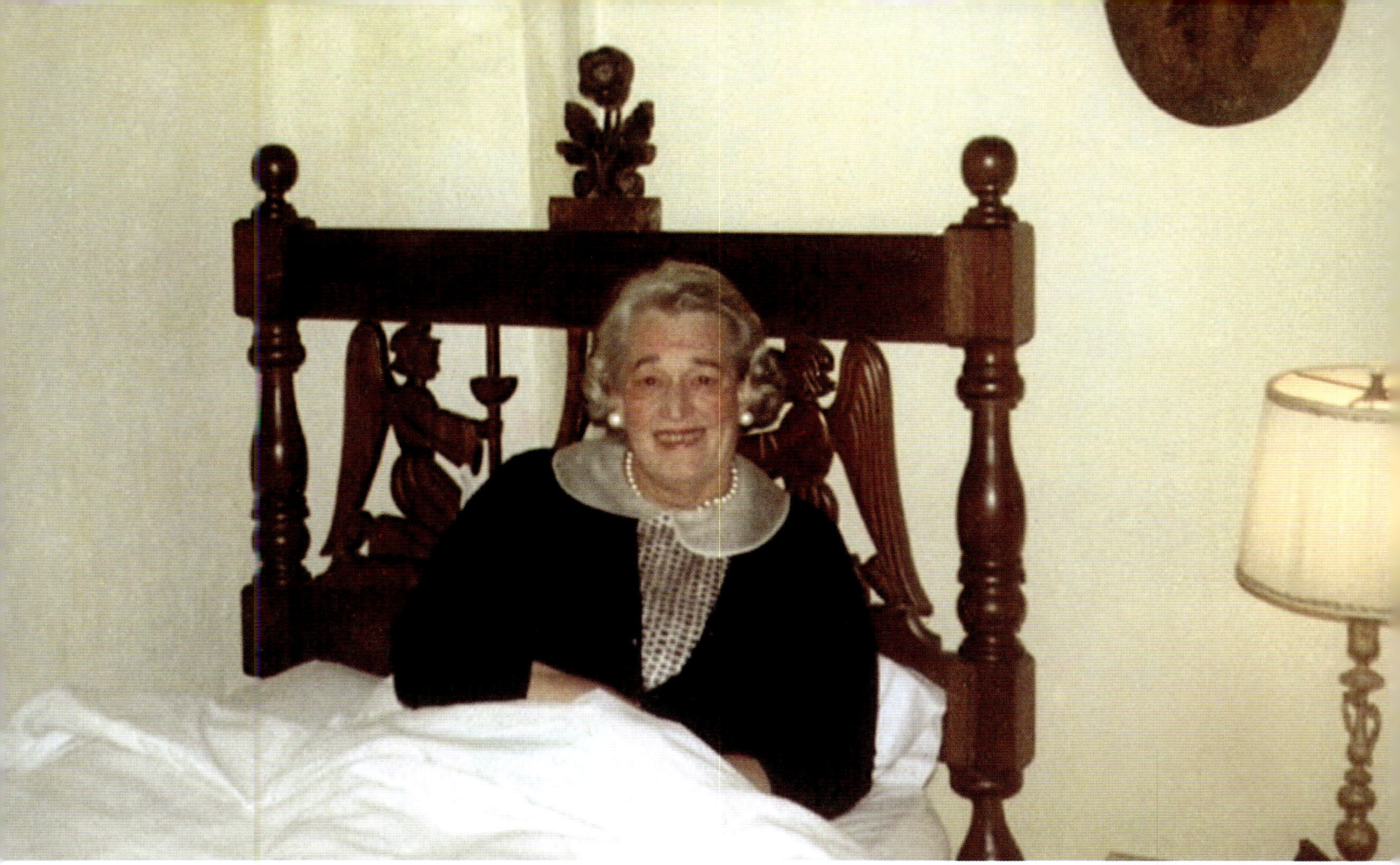

PREVIOUS PAGE: A watercolor that Albert Hadley left on my desk of a client's living room in New York City. Often, I would come to work and find one of his drawings on my desk. He would paint wonderful renderings of rooms after discussions from the evening before.

ABOVE: Sister Parish in bed in Antigua, Guatemala.

RIGHT: Mrs. Parish often worked in either her bathroom or in her bed. She is seen here with her Pekingese dog Honey.

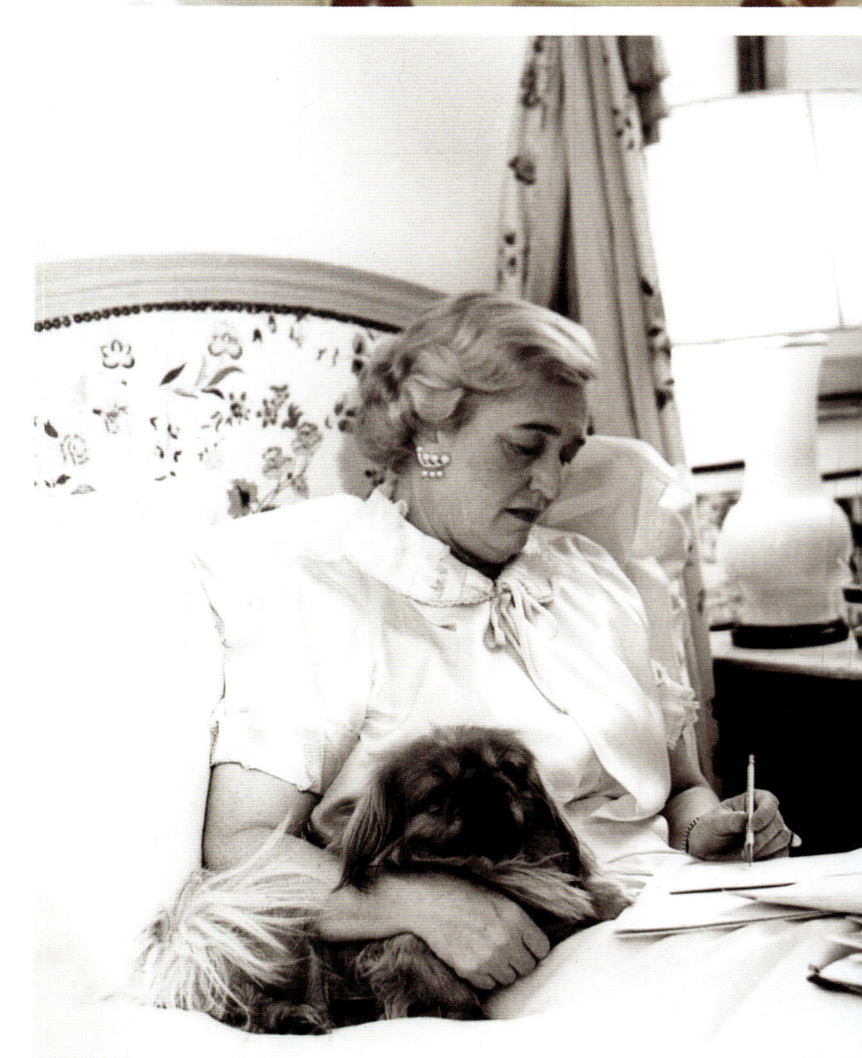

Mrs. Parish was very different from Albert in her approach. She followed her intuition and instincts. She didn't pore over plans like Albert did but would see something and know right away if it worked. She didn't have any formal schooling; she chose and worked around what she loved and was drawn to. The floor plans she drew were never to scale. Sometimes during a conversation about a job, she would sketch out a plan, usually on the back of an envelope or on a Don't Forget pad. The crescent-shaped sofa she drew would be the size of an apple seed and the chairs four times that size and in odd shapes. Tables were never to scale and lamps were suggested by tiny little x's on the paper. Nothing made sense as she drew it and you really would not have known what each shape was meant to be unless you had been sitting there with her while she explained her thinking. But in her head, it was all to scale and just right. When the moving trucks arrived everything fit perfectly.

Mrs. Parish had a great sense of humor and a very mischievous side. Driving back from Far Hills, New Jersey, one day, she told me about her drive to Maine the spring before. Somewhere along the Maine Turnpike she started to think about her final years. She realized that she had been so mean to so many people that perhaps nobody would even come to her funeral. She envisioned an empty church. She said that she had to pull over because she started crying so hard. Needless to say, the church was completely filled at her funeral in Maine and absolutely packed at St. James's Church in New York.

Sister Parish and I got along well and we became close. She looked out for me, and I felt she understood me, although she chided me daily about the way I dressed—the length of my skirts and the need for more polish on my shoes.

Often I would pass her office and see her struggling with her skirt. She usually wore knit skirts with a silk blouse and cardigans from the women's clothing store Worldly Things. Her skirt would have gotten all twisted around somehow so I would go in to help her untangle it and straighten her slip. She was very self-assured and direct and could be very funny. We had many good laughs. I remember one cold, rainy day in the late fall that didn't have much sunlight to begin with. It was the sort of day when you have no energy and the office lights glare and everything feels off. She called me into her office and asked what I was doing that afternoon. I didn't have appointments, so she said, "Good, let's go to the movies." I was so surprised, and for a minute even felt a pang of guilt, but it was she who was inviting me to join her, and what could be more fun than going to the movies with Mrs. Parish? We went to the 2:00 matinee of *Fried Green Tomatoes*, which is still one of my favorite movies to this day.

My telephone would ring every morning around 6:30 a.m. and it would be Mrs. Parish, who would immediately say, "What is your day?" Somewhere along the way, I ended up working as closely with her as with Albert. Mrs. Parish was always very protective of me. She would ask the office's driver, Samuel Bell, to pick me up in the morning before or just after he had dropped Albert off at the office. I never understood why, but in retrospect, I think she was absolutely appalled that I lived downtown.

There were four decorators when I began at Parish-Hadley: Bunny Williams, Gary Hager, David Kleinberg, and Nicholas Pentecost. Each of them had a "team," which was a secretary or coordinator for their jobs and an assistant. Albert Hadley and Mrs. Parish were involved in every job to some extent, editing and often joining in the client meetings depending on their schedules. When I was there, Harold Simmons was in charge of the architectural department and wasn't really decorating anymore. Mark Ferguson, Oscar Shamamian, John Murray, David McMahon, Michael Schell, John Tackett, and Paul Engle made up the architectural department, each of them working on various projects.

Every day was different. I went with either Mrs. Parish or Mr. Hadley to the various workrooms to check on things—upholstery, curtains, or furniture—or to visit job sites. I shopped for everything—lighting, furniture, rugs, fabrics, and trimmings for them both even though Parish-Hadley had a room filled with fabrics and rug samples. The D&D (Decoration and Design building) was just around the corner from the 63rd Street office, so it was easy to run over and hunt for whatever was needed. It was a bustling building back then, before the Internet made it so you could see everything online. I still like to actually see and touch everything and not work from pictures.

The design of a room always started with the rug and fabrics, and often what a client already owned and loved determined the initial direction of a job. Editing what people had, and incorporating it into the floor plans, was sometimes a challenge and could be a delicate process. You couldn't just dismiss what someone owned, loved, or had collected. But clients wanted the help and direction that Parish-Hadley gave them and would usually listen to recommendations. Albert always quoted Diana Vreeland, "Give them what they never knew they wanted!" It was always thrilling to see projects come together, and to see their hand in the final result. Both Albert Hadley and Sister Parish had an innate sense for creating inviting, practical, and often spectacular spaces. It was a privilege to

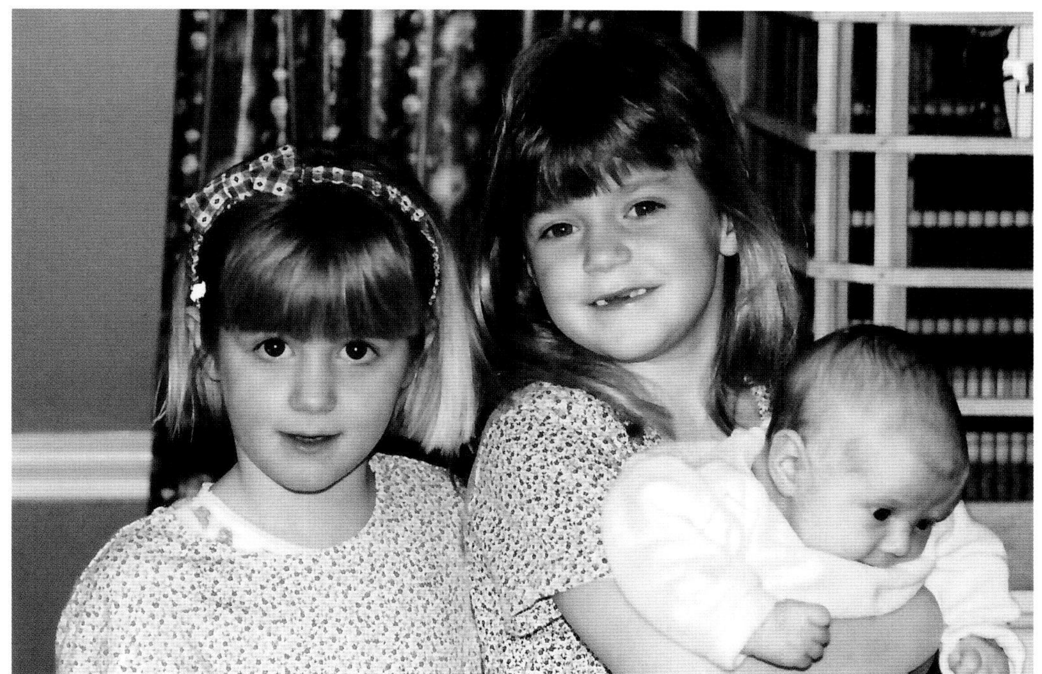

My three children in 1995. From left to right: Charlotte, Flora, and Bean.

have worked with them both, and I am grateful to them for giving me so much and for teaching me all that they did.

My life has changed as much as I have over the past forty-two years. After Mrs. Parish died, I opened my own office in 1995. At that time, my three children were young and the commute from Larchmont to the city every day was just too much and too frazzling. I wanted to be with my children for that important time in their lives. Since then, the children have grown and gone on with their own lives. My marriage ended after thirty-two years. My family, my animals, and my career have always been my mainstay, and always will be.

At this point in my life, I do what I love: I spend time with and fuss over my children and my grandchildren and work on houses in many different locations. I occasionally breed one of my beloved Labradors. There is nothing more wonderful than a litter of puppies—new life, and the innocence and magic of their birth.

I realize there is still so much to learn as I get older. It seems like my life has been the work of settling the unsettled on so many levels, of racing against time to get everything done. My values have changed over the years. I now long for a slower life and a world that is more simplified and peaceful, one that is manageable and cozy—a world that allows for the pleasures of everyday life.

A

PLACE

ONE'S

OF OWN

> "I try not to clutter my life with things that aren't meaningful. Instead, I surround myself with the things that I love."
>
> —LIBBY CAMERON

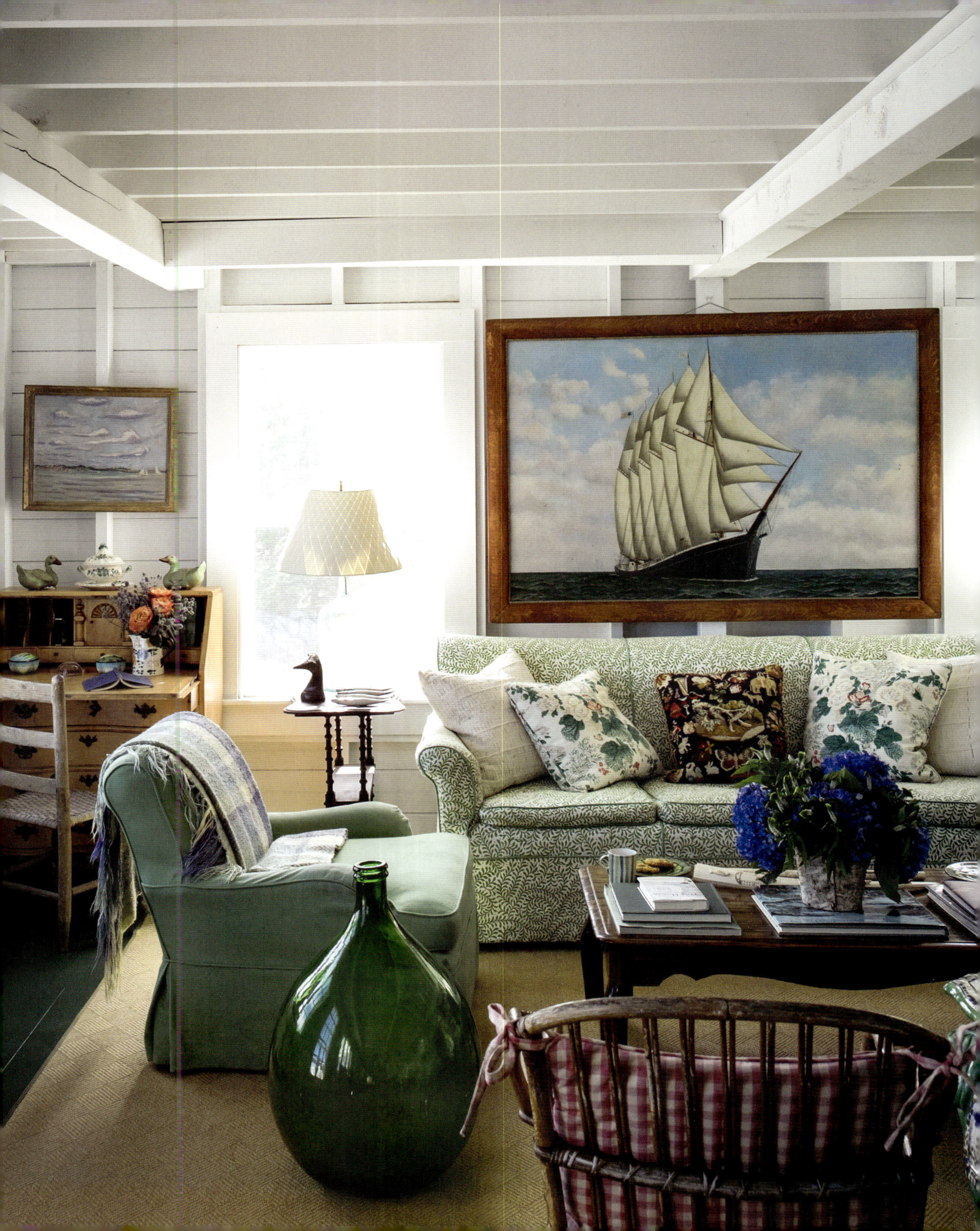

Someone once said to me that a designer's own house is their best work. I don't know if that is always true but there are fewer restrictions when working on your own place than when working with a client, and you can use what you want and like freely. A decorator's house is a far better reflection of their own taste than anything done for a client. I am a homebody and love being in my own peaceful space. I often putter around, moving pictures or furniture about—swapping one thing out for another—but for the most part, there is an eclectic consistency in my house.

I love color and pattern, using old pieces with newer pieces, and bringing things together that are compatible but not necessarily of the same period. A room can have a few high-quality things in it and can then be filled in with more humble, less expensive things. The quality of what is used is so important but the provenance isn't essential. Good furniture will last. A nice finish on a decent type of wood does matter, and well-made furniture is so much better than a bad copy.

Comfortable upholstery is a big investment and, in my mind, the most important investment one can make. There is nothing worse than sitting on a sofa that is so deep that your legs stick straight out or that you can't easily get out of, or a sofa that pitches you down and forward so you feel like you are slipping off and might land on the floor at any minute! A good piece of upholstery will last forever. My favorite sofa is one that belonged to my great-aunt and was made in the 1940s. I can't imagine how many times it has been recovered, but it has lasted for longer than I have been alive.

I try not to clutter my life with things that aren't meaningful. Instead, I surround myself with the things that I love—things that make me feel settled and safe. There is a happy feeling that familiar things can bring. Surround yourself with the things that you love; seeing them will bring you comfort.

PREVIOUS PAGE: The south end of the living room at our house in Newagen. The painting of the schooner is by Thomas Birch.

RIGHT: The two fireplaces in the house are both made with the rounded granite rocks from our cove beside the house. The grout in the mantel is made with tiny pebbles, sand, and periwinkle shells.

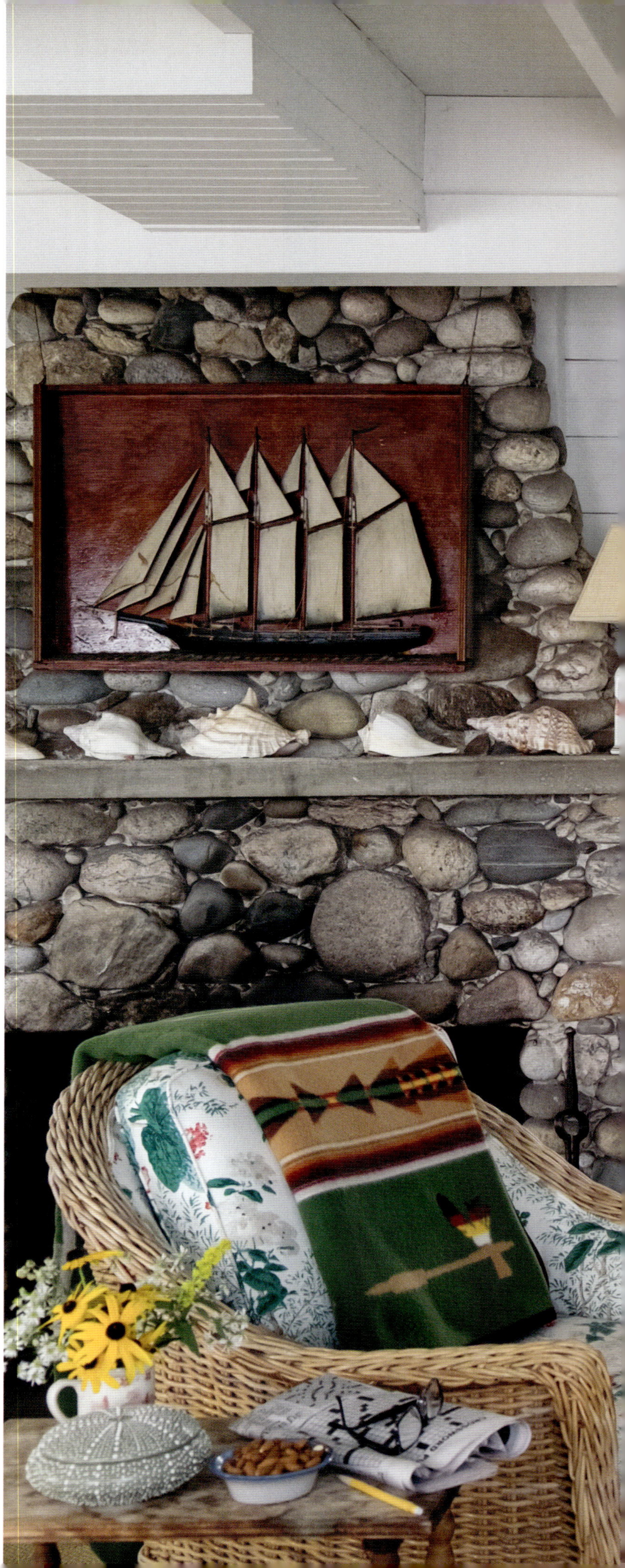

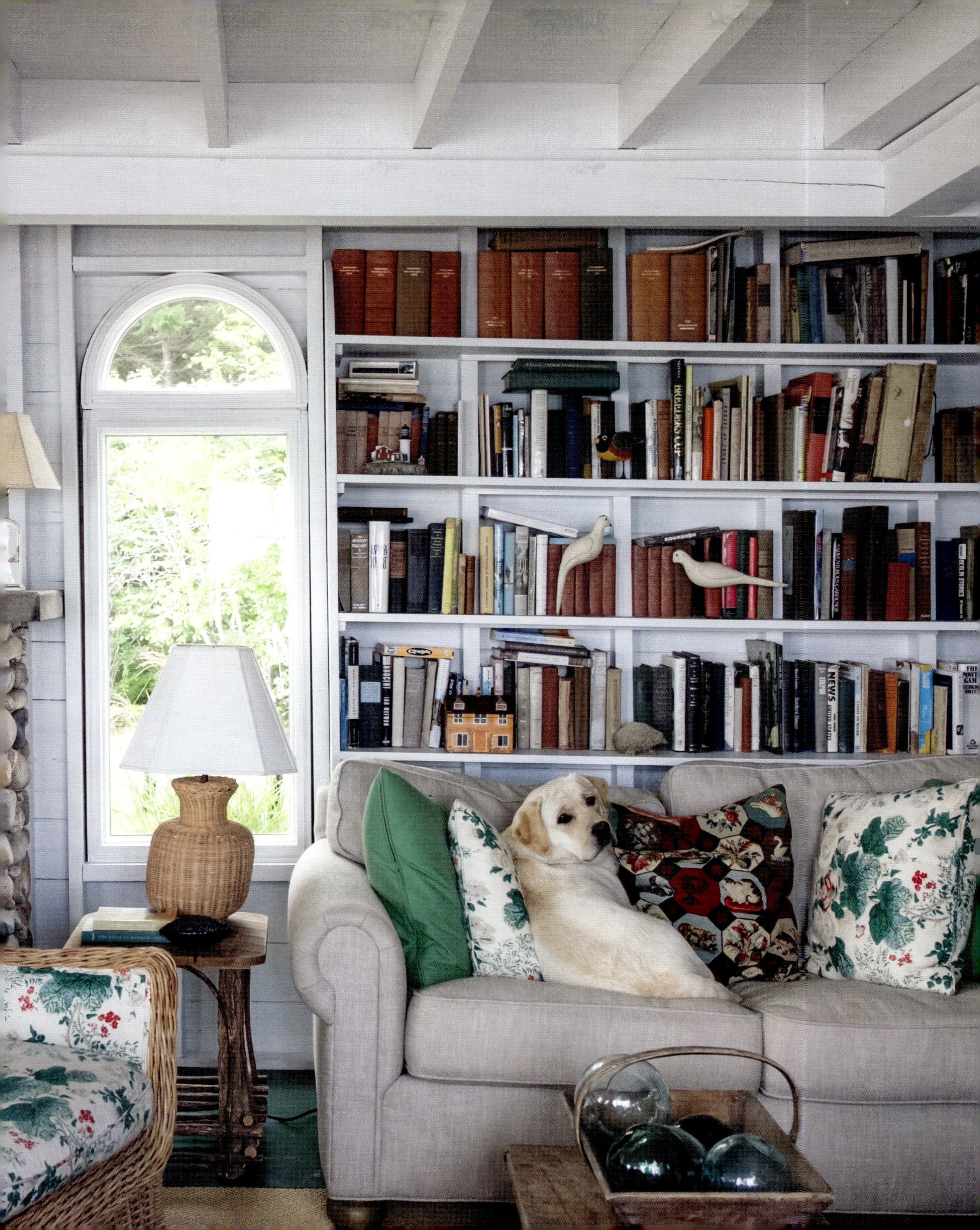
BERLIN STORIES
NEWS
UNITED STATES
COAST OF MAINE

Maine

The most constant place in my life has been my family's summer house in Maine. Maine is a very beautiful and peaceful part of the world where time moves at a very different pace. I spent every summer there growing up, and now I return every year with my brothers and sister, all of our children, and my grandchildren. We all love it there, and it goes without saying that we all plan to be there at the same time together. The view out over the water is just the same as it has been since I was very small, as are the sounds of the seagull and osprey calls, and of the lobster boat engines puttering as the lobstermen check their pots in the early morning.

The screen porch faces due east and the sun creates a sparkly, shimmering reflection on the water. Tatie, the wonderful woman who raised me, used to sit there, and would always tell me that those sparkling ripples of light on the water were the mermaids playing.

The islands we look out at today haven't really changed at all. Fisherman's Island has an additional house or two. Outer Heron is owned by the state of Maine and only allows day visitors. The same is true of the island of Seguin, which is farther out and now has an automated lighthouse with lighthouse keepers living there only during the summer. The Cuckholds Light Station has also been automated. At one point, Cuckholds was turned into a very snappy spot for an overnight romantic getaway, but it proved too hard to maintain and difficult to access in bad weather, so once again it is a lovely old lighthouse standing proudly on a spit of granite rock, weathering the sea and the storms. One can hear the Cuckholds horn on cloudy and foggy days, a sound I have always loved. Donald Duncan, our neighbor whose family has been there as long as ours, used to play his bagpipes on the rocks toward dusk and the sound would carry across the water.

My paternal grandparents built the house literally on the water's edge, atop a granite ledge in 1904. The house isn't winterized so it can only be used from the end of May until the beginning of October when the water gets turned off. The house itself hasn't changed a great deal since it was built. Some of the furniture has been replaced or repainted or has just been moved to another spot. The kitchen hasn't really been

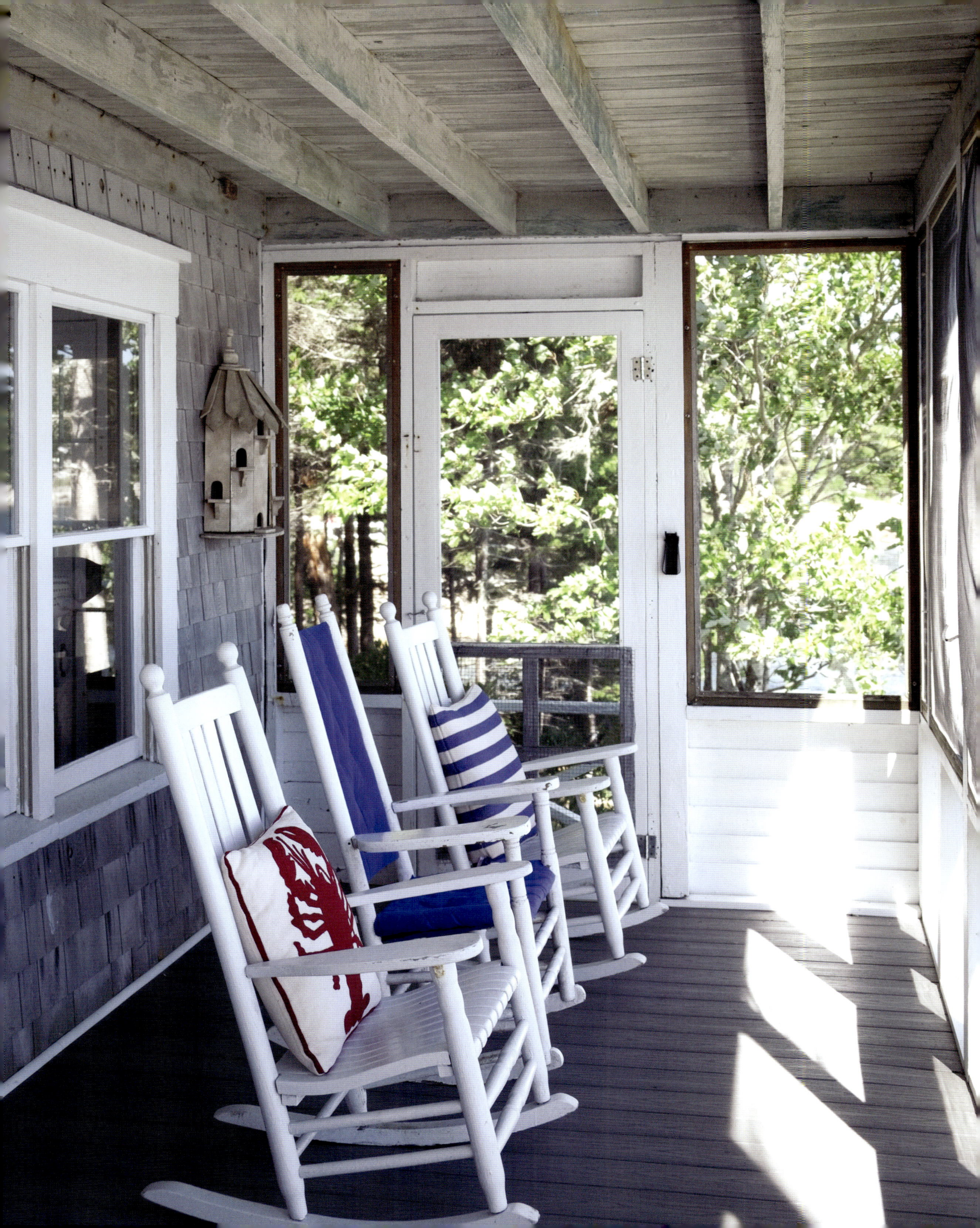

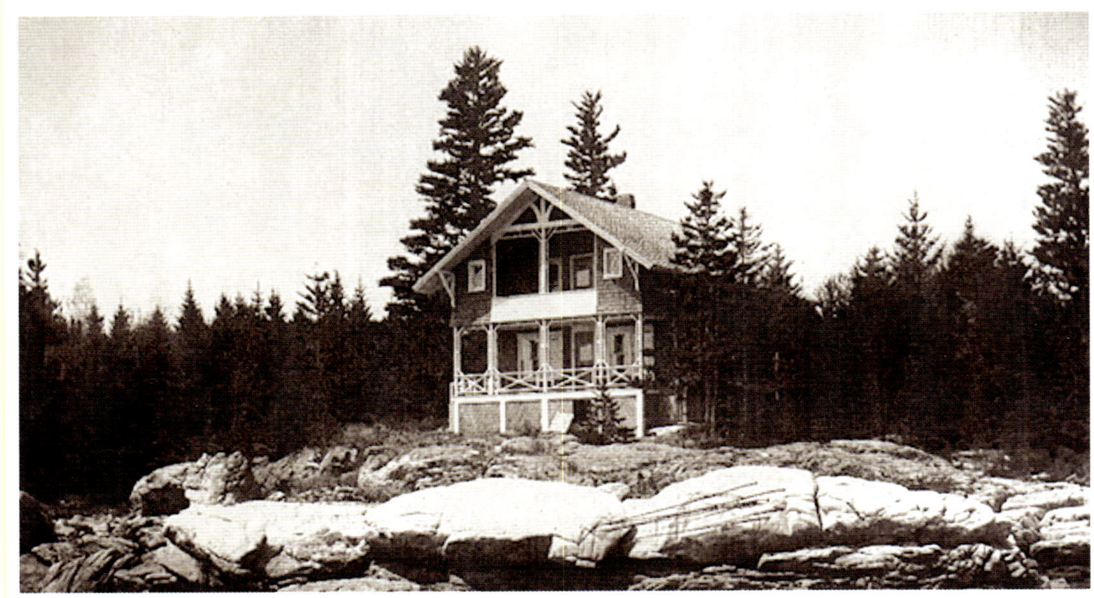

PREVIOUS PAGE: The screen porch is filled with light and is a great place to sit and relax.

ABOVE: The original exterior of my family's house in Maine, circa 1904. The architect is unknown.

BELOW: Here the house is shown with the living room addition on the left side.

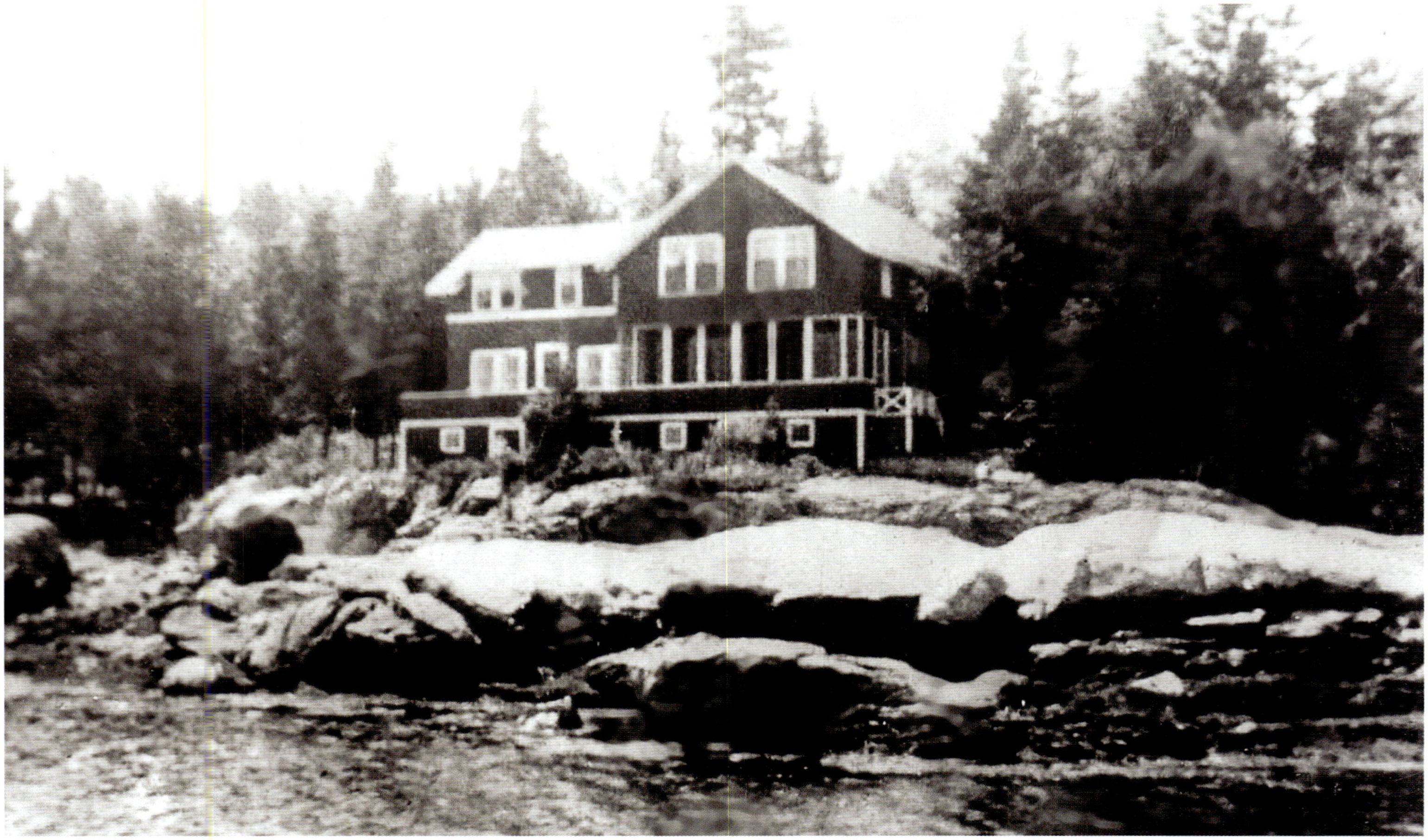

updated except for a new icebox or stove from time to time. The rugs get replaced periodically. The piano that was in the living room is gone—it didn't do well over the cold, damp winters. The house is too small for all of us now. I am one of six siblings, and three of us still own and use the house together. I love being there with my brothers and their families. There are six bedrooms but with all our children and the beginning of the next generation, it is getting a bit too cozy.

My paternal grandmother loved the house. She would stay until late into October every fall for duck hunting season. She passed the love of Maine on to my father, and I am so grateful to my father for passing it on to me. The house is filled with its past: old furniture, paintings, books, and the china and teacups that belonged to my grandparents. There are scrapbooks with old photographs of the family and the house as it was in the beginning.

Today, the façade is quite different. A wing with a big living room downstairs facing the water and a bedroom upstairs was added long before I was born. An upstairs bedroom we call the Yellow Room was most likely once a sleeping porch. The stairs to the second floor are narrow and steep, and the railing has a wonderful, somewhat crude version of a Gothic-shaped cutout on it. The two fireplace mantels downstairs are made from the rounded granite stones found on the rocky little beach in a cove beside the house. The grout is a pebbly, sandy grout with periwinkle shells set in it. The floors are all painted a dark green. The walls are open with horizontal boards between the vertical studs.

It is all very simple and basic. The house is colorful with lots of deep greens and blues, and there is a very eclectic mixture of furniture. Some of it has been there forever and has been able to survive the cold and damp winters right on the water. My favorite thing in the house is a big painting over the sofa at the far end of the living room of a six-masted ship. It has been there my entire life. Everything else there has little value but it works and it doesn't matter that it has been painted over and over again.

Maine is ingrained in me: the smell of the pines through the fog or sunshine, the salty clean air, the sound of the waves lapping up against the rocks, the clusters of ferns everywhere, and the soft mossy paths through the woods. The sea is still cold

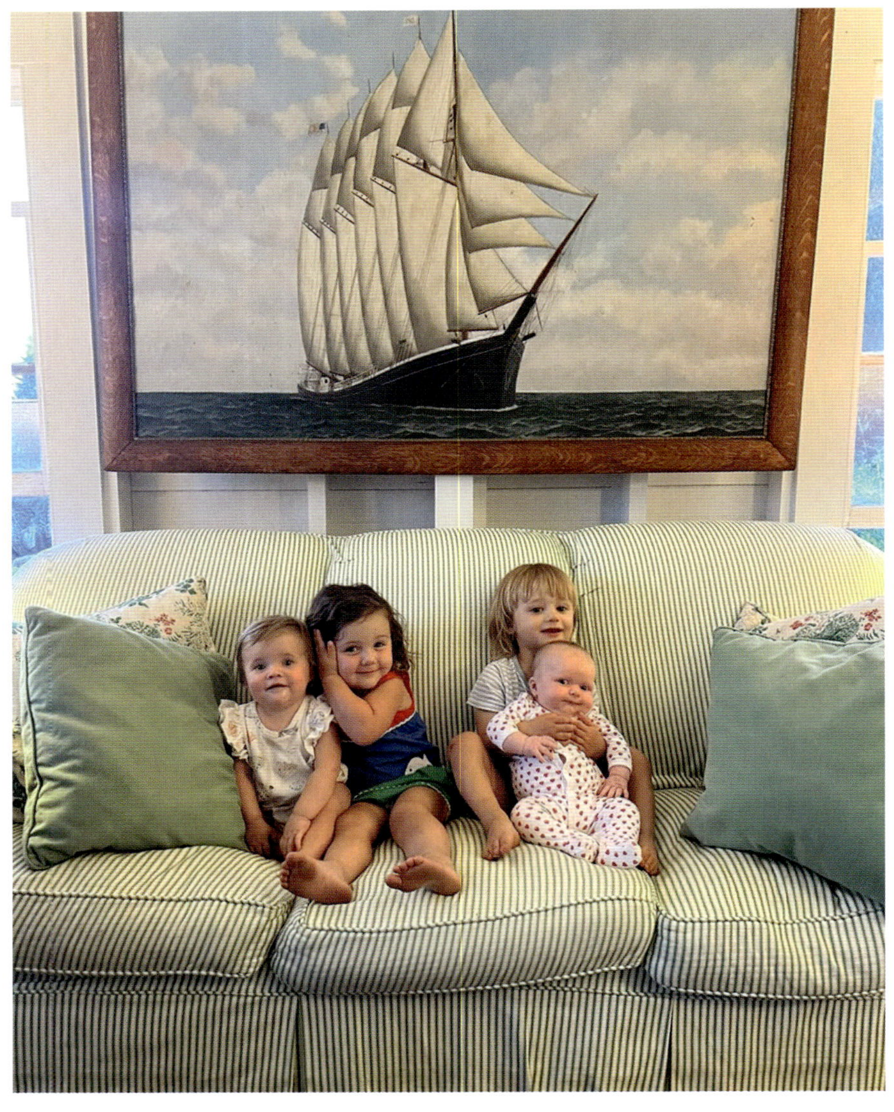

ABOVE: The youngest and next generation in Maine. From left to right: Cakie, Elizabeth, and Cully holding Jane.

OPPOSITE: An extra bed for whoever won't sleep in their own is in the alcove.

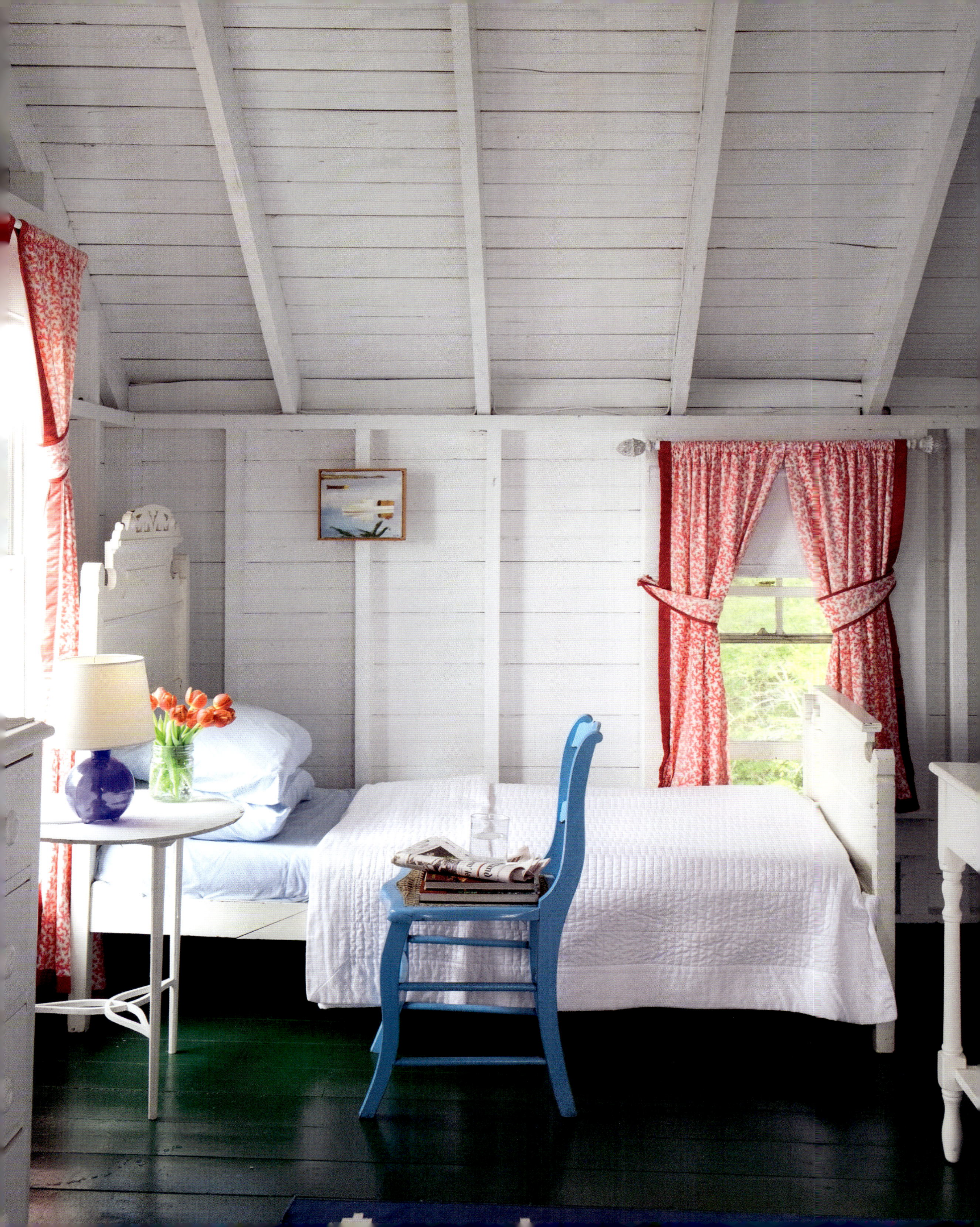

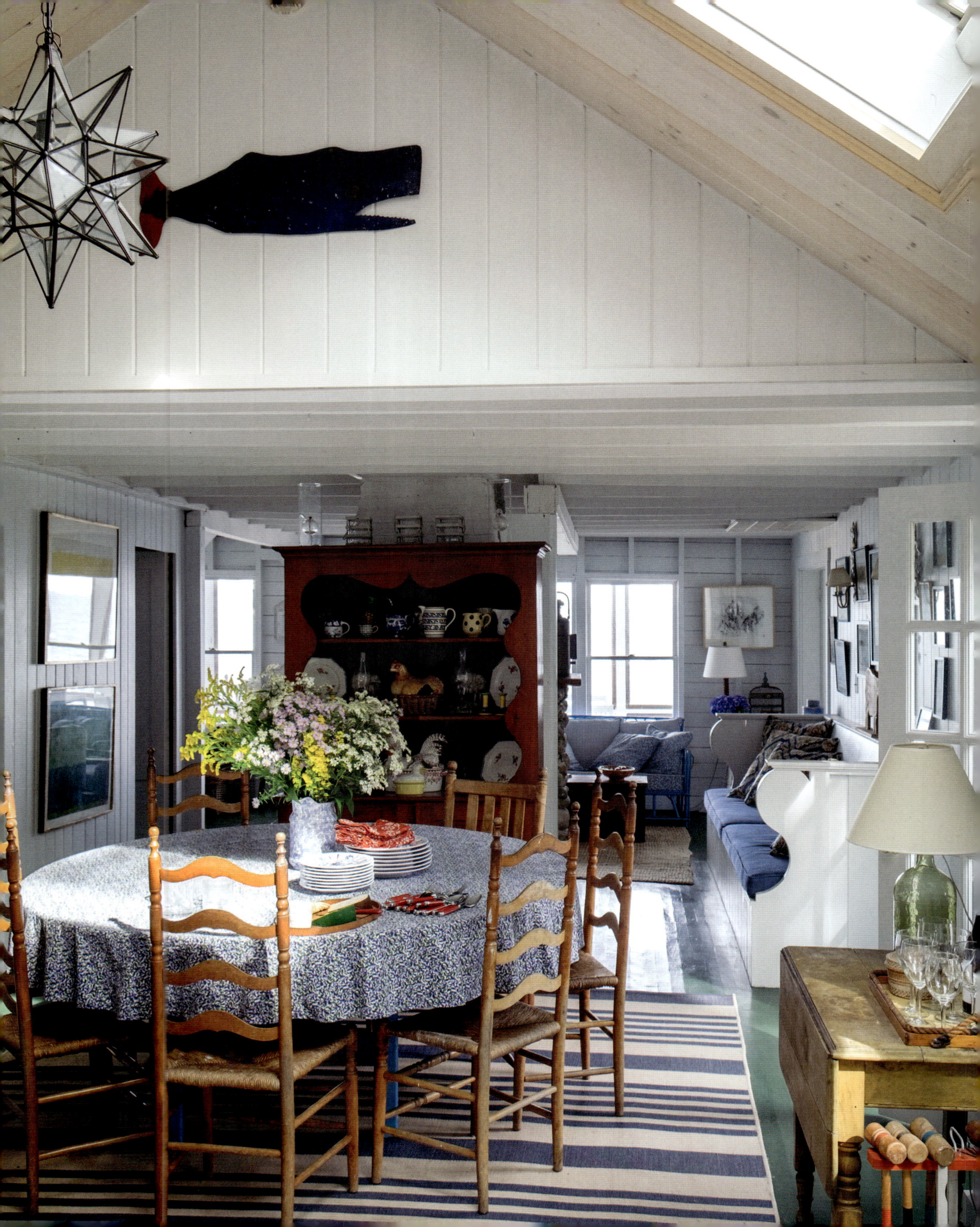

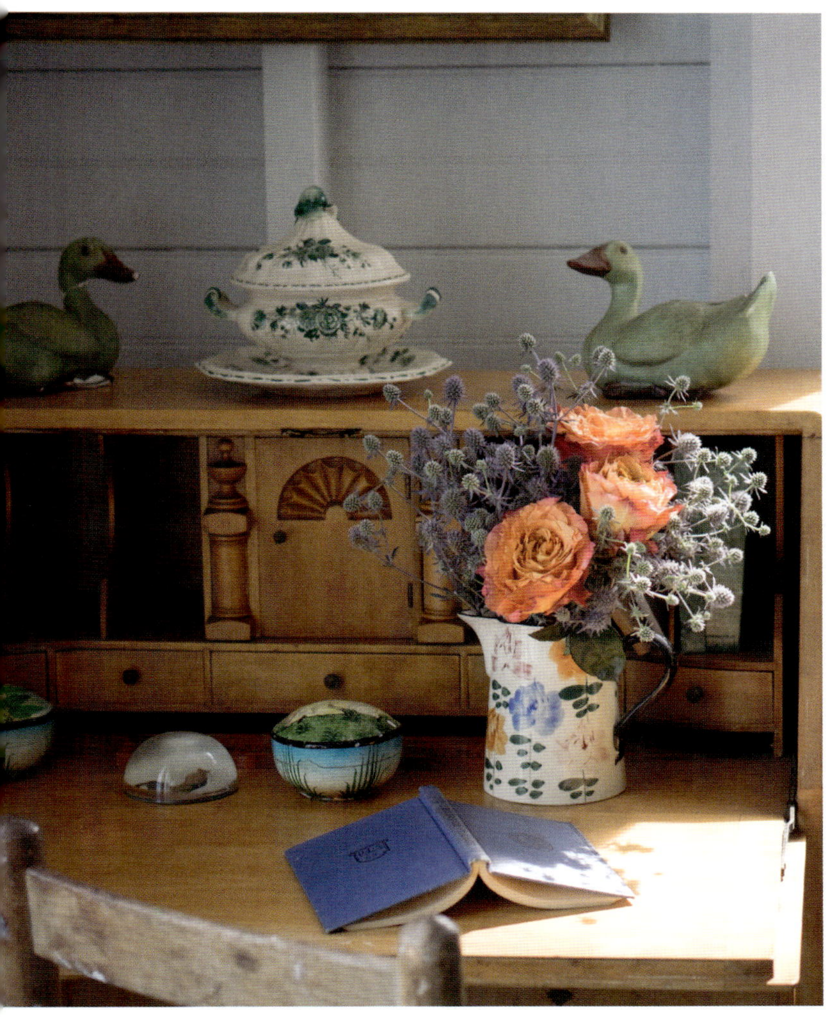

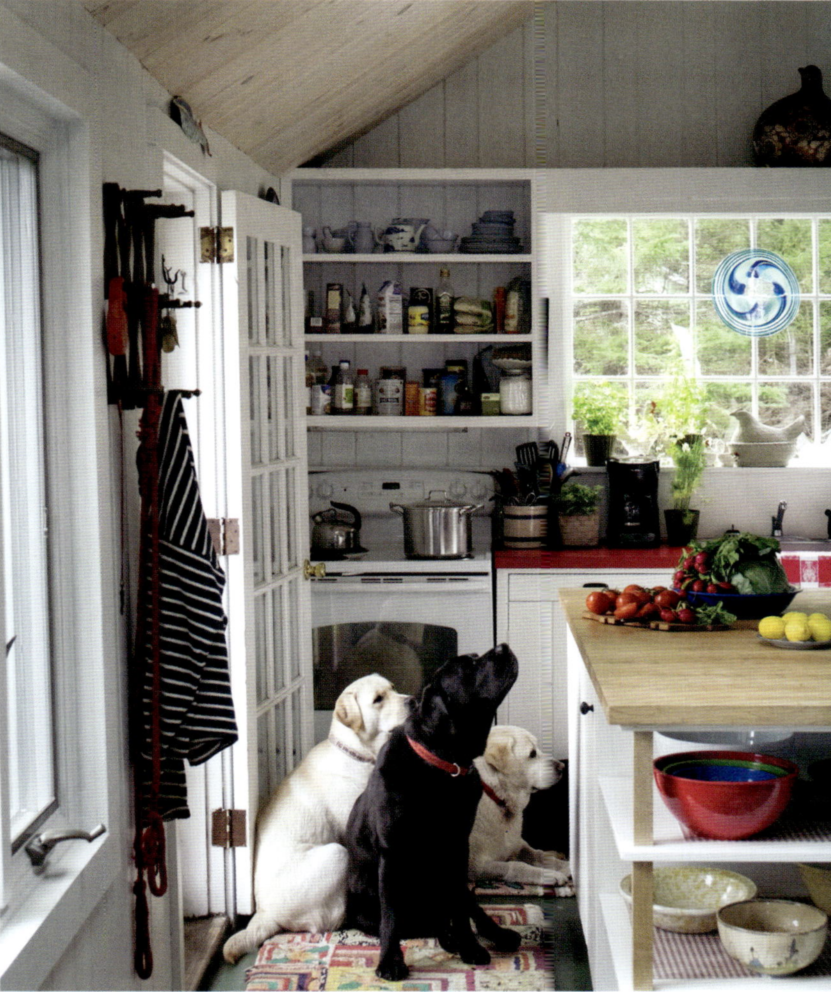

OPPOSITE: The dining room faces due east and looks toward the water through the screen porch.

ABOVE, LEFT: My father spent hours working at this desk in the corner of the living room.

ABOVE, RIGHT: Fig, Skyler, and Logan in the Newagen kitchen. The dogs are always near the kitchen hoping to get fed anything at all.

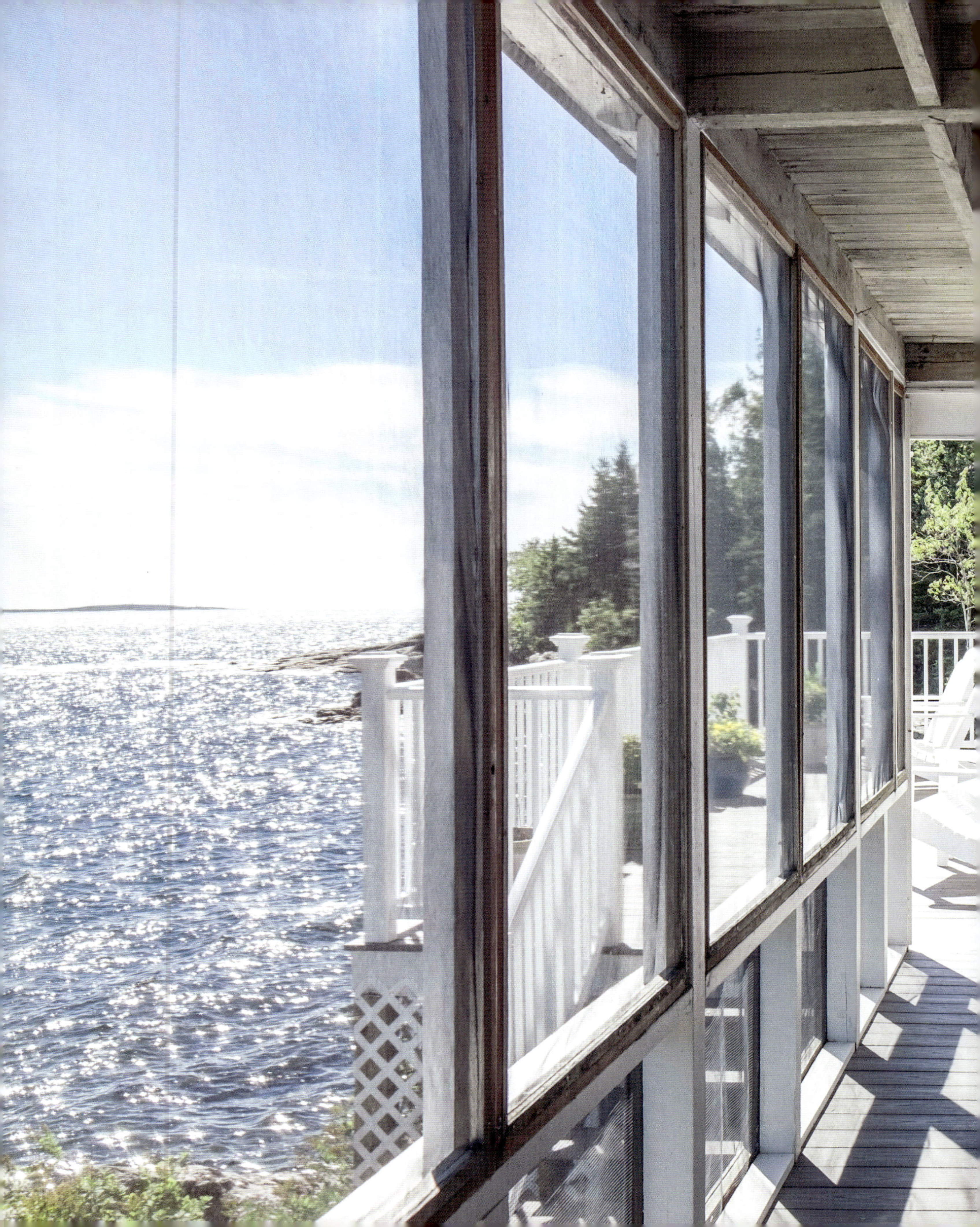

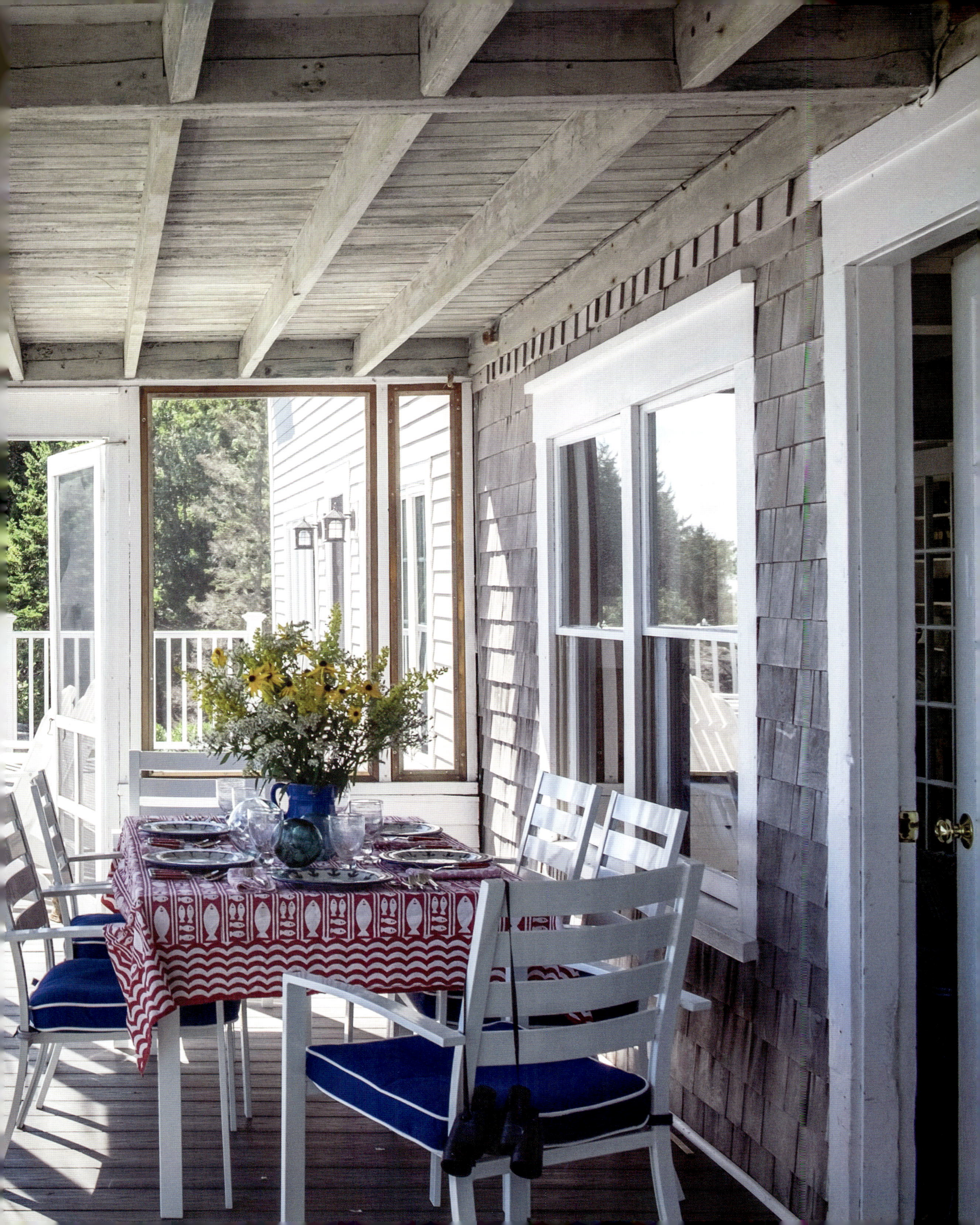

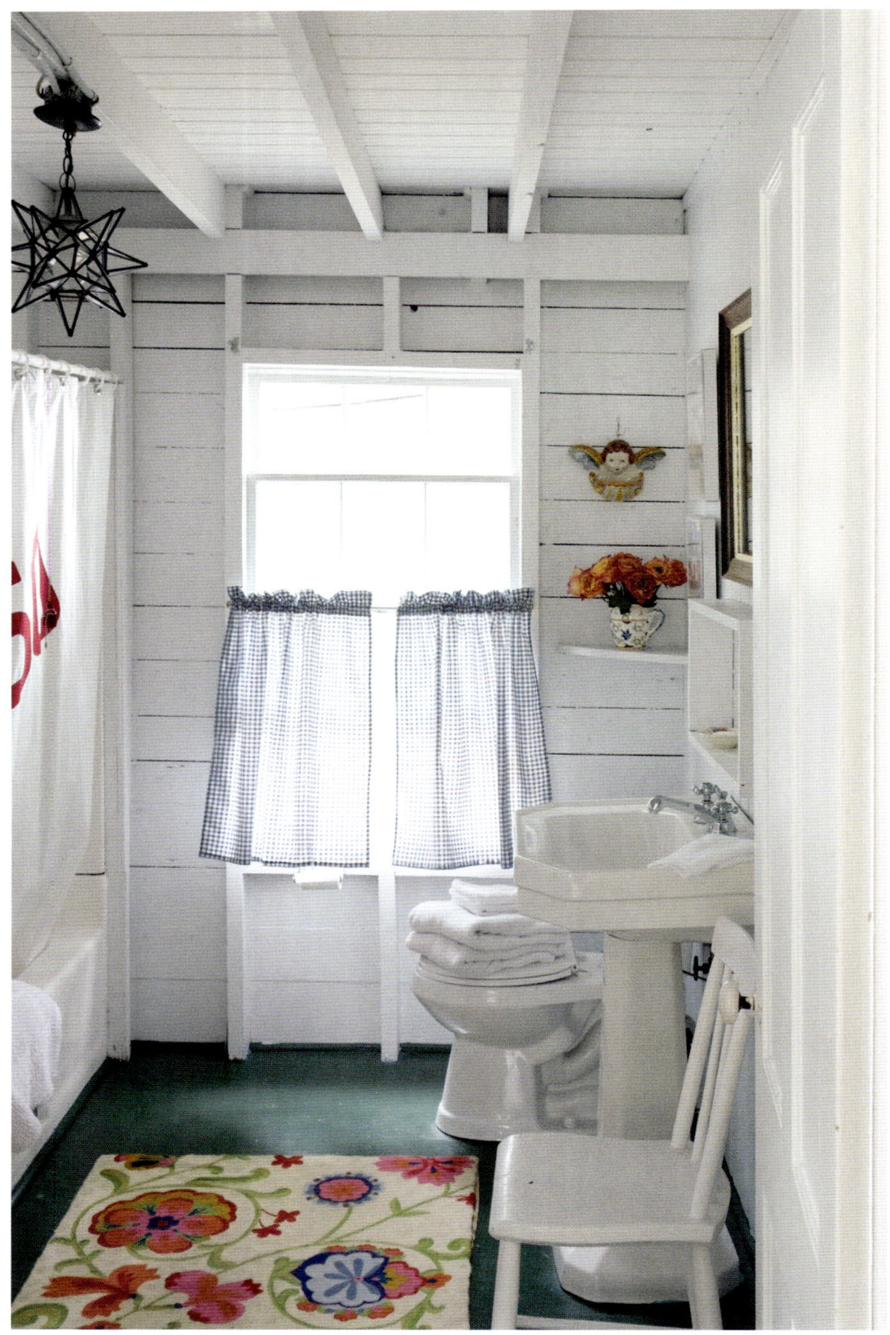

PREVIOUS PAGE: The screen porch in Maine has always been one of my favorite places to spend time reading and watching the sea.

ABOVE: This bathroom is cheery and light-filled.

OPPOSITE: All the furniture in this room was painted blue with leftover paint from our turnabout sailboat.

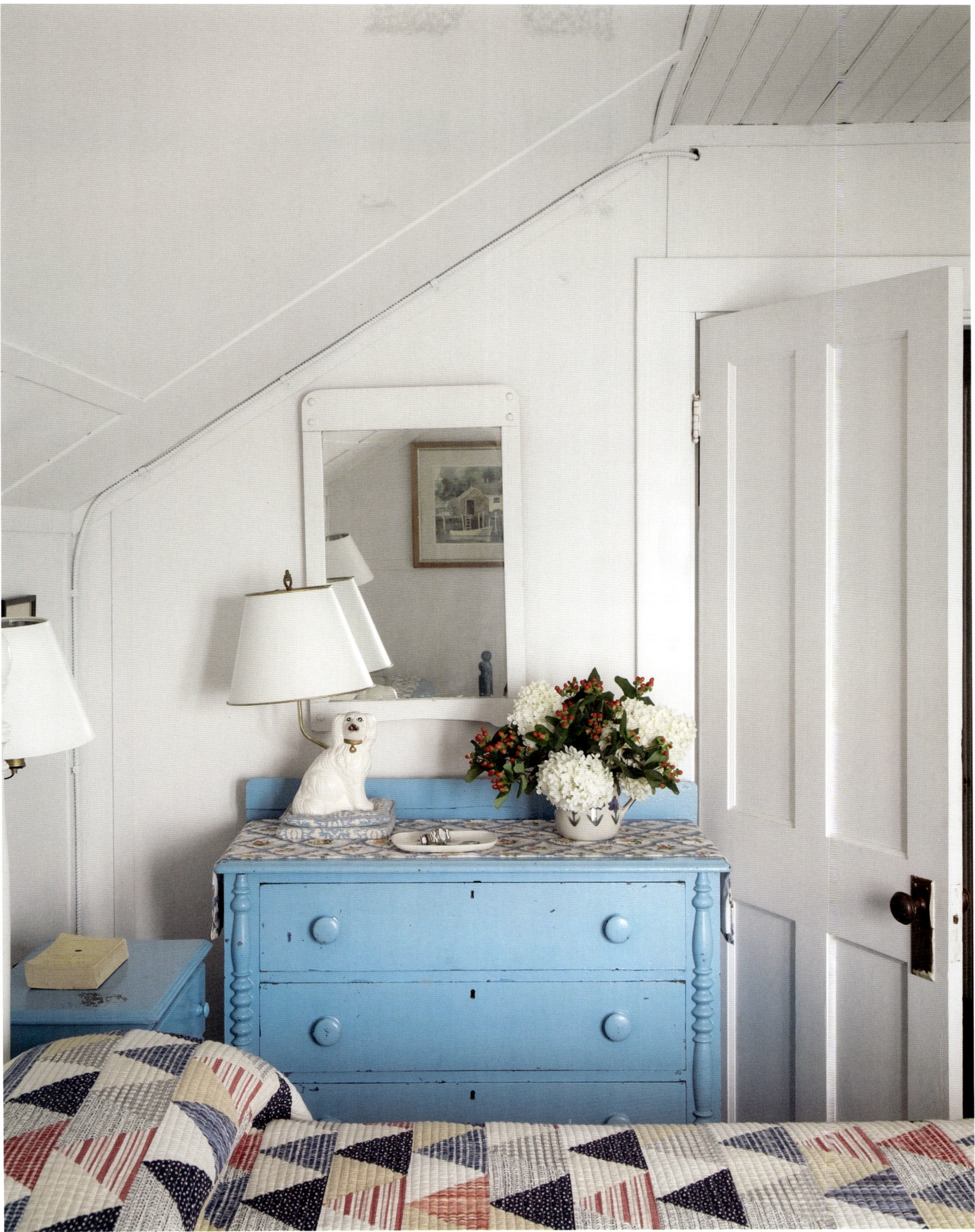

enough that most people jump in and jump right back out, but it is not as frigid as it used to be. I try to swim every day around the big rock in front of the house or across the cove with all of my dogs in tow. This is a place I will always come back to, no matter how long I have to be away. This will always be home.

A corner in the living room that looks out toward the water. The bookcases in our Maine home are very basic, and books sit between the vertical studs. The walls are open and the framing is exposed.

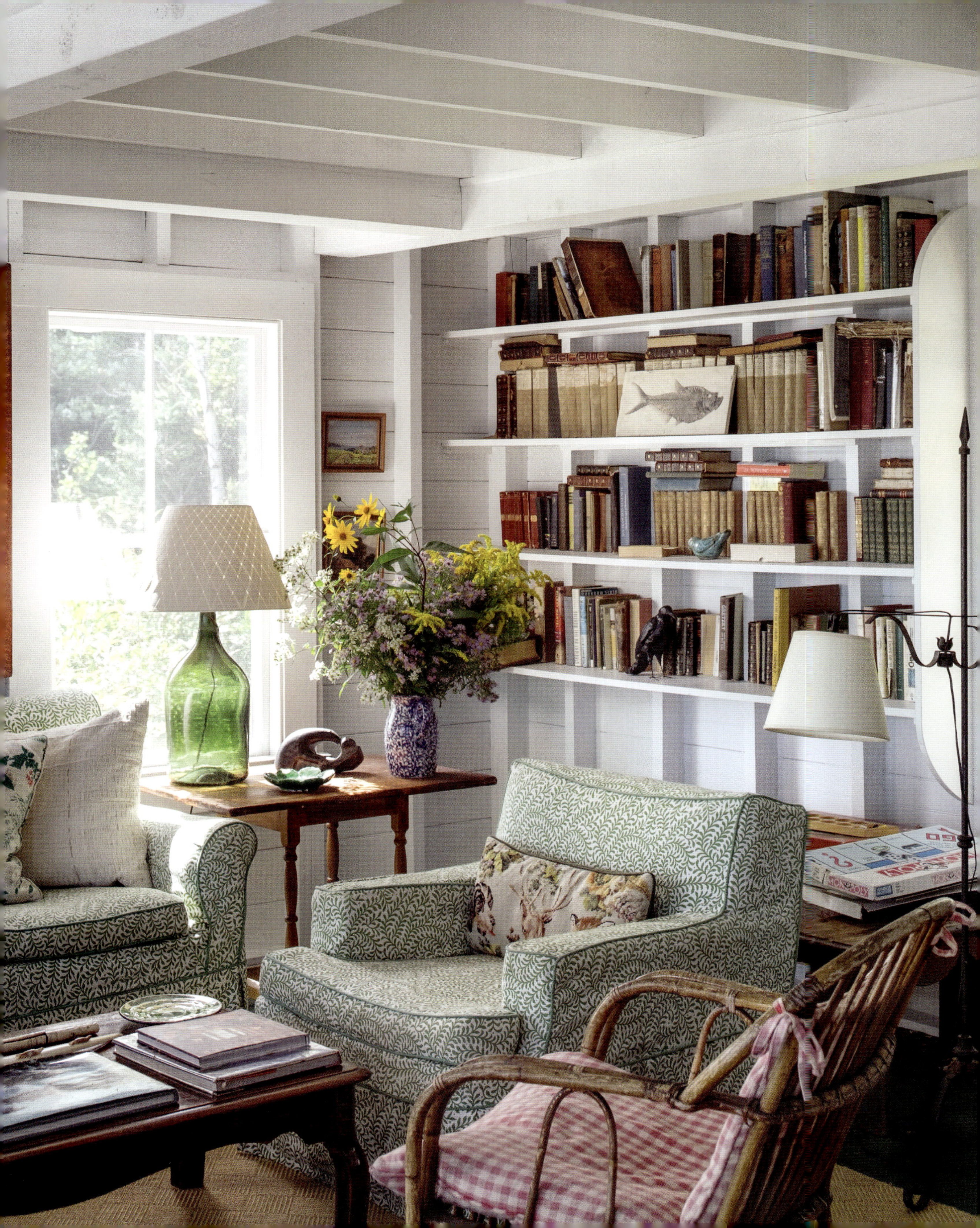

Lofts

When I moved to New York in 1981, I lived for years in a loft on the fourth floor on the corner of Broome and Wooster Street. Soho was very, very different then. At that point, New York City required that many (if not all) of the buildings in Soho have only certified artists living in the lofts, so it was hard to find a loft to rent or to simply get a lease on a space. The loft I lived in had been sold to my roommate, who later became my sister-in-law. She had bought the "fixtures" from an artist who had lived there—the "fixtures" meaning quite literally everything inside the loft but not the piece of real estate itself.

The neighborhood was incredibly dilapidated when I lived there—run-down, gritty, and wonderful. Broome Street was—and still is—the main truck route out of Lower Manhattan to the Holland Tunnel. The sound in the early morning of the trucks with their empty trailers bouncing over bumps and potholes was deafening, but I got used to it. There were many kitchen supply stores, small family-owned shops, and some not very impressive fabric stores. Where Broome Street forked left toward the Holland Tunnel one block away, there was a store that sold live chickens.

West Broadway was home to a great many art galleries, including Leo Castelli, Mary Boone, and Sonnabend. The loft was close to Little Italy and Chinatown and there were still wonderful Italian food shops in Soho and Little Italy. Vesuvio's was a favorite of mine and it was right around the corner. They made their own mozzarella, as well as pastas and bread, each morning. The floors were covered in a thick layer of sawdust as a way to keep the floors clean and dry. It was run by an older Italian couple who both spoke with heavy accents. She would always smile at me and be so welcoming, and she used to pinch my cheek.

It has all changed so much since then. There are no longer restrictions requiring that only working artists live in the lofts, and lofts and apartments now sell for many millions of dollars.

I lived in that wonderful loft for five years. It was on a corner and had a bedroom, bath, and kitchen with a loft space above it at one end. The rest was one huge open space with big windows along the south and east walls. It was painted all white, and furnished with mostly wood furniture gathered from our families, so it had a more traditional feel. Some of the pieces were street finds—the street finds were one of my

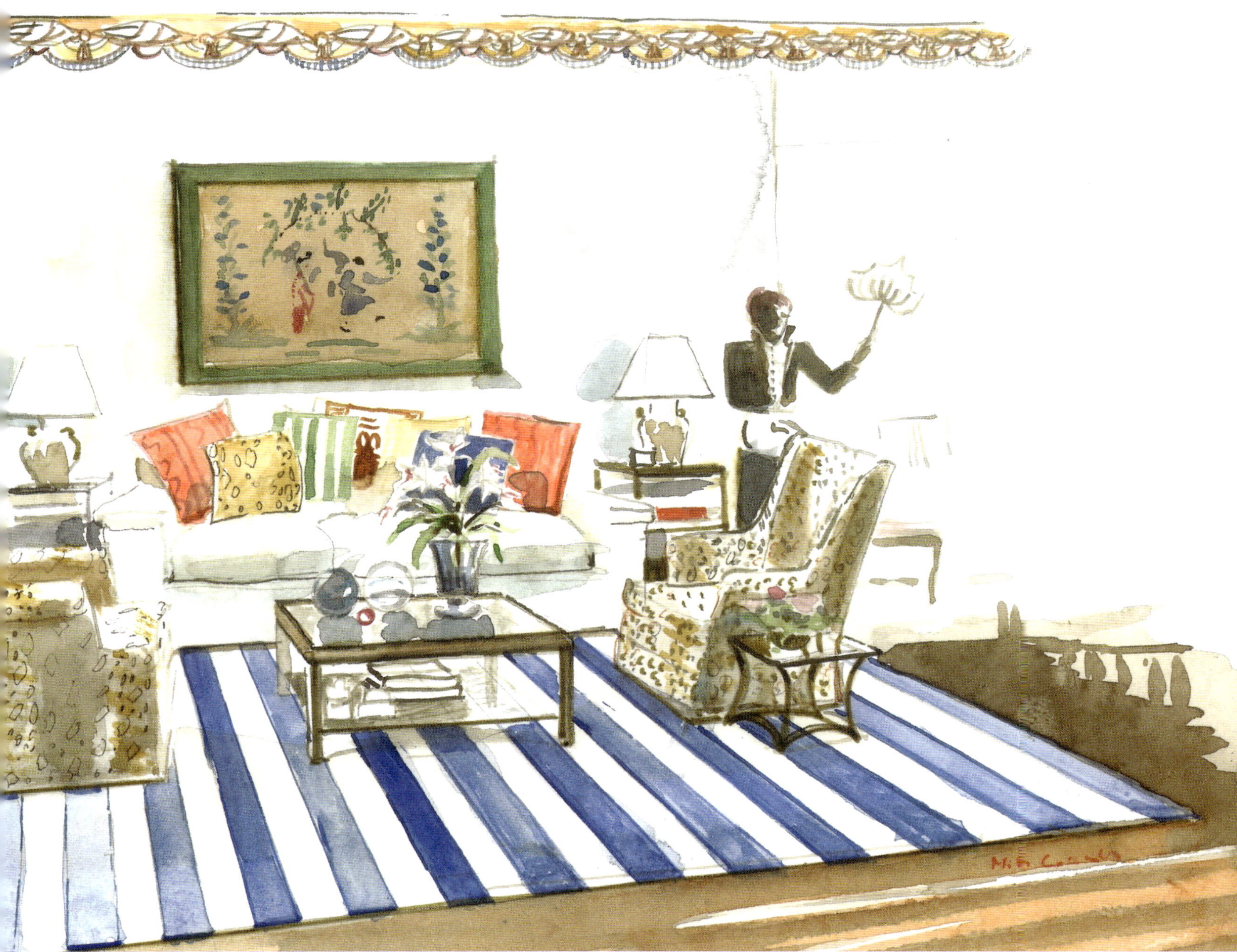

A watercolor painted by Mita Corsini Bland of the Bond Street loft living room.

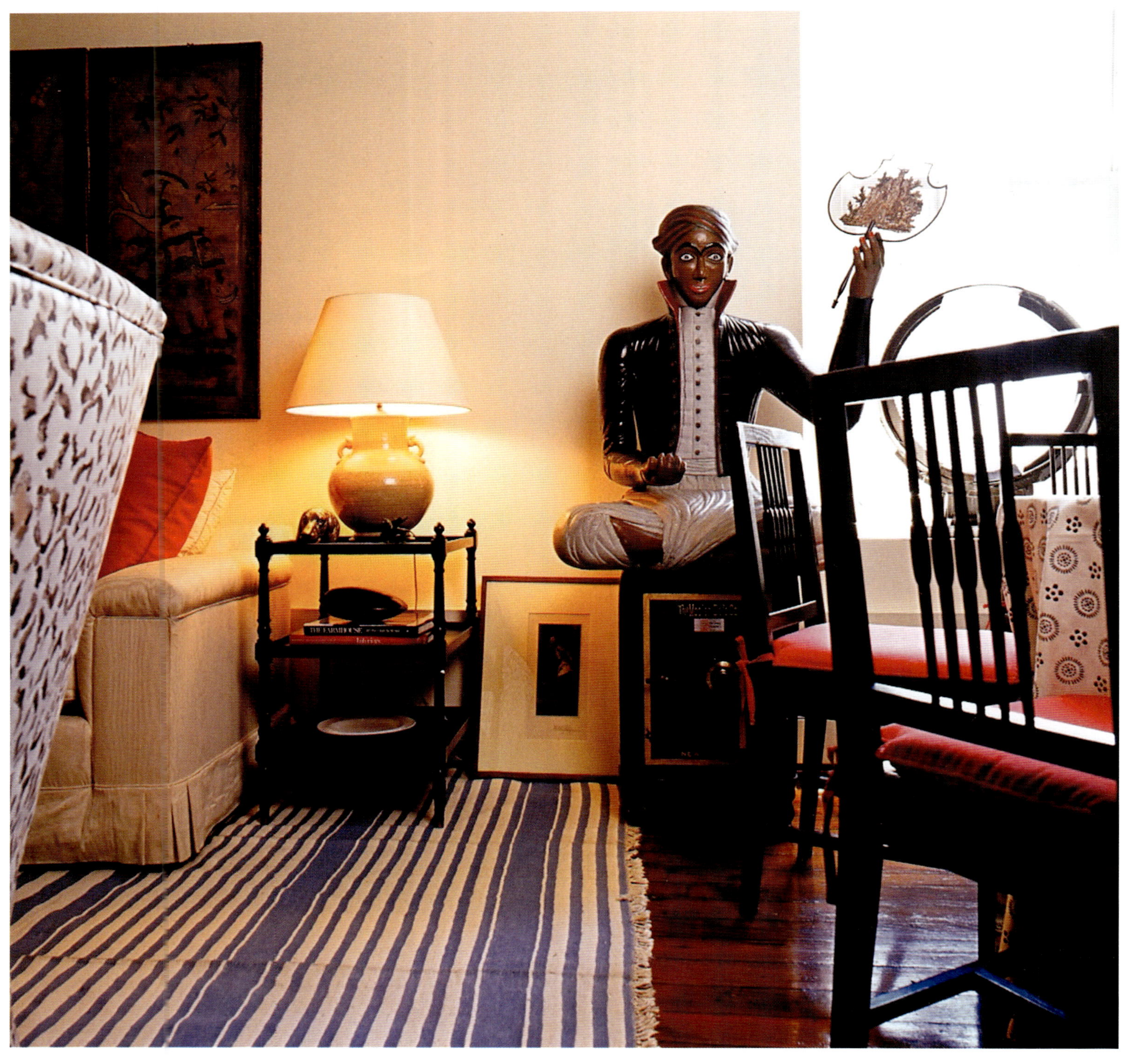

This Indian palace guard statue, who lived on a screen porch in Old Westbury, is somewhat of a mystery. He is believed to have been brought by Gertrude Vanderbilt Whitney to her house on Long Island from her travels abroad and ended up on her daughter Flora Whitney Miller's porch. When Flora Miller died, he came to live with us. He is almost life-size and was partially repainted at some point. His scepter has always been missing.

favorite things about living in New York. In the time that I lived there, I got married, started working at Parish-Hadley, and we started a family. When our first child, Flora, was born, we needed another bedroom and the steep, straight run of ninety-seven stairs up to the fourth floor became a daunting daily prospect with a new baby and a stroller. It was time to move.

We found a loft floor nearby so we moved to Bond Street into another sunny space that had once been a button factory. There was a creaky manual elevator in the building, which rarely worked (our landlord often neglected to pay the monthly maintenance bills) but still it was such a luxury to have. It had an accordion door behind great big steel doors with a huge sliding iron bar. We moved to Bond Street when Flora was tiny and Charlotte arrived shortly thereafter. The fourth-floor loft had windows on three sides of the building, which I loved. We bought and renovated the raw space with Michael Schell's guidance and plans, adding three bedrooms, two bathrooms, and a kitchen. It was a great place to live. Once upstairs and inside, you were in a different world, surrounded by family heirlooms and the comfort of home. The loft was filled with light and our little girls had plenty of space to play—they could ride their tiny tricycles around and make wonderful forts with pillows and blankets. It had high ceilings and was very quiet in comparison to the old loft on Broome Street.

The three bedrooms in this loft were all painted. The girls' room was pale pink, the guest room was a creamy white, and our room was a peach color. The center and main section of the space was white and had one of my favorite Brunschwig & Fils wallpaper borders, "Bosphore," pasted along the ceiling line. It was a coral-and-blue historical document border, which is not what one would expect to find in a loft space. There was a big, round skirted dining table, and the two pyramid-shaped bookcases that I had had made for the first loft. A big creamy white sofa was flanked by two Rose Cummings leopard-print cotton chintz chairs, and a big blue-and-cream Dhurrie rug filled the floor in the middle.

The neighborhood between Lafayette Street and the Bowery was dirty—dicey at best. It was teaming with crack addicts. Crack was the new, cheap drug of choice then, and there were always little plastic vials all over the ground. At the corner of Lafayette and across the street there was a women's shelter and there was always some sort of commotion going on there. It was rough but I always felt safe there—even when out at night walking our dog, Tiny. Most of the street addicts knew Tiny by name and always wanted to talk her. Like most Labradors, she had a tail that wagged a mile a minute and she wasn't very discerning. Once the children got older and it was time for school, we decided to leave the city. Today that neighborhood is one of the fanciest areas in downtown Manhattan, with expensive real estate, stores, and great restaurants.

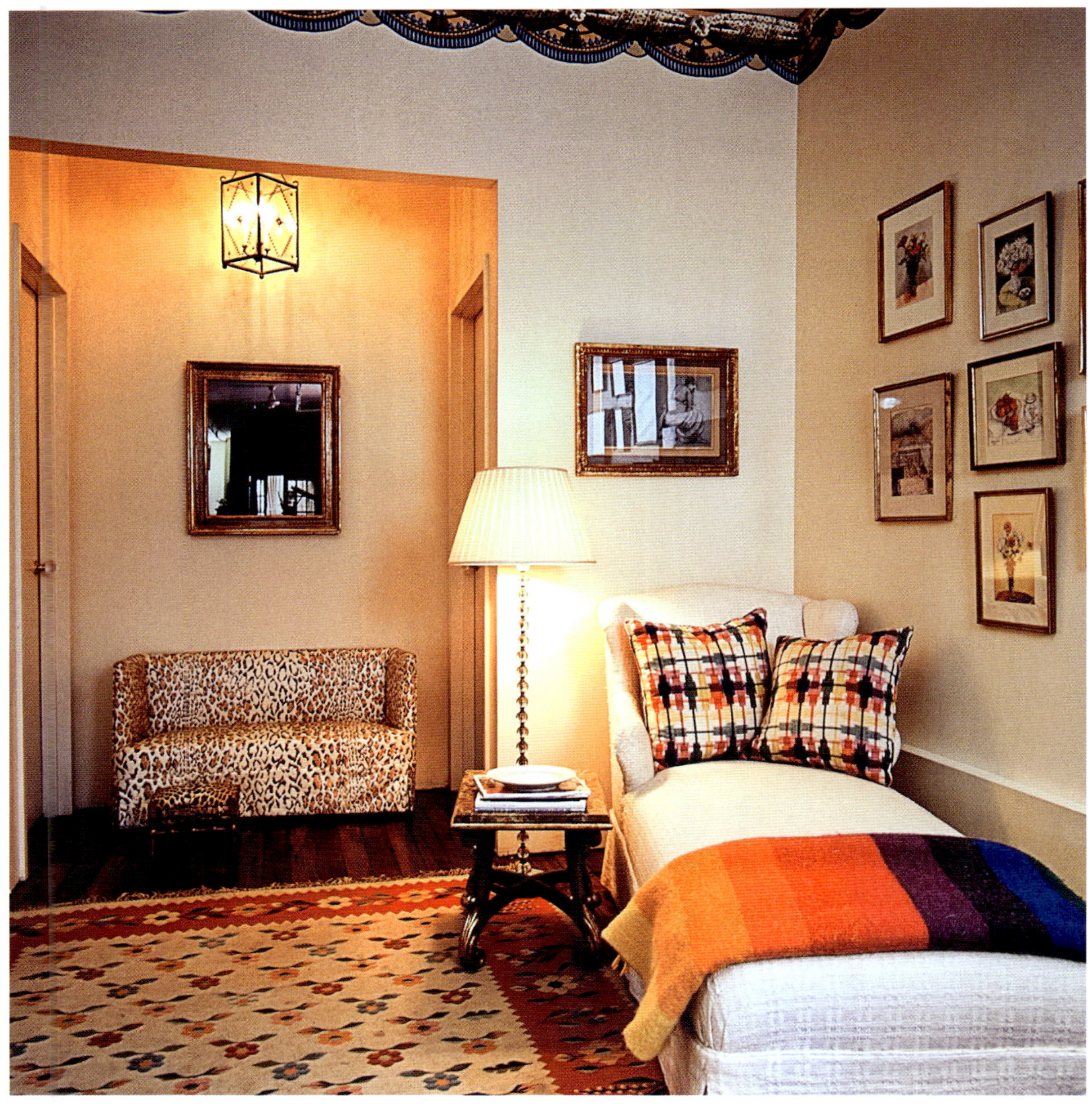

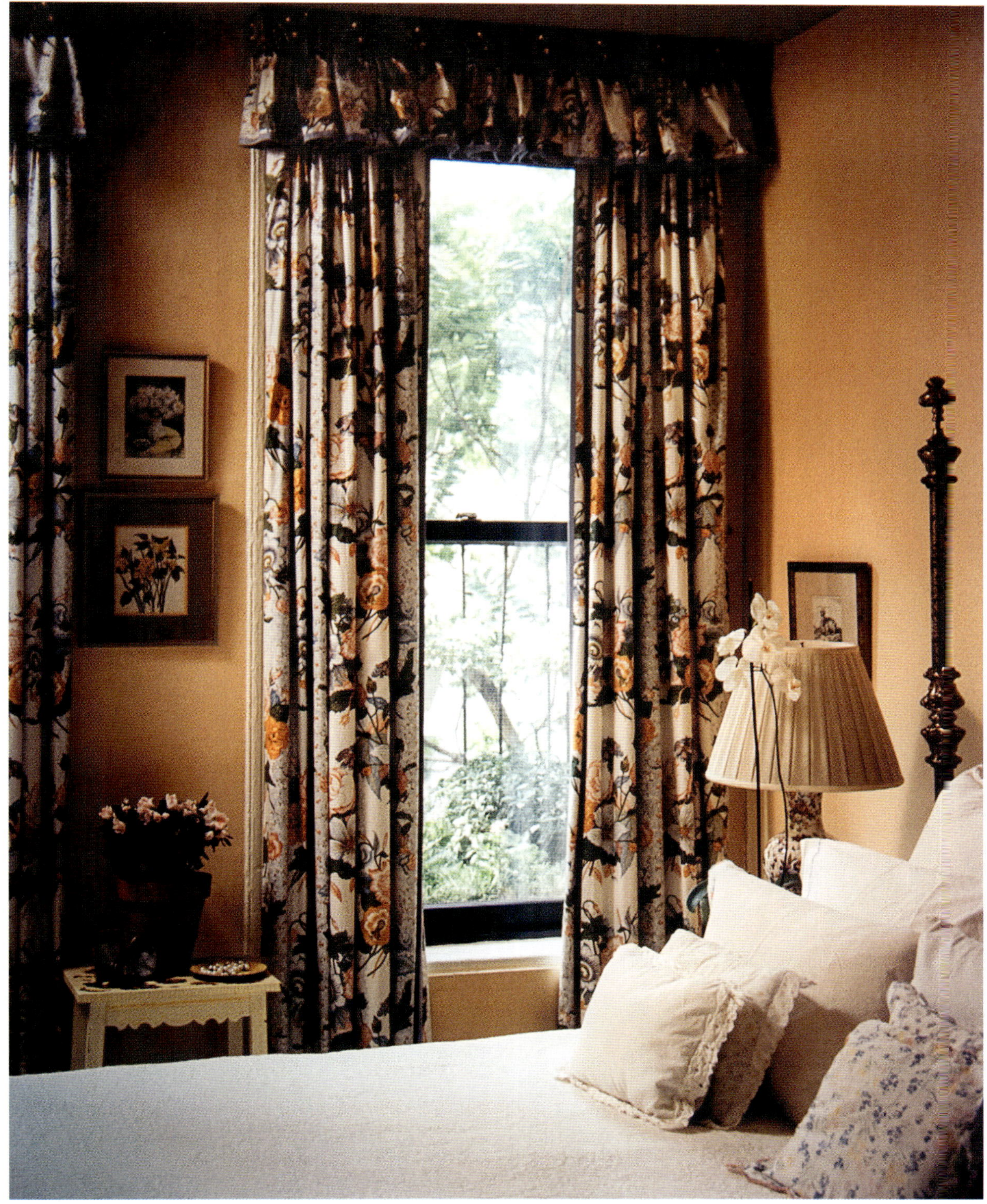

OPPOSITE: The vestibule at the north end of the loft led to two of the bedrooms. Albert Hadley gave me the little sofa, which I still have and love.

ABOVE: Our bedroom on Bond Street faced north and looked out over some lower buildings, so it was quiet and felt calm.

Larchmont

We moved to Larchmont in 1992, into a simple, little, white colonial house on a postage-stamp-sized piece of land a block away from Long Island Sound. The house was sweet but was very dated when we bought it. An ugly floral wallpaper covered the living room walls, and the dining room was painted an acidy lime green. There were four bedrooms and a little, orange-colored, pine-paneled library. It was a very cozy house—the rooms were all small and spilled into each other.

Nothing could be done to the house before we signed the closing papers, so we moved into it as it was. I went right to work. I had in my head what the various color of each room should be and then used coral as a thread to tie all of the downstairs rooms together. The colors for the house all came from a snippet of fabric I had found at Far Eastern Fabrics on Madison Avenue and 32nd Street. The cutting was from an Indian madras fabric but the colors were clear and bright, quite different from most madras materials. It had a soft, clear yellow without any hint of green, a lovely bachelor's buttons blue, and a warm soft coral color. The living room became yellow, the library's pine paneling was painted blue, and the dining room was glazed in coral. The hall in between that connected the downstairs rooms was wallpapered in a coral color with a Parish-Hadley-designed wallpaper called "Sue Ellen" with cerulean blue stars. The Brunschwig & Fils wallpaper border "Bosphore" with swags in blues and coral tones—the same one I used in our Bond Street loft—wrapped around the ceiling line. It was such a happy, fun house full of energy and warm colors. My girls shared a room and, of course, they wanted a pink bedroom. Another bedroom was painted a true bright orange and became Bean's, our third baby's room.

It was so exciting to move into a real house as a young family! We had a yard, a swing set, and a wonderful screen porch. I planted New Dawn roses along the picket fence in the front.

Flora and Charlotte painting "pixie dust" on the picket fence for a *House Beautiful* photo shoot.

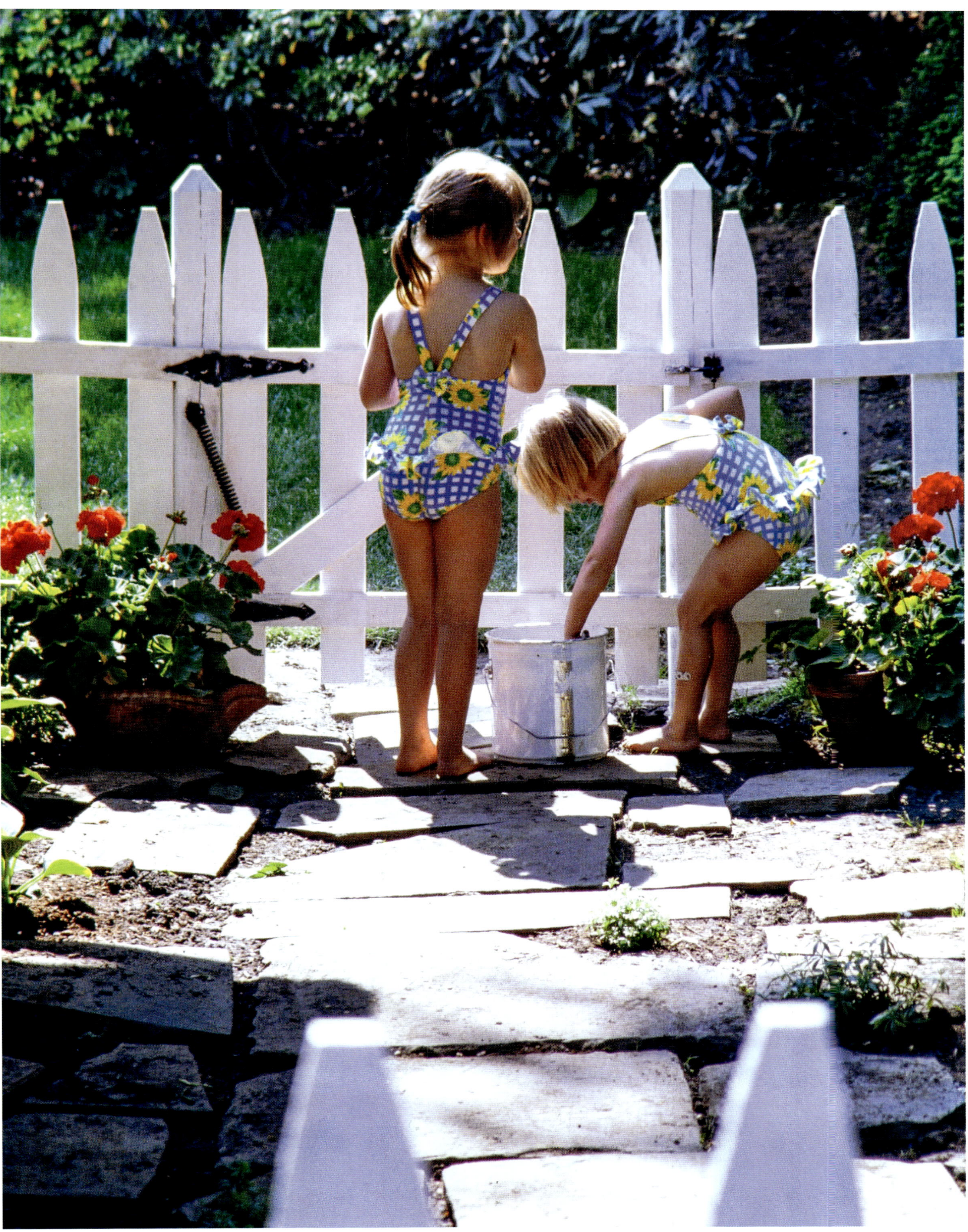

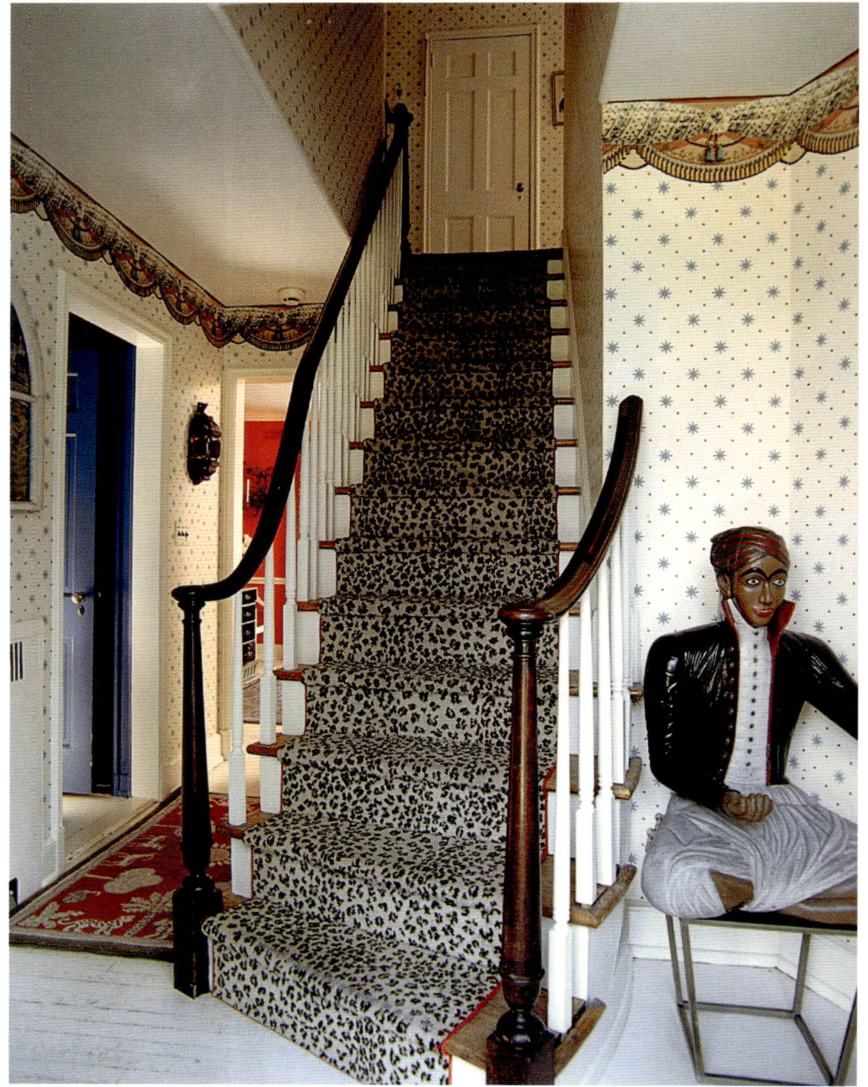

ABOVE: The entrance hall in the house in Larchmont is guarded by this Indian guard statue.

OPPOSITE: The walls in this room were pine when we bought the house. The color of the pinewood was too orange for my taste and the finish needed a little TLC, so I painted the room a shiny blue.

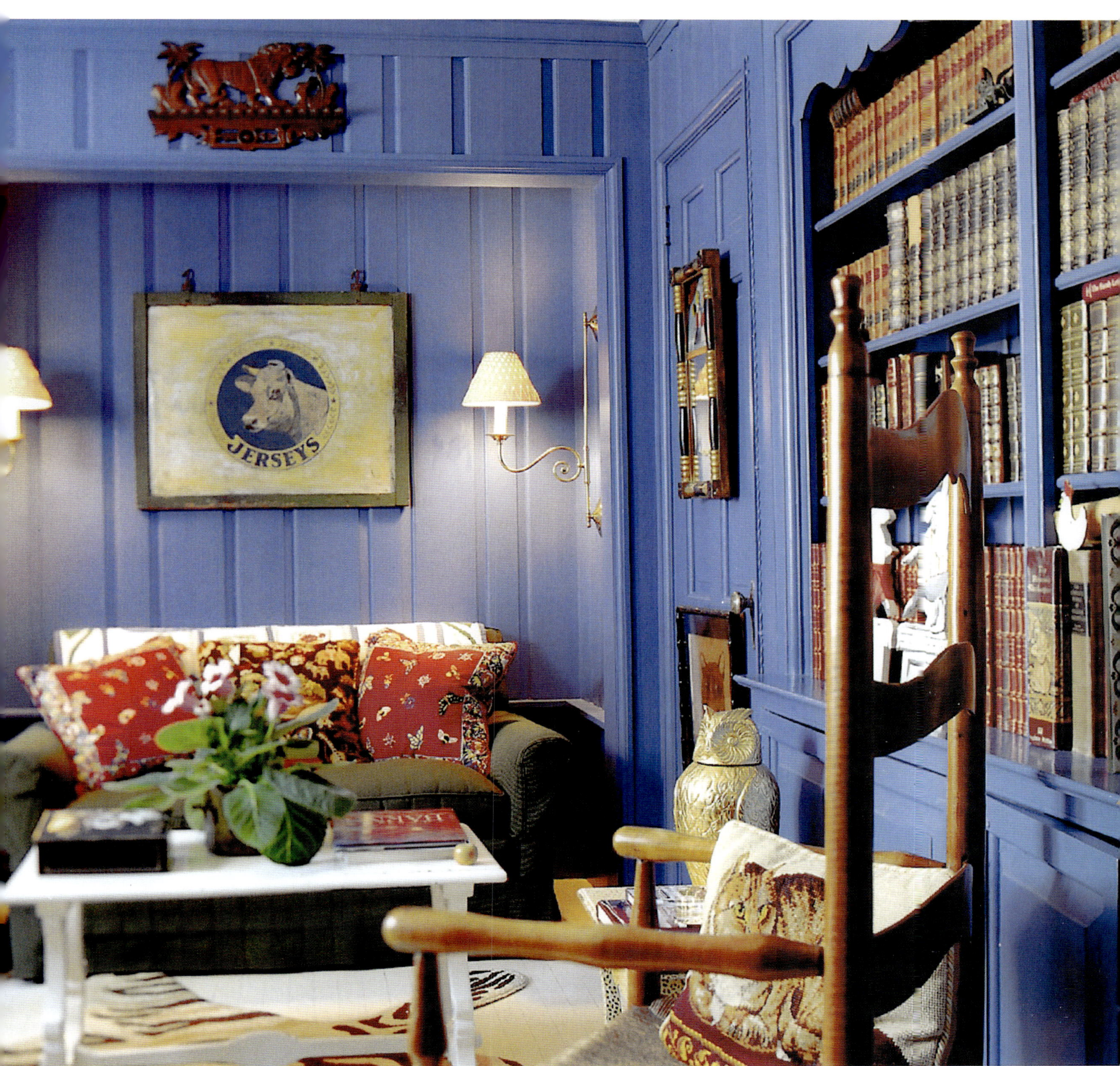
JERSEYS

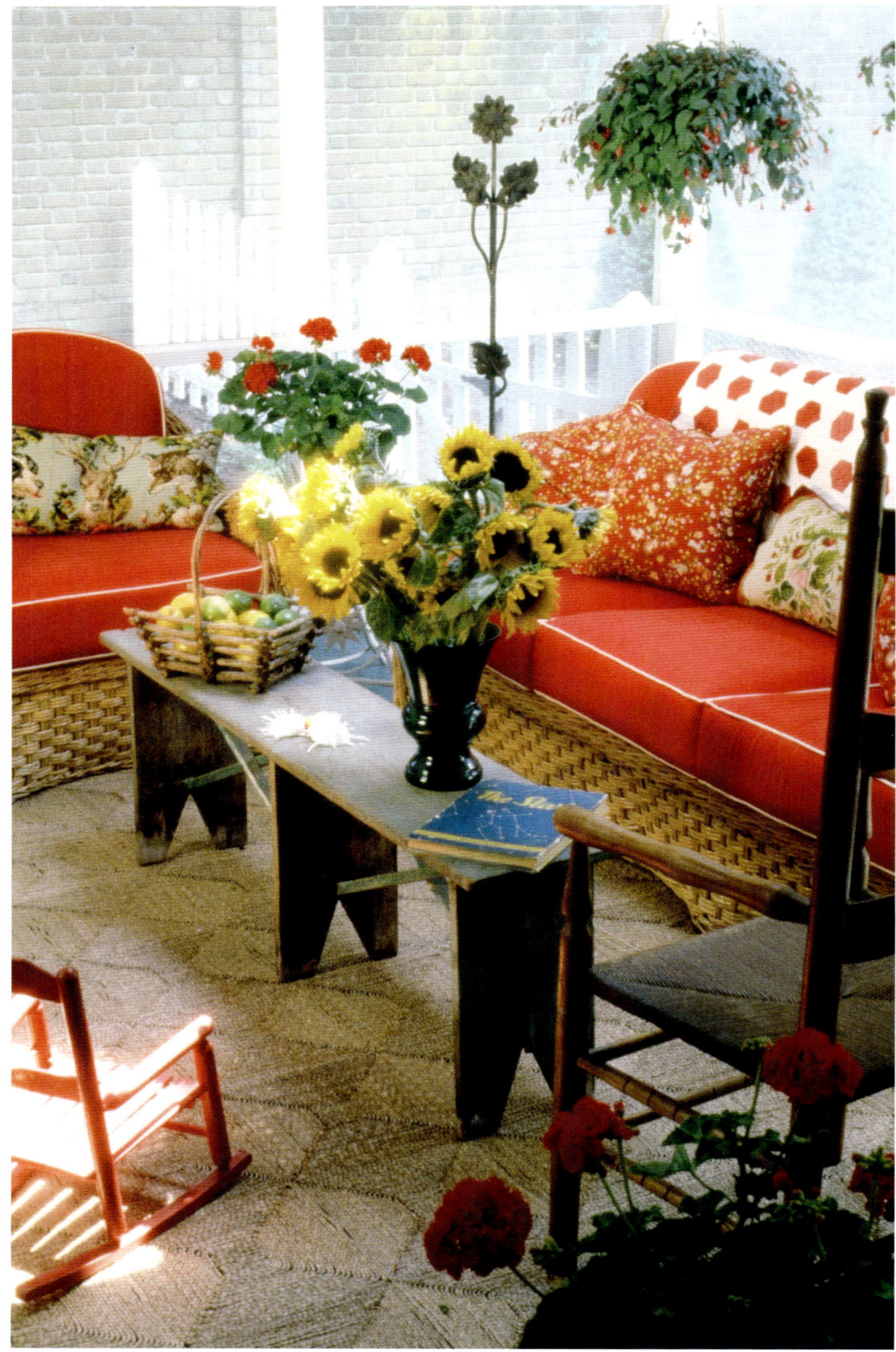

ABOVE: The screen porch in Larchmont was another room for us. It was a very private and comfortable spot for naps.

OPPOSITE: Mita Corsini Bland painted this watercolor of a corner of the living room in Larchmont, showing one of the pyramid bookcases I had made for our first loft on Broome Street. These bookcases have traveled with me to each house.

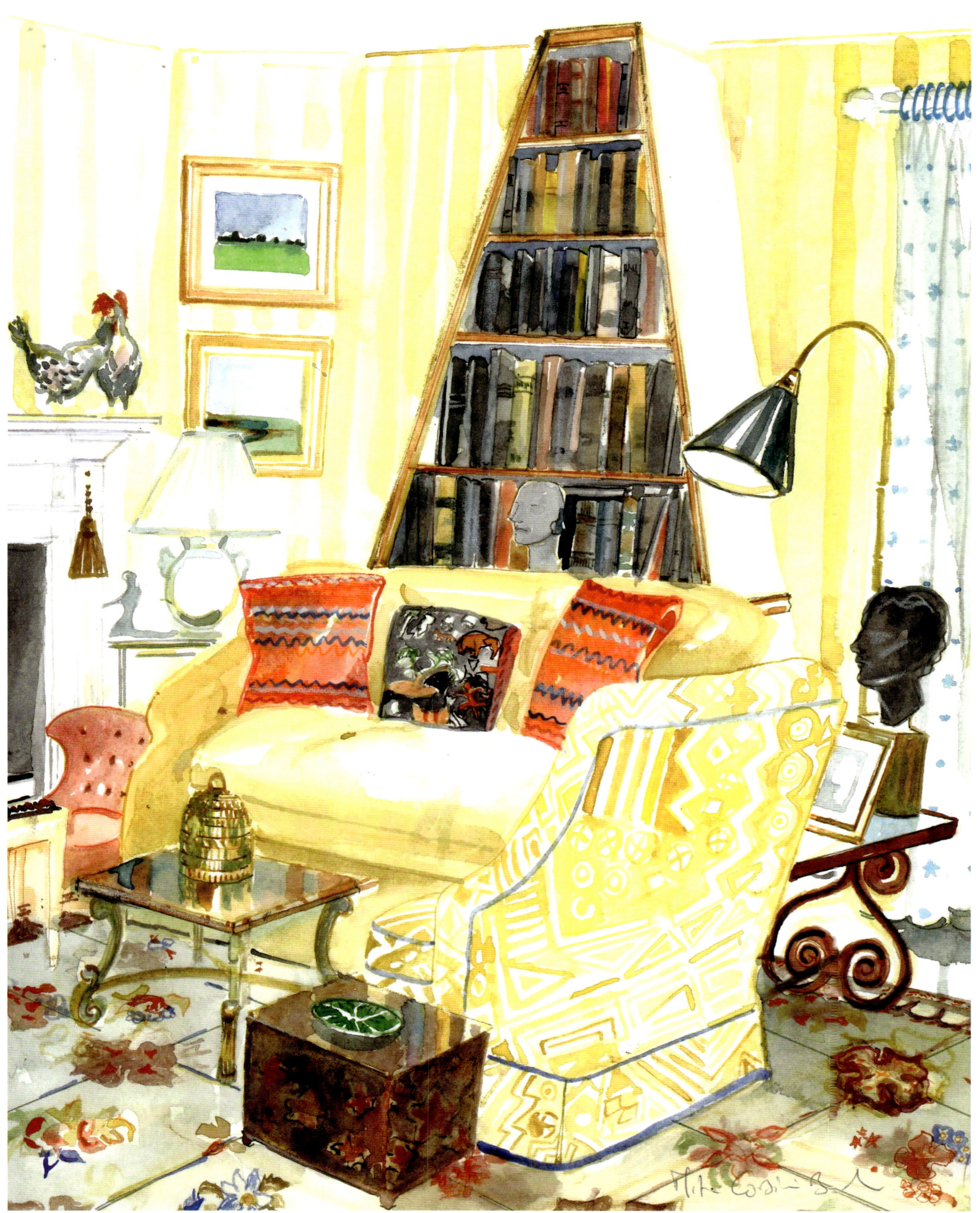

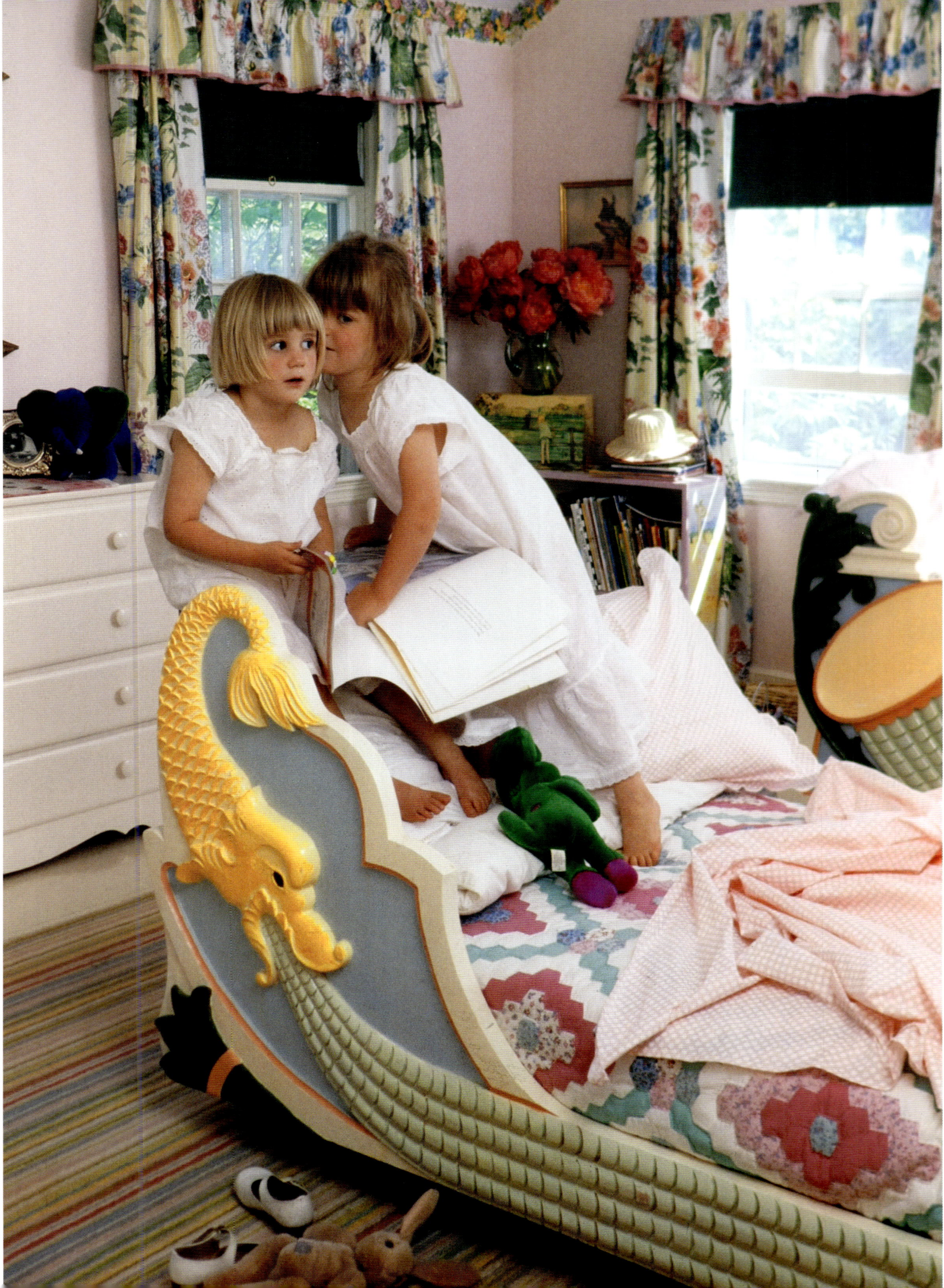

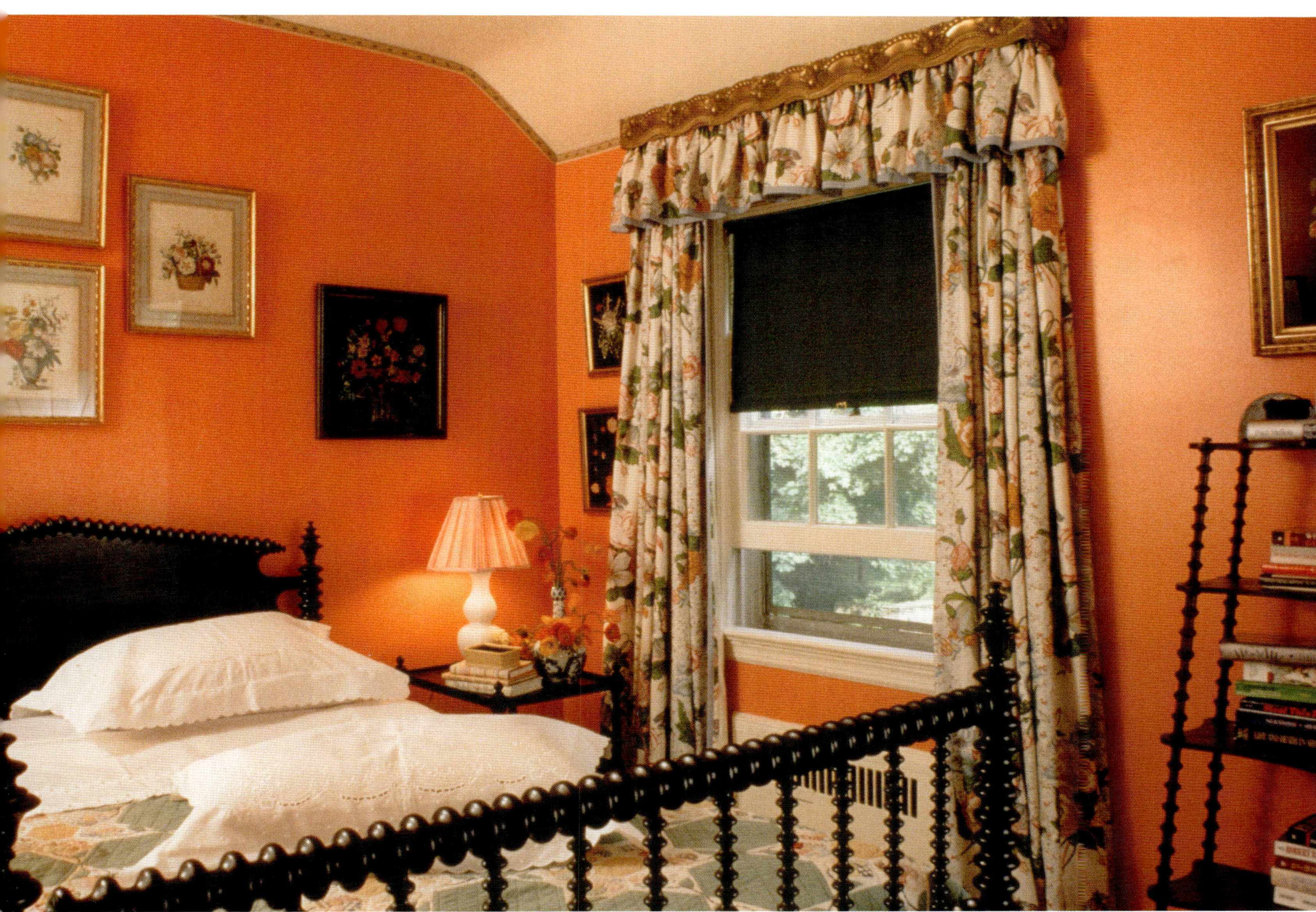

OPPOSITE: Charlotte and Flora playing on one of the sleigh beds I had made by Bill Sullivan. The original sleigh beds were from a carousel in Paris and had been converted into twin beds. They were quite short, so I had them copied and made longer for the children.

ABOVE: This was our youngest child Bean's bedroom. It was a wonderful orange color and had a thin Colefax & Fowler wallpaper border set around the ceiling line, doors, and windows. The press brass cornices were given to me by Albert Hadley as was the spool bed.

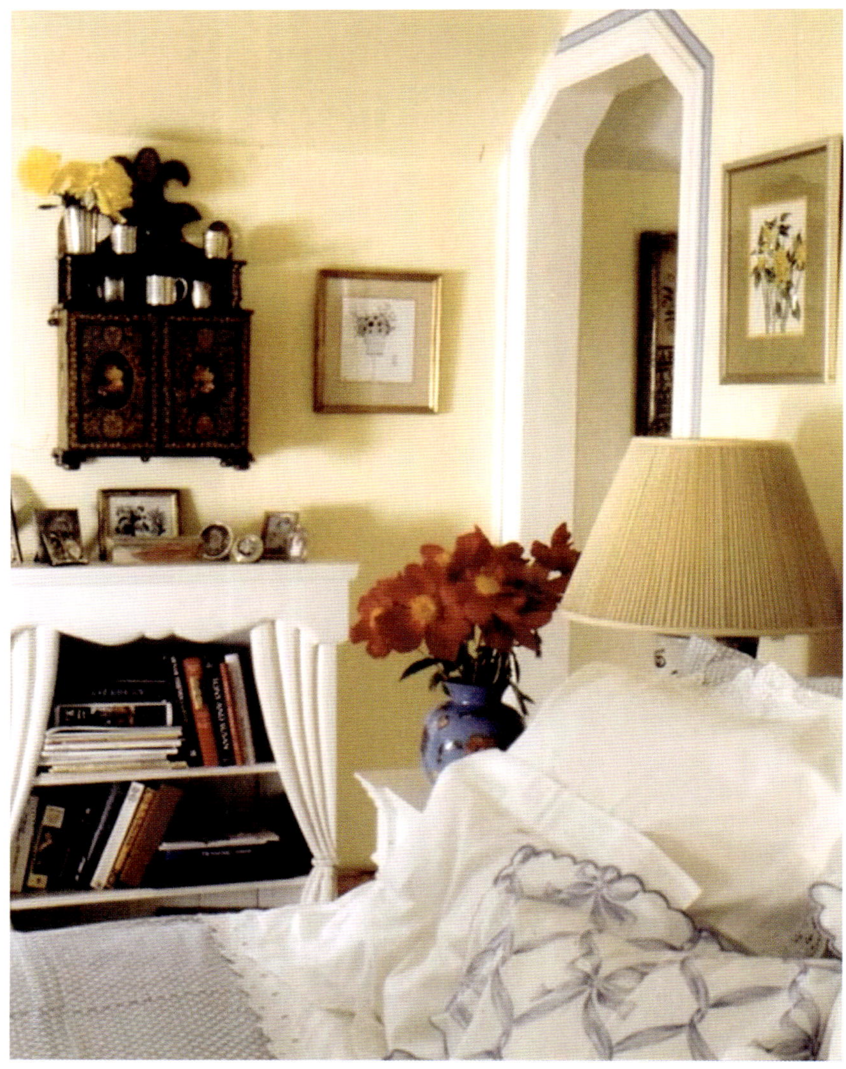

The carved wood curtain bookcase was given to me by Albert Hadley and is flanked here by a drawing he did for me. The black hanging cabinet is a decoupage piece given to me by Mrs. Parish.

My husband and I both commuted to the city, so weekends were the only time we could entertain. Albert Hadley was so generous to me when we moved and gave me some great furniture and things for the house and, of course, his invaluable advice. Mrs. Parish wanted to see the house, so shortly after we had moved in I invited Alan Campbell, Sister Parish, and Albert Hadley to lunch one Sunday. The girls were very excited to have people visiting and insisted on dancing and doing cartwheels to entertain us. When we went in to sit down for lunch, the children went upstairs. It became very quiet—almost too quiet. Halfway through lunch, I went upstairs to check on them, only to find them connecting the gold dots in the "Sue Ellen" wallpaper with crayons. Can you blame them? We have to connect the dots in life, one way or another.

I have always been fearless with a paintbrush in hand. As a child, I spent hours with my father painting things—sometimes furniture, but mostly boats. I grew up with painted furniture and have never thought twice about adding a coat of paint to spruce up an old piece of furniture. The sanctity of natural wood means less to me than to most people. Painting the dull pine paneling bright blue in the Larchmont library was an exciting prospect. A shiny finish on the walls opened up the room and brought in light even though the color wasn't a light blue but instead, a bright, strong bachelor's button blue.

Albert Hadley went to Nashville several times a year to visit his family and always came back with the best furniture, treasures, and finds. He found a wonderful armchair that had a flower cutout back, which I instantly fell in love with. I had eight chairs made by Ahmed, a wonderful Egyptian furniture maker who used a nice mahogany wood for the chairs. Ahmed was so proud of the chairs he had made and they were just beautiful, but I wanted them to feel lighter and more playful, so I painted them white. I still do not have any regrets about painting those chairs, and they still look so fresh and happy in my dining room today.

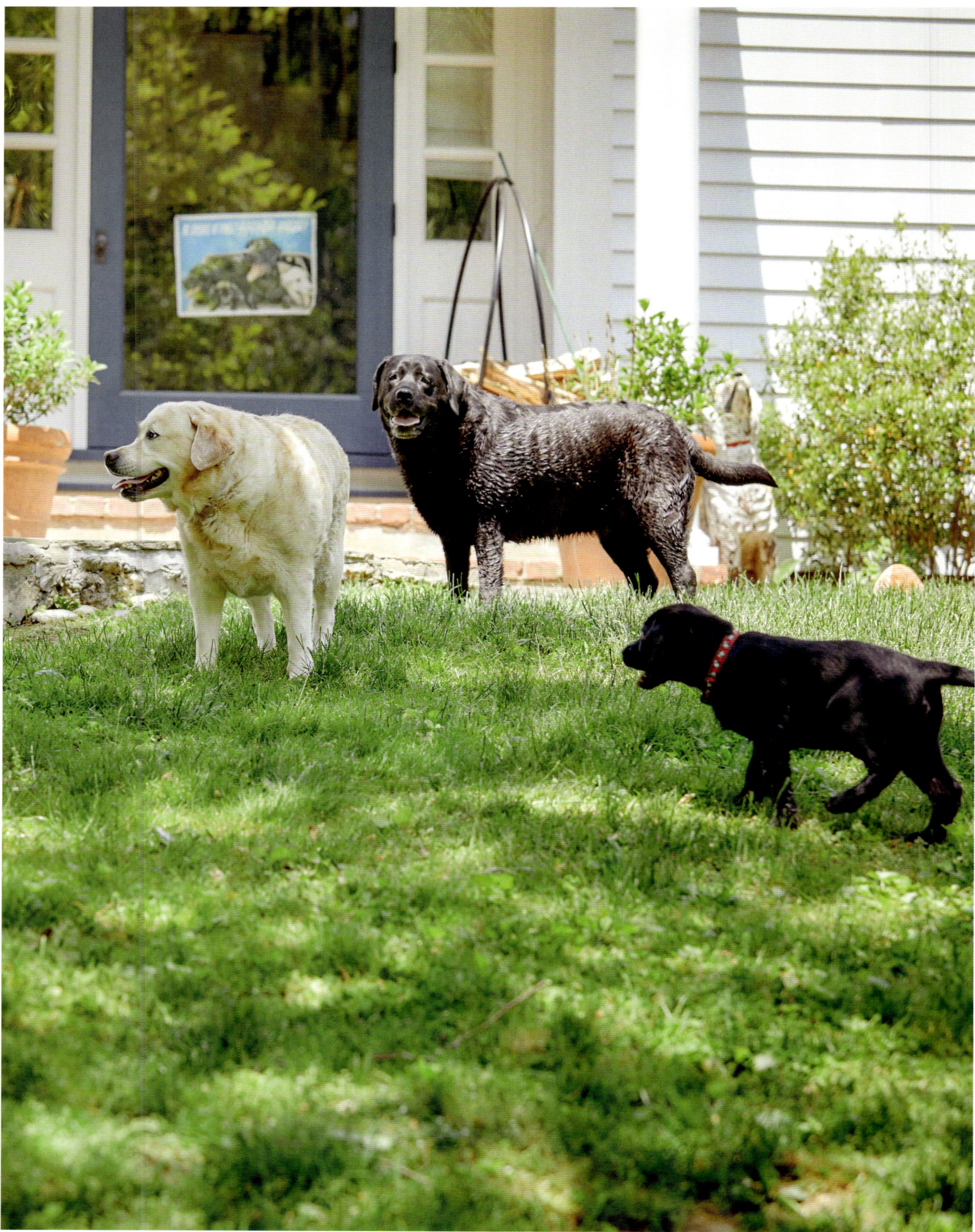

Connecticut

When the children got older and my marriage ended, I got bolder and moved on my own to Connecticut. It was time for a new start. I wanted more land and space for my animals (and lower taxes). I wanted to be close enough to the city for work but not too far out. I hate to admit that I usually drive into town rather than take the train, but my car is always filled with bags, rugs, or furniture.

I got an email from one of the real estate websites for a house that I must have put a "like" tag on but I didn't remember ever seeing any pictures of it. It was a simple, unexciting, red colonial. Sadly, it had been neglected and needed a lot of work, mostly cosmetic work and updating. Yet I knew it had potential.

One of my best friends is a Realtor in Greenwich, and she desperately tried to dissuade me from buying the house; it was a wreck and the land had been let go. The pond was a swamp. But this was exactly the sort of project I needed at that point. The dreamy, romantic side of me didn't even think about the pond, or what havoc my four muddy but ecstatic Labradors would wreak on the house with their own water to swim in. I immediately had to buy a dog bathtub just to let them back inside.

It was more the land that I loved than the house itself—two acres and a pond for the dogs. There is so much wildlife—great blue herons, hawks, egrets, mallards and their ducklings, a gaggle of geese and their goslings every spring. There are so many different types of birds, and I feed them all religiously. There are fox, coyotes, deer, and even an occasional bear. The sound of the frogs at night in the summer is just wonderful.

Both the house and the land needed an overhaul, and a good deal of attention and restoration.

Being a decorator for the last four decades has made me both more discerning and more capable of imagining what is possible. I started with wallpapers and paint, choosing warm colors and knowing I would use lots of both. When I bought the house,

A few of the dogs—Leisl, Marta, and Fern—after a swim in the pond.

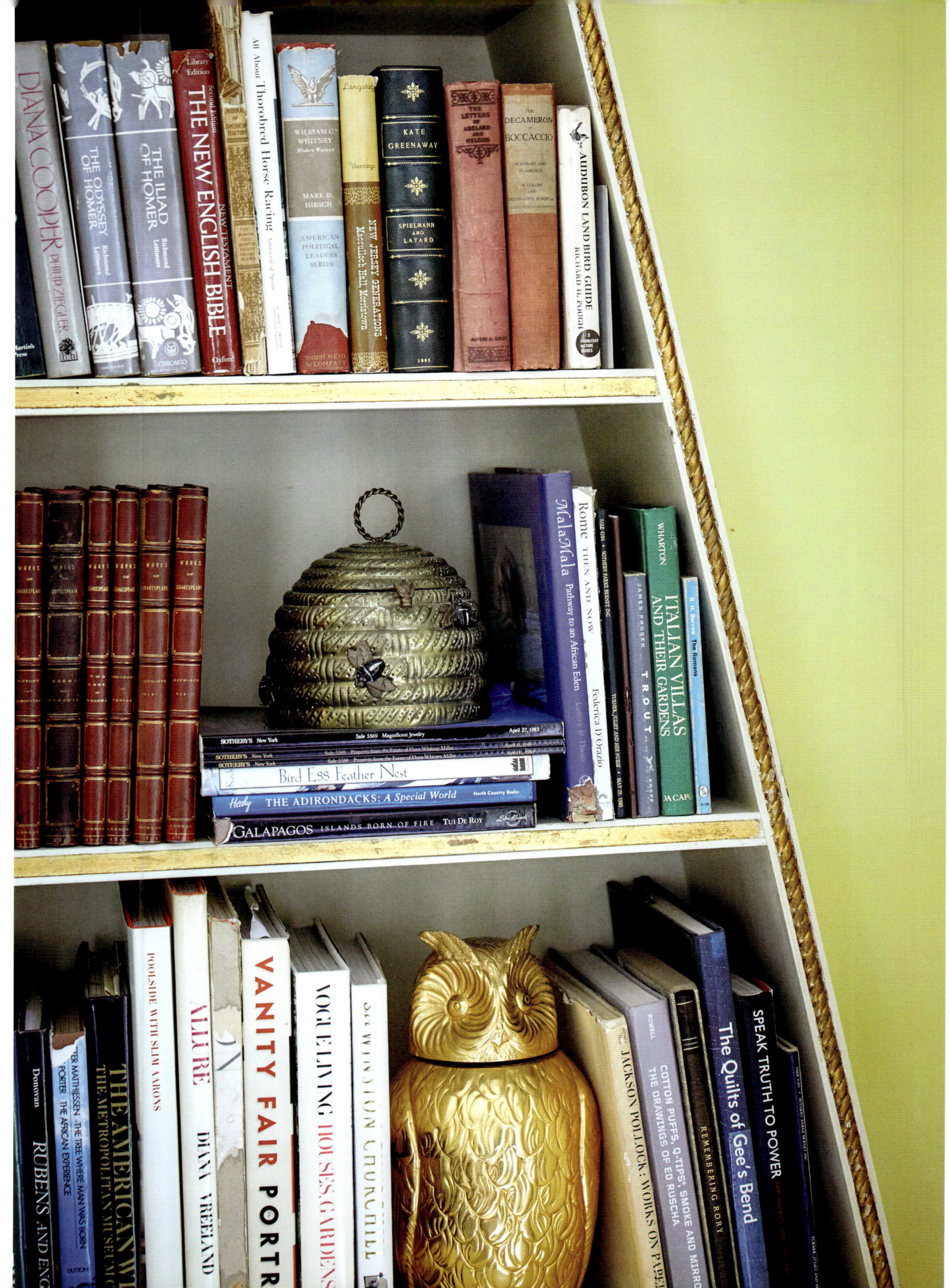

DIANA COOPER PHILIP ZIEGLER
THE ODYSSEY OF HOMER Richmond Lattimore
THE ILIAD OF HOMER Richmond Lattimore CHICAGO
Library Edition Second Edition THE NEW ENGLISH BIBLE NEW TESTAMENT Oxford
All About Thorobred Horse Racing
WILLIAM C. WHITNEY Modern Warwick MARK D. HIRSCH AMERICAN POLITICAL LEADERS SERIES DODD MEAD & COMPANY
Vantage
NEW JERSEY GENERATIONS Macculloch Hall, Morristown
KATE GREENAWAY SPIELMANN AND LAYARD
THE LETTERS OF ABELARD AND HELOISE
THE DECAMERON OF BOCCACCIO
AUDUBON LAND BIRD GUIDE RICHARD H. POUGH
WORKS OF SHAKESPEARE
MalaMala Pathway to an African Eden
Rome THEN AND NOW Federica D'Orizio
SOTHEBY PARKE BERNET INC
JAMES PROSEK TROUT KNOPF
WHARTON ITALIAN VILLAS AND THEIR GARDENS DA CAPO
R. H. Barrow The Romans
SOTHEBY'S New York Sale 5569 Magnificent Jewelry April 27, 1987
Bird Egg Feather Nest
Hardy THE ADIRONDACKS: A Special World North Country Books
GALAPAGOS ISLANDS BORN OF FIRE TUI DE ROY
Donovan
THE TREE WHERE MAN WAS BORN THE AFRICAN EXPERIENCE PORTER
THE METROPOLITAN MUSEUM
POOLSIDE WITH SLIM AARONS
ALLURE DIANA VREELAND
VANITY FAIR
VOGUE LIVING HOUSES GARDENS
WINSTON CHURCHILL
JACKSON POLLOCK: WORKS ON
COTTON PUFFS, Q-TIPS, SMOKE AND THE DRAWINGS OF ED RUSCHA
REMEMBERING RORY
The Quilts of Gee's Bend
SPEAK TRUTH TO POWER

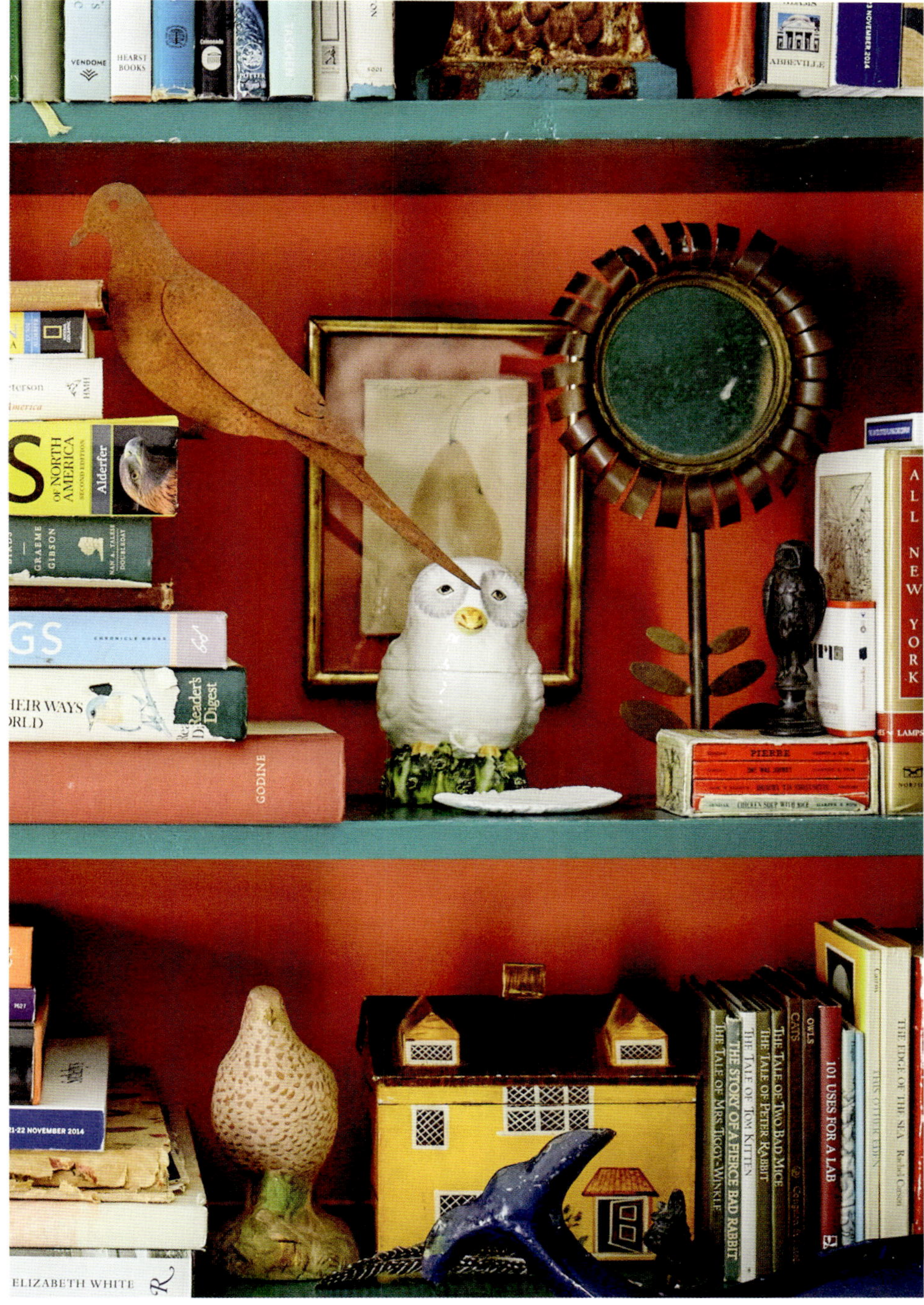

OPPOSITE: A detail of one of the living room's pyramid-shaped bookcases. I always include different things on bookshelves and like books to be stacked as well as standing upright.

ABOVE: The library bookcases are filled with many pieces from my animal collection along with items from my other collections.

there were a pair of entry doors with a transom above that did not really allow for much light to come in on the front and sunniest side of the house. Natural light is something I always crave. The front doors had to go. I had a Dutch door made with sidelights so that the top half of the door could be left open during the day and let light in.

In general the hall had far too many doors: double closet doors, double doors going into the dining room, and double doors going into the living room. I wanted walls to hang paintings on and a wall for a front hall table with a lamp on it and a mirror above to open up the space and bring in light. It is essential for me to have a surface as I walk in to put down whatever it is that I am inevitably carrying, including the mail and my keys.

The floor was slate and not a pretty slate. It was also an acoustical nightmare, so I replaced it with wood and then painted it white. It has since been painted by Matthew Tyrrell, a wonderful old friend who I first met when he painted wavy stripes in Mrs. Parish's foyer in her last New York apartment. It's an open crisscross design with fun colors. Matthew started on a beige glazed ground and added a fantasy of marbleized squares on the diagonal with jewel-colored veining and red squares connecting the diamonds. The rest of the floors in the house are still painted white—perhaps not a great choice with black Labradors, but it makes the house feel light and bright. After a few years, the floors have started to wear, giving them a softer quality, which makes them even better.

I replaced the 1960s iron railing with a wooden railing of very simple square spindles. I hung the same "Sue Ellen" wallpaper designed by Albert Hadley that I used in the old house. It's one of my favorite wallpapers—whimsical, playful, not too serious. It always amazes me to see a space get transformed as you make changes. The entrance hall is now a bright and cheerful space. It's filled with light and sets the tone for the house. An old wooden cow that belonged to John Rosselli sits in the front hall on a bright red table. A leopard-spotted runner on the stairs is very forgiving and makes sense in a house full of dogs. I added a small

This library has most of the animal pieces that I have collected over the years. The Steiff giraffe has been with me for decades. The wooden seal was carved by John Bryan. Each time I find an owl, it inevitably comes to live with me. Our dog, Fig, loved to pose for photographs.

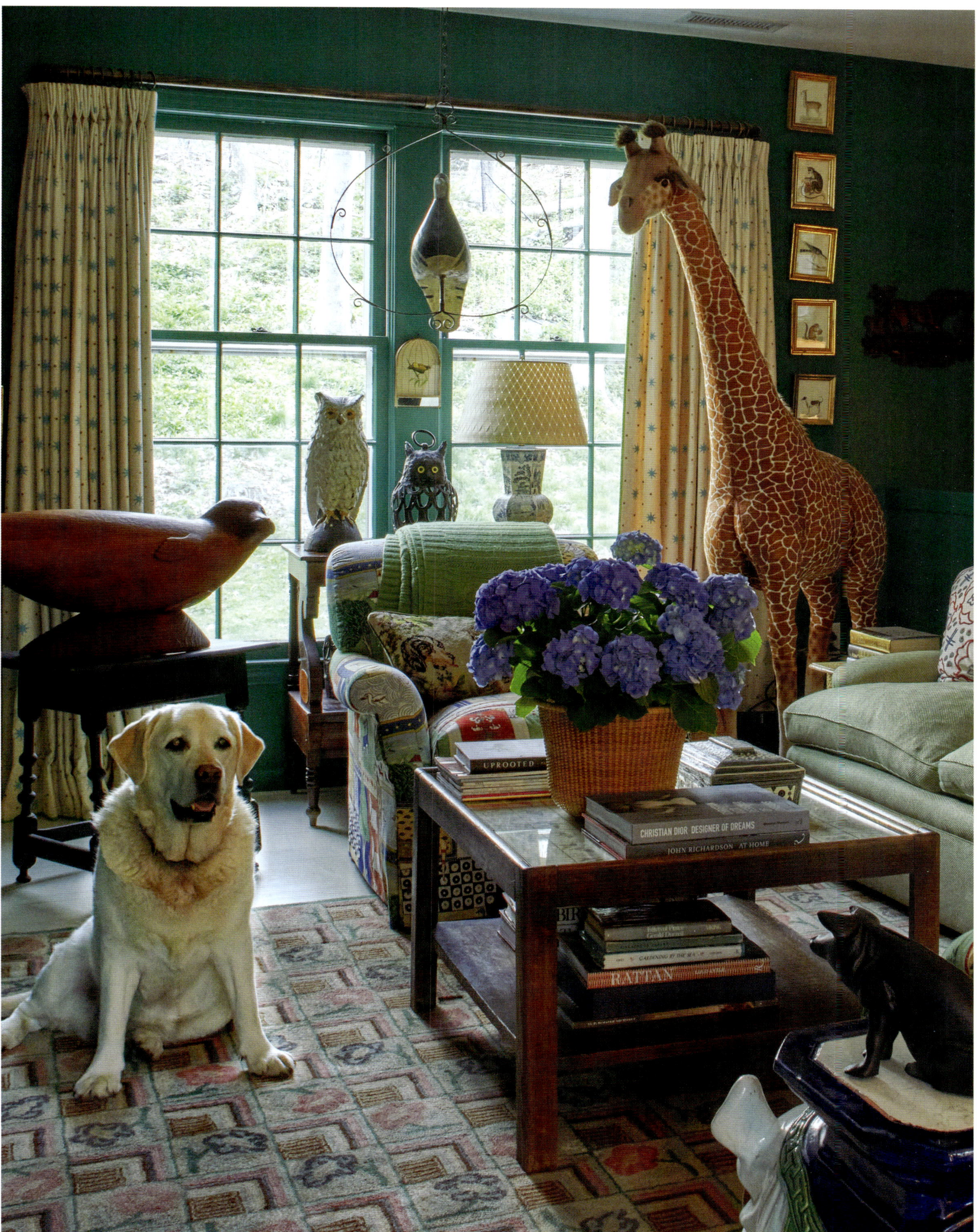
UPROOTED
CHRISTIAN DIOR DESIGNER OF DREAMS
JOHN RICHARDSON AT HOME
GARDENING BY THE SEA
RATTAN

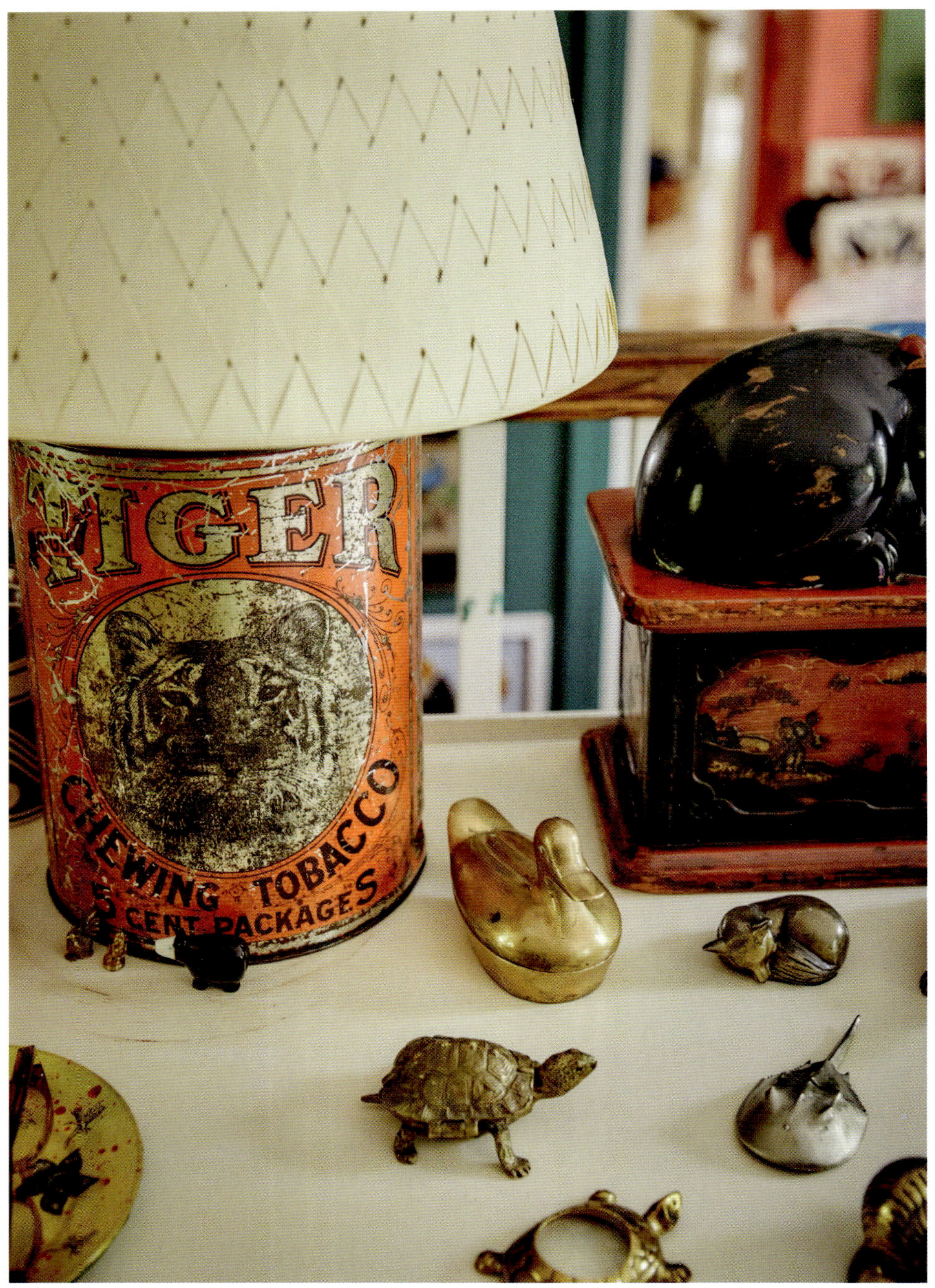

ABOVE: The Tiger tea cannister is from Woodard & Greenstein (once simply Thomas Woodard) and is one of the very first things I bought when I moved to New York. The sleeping cat piece next to it was given to me by Albert Hadley—it was always next to his bed in the city. The little brass animals are part of an ever-growing collection.

OPPOSITE: The Jersey cow sign has been with me since 1977 and was the beginning of my animal collection. It is from a barn in Concord, Massachusetts. The paper geraniums were made by Livia Cetti at the Green Vase. Chuck Fischer painted the tin valance.

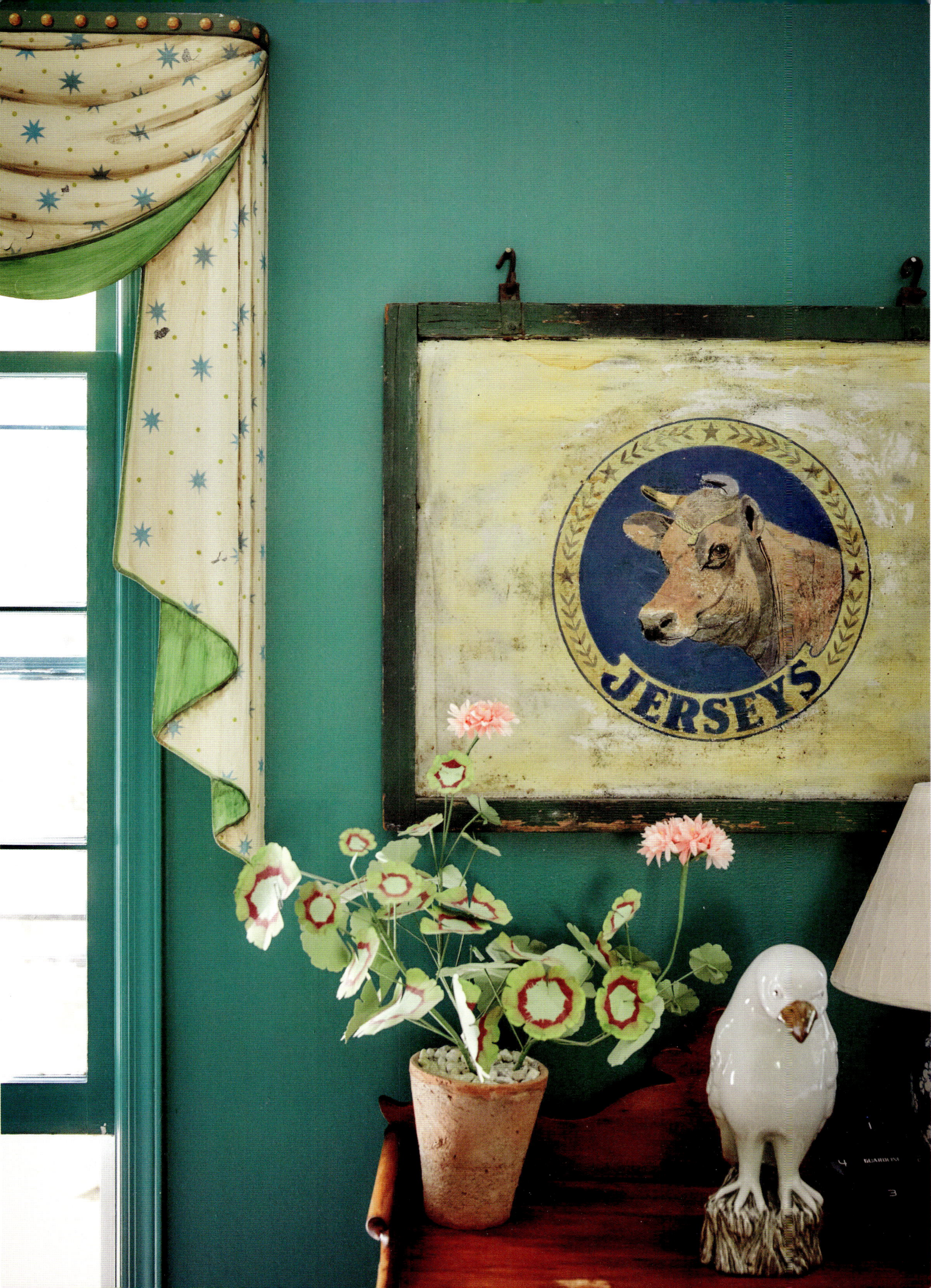
JERSEYS

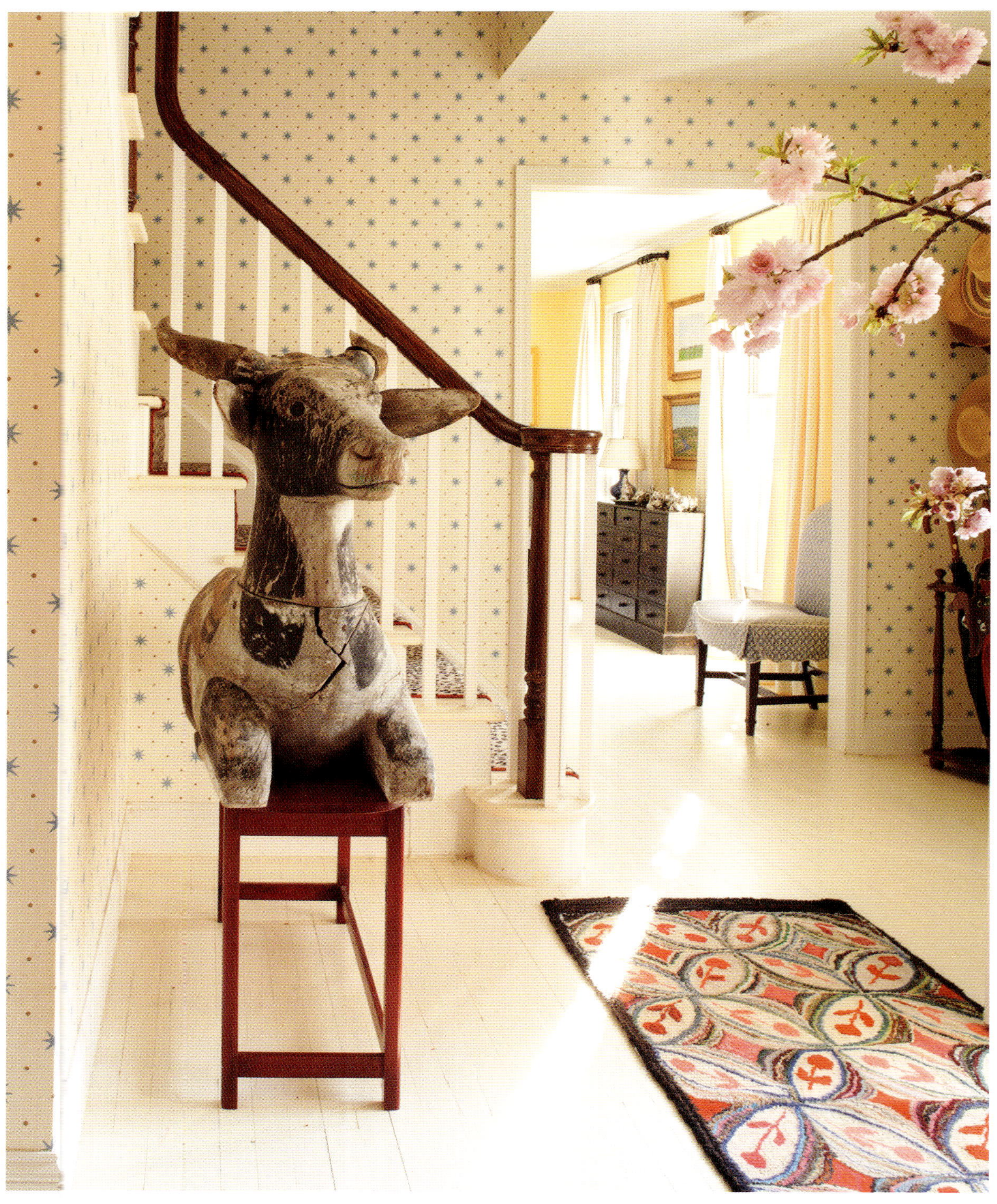

I installed a white painted wood floor in the entrance hall of my Connecticut house to replace a slate floor. The acoustics are much better with a wooden floor. The large wooden cow was a gift from John Rosselli.

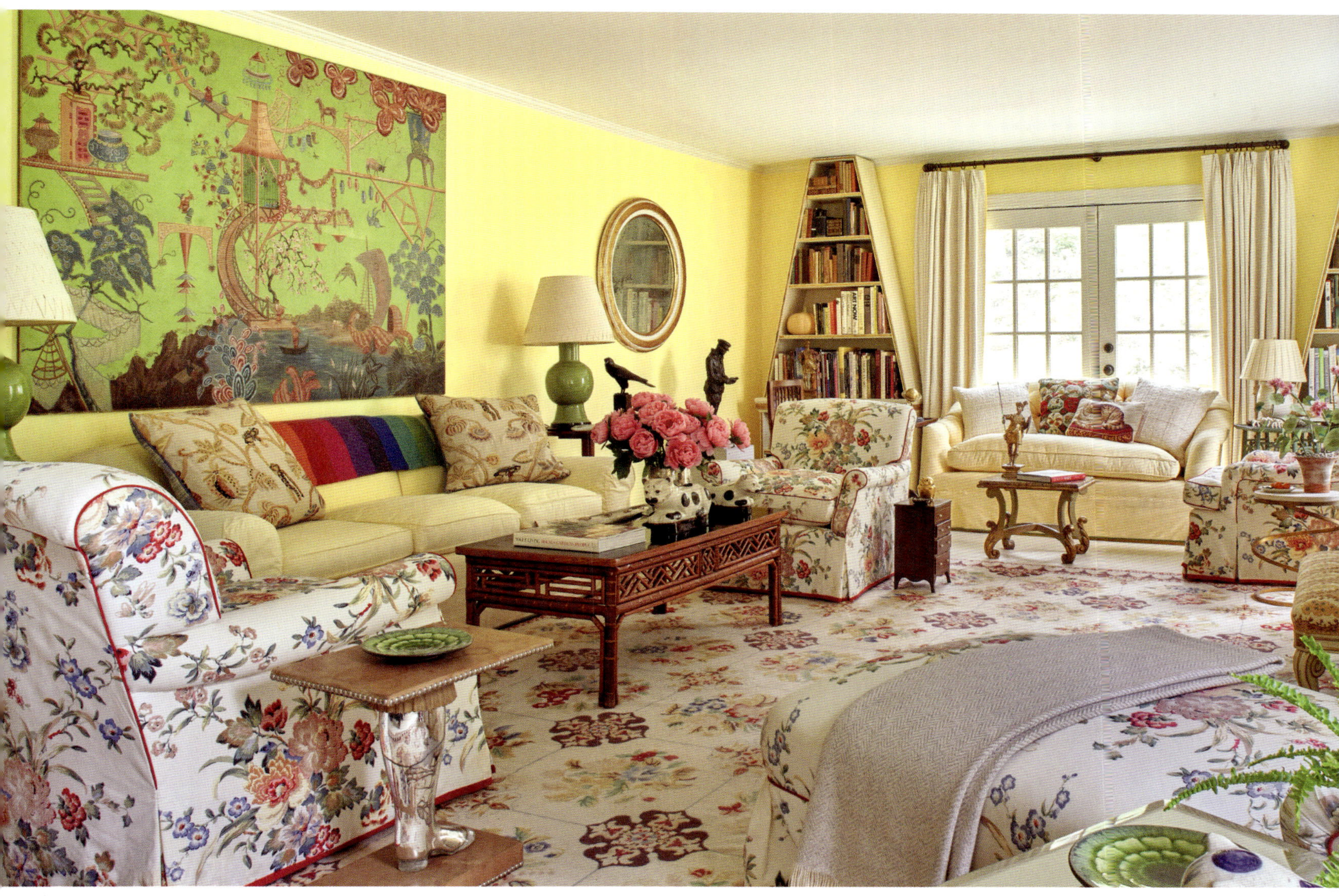

In my Connecticut living room, the pyramid bookcases flank the doors to the terrace. The placement of a sofa at the far end of the room means the doors to the terrace cannot be opened, but the room feels more usable and has more seating.

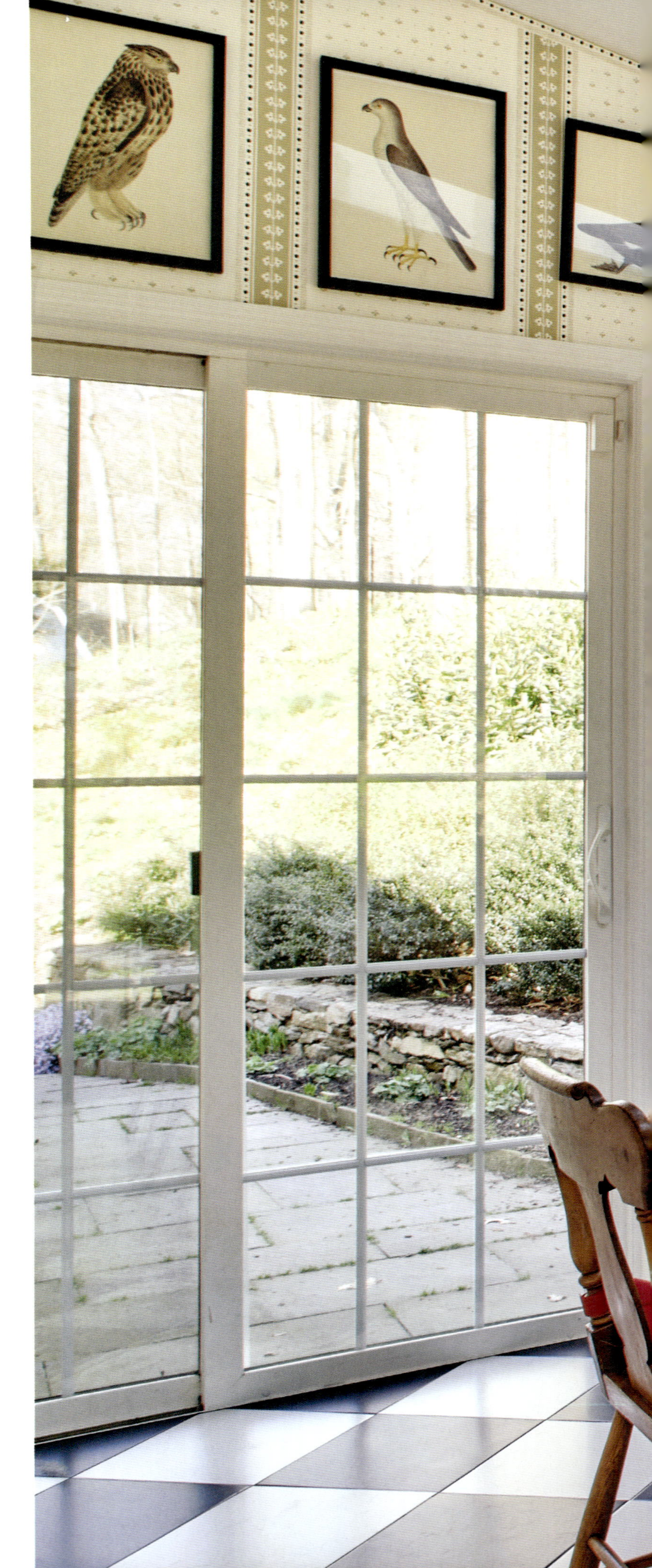

The breakfast area in the kitchen houses a collection of Olof Rudbeck bird prints, a hanging parrot, and ceramic nesting hens—all part of the animal collection.

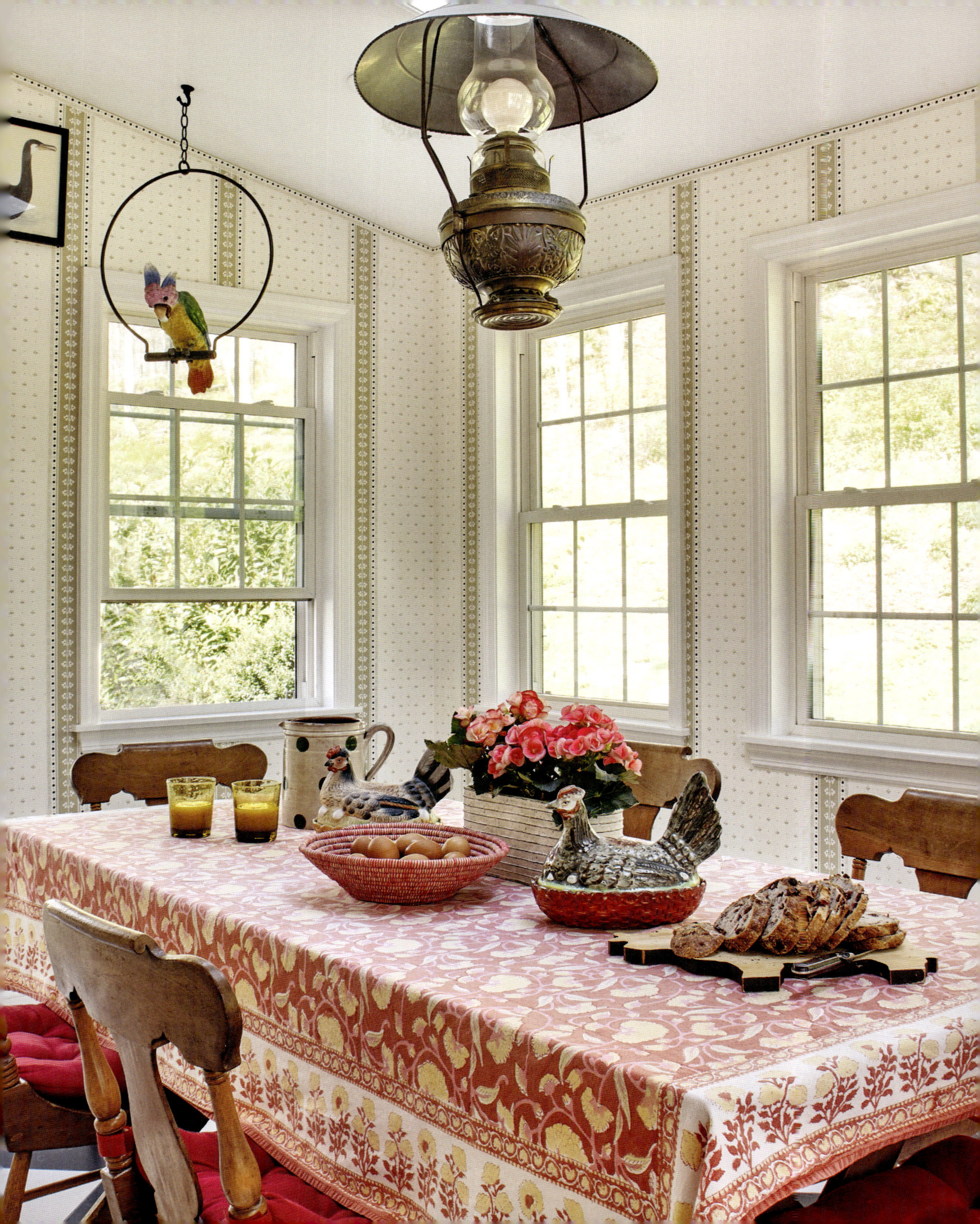

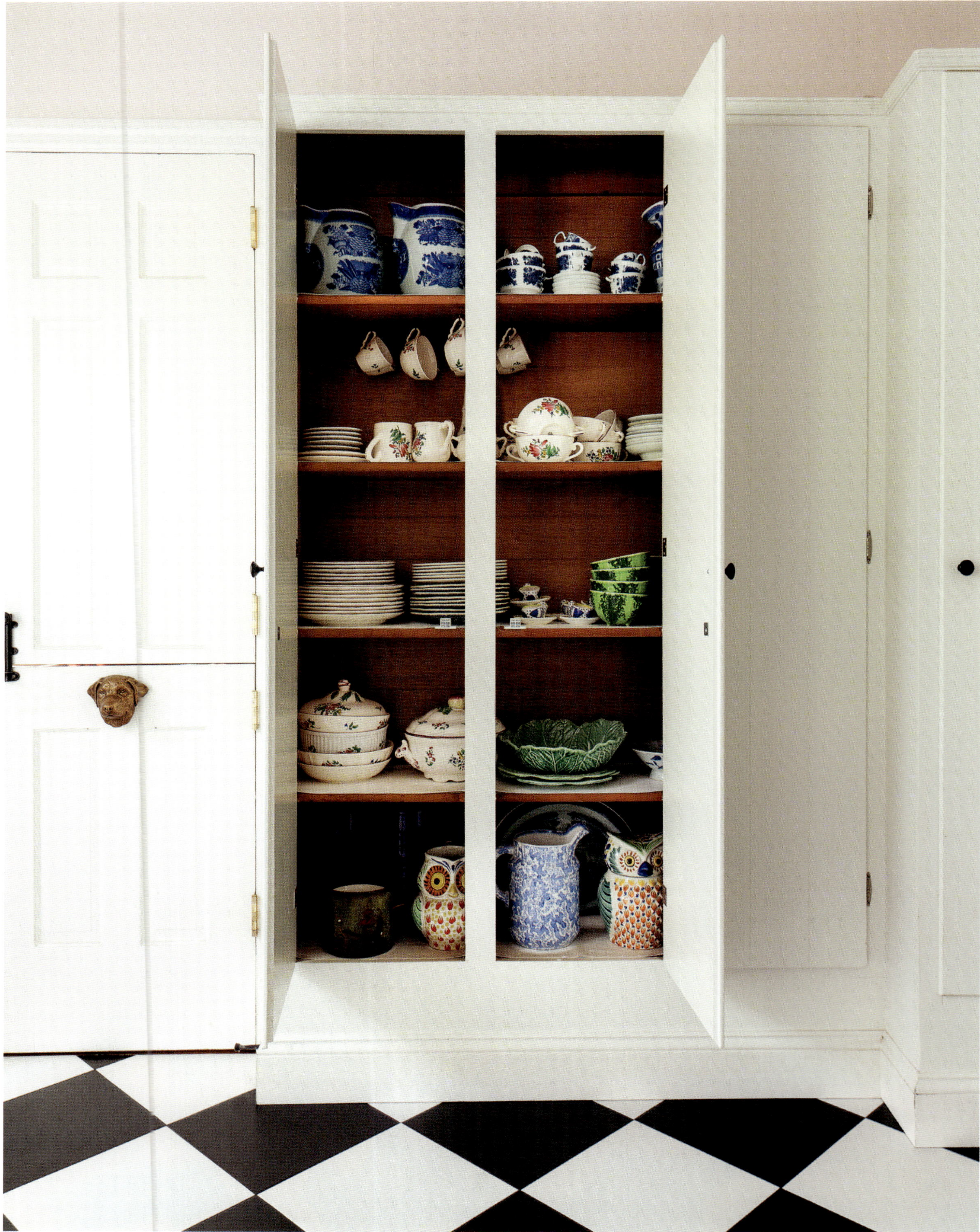

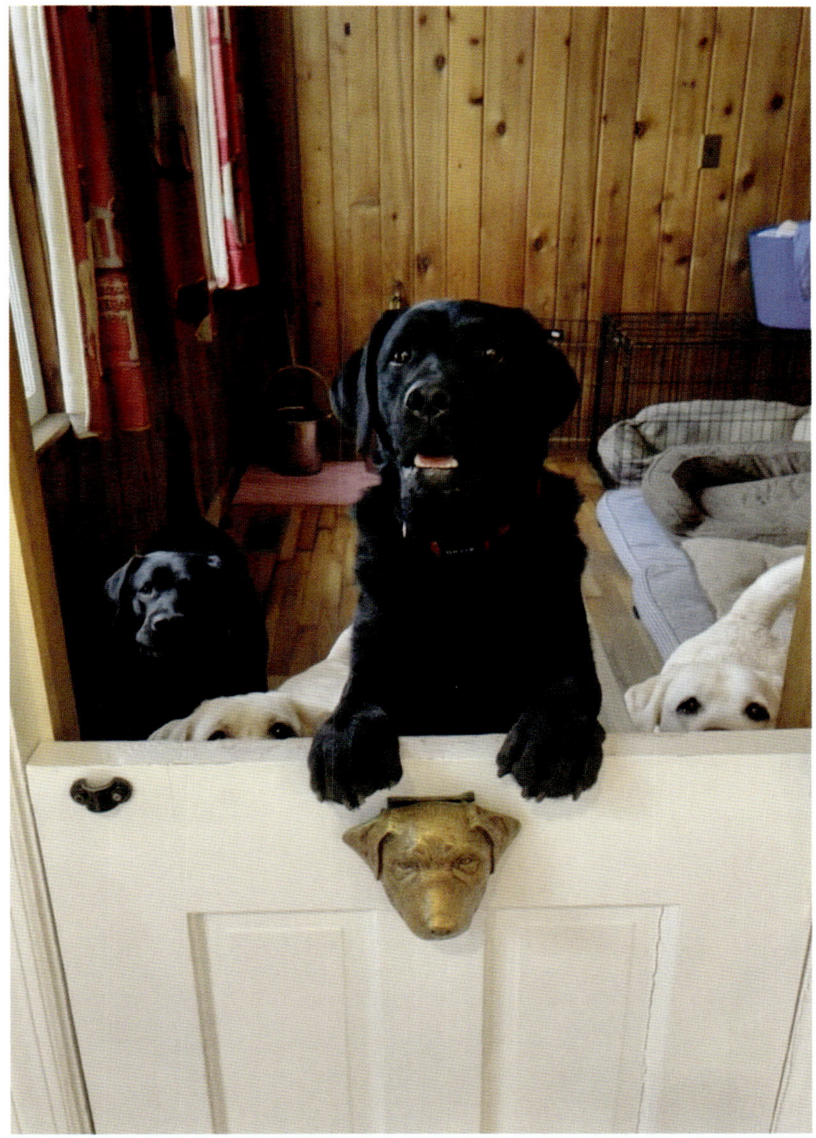

OPPOSITE: These tall cabinets hold pitchers and plates. Nothing is better than lots of storage in a kitchen.

ABOVE: The dogs—especially Henry—love to look out over the bottom half of the kitchen's Dutch door. My children gave me the bronze Labrador retriever door knocker. The curtains at the two windows keep the dogs from seeing the wildlife at night.

band of red at the edge of the stair rug. Details like these make such a difference and everything is always better with a finished edge.

The living room, dining room, and kitchen all needed work and warming up. In the living room, the six-over-nine pane double-hung windows are low to the floor and bring in lots of light. They are the perfect height for the dogs to look out of. The living room is a long and somewhat narrow room with a fireplace on the long outside wall in between two windows. I ended up putting a love seat at the far end of the room in front of doors that lead to a terrace on the back of the house. Even though having a seating area at that end of the room makes access to the outside impossible, the multiple seating groups make for a much better, cozier room.

The room is painted a canary yellow and the two pyramid-shape bookcases that I had made in the early 1980s—inspired by Rory Cameron's own bookcases in France—flank the doors to the terrace. Everything that I already had has found a place and works in this new space; some pieces have ended up in a very different sort of room, and have been painted or recovered. I love it when pieces can be repurposed and work in a new space.

I decided to glaze the dining room a coral color that my friend Adreano, who worked at Weidl for years, mixed on-site with me. Albert used to always say that red- and coral-colored dining rooms made for better dinner conversation and brought out the best in people's coloring. Reds and corals are tricky and can easily veer in a blue or orange direction. A true coral is a lovely color and evokes both energy and happiness. Years ago I went to John Rosselli's shop when it was on 73rd Street at just the right moment. A shipment was being unloaded and there was a very large painted linen panel of an Indian elephant dressed for a celebration of sorts, adorned with beads and necklaces and a beautiful saddle cloth. I had to have that elephant and it has been in my dining rooms for years now. There is also a decoupage panel of two elephants in the dining room, which was made by the incredibly talented Apple Bartlett, Sister Parish's daughter. I love her work and have many of her things. The first decoupage piece I ever bought of Apple's is also in this room, and it is the first thing you see when you walk through the front door. It is of a yellow house with a walkway with flowers and animals in the garden. There is a blue art deco mirrored chest of drawers, which is a family piece, and the bright green painting of a ram is from Mario Buatta's estate sale by STAIR Galleries. I bought him at the beginning of the COVID-19 pandemic, so he is named Covid.

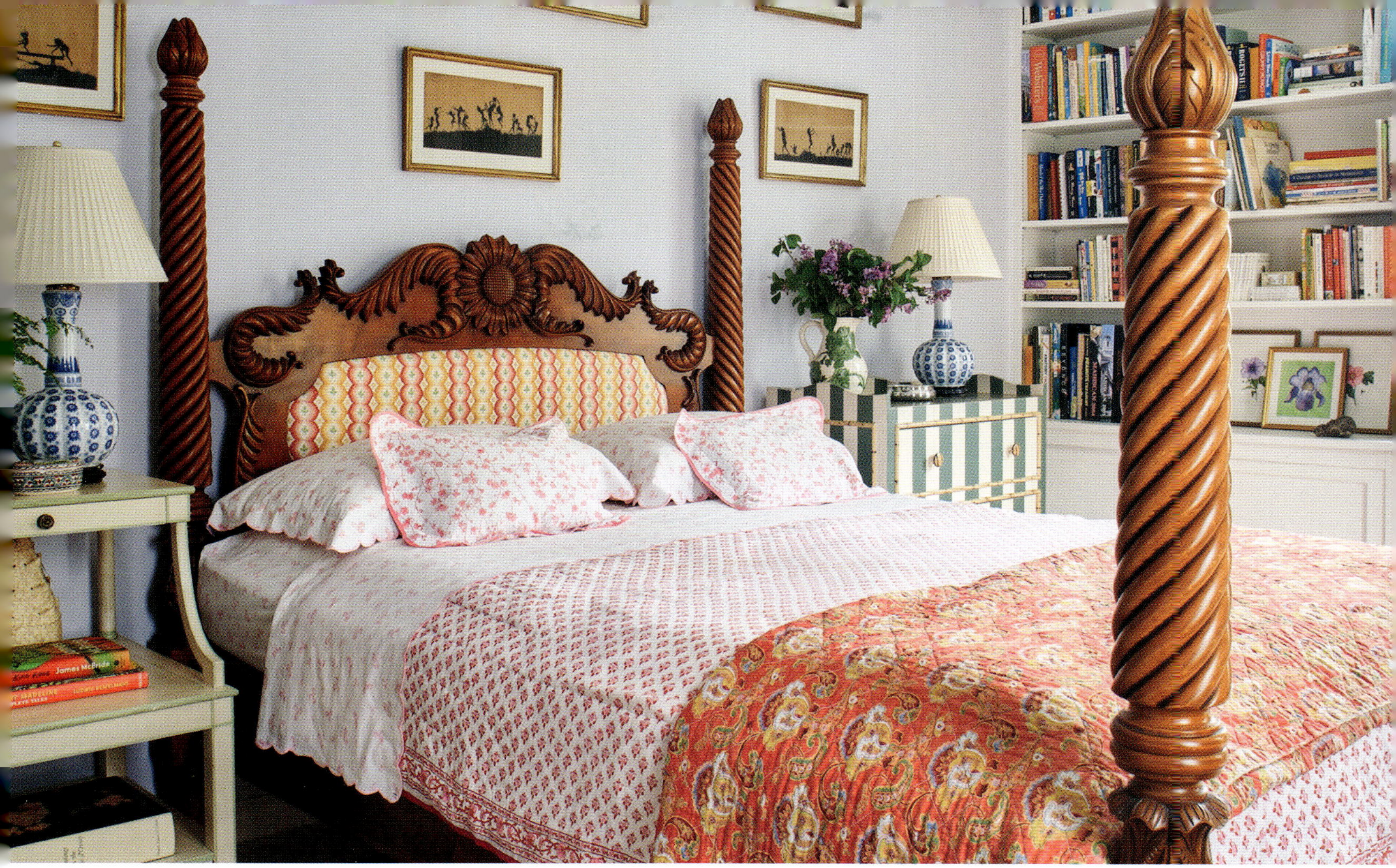

ABOVE: Charlotte's bedroom has the silhouettes that were in my room when I was a little girl. The walls are painted a soft lavender color; the wonderful carved bed was made by Robert Huggins in Rhode Island.

RIGHT: Flora's bed is tucked between two bookcases. The Guatemalan tin mirror above her bed is from Tucker Robbins; the black-and-white photographs are of her great and great-great grandmothers.

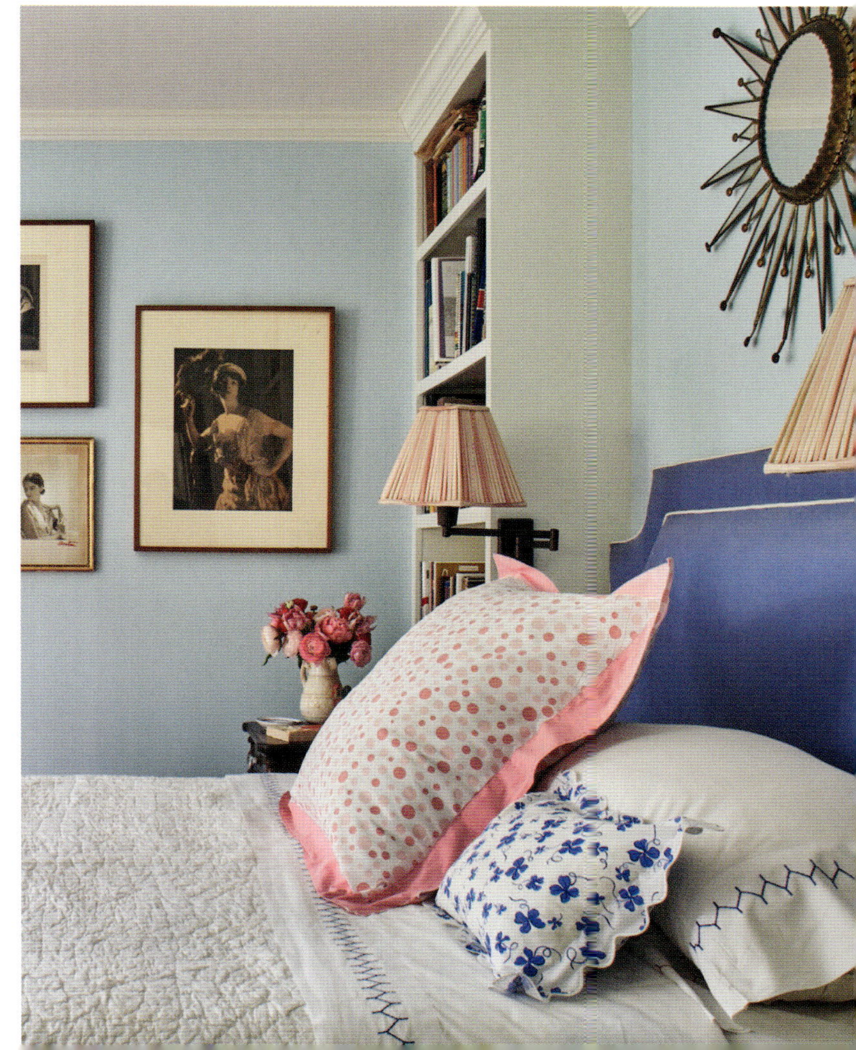

The kitchen in the house was dated, boring, and very bland with beige tiles, beige counters, and beige backsplashes—all quite indistinct and unattractive. It felt as though you were inside of a cardboard box. The actual layout of the space isn't bad, and the working space in the kitchen is fine with plenty of counter space. Previous owners must have closed in a porch on the back of the house at one point, and it is now a nice sunny breakfast room. It has wall-to-wall windows and I added a couple of skylights for even more light. There is nothing better in my mind than a bright sunny kitchen. The floors were a beige tile that looked like travertine, installed in a subway pattern. I replaced that floor with a black-and-white ceramic checkerboard tile floor, which is graphically strong. The counters are now a honed Black Absolute stone and the cabinets are all painted white and have black knobs. The backsplash is made of white Thassos subway tile, which adds another texture. The little bit of wall in the space is painted a pale pink. I loved Diane Keaton's kitchen in the movie *Something's Gotta Give* and it became the inspiration for this kitchen.

There was a small room with stained pine beadboard walls that was only accessible from the living room and had been used as an office. I ended up closing up the entrance to this little room on the living room side and opening it up on the kitchen side instead, giving up a section of floor-to-ceiling cabinets. I used this space to create the "Dog Dorm," which is almost the best room in the house. It is lined with comfy dog beds and doorless crates. There is a Dutch door into their room so they can see and know what is happening in the kitchen without being underfoot.

There are two rooms past the kitchen above the garage: my office and a library. The green library has all of my design books as well as the many animal prints and sculptures I have collected. The room has dark green walls that almost envelop you; the dark color leads your eyes right out the windows, bringing the outdoors in. I have the wonderful painted tin trompe l'oeil valances that Chuck Fischer painted for a room I did at the Kips Bay Show House. They fit and frame the windows perfectly and add whimsy to the room.

Charlotte chose to have a lavender bedroom in Connecticut, which is not a color I often use but it works nicely here and makes the room feel soothing.

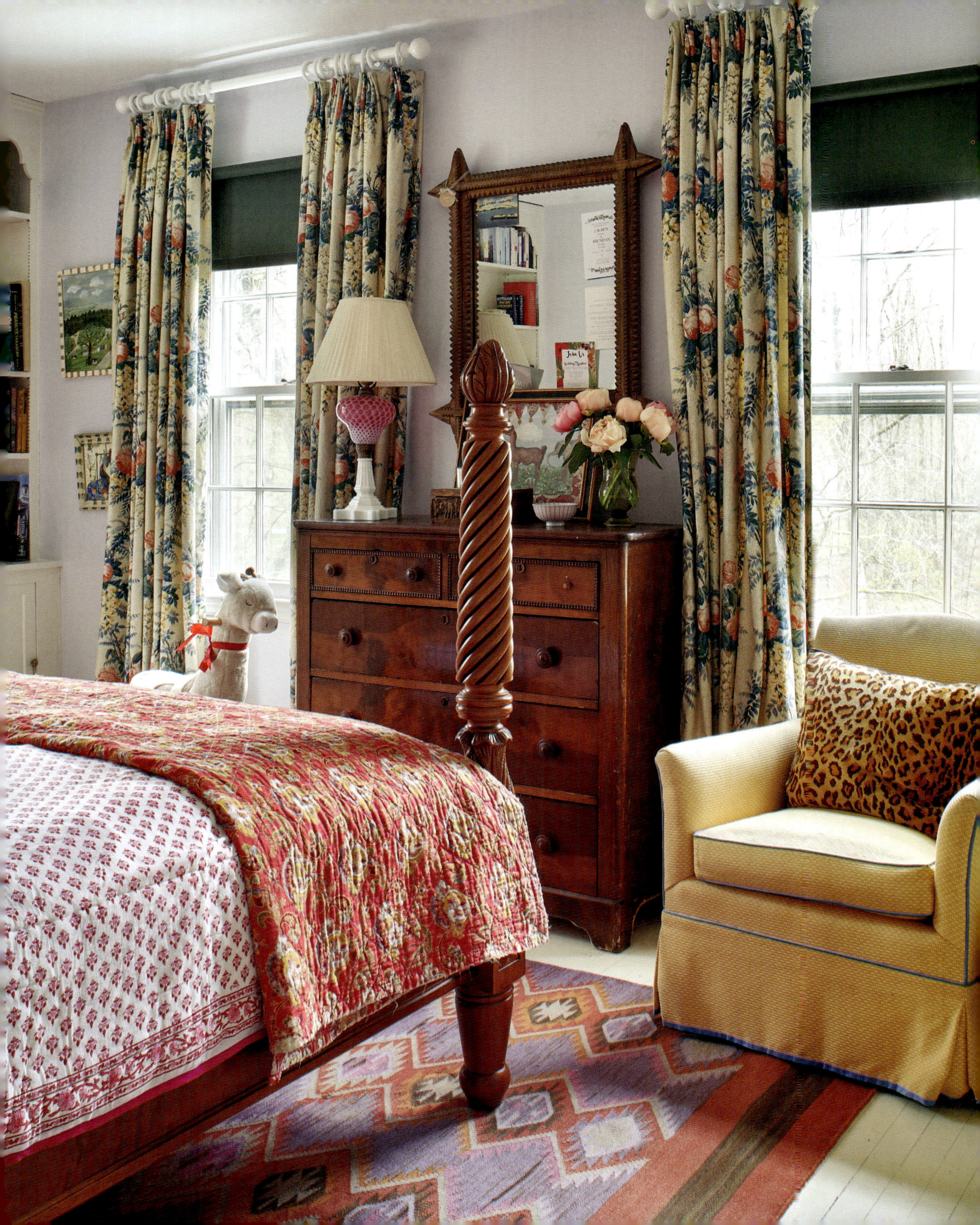

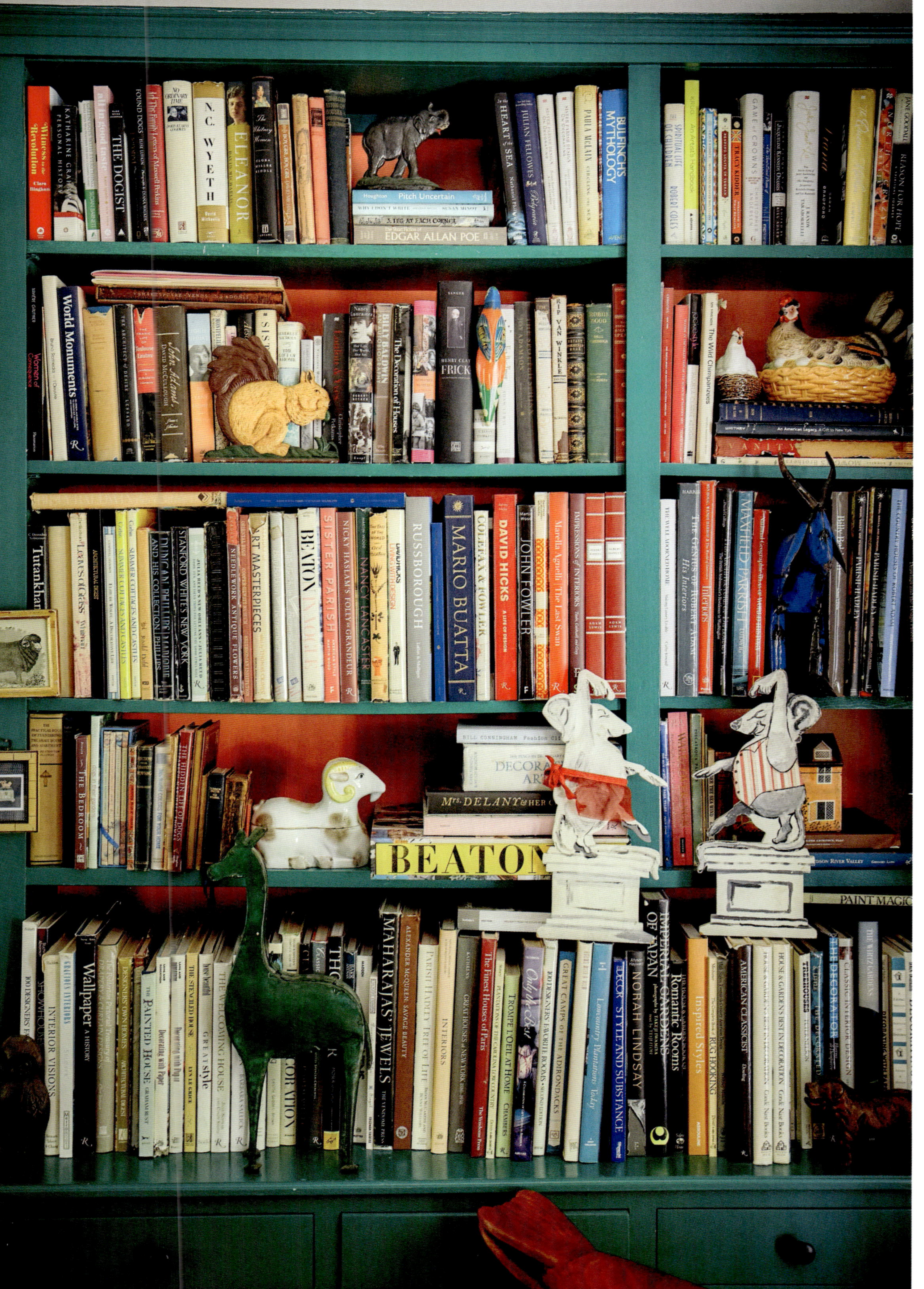

Witness to the Revolution
KATHARINE GRAHAM PERSONAL HISTORY
THE DOGIST
N. C. WYETH
ELEANOR
Pitch Uncertain
A FIG AT EACH CORNER
EDGAR ALLAN POE
JULIAN FELLOWES Belgravia
PAULA MCLAIN
BULFINCH'S MYTHOLOGY
GAME of CROWNS
TRACY KIDDER
REASON FOR HOPE
World Monuments
Women of Consequence
John Adams DAVID McCULLOUGH
BILLY BALDWIN
The Decoration of Houses
FRICK
RIP VAN WINKLE
The Wild Chimpanzees
An American Legacy
Tutankhamun
SUMMER COTTAGES AND CASTLES
DUNCAN PHYFE AND HIS CIRCLE
STANFORD WHITE'S NEW YORK
NEEDLEWORK ANTIQUE FLOWERS
ART MASTERPIECES
BEATON
SISTER PARISH
NICKY HASLAM'S FOLLY DE GRANDEUR
NANCY LANCASTER
RUSSBOROUGH
MARIO BUATTA
COLEFAX & FOWLER
DAVID HICKS A LIFE OF DESIGN
JOHN FOWLER
Marella Agnelli The Last Swan
IMPRESSIONS of INTERIORS
ROBERT ADAM
MAXWELL PARRISH
THE BEDROOM
BILL CUNNINGHAM
DECORATIVE ART
MRS. DELANY & HER CIRCLE
BEATON
PAINT MAGIC
Wallpaper A HISTORY
INTERIOR VISIONS
THE PAINTED HOUSE
THE WELCOMING HOUSE
MAHARAJAS' JEWELS
ALEXANDER MCQUEEN SAVAGE BEAUTY
The Finest Houses of Paris
TROMPE L'OEIL AT HOME
GREAT CAMPS OF THE ADIRONDACKS
DECOR STYLE AND SUBSTANCE
NORAH LINDSAY
IMPERIAL GARDENS OF JAPAN
Romantic Rooms
Inspired Styles
RUG HOOKING
AMERICAN CLASSICIST
THE DECORATOR

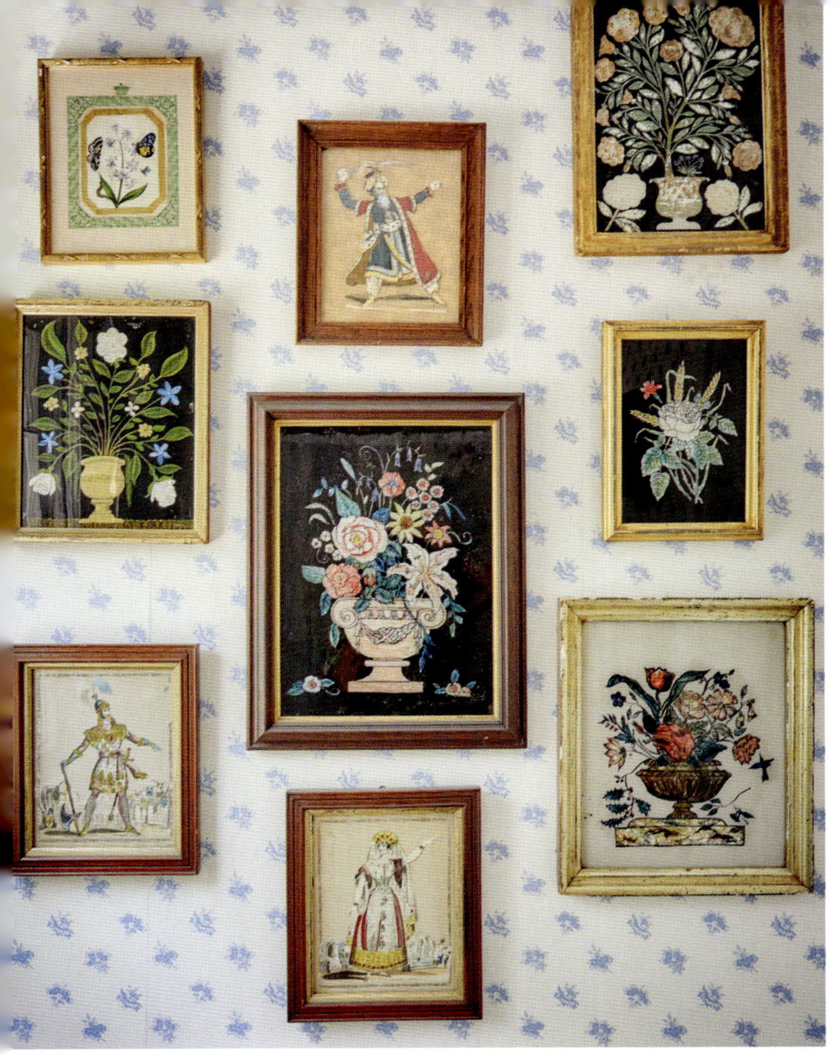

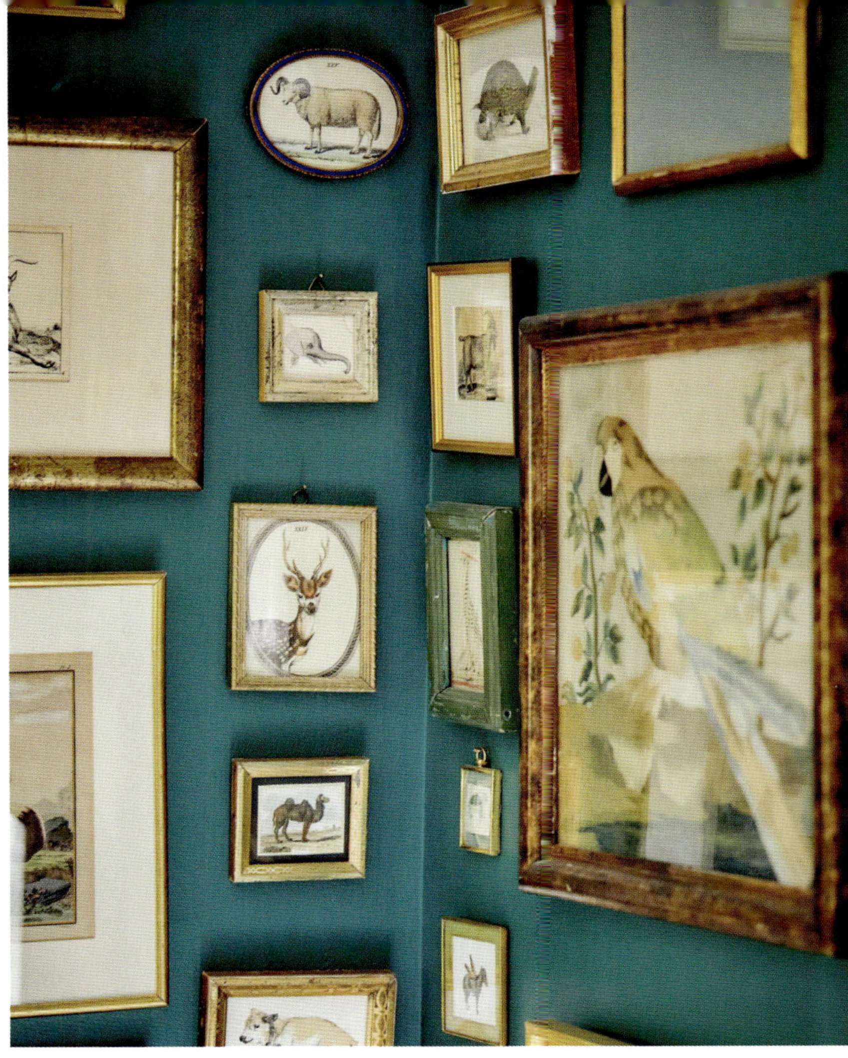

OPPOSITE: The bookcase shelves in my Connecticut library are filled with design books along with various pieces from my animal collection. The dancing mice were made by some of us at Parish-Hadley to be used as centerpieces for an American Ballet Theatre benefit.

ABOVE LEFT: A collection of tinsel art. Albert Hadley loved tinsel art and gave me several of these pieces.

ABOVE RIGHT: This corner of my library features some of my animal print collection. The parrot wool work was a gift from my father-in-law.

RIGHT: The shadowbox of a beaded pot of flowers has always been one of my favorite finds. The owl hand towels add a bit of whimsy.

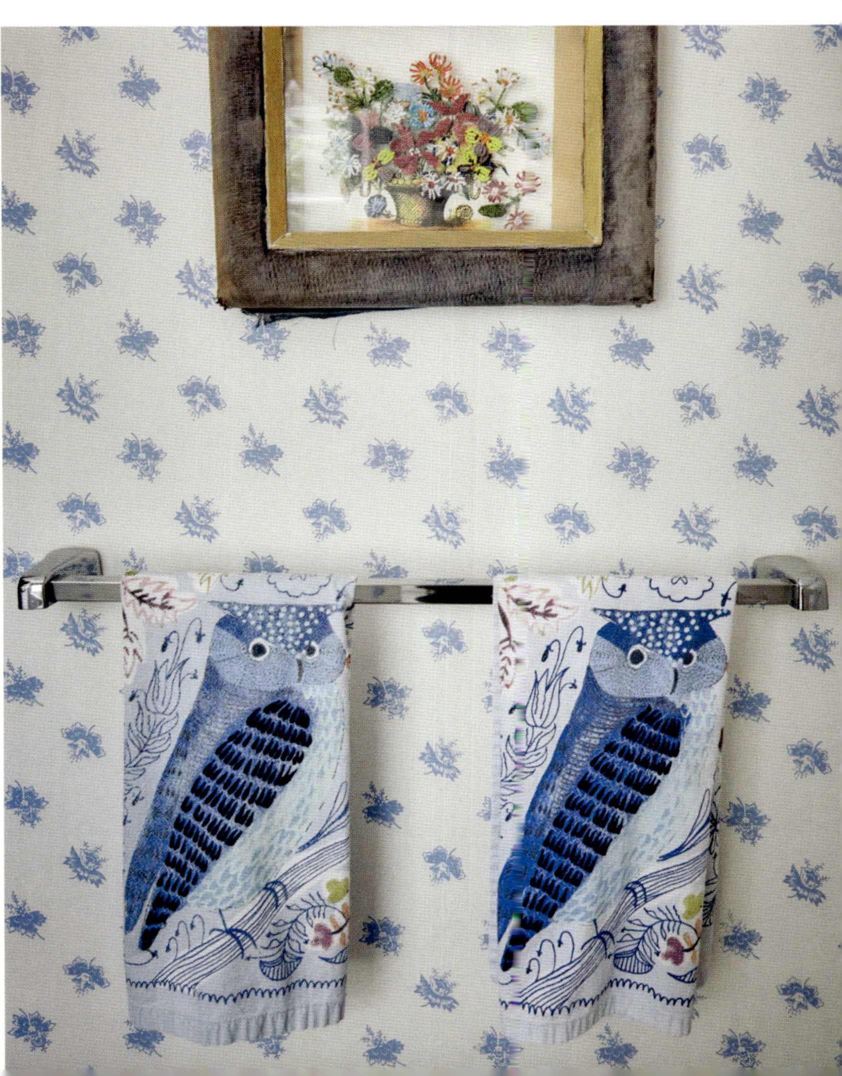

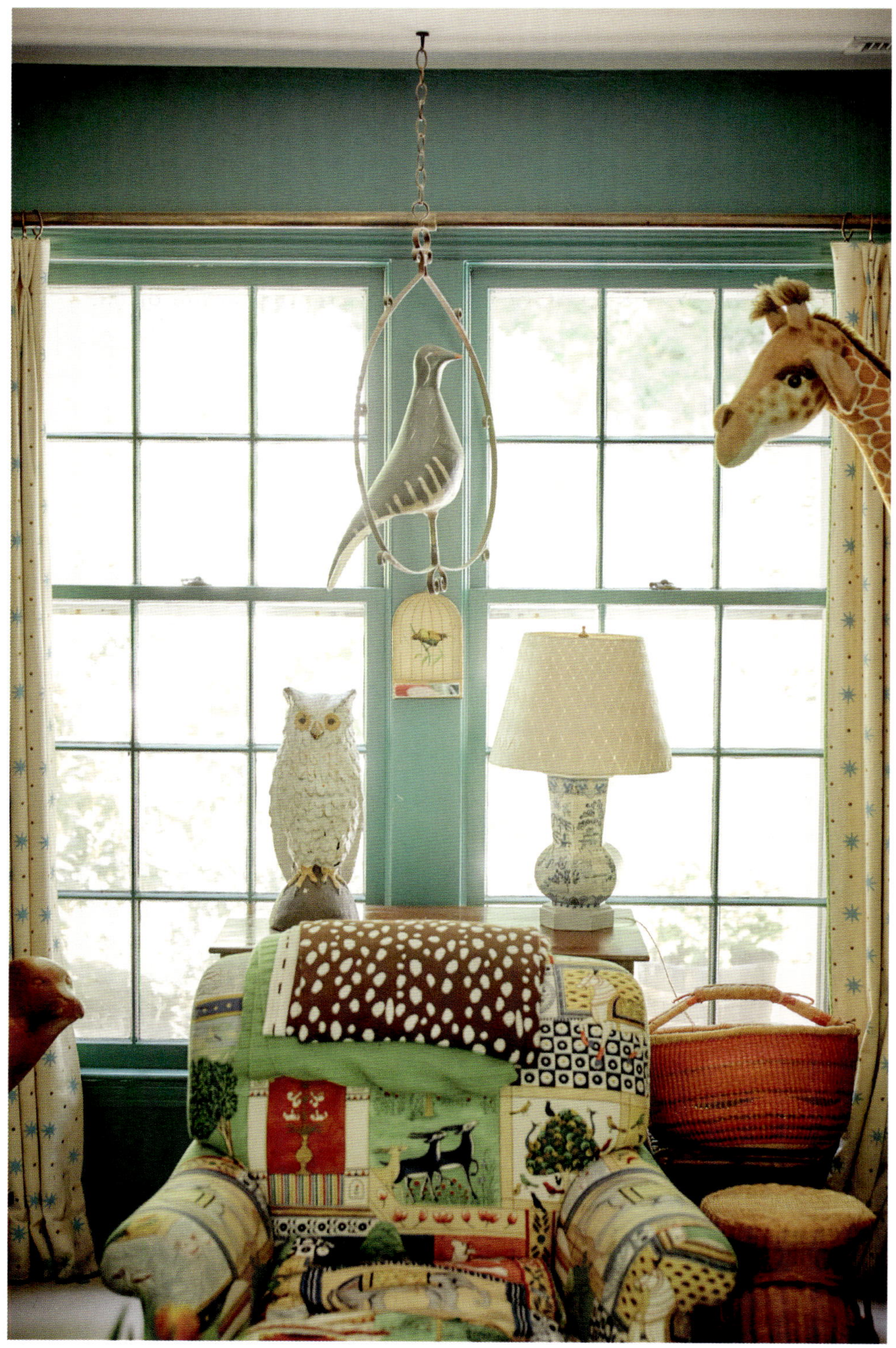

The painted cement owl used to be in Albert Hadley's garden.

The bedrooms in the house are all in soft tones of blues, lavender, and pink, except for my bedroom, which has a wallpaper stripe from Twigs. I have watercolors that I love in my room painted by Albert Hadley, my mother, and Mita Corsini Bland.

I like strong beds—beds with character to anchor a room and give it focus. The bed in my room is a French brass-and-enamel bed. It was Gertrude Vanderbilt Whitney's bed from her bedroom at her "Studio" in Old Westbury, Long Island. I like to use patterned coverlets and quilts on beds along with pretty sheets and pillowcases. Good night tables are always a must, as is good light to read by. I tend to use more pattern in bedrooms than in other rooms, as pattern tends to add warmth for me.

I think it is important to use what means something to you personally. There are family pieces in this house along with pieces I have bought over the years, including some incredible street finds. It has always amazed me to see what people put out on the street, in New York City as well as in the suburbs. I have never been shy about pulling over and putting things in my car. Albert Hadley found some amazing pieces on the street and fearlessly squashed any sense of disdain I had for liking someone else's cast-offs. Almost nothing gives me greater pleasure than a great street find, except perhaps finding a parking spot on the street in New York City.

Several years after buying this house, I have settled in. Architecturally, it has changed very little, but the interior is very different from when I bought it. The grounds are different too. Many trees have had to come down and the property is now filled with light. I love coming down the driveway and hearing the crunching sound of the gravel. I have come to have a calming sense of belonging here; there is a sense of timelessness. I love that this house is a place for my children and their children to come to. It is my safe haven and I hope that it is theirs as well. I love being surrounded by things that have meaning to me, that I have inherited and that I can pass on. It is never just about a house—it's about creating a place to be a family.

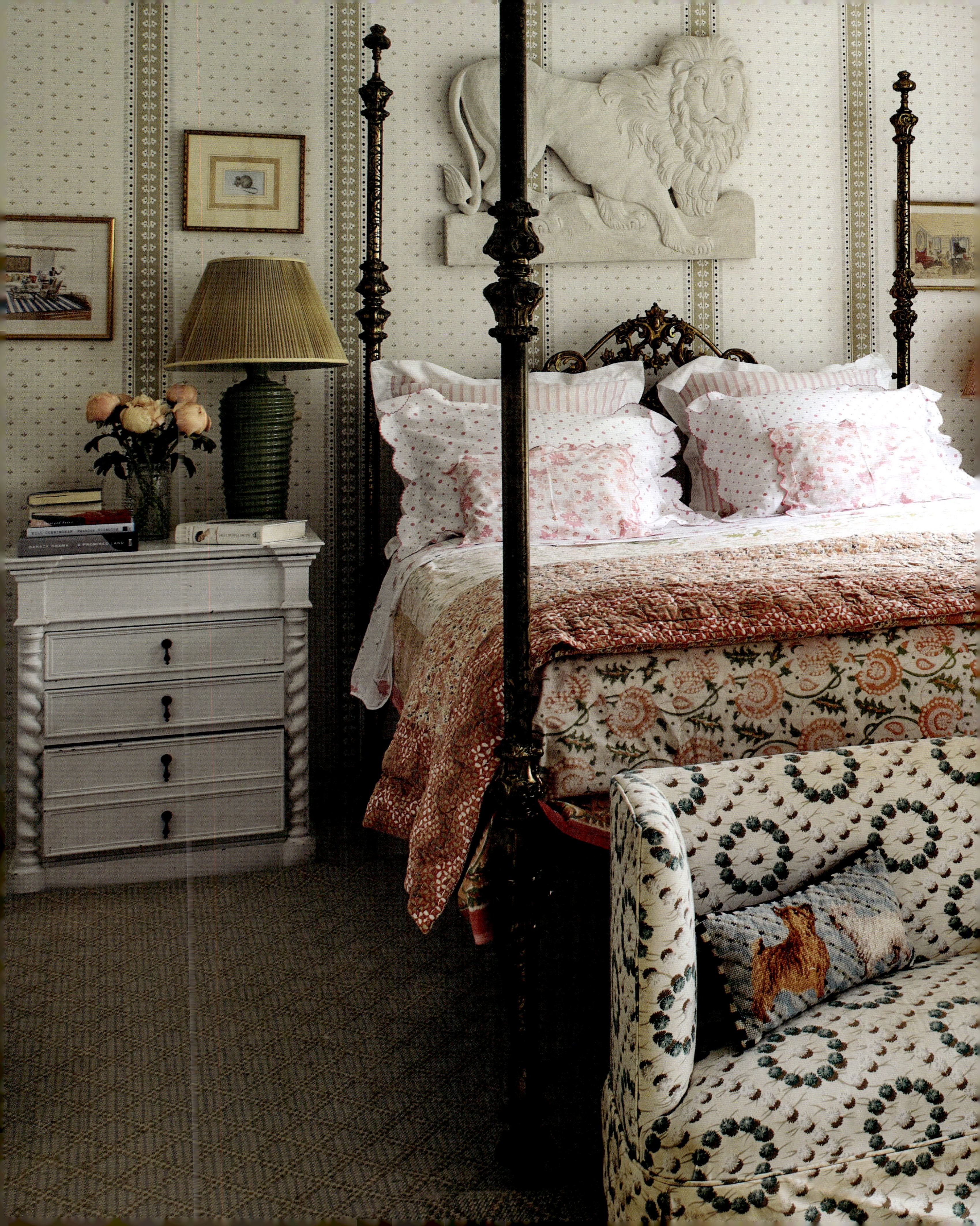
BILL CUNNINGHAM Fashion Climbing
BARACK OBAMA A PROMISED LAND
SALLY BEDELL SMITH

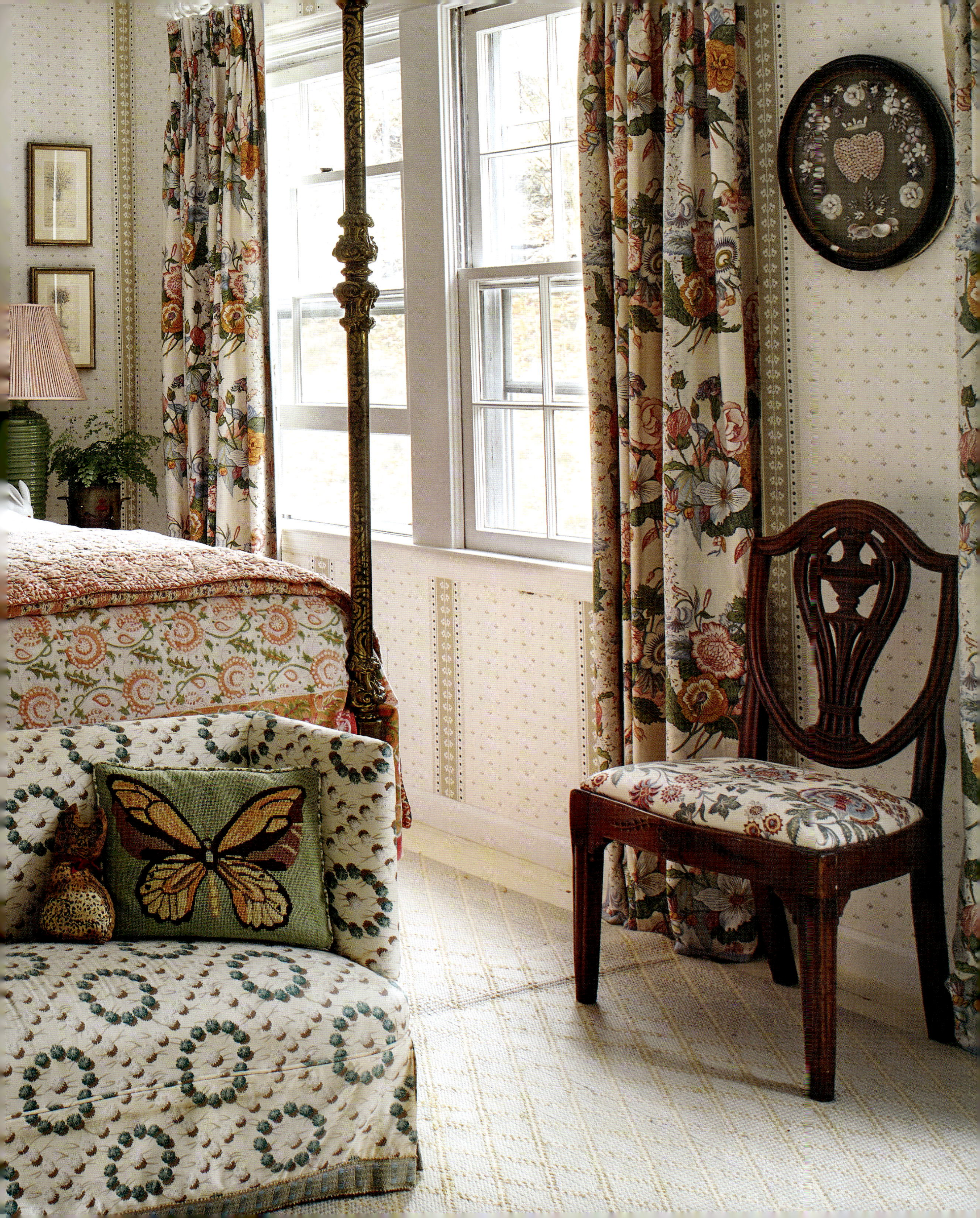

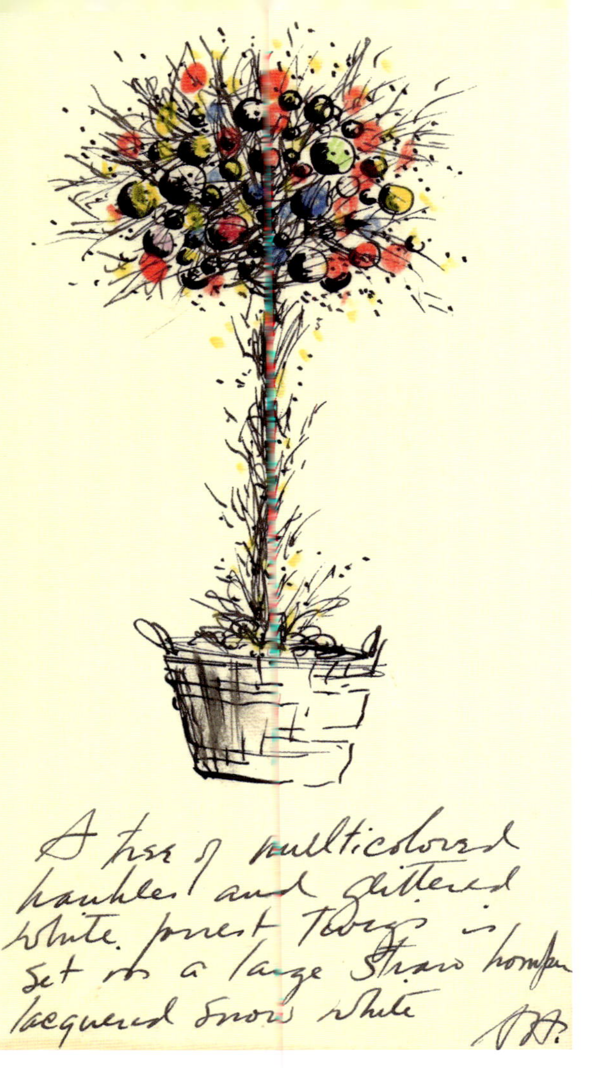

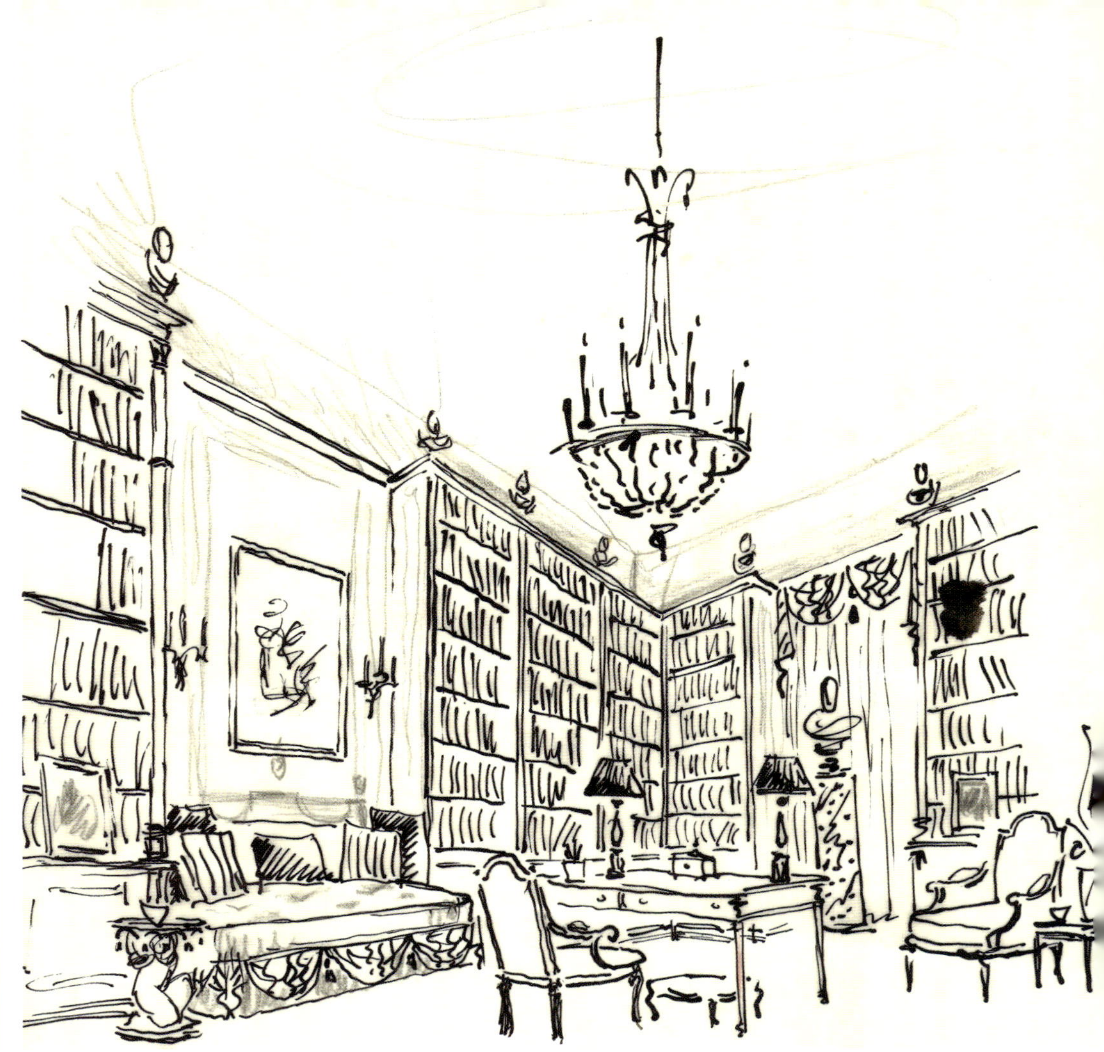

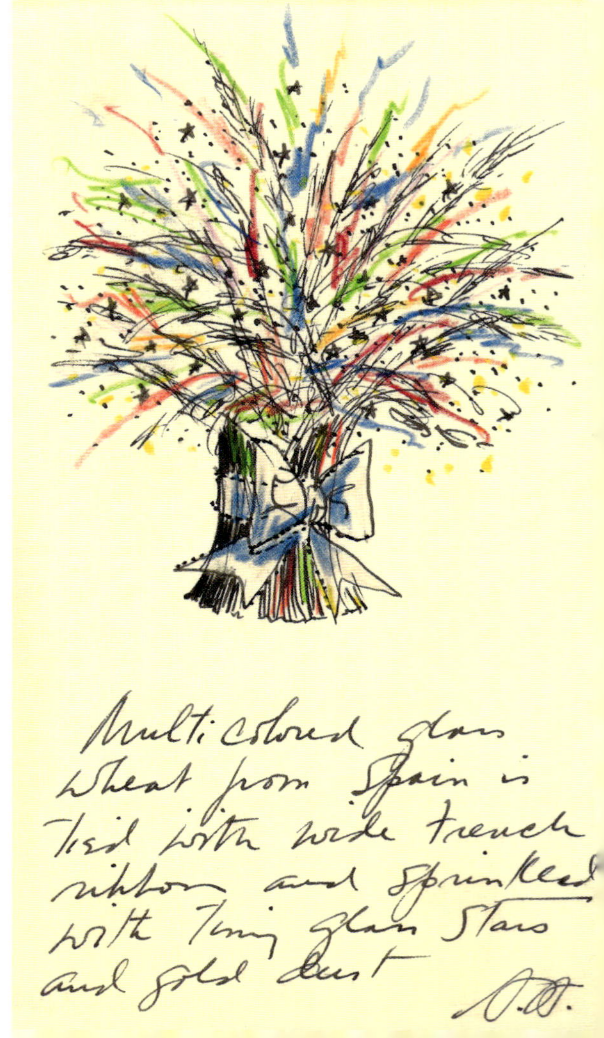

PREVIOUS PAGE: The bed is from Gertrude Vanderbilt Whitney's studio on Long Island. The frame for the small sofa at the end of the bed was found when antiquing one Saturday with Albert Hadley. The white night table to the left of the bed was given to me by Albert Hadley. The bedside lamps are by Christopher Spitzmiller.

ABOVE LEFT: The sketch from Albert Hadley includes this description: "A tree of multicolored branches and glittered white forest twigs inset in a large straw basket lacquered snow white."

ABOVE RIGHT: A room sketch by Albert Hadley.

RIGHT: The description on this sketch by Albert Hadley reads: "Multicolored glass wheat from Spain is tied with wide French ribbon and sprinkled with tiny glass stars and gold dust."

OPPOSITE: My bedroom desk is filled with things made by my children and photographs of people I love.

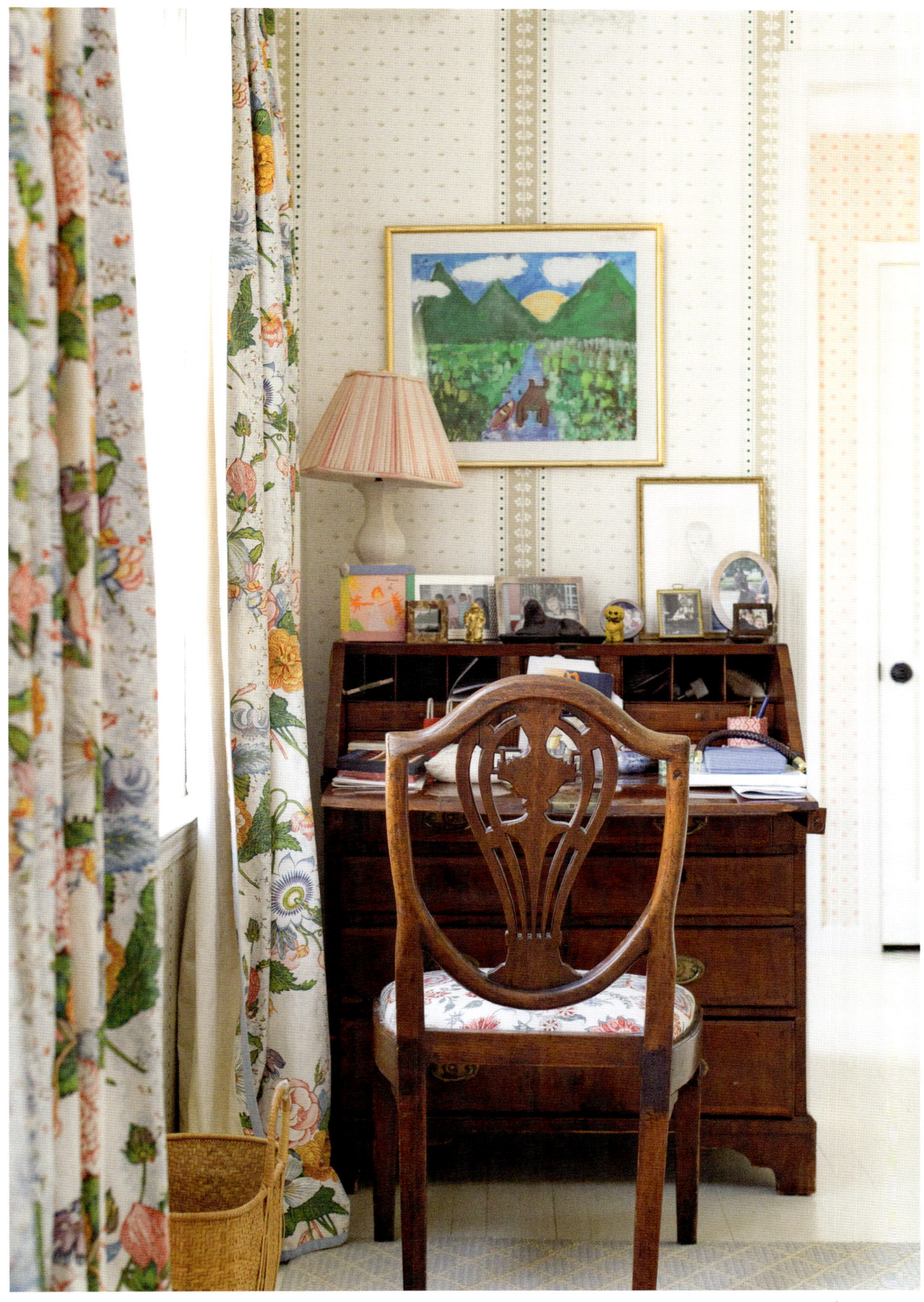

THE AMER HOUSE

ICAN

“When a person has flair, a grounding in the principle of design, and self-discipline, that person has the potential of being an outstanding designer.”

—ALBERT HADLEY

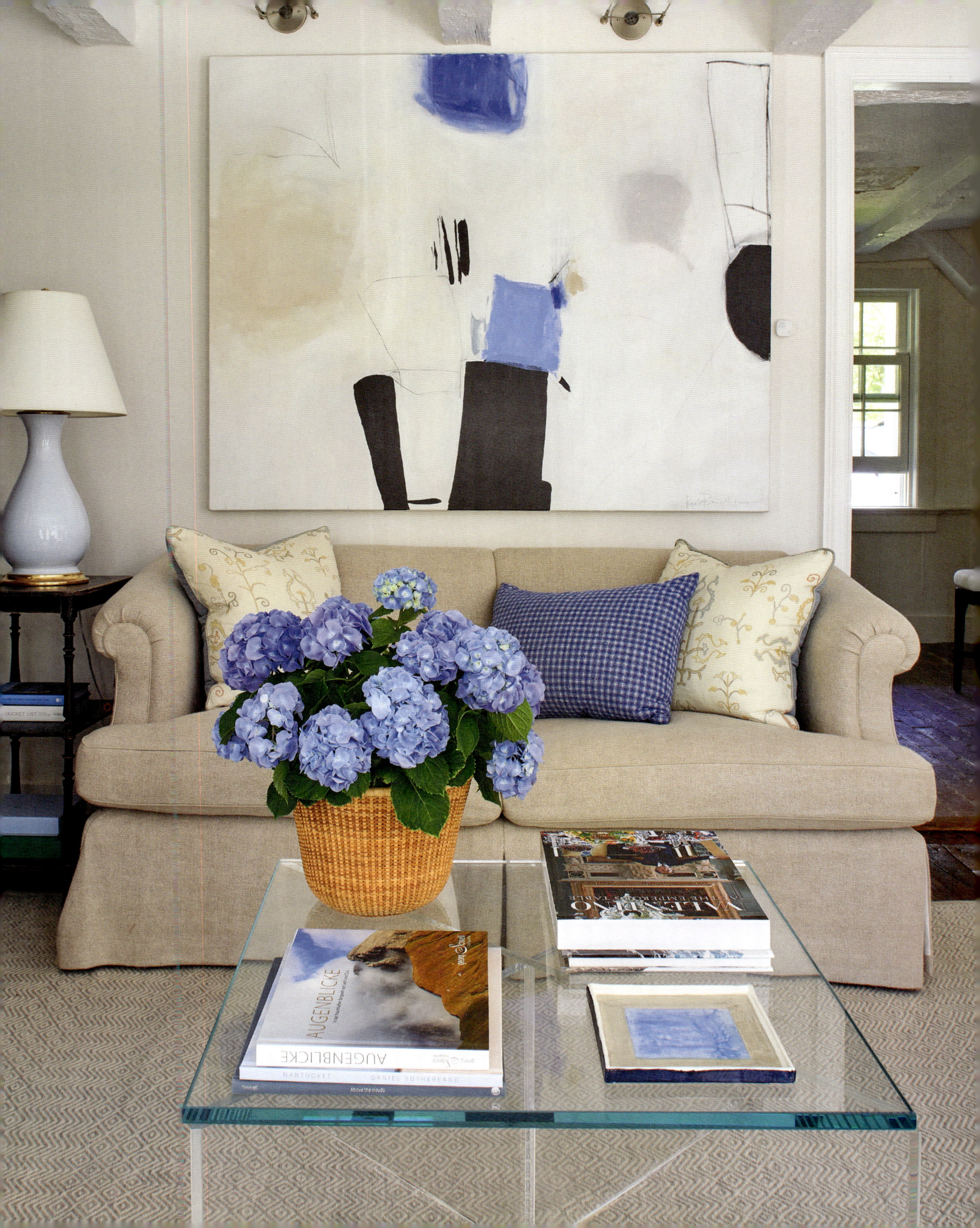
AUGENBLICKE
AUGENBLICKE
NANTUCKET
DANIEL SUTHERLAND
Above the clouds

Years ago, architects defined the interior style of the houses they designed. The architecture of McKim, Mead & White's buildings precluded a differing style on the interior than what you saw on the exterior. This was true of a house as grand as The Breakers in Newport in Rhode Island: its architecture dictated the interior style of that ornate marble and gilded mansion by the sea. Exteriors and interiors went hand in hand. There were fewer textile sources until well into the twentieth century in America, so this limited interior design options as well. Furniture and furnishings had to be commissioned or imported as inventories of any sort did not exist. Most often, suites of brown furniture were the only choice. For the most part, American furniture was simply a reinterpretation of various European styles; the predominant influence for interiors and furniture emphasized Italian, French, and English. Nobody would have dreamt of mixing one style of architecture with a different style of interior design, but today styles are usually blended and combined.

At the beginning of the twentieth century, the role of an interior decorator didn't exist. Nor was there a particular or predominant style that could be attributed to America. Elsie de Wolfe is considered to be the first American decorator. Originally, she was an actress and antiques dealer; later she became a prominent female interior designer. She wrote *A House in Good Taste*, the first book on interior design. She replaced dark and ornate Victorian décor with simpler, lighter, and less cluttered rooms.

The American style grew out of the English Country House style that was epitomized by the English firm Colefax and Fowler. Sybil Colefax was a preeminent English interior decorator who greatly influenced Mrs. Parish. Mrs. Parish loved the English Country House style and she coveted Haseley House, the country house of her American ex-pat friend, Nancy Lancaster. Nancy bought the design company Colefax and Fowler when Sybil Colefax retired. Mrs. Parish worked with John Fowler for years, furthering the English Country House style in the United States. She included the Colefax and Fowler fabrics and patterns in her own work. John Fowler said that what was significant about Sister Parish was "not only what was done but what not done. Chintzes and silks were freely mixed; there was an avoidance of materials and colors matching and sets of furniture that would give a static character, or indeed a 'period' feeling."

Early rooms in America were filled with wood furniture, pastoral paintings, and animal heads hung as decoration. It was Sister Parish who embodied the sensibility of "Americana" without a colonial feel. She used indigenous crafts, rugs, and furniture to create warm environments, combining old and new, along with naive and sophisticated pieces. Much of the wood furniture she used she had painted either white or in a more elaborate, decorative manner by artists. Her American style became a look as distinctive as the English Country House style, and the houses she worked on suggested that families had been living in them for generations. The houses she did were quaint and cluttered, all-inclusive and not prescriptive, modest but with moments of diminutive grandeur. She arranged furniture where it was most comfortable and looked best, using a mixture of styles instead of a uniform whole. Her rooms were romantic without being sentimental or too sweet.

I worked on an old farmhouse in Connecticut that was full of charm. It was on a lovely piece of property with an apple orchard sloping down the hill toward a swimming pool. The house had beautiful, old, wide floorboards and lovely, old wavy glass in the windows. Its layout was logical and practical with fireplaces in all of the upstairs and downstairs rooms. A separate building, which they called the "Big Room," was a simple barn-like structure just a few steps away. It felt like the original farmhouse and the family loved it. It had a large, tall living room and a small kitchen. This was really where the family

PREVIOUS PAGE: A living room in a 19th-century farmhouse in Connecticut has modern art and furniture. Lamp by Christopher Spitzmiller; coffee table by Hugh Newell Jacobsen; painting by Renee Bouchon; rug by Elizabeth Eakins.

OPPOSITE: The carpet from Beauvais was the starting point for this room. The colors of the Marthe Armitage wallpaper "Gardeners" were custom and based on a rug replicated from an antique rug we had seen but that was the wrong size for the room. The trim and the fireplace mantel were glazed.

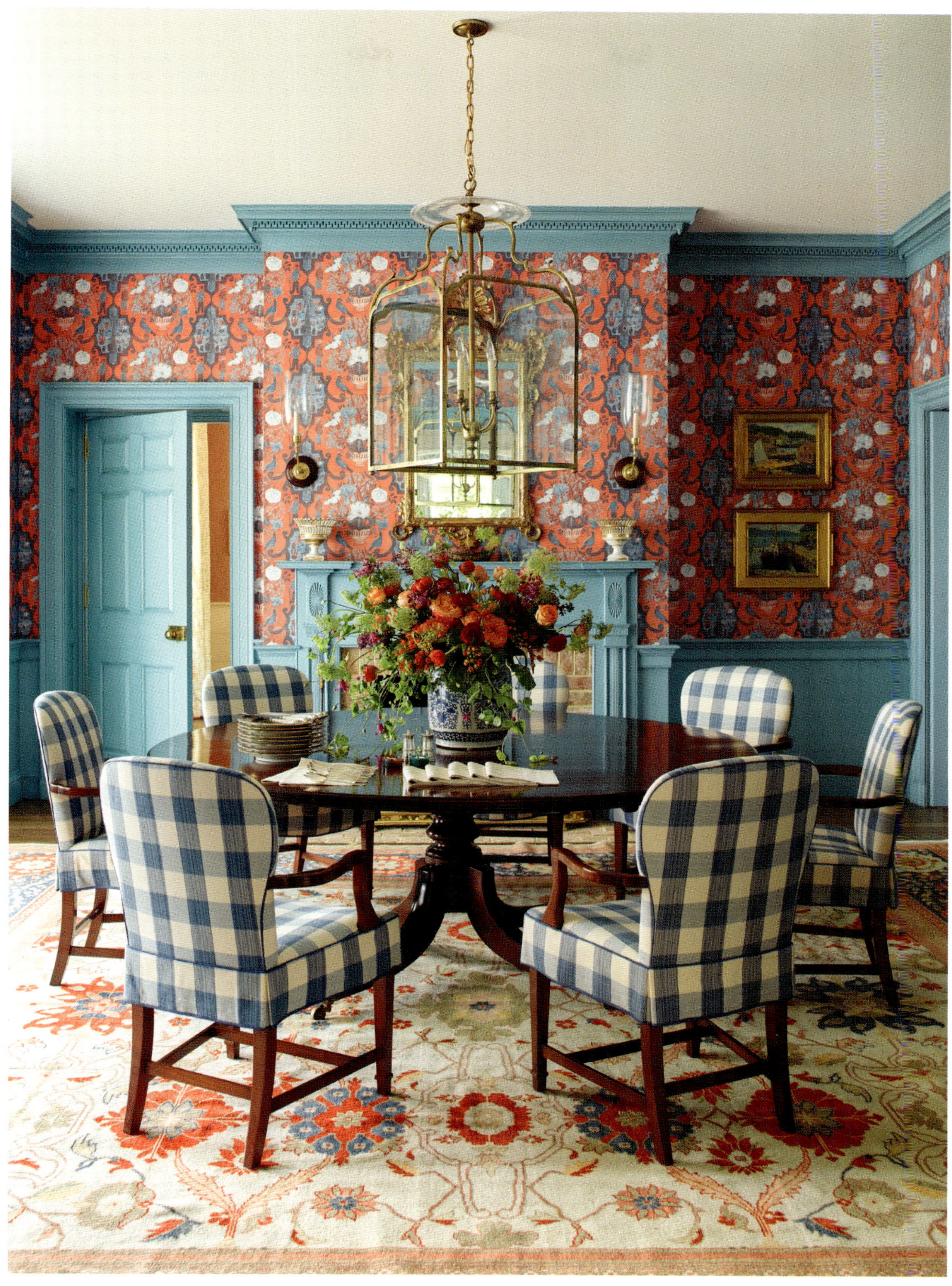

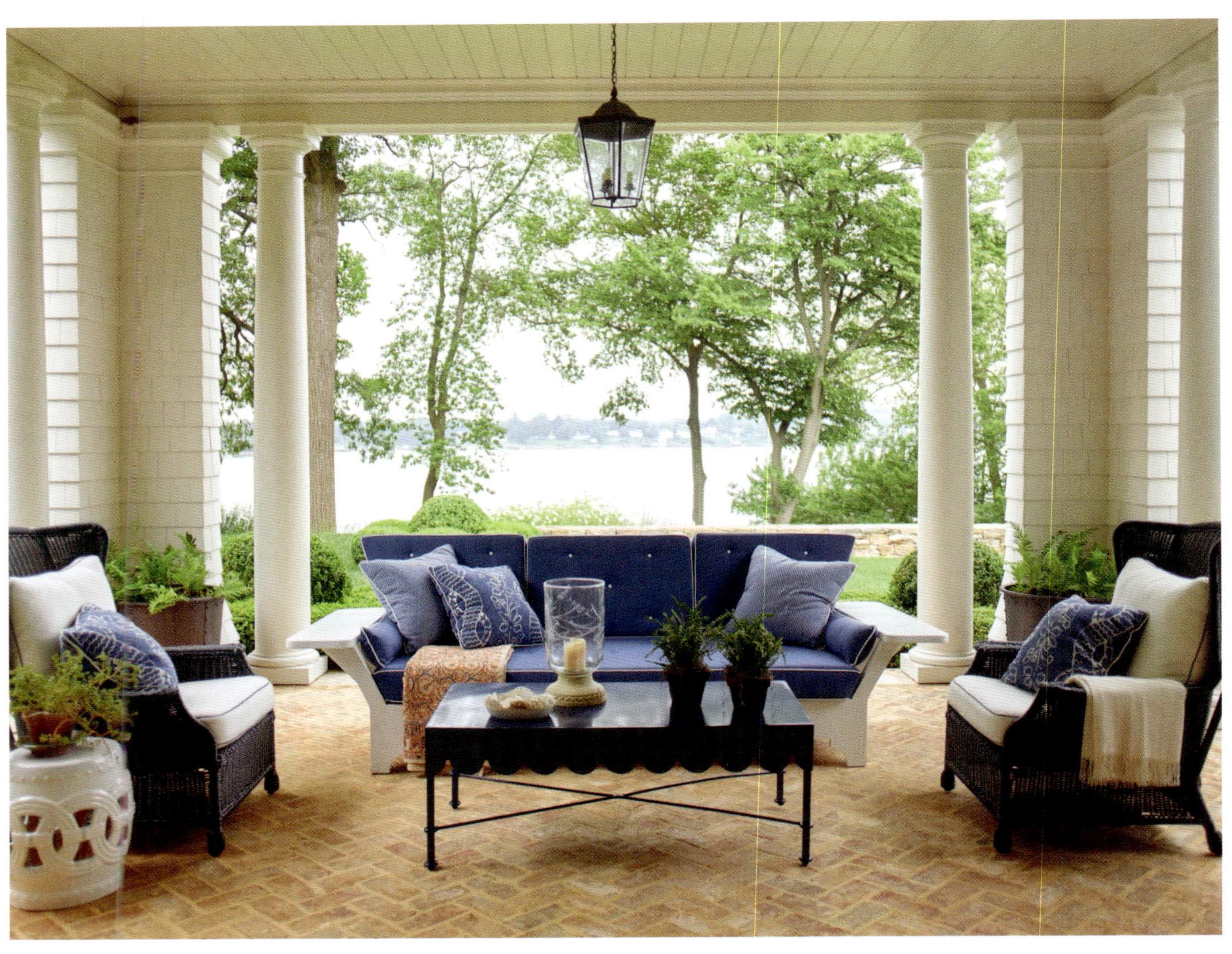

An open porch on a house in New Jersey designed by Gil Schafer.

lived, entertained, and spent most of their time. Sadly, it burned down in a fire.

My client was very involved with the university he had attended and was on the board. He admired the work of the more modern architectural firm that was designing some of the university's newer buildings, and asked them to design a new "Big Room." It was an interesting addition to the property—very different architecturally from their sweet little farmhouse.

The new entrance had a double-height, square tower with a pretty, old brick patterned floor that led through into the large, new, proper entrance hall; it was this hallway that connected the old farmhouse and the new addition. The original farmhouse was to the left and the added wing was ahead and to the right. The addition had a living room, dining room, large kitchen, and a primary bedroom area with two full baths and dressing rooms.

The living room was two steps down from the entrance hall. It had an elliptical-shaped wall of floor-to-ceiling windows that overlooked the orchard. The kitchen and dining room were set behind the living room and the bedroom wing was to the side. The dining room was an oval shape. Trying to figure out the floor plan—how to connect the rooms and to make sense of the old and new—was a challenge. It was a meandering, amorphous space without true delineations between rooms. Chuck Fischer painted the entrance hall and dining room floors in quite different geometric patterns—all in neutral colors and with borders to clearly differentiate the spaces. It was only the shape of the area and the furniture placement that created "rooms."

Classicism can be defined as reaching back to the past, adhering to essential traditional standards and principles of simplicity, restraint, and proportion. Decorating in a classical style doesn't preclude modernizing a house for comfort. As much as we admire historic and classical American houses, imitating or trying to replicate and re-create historical houses doesn't always make sense. Our lives are so different today; life has changed and so has the nature and proportion of the rooms we live in.

Years ago, big porches allowed for shade and helped to keep rooms cool. Houses were often only one room deep with windows on multiple sides allowing for both good ventilation and light. Windows were placed low, allowing for airflow and for the house to feel more connected to the gardens. It was well thought out and very practical, utilizing natural resources for a far "greener" way of living. Many of the houses built today are stacked deep with rooms behind each other like a Rubik's Cube.

A successful house today connects what was once the formal rooms and the informal rooms and updates them to suit one's needs. Few people have full kitchen staff anymore, so having kitchens at the far end and on the other side of the house doesn't make sense. People congregate in their kitchens. Modernizing bathrooms and kitchens only makes a house more comfortable, usable, and enjoyable. Understanding houses—how they should be sited, how they should relate to their surrounding—is the talent of a good architect. Yet knowing how a house should work and flow from a practical standpoint is an entirely different consideration. The architecture of a house can be formal or informal as long as it can adapt to contemporary conditions and be realistic; we can respect history while reinterpreting it to meet the needs and tastes of people today. It is the furnishings that make a house comfortable, softening spaces so they suit the way people like to live. The importance of comfort is essential to a successfully designed house.

One of my clients built a very modern house in Corning, New York. Originally, they furnished it in a way that was appropriate for a new modern house built in the early 1970s—clean, monochromatic, and filled with mid-century modern furniture. They both were raised in traditional New England houses and envisioned their new life as newlyweds in a very different way. The house was built of glass and cement and was based on the modernist Sarasota School of Architecture. By the

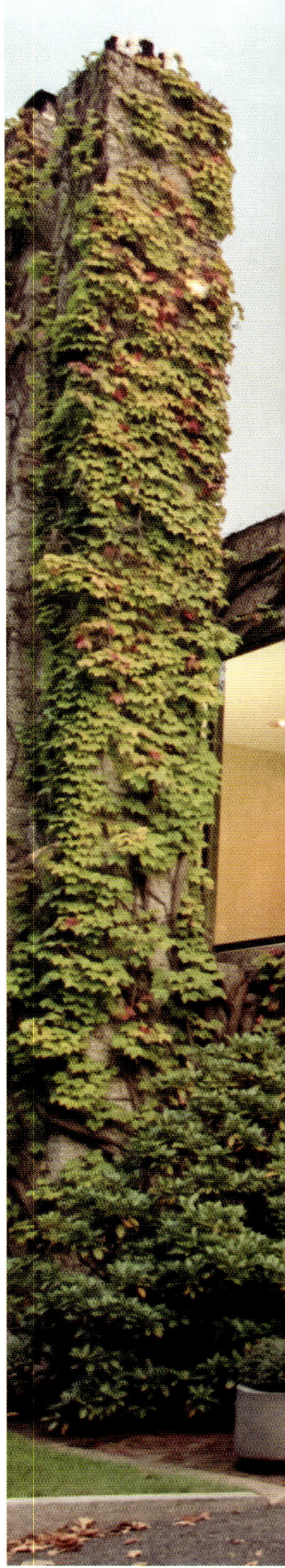

The exterior of this house in Corning, New York, was designed by Terry Twitchell and Nancy Miao of the Sarasota School of Architecture, with the help of David Beer, a family friend.

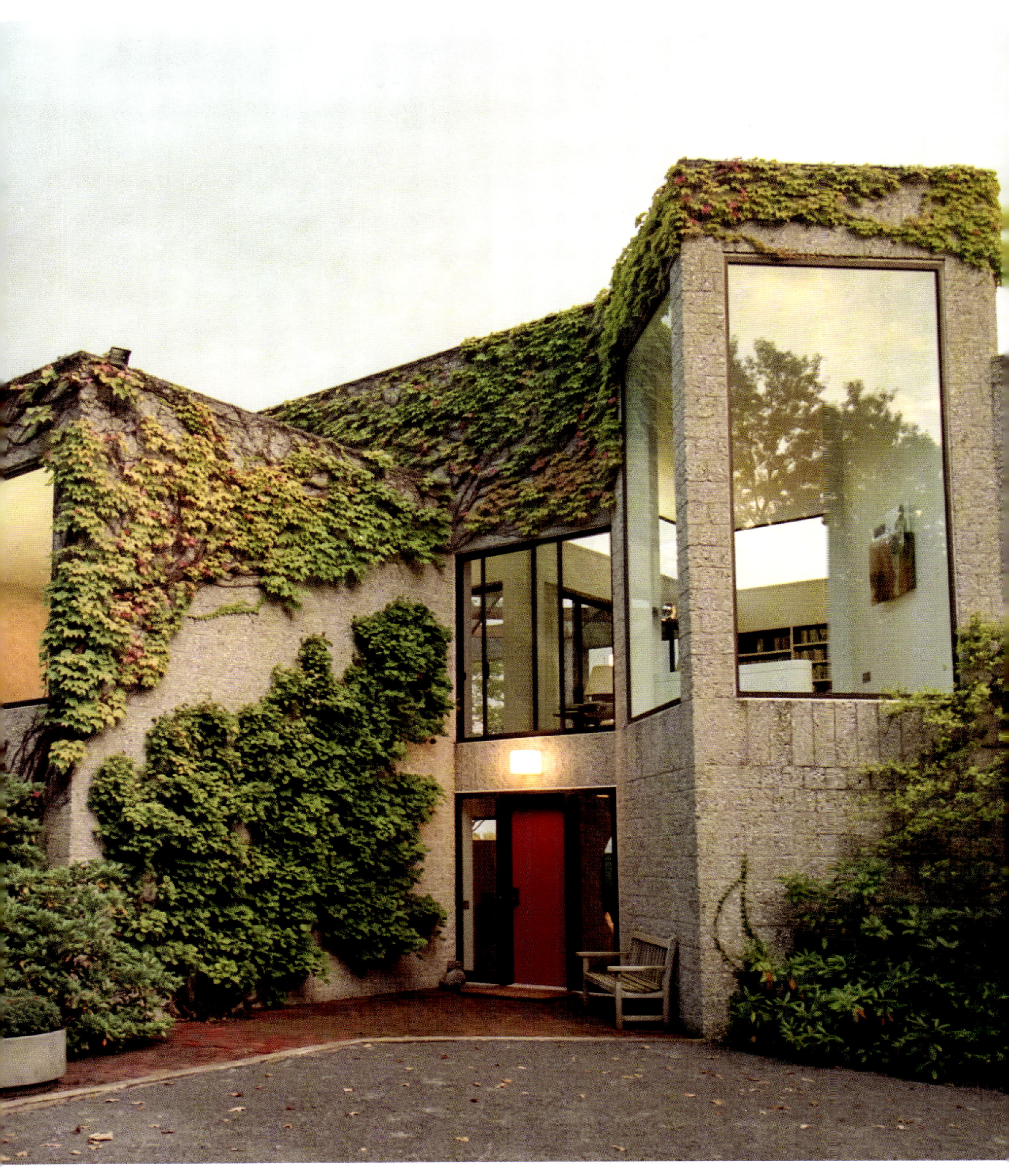

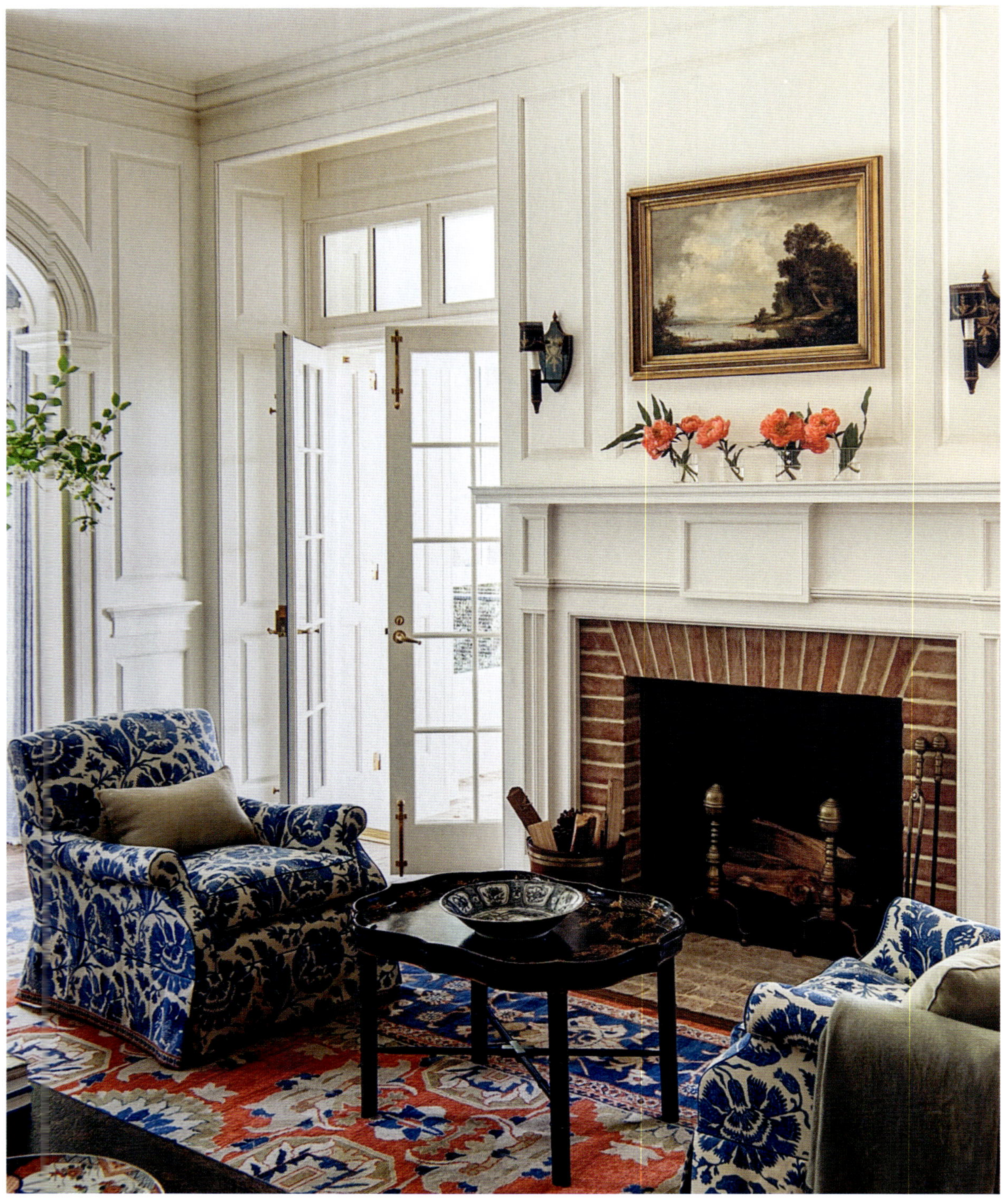

A paneled living room in New Jersey with a seating area by the fireplace.

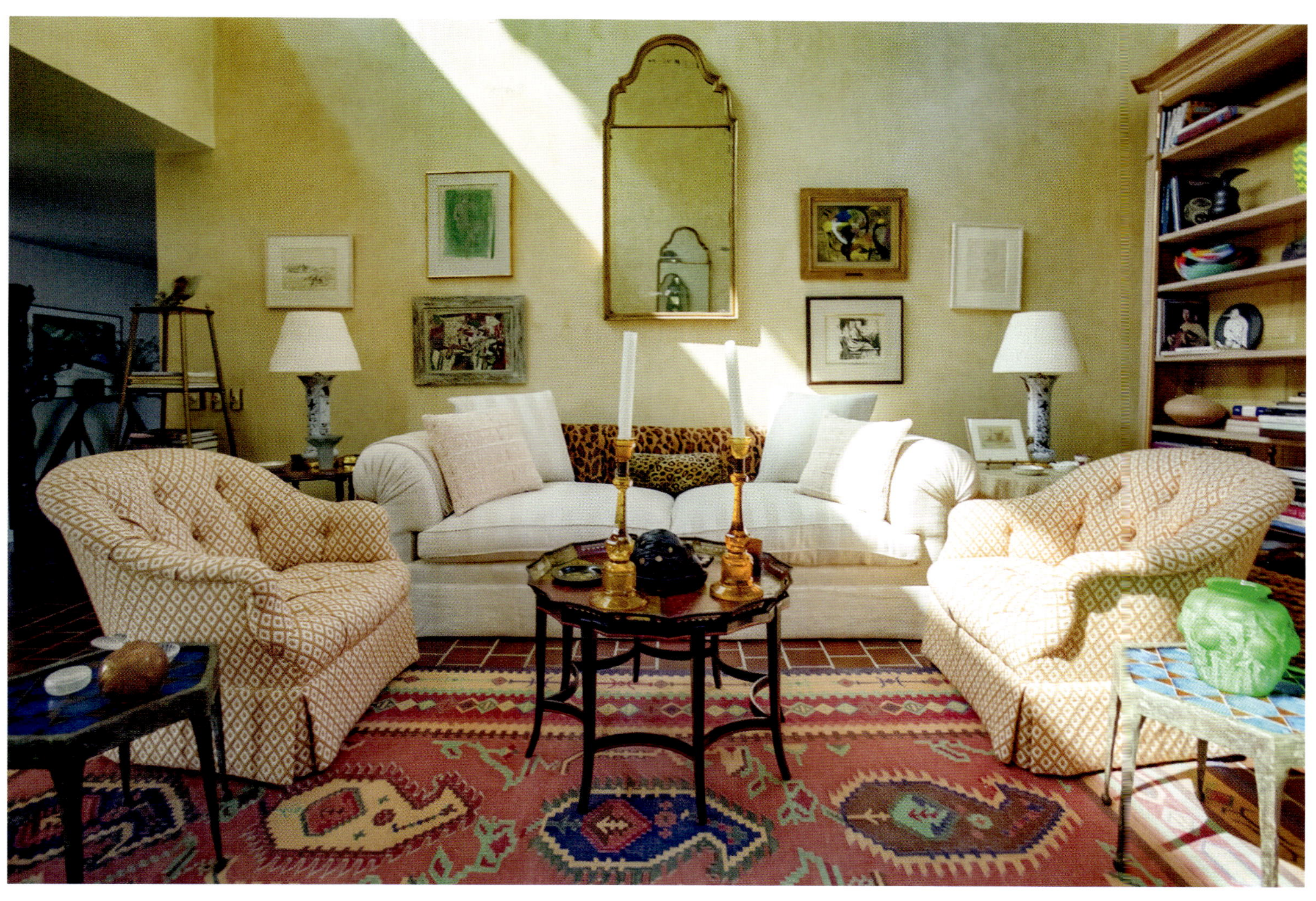

This living room in upstate New York has high windows and a double-height ceiling; the light floods down from the upstairs.

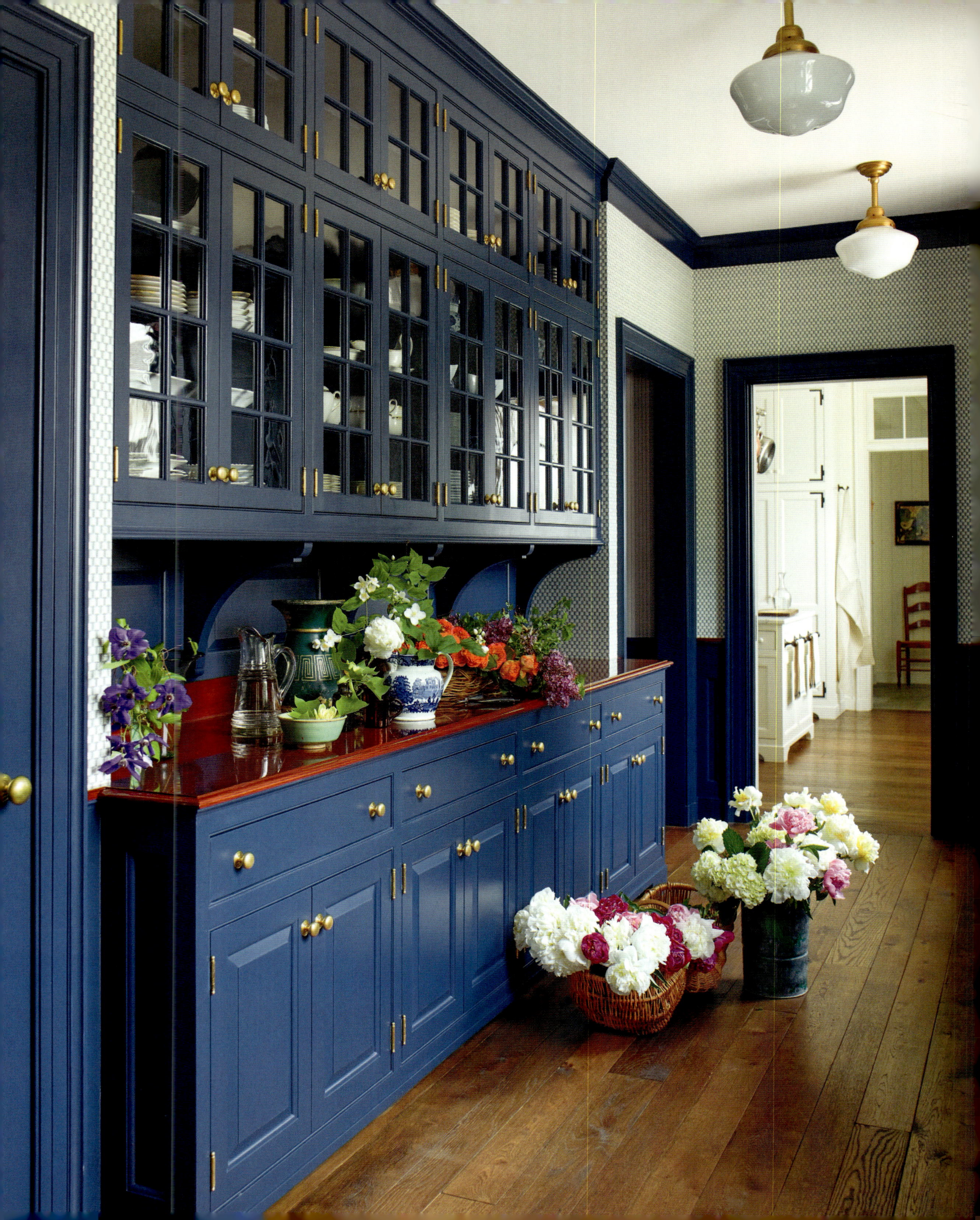

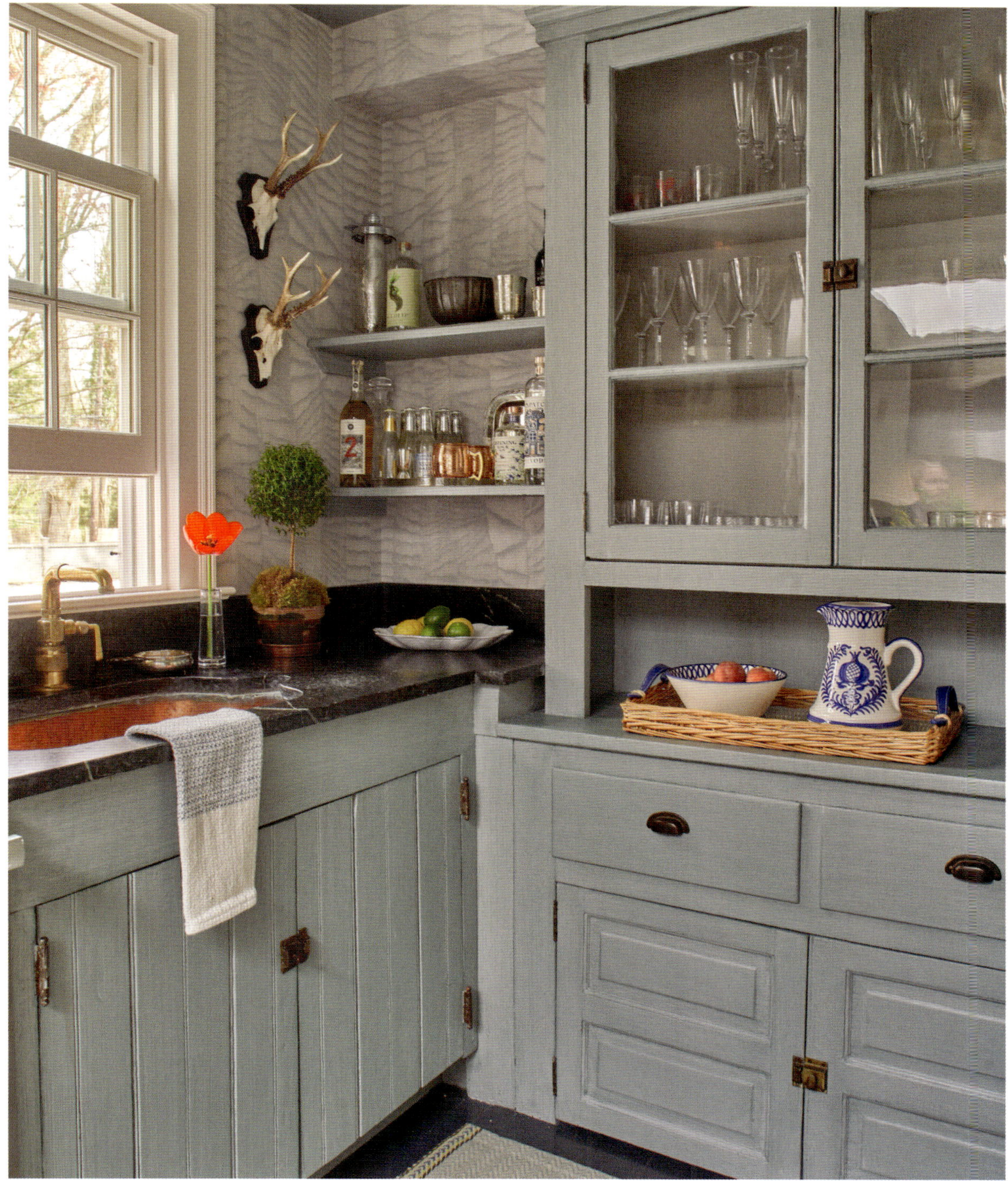

OPPOSITE: The high-gloss cabinetry in this butler's pantry is painted in a deep royal blue. The countertops are a stained mahogany and have a shiny finish. The walls are covered in Robert Kime's "Wattle Blue" wallpaper.

ABOVE: The painted cabinetry in a butler's pantry in this farmhouse is painted a soft gray-blue, and an abstract textured wallpaper is used on the small bit of wall space. The floors are painted a deep glossy blue.

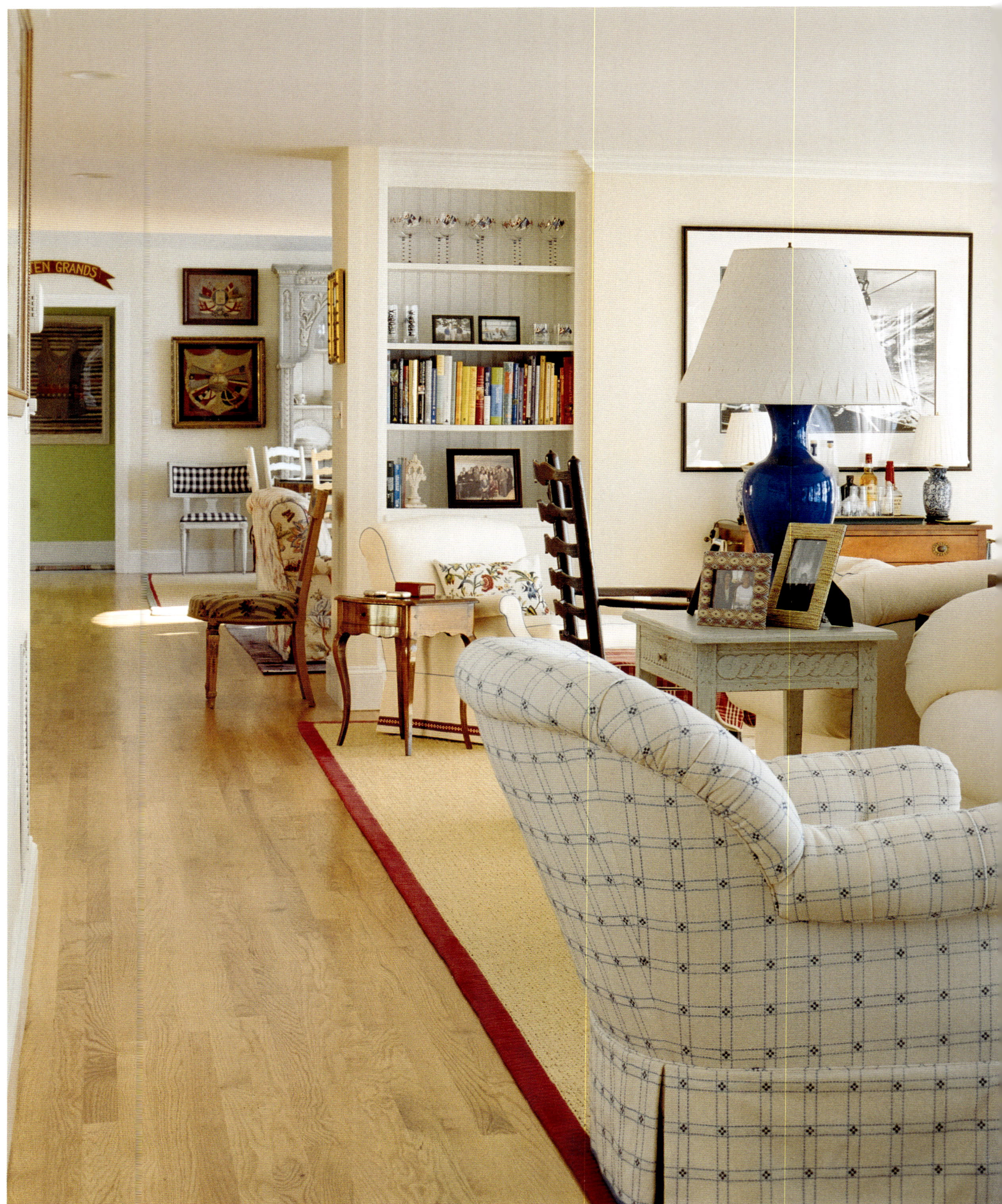

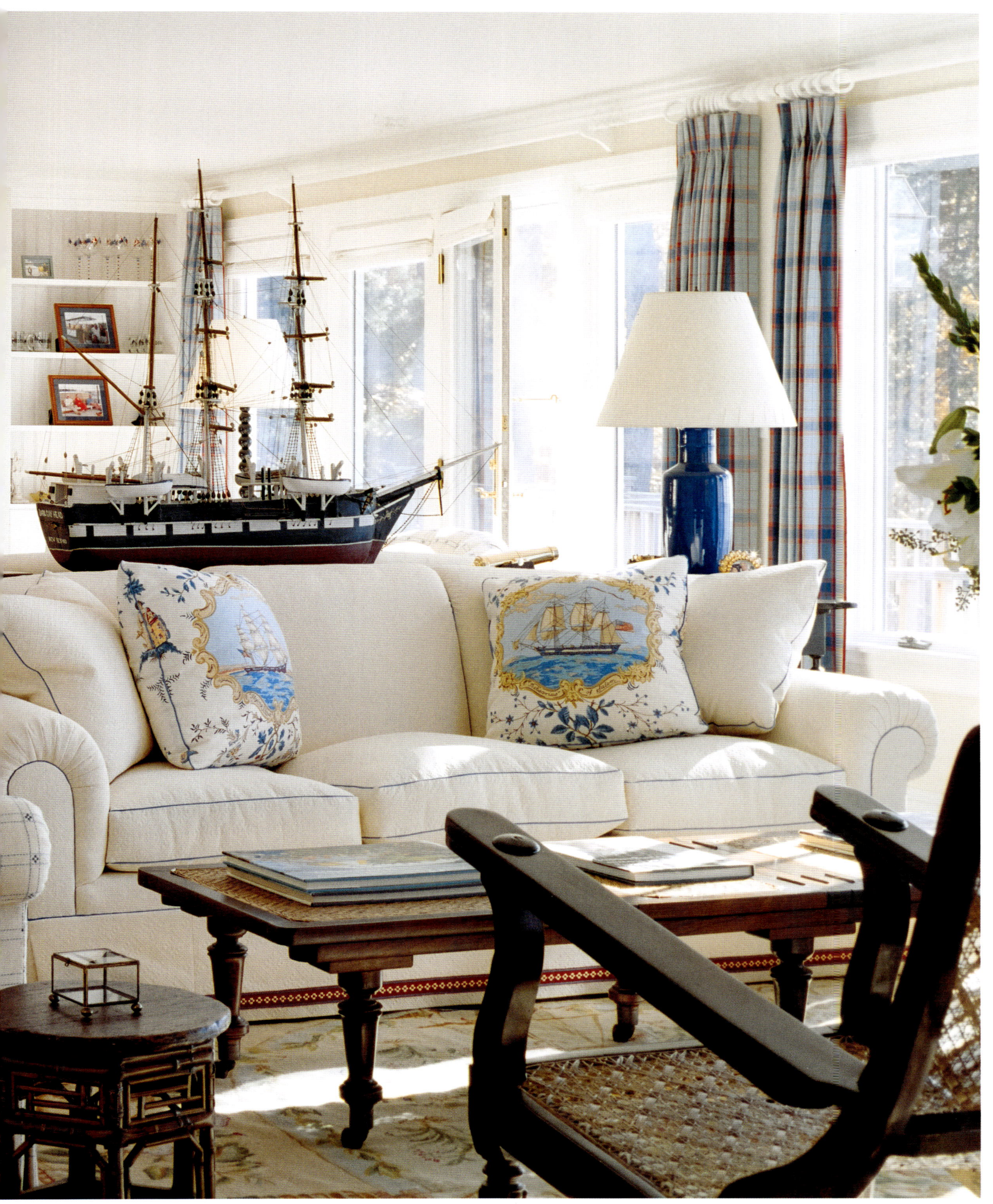

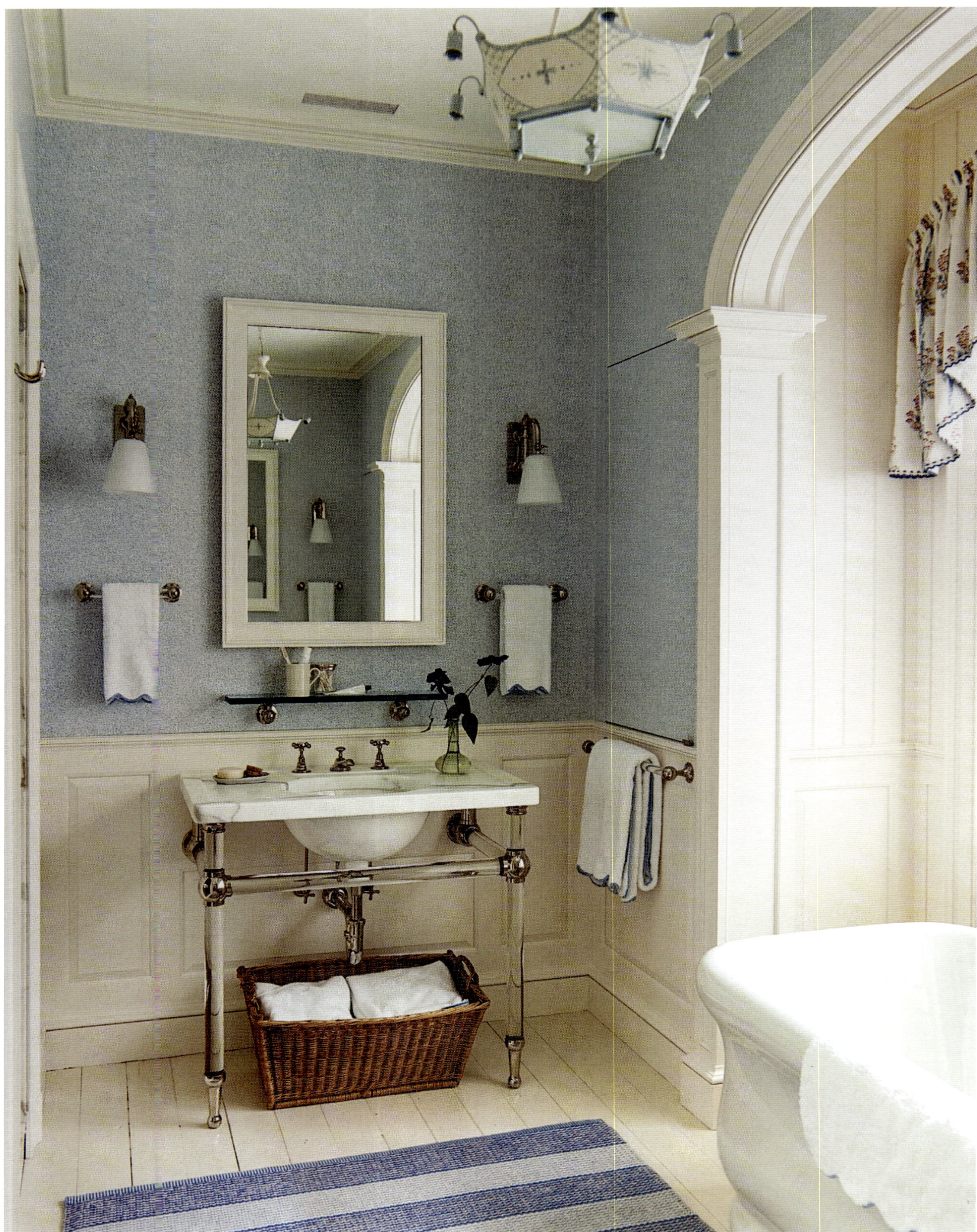

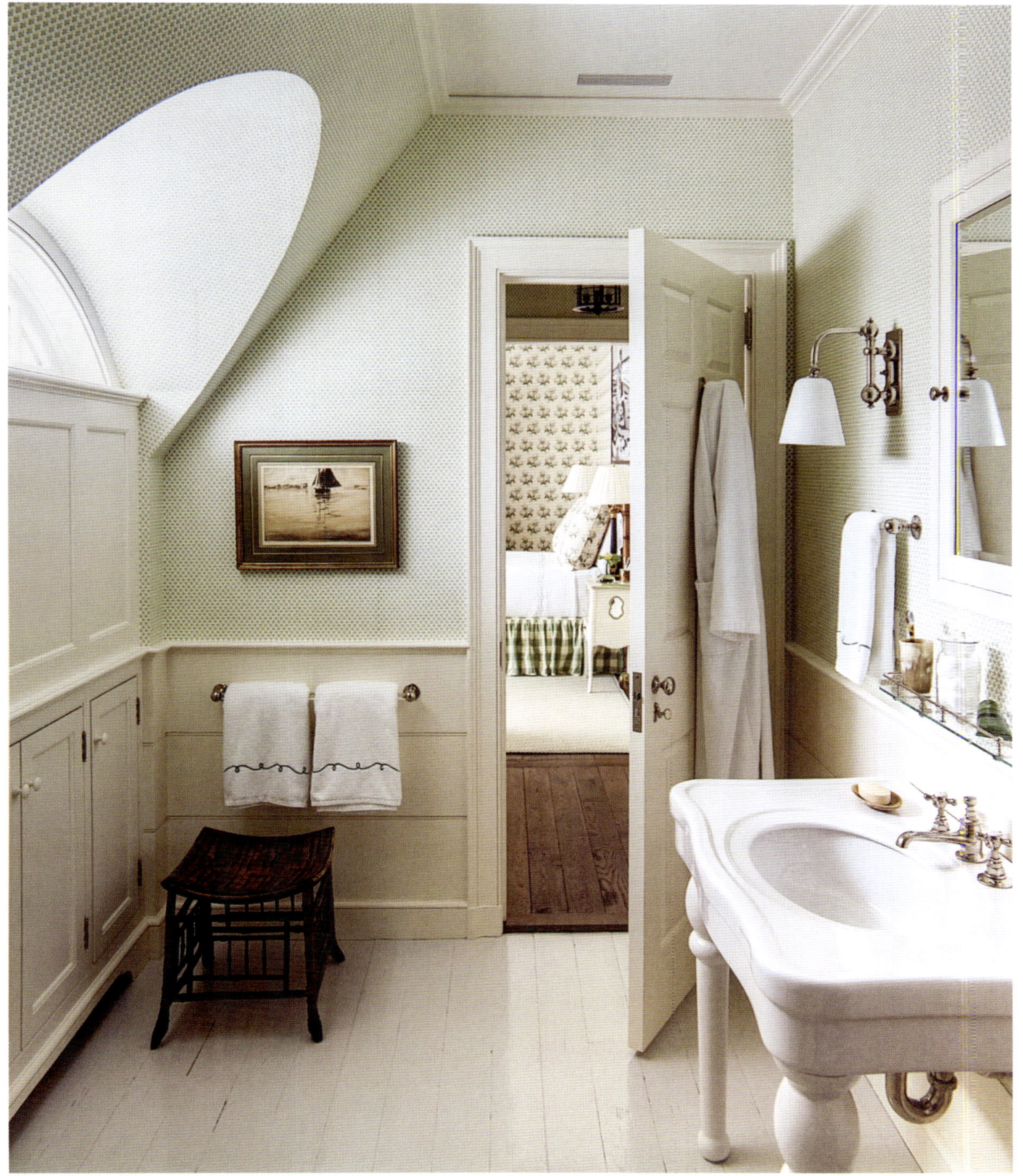

PREVIOUS PAGE: A long living room in Maine is divided by two back-to-back sofas, creating two comfortable seating areas. The table between the two sofas has a wonderful ship model.

OPPOSITE: The bathtub sits in an arched niche with windows to let in lots of light. There are sinks at either end of the room. The wide floorboards in the room are painted creamy white.

ABOVE: An eyebrow window in this guest bath allows for a wonderful soft light and total privacy.

nineties, their children had grown and moved away, so they decided to redecorate. Albert Hadley had designed the original interior, but their taste had evolved after so many years. They wanted a less stark, modern feel and leaned toward more comfortably furnished rooms. We ended up combining more traditional furniture with some of the original pieces, bringing together many styles and time periods. It ended up being an interesting mix of furnishings instead of a uniform house. The antique pieces that we added were as sculptural and defined against the backdrop of the house as their modern furniture had been. The rooms were elegant but cozy, relaxed, and appropriate.

Albert Hadley's design masterpiece was the red lacquer library that he created for Brooke Astor. It is one of the most iconic rooms in American interior design. Pictures of this room have been published in magazines, journals, and books around the world, and it is the most photographed room in the history of American interior decorating. It was an extraordinarily beautiful room to be in and it embodied everything that Brooke Astor cared about: classicism and an emphasis on continuity and tradition. It housed her most important treasures, including her late husband's book collection and the Childe Hassam painting she loved. This elegant room is a perfect example of Albert Hadley's genius.

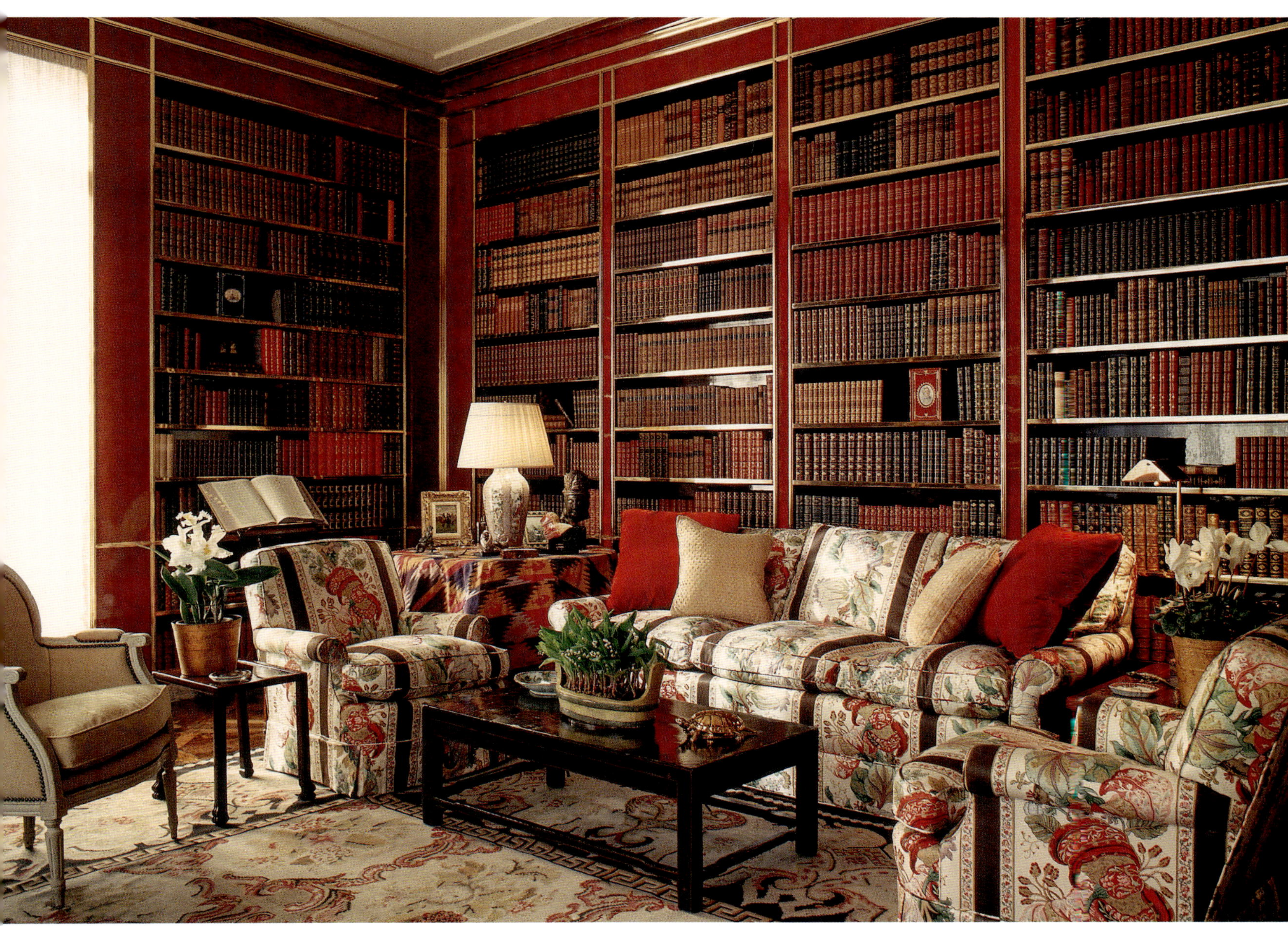

A red lacquer library designed for Brooke Astor by Albert Hadley. It is the most photographed and published room in the history of American interior decorating.

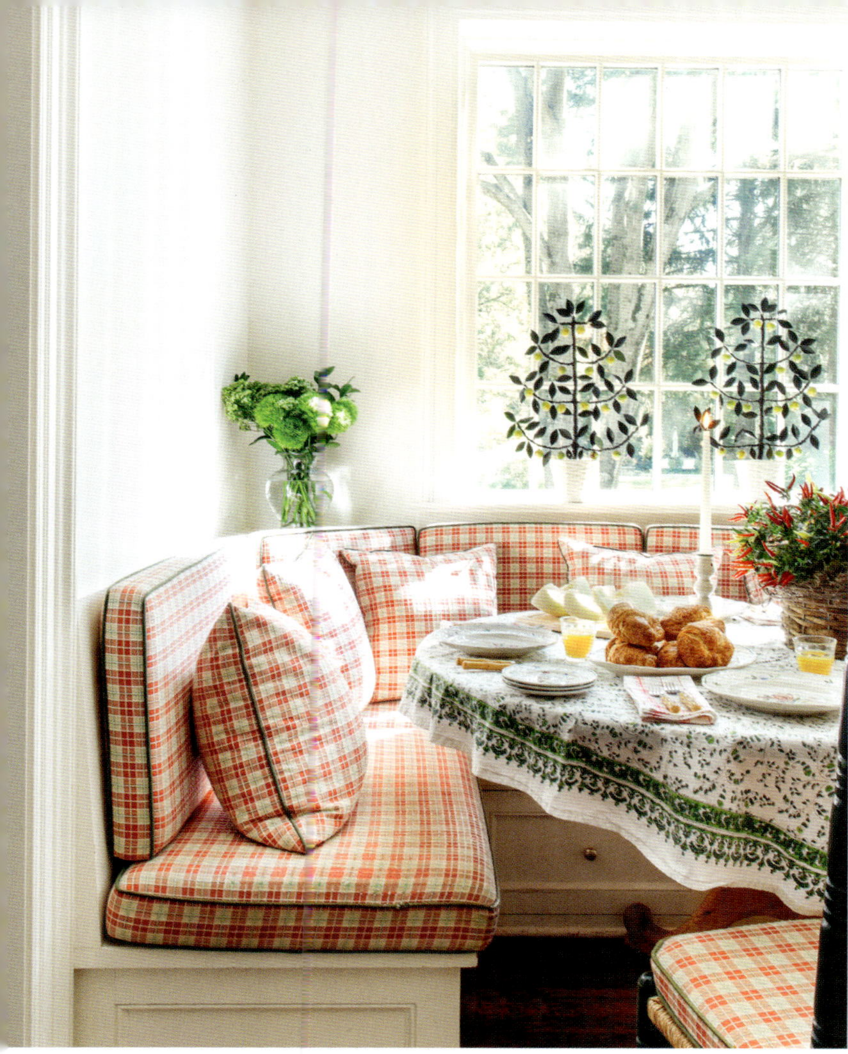

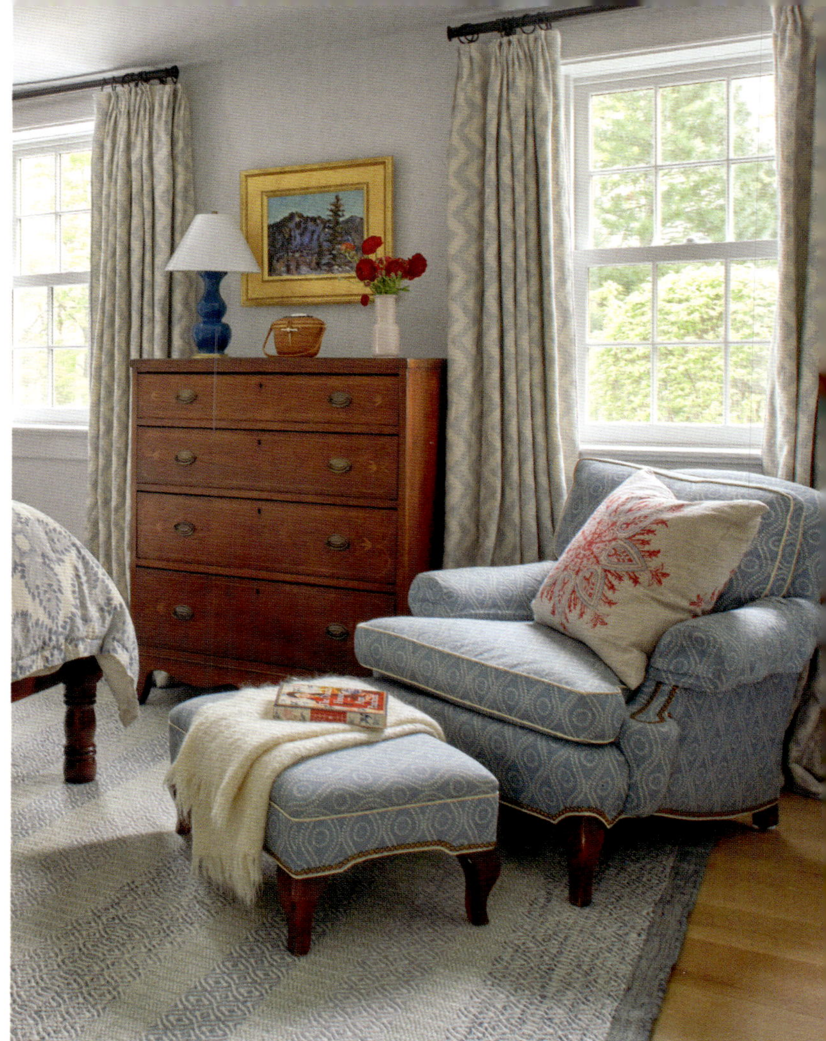

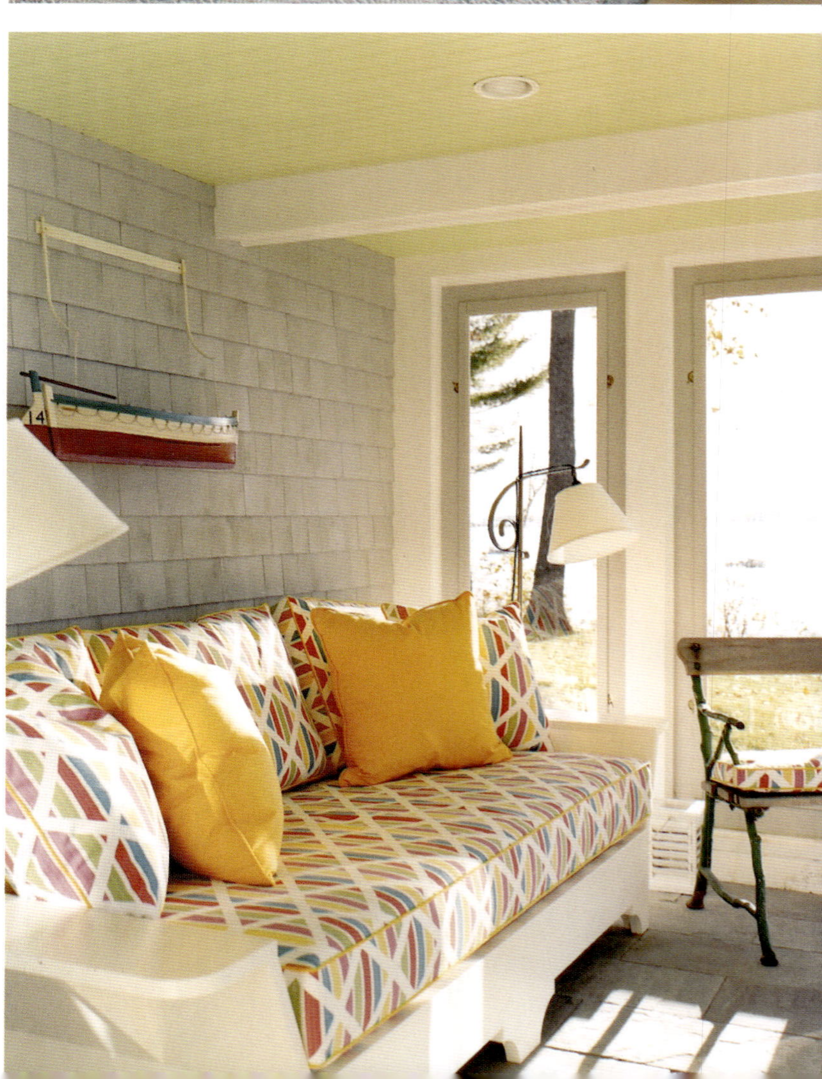

ABOVE LEFT: A cozy breakfast room banquette in Connecticut.

ABOVE RIGHT: A comfortable corner in a guest room with Blithfield curtain fabric and an Elizabeth Eakins rug.

RIGHT: A porch in Maine which overlooks the thoroughfare between Yarmouth and Cousins Island.

I go back to my memories of houses and the places that have had meaning for me. I remember the smells of a house, the color of a room, the way it is furnished, and how it is all arranged. It's the quirky things that I think of most that make that place a home, like the sagging, rolling floors in our house in Maine. It is the layers of a house that make me feel rooted and add unexpected joy.

I think about the porch I love in Maine, and the light, the breeze, and the sounds of the ocean. It is my favorite place to be, watching the sun come up over distant islands, watching it turn from a soft glow into a strong glare only to gradually soften into diffused light over the course of a day. The southern light lingers and the western light diffuses. The house is so filled with memories and I suppose that is what I know and love about it so. A house is a reflection of who lives in it—the children and the dogs gathered around a wood-burning fireplace. Things don't have to match perfectly, but they do need to work together; it is all about balance and juxtaposition. Isn't it about not taking it all too seriously?

CULTI
TASTE

VATING

"He had an infallible sense of what to do with a house and always made life more interesting and beautiful."

—LIBBY CAMERON

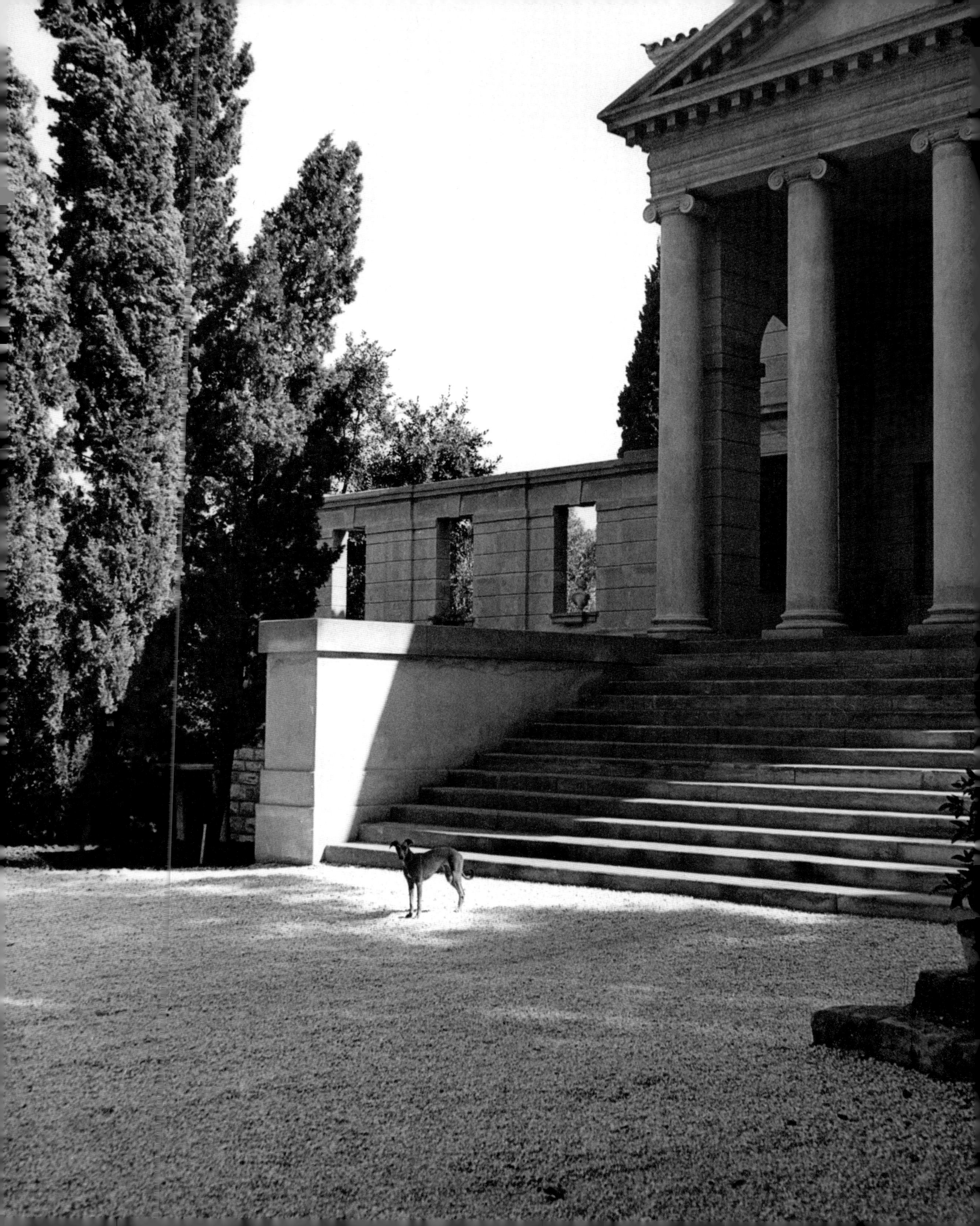

There are many illusions about decorating—the supposed glamour, the travel, carte blanche spending, endless shopping and parties—but the reality of decorating dashes those illusions rather quickly. It is detailed work, and the search to find and deliver all of the pieces of the puzzle takes time and is sometimes quite exasperating. There seem to be endless delays and necessary changes. Sometimes curtains or rugs need to be adjusted; sometimes damaged and broken pieces arrive and need to be replaced. You need patience and perseverance. But when a house is done, there is nothing better than a happy client and that feeling of pride.

I was lucky enough to have grown up living with antiques. None of the pieces were priceless by any means and they were all a little the worse for wear. But everything had character. Someone years ago must have had a good eye and put a great deal of thought into what they bought. As a child, I didn't realize that I was surrounded by artwork and antiques, nor the importance of that. Nor did I think about who had been instrumental in combining them to make wonderful rooms and spaces.

Every summer on the way to Maine, we stayed at my great-aunt Katherine Coolidge's property on the North Shore outside of Boston. Her house was beautiful—light, lively, cheerful, and calm. It was built on the most perfect spot. It was tucked into the slope of the land so it appeared to be one level as you drove up to the front courtyard. The round entrance hall had a domed ceiling, and there was a stone fireplace across from the front door. Five portraits of the first five presidents of the United States painted by Gilbert Stuart, one of America's foremost portraitists, were hung in this circular room. As a child, I did not have a clue about the importance of those paintings. They now hang in the National Portrait Gallery in Washington, DC. It was the entrance hall's floor—a patterned pinky beige marble—that captivated me. I loved to practice my tap

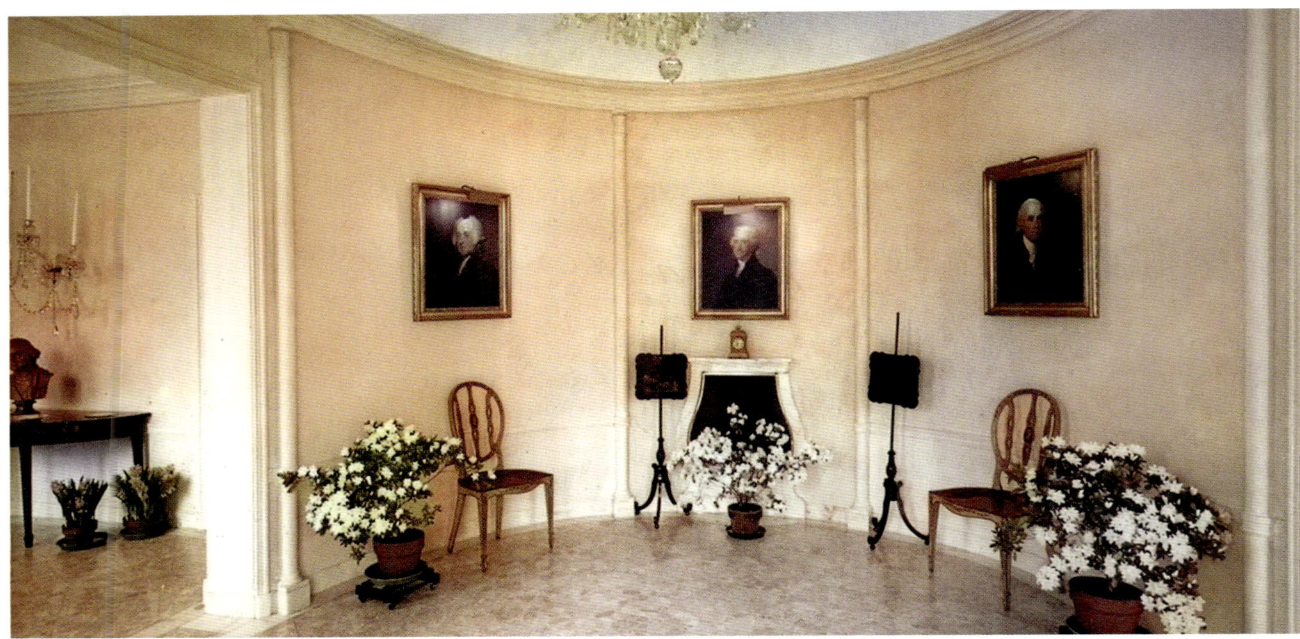

PREVIOUS PAGE: La Fiorentina in St. Jean Cap Ferrat was originally built in 1917. During the war, the villa was occupied by the Nazis who left it in ruins before Lady Kenmare and her son Rory Cameron restored it. Rory oversaw the large modifications to the villa and transformed it into a house with extensive, beautiful gardens and interiors.

ABOVE: The round entrance hall at Coolidge Point had a domed ceiling with hallways that went off to the left and right. Portraits of the first five presidents of the United States, painted by Gilbert Stuart, hung in this room.

BELOW: This black-and-white photograph doesn't show the wonderful color palette of pale yellows, tangerines, light blue, and sand that graced this living room. It was a wonderfully proportioned room and looked out toward Cape Ann.

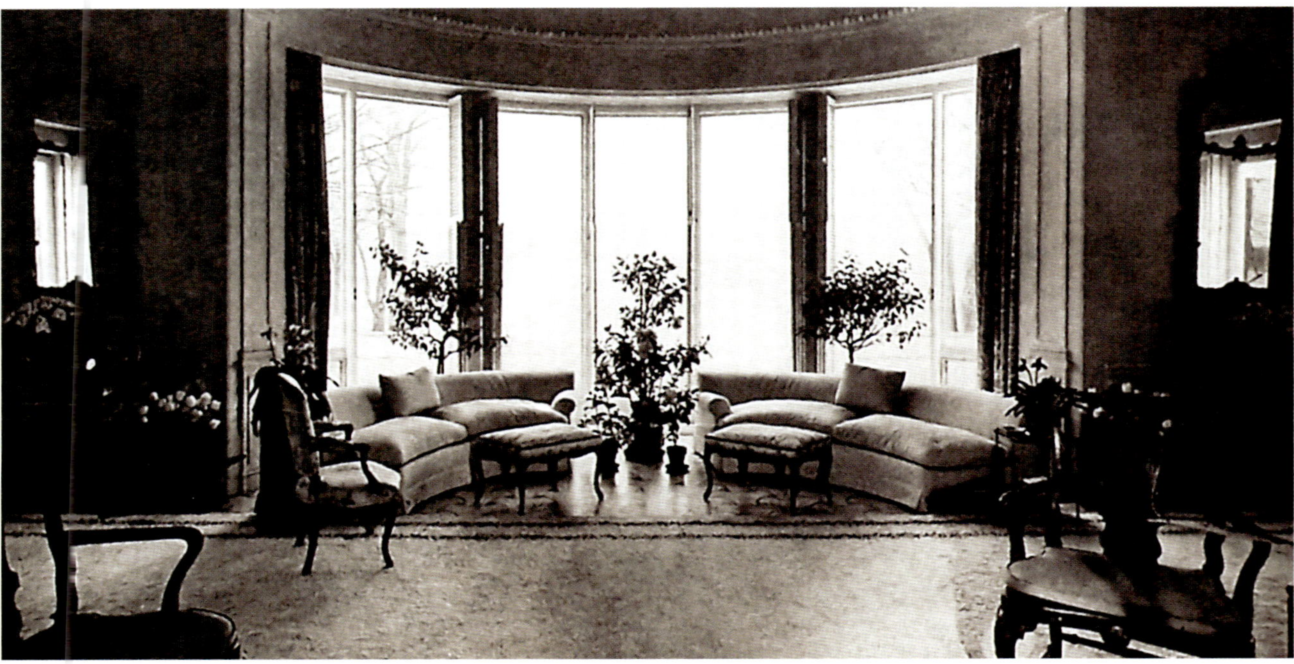

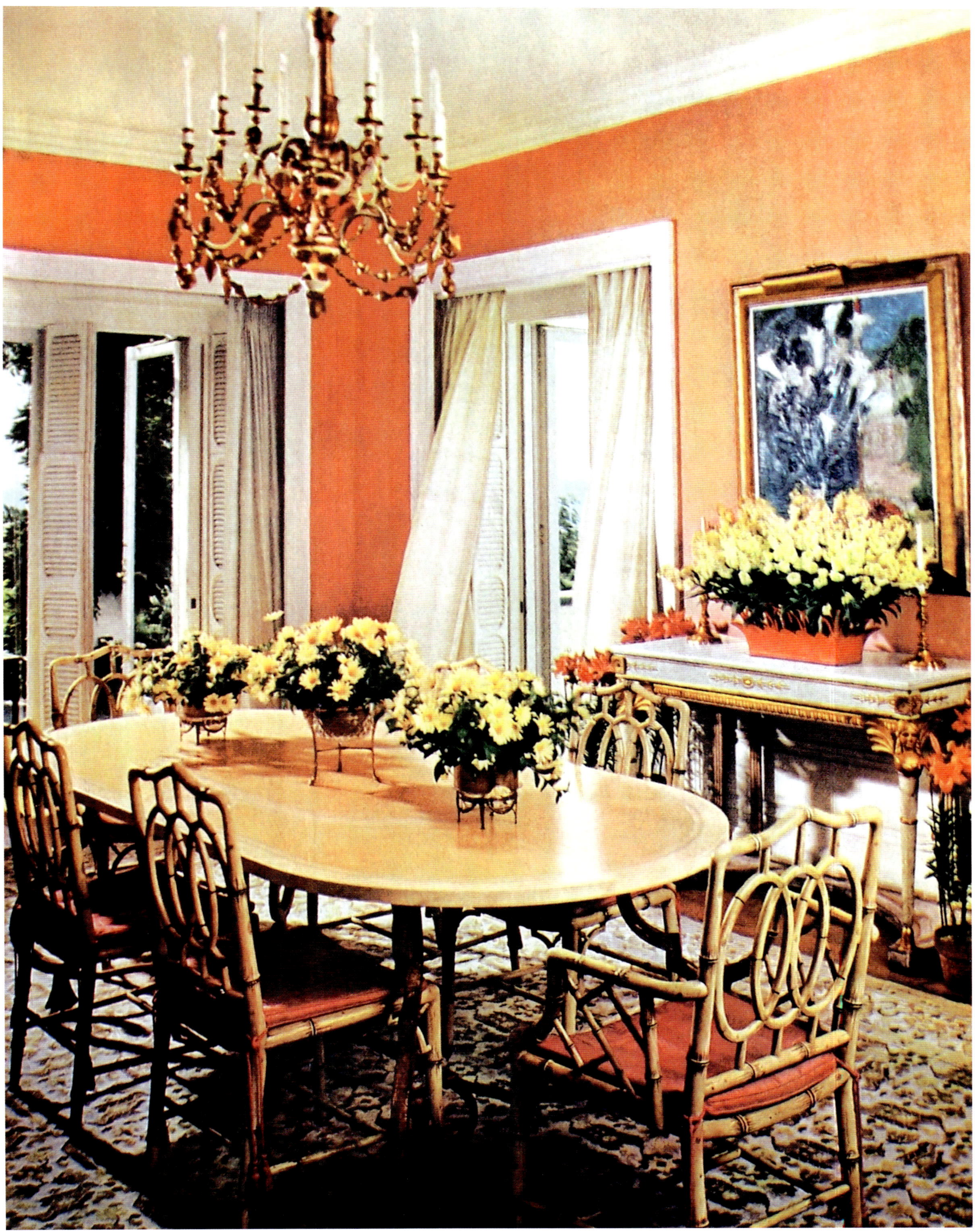

dancing there. The sound and echo my shoes made was just perfect. Auntie Katherine had Thomas Jefferson's eyeglasses, his desk paperweights, and one of his letter openers in her library, which was a cozy room that always smelled so good. The living room was on the side of the house that looked out toward the sea. It was filled with a combination of French and English furniture and was done in hues of pale yellow, tangerine, light blue, and sand. A big tangerine-colored sofa sat in the rounded bay window. The floor was bleached and had a subtle overlapping scallop design with an incised line outlining the pattern overtop of a pickled floor. The house was long and low, and rambled with turns in the hallways taking you to other rooms beyond. It was very serene and always smelled of flowers.

Auntie Katherine had a passion for flowers. The greenhouse was always full to the brim; it was overseen by Bruno. He was a lovely man with a big, beautiful smile. The house was filled with orchids, lilies, and flowering plants in mostly yellows, strong pinks, and whites. Every once in a while I will smell a flower that will take me right back to Auntie Katherine's house and my memories of being there.

Rory Cameron played an important role in my life. He was very curious with a creative spirit and a great enthusiasm for and knowledge of so many things—the pre-Raphaelites, Mies van der Rohe, flowers, photographers, designers, writers, clothing, restaurants, exhibitions, travel, antiques, houses, and interesting people. He had an extraordinary gift for friendship and loved beauty. He took me to many places to see all different types of things. John Fairchild of *Women's Wear Daily* dubbed him "A Man of Taste." Rory would pick things up and lift the lids on boxes as he walked through a room, and touch things in a shop or in a garden just to know what they felt like. He loved to share his taste and thoughts. Everything Rory had, whether it was a piece of furniture, an object, or a picture was something you'd covet for yourself. He had an infallible sense of what to do with a house and always made life more interesting and beautiful.

I was lucky enough to spend a lot of time with Uncle Rory when he visited my family in Washington, DC. After I moved to New York we got together every time he was in New York, which was often as he was working on a few projects there. I spent a summer at his house in Donegal, Ireland, which had been an Irish rectory. His house there was

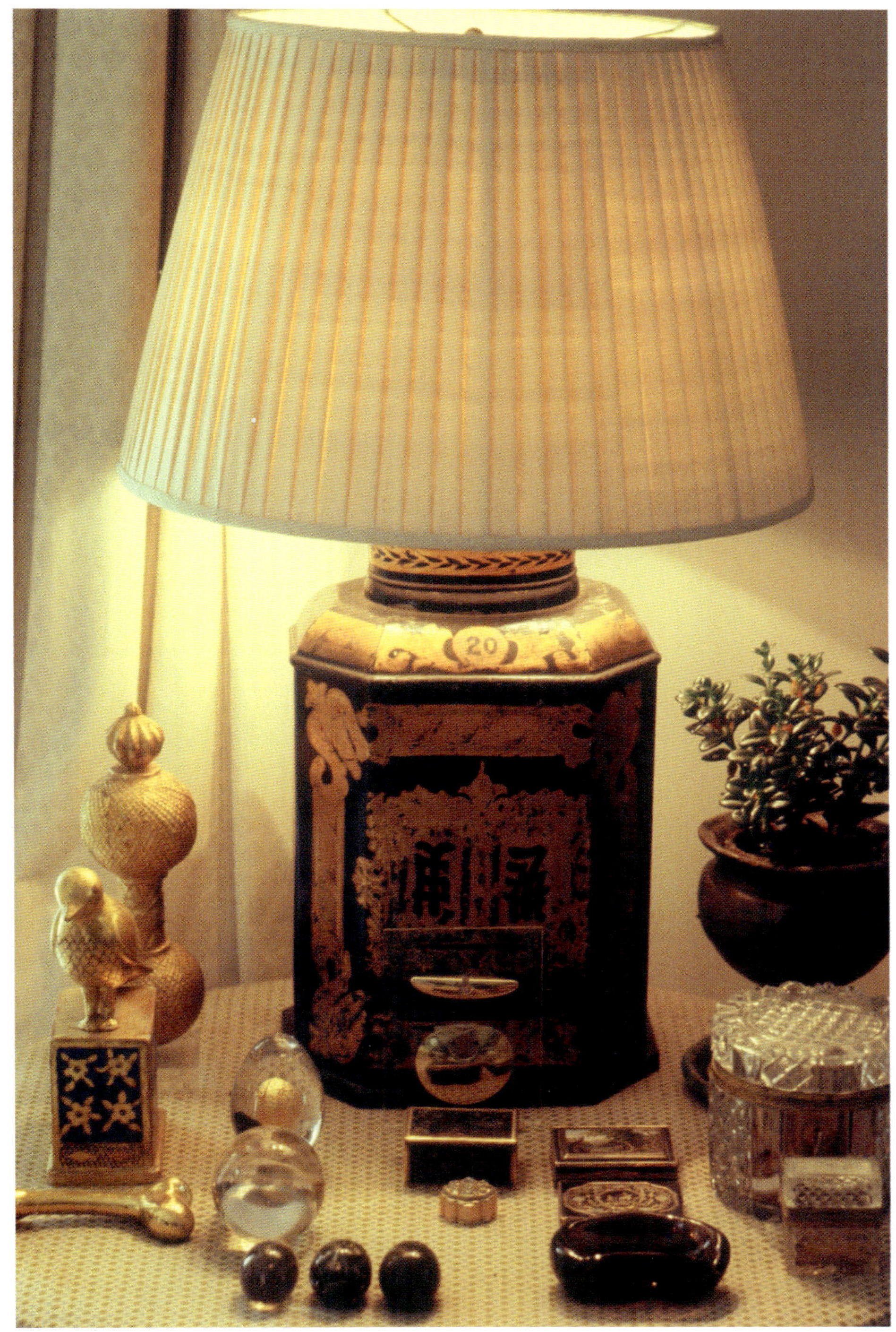

PREVIOUS PAGE, RIGHT: The dining room at Coolidge Point was painted a tangerine color and had both shutters and cream-colored, lightweight curtains at the windows. The contemporary oval dining table had a gilded metal base, a painted top, and was surrounded by faux bamboo dining chairs.

ABOVE: A table with items from one of Rory Cameron's many collections at Les Quatres Sources in France. He had lovely things and a discerning eye.

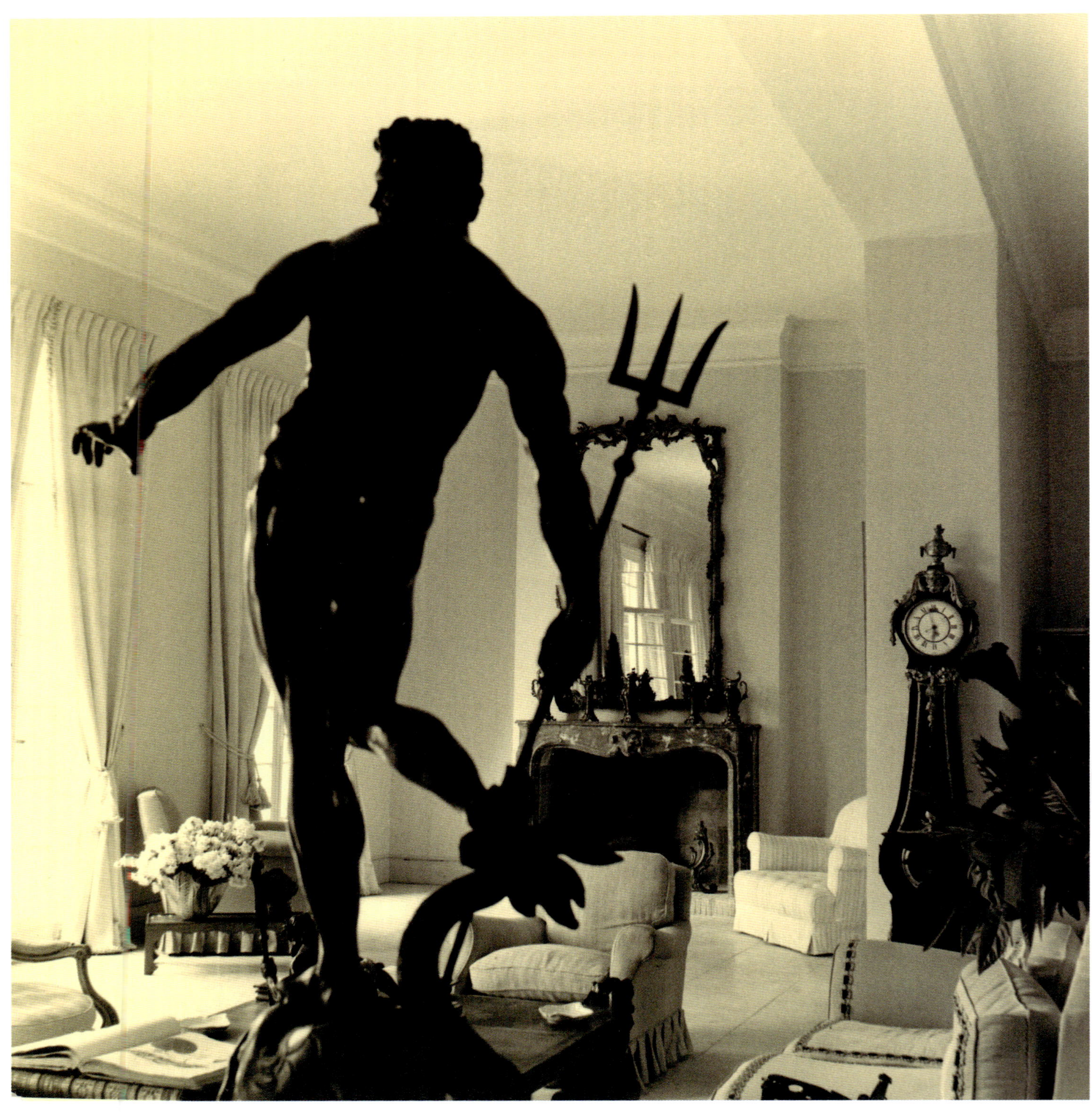

Detail of a bronze statue of Poseidon in the living room at La Fiorentina, photographed by Lord Snowdon.

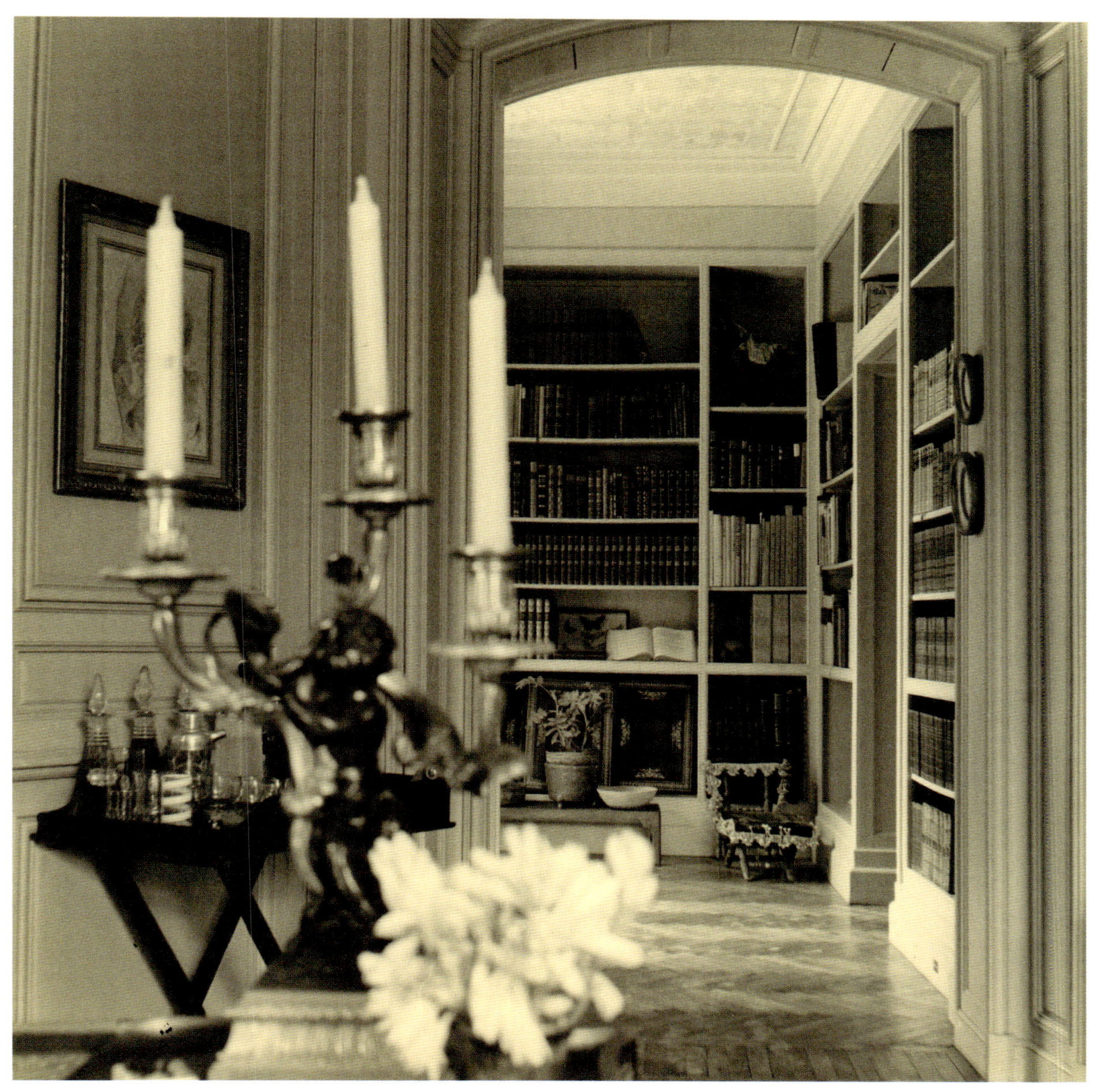

The hallway to the library at La Fiorentina.

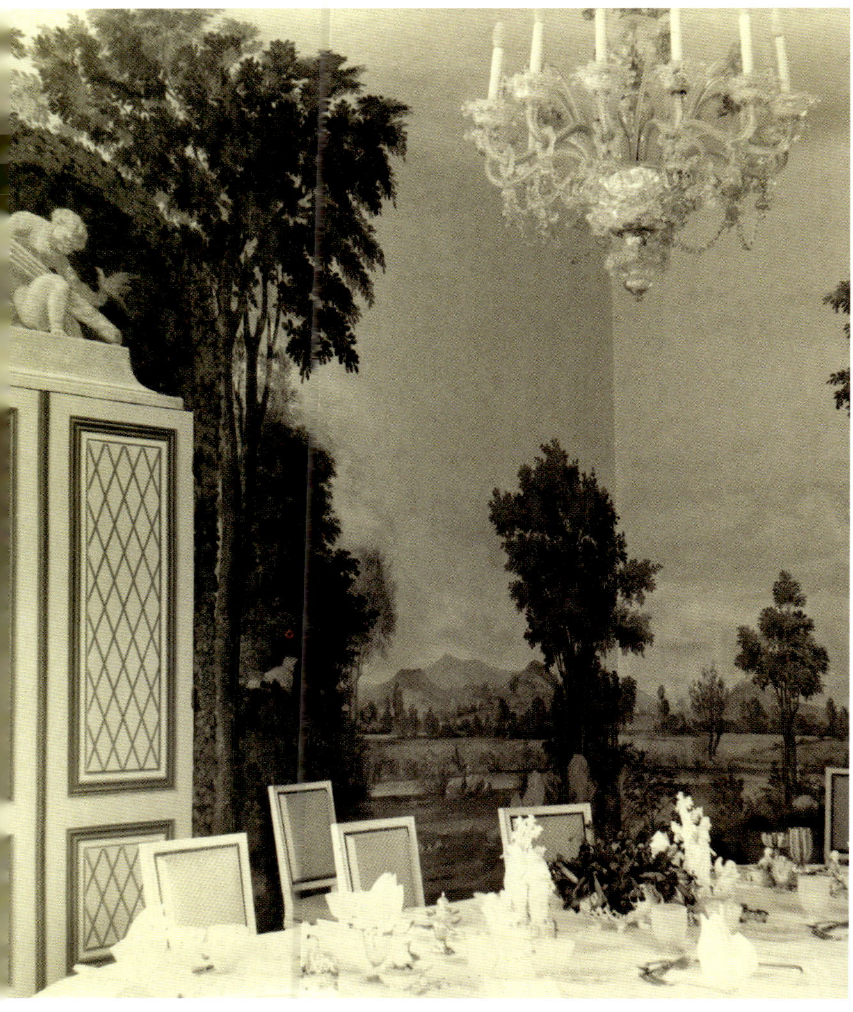

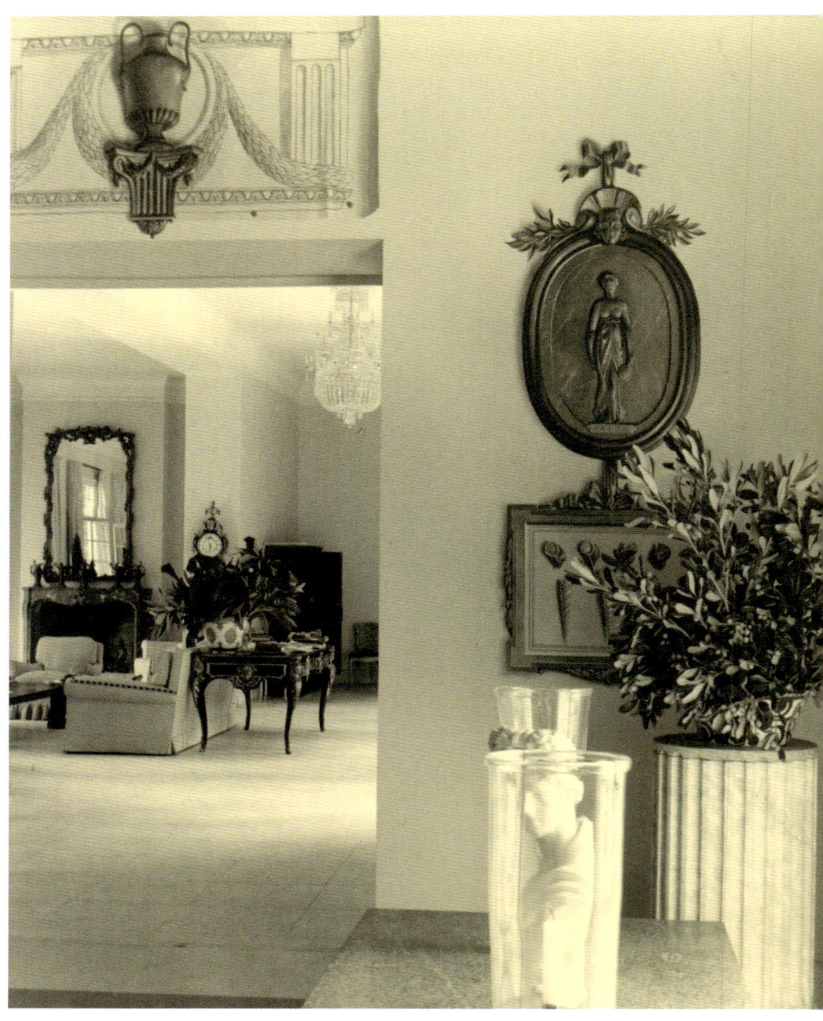

ABOVE LEFT: The grisaille dining room at La Fiorentina.

ABOVE RIGHT: A view into the living room at La Fiorentina from the entrance hall that had been painted in trompe l'oeil by Martin Battersby.

OPPOSITE: A living room detail over the books table at La Fiorentina.

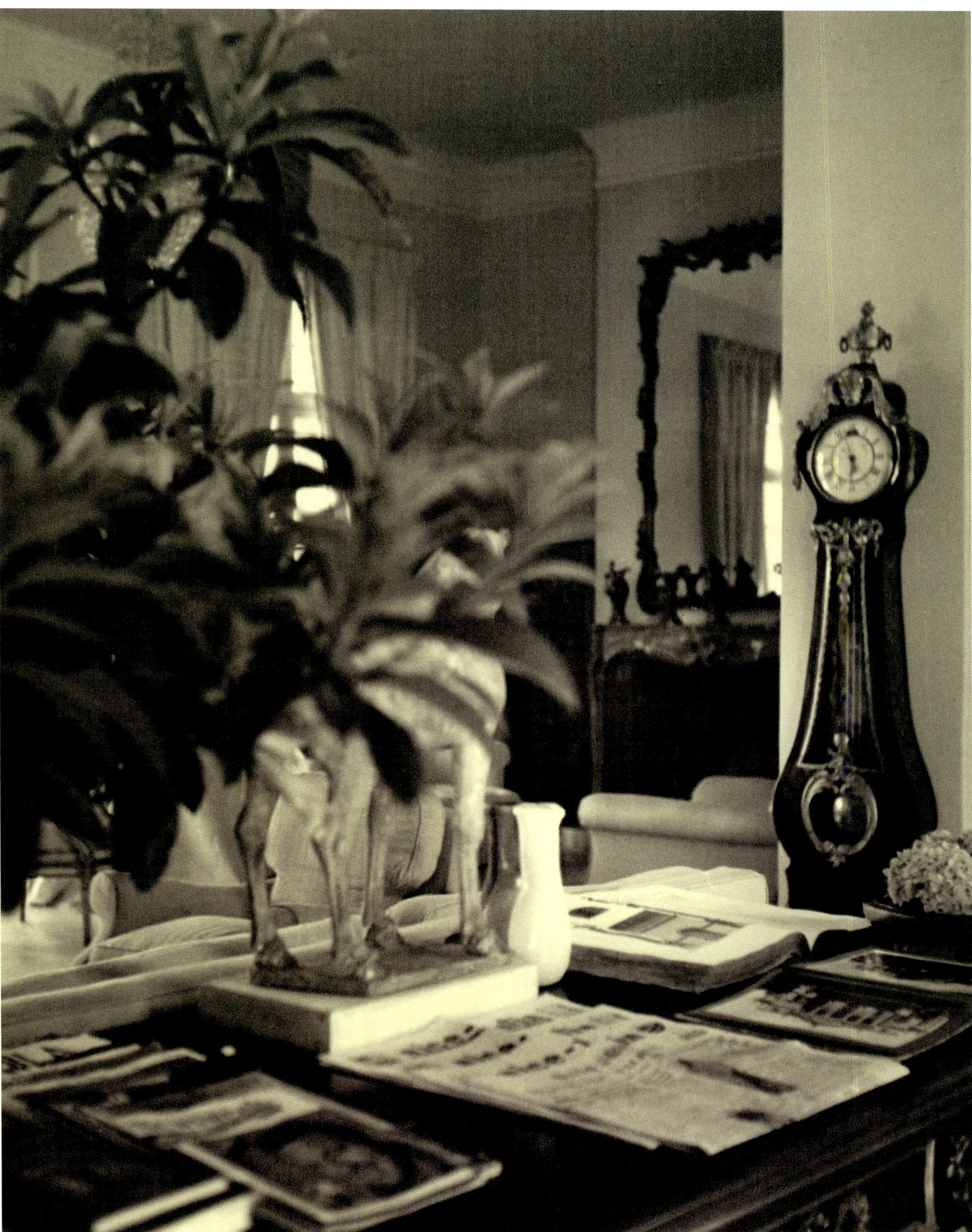

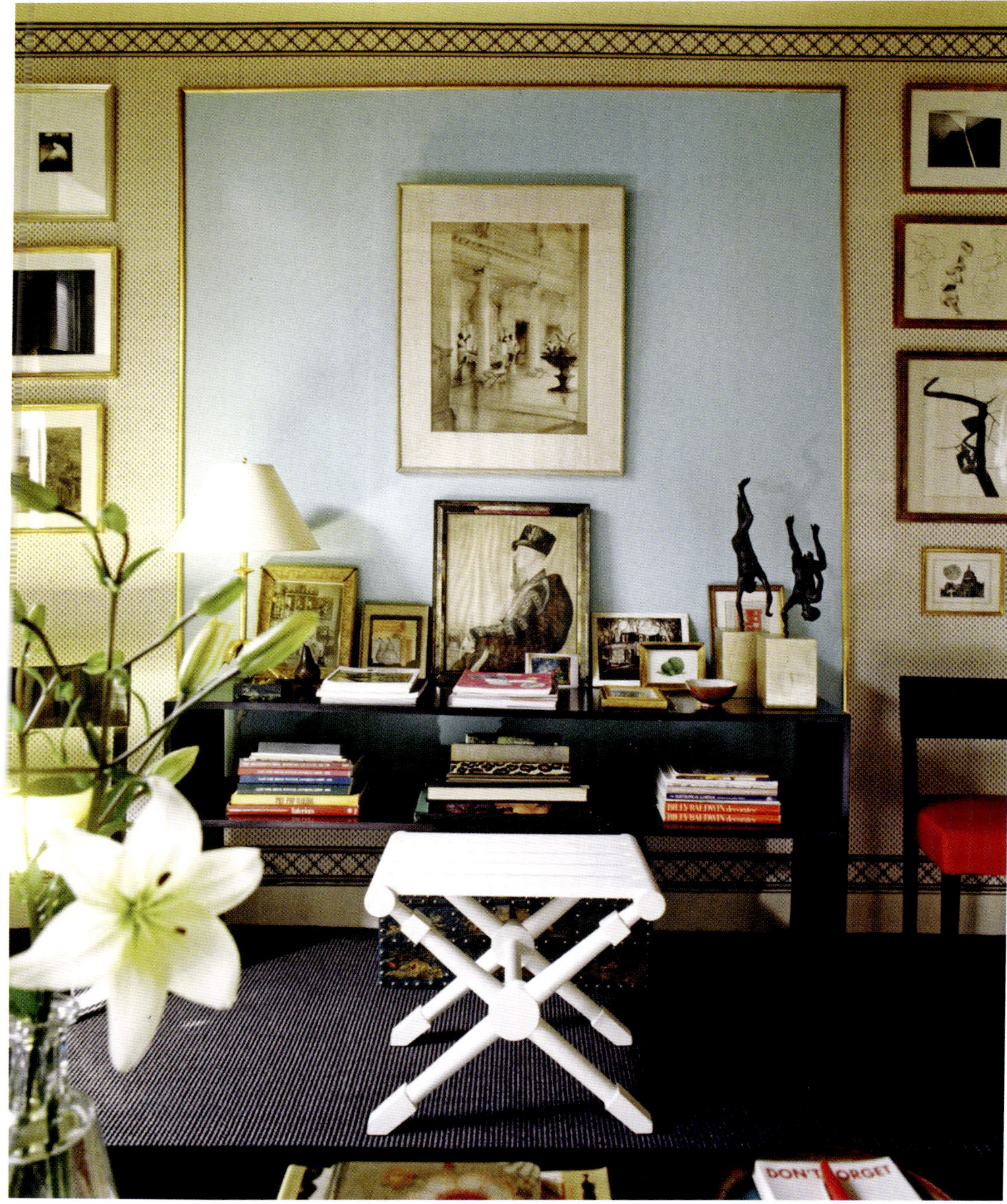

The "middle room" in Mr. Hadley's apartment was used as a living room. The walls were wallpapered in a small black-and-beige pattern called "Truex" and then covered with gouache-and-ink drawings. The bulletin board is painted a robin's-egg blue that Albert loved and is framed with a thin gilt molding. The drawing of the woman in profile is of Ruby Ross Wood.

beautiful and filled with objects from his travels around the world. It had William Morris wallpapers in a few of the rooms, which was in such contrast to his house in France. Les Quatres Source in Provence was decorated in a palette of creams, beiges, soft yellows, and a green that Rory said was taken from the underside of an olive leaf.

Visiting Rory's house, Les Quatres Source, was an education. We spent time with his friend Van Day Truex who had an old house that was quite literally built into the side of the hill town of Ménerbes, and overlooked the endless acres of vineyards below. I honestly didn't have a clue that Van Day Truex was one of the greatest designers in America. I only knew that he was wonderful to me. His lovely ink-and-gouache drawings hung on the walls, and the house was, of course, very beautiful, serene, and orderly. It was filled with indigenous materials including chalky limestone, raffia, and rattan. He had all of the furniture for his house made locally. His table lamps were made from old aubergine-colored wine bottles from the local vineyards. Everything was of a natural texture or a shade of white or beige except for the lovely yellow plates that we had lunch on. He used raffia woven shades at the windows and had nubbly sisal rugs, which I had never seen used before. I asked him about the sisal, which was not yet in vogue or readily available in the United States. I still have the pale blue octagonal plates from the town of Apt that Van Day Truex and Rory bought for me one afternoon.

Interesting people were always coming and going when I stayed with Rory. The poet Stephen Spender as well as Peter Quennell, David Niven, Hubert de Givenchy, Marguerite Littman, Barry Sainsbury, David Hicks, and, of course, Rory's partner, Gilbert Occelli. Gilbert was a beautiful man—he looked like Omar Sharif. He spoke mostly French and my French was far from good, but we understood the gist of what we were trying to say to each other and always laughed and had fun together.

Rory's gardens were just as beautiful as the interior of his house. Lunch at Rory's in Ménerbes was almost always served on the terrace. He fed his dogs from the table, which often resulted in a scuffle. It amused Rory, although it was unnerving for the rest of us.

Rory took me to see wonderful houses and apartments. One night in Paris, he

NEXT PAGE, LEFT: Enid Kenmare photographed by Lord Snowdon.

NEXT PAGE, RIGHT: Rory Cameron photographed by Guy Marcineau at Les Quatres Sources.

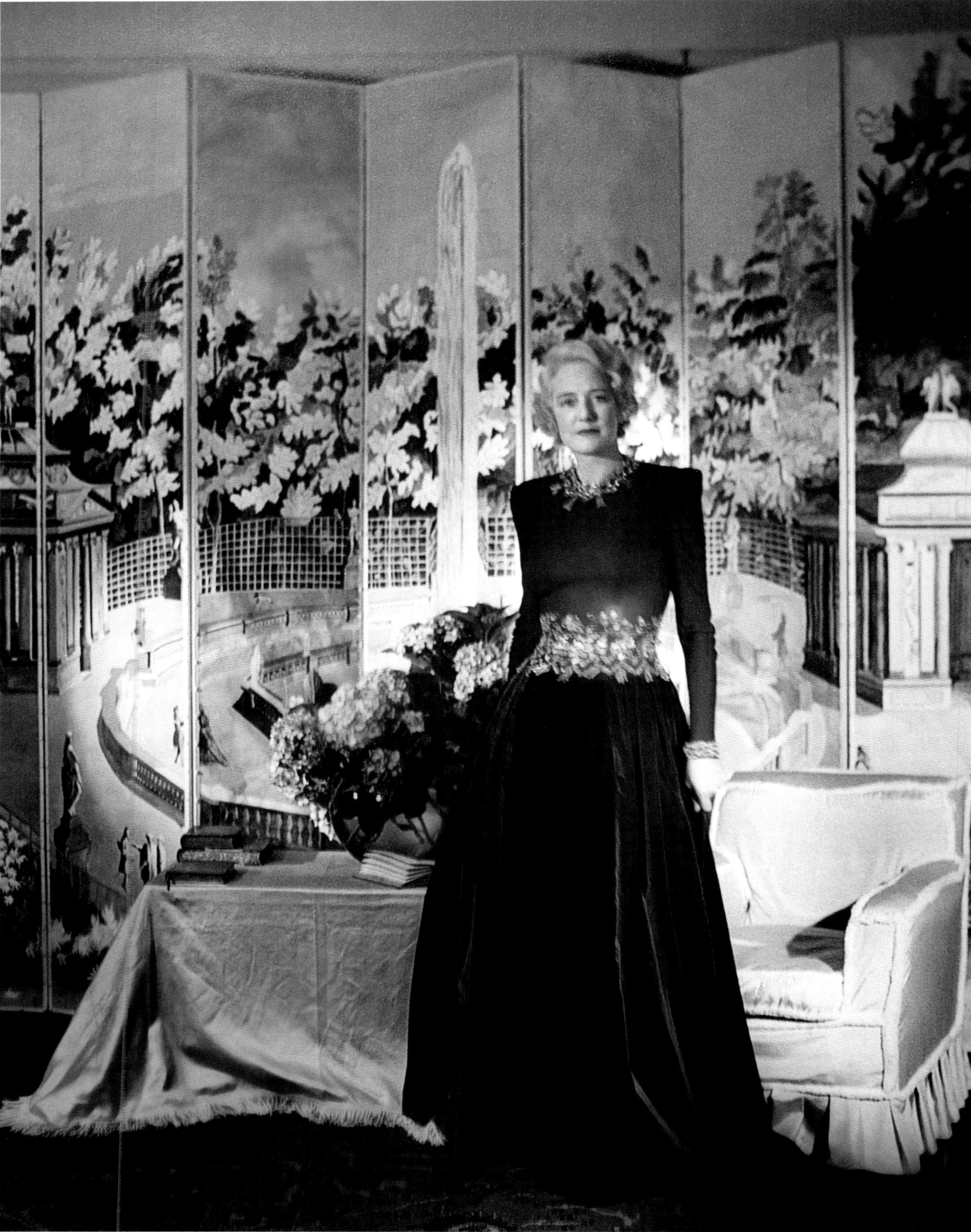

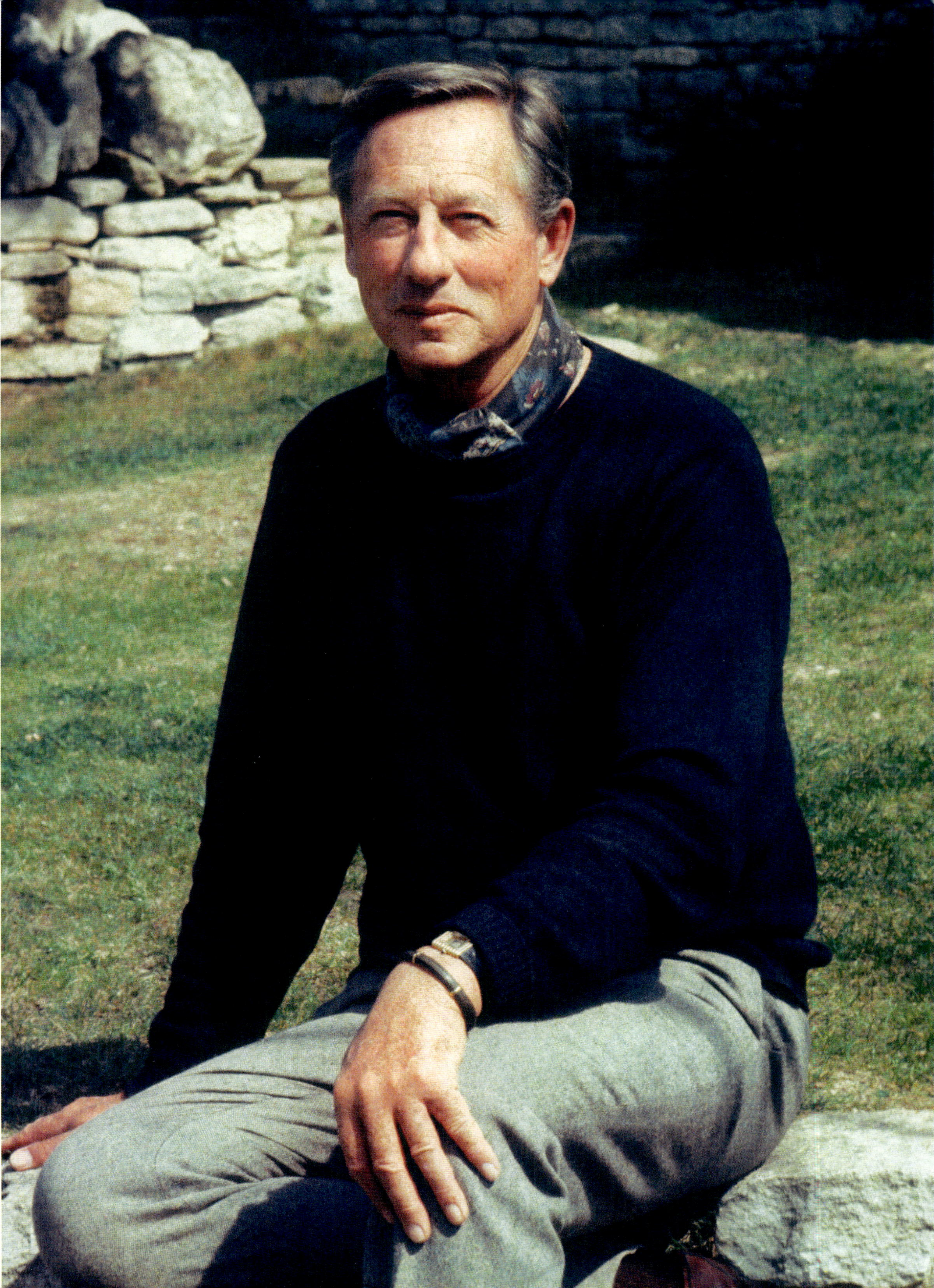

took me to his friend Walter Lees's apartment. To get into Walter's top floor apartment you had to climb up an exterior metal staircase on the side of the building. I was absolutely awestruck when we walked in—I had never been in such a beautiful place. It was spectacular; it overlooked Les Invalides, which at night with the lights on, was just magical.

Rory adored his mother, Enid, the Countess of Kenmare, who was married and widowed four times. She was one of the great beauties of her era—elegant and exotic, with sapphire blue eyes. She was a great animal lover and often had a large parrot or a hyrax sitting on her shoulder. I remember sitting at her feet when I was a little girl and asking her about the spots on her legs. She told me that she had wrestled with a large octopus in the Mediterranean that had tried to pull her under, and that those were the scars left from her encounter. Of course I believed her—why wouldn't a child believe that amazing tale? In reality, the spots were just the pattern on her stockings. She was entrancing, quiet, and demure. Originally from Australia, Enid first married Sir Roderick Cameron. Roderick died not long after Rory was born. She then married Frederick Cavendish, then Lord Furness, and finally, Lord Kenmare. Her friend Somerset Maugham jokingly referred to her as "Lady Killmore," since all four of her husbands had died. His book *The Razor's Edge* is based on my father who stayed with Enid and Rory often.

Rory told me about going to the Valley of the Kings with his mother and Howard Carter—a beau of hers—to see the tomb of King Tutankhamen, which had just been discovered. They went the day after the tomb was found and opened. There were still untouched footprints in the sand. Can you imagine?

Rory's sister, Patricia Cavendish O'Neill, was a breeder and trainer of thoroughbred horses. She lived on a farm called Broadlands Stud near Sir Lowry's Pass outside of Cape Town in South Africa. Pat and Enid settled in Kenya after they left La Fiorentina on Cap Ferrat and the French Riviera. Pat spent many years in Kenya living with her

These are stills taken from a video when we were staying with Pat O'Neill, Rory Cameron's sister, at Broadlands Stud outside of Cape Town in South Africa. Pat's baby baboons were fascinated by the braces Flora and Charlotte had on their teeth and tried to pull them off.

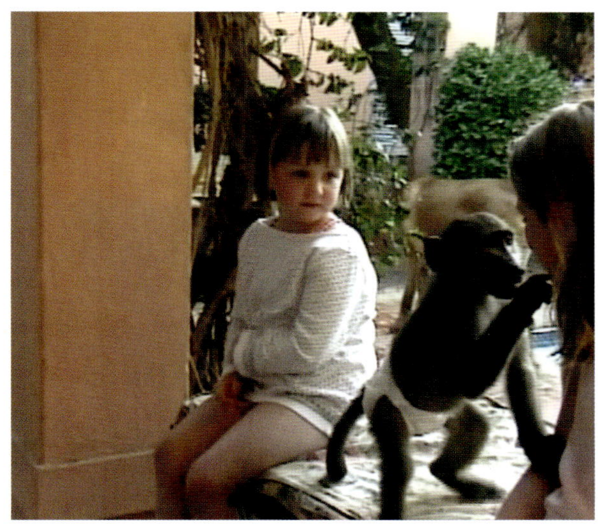
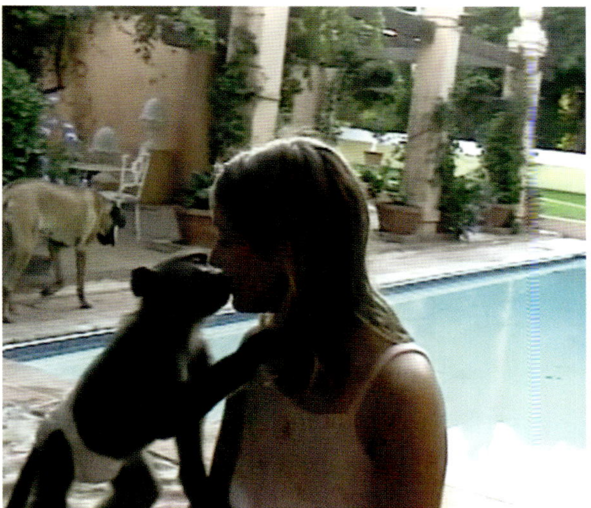
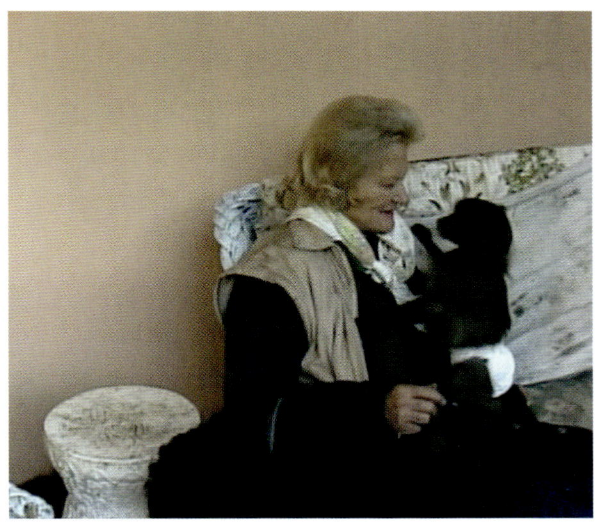
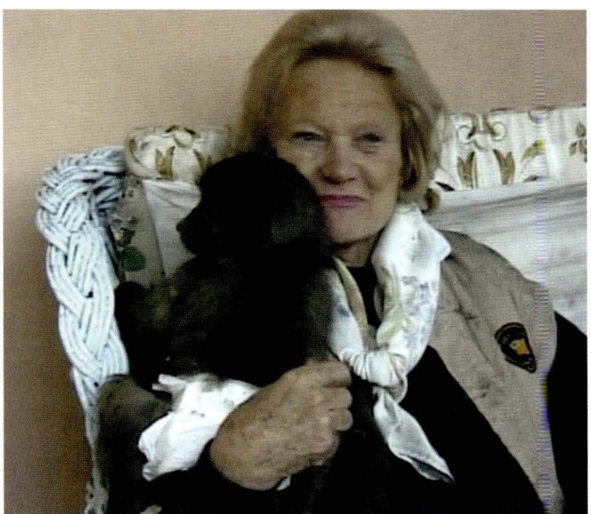
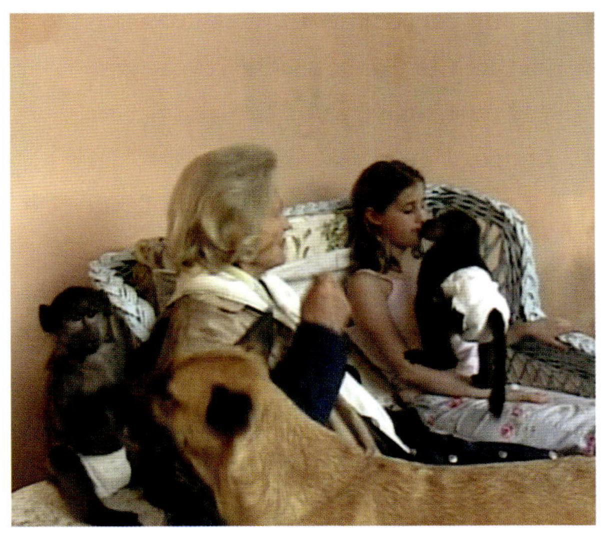
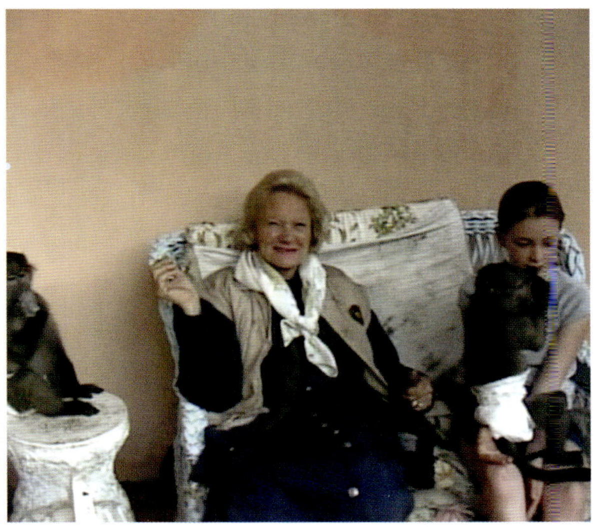

mother on Equator Farm where together they had a stud farm. But the altitude in Kenya was too much for Enid, so she decided to move farther south.

Enid was great friends with Beryl Markham, the pilot and author. Together they flew down the east coast of Africa and found a piece of land outside of Cape Town that overlooked False Bay. The land ran down to the water's edge and became Broadlands Stud. Pat eventually came from Kenya to oversee Broadlands. The farm later became an animal sanctuary, and was filled with baboons, exotic birds, a chimpanzee, and a herd of rescued donkeys in addition to the racehorses. When I was last there, there were twenty-seven dogs. The front gate was not automated and had a pulley system of weights that allowed it to open and close. The sign at the entrance read: "Beware of Wild Agapanthus." It was meant to be a deterrent to unwanted guests, and an agapanthus does sound frightening if you don't know much about plants. Upon arrival, one was always greeted by a large pack of dogs and occasionally one of Pat's baboons that had gotten loose. There were many peacocks that roamed about, and the sound of Pat's rescued parrots and birds could also be heard from their enclosures behind the house. Pat was wonderful and quite a bit like Rory in her quiet, unassuming, kind way. She was totally devoted to her animals. She wrote two wonderful books, *A Lion in the Bedroom* and *A Chimpanzee in the Wine Cellar* about her animals and life in Africa.

I feel so grateful to have had all these people, and particularly Rory, as influences in my life. Rory's beautiful houses, La Fiorentina, Le Clos, and Les Quatres Source, inspired me. He taught me about taste and style. I miss sitting with him and having him twirl the rings on my fingers around and around. I miss his laughter and smile, and how he would flutter just the tips of his fingers while simultaneously running his thumb across his hand. He was a lovely person.

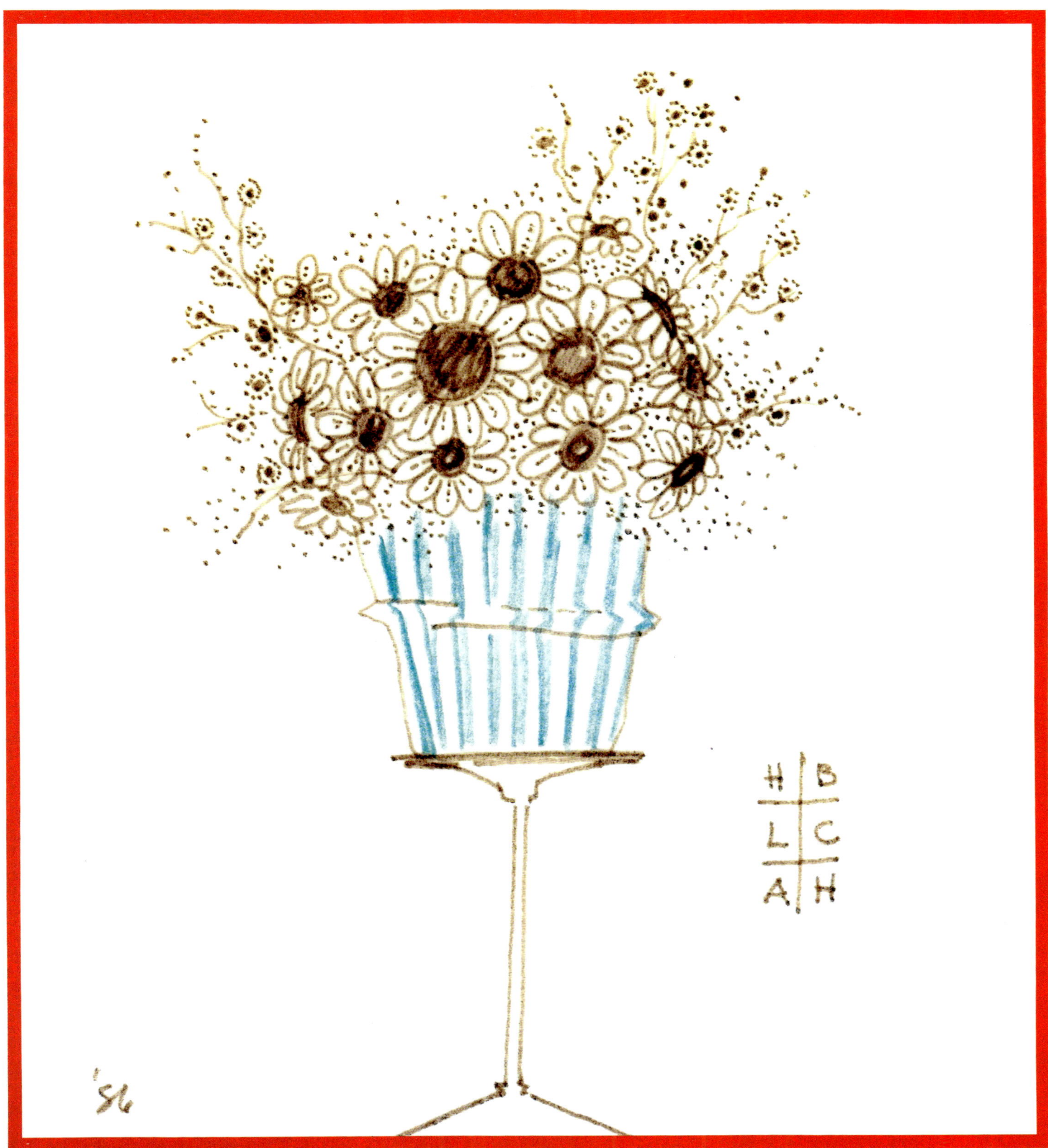

Albert Hadley gave me this drawing for my birthday.

CREA
BALA

TING

NCE

"Balance is what makes a room really work."

—LIBBY CAMERON

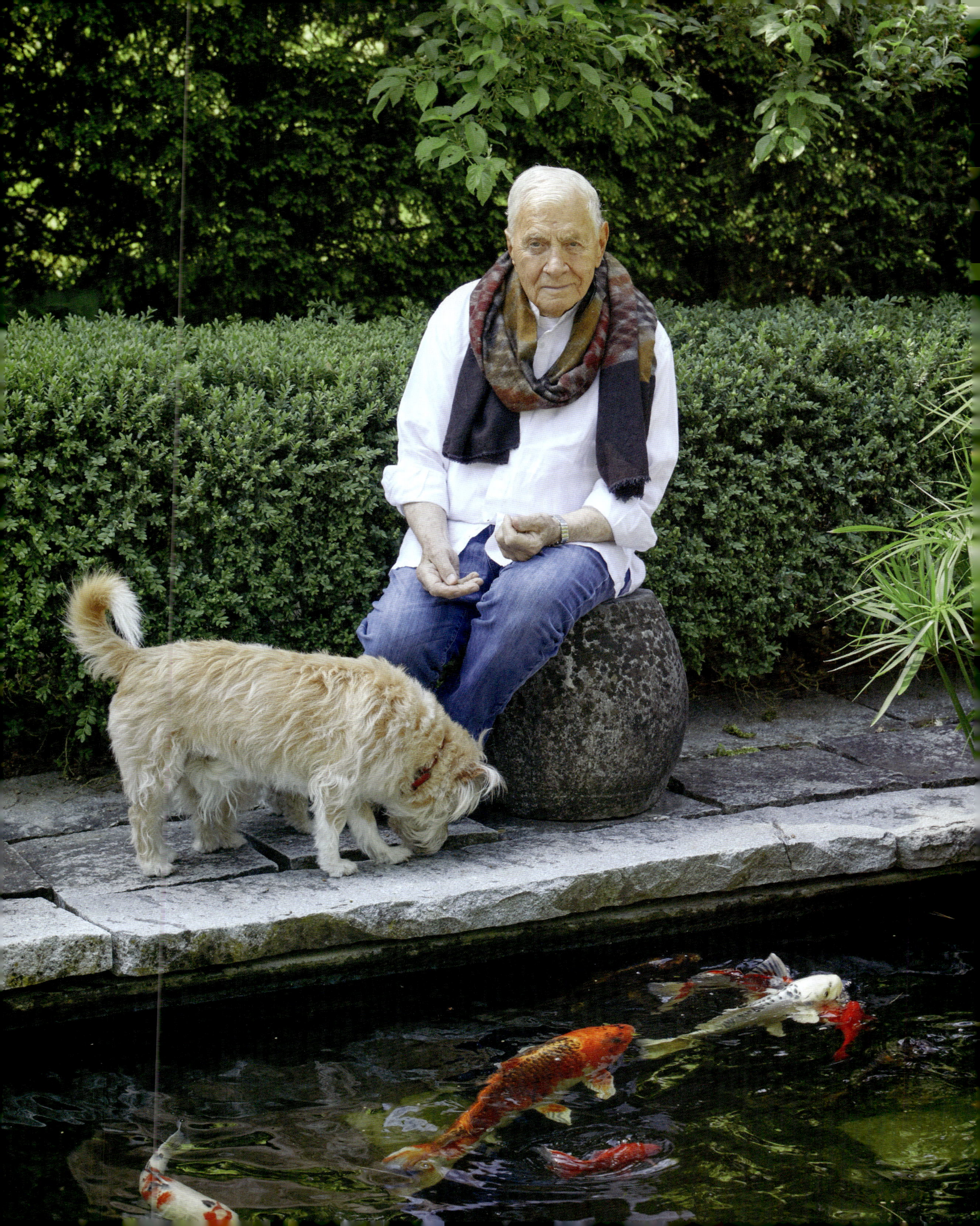

At the age of twenty-four, a very different sort of learning began for me when I started working at Parish-Hadley. I gained an understanding of how and why certain things work and learned what needed to be changed and why in order to make a space better. I learned how to create a flow and balance to the rooms in a home. In the quest to create perfect rooms and houses, there were always many discussions in the office about the projects we were all working on, and what changes would be best made to an existing space. If something were to change, what would be required to make the room better, more architecturally correct, and livable?

There are many preconceived notions about rooms and how they should be furnished. Asymmetrical rooms can certainly be intriguing and usually make for a more interesting space as asymmetry is unexpected, but balance is what makes a room really work. You don't want one end of a room to end abruptly or fade out. It's important to think about the weight of furniture and where and how it is placed. You don't want to place furniture in such a way that other parts of a room are blocked off or less accessible, or that will make a section of a room feel disconnected. Empty spaces are just as important as filled spaces.

But it is not just furniture that fills a room. Balanced lighting, mirrors, and art can help to anchor a room. Walls without artwork, photographs, or mirrors feel naked to me. I always want to fill that void. Mirrors are great because they reflect other things in a room and reflections add another dimension. How the pieces in a room work together is also important. I like combining the old and the new, whether its fabrics, art, or furniture, as long as the various pieces work together. As Mrs. Parish used to say, you don't want the things in a room to "swear at each other."

Rooms have different needs depending on their size and shape. Rooms with low ceilings need height as opposed to rooms with high ceilings, which need anchoring;

darker rooms and sun-filled rooms also function differently. If you are looking to add a sense of ceiling height, use a vertical stripe on the wall or floor-length curtains set just at the ceiling line. Low furniture in a high room can make the space feel squat. Small rooms feel larger when you can look from one room into another. Avoiding color is not a way to make a room seem bigger; just use color effectively. I find it best to choose and start with just a few colors. By having a constant tone or color in the room, you create balance and have a good starting base for how other things will be placed.

I like things in a room to feel settled, as if everything has always been there. I've learned that one change in a room starts the progression of another change. One change can lead to many changes, like dominoes. I am always moving things around including furniture, lamps and lighting, artwork, plants, and flowers. I prioritize comfort and what is appropriate for a space. Visual comfort matters as much as practical comfort, and that includes welcoming, comfortable seating areas. Chairs and sofas need tables next to them on which to put down your things. There should never be one thing in a room that towers over everything else and dominates a space. Albert Hadley always talked about the importance of a "skyline" in a room. Your eye needs to be able to scan up and down and around a room and not see everything at the same level. Furniture placement and size, artwork, and curtains will create that skyline. Mixing up how art is hung, such as a large picture or mirror on a wall with a collection of smaller ones next to it, balances out large wall surfaces and adds visual interest.

A play of scale is another way to create balanced walls in a room. Small things above or below something bigger always add interest, as does using a mixture of simple and grand, fancy and humble. In my decorating, I am not on a quest for the best of everything. I prefer to work with things that I love, and with things that are a reminder of a time or person. For me, the sense of association matters—the story of where I found something, who gave it to me, or to whom it once belonged.

There are so many great treasures to find in the world, and with a good eye you can find amazing pieces that have character and charm. Not everything has to be absolutely perfect—imperfection and quirkiness can add magic. And, as with anything in life, too much of a good thing can spoil a space.

The first thing that always catches my eye going into any store has to do in some way with an animal—be it a print or a painting or an object. I have been collecting almost anything I can find to do with animals for more than fifty years now. I'm discriminating in what I choose: I don't like sad-looking creatures, or ones that are

PREVIOUS PAGE: John Rosselli at his house in Falls Village, Connecticut.

overly stylized or too serious. Combining some good and other simply decorative things, and using found objects adds character to a room.

Rooms are to be lived in and furnished in a way that they can be used and not just admired. A room should be beautiful, comfortable, welcoming and functional, filled with energy and interest. Is there anything better than going into a room where you feel drawn or pulled in and want to explore every corner? I love looking around and getting both an understanding of the person who lives there and admiring what they have chosen.

I have learned so much about design from John Rosselli. When I first began at Parish-Hadley, John had a small store on the northwest corner of 72nd Street at Second Avenue. It was tiny and filled to the rafters with amazing, interesting, unique things. He has an incredible eye and likes practical furniture and pieces as well as unusual ones. I have always loved visiting him in his various shops. He moved from 72nd to 73rd Street, and then finally to 61st Street. The 73rd Street shop was two floors full, and I would find almost any excuse to visit. The shop was a wonderful source: he had absolutely everything from furniture to lamps, mirrors, tabletop objects and accessories, and artwork. It was such a treasure trove, and I doubt there were many times that I left empty-handed. His dogs would be asleep on the chairs and sofas. I remember Flora, one of the especially sweet whippets. She always greeted me when I came in. John's stores were a beehive of activity: people carrying things up and down the stairs, art and objects being hung on the walls, or things being moved around or rearranged to fill the empty spots left by something that had just sold. It had great energy and was always changing.

John and Bunny Williams opened Treillage together, an equally wonderful store filled with amazing and beautiful things. I miss their shops—nothing quite like them exists in the city any longer.

Taste is not a standard but the power to discern—to know what works and what doesn't work—and why. It's important to understand a room's purpose to understand what is suitable for a room and why. There has to be an appreciation of order and relevance, and a sense of logic for one's eye. As a decorator, you can suggest and guide people, but a client must find their own logic in their space. Just as a really "done up" room can be fun in the moment, it can sometimes lack substance, and a perfect or pristine room can lack soul, or feel cold and unwelcoming. To me, the essence of interior design is people and how they live, and what makes for a meaningful space. Decorating is about how to make a room work by creating a quality of life.

INCORPO
COLOR

RATING

> “I love color and mix it fearlessly, using different patterns, textures, and textiles.”
>
> —LIBBY CAMERON

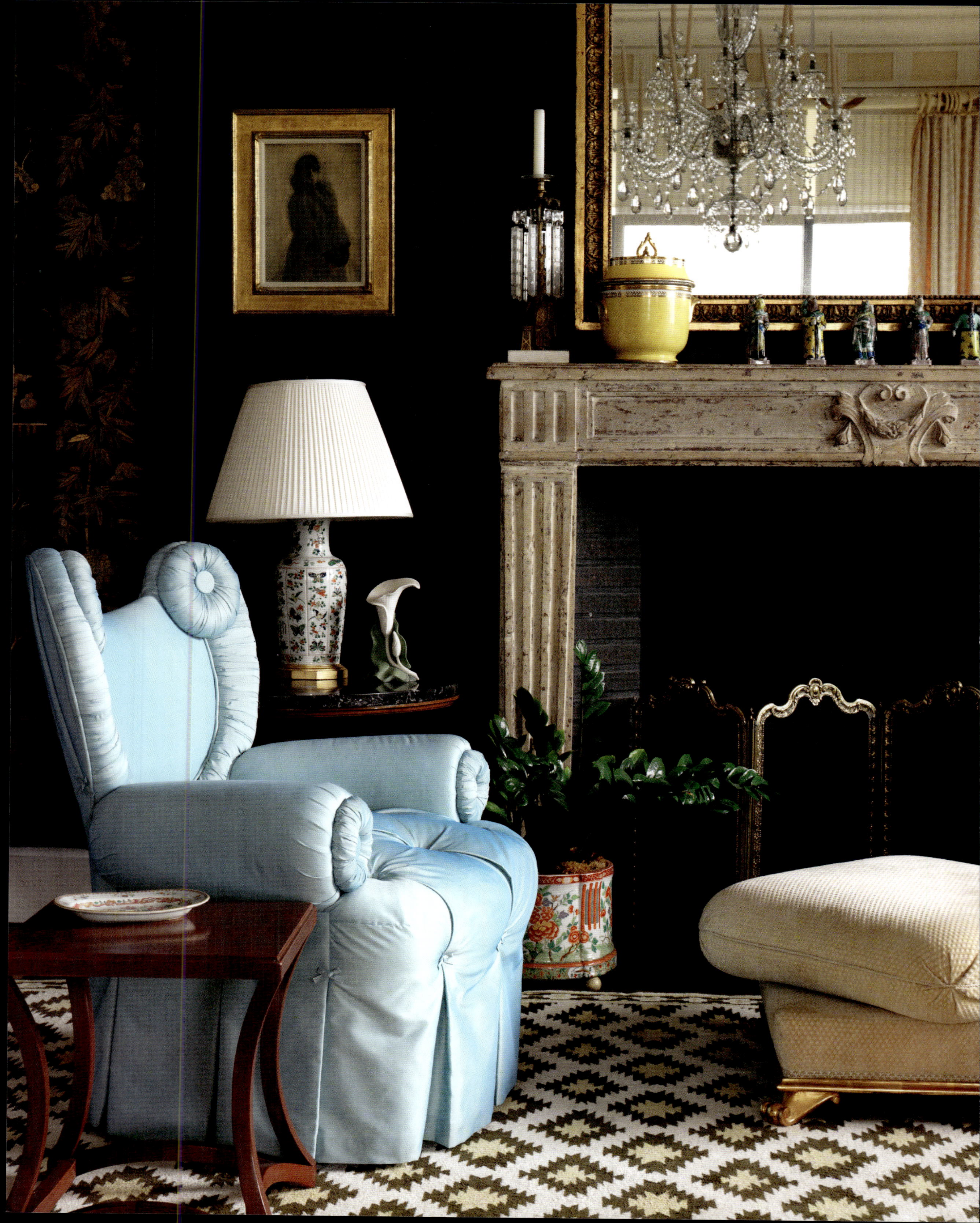

Color, pattern, and texture make such a difference, and it always amazes me to see how they can completely change a space. When a room is wallpapered or painted in a different color, it takes on a new personality. Color is exciting and, if used well, can create allure. It invites you into a room and makes a welcoming space. I love color and mix it fearlessly, using different patterns, textures, and textiles.

Varying textures in a room is important, as is using different scales of pattern. This can be what lifts a room. The unexpected adds a new dimension to a room and makes it come alive. Balancing the old with the new—either furniture or fabric—will add a patina to a space.

John Fowler said, “Often an ugly color is introduced such as a faded black or drab, to give counterpoint to colors that are sweet and clean.”

Years ago, I worked on a project in Washington, DC. My client had a Federal brick house surrounded by pachysandra plants. The house was at the top of a steep staircase. There were two adjoining living rooms; one of them had a fireplace in it and was a bit more formal than the other. The plan was to use all of the same fabrics and patterns between the two rooms in order to connect them, but to use the fabrics in different ways with a different emphasis. The floors were pickled and stenciled in an overlapping open square design by the wonderful artist Chuck Fischer. My client had a collection of very pretty furniture and, understandably, wanted to reuse it all. There were three sofas between the two rooms, all covered in a pretty Rose Cummings’s chintz fabric that had a wonderful border; the border was cut off, turned, and then used for the sofa skirts. Two different neutral, small-scale textures were used on the upholstered club chairs, and a lovely jade green silk striae velvet was on a high-back frame chair. A cocoa brown suede was used on a French slipper chair beside the fireplace. New curtains were made with a pretty celadon, raspberry, and cream silk stripe. The rooms included lacquer and Japanned tables, painted furniture, as well as walnut and some mahogany pieces. Modern painted coffee tables were used in front of two of the sofas, and a low, stylized lacquer table was in front of the sofa in the bay window.

My client had two small "spare" side chairs, which were to sit on either side of a low bookcase. Because there were already quite a few fabrics being used, repeating the curtain fabric for those spare chairs made sense. The colorful curtain stripe tied all of the fabrics together and balanced out the varying tones in the room, but it was too big in scale for those small chair seats. We decided to cut the striped silk, and to only use the smaller-scaled sections of the stripe, sewing the strips together thereby creating an overall small stripe. The seams were hidden naturally.

There used to be an antique fabric shop on East 78th Street owned by Elinor Merrell, who collected and sold the most beautiful old textiles. I found a small floral English quilt there in just the right colors; the quilt was cut and used to recover a bench beside a coffee table. Miss Merrell's shop was in her apartment, and she had gathered an impressive major collection of fabrics, many of which were museum quality. She was a specialist in seventeenth- and eighteenth-century French textiles and sold her patterns to fabric houses to be copied. I loved to go hunting in her shop and listen to her talk about what she had collected.

Layers are ultimately what give a room depth, character, and warmth. Yet there are combinations of color that don't appeal to me when used together. Mrs. Parish used to say that colors in a room needed to be in harmony with each other but not necessarily match. On the other hand, Albert Hadley would say that there aren't any colors that don't get along. "When you combine a bunch of mixed flowers—in a garden, in a meadow, or in an arrangement—without any two alike colors, you will see that they do all work together."

PREVIOUS PAGE: A blue cotton taffeta chair that can certainly be called a "personality chair" in a Boston apartment.

OPPOSITE: A powder room in a Washington, DC, home is wallpapered in "Dune" by Hermés.

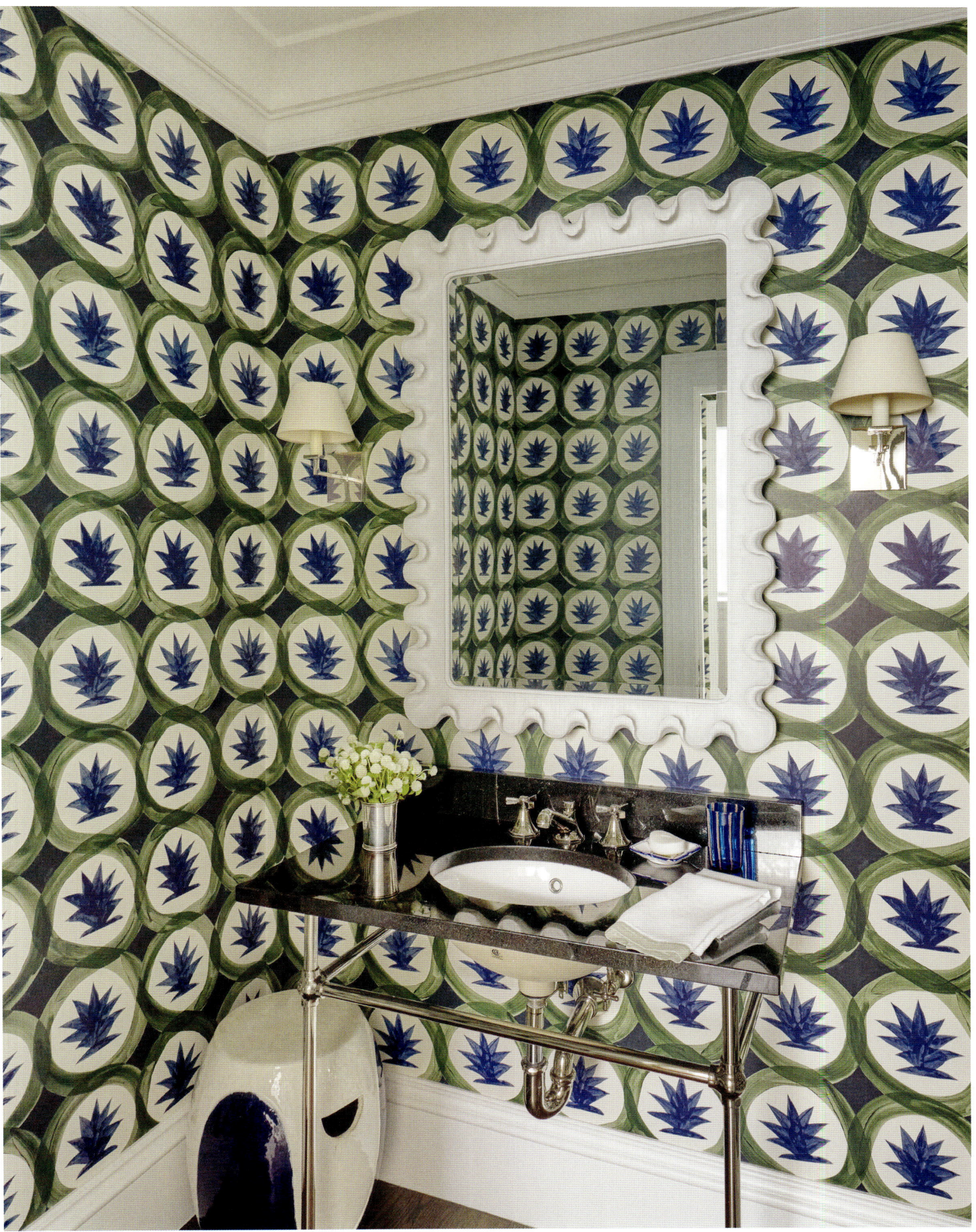

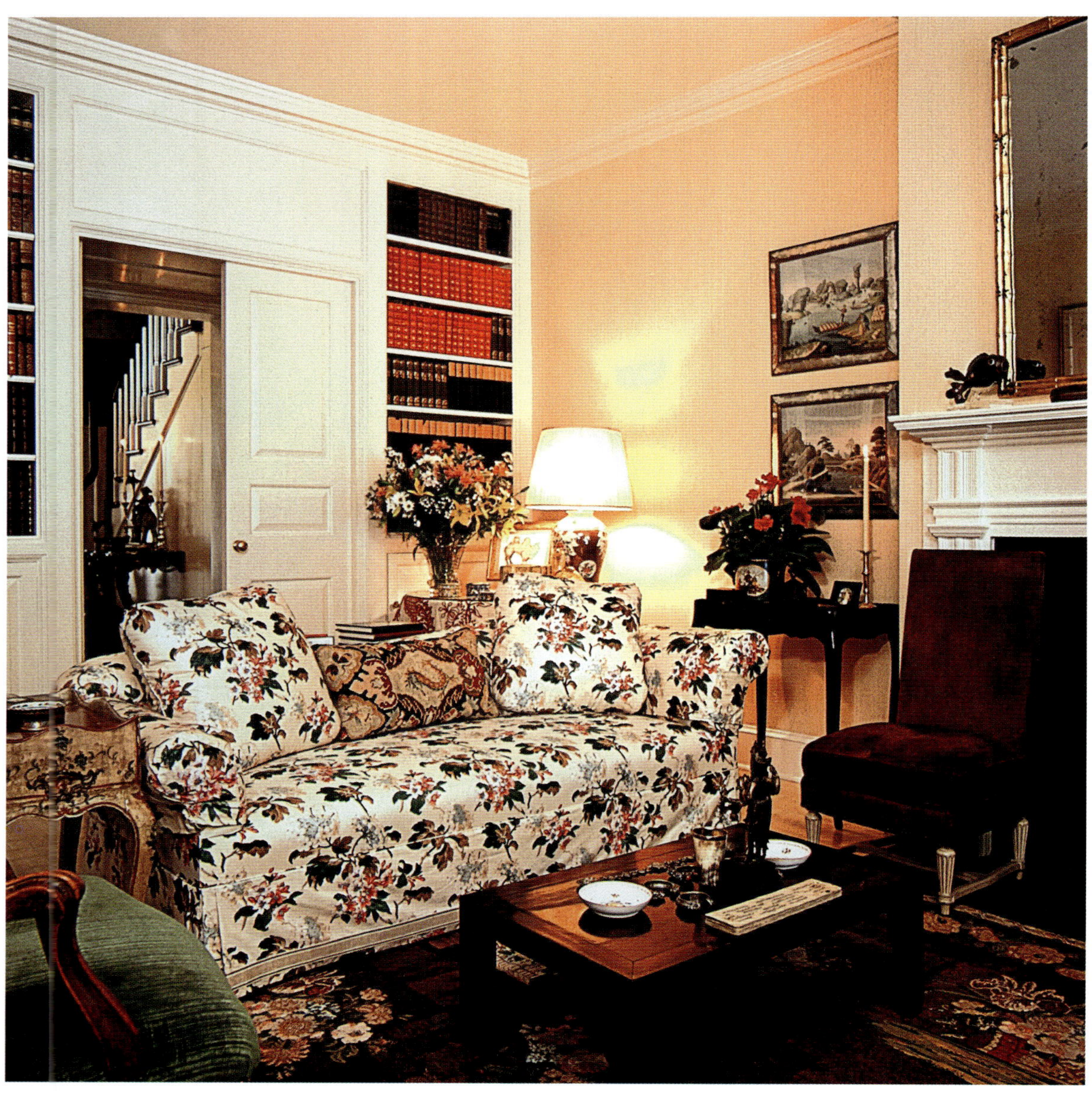

The more formal of the two living rooms in a townhouse in Washington includes a fireplace. The book collections add color and warmth to the room.

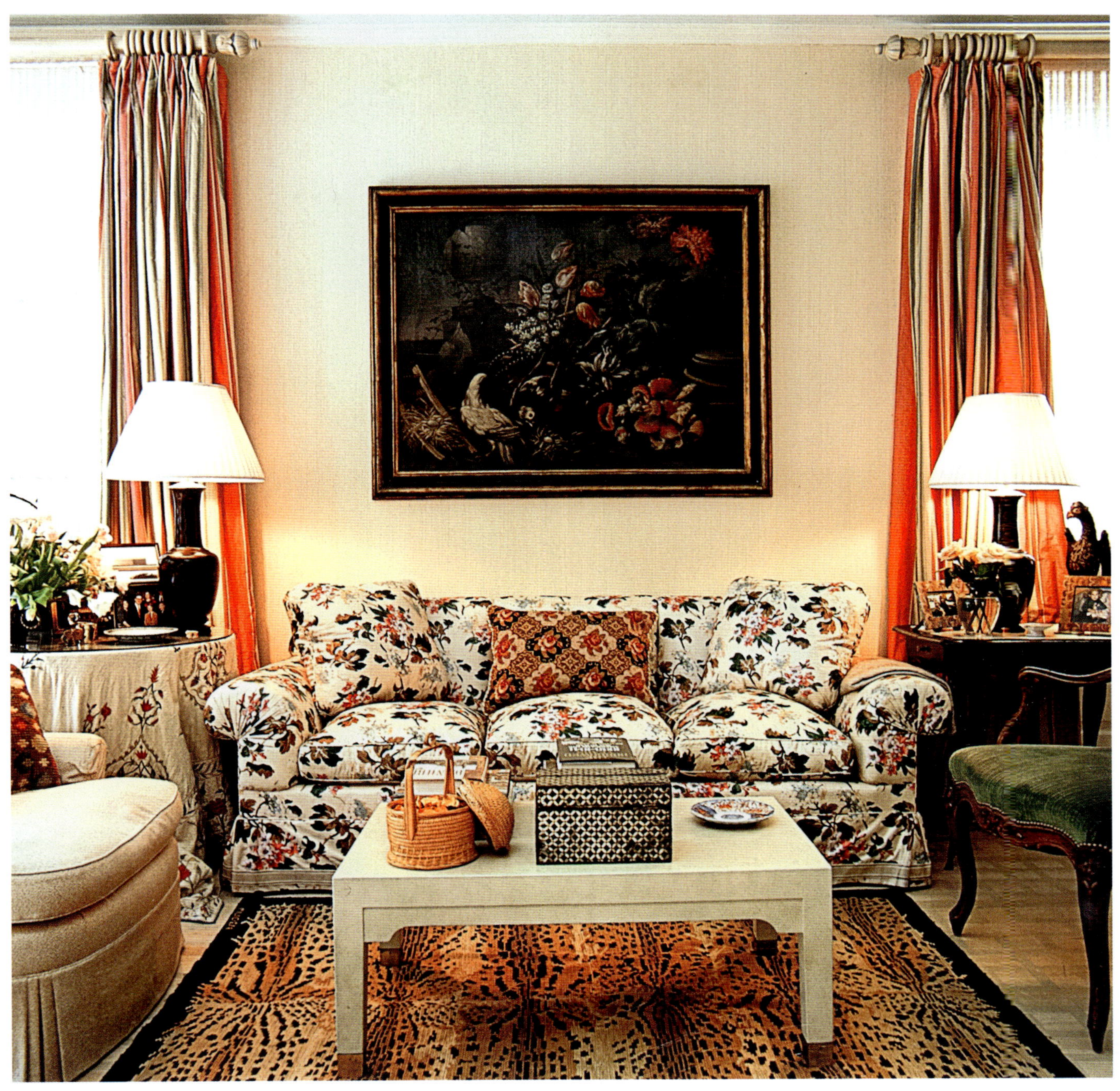

The adjacent living room is more casual.

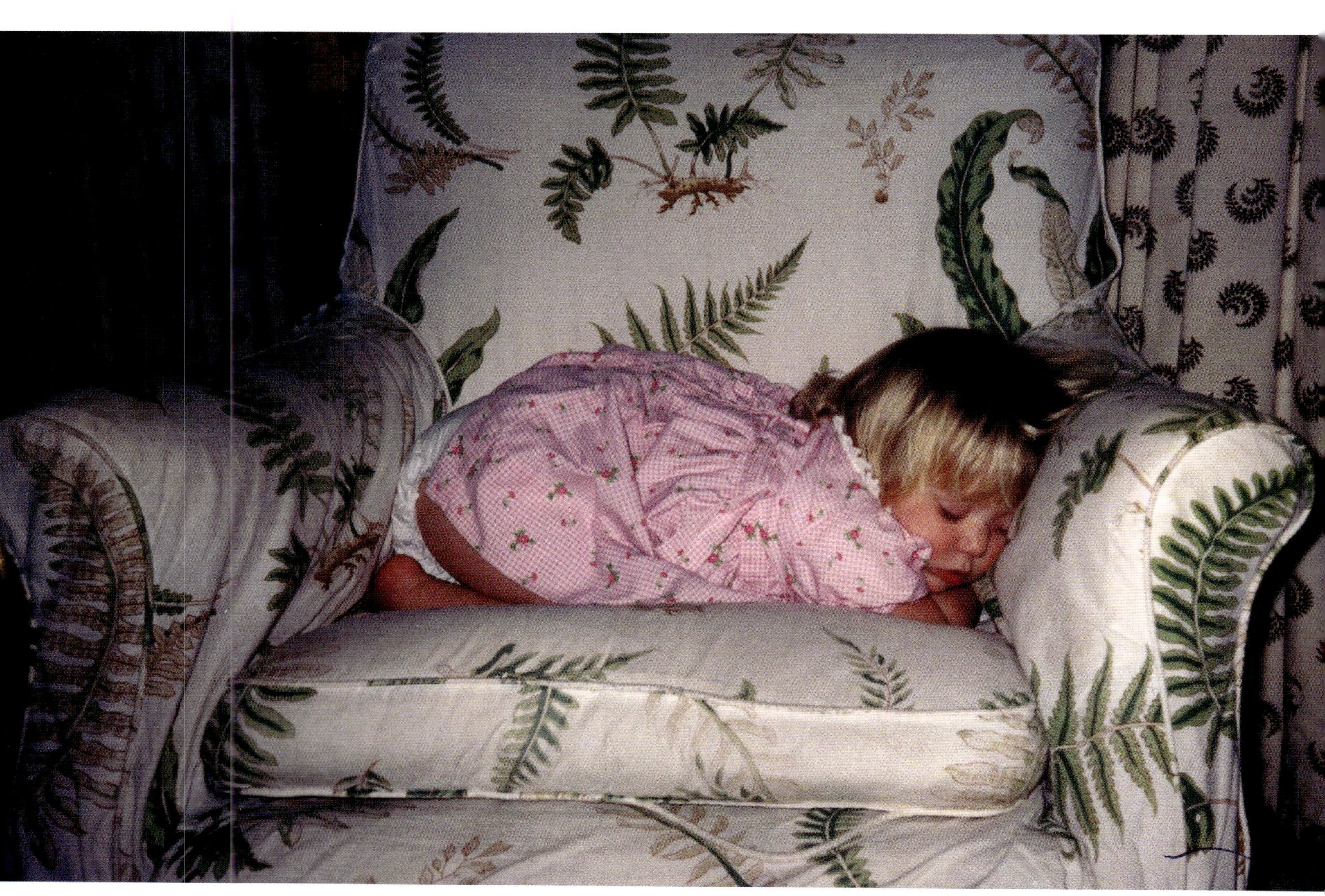

Bean napping in a chair covered in Lee Jofa's "Ferns" fabric, which has always been one of my favorite prints.

Some colors do just naturally feel right together, but everyone has their own preference for color combinations and compatibility. Corals and blues, as well as pinks and browns, are soothing to my eye, and I always love deep greens and blues. I wouldn't say that there are any colors I don't like—perhaps with the exception of mauve.

When we were moving out of New York City, my mother asked me what colors and fabrics I was going to use in the new house in Larchmont. I described the rooms but the scheme in the library gave her pause. She questioned why I would chose to paint a pine-paneled room, and then she questioned how a deep green love seat, blue walls, a chintz on the upholstered chair, the Parish-Hadley print "Josephine" fabric on the curtains, and a hooked zebra rug that Albert had given me made any sense when all used altogether. Yet when it was finished, I got so much positive feedback and so many compliments on that room. One talent designers have is to envision things before they can actually see them.

I miss the days before the introduction of "smart technology," when life was slower and there was more time to spend being creative and using one's imagination. I can still remember old telephone numbers from before cell phones and Siri came along—before the ability to just say a name or push a button to call anyone you want. I remember colors in the same way. Re-creating colors you have seen and loved is not always easy. Light is so important, and the way a color looks in one room as opposed to another room or in another house can be so different. It can be very difficult to capture the same exact color in different settings. Colors don't have the same quality in different lights. Often, a client will say to me, "I love the color of so-and-so's dining room," and want just that color. Really talented painters can re-create colors but it is still never going to be exactly the same.

Glazed walls are harder to replicate as they have a second dimension and depth, especially if there is a strong contrast between the base color and the color of the actual glaze that is finally added. I once worked on an ivory-glazed bedroom and it was the hardest color to achieve. It took so many samples and tries to get it just right. In the end, the painter used a glaze color that was a soft, chalky hue on a parchment, pinkish-colored base coat. A dining room I worked on in Washington took nine coats of glaze to get it just the color my client wanted. It is not easy to find exceptional painters anymore who have worked as an apprentice and have truly learned on the job, painters who have an artistic bent and really understand color. Any paint store can computer match a sample that is brought in, but color works differently on every surface. You can achieve a lot of control with paint depending on how it is used, but you need to consider how a room will look in the morning, at midday, and in the evening as the light changes so much.

It is a given that dark colors are best on walls when they have a shiny finish, but the walls have to be completely smooth. There is nothing worse than a sheen on marred walls, where every scratch, dent, blister, and stray paintbrush hair jumps out at you. The shine on a wall allows for light to reflect off of it and it opens up a room, adding vitality to the space. Soft colors are usually better in a less shiny, flatter finish. Regardless of the color you use, the wall preparation is really the most important part of painting any room.

Not that long ago, I decorated an apartment in Boston that Parish-Hadley had done in the 1960s. You could see how incredible and unique it must have been when it was completed so many years before. In many ways it had become dated—the bathrooms and kitchen needed upgrading—but the gist of what it was sixty years ago remained. The living room walls had been covered in a coarse burlap and painted a semisweet chocolate brown, with a slight sheen, and the trim and crown molding were glazed in a creamy white and beige. The wall color was wonderful; I would not have dreamed of changing it, especially given that the high-ceilinged room was on the top floor surrounded by a terrace that had a north and western exposure and was flooded with light. The burlap creates such a lovely texture on the walls and the contrast of the trim brings a liveliness to the room. The furniture is all covered in neutral materials—creams and beiges—and the two area rugs are a linen geometric design of brown, taupe, and cream. Pops of color in the room come from an end-of-summer corn yellow on pillows and a robin's-egg blue on a fanciful chair by the fireplace. Other objects and accessories bring in color as well. The shape of this square room, its ceiling height, and color palette, make it quite dramatic. The rest of the apartment is filled with patterned wallpapers and colored patterned rugs. It is a lovely apartment, overlooking the Charles River and Harvard University's ivy-covered brick buildings along the opposite riverbank.

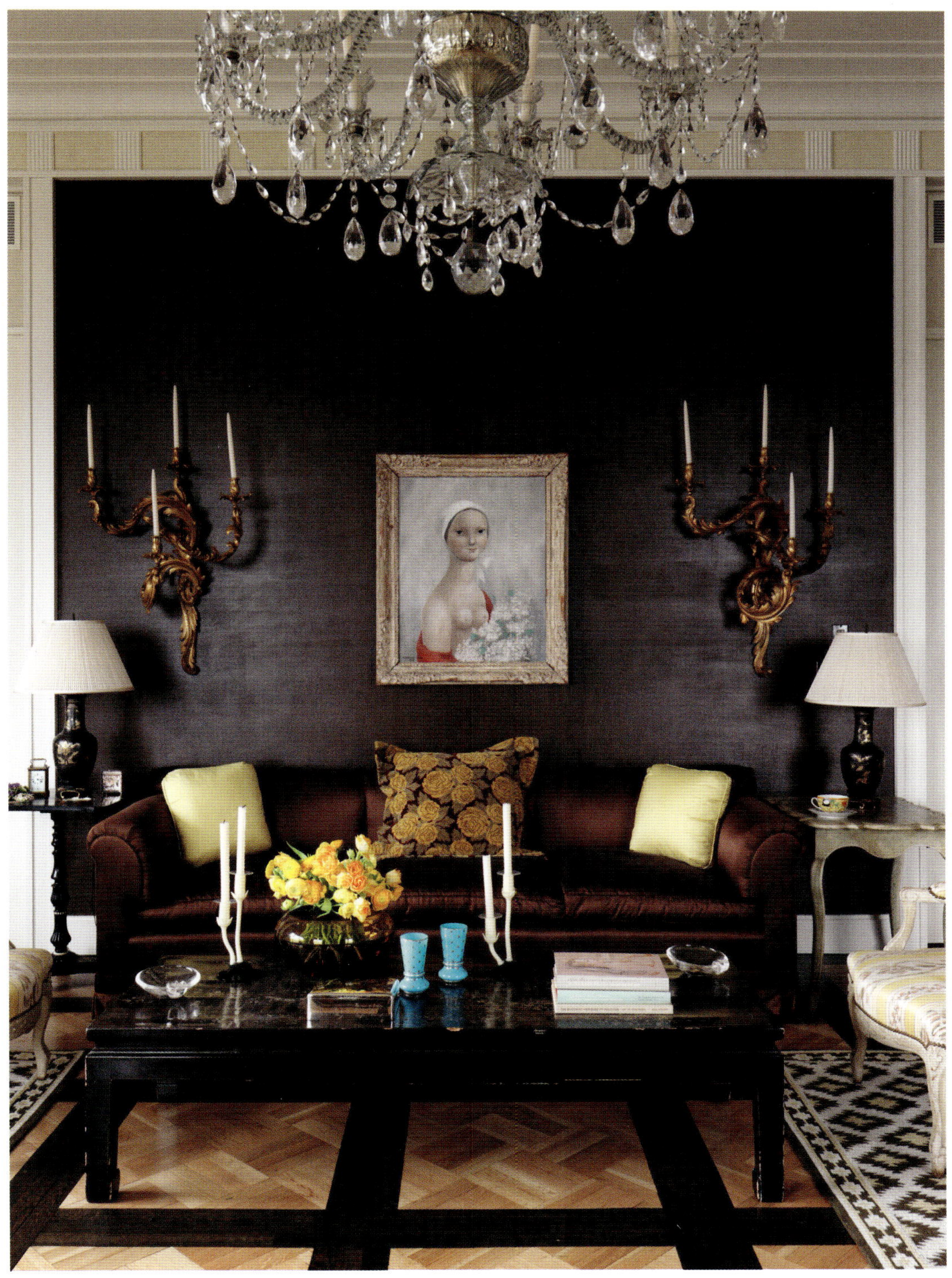

ABOVE: The floors here are parquet de Versailles and the border boards are stained a darker color, which frames the inset panels.

NEXT PAGE: The walls in this living room are painted a semisweet chocolate brown; the texture of burlap on the walls has a slight sheen. The room is square and dramatic with very high ceilings.

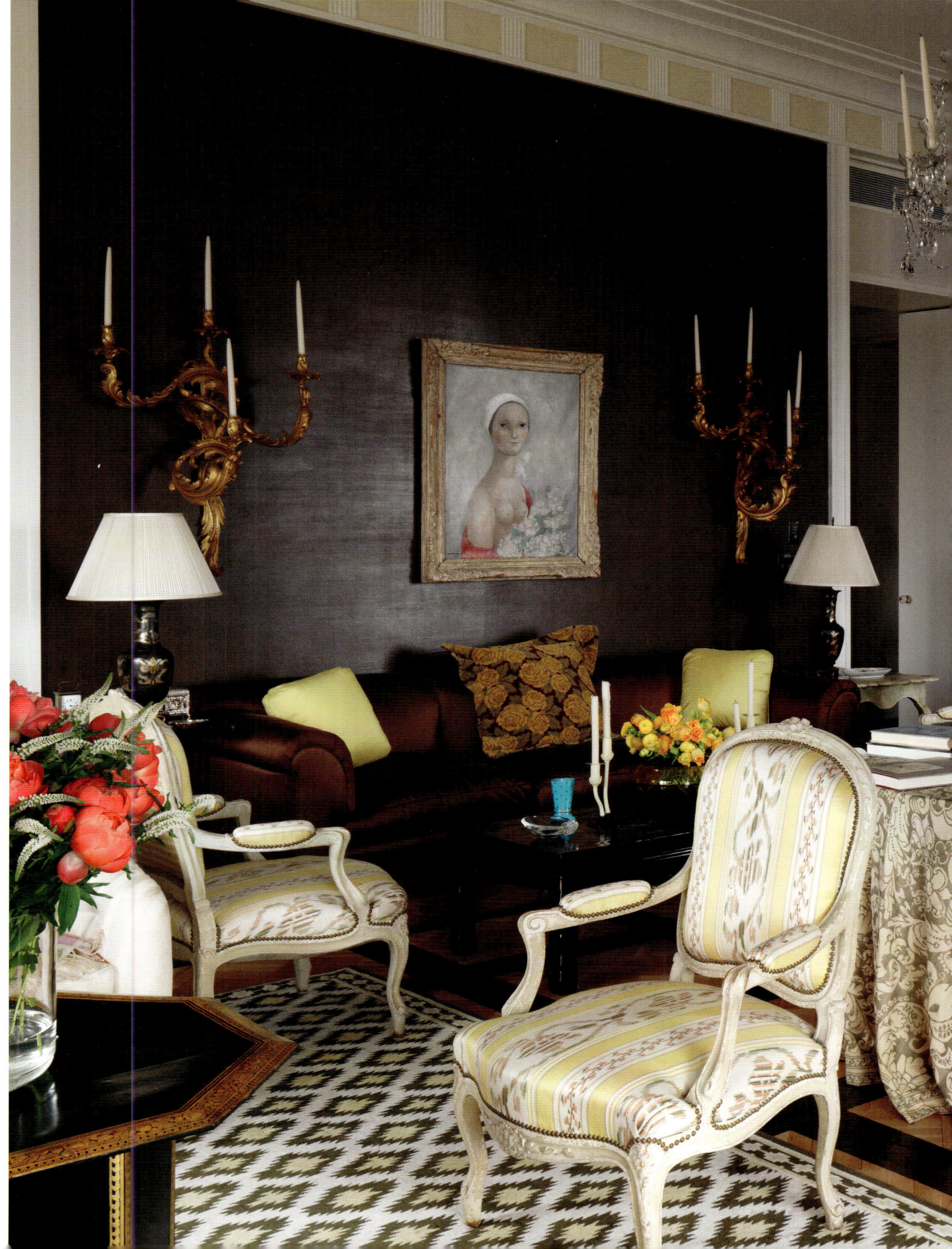

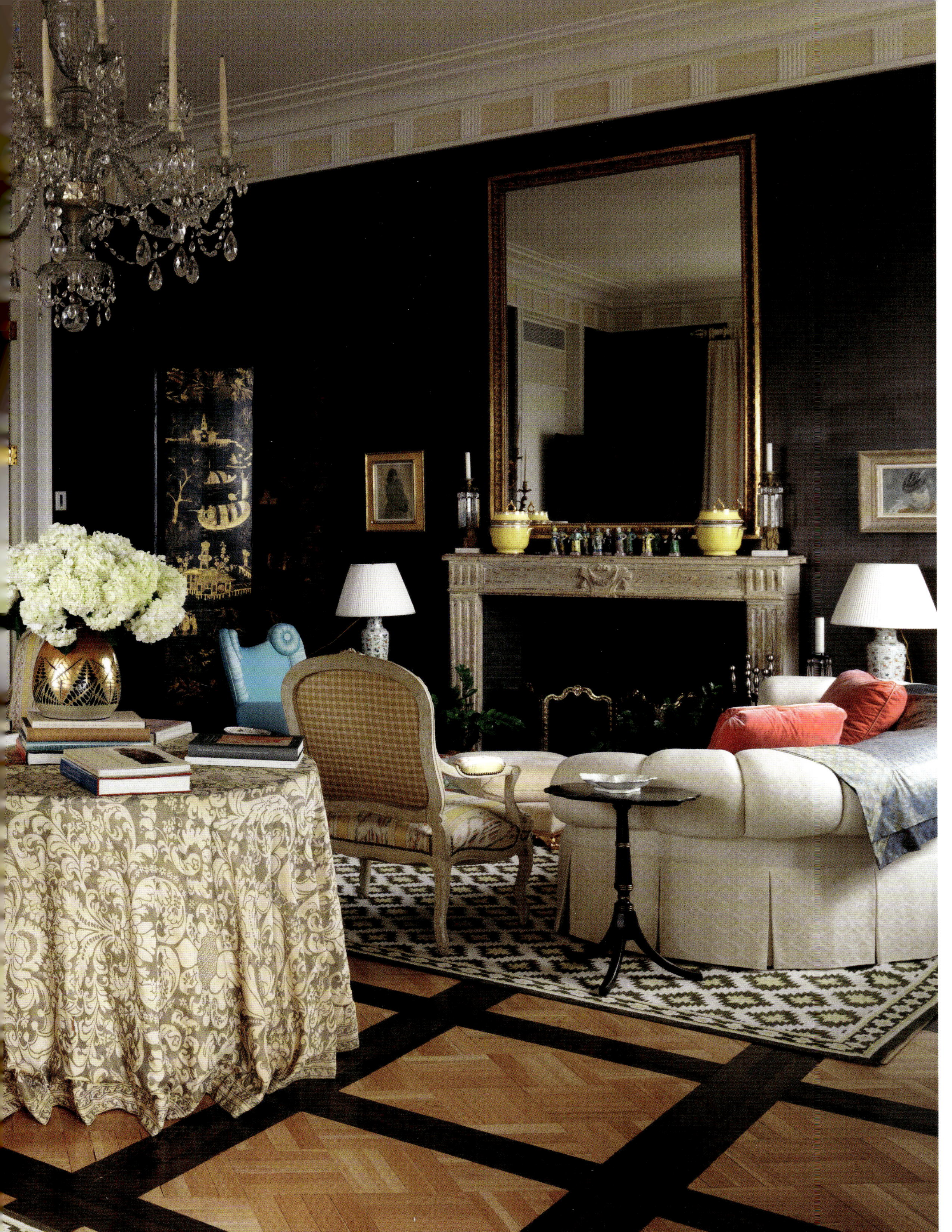

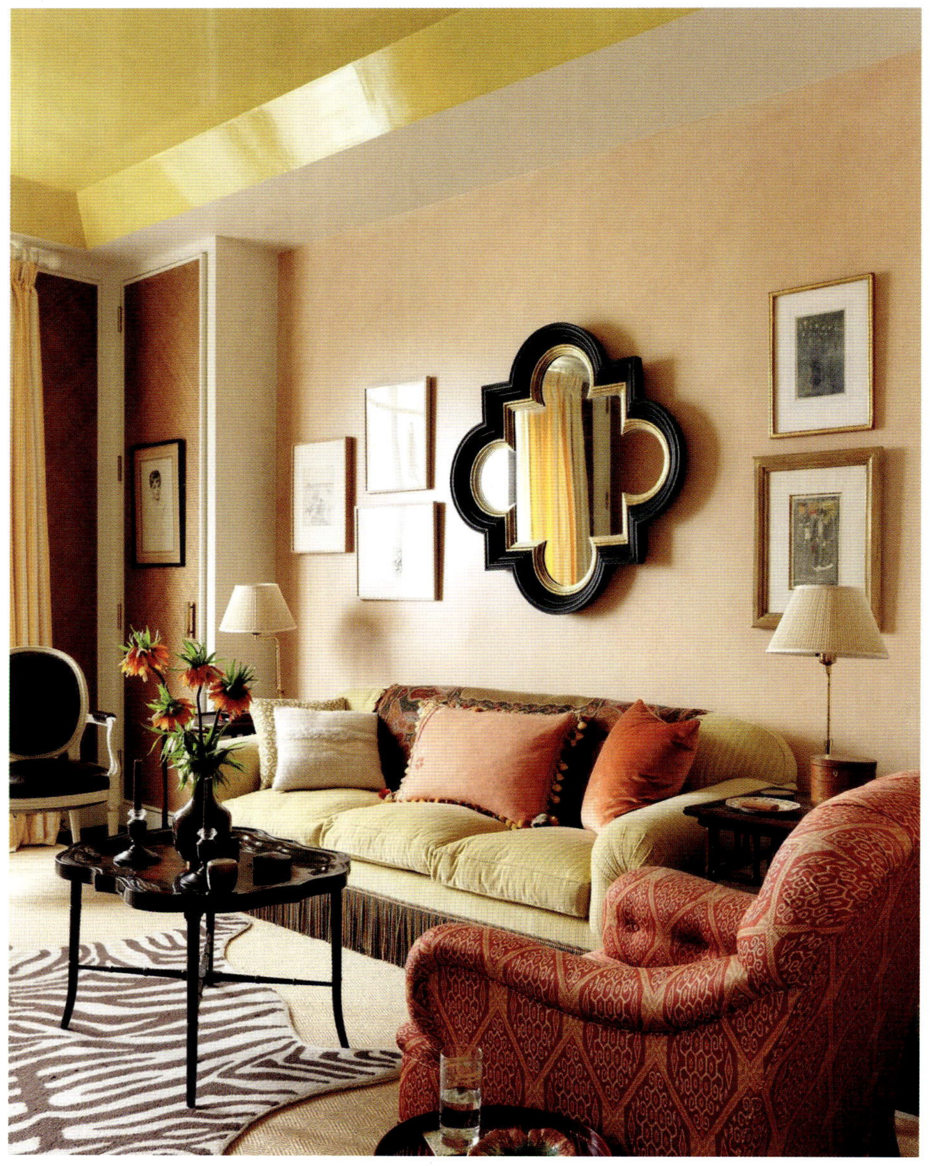

Several textures and finishes in this room add a wonderful, layered look: the walls are glazed a pale apricot and the ceiling is painted in a shiny yellow finish. The built-in cabinet's doors are all covered in a rough, natural colored raffia.

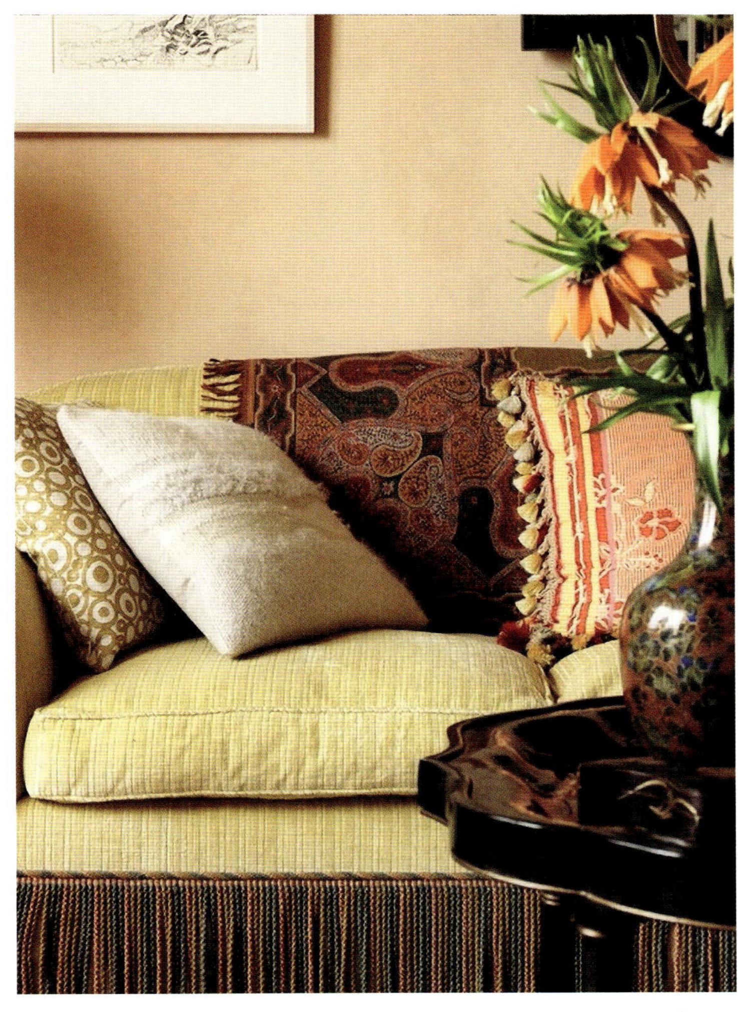

A detail from this room shows the yellow linen velvet on a sofa with a green, red, and yellow bullion fringe.

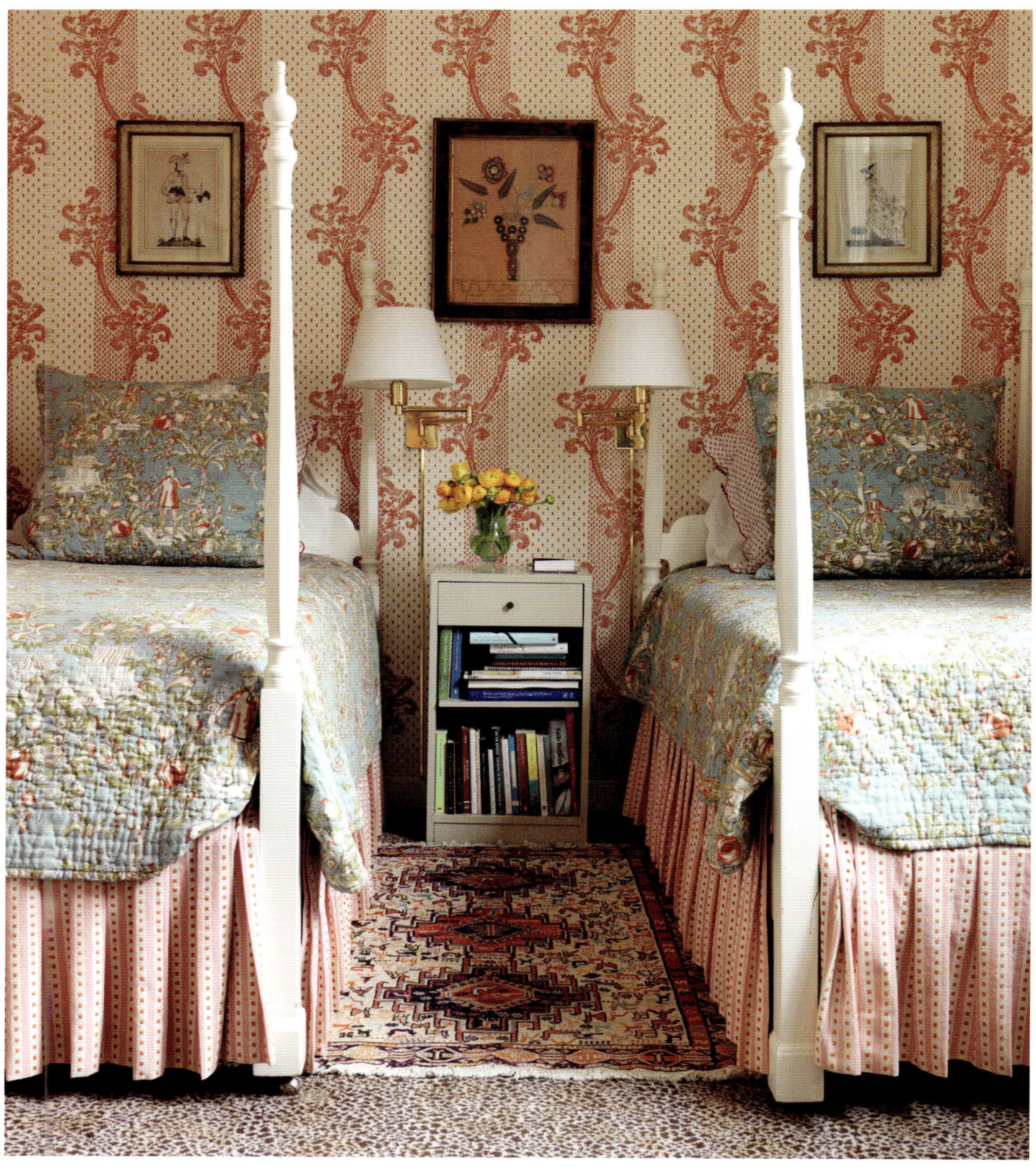

ABOVE: A guest room wallpapered in Sister Parish Kinnicutt Wallpaper with Toile de Jouy quilts and bedding. The "Ocelot" wall-to-wall carpeting is by STARK Carpet.

OPPOSITE: A bedroom in Maine with wallpaper from Zina Studios, "Wavy Lines," and a carved bed by Robert Huggins.

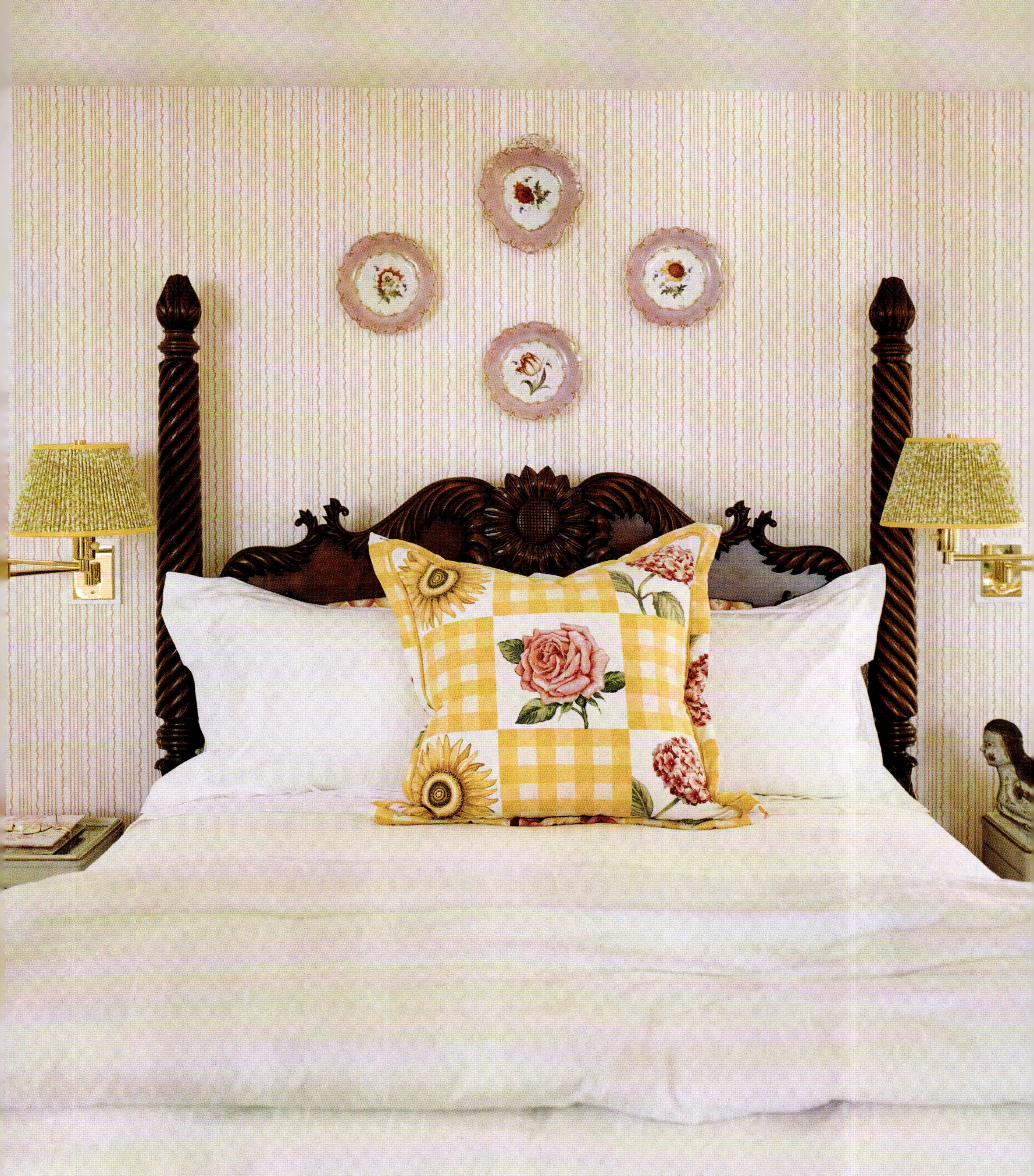

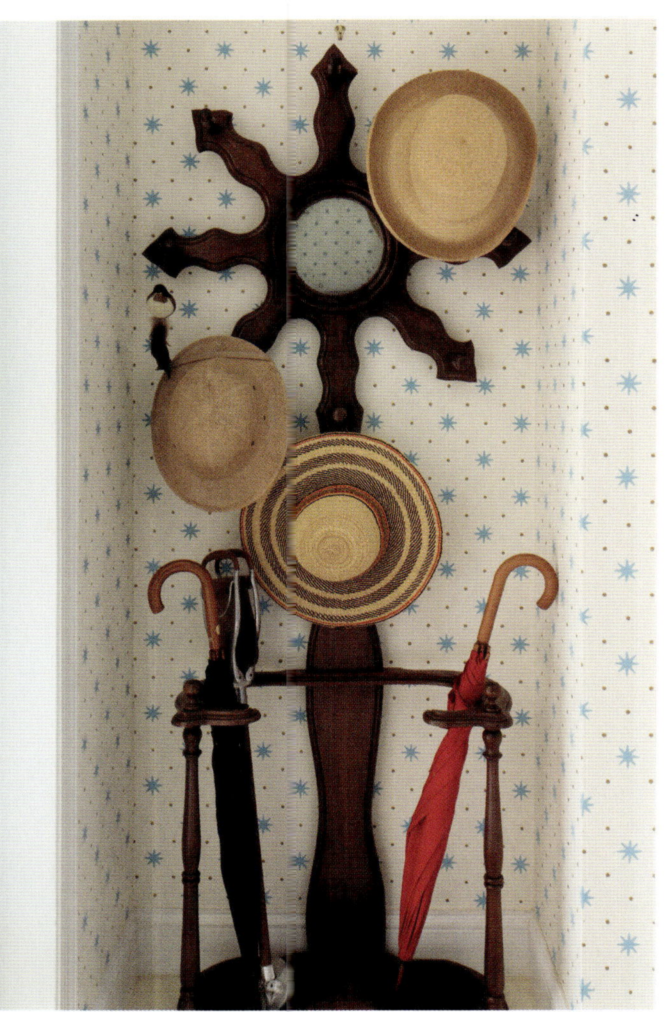

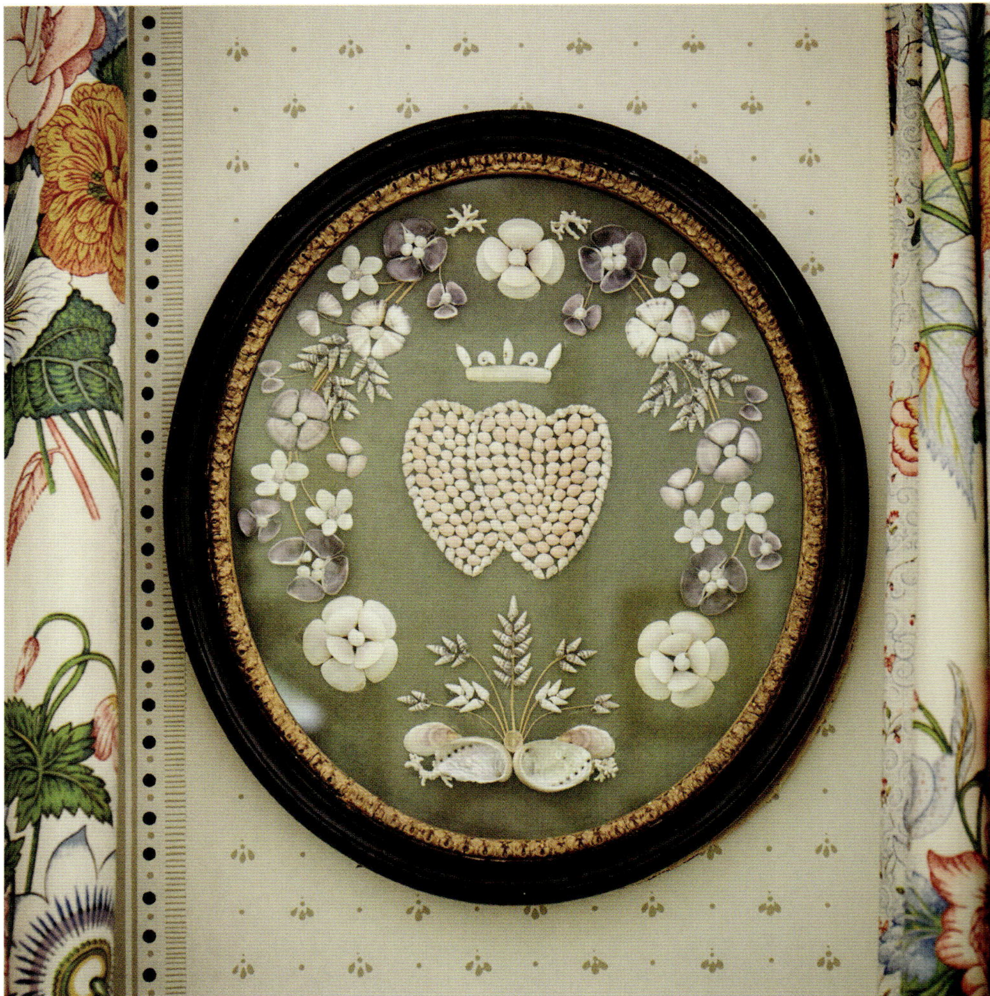

ABOVE, LEFT: I found this hat stand at Lilac Cottage Antiques in Wiscasset, Maine. It fits perfectly in the niche in my front hall.

ABOVE, RIGHT: This sailor's valentine, made of seashells, was in my grandparents' house in Maine for years, and I always loved it as a child.

OPPOSITE: I fell in love with this ram painting from Mario Buatta's estate sale at STAIR Galleries.

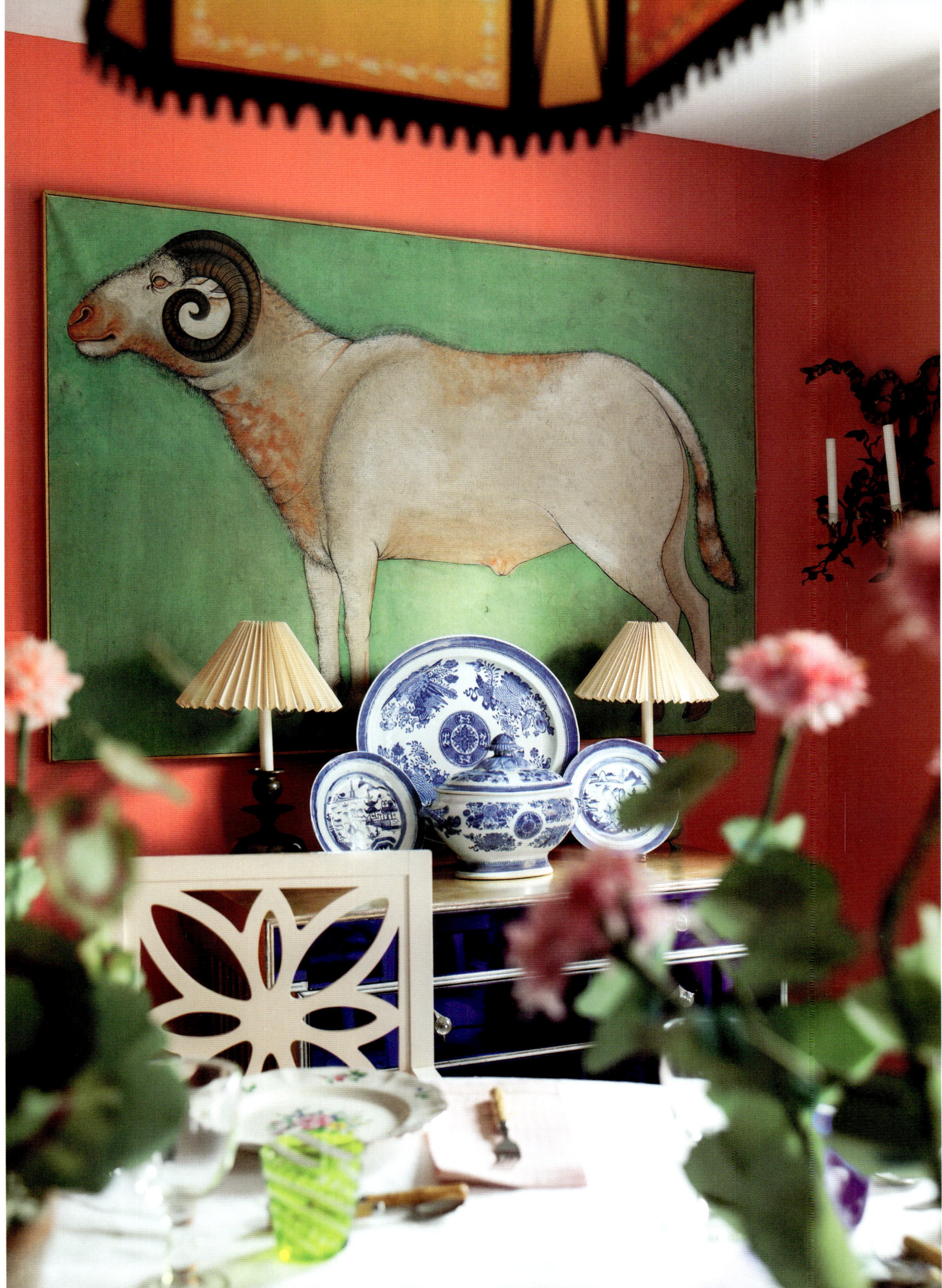

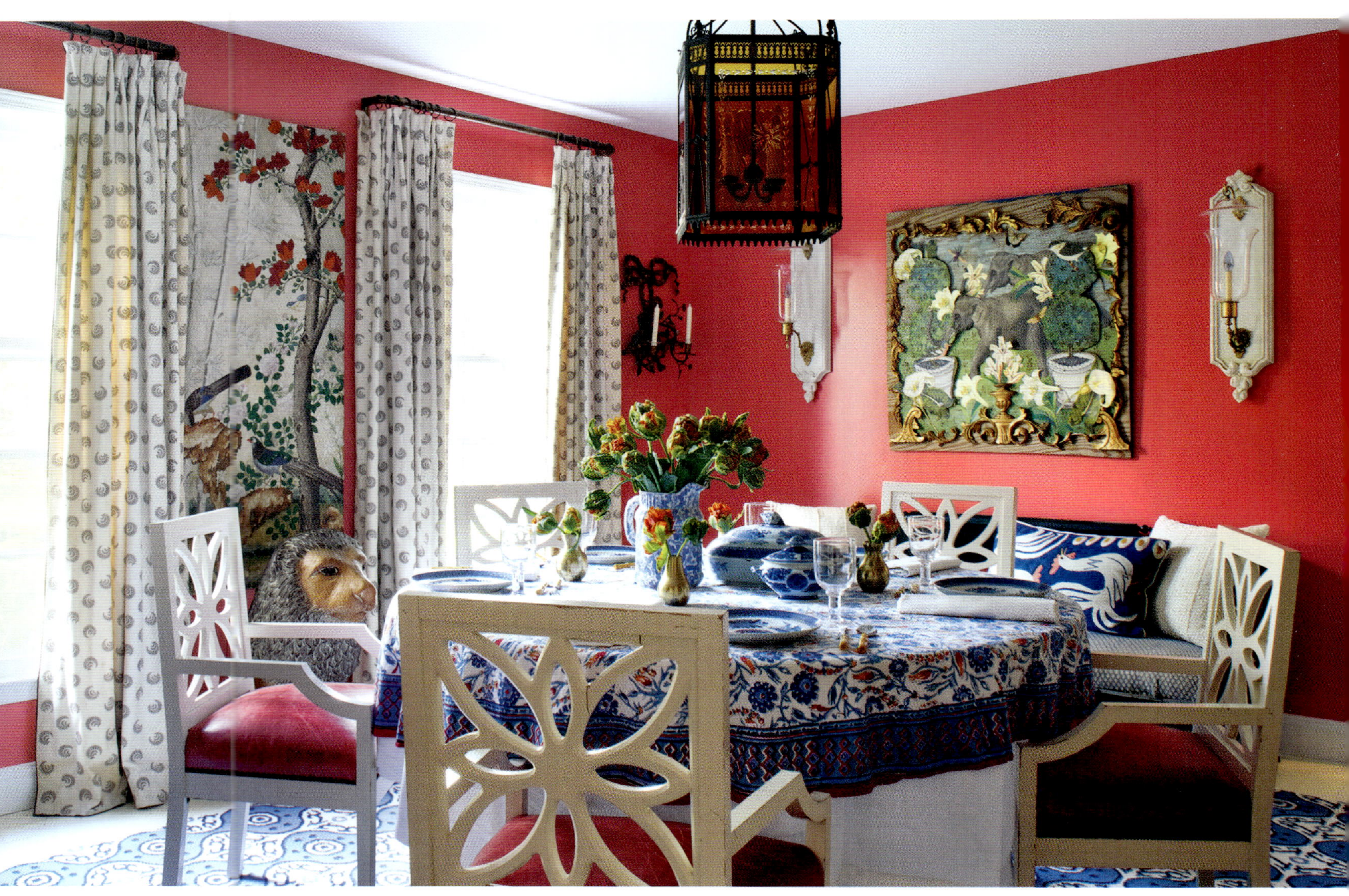

The dining room in my Connecticut house is glazed a coral color. The bench under the decoupage elephants is one I found on the street. I painted it and had the seat recovered; it is one of my favorite pieces. There is nothing better than a good street find.

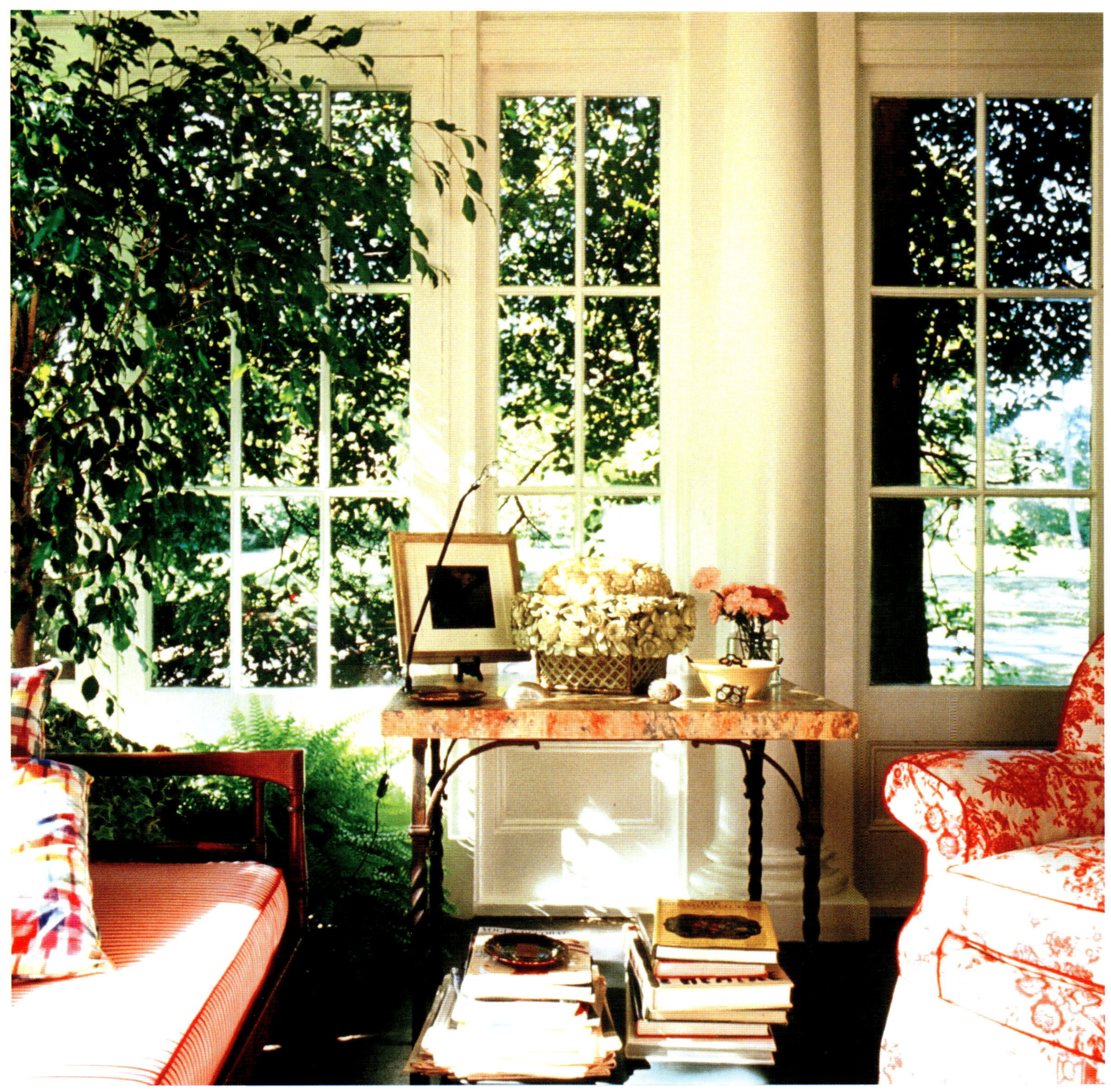

A garden room in Greenwich, Connecticut, had high windows on three sides.

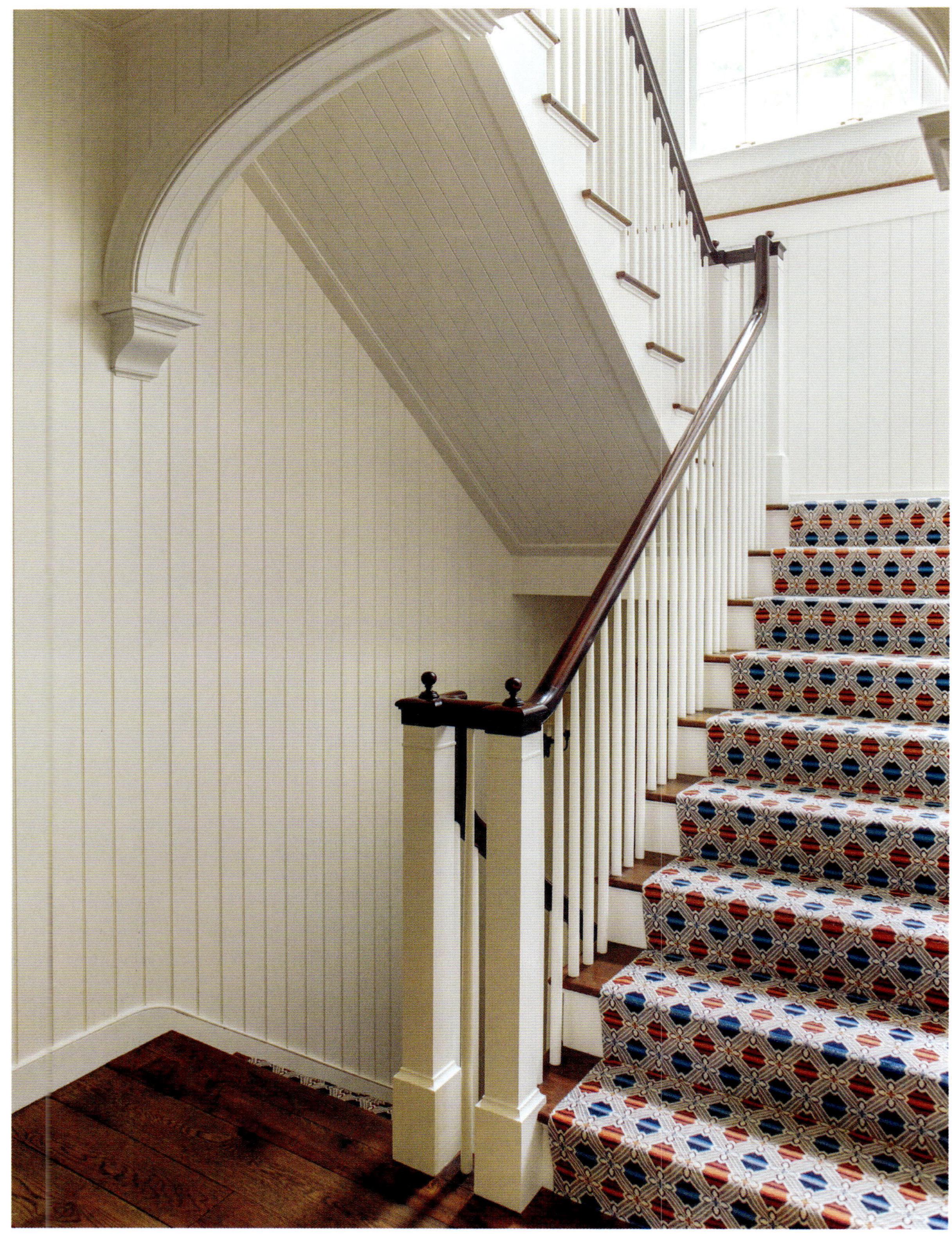

A jacquard weave stair carpet adds a bit of color and texture to a back hallway and stairs.

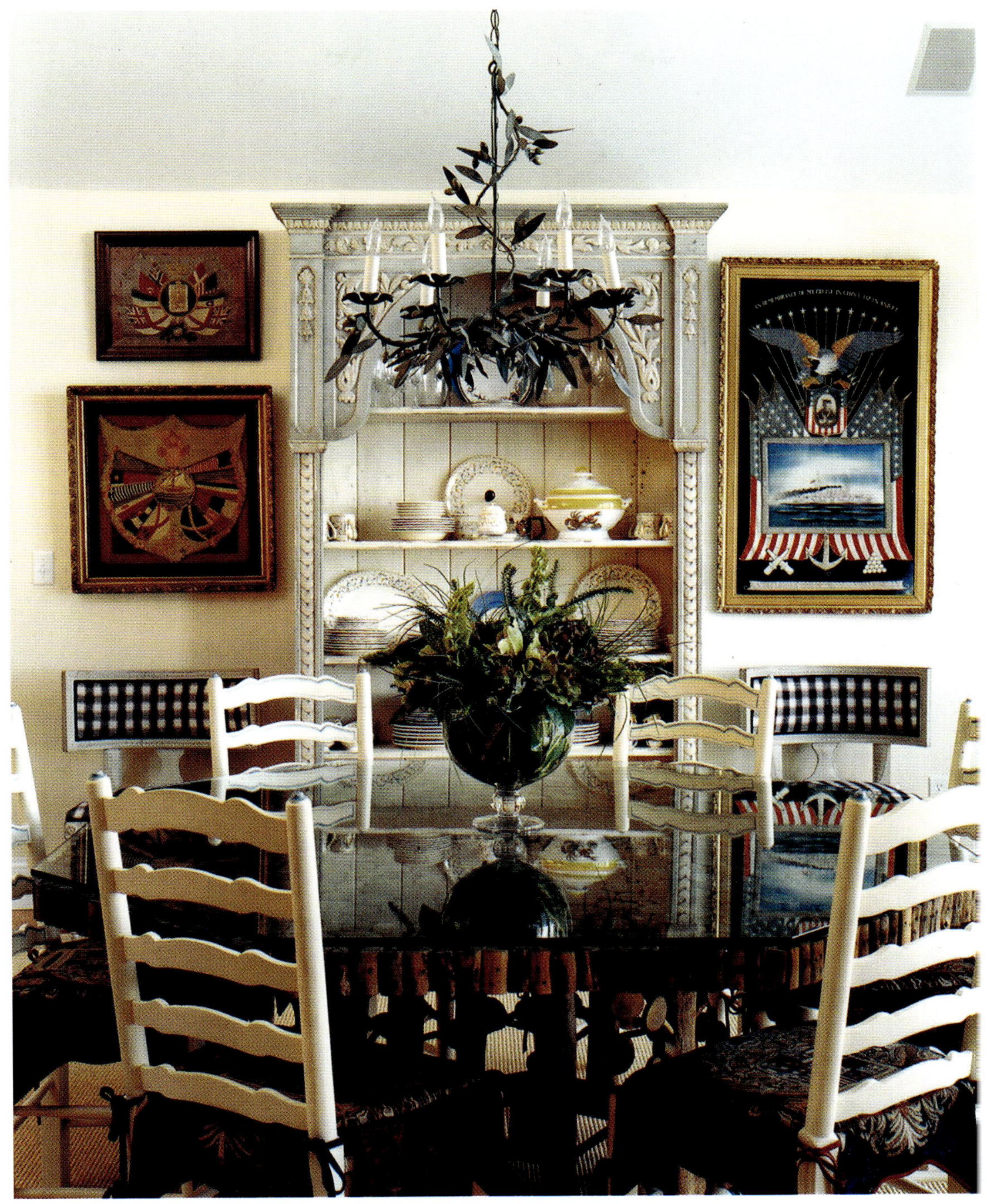

A dining room in Maine with an eclectic mix of furniture. This client loved "woolies," wool works that were made by British Navy and Royal Marine sailors during the long periods away from home; it was a popular pastime for the months at sea. This room includes a combination of Swedish and English furniture; the dining table base is made of wood and twigs with the ends of the wood pieces purposely showing.

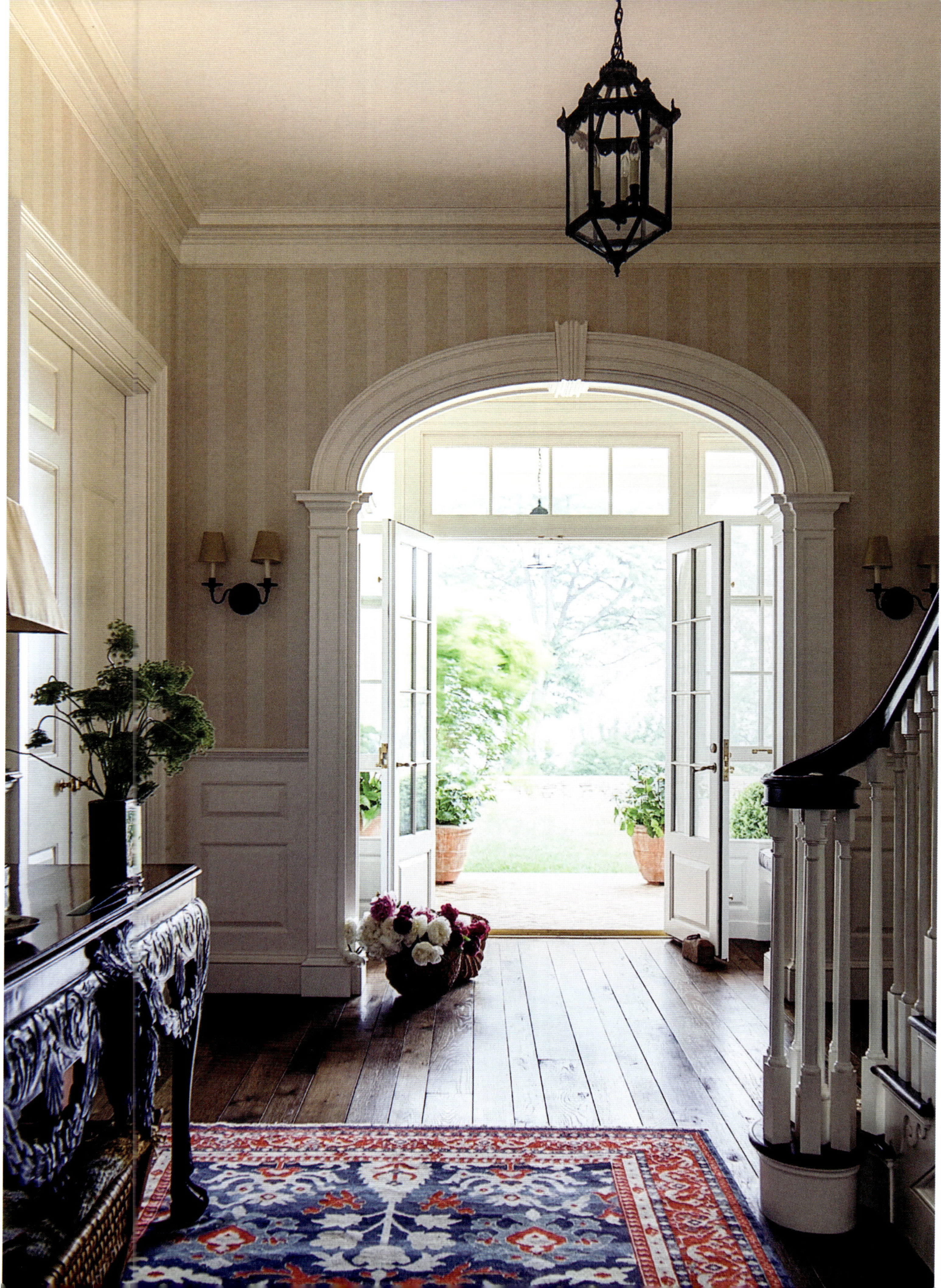

I have a wonderful client who is unafraid of color and pattern, which made the process of working on her house so much fun. She loves blues and oranges so we used quite a bit of those colors throughout the house. She knows what she likes and thinks through her decisions carefully, which I truly admire. Rushing to finish and fill a house can be a mistake.

Everything that is combined and used together in a house—the colors and furniture and its finishes—should be compatible and have an innate sense of belonging together. Some things just don't work and shouldn't coexist in a room. Ultimately, it's a personal decision but I try to guide people as to what is suitable and appropriate. While some things can clash and feel uncomfortable, there is nothing better than a pleasing mixture of pieces—an English chair, a French chair, a Chinese vase, or an Oriental rug—all working together in the same room. Painted pieces and lacquered furniture along with wooden pieces all combined in a room can work well. Every piece of furniture has its own personality and character.

There has to be balance in the juxtaposition of objects and furniture. The types of pieces that you have either inherited or collected over the years (without putting any thought into them being used side by side) is what makes for an interesting room. Things that don't necessarily match yet work together create interest. A piece that is collected simply because it appealed to you or meant something to you is always worth having.

I am always on the hunt to find pieces that are quirky and stylish. The value matters less to me than how it looks, and a piece's association is by far the most important aspect for me. One always forgets that small things can also have a large presence. For me, a room feels best when it isn't too formal and is filled with character furniture. I choose things for warmth and style, and always think that not taking nice things too seriously is important in making a room more inviting. The perfectly imperfect can be just as wonderful. Sometimes, it simply comes down to being intuitive about a room, trusting your taste, and bonding with what you have.

Constantly struggling to make choices—and second guessing your choices—is so stressful and exhausting. The atmosphere in your environment should be restorative. For me, that comes with choosing the right colors and the juxtaposition of things that matter to me. By reusing what I have and what I love, there is a sense of continuity in my home. I like to preserve the positive stories, history, and associations that come with pieces. Making order out of chaos, creating comfort in unpretentious rooms, and choosing things for warmth and style is what makes a house a home.

I agree with Billy Baldwin, who said this of overdecorating: "The whole business has gone berserk. There's an absurd overemphasis on decoration. Decorating is not an end in itself—in fact if it turns out to be, that is the end. Take as simple a thing as a chair. A chair, for God's sake, is to sit in. If your hostess gives you the look that makes you feel that you shouldn't sit in it, it should go. The only place I will permit a chair like that is in a bedroom and rarely there. If it's worth anything it should go to a museum. If not, it should go into the ashcan."

Mixing everything up creates texture. You can mix up finishes, shapes (both big and small), and important and less important pieces. Some think of texture as being only that which you touch, but it is more than that. Curtains, window shades, shutters, rug patterns, objects, artwork, and walls of books all add texture to a room. Shiny surfaces are a good contrast to soft, smooth wood. Color has to keep pace with a room. A brightly colored room cannot work with dreary, mousy furniture; a room also needs character pieces with visual importance. There should be a sense of lightness and whimsy in rooms. I like to add funny little chairs, some quirky shaped tables, or tables with just three legs. Even a little bit of ugly helps a stilted or too-perfect room become comfortable.

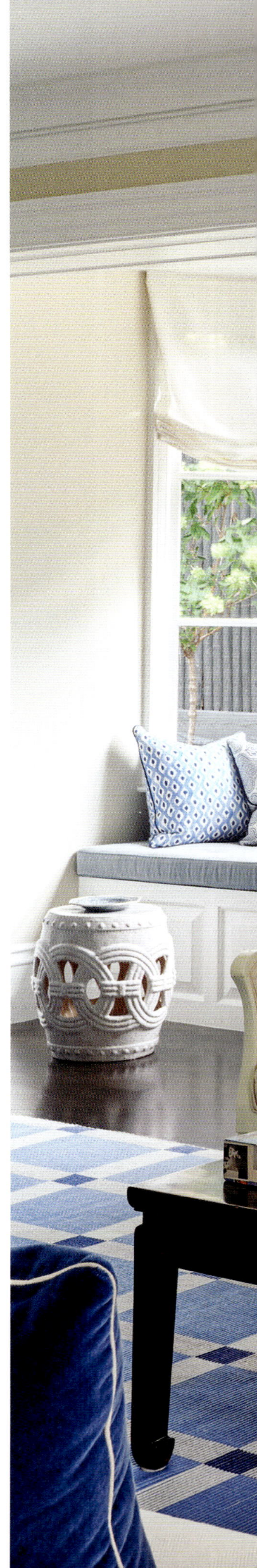

PREVIOUS PAGE: A view from the front hall looking out toward the Navesink River.

OPPOSITE: This living room has more contemporary art and furnishings and is long and not very deep.

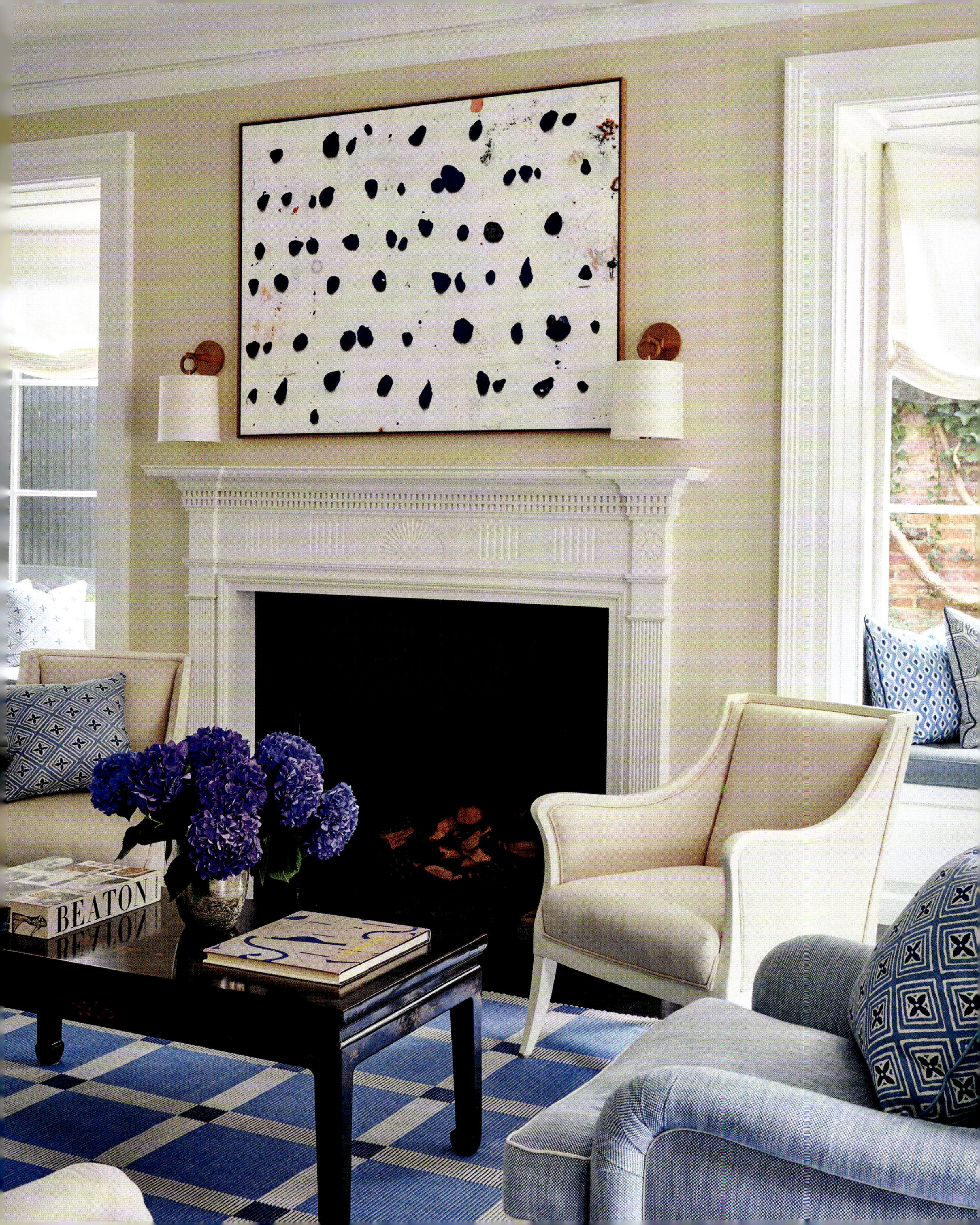
BEATON

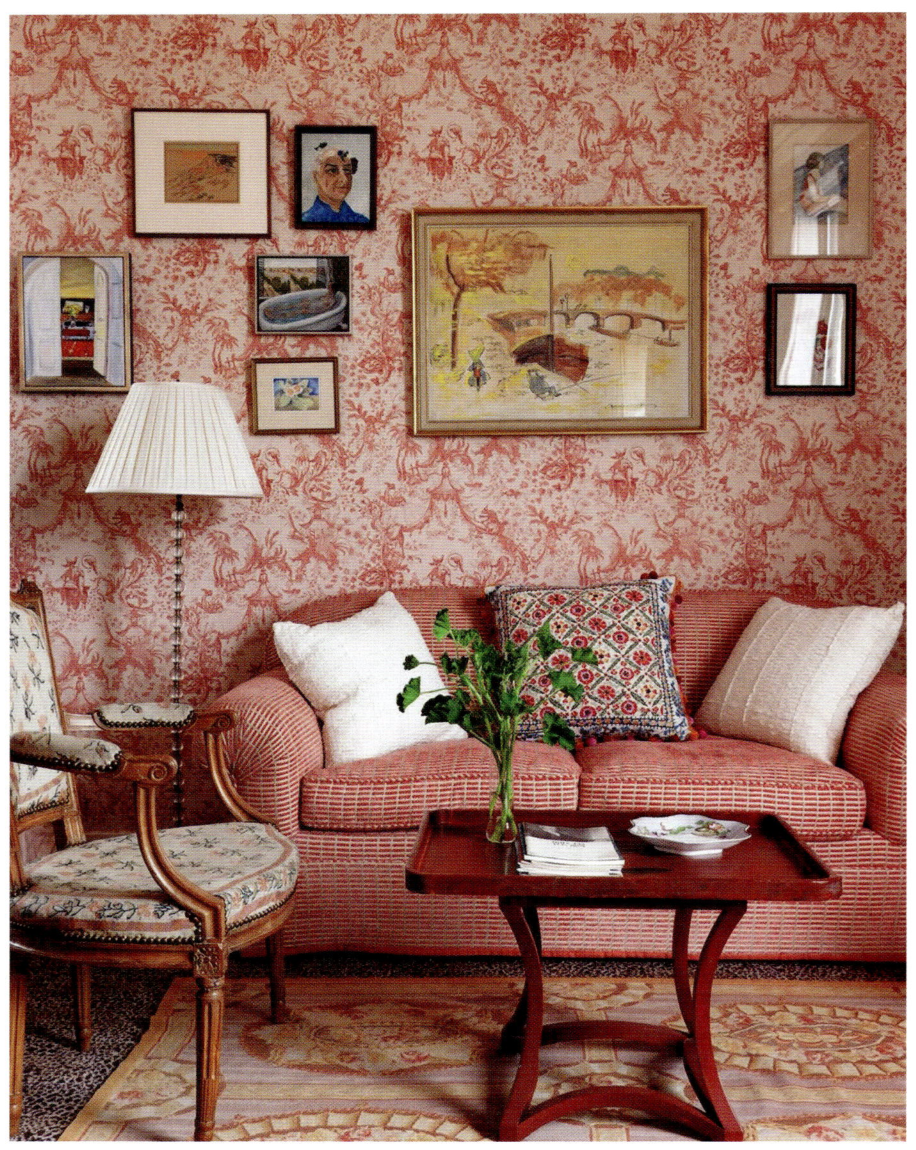

A corner seating area of a bedroom in Boston. Both the wallpaper and curtains are of an Osborne & Little pattern.

The logic of one's eye is very different from the logic of one's mind. I choose things for warmth and style, not the latest trends. Trends come and go and most often are overdone; at the end of the day following trends is a mistake. Rooms that are built around comfort first are the best sorts of rooms. Fabrics do not have to be intricate and expensive. The fabrics you use don't have to be a museum reproduction that is stylistically like the piece it is being used on. Albert Hadley used one of Alan Campbell's modern pastel geometric prints on Brooke Astor's antique Bergère chair in her bedroom. I am always happy choosing a ticking stripe or a simple pattern over a brocade or gauffrage fabric any day.

Years ago, Albert Hadley asked me to go antiquing with him in Connecticut on an autumn Saturday with Gary Hager. We left the city in Albert's bottle green Camaro and headed north, all the while talking and admiring the colors of the fall foliage. Something that has stayed with me visually is Albert's description about using black and red together—a combination he certainly appreciated. He said to think about a rowboat, what it would look like if just the outside of the boat, the seats, and the frame piece around the top of the inside were painted black, and the inside of the boat were painted red. Then he asked me to imagine a red hull, red seats and trim, and a black interior. It was such a great visual exercise—the two versions of the same color scheme being used so differently. I have always wondered why Albert knew and thought so much about how a rowboat is made.

Excess—not excessiveness—makes a room. I like to include soft, cushioned upholstery and find beautiful things to add in everywhere. A house evolves and lifestyles evolve; a home can be an escape from life and become your safe haven. My house is certainly that for me. Happy houses make you feel good—they make you feel that this is where you want to be and where you belong. The more a house is cared for, maintained, and loved, the better it is and becomes.

NEXT PAGE: A garden room in Connecticut has windows on three sides, which allows for plenty of natural light and makes the room feel very connected to the outdoors.

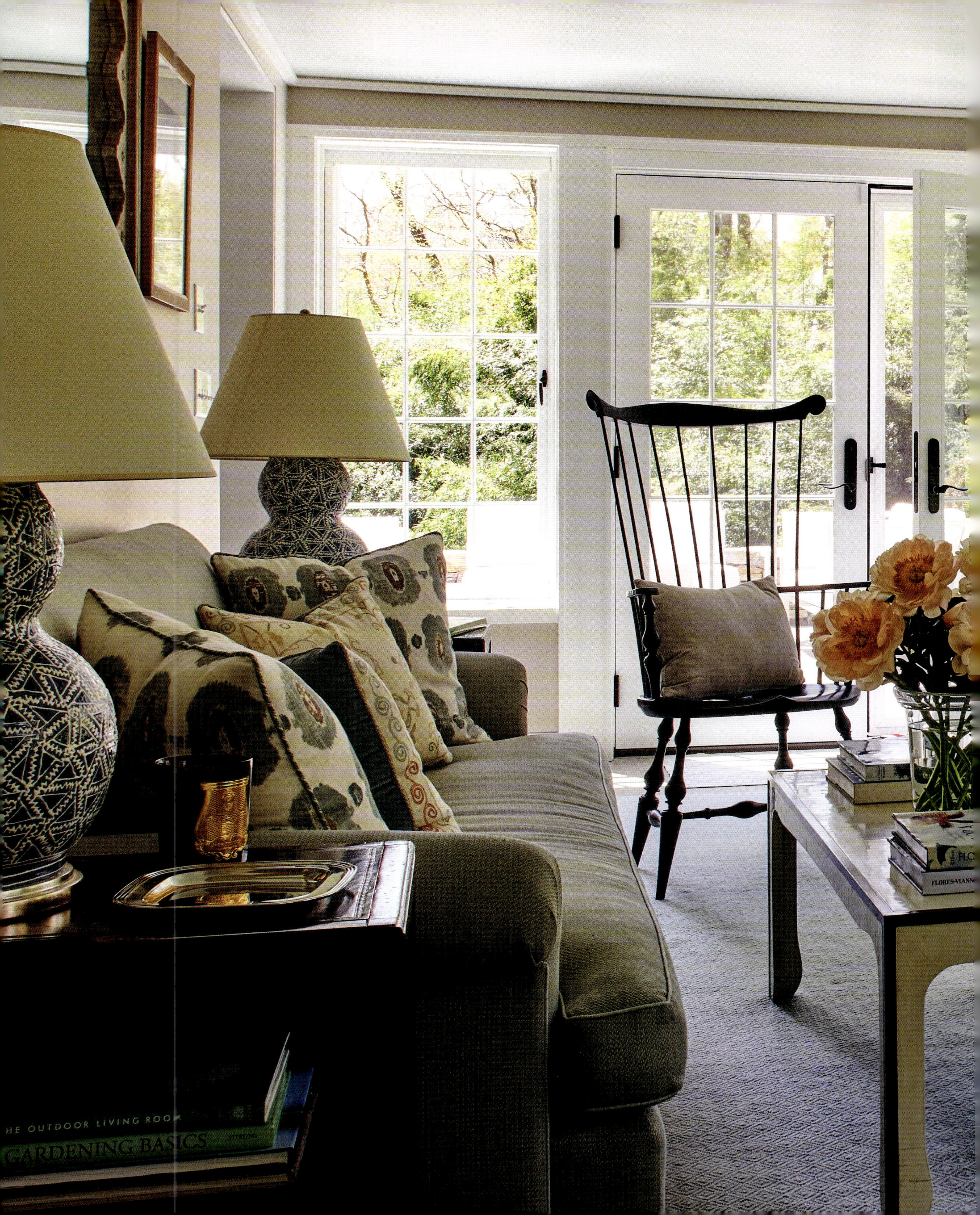
HE OUTDOOR LIVING ROOM
GARDENING BASICS

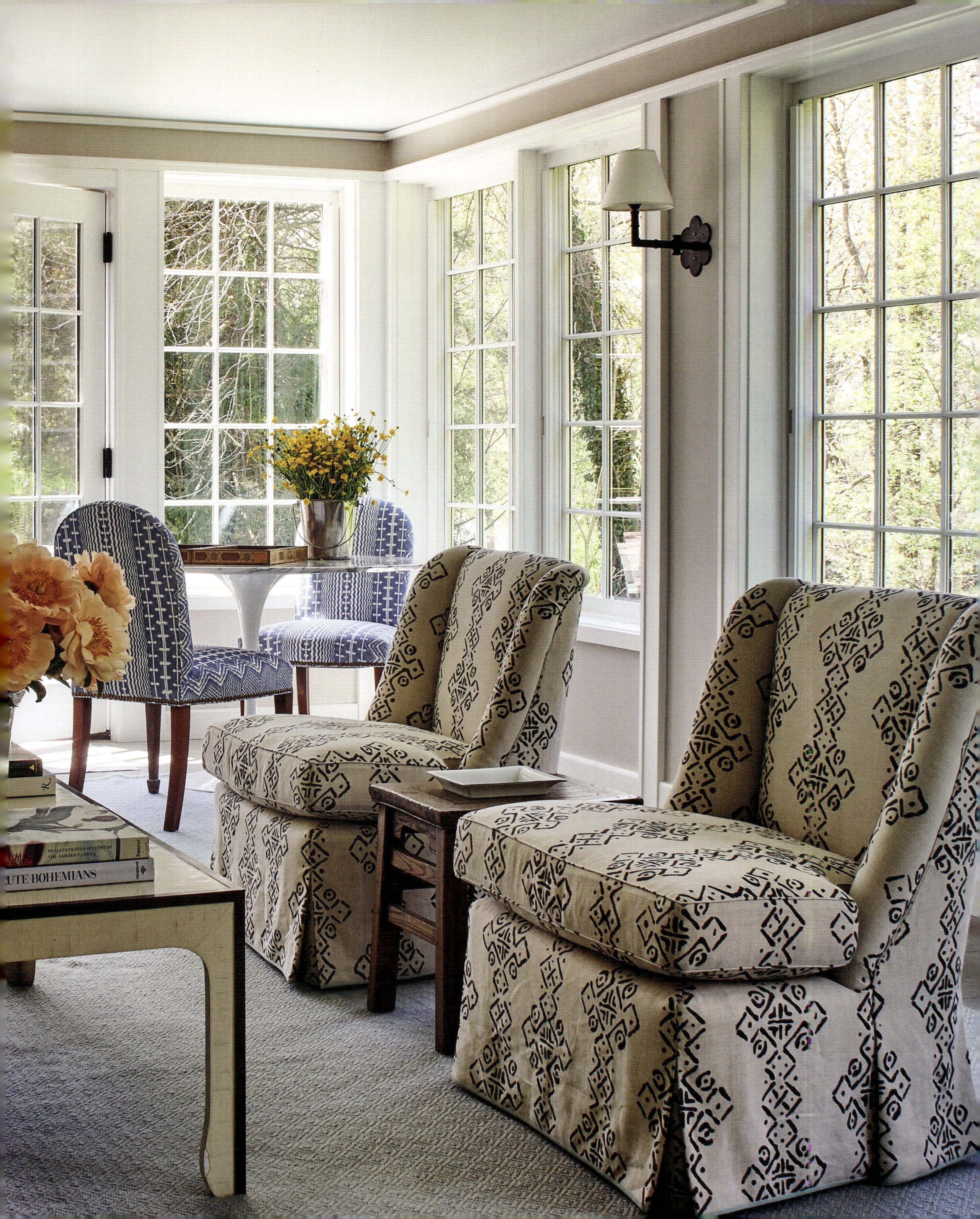
AN ILLUSTRATED HISTORY OF
THE GARDEN FLOWER
UTE BOHEMIANS
VENDOME

CELEB

IMPERF

RATING

ECTION

"So many people feel that perfection is essential to making a room work, but it is the imperfections that give a room character."

—LIBBY CAMERON

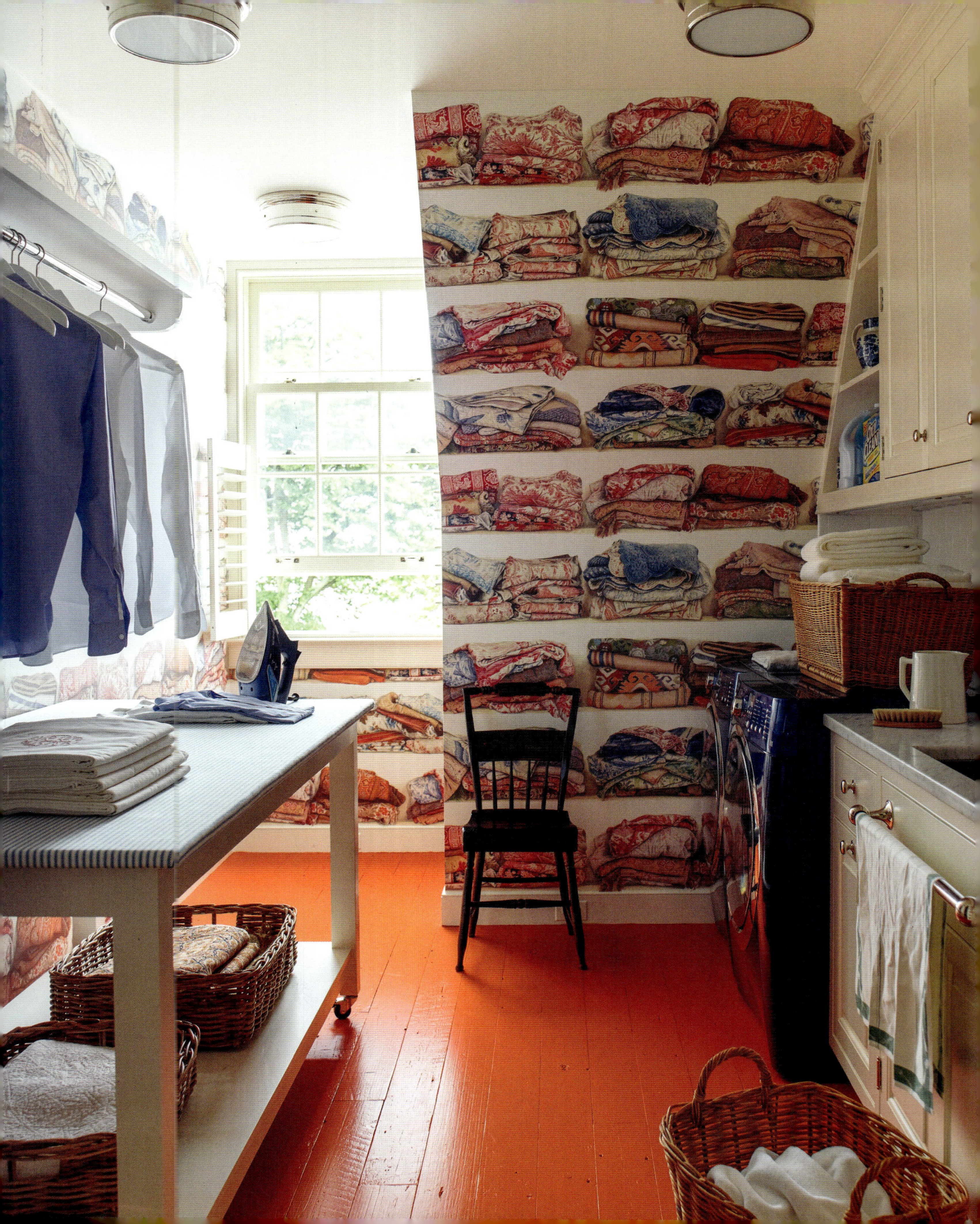

Mario Buatta said, "I have a particular way of decorating. Composing a room is like taking a canvas and putting colors on a little bit at a time. Most clients don't understand this and want to see a rendering of exactly how it is going to look when you're finished. They also don't understand that you have to have varying sizes of things in a room; everything can't be at the same level or it will look like a sea. It should be like a garden where things are growing at all different heights. I always say that I am bringing the outdoors in and that a room grows like a garden over the years. You continue to add to it, you subtract from it, you add things you've been left, add things you have found, better things than you had before. No room is ever finished—it's continually evolving and changes as you change."

It is so true that a home grows along with you—it evolves and changes and becomes more layered and filled with the things you love and care about. There is not a formula for decorating—it is not a precise science, and there is certainly not only one way to design a room. It is all subjective, but getting the layout and the flow the way it makes the most sense and feels right is the best place to start.

The first thing to consider is the architecture. Does it work given the way you live and use the house? Changes should be made if needed before any decorative work is started. Addressing the architectural elements you want to change should be done at the beginning and not later in the game as it is prohibitively expensive to redo what has already been done. Every so often a client does change their mind and voices their thoughts after the fact, maybe not realizing the delays it causes as well as additional costs. Envisioning how something might look is not easy for everyone.

I have had so many clients who simply cannot read two-dimensional floor plans. In fairness, these drawings are very different from pictures or renderings of rooms. The beginning of a project is the time to comb through drawings and plans and to perhaps rethink what is realistic. It's better to do less but do it well. If the scale and proportion in a room is right, it will last forever, and the space will feel the best it can be. How you will be using the room is so important to consider. I've worked with many architects over the years and I love the process, weighing in and working on the evolution of someone's home. It helps to not be too stodgy and restricted in the design process and be open to moving things around. Often the importance of a room and its purpose are overlooked or not properly considered. Houses have many tasks and even utilitarian, practical spaces should be enjoyable and pleasing to be in.

Some houses are quirky to begin with and you just have to live with it. If a house has had several additions and some questionable changes made to it over the years, it can add a lot of charm. In the many hours I spend driving going to see clients and looking for things to fill houses, I always try to look at the houses I drive past. If I see one I like I will stop, get out of my car, and take pictures. People driving by must think I am either crazy or casing the joint. There are some amazing places out there, some wonderful and some simply awful!

Older houses and cottages always appeal to me; some beautifully designed contemporary houses do as well. Although I can appreciate a pleasing sort of decay with furniture up to a point, I don't feel that way about houses. It always makes me sad to see houses when they have not been maintained or kept up properly—when the paint is peeling or when a house has lost its structural integrity. It can all fall apart so quickly and then spiral out of control before the house has to be taken down. On the interior, dilapidated elegance, a bit of wear and tear, or marks, scratches, and scars that reflect our lives and lifestyle are okay—that's just what happens over time and are the signs of

PREVIOUS PAGE: Even utilitarian rooms can be pretty and fun. The Pierre Frey wallpaper feels like it was made for this laundry room. The big table works for both folding and ironing, and the bright orange floor is playful.

OPPOSITE: Although a mudroom feels like a luxury, it is honestly necessary in a home. Having a place to put, hang, and keep everything on your way in and out is essential.

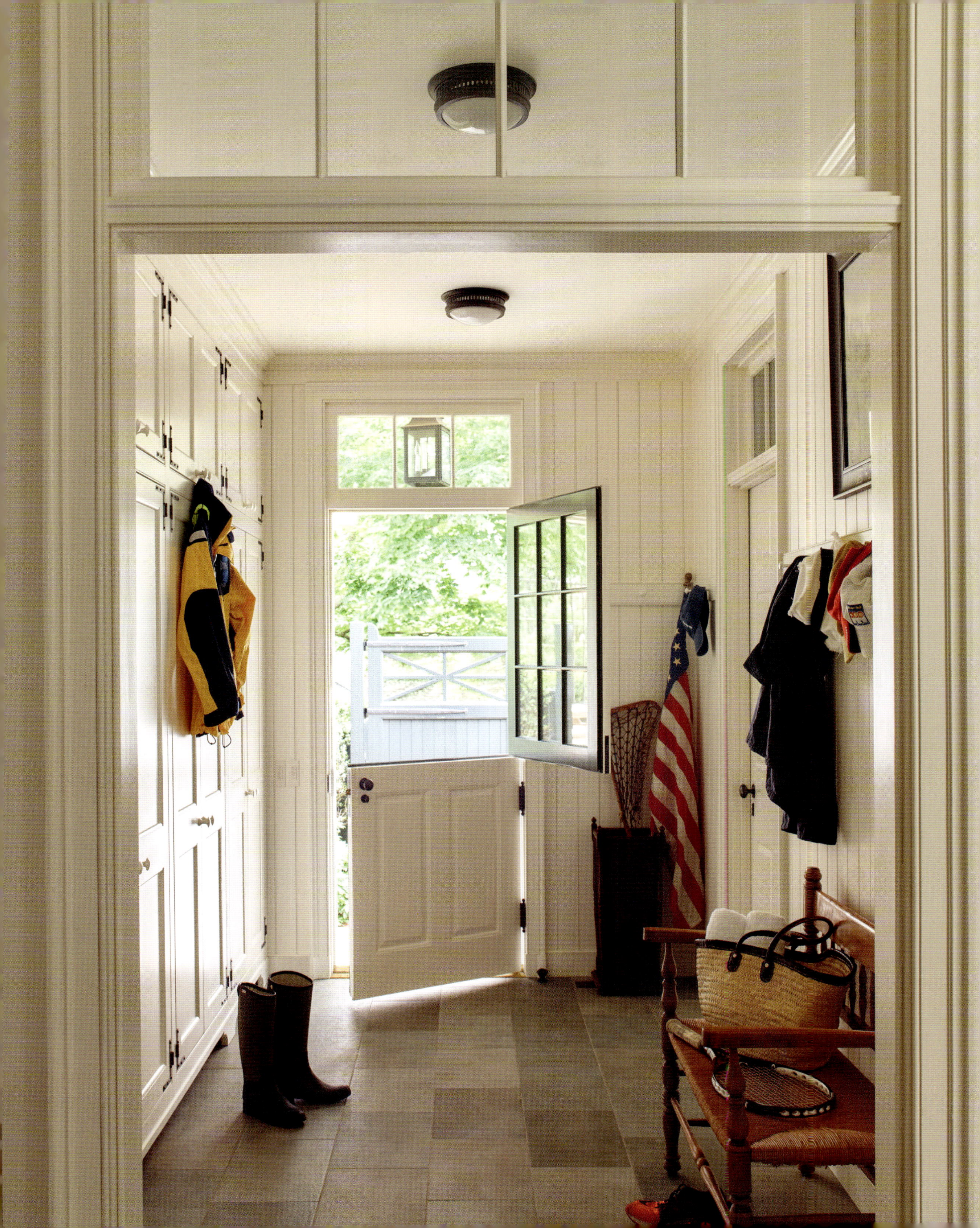

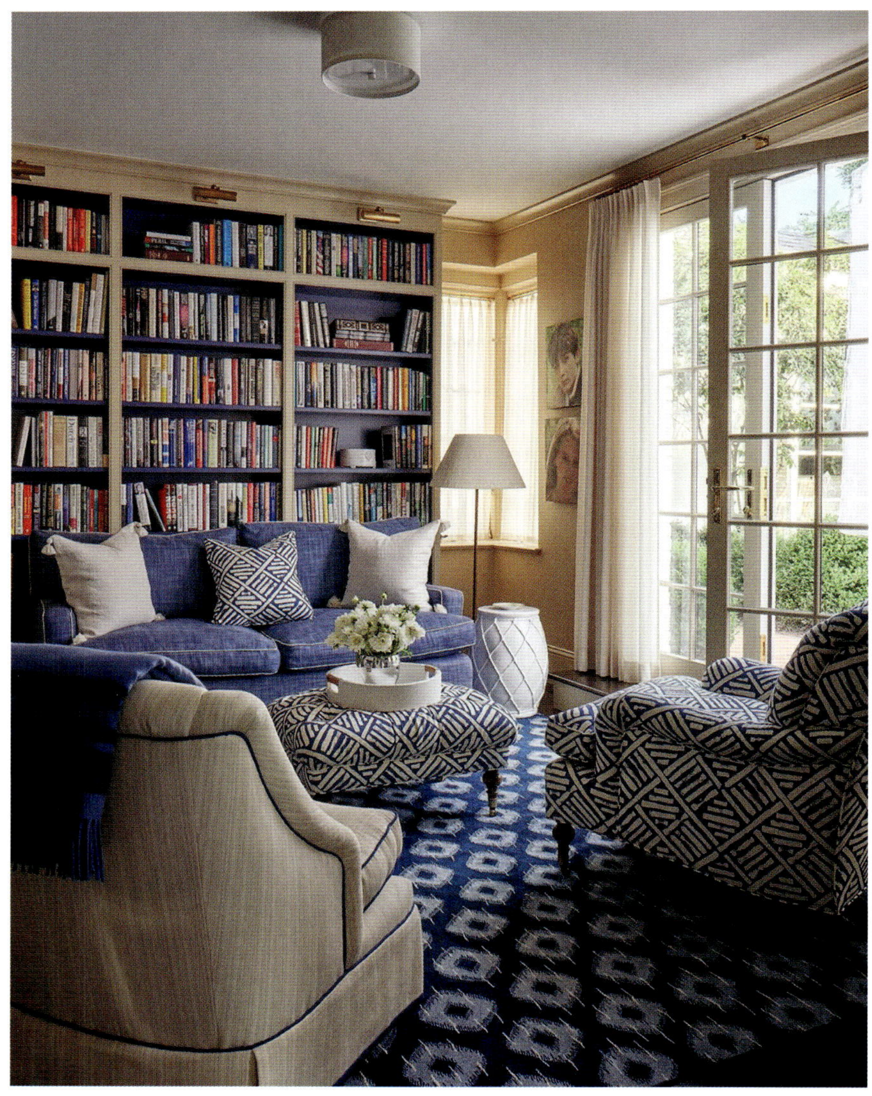

This small, cozy library in Washington, DC, looks out on a wonderful garden.

a well-loved and lived-in house. Every time I look at the lantern above the dining room table in my house, I think of my daughter, and telling her, "Please don't play with that ball in the house." Minutes later I heard the sound of glass breaking. I thought I had carefully put the piece of amber-colored glass from the broken lantern in a drawer so that I could have it fixed or duplicated later, but it is nowhere to be found. The missing piece of glass is the sort of scar I can live with.

I worked on a house in Washington, DC, that was completely renovated. The staircase was moved—which changed the entire layout—and an atrium room on the back of the house needed to be completely removed and reworked. There was plenty of open living space downstairs with a proper living room and family room and garden room. The breakfast room had a fireplace and seating at one end and a table and chairs in a bay window at the other. Those rooms were all done in tones of blue and cream.

At the side and on the back of the house was a little room with floor-to-ceiling bookcases. It was my favorite room, but then I always love small, cozy rooms. This room had doors that opened to the garden and the pool house. Fitting enough good, comfortable upholstery in the space was a challenge. The compromise was a sofa up against the bookcase, a slipper chair as you walk in, and a bigger comfortable chair in the corner; the ottoman for the most part became the coffee table. (I am always wary of using an ottoman as a coffee table, but a tray in the middle helps to stabilize what is put on it as well as breaking up the fabric surface.) The room was deep blue, cream, and white. There wasn't enough space for end tables and lamps beside the sofa, so standing lamps were used instead. There weren't any real tables or any wooden furniture in the room—there just wasn't enough space for anything but a ceramic garden stool, so everything was soft and upholstered. The view out to the courtyard garden is lovely. When in that room, you feel like you are in a little jewel box surrounded by books and the greenery of the garden. Sometimes a room is not the perfect size but then lends itself to something special you would not have created otherwise.

While some people get frazzled by too much pattern, it energizes me. One of my sons-in-law is Danish and likes a serene environment with the clean, minimal palette of Denmark's renowned style. He must have been reeling the first time he came to my house! Between the initial chaos of the dogs' excitement over a new visitor, the myriad of colors, and the abundance of things I have collected, it is certainly very different from what he's known!

So many people feel that perfection is essential to making a room work, but it is the imperfections that give a room character. What is unexpected adds soul to a room. Trying to reign in any imperfection and have everything be perfect at all times is a big job—and it is impossible. The bottom line is that all of our lives are imperfect, and there is imperfection everywhere you look. I suppose that is what makes each of us and every place unique. As William Norwich once said, "The world of interiors isn't perfect. Things fall apart. Consoles don't console. Chintz happens."

There are many preconceived notions of how a room should be furnished. The goal is to make a room feel inviting, sensible, and warm—without a clash of scale or proportion. Some people think that by creating a "main" area within a room—one central, most used and furnished section—that the room is finished. But a room falls apart when corners can't hold their own. Corner banquettes can often solve the problem of a dead corner and are cozier than just two chairs with a table in between. But, in the same breath, a completely symmetrical room can be quite boring; asymmetry in a room can work as long as there is something to create a balance. Artwork can balance out a room visually by filling walls with one large painting or a combination of paintings of all sizes. I always think of the amazing English country houses and the paintings of all sizes hung at varying levels covering the walls.

My dear friends Sally and Victor Ganz were renowned collectors of contemporary art. They lived uptown beside the East River in New York City and had an impressive and important collection of twentieth-century contemporary art. Victor had always appreciated art, even as a teenager, and started seriously collecting in 1941. After he and Sally married, it became their passion. The Ganzes were recognized for their ability to choose art; they never seemed to make a mistake in what they chose. Their art collection included work by Jasper Johns, Robert Rauschenberg, Frank Stella and Eva Hesse. All of this artwork was hanging amid a relatively traditional mix of furniture. Their extraordinary collection included several large Picassos.

My idea of heaven is an organized linen closet with a glass door front where everything can be seen and is easily accessible.

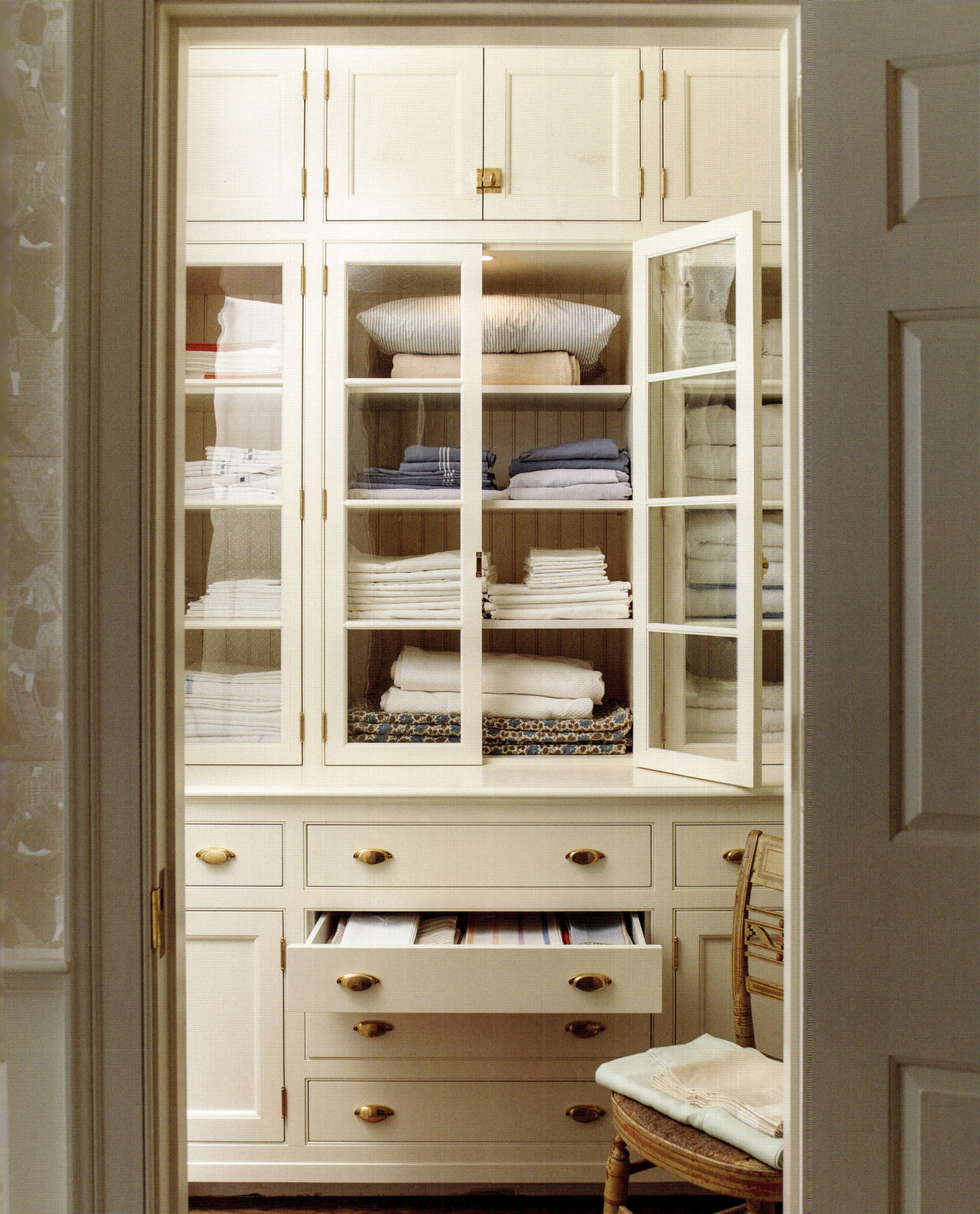

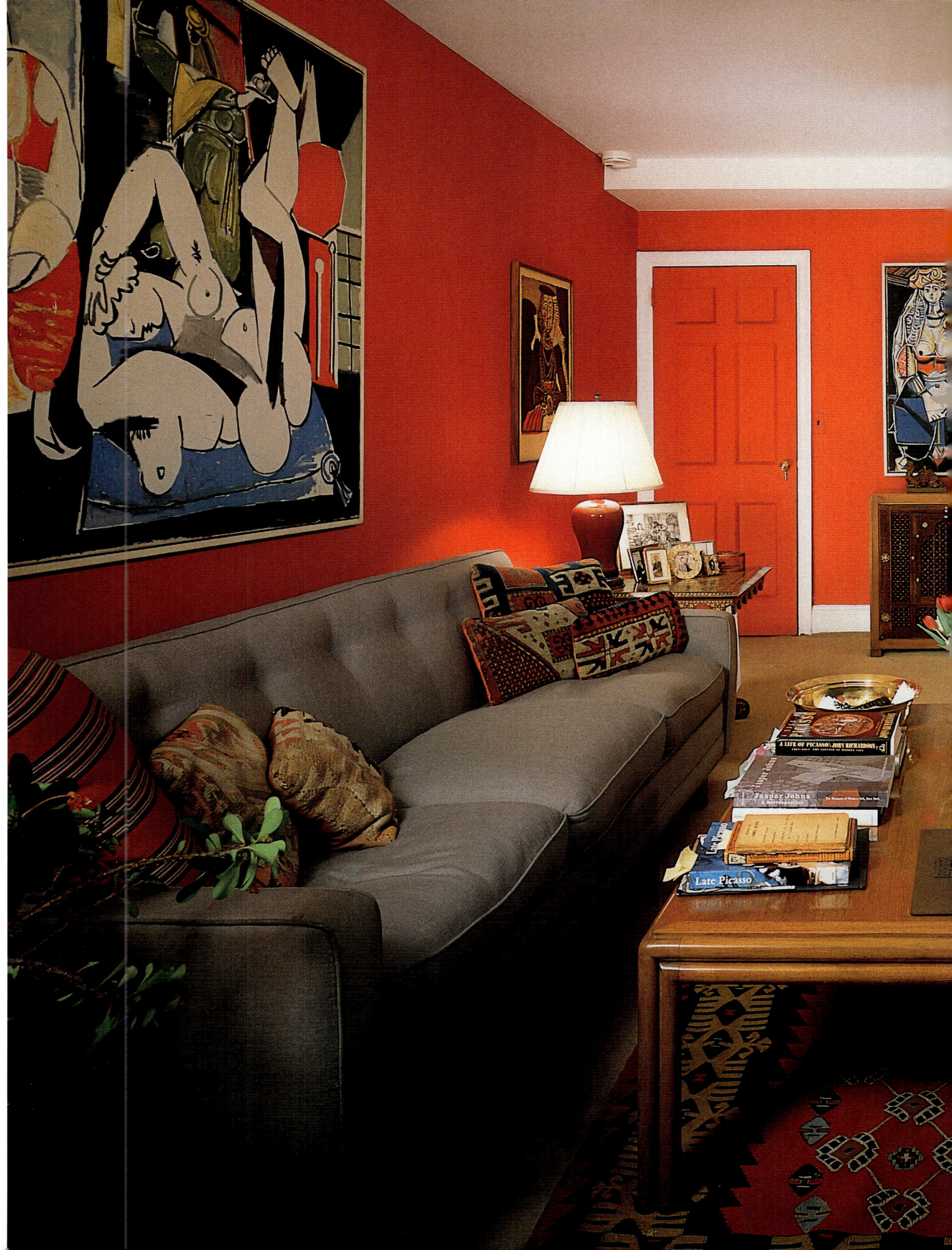
A LIFE OF PICASSO | JOHN RICHARDSON
Jasper Johns
Late Picasso

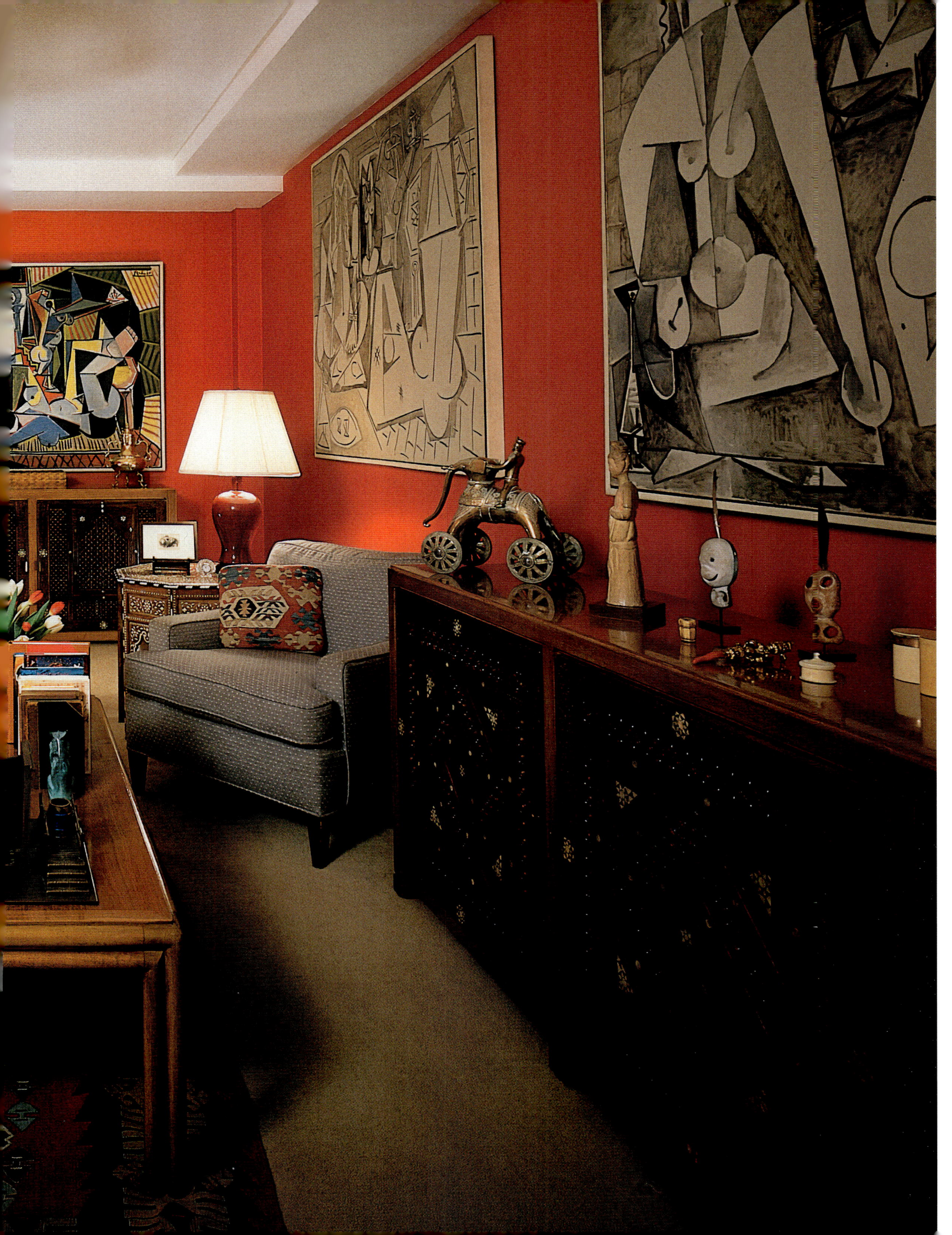

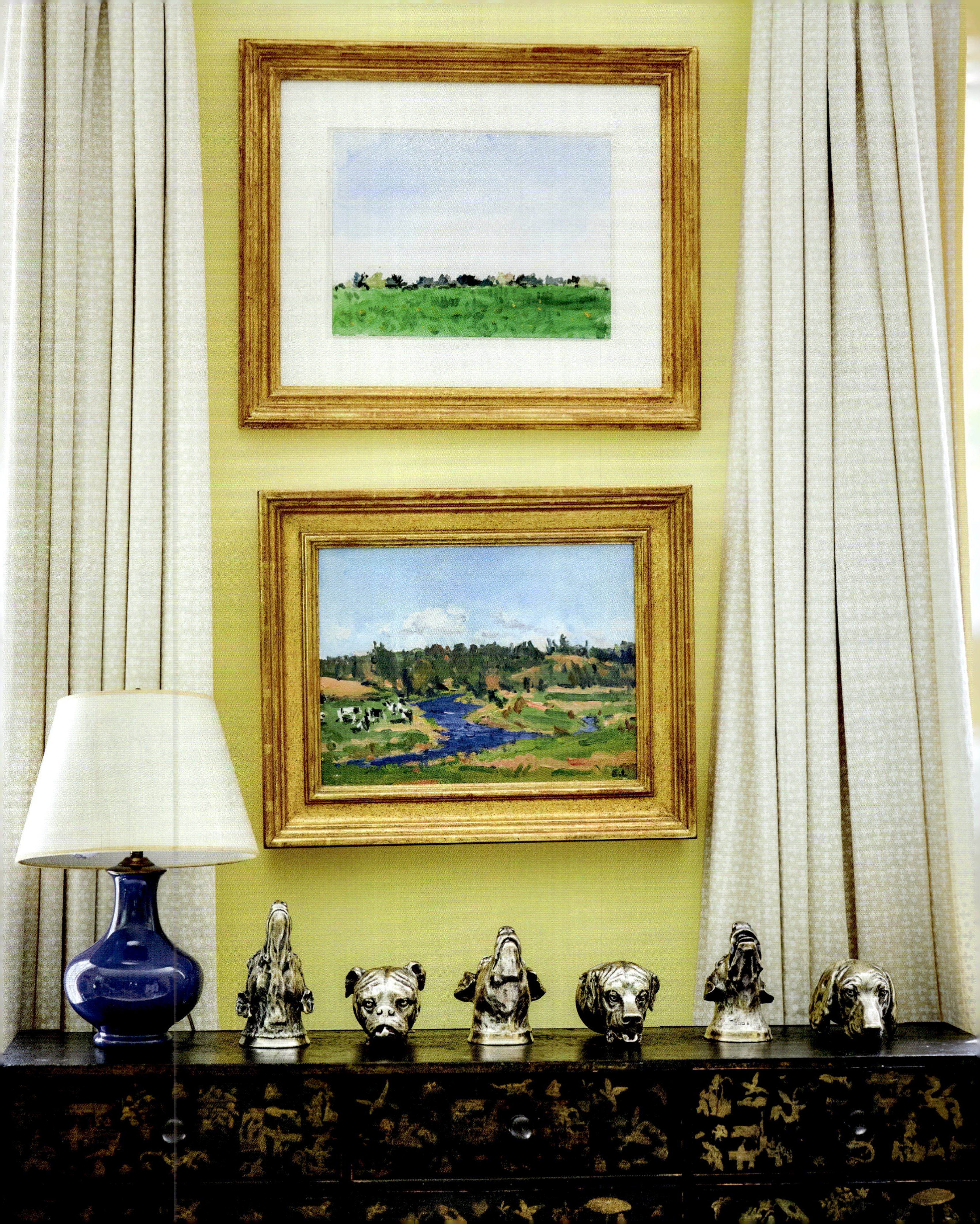

Sally asked me to help her "freshen up" their small red sitting room in which there were several very large paintings of Picasso's *Les Femmes d'Alger* in variations and different tones. It was without doubt my favorite room in their apartment because of the big, bold, important paintings in such a tiny room and because that red was the most beautiful color. That little red room taught me so much: I learned that boldness and appropriateness can and do coexist, and colors and textures that might clash can end up being something to be celebrated. When it was just the two of them, this was the room Sally and Victor spent most of their time in. It goes to show that private worlds provide us with peace and pleasure.

Sally and I met for lunch almost every Friday. We would walk together from her apartment to the coffee shop at the corner on East End Avenue and she would always order a grilled cheese sandwich. She was so fun to be with and could be so funny. Each and every time we walked to and from the coffee shop, she would say that there were too many impatiens planted in the tree wells and called them "insipid little flowers." I never understood why those little flowers exasperated her so!

There always seem to be comfort zones in a house, where the things that you love most are. Everything I own has personal meaning, and my house is filled with things I have had for a long time—things that have come from my family and friends, or that I have collected. A home really is a scrapbook of one's past, filled with what we've collected over the years without any thought given to them matching but only because they were appealing to us in the first place. I am always drawn to pretty antiques but am not driven by museum-quality pieces or swayed by the names of who made what or what is important because of its provenance. Who designed or made something can increase its value if the maker was important, but how something speaks to me is what motivates me to buy it. The pieces don't have to be perfect or fit together perfectly to make a room work.

PREVIOUS PAGE: A small, narrow sitting room in an apartment in New York City had big paintings from Picasso's *Les Femmes d'Alger* series.

OPPOSITE: The sterling stirrup cups were given to me by my father when I got married. The two pastural paintings are by Eugene Leake.

So many things are copied and there are knockoffs of practically everything. Most people in the decorating world are guilty of copying or "modifying" the designs of others but stating a piece was made by a renowned designer when it was not is too much of a stretch. There is a fine line between reinventing and overdoing. Of course, all inspiration comes from the past—designs and patterns, faux painting, faux finishes, painted floors, parquetry, marquetry, elaborate designs, and painted patterns—but they can only be replicated. Having the imagination to see the potential of a design or shape is the interesting and exciting part. Proportion and scale can get lost in translation—as can the original beauty of a shape or form when it is reproduced, not to mention the resulting horror when inferior materials are used.

Having the imagination and willingness to experiment with color, rugs, and textiles can be surprisingly pleasing. Some people use color to make up for a lack of fine furniture and antiques. Strong rugs can compensate for a pale color scheme, while a soft rug can balance out a strong room's color. A monochromatic room can be enlivened with a rug or art. And even pattern upon pattern can be intriguing. Again, it doesn't have to fit perfectly to work well together. The unexpected always seems to add charm and interest—it's much more interesting to have things that have a quirky personality than things that are formally "correct." Some of my very favorite pillows were ones I had made from red handkerchiefs I found from the Gap. It's much more interesting to have a home with the things that are pleasing to you.

After Angelo Donghia died, Albert was asked to go and see Ralph Lauren at his apartment on the upper East Side. Donghia had done the apartment for the Laurens in all whites and creams using boxy modern furniture. Albert was excited to see the actual apartment and not just photographs; he was honored to have gotten the phone call to come and consult with the Laurens. When he got back to the office, he described the apartment in detail. He told the funniest story about using the powder room and described the completely mirrored room. All four sides and even the ceiling was mirrored. It was all smooth mirror without any seams. He said that he had the hardest time finding his way out of the bathroom—he couldn't figure out which wall the door was on, and said, "Can you imagine having had a couple of gins and using the bathroom—I would have never gotten out of there!"

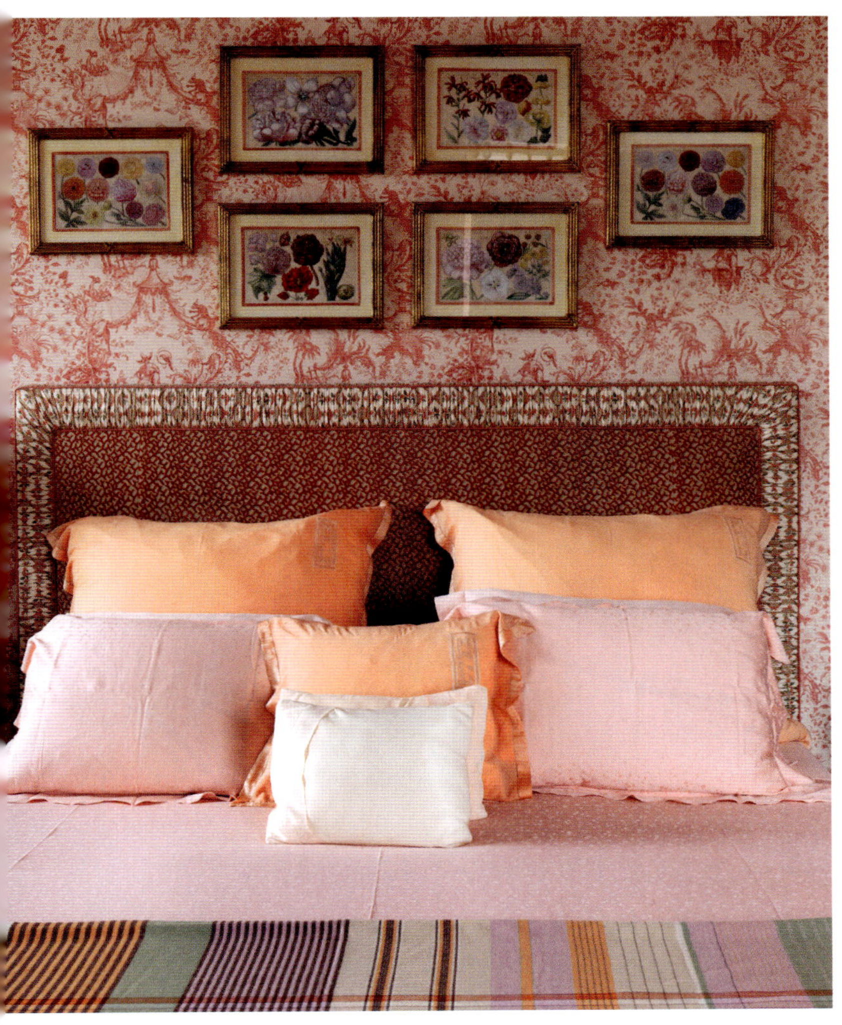

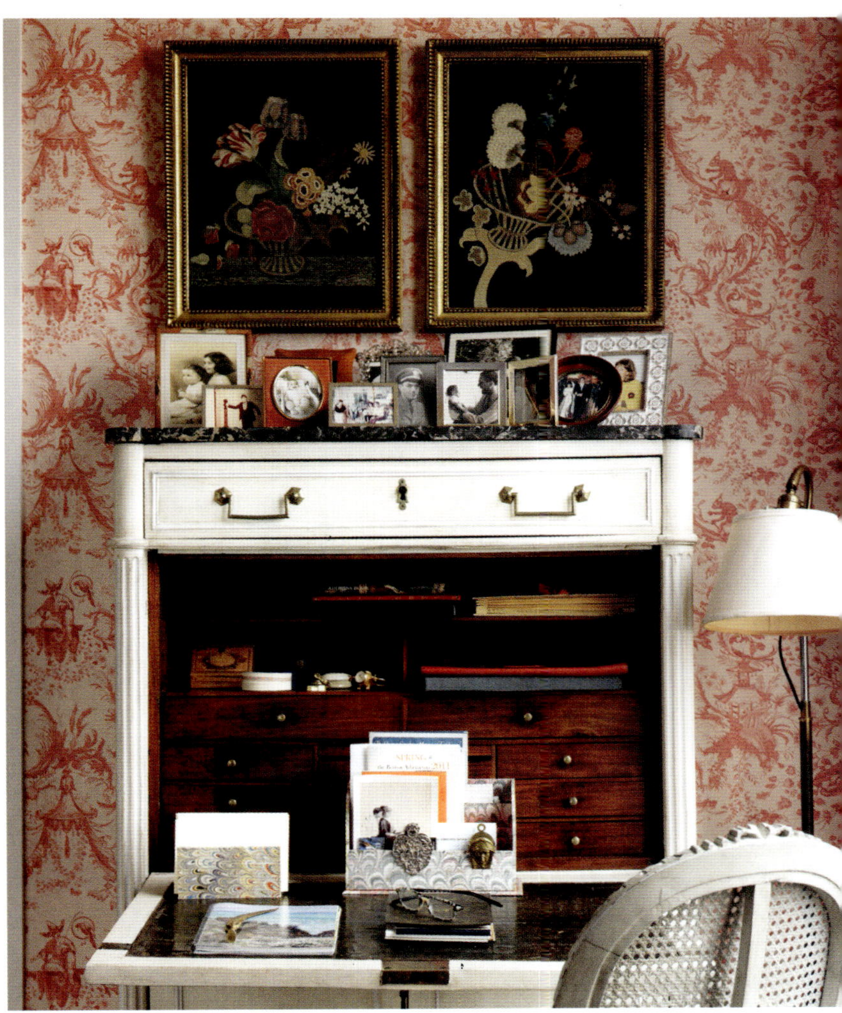

A bedroom in Boston with walls covered in Nina Campbell wallpaper.

EMBRACING
COLLABO

RATION

"None of what I have done could have be possible without the help of artisans and craftsmen."

—LIBBY CAMERON

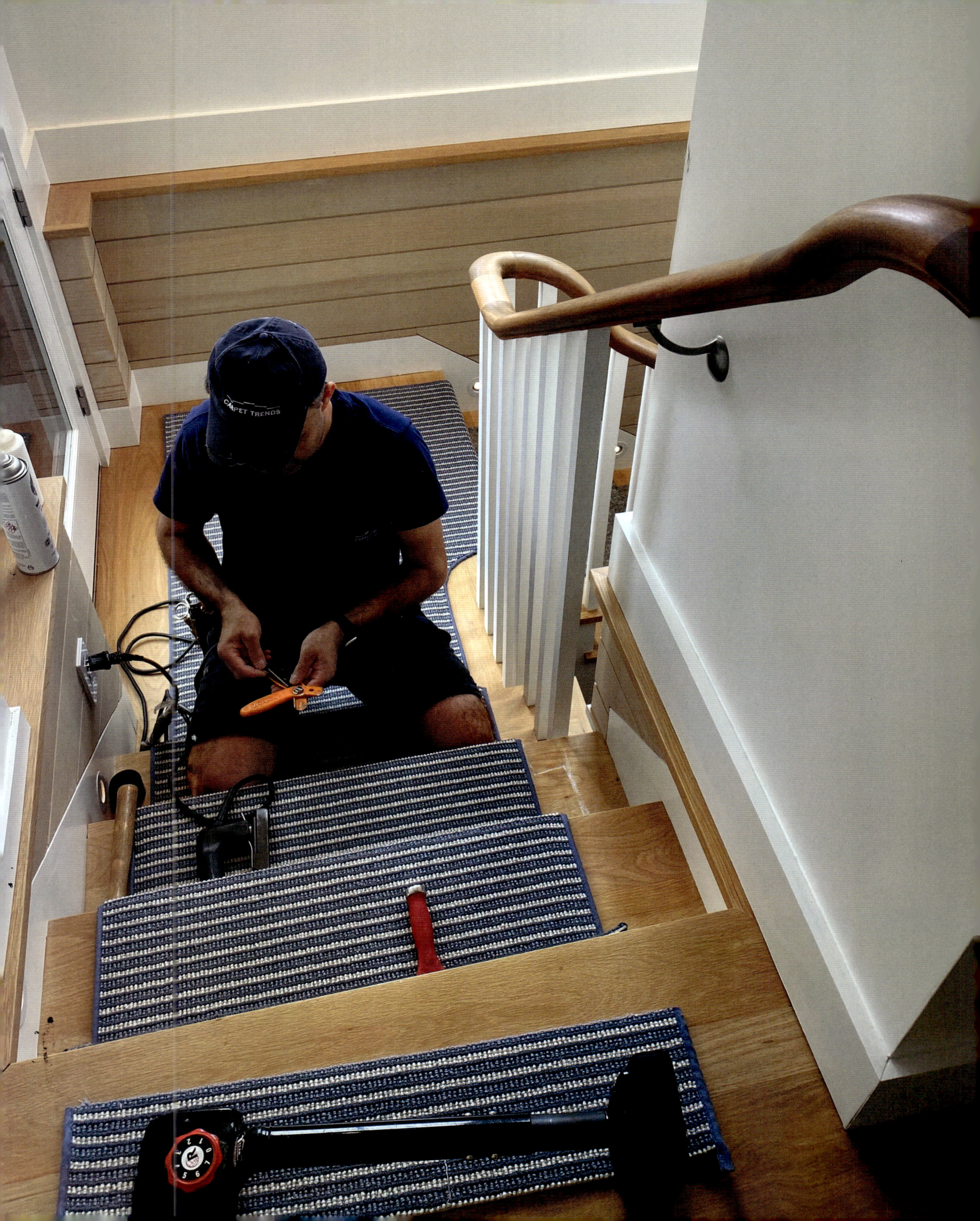

Working in an office with other decorators, assistants, and an architectural department was a wonderful luxury and experience. The team needed for a project is much bigger than you would imagine and it is the people who work behind the scenes that make everything come together. Some of the people I have been lucky enough to work with are incredible artisans—for instance, the painters and decorative painters who can mix the most beautiful glazes for walls and create the most wonderful fantasy finishes. I've loved working with the people who can cut and make the most beautiful curtains, the talented cabinetmakers who are so precise, the hardware makers who can re-create almost anything, the landscape architects, the contractors, the amazing electricians who understand how a light fixture should be hung, the carpet installers, and the truckers who can carefully move pieces from one place to another. These are the people who are essential to a good working team.

Once there is a plan in place for a house of what needs to be altered or kept, it's off to the races. The beginning of a project is exciting on so many levels—it's like a puzzle to solve and put together. The planning stage always fascinates and captivates me. I love having to think through some of the nuts and bolts of an existing space, why something will work or why not, and how to hide some of the uglier elements like HVAC grills and structural beams. One has to determine where the plumbing goes and carefully review a light switching plan so you can walk through a space easily switching lights on and off. Nothing is more annoying than having to get out of bed and go downstairs to turn off a hall light then head back to bed in the dark! All of these essential but not very glamorous elements are a part of a renovation and how a house works. A multilayered process of thought and collaboration is needed to get the best results.

Weekly site meetings are important for a renovation. If a project is local, those meetings are usually early in the day. They give everyone involved updates about what stage the job is at, who needs to supply what information next, and which answers are still needed. It is good to have all-hands-on-deck at these meetings—it keeps the work schedule up to date so the client's needs and thoughts can continuously be addressed. Today, these calls often happen over Zoom, but I prefer the meetings in person and on-site. Too often I have been called in to work on a project when the important decisions have been made without the proper thought to detail—then the layout has to be tweaked because of the logic of the room's circulation, or the placement of lights has to be changed. Changes are not only expensive but cost time delays as well. I think the most crucial piece to it all is a mutual trust and the assurance that the team can and will work together to create the best space possible.

There is the very practical side of me that first thinks about sustainability, and what will last both aesthetically and practically. I think about the future of a house—what will make it work best and remain appealing to multiple generations as well as in this moment. A house needs its own character and personality. The style of the house and the interior set that direction.

When possible, I like to keep the original elements in a house. I think there is something lovely in the notion about how it all started that should be honored. A space can be modernized without stripping it of all that was. I've seen so many disastrous renovations in which the defining and appealing elements in a room have been simply removed—which then completely changes the feel of a space. Taking out old moldings can also take out the charm and soul of a house if done without a careful, thoughtful approach. Houses should be loved.

Billy Baldwin said, "Any house or room remembered with pleasure has the look of being loved by those living in it."

A floor plan is absolutely the starting point. It's important to spread out the floor plans and pore over them to figure out what will work, what will fit, and what needs to find a home in another room or house. The answers aren't always obvious. You need to decide how to incorporate what someone already has and wants to use and then figure out what is missing and needs to be added. I have worked on a few houses that had

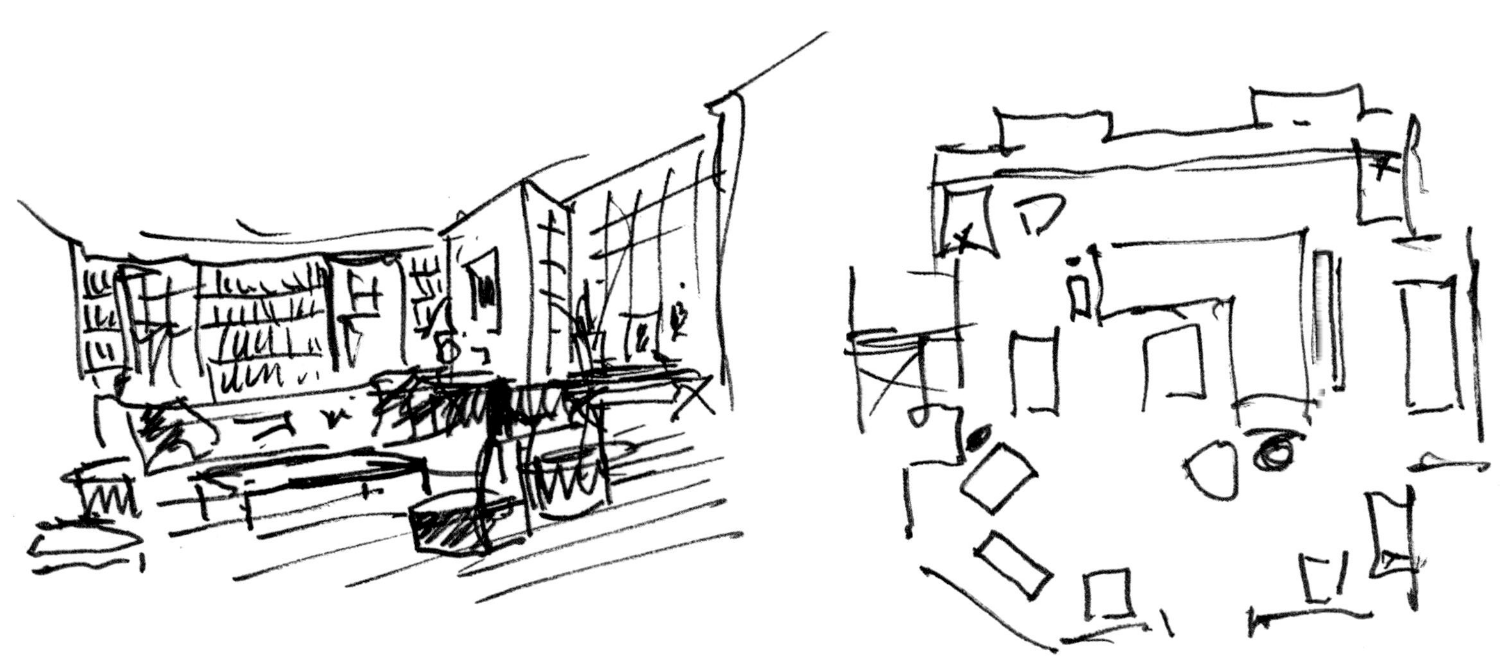

PREVIOUS PAGE: A stair carpet being installed in a home in Rhode Island.

ABOVE: Quick room sketches by Albert Hadley.

rambling hallways and disconnected rooms, so making sense and creating connections between rooms is the first step.

Often an overall patterned painted floor can unify an unorganized space. One of my clients bought an island in Maine that had a large summer "cottage" on it that was long and essentially one room deep. There was a small living room and dining room on the first floor, both with single facing views to the east, and there were a couple of very small bedrooms beyond the living room at the end of the house. Mark Ferguson of Ferguson & Shamamian changed the ground floor of the house by removing the bedrooms at the southern end and creating a large living room instead with three pairs of French doors on each of the long sides of the room. He added a fireplace at one end of the room and built bookcases on the opposite wall. Mark created a sun-filled, balanced room. It was a challenge to work up there. The island was small with one working dock that led up and over a hill to the house so it was hard to get to, especially during the winter. Everything had to be taken over by boat or by barge and then carried up to the house. Unfortunately, a barge that was stacked high with unopened boxes of hardware got swamped during a storm; the boxes fell overboard and the hardware is still somewhere at the bottom of the brink. That house was one of my favorite projects because the crew who worked on it with me were so great and fun to work with. And Maine is as beautiful in the dead of winter as it is in the summertime with the sun rippling across the water with each gust of wind.

After the rooms had been rearranged and a big living room had been added, a long hall now ran from one end of the house to the other. The hall was wide, then narrow, and then wide again. It was in need of something to help its length and odd shape make sense. I worked with Matthew Tyrrell and Chris Butler to paint the floor. We had figured out on the floor plans what sort of painted floor pattern would work best to marry the first-floor rooms. The painting had to be done in stages—the oil paint needed to dry in between the different layers, which was all part of the process. I went up there while they were working. Those are some of the best moments in my work—figuring out solutions and working on colors with artists. Matthew is a hoot—he loves to laugh and have a good time and can be very, very funny. Everyone's opinion and take on the job at hand matters in a situation like that even though everyone's thought process is different. We all imagine and envision different solutions and together we create an appropriate design in the right scale and proportion for the space.

I have loved working with the painting company John Weidl Associates for my entire career. They can do the most amazing specialized painting work of all kinds, and they create the most beautiful backgrounds on which any room can begin. Pete was one of the first of their painters who I worked with and got to know. He knew instantly how to make the perfect color, what to add, and how to give more depth and dimension to any finish. That sort of understanding is instinctive—it's not something you can go to school for. One can learn techniques with a great mentor, but knowing exactly just how to create a color, how much of what to add, and what colored ground to use it on is innate. Many of the talented people I have worked with came from Weidl—Sammy, Antonio, Paul, Adreano, and Cristopher. They each had their own way of working and their own techniques.

There is nothing better than the look and smell of a painting studio. I will find almost any excuse to go to Zina Studios in Mount Vernon whenever I can. It was once owned and run by Count and Countess Nicholas Bobrinskoy. Nicholas was the great-great-great grandson of Empress Catherine the Great of Russia. He and his wife Tania, also of Russian descent, hand printed fabrics and wallpapers for Parish-Hadley's clients for years, all custom colored. Nicholas was a very talented artist and designed some wonderful patterns that are still printed by Zina Studios today. Tania was a wonderful, smart woman—small but mighty—and one who did not hold back her opinions. I learned a lot from her and have always been grateful for her kindness and teaching. The studio was filled with glass jars of paint with lids and paint drips running down the side. The printing is still done on long tables with framed screens that get moved down the table in increments. The printing is done layer after layer and in sections, and the design is hand applied with silk screens. Now owned by Scott Sloat and Jorges Tan, Zina is always a very busy workroom. I love the smell of that studio. Sadly, printing textiles by hand is a dying art, as so much is done now with rotary and digital printers. I love that the old style of textile printing is still going strong.

RIGHT: A proposed rendering for a painted center of a floor by Franklin Tartaglione.

BELOW: An idea for a mural painting by Chuck Fischer for a dining room in South Carolina.

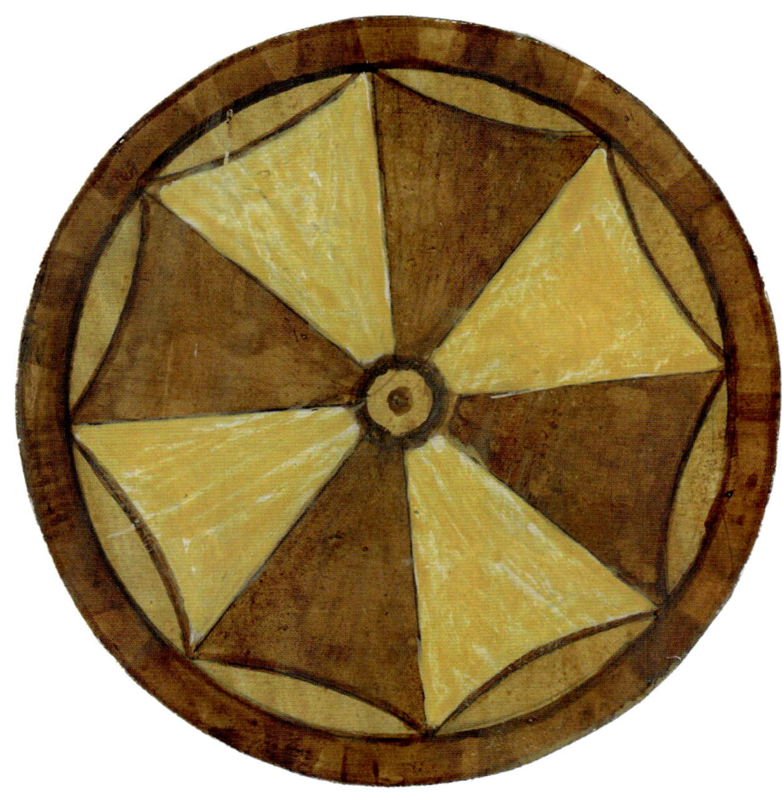

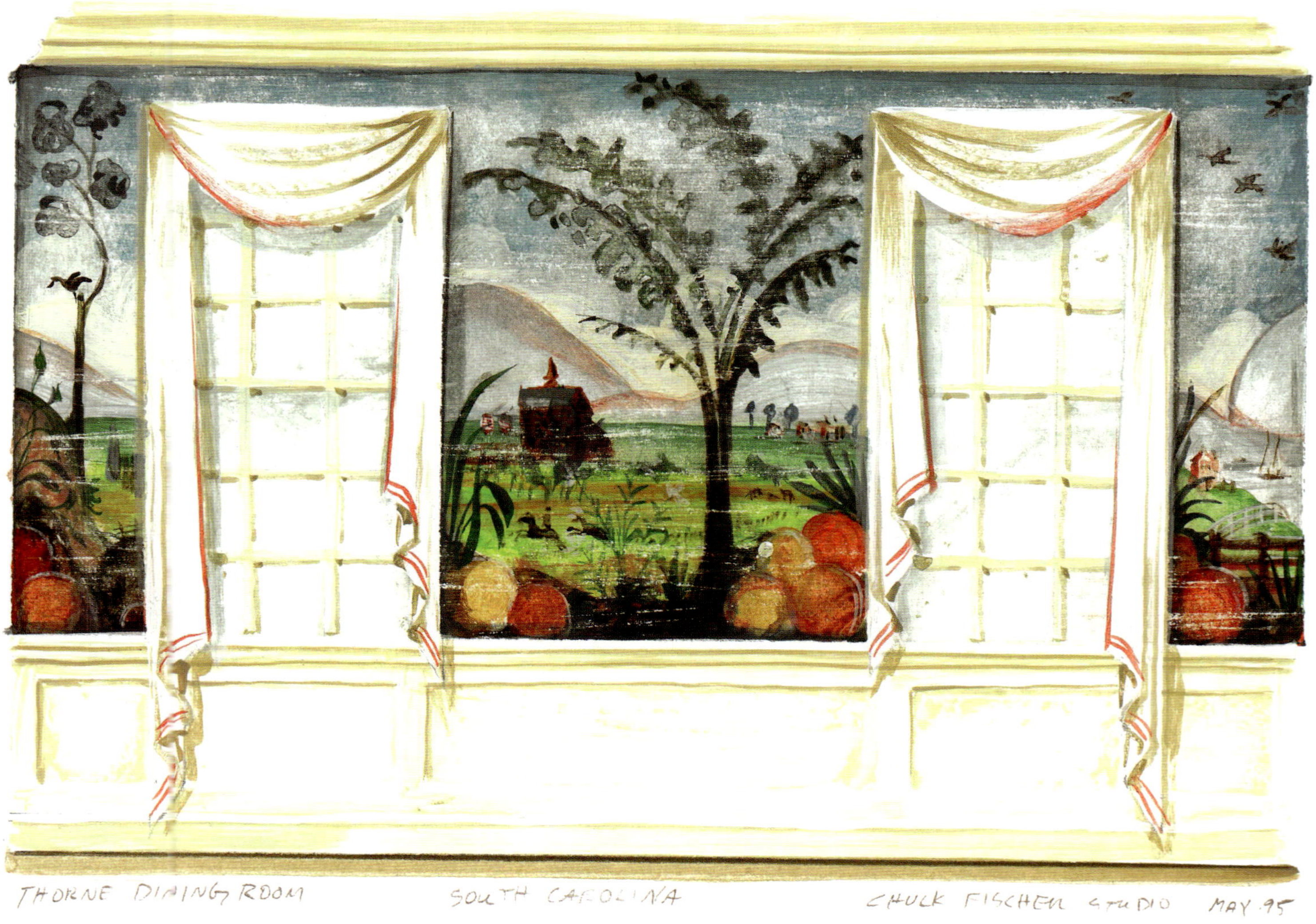

THORNE DINING ROOM SOUTH CAROLINA CHUCK FISCHER STUDIO MAY 95

Peter Fasano and Elizabeth Hamilton have been great friends of mine for years. They created beautiful fabrics and their studio in the Berkshires had jars everywhere and that same wonderful smell of paint. When they lived in the city, Peter's studio was one floor below the apartment where he and Elizabeth lived on Madison Avenue in Carnegie Hill. He worked on the second floor of one of those low buildings that have huge plate glass windows that look west out on to Madison near the Corner Bookstore. Peter hand painted and printed his own designs. He made beautiful floor cloths and wonderful painted geometric patterns in clear pastels and bright colors. His work was all free hand. I used his work as often as I could. Peter is enormously talented; he still paints but not on fabrics anymore. He and Elizabeth moved to Great Barrington, Massachusetts, in the late 1980s. Elizabeth started her own textile company, Elizabeth Hamilton, and created some very beautiful designs. They have since sold both of their companies and are now living in Santa Fe.

Any handwork impresses me because it is not easy to do. I have such respect for people who make things in a seemingly effortless manner, and who are unflappable in the process. Mr. Biunno had a small shop in the East Twenties and his was the first workroom I ever visited when I started at Parish-Hadley. Mr. Biunno was such a lovely man and he had a magic touch when refinishing furniture. The smell of his shop—the lacquer, wax, and turpentine—stays with me. His son, Joe, took over his business when he died. Joe later expanded his business to include curtain hardware. In the 1990s, his business focused more on finishing furniture, gilding, and making curtain hardware, including poles, finials, and rings, so he opened Finials Unlimited. His work is just beautiful. He reminded me the other day of when I came to him asking if he could copy a Chippendale-style dining chair for a client. I needed sixteen chairs because my client had two tables for eight in her dining room. Joe happily took on the job, made the chairs, and has been making furniture and carving pieces ever since. Joe no longer does finishing work himself but makes and restores furniture. The gilding, staining, and faux finishes are done by his neighbors, Osmundo Echevarria and Oliver Westermeier, who are incredibly talented. There is a cluster of workrooms on the second floor of a building in Long Island City where Freddie Victoria, Joe Biunno, Osmundo Echevarria,

Oliver Westermeier, and Bill Sullivan all work. Visiting the workrooms is still one of my very favorite things to do and one of the best parts of my work. I can't imagine how many hours of my time is taken up visiting all of the various artisans involved in a project. The people are all so talented. It still amazes me to see them transform broken, dull furniture and objects into things of beauty.

Is there anything prettier than well-made curtains? I have always loved going to the various workrooms and watching curtains being made, or chairs and sofas being recovered or made from scratch. It's not easy to create well-made curtains that fall just right and are the perfect weight and volume. You can add tassels and trims and use beautiful fabrics, but how they are cut and sewn is really what matters. I am not a big fan of curtains that puddle on the floor; I like it when they just brush the floor and have lovely detailing on the edges. I remember sitting in Mrs. Parish's office years ago and reviewing a job with her, explaining which fabrics were to go where in a room, and how the various pieces were to be finished. I hadn't planned for any trimming on the curtains; they were going to be made of a stripe and I thought the dominant color in the stripe could be used on the inside lead edge of the curtains. I hadn't thought that a different edging would be needed. Mrs. Parish very sternly said that everything needs a finished edge—be it a self-contrast, a self-bias, a tape or a fringe. I took her message to heart, and to this day, there is a finished edge on all of the work that is done for me unless otherwise called for. Albert Hadley always spoke about "dressmaker" details; it is the subtle and elegant details that make all the difference.

Not every workroom can cut curtains the right way. Mike Milillo was the most wonderful man and did a great deal of work for me. His was a small workroom without a formal name, but he knew how to cut fabric and always made pretty curtains. Mike really understood how fabric would fall based on what it was made of—its content and weight. The scissors people use for cutting curtain and upholstery fabric are very big and heavy, and you have to know which way to cut—with or against the weave.

DeAngelis has always made lovely curtains and upholstery and thankfully, Kayel Jr. and Christine still carry on their family's workroom. There are many talented people and workrooms but I fear the great teachers are becoming fewer and farther between.

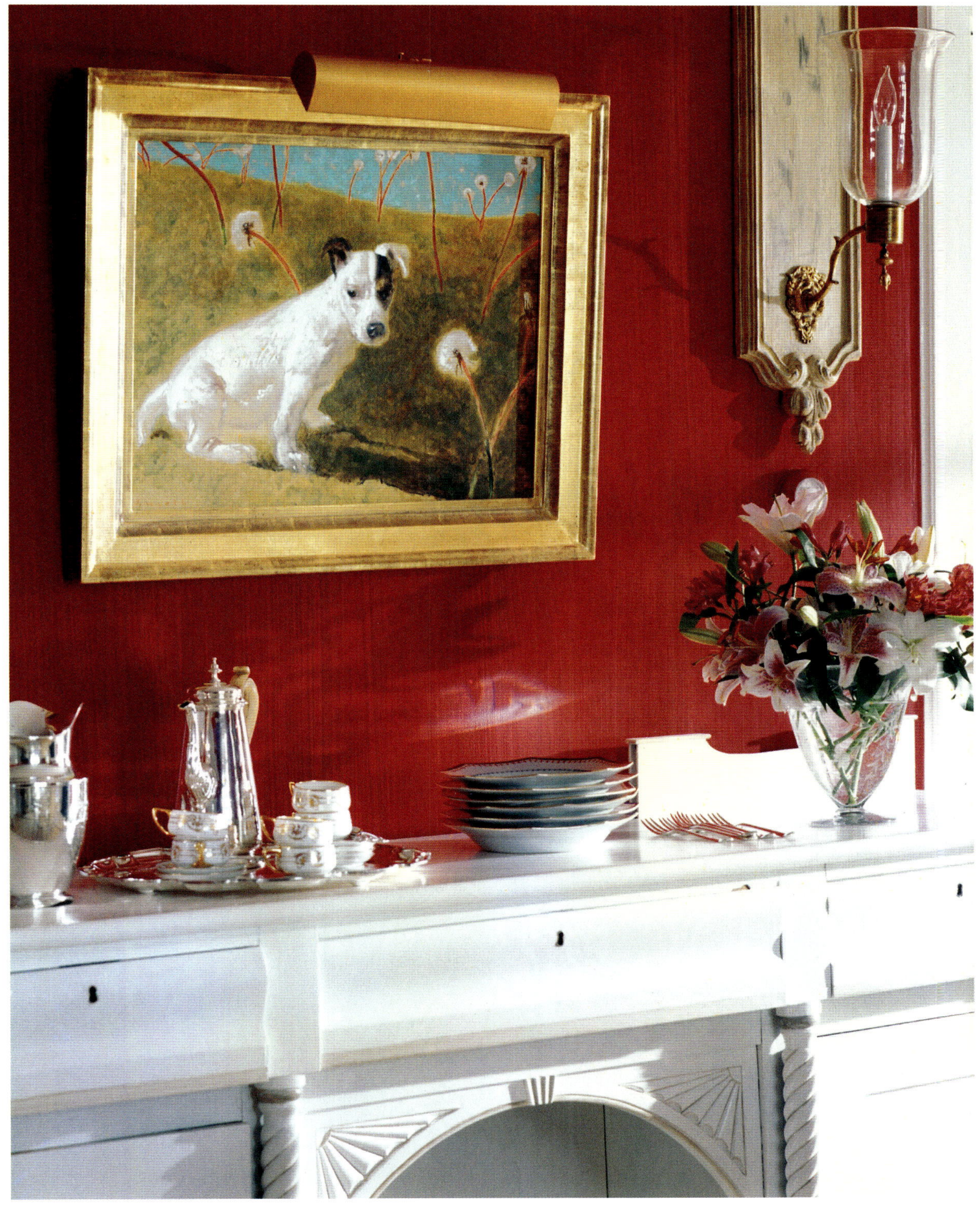

Detail from a dining room in Maine glazed in a red striae finish with shiny, bright white trim. The room feels very crisp. Furniture that had been left by the previous owners was painted white.

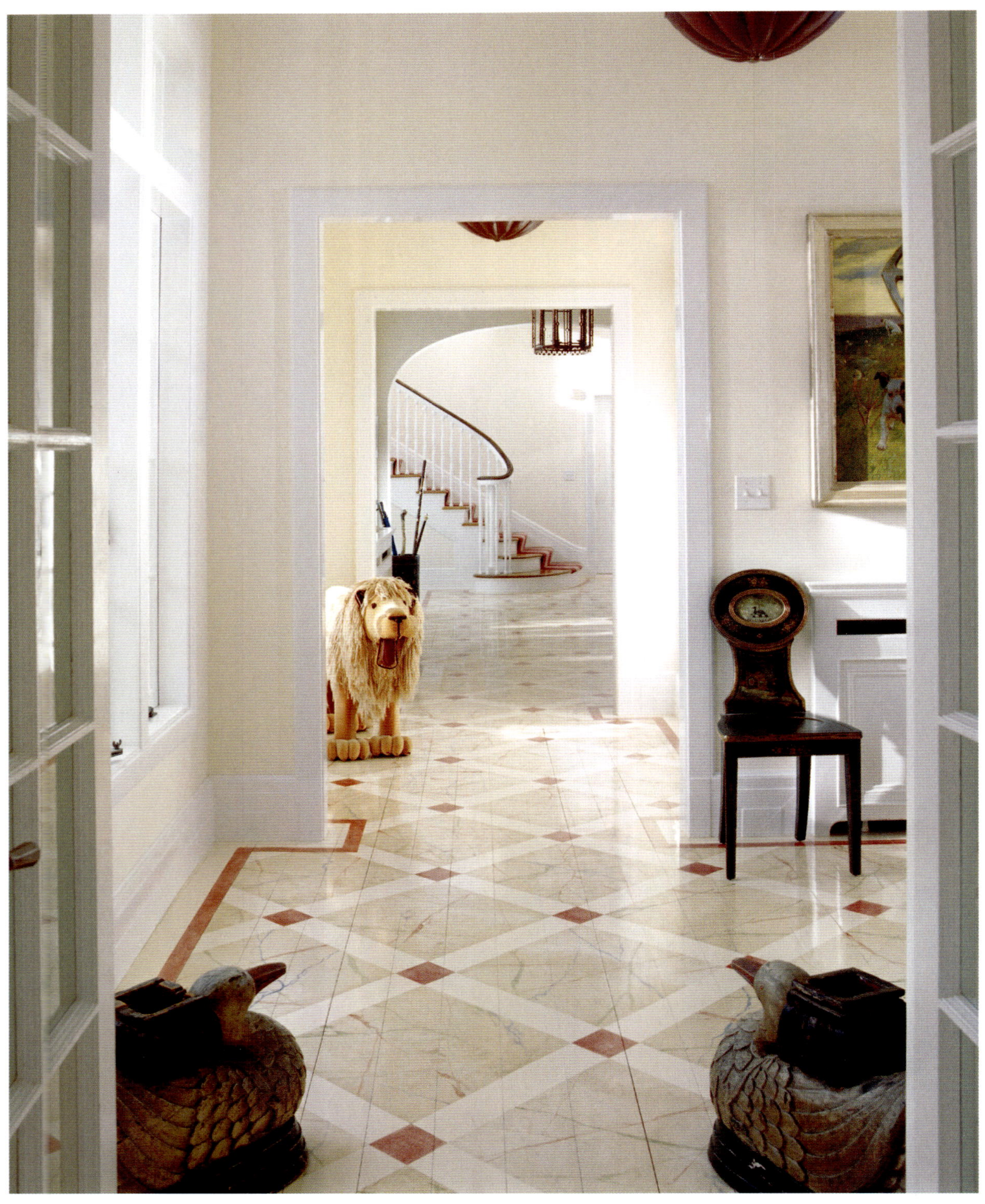

ABOVE: A painted floor by Matthew Tyrrell and Chris Butler was the solution for a hallway that passed the downstairs rooms.

NEXT PAGE: Sketches of furniture and curtain ideas by Albert Hadley.

There are many hiccups in the work of decorating—delays, dye lot differences in fabrics, chips on furniture, cracked finishes, and missing or broken pieces. Someone who knows how to move things carefully is a godsend. It is not always simple. The days of bringing big pieces up on top of an elevator car are over—insurance companies won't cover that anymore. If something can't be taken apart and fit into an elevator or if it can't make the turn in a staircase, it has to be hauled up by a crane and brought in through a window.

I recently worked on a house in Rhode Island. My clients bought a lovely, big painted antique French cabinet to go along a wall in the dining area with big windows and doors that look out at Newport Harbor. The house was recently built and there are two staircases. The cabinet does come apart into two pieces but that didn't solve the problem of getting the top part of the cabinet upstairs. Josh, a mover I have worked with for years, tried every which way to get the glass door half of the cabinet up the back stairs. Josh finally gave up on the staircase and with many moving straps all tied together, and the power of the six men who had come to help with the move, was able to bring the cabinet up and over the railing onto the upper porch from the outside and then into the house. It was a Herculean effort on Josh's part and I am eternally grateful. I only hope my client doesn't decide to move any time soon!

When people have pride in their work, when they really care and have an enthusiasm for what they do, it makes all the difference. Not many people in life truly love what they do for work. I have been blessed to work with the best, kindest, most loyal, and hardworking people who are immensely responsible. They care about what they do and have respect not only for their trade but for their customers. Maybe it all comes down to manners and respect. I was taught as a child that it was essential to be polite; I have learned to always lean on the manners that were taught to me. Anne Tiffany (Aunt Nanny to us) was the matriarch in my family. My father was very close to her, as was Rory Cameron, and she was in charge, especially when it came to manners. I remember reaching across the table as a child to get bread out of a breadbasket during a Sunday lunch. She stabbed the top of my hand with her fork—not too hard but it was terrifying and she certainly made her point. To this day, I always ask politely. My parents were always drilling in manners—telling me to open and hold doors open for others, to stand up when someone walked into a room, to say hello while being certain to look someone in the eye as I did so, and, of course, to always acknowledge someone's help by thanking them. They were less strict about other things, but, to this day, I am very grateful for knowing manners and, in turn, I have tried to instill the same values in my own children. Above all else, it matters to be kind to the people you work with. We all have to be kind and work as a team, otherwise life falls apart.

The home furnishings and antiques market is forever changing. I am always searching for new, exciting, and beautiful things. I have known many wonderful vendors in my years, some of whom have become good friends. None of what I have done could have been possible without the help of artisans and craftsmen. It's important to know the best people—exceptional cabinetmakers, furniture restorers, and artists who can make beautiful things and produce such special finishes as lacquer, shagreen, tortoise shell, and faux marble. It is so important to work with people who understand what you are trying to achieve. If something is not done right, it doesn't look right. I have been lucky enough to work with people who have done whatever was necessary to get the job done properly even if it required working nights or on weekends. We can hope and plan and have expectations about how something will happen, but it is those who help along the way that get the job done.

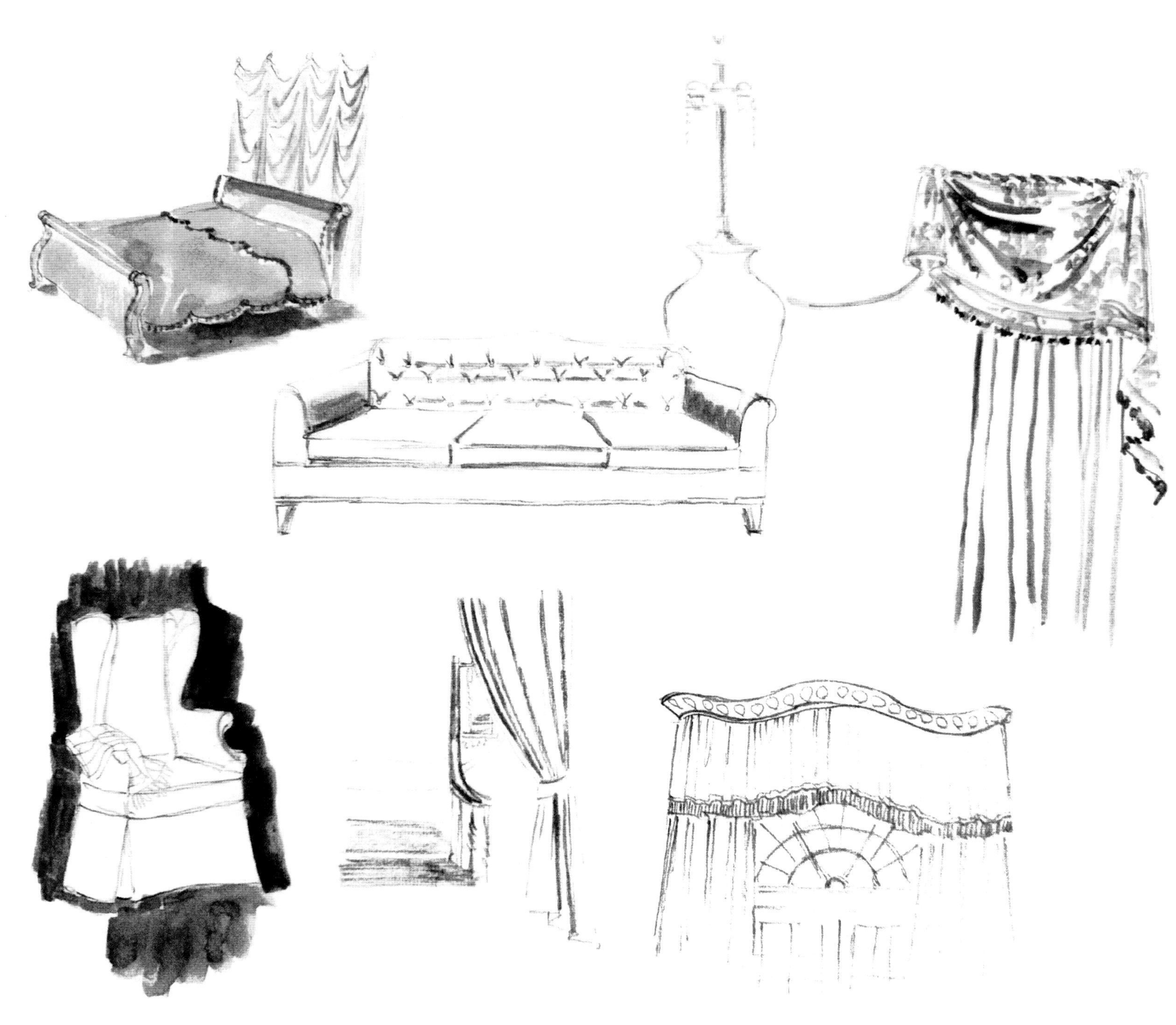

CHOOSING
COMF

ORT

"Luxury is not only expense and grandeur; luxury is also style."

—LIBBY CAMERON

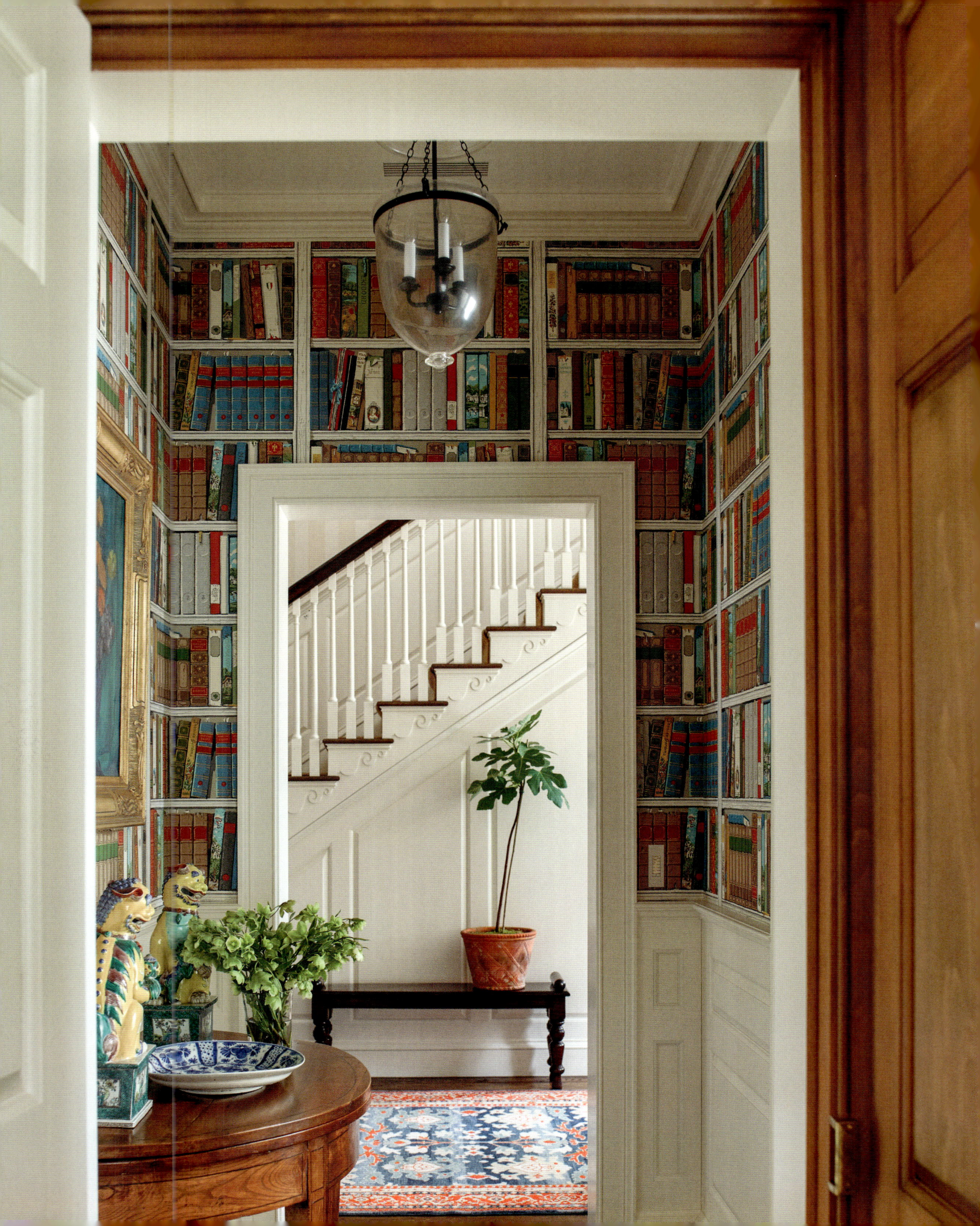

Today the world is so unsettled and full of chaos that having a safe haven is absolutely essential. It is so important to arrange our lives around comfort, well-being, and pleasure. Although we need some sort of expectation of how we want to live in our rooms, some people start with such prescriptive preconceived notions of how their house should be that it limits them in what their house can become.

My hope in decorating is to make rooms that are warm and inviting, and as usable and comfortable for just one person as for many. Houses can and should have character and personality. Being able to listen and reinterpret a client's wants, needs, and dreams is the starting point. It is much more fulfilling to work with someone who has some idea of what they like and don't like, and who knows how they want to live; it's more difficult to give a client's house personality when they don't think it through themselves. The process of decorating a house follows a certain logic, and a client needs to be open to moving things about and rearranging furniture. Furniture placement may look better on paper than it does in reality, so being open-minded is important. Rooms should look lived in and every corner should be usable. You should want to spend time in your house!

We have an illusion that life should be perfect, but life is never perfect. Some people have the idea that their house should be just so and just right, but the fact is, it doesn't have to be perfect. What works, what feels good, and what draws you in is really all that matters. Rooms are for people and should be comfortable, comforting, and cozy. It helps to instinctively have good taste and an innate sense of what a well-ordered house can be. And it goes without saying that you need to have confidence in yourself—in your choices and ultimate decisions about how to set up your environment.

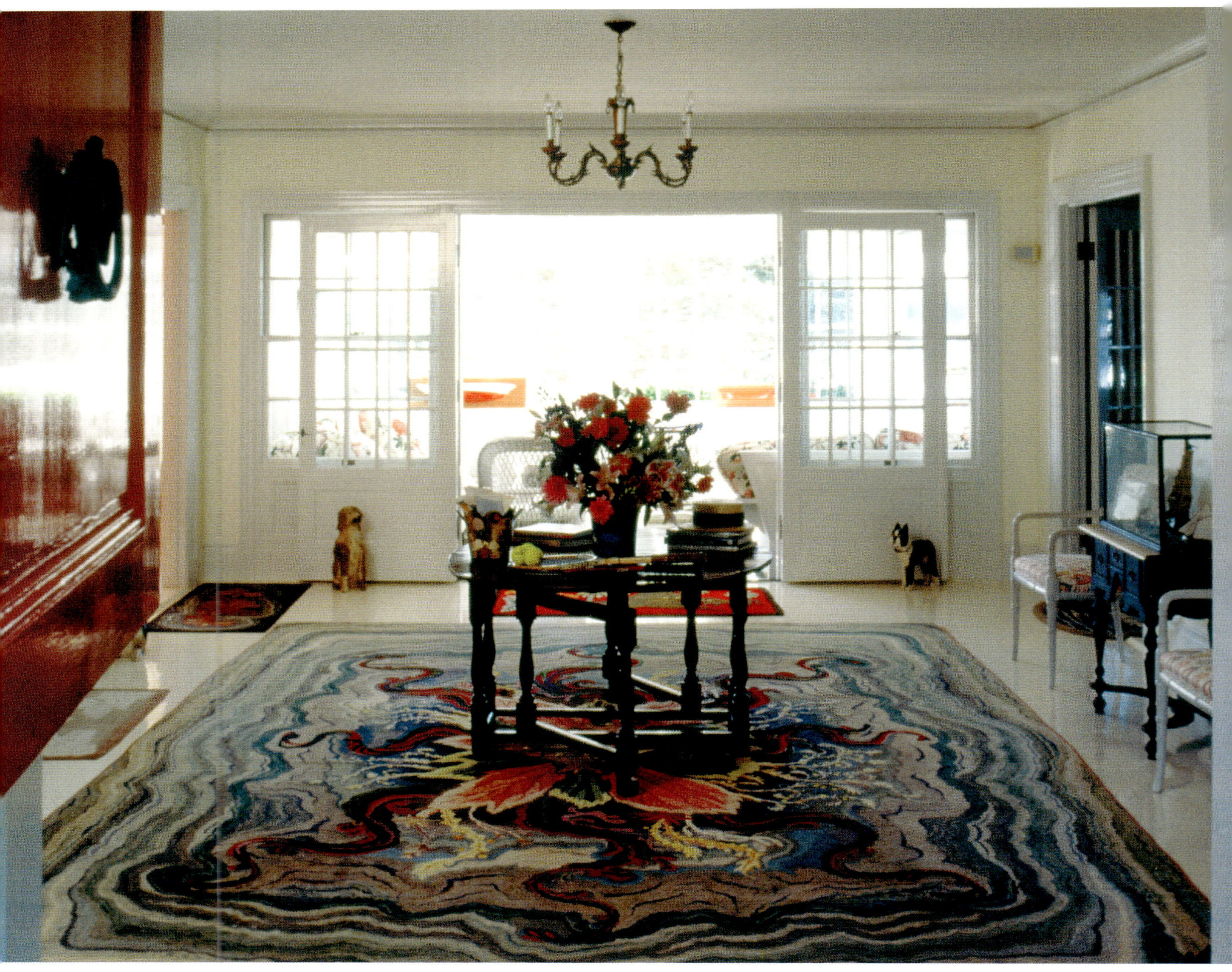

PREVIOUS PAGE: A vestibule between an entrance hall and library covered in Brunschwig & Fils "Bibliothèque" wallpaper.

ABOVE: A square entrance hall in a house in Maine. This wonderful antique hooked rug showing waves, water, and coral was just right for this spot.

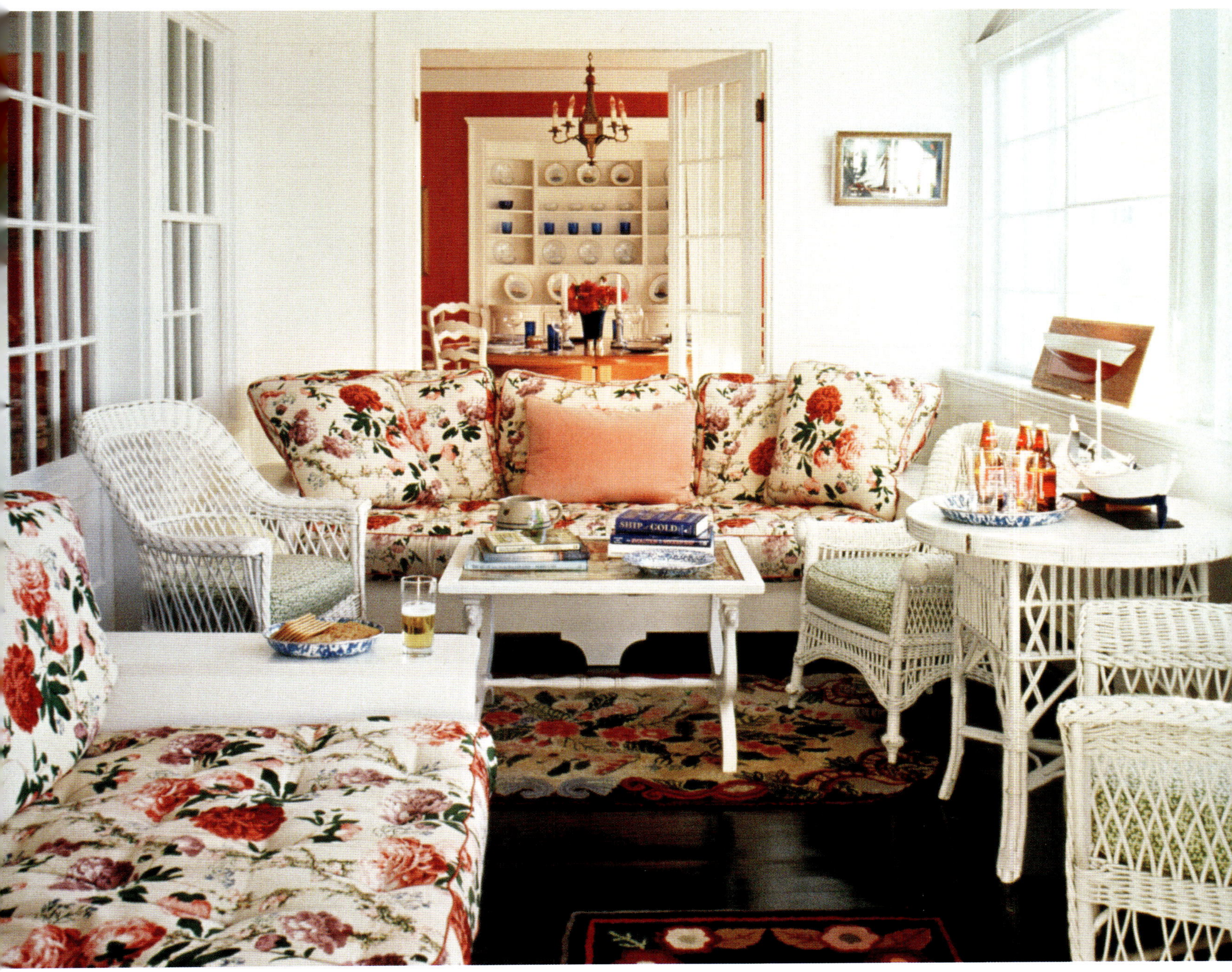

A porch in Maine has two Aiken sofas that are deep and wonderful for naps.

Houses should have their own character and a personality that represents whoever lives there. In my opinion, rooms that are filled with interesting objects and wonderful colors are the best rooms. It takes time to properly furnish and complete a house; it is not that simple for a multitude of reasons. Unforeseen snags in decorating cause delays, and it simply takes time to find the right things to fill a house. People evolve during the process and change their minds. To me, it seems like such a mistake to buy something just to fill an empty spot—you should buy what you love. I love rescuing things from people's attics and basements and always want to leave room for filling in here and there, to add my client's smaller and favorite things. You can always change or rework something if needed or replace an object or piece of furniture with something better later on. People should be surrounded by the things that make them feel happy and comfortable.

As a decorator, getting to know and really understand who you are working with is the biggest part of the whole process. To work well with someone you need an understanding of what matters most to them. It's essential to be attuned to your clients—getting to really know them, understand what they want, and make them feel safe with you. Diplomacy is an art; you have to be tactful while simultaneously having the courage to say what you think. Ultimately, decorators should remember that your clients will be living there, not you!

I invited Albert Hadley and Zoran Ladicorbic over for dinner one night. Zoran is a clothing designer who made beautiful clothing out of the finest materials—silk, satin, chiffon, linen, and cashmere—all very minimal and without buttons or zippers. All of his clothing was made in solid colors and in a quite restricted palette. I knew him best when he lived on Sullivan Street in the Village, in a space where absolutely everything was painted white—the floors, walls, and ceiling. It was an amazing studio

Almost anything made of tole appeals to me. These sconces were given to me years ago and are wonderful just as they are and especially when the candles are lit.

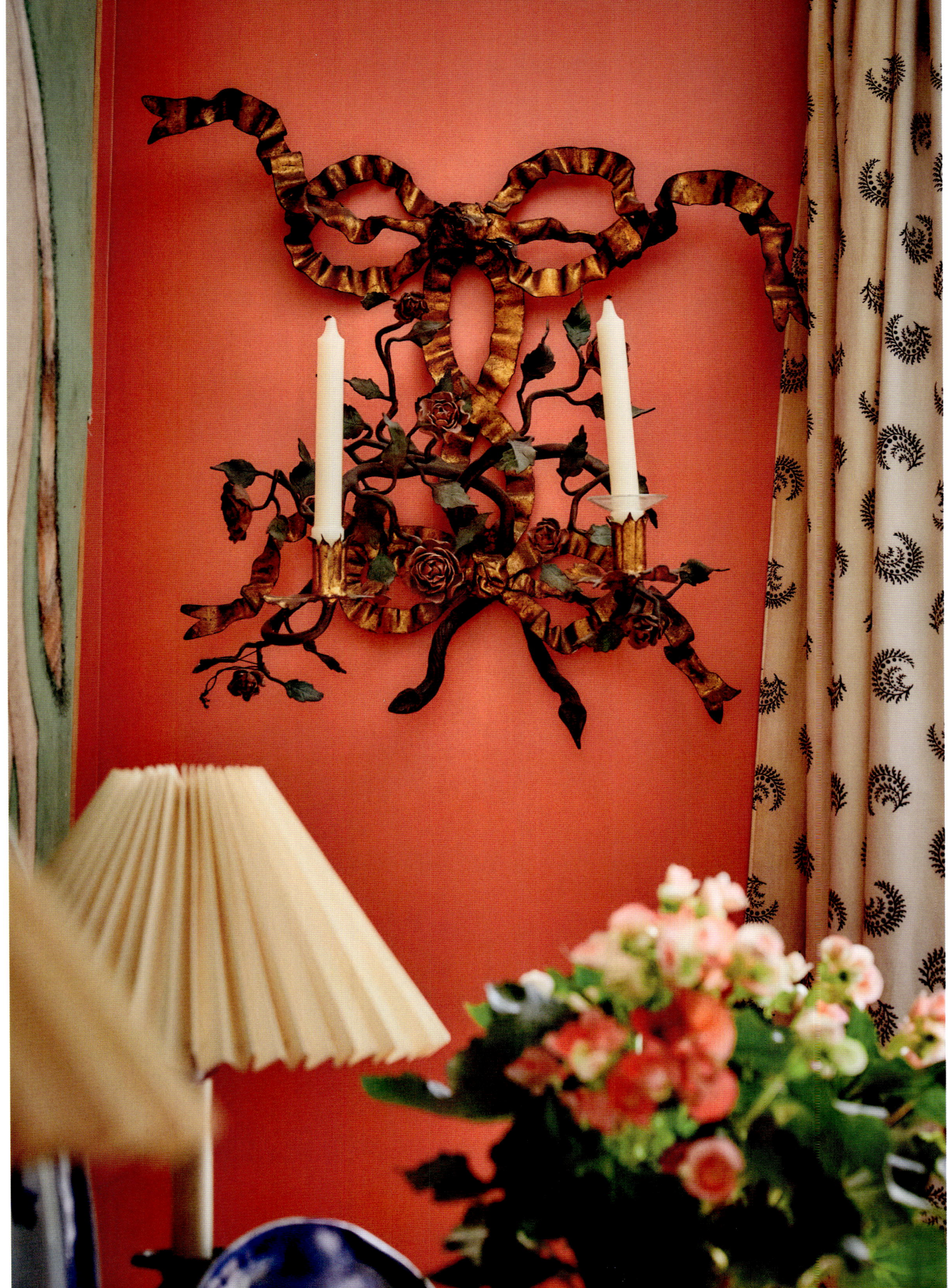

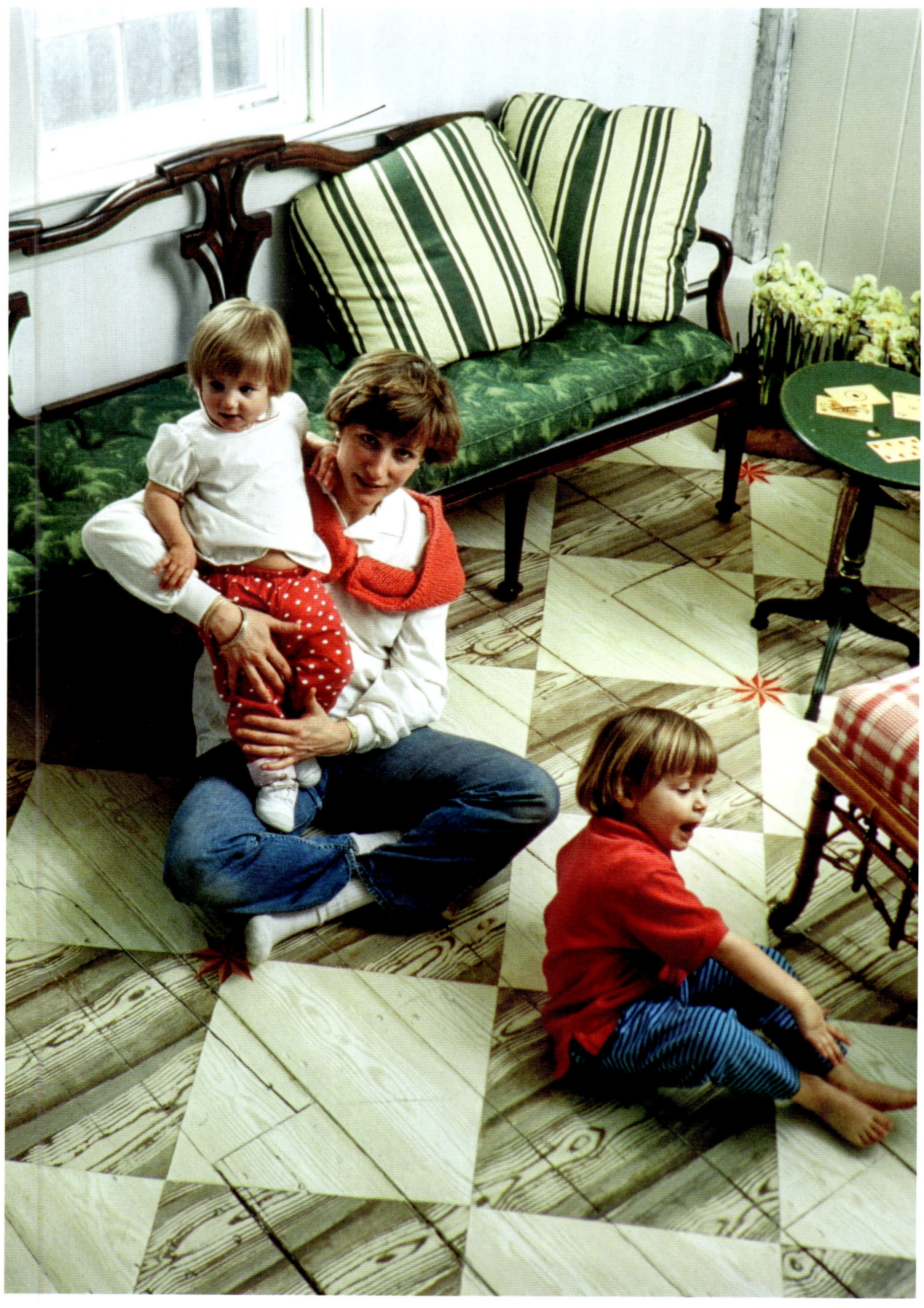

to visit, and Zoran is such a character. Albert had commented on what I was wearing one day and I knew that they would get on like a house on fire, so I invited them to our loft on Broome Street for dinner. What we ate was of no importance to either of them—they both were uninterested in food for the most part. Albert only drank gin and Zoran only drinks vodka so I had plenty of both. A few drinks in, we were talking about clean, uncluttered spaces. I must have said that I didn't like too much clutter, yet as I looked around the loft I noticed that every surface had something on it, and we all started to laugh. There were plants and books and boxes and sculptures, just too much of everything everywhere—too many objects—too much of nothing and of everything. I don't remember how much either of them had had to drink by that time, but both of them were very animated and jolly, and the night was getting on. Zoran asked me if I had any boxes or paper bags, and then like Rasputin with his wicked, peevish smile, he proceeded to clear off virtually every tabletop and shelf in the loft. Albert and I joined in right behind him. Within minutes the loft was cleared and much more minimal. I kept it that way for a time and it did feel much better but I have regressed since then and have collections of things everywhere.

When thinking about a welcoming space, it is important to consider the entrance hall or foyer because it introduces you and sets the tone for a house. Usually, there is less space for furniture in halls or foyers as they are passageways and not actual "rooms." But just because there isn't a proper seating area doesn't mean that the space should be less welcoming or friendly. A foyer or entrance hall sets the tone for the entire house and should have allure and vitality. It's good to have a place to set your gloves, bags, keys, or a dog leash, and it's important to have a mirror. A mirror will bring in light and open up a space. You can add texture or make a statement with wallpaper. Decorative floors will create interest. I happen to love painted floors of almost any sort—plain colors, stenciled, or painted patterned. They are often a good solution for meandering hallways when it is a challenge to find a rug that works. If more halls were considered to be living spaces it would add more warmth and personality to homes.

My children Charlotte and Flora were with me the day of this photo shoot in Waccabuc for an article on painted floors for *House Beautiful*.

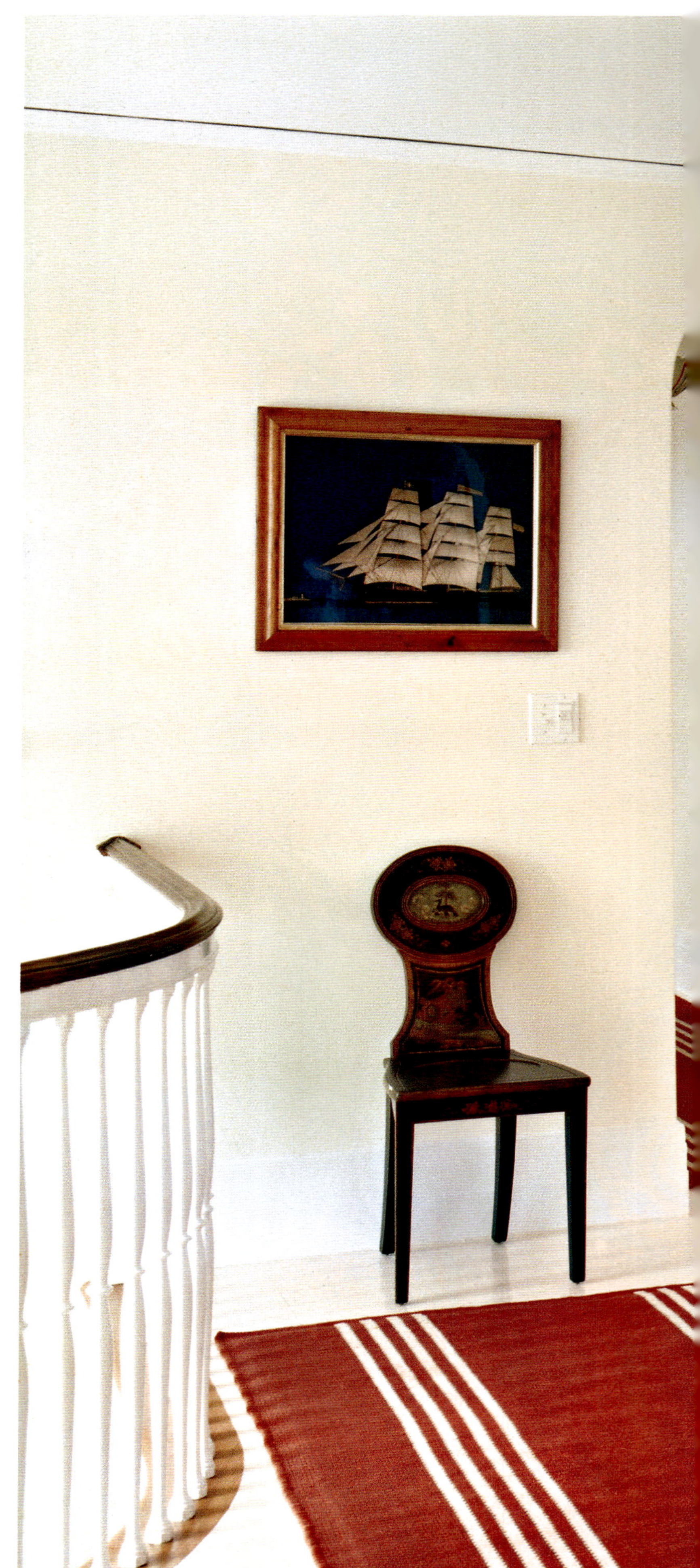

The second-floor landing in a house in Maine with "Reading Stripe" rugs from Woodard Weave. The built-in bookcase has a wonderful boat model on it; the house still has a good deal of maritime art.

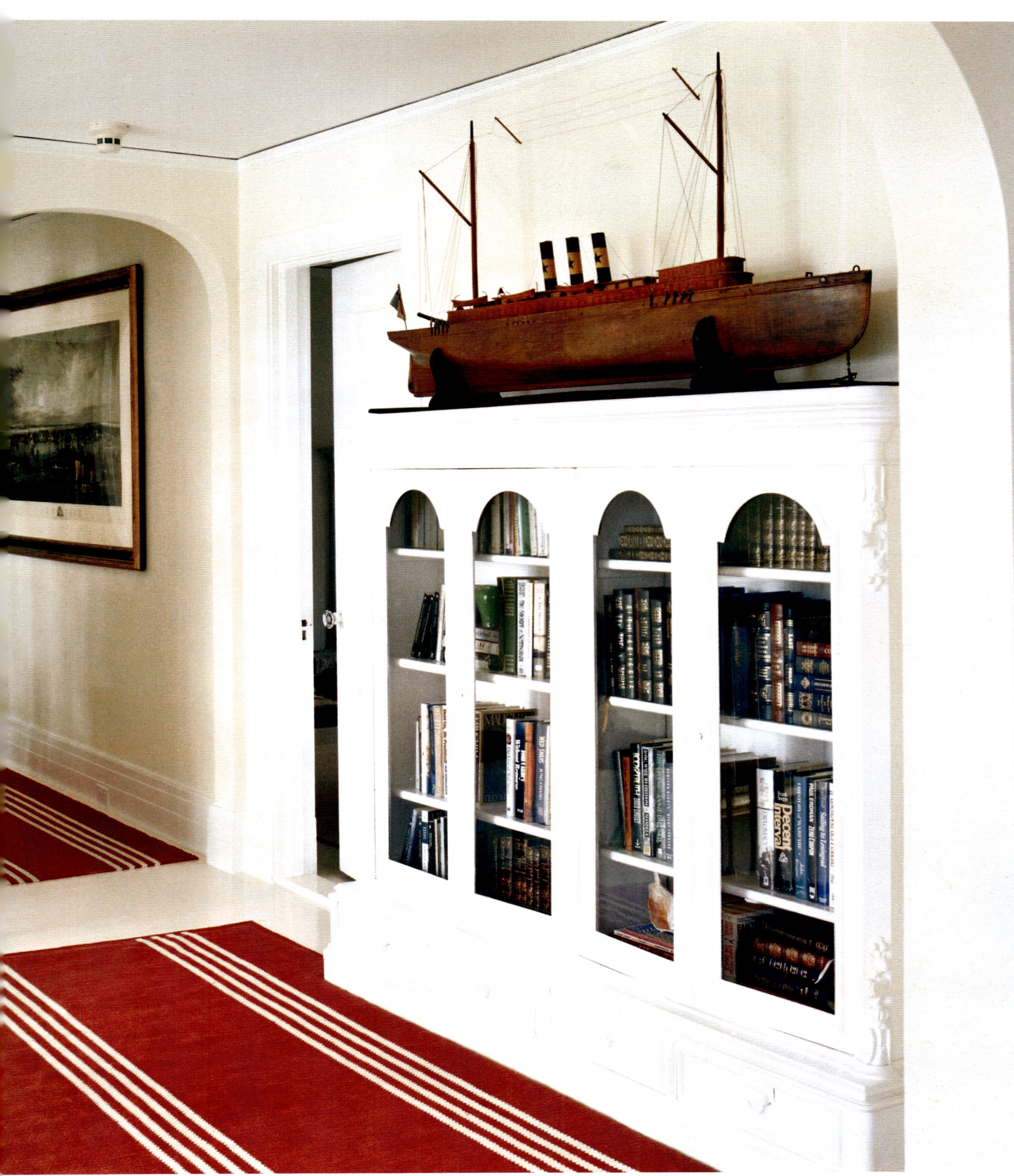
Decent Interval
PAUL ERDMAN

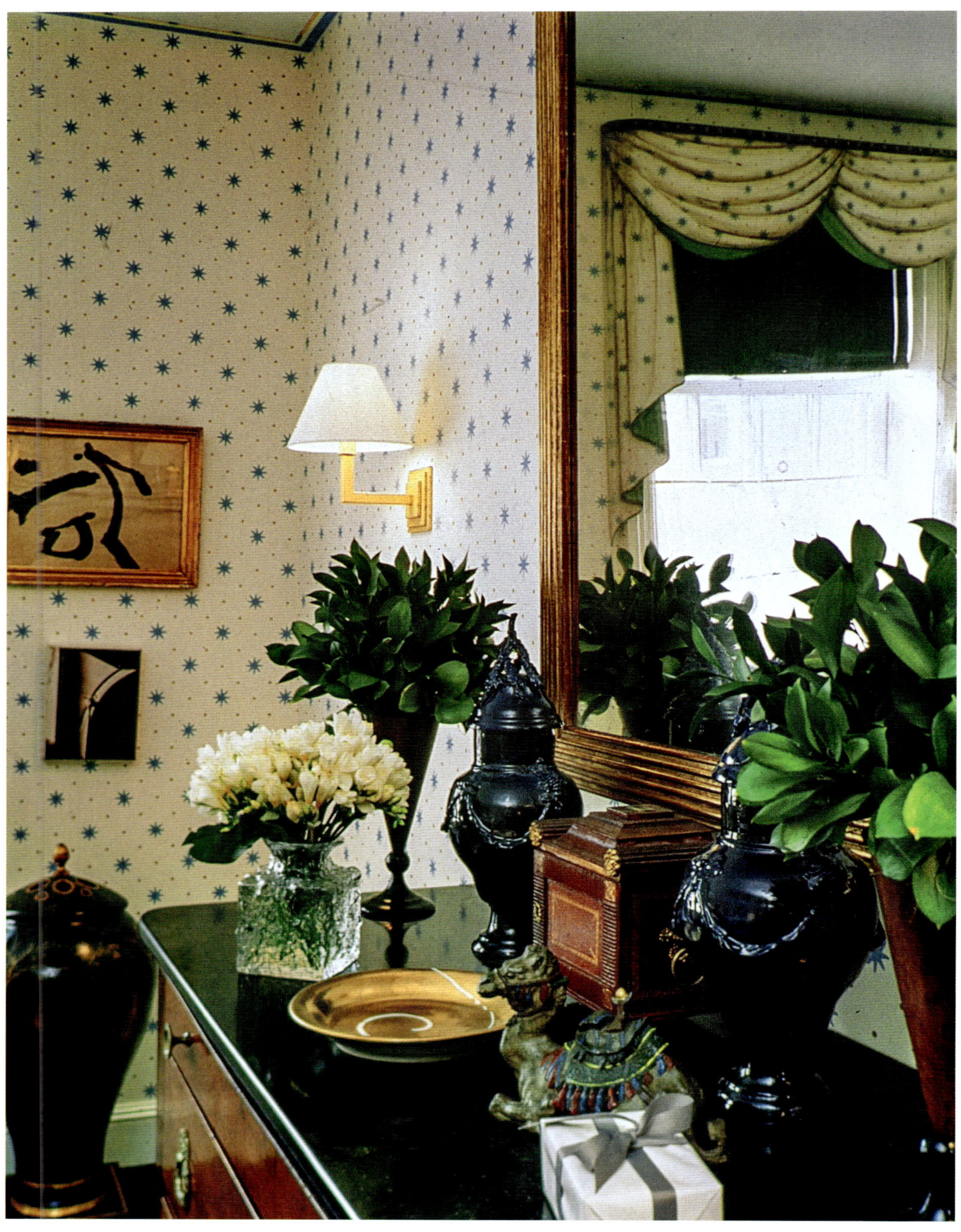

This room at Kips Bay incorporates the "Sue Ellen" wallpaper from Parish-Hadley. Chuck Fischer painted the tin valances, which were made by an auto body shop to get the curve on the ends.

Living rooms are so often filled with the very best furniture and objects that a person has, but sometimes that can make the room feel less friendly. As a child, my mother did not encourage us to use the living room, but instead we spent time in a glassed-in garden room or in the library. Neither of these rooms was wildly comfortable but they were pretty. There is a big difference between a room being arranged for comfort versus a room that is only to be seen and not lived in. I always go for comfort.

If you have something and went to the cost and trouble of bringing it home, then you should use it or take it away. Anything you are afraid to use in your home is a mistake. I find that fragile furniture and fabrics that pull or stain easily make everyone uncomfortable. Inviting rooms are the best, with multiple seating areas; small groupings with easily movable chairs make for a better room along with seating groups that talk to each other. At least two very comfortable chairs are a must. Having tables at the same height so the lamps are at the same height balances out a room. What it really all boils down to is how you live. A room should be able to be used by just one person or by many.

Dining rooms can be quieter rooms with good, soft lighting, and should never be too hot. A bright color doesn't preclude quiet or a sense of tranquility, and can even add warmth to a space. Flowers add so much and are so beautiful but too many flowers in any space can be a mistake and this is especially true in a dining room. If you can't see the person sitting across from you the flowers are too tall, and if they are too fragrant, it can be distracting when you are eating. Setting a table is full of endless possibilities, and there aren't any rules about how to combine and use what you love—so go for it! It's always fun to see what people use as centerpieces on dining tables.

If you are faced with space constraints, a dining room and library can be quite wonderful combined together as one room. Being surrounded by books is my idea of heaven, and books bring in color and texture, and create a more relaxed, cozy atmosphere. Your eye needs something to see and feed on, and books will do just that. I like to fill my bookshelves with pictures and objects in addition to books, and to have some books lying on their side looking like they are almost holding up the other books.

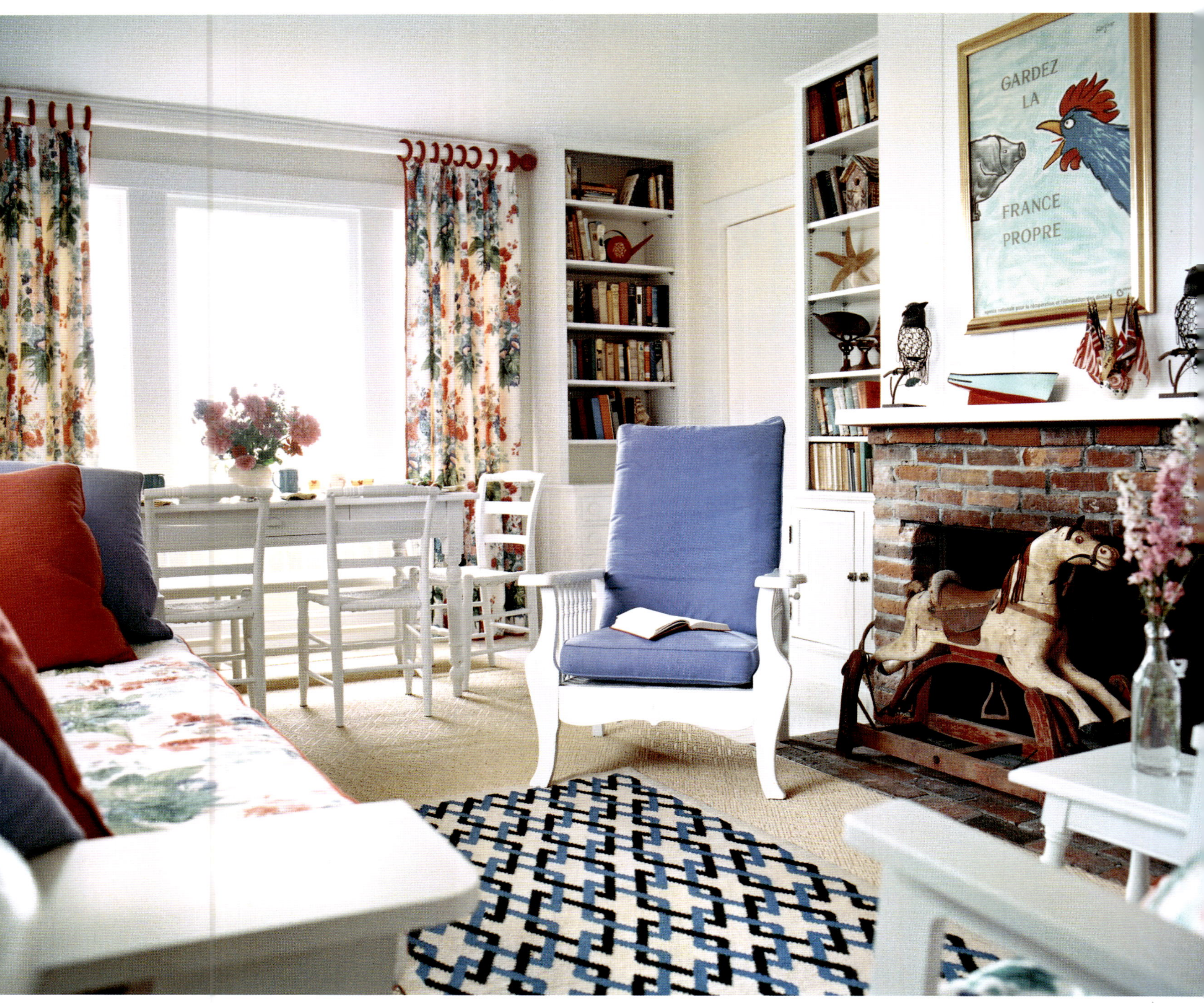

The living room in this cottage on an island in Maine is light-filled and welcoming.

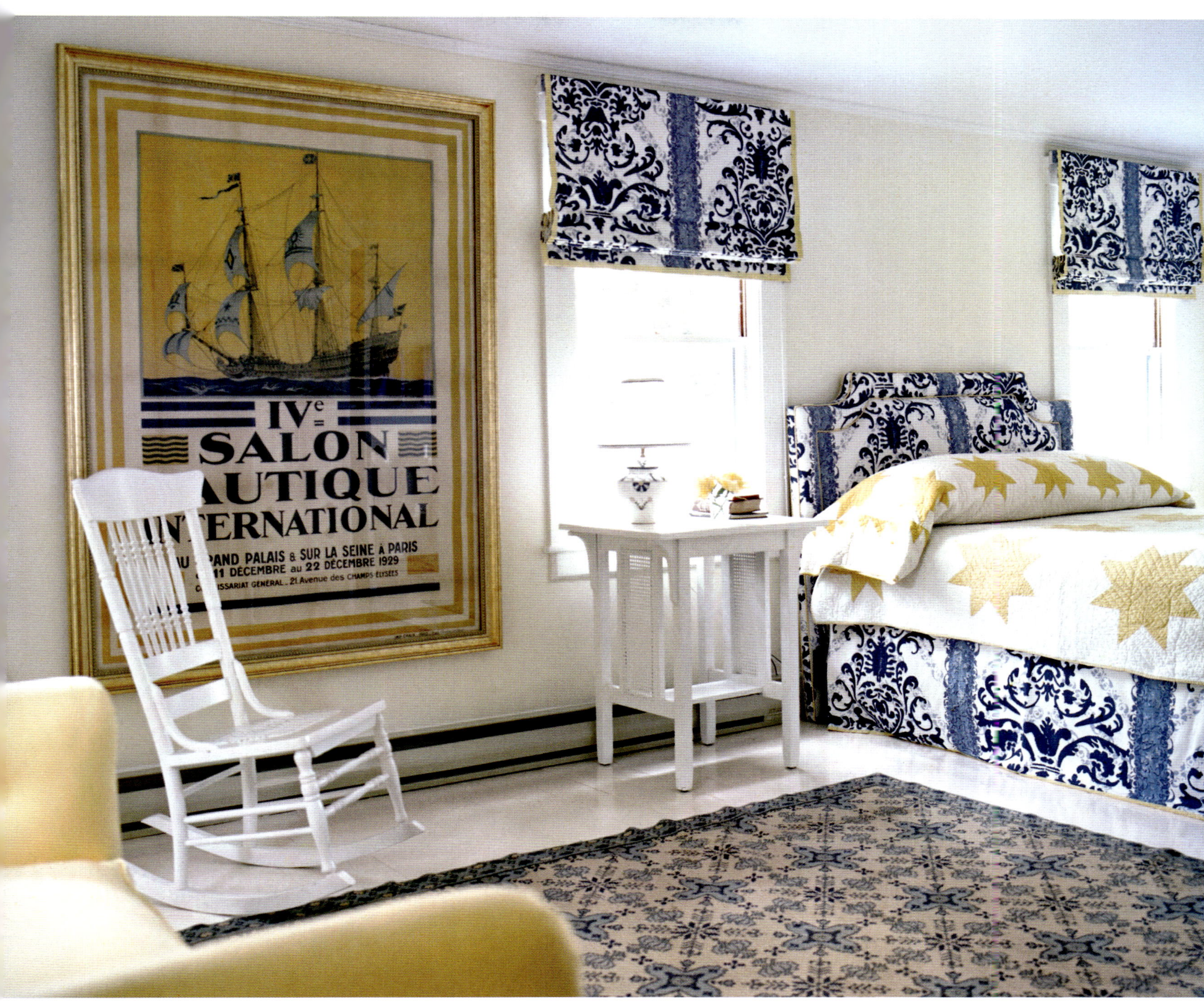

A blue-and-white guest room in Maine includes a Portuguese needlepoint rug and yellow accents in the art and furnishings.

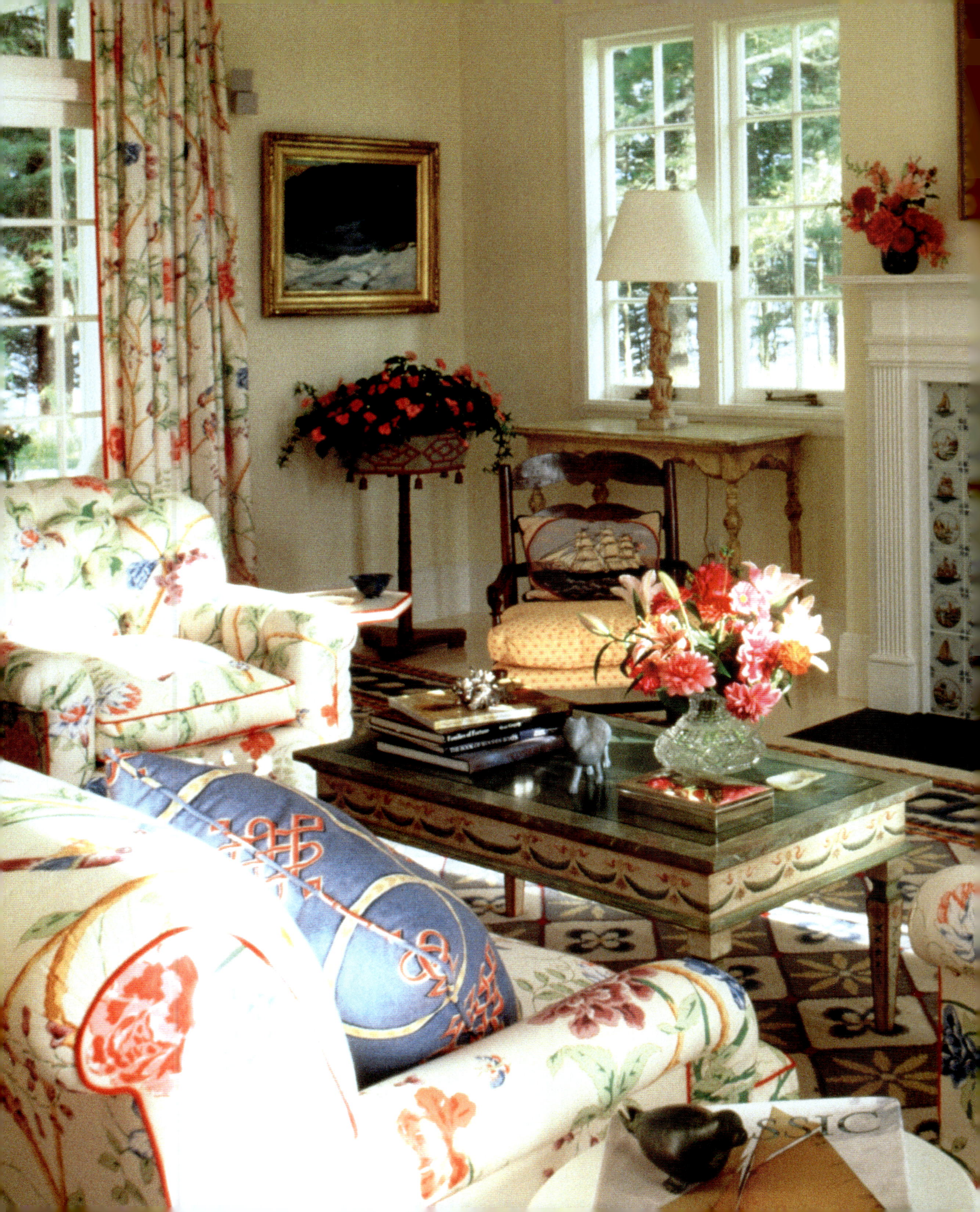

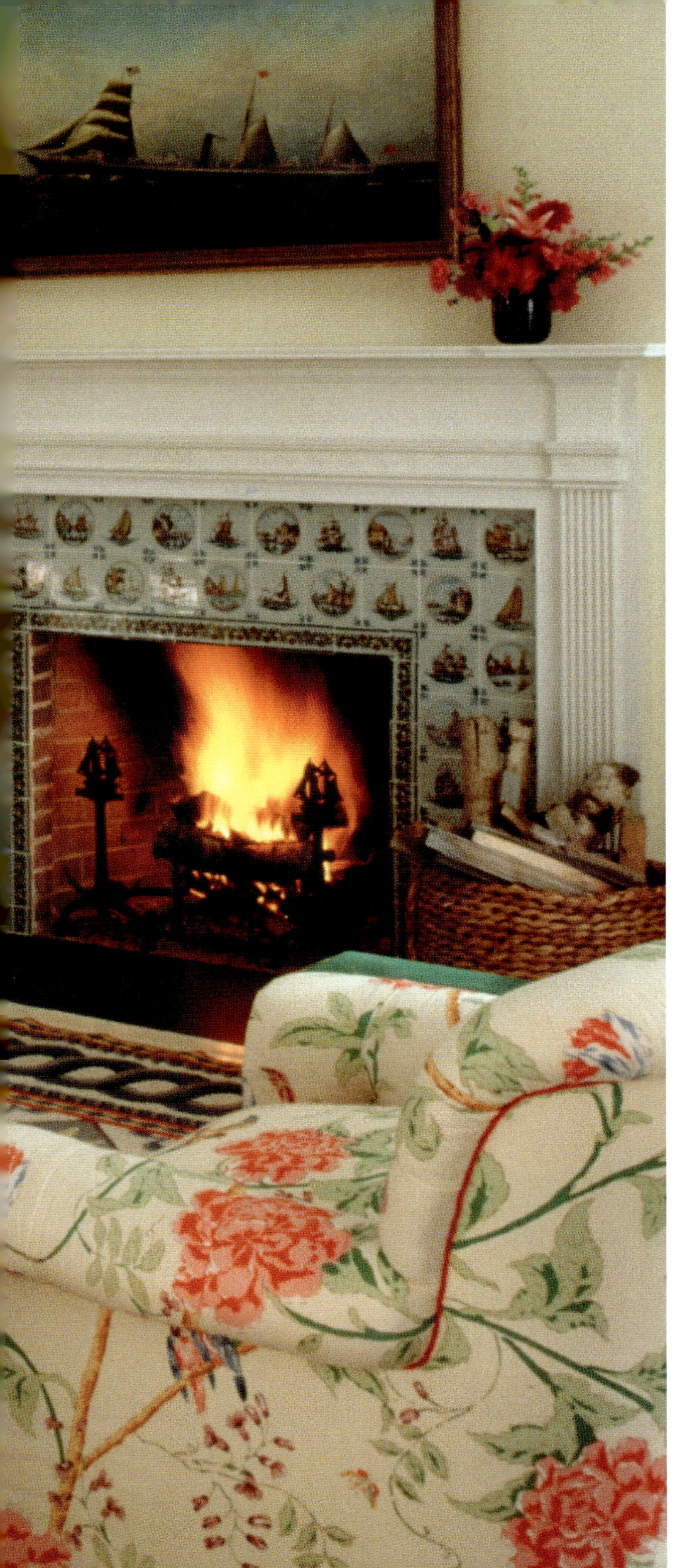

This living room in Maine has pairs of French doors running along both sides of the room. The delft tile on the firebox surround features sailboats and came from Country Floors.

There are all sorts of things on my bookshelves; miniature pictures and prints are hung on the frames of the bookcases, and papier-mâché, tole, bronze, and porcelain animals peek out between the books. These are all things that I have collected or that have been given to me over the years. My books are vaguely arranged by subject but are not in alphabetical order nor placed by color. There is a whimsy to my bookcases. The whole world is full of pattern on pattern, and bookcases can create another wonderful layer of interest.

Bedrooms are in another category altogether because, although they are another living space and an equally important one, a bedroom is a private space. Personal space should be romantic as well as just comfortable. Our bedrooms are a place to focus on our comfort and pleasure in every detail. As the most personal space in a home, a bedroom should be arranged to take care of us, to be a room in which you can indulge yourself. Bedrooms have to be a place you can retreat to and be in peace. This doesn't mean the room has to be Zen. I love a fun bed, with a great quilt in a pattern that is cheerful and warm. Wallpaper can also be happy and fun and add interest.

There is not one set or right way to use what you have, and it's helpful to have the flexibility to imagine different uses for things. Actually using rooms will take you there. Sleeping in your guest room, for example, will tell you what is missing or needed in that room, and what would make it better and more comfortable. A guest room should feel like a permanently occupied and loved room, with thought given to where you put your things. However, if the night tables are too filled with your own things, then the guests won't have a place to put their things. There is nothing better than staying with someone who has left wonderful magazines to read and look at. I recently stayed with friends on their farm and ended up staying up far too late reading the English magazines that they had left in the room. They also had placed the most beautiful flowers everywhere—using flowers well in a home can make a room come alive.

Part of being comfortable is having fun things to look at. Interesting objects and whimsy should catch your eye, but not be too heavy handed. An overly decorated room

In this sleepover room, there is just enough space for twin beds to tuck into the dormers. The beams have been whitewashed, and the walls are covered in Michael Smith's "Indian Flower" wallpaper.

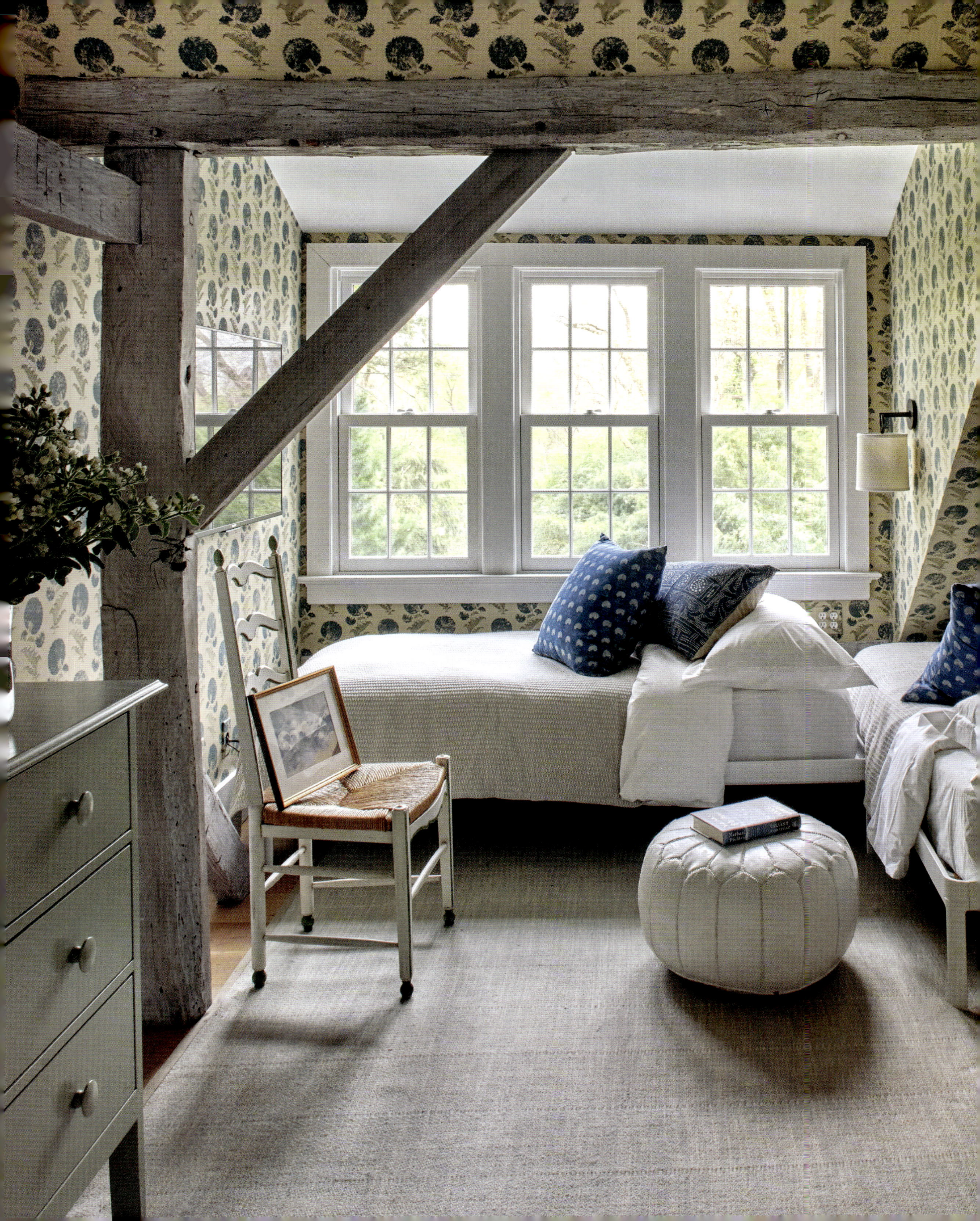

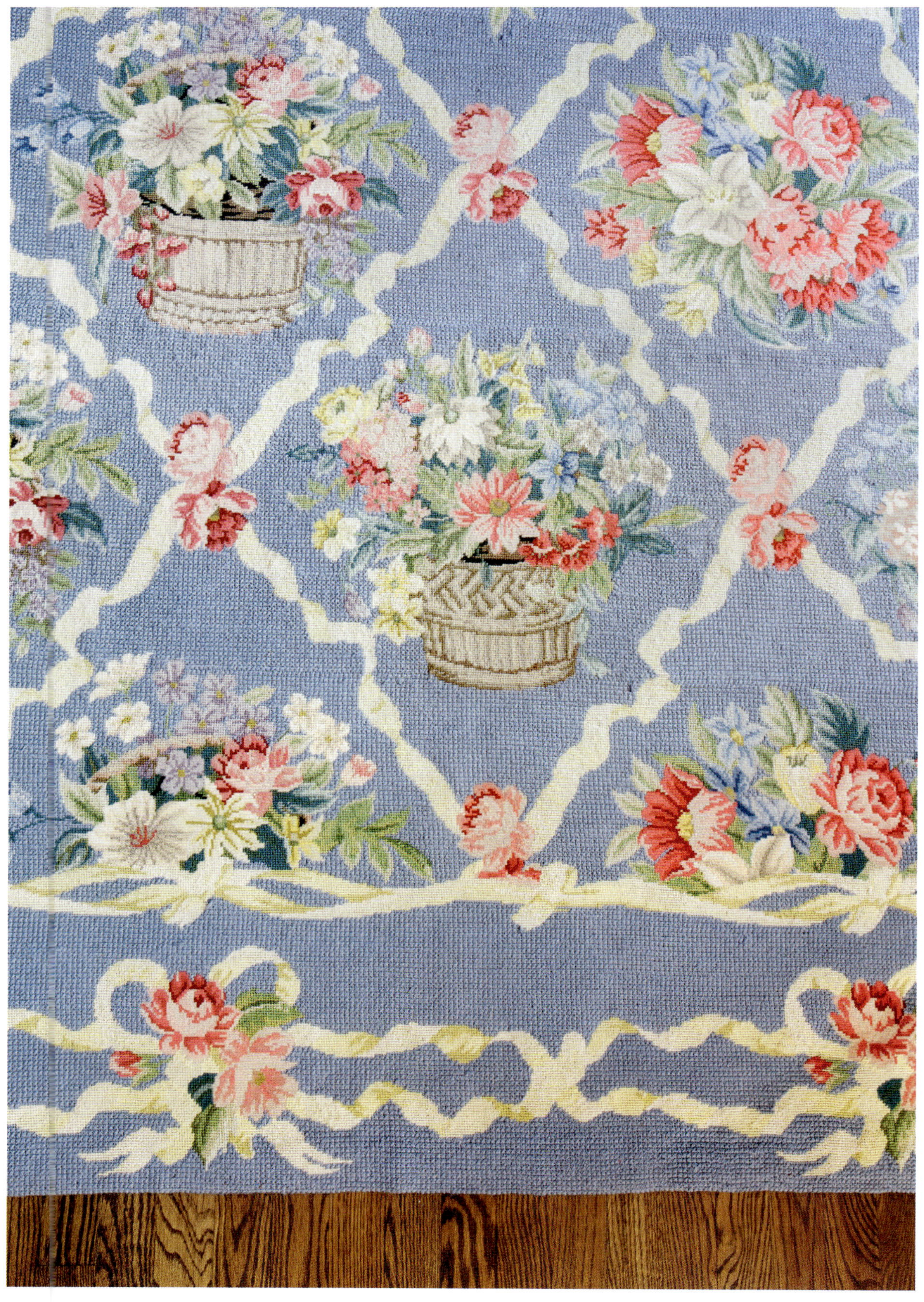

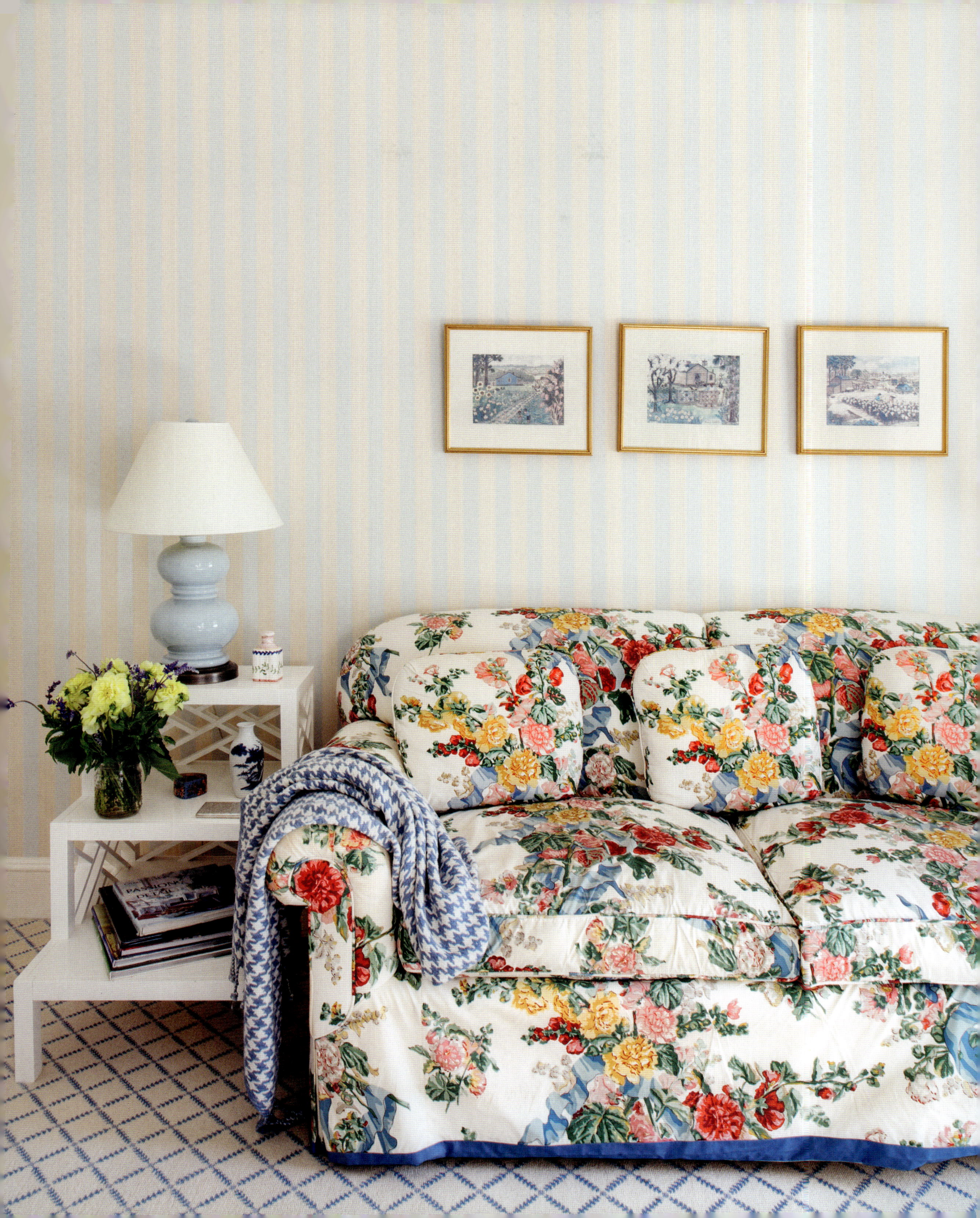

can sometimes be just too much, exhausting rather than relaxing. Empty spaces are just as important as spaces that are filled, and there needs to be balance within a room. Filling and decorating a house is like a puzzle but eventually you will find all of what is needed. It takes time to create a house that is filled with character and soul. Stay with what you love, have rooms that you can live in, and you will be on your way.

For some people, it is better to focus on only a few rooms at a time and to buy what you can afford and enjoy it. Furniture moves easily. I had a client who moved from a smaller house to a larger one. We used virtually every stick of furniture that they had but still needed more to fill the new house. The first floor was done just right—rugs made and laid, light fixtures placed and installed, curtains at every window, and furniture arranged. The children's bedrooms were carefully planned out and the guest room had everything a visitor could possibly need. Their bedroom had some holes in it and needed more furniture, but by then they were tired of writing checks. We needed to search for the few remaining things for their bedroom in the most economical way possible.

The primary bedroom was a large room. The sofa from the old house's living room found a spot against one wall across from a bureau, and we had an armoire made for the television across from the foot of the bed. But we still needed end tables beside the sofa, two lamps, a coffee table, and ideally, some small pull-up chairs. It was fun looking and finding things without a preconceived notion of what it "had to be." We found things that would work and would feel right in the room that were readily available. The end tables beside the sofa came from Pottery Barn and are still stylish. We found lamps that are a great color and a good size to balance out that side of the room. Through scouring the online sources and visiting some lesser-known shops, we found some great things.

Arranging a room for practicality and how it is used matters just as much as how a room looks and feels. In fact, by arranging a room in this way you can achieve the right look and feel. By practicality, I mean things like a good reading light and comfortable furniture. I am drawn to versatile furniture—simple, elegant furniture—that seems singular in its purpose but affords you many options. There are so many pretty

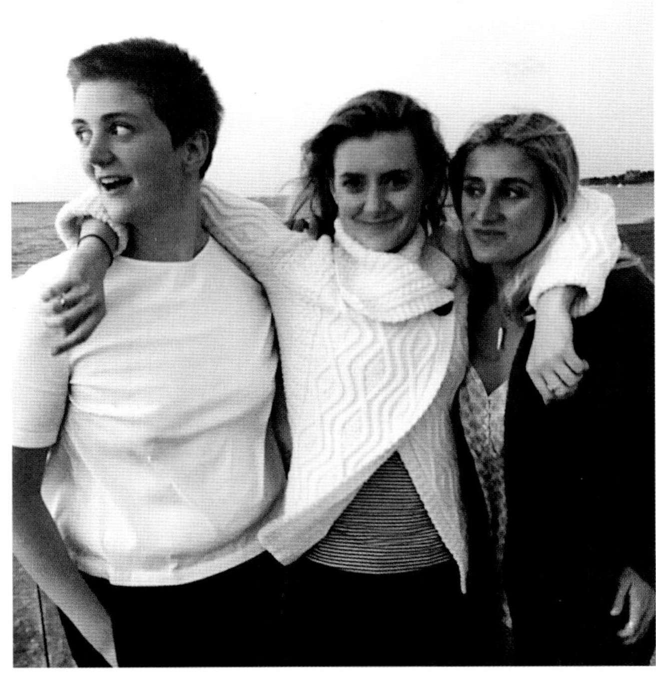

PREVIOUS PAGE, LEFT: A detail of a needlepoint rug with baskets of flowers made by STARK for a client in Connecticut.

PREVIOUS PAGE, RIGHT: This bedroom was big enough to have a sofa against one wall.

ABOVE: My children Bean, Flora, and Charlotte at Pimny's Point.

tables out there that can work in many capacities. One can learn to make a room functional as well as beautiful and have it be filled with energy. Incorporate color, interesting objects, and art. One of my favorite things I own is a tiny seal paperweight I found at an auction. It does not have any particular value but it simply appeals to me. Adding things with sentimental value to a home will make it your own. If you see something that appeals to you—get it. Houses that lacking gaiety, comfort, or charm feel neglected.

Decorating can be life enhancing, and I like to wake up and feel inspired by something in the room, be it a color or an object or the memory of where it came from, even if it's something that is flavored by a wicked wit or a degree of jovial irreverence. It's all about the art of living and the art of home. A stylish home is highly functional and reflective of your life, your budget, and your way of living. Luxury is not only expense and grandeur; luxury is also style, and style is what makes you happy. Comfort is what makes us feel taken care of and creates a loved house that is well lived in.

When my children were grown and had left, there was a big hole in my life. The crazy negativity of sparring politicians, the wars, and the injustices in this world made me think beyond just the pleasure and protection my own house can give. One way I have filled that hole is with animals. I have always had many dogs and each one is wonderful, loving, and loyal a different way. There have been nineteen dogs in my life. Sixteen of them have been Labrador retrievers and there have been many litters of puppies. With their soulful, pleading eyes, my dogs have shepherded me through childhood, adolescence, and into adulthood. They are my best companions and give me hope and support through the hardest times—giving their unconditional and faithful love. They have been by my side for every pivotal moment in my life. If you say something out loud to a dog, they do not judge you. Dogs don't chase illusionary goals or worry about what will happen tomorrow: they live in the moment. Their lives are short but they live it with so much gusto and they enjoy the simplest things in life and almost every moment of each day. It's so heartbreaking to lose a dog. When a person you love is dying, you can tell them how much you love them and hopefully they can both hear and understand you. You can remember the happy, wonderful moments you have had together and the accumulation of memories you have shared. A dog's death is so different—there isn't any sort of conversation, just a level of grief that cannot be put into words. Maybe the reason I love animals so much is because the only time they have broken my heart is when theirs have stopped beating. It is just as sad and equally devastating each time I lose one of my animals. After I settle when they are gone, I realize how grateful I am for having had them in my life and for all that they taught me. The miracle of animals is that they love us unconditionally and more than they love themselves. We think we are caring for them but in fact they are looking after us.

George was the most beautiful creature and had a side to him that many of my other dogs haven't. He was the sweetest, most loyal, and affectionate boy. I decided to breed him and keep his line going so I got him a wife, Fig. She is still with me and her face has turned white over the years. I like to think that my kisses have rubbed off all of the color. I have had the joy of her litters with George as well as litters from

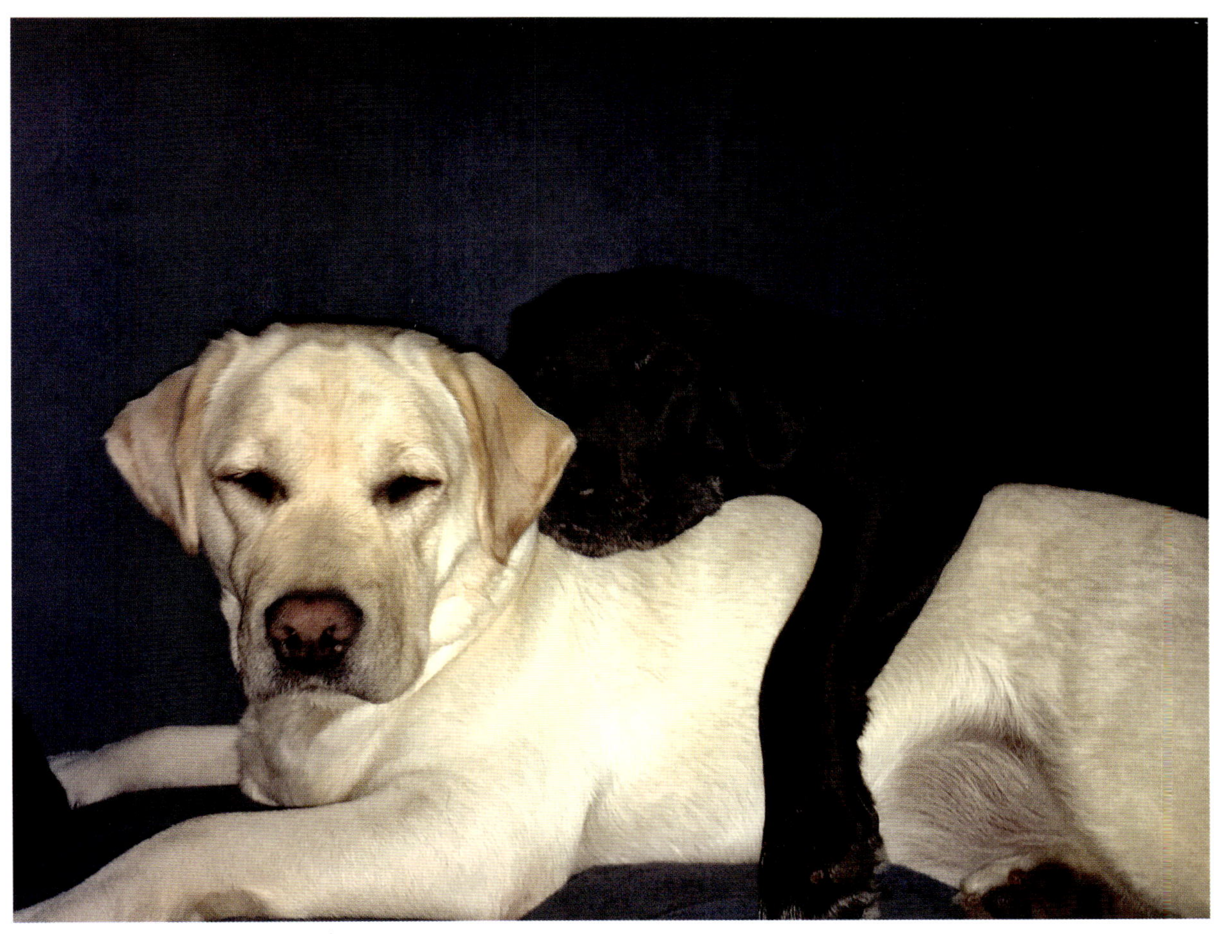

George, who has his arm around Fig in this photo, is the reason I started breeding Labradors.

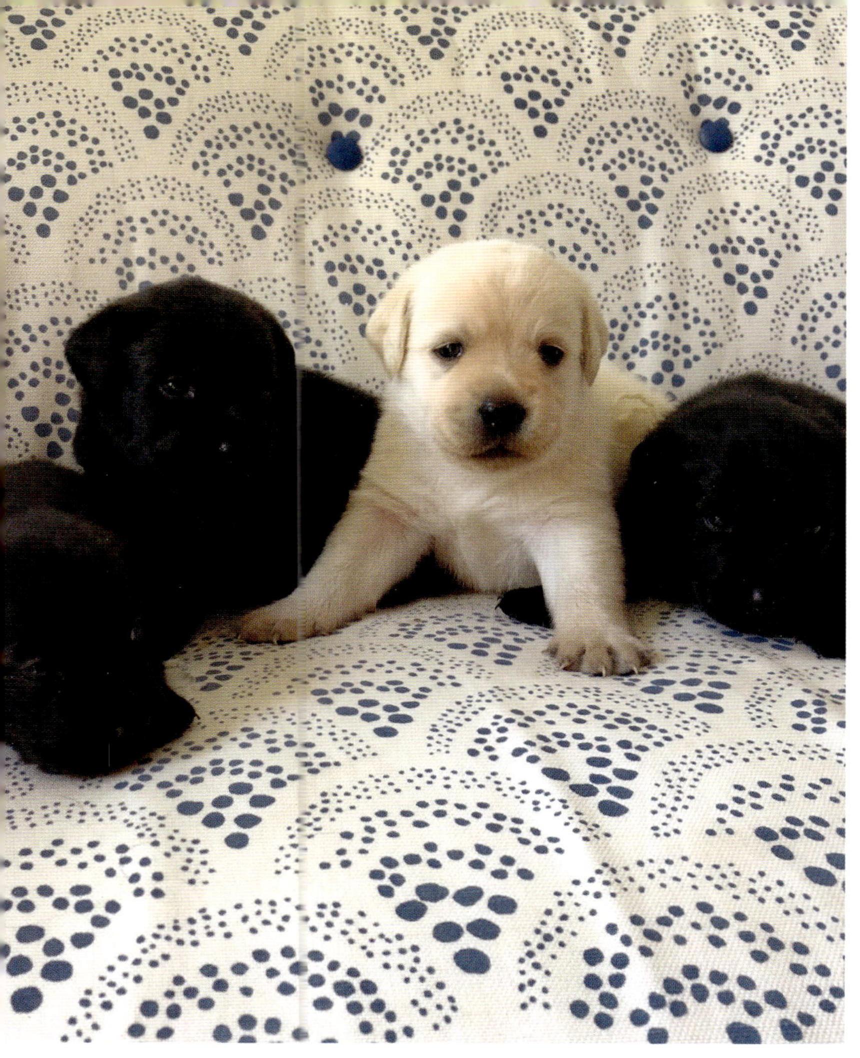

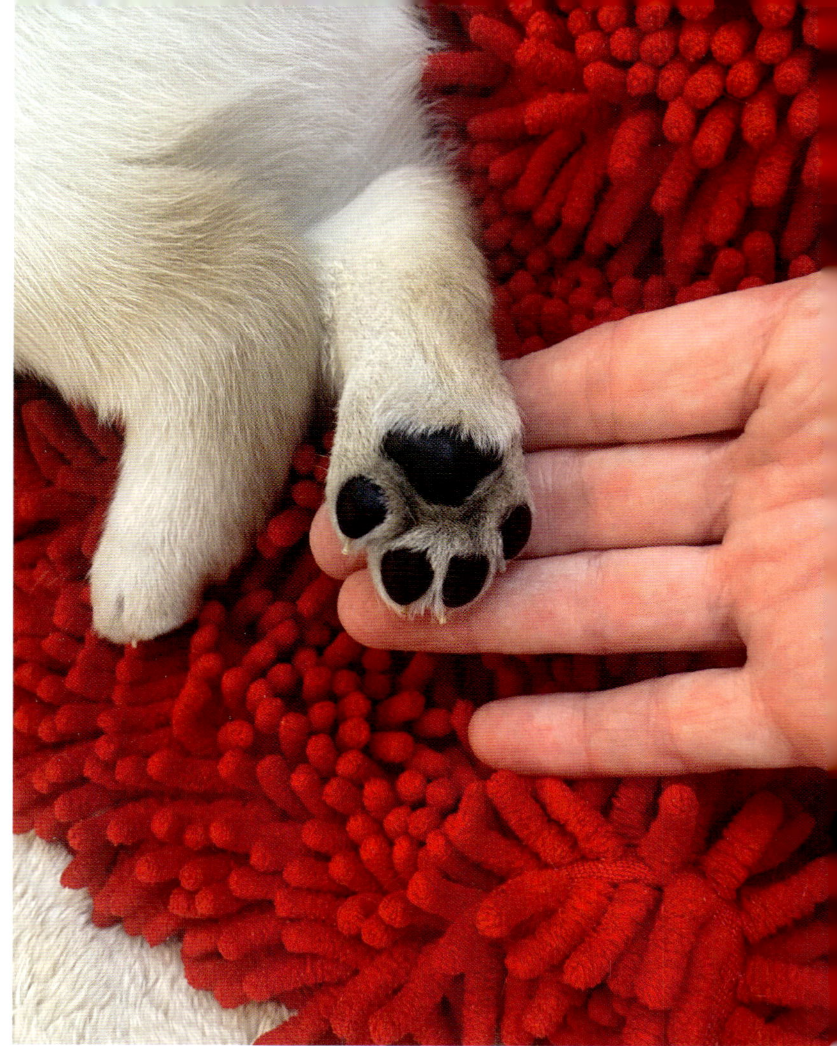

ABOVE LEFT: A litter of Brie's puppies.

ABOVE RIGHT: A very small paw. Yellow Labradors' skin pigment begins to show a few days after they are born; their noses and paw pads turn from pink to black.

BOTTOM RIGHT: Fern and her brother Bear in the geraniums.

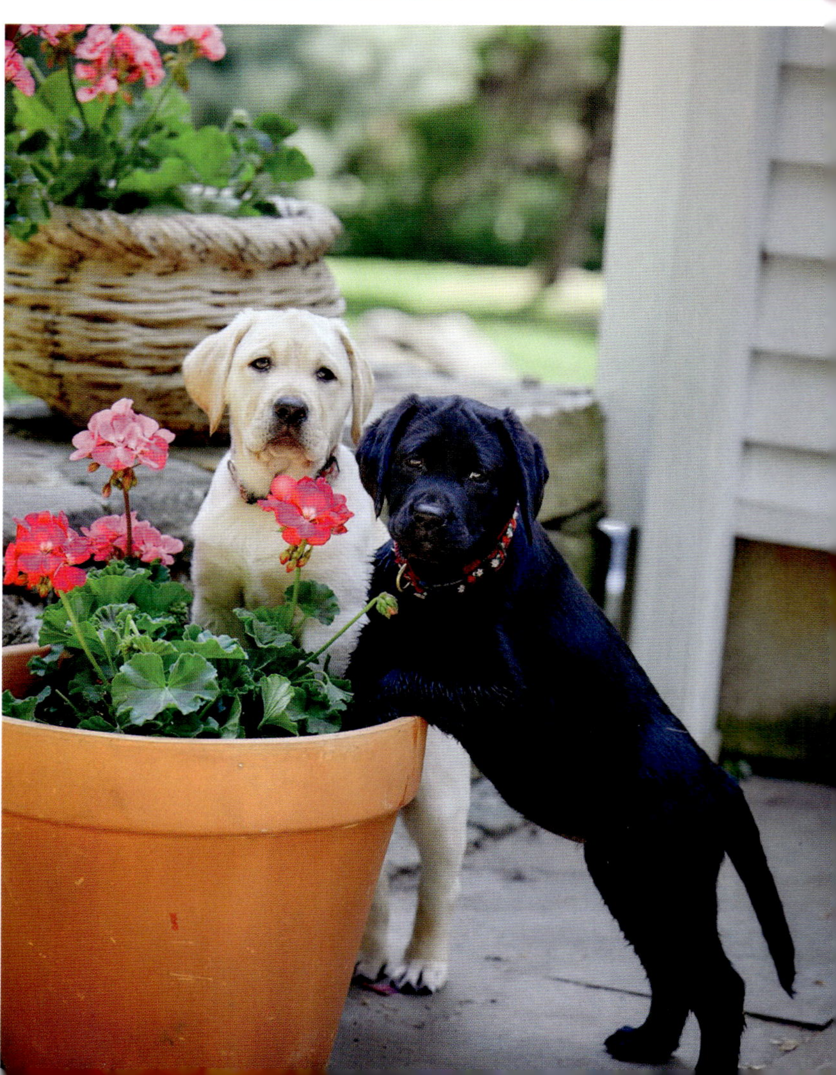

her daughter, Marta, and granddaughter, Brie, and hopefully her great-granddaughter, Fern—when she is ready. Puppies are magical. It is such a pure experience; for me, it is life at its best. It's a lot of work raising a litter even if only for eight weeks or so, but it is also so wonderful to watch them develop and grow, and to know about their lives in their new homes. Helping a new mother with her puppies creates such a bond; it's all about trust and support and being gentle.

Whether I am sharing a room with my dogs, my family, or friends, it is fundamentally important to me to be aware of who I am enjoying the room with, not simply how the room looks. A room can be lovely to be in, but if the person you are with doesn't have the same sense of life or joy that you have, then the rooms can't help, and none of it really matters. I admit that I enjoy my solitude and have surrounded myself with what matters to me. And at the end of the day, what could be better than a cheerful house filled with the things that matter most?

PHOTO CREDITS

ARS-Bridgeman Imaging: pages 190–91

Fernando Bengoechea: pages 25 (bottom left), 134, 224

James Calderaldo: page 22 (top)

Linzee Coolidge, courtesy of: page 126

Julia D'Agostino: pages 82, 99

Libby Cameron: pages 139 (stills from video), 156, 198, 237, 238 (top left and top right)

Roger Davies: pages 114–15, 120 (bottom right), 165, 171

Philip Ennis: pages 66, 67

Porter Gifford: pages 108–9, 111

John Hall: pages 60, 62, 63

Lizzie Himmel: pages 65, 68, 70, 71, 72, 220

Flora Irving: page 48

Kevin Kerr: pages 6, 14–15, 79, 83, 84–85, 87, 89 (top and bottom), 91, 96–97, 102, 113, 120 (top left and top right), 153, 168, 174–175, 178–79, 186, 231, 232, 233

Erin Kestenbaum: pages 86, 167

Dennis Krukowski: pages 154, 155

Guy Marcineau: pages 22 (bottom), 129, 137

Jeff McNamara: pages 207, 208, 216, 217, 222–23, 226, 227, 228–29

James Merrell: pages 4–5, 40, 42–43, 45, 50, 51 (left and right), 52–53, 54, 55, 57

Parish-Hadley Archives: pages 25 (top), 34 (top)

Eric Piasecki: pages 2, 8, 11, 105, 106, 110, 112, 116, 117, 170, 172, 182, 185, 189, 214

Walter Pippin, courtesy Parish-Hadley Archives: page 34 (bottom)

Annie Schlecter: page 144

Lord Snowdon: pages 124, 130, 131, 132 (left and right), 133, 136

William P. Steele, courtesy of Brunschwig & Fils: page 119

Jonny Valiant: pages 150, 159, 160–61, 162, 163, 164, 176, 195 (left and right)

Daphne Youree: pages 74, 76, 77, 80, 81, 92, 93 (all), 94, 166 (left and right), 192, 219, 238 (bottom right)